HANDBOOK OF CRITICAL AGRARIAN STUDIES

T0313701

Handbook of Critical Agrarian Studies

Edited by

A. Haroon Akram-Lodhi

Department of International Development Studies, Trent University, Canada

Kristina Dietz

Faculty of Social Sciences, University of Kassel, Germany

Bettina Engels

Otto Suhr Institute of Political Science, Department of Political and Social Sciences, Freie Universität Berlin, Germany

Ben M. McKay

Department of Anthropology and Archaeology, University of Calgary, Canada

EE Edward **Elgar**
PUBLISHING

Cheltenham, UK • Northampton, MA, USA

Published by
Edward Elgar Publishing Limited
The Lypiatts
15 Lansdown Road
Cheltenham
Glos GL50 2JA
UK

Edward Elgar Publishing, Inc.
William Pratt House
9 Dewey Court
Northampton
Massachusetts 01060
USA

Paperback edition 2023

A catalogue record for this book
is available from the British Library

Library of Congress Control Number: 2021947686

This book is available electronically in the **Elgar**online
Geography, Planning and Tourism subject collection
http://dx.doi.org/10.4337/9781788972468

ISBN 978 1 78897 245 1 (cased)
ISBN 978 1 78897 246 8 (eBook)
ISBN 978 1 0353 1888 9 (paperback)

Printed and bound by CPI Group (UK) Ltd, Croydon, CR0 4YY

Contents

PART III   METHODOLOGIES

PART IV   REGIONAL PERSPECTIVES

PART V   DEBATES

Contributors

Lincoln Addison is Associate Professor in the Department of Anthropology at the Memorial University of Newfoundland. His research focuses on the gender and labour impacts of agricultural intensification in southern Africa. He is the author of *Chiefs of the Plantation: Authority and Contestation on the South Africa-Zimbabwe Border* (2019).

A. Haroon Akram-Lodhi teaches agrarian political economy. He is Professor of Economics and International Development Studies at Trent University in Peterborough, Canada. He is the former editor-in-chief of the *Canadian Journal of Development Studies*, an associate editor of *Feminist Economics*, and was a member of the advisory board for the Women's Rights Programme of the Open Society Foundations in New York City. Haroon Akram-Lodhi has provided policy and programme advice to eight United Nations organizations.

Samir Amin was amongst the most distinguished writers, not just in the field of critical agrarian studies but in political economy, global history and development studies in general. His critiques of imperialism and neo-colonialism have influenced more than a generation of scholars and activists. He received a PhD in political economy in Paris (1957), as well as degrees from the Institut de Statistiques and from the Institut d'Etudes Politiques. He was a full professor in France from 1966 and then for 10 years (1970–1980) the director of the United Nations African Institute for Economic Development and Planning in Dakar. From 1980 he directed the African Office of the Third World Forum, an international non-governmental association for research and debate. He passed away, at the age of 86, in August 2018.

Bimbika Sijapati Basnett is a researcher and practitioner interested in the intersection between gender theories and development policy. At the time of contributing to this chapter, Bimbika was a social scientist and gender coordinator for the Center for International Forestry Research. Since 2019, she has been working as a senior gender and social inclusion advisor for an Australian government-funded economic governance facility that advises Indonesian central government agencies. Bimbika holds an MSc and PhD in development studies from the London School of Economics and Political Science, United Kingdom and Bachelor in economics and environmental studies from Macalester College, United States.

Sara Berry is a retired professor of history at Johns Hopkins University. She has done research on land, development, agrarian change, political economy and socio-economic history in sub-Saharan Africa, with primary emphasis on Nigeria and Ghana. Principal publications include *Fathers Work for Their Sons: Accumulation, Mobility and Class Formation in an Extended Yoruba Community* (1985), *No Condition Is Permanent: The Social Dynamics of Agrarian Change in Sub-Saharan Africa* (1993) and *Chiefs Know Their Boundaries: Essays on Property, Power and the Past in Asante, 1896–1996* (2001).

Ulbe Bosma is Senior Researcher at the International Institute of Social History in Amsterdam and Professor of International Comparative Social History at the Free University of Amsterdam. His main fields of interest are the histories of labour and commodity production, especially sugar and international labour migration. His most recent publication is *The Making* *of a Periphery: How Island Southeast Asia Became a Mass Exporter of Labor* (2019). Ulbe Bosma and Eric Vanhaute are co-founders of the *Commodity Frontiers Initiative*.

Ray Bush is Professor Emeritus of African Studies and Development Politics at the University of Leeds. He is Briefings and Debates editor of the *Review of African Political Economy* and works on the political economy of radical transformation. His recent publications include *Food Insecurity and Revolution in the Middle East and North Africa* (with Habib Ayeb, 2019).

Liam Campling is Professor of International Business and Development at Queen Mary University of London where he works collectively at the Centre on Labour and Global Production. He is co-author of *Capitalism and the Sea* (2021) and *Free Trade Agreements and Global Labour Governance* (2021) and an editor of the *Journal of Agrarian Change*.

Robert Chernomas is Professor of Economics at University of Manitoba. His most recent book is *Neoliberal Lives* (with Ian and Mark Hudson, 2019). Further publications are *Economics in the 21st Century: A Critical Perspective* (with Ian Hudson, 2016) and *The American Gene: Unnatural Selection* (with Ian Hudson and Greg Chernomas, forthcoming). He has published articles in the *Cambridge Journal of Economics*, *Review of Radical Political Economics* and *International Journal of Health Services*.

Priscilla Claeys is Associate Professor in Food Sovereignty, Human Rights and Resilience at the Centre for Agroecology, Water and Resilience at Coventry University, United Kingdom. Priscilla's main research focus concerns human rights and social movements. She is particularly interested in understanding processes of legal mobilizations by which social actors use and seek to transform the law to advance their claims. She is also passionate about food security governance, feminism and gender equality and ways to encourage inclusion and diversity in policy-making spaces.

Jennifer Clapp is Canada Research Chair in Global Food Security and Sustainability and Professor in the School of Environment, Resources and Sustainability at the University of Waterloo, Canada. She has published widely on the global governance of problems that arise at the intersection of the global economy, food security and food systems and the natural environment. Her most recent books include *Food*, third edition (2020), *Speculative Harvests: Financialization, Food, and Agriculture* (with S. Ryan Isakson, 2018) and *Hunger in the Balance: The New Politics of International Food Aid* (2012).

Nicholas Copeland is a cultural anthropologist and teaches courses in social theory and American Indian studies in the Department of History at Virginia Tech. He has studied political dynamics in rural Guatemala since the early 2000s and is a member of the Guatemalan Water Network REDAGUA. He is the author of *The Democracy Development Machine: Neoliberalism, Radical Pessimism, and Authoritarian Populism in Mayan Guatemala* (2019).

Sergio Coronado is a PhD candidate at the International Institute of Social Studies, The Hague, The Netherlands, and at the University of Kassel, Germany and Associate Researcher at Centro de Investigación y Educación Popular, Bogota. He holds a Bachelor degree in law and MA degrees in rural development and constitutional law.

Ben Cousins is Emeritus Professor at the Institute for Poverty, Land and Agrarian Studies (PLAAS) at the University of the Western Cape. He established PLAAS in 1995 and was its director until 2010, when he was awarded a research chair. He holds a DPhil in applied social studies from the University of Zimbabwe, and was in exile between 1972 and 1991. He is the author of 80 articles and chapters and has edited or co-edited 12 books.

Federico Demaria is Assistant Professor of Ecological Economics and Political Ecology at the University of Barcelona. His work aims to inform theory on how environments are shaped, politicized and contested. He published: *Degrowth: A Vocabulary for a New Era* (with Giorgos Kallis and Giacomo D'Alisa, 2014), translated into more than 10 languages; *Pluriverse: A Post-Development Dictionary* (with Ashish Kothari, Arturo Escobar, Ariel Salleh and Alberto Acosta, 2019); and *The Case for Degrowth* (with Giorgos Kallis, Susan Paulson and Giacomo D'Alisa, 2020).

Annette Aurélie Desmarais is Canada Research Chair in Human Rights, Social Justice and Food Sovereignty at the University of Manitoba, Canada. Annette is the author of *La Vía Campesina: Globalization and the Power of Peasants* (2007), co-editor of three books on food sovereignty and editor of *Frontline Farmers: How the National Farmers Union Resists Agribusiness and Creates our New Food Future* (2019). Prior to obtaining a doctorate, she was a farmer and she also worked as technical support to La Via Campesina. Her research centres on agrarian change, rural social movements and food sovereignty. Desmarais' research on food sovereignty is made possible with support from the Canada Research Chair Program.

Kristina Dietz is Substitute Professor for International and Intersocietal Relations at the University of Kassel, Germany. From 2022, she will be Professor of International Development at the University of Vienna. Together with Bettina Engels, she is Director of the research group, Global Change – Local Conflicts? Her research and teaching focuses on conflicts over land and mining, democracy and institutional changes, radical transformation and political ecology with a regional focus on Latin America.

J. Paul Dunne is Emeritus Professor of Economics at the University of Cape Town and Emeritus Professor of Economics at the University of the West of England. He has held positions at Middlesex University, the University of Leeds, University of Cambridge, University of Warwick and Birkbeck College, University of London. He is co-editor with Mike Brown of the online *Economics of Peace and Security* journal and has published widely on economics and security.

Franza Drechsel is Project Manager and Advisor in the Africa Unit of the Rosa Luxemburg Stiftung. Before she was a junior researcher in the research group Global Change – Local Conflicts? at Freie Universität Berlin. In her work and research, she focuses on conflicts over gold mining in Burkina Faso as well as state–society relations and postcoloniality in Africa.

Bettina Engels is Substitute Professor on contemporary politics and societies in Africa at the Department of Political and Social Sciences, Freie Universität Berlin, Germany. Together with Kristina Dietz, she is Director of the research group Global Change – Local Conflicts? Her research and teaching focuses on political economy in Africa, agrarian change and social transformation.

Irmak Ertör is Assistant Professor in the interdisciplinary Ataturk Institute for Modern Turkish History, Boğaziçi University, Istanbul. She wrote her PhD (as part of the European Network of Political Ecology project) in the Institute of Environmental Sciences and

Technology on the political ecology of aquaculture. As a postdoctoral researcher, she continued investigating environmental justice and socio-environmental conflicts related to fisher folks in the Environmental Justice Project. Her current research interests include agroecology and food sovereignty in small-scale fisheries, blue degrowth as well as community-supported fisheries.

Jennifer C. Franco is a research associate in the Agrarian and Environmental Justice and the Myanmar in Focus Programmes of the Transnational Institute and Adjunct Professor at the College of Humanities and Development Studies of the China Agricultural University in Beijing. She has been a member of the International Panel of Experts on Sustainable Food Systems and currently serves on the editorial advisory board of the journal *Environment and Planning* and the journal *Agriculture and Human Values*. She has a PhD in political science and works in a scholar-activist tradition. Her research interests are on the politics of natural resources and rural politics in broader democratization processes.

Harriet Friedmann is Professor Emerita of Sociology, University of Toronto. Her publications include history (food regimes and metabolism of global cities), eco-social theory and agriculture. Her current project is Political Ecology of Food. Friedmann is a Toronto Food Policy Councillor and former chair. She serves on editorial boards of food, agriculture, and global change journals and has served on non-profit boards related to seed sovereignty and city-food regions. She received the 2011 Lifetime Achievement award from the Canadian Association of Food Studies.

Julien-François Gerber is Assistant Professor at the International Institute of Social Studies in The Hague. After completing his PhD in Barcelona and postdoc at Harvard University, he lived and worked in India and Bhutan before moving to the Low Countries. He has published on the expansion of capitalism in the rural sphere, particularly through the lenses of ownership, credit/debt, social conflict and plantation studies. He is also interested in bridging science and activism and has been active in the degrowth movement.

Ariane Goetz is Researcher and Lecturer in the Department of International Agricultural Policy and Environmental Governance at the University of Kassel, Germany. Her research deals with the political economy of agrarian-environmental transformation in the context of national development strategies, international restructuring and global sustainability politics. She is the author of *Land Grabbing and Home Country Development* (2019).

Elisa Greco is Associate Professor in International Political Economy and Development at the European School of Political and Social Sciences, Catholic University of Lille, France and Visiting Fellow at the Sustainability Research Institute, University of Leeds, United Kingdom. She works on critical political economy and the political economy of agrarian change in the Global South. Elisa researches on land grabs in Africa, class dynamics and rural resistance, labour questions and labour regimes in African farming and finance, and on developing a Marxist analysis of rent, value and natural resources through ethnographic research in Tanzania and Uganda.

Severin Halder is currently coordinating the UrbanLab at the Faculty of Geosciences at the University of Münster, Germany. His activist geography is inspired by the everyday resistance of urban peasants in Rio de Janeiro, Bogota, Maputo and the *Allmende-Kontor* Network in

Berlin. His work is generated from within the popular education collective *orangotango*. The research aims towards the creation and critical reflection of solidarity relationships, horizontal knowledge exchange and self-organized struggles. He holds a PhD, co-edited 'This Is Not an Atlas' (2018), worked at the Centre for Rural Development at the Humboldt University of Berlin but still plants only sufficient food for some meals every year.

Derek Hall is Associate Professor in the Department of Political Science and the Balsillie School of International Affairs at Wilfrid Laurier University. His research focuses on the political economy of food, agriculture, land and environment in Japan and Southeast Asia, and on the history and theory of capitalism. He is the author of *Land* (2013) and *Powers of Exclusion: Land Dilemmas in Southeast Asia* (with Philip Hirsch and Tania Murray Li, 2011).

Wendy Harcourt is Full Professor and Westerdijk Professor with an endowed Chair of Gender, Diversity and Sustainable Development at the International Institute of Social Studies of the Erasmus University Rotterdam in The Hague. She is Coordinator of the European Union H2020-MSCA-ITN-2017 Marie Sklodowska-Curie Innovative Training Networks on Well-Being, Ecology, Gender and Community, awarded in May 2017. She has written extensively in critical development theory, feminist political ecology and body politics.

John Harriss, Fellow of the Royal Society of Canada, is Professor Emeritus of International Studies at Simon Fraser University in Vancouver and formerly Professor of Development Studies at the London School of Economics. He is the author of *Capitalism and Peasant Farming: Agrarian Structure and Ideology in Northern Tamil Nadu* (1982) and of *Power Matters* (2006); co-author of *Reinventing India* (with Stuart Corbridge, 2000) and most recently of *India: Continuity and Change in the 21st Century* (with Craig Jeffrey and Trent Brown, 2020).

Barbara Harriss-White drove from Cambridge to New Delhi in 1969 and has studied and taught about India ever since, working in political economy and economic anthropology. Her research fields are agrarian transformations, agricultural markets and the food economy: *Rural Commercial Capitalism: Agricultural Markets in West Bengal* (2008); India's informal and criminal capitalism: *The Wild East: Criminal Political Economies in South Asia* (with Lucia Michelutti, 2019); aspects of deprivation: *Dalits and Adivasis in India's Business Economy: Three Essays and an Atlas* (2013); the economy as a waste-producing system; aspects of policy in these fields and the long-term study of a market town: *Middle India and Urban Rural-Development: Four Decades of Change* (2013). She has advised seven United Nations agencies, published or co-published 40 books and research reports, over 270 papers and chapters, 115 working papers and has supervised 40 doctoral students. In Oxford, she is Emeritus Professor of Development Studies and Emeritus Fellow of Wolfson College.

Elizabeth Havice is Professor of Geography at University of North Carolina at Chapel Hill. Her work explores intersections among states, firms, non-state organizations, science and nature in the global economy. Current projects include a *Handbook on Critical Resource Geography* (with G. Valdivia and M. Himley, forthcoming) and research on the intersection of data and oceans governance.

Ian Hudson is Professor of Economics at the University of Manitoba. His research is in the areas of political economy and ethical consumption. His most recent book is *Neoliberal*

Lives: Work, Politics, Nature and Health in the Contemporary United States (with Robert Chernomas and Mark Hudson, 2019). His articles have appeared in the *Review of Social Economy*, *Canadian Journal of Development Studies*, *Cambridge Journal of Economics*, *Review of Radical Political Economics* and the *Journal of Economic Issues*.

Carol Hunsberger is Associate Professor in the Department of Geography and Environment at the University of Western Ontario, Canada. Her research explores energy justice in the context of anti-pipeline struggles, the governance of biofuels and the spatial politics of energy conflicts.

Markus Ihalainen has recently moved on to a new position. At the time of contributing to his chapter, Markus was Senior Research and Engagement Officer and Gender Co-Coordinator at the Center for International Forestry Research. He is particularly interested in enhancing conceptual approaches to understanding gender dynamics in forested landscapes. His work is mainly focused on sub-Saharan Africa, with a particular emphasis on assessing and addressing gender inequities in various forest-based value chains as well as in forest and landscape restoration.

S. Ryan Isakson is Associate Professor of Global Development Studies and Geography at the University of Toronto. His research focuses upon the political economy of food systems and agrarian change, particularly in Latin American contexts. His current research explores how contemporary initiatives promoting financial inclusion and the financialization of agricultural risk management in rural Guatemala interplay with gender relations and the differentiated vulnerabilities of peasant farming households to economic and environmental stresses. He is the co-author of *Speculative Harvests: Financialization, Food, and Agriculture* (with Jennifer Clapp, 2018).

Muhammad Ali Jan is Assistant Professor in Economics and Development Studies at the Information Technology University in Lahore, Pakistan. He is also a research associate of the Contemporary South Asian Studies Programme at the Oxford School of Global and Area Studies, where he has taught political economy. He works on the political economy of agricultural markets and agrarian change in the Pakistani Punjab and his articles have been published in the *Journal of Agrarian Change* and *Economic and Political Weekly*. He is currently preparing a manuscript on the agrarian sociology of the Pakistani Punjab, through the class and status struggles between merchants, landlords and peasants in two districts of the province.

Kees Jansen is Associate Professor in the Rural Sociology group at Wageningen University in the Netherlands. His work connects the fields of political ecology, critical agrarian studies and international development. His current research focuses on pesticide risk governance and social movements concerned about pesticides.

Petr Jehlička has recently moved to his native Czechia after 20 years at the Department of Geography at the Open University, United Kingdom. He is Senior Researcher at the Institute of Ethnology of the Czech Academy of Sciences in Prague. His research is located in agro-food studies and revolves around everyday environmentalism and sustainable food consumption at the intersection of formal and informal food economies. More recently he has explored these topics in relation to the geopolitics of knowledge production.

Praveen Jha is Professor of Economics at the Centre for Economic Studies and Planning and Adjunct Professor at the Centre for Informal Sector and Labour Studies, Jawaharlal Nehru University, New Delhi, India. He is editor of *Agrarian South: Journal of Political Economy*.

Joost Jongerden is Associate Professor at Rural Sociology, Wageningen University, the Netherlands and Project Professor at the Asian Platform for Global Sustainability and Transcultural Studies at Kyoto University, Japan. He studies the ways in which people develop alternatives to market- and state-induced insecurities. This he refers to as 'do-it-yourself development'.

Cristóbal Kay is Emeritus Professor in Rural Development and Development Studies at the International Institute of Social Studies of Erasmus University Rotterdam and Professorial Research Associate at the Department of Development Studies, SOAS, University of London. He is an editor of the *Journal of Agrarian Change*.

Benedict J. Tria Kerkvliet's research has emphasized agrarian politics and state–society relations in Southeast Asia, particularly the Philippines and Vietnam. His most recent book is *Speaking Out in Vietnam: Public Political Criticism in a Communist Party-Ruled Nation* (2019). He is an emeritus professor at the Australian National University and an affiliate graduate faculty member at the University of Hawai'i at Mānoa.

Markus Kröger is Associate Professor of Global Development Studies at the University of Helsinki and a fellow at the Academy of Finland. He has written extensively on global natural resource politics, conflicts and social resistance movements and their economic outcomes, especially in relation to mining and forestry. He is an expert on the political economy, development and globalization in Latin America, India and the Arctic. Currently he focuses on the world ecology and political ontology of global extractivisms and deforestation.

Brian Kuns is Associate Senior Lecturer at the Swedish University of Agricultural Sciences in the Department of Rural and Urban Development. He received his PhD in human geography from Stockholm University and studies questions of agricultural financialization and corporatization, changing agrarian structure, smallholders and farm labour, mostly with respect to Eastern Europe and the Nordic countries.

Xavier Lafrance is Associate Professor of Political Science at the Université du Québec à Montréal. He is the author of *The Making of Capitalism in France: Class Structures, Economic Development, the State and the Formation of the French Working Class, 1750–1914* (2019). He is the co-editor of *Case Studies in the Origins of Capitalism* (with Charles Post, 2019).

Johanna Leinius is a social scientist at the Faculty of Social Sciences, University of Kassel, Germany. She has been spokeswoman for the section Politics and Gender of the German Political Science Association and is speaker for the working group Poststructuralist Perspectives on Social Movements of the Institute for Social Movement Studies. Her research interests include postcolonial feminist theory, social movement research, socio-ecological transformations and political ontology.

Christian Lund is Professor at the University of Copenhagen, Denmark. He works on land and politics issues in West Africa and Indonesia. He is the author of *Law, Power, and Politics* *in Niger* (1998), *Local Politics and the Dynamics of Property in Africa* (2008) and *Nine-Tenths of the Law: Enduring Dispossession in Indonesia* (2020).

Facundo Martín is Assistant Professor at the Department of Geography, Universidad Nacional de Cuyo (Mendoza) and Researcher at the National Council for Scientific and Technological Research in Argentina.

Giuliano Martiniello is Associate Professor of Political Science and Political Economy at Sciences Po Rabat, International University of Rabat and Adjunct Assistant Professor at the Faculty of Agricultural and Food Sciences, American University of Beirut. He is broadly interested in the political economy, political sociology and political ecology of agrarian and environmental change. His research interests include land questions and reforms, food and farming systems, large-scale land enclosures and contract farming, conservation and deforestation, rural social conflicts and agrarian movements in Africa and the Middle East.

Nils McCune is Research Associate at the Agroecology and Livelihoods Collaborative at the University of Vermont, and Visiting Scholar at ECOSUR, Mexico. His research interests include power and politics in food and agrarian systems, peasant economies, agroecology pedagogy, and social movements in Latin America and the Caribbean.

Ben M. McKay is Associate Professor of Development and Sustainability in the Department of Anthropology and Archaeology at the University of Calgary in Canada. His research focuses on the political economy and ecology of agrarian change in Latin America, agrarian extractivism and food sovereignty alternatives. He is the author of *The Political Economy of Agrarian Extractivism: Lessons from Bolivia* (2020) and co-editor of *Agrarian Extractivism in Latin America* (2021) and *Rural Transformations and Agro-Food Systems* (2018).

Philip McMichael is Emeritus Professor of Global Development at Cornell University. He is author of *Development and Social Change: A Global Perspective* (2017), *Food Regimes and Agrarian Questions* (2013) and the award-winning *Settlers and the Agrarian Question* (1984). He co-edited *Finance or Food? The Role of Cultures, Values and Ethics in Land Use Negotiations* (with Hilde Bjørkhaug and Bruce Muirhead, 2020). He works with civil society in the United Nations Committee on World Food Security.

Sofía Monsalve Suárez is Secretary General of Food First Information and Action Network (FIAN International). FIAN International is an international human rights organization working for the right to food and nutrition. Her work focuses largely on the intersection between human rights and land and natural resources governance.

Avanti Mukherjee is Assistant Professor of Economics at State University of New York College at Cortland, United States, whose research uses a feminist political economy lens informed by institutional bargaining and Marxian theories to study issues of labour, gender and development. She is also engaged in popular dissemination and policy advocacy on these issues, most recently with the United Nations Entity for Gender Equality and the Empowerment of Women. Such experience informs her teaching of labour economics, development, political economy of women and microeconomic theory.

Ryan Nehring is a postdoctoral research associate in the Department of History and Philosophy of Science at the University of Cambridge and holds a PhD in Development

Sociology from Cornell University. His research looks at the relationship between the political economy of development and the bureaucratic politics of public agricultural science in Brazil. Some of his past research has been published in the *Journal of Peasant Studies*, *Geoforum*, *Global Food Security* and the *Canadian Journal of Development Studies*.

Andrea J. Nightingale is Professor of Geography at the University of Oslo and Senior Researcher at the Swedish University of Agricultural Sciences where she previously held a Chair in Rural Development. Her research interests span political violence, public authority and state formation in relation to climate change programmes; and feminist work on emotion and subjectivity in relation to theories of development, transformation and collective action. She is the author of *Environment and Sustainability in a Globalizing World* (2019).

Gustavo de L.T. Oliveira obtained his PhD in geography from University of California, Berkeley and is now Assistant Professor in the Department of Global and International Studies at the University of California, Irvine. He is co-editor of *Soy, Globalization, and Environmental Politics in South America* (2018) and *Beyond the Global Land Grab: New Directions for Research on Land Struggles and Global Agrarian Change* (2021). His current research focuses on Chinese investments in Brazilian agribusiness, finance and infrastructure.

Gerardo Otero, Fellow of the Royal Society of Canada, is president (2021–2022) of the Latin American Studies Association (LASA). He is a sociologist and political economist, and is Professor of International Studies at Simon Fraser University in Vancouver, Canada. He has published over 100 scholarly articles, chapters and books, including *Farewell to the Peasantry? Political Class Formation in Rural Mexico* (1999; reissued in 2018) and *The Neoliberal Diet: Healthy Profits, Unhealthy People* (2018).

Carlos Oya is Professor of Political Economy of Development at SOAS, University of London, and a development economist by training. He has extensively published on agrarian capital, labour relations, rural poverty, and development policy with a focus on Sub-Saharan Africa. He also teaches at China Agricultural University in Beijing, Graduate Institute of International Development Studies in Geneva, and Universidad Complutense Madrid. He has been co-editor of the *Journal of Agrarian Change* since 2008.

Prabhat Patnaik has taught at the University of Cambridge and at Jawaharlal Nehru University, New Delhi, from where he retired in 2010 and where he is currently Professor Emeritus. His areas of interest are macroeconomics and development economics, in which he has written a number of books. He is the editor of the journal *Social Scientist*.

Utsa Patnaik is Professor Emeritus at Jawaharlal Nehru University, Delhi. She has written extensively on theorizing the transition from agricultural, peasant-predominant societies to industrial society; on imperialism and the drain of wealth; and on food security and poverty. Her most recent books are *A Theory of Imperialism* (with P. Patnaik, 2016) and *Capital and Imperialism: Theory, History and the Present* (with P. Patnaik, 2021).

Jonathan Pattenden is Associate Professor of Political Economy and Sociology of Development at the University of East Anglia, United Kingdom. He is author of *Labour, State and Society in Rural India: A Class-Relational Approach* (2016), lead editor of *Class Dynamics of Development* (2017), and an editor of the *Journal of Agrarian Change*.

Nancy Lee Peluso is Professor of Society & Environment in the Department of Environmental Science, Policy, and Management at the University of California, Berkeley, where she held the Henry J. Vaux Research Chair from 2009–2019. Her three decades of research in Indonesia on the political ecologies of forests, gold-mining, and other land-based resources have received numerous awards, including the John Simon Guggenheim Fellowship and the Al-Moumin prize in Environmental Peacemaking. She is currently Chair of the Center for Southeast Asia Studies at Berkeley, a member of the *Journal of Peasant Studies Editorial Collective*, and co-editor of the Cornell University Press Series, 'On Land: New Perspectives on Territory, Environment, and Development'. Her latest research explores the mutual constitution of mobile labour and agrarian transformation in montane Java.

Pauline E. Peters is a social anthropologist and retired faculty member of the Department of Anthropology and the Kennedy School, Harvard University. Since her retirement from teaching in 2008, she has continued her research as a Faculty Fellow at the Center for International Development and a Fellow of the Center for African Studies, Harvard. Her research has concentrated on southern Africa, particularly Malawi, and her publications are on land, rural economy, kinship and gender.

Helena Pérez Niño is an Assistant Professor at the International Institute of Social Studies of the Erasmus University Rotterdam in The Hague. Before joining ISS she was a research fellow at the Institute for Poverty, Land and Agrarian Studies, a visiting researcher at the Institute of Social and Economic Studies in Mozambique, and a lecturer at SOAS and Cambridge. She serves on the board of the *Journal of Southern African Studies* and is an editor of the *Journal of Agrarian Change*.

Carol J. Pierce Colfer is a cultural anthropologist whose work has been interdisciplinary in nature. For the past 25 years she has been affiliated with the Center for International Forestry Research in Bogor, Indonesia, where she participated in and led teams of researchers on forest–people interactions in the tropics, including developing a programme on adaptive collaborative management. She is author of *Masculinities in Forests: Representations of Diversity* (2020), co-editor (Colfer, Ravi Prabhu and Anne Larson, eds) of *Adaptive Collaborative Management of Forest Landscapes: Villagers, Bureaucrats and Civil Society* (2022), and is also connected with Cornell University's Southeast Asia Program.

Oliver Pye is Associate Professor of Southeast Asian Studies at Bonn University, with a research focus on political ecology and social movements. He borrows extensively from human and economic geography in his work. At the moment, he is developing a labour geography perspective of the palm oil industry.

Smriti Rao is Professor of Economics and Global Studies at Assumption University, United States and Affiliated Scholar, Women's Studies Research Center at Brandeis University, United States. She works on feminist political economy analyses of developing country contexts, particularly India.

Mattias Borg Rasmussen is Associate Professor at the University of Copenhagen, Denmark. He works on territory, resources and politics in Peru and Argentina. He is the author of *Andean Waterways: Resource Politics in Highland Peru* (2015).

Peter Rosset has written extensively on food sovereignty, peasant movements, agroecology, agrarian reform and the collective defense of land and territory. He is a Professor in the Department of Agriculture, Environment and Society of El Colegio de la Frontera Sur (ECOSUR), in Chiapas, Mexico. He is also BPV-FUNCAP Professor of the Graduate Program on Sociology (PPGS) of the Universidade Estadual do Ceará (UECE) and Collaborating Professor of the Graduate Program on Territorial Development (TerritoriAL) of the Universidade Paulista (UNESP), both in Brazil, as well as Visiting Professor of the Social Research Institute (CUSRI) of Chulalongkorn University in Thailand. Among his books are *Agroecology* (with C.R. Carroll and J.H. Vandermeer, 1990), *Promised Land: Competing Visions of Agrarian Reform* (with M. Courville and R. Patel, 2006), *Food Is Different* (2006), *Agroecological Revolution* (with B. Machín Sosa, A.M. Roque Jaime and D.R. Ávila Lozano, 2010) and *Agroecology: Science and Politics* (with M.A. Altieri, 2017).

Arnim Scheidel is a Beatriu de Pinós research fellow at the Institute of Environmental Science and Technology, Universitat Autònoma de Barcelona. His research focuses on the political ecology of development, agrarian and environmental change, environmental justice, and the sustainability of agriculture and land use change. He is a member of the Direction and Coordination Group of the *Global Environmental Justice Atlas* and part of the editorial collective of the journal *Sustainability Science*.

Matthew A. Schnurr is Associate Professor in the Department of International Development Studies at Dalhousie University. His research focuses on the potential for new agricultural technologies to alleviate poverty and hunger in sub-Saharan Africa. He is the author of *Africa's Gene Revolution: Genetically Modified Crops and the Future of African Agriculture* (2019).

Annie Shattuck is Assistant Professor of Geography at Indiana University. Her work engages agrarian change, food sovereignty and critical approaches to rural health.

Jasber Singh has several years of experience designing, delivering and evaluating community participation projects on social and environmental justice. He is currently Associate Professor in Participatory Practice at the Centre for Agroecology, Water and Resilience at Coventry University. Jasber is interested in the way that the right to food, food sovereignty and environmental actions engage with the politics of difference. Before joining academia, Jasber worked with several non-governmental organizations and passionately tackled racism and other forms of discrimination.

Maristella Svampa is an Argentine sociologist. She is Full Professor at the Universidad Nacional de La Plata, Buenos Aires and Researcher at the Consejo Nacional de Investigaciones Científicas y Técnicas. Her research focuses on social movements and collective action, socio-ecological crisis, critical thinking and Latin American social theory. She is author of *Chacra 51. Regreso a la Patagonia en los tiempos del fracking* (2018) and *Las fronteras del neoextractivismo en América Latina* (2018). In 2020 she published *El colapso ecológico ya llegó. Una brújula para salir del (mal)Desarrollo* (with Enrique Viale).

Larry A. Swatuk is Full Professor in the School of Environment, Enterprise and Development at the University of Waterloo in Canada. Prior to his appointment at Waterloo, Dr Swatuk spent 11 years at the University of Botswana where he was Lecturer in the Department of Political and Administrative Studies, University of Botswana and Associate Professor of

Natural Resources Governance at the Okavango Research Institute. Among his most recent publications are the monograph *Water in Southern Africa* (2017) and two co-edited collections: *Water, Energy, Food and People: The Nexus in an Era of Climate Change* (with Corrine Cash, 2017) and *Water, Climate Change and the Boomerang Effect: Unintentional Consequences for Resource Insecurity* (with Lars Wirkus, 2018).

Marcus Taylor is Associate Professor in the Department of Global Development Studies at Queen's University, Kingston, Canada. He researches and teaches on the political ecology of development, with a focus on agriculture, labour and livelihoods. His recent books include *The Political Ecology of Climate Change Adaptation* (2015) and *Global Labour Studies* (with Sébastien Rioux, 2018).

Robin Thiers obtained his PhD in political science from Ghent University. His research interests lie at the crossroads of agrarian political economy, political ecology and actor network theory. His forthcoming book is *Tales of the Post-Plantation. Unlikely Protagonists of Modern Philippe Banana History* (2022).

Chiara Tornaghi is Associate Professor in Urban Food Sovereignty and Resilience at the Centre for Agroecology, Water and Resilience, Coventry University, United Kingdom. A scholar-activist in the field of critical urban studies, her current work revolves around urban political agroecology, grassroots pedagogies, soil care and the conceptualization of an agroecological urbanism.

Jan Douwe van der Ploeg is Emeritus Professor of Wageningen University in the Netherlands where he was Chair of Rural Sociology and, later, of Transition Studies. Currently he is Adjunct Professor at the College of Humanities and Development Studies of China Agricultural University in Beijing. He worked in Latin America, Africa, Europe and Asia and likes to operate at the interface of science, social movements and politics. His main publications include *The New Peasantries* and *Peasants and the Art of Farming* (2013).

Eric Vanhaute is Professor Economic and Social History and World History at Ghent University. He has published extensively on the history of peasantries and rural societies. His latest book is *Peasants in World History* (2021). Ulbe Bosma and Eric Vanhaute are co-founders of the *Commodity Frontiers Initiative*.

Henry Veltmeyer is Senior Research Professor at the Universidad Autónoma de Zacatecas, Mexico; Senior Research Fellow at the Centre for Advanced Latin American Studies at the Universidad de Guadalajara; and Professor Emeritus of International Development Studies at Saint Mary's University, Canada. He has authored and edited over 60 books in the area of Latin American studies, the political economy of development and globalization and social movements in the Latin American context. Recent publications include *The Essential Guide to Critical Development Studies* (2021) and *Latin America in the Vortex of Social Change* (2019).

Boris Verbrugge is a senior researcher at the HIVA Research Institute for Work and Society at the Katholieke Universiteit Leuven (HIVA-KU Leuven). For several years, Boris has worked on labour governance in informal gold mining. His current research interests revolve around the political economy of sustainability, and particularly the distributional impacts of efforts to make global value chains more inclusive and more sustainable.

Leandro Vergara-Camus is Associate Professor and Head of Programme in Economy and Social Innovation at the Université de l'Ontario Français in Toronto. He has published on land struggles, peasant movements, alternative development, sugarcane ethanol, the left and state formation in Latin America. He has published two books: *Land and Freedom: The MST, the Zapatistas and Peasant Alternatives to Neoliberalism* (2014) and *La cuestión agraria y los gobiernos de izquierda en América Latina* (with Cristóbal Kay, 2018). His current research is on energy transition, the appropriation of nature, the state/business nexus and climate change as an accumulation strategy of renewable energy companies across the globe.

Oane Visser is Associate Professor at the International Institute of Social Studies and a Fellow of the Independent Social Research Foundation, United Kingdom. He has been a visiting scholar at the University of Oxford, City University of New York, Cornell University and the University of Toronto. His research focuses on farmland investment, large-scale farms, digital farming, interactions between small and large farms and rural movements, particularly in Russia, Ukraine and the European Union. European Research Council laureate and *Focaal* editor, Visser has (co-)edited five special issues, including two on the financialization of agriculture, on land imaginaries and postsocialist smallholders.

Michael Watts is Professor Emeritus of Geography and Development Studies at the University of California, Berkeley. His research focuses on the political economy of development and in particular on the energy and agro-food sectors in Africa. He also works on contemporary geopolitics and social movements. Michael has published extensively on Nigeria and the Niger Delta.

Tony Weis is Professor of Geography at the University of Western Ontario. He is the author of *The Ecological Hoofprint: The Global Burden of Industrial Livestock* (2013) and *The Global Food Economy: The Battle for the Future of Farming* (2007). His research is broadly located in the field of political ecology and has focused heavily on industrial livestock production over the past decade.

Ben White is Emeritus Professor of Rural Sociology at the International Institute of Social Studies, The Hague. His research and teaching have focused on agrarian change and the anthropology and history of childhood and youth. He has been engaged in research on these topics since the early 1970s, primarily in Indonesia. His most recent book is *Agriculture and the Generation Problem* (2020).

Paris Yeros is Professor at the Federal University of ABC, São Paulo, Brazil, and member of the faculties of Economic Sciences, Sciences and Humanities, and World Political Economy. He is editor of *Agrarian South: Journal of Political Economy*.

Qian Forrest Zhang received his PhD in sociology from Yale University. He has been teaching at Singapore Management University since 2005 and is currently Associate Professor of Sociology and Associate Dean for Research at the School of Social Sciences. His research focuses on China's agrarian political economy. His recent works have investigated agricultural cooperatives, industrial pig farming, the agrarian capitalist class and land politics.

Foreword
Tania Murray Li

Let me begin with a stark but simple fact: more people than ever before make their homes in rural areas and depend on agriculture for their livelihoods, in whole or in part. Although the percentage of the global population classified as rural is declining, World Bank data show that the net number of people who live in rural areas continues to increase: from 2 billion in 1960 to 3 billion in 1990 and 3.4 billion in 2020. Anyone interested in global affairs should seek to be informed about the rural half of the global population, and yet rural people are largely absent from public and academic discourse, except perhaps at election time. A key reason for their absence is the stubbornly persistent modernization narrative which suggests that rural populations are anachronistic: they belong to the past, and sooner or later they too will move to cities and join the march of progress, enlightenment-style. From this perspective it is not worth worrying too much about who they are or how they live, how national and global currents affect them or their aspirations for themselves or their children. The only question seems to be how to move them more quickly along the transition path – out of their small farms and businesses into bigger, more capital-intensive ones; or off the land altogether, in order to free up space for large-scale corporate agriculture, extractive industries, conservation schemes or urban sprawl.

Critical agrarian studies, the subject of this volume, begins from a different premise: rural people will continue to occupy the countryside for many generations to come, and their actions will shape the course of history in the future, as they did in the past. Critical agrarian studies is *critical* of versions of modernization and Marxian theory which endlessly rehearse transition narratives in which all the people of the world will travel along a single pathway whose destination is known in advance. Its focus is *agrarian* in the sense that it foregrounds the people, processes and powers at play in the rural or peri-urban spaces where food, fuel and fodder are produced; and where different actors compete over land, water and other resources. Most significantly it is a rich field of *study* animated by a sense that – shorn of transition narratives – there is a great deal we should know about rural people and rural spaces, and their radically heterogeneous trajectories in different parts of the world.

Core questions posed by scholars working in the tradition of critical agrarian studies are empirical, conceptual and political. Empirically, if we do not assume that rural populations are disappearing or that the trajectory of change is the same world-over, some important questions follow. For example: How do rural people use land and how is their access to (and exclusion from) land and water changing? What are the resources they rely on to sustain themselves (e.g. farms, wages, remittances, transfers, rent)? How do they mobilize to defend their livelihoods or to improve upon their situation? How does competition over resources play out? The conceptual questions stem from the challenge of pursuing empirical research that is theoretically guided but open-ended. Scholars work with theories that raise questions about how capital, class, caste, race, gender, generation and ecology shape rural trajectories, while remaining alert to their intersections and site-specific constellations. The political questions are perhaps the most urgent. Many scholars in the critical agrarian studies tradition are 'scholar-activists' who work closely with agrarian social movements, or who move between activist and scholarly positions. Their questions concern the transformational possibilities that emerge when rural people are recognized as actors who are always already engaged in the production of new worlds. These worlds are shaped – but not determined – by national and global flows of capital, legal and policy regimes, and political alliances; understanding them demands the kinds of multi-scalar and multi-disciplinary analyses at which many agrarian scholars excel. By assembling leading-edge scholarship on these topics and more, this volume makes an essential contribution.

Acknowledgements

In May 2017 Harry Fabian of Edward Elgar Publishing approached A. Haroon Akram-Lodhi to enquire whether he would be interested in editing a volume on contemporary research agendas in agrarian studies. Over the next couple of months this idea developed into something somewhat different: a handbook of critical agrarian studies. Knowing the scale of a project designed in part to define the undefined, Ben McKay agreed to join as a co-editor in June, and Kristina Dietz and Bettina Engels joined the project in November. A first draft of the proposed contents and the contributors to be invited was agreed in February 2018. When invitations to contribute started to go out in the late winter of 2018 what was striking was the speed with which contributors agreed to participate, reflecting the extent of the excitement generated by the prospect of this *Handbook*. In May 2019, under the auspices of the Global Change – Local Conflicts (GLOCON) research programme at the Freie Universität in Berlin, a small selection of the contributions to the *Handbook* were reviewed by peers within the field. Similarly, in July 2019, under the auspices of the University of Waterloo and the Balsillie School of International Affairs in Kitchener/Waterloo, Canada, a second small selection of contributions to the *Handbook* were peer reviewed. What was notable about both was the level of engagement of the contributors with the project; debates were vigorous, rigorous and yet exceptionally good-natured. Yet, as with all such projects, there was still a great deal of work to be done before the final manuscript was ready to be delivered to Edward Elgar Publishing in March 2021. While it is the contributors, first of all, to which we owe our thanks, for their willingness and effort to have made this *Handbook* possible and – hopefully – a success, we would like to more generally thank all those colleagues who have contributed, in different ways, to this *Handbook*. We owe many thanks to Commissioning Editor Katy Crossan, Senior Assistant Editor Stephanie Hartley, Senior Desk Editor Christine Gowen, proofreader Gill Wheatley and the entire production team at Edward Elgar Publishing for their excellent work and acceptance of a manuscript that turned out to be much, much larger than originally anticipated.

A. Haroon Akram-Lodhi would like to thank generations of undergraduate and graduate students at London South Bank University, the International Institute of Social Studies of Erasmus University Rotterdam and Trent University in Peterborough, Canada for the contributions that they have made to establishing the need for this *Handbook*. Their engagement with and questioning of agrarian political economy and critical agrarian studies has made him a better scholar, and for that he is in their debt. He would also like to thank Catherine, Cameron and Ròisìn, who have been exceptionally gracious in accepting the absences that work on a project like this entails. Finally, he would like to dedicate his work on this project to his sister, Soraiya, who died while it was being steered toward completion. Ben McKay is grateful to the network of critical agrarian scholar-activists at the International Institute of Social Studies, as well as his colleagues from the BRICS Initiative for Critical Agrarian Studies, the Emancipatory Rural Politics Initiative and the Land Deal Politics Initiative for their rigorous work, vibrant discussions and debates over the years, which have certainly shaped and helped define this emerging field of study. He would also like to thank Chelsea Klinke for her excellent copy-editing work. Finally, a very special thanks to his support team – Carolina, Sophia and Thomas. Kristina Dietz and Bettina Engels are indebted to the fantastic GLOCON team and GLOCON's extended family all over the world, who have sustained and accompanied this and many other joint projects. A huge thanks also to Robin Faißt, Zoe Goldstein, Alina Heuser, Karin Hülsmann, Isabella Pfusterer and Mirka Schäfer for invaluable support in copy-editing the chapters.

1.　An introduction to the *Handbook of Critical Agrarian Studies*

A. Haroon Akram-Lodhi, Kristina Dietz, Bettina Engels and Ben M. McKay

When Marc Edelman and Wendy Wolford (2017) published 'Introduction: Critical Agrarian Studies in Theory and Practice', it represented a significant intervention to seek to realign a number of heterodox strands of rural development theory and practice. Strikingly, none of the references in their article actually contained the phrase 'critical agrarian studies'. The phrase itself has its most direct origin in the creation, in 2009, of the Initiatives in Critical Agrarian Studies at the International Institute of Social Studies in The Hague. The Initiative describes itself as:

> a community of like-minded critical scholars, development practitioners and movement activists from different parts of the world who are working on agrarian issues. It responds to the need for an initiative that builds and focuses on linkages, and advocates a mutually reinforcing co-production and mutually beneficial sharing of knowledge. (ISS n.d.)

This description, however, does not actually state what is meant by critical agrarian studies. In this light, Edelman and Wolford's paper represents the first attempt to map out the meaning of the field and, as such, it ambitiously seeks to shape the future of a pluralist field of study, action and advocacy rooted in peasant studies and the broader field of critical development studies (Veltmeyer, this volume). Critical agrarian studies represents a field of research that unites critical scholars from various disciplines concerned with understanding agrarian life, livelihoods, formations and their processes of change. It is 'critical' in the sense that it seeks to challenge dominant frameworks and ideas in order to reveal and challenge power structures and thus open up the possibilities for change. Claiming to combine research and activism, it is 'an institutionalized academic field, and an informal network (or various networks) that links professional intellectuals, agriculturalists, scientific journals and alternative media, and non-governmental development organizations, as well as activists' (Edelman and Wolford 2017, 962).

Edelman and Wolford (2017) stress that 'critical frameworks ... call into question dominant paradigms'. In international development studies, the dominant paradigm remains, still, modernization theory, which emerged in the 1950s. It is predicated on a dualism: that 'traditional' small-scale subsistence-oriented agriculture must be transformed into 'modern' capital-intensive market-oriented agriculture, and that this requires that the bulk of farmers eventually seek out off-farm livelihoods as waged workers or entrepreneurs in manufacturing and services. This approach to rural development remains predominant within the management of the World Bank; it is implicit within some strands of the United Nations such as divisions of the Food and Agriculture Organization; it lies behind the contemporary teaching of agricultural economics in most universities around the world; and in many countries, it is the foundation upon which ministries of agriculture and their 'partners' from bi- and multilateral donor agencies operate. Scholars from critical agrarian studies do not accept this paradigm, suggesting that it is predicated on the need to subsume everything to the market, to transform labour, natural resources, the means of production, goods and services into commodities, based on taken-for-granted principles of private property rights, money and competition—in short: capitalism (van der Linden 2016, 256f.). These values and principles are, in mainstream development theory and politics, associated with modernity, but are historically such recent social constructions that they are a dramatic 'break with the past' (Edelman and Wolford 2017, 961), in that the forms of knowledge they promote are not open-ended but rather closed-off. Closed bodies of knowledge make historically constructed social structures and institutions appear to be the inevitable way societies must be ordered. As opposed to this, the identification and analysis of biases within dominant paradigms in social science is done in order to construct 'alternative forms of knowing and of acting in the world' (Edelman and Wolford 2017, 962). This is the overarching purpose of critical agrarian studies.

In the remainder of this introductory chapter, we review the emergence of critical agrarian studies vis-à-vis its relationship with peasant studies. We then discuss the relationship between agrarian political economy and critical agrarian studies. Finally, the concluding section presents the structure of this *Handbook*.

FROM PEASANT STUDIES TO CRITICAL AGRARIAN STUDIES

As a field of study, the origin of critical agrarian studies lies in peasant studies, which as a distinct field of investigation emerged during the 1960s and early 1970s, rooted in various complementary but distinct epistemological approaches: theories of agrarian change derived from the classical analysis of the agrarian question (originally tracing back to Kautsky 1899; see Akram-Lodhi and Kay 2010; Watts, this volume); agrarian Marxism (Levien et al. 2018; Akram-Lodhi and Kay, this volume); the Indian 'mode of production' debate (Patnaik 1990); quantitative analysis of agricultural data sets that featured in the analysis of the Organization and Production School (Chayanov 1986 [1925]); and the finely grained, intimately detailed ethnographic analysis that featured in the work of anthropologists who often took their initial impetus from the work of such luminaries as Eric Wolf, Maurice Godelier, Jack Goody and Sidney Mintz. In the field of peasant studies, Marxist agrarian political economy or radical agrarian populist lenses often framed central research questions and empirical knowledge was generated drawing on various research approaches and methods from sociology, political science, economics, human geography and social anthropology. Cumulatively, manifold insights into and analysis of social change in rural societies around the world were established in the peasant studies literature.

In the past 25 years, this thread of theoretical and methodological approaches has, to a degree, unravelled. Rural research framed by the central concerns of the agrarian question has declined as social science orthodoxies tend to marginalize critical analysis, particularly in undergraduate university programmes and in policy-oriented research by think tanks, consultancies and international agencies. The agrarian question is fundamentally concerned with whether and to what extent capitalism is emerging in farming and agriculture, and the forms by which it does or does not emerge. However, in much of orthodox social science, capitalism is now taken for granted. The quantitative analysis of large data sets has now become the preserve of resolutely neoclassical economists, who have shaped statistical tools to reflect their concerns, in ways that can seriously compromise the reliability of the data that are collected and the resulting analysis that is produced (Akram-Lodhi 2010, 570–571; Oya and Pontara 2015). Many contemporary ethnographers are less interested in the rural, and those that are face significant personal, professional and financial constraints if they want to engage in the serious long-term work of understanding the detailed nuances of a rural social formation and the processes of change within which it is enmeshed (Greco, this volume).

The emergence of critical agrarian studies as a field of study is a response to the unravelling of the diverse approaches that have constituted peasant studies. With the latter, it shares Marxism as one of its common theoretical grounds, and thus engages with the processes, implications and limitations of pervasive capitalist insinuation into the agricultural sector; i.e. its transformation from subsistence and small-holder to capitalist production, including the separation of labour and the means of production, and its effects on class structure (Akram-Lodhi and Kay 2010, 179). Class is a key, though of course not the only, category of social structure and identity. How agrarian classes are historically and contemporarily formed, reproduced, transformed and cease to be is a central component of the analytical framework of critical agrarian studies. Class analysis is clearly more nuanced if it is multidimensional, identifying and exploring the cultural, ecological, social, political and economic factors and forces that facilitate or impede class formation.

Critical agrarian studies often combines micro- and macro-level analyses, connecting individual and local dynamics with the global political economy, and by embedding its analysis and findings within the context of global processes such as the ecological, climate and energy crisis, financialization, COVID-19 or geopolitical transformations (see Hunsberger; Clapp and Isakson; Akram-Lodhi, Oliveira and McKay, all in this volume). In providing this macro and global context, critical agrarian studies goes significantly beyond the terrain of peasant studies as it developed in the 1970s. It connects the local to the global, in terms of both structures and agency, incorporates a plurality of perspectives and this, in an era of neoliberal globalization, allows it to ask a broad set of questions that point toward alternatives (see Bush; Dietz and Engels, this volume).

Critical agrarian studies starts from a critique of 'peasant essentialism' that was widespread, including among critical scholars, in the 1970s and 1980s. Peasants do not form a homogenous class, nor are rural populations limited to peasants. Rather, the livelihoods of people living in the countryside build on animal husbandry and pastoralism, fisheries, paid labour in both the agricultural and non-agricultural sectors, both formal and informal, crafts, trading, artisanal mining and many others. Analyses of agrarian structures and change reveal how the peasantry relates to other social classes in terms of property relations, capital–labour relations and rural–urban relations (Bernstein and Byres 2001, 8). Whereas historical debates on agrarian questions were based on a much sharper line between the city and the countryside, it has now become a key assumption of critical agrarian studies that the rural and the urban are mutually constitutive of each other, in particular concerning patterns and linkages of production, distribution and consumption that increasingly transcend national borders.

FROM AGRARIAN POLITICAL ECONOMY TO CRITICAL AGRARIAN STUDIES

Scholars in critical agrarian studies often analyse agrarian change through an agrarian political economy lens by focusing on patterns of accumulation; on processes of production, i.e. the distribution of the means of production, technological changes and labour commodification; and on how agrarian politics interact with processes of accumulation and production. As defined in the mission statement of one of the leading journals in the field, the *Journal of Agrarian Change*, agrarian political economy investigates 'the social relations and dynamics of production and reproduction, property and power in agrarian formations and their processes of change, both historical and contemporary' (Bernstein 2010, 1). Henry Bernstein, in his fundamental 'small' book on *Class Dynamics of Agrarian Change*, summarizes this focus through four guiding questions (Bernstein 2010, 22–24): Who owns what? Who does what? Who gets what? What do they do with it? These four questions align with changes in: access and control over resources; agricultural production, most notably the distribution of assets, the capture of the benefits of technical change by social forces, and processes of commodification; the accumulation that emerges out of changing technical coefficients of production; and the political implications, across a myriad variety of forms, of changing patterns of production and growth. Cumulatively, these changes may or may not facilitate the rural transformation that is the object of knowledge among scholars and the purpose of action among advocates. However, the analysis of actually existing rural societies cannot limit itself to what was, within the agrarian question literature, an evaluation of the political economy of production, distribution, accumulation, consumption and the structural and institutional governance of these stocks and flows, but must also, critically, integrate within its arguments the socio-cultural dimensions of these processes.

Critical agrarian studies has a broader approach to agrarian questions, reflective of its more open and pluralist lines of inquiry. More recent contributions to the field emphasize the importance of 'local and national dynamics' (Bush and Martiniello 2017, 200). These studies investigate the respective histories of social struggles related to the economic valuation of agriculture under different systems (colonialism, capitalism, socialism) and the historical production of the social world. They look at the various dimensions of structural change in the countryside, and at human–nature and nature–culture relations (see Nightingale and Harcourt; Copeland, this volume). They go beyond rural–urban linkages by exploring 'nature in the city' and similar planning logics in urban and rural settings (Edelman and Wolford 2017; Watts 2009; Tornaghi and Halder, this volume).

As Edelman and Wolford (2017, 963) put it, '[c]ritical agrarian studies, like the Marxism on which it draws, is not a consensus field'. However, Marxist perspectives still remain a central theoretical foundation to critical agrarian studies, though not all empirical studies in the field explicitly refer to it. As Edelman and Wolford (2017, 965) note, the 'institutional forms' that critical agrarian studies takes are epitomized by the *Journal of Peasant Studies* and the *Journal of Agrarian Change*. Both of these journals were founded by Terence J. Byres, who co-edited both with Henry Bernstein. Under their editorships, both journals utilized explicitly Marxist theoretical frameworks to guide the empirical studies that they published. However, when the editorship of the *Journal of Peasant Studies* passed to Saturnino M. Borras, Jr., the journal adopted a more pluralist heterodox standpoint, continuing to publish papers within a Marxist framework but also publishing work rooted in critical non-Marxist social theory, such as radical agrarian populism, among others. However, while there are diverse analytical categories, class dynamics around land and labour remain central, as is reflected in this *Handbook*. In line with critical agrarian studies in general, the way categories are conceptualized vary depending on epistemological approaches and analytical aims. But beyond theoretical and methodological variation, scholars in the field are increasingly united by the claim that research and activism need to be linked to each other. This is equally reflected in the way Marxism is understood in critical agrarian studies: not as a theory for its own sake, but as a political intervention.

THE EDWARD ELGAR *HANDBOOK OF CRITICAL AGRARIAN STUDIES*

Critical agrarian studies is an emerging rather than an established field. Far from being a monolithic theory on agrarian issues, it is characterized by theoretical and methodological pluralism and innovation. Its internal variety, controversies and even contradictions represent its strengths rather than a weakness. This *Handbook* does not try to impose any theoretical standpoint but rather it seeks to bring together a wide range of contributions from scholars of various backgrounds and perspectives who are united by their enthusiasm for critical analysis of, and controversies about, historical and contemporary social structures and processes in agrarian and rural settings. The *Handbook* consists of 72 chapters, including this introduction. It brings together many of the leading scholars in critical agrarian studies, and attempts to lay down the key parameters of an emerging field by subdividing the chapters into six parts:

I. Origins: although critical agrarian studies has emerged out of an encounter with peasant studies, the historical origins of both lie in the late nineteenth century, and in the evolution of a set of ideas through the twentieth century in various world regions. The evolution of the ideas underpinning critical agrarian studies demonstrates its historically innovative character, its diversity, its pluralism and its willingness to fundamentally rethink perceived orthodoxies.

II. Concepts: underpinning the diverse theoretical approaches of critical agrarian studies lie a set of central concepts that are deployed in work that falls within it. Concepts explicitly or implicitly lie behind the analytical explanations and advocacy that are witnessed in the field of critical agrarian studies and understanding and interrogating such concepts is of central importance in evaluating the claims that are made within the field about understanding processes of social change.

III. Methodologies: the way in which those that work within critical agrarian studies come to 'know' and understand a contemporary rural setting and the changes that are being witnessed starts from different epistemologies and disciplines and the methodologies that different epistemologies and disciplines rely upon. At the same time, however, critical agrarian studies explicitly confronts the strengths and weaknesses of the epistemologies and methodologies that are adopted in order to produce understandings and explanations of social development and change that are both stronger and more finely grained.

IV. Regional perspectives: the central concerns of critical agrarian studies demonstrate both overlapping domains of investigation and debate and unique specificities when examined at the regional and subregional levels. This part of the *Handbook* therefore offers a limited number of perspectives from major regions and countries in order to introduce readers to how agrarian change is playing out in both similar and different ways in important contemporary rural settings.

V. Debates: the key areas of contemporary investigation and analysis within critical agrarian studies are wide-ranging and diverse. This part of the *Handbook* deploys both the key concepts within the field and the epistemologies engendered by such concepts to provide insights and arguments into some of the key domains of contemporary research and advocacy within critical agrarian studies. Thorough but by no means exclusive, this part of the *Handbook* will facilitate the capacity of readers to quickly come to understand a broad array of key analytical perspectives within critical agrarian studies.

VI. Trajectories: as an open-ended field of investigation and advocacy, future developments within critical agrarian studies will emerge out of both its action-oriented research as well as an intersection with and dialogue between it and other fields of research and activism. By opening up a number of intersections between critical agrarian studies and other fields it becomes clear that the forward trajectories of it remain to be defined and as such produce a rich and often yet-to-be unearthed terrain for future research and engagement.

Many of the chapters could, indeed, fit into more than one section. However, by suggesting this structure, we hope to contribute to the systematization of an otherwise heterogeneous and exciting field of research. While we have attempted to be extensive in our coverage, there will no doubt be shortcomings and gaps as critical agrarian studies remains a highly diverse and emerging interdisciplinary field of study.

This *Handbook* seeks to provide students, scholars and activists with an overview of the field of critical agrarian studies and insights into its variety of epistemologies, methodologies, theoretical questions, empirical issues and contemporary debates. It will be suitable, we hope, as a book of reference and as a resource for teaching at all levels. It is also aimed at readers not yet familiar with critical agrarian studies—and if flipping through this *Handbook* sparks interest and motivates readers to delve deeper into the field, this joint project by a considerable number of authors will have accomplished its goal.

REFERENCES

Akram-Lodhi, A.H. (2010), Land, labour and agrarian transition in Vietnam, *Journal of Agrarian Change*, 10(4), 564–580.

Akram-Lodhi, A.H.; Kay, C. (2010), Surveying the agrarian question (Part 1): Unearthing foundations, exploring diversity, *Journal of Peasant Studies*, 37(1), 177–202.

Bernstein, H. (2010), *Class Dynamics of Agrarian Change*, Halifax: Fernwood.

Bernstein, H.; Byres, T.J. (2001), From peasant studies to agrarian change, *Journal of Agrarian Change*, 1(1), 1–56.

Bush, R.; Martiniello, G. (2017), Food riots and protest: Agrarian modernizations and structural crises, *World Development*, 91, 193–207.

Chayanov, A.V. (1986 [1925]), *The Theory of Peasant Economy*, Madison, WI: University of Wisconsin Press.

Edelman, M.; Wolford, W. (2017), Introduction: Critical agrarian studies in theory and practice, *Antipode*, 49(4), 1–18.

ISS (n.d.), *Initiatives in Critical Agrarian Studies (ICAS)*, The Hague: International Institute of Social Studies, accessed 26 September 2020 at www.iss.nl/en/research/research-networks/initiatives-critical -agrarian-studies.

Kautsky, K. (1899), *Die Agrarfrage: Eine Uebersicht über die Tendenzen der modernen Landwirthschaft und die Agrarpolitik der Sozialdemokratie*, Stuttgart: Dietz.

Levien, M.; Watts, M.; Yan, H. (2018), Agrarian Marxism, *Journal of Peasant Studies*, 45(5–6), 853–883.

Oya, C.; Pontara, N. (2015), *Rural Wage Employment in Developing Countries: Theory, Evidence, and Policy*, London: Routledge.

Patnaik, U. (1990), *Agrarian Relations and Accumulation: The 'Mode of Production' Debate in India*, Mumbai: Sameeksha Trust.

van der Linden, M. (2016), Final thoughts, in Kocka, J.; van der Linden, M. (eds), *Capitalism: The Reemergence of a Historical Concept*, London: Bloomsbury, 251–266.

Watts, M. (2009), The Southern question: Agrarian questions of labour and capital, in Akram-Lodhi, A.H.; Kay, C. (eds), *Peasants and Globalization: Political Economy, Rural Transformation and the Agrarian Question*, London: Routledge, 262–287.

PART I

ORIGINS

2. Frontiers, regimes and learning from history

Ulbe Bosma and Eric Vanhaute

Today's world knows a wide patchwork of social and environmental regimes; some are agrarian – this pertains particularly to the poorest areas of the world – whereas others have reached the state of post-industrial societies. This global landscape of different socio-metabolic regimes constitutes a deep source of contention. It reflects huge global inequalities and is the outcome of different roles in the rise of the capitalist world economy. This contention includes questions about ecologically unequal exchange – the unequal flows of the proceeds of land and nature – the disproportionate utilization of ecological systems and the externalization of negative environmental costs by core industrializing and industrialized countries. In sum, it pertains to the prevalence of history.

Global capitalist expansion derived much of its impetus from the unstinting expansion of vast rural and agrarian frontiers of labour, food, energy and raw materials. Slave-based sugar and cotton production, for example, supplied the calories and clothing that industrializing Britain could never have procured from its own soil, providing so-called 'ecological relief' at the expense of others (Mintz 1985; Pomeranz 2000; Bosma 2019). Up to now, capitalist growth has overcome problems related to the declining resilience of its production system thanks to the progressive incorporation and appropriation of natural resources and labour through the constant opening up of new frontier zones. Boundless accumulation and geographical appropriation have driven capitalism's extension to new, not yet fully commodified, zones.

Capitalism's dependence on external resources increases over time, as it requires ever larger energy inputs in order to reproduce itself. Historically natural limits have been overcome mainly through geographical expansion and production intensification. This occurs in a very unequal way. The accumulation strategies that work at the beginning of a cycle of expansion, through particular forms of science, technology, territoriality and governance, create new forms of exhaustion, which in turn increase production costs and commodity prices and reduce profits. The effects can be highly contradictory.

The study of multiple commodity frontiers throughout the history of capitalism helps us to map its relentless expansion, but also the unevenness and diversity of that expansion (Moore 2000, 2015; Beckert et al. 2021). The concept of the commodity frontier explains how place-specific commodity production shapes and is shaped by the socio-spatial expansion, as well as the deepening and widening, of capitalism's social division of labour (see also Lund and Borg Rasmussen 2021). Commodity frontier expansion is the classic instance of capitalism's 'metabolic rift', whereby the nutrient cycle between town and country is progressively disrupted, leading to ecological exhaustion in the countryside and worsening pollution in cities (Foster 1999).

The commodity frontier is a conceptual device that enables an integrated, historically informed approach to the transformation of the global countryside. It deals with the dynamics of capitalist commodity production in relation to social, economic and ecological inequality, depletion and resilience. It provides a multi-scalar and *longue durée* understanding of the workings of capitalism, its immense transformative capabilities and flexibility, but also its limits, and the feedbacks and resistances it provokes.

In this chapter we argue that the complex relationship between capitalist development and rural transformation requires a global historical-comparative approach that takes into account both historical variation and spatial divergences. We propose the analytical devices of commodity regimes and commodity frontiers to link structural changes with local resistance and accommodation.

REGIMES OF COMMODITY FRONTIER EXPANSION

To systematically analyse how processes of value extraction vary across time and place, how and why such variations are patterned and how and why key dynamics change, we need to reflect upon the periodization of capitalism. An influential approach is Friedmann's (2009) and McMichael's (2013, 2021) work on successive food regimes. Thinking about food regimes has developed into a device for periodization, and a proposal for a comparative historical method that links broad political economic change to local agency and contestation. The regime concept is a meta-historical device that allows us to capture the ways in which different societal domains at commodity frontiers (ecological, technological, social and political) are organized and related to one another. Every commodity regime is characterized by particular labour relations, particular patterns of land ownership, particular forms of the insertion of capital, as well as particular sets of technologies and state policies.

While capitalism has to be understood as a singular historical system, the ways in which frontiers have become integrated into globalizing markets vary greatly over space and time. About five to six centuries ago, global commodity trade began to involve large populations in production and processing, exerting a significant impact on local, and increasingly global, social and ecological systems (De Zwart and Van Zanden 2018). By and large, one can identify three, maybe four, different regimes in the advancement of global commodity production: an early capitalist regime, which lasted until the Industrial Revolution gained traction (by the mid-nineteenth century); an industrial regime, marked by the prominent roles of industrial markets and the state from the mid-nineteenth century to the 1970s; a corporate regime, dominated by a new market ideology and transnational businesses; and, conditionally, a still unfolding contemporary regime from the early 2000s onward (Beckert et al. 2021). Each regime had its own trajectory of labour relations, property relations, technological progress, roles of the state, degrees of vertical integration between countryside and end producers and movements of reaction and resistance. The two key transformations demarcating these regimes were the Industrial Revolution, as it became transnational by the mid-nineteenth century, and the emergence of exceptionally powerful transnational businesses beginning in the 1970s. These two transitions coincided with the changing role of the state, which was more prominent in economic life between the 1850s and 1970s than either before or since.

The first regime, which lasted from the 1450s to the 1850s, was characterized by the direct and violent dispossession of people from land and nature, as well as unfree labour systems with a proliferation of chattel slavery, peonage and subcontracting. Its forceful expansion was sanctioned by states, but its principal expansionary driver was merchant capital (Wallerstein 1974; Beckert 2014). In the second regime, which lasted from the 1850s to the 1970s, industrial markets and interventionist states gained prominent roles, as did multinational capital, global bulk commodity markets and new transport and communication technologies. This thoroughly reinforced the infrastructural capabilities to shape the conditions under which frontiers expanded. In the 1970s, a new so-called corporate commodity regime emerged, driven by a refurbished ideology of free commodity markets and the concentration of transnational corporate power. This was reinforced by the changing role of the state vis-à-vis transnational corporations and financial institutions, and new global political divisions among and between North and South, reproducing and in some ways remapping imperial, colonial and Cold War political geographies. The concentration of power in the hands of a few producers took a quantum leap as commodity trade and financial institutions became tightly connected from the 1980s on. Since the early 2000s, firms and financial actors looking for new investment opportunities have come to own or finance increasing amounts of land around the world, largely through dispossession, and often with the assistance of state power. Rising authoritarianism around the world is pressuring people and environments at commodity frontiers in South America, the United States, South East Asia and elsewhere. Companies, often with states' assistance, are expanding into radically new production and information technologies (Srnicek 2016). As a still-unfolding regime, many questions remain about which processes and relations will be most important in this phase of capitalism, which ones will spur or encounter the most resistance and what forms will this resistance take.

Clearly, there are overlaps between the different regimes, which underscores the fact that each regime sets at least some of the conditions for the one that follows. Over time, these historical movements became increasingly interwoven, revolutionizing the preceding production systems and incorporating new commodity frontiers. This continual process of frontier expansion has transformed former rural societies and configured the world of today.

Commodity regimes have been the subject of profound social and political contestation. Together with the physical limits to further expansion, contestation has been a destabilizing force, eventually leading to a transition towards a new regime. This speaks against a teleological or linear interpretation of capitalist expansion and urges us to try to uncover its historical and spatial logic. Historical research shows us that each commodity regime exhibits particular frictions in the realms of nature, land and labour, inciting resistance and counter narratives (Mintz 1985; Bosma 2019). It also shows us that capitalism at a global scale has, so far, overcome these frictions by various fixes; using 'fixes' as a metaphor for particular sets of solutions to capitalist social and ecological crises. The most well known is the spatial fix (Harvey 2001), but we can also discern technological fixes (particularly since the Industrial Revolution), state-led fixes (with the rise of nineteenth-century bureaucracies) and since the 1970s corporate fixes (Arrighi 2004). These fixes are cumulative and become entangled over time.

Since capitalism inherently seeks the cheapest answers to environmental and resource problems, it often comes down to the export of these problems from richer and more powerful countries to poorer and more peripheral countries, through the opening up of new frontiers of commodity cultivation or extraction and even waste disposal. This can be regarded as a spatial fix. It can lead to robber capitalism, the extraction of resources by the dispossession of local communities, resulting in highly uneven development. Global treaties on environmental protection (a state-led fix) and technological progress (a technological fix) may shift some parameters, but they will not change the basic contradictions of capitalism and its hunger for cheap labour, nature and land. Historical configurations, rather than objective physical conditions and technological limits, endanger our common future. The problem is not about a lack of technology to ensure global survival. It is about the political will to change the param-eters of human survival, despite the fact that most politicians, for instance, agree that global warming is human-caused and poses an existential threat. Moreover, even if political blaming and anxieties can be overcome in the international political arena, there is no guarantee that the burden of the resulting political arrangements will not fall on the shoulders of the world's poorest rural communities.

The prospect is real that these communities will be shorthanded in the geopolitical tussles over ecological survival. History has many grim lessons to teach in this regard. The past centuries are marked by stronger societies, colonial powers usually, who compensated their ecological deficits through colonial exploitation. And as recently as the 1980s and 1990s, the World Bank and International Monetary Fund forced governments of the Global South out of their national food markets, while at the same time the protection of farmers in the United States and the European Union reached staggering heights. Meanwhile, the most powerful countries of the world still import far more biomaterial than they export, and in addition they tend to export their most polluting industries. This approach to historical regimes, through the lens of multiple frictions and fixes, surpasses single-factor explanations. This in turn is pivotal for grasping present socio-ecological conditions and contestations, and the future options we have towards engendering more equal societies.

THE IMPORTANCE OF HISTORY

Historical concepts are crucial for understanding present issues in longer trajectories. For a long time, social scientists have argued that global capitalism emerged on the eve of the Columbian voyages across the Atlantic; that capitalism, in fact, was born global. Commodity frontier expansion and the transformation of the countryside was hence one of its key features from the very beginning, and the historical perspective illuminates its determining impact. Global historians have picked up on some of these ideas. Studies of the history of commod-ities and of commodity chains have persuasively shown the deep links between agriculture and industry, between the countryside and the city and between the household and expanding production systems (Gereffi and Korzeniewicz 1994; Collins 2014). These studies reveal how the global has emerged from local configurations, and they show the essential role played by the politics, ideas and collective actions of rural cultivators, especially in the Global South, who have been central in shaping commodity frontiers and thus the political economy of global capitalism. Similarly, many historians have been sensitive to the ecological dimension of the economic and technological divergence between core and periphery (Hornborg et al. 2007; Ross 2017). Since for most of human history technological advances were slow and piecemeal, the global economy derived much of its growth from the unflagging expansion of vast frontiers of labour, food, energy and raw materials. This started as early as the fourteenth century, when the Baltics began to provide timber and wheat for the relatively densely popu-lated and urbanized coastal provinces of the Low Countries.

Throughout its history, global capitalism has been organized through frontiers, transforming socio-ecological relations and producing more and more goods and services that circulate through an expanding series of exchanges. The commodity frontier approach, which devel-oped from world-system analysis, moves analytically from chains of commodities, to labour relations, to frontiers of spatial expansion that include not only land and labour but also the incorporation and extraction of non-human nature (Moore 2015). Over time, commodity frontiers have exhibited regularly shifting combinations of labour systems, property regimes, technology and state interventions. Any systematic analysis of the long history of these frontiers thus needs to begin by acknowledging this diversity. Yet we also need to acknowledge that despite diversity, we can see certain patterns. Properly analysed, these patterns help us to understand the historical development of capitalism and the transformation of the global countryside. Applying the conceptual device of regimes, we learn that historical capitalism developed in a very unequal way. It engendered widely divergent forms of expansion and exploitation, marking capitalism as a highly adaptive and flexible system. And just like capitalism more broadly, each regime contains profound tensions, with dynamics that were (and are) the subject of fierce contestation.

There are compelling reasons to shift academic attention to the global countryside: global poverty is overwhelmingly concentrated in rural areas, while a considerable share of global warming is caused by industrial agriculture, and the loss of biodiversity leads to a decreasing capacity for ecological regeneration. Current debates on 'sustainability' are unduly optimistic, as they leave out the historical trajectory of capitalist commodity regimes and tend to overlook the fact that centuries of global commodity production have seriously weakened institutional capabilities in the global peripheries. Meanwhile, structural approaches tend to homogenize the global countryside, ignoring agency that might change these regimes.

There is an urgent need to 'learn from history', to uncover the rootedness of sequential commodity regimes in a history of six centuries of global capitalism which has created massive inequalities. The complexities of this global condition require an historically informed and comparative analytical approach that unites the myriad case studies which reveal how local rural populations and societies resist, accommodate or even benefit from capitalism. By doing so, we can address an urgent and unresolved question within the current debates on global growth, inequality and sustainability, namely how to avoid simply applying another set of fixes that would allow the relentless exploitation of the global countryside to continue.

FURTHER READING

Barbier, E.B. (2011), *Scarcity and Frontiers: How Economies Have Developed through Natural Resource Exploitation*, Cambridge: Cambridge University Press.

Beckert, S. (2014), *Empire of Cotton: A Global History*, New York: Alfred A. Knopf.

Beckert, S.; Bosma, U.; Schneider, M.; Vanhaute, E. (2021), Commodity frontiers and the transformation of the global countryside: A research agenda, *Journal of Global History*, open access, https://doi.org/10.1017/S1740022820000455.

Bosma, U. (2019), *The Making of a Periphery: How Island Southeast Asia Became a Mass Exporter of Labor*, New York: Columbia University Press.

Moore, J. (2015), *Capitalism in the Web of Life: Ecology and the Accumulation of Capital*, London: Verso.

REFERENCES

Arrighi, G. (2004), Spatial and other fixes of historical capitalism, *Journal of World-Systems Research*, 10(2), 527–539.

Beckert, S. (2014), *Empire of Cotton: A Global History*, New York: Alfred A. Knopf.

Beckert, S.; Bosma, U.; Schneider, M.; Vanhaute, E. (2021), Commodity frontiers and the transformation of the global countryside: A research agenda, *Journal of Global History*, open access, https://doi.org/10.1017/S1740022820000455.

Bosma, U. (2019), *The Making of a Periphery: How Island Southeast Asia Became a Mass Exporter of Labor*, New York: Columbia University Press.

Collins, J. (2014), A Feminist approach to overcoming the closed boxes of the commodity chain, in Dunaway, W.A. (ed.), *Gendered Commodity Chains: Seeing Women's Work and Households in Global Production*, Stanford, CA: Stanford University Press, 27–37.

De Zwart, P.; Van Zanden, J. (2018), *The Origins of Globalization: World Trade in the Making of the Global Economy, 1500–1800*, Cambridge: Cambridge University Press.

Foster, J.B. (1999), Marx's theory of metabolic rift: Classical foundations for environmental sociology, *American Journal of Sociology*, 105(2), 366–405.

Friedmann, H. (2009), Moving food regimes forward: Reflections on symposium essays, *Agriculture and Human Values*, 26(4), 335–344.

Gereffi, G.; Korzeniewicz, M. (eds) (1994), *Commodity Chains and Global Capitalism*, Westport, CT: Praeger.

Harvey, D. (2001), Globalization and the 'spatial fix', *Geographische Revue*, 2, 23–30.

Hornborg, A.; McNeill, J.R.; Martinez-Alier, J. (eds) (2007), *Rethinking Environmental History: World-System History and Global Environmental Change*, Lanham, MD: Altamira Press.

Lund, C.; Borg Rasmussen, M. (2021), Frontiers, in Akram-Lodhi, A.H.; Dietz, K.; Engels, B.; McKay, B.M. (eds), *Handbook of Critical Agrarian Studies*, Cheltenham, UK and Northampton, MA, USA: Edward Elgar Publishing.

McMichael, P. (2013), *Food Regimes and Agrarian Questions*, Halifax: Fernwood Books.

McMichael, P. (2021), Food regimes, in Akram-Lodhi, A.H.; Dietz, K.; Engels, B.; McKay, B.M. (eds), *Handbook of Critical Agrarian Studies*, Cheltenham, UK and Northampton, MA, USA: Edward Elgar Publishing.

Mintz, S.W. (1985), *Sweetness and Power: The Place of Sugar in Modern History*, New York: Viking.

Moore, J. (2000), Sugar and the expansion of the early modern world-economy commodity frontiers, ecological transformation, and industrialization, *Review: A Journal of the Fernand Braudel Center*, 23(3), 409–433.

Moore, J. (2015), *Capitalism in the Web of Life: Ecology and the Accumulation of Capital*, London: Verso.

Pomeranz, K. (2000), *The Great Divergence: China, Europe and the Making of the Modern World Economy*, Princeton, NJ: Princeton University Press.

Ross, C. (2017), *Ecology and Power in the Age of Empire: Europe and the Transformation of the Tropical World*, Oxford: Oxford University Press.

Srnicek, N. (2016), *Platform Capitalism*, Cambridge: Polity.

Wallerstein, I. (1974), *The Modern World-System, Vol. I: Capitalist Agriculture and the Origins of the European World-Economy in the Sixteenth Century*, New York: Academic Press.

3. Origins of peasant studies

Harriet Friedmann

INTRODUCTION

Peasant studies emerged in the context of debates about development and agriculture. Were peasants doomed to disappear, as both dominant and Marxist development theories posited? If so, how could we explain their 'persistence' theoretically and practically, and how could we understand the particularities of rural people in each country? If the term *peasants* was used at all in the 1950s and early 1960s, it was mainly by anthropologists who understood them as remnants of 'traditional' lifeways, and by political organizers in colonial and post-colonial societies organizing national liberation struggles among majority agrarian populations. Most shared the belief that peasant life and peasant struggles were part of a journey towards industrial and urban societies. This hegemonic belief was reinforced by competition between Cold War blocs, which asked not *whether* but *how* peasants would give way to modern agriculture.

The study of peasants required first that they be defined, a project that is still underway. This openness is one of the strengths of what came to be called *peasant studies* and later *agrarian studies*. At the time, it was innovative simply to use the word positively, to look at land-based communities as active agents in constructing the world rather than exotic leftovers from an amorphous past called 'traditional'. The new field was led by researchers studying agrarian countries struggling for independence from colonial rule or against international relations that seemed to reinforce dependence even after formal independence. Early on, it was clear that historical cases, first of all Russia, but also early transitions to capitalism in Europe, and settler colonial agriculture were relevant. Those engaged in these debates realized that comparative empirical research was crucial and that it had to embrace histories of all places.

This chapter opens with the context in which peasant studies emerged in the early 1970s. The key themes are *development* and *Cold War* as contexts for anti-colonial struggles, especially the defining struggle of the time, the Vietnam War. It then turns to the (re)discovery of *peasants* as key agents of present history, not simply, for instance, of past revolutions in Russia or France. Peasant studies recognized rural people as diverse and living in particular places, not simply a leftover of an amorphous past. Once begun, careful comparative research inquired into what we might now call the 'resilience' but was then called the 'persistence' of households as farming enterprises and parts of communities, even when participating in wage work. The next section summarizes the specific history of the Peasants Seminar and the *Journal of Peasant Studies* (JPS) in 1972 (Byres 2001), which created the first fora for scholars to engage across disciplines in an ever widening sphere of contexts and issues, eventually linking to emerging studies of family, gender and patriarchy. I conclude with a brief reflection on the opening of world politics and of scholarship to the centrality of food, farming and land to social and ecological politics, and thus to critical agrarian studies.

CONTEXT: DEVELOPMENT AND ITS CRITICS

In the 1960s a veil began to be lifted from modernist ideas about peasantries. National states struggling against colonial rule and international policies of *development* were premised on the role of rural dwellers as providers of food and labour for industries and cities. The idea of *development* was understood as growth of *industry*, which in the period was measured as one of three national economic sectors; the others were *agriculture* – destined to decline – and *services* – destined also to rise. The conflation of *development* with *industry* has since extended to industrial agriculture. However, the tripartite division of sectors was an obstacle to seeing the emerging agro-food system, which caught farmers between what were called *upstream* and *downstream* industries and services (Chombart de Lauwe 1979; Malassis 1979; Busch and Lacy 1984).

In the modernist view, rural dwellers were to be concentrated into fewer, larger and more specialized farms, to increase productivity for a few crops and to send those specific foods (mostly grains) and labour to cities. For tropical colonial and post-colonial export crops, the goal was to bring in foreign exchange to support domestic industrialization. It was assumed, based on theories of political economy prevalent since the English enclosures of the sixteenth to eighteenth centuries, that land appropriation and rural exodus would lead to the 'end of peasants' in favour of modern agriculture (Mendras 1970). This would improve the wealth of nations.

Classical Marxist texts assumed the same, seeing capitalist development as the creation of a proletariat destined to revolution. They focused on Lenin's (1899) analysis of differentiation of peasantries into classes of agricultural owners and labourers, and Kautsky's (1988 [1899]) exploration of complex ways they might contribute to capitalism as a path toward socialism (see Watts, this volume).

The main disagreements within the development paradigm were about which 'path' from agrarian to industrial society was most effective: the 'collectivization' model of the Soviet Union versus the 'family farm' model of the United States (US). The two sides of the Cold War competed over how best to *modernize* land and labour by replacing human and animal energy with industrial methods based on chemicals, machines and cheap fossil energy.[1] *Modernization*, the prevailing idea in social sciences, imagined that with the help of foreign aid and expert advice to the 'backward' countries in Latin America, Africa and Asia, urban industries would emerge based on labour released or expelled from countrysides and supply food to growing urban proletariats. Even in the US, farmers who refused to adopt new technologies (and attendant debts and dependence) were understood to resist the 'diffusion of innovation' (Rogers 1962). And even the influential comparative study of rural uprisings by Marxist historian Eric Hobsbawm (1959) was called *Primitive Rebels: Studies in Archaic Forms of Social Movement*.

Threats of peasant unrest were interpreted by modernizers within a Cold War framework. Selective and partial land reform initiatives in the US-led bloc were more thoroughly implemented in countries thought to be vulnerable to following the Chinese revolutionary example. Technological innovations were called a *Green Revolution*, as an alternative to a potential *Red Revolution*, understood as an alliance with the Soviet Union or China. Following the idea that so-called underdeveloped countries were on a train whose tracks led toward industrial economies, land reforms in the capitalist bloc were intended to create commercial 'family farms' on an idealized US model; to replace human and animal power by machines, the Green

Revolution introduced laboratory-bred seeds, chemical fertilizers and pesticides and machinery to change from mixed, labour-intensive *farms* into specialized rice or wheat *enterprises*.

It is good to remember that in its early days *development* included a focus on wellbeing, always rhetorically and partly in practice. Development projects built institutions for education and health care, and public infrastructure such as roads and bureaucracies to deliver them to society (as well as to connect to mines and otherwise serve capital). At the time, these were understood to be part of the path toward industrial and democratic societies.[2] With many variations, development policies often included government support for farmers to *modernize* themselves through marketing boards, cooperatives, farm organizations and credit. The most extensive of these outside the Soviet bloc were in Mexico, which had experienced a successful peasant-led revolution in the early twentieth century, and which for the US reinforced the need to manage rural unrest likely to accompany a deep transition imposed on rural societies.

Critics of *development* arose in a hopeful context. National liberation struggles, for instance in India, Ghana, Indonesia and Egypt, had led to independent states, but these came to be caught in the political dilemma of promoting industrialization in societies whose peasants had provided much of the political and military energy for independence struggles. In the United Nations (UN), a growing number of states called themselves the *Third World* – to oppose a forced choice between First (US-led) and Second (USSR-led) worlds. They soon became a majority (Hoogvelt 1982) and created a new UN agency in 1966 to represent their shared interest, the UN Conference on Trade and Development. However, the new agency shared the view of *development* as industrial growth. The movement it promoted for a New International Division of Labour proposed new trade institutions in place of unfair practices by already industrial countries, especially import controls against Third World agricultural exports, which limited foreign exchange earnings to support industrialization (Toye 2014). The project had support in progressive parties then in power in Europe, which eventually took the form of the Brandt Report *North-South* (Brandt Commission 1983 [1980]). The regime they proposed to change – unsuccessfully – was one in which new states had little choice but to welcome non-emergency food aid, despite its negative impact on domestic farmers and food markets (Friedmann 1993).

REDISCOVERING PEASANTS

Critics of *development* in the West and Third World were challenged to explain two policies: land reform and the Green Revolution. Both were designed to manage a transition to cities and industries without unrest or revolution. Were these social and technical projects part of a deepening of capitalism through proletarianization, and thus potentially a step in the direction of socialism? Or were they something else? Marx had compared peasants to 'a sack of potatoes' with no internal relations and therefore incapable of collective agency (Marx 1851–1852). Although he wrote differently elsewhere, the sack of potatoes analogy was influential. It converged with the disregard, even contempt, by modernist social science for rural dwellers as exotic remnants of 'traditional societies'. How then could the 'persistence of peasants', not only as rural dwellers, but as active creators of contemporary capitalist and socialist societies, be explained?

Eric Wolf's (1966) ground-breaking small book *Peasants* broke with the then dominant anthropological approach to peasants as trapped in precapitalist/premodern stasis. He defined peasants as classes in relation to ruling classes and states in each nation. In his next book, Wolf (1969) reframed Mexican, Russian, Chinese, Vietnamese, Algerian and Cuban revolutions as *Peasant Wars of the Twentieth Century*. These crossed the categorical lines of *socialist revolution* and anti-colonial *national liberation struggles*. Like many of the founders (and later practitioners) of peasant studies, Wolf cited the Vietnamese and Chinese revolutions especially as inspirations (see Bernstein and Byres 2001; Bernstein et al. 2018). The Vietnam War was difficult to understand in relation to dominant modernist ideas, since an agrarian country was sustaining a long war of independence against the greatest military power in the world, eventually defeating the US after earlier defeating its French colonial rulers. Across disciplines, scholars were asking how peasants fit into prevailing debates about modes of production, social formations and, more widely, the emergence of capitalism past and present. Especially influential were the writings of James Scott (1977, 1985) on the moral economy of peasants and their everyday resistance to power.

The appearance of A.V. Chayanov's *Theory of Peasant Economy* in English translation in 1966 exhilarated (and infuriated) scholars struggling with dynamics of past and present family farms and villages. Chayanov and his colleagues had created a comprehensive body of ethnographic and statistical studies of farm and village households in Russia in the decades before the Revolution of 1917 and in the Soviet Union in the early creative decade before forced collectivization. Chayanov was the leading member of the 'neo-populist school' of Russia and Eastern Europe in the 1920s, where well-developed intellectual institutions existed in social contexts of massive peasantries, quite different from those of Western Europe (Bernstein et al. 2018). Their detailed ethnographic and statistical studies of peasant households and communities are arguably still unmatched. Their approach, summarized by Mark Harrison (1975, 390), 'emphasised the viability of peasant agriculture and its ability to survive and prosper under any circumstances'. Since peasants had no necessary tendency to divide into classes of rich and poor, they could raise the technical levels of agricultural production through cooperation and support by experts. They did not have to follow either a capitalist or socialist 'road', but could forge a distinct 'peasant path' building on family small holdings. Bernstein and Byres (2001, 4) later reflected that:

> The Russian debates from the 1890s to the moment of Stalin's collectivization of agriculture in 1929 were probably the most important single source of subsequent Marxist thought about agrarian questions in poor countries, notably for communist parties in Asia.

The English translation of Chayanov's work entered wider debates of the 1970s on history, development, dependency, social formations and transition between modes of production (Bernstein 2015). Chayanov (1966 [1925]) demonstrated the existence of two types of social differentiation. One was cyclical mobility (or 'demographic differentiation') based on the changing balance of workers and consumers within patriarchal households. This was a centripetal force, leading to the stability of peasantry as a whole. The other dynamic was centrifugal, namely the permanent differentiation of peasants into classes of owners, workers and 'middle peasants'. Class differentiation was the only one expected by most analysts across the political spectrum, including Lenin (1899). Thus, Bernstein (1979) analysed peasant household persistence (or dissolution) in light of penetration (or not) of commodity relations into their social and material reproduction. Whether cyclical mobility or class differentiation would prevail became an empirical question.

Even before his magisterial writings on Chayanov, Shanin (1971; cf. 1987) had collected a wide set of writings from many disciplines in the first edition of *Peasants and Peasant Societies*. In *The Awkward Class*, Shanin (1972) elaborated Chayanov's data and interpretation to show that Russian peasant communities could and did resist modernization, both before and after the Revolution. They did so in the context of particular land laws of pre-revolutionary Russia, which allowed for reallocation by (patriarchal) village councils according to changing demographic cycles. Resistance to collectivization could be explained by the intersection of peasant logic with specific historical events. The logic of peasant societies, including participation in markets and occasional wage labour, privileged household reproduction. Therefore, monetary income could support rather than undermine family and village relations (Chayanov 1966 [1925]). By extension, this could apply to understanding politics in all societies with large peasantries – what later came to be called *agrarian societies*.

As Shanin (1986, 2009) explained later, Chayanov's bottom-up conception of 'Theory of Vertical Cooperation' was a challenge to the forced collectivization of agriculture. Official Soviet ideology was threatened by this insight. The murder of Chayanov and suppression of these important studies by the Stalin regime in 1937 enforced silence until Chayanov's writings were finally made available in the West.

New theories of *peasants* opened Marxist theory in the 1970s to complexities of a capitalist world, especially in countries emerging from colonial empires. Although much debate in early peasant studies presumed a conflict between the theories of Lenin and Chayanov, Banaji (1976a) argued that the two were compatible. Based on empirical research in India, he wrote, 'Chayanov's theories ... impart a logical and truly historical content to those assumptions of Marxist tradition which form the theoretical foundation of the work of Kautsky and Lenin' (see Watts, this volume). In the same year, Banaji (1976b) had translated from the original German a summary of the classical Marxist interpretation by Kautsky (1988 [1899]), called *The Agrarian Question*. An influential argument by Bernstein (1979) drew on Banaji's (1977) concept of 'wage-labour equivalents' to analyse 'subsumption of peasant simple commodity production in the circuit of capital' in African (and by extension other) post-colonial societies. This analytical move connected rural populations of the Third World to the precapitalist histories of peasants in societies that had become industrial (Moore 1966; Skocpol 1979), and to the present of farmers under pressure from change in industrial capitalist countries.

Analysts of the history of family agriculture drew on Chayanov to explain, for instance, how risk worked in decisions to balance commodity crops with self-provisioning by sharecroppers in the US South (Wright 1975), and how settler farms in the US and other settler colonies outcompeted capitalist farms in England and Prussia through the 'self-exploitation' of family labour (Friedmann 1978). Rural sociologists, first in France (Servolin 1972) and later in North America and England (Newby 1979; Buttel 2001), began to introduce sociology of agriculture into rural sociology, which had so far devoted itself to studies of the supposed inevitable decline of rural populations and communities. Sociology of agriculture in the US had until then focused on labour studies, drawing on theories of (implicitly urban) industrial labour to study capitalist agriculture in California, which was dominated by large landowning capitalists and armies of (mainly migrant) workers (Berry 1977; Friedland et al. 1981).

Sociologists of agriculture began to also study 'family farmers' in grain and livestock. They inquired into the forces leading to differentiation or persistence of family enterprises through processes of concentration, legal incorporation, participation in world markets and domination over supposedly independent farmers by a handful of corporations in agricultural trade and means of production (machines and chemicals). They also analysed the political organizations of farmers such as cooperatives, populist movements and commodity lobby groups. Building on the insights of emerging gender studies, in the later 1980s peasant studies (and international institutions such as the World Bank) recognized households as male-headed enterprises, and 'women in agriculture' became an important topic of research and policy. For peasant studies, which continued to challenge the *development* paradigm, this meant at least two things: that women were often drawn into labour for capitalist agriculture; and that gender and generation were in effect 'relations of production' in family farming and subject to the wider challenges to patriarchy by women and youth (Friedmann 1986).

A PLACE AND VOICES FOR PEASANT STUDIES

The Peasants Seminar established in 1972 by Terence J. Byres and Charles Curwen was a brave and creative name for a new interdisciplinary seminar at the School of Oriental and African Studies in London (Byres 2001). Attendance overflowed the halls to hear papers by eminent historian Eric Hobsbawm and newly minted PhD and interpreter of Chayanov, Teodor Shanin. The enthusiastic response by scholars from fields as diverse as ancient history and literature, as well as the social sciences, led Byres and Curwen to found the JPS the same year, and its early volumes were filled with papers from the seminar. The alternative name considered by two of the co-founders had been 'Imperialism', a word current in progressive publications of the time, which reflected the original focus on anti-colonial social movements. Their respective research on India and China had raised questions of economic development in agrarian societies with very different political systems, and recognition that different disciplines would need to engage in exploring many empirical and theoretical questions. According to Byres's (2001, 357) history of the Peasants Seminar, the differentiation of the peasantry, which formed the majority in anti-colonial struggles, immediately emerged out of the original focus. Its wider embrace allowed both seminar and journal to include luminaries and new scholars from history, literature, anthropology, sociology, economics, classics and more, and to broach themes that were only later to become central, especially gender.

The focus on peasants led to the inclusion of Teodor Shanin as a third editor of the JPS. Shanin's mentor, Daniel Thorner, had translated Chayanov. Shanin's (1972) *The Awkward Class: Political Sociology of Peasantry in a Developing Society, Russia 1910–25*, which appeared in the same year, established the link between peasants, development and history that characterized the journal; Shanin's two-part article (1973, 1974) in the first two issues of the JPS were general introductions to Chayanov. Shanin's edited volume *Peasants and Peasant Societies* in 1971, followed by a second edition in 1987, reflected the breadth and depth achieved by both the seminar and the journal. Shanin left the JPS in 1975 and Curwen in 1984. Henry Bernstein joined Byres as co-editor in 1985. In 2001, by which time there was plenty of space for two journals, the two became founding editors of the *Journal of Agrarian Change* (JAC). The two journals evolved in parallel until 2008, when Jun Borras became editor of the JPS.

The JPS and JAC henceforth evolved with intentional complementarity. The JPS came to represent a more thorough mixture of research, theory and political engagement, especially with the growing food sovereignty movement, while the JAC focused on rigorous intellectual debates whose spine was – and remains since the retirement of Byres and Bernstein – agrarian political economy.

By this time, there was mutual engagement between what had at first been separate English-language and continental European research connecting peasants in industrial societies to those in the Third World – or as it came to be called, the Global South (van der Ploeg 2008). Not only the JAC and the JPS, but also many older disciplinary journals and new interdisciplinary ones now include farming and food. Peasant studies, by whatever name or no name at all, had by then come to embrace an increasingly widespread appreciation of farmer agency, past and present.

CONCLUSION

Studies of the agro-food system, of food sovereignty, of indigenous and other types of knowledge, of women in farming, among others, are now widely embraced as food and farming moves ever closer to the centre of capitalism, of policy, of social science and of politics. The origins of peasant studies in the context of modernist obsession with industry and cities, both liberal and Marxist, led with questions about how agrarian societies might become like idealized economies called *industrial* or *developed*. By focusing on agrarian societies, early peasant studies embraced historical and ethnographic research in exploring tensions not visible to dominant disciplines, such as the complex relations between family labour and wage labour. This became relevant to the slow realization among the wider research and policy world that – beginning in the early 1970s, at the same time as peasant studies was emerging – industries were beginning to move 'off-shore' from so-called *developed* countries to low-wage countries; the latter were becoming 'industrial' without 'developing'.

Peasant studies thus opened new questions and new avenues of research and paved the way for interdisciplinary journals on food and farming. This openness allowed peasant studies to incorporate other cross-cutting issues as they arose: gender, generation, ecology and much more.

The new field of critical agrarian studies became more all-embracing as old paradigms cracked, and as contradictions of capitalism came to be more visibly centred in land use, food supplies, livelihoods and crises of biological diversity and climate. Peasant studies retain the old questions in new ways: for instance, the relation between 'depeasantization' and 'repeasantization' (now in all countries); the viability, even possible superiority, of small farms (now including much more fluid gender relations than 'male-headed households') and indigenous and other farming communities now claiming food sovereignty and recognition of diverse forms of knowledge; the changing connections between cities and peri-urban and rural areas; mobility of many kinds, not simply linear 'urbanization', involving multiple kinship and labour strategies (Bosc et al. 2018); and deepening conflicts between ever larger concentrations of land, often by distant finance capital, with the livelihoods and ecologies that connect people to places (see Clapp and Isakson, this volume). Since the first 'food crisis' of 1973–1974, which coincided with the origins of peasant studies, it has gradually become clear that food systems and ways of organizing land are by no means part of a distant past. They are central to the world and how we understand it.

NOTES

1.   China was the very important exception, which decades later (in the 1990s) joined international institutions and international trade, and also embraced industrial agriculture, but was isolated during the Cold War – from the US-led capitalist bloc after 1949 and from the Soviet bloc after 1969.
2.   It was these social institutions built up during the early post-war period that were 'deregulated' under what came to be called structural adjustment policies beginning in the 1980s.

FURTHER READING

Shanin, T. (1971), *Peasants and Peasant Societies: Selected Readings*, Harmondsworth: Penguin.
Shanin, T. (1987), *Peasants and Peasant Societies: Selected Readings*, second edition, Oxford: Blackwell.
van der Ploeg, J.D. (2008), *The New Peasantries: Struggles for Autonomy and Sustainability in an Era of Empire and Globalization*, London: Earthscan.
Wolf, E. (1966), *Peasants*, Englewood Cliffs, NJ: Prentice-Hall.
Wolf, E. (1969), *Peasant Wars of the Twentieth Century*, New York: Harper and Row.

REFERENCES

Banaji, J. (1976a), Summary of selected parts of Kautsky's 'The Agrarian Question', *Economy and Society*, 5(1), 1–49.
Banaji, J. (1976b), Chayanov, Kautsky, Lenin: Considerations towards a synthesis, *Economic and Political Weekly*, 11(40), 1594–1607.
Banaji, J. (1977), Modes of production in a materialist conception of history, *Capital and Class*, 3.
Bernstein, H. (1979), African peasantries: A theoretical framework, *Journal of Peasant Studies*, 6(4), 421–443.
Bernstein, H. (2015), Agrarian political economy, in Wright, J. (ed.), *International Encyclopedia of the Social and Behavioral Sciences*, second edition, Amsterdam: Elsevier, 456–462.
Bernstein, H.; Byres, T. (2001), From peasant studies to agrarian change, *Journal of Agrarian Change*, 1(1), 1–5.
Bernstein, H.; Friedmann, H.; Ploeg, J.V.; Shanin, T.; White, B. (2018), Forum: Fifty years of debate on peasantries, 1966–2016, *Journal of Peasant Studies*, 45(4), 689–714.
Berry, W. (1977), *The Unsettling of America: Culture and Agriculture*, San Francisco, CA: Sierra Club Books.
Bosc, P.-M.; Sourisseau, J.-M.; Bonnal, P.; Gasselin, P.; Valette, E.; Bélières, J.-F. (eds) (2018), *Diversity of Family Farming around the World: Existence, Transformations and Possible Futures of Family Farms*, New York: Springer.
Brandt Commission (1983 [1980]), *Common Crisis North-South: Cooperation for World Recovery*, Cambridge, MA: MIT Press.
Busch, L.; Lacy, W.B. (eds) (1984), *Food Security in the United States*, Boulder, CO: Westview Press.
Buttel, F.H. (2001), Some reflections on late twentieth century agrarian political economy, *Sociologia Ruralis*, 41(2), 165–181.
Byres, T.J. (2001), The Peasants Seminar of the University of London, 1972–1989: A memoir, *Journal of Agrarian Change*, 1(3), 343–388.
Chayanov, A.V. (1966 [1925]), *Theory of Peasant Economy*, edited by Thorner, D.; Kerblay, B.; Smith, R.E.F., Homewood, IL: American Economic Association.
Chombart de Lauwe, J. (1979), *L'aventure agricole de la France, de 1945 à nos jours*, Paris: Presses Universitaires de France.
Friedland, W.H.; Barton, A.E.; Thomas, R.J. (1981), *Manufacturing Green Gold: Capital, Labor, and Technology in the Lettuce Industry*, New York: Cambridge University Press.

Friedmann, H. (1978), World market, state, and family farm: Social bases of household production in the era of wage labour, *Comparative Studies in Society and History*, 20(4), 545–586.

Friedmann, H. (1986), Family farming in capitalist agriculture: Structural limits and political possibilities, in Cox, G.; Lowe, P.; Winter, M. (eds), *Agriculture: Policies and People*, London: George Allen and Unwin, 41–46.

Friedmann, H. (1993), The political economy of food: A global crisis, *New Left Review*, 197, 29–57.

Harrison, M. (1975), Chayanov and the economics of the Russian peasantry, *Journal of Peasant Studies*, 2(4), 389–417.

Hobsbawm, E.J. (1959), *Primitive Rebels: Studies in Archaic Forms of Social Movement in the 19th and 20th Centuries*, Manchester: Manchester University Press.

Hoogvelt, A. (1982), *The Third World in Global Development*, London: Macmillan.

Kautsky, K. (1988 [1899]), *The Agrarian Question*, 2 volumes, translated by Burgess, P., London: Zwan Publications.

Lenin, V.I. (1899), *The Development of Capitalism in Russia: The Process of the Formation of a Home Market for Large-Scale Industry*, accessed 18 July 2020 at www.marxists.org/archive/lenin/works/1899/devel/.

Malassis, L. (1979), *Économie agro-alimentaire*, Paris: Éditions Cujas.

Marx, K. (1851–1852), *The 18th Brumaire of Louis Bonaparte*, accessed 29 June 2020 at www.marxists.org/archive/marx/works/subject/hist-mat/18-brum/ch07.htm.

Mendras, H. (1970), *La fin des paysans; changement et innovations dans les sociétés rurales françaises*, Paris: A. Colin.

Moore, B. (1966), *Social Origins of Dictatorship and Democracy: Lord and Peasant in the Making of the Modern World*, Boston, MA: Beacon Press.

Newby, H. (1979), *Green and Pleasant Land? Social Change in Rural England*, London: Hutchinson.

Rogers, E.M. (1962), *Diffusion of Innovations*, New York: Free Press.

Scott, J.C. (1977), *The Moral Economy of the Peasant: Rebellion and Subsistence in Southeast Asia*, New Haven, CT: Yale University Press.

Scott, J.C. (1985), *Weapons of the Weak: Everyday Forms of Peasant Resistance*, New Haven, CT: Yale University Press.

Servolin, C. (1972), L'absorption de l'agriculture dans le mode de production capitaliste, in Tavernier, Y.; Gervais, M.; Servolin, C. (eds), *L'univers politique des paysans dans la France contemporaine*, Paris: Editions Science-Po., 41–77, accessed 6 July 2019 at www.cairn.info/l-univers-politique-des-paysans-dans-la-france--9782724602285-page-41.htm?try_download=1.

Shanin, T. (1971), *Peasants and Peasant Societies: Selected Readings*, Harmondsworth: Penguin.

Shanin, T. (1972), *The Awkward Class: Political Sociology of Peasantry in a Developing Society, Russia 1910–25*, Oxford: Oxford University Press.

Shanin, T. (1973), The nature and logic of peasant economy 1: A generalization, *Journal of Peasant Studies* 1(1), 63–80.

Shanin, T. (1974), The nature and logic of peasant economy II: Diversity and change; III: Policy and intervention, *Journal of Peasant Studies*, 1(2), 186–206.

Shanin, T. (1986), Chayanov's message: Illuminations, miscomprehensions, and the contemporary 'development theory', in Thorner, D.; Kerblay, B.; Smith, R.E.F. (eds), *The Theory of Peasant Economy*, second edition, Madison, WI: University of Wisconsin Press, 1–24.

Shanin, T. (1987), *Peasants and Peasant Societies: Selected Readings*, second edition, Oxford: Blackwell.

Shanin, T. (2009), Chayanov's treble death and tenuous resurrection: An essay about understanding, about roots of plausibility and about rural Russia, *Journal of Peasant Studies*, 36(1), 83–101.

Skocpol, T. (1979), *States and Social Revolutions: A Comparative Analysis of France, Russia, and China*, New York: Cambridge University Press.

Toye, J. (2014), *UNCTAD at 50*, New York: United Nations, accessed 5 July 2019 at https://unctad.org/en/PublicationsLibrary/osg2014d1_en.pdf.

van der Ploeg, J.D. (2008), *The New Peasantries: Struggles for Autonomy and Sustainability in an Era of Empire and Globalization*, London: Earthscan.

Wolf, E. (1966), *Peasants*, Englewood Cliffs, NJ: Prentice-Hall.

Wolf, E. (1969), *Peasant Wars of the Twentieth Century*, New York: Harper and Row.

Wright, G. (1975), Cotton, corn and risk in the nineteenth century, *Journal of Economic History*, 35(3), 526–551.

4.   The diversity of classical agrarian Marxism

A. Haroon Akram-Lodhi and Cristóbal Kay

INTRODUCTION

Critical agrarian studies is predicated upon developing theory and empirics that emphasize the social dimensions of rural identities and power relations. Thus, rural behaviour can reflect a continuum of possibilities, from the rigid dictates of social structure and the ways in which this can socialize individuals, to the social autonomy of the person. However, in actually-existing rural worlds power is asymmetrical and relational, and thus the social dimensions of identity are reflected in sources of social power. While assets, incomes and their distribution may be an important determinant of power, critical agrarian studies stresses intersectionality, in terms of gender, generation, ecology, space and landscapes, among others, and in so doing does not exclusively focus upon assets, incomes and their distribution as the sole basis or expression of power in each and every instance.

Agrarian Marxism is an important current within critical agrarian studies. Agrarian Marxism refers 'to over a century of work in the Marxist theoretical tradition on the "agrarian question"' (Levien et al. 2018, 854), which consists of three interrelated issues: the terms and conditions by which capitalism does or does not transform agricultural activities by subsuming them to the market imperatives of the capitalist mode of production; the contribution of agriculture in facilitating the emergence and consolidation of capital accumulation both within and beyond the sector; and the impact of these processes on the political agency of rural peoples (Akram-Lodhi and Kay 2010). As such, it approaches issues of structure and agency in a way that is consistent with critical agrarian studies, but from within a specific theoretical tradition and a unique methodological perspective. 'Classical' agrarian Marxism focuses upon the ground-breaking insights into the agrarian question offered by Marx and Engels and the development of these insights in writings by Kautsky and Lenin in the late nineteenth century. It also uses the wide variety of theoretical, methodological and empirical innovations developed in the Soviet Union during the 1920s that explicitly drew upon earlier understanding of the agrarian question. The literature that emerged in just over 50 years is voluminous, but what is especially striking about it is the breadth and depth of rigorous intellectual creativity that can be found within it, the substantive diversity of the arguments that can be identified, as well as the pluralism that was central to its creative diversity. Thus, many of the central concerns of contemporary critical agrarian studies have their origin in classical agrarian Marxism: processes of enclosure, class formation and fragmentation, the challenges facing rural labour, the social origins of difference, the drivers of rural growth and social change in the countryside and the political responses of rural peoples. Therefore, this contribution will offer a selective summary of the key arguments made by some of the central theorists in the classical agrarian Marxism tradition. It will demonstrate that classical agrarian Marxism did not identify unilinear social processes but rather diverse, dynamic and recurrent manifestations of multifaceted and contradictorily changing patterns of social and economic relations that continually and complexly reconfigured rural labour regimes subject to multiple determinations and contingencies. As such, classical agrarian Marxism remains remarkably theoretically and empirically coherent, providing the analytical tools and sensitivity necessary to understand continuing and ongoing processes of agrarian change in the contemporary world. For this reason, many within critical agrarian studies continue to rely upon the theories, methods and evidentiary techniques of classical agrarian Marxism.

MARX AND ENGELS

Marx's analysis of the agrarian question was principally concerned with how agriculture did or did not facilitate the emergence of capital and hence capitalism in the rural world and beyond. Thus, as Henry Bernstein (2006) emphasizes, his focus was on the agrarian question of capital. To do this, as early as the *Grundrisse* and the notes that comprised the third volume of *Capital*, Marx carefully considered the relationship between small-scale pre-capitalist peasant farming and small-scale peasant production that is subsumed to capitalism. In particular, Marx focused upon how, through the transformation of the former into the latter, the emergence of agrarian capital took place (Marx 1973 [1939–1941]; Marx 1981 [1894]). In this reading, historical and contemporary peasants can be analytically approached as female and male agricultural workers whose livelihoods are primarily but not exclusively based on having access to land that is either owned or rented, who have diminutive amounts of basic tools and equipment and who use mostly their own labour and the labour of other family members to work that land. So, allocating small stocks of both capital and labour peasants are 'petty commodity producers', operating within capitalism as both a petty capitalist of little consequence and as a worker with little power over the terms and conditions of their employment (Bernstein 1991; Gibbon and Neocosmos 1985).

Marx identified three 'paths' of transition from pre-capitalist farming to peasant farming subsumed to capitalism (Akram-Lodhi and Kay 2016). The first and most fully developed analysis of the development of capitalism in agriculture is that which was published in the first volume of *Capital* (Marx 1976 [1867]). There, the so-called 'primitive accumulation' that was witnessed in England used dispossessory enclosures by predatory feudal landlords, later supported by the state, to reconfigure the relations of production in order to physically expel a relatively prosperous rich peasantry from land that they did not own. This created a property-less class of rural waged labour that faced a class of capitalist tenant-farmers, beneath the dominant landlord class (Byres 2009). For decades this 'landlord-mediated capitalism from below' (Byres 2009, 57) was seen by many as the sole analysis offered by Marx of the development of capitalist agriculture, but it was not. In the third volume of *Capital* Marx identified a second 'path' of agrarian transition, namely peasant class differentiation, which is witnessed when:

> the custom necessarily develops, among the better-off rent paying peasants, of exploiting agricultural wage-labourers on their own account … In this way it gradually becomes possible for them to build up a certain degree of wealth and transform themselves into future capitalists. Among the old possessors of the land, working for themselves, there arises a seedbed for the nurturing of capitalist farmers, whose development is conditioned by the development of capitalist production. (Marx 1981 [1894], 935)

Thus, peasant petty commodity producers can stratify into distinct classes based upon their position as buyers or sellers of labour-power, a process that is driven by the market imperatives of capitalism to exploit labour, improve productivity and cut the costs of production (Wood 2009).

Finally, the third path of agrarian transition was identified by Marx late in his life in a reply to a letter from Vera Zasulich (Shanin 2018). This path would witness the peasant community collectively slowly transforming itself into 'an element of collective production on a national scale' (Marx 1983 [1925], 106). For this to occur, land would have to be held in common, all community members would have access to the land necessary to produce their subsistence, membership of the community would not be based solely on kinship and collectivism would have to be capable of overriding private property. In such settings, peasant communities witnessed 'dualism' (ibid., 104) between, on the one hand, land that was owned in common, such as pastures and forests, and on the other hand individual peasant plots. With the emergence of capitalism communal areas were being encroached upon, and it was this that the peasant community could collectively prevent. As a result, the third path had a set of social relations that unevenly combined the progressive features of capitalism with a set of features derived from historically adaptable peasant social relations. Conditional on the emergence and introduction of new technologies that developed the forces of production in a way that sustained the position of small-scale peasant farming, and conditional on state support for small-scale peasant farming, cumulatively these social relations would allow the community to 'reap the fruits with which capitalist production has enriched humanity without passing through the capitalist regime' (ibid., 112).

Marx therefore argued that processes of capitalist development could, in agriculture, create 'peasant dispossession by displacement', or enclosure, 'peasant dispossession by differentiation', or sustain a 'hybrid' form of peasant subsumption to capital that maintains and sustains peasant communities where collective tendencies dominate because 'smallholding and petty landownership ... production ... proceeds without being governed by the general rate of profit' (Marx 1981 [1894], 946; Araghi 2009, 118). Moreover, Marx's third path of transition demonstrated the highly political character of his analysis, in that collective political agency could transcend the structural processes facilitating the development of capitalism in agriculture.

A decade and a half after Marx published the first volume of *Capital* Friedrich Engels turned his attention specifically to this. In *The Peasant Question in France and Germany*, Engels (1950 [1894], 381) argued that cheap grain imports into Europe in the last 20 years of the nineteenth century had undermined rural livelihoods and created an agrarian crisis that was resulting in the slow dissolution of most European peasantries. For Engels, the only possible response to the agrarian crisis was a political one; however, 'the doomed peasant (was) in the hands of his false protectors'—big landowners that 'assume the role of champions of the interests of the small peasants' (Engels 1950 [1894], 382). It was therefore necessary for urban working-class parties to become a 'power in the countryside' by producing a political programme that reflected the needs of the peasantry and, in so doing, create the foundations of a peasant-worker alliance. Engels' emphasis was thus that the agrarian question must ultimately be about the position of labour and the expression of its agency. His concern was not with the issue of the emergence of agrarian capital, rural capital accumulation or capital more generally, as had been Marx's central concern. These more structural concerns were however taken up by Vladimir Lenin and Karl Kautsky in the late 1890s.

LENIN AND KAUTSKY

Lenin (1964 [1899]) argued that the capitalist industrialization of Russia was breaking the historical interrelationship of rural agriculture and rural petty manufacturing as cheaper capitalist commodity manufactures for the rural economy created a need for money that could only be met by commodifying subsistence production. As subsistence food crops were commodified the disciplines of capitalist competition were introduced into rural society. Notably, as more was produced to be sold, the need to sell resulted in increasing specialization as a means of controlling costs, which further heightened dependence upon the market even as those producers that sought to sustain their market competitiveness found that markets could provide the basis of agrarian accumulation if the principles of capitalism were followed: expansion, innovation and a lowering of unit costs through scale economies. By way of contrast, those peasants unable or unwilling to compete in markets found that attempts to use markets to sustain or increase consumption while not being able to be competitive generated cash deficits which were only reinforced by the distress sales of output and the accrual of debt. In order to meet the costs of increasing market dependence deficit households would therefore increasingly engage in waged labour in an effort to avoid immiserization, which was performed both for the more dynamic agrarian producers and for industrial capital.

As agricultural commodity production expanded, peasants became subordinated to product and labour markets even as some producers produced for the purpose of accumulation. The result was the emergence, as Marx had indicated, of qualitatively distinct types of rural holdings which differed in their purpose of production and in their technical coefficients of production. One group produced for markets and for accumulation, while the other strove to maintain subsistence in increasingly arduous and tenuous circumstances. Accumulating peasant households sought to increase their control over productive assets in order to give a further impetus to accumulation. Deficit peasant households were eventually forced to liquidate their assets by selling them to more dynamic producers, in order to be able to cope. So a change in the distribution of productive assets—both means of production and labour-power—took place. For Lenin, petty commodity production would be torn asunder as the development of capitalism in agriculture proceeded with the emergence of capitalist exploitation, defined in its strict sense as the appropriation by capital of the surplus value produced by classes of rural waged labour. However, Lenin also recognized the substantive diversity that can be witnessed in processes of agrarian change, writing that 'a theoretical economic analysis can, in general, only deal with tendencies' and as such cannot uncover 'a law for all individual cases' (Lenin 1964 [1899], 111, 117). Lenin himself identified two paths of transition to agrarian capitalism. One, capitalism from above, saw the process of differentiation and the emergence of rural classes being driven by rural dominant classes as landlords transformed themselves into capitalists and forced tenants to turn themselves into waged labour. The other, capitalism from below, saw the process of market-mediated differentiation driving the emergence of rural classes of agrarian capital and waged labour in a process of peasant social differentiation.

It was in fact Kautsky who first coined the phrase 'agrarian question', enquiring 'whether and how capital is seizing hold of agriculture, revolutionizing it, making old forms of production and property untenable and creating the necessity for new ones' (1988 [1899], 12). Herewith, he wanted to get a better understanding of 'the role of pre-capitalist and non-capitalist forms of agriculture in capitalist society' (ibid., 3). Kautsky emphasized a point made by Marx: family-based petty commodity farm production could depress living standards by working longer and harder, and in so doing could use underconsumption to sustain an ability to compete with agrarian capital driven by market imperatives. In such circumstances, according to Kautsky, capital need not wholly transform agriculture in a capitalist direction. Rather, agro-industrial capital could restrict itself to food processing, farm inputs and rural financial systems, using science, technology and money to subsume smallholder petty commodity production to the demands of agro-industrial capital while at the same time sustaining the persistence of petty commodity production. Indeed, the state might intervene to specifically support petty commodity production because of the political importance of rural interests, as the slow extension of the democratic franchise took place. For Kautsky (ibid., 59–197), this could be sustained over time, and would facilitate the persistence of the peasantry, notwithstanding the emergence of capitalism across the economy as a whole. Thus, the place of peasants in processes of social change need not be immutable; it was contingent.

CHAYANOV AND KRITSMAN

Given this contingency, Soviet debates in the 1920s on the place of the peasantry in the process of social change pivoted around two prevailing approaches. The first was the theory of the peasant household developed by A.V. Chayanov and the Organization and Production School. The second was the approach associated with Lev N. Kritsman and the Agrarian Marxists. Both men were theoretically informed and empirically minded agrarian political economists who sought to understand the realities of the Soviet countryside. Although Chayanov was not a Marxist, there is no doubt that part of his analysis derived from the insight of Marx (and Kautsky) that peasants could depress the rate of return to their work in order to sustain the survival of the farm; Chayanov called this 'self-exploitation'. Nor is there any doubt that in his writing Chayanov explicitly argued that he was developing insights originally found in the writings of Marx and Lenin.

Chayanov offered an analysis of peasant farming in which intrahousehold resource allocation was determined by a trade-off between 'the family's single indivisible labour-product' (Chayanov 1986 [1925], 8) and the effort required to obtain such 'material results' (ibid., 41) in light of a socially determined acceptable consumption level. Chayanov wrote that 'there comes a moment at a certain level of rising labour income when the drudgery of the marginal labour will equal the subjective evaluation of the marginal utility of the sum obtained by this labour' (ibid., 81). Chayanov called this the household's labour–consumer balance. Clearly, family size and household generational structure would be a major determinant of the labour–consumer balance. For larger families a higher consumer-worker ratio might require an increase in the degree of self-exploitation. The need to restore the labour–consumer balance could then necessitate the acquisition of more productive assets, and in particular more land to work with family labour, so that household consumption demand could be satisfied. By way of contrast, smaller families' ability to achieve household consumption demand and maintain their labour–consumer balance might permit them to shed redundant land. Thus, the attempt to maintain the labour–consumer balance in the context of changing family size would give rise to changes in the productive assets held by the family. *Contra* Lenin, rural inequalities would not be the result of socio-economic differentiation but would be the result of the pressures of generational cycles. This is called demographic differentiation.

Unlike Chayanov, who identified a seemingly unique peasant mode of production, Kritsman and the Agrarian Marxists argued that stratification over time would result in one dominant structure of rural class relations imposing a new pattern of social and economic development. In the early stages of social transformation, however, Kritsman argued that the situation was both fluid and volatile. While peasant farm households faced different opportunities, incentives and contradictions, Kritsman believed that in the early stages of social change the majority of peasant farms found themselves entwined within simultaneous relations in which they exploited and were in turn exploited. It was therefore necessary to trace emerging dominant patterns of surplus appropriation because these cut across the contradictory class location in which many peasant households found themselves. In so doing, direct class indicators such as the hire and sale of labour-power, the rental or leasing of land and the rental or leasing of capital stock including working animals would be important to document because they reflected surplus appropriation. They would not be sufficient, however. Kritsman argued that 'the hiring of rural wage-workers ... appears ... in covert form' (Kritsman 1984 [1926–1927], 140), that 'an index of the growth of the economic power of the capitalist part of the peasantry is the growth of rented land, relieving the poor of their land' (ibid., 141), that stratification might be driven not by concentration of land but by concentration of livestock and that usury and trade were important channels by which surplus was extracted. In other words, Kritsman and the Agrarian Marxists sought to identify the 'growth of hidden capitalist exploitation' (ibid., 128) that was transforming the countryside.

BUKHARIN AND PREOBRAZHENSKY

Chayanov's and Kritsman's central arguments on the extent to which peasants could be self-sufficient, producing their subsistence with their own resources, continue to resonate within critical agrarian studies. However, these arguments were embedded within the more general issue of the role of the peasantry in the process of accumulation in the new Soviet state. Nicolai Bukharin, one of the key theoreticians of the Bolsheviks, argued in the mid-1920s that a socialist transformation could only be achieved by strengthening the political alliance of the peasantry and the working class because of the agrarian character of the country (Bukharin 1982 [1925]). Generating the active consent of the peasantry to their being governed by the Soviet state in turn required improving the livelihoods of the peasantry by creating the commercial circumstances in which peasants could and would produce the agricultural food and non-food surpluses needed for the cities and for industry. Therefore, Bukharin envisaged an active role for rural markets. However, as Bukharin was well aware, this would encourage the development of agrarian capital and relations of exploitation. Therefore, Bukharin argued that democratic peasant cooperatives had to be strengthened as a means of offsetting the imperatives of rural markets, improving the livelihoods of all peasants including the poorest, and constructing political support for the Soviet state even as that state controlled key aspects of the non-rural economy, most especially finance. For Bukharin, social transformation would have to proceed gradually, by increasing balanced trade between agriculture and industry, in order to 'guarantee first and foremost a development of the productive forces ... of the peasant economy' (Bukharin 1982 [1925], 243) so that increases in voluntary savings could serve as the basis for social transformation.

Evgeny Preobrazhensky (1965 [1926]) challenged Bukharin, developing the concept of primitive socialist accumulation, which he defined as 'accumulation in the hands of the state of material resources mainly or partly from sources lying outside the complex of state economy' during the period of structural transformation (ibid., 132). Primitive socialist accumulation required 'the alienation in favour of socialism as part of the surplus product of all the pre-socialist economic forms' (ibid., 133). In the Soviet Union in the 1920s the bulk of the surplus produced under 'pre-socialist economic forms' would have been produced by the petty commodity producing peasantry. So Preobrazhensky's primitive socialist accumulation required the appropriation of the agricultural surplus of the peasantry in order to underpin structural transformation. According to Preobrazhensky this appropriation could occur in two main ways: through taxation and through the manipulation of the intersectoral terms of trade between agriculture and industry (Dobb 1966). The principal mechanism by which the intersectoral terms of trade could be manipulated was to be state trading monopolies that would buy farm products at below-market prices and sell industrial products at above-market prices; unequal exchange would capture the agricultural surplus of the Soviet peasantry for socialist development. Thus, whereas Bukharin saw peasants as the source of the political support needed for social change, Preobrazhensky saw peasants as the source of the resources needed for social change through rapid industrialization. Preobrazhensky favoured rapid industrialization so as to enlarge and strengthen the industrial working class, which he saw as the main source of political support for socialist transformation (Erlich 1960). The two, like Lenin and Kautsky and Chayanov and Kritsman, had strongly contrasting views on the place of peasants in processes of social transformation, the emergence of agrarian capital, accumulation and the political implications of such structural changes.

CONCLUSIONS

Clearly, classical agrarian Marxism demonstrated substantive diversity in the arguments that it developed. This diversity is demonstrated in the theoretical, methodological and empirical innovations that can be found within it, which in turn shows the extent to which pluralism was central to its creative diversity. Moreover, the central concerns of classical agrarian Marxism, of rural class formation and dissolution, accumulation and the political relationships within and between rural and non-rural classes, are those of critical agrarian studies, which suggest why agrarian Marxism is an important current within critical agrarian studies. So: in what ways are critical agrarian studies and classical agrarian Marxism different? Here, it is possible to identify two clear divides.

First, critical agrarian studies tends to understand contemporary capital as national and international phenomena, subsuming the rural and imposing processes upon rural dynamics. As a result, within critical agrarian studies the emphasis of many academics and activists is now squarely upon understanding the agrarian question of rural labour. The formation of agrarian capital, processes of exclusively rural accumulation and the role of industrialization in social transformation are the province of only a minority of those working within critical agrarian studies.

Classical agrarian Marxism offers a different perspective. It recognizes that newly emergent capital is always local, and that it is itself subsumed to sub-national capital, which is itself subsumed to national capital, which is in turn subsumed to global capital. In other words, capital is stratified, and this has implications understanding agrarian change. While peasants and rural labour are subsumed to global capital the first site of that subsumption is usually sub-national and newly emergent local capital that arises in local towns, their peripheries and in the countryside, and thus relations of exploitation that result from local capital–labour relations continue to shape the lives and livelihoods of rural peoples around the world. In this straightforward sense, then, agrarian questions of capital and labour still need to be addressed in the countryside.

The second divergence lies within the realm of intersectionality. Intersectionality is central to critical agrarian studies, with both structures and agency being understood through the multidimensional angles of class, gender, generation, ability, ethnicity, race, social status and other markers of identity. By way of contrast, many working in the classical agrarian Marxist tradition have not seriously integrated into their analysis any other category of social differentiation but class. Yet the interrelationships between class and gender, generation, ethnicity, race and other markers of social status and identity can be integral to understanding the political economy of processes of agrarian class formation and dissolution, rural accumulation and politics. By way of example, the central issue of the role of intrahousehold social reproduction and its relationship to the political economy of processes of agrarian class formation and dissolution remains, within agrarian Marxism, far too marginal to much of the analysis that is done (Deere 1995; O'Laughlin 2009). As such, it is clear that both classical agrarian Marxism and critical agrarian studies still have much to learn from each other.

FURTHER READING

Akram-Lodhi, A.H.; Kay, C. (2010), Surveying the agrarian question (I): Unearthing foundations, exploring diversity, *Journal of Peasant Studies*, 37(1), 177–202.

Bernstein, H. (2006), Is there an agrarian question in the 21st century?, *Canadian Journal of Development Studies*, 27(4), 449–460.

Deere, C.D. (1995), What difference does gender make? Rethinking peasant studies, *Feminist Economics* 1(1), 53–72.

Levien, M.; Watts, M.; Hairong, Y. (2018), Agrarian Marxism, *Journal of Peasant Studies*, 45(5–6), 853–883.

Shanin, T. (2018), 1881 Letters of Vera Zasulich and Karl Marx, *Journal of Peasant Studies*, 45(7), 1183–1202.

REFERENCES

Akram-Lodhi, A.H.; Kay, C. (2010), Surveying the agrarian question (I): Unearthing foundations, exploring diversity, *Journal of Peasant Studies*, 37(1), 177–202.

Akram-Lodhi, A.H.; Kay, C. (2016), Back to the future? Marx, modes of production and the agrarian question, in Mohanty, B.B. (ed.), *Critical Perspectives on Agrarian Transition: India in the Global Debate*, London: Routledge, 43–66.

Araghi, F. (2009), The invisible hand and the visible foot: Peasants, dispossession and globalization, in Akram-Lodhi, A.H.; Kay, C. (eds), *Peasants and Globalization: Political Economy, Rural Transformation and the Agrarian Question*, London: Routledge, 111–147.

Bernstein, H. (1991), Petty commodity production, in Bottomore, T.; Harris, L.; Kiernan, V.G.; Miliband, R. (eds), *A Dictionary of Marxist Thought*, second edition, Oxford: Blackwell, 417–419.

Bernstein, H. (2006), Is there an agrarian question in the 21st century?, *Canadian Journal of Development Studies*, 27(4), 449–460.

Bukharin, N. (1982 [1925]), The road to socialism and the worker-peasant alliance, in Day, R.B. (ed.), *Selected Writings on the State and the Transition to Socialism*, White Plains, NY: M.E. Sharpe, 209–294.

Byres, T.J. (2009), The landlord class, peasant differentiation, class struggle and the transition to capitalism, in Akram-Lodhi, A.H.; Kay, C. (eds), *Peasants and Globalization: Political Economy, Rural Transformation and the Agrarian Question*, London: Routledge, 57–82.

Chayanov, A.V. (1986 [1925]), *The Theory of Peasant Economy*, edited by Thorner, D.; Kerblay, B.; Smith, R.E.F., Homewood, IL: Richard Irwin.

Deere, C.D. (1995), What difference does gender make? Rethinking peasant studies, *Feminist Economics* 1(1), 53–72.

Dobb, M. (1966), *Soviet Development since 1917*, London: Routledge and Kegan Paul.

Engels, F. (1950 [1894]), The peasant question in France and Germany, in Marx, K.; Engels, F., *Selected Works*, vol. 2, London: Lawrence and Wishart.

Erlich, A. (1960), *The Soviet Industrialization Debate, 1924–1928*, Cambridge, MA: Harvard University Press.

Gibbon, P.; Neocosmos, M. (1985), Some problems in the political economy of 'African socialism', in Bernstein, H.; Campbell, B. (eds), *Contradictions of Accumulation in Africa: Studies in Economy and State*, Beverly Hills, CA: Sage, 153–206.

Kautsky, K. (1988 [1899]), *The Agrarian Question*, 2 vols, London: Zwan Publications.

Kritsman, L.N. (1984 [1926–1927]), Class stratification of the Soviet countryside, in Cox, T.; Littlejohn, G. (eds), *Kritsman and the Agrarian Marxists*, London: Frank Cass, 85–143.

Lenin, V.I. (1964 [1899]), *The Development of Capitalism in Russia*, Moscow: Progress Publishers.

Levien, M.; Watts, M.; Hairong, Y. (2018), Agrarian Marxism, *Journal of Peasant Studies*, 45(5–6), 853–883.

Marx, K. (1973 [1939–1941]), *Grundrisse: Foundations of the Critique of Political Economy*, Harmondsworth: Penguin Books.

Marx, K. (1976 [1867]), *Capital: A Critique of Political Economy*, vol. 1, Harmondsworth: Penguin Books.

Marx, K. (1981 [1894]), *Capital: A Critique of Political Economy*, vol. 3, Harmondsworth: Penguin Books.

Marx, K. (1983 [1925]), Marx-Zasulich correspondence: Letters and drafts, in: Shanin, T. (ed.), *Late Marx and the Russian Road: Marx and 'the Peripheries of Capitalism'*, London: Routledge and Kegan Paul, 97–126.

O'Laughlin, B. (2009), Gender justice, land and the agrarian question in Southern Africa, in Akram-Lodhi, A.H.; Kay, C. (eds), *Peasants and Globalization: Political Economy, Rural Transformation and the Agrarian Question*, London: Routledge, 190–213.

Preobrazhensky, E. (1965 [1926]), *The New Economics*, Oxford: Clarendon Press.

Shanin, T. (2018), 1881 Letters of Vera Zasulich and Karl Marx, *Journal of Peasant Studies*, 45(7), 1183–1202.

Wood, E.M. (2009), Peasants and the market imperative: The origins of capitalism, in Akram-Lodhi, A.H.; Kay, C. (eds), *Peasants and Globalization: Political Economy, Rural Transformation and the Agrarian Question*, London: Routledge, 37–56.

5.   Debates on the historical origins of agrarian capitalism

Xavier Lafrance

INTRODUCTION

The theme of the origins of agrarian capitalism offers a fertile purview for a theoretically controlled empirical exploration of the social dimensions of rural agencies, productive structures and power relations. It provides an entry point into the relationship between agency and structure in agrarian settings and allows us to see how their interplay orients agrarian production and can lead to a variety of sometimes profoundly divergent patterns of development. As such, the transition to capitalism represents an important research field within critical agrarian studies, and agrarian Marxism more specifically.[1]

While works on the origins of capitalism have operated from different theoretical perspectives – from Smithian to Weberian – Marxist authors have engaged in especially rich debates on the agrarian dimensions of the transition from non-capitalist to capitalist societies. This chapter offers an overview of these exchanges structured around the important contributions of Robert Brenner and Ellen Meiksins Wood to our understanding of agrarian capitalism as a socio-historically specific phenomenon. As will be shown in what follows, their contributions have formed together a lynchpin of the debate on these issues over the last four decades.

As an ongoing dominant paradigm in the field of rural international development studies, neoclassical agrarian political economy has intellectual roots in Adam Smith's analysis of capitalist development. Smith developed the classical version of the 'commercialization model' of the origins of capitalism. He explains how humans have a natural tendency to 'truck, barter and trade'. Historically, these tendencies produced the growth of the division of labour and greater trade. In the absence of 'obstacles' (political and customary restrictions on trade) to the deepening of the division of labour, producers would rationally take advantage of the opportunities presented by the market to specialize output, technically innovate and accumulate. This process, fueling a primitive 'accumulation of stock', would lead to the emergence of agrarian (and eventually industrial) capitalism that characterize what Smith (2003 [1776]) called 'commercial societies'. Smith's theory of the transition has informed – and continues to inform – much of the analyses on the capitalist transformation of agriculture. Indeed, as will be discussed below, some authors associated with Marxism are in fact arguably influenced by Smithian notions.

As will be shown in this chapter, agrarian Marxism offers the main alternative to Smith's perspective and allows us to break with the rationality and methodological individualism assumed by neoclassical agrarian political economy. Doing so, this approach fits within the broader perspective of critical agrarian studies. Brenner and Wood's works are especially effective at building upon Marx's insights to develop a historical explanation of the origins of capitalism. Doing this, these authors developed a theoretical framework that has been called 'political Marxism', but which might be more aptly named '*Capital*-centric Marxism', given its reliance on Marx's mature work. Brenner and Wood show how agrarian economic actors do not naturally adopt 'Smithian' economic behaviours. These actors will act as self-interested maximizers only when embedded in a specific social context that cannot be naturalized and universalized – one in which distinct social property relations and attendant market impera- tives compel actors to adopt profit-maximizing behaviours, leading to epoch-making patterns of agrarian development.

In what follows, Brenner and Wood's interventions are presented as a critical answer to different contributions – both non-Marxist and Marxist – on the issue of the origins of capital- ism. The chapter then critically engages with different responses to their work. We begin with a discussion of debates on the transition to capitalism among Marxist scholars that preceded Brenner's original intervention of the mid-1970s.

FROM MARX TO THE DOBB-SWEEZY DEBATE ON THE TRANSITION FROM FEUDALISM TO CAPITALISM

The younger Marx stuck to Smith's paradigm, and saw capitalism as arising in the interstices of feudalism and maturing in the follow up to a bourgeois revolution that broke down remain- ing obstacles to a fully developed capitalist economy. Marx later broke with Smithian notions, however, especially in the *Grundrisse* and in *Capital*. There, Marx unequivocally rejected classical political economy's notion of a 'primitive accumulation' of capital stock enabling a shift to a capitalist society. Capital, Marx explains, is not a thing but a 'social relation' that originated in 'the historical process of divorcing the producer from the means of production', first in the early modern English countryside (Marx 1990 [1867], 908, 932). This is why Marx spoke of a 'so-called primitive accumulation', in part eight of the first volume of *Capital*, so as to present the mass dispossession of peasants – as opposed to a mere accumulation of wealth – and the transformation of agrarian class relations that ensued, as fundamental conditions for the formation of new capitalist dynamics.

In the new agrarian context that emerged out of this process of expropriation, English land- lords increasingly relied on economic as opposed to extra-economic forms of appropriation, as growing numbers collected rents out of the commercial profits of tenants who employed dispossessed wage labourers. This resulted in sustained economic development since, as Marx (1990 [1867], 908) notes, 'the revolution in property relations on the land was accompanied by improved methods of cultivation, greater co-operation, a higher concentration of the means of production and so on, and because the agricultural wage-labourers were made to work at a higher level of intensity'.

For nearly eight decades after the publication of the first volume of *Capital* theorists ignored, for the most part, the 'late Marx's' account of the origins of capitalism; discussion of the origins of capitalism after Marx reverted back to his earlier formulations based on Smith's version of the 'commercialization model'. When the question of the origins of capitalism was directly addressed, as for example by the Soviet historian M.N. Pokrovsky (1933), the Smithian narrative of *The German Ideology* and *The Communist Manifesto* was reproduced in its entirety.

The publication of *Studies in the Development of Capitalism* (1946), authored by the leader of the Communist Party of Great Britain's Historians Group, the economist Maurice Dobb, marked an important if partial break with the Marxian variants of the commercialization model.[2] Dobb rejected the notion that the reproduction of non-capitalist social property relations, in particular those of European feudalism, was incompatible with the growth of trade and urban centres. Instead, feudalism, distinguished by lordly expropriation of rents (in labour, kind or cash) from an unfree peasantry (serfs) through political and juridical mechanisms, had its own distinctive, non-capitalist logic. The systematic obstacles to either the lords or peasants developing the productivity of labour through specialization, technical innovation and accumulation of land and tools resulted in an internally generated crisis of feudalism in the form of subdivision of landholdings and declining yields per acre and per worker. By the mid-fourteenth century, the feudal crisis produced a massive demographic collapse across Europe, which opened the road to the transition to capitalism. For Dobb, the abolition of serfdom and urban guilds marked the end of extra-economic extraction of surpluses. As the 'petty mode of production' – rural and urban household production – was freed from feudal 'super-structures', peasants and artisans were able to respond to market signals, specialize output, innovate and accumulate. As early industrial and agrarian capitalism spread, it confronted the remnants of feudal relations in the countryside and feudal power organized through the Absolutist states. The bourgeois revolutions in England (1640–1660) and France (1789–1799), led by urban and rural capitalists, overthrew Absolutism, established capitalist rule and eliminated the last vestiges of feudalism, completing the transition to capitalism.

The United States Marxist economist Paul Sweezy's review of Dobb's book in *Science and Society* initiated the first debate on the transition to capitalism among Marxists. Sweezy (1976a, 1976b) insisted that feudalism, as a form of non-commercial 'natural economy', was highly resistant to change. Instead, the impetus for the transition to capitalism had to come from external developments – most importantly the growth of towns and trade after around 1000 CE. Relying on the work of Henri Pirenne, Sweezy argued that the growth of trade and towns dissolved feudalism – monetizing rents and undermining serfdom and promoting the growth of markets that destabilized guilds and other restrictions on production and trade. Sweezy (1976a, 1976b) argued that the trade-induced collapse of feudalism initiated a period of 'pre-capitalist commodity production' which was not governed by capitalist dynamics of specialization, innovation and accumulation. Instead, this distinct phase prepared the way for the emergence of capitalism in the seventeenth and eighteenth centuries.

Throughout their debate, Sweezy and Dobb both continued to assume, albeit in different ways, that capitalism remains present in the interstices of feudalism, awaiting its liberation from non-market constraints. This assumption was subsequently radically challenged by Brenner.

THE BRENNER DEBATE

The publication of Brenner's 'Agrarian class structure and economic development in pre-industrial Europe' in *Past and Present* in 1976 fundamentally transformed the discussion of the origins of capitalism.[3] While engaging the main non-Marxian explanations of the transition to capitalism in Europe – the 'commercialization model' associated with North and Thomas (1973) and the 'demographic model' associated with M.M. Postan (1966) and Emmanuel Le Roy Ladurie (1974) – Brenner's essay would also reshape Marxian discussions over the next 40 years. Differing on the relative importance of the spread of markets or long-term population movements, both models however assume that the early modern agrarian economy responded in a basically automatic manner to changes in the supply and demand of land and labour. Not only did these models assume that specifically capitalist dynamics – the necessity of producers to specialize, innovate and accumulate in response to market signals – existed trans-historically, but they were unable to account for the divergent paths of development across Europe in the fifteenth century. Brenner pointed out that the spread of towns and trade beginning in the eleventh century and the demographic collapse of the fourteenth century were cross-European phenomena. However, these relatively uniform processes produced very different outcomes – the reduction of a formerly free peasantry to serfdom in Eastern Europe, the emergence of a free, subsistence-oriented peasantry in most of continental Western Europe and the emergence of the distinctive relationship between capitalist landlords, capitalist tenant farmers and wage labourers in England alone.

Brenner's alternative explanation began, as did Dobb, with the specificity of feudal social property relations and its specific crisis tendencies. The ability of the lords to use extra-economic coercion to extract rents in labour, kind or cash from the peasantry, and the peasantry's ability to reproduce their possession of land outside of market competition, ruled out the systematic development of productivity through improved methods and labour-saving techniques. As the population rose in the face of relatively stagnant agrarian productivity, the tendency toward the parcellization of landholdings through partible inheritance led to declining yields per acre and labour input, and, eventually, to demographic collapse. The outcome of the feudal crisis, however, was not pre-determined. Instead the intensified struggle between lords and peasants in different zones of Europe shaped the divergent results of the crisis. Across Europe lords and peasants struggled to reproduce their existing class position – the lords' access to peasant surpluses and the peasants' effective possession of landed property. The differing conditions faced by lords and peasants in varied parts of Europe produced a variety of outcomes of the feudal crisis, with the emergence of capitalist social property relations occurring in England alone, as the unintended consequence of the struggle of lords and peasants to reproduce themselves.

In Eastern Europe, where the legally free peasants possessed large plots of land but did not develop strong communal village organization, the lords were able to defeat peasant revolts and establish a 'second serfdom'. In Western Europe, the stronger peasant villages were able to free themselves from serfdom and monetize rents. However, the 'liberation of the petty mode of production' – the abolition of serfdom – did not lead automatically to capitalism. Instead, the peasants preserved their effective possession of their plots through stable, customary rents and taxes. The Western peasantry engaged in 'safety-first' agriculture – marketing only physical surpluses after the consumption needs of household members and villagers were satisfied. The consolidation of Absolutist monarchies, whose main source of revenue was taxes on the peasants, short-circuited lordly attempts to consolidate leaseholds and raise rents in response to increased agricultural prices. Only in England were the peasants able to gain their legal freedom, while the lords – in possession of larger *demesne* and backed by a more centralized state – were able to impose commercial, capitalist leases on their tenant farmers. Thus, the breakthrough to specifically capitalist social property relations – in which capitalist tenant farmers were compelled to specialize, innovate and accumulate in order to pay rising rents – was the unintended consequence of the feudal crisis.

The ensuing debate on Brenner's essay involved a variety of prominent medieval and early modern European historians. Brenner faced two major criticisms. On the one hand, Le Roy Ladurie (1985) accused Brenner of conflating 'surplus extracting' classes and 'ruling classes' in pre-industrial Europe as if they were one and the same. While acknowledging that the demographic collapse produced a different result in Eastern Europe, Le Roy Ladurie continued to insist that objective economic and demographic trends produced uniform results across Western Europe, including England. As Brenner (1985, 246–253) pointed out, however, this left Ladurie incapable of explaining how England alone broke out of the Malthusian population cycle – supporting a growing population with an increasingly productive agriculture based on capitalist social property relations. Only the historic divergence in social property relations, between capitalist and peasant (independent household) production, could explain the difference.

On the other hand, Guy Bois (1985) and Rodney Hilton (1985) accused Brenner of giving excessive weight to political factors – the class struggle – in analysing the feudal crisis and its outcome across early modern Europe. It was Bois who first levelled the charge that Brenner's was a 'political Marxism'. Specifically he argued that Brenner underestimated what Marx, in the 1859 preface to *A Contribution to the Critique of Political Economy*, called the 'contradiction between the forces and relations of production' under feudalism that manifested itself in a 'falling rate of seigneurial revenue'. Brenner (1985, 242–253) pointed out that Bois was correct that rents and taxes were declining in northern France in the thirteenth century. However, in the same period seigneurial incomes rose in England. Brenner argued that the relative organization and strength of lords and peasants in England and France – English lords possessed larger *demesnes* in relation to lands regulated by village communities than their French counterparts – explained the divergent trends in seigneurial revenues in the thirteenth century. Moreover, as Wood (2017, 55) pointed out, 'the criticisms levelled by Bois and Le Roy Ladurie were quite substantially beside the point, and both … took for granted a separation between the "political" and the "economic" that is specific to capitalism'. Under feudalism and other non-capitalist forms of social labour, surplus was extracted from the peasantry through extra-economic means – via political, juridical and military power. Class struggle was therefore directly political, and the evolution of political power had a direct impact on social relations of production and distribution of (mostly agrarian) surpluses.

WORLD SYSTEMS THEORY AND THE CRITIQUE OF 'NEO-SMITHIAN' MARXISM

At the same time that Brenner was intervening in the wider debate among historians over the different trajectories of economic development in early modern Europe, he engaged with a new work that had rekindled interest in the transition to capitalism among Marxists – Immanuel Wallerstein's *The Modern World System* (1974). Wallerstein came to see the limits of 'modernization theory' (Rostow 1960) which posited a universal sequence of economic stages that each society, defined by the nation-state, would traverse over time. Instead, Wallerstein concluded that the tremendous social and economic inequalities between societies was not the product of their being at different 'stages' of development, but the products of the workings of a single, capitalist world-economy. Wallerstein embraced the work of the Marxian dependency theorist, Andre Gunder Frank, who argued that 'economic development and underdevelopment are the opposite face of the same coin. Both are the necessary result and contemporary manifestations of internal contradictions in the world capitalist system' (Frank 1967, 9).

In *The Modern World System*, Wallerstein synthesized Sweezy's account of the transition to capitalism with Gunder Frank's analysis of the unity of development and underdevelopment in the capitalist world-economy. At the centre of Wallerstein's historical analysis is the distinction between world-empires and world-economies. While world-empires like China often began at a much higher level of agrarian labour productivity, their single polity often appropriated the lion's share of surplus product and blocked the spread of markets. World-economies like Europe, with their multiple states, left surpluses in the hands of local rulers who could reinvest them in productive activities and allowed the growth of a trade-based division of labour after 1000 CE. As had Sweezy, Wallerstein argued that the expansion of markets was the main solvent of feudalism and the development of capitalism. Following Gunder Frank, he argued that all of the varied forms of 'labour control' – wage labour in the north-western European 'core', sharecropping and serfdom in the European 'semi-periphery' and slavery and peonage in the New World 'periphery' – were regional market responses to the relative supplies of land and labour. All of these forms were capitalist from birth, part of a world-economy in which surpluses were transferred from the periphery and semi-periphery to the core. This process of surplus transfer, through mechanisms of 'unequal exchange' (Emmanuel 1972), guaranteed the economic development of the core through the underdevelopment of the periphery and semi-periphery.

Brenner's essay, 'The origins of capitalist development: A critique of neo-Smithian Marxism', located the roots of Sweezy, Gunder Frank and Wallerstein's arguments in the work of Adam Smith. Brenner (1977, 22–92), following Marx, demonstrated that producers could be compelled to respond to market signals in ways that systematically developed the productive forces only if certain social property relations existed. These relations allow direct producers to move from one branch of production to another; non-producers are able to expel labour from production to introduce more efficient tools and machinery; and producers who do not lower costs through specialization, innovation and accumulation face the loss of their means of production through market competition. Put simply, neo-Smithians like Sweezy, Gunder Frank and Wallerstein assume what needs to be explained – the existence of capitalist social property relations and their distinctive 'rules of reproduction', or laws of motion.

In painstaking historical detail, Brenner demonstrates that different social–property relations in different regions of the emerging world market of the 'long sixteenth century' (1450–1640) were not regional responses to the relative supply of land and labour, but the products of divergent class conflicts in various parts of Europe and the Americas. Neither the 'underdevelopment' of the semi-periphery and periphery nor the 'development' of the core were the products of surplus transfers through unequal exchange. Instead, it was the logic of their specific social property relations that shaped their pattern of development – with non-capitalist forms like sharecropping, peasant production, serfdom and slavery structurally ruling out the continuous development of the productivity of labour through technical innovation; and the specifically capitalist agriculture in England uniquely requiring the continuous development of the productive forces.

LATER DEBATES ON THE TRANSITION

Since Brenner's breakthrough contributions in the mid-1970s, his thesis on the centrality of the transformation of social property relations to the origins of capitalism has been challenged by different historians. They have, for the most part, concentrated their criticisms on Brenner's account of the origins of capitalism in England in the fifteenth and sixteenth centuries. Two distinct currents have emerged among these historians. John Hatcher and Mark Bailey (2001) and S.P. Rigby (1995) have accused Brenner of a form of 'class' reductionism that essentially ignores the role of demographic factors and the spread of markets in the dissolution of English feudalism and the emergence of capitalist agriculture. They defend a causal pluralism that gives equal weight to population collapse, the growth of commerce and changes in class relations. As Spencer Dimmock (2014, 34–48) points out, these arguments both misinterpret Brenner and face the same problems as the earlier demographic and commercialization models. On the one hand, Brenner did not dismiss or ignore demographic and commercial factors. Brenner acknowledged both the growth of markets since the eleventh century and the demographic collapse of the fourteenth century. However, he argued that different social property relations ultimately determined their impact on the varied regions of Europe. Their failure to give causal primacy to social property relations leads them to be unable, as did Le Roy Ladurie as well as North and Thomas, to explain how uniform population and trade developments led to divergent outcomes in England, Western and Eastern Europe.

The second trend among historians critical of Brenner has been a new 'Smithian' historiography that gives explanatory primacy to the growth of markets in the origins of capitalist agriculture in England. Claiming that Brenner's analysis lacks a 'prime mover' in explaining the emergence of agrarian capitalism, S.R. Epstein (2000) argued that the removal of feudal political constraints on trade and the resultant centralization of political authority led to an unprecedented level of market integration in England. Epstein, along with J.R. French and R.W. Hoyle (2007), argued that the newly liberated peasantry seized the new opportunities presented by the growth of markets to specialize, innovate and accumulate. Like Epstein, French and Hoyle – and Dobb and Hilton before them – Jane Whittle also argued that the abolition of serfdom freed the peasantry to take advantage of new market opportunities and eventually 'merge into capitalism'. In Whittle's account, the peasantry 'expropriated themselves' without any interference by landlords (Whittle 2000, 305–313). In other words, peasants voluntarily opted to specialize output, innovate technologically and accumulate land and tools, rather than being compelled to do so by increasingly insecure leases imposed by the landlords.

The new Smithian historians' claims reproduce many of the same problems of earlier versions of the 'commercialization' model. As Wood (2017, 6–8) points out, all variants of the claim that capitalism emerges from the spread of markets fundamentally view the market as a realm of opportunity rather than coercion. This notion fundamentally ignores the dangers that come when producers specialize output in order to take advantage of market 'opportunities'. Put simply, rural producers who forgo the production of their own subsistence put themselves at the risk of starvation in the case of bad harvests, falling prices and the like. Except for a minority of wealthy peasants in exceptional settings, rural households opt whenever possible for safety-first agriculture – the marketing of physical surpluses after the subsistence needs of household members and neighbours are met.

While developing a more nuanced argument and being more sympathetic toward his general thesis, Terence J. Byres (2006) also criticizes Brenner for not recognizing the extent of the social and economic differentiation of the English peasantry that had been revealed by Rodney Hilton. According to Byres this led Brenner to conceive the transition to agrarian capitalism as the result of a top-down imposition of commercial leases on a passive peasantry by an all-powerful class of landlords. Byres offers an alternative argument according to which a proto-capitalist layer of rich peasants, which already existed prior to the Black Death of the mid-fourteenth century, took commercial leases, and thus became the driving force that generated capitalism from below in England.

Brenner's argument, however, is more complex – for him, capitalism was neither imposed from above nor developed from below in the English case. While it is true that Brenner might not have given enough explicit attention to peasant differentiation prior to the transition to agrarian capitalism, he did recognize a process of accumulation and of consolidation of a middling peasantry during the late medieval period in both England and France. But central to Brenner's argument was that a polarization of tenancies took place in England from the mid-fifteenth century while France experienced a fragmentation of tenancies over the same period. The reason for this was that English landlords were compelled by their declining coercive power over peasants, and an ensuing fall of their revenues, in the wake of the plague, to offer leases on their *demesnes*. A small layer of wealthy peasants seized this new opportunity to farm extensive new lands – tentatively at first, and while still having their own lands to fall back on if things went wrong. Meanwhile, the vast majority of the peasantry struggled to stick to subsistence-based agriculture and fought against the unleashing of agrarian capitalist social property relations over the early modern period (Dimmock 2014, 180–195).

Before this momentous transference by lords of the leases of their *demesnes* from around the turn of the fifteenth century, while significant economic differentiation existed within the peasantry, there was no class of capitalist farmers to be found in England. Taking commercial leases, and thus facing new market imperatives and rules of reproduction, wealthy peasants coalesced into a consolidated and separate class of capitalist yeomen farmers. This new class formed a political alliance with landlords so as to remodel social property relations through an enclosure movement that evicted peasants from their lands and turned an increasing proportion into wage labourers. The lesser landlords – the 'gentry' – were also a core force evicting small peasants and consolidating landholdings that they then rented through commercial leases. Enclosures began to eat away mounting portions of the peasants' lands from the later part of the fifteenth century and culminated with the 'parliamentary enclosures' of the eighteenth and nineteenth centuries. This process implied not only the physical enclosing of peasant lands and commons, but also, and more fundamentally, the extinguishing of secular customs that had been ordering farming practices and community relationships from time immemorial. As such, enclosures were intensively resisted by English peasant communities.

CAPITALISM AND EUROCENTRISM

More recently, a new account of the origins of capitalism has emerged that disapproves of both the overly 'externalist' account of Wallerstein and the alleged 'internalist' and Eurocentric theoretical leanings of 'political Marxism', with a critique that has been formulated by Alex Anievas and Kerem Nisancioglu (2015). Their book *How the West Came to Rule* offers an alternative reading of the rise of capitalism based on the theory of 'uneven and combined development', originally formulated by Trotsky in his *History of the Russian Revolution* (1932). Anievas and Nisancioglu argue that uneven and combined development, as manifested through intersocietal relations, is central to accounting for the emergence of capitalism in England and parts of Western Europe in the sixteenth and seventeenth centuries. They provide a sweeping history of the varied impacts of intersocietal interactions that created the conditions for capitalism, attempting to account for historical processes ranging from the expansion of the Mongol trading empire in the thirteenth century to the European colonization of the Americas and the establishment of plantation slavery.

Anievas and Nisancioglu present conceptual and historical problems.[4] First, the 'law of uneven and combined development' is specific to capitalism, not a general law of history, as Anievas and Nisancioglu would have us believe. While uneven development characterizes all of human history, the process of more 'backward' groups appropriating productive methods from more 'advanced' groups did not lead to their 'combination' – the introduction of the capital–wage labour relation and the systematic development of labour productivity through labour-saving devices – before the advent of industrial capitalist production (Ashman 2009, 29–46). Attempts to use uneven and combined development to explain the origins of capitalism reproduce the errors of the 'commercialization model' – assuming the existence of capitalist rules of reproduction to explain the emergence of capitalist social property relations. Anievas and Nisancioglu's work also offers a variety of problematic historical claims that, again, reproduce many of the questionable assertions of both the demographic and commercialization models.

Following Wood (2001), it can be argued that '*Capital*-centric Marxism' actually offers a deeply powerful response to Western chauvinism while, paradoxically, most anti-Eurocentric theories are based on Eurocentric assumptions. Eurocentrists tend to explain the transition to capitalism in Western Europe by its capacity to remove obstacles to the maturation of commercial activities into modern capitalism; obstacles that remain in place and consequently stall the development of non-Western civilizations. Most anti-Eurocentric responses reverse the argument while sticking to a similar conception of capitalism, claiming that the failure of non-European societies that had reached high levels of commercial development – in many cases superior to European societies – to transit toward mature modern development derives from impediments stemming from Western imperialism. This line of argument assumes that non-Western societies ought to be judged according to their capacity to follow the path of development trailed before them by Western society, as if capitalism was the natural order of things. As Wood puts it, there is 'no more effective way to puncture the Western sense of superiority than to challenge the triumphalist conviction that the Western path of historical development is the natural and inevitable way of things', and doing this implies stressing the historical specificity of capitalism.

CONCLUSION

The theoretical framework and problematizing of capitalist agrarian development developed by Brenner and Wood has now inspired a series of new contributions that go beyond the English case. Charles Post (2012), for instance, has tracked the American road to capitalism. He challenges the notion that North America was capitalist from the beginnings of English colonial settlement in the seventeenth century. While English colonialism in the seventeenth and eighteenth centuries was fuelled by the dynamics of capitalism, the inability to establish a social monopoly of land led to the establishment of two distinctive non-capitalist forms in colonial North America – independent household ('peasant') production in the North and plantation slavery in the South, bound together and with England through the activities of seaboard merchants. Post shows how the unintended consequences of the American Revolution transformed Northern agriculture into petty-capitalist farming through the establishment of a competitive market for land, while preserving and reviving Southern plantation slavery.

Similar critical historicizing of the origins of capitalism has inspired analysis of the historical evolution of agrarian social relations in France, Catalonia, Japan, Brazil, the Ottoman Empire and Turkey and Taiwan.[5] This critical perspective can and should also inform analyses of contemporary agrarian societies. Indeed, the problematizing of capitalist agrarian development as a historically distinct phenomenon remains a highly relevant issue today for critical agrarian studies.

NOTES

1. See Akram-Lodhi and Kay's contribution to this volume.
2. Chapters I–IV in particular.
3. Brenner's original article and the contributions that followed in the pages of *Past and Present* were subsequently collected and published as a book (Aston and Philpin 1985). Our assessment of the 'Brenner Debate' is shaped by Wood (2017, 50–61).
4. My criticisms of Anievas and Nisancioglu are based upon Dimmock (2016), Rioux (2015) and Post (2018).
5. Many of these contributions can be found in Lafrance and Post (2018).

FURTHER READING

Aston, T.H.; Philpin, C.H.E. (eds) (1985), *The Brenner Debate: Agrarian Class Structure and Economic Development in Pre-Industrial Europe*, New York: Cambridge University Press.
Lafrance, X.; Post, C. (eds) (2019), *Case Studies in the Origins of Capitalism*, New York: Palgrave.
Wood, E.M. (2017), *The Origin of Capitalism*, New York: Verso.

REFERENCES

Anievas, A.; Nisancioglu, K. (2015), *How the West Came to Rule: The Geopolitical Origins of Capitalism*, London: Pluto Press.
Ashman, S. (2009), Capitalism, uneven and combined development and the transhistoric, *Cambridge Review of International Affairs*, 22(1), 29–46.
Aston, T.H.; Philpin, C.H.E. (eds) (1985), *The Brenner Debate: Agrarian Class Structure and Economic Development in Pre-Industrial Europe*, New York: Cambridge University Press.
Bois, G. (1985), Against the neo-Malthusian orthodoxy, in Aston, T.H.; Philpin, C.H.E. (eds), *The Brenner Debate*, New York: Cambridge University Press, 107–118.
Brenner, R.P. (1977), The origins of capitalist development: A critique of neo-Smithian Marxism, *New Left Review*, 1(104), 27–92.
Brenner, R.P. (1985), Agrarian roots of European capitalism, in Aston, T.H.; Philpin, C.H.E. (eds), *The Brenner Debate*, New York: Cambridge University Press, 213–328.
Byres, T.J. (2006), Differentiation of the peasantry under feudalism and the transition to capitalism: In defence of Rodney Hilton, *Journal of Agrarian Change*, 6(1), 17–68.
Dimmock, S. (2014), *The Origin of Capitalism in England, 1400–1600*, Leiden: Brill.
Dimmock, S. (2016), The eastern origins of capitalism?, *Historical Materialism Blog*, accessed 5 June 2020 at www.historicalmaterialism.org/blog/eastern-origins-capitalism.
Dobb, M. (1946), *Studies in the Development of Capitalism*, New York: International Publishers.

Emmanuel, A. (1972), *Unequal Exchange: A Study of the Imperialism of Trade*, New York: Monthly Review Press.

Epstein, S.R. (2000), *Freedom and Growth: The Rise of States and Markets in Europe, 1300–1750*, London: Routledge.

Frank, A.G. (1967), *Capitalism and Underdevelopment in Latin America*, New York: Monthly Review Press.

French, H.R.; Hoyle, R.W. (2007), *The Character of English Rural Society: Earls Colne, 1550–1750*, Manchester: Manchester University Press.

Hatcher, J.; Bailey, M. (2001), *Modelling the Middle Ages: The History and Theory of England's Economic Development*, Oxford: Oxford University Press.

Hilton, R. (1985), A crisis of feudalism, in Aston, T.H.; Philpin, C.H.E. (eds), *The Brenner Debate*, New York: Cambridge University Press, 119–137.

Lafrance, X.; Post, C. (eds) (2018), *Case Studies in the Origins of Capitalism*, New York: Palgrave.

Le Roy Ladurie, E. (1974), *The Peasants of Languedoc*, Champaign, IL: University of Illinois Press.

Le Roy Ladurie, E. (1985), A reply to Robert Brenner, in Aston, T.H.; Philpin, C.H.E. (eds), *The Brenner Debate*, New York: Cambridge University Press, 101–106.

Marx, K. (1990 [1867]), *Capital*, vol. 1, London: Penguin Books.

North, D. and Thomas, R.P. (1973), *The Rise of the Western World: A New Economic History*, New York: Cambridge University Press.

Pokrovsky, N. (1933), *Brief History of Russia*, vol. 2, New York: International Publishers.

Post, C. (2012), *The American Road to Capitalism*, Chicago, IL: Haymarket Books.

Post, C. (2018), The use and misuse of uneven and combined development: A critique of Anievas and Nisancioglu, *Historical Materialism* 26(3), 79–98.

Postan, M.M. (1966), Medieval agrarian society in its prime: England, in Postan, M.M. (ed.), *Cambridge Economic History of Europe from the Decline of the Roman Empire, Volume 1: Agrarian Life of the Middle Ages*, New York: Cambridge University Press, 548–632.

Rigby, S.H. (1995), *English Society in the Later Middle Ages: Class, Status and Gender*, Basingstoke: Macmillan.

Rioux, S. (2015), Mind the (theoretical) gap: On the poverty of international relations theorising of uneven and combined development, *Global Society*, 29(4), 481–509.

Rostow, W.W. (1960), *Stages of Economic Growth: A Non-Communist Manifesto*, New York: Cambridge University Press.

Smith, A. (2003 [1776]), *The Wealth of Nations*, New York: Bantam Books.

Sweezy, P. (1976a), A critique, in Hilton, R. (ed.), *The Transition from Feudalism to Capitalism*, London: New Left Books, 33–56.

Sweezy, P. (1976b), A rejoinder, in Hilton, R. (ed.), *The Transition from Feudalism to Capitalism*, London: New Left Books, 102–108.

Trotsky, L. (1932), *The History of the Russian Revolution*, London: Victor Gollancz.

Wallerstein, I. (1974), *The Modern World System, Volume 1: Capitalist Agriculture and the Origins of the European World-Economy in the Sixteenth Century*, New York: Academic Press.

Whittle, J. (2000), *The Development of Agrarian Capitalism: Land and Labour in Norfolk, 1440–1580*, Oxford: Clarendon Press.

Wood, E.M. (2001), Eurocentric anti-Eurocentrism, *Against the Current*, May–June, accessed 5 June at https://solidarity-us.org/atc/92/p993/.

Wood, E.M. (2017), *The Origin of Capitalism*, New York: Verso.

6. An alternative perspective on the agrarian question in Europe and in the developing countries

Utsa Patnaik

INTRODUCTION

The classical discussion of the agrarian question was premised on an accepted narrative regarding the path of industrialization followed first by Britain and generalized to Western Europe. This narrative spoke first of the break-up of feudal relations of production in the European heartland, with a debate turning on the relative causative importance of internal contradictions within the disintegrating feudal system, on the one hand, and on the other the impact of long-distance trade. Second, it assumed that industrial capitalism was necessarily predicated on the displacement of peasant petty producers from the land, their conversion to a class of property-less, wage-dependent workers and the consolidation of land into larger, more productive units under emerging capitalist tenant farmers, inducing a successful 'agricultural revolution'. Third, it assumed that unemployment of displaced peasants was only a transitional problem and that they would be absorbed eventually partly into capitalist agriculture and mainly into expanding factory production.

This narrative was widely accepted by academics in developing countries too, as not only providing a correct perspective on industrial transition in history, but also as providing a suggestive map for the developing countries in the Global South that had recently emerged from their colonial status into independence. Subsequent academic work has followed this accepted narrative in its broad outlines while deviating from it only to stress the particularities of the transition in different countries. From Maurice Dobb (1946) to Robert Brenner (1988), the question of transition from a mainly agrarian economy in Europe has been viewed as driven by a purely internal dynamic, with the destruction of small-scale peasant production as a necessary condition of development. More recent work on the agrarian question, while more sympathetic than earlier to the idea of the importance of imperialism, has continued in the same dominant tradition. Above all, none of the authors have at any point integrated the reality of the possession by the Western European nations of first colonies and then empire into their narrative – a reality that was crucial in defusing the class tensions arising from internal displacement and pauperization. Given the hegemony exercised by the writings from Northern universities, scholars from developing countries too when addressing the agrarian question in their own countries adhere to theoretical frameworks that are not appropriate for their conditions, and this includes the idea of extracting surplus from agriculture for industrial growth through new processes of primitive accumulation.

This author was persuaded by the dominant discourse for some years before realizing that it was seriously flawed, a realization that emerged from studying the history of trade and industrial growth in Britain, which indicated a very close economic link with the transfers it enjoyed from its largest colony, India. Accepted trade theory derived from comparative advantage was found to be based on the factually incorrect premise that all countries could produce all goods.

Neither external sources of primitive accumulation nor massive international migration from Europe had ever been related to its successful industrial transition. But the problems faced by the peasantry in the Global South today cannot be understood within the accepted narrative that, by ignoring colonial transfers, one also thereby ignores the reason for the present-day continuing thrust of Northern countries using new free trade regimes and income-deflating policies to access the products of the Global South, thereby undermining severely the latter's food security.

AGRICULTURAL PRODUCTIVITY AND 'AGRICULTURAL REVOLUTION' IN THE FIRST INDUSTRIAL COUNTRY

The striking feature of the transition to capitalism in Western Europe during the eighteenth and nineteenth centuries was the drive to acquire primary resources from distant lands, first through trade and later through conquest. In academic writing from Northern universities, including those informed by a Marxist perspective, the question was never asked as to why a handful of maritime European nations found it necessary to undertake 'external primitive accumulation' through armed expansion beyond their own borders, followed by either the complete expropriation of small producers there, or their political subjugation as a prelude to extraction of slave rent or taxes from them. The limited primary resource base in Europe and North America, and the inability of their populations to produce a range of goods producible only abroad, has been ignored; mainstream trade theory, including its more modern variants, is based on the factually incorrect Ricardian assumption that all countries could produce all primary goods.

In reality, since cost of production could not be defined for tropical goods in temperate countries where the output of these goods was in the past, is at present and will always be zero, Ricardo's theory contained a material fallacy: the 'fallacy of converse accident' explained by this author in detail elsewhere (Patnaik 2005). One of the main drivers of external expansion, which is the accessing of those products of peasant labour in the South that are not producible at all in cold temperate lands, has been explicitly assumed away by accepted trade theory. The thrust of standard analysis has always been on the internal sources of primitive accumulation; namely, the displacement of small-scale production, the formation of a proletariat and the rise of an assumed efficient farm sector of large-scale capitalist production. Long-distance trade was indeed discussed at length, for example by Dobb (1946), but only in terms of high profit rates for monopoly trading companies. There is no discussion at all of the much more lucrative source of accumulation arising from conquest; the use of colonial budgetary revenues to purchase export goods in India or importing goods that embodied slave rent from the Caribbean colonies meant that the rising trade deficit of Britain with these regions created no external payment liability, unlike its trade with sovereign countries. Transfers in commodity form, of slave rent, land rent, taxes or a combination of the last two, as in Ireland, were very large. The transfer from Asia and the West Indies to Britain estimated in Patnaik (2006) ranged from 5.5 to 6 per cent of Britain's gross domestic product (GDP) during 1780 to 1820, the period of the Industrial Revolution, and nearly doubled the rate of capital formation out of domestic savings.

There are two completely separate aspects of the internal 'primitive accumulation of capital': the first is the class structure-altering aspects of the process; and the second is the alleged rise in productivity (the 'agricultural revolution') required to supply food and raw materials as the labour force shifts toward factory production. While the social changes in class structure brought about by the redistribution of the land were undoubtedly, as described by Karl Marx (and later by Richard H. Tawney, John L. and Barbara Hammond and Paul Mantoux, among others), the narrative of higher productivity departs from the actual facts. In reality, in England, there was absolute decline of grain production per head of population, as a result of which the availability of bread, the main 'wage-good', declined after 1750 for eight decades, which was precisely the period of transition to capitalist farming. The raw material of the Industrial Revolution, raw cotton, was of course entirely imported.

Over the entire eighteenth century there was only a 43 per cent rise in cereal output according to Chambers and Mingay (1966), and this is confirmed by later detailed empirical studies (Allen 1999; Turner et al. 2001; Clark 2002). Yield net of seed per unit of area did rise (see table 7.1 in Turner et al. 2001) but this rise was not enough to maintain even the level of per capita grain availability found in 1700. Using alternative population estimates, ranging from those of Schofield (1981) to Maddison (2006), we have found that cereal output per capita declined by between 12.5 and 17.5 per cent from 1750 to the end of the century (Patnaik 2011, table 2b). Wheat output per head of that part of the population estimated as consuming wheaten bread was 223 kg in 1750, which fell to only 168 kg by 1800, before rising by 1850 to 190 kg. This latter amount still left the figure well below that of the developing countries today. Overton (1996) is the main proponent of the 'successful agricultural revolution' narrative, but he contradicted his own position, saying that from 1750 to 1850 population grew at an average of 1.07 per cent per annum and the estimates of agricultural output growth ranged from 0.77 to 0.82 per cent per annum; this means that output per capita declined.

Despite a yield-raising transition to capitalist agriculture, Britain failed to feed its population. Little wonder that the cry for cheap bread became the principal political economy demand of the working class for many decades starting from the 1790s. Obdurate landlords using the Corn Laws to prevent imports, rapid wartime food price inflation and bad harvests in the 1790s all combined to reduce the rioting working class to starvation. France saw the same trend of mass hunger preceding its Revolution. Taking 10-year averages, Britain's grain imports increased more than five-fold during the period between 1800–1809 and 1850–1859 (Patnaik 2011, table 3a) and nearly quadrupled over the following three decades. Indeed, by 1855 Britain's retained imports of all primary products by value exceeded the value of its own domestic primary sector output (Davis 1979, table 31).

Imports of primary products exceeding domestic output was only possible because most of the imports represented tax-financed transfers from the colonies. George Wingate, who set up the land revenue system in the Bombay presidency in 1818, deplored the 'tribute' that India was forced to pay every year to Britain: from 1765 onwards, one-third of net budgetary revenues was not spent within the country but was set aside as 'expenditure abroad' for purchasing export goods from the peasants and artisans, from whom the taxes in cash had been extracted in the first place. These producers, though appearing to be paid, were not actually paid for their export products, for a large part of their own taxes, without their knowledge, simply changed its form from cash to export goods. The producers were taxed out of their goods, and the foreign ruler thereby obtained a vast inflow of completely free tropical goods and textiles which it partly retained for use in the home country and partly re-exported to other temperate lands against the imports of food grains and strategic naval materials in which it was deficient. In the West Indies costless imports were embodied in slave rent, namely the excess of output net of material costs over the bare subsistence of enslaved labour, while in Ireland tenants subsisted on cheap potatoes while rents plus taxes extracted from them were embodied in exports of wheat and animal products to Britain.

An inverse relation always emerged between primary-sector exports and domestic consumption. As very little investment was put in place to raise productivity, the sown area of tropical land remained virtually fixed but it was made to provide increasing volumes of foodstuffs and raw materials to the industrializing world. This always led to declining grain supplies for the domestic population. In India commercial crops exported to the Global North grew 10 times faster than food grains (superior grains were also exported), and domestic per capita grain availability declined from 200 kg in 1900 to 137 kg by 1946; similar declines took place in Java under the Dutch and in Korea under Japan (Patnaik 2008).

UNDERESTIMATING COLONIAL TRADE AND IGNORING UNILATERAL TRANSFERS

The obligations placed on the colonies through the extraction of taxes and rents to meet the insatiable demand for primary goods in the metropolitan countries, and given inadequate investment, forced colonized populations to reduce their level of consumption and profoundly affected the cropping pattern, which shifted toward export crops at the expense of food staples consumed locally. The major metropolitan countries always imported much larger volumes of tropical goods from their colonies than they required for their own use. This was done in order to re-export the substantial balance, because these goods represented international purchasing power and commanded a ready market in the other temperate lands of Europe and North America that were equally unable to produce these goods and which did not have tropical colonies.

Yet in the metropolitan literature colonial trade is systematically downplayed, to the extent of many scholars presenting conceptually incorrect trade estimates, and transfers from colonies to the metropolis are ignored entirely. Estimates of 'the volume of British trade' presented by Phyllis Deane and W.A. Cole (1969, table 14) were incorrect because the authors excluded re-exported imports entirely from the series of both imports into and exports from Britain. They simply added up imports retained within the country and exports of its domestically produced goods, with no explanation for their procedure. This was particularly inexplicable because earlier Deane (1965) had emphasized the importance of re-exports for Britain. In open economy macroeconomic theory, and in the actual practice followed by all international organizations (namely the World Bank, International Monetary Fund and United Nations) that present country-wise trade data, total trade comprises total imports plus total exports, with re-exported imports being included both in imports and in exports. This is conceptually correct because re-exported goods finance imports of goods from other countries, just like a country's domestic exports. Using this correct trade concept we find that Britain's total trade to GDP ratio reached 58 per cent in the three years ending in 1801, compared to the 36 per cent presented in Deane and Cole (1969). Similar underestimates of Britain's trade are presented by later authors such as Crafts (1985) and Harley and McCloskey (1981). Excluding re-exported imports without any explicit mention of such exclusion results in lower and factually incorrect ratios of imports and exports to GDP.

From 1765 to 1836, and then from 1837 to 1900, the gold and foreign exchange earnings from India's global commodity export surplus were £316.25 million and £620 million, respectively. These earnings were entirely taken by Britain for its own use while 'paying' the local peasant and artisan producers out of their own taxes, which in practice of course meant not paying them at all (Patnaik 2017). Compounded at 5 per cent interest to the year of independence, 1947, the estimate of this drain from India to Britain amounts to £440 billion, which is more than 40 times the United Kingdom's GDP in 1947.

It was not a more productive domestic capitalist agriculture that satisfied growing food and raw material requirements, unlike the *jejune* accounts in the standard works. It was primarily tax-financed and rent-financed transfers from the colonies. As the transfers increased, famines became endemic: one-eighth of Ireland's population perished in the famine of 1846–1847, even as wheat exports to England continued. India suffered several colonial famines of great severity, culminating in the 1943–1944 Bengal famine when 3 million civilians, of whom one-third were children aged 14 years and less, starved to death (Patnaik 2018). Civilian mortality during the two years of the famine was more than six times the total estimated for British civilians and armed forces personnel combined for the entire period of the war, which was below half a million. Yet we find no reference to agrarian distress in Ireland or India in standard works or by leading economic historians on the agrarian question: in their idyllic world it appears that lord, peasant and merchant played out their roles as though the colonial exploitation of today's Global South or of Ireland simply did not exist.

Similarly, the economic effects of out-migration by Europeans to overseas lands they had seized from indigenous populations is ignored completely. The vast land, timber and mineral resources of North America, Argentina, South Africa and Australasia were permanently appropriated by European settlers. For nearly a century after 1821 more persons emigrated permanently from Britain (16 million) than its initial population (12 million), not counting Irish emigration after its famine, and they were followed by other Europeans. The metropolitan reserve army declined and workers could unite effectively to demand better working and living conditions.

In the compulsorily trade-open colonies, however, the opposite process operated. Peasants and artisans, defrauded of their own export surplus earnings by the linkage of taxes and rents with trade, were pauperized into undernutrition and often into actual starvation; when the dumping of textiles simultaneously displaced local manufactures, these two factors combined to swell the reserve army of labour. Only a small fraction of this vast reserve army was transported under indentured labour systems to work on plantations in other regions of the world. During the interwar Great Depression, as primary product prices declined conditions worsened further, with substantial losses by peasants of their mortgaged assets against debt; in India, 38 per cent of rural workers declared themselves as mainly working for wages in the 1931 Census, compared to 26 per cent in 1921.

The gravest problems facing developing economies today are unemployment and declining nutritional standards for the masses, and both are endemic to capitalism as an economic system. Developing countries do not have the options today that Europeans used in the past, albeit in a ruthless manner, to overcome the same problems. After gaining independence developing countries protected their agriculture and stabilized incomes to some extent, but this ended with the inception of the neoliberal reforms that reduced state expenditure and renewed free trade. External demands on developing countries' peasant producers were revived in an even more intensive form via transnational companies and the world trade regime to supply the North with the primary products in which they are permanently deficient. Under the neoliberal regime of sharp cut-backs in state spending on investment and rural development, it has proved impossible to raise enough yields to maintain per capita grain availability in these countries as well as supply the growing demands of the Global North for primary products they cannot produce at all. While under the protectionist regime from 1950 to 1990 per capita food grain availability in India had risen, under the trade-open regime since then it has declined again to the level of 1937. In advanced countries capitalist agricultural production is inefficient by global standards but is sustained by massive state subsidies every year that amount to half or more of the value of their entire farm output. This output however can only supply a part of the diversified consumption basket of their rich populations.

In developing countries, the real facts of rising unemployment and declining nutrition for the masses have been camouflaged behind figures of high service-based GDP growth rates and spurious claims of decline in poverty. In India, growth in the material production of agriculture plus industry has declined, and they now provide less than two-fifths of GDP compared to two-thirds a few decades ago. Reliable official data on nutrition (National Sample Survey Organization 2013) show that per capita energy intake in kilocalories per day and protein intake have been declining during the decades of neoliberal reform, and have declined faster in rural areas. With trade liberalization farmers, exposed to price volatility as in the colonial past, have again fallen into the trap of cumulating debt: over 320,000 farmers have committed debt-induced suicide since 1997 (Nagaraj et al. 2014). Concentration of land ownership has increased as assets have been sold to repay debt, and the near-forcible acquisition of productive agricultural land by corporate interests facilitated by the state has induced waves of farmer protests. Technological change in manufacturing, mandatory in a competitive world, has meant that positive growth in manufacturing output is producing negative growth in employment.

The long-term solution for developing countries is not the promotion of labour-displacing capitalist or corporate agriculture, for the displaced have nowhere to go, but ensuring the viability of small-scale production, which continues to be the main source of livelihood for the majority, and ensuring work and wages for rural labour. A reversal of income-deflating fiscal and monetary policies, and the protection of farmers through price stabilization measures combined with the provision of affordable credit, are all eminently feasible. Reaping the benefits of economies of scale and improving livelihoods requires that small-scale units of peasant and artisan production enter into voluntary co-operation. Some successful experiments have been undertaken already in India, such as women's co-operative groups in Kerala engaged in paddy cultivation and fisheries co-operatives in a number of states, both of which point the way to a more viable future.

FURTHER READING

Bagchi, A.K. (2006), *Perilous Passage: Mankind and the Global Ascendancy of Capital*, New Delhi: Oxford University Press.
Byres, T.J. (2014), In pursuit of capitalist agrarian transition, *Journal of Agrarian Change*, 16(3), 432–451.
Patnaik, U.; Patnaik, P. (2016), *A Theory of Imperialism*, New York: Columbia University Press; Delhi: Tulika Books.

Patnaik, U.; Patnaik, P. (2021), *Capitalism and Imperialism: Theory, History and the Present*, New York: Monthly Review Press.

REFERENCES

Allen, R.C. (1999), Tracking the agricultural revolution in England, *Economic History Review*, 42(2), 209–235.

Brenner, R. (1988), Agrarian class structure and economic development in pre-industrial Europe, in Aston, T.H.; Philpin, C.H.E. (eds), *The Brenner Debate*, Cambridge: Cambridge University Press, 10–63.

Chambers, J.D.; Mingay, G.E. (1966), *The Agricultural Revolution 1750–1880*, London: Batsford.

Clark, G. (2002), The agricultural revolution and the Industrial Revolution: England 1500–1912, accessed 22 June 2020 at http://faculty.econ.ucdavis.edu/faculty/gclark/papers/prod2002.pdf.

Crafts, N.C.R. (1985), *British Economic Growth during the Industrial Revolution*, Oxford: Oxford University Press.

Davis, R. (1979), *The Industrial Revolution and British Overseas Trade*, Leicester: Leicester University Press.

Deane, P. (1965), *The First Industrial Revolution*, Cambridge: Cambridge University Press.

Deane, P.; Cole, J.A. (1969), *British Economic Growth 1688–1959: Trends and Structure*, second edition, Cambridge: Cambridge University Press.

Dobb, M.H. (1946), *Studies in the Development of Capitalism*, London: Routledge and Kegan Paul.

Harley, C.K.; McCloskey, D.N. (1981), Foreign trade: Competition and the expanding international economy, in Floud, R. and McCloskey, D.N. (eds), *The Economic History of Britain since 1700*, vol. 2, Cambridge: Cambridge University Press, 50–69.

Maddison, A. (2006), *The World Economy*, vols 1 and 2, Paris: OECD Publishing.

Nagaraj, K.; Sainath, P.; Rukmani, R.; Gopinath, R. (2014), Farmers' suicides in India: Magnitudes, trends, and spatial patterns, 1997–2012, *Review of Agrarian Studies*, 4(2), accessed 1 July 2021 at http://ras.org.in/farmers_suicides_in_india.

National Sample Survey Organization (2013), *Nutritional Intake in India 2011–12*, Report No. 560, Government of India, Ministry of Statistics and Programme Implementation.

Overton, M. (1996), Re-establishing the English agricultural revolution, *Agricultural History Review*, 44(1), 1–20.

Patnaik, U. (2005), Ricardo's fallacy, in Jomo, K.S. (ed.), *The Pioneers of Development Economics*, Delhi: Tulika Books; London: Zed Books, 31–41.

Patnaik, U. (2006), The free lunch: Transfers from the tropical colonies and their role in capital formation in Britain during the Industrial Revolution, in Jomo, K.S. (ed.), *Globalization under Hegemony: The Changing World Economy*, Oxford: Oxford University Press.

Patnaik, U. (2008), *The Republic of Hunger*, Delhi: Three Essays Collective and (2009) London: Merlin Press.

Patnaik, U. (2011), The 'agricultural revolution' in England, in Moosvi, S. (ed.), *Capitalism, Colonialism and Globalization*, Delhi: Tulika Books, 17–27.

Patnaik, U. (2017), Revisiting the 'drain' or transfers from India to Britain in the context of global diffusion of capitalism, in Chakrabarti, S.; Patnaik, U. (eds), *Agrarian and Other Histories: Essays for Benoy Bhushan Chaudhuri*, Delhi: Tulika Books, 277–313.

Patnaik, U. (2018), Profit inflation, Keynes and the holocaust in Bengal 1943–44, *Economic and Political Weekly*, 43(42), 33–43; also in Narayanamoorthy, A.; Bhavani, R.V.; Sujatha, R. (eds) (2019), *Whither Rural India? A festschrift for Venkatesh Athreya*, Delhi: Tulika Books.

Schofield, R. (1981), British population change, 1700–1871, in Floud, R.; McCloskey, D.N. (eds), *The Economic History of Britain since 1700*, vol. 1, Cambridge: Cambridge University Press, 60–95.

Turner, M.F.; Beckett, J.V.; Afton, R. (2001), *Farm Production in England 1700–1914*, Cambridge: Cambridge University Press.

PART II

CONCEPTS

7. The agrarian question

Michael Watts[1]

[The agrarian question is] ... whether and how capital is seizing hold of agriculture, revolutionizing it, making old forms of production and property untenable and creating the necessity for new ones. (Kautsky 1988 [1899], 12)

INTRODUCTION

The agrarian question – whether and how agriculture provides surpluses over and above subsistence; the differing forms of agrarian production; and the relations between agriculture and the accumulation of capital, between land-based resources and empire – is capacious and wide ranging. It represents a sort of red thread running across the *longue durée* of human history. There is, however, a modern or 'classical' sense in which the term 'the agrarian question' is customarily deployed, which can be traced back to Adam Smith and the Scottish Enlightenment political economists, and to Karl Marx (1976/1867) in his famous chapter on primitive accumulation in Volume 1 of *Capital*. All of these thinkers were concerned with the origins of capitalism, the forms of capitalist agriculture and the transition from feudalism to capitalist modes of production. By the late nineteenth and early twentieth centuries, the agrarian question took on a new lease of life shaped by deepening demands for wage foods (staples), as European economies entered into the Second Industrial Revolution (marked by an increase in the scale and scope of industrial manufacture in Europe), by the emergence of a global grains trade and the related struggles among landlords, industrialists and workers over free trade and protectionism, and not least by the extension of the political franchise into rural areas still dominated by peasant and family forms of agrarian production (Akram-Lodhi and Kay 2010).

The canonical text addressing this issue is Karl Kautsky's *The Agrarian Question (Die Agrarfrage)*, published originally in 1899, which was central to a wide-ranging debate within Marxist and socialist circles on the future of European smallholders, the relation of agricultural production to industry and capitalist accumulation and the political prospect of alliances between workers and peasants. At stake was the very look of agriculture: What constituted an identifiable agrarian capitalism and its forms of production, what was the trajectory of agrarian capital in the heartlands of Western European late nineteenth-century industrial capitalism during the Age of Classical Empire and what did a commercial and globalizing agro-food system – what Harriet Friedmann (1993) calls the 'first world food regime' – portend for the future of the varied scales and forms of production, livelihood and political struggle in relation to the land?

This chapter consists of four parts. First, I provide a rather condensed synopsis of the so-called classical debates over the agrarian question (see Kay and Akram-Lodhi 2021), following which I present some of the subsequent research which examines the various paths of agrarian transitions in the Global North and South (Byres 1991). Second, I focus on two important contemporary questions, namely: How has the emergence in the twentieth century of a global corporate-dominated agro-food system (McMichael 2015; Bernstein 2016) challenged and extended some of the classical agrarian debates? And does the hegemony of global capitalism in its current neoliberal form signal the end or the resolution of the agrarian question (Bernstein and Byers 2001; Bernstein 2006)? Third, I offer some brief remarks on why the agrarian question remains a vital one and an important focus for theoretical debate and reflection.

CLASSICAL AGRARIAN QUESTIONS

Upon its publication, Kautsky's *The Agrarian Question* (1988 [1899]) defined the contours of the debate over the political economy of agriculture in the late nineteenth and twentieth centuries. Kautsky was not the first political economist within the Marxist tradition to address peasant or smallholder agriculture. Marx himself had described in his notebooks – the *Grundrisse* (1993 [1857–1858]) – the variety of conditions under which agrarian capitalism could emerge from the 'swamp' of pre-capitalist relations. Surveying European economies at the turn of the century, Friedrich Engels noted in 1894 in his *The Peasant Question in France and Germany* that peasants were 'a very essential factor of the population, production and political power' (Engels 1951 [1894], 2). Neither capitalist exploiter nor dispossessed prole-tarian, the peasant farmer occupied a politically ambiguous space. Bifurcated class positions among the peasantry produced contradictory interests and, according to Engels, the possibility of being subverted or diverted by powerful class interests. Peasant political impulses, said Engels, were distorted by a 'deep rooted sense of property' and their political allegiances could be easily manipulated by the 'wolf in sheep's clothing' (ibid.), namely 'the big landowner' and 'the bourgeoisie'.

In Kautsky's book, the figure (and future) of the smallholder commanded centre stage, not least in terms of whether the ubiquity of peasants (and indeed their numerical and geographical expansion) was a sign of their ability to resist competition, and in doing so to represent a chal-lenge to classical conceptions of agrarian capitalism and large-scale wage-based production. In contrast, for the likes of Engels (and subsequently Lenin), neither the peasants nor their holdings could or should be preserved; locked in a losing battle to save their land in the face of global competition, their 'antiquated' mode of production would inevitably be superseded by 'capitalist large-scale production'. Like every relic of the past, the peasant was 'hopelessly doomed'; she is, and can only be, 'a future proletarian' (Engels 1951 [1894], 5).

Kautsky's intervention posited this tendency as a question. The peasantry and family farmers in *The Agrarian Question* were not granted an inevitable historical fate. The book rather examined the relations between agriculture and industry, what capitalist forms of agrarian production might look like and what sorts of political struggles were to be waged. Kautsky, like Engels and most Marxist analysts, rested upon two fundamental premises. The first was the economic and social differentiation among peasant households and communities. The second was a process of historical elimination, namely that peasants would suffer the same fate as petty commodity producers (artisanal industrial producers) when confronting the competitive forces unleashed by the large-scale industrial manufacturing sector. Capitalist accumulation would drive consolidation and concentration among smallholders into larger capitalist enterprises, and would therefore provide the conditions of possibility for the development of a rural and agrarian bourgeoisie. In short, what was at stake in the agrarian question was the imminent (and strategically necessary) demise of the peasant and the family farm.

If Kautsky held to some form of Marxist orthodoxy when he began to draft *The Agrarian Question*, by chapter 7 he was already going in the opposite direction, citing the 1895 German Census which indicated that the small farm had not lost ground since the 1850s and in some areas was even flourishing. Why then did the peasantry persist, why and how did what Kautsky called 'the limited nature of the soil' (Kautsky 1988 [1899], 145) (land as non-reproducible) retard the processes of concentration of land and capital, and why (and how) was household production in agriculture structurally different from manufacturing, with its own logic and dynamics? Kautsky's answer was in many respects heretical. As he put it, agriculture 'does not develop according to the pattern of industry: *it follows its own laws*' (ibid., 15, emphasis added). The obstacles to agrarian transition were based in part in nature: seasonality, climatic and other risks, and the limits to mechanization for some crops made factories in the field difficult and in some respects undesirable for capital. Peasants could, moreover, overexploit their own labour, accepting 'under-consumption' and 'excessive labour' and underbidding permanent wage workers, thereby providing a source of 'continuous primitive accumulation' (Alavi and Shanin 1988, xvi).

In sum, Kautsky's intervention proved to be brilliantly prescient and a sort of theoretical and political challenge to Marxist orthodoxy. Yet the work was 'forgotten within barely a decade' (Alavi and Shanin 1988, xviii). Half a century later in the 1960s and 1970s, as the figure of the peasant, as well as the concepts of peasant revolution and agrarian transition – both capitalist and socialist – in the post-colonial world returned to centre stage, *The Agrarian Question* came back into vivid focus. Kautsky in particular took the material world (nature) seriously (the immovability of land, the perturbations and risks associated with biology and climate), and while he did not address the question of agro-ecology or sustainability at length, it is not a stretch to see glimmers of what was to become political ecology (Dietz 2021). He was also attentive to how global forces shape national and local agrarian systems. While he did not assign them an active role in any assessment of the coming socialist revolution, Kautsky saw 'two souls' in the breast of the peasant – the worker and the property owner – which implied that the smallholder might under some circumstances align with revolutionary movements and proletarian parties. All of this was to have powerful relevance when the struggles and conflicts surrounding 'development' in the post-colonial world shattered.

Beyond Kautsky and his focus on Germany, Russia too saw a robust debate on the agrarian question toward the end of the nineteenth century. Indeed, the three other canonical texts which shaped thinking about agriculture and capitalism in the early twentieth century were all authored by Russians: V.I. Lenin's *The Development of Capitalism in Russia* (1964 [1899]), Alexander Chayanov's *The Theory of Peasant Economy* (1966 [1924]) and Evgenii Preobrazhensky's *The New Economics* (1967 [1926]). Lenin's focus was on the prismatic ways in which the social differentiation of peasants – from the allotment-holding worker to the rich *kulak* (a peasant in Russia wealthy enough to own a farm and hire labour) – marked a hegemony of wage relations, the remaking of the countryside and the development of a home market. Lenin developed two lines of thinking which departed from Kautsky. One acknowledged Kautsky's insights into the unique character of agriculture and the spatial heterogeneity of farming systems, yet provided a more systematic account of differing trajectories of capitalist dynamics. Lenin discerned two basic paths of capitalist agrarian transition: the Prussian path and the American path. In the former, the feudal landlord economy slowly and gradually evolved into a capitalist Junker landlord economy, which 'condemns the peasants to harrowing exploitation and bondage while a small minority of *Grossbauern* ['big peasants'] arises' (Lenin 1964 [1899], 239). Conversely, in the American path, there is no landlord economy, or 'it is broken up by revolution' and the peasant 'predominates, becomes the sole agent of agriculture and evolves into a capitalist farmer' (ibid.).

Lenin's second departure from Kautsky was political, as he took issue with the populist Narodnik economist who believed that landlord farming was the only source of agrarian capitalism. Lenin's analysis revealed the ways in which peasant life was being torn asunder; the countryside was being parcellized into a rural bourgeoisie and a rural proletariat. Self-exploitation by peasants still mired in some of the extra-economic trappings of serfdom was untenable. In the face of technological change, global competition and deepening indebtedness, such conditions offered the possibility that peasants (many of whom were in fact semi-proletarians) and workers might constitute a revolutionary class and provide the foundation for the overthrow of a corrupt and weak Russian capitalism.

Two other towering figures emerged from the foundry of the Russian Revolution and its aftermath, Yvgeni Preobrazhensky and Alexander Chayanov, each of whom made lasting contributions to the agrarian question, and both were casualties of the Stalinist purges, executed during the 1930s. As a leading figure in the People's Commissariat of Finance, Preobrazhensky became deeply involved in the problems of taxation and economic planning for the industrialization of peasant Russia and published a series of articles on the topic in 1924, detailing the argument that the money to finance mass industrialization would necessarily have to come from the country's rural peasantry, which comprised about 80 per cent of the nation's population. Preobrazhensky advocated for a rapid pace of industrialization, arguing that the Communist Party faced a grave danger of being held hostage by nascent rural capitalists (*kulaks*), who were effectively smuggling in capitalist relations and undermining socialist agriculture. Without forcing industrialization on the backs of the peasants, the socialist state was 'doomed' (Preobrazhensky 1967 [1926], 89).

Chayanov's writing represented a break with both Marx and Lenin, though he was careful to never make this rupture explicit or to politicize his differences. Chayanov can be read as an alternative to Lenin's unilinear differentiation theory of agrarian capitalism. Lenin saw the Russian countryside as already capitalist; the key marker was the resort to the hiring of workers (Lenin 1964 [1899], 52). Chayanov, conversely, argued that 90 per cent of farms hired no farm labour. His goal was to show the viability of peasant farming for Russia's socialist future. Chayanov emphasized two things: that the family farm was not a capitalist enterprise and operated on a different logic; and that a system (an economy) constituted of peasant farms ought to be treated as a separate form of economy, a non-capitalist national economy – and in principle, as he explained in his discussion of vertically state-integrated and controlled co-operatives, was consistent with a notion of socialist agriculture.

Another figure is worthy of note in these Marxian and populist debates on agrarian capitalism and the peasantry. In a different register, Rosa Luxemburg, in *The Accumulation of Capital* published in 1913, self-consciously saw the agrarian question in global (and imperialist) terms, and specifically emphasized the structural need for the competitive struggle of capital on the international stage to invade and break down what she called 'the natural economy' (Luxemburg 1968 [1913], 348) of the peasantry (this is brilliantly elucidated in chapter 29 of *The Accumulation of Capital* entitled 'The struggle against the peasant economy'). Luxemburg saw the peasantry as capitalism's victim as a consequence of 'capital in power', namely 'modern colonial policy' (ibid., 350). She provided two new insights. The first (and here there was an echo of Marx's writings on primitive accumulation) was that the transformation from a natural to a commodity economy could not rest upon what she called 'slow internal disintegration' which would take 'centuries'. Rather, the breakdown of the 'rigid barriers' of the natural economy required massive force and violence, oppressive state taxation and cheap goods (ibid., 350). The second was that capitalism was a sort of frontier process, requiring non-capitalisms of various sorts to accumulate. Capital accumulation was not an internal process linking branches of the economy, but a relation between inside and outside (capitalist and non-capitalist, core and periphery). What Luxemburg flagged was not simply the global character of the agrarian question, but the contradictory ways in which the non-capitalist system (the peasant natural economy, for example) is simultaneously preserved and destroyed – ideas which were to resurface in the 1970s with discussions of the articulation of modes of production and the so-called 'conservation-dissolution' thesis (see Vergopolous 1978).

THE REBIRTH OF THE AGRARIAN QUESTION

The historical debates surrounding Kautsky, Lenin and Chayanov, and the various forms of what is often referred to as 'peasantism' or agrarian populism (see Brass 2000; Bernstein 2016), may seem somewhat arcane, occupying the higher elevations of academic theory. In many respects, the debate largely disappeared in the 1930s and 1940s. It was not until the 1960s, and especially the 1970s and 1980s, that the agrarian question reappeared in what has been referred to as 'the peasant studies boom'.

How might one account for this rebirth? One reason was the publication of a series of key texts which did much to draw scholarly attention to peasants, landlords and agrarian conditions, both historical and contemporary, in all 'three worlds', but especially in relation to the raft of newly independent post-colonial states. Eric Wolf's *Peasants* (1966) and *Peasant Wars of the Twentieth Century* (1969), Barrington Moore, Jr.'s *The Social Origins of Dictatorship and Democracy* (1966), Moshe Lewin's *Russian Peasants and Soviet Power* (1968), Christopher Hill's *From Reformation to Industrial Revolution* (1967) and not least the translation into English of Chayanov's *The Theory of the Peasant Economy* (1966) appeared almost simultaneously in the run-up to the Vietnam War and the turbulent late 1960s. These books galvanized attention to the intersections of agrarian transitions and political economy in an era in which both anti-colonial nationalist movements (which included an active role of peasantries) and the challenges of post-colonial state building and development on the back of largely agrarian (and peasant) societies took centre stage.

Another lineament of the peasant studies boom was a generation of post-1945 Third World intellectuals and revolutionaries. The likes of Nehru, Nasser, Castro, Nkrumah, Ho Chi Minh and Sukarno had their eyes keenly focused on questions of anti-imperialism, non-alignment and post-colonial autonomy. But the peasant question – its size, condition, political leanings and relations to the common aspiration toward rapid industrialization – was always a red thread (literal and metaphorical) which ran through these earliest expressions of Third World solidarity and emancipatory politics. Of course, some of these towering figures of this generation took on the peasant question as a practical political question – Ho Chi Minh, Mao-se-Tung and Amilcar Cabral, for example – and wrote extensively in a tradition which echoed the classical interventions of Luxemburg, Lenin and Kautsky. Perhaps the most compelling figure in this regard was Frantz Fanon, who had much to say about the role of peasants in revolutionary change and the pitfalls of what he called national consciousness, both of which had pride of place in his influential *The Wretched of the Earth* (1963). For Fanon, there were only two roads from colonial subjugation: national liberation based on peasant revolution leading to a socialist participatory democracy, or the national bourgeois road that would bring progressive degradation to political order, ending in dictatorship and repression.

Finally, there is the matter of the historical conjuncture of the Cold War; the chilling effects of which, as well as the threat of what was perceived as peasant communism, left-inspired peasant revolution and/or anti-imperialism, increasingly pushed agriculture to the centre of the development agenda. The Green Revolution, and the World Bank's focus on promoting 'smallholder development', further invigorated agrarian questions. This geopolitical conjuncture provided a key condition of possibility – intellectual, political, developmental – for the rebirth of the agrarian question.

The explosion of research on peasantries and the agrarian question in the 1970s and 1980s contributed to, and drew strength from, the emergence of Marxist-inspired theories of political economy. The arrival of dependency theory from the Americas, the genesis of world systems thinking, the wide-ranging debates over modes of production and the resurgence of theories of imperialism addressing uneven development, unequal trade and post-colonial state formation all contributed to a body of critical theory on class, state and capitalism, which provided the wider canvas on which the agrarian question could flourish. The 1970s and 1980s was a period of assertive nationalism in the Global South and in some countries undergoing revolutionary change. Not only did the majority of the world's population live in self-identified socialist states, but a number of Global South countries – for example Laos, Angola, Mozambique, Nicaragua and Chile – emerged as fully fledged revolutionary states, and a raft of others were marked by (often debilitating) struggles involving powerful left revolutionary (and often peasant-based) movements (for instance, El Salvador, Indonesia, Vietnam).

THREE PROBLEMATICS IN THE AGRARIAN QUESTION BOOM

The conjuncture of the peasant and critical agrarian studies boom brought forth an enormous flowering of research engaging with a variety of different theoretical registers on the three problematics of the classical agrarian question. One was the peasant differentiation question, and the return to ethnographically and historically rich examinations of the Lenin-Chayanov debate – and the purported weaknesses, romanticism or untenable natures of peasant populisms (Shanin 1986; Brass 2000; Bernstein 2010). Studies examined the complex ways in which rural differentiation and commodification were proceeding, often triggered by the Green Revolution and related development interventions (Harriss 1982; for more recent work see Moore 2005; Li 2007). Another issue was the emergence of forms of wage labour, sometimes alongside the persistence of forms of unfree labour (see Ramachandran 1990), and in particular how seasonal or permanent rural out-migration, which fostered conditions in which rural households in effect subsidized the costs of the reproduction of labour power, was functional to capital. The processes of commodification and the effects of markets and price variation on household reproduction (see Bernstein 1977; Deere and De Janvry 1979) were especially important themes and contributed to a body of work which questioned peasants as a distinctive and unique form of production and rather theorized households as forms of petty commodity production (Friedmann 1978; Gibbon and Neocosmos 1985; Scott 1986).

The variety of forms and paths of differentiation was astounding, from the role of usury and merchant capital, which often kept peasants and tenants on the land, albeit in penury, rather than stimulating land dispossession, to the ways in which so-called traditional institutions (youth groups in Africa or village chieftaincies) could be repurposed in the circuits of agrarian accumulation (Berry 1989, 2009). The larger question once again was, as the title of one book put it, 'disappearing peasantries' (see Bryceson et al. 2000). But the focus on household differentiation also opened up a second problematic, namely the black box of the domestic sphere, which of course raised questions of patriarchy and its relation to property, as well as the dynamics of household social reproduction (see Friedmann 1978; Guyer and Peters 1987). The household and gender then emerged as a terrain of struggle and the debate moved away from relations of production narrowly construed to social reproduction.

Land rights and land struggles – and the complex overlapping, nested and contested intersections of customary, private and state forms of property – became an object of considerable scrutiny (see De Janvry 1981; Lund 2008; Berry 2009). Not surprisingly, the ecological question loomed large in a way that was essentially absent in the classical formulation of the agrarian question. Issues such as soil erosion, the assault on common property resources, the contradictions between state forest or national park projects and peasant communities, forms of peasant science and indigenous knowledge and the vulnerabilities of the agrarian ways of life to environmental threats such as drought all generated a large body of work on famine, food security and agro-ecology (Watts 1983; Richards 1985).

A BOOM IN HISTORICALLY ORIENTED FIELD-BASED PEASANT STUDIES

One of the hallmarks of the 1970s and 1980s was the richness, diversity and comparative scope of historically oriented and field-based studies of peasants and agrarian conditions in the Global South. There was a quartet of major interventions that explicitly and directly engaged with the classical agrarian question, which deserve mention because of their profound impact on the field. The first was Alain De Janvry's *Agrarian Question and Reformism in Latin America* (1981), a brilliant *tour d'horizon* of agrarian dynamics in Latin America prior to the onset of the neoliberal revolution. De Janvry returned explicitly to the Lenin-Kautsky-Chayanov works, but situated them on a much larger canvas of globally uneven capitalism, drawing upon theories of imperialism and Samir Amin's book *Unequal Development* (1976) in particular.

The second was a book, also with a strong Latin American focus, by David Goodman et al., entitled *From Farming to Biotechnology* (1987), which returned to Kautsky's insights into the consequences of the biological character of agriculture, but also linked in a powerful way tendencies in both the Global North and South. Agriculture, the authors argued, 'confronts capitalism as a natural production process' (Goodman et al. 1987, 1), including the biological character and risks associated with agriculture, such as the fixity of land, seasonality, uneven fertility, crop-specific biophysical constraints on mechanization and climatic and other on-farm risks. Unable to remove these constraints directly, industrial capital adapts to nature through two mechanisms which are in tension with each other. One is appropriationism, by which discrete elements of the production process are taken over by industry (without necessarily radically transforming the land-based forms of production). The other is substitutionism, also a discontinuous and persistent process by which key agricultural crops (foods and fibres) can be substituted by industrial products (synthetic sugars, for example). Both of these tendencies take on new and distinctive forms through the biotechnological and genetic revolutions of the late twentieth century, and each can be associated with very different fractions of capital and institutional forms of entry into agriculture (pharmaceutical companies, agro-food integrators, retailers and so on). The central issue – again an echo of Kautsky – is the industrialization of agriculture through a series of 'partial, discontinuous appropriations of rural labour and biological production processes and parallel substitutions of rural products' (Goodman et al. 1987, 2); processes often propelled by state support (research and development, credit, extension). As Goodman et al. put it, 'capitalist development has found expression neither in the factory farm nor the subsumed family farm' (ibid.).

The final two books are marked by a deep historical sensibility. Terry Byres's capacious and wide-ranging comparative historical study of the differing paths of agrarian transition, entitled *Capitalism from Above and Capitalism from Below: An Essay in Comparative Political Economy* (1996), addressed the apparent historical anomalies and puzzles associated with differing paths of transition, both complicating and resituating the roads outlined by Lenin. And in a completely different theoretical register is Silvia Federici's feminist account of primitive accumulation and the transition from feudalism to capitalism, entitled *Caliban and the Witch: Women, the Body and Primitive Accumulation* (2004). Federici sought to rethink primitive accumulation from a feminist vantage point, offering a critique of both Marx and Michel Foucault. For Federici, primitive accumulation – and hence the agrarian question – was less about the process of creating the waged male proletariat (forged in the foundry of the enclosures) than about the transformation of the social position of women and the reproduction of labour power.

A GLOBAL AGRARIAN QUESTION OR THE END OF THE AGRARIAN QUESTION?

One of the great strengths of Kautsky's *The Agrarian Question* was its sensitivity to historical context, to the global conjuncture and centrality of class struggles and to the expansive powers of capital and empire. The need to historicize the agrarian question highlights the challenges of contemporary agrarian transitions in a very different phase of globalization (military neoliberalism), with a different configuration of capitalist and geopolitical forces at play (sometimes called the corporate food regime). Once again there has been an explosion of work examining differing aspects of the twenty-first-century global agrarian question: the growing role of finance capital and of commodity price speculation through the transnational commodity trading of houses (Gunvor, Mercuria, Trafigura) (see Clapp and Isakson 2018); the new wave of global enclosures and land grabs, especially in the run-up to and aftermath of the 2008 financial crisis (see Borras and Franco 2012, and various special issues of the *Journal of Peasant Studies* devoted to land grabs); the diverse impacts of new waves of biotechnologies on the farm sector (from cell phones to drones to genetically engineered crops); the proliferation of contract farming (Oya 2012) as a central vehicle for agri-food global commodity chains, some of which are dominated by large retailers such as Sainsbury's and

Carrefour (Selwyn 2014); the growing presence of agri-capital (both private and state) from the Global South (Brazil, China, India), which is investing in new frontier settings in Africa, Latin America, South East Asia and elsewhere (Oliveira and Schneider 2016); and last but not least, a new wave of peasant and farmers' movements operating under the sign of the food sovereignty movement (McMichael 2015). The diversity and dynamism of agrarian questions in both the Global North and South seem as vital as ever.

At the same time, there is a sort of counter-discourse which points to the end or 'resolution' of the agrarian question in its classical sense, which turns precisely on globalization and a world dominated by capitalism and capital flows. Specifically, the historical necessity for agriculture to contribute surpluses (cheap food) and capital to industrialization is now moot because of 'external sources of accumulation' (Bernstein 1996, 32). The most prominent version of this latter argument comes from Henry Bernstein (1996, 2010), who argues that industrialization in the developing world no longer depends to any significant extent on inter-sectoral linkages to agriculture, because other sources of investment capital and markets, both international and non-agricultural, are readily available. In short, industrialization can proceed without agriculture or agrarian transitions as a necessary precondition for capital accumulation. Instead, Bernstein argues, industrial development only presumes linkages to international circuits of capital and to the capacities of developmental states.

Bernstein's argument and related work turns on two important sets of arguments which reflect the dominance of capital and the penetration of capital into all corners of the earth. One assumption is that by the end of the colonial era, agrarian societies were permeated by 'generalized commodity production' and were increasingly integrated into international divisions of labour and world markets. In the wake of the Green Revolution, past forms of 'predatory landed property' and other types of pre-capitalist social formations, including the peasantry (who were now fully fledged petty commodity producers), had largely disappeared across the Global South. This view is consistent with a capital logic position in which the entire world is governed by capitalist social relations due to their increasing integration in global markets and commodity chains. McMichael (2015), for example, argues that agriculture in the South has become subjected to a global 'corporate food regime' which determines the conditions of production and distribution on a world scale. Not only are peasants unable to compete, but they are in effect no longer peasants or petty commodity producers as such, and are seen as semi-proletarianized rural producers: they are more like wage labourers than family farmers, insofar as their dynamics of social reproduction rely more on off-farm income (working for wages in other sectors of the economy) than on land-based production (Akram-Lodhi and Kay 2010). In practice, not all aspects of family farming systems have been commodified, but households are indeed unable to secure their social reproduction outside of the market (and the reach of capital).

The second assumption (often not so starkly put) is regarding the untrammelled hegemony of global capital and its unrestrained universalism. It is in many respects a Leninist vision and one in which there is a world systemic capitalist domination and a sense of historical closure and inevitability: the great clanking and unstoppable gears of capitalism (now in corporate agri-business form) roll over agriculture, churning out proletarians at a rapid clip (for a critique of this assumption in the work of Bernstein, see Byres 2016). For Bernstein (2006, 2010), producers in the South are now subject to the same fundamental forces of capitalist class relations and differentiation as their counterparts in Europe or North America, as well as to imperialism or globalization, with industrialized 'backward' agrarian formations. For global capitalism, there is no agrarian question; we have 'the end of the agrarian question without its resolution' (Bernstein 1996, 50). Linkages to agriculture and the agrarian question, and questions of agrarian transition, are of no consequence to economic development in the Global South. What remains, says Bernstein, is the agrarian question of labour (which, he argues, does not have the same significance as the agrarian question of capital). It includes the global reserve of migratory labour (Araghi 2012) and the ways in which differing forms of labour are emerging from the variegated and heterogeneous conditions of contemporary agriculture. The agrarian question of labour in this account places land rights and land struggles – particularly in Africa, India and South East Asia – at the heart of contemporary politics.

The notion of the end of the agrarian question is, to put it mildly, quite controversial (see Carlson 2017). The very idea that all states would have untrammelled access to capital (money is not exactly pouring into Mali or Mauretania) is questionable; and the notion that the developmental state assists in the process is precisely the weak reed of so much development theorizing. But there is also the question of whether capitalist property – given the 'persistence' of family farms and a complex picture of trends in farm size and land consolidation – has fully saturated the rural worlds of the Global South. Last but not least, there are the contributions of the agrarian question to the challenges of national food provisioning and industrial development, especially in terms of the home market. Many states would be loath to depend every year on the Russian roulette of the global grain market; indeed, the whole issue of whether and how ecological questions might give cause to rethink the end of the agrarian question is often passed over.

FINAL REFLECTIONS

The agrarian question is very much alive and kicking in the twenty-first century (see Amin 2017; Li 2017; Levien et al. 2019). A recent report by the United States (US) Department of Agriculture (2018), for example, looking at the year 2017, shows that in the heartland of North American corporate agri-business, family farms of various types together accounted for 98 per cent of farms and 87 per cent of production; furthermore, 89 per cent of farms were small, and these farms accounted for 52 per cent of the land operated by farms. The US's 'large-scale family farms' accounted for the largest share of production at 39 per cent, which of course points to the considerable heterogeneity in what constitutes a family farm. Yet the fact remains that capitalist agriculture, both in its forms of land-based production and the degree of corporate control, varies by region, by crop and by livestock sector. Some form of family-based production – fully commodified, often with substantial land holdings – continues to play a central role in contemporary US agriculture, and in some sectors smaller family farmers are the backbone of the agro-industrial value chain (for example, contract production in hogs, poultry and a number of fruits and vegetables). Even in California, the capitalist breadbasket of the US, capitalist agriculture does not look necessarily like a classic form of large-scale 'factories in the fields'.

The *New York Times* (5 October 2018) recently ran a story on China's 'fading family farms'. China does, of course, represent a peculiar sort of agrarian transition: historically speaking, its quasi-feudal agrarian sector was socialized following the Revolution, but the Maoist communal model was in turn reformed starting in the late 1970s during the Deng period. The government broke up the giant communes and redistributed the rights to farm individual plots to households, while further changes in government policy in the mid-1990s made those land rights secure enough for farmers and others to have the confidence to rent land out on a wide scale. China's agriculture sector is far from being dominated by big commercial farms, but the process has begun. Yet the agrarian picture in China is also enormously varied. The central government has pursued policies which direct farm subsidies and the acquisition and accumulation of land (quite unlike in the US and Germany). Special large households have emerged around particular crops, rural co-operatives (with differing degrees of private and state control) have mushroomed (accounting for 30 per cent of rural households) and state-sponsored (but private) agri-businesses that contract to tenants and small farmers now cover 40 per cent of rural households (owning over 10 per cent of the land) (see *New York Times*, 2018). Rather like the US, peasants and family farms play a central role in farming in China, but the institutional forms by which they are linked to state and capital are numerous, complex and dynamic.

Such examples reinforce the notion of the seemingly infinite variety of agrarian transitions. The ceaseless search for newer and cheaper resources at the very least means that new agrarian frontiers are opening up all the time, unleashing new rounds of enclosure, primitive accumulation and political struggle.

The vitality of the agrarian question takes on particular significance when placed on the larger canvas of global climate change on the one hand and the biotechnological revolution on the other. To return to Kautsky, the look of agriculture in the Anthropocene and in the face of (one hopes) some sort of transition to a low-carbon economy will doubtless call forth a variety of new and different forms of agrarian transition. Some of the classical questions described by Kautsky are surely still with us: the growing centrality of land struggles in the Global South (Hall 2013; Moyo 2018; Levien et al. 2019), the oscillations between appropriation and substitution and the growing centrality of finance capital in shaping global commodity chains. If there are fundamentally new challenges to which the contemporary agrarian question points us, it is surely the question of ecology and sustainability in the Anthropocene. A red thread through the agrarian question has always been accumulation, property and peasant survival – issues which are still with us; but equally, it has necessitated an engagement with nature and ecology, namely the biological basis of agriculture and the contradictions between capitalist growth and ecological survival.

The classic question was expressed in terms of obstacles and constraints imposed by biology, and the tendencies of capital to withdraw from production and/or to dominate non-land-based aspects of the global agro-food supply chain. If these dynamics are still in play, they are now profoundly shaped by the crises derived from what Jason Moore (2015) calls the ceaseless search for the 'four cheaps' (labour power, food, energy, raw materials) and the larger crisis of hydro-carbon capitalism. In the same way that the classic agrarian question looked backward to the origins of capitalism and forward to the futures of agrarian capitalism, the contemporary agrarian question alerts us to the damages and costs of industrial agriculture and brings into sharp focus the enormous challenges of building an agrarian system that is congruent with the Anthropocenic world we now inhabit.

NOTE

1.   Many thanks to Cris Kay, Bettina Engels and Kristina Dietz for their many critical inputs and insights.

FURTHER READING

Akram-Lodhi, A.H.; Kay, C. (2010), Surveying the agrarian question (Part 1): Unearthing foundations, exploring diversity, *Journal of Peasant Studies*, 37(1), 177–202.
Kautsky, K. (1988 [1899]), *The Agrarian Question*, London: Zwan.
Levien, M.; Watts, M.; Hairong, Y. (eds) (2019), *Agrarian Marxism*, London: Routledge.
Wolf, E. (1969), *Peasant Wars of the Twentieth Century*, New York: Harper and Row.

REFERENCES

Akram-Lodhi, A.H.; Kay, C. (2010), Surveying the agrarian question (Part 1): Unearthing foundations, exploring diversity, *Journal of Peasant Studies*, 37(1), 177–202.
Alavi, H.; Shanin, T. (1988), Introduction, in Kautsky, K., *The Agrarian Question*. 2 vols, London: Zwan, xi–xxxix.
Amin, S. (1976), *Unequal Development*, New York: Monthly Review Press.
Amin, S. (2017), The agrarian question a century after the October Revolution, *Agrarian South: Journal of Political Economy*, 6(2), 149–174.
Araghi, G. (2012), The invisible hand and the visible foot: Peasants, dispossession and globalization, in Akram-Lodhi, A.H.; Kay, C. (eds), *Peasants and Globalization*, London: Routledge, 123–159.
Bernstein, H. (1977), Notes on capital and peasantry, *Review of African Political Economy*, 4(10), 60–73.
Bernstein, H. (1996), Agrarian questions then and now, *Journal of Peasant Studies*, 24(1/2), 22–59.
Bernstein, H. (2006), Is there an agrarian question in the 21st century?, *Canadian Journal of Development Studies/Revue Canadienne d'Études Du Développement*, 27(4), 449–460.
Bernstein, H. (2010), *Class Dynamics of Agrarian Change*, Halifax: Fernwood Publishing.
Bernstein, H. (2016), Agrarian political economy and modern world capitalism: The contributions of food regime analysis, *Journal of Peasant Studies*, 43(3), 611–647.
Bernstein, H.; Byres, T. (2001), From peasant studies to agrarian change, *Journal of Agrarian Change*, 1(1), 1–56.
Berry, S. (1989), Social institutions and access to resources, *Africa*, 59(1), 41–55.
Berry, S. (2009), Property, authority and citizenship: Land claims, politics and the dynamics of social division in West Africa, *Development and Change*, 40(1), 23–45.
Borras, Jr., S.M.; Franco, J.C. (2012), Global land grabbing and trajectories of agrarian change: A preliminary analysis, *Journal of Agrarian Change*, 12(1), 34–59.
Brass, T. (2000), *Peasants, Populism and Postmodernism: The Return of the Agrarian Myth*, London: Routledge.
Bryceson, D.F.; Kay, T.; Mooji, J. (2000), *Disappearing Peasantries? Rural Labour in Africa, Asia and Latin America*, London: Intermediate Technology Publications.
Byres, T. (1991), The agrarian question and differing forms of capitalist agrarian transition: An essay with reference to Asia, in Breman, J. (ed.), *Rural Transformation in Asia*, New Delhi: Oxford University Press, 3–76.
Byres, T. (1996), *Capitalism from Above and Capitalism from Below: An Essay in Comparative Political Economy*, London: Macmillan.
Byres, T. (2016), In pursuit of capitalist agrarian transition, *Journal of Agrarian Change*, 16(3), 432–451.
Carlson, C. (2017), Rethinking the agrarian question, *Journal of Agrarian Change*, 18(4), 703–721.
Chayanov, A.V. (1966 [1924]), Peasant farm organization, in Thorner, D.; Kerblay, B.; Smith, R.E.F. (eds), *The Theory of Peasant Economy*, Homewood, IL: Richard D. Irwin for the American Economic Association.
Clapp, J.; Isakson, R. (2018), *Speculative Harvests*, Halifax: Fernwood.
De Janvry, A. (1981), *The Agrarian Question and Reformism in Latin America*, Baltimore, MD: Johns Hopkins University Press.
Deere, C.D.; De Janvry, A. (1979), A conceptual framework for the empirical analysis of peasants, *American Journal of Agricultural Economics*, 89, 601–611.

Dietz, K. (2021), Political ecology, in Akram-Lodhi, A.H.; Dietz, K.; Engels, B.; McKay, B.M. (eds), *Handbook of Critical Agrarian Studies*, Cheltenham, UK and Northampton, MA, USA: Edward Elgar Publishing.

Engels, F. (1951 [1894]), The peasant question in France and Germany, in Marx, K.; Engels, F., *Selected Works*, vol. 2, Moscow: Foreign Languages Publishing House, 381–399.

Fanon, F. (1963), *The Wretched of the Earth*, London: Penguin.

Federici, S. (2004), *Caliban and the Witch: Women, the Body and Primitive Accumulation*, Brooklyn, NY: Autonomedia.

Friedmann, H. (1978), World market, state, and family farm: Social bases of household production in the era of wage labor, *Comparative Studies in Society and History*, 20(4), 545–586.

Friedmann, H. (1993), The political economy of food: A global crisis, *New Left Review*, 197, 29–57.

Gibbon, P.; Neocosmos, M. (1985), Some problems in the political economy of 'African socialism', in Campbell, B.; Bernstein, H. (eds), *Contradictions of Accumulation in Africa: Studies in Economy and State*, London: Sage, 153–206.

Goodman, D.; Sorj, B.; Wilkinson, J. (1987), *From Farming to Biotechnology: A Theory of Agro-Industrial Development*, Oxford: Basil Blackwell.

Guyer, J.; Peters, P. (1987), Conceptualizing the household: Issues of theory and policy in Africa, *Development and Change*, 18(2), 197–213.

Hall, D. (2013), Primitive accumulation, accumulation by dispossession and the global land grab, *Third World Quarterly*, 34(9), 1582–1604.

Harriss, J. (1982), *Capitalism and Peasant Farming: Agrarian Structure and Ideology in Northern Tamil Nadu*, London: Oxford University Press.

Hill, C. (1967), *From Reformation to Industrial Revolution*, London: Penguin Books.

Kautsky, K. (1988 [1899]), *The Agrarian Question*, London: Zwan.

Kay, C.; Akram-Lodhi, A.H. (2021), The diversity of classical agrarian Marxism, in Akram-Lodhi, A.H.; Dietz, K.; Engels, B.; McKay, B.M. (eds), *Handbook of Critical Agrarian Studies*, Cheltenham, UK and Northampton, MA, USA: Edward Elgar Publishing.

Lenin, V. (1964 [1899]), *The Development of Capitalism in Russia*, Moscow: Progress Publishers.

Levien, M.; Watts, M.; Hairong, Y. (eds) (2019), *Agrarian Marxism*, London: Routledge.

Lewin, M. (1968), *Russian Peasants and Soviet Power*, New York: Norton.

Li, M. (2017), Barbarism or socialism?, *Agrarian South: Journal of Political Economy*, 6(2), 263–286.

Li, T.M. (2007), *The Will to Improve: Governmentality, Development, and the Practice of Politics*, Raleigh, NC: Duke University Press.

Lund, C. (2008), *Local Politics and the Dynamics of Property in Africa*, London: Cambridge University Press.

Luxemburg, R. (1968 [1913]), *The Accumulation of Capital*, New York: Monthly Review Press.

Marx, K. (1976/1867), *Capital*, vol. 1, London: Vintage.

Marx, K. (1993 [1857–1858]), *Grundrisse: Foundations of Critique of Political Economy*, London: Penguin.

McMichael, P. (2015), A comment on Henry Bernstein's way with peasants, and food sovereignty, *Journal of Peasant Studies*, 42(1), 193–204.

Moore, B., Jr. (1966), *The Social Origins of Dictatorship and Democracy: Lord and Peasant in the Making of the Modern World*, Boston, MA: Beacon Press.

Moore, D. (2005), *Suffering for Territory: Race, Place, and Power in Zimbabwe*, Raleigh, NC: Duke University Press.

Moore, J. (2015), *Capitalism in the Web of Life: Ecology and the Accumulation of Capital*, London: Verso Books.

Moyo, S. (2018), Debating the land question in Africa with Archie Mafeje, *Agrarian South: Journal of Political Economy*, 7(2), 211–233.

New York Times (2018), China's family farms are fading, *New York Times*, 18 October, accessed 26 February 2020 at www.nytimes.com/2018/10/05/business/china-small-farms-urbanization.html.

Oliveira, G.; Schneider, M. (2016), The politics of flexing soybeans: China, Brazil and global agroindustrial restructuring, *Journal of Peasant Studies*, 43(1), 167–194.

Oya, C. (2012), Contract farming in sub-Saharan Africa: A survey of approaches, debates and issues, *Journal of Agrarian Change*, 12(1), 1–33.

Preobrazhensky, E. (1967 [1926]), *The New Economics*, Oxford: Clarendon Press.

Ramachandran, V.K. (1990), *Wage Labour and Unfreedom in Agriculture: An Indian Case Study*, Oxford: Clarendon Press.

Richards, P. (1985), *Indigenous Agricultural Revolution: Ecology and Food Production in West Africa*, London: Methuen.

Scott, A. (1986), Introduction: Why rethink petty commodity production?, *Social Analysis: International Journal of Social and Cultural Practice*, 20, 3–10.

Selwyn, B. (2014), Capital–labour and state dynamics in export horticulture in north-east Brazil, *Development and Change*, 45(5), 1019–1036.

Shanin, T. (1986), Chayanov's message: Illuminations, miscomprehensions, and the contemporary 'development theory', in: Chayanov, A.V., *The Theory of Peasant Economy*, second edition, edited by Thorner, D.; Kerblay, B.; Smith, R.E.F., Madison, WI: University of Wisconsin Press, 1–24.

United States Department of Agriculture (2018), *America's Diverse Family Farms*, Washington, DC: United States Department of Agriculture.

Vergopoulos, K. (1978), Capitalism and peasant productivity, *Journal of Peasant Studies*, 5(4), 446–465.

Watts, M. (1983), *Silent Violence*, Berkeley, CA: University of California Press.

Wolf, E. (1966), *Peasants*, Englewood Cliffs, NJ: Prentice Hall.

Wolf, E. (1969), *Peasant Wars of the Twentieth Century*, New York: Harper and Row.

8. Class

Sara Berry

Agrarian societies have changed a great deal since the early twentieth century, and so have the uses and meanings of class in agrarian studies. Broadly speaking, 'class' refers to categories of people distinguished by income, wealth, occupation, lifestyle and/or their roles in relation to agrarian production. For some observers, class serves as a description of socioeconomic inequality—a quantitative indicator that can be used to compare patterns of differentiation in different times and places. For others, class denotes relations of production—interactions between workers and accumulators, for example, or coordinated actions undertaken collectively by groups of people to transform or reinforce the conditions under which they live, work and try to get ahead. The present discussion focuses on the role of class in processes of agrarian change.

AGRARIAN TRANSFORMATIONS

Agricultural production has changed dramatically in the last hundred years, prompted by changes in the structure of markets and commodity chains, the industrialization of agricultural processing and the uses of agricultural products. Intertwined with transformations in structures of agrarian activity and relations among agrarian classes, these changes have been reflected, *inter alia*, in the terminology used to describe them. Plantation owners have become (or been replaced by) capitalist farmers; peasants by smallholder farmers; slaves and serfs by 'free' workers—wage earners, labour tenants, outgrowers and farm managers, many of whom are obliged to work, but by circumstance rather than direct coercion. Transhumant pastoralism still exists—notably in the African savanna and Sahelian regions—but is increasingly replaced or marginalized, in many areas, by ranches or by smallholder farms that keep a few livestock on the side.

Each of these agrarian classes may be further subdivided, according to size, ownership, terms of employment, mobility and so forth. Older forms of enterprise and relations of production continue to exist, especially in poorer economies, alongside more commercialized or technologically complex enterprises, and many agrarian societies remain (or have become) deeply divided between prosperous farm owners, including corporations, and low-paid skilled and unskilled workers, many of them seasonal migrants, who earn little and often live in poor conditions.

Changes in the social character of agrarian classes have resulted from, or accompanied, transformations in the structure and dynamics of agrarian economies and societies. The following paragraphs discuss several of the principal forces of agrarian change in the twentieth and early twenty-first centuries—commercialization, technological change, diversification and dependencies—asking how far class relations help account for the realities of contemporary agrarian life, and shifts in the roles of agricultural goods and agrarian societies in national and international political economies.

COMMERCIALIZATION

Over time, agrarian enterprises and societies have become steadily more commercialized and more complex, especially in recent decades. For demographic, ecological and economic reasons, labour relations and access to land and credit have steadily become more monetized, with terms of access and employment determined primarily by market conditions rather than social relationships. Cropping patterns, methods of cultivation, disposal of output and lifestyles of people engaged in agriculture are also increasingly geared to market conditions. Patterns of work and production have become more specialized—both within agricultural enterprises and between farmers and those who supply them with inputs and services. For example, people who operate combine harvesters and other complex machines do different work and earn very different wages than casual labourers who pick perishable fruits and vegetables by hand.

Both large- and small-scale farms are involved in an increasing number and variety of commercial transactions with merchants and brokers, who supply farmers with inputs and consumer goods and market their crops and animals; with service providers such as mechanics, accountants, extension agents, veterinarians; and with financial institutions (banks, moneylenders, credit societies, microfinance groups, state lending agencies), transporters, processors and storage facilities at home and abroad (see for example Reardon et al. 2009). Some enterprises and individuals specialize in providing one commodity or service, but others are involved in several activities. And whether specialized or diversified, agrarian producers, suppliers and marketers earn very different levels of income and have varying degrees of control over terms of exchange.

Commercialization both expands the range of opportunities available to agrarian producers and compounds the risks they face from weather and disease. For example, agricultural extension workers and other civil servants are often treated as members of the bourgeoisie. If a state is strapped for revenue, however, and has exhausted its ability to borrow from financial institutions at home and abroad, government employees may go unpaid for months at a time or receive salaries so eroded by inflation that they fall below earnings from modest-sized farms. In contrast, people who work for donor governments or international non-governmental organizations may earn far more than their counterparts in developing economies, regardless of experience or educational qualifications. Similarly, traders operating on razor-thin margins in markets beset by unstable prices may earn less than larger farmers whose output they buy and resell to wholesalers, processors or state agents. Even relatively prosperous farmers can be wiped out by a series of poor harvests, especially in economies where credit and/or insurance are unavailable or prohibitively expensive.

TECHNOLOGICAL CHANGE

Many changes in methods of agricultural production and livestock raising have substituted capital (equipment and manufactured fertilizer, pesticides, herbicides and so on) for labour, sought to counteract the declining quality of natural resources (for example soil fertility) or worked to meet rising standards of quality for marketed produce. Mechanization and the use of chemical inputs have spread most widely, but farmers have also adopted irrigation, conservationist measures (zero tillage, intercropping, composting, agroforestry), land-saving practices (double or triple cropping) and practices such as monocropping designed to facilitate mechanization. Since the beginning of the twenty-first century, genetic engineering has emerged as a new and powerful driver of rising productivity and market concentration.

Technological change both enables and reduces economic and social mobility. In his classic study, *The Seed is Mine*, van Onselen (2005 [1996]) chronicles the life of a black South African sharecropper who prospered using his own draught animals and family labour, but was reduced to near poverty when his oxen were replaced by tractors, eliminating his principal source of leverage in negotiations with white land-owning farmers. Similarly, farmers' expanding use of manufactured inputs (seed, fertilizer, pesticides) may increase their yields, but leave them more dependent on oligopolistic markets where their earnings are squeezed from both directions. Pastoralists also face rising costs of production when restricted access to grazing land limits animals' access to fresh pasture and water, forcing livestock owners to bring feed and water to their animals, rather than letting them forage or move to new grazing areas.

For farmers and livestock raisers alike, the adoption of capital- and/or input-intensive techniques of production has allowed some to expand the size of their farms or herds, moving upward in income and wealth. For many others, expensive or irregular input supplies, bad weather or an outbreak of disease may force them to sell land, equipment or stock and hire themselves out, re-enacting the classic Leninist story of the division of the peasantry into capitalists and proletarians. Together with deepening financialization, the development of increasingly complex technologies has facilitated the concentration of economic and political power in global agricultural markets that, in turn, set conditions for both producers and consumers in rich countries and poor. In response, global agriculture seems to be moving toward a dual class system: (1) characterized by a growing gap between small, medium and even large independent or 'family' farms on one hand and mega-corporations on the other, and (2) a corporate agribusiness sector internally divided between a class of corporate owners and executives, and the contract farmers, skilled workers, casual labourers and others who do the actual work of agricultural production, processing and marketing.

DIVERSIFICATION

Commercialization, uncertainty and technical change have contributed to the emergence of a growing population of agrarian producers who own small amounts of land or equipment, but also sell (some of) their labour in order to make ends meet. Ironically, increased specialization in the production of agricultural commodities, inputs and related services has gone hand in hand with a long-term trend toward diversification of livelihoods. Declining yields, unstable prices and constraints on access to land and credit combine to erode farmers' livelihoods, leading many to supplement farm incomes through petty trade, artisanal enterprises, artisanal mining and/or hiring themselves out. Diversification is not limited to small farmers. Poorly paid civil servants and professionals, such as schoolteachers or health-care workers, who face similar pressures also combine their meagre earnings with other occupations—farming and animal husbandry, trading, artisanal mining, carpentry, metalworking, tailoring, selling cooked food, styling hair or foraging.

Sometimes referred to as 'straddling', the diversification of occupations and livelihoods has increased spatial mobility and accelerated the tempo of rural economic and social life. People do one job in the day and another at night, or oscillate between one occupation and another.

Many rural women harvest a few crops from their own or their households' fields, cook them and transport the cooked food to a nearby town to sell to urban dwellers who do not have time to prepare meals for themselves. Others change jobs on a daily or seasonal basis—shifting from farm work to trade, transport, construction or artisanal pursuits when it's too dark, dry or cold to farm. In the process, many travel between farms, firms, marketplaces, rural areas and cities or across borders to find employment or practise a trade.

People who derive income from a variety of activities, using their own capital and selling their labour power, do not fit easily into conventional class categories such as peasant, capitalist and proletarian. Since the late twentieth century, concentrations of economic and political power have led to stark increases in economic inequality within nation states and among them, along with rising levels of financialization that leave many with debts they cannot pay off, but may also threaten the stability of wealthy and powerful enterprises and individuals. Scrambling to amass wealth or put together a livelihood from a variety of sources, growing numbers of people are neither peasants, capitalists nor proletarians, but share characteristics of all three. Embracing their diversity, Marxists describe them as 'petty commodity producers' (Bernstein 2010). Sidestepping the question of class formation, neoliberal analysts prefer more neutral terms such as farmers, traders, artisans or economic 'agents'.

Facing uncertain job prospects and precarious earnings, many low- and even middle-income people invest what little surplus they have in the means of security rather than productive but risky undertakings. In countries where wealth and power are controlled by the state, small-scale producers may compete for political patrons, rather than allying with fellow producers to advance common interests (Meagher 2010). Others attach themselves to persons with work or residence permits to gain access to land, markets or employment (Bolt 2015). Even rich and powerful people may seek protection in volatile times.

Rising inequality, reduced mobility and the uncertainty of markets and livelihoods lead to persistent differences in income and wealth. As unstable markets, turbulent politics and social relations shift patterns of accumulation towards land, financial capital and security, rather than public goods (such as infrastructure or environmental protection), class categories no longer mean quite what they used to. Investment in social relations may substitute for capital or lines of credit in gaining access to resources, jobs and means of recovery as well as accumulation, but also it increases people's dependence on the fortunes and good will of others. If your kin, colleagues and neighbours are poor too, they cannot help you much even if they'd like to. On the other hand, investing in networks or patrons can be risky or even futile as well as rewarding. Facing precarious livelihoods and global markets together with an increasingly unpredictable climate, people tend to allocate time and resources to pursuing security for themselves and their immediate dependents, undercutting the socially transformative power of class mobilization. In a sense, people are exploited by the political, economic and social world they live in as well as by members of a particular class.

FURTHER READING

Bernstein, H. (2010), *The Class Dynamics of Agrarian Change*, Sterling, VA: Kumarian Press.
Hall, R.; Edelman, M.; Borras, S.M.; Scoones, I.; White, B.; Wolford, W. (2015), Resistance, acquiescence or incorporation? An introduction to land grabbing and political reactions 'from below', *Journal of Peasant Studies*, 42(3–4), 467–488.

Meagher, K. (2010), *Identity Economics: Social Networks and the Informal Economy in Nigeria*, Cambridge: Cambridge University Press.

Pauline, P. (2004), Inequality and social conflict over land in Africa, *Journal of Agrarian Change*, 4(3), 269–314.

Southall, R. (2018), (Middle-)class analysis in Africa: Does it work? *Review of African Political Economy*, 45(3), 467–477.

REFERENCES

Bernstein, H. (2010), *Class Dynamics of Agrarian Change*, Sterling, VA: Kumarian Press.

Bolt, M. (2015), *Zimbabwe's Migrants and South Africa's Border Farms: The Roots of Impermanence*, Cambridge: Cambridge University Press.

Meagher, K. (2010), *Identity Economics: Social Networks and the Informal Economy in Nigeria*, Cambridge: Cambridge University Press.

Reardon, T.; Barrett, C.B.; Berdegué, J.A.; Swinnen, J.F.M. (2009), Agrifood industry transformation and farmers in developing countries, Special issue of *World Development*, 37(11), 1717–1727.

van Onselen, C. (2005 [1996]), *The Seed is Mine: The Life of Kas Maine, a South African Sharecropper, 1894–1985*, Johannesburg: Ball Publishers.

9. Land

A. Haroon Akram-Lodhi

LAND IN THE WEB OF LIFE

'Land' is one of the most commonly used words within critical agrarian studies, but is also a word whose meaning is more often than not treated as being self-evident. Scanning the indices of books with 'land' in the title reveals that the word fails to be analytically problematized in and of itself but is rather usually conjoined with a second word, such as 'land reform' or 'land market', in order to create a concept (see, for example, Cousins, this volume and Goetz, this volume). Granted, there is an extensive literature that problematizes both landscapes and territory. Social geographers and anthropologists approach landscapes as socially constructed but culturally variable spaces (Mitchell 2000). Territory refers to landscapes that have been constituted and demarcated by peoples in ways that not only define those very same people but which also confer some degree of authority over the said territory (Shattuck and Peluso, this volume). Both thus allow us to recognize how land has simultaneously an independent existence while being a cultural construction. Yet both concepts do not go into the meaning of land in and of itself. Moreover, it is apparent that land means very different things to different people, and to different groups of people; the farmer, the rural waged labourer, the agronomist, the property developer, the local religious authority, the social scientist, the artist: all 'see' land in radically different ways. Yet it is only by recognizing that, across the diversity of vernaculars, there are common conceptual underpinnings around the meaning of land that critical agrarian studies can start to interrogate the centrality of land in rural lives, and as a result its power in rural mobilization and agrarian politics.

A starting point must be to try and understand what, if anything, is universal about land. Here, Derek Hall (2013, 7) stresses that land is simultaneously concrete and abstract. It is concrete in the sense that it is 'the ground beneath our feet' from which our vernaculars arise. It is abstract in the sense that it is possible to strip away the ground beneath our feet and yet still have land in the very same space even though it has become something quite different from that which it was. This fusion of the concrete and the abstract might render land a 'chaotic conception', in Marx's (1973 [1939], 100) memorable phrase, but Hall provides a way to start to cut through the chaos. Land is fixed; it does not move, but also, barring small amounts that give way to water or are reclaimed, the amount that is available is also fixed. Yet even though it is fixed in place and quantity, land is not defined by its uniformity but rather by its difference; land is a patchwork of difference. Indeed, heterogeneous difference is central to one of the key characteristics of land: that 'land is indispensable to almost all human activity' (Hall 2013, 9).

Hall's reflections focus upon land's materiality. However, the concepts of landscapes and territory, which are intimately entwined with land, suggest that land itself is more than the material. This is because land shapes and is shaped by peoples and their social relations, practices and identities. This is one reason why Polanyi (2001 [1944]) considered land a 'fictitious commodity'; it is socially embedded, and it is its social embeddedness from which its meaning is both derived and driven. Consider a thought experiment involving a stream running through arable fields. That social relations shape how those fields and water are used, and the characteristics of power and subordination that might be observed around those fields and water, would be axiomatic to practitioners of critical agrarian studies; but that the fields and water are mutually co-constitutive in shaping those social relations of power and subordination might not be recognized so clearly. Yet change the parameters of the thought experiment by taking away the water and most would expect to encounter quite different relations of power and subordination. Land is integral to the web of life; and paraphrasing Jason Moore (2015), while human activity works in and through land, land also works in and through human activity.

Indeed, it is because of the mutually co-constitutive character of land and the peoples of the land that for most of human history land has been thoroughly embedded within both material practices and the symbolic cultures that they foster. Notwithstanding the modern world, for the peoples of the land across the span of human history, the biologies, chemistries, geologies, geographies and temporal mechanics that populate land themselves produce a meaning that emerges from historically embedded encounters with it. These encounters give rise to behaviour around cultivation, hunting, gathering and diet that regulates land through social practice and convention, structures the process of social reproduction and through consistent event regularities establishes persistent individual and collective patterns of expectation that shape cognitive impressions, feelings and beliefs. In so doing, it is land that has historically mediated the physical, conceptual and imaginative relationships between people and the powers that preside over them. Material processes are thus the foundations of values and morals that are usually grounded in cosmologies that articulate a relationship between the natural and the supernatural and the sacred and the secular. So, while land is something that is constructed by humans over their daily lives, both physically and symbolically, by being invested with meaning, memory and value, land is also something that constructs humans as social beings. Land has thus been, for most of human history, a central component in producing the 'common sense', in Gramsci's (1971, 422) sense of the phrase, that anchors the identity, perception, emotion and agency needed to be conscious of one's position within a broader social structure and in relation to nature. At the same time, the common sense that is produced in relation to land is also a way of perceiving the land. Since time immemorial, then, people have not only used and interpreted the land that they occupy as a part of their life but also as an integral means of understanding themselves, their position in the world and their cosmological role. Land intimately infuses being and belonging with what potentially could be. So, people act in relation to land, but land acts upon people, mediating, shaping and embodying individual common sense as well as the collective knowledge expressed in social rules, norms and values.

In the contemporary world the mutually co-constitutive character of land and people is most clearly seen in Indigenous communities. As Thomas King (2012, 218) writes:

> Land has always been a defining element of Aboriginal culture. Land contains the languages, the stories, and the histories of a people. It provides water, air, shelter, and food. Land participates in the ceremonies and the songs. And land is home. Not in an abstract way … The mountain is a special place … and friends … have told me more than once that, as long as they can see the mountain, they know they are home.

Similarly, for most rural populations across the span of historical time, confined to the very limited spaces of their farms, their villages and their hinterlands, land is a two-way relationship; the meaning of burial places to most human cultures as places that stimulate emotion in people even as emotion is bestowed upon a space embodies the reciprocal relationship of people to land. So historically land use practices reflect the emergence of social institutions that embody the materiality of the powerful and deep cultural and symbolic meanings attached to land when it is organized as a physical reality. In this light, it is not in the least surprising that access to land has been the central demand of peasant movements since time immemorial; peasants seek land because they seek to understand themselves.

LAND AND PRE-CAPITALIST AGRICULTURE

The pre-capitalist social institutions that organized land use practices in both subsistence-oriented communities and pre-capitalist states reflected a key characteristic of agriculture. This is the capacity of agriculture to supply a surplus: production by peasant farmers of food and non-food crops that they themselves neither needed to eat nor to store as seed for the following growing season. The production of surplus meant that, for the first time in human history, people could eat when their own production was inadequate or without being directly involved in hunting, gathering or producing food (Paxson 1932). In order to do this, the terms and conditions governing the distribution of surplus had to be such as to allow those in need of surplus to be able to secure the food they needed from a food producer. Thus, surplus opened up two distinct possibilities: first, the possibility of sustaining life even when a farmer's own food production was inadequate; and second, the possibility of sustaining non-food producers – soldiers, servants and artisans, as well as an elite class of lords, bureaucrats and priests.

With regard to the first possibility, early agriculturalists developed what James C. Scott (1976) has called a 'subsistence ethic', a social relationship that is a marker of some peasant and Indigenous societies up to the present day. The subsistence ethic resulted in extended kinship groups and early agricultural villages developing technical arrangements around farm production processes and social arrangements around food distribution mechanisms that ensured that all within a community were able to obtain their basic food needs regardless of the success or failure of their food production processes or their social status within their communities. For example, communities developed work-sharing arrangements at important stages of the farm production cycle, such as harvesting; such reciprocal labour exchanges would entitle members of communities, if necessary, to make claims on the farm production of those for whom they had worked. Similarly, the celebration of communal feasts at different times of the calendar were social arrangements that could serve as a means of collective redistribution from those producing surplus to those that had underproduced, allowing them to maintain a minimum standard of living when production was less than that which was necessary. Thus, the subsistence ethic produced reciprocal dependence within and between households in villages, ensuring a socially constructed right to adequate food within a community. In subsistence-oriented societies, which were organized around kinship relations, it was the surplus, the subsistence ethic and reciprocal dependence that allowed the emergence of divisions of labour, and particularly artisans, religious figures and warriors.

With regard to the second possibility, a key issue facing the elite in a pre-capitalist state was: what were the terms and conditions by which they obtained the food they needed? Food has historically been the principal source of wealth because it is essential to life; so, obtaining surpluses from the actual producer was, in effect, the extraction of wealth. In order to extract this wealth in a way that was deemed to be legitimate the control of the food that was produced had to be socially recognized to be the enforceable right of the elite class. Here, Scott (2017) maintains that grains were particularly important because unlike other food crops grains are visible, divisible, assessable, storable and transportable. Centring agricultural production around grains gave rise to the complex hierarchies of pre-capitalist states, divisions of labour and specialist jobs such as soldiers, servants and artisans, as well as the elite class of lords, bureaucrats and priests presiding over society.

However, even in farming communities characterized by complex hierarchies, peasants, as 'clients', provided seasonal labour services and grain to a lord, their 'patron', who in a bad season ensured that the peasant and their family received the food that they needed but had not been able to produce. Thus, even in communities with significantly marked differences in social status members of a community had an entitlement to a socially acceptable standard of living, even if it was obtained through their loss of autonomy and its replacement with dependence upon those perceived to be social superiors. Scott (1976) calls this the 'moral economy' of the peasant:[1] what women and men engaged in farming deemed to be just and what they deemed to be unjust was predicated upon the maintenance of the subsistence ethic through patron–client relations.

In this way, the redistribution of food through social mechanisms of reciprocity were, over millennia in antiquity, found across subsistence-oriented societies and pre-capitalist states. Reciprocity could be symmetrical, when it took place in relatively more egalitarian settings, and it could be asymmetrical, as between clients and patrons, in settings characterized by complex hierarchies. In either case, the moral economy was predicated upon socially constructed and sanctioned rights between and across households and societies to make claims over the surplus products of land and of labour. As a result, rights to claim-making over the products of land in both relatively more and relatively less egalitarian settings were far more important than the private ownership of land, as this was what sustained livelihoods and a social order constructed around the subsistence ethic. This in turn was the material basis by which powerful emotional and cultural attachments and social meanings were fused into and reflected the common sense that was constructed around land.

Moreover, even when land was privately owned in pre-capitalist societies, the explicit and implicit rights conferred on the basis of such ownership were very different from those assigned to contemporary owners of private property. Socially sanctioned rights between and across households and communities were overlapping, perpetual and applied within and between households and thus across communities (Piketty 2020, 106). As a result, even when land was privately owned such ownership did not necessarily convey a right to all the products of land in perpetuity – and indeed the subsistence ethic precluded this. It was instead more commonly the case that the explicit right to own land in perpetuity overlapped with the different implicit or explicit right to use land in perpetuity, which in turn overlapped with the different implicit or explicit right to obtain a payment from land in perpetuity, which in turn further overlapped with the different implicit or explicit right to benefit from a transaction in perpetuity, and so on. For peasants in both subsistence-oriented societies and pre-capitalist states the conferral of explicit and implicit rights in perpetuity over both the use of land and the control the products of land was integral to the common sense constructed around land.

CAPITALISM, PRIVATE PROPERTY AND LAND

The emergence of capitalism reconfigured the relationship between rights, control and owner-ship. Capitalism is a system of commodity production seeking profit. The centrality of com-modity production is predicated upon private property as the basis of any explicit right to make claims over the distribution of the product, including, most centrally, the distribution of the net product between wages, rents and profits. More specifically, capitalism requires the owners of private property to be able to make exclusive explicit claims upon the products of private property because of such ownership (Akram-Lodhi 2018). As a result, the only perpetual rights attached to property with the emergence of capitalism were those that became explicitly attached to private ownership; all other rights became contingent on the action of the private property owner. Capitalism structured social relations around private property rights, and the private property owner became the central actor in capitalist society.

The centrality of private property in capitalism emerged as the decline of feudalism in Western Europe fuelled the rise of colonialism. Hard-wired into colonialism from its inception were four principles that were grounded in a set of exclusive explicit rights conferred upon private property: that the peoples indigenous to colonized lands were infidels to be enslaved, and thus become private property; that the infidels had no claim over their land and natural resources, because these were gifts from God for believers; that because such lands were empty of believers they were in principle empty and could be seized, enclosed and bestowed upon Christians as private property; and that the non-land resources of non-Christian peoples and lands that were confiscated by believers could be commercially transported to Europe as private property, for use and profit. Since the 1500s, then, the messianic zeal that underwrote colonial expansion promoted private property ownership as the economic foundation of indi-vidualistic explicit rights – over enslaved peoples, over land, over natural resources and over goods and services (Bhandar 2018).

Private property rights were especially important in the early history of capitalism for two reasons. First, private ownership both legitimized and obscured the theft that had taken place under colonialism; and second, it allowed private owners to exclusively benefit from the exploitation of people and resources on and beneath their land (Rubin and Klumpp 2012). These resources were both in the metropolitan colonial countries in Europe and in their colonies. In metropolitan Britain coal was the essential resource needed to fuel the Industrial Revolution, while in the colonies of the western hemisphere sugar and then cotton were the essential resources needed to grow industrial manufacturing. The exercise of explicit rights over these resources required private property in land and the exclusive control of the products of the land as a consequence of those rights. In this way, the exclusivity of capitalist private property optimized resource exploitation and facilitated the Industrial Revolution.

It was classical political economy that provided the intellectual underpinnings for the ele-vation of the individual and exclusive private property rights that replaced understandings of overlapping and perpetual rights. In this way, classical political economy incorporated private property into everyday common sense in a way that had historically probably never been the case. The scarcity paradigm of Thomas Malthus, the utilitarianism of James and John Stuart Mill and Jeremy Bentham, John Locke's sacralization of private property and Adam Smith's and David Ricardo's analysis of the mutual benefits from free exchanges in unencumbered markets: these, and many others, served to reify the role of and benefits from the private property owner in capitalist societies.[2] In so doing, it also served to demonstrate the scientific modernity of the rational capitalist property owner and the unscientific and anti-modern attitudes of rural peasants and Indigenous peoples rooted in moral economies. Indeed, the sanctity accorded to the ownership of private property over more than a century resulted in the portrayal of any resulting inequality as a reflection of a natural – and indeed cosmologically ordained – order (Pujol 1992), which of course completely ignored a history of national and intercontinental class relations and the role played by colonial enclosures in reinforcing structures of power and privilege.

As land across Europe was enclosed during the transition from feudalism to capitalism, it ceased to be socially embedded. So too when land was enclosed in the colonies. The depersonalization of relations between people and the land served capitalism well because it undermined the moral economy and the social mechanisms of reciprocity that underwrote pre-capitalism. Such social structures and norms were incompatible with capitalist rationality – while the process further disempowered those who were already socially subordinate.

It was within this context that land assumed some of the dimensions with which it is associated today. Land became a 'natural resource' that was unique, in part because it encompassed other natural resources such as minerals, water and forests. Land became territory, and as territory became a way of demarcating populations that worked on the land. Intellectually, land became a 'factor of production' that, while unique, was theoretically specified as being interchangeable with other factors of production. In these ways, land assumed the guise that it has taken on in modernity. The common sense that had historically emerged in and through the encounter with land was replaced by objective commodification and the separation of direct producers from the land; and it was no coincidence that alienation from the land was a direct function of being separated from it. Alienation from the land served as the foundation upon which the destruction of nature could be unleashed by the emergent capitalist order, as land was only a resource to be used and exploited, a 'factor of production' substitutable with any other such factor.

For the peasant and Indigenous communities that became detached from the land that had structured their intimate and social life for millennia, the exploitation of land as a natural resource was in fact a source of social upheaval as communities became disarticulated with the land around them. Yet because of combined and uneven development across time and space not all became detached; remnants of the subsistence ethic mean that there remain many communities around the world for which land remains socially embedded. For those, and for some of those that have become alienated from the land, struggles over land by peasants and Indigenous peoples in effect seek, in a Polanyian sense, to transcend the contemporary modernist meaning of land and re-embed both the material practices and the symbolic cultures of it within the social. In this process, land can exert a form of 'agency' in the resistance struggles of peasant movements through both its physicality, which, for example, shapes movement through the barriers that it may create, as well as through its symbolic associations. In some instances, this re-embedding is proposed through decommodification; and in some instances, it is proposed through state intervention that renders commodification processes highly contingent. Nonetheless, the purpose of these struggles is to reassert the plurality of materialities, and hence of meanings, attached to land, far beyond it as a mere factor of production.

CONTEMPORARY COMMON SENSE ABOUT LAND

As a result, there are currently two qualitatively different overarching sets of common sense attached to land and 'land-based social relations' (Borras and Franco 2012). The dominant one is that of enlightenment modernism, in which land is a scarce resource to be scientifically exploited for social gain and private profit. This dominant view has been internalized as a common sense of modernity, not only by urbanized populations but also by many farmers in both the agrarian North and the agrarian South, even though this view is historically very recent. This common sense continues to propel ecologically destructive capitalist development. Yet a minority worldview predicated upon how people work through land, how land works through people and how land can sustain the remnants of a moral economy, persist, unable to yet be fully captured by the dynamics of enclosure so central to capitalist development. This common sense reflects a degree of attachment to land that embodies the ways in which land continues to reflect and affect social relations and identities because of the ways in which the terms and conditions by which people work in and through the land shapes their understanding of themselves and their place in nature (Manuel 2017). This is the common sense of the peoples of the land who struggle for the land; it is the common sense of global transnational peasant and Indigenous movements; and it is a common sense that in its essence is antithetical to the logic of capitalist development. These contrasting common senses have, following Lefebvre (1992), fundamental differences over the lived, the perceived and the conceived experience of land, and are reproduced in social sciences: cultural anthropology and economics understand the meaning of land in very different ways. These contradictory common senses can be captured very succinctly in a saying that I have never been able to source: 'The farmer owns the land; the land owns the peasant.'[3] These contrasting common senses underpin different conceptualizations of what the future looks like for contemporary inhabitants of the rural world, and the world at large, in both the agrarian South and the agrarian North.

NOTES

1.   Scott's understanding of the moral economy is quite different from that of Thompson (1971), who first coined the phrase.
2.   The references here would be too extensive to list, but see Hunt (1979) for a very useful overview.
3.   The second half of the saying is attributable to Ryazanoff (1944, 120).

FURTHER READING

Hall, D. (2013), *Land*, Cambridge: Polity Press.
King, T. (2012), *The Inconvenient Indian: A Curious Account of Native People in North America*, Toronto: Anchor Canada.
Manuel, A. (2017), *The Reconciliation Manifesto: Recovering the Land, Rebuilding the Economy*, Toronto: James Lorimer and Company.

REFERENCES

Akram-Lodhi, A.H. (2018), 'Old wine in new bottles': Enclosure, neoliberal capitalism and postcolonial politics, in Rutazibwa, O.; Shilliam, R. (eds), *Routledge Handbook of Postcolonial Politics*, London: Routledge, 274–288.

Bhandar, B. (2018), *Colonial Lives of Property: Law, Land, and Racial Regimes of Ownership*, Durham, NC: Duke University Press.

Borras, Jr., S.M.; Franco, J. (2012), Global land grabbing and trajectories of agrarian change: A preliminary analysis, *Journal of Agrarian Change*, 12(1), 34–59.

Gramsci, A. (1971), *Selections from Prison Notebooks*, London: Lawrence and Wishart.

Hall, D. (2013), *Land*, Cambridge: Polity Press.

Hunt, E.V.K. (1979), *History of Economic Thought: A Critical Perspective*, Belmont, CA: Wadsworth Publishing Company.

King, T. (2012), *The Inconvenient Indian: A Curious Account of Native People in North America*, Toronto: Anchor Canada.

Lefebvre, H. (1992), *The Production of Space*, Oxford: Blackwell Publishers.

Manuel, A. (2017), *The Reconciliation Manifesto: Recovering the Land, Rebuilding the Economy*, Toronto: James Lorimer and Company.

Marx, K. (1973 [1939]), *Grundrisse*, Harmondsworth: Penguin Book.

Mitchell, D. (2000), *Cultural Geography: A Critical Introduction*, Oxford: Blackwell.

Moore, J. (2015), *Capitalism in the Web of Life: Ecology and the Accumulation of Capital*, London: Verso.

Paxson, F. (1932), The agricultural surplus: A problem in history, *Agricultural History*, 6(2), 51–68.

Piketty, T. (2020), *Capital and Ideology*, Cambridge, MA: The Belknap Press.

Polanyi, K. (2001 [1944]), *The Great Transformation: The Political and Economic Origins of Our Time*, Boston, MA: Beacon Press.

Pujol, M. (1992), *Feminism and Anti-Feminism in Early Economic Thought*, Cheltenham, UK and Northampton, MA, USA: Edward Elgar Publishing.

Rubin, P.; Klumpp, T. (2012), Property rights and capitalism, in Mueller, D. (ed.), *The Oxford Handbook of Capitalism*, Oxford: Oxford University Press, 204–219.

Ryazanoff, D. (1944), 'Explanatory notes', in Marx, K.; Engels, F., *The Communist Manifesto*, Calcutta: Bose Press, accessed 21 September 2020 at https://universallibrary.org/details/in.ernet.dli.2015 .501746/page/n3/mode/2up?q=land+owns.

Scott, J.C. (1976), *The Moral Economy of the Peasant: Rebellion and Subsistence in Southeast Asia*, New Haven, CT: Yale University Press.

Scott, J.C. (2017), *Against the Grain: A Deep History of the Earliest States*, New Haven, CT: Yale University Press.

Thompson, E.P. (1971), The moral economy of the English crowd in the eighteenth century, *Past and Present*, 50(November), 76–136.

10. Frontiers: Commodification and territorialization

Mattias Borg Rasmussen and Christian Lund

Frontiers conjure up images of vast expanses of untouched nature, ready to be subjugated and domesticated, processed and commodified. They also evoke notions of heroic conquest in the past. However, few spaces are truly empty and unclaimed no-man's-lands. In fact, frontier tales seem to always include the primitive, the savage and the irrational, whose destruction is inevitable in order for the frontier to be conquered. What is more, frontiers involve recurrent dynamics of transformation regarding resource access, and are thus neither empty nor exclusively of the past.

This chapter selectively reviews different positions on the frontier, moving from the historically specific analysis and foundational narrative of the United States (US) frontier exposed by F.J. Turner to analyses informed by contemporary debates within Marxist political economy, environmental history, ecological economics and new institutional economics. We suggest that frontiers can fruitfully be rescaled in our analysis to encompass local institutional competitions over resource control, legitimacy and authority. Frontiers are therefore not only about the unmaking of existing institutional arrangements and legitimate resource use through discursive and physical violence, but are also about the reconstitution and negotiation of new territorial orders. State and government may play a double role in this process: not only do they territorialize, but they may also be implicated by intention or happenstance in the production of frontiers, even within their own sovereign space.

We end the discussion with the example of Patagonia. This vast terrain was for centuries outside the control of colonial and postcolonial governments. It was only after the military campaigns of the late nineteenth century that the young states of Argentina and Chile were able to successfully subdue, stabilize and consolidate these territories. The history of Patagonia is one of recursive movements of resource extraction and intense imaginations of bounties awaiting discovery and productive use. Wool, forestry, hydropower, scenery and hydrocarbons all rely on and reinforce imaginaries of vacant, idle and unproductive lands that can be made productive by the movement of capital, human ingenuity and labour. The discovery – or rather, the production – of a new resource, often enabled by new technologies and market demands, opens up spaces for institutional competition and negotiation over the rights to reap the benefits. Reterritorialization of these resource frontiers involves the wilful crafting and circumstantial emergence of institutional arrangements for establishing legitimate authority. The case of Patagonia shows how frontiers are contact zones between dynamics in different regimes of value.

FRONTIER DEBATES

Over the past decades, academic interest in frontiers has swelled.[1] Different elements of the dynamic process have enjoyed varied attention and a set of vantage points and approaches can be identified, with some crosscutting connections and overlaps. In this section, we outline key positions and insights on frontiers. We thus locate our understanding of frontier at the intersections between different approaches, each emphasizing a different perspective: history and conquest, representation, political economy, resistance and conjuncture. This suggests that we understand frontiers as multi-scalar, historically conditioned, spatio-temporal arrangements imbued with considerable amounts of human agency, institutional dynamics and navigational forms.

In 1893, F.J. Turner (2010 [1893]) published *The Frontier in American History*. It marks one of the first consolidated efforts to narrate and understand the history of the US through the expansion of the frontier, the settlement of territories beyond the control of state and capital: 'the existence of an area of free land, its continuous recession and the advance of American settlement westward, explain American development' (ibid., 1). To Turner, then, the frontier moves forward. It denotes the expansion of Euro-American settlement, economies and institutions. 'The most significant thing about the American frontier is,' writes Turner, 'that it lies at the hither edge of free land' (ibid., 2–3). The frontier stands in relation to the centre. The first frontier in America – that on the east coast – was more European than American. It was only as it advanced inland and westward that the frontier *became* American. Beyond Turner's American frontier lies free land; inhabited by Native Americans, but conceptually uninhabited. 'Indian country' and the presence of a group which stood in antagonistic relation to the project of expansion, conquest and settlement, created a basis for a unified idea of America. To Turner, the frontier is a constituent element of what America is. The movement of traders, trappers, settlers, merchants, soldiers and farmers – the 'procession of civilization' (ibid., 9) – came in different waves, which combined to consolidate the country economically and socially.

Within this reading of American history, the advancing frontier as a civilizing project relates to the stabilization of American institutions. Where Turner offers a reading from the centre, where legislation and rights descend from above, albeit crucially shaped by 'frontier ideas and needs' (Turner 2010 [1893], 22), Anderson and Hill (2004) suggest a subtler set of dynamics, where property rights emerge from the interactions between different stakeholders at the local level. Rooted in new institutional economics, these authors go against the dominant narrative of the *Wild West* and suggest that frontiersmen acted rationally to devise rules and regulations to enhance the profitability of frontier life. Conditioned by rent-seeking actors, according to Anderson and Hill, the American frontier was a less violent place than imagined. This perspective is suggestive of the ways in which institutions come into being *in* context, however, it also airbrushes out the violent elimination of prior modes of existence. What is equally redacted from Turner and his followers' analyses is the role of government and the state. Turner's idealized sequence of a frontier goes like this:

> First, there is nature, either in its raw, untouched state or cut through by Indian trails. Then come the settler families, who apply their labour to wrest a clearing in the woods and create fields and pastures. As they do this work, individual families begin to aggregate, forming communities and voluntary associations, including law-and-order vigilante groups … Dispersed communities begin to 'touch hands with each other', along old indigenous roads or along river valleys, creating … civil society. (Grandin 2019, 123)

Grandin argues, however, that in reality and well known to Turner at the time, the state preceded the frontiersmen: the government and army had already removed the Native Americans and Mexicans from the settlers' paths in the most violent way.

The frontier relates to distinctions between wilderness and civilization. William Cronon (1991) discusses the relationship between the city of Chicago and the countryside, showing how the two are intimately linked. Contrary to Turner, who sees the frontier as consisting of fundamentally rural spaces which were then followed by the evolution of towns and cities in an ever more developed form, to Cronon these spatial forms are co-constitutive. Cronon (1996) further argues that imaginaries about the frontier and, more specifically, about wilderness, reveal more about understandings of civilization than they do about the actual conditions beyond the so-called frontier. Wilderness and civilization cannot be understood independently. Similarly, the frontier exists only in its relationship to something else: a centre and a beyond.

Consequently, imageries of frontier modes of existence enable their domestication and legitimize territorializations. America's frontier myth is heavily loaded with iconography, which has been widely reproduced in popular culture, art and literature (White 1994). Otherings, through representations of landscapes as idle and of Native Americans as savage, have thus been nurtured and reinforced by Turner's and others' frontier narratives, where the idea of America and American exceptionalism is predicated upon the domestication of the frontier. In Turner, we see a certain nostalgia for the rural, but also a justification – indeed, a compulsion – for its transformation. It is through advancement and evolution that the frontier creates the foundation of America as a country and an idea. Frontier imaginaries thus resemble what Navaro-Yashin (2012) calls the make-believe space where imaginative and material practices combine to produce frontiers as affective geographies. They rest upon representations and discursive formations that enable resource extraction and territorial control.

Representations of wilderness are not the exclusive domain of US history, however. Frontier imaginaries such as Green Hells or the El Dorado can be found in many locations, and the Othering of landscapes and people is a well-known theme from both travel literature and colonial records. The Wild West frontier is a particular historical moment, but it raises questions about the nature of resource extraction and commodification that extend far beyond it in time and place. It is a concept, an analysis and an imaginary which travels well.

Another recurrent figure in depictions of the frontier in the US and beyond is the idea of primitive accumulation. Here, the control of natural resources, their commodification and insertion into capitalist circulation, dominate. Environmental historian Jason Moore (2000) has suggested the term 'commodity frontier' in his analysis of the globalization and restlessness of sugar production. Regardless of whether sugar is produced in Madeira, Brazil, the Caribbean or Peru, it transforms ecologies, labour relations and social structures. The commodity frontier is a spatial relation of the world system, an unequal ecological exchange which transports resources from the periphery to the centre.

The commodity frontier is intellectually indebted to Marx's idea of primitive accumulation (1954 [1887]) and Neil Smith's 'uneven development' (1984), and bears a family resemblance to David Harvey's reformulation of Marx into 'accumulation by dispossession' (2003). To Moore, the production and distribution of specific commodities, in particular primary goods, have 'restructured geographical space at the margins of the system in such a way as to require further expansion' (Moore 2000, 410). In Harvey's terms, capital is highly capable of moving around. As was even (partly) suggested by Turner, the commodity frontier therefore relates to particular commodities like silver, gold, cotton and, as analysed by Moore, sugar; indeed, it exists only in relation to capitalist expansion. It is 'a *zone beyond which further expansion is possible* in a way that is limited primarily by physical geography and the contradictions of capitalism rather than the opposition of powerful world empires' (Moore 2000, 412, emphasis in original).

The metabolic rift – that is, the separation between sites of production and sites of extraction, with the concomitant uneven exchange and development – suggests the steady emptying of commodity frontiers to the benefit of those living elsewhere (Moore 2011). Commodity frontiers are not just produced at the frontier itself (Kaur 2018). The 'liberalization' of regulation and similar institutional work which make frontiers, the 'third world' or emerging markets attractive for investment is often cooked up by global financial institutions. The packaging and labelling of entire nations as investment destinations commodifies countries, populations and their natural resources in one elegant sweep. Ecological economists have reached similar conclusions to those of the environmental historians cited above, and have, for example, suggested that we understand environmental conflicts in terms of an uneven global metabolism, where energy and resources are transported from the sites of production to the centres of consumption (Martinez-Alier et al. 2010).

A different perspective focuses on frontiers as contact zones. This has especially emerged from studies on the hills of South and South East Asia, where historically, societies developed conscious, ingenious and deliberate responses to the threat of being governed (Scott 2009). The contact zone between hill people and valley states was one of conflict and resistance, where autonomy and incorporation, freedom and subjugation, were at odds. The frontier was a place of refuge for people who wished to escape the control of government and a central state. These were runaway communities which, over time, had fled the oppression of state-making projects in the valleys by moving to a frontier beyond political control. Slavery, conscription, taxes, forced labour, epidemics and warfare made up the list of incentives to flee.

The perspective of the frontier as something not yet domesticated combines with the natural topographical features of the landscape, the technology to inhabit it versus the technology to dominate it, and political institutions to order access to it. Hill people living in these frontiers developed subsistence routines that proved difficult to concentrate and accumulate. By engaging in shifting cultivation and by cultivating and foraging a broad range of crops that matured at different times over the year, it was difficult for the state to appropriate their fruits of production. The rugged terrain added friction to distance; what was only a short distance to travel in a flat landscape became, in this instance, very difficult, expensive and dangerous for a state – an army – to navigate in the pursuit of taxes and labour. To escape the reach of the state, people simply moved up in the landscape. The further away they were in terms of the friction of the terrain, the argument runs, the more likely they were to remain outside of the oppressive reach of the state (modern technology has, however, reduced and redefined such distances). Thus, hill peoples who were historically not incorporated into states controlled by valley and lowland communities were – and are – not *remnants* of pre-state people but rather a *living testimony* to the past of the – now – civilized valley societies. Furthermore, hill peoples, their production, their social organization and their understanding of themselves in terms of norms and history have been the result of, and a reaction to, state formation in the valleys.

A further perspective is to see frontiers as zones of friction between contradictory forces. This owes a debt to the perspectives of primitive accumulation and the commodification of nature and focuses on the complexities of institutional encounters, competition and amalgamation. To writers like Campbell (2015), Eilenberg (2012), Li (2014) and Tsing (2005), frontiers represent the conjuncture of interests and ideas, claims and conflict, where people try to make sense of the creative destruction around them. While different in several ways, these authors share an insistence on the simultaneity of destruction and creation. The attention to simultaneity provides a multi-chromatic analysis of actors, their constellations and means of interaction. Campbell, for example, shows how statutory legislation endorses and encourages the conquest and transformation of forest landscapes in the Amazon. This opportunity is seized very differently by different groups, who, in turn, engage very differently with indigenous groups and government agencies and produce different forms of legalization.

Tsing (2005) brings indigenous people and developers, the military and local and international social movements together with global capital. All of these actors negotiate prosperity, knowledge and freedom in a 'zone of awkward engagement', and what appears, at first glance, to be small against big, weak against strong, good against evil, soon becomes more complicated: '[T]he closer one looks, the more confusing the story becomes' (ibid., 248). Alliances crisscross, while discourse, the law and force do not align neatly into simple categories (Eilenberg 2012; Li 2014).

In this way, frontier dynamics in relation to land spill over to another resource: labour. The great transformation may well be propelled by world market cravings for space, but it is acted out among kin regarding control over bodily effort, while the state's control over vanquished people's time and lives through slave or wage labour often redirects the resource of work towards capitalist expansion. At the larger scale, as examined by Eilenberg (2012) in Indonesia, indigenous Dayak groups, the army's counter-insurgency actions, transmigration settlement programmes and the enforcement of sovereignty *vis-à-vis* neighbouring Malaysia, all crowd the frontier proportionally. This creates a combination of frontier constellations where indigenous swidden agriculture becomes a security issue, and the transmigration of labour from Java to oil palm plantations in Kalimantan becomes an issue of sovereignty. This simultaneity makes the different frontier issues connect and become one another.

There is not one single conceptualization of the frontier. Yet despite the different foci – on a forward-moving line of conquest and accumulation; a contact zone of civilizations and modes of production; or areas of complex institutional interaction – all of these conceptualizations conjure up images of change, contact and confrontation, as well as competition over resources and revolutions in their use. In the following, we conceptualize frontiers as a production of a particular space-time, capturing this diversity while, all the same, proposing some simple precisions on the relationship between frontiers and resource control, rights and the constitution of authority.

CONTEMPORARY FRONTIER SPACES

The notion of frontiers is as relevant now as it was in the nineteenth and seventeenth centuries.[2] The commodification of nature, the scramble for land and resources, the imaginaries of self and others, the erasure of existing orders and the establishment of new patterns of governance and regimes of access may take on new forms, but the dynamic persists. While frontiers have conventionally been seen as linear movements across space, we see them as particular dynamics related to the discovery or invention of new resources. Frontiers have conventionally had a spatial or material appearance, but it is not the spatiality or materiality of the resources in themselves that make them frontiers. It is, rather, the reconfiguration of the relationship between a resource and institutional orders that makes it relevant to talk in terms of frontiers. Indeed, frontier dynamics may take place in what is not a geographical expanse. Think, for example, of the human body and the medical technology that has enabled us to harvest stem cells – a new resource – a situation which produces a series of new ethical, legal and commercial considerations. As stem cells are no longer exclusively an integral part of the body, is their use reprehensible, are they now a commodity, should their use be regulated and how will such use become clandestine, and so on? Thus, rather than a 'tidal wave', frontiers mushroom across the globe as an institutional transformation of our intercourse with nature. A frontier is not space or a resource itself, but a space or resource characterized by a set of dynamics of institutional destruction.

Frontier dynamics and territorialization are co-constitutive. Frontier dynamics dissolve existing social orders – property systems, political jurisdictions, rights and social contracts – while territorialization is shorthand for all the dynamics that establish frontiers' new social orders and reorder space anew. This sequence involves, in principle, recursive movements of destruction and consolidation: frontier-territorialization-frontier-territorialization. It follows that frontiers are particular space-time configurations. A frontier emerges when a new resource is identified, defined and becomes subject to extraction and commodification. The discovery and production of new resources – oil, gold, new crops like soy or palm oil, carbon storage, space for urban growth, 'scenery' – opens up frontiers and challenges established rights and institutions. New resource frontiers emerge in different places around the globe. They do not exist as a function of geography *per se*, but can be experienced in informal urban settlements as well as in rural backwaters. They are brought about because new possibilities for resource use and extraction prompt new and competing claims to access, authority and legitimacy.

Technological development, demographic change and movements in market price differentials all ensure that particular geographical spaces can host recurrent frontier moments of capitalist extraction. Frontiers link to processes of land and resource control and are actively created through social and political struggles. Frontier dynamics are the discursive, political and physical operations that classify space and resources as 'vacant', 'free', 'ungoverned', 'natural' or 'uninhabited'. This happens by expunging existing systems of rights and use, often through the dislocation of previous users. Through processes of dispossession, enclosures, land grabbing and other forms of primitive accumulation, previously accepted rights are criminalized, dwellers are turned into squatters and their land uses relabelled as destructive behaviour. Frontier dynamics do not take place in an empty wild; rather, frontiers *make* territorialized spaces 'wild' or 'free'. Frontiers thus pave the way for new acts of territorialization.

Territorialization, in turn, is the creation of systems of resource control, rights, authorities, jurisdictions and their spatial representations (see Shattuck and Peluso, this volume). However, when new resources come within reach, new acts of frontier-making are mobilized to undo established territorial orders. This constant process of formation and the erosion of a social order of property rights, socio-legal identities and political institutions constitute a dynamic where governing institutions build, maintain or lose their authority, and people become, or disappear as, enfranchised rights.

States and governments have obvious roles in territorialization. It is also important, however, to acknowledge their roles in the production of the frontier. Frontier spaces can emerge in any place where a government sometimes unwillingly – but often deliberately and selectively – refrains from intervention and thereby 'promotes an unregulated process of violent dispossession' (Weizman 2007, 5). In his work on the state of exception, Agamben

(2005) describes how governments can assume sovereignty to suspend rights and institutional predictability, only to 'return' to what is now a new emerging structure of rights and authorities. This creates a frontier dynamic different from the one described by Turner: the sovereign can vacate previously ordered spaces in order to allow extraction and commodification to occur beyond the usual regulatory frameworks. This involves the suspension of control, social protections and the rule of law (Mattei and Nader 2008).

We will exemplify this conceptualization of frontiers and territorialization with an analysis of Patagonia.

FRONTIER DYNAMICS IN PATAGONIA: AN EXEMPLARY CASE

Patagonia lends itself easily to a Turneresque interpretation of the frontier foreshadowing civilization. It has a history of wild capitalism, contradictory political projects and banal brutality. It is an extensive space, open to fanciful imaginations of the radical Other, and to commodity exploration and exploitation. During the colonial era and well into the first century of the young independent Latin American states of Argentina and Chile, the vast, windblown and dry lands of the south with their rugged mountains, icecaps and 'savage' peoples remained outside the control of the governments of Santiago de Chile and Buenos Aires (Bandieri 2005). Today, imaginaries of Patagonia as a pristine and people-less wilderness not only condition resource exploitation but also green environmentalisms and corporate philanthropies (Mendoza et al. 2017). The contradictions of the frontier dynamics continue to shape Patagonia through the co-production of frontier imaginaries and resource extraction, and hence also the persistent replay of violent erasures which literally and figuratively confine rural communities to ever more marginal lands.

Patagonia and similar spaces continue to stir our imagination. The mere name *Patagonia* – the land of a mythical race of people with big feet – conjures up images of the untamed. Literary historian Gabriela Nouzeilles (2007) points to contemporary representations in media, art and literature which often consist of replays of the imaginary of Patagonia as a barren desert, a place of solitude and a potential source of wealth. It suggests that the territorial fantasy of Patagonia not only represents reality, but contributes to *producing* it. So it has been historically, and so it is today. It is significant that Thomas More's 'Utopia' of a dream society of the New World, published in 1516, shortly after the 'discovery' of the Americas, was located on the coast of southern South America. Later, travelogues from explorers and scientists, perhaps most notably Charles Darwin in 1859, contributed to the production of Patagonia as a wilderness and its people as barbarians. Similar stories emerged from explorers and solitary peoples of wanderlust throughout the twentieth century.

The 'conquest of the desert' was a territorializing project that stood in relation to the emerging nation state. It was through the violence of the military campaigns of the 1880s that Patagonia became nationalized territory, and as a civilizing project, it relied on the racialized policies of the central government. Following the military campaigns and the diminution of the native population, great portions of Patagonia were awarded to the military elite veterans for their role in its conquest (Bandieri 2005), while British capital and scores of settlers also arrived to populate the newly established colonies. The sediments of these skewed territorial arrangements continue to shape Patagonian spaces to this day. The economy required legal underpinning to enforce private property and to secure commerce and physical infrastructures in terms of fences and roads, all of which served to further bring to bay rural communities.

Frontier dynamics have not ceased to shape Patagonian spaces, as the invention and discovery of new resources continue to emerge. The effective utilization of such resources requires previous social contracts to be renegotiated by force, stealth, cunning and co-optation. Different commodities have thus shaped recent Patagonian history. Wool and meat were the prime commodities in the second half of the nineteenth century, but the First World War deflated these economies (Bandieri 2005). In the first decade of the twentieth century, a new commodity, oil, was discovered in Patagonia, inaugurating new movements of resource extraction, with institutional and political implications. In recent years, the privatization and renationalization of the national energy company restructured the relationship between workers and the company, as well as the role of the company in the regional economy. At the same time, hydrocarbons have been pitched in a discourse on national energy sovereignty, and technological innovations have made the hydraulic fracturing of unconventional shale gas a viable economic option (Svampa and Viale 2014).

Currently, Patagonia is home to two seemingly contradictory frontier movements. Energy sovereignty based on the most environmentally harmful hydrocarbon extraction process coexists with the green imaginary. At the same time as environments and bodies are being exposed to lethal substances and legislations, Patagonia is being promoted as the true wilderness, a pristine Eden to be explored (Mendoza et al. 2017). Green development, environmentalism and sustainability appear to have found a home on the southern tip of South America. Ironically, both economies rely on and reinforce imaginaries of pristine wilderness in the Andean region, as hydrocarbon extraction also relies on representations of Patagonia as idle and free land, an apt sacrifice zone for national progress (Svampa and Viale 2014).

A FRONTIER FRAMEWORK: EMERGENT INSTITUTIONAL ORDERS

Arguably, in Patagonia, the current frontier dynamics and concomitant territorializations are no less racialized than the initial domestication of the southern frontiers. For both green and black economic development, commodity rents travel far from the sites of extraction, while the local costs of living increase. The commodity frontiers rest on a valuation of the environment which runs counter to local, indigenous and otherwise place-based ways of perceiving it.

Significant institutional transformations have followed the discovery of resources in Patagonia and the local-level negotiations over access to their benefits. The early agro-pastoral colonies were social experiments that combined customs from settlers' places of origin with the rules and conditions of the local context. More recently, we also see rules enacted that respond to current commodity territories that are neither recycled nor total reinventions. Hence, in Añelo, the ground zero of the fracking industries in Patagonia, the local populations are struggling with the institutional and social innovations that follow from intensified extraction (Svampa and Viale 2014). Furthermore, in relation to Patagonia's protected areas, we see a number of institutional arrangements that build upon existing claims and entail contests over who is a rights subject within these segregated geographies (Rasmussen 2021).

In Patagonia, the concentration of land in the hands of relatively few people and companies is remarkable, and the introduction of private property has been instrumental in the stabilization of Patagonian spaces (Bandieri 2005). The central government has had an ambiguous relationship to private property. Private ownership was already distributed along ethnic lines at the outset of the conquest of the desert. The short-lived settler colonies formed by the government entailed lands held under fairly precarious conditions, and with settler families being granted only conditional user rights. On the other hand, the descendants of veterans and members of the Buenos Aires economic and social elite were able to secure permanent, exclusive and alienable rights to vast territories. Subsequent land legislations only served to further enforce the parcelling out of Patagonia. These earlier processes of propertization continue to shape the production of space to this day.

Across Patagonia, indigenous communities struggle to maintain control over their resources and territories, in what they refer to as the 'second conquest of the desert'. The scramble for land and resources produces contests over their legitimate use and rent control. In Patagonia, each resource frontier has been accompanied by a host of claims to authority, new jurisdictions and fixed spatial representations that serve to legitimate extraction. Such movements not only enable particular forms of extraction, but also serve to erase prior systems of resource control. Historically, this has happened by force and exclusion as well as through forms of recognition, concession and conditioned inclusion. Some people have thereby become disenfranchised as rights subjects within a moribund system, while others have been granted rights in an emerging one.

Current maps of Patagonia depict different logics of zoning: natural resources for extraction, wind or hydropower potentials, protected areas and adventure tourism and indigenous territories. All of these produce abstract spaces in particular ways, by referring to the potential that these territories are imagined to possess. Such spatial representations are accompanied by legislation, which enable some forms of resource use and marginalize others. While their territorial imprints differ dramatically, both zoning for conservation and zoning for extraction serve to limit local user rights and redefine proper rights subjects. There is a spatial division in Patagonia: whereas the Andean region is predominantly reserved for nature protection and adventure tourism, the steppes and Atlantic coastline are used to ensure Argentina's energy sovereignty aspirations. Both serve as attractors to foreign capital investment. The co-existence and simultaneity of multiple frontier spaces in Patagonia, each with their own spatio-temporal qualities, suggest that frontiers are deeply embedded in both local struggles over resource control and authority, as well as larger political economies and global flows of capital, labour and technologies.

CONCLUSION

The global expansion of markets produces frontiers of contestation over the definition and control of resources. In a world of increasing competition between different actors making their own claims and concessions to resources, the frontier has re-emerged as both an analytical perspective and a diagnosis of current struggles over land and resources. The concept of the frontier underlines the transient nature of any resource system. It definitely puts an end to the notion of the innocence of territorialization by highlighting the inevitable destructive elements of new forms of resource control. Frontier imaginaries, new technologies and market demands enable and promote the discovery and invention of new resources to territorialize and command. Frontier spaces are transitional, spaces in which existing regimes of resource control are suspended, making way for new ones. Hence, frontier dynamics mean the end of worlds at the end of the world. The subsequent new territorialization of resource control in a frontier space fundamentally challenges and replaces existing patterns of spatial control, authority and institutional orders. New patterns of resource exploration, extraction and commodification involve the wilful crafting and circumstantial emergence of institutional arrangements for establishing legitimate authority over new territories.

NOTES

1. A SCOPUS search on 'frontiers' and 'capital*' shows an increase in publications from between 1 and 16 annually in the 1990s, to between 46 and 92 annually in the 2010s (Social Science and Art and Humanities).
2. This section draws on Lund (2020), Rasmussen (2021), Rasmussen and Lund (2018) and Peluso and Lund (2011).

ACKNOWLEDGEMENTS

We are grateful for the generous comments on an earlier draft given by Kristina Dietz, Bettina Engels and Michael Watts. Funding for the research was provided by the Carlsberg Foundation, Julie von Mullens Foundation, Independent Research Fund Denmark (FSE-132262, FKK 102-0579/19-5480) and European Research Council (State Formation through the Local Production of Property and Citizenship (Ares (2015) 2785650-ERC-2014-AdG-662770-Local State)).

FURTHER READING

Chari, S.; Freidberg, S.; Gidwani, V.; Ribot, J.; Wolford, W. (eds) (2017), *Other Geographies: The Influences of Michael Watts*, London: John Wiley & Sons.
Geiger, D. (2008), Turner in the tropics: The frontier concept revisited, in D. Geiger (ed.), *Frontier Encounters. Indigenous Communities and Settlers in Asia and Latin America*, Copenhagen: IWGIA, 75–215.
Lefebvre, H. (1974), *The Production of Space*, London: Blackwell.
Mattei, U.; Nader, L. (2008), *Plunder: When the Rule of Law is Illegal*, London: Blackwell.
Rasmussen, M.B.; Lund, C. (2018), Reconfiguring frontier spaces: The territorialisation of resource control, *World Development*, 101, 388–399.

REFERENCES

Agamben, G. (2005), *State of Exception*, Chicago, IL: University of Chicago Press.
Anderson, T.L.; Hill, P.J. (2004), *The Not so Wild, Wild West: Property Rights on the Frontier*, Stanford, CA: Stanford University Press.
Bandieri, S. (2005), *Historia de la Patagonia*, Buenos Aires: Editorial Sudamericana.
Campbell, J. (2015), *Conjuring Property. Speculation and Environmental Futures in the Brazilian Amazon*, Seattle, WA: University of Washington Press.
Cronon, W. (1991), *Nature's Metropolis: Chicago and the Great West*, New York: WW Norton & Company.

Cronon, W. (1996), The trouble with wilderness: Or, getting back to the wrong nature, *Environmental History*, 1(1), 7–28.

Darwin, C. (2009 [1859]), *The Origin of Species*, 150th anniversary edition, Alachua, FL: Bridge-Logos.

Eilenberg, M. (2012), *At the Edges of States: Dynamics of State Formation in the Indonesian Borderlands*, Leiden: KITLV Press.

Grandin, G. (2019), *The End of the Myth: From the Frontier to the Border Wall in the Mind of America*, New York: Henry Holt and Company.

Harvey, D. (2003), *The New Imperialism*, Oxford, Oxford University Press.

Kaur, R. (2018), World as commodity. Or, how the 'Third World' became an 'emerging market', *Comparative Studies of South Asia, Africa and the Middle East*, 38(2), 377–395.

Li, T.M. (2014), *Land's End: Capitalist Relations on an Indigenous Frontier*, Durham, NC: Duke University Press.

Lund, C. (2020), *Nine-Tenths of the Law: Enduring Dispossession in Indonesia*, New Haven, CT: Yale University Press.

Martinez-Alier, J.; Kallis, G.; Veuthey, S.; Walter, M.; Temper, L. (2010), Social metabolism, ecological distribution conflicts, and valuation languages, *Ecological Economics*, 70(2), 153–158.

Marx, K. (1954 [1887]), *Capital*, vols 1–3, Moscow: Progress Publishers.

Mattei, U.; Nader, L. (2008), *Plunder: When the Rule of Law is Illegal*, London: Blackwell.

Mendoza, M.; Fletcher, R.; Holmes, G.; Ogden, L.A.; Schaeffer, C. (2017), The Patagonian imaginary: Natural resources and global capitalism at the far end of the world, *Journal of Latin American Geography*, 16(2), 93–116.

Moore, J.W. (2000), Sugar and the expansion of the early modern world-economy: Commodity frontiers, ecological transformation, and industrialization, *Review (Fernand Braudel Center)*, 409–433.

Moore, J.W. (2011), Transcending the metabolic rift: A theory of crises in the capitalist world-ecology, *Journal of Peasant Studies*, 38(1), 1–46.

More, T. (1992 [1516]), *Utopia*, New York: Alfred A. Knopf.

Navaro-Yashin, Y. (2012), *The Make-Believe Space: Affective Geography in a Postwar Polity*, Durham, NC: Duke University Press.

Nouzeilles, G. (2007), The iconography of desolation: Patagonia and the ruins of nature, *Review: Literature and Arts of the Americas*, 40(2), 252–262.

Peluso, N.; Lund, C. (2011), New frontiers of land control, *Journal of Peasant Studies*, 38(4), 667–681.

Rasmussen, M.B. (2021), Institutionalizing precarity: Settler identities, national parks and the containment of political space in Patagonia, *Geoforum*, 119, 289–297.

Rasmussen, M.B.; Lund, C. (2018), Reconfiguring frontier spaces: The territoriality of resource control, *World Development*, 101, 388–399.

Scott, J. (2009), *The Art of Not Being Governed: An Anarchist History of Upland Southeast Asia*, New Haven, CT: Yale University Press.

Smith, N. (1984), *Uneven Development. Nature, Capital and the Production of Space*, London: Verso.

Svampa, M.; Viale, E. (2014), *Maldesarrollo. La Argentina del extractivismo y el despojo*, Buenos Aires: Katz.

Tsing, A. (2005), *Friction. An Ethnography of Global Connection*, Princeton, NJ: Princeton University Press.

Turner, F.J. (2010 [1893]), *The Frontier in American History*, New York: Courier Corporation.

Weizman, E. (2007), *The Hollow Land: Israel's Architecture of Occupation*, London: Verso.

White, R. (1994), Frederic Jackson Turner and Buffalo Bill, in J.R. Grossman (ed.), *The Frontier in American Culture*, Berkeley, CA: University of California Press.

11. Labour

Jonathan Pattenden

Labour, in both its paid and unpaid forms, is central to capitalism and agrarian change in four fundamental ways: as the basis of the reproduction of social life; as the primary basis of the livelihoods of most of the world's population; as the source of surplus value that is the foundation of profit and accumulation; and, this chapter will argue, as the driving force of politics. In its most visible and concrete form, labour is the act of exerting energy to produce commodities or services within the 'labour process'. As well as production sites, it is expended in the extraction of natural resources that provide the means of production; along the value chains through which commodities are circulated; in the call centres and at the keyboards where services are shaped and sold; and within the many private and public spaces (homes, schools, hospitals and so on) where reproductive labour prepares and repairs the workforce. Past exertions are embedded in the infrastructures of the present.

Labour can, therefore, be observed in congealed and active forms in our homes and workplaces, and all around us in the built environment. But in order to understand why it is so central to social and political life under capitalism, and to possibilities for transcending capitalism, it has to be understood as lying at the centre of a complex web of relations. This chapter sketches some of the contours of that web – firstly by discussing the forms of labour exertion in the spheres of reproduction and production, and then by focusing on the politics of its antagonistic relations with capital.

LABOUR AND THE REPRODUCTION OF SOCIAL LIFE

The more visible forms of labour that take place in the production process (the moment of exploitation) obscure reproductive labour and the fact that capitalism is reproduced through social life as a whole (the process of exploitation). Social reproduction is the set of private and public activities, institutions and unpaid and paid forms of work that are largely carried out by women in the home and in social institutions like schools and hospitals, which prepare and repair labourers physically and emotionally. Without it there can be no labour-power, no production process and no accumulation.

Capitalism integrates reproductive labour into the process of exploitation in historically specific ways (Fraser 2017). In late medieval and early modern Europe, widespread violence in the form of 'witch hunts' sought to erode women's control over their bodies and intensify the biological aspects of reproductive labour to compensate for post-plague labour shortfalls (Federici 2004). In Victorian Britain, women were increasingly pressed into highly exploitative wage labour, without reducing their reproductive labour burdens, producing 'a crisis of social reproduction' as working-class 'capacities for sustenance and replenishment were stretched to breaking point' (Fraser 2017, 26). Capitalism sought to reset its appropriation of reproductive labour through discourses of 'housewifeization' (Mies 1986), which hive off the 'domestic sphere', imbue it with 'ideals of femininity' and render it 'structurally subordinate' to waged work (Fraser 2017, 24).

The sharpened differentiation of homeplace and workplace has also served to divide male and female labourers, and justify a systematic underpayment of women for equivalent work. Throughout, capital and the state have used social welfare practices and ideological signifiers to champion the 'privatized household' as the primary foundation of social reproduction – all part of the 'ways in which a capitalist totality inflects our institutions, interactions and relations' (Ferguson 2016, 50–51). More recently, neoliberalism's erosion of state support for social reproduction (which was only ever threadbare in many countries) has led to better-off households buying in care work from lower-income households in often racialized 'chains of reproductive labour' (Fraser 2017, 34).

If labour is understood as all those activities through which individuals and groups reproduce themselves and society as a whole, it becomes 'the ontological premise of an integrated (albeit diverse) unity' (Ferguson 2016, 49). As Gramsci (1971, 34–35) put it, it is,

> the discovery that the relations between the social and natural orders are mediated by work ... [that] provides a basis for the subsequent development of an historical, dialectical conception of the world, which understands movements and change.

This is significant analytically, methodologically and politically, because it counters mainstream social science's analytical fragmentation of social life under capitalism, which undermines understandings of capitalism's co-constitution by capital and labour (and nature), and makes possibilities for progressive change less intelligible.

LABOUR WITHIN AND BEYOND THE LABOUR PROCESS

Just as reproductive labour is obscured, so too is capitalism's central process, the extraction of surplus labour from the worker (the moment of exploitation), masked by the fact that wages appear to compensate the worker for all of the time spent in the production process. Surplus value is extracted from workers during surplus labour time – that part of the working day when the labourer no longer works for her wages, but directly for her employer by generating additional, or 'surplus', value. This surplus value becomes profit when the commodities labour has produced are traded in the market. Labour, then, has to be understood simultaneously in relation to social life as a whole *and* in relation to the labour process. The labour expended in the labour process lies at the heart of capitalism, while the labour-power (or capacity to work) that workers possess, and which capital accumulates through, is generated by reproductive labour.

Wage labourers sell their labour-power because they lack sufficient means of production for their own livelihood, itself the result of historical and contemporary acts of dispossession by private and state actors seeking resources as bases for accumulation – be it the eighteenth-century enclosures of public land by British aristocrats, contemporary government-facilitated appropriations of land in north-eastern Cambodia for rubber production (Milne 2015) or the submerging of villages along the Narmada river two decades ago following the construction of the Sardar Sarovar dam (Nilsen 2011).

As well as dispossession, labour is made available to capitalists through processes of socio-economic differentiation, whereby the asset base of some expands, while that of others becomes insufficient for reproduction or disappears altogether. This process takes place through an array of unequal social, economic and political relations, including the unequal exchange relations experienced by smaller and larger farmers (Bharadwaj 1985).

Most of the world's population primarily depends on wage labour (Selwyn 2014), and under neoliberalism wage labour has become increasingly precarious (insecure and often short-lived) and informal (unregulated). Recent ILO (2018, 16) estimates indicate that 61.2 per cent of employment worldwide is informal. A continuum of working conditions ranges from the formal and contracted, through informal and precarious, to forced labour, where exit is prevented, conditions are at their worst and surplus labour time is at its longest. Debt – which results from capitalists not paying sufficient wages to cover the requirements of simple reproduction – acts as a widespread form of control and a key means of intensifying and extending the working day (Breman 2016). Surplus value, though, is extracted from labour irrespective of the degree of freedom that workers have to move between employers.

Those who experience the most oppressive forms of exploitation are more likely to come from racial and ethnic minorities and 'lower' castes. This has long been the case, most famously in the mass murder that took place on European slave boats and in American cotton and sugarcane fields. Social differences are constructed and manipulated by the dominant classes through racism, sexism and other forms of ideological subterfuge intended to maintain control and foster accumulation. This was the case in European empires that used racism to divide, rule and facilitate violent forms of exploitation and natural resource extraction. Such practices have since been reproduced through international wars, through violence linked to many transnational corporations, and through contemporary crudely pro-capital governments like that of Bolsonaro in Brazil as it intensifies the deforestation of the Amazon. In addition to highly oppressive forms of exploitation, racial and ethnic minorities also experience higher rates of dispossession.

THE CRISIS OF REPRODUCTION AND THE FRAGMENTATION OF LABOUR

As the basis of surplus value and accumulation, labour has always been at the centre of agrarian questions focused on the development of capitalism in agriculture and the role of agricultural surpluses in the broader economy. Intricately linked to these questions of expanded reproduction is the question of simple reproduction, or the meeting of a household's material, social and cultural needs.

A declining share of rural dwellers are able to make a living from their own land, while levels of non-agricultural employment are insufficient to absorb the labour surplus. Ongoing appropriations of land (for plantations, mines, special economic zones and so on) and the unequal social relations that generate socio-economic differentiation continue to erode livelihoods. And technological change within and beyond the countryside increases underemployment by reducing capital's need for physical and mental labour.

The scarcity of work stretches households across different sites of wage labour and different forms of petty self-employment, such as small-scale farming and the making and selling of snacks. Such petty commodity producers may be disguised wage labourers (because the households concerned neither have nor accumulate assets) or combine the positions of capital and labour in an unsteady relationship, where some households are petty capitalists in the making, while others increasingly depend on wage labour.

This 'crisis of reproduction', whereby capitalism is unable to provide for the simple reproduction of the growing global labour force, means that hundreds of millions of rural people across the global south commute and migrate to cities for work (Zhang 2015). Many are part of a 'reserve army of labour' that holds down wages and disciplines those in work. Other labourers are surplus even to the strategic requirements of capital, languishing as latent labour away from capital flows or in places where capital has little need for labour-power, and migration streams have not drawn them into wage labour elsewhere (Li 2013).

This spatial fragmentation meshes with social fragmentations of race, caste and gender. In turn, both mesh with a fragmentation of the labour process by task, experience and wage level; of the production process across principal contractors or subcontractors; and of commodity chains between those who extract primary resources, manufacture and transport goods, or provide 'services'. They are also fragmented by scale between, for example, those working in groups in larger factories, or alone as homeworkers, and between those who work in sites of production and reproduction.

Labour's multiple fragmentations make it more pliable. This strengthens capital's dominance of class relations as owners of the means of production, and its tendency to control mediating institutions, including the state. Bernstein's (2006) concept of 'classes of labour' allows space for the complexities of fragmentation, while underlining that all households that primarily depend on wage labour for their simple reproduction or which depend on it in combination with forms of petty self-employment share a position as members of the exploited classes. This is politically significant.

CRITICAL AGRARIAN STUDIES AND LABOUR STRUGGLES

This final section fuses two central aspects of the 'agrarian question of labour': how is labour reproduced under contemporary capitalism, and how can political struggles transform its conditions? In other words, what is the relationship between simple reproduction and 'the role of agrarian classes of labour – peasant classes, small farmers and agricultural workers – in struggles for democracy and socialism' (Bernstein 2009, 241)?

This is part of a broader set of well-worn questions about the dynamics of labour's political agency across time and place (Burawoy 1985; Gramsci 1971; Harvey 1989). Where do and where will rural-based labourers organize, and with whom? Do they do so in the city or the countryside, as labourers or as farmers, in sites of production or reproduction? And do they act in direct opposition to capital or are their struggles channelled through the state? Are their struggles sporadic or sustained, place-bound or networked? And are they more likely to be focused on land or wage labour?

The multitude of case studies in the literature underline that all of these forms of struggle are at play (see McNally 2013) – be it decades-long struggles against dispossession (Nilsen 2011), everyday contestation of work intensity (Swider 2015), short-lived mass mobilizations that underline labour's capacity to disrupt production and undermine accumulation or networked movements against transnational corporations (Brookes 2019). Fragmentation impedes labour's collective action, but also generates connections that provide moments and places where collective action can flourish – at critical moments in the production and circulation of commodities, or when the spotlight on well-known brands reveals harsh working conditions.

If labour's antagonistic relations with capital are the driving force of politics, then how can the patterns and forms of its collective action be understood? When and why does labour organize primarily in relation to land or wage labour? When and why does it orientate its actions towards capital or the state? When and why does it primarily act in the spheres of production or reproduction? And when and why are its actions sporadic or sustained, isolated or networked?

These variables combine in different ways too. So, for example, labour may mobilize in relation to land by targeting the state in sustained networked campaigns that encompass the spheres of production and reproduction, or it may target capital in short-lived isolated campaigns with particular objectives related to working conditions. The point is that where labour lives and works (its locations of production and reproduction), and the forms of control and fragmentation that it experiences, influence the patterns and forms of its collective action.

Where classes of labour remain primarily dependent on small-scale farming and common property resources, they are more likely to mobilize around those aspects of their livelihoods – especially when their access to land is threatened by plantations or industrial zones (Le Mons Walker 2008). Where labourers mobilize around land and farming, the political dynamics are shaped in part by whether the movement is dominated by labourers, as was the case with Brazil's Movement of Landless Workers, or by petty capitalist farmers, as was the case with India's Karnataka State Farmers Association. The latter was a cross-class political formation in which the interests of classes of labour were systematically marginalized (Assadi 1997). Cross-class alliances cannot be rejected *a priori*, but can only be persisted with where they progressively expand rather than shrink the political space for classes of labour (Alavi 1973).

Where classes of labour consist mostly of wage labour, they are more likely to mobilize in relation to wages or workplace conditions, access to housing, healthcare, education, crèches and water, or to target government institutions over precarity and state regulation (see McNally 2013). State regulation, or the lack of it, directly impacts the intensity and extent of the working day. Government programmes (from workfare to subsidized foodstuffs) subsidize labour's simple reproduction and also capital as the state in effect pays that portion of the costs of simple reproduction that capital does not meet. Primarily controlled by capital in most cases, the state seeks social stability as well as the expanded reproduction of capital. Government welfare programmes reduce workers' dependence on wage labour, which has contradictory implications. It can expand labourers' 'political space', but also tends to divide and control labour.

Informality and spatial fragmentation reduce workplace-based mobilizations and increase the frequency of those focused on social reproduction. Nevertheless, the former remain widespread in momentary, networked and sustained forms (Bank Munoz 2017; Brookes 2019; Swider 2015). And so the move from workplace to 'community' or neighbourhood-based mobilization should not be overplayed – not least because of the often hierarchical nature of social relations in hamlets and villages. Where community hierarchies are steeper, the importance of mobilization and conscientization during the process of migration becomes more important.

The political aspects of the agrarian question of labour arguably, then, have three principal bases: the first is concerned with dispossession and 'popular struggles over land', the second with state mediation of the capital–labour relation and the conditions of material reproduction and the third with the forms of wage labour. But these are increasingly intertwined. When labourers move between sites of production, they also move between 'local labour control regimes' – an intermediate concept intended to facilitate understanding of the geography of labour's conditions and its ability to act collectively (Jonas 1996; Pattenden 2018).

Rural-based labourers, both when they are in the countryside or circulating through the city, usually face greater restraints on their mobilization than their urban counterparts, not least because they tend to be more spatially fragmented and have more frequent interactions with members of dominant social groups. Socio-political hierarchies are (re-)enacted through everyday meetings in the common spaces of multi-class villages, as well as through the more tangible forms of domination and exploitation that mark wage labour and debt relations.

This contrasts with living places where workers are 'concentrated together, and in relative physical and social isolation from the influences of the dominant social classes' (Petras and Zeitlin 1967, 580). It is in such places, Petras and Zeitlin have argued in relation to Chilean miners, that conditions for developing a collective consciousness are greater. They decline as everyday social and workplace dynamics become more hierarchical, and are more systematically strengthened by the ideological machinations of the state (school history syllabuses, for example), religious institutions preaching sobriety and discipline and the digitalized flows of big capital's messages on social media feeds.

The ways in which labour is the driving force of politics are also highly gendered. For example, in some contexts men's social and political interactions with dominant actors may be more numerous than those of women, leaving men more divided by vertical connections and less open to horizontal solidarities than women (Park and Maffii 2017; Phan 2018). Meanwhile, women workers confined to agricultural work in patriarchal home villages have little scope for collective action, while those who migrate to work in urban industries may be able to organize – depending on their relationships with other workers, and the ways in which the industries that they work in are integrated into local, national and international economies (Silvey 2003).

CONCLUSION

Labour's agency and the ebb and flow of labour movements exist within the broader structural dynamics of world-historical capitalism (Silver 2003). It is not simply about labour's relations with capital, or with other labourers, but also about competition between capitals in their search for expanded reproduction. Where labour's mobilizations increase its share of the value produced, capital can bring in more pliant workers from elsewhere or relocate. Put another way, labour's collective action under capitalism operates within structural limits.

The study of labour as a political actor should always focus on the dynamic inter-reaction of labouring and capitalist class agencies in individual and collective forms at multiple levels, and in more direct or mediated forms. Labour, as was argued at the outset, provides the basis of social life, and simple and expanded reproduction, and is also the driving force of politics. Its latent power is vast, and somewhere in the dialectics of patterns of control, reproduction, conscientization and collective action lie clues about how and where it might mobilize, not simply to improve its conditions, but to transcend them in search of systemic change.

FURTHER READING

Bernstein, H. (2010), *The Class Dynamics of Agrarian Change*, Hertford, CT: Kumarian and Winnipeg: Fernwood.
Bhattacharya, T. (ed.) (2017), *Social Reproduction Theory: Remapping Class, Recentering Oppression*, London: Pluto.
Breman, J. (2016), *At Work in the Informal Economy: A View from the Bottom Up*, New Delhi: Oxford University Press.
Oya, C.; Pontara, N. (2015), *Rural Wage Employment in Developing Countries: Theory, Evidence and Policy*, London: Routledge.
Taylor, M.; Rioux, S. (2018), *Global Labour Studies*, Cambridge: Polity.

REFERENCES

Alavi, H. (1973), Peasants and revolution, in Gough, K.; Sharma, H.P. (eds), *Imperialism and Revolution in South Asia*, London: Monthly Review Press, 291–337.
Assadi, M. (1997), *Peasant Movement in Karnataka 1980–1994*, Delhi: Shipra.
Bank Munoz, C. (2017), *Building Power from Below: Chilean Workers Take on Walmart*, Ithaca, NY: Cornell University Press.
Bernstein, H. (2006), Is there an agrarian question in the twenty-first century?, *Canadian Journal of Development Studies*, 27(4), 449–460.
Bernstein, H. (2009), Agrarian questions from transition to globalization, in Akram-Lodhi, A.H.; Kay, C. (eds), *Peasants and Globalization: Political Economy, Rural Transformation and the Agrarian Question*, London: Routledge, 239–692.
Bharadwaj, K. (1985), A view on commercialisation in Indian agriculture and the development of capitalism, *Journal of Peasant Studies*, 12(4), 7–25.
Breman, J. (2016), *At Work in the Informal Economy of India: A Perspective from the Bottom Up*, New Delhi: Oxford University Press.
Brookes, M. (2019), *The New Politics of Transnational Labor*, Ithaca, NY: Cornell University Press.
Burawoy, M. (1985), *The Politics of Production: Factory Regimes under Capitalism and Socialism*, London: Verso.
Federici, S. (2004), *Caliban and the Witch: Women, the Body and Primitive Accumulation*, Brooklyn, NY: Autonomedia.
Ferguson, S. (2016), Intersectionality and social-reproduction feminisms, *Historical Materialism*, 24(2), 38–60.
Fraser, N. (2017), Crisis of care? On the social-reproductive contradictions of contemporary capitalism, in Bhattacharya, T. (ed.), *Social Reproduction Theory: Remapping Class, Recentering Oppression*, London: Pluto, 21–36.
Gramsci, A. (1971), *Selections from the Prison Notebooks*, London: Lawrence and Wishart.
Harvey, D. (1989), *The Urban Experience*, Baltimore, MD: Johns Hopkins University Press.
ILO (2018), *Women and Men in the Informal Economy: A Statistical Picture*, Geneva: ILO.
Jonas, A. (1996), Local labour control regimes: Uneven development and the social regulation of production, *Regional Studies*, 30(4), 323–338.
Le Mons Walker, K. (2008), From covert to overt: Everyday peasant politics in China and the implications for transnational agrarian movements, *Journal of Agrarian Change*, 8(2), 462–488.
Li, T. (2013), *Land's End*, Durham, NC: Duke University Press.
McNally, D. (2013), Unity of the diverse: Working-class formations and popular uprisings from Cochabamba to Cairo, in Barker, C.; Cox, L.; Krinsky, J.; Nilsen, A.G. (eds), *Marxism and Social Movements*, Chicago, IL: Haymarket, 401–424.
Mies, M. (1986), *Patriarchy and Accumulation on a World Scale*, London: Zed Books.
Milne, S. (2015), Cambodia's unofficial regime of extraction: Illegal logging in the shadow of transnational governance and investment, *Critical Asian Studies*, 47(2), 200–228.
Nilsen, A. (2011), *The River and the Rage*, London: Routledge.

Park, C.; Maffii, M. (2017), We are not afraid to die: Gender dynamics of agrarian change, Ratanakiri Province, Cambodia, *Journal of Peasant Studies*, 44(6), 1235–1254.

Pattenden, J. (2018), The politics of classes of labour: Fragmentation, reproduction zones and collective action in Karnataka, India, *Journal of Peasant Studies*, 45(5–6), 1039–1059.

Petras, J.; Zeitlin, M. (1967), Miners and agrarian radicalism, *American Sociological Review*, 32(4), 578–586.

Phan, H.P. (2018), *Gendered Access to Resources and its Implications for REDD+: A Case Study from the Central Highlands, Vietnam*, Unpublished PhD thesis, Norwich: University of Anglia.

Selwyn, B. (2014), *The Global Development Crisis*, Cambridge: Polity Press.

Silver, B. (2003), *Forces of Labour*, Cambridge: Cambridge University Press.

Silvey, R. (2003), Spaces of protest: Gendered migration, social networks, and labor activism in West Java, Indonesia, *Political Geography*, 22, 129–155.

Swider, S. (2015), Building China: Precarious employment among migrant construction workers, *Work, Employment and Society*, 29(1), 41–59.

Zhang, F.Q. (2015), Rural households' social reproduction in China's agrarian transition: Wage employment and family farming, in Oya, C.; Pontara, N. (eds), *Rural Wage Employment in Developing Countries: Theory, Evidence and Policy*, London: Routledge, 230–253.

12. Labor and social reproduction

Smriti Rao

INTRODUCTION

Marx (1976) used the term 'social reproduction' to mean the cultural, economic and political processes required to maintain and perpetuate particular social relations of production. But Marx's definition of the term ignored the reproduction of labor power itself, and focused too narrowly on relations of production alone (Hartmann 2010). Feminist critiques have helped generate a more expansive definition of social reproduction as the study of 'the material and discursive practices which enable the reproduction of a social formation (including the relations between social groups) and its members over time' (Wells 2009, 78; White, this volume).

The feminist political economy stream of this now vast literature on social reproduction establishes perhaps the most direct connection between labor and social reproduction. This literature closely examines the processes involved in the production and maintenance of life and thus labor power itself (Benería and Sen 1981; Federici 2012). It has helped us see the capacity to labor as something that must be produced, while also extending our understanding of labor to include forms of labor, such as the labor of care, that were invisible to much of political economy, and are still undertheorized within agrarian studies. The fact that the labor of life-making (Bhattacharya 2017a), or the labor of social reproduction, is so often performed by groups marginalized by gender, race, ethnicity and caste, forces us to confront how these different axes of power constitute each other and constitute class relations (Fraser 2016).

This chapter thus narrows its focus to feminist political economy analyses of social reproduction, which is most consistent with the concerns of critical agrarian studies, and which have re-emerged as particularly vibrant areas of inquiry in the aftermath of the Great Recession. I begin by reviewing the debate over the term social reproduction within feminist political economy and then discuss what we know about the possible specificities of social reproduction in agrarian societies of the Global South. I argue that current feminist theorizations of social reproduction fail to sufficiently address contexts where (1) wage labor is one of many forms, rather than the primary form, of livelihood generation; (2) the penetration of both state and the market in the realm of social reproduction is shallow and thus (3) the labor of social reproduction is dominated by what is sometimes termed 'indirect care work': cooking, cleaning or fetching fuel and water in ways that are less mediated by technology and highly dependent upon access to the commons.

Many dominant narratives of economic development have dismissed lives and livelihoods built around agricultural labor as no longer capable of history-making. This chapter, like the others in this collection, instead foregrounds agrarian society as the stage upon which some of the key political, economic and cultural conflicts of our time are playing out (Akram-Lodhi and Kay 2010). Laboring in agriculture is certainly not the only form of livelihood generation in much of the Global South, and it has become much less important to understanding profit-making. But agriculture remains critical to the survival and reproduction of working people across the Global South, with no sign that the workers of the Global South are going to experience anything like the European transition away from agriculture (Bernstein 1996). Thus social reproduction cannot be fully understood without grappling with the agrarian nature of many societies in the South. And societal transformations in the contemporary agrarian South may be usefully understood 'from below' as the unfolding of the dynamics of social reproduction, including changes in the labor of social reproduction. If that is the case, a successful politics will have to take this labor, and those who perform it, into account.

THE EVOLUTION OF FEMINIST SOCIAL REPRODUCTION THEORY

The current feminist understanding of social reproduction emerges from three intertwined debates conducted in the 1970s and 1980s, and led by Marxist or socialist feminists. In her review of these debates, Luxton (2006) terms them the production/reproduction debate, the sex/gender debate and the domestic labor debate, a classification that I follow here.

The production/reproduction debate was an initial attempt to explore the production and maintenance of labor power within the framework of Marxist theory. Marxist feminists debated whether to conceptualize a separate sphere of reproduction, and if so, whether to characterize it as surplus producing itself, a debate that became increasingly caught up in technical questions about the labor theory of value. In the process it became clear that Marxian theory alone could not explain why it was women who were often assigned the labor of reproduction, leading to the theorization of a 'mode of patriarchy' that interacted with the 'mode of production' (Hartmann 2010). However, the project of replicating a 'mode'-like analysis of patriarchy proved to be difficult to sustain and, eventually, not entirely productive (Rowbotham 1981). This in turn led to the domestic/household labor debate, which examined the labor of reproduction without embedding in it any systematic 'mode of patriarchy'.

Participants in the domestic/household labor debate helped us develop an understanding of the gender division of labor as historically specific and mutually constitutive of capitalist processes. But the term 'domestic labor' was, and is, apolitical enough that it could be coopted into liberal or conservative analyses that divorced it from questions of class as well as race or ethnicity. And while using the term 'domestic' does focus attention on the relatively understudied sphere of the household-family, it also allows us to remain there, accepting a particular division between domestic and non-domestic, and documenting what happens within the 'domestic' without going any further.

Both these debates were conducted alongside a third, which revolved around the terms sex and gender, and led to increasingly sophisticated feminist formulations of gender as the social construction of biological difference (Scott 1988). Much of this theorization failed to account for race, ethnicity and the 'third world difference' (Mohanty 2003). But this debate may have had the most widespread, if often problematic, influence. Concepts of gender that emerged from this debate quickly became central to liberal 'lean in' feminism in ways that entirely divorced gender from class (Fraser 2016). And of course we are all familiar with the completely apolitical mainstream use of 'gender' as simply a stand-in for the word 'women' (Luxton 2006). Nevertheless, the fact that it is now relatively uncontroversial, at least in the realm of theory, to state that biological difference does not explain economic, political or cultural power is a critical accomplishment, the importance of which cannot be overstated.

At the intersection of these debates lay the question of the extent to which women's assignment to the sphere of reproduction helped to explain their subordination under capitalism. Peasant societies, which were largely considered to be pre-capitalist, were seen as interesting case studies of women's status under alternative economic systems. Two features of peasant pre-capitalist societies were considered particularly noteworthy: (1) a greater articulation between production and reproduction than under capitalism, with less subordination of the latter and (2) the fact that reproductive activities were not entirely relegated to women (Benería and Sen 1981). One possible argument was therefore that the development of capitalism in these societies would result in a decrease in women's status, because capitalism tended to push women into an increasingly subordinated reproductive sphere (Deere 1976). On the other hand, there was also a tendency for the debates within Northern feminism to be inflected with orientalism. The realm of reproduction, considered to be relatively dominant in peasant societies, was cast as the primary site of 'tradition' and was thus often assumed to be particularly oppressive to women. This then meant that women's condition could be improved by the expansion of the productive, capitalist sphere, and of course the interventions of western feminism itself (Mohanty 2003).

Empirical work in the agrarian South made it clear, however, that the development of capitalism had contradictory effects for women – in some cases enhancing women's status, and in others reducing it (Mies 1982; Hart 1995; Kapadia 1995). Furthermore, feminists argued that the development (or not) of capitalism intersected in contextually specific ways with 'household relations', forms of family-household and kinship systems that shaped gender divisions of labor constitutively with changes in the forces and relations of production (Deere 1990). Empirical work in the agrarian South showed that the household took different forms in different contexts, often varying significantly from the male-headed, nuclear family assumed in the North (Hart 1995; Ruwanpura 2006; Razavi 2009). This work challenged assumptions about public–private divides, and pointed out that in some contexts reproductive work was better understood as the responsibility of the community or neighborhood rather than the family unit (Katz 2001). Changes in the form and extent of reproductive labor could not therefore be understood by merely looking 'within' the household. This work also pointed out that the agrarian question, in so far as it examined the persistence of the peasantry, *was* a question of social reproduction and could not be understood by merely examining the 'productive' sphere (Deere 1995).

The explicitly Marxist feminist orientation of these debates in the 1970s and 1980s faded as both feminism and social theory more generally turned away from Marxism. But the debates influenced later feminist work on time use, 'double burdens' and time poverty which echoed themes that emerged in these earlier debates (Kongar and Connelly 2017), without using the language of social reproduction, or directly linking questions of 'time poverty' to capitalist accumulation processes. On the one hand, the methodologies developed to generate time use data return labor time to the center of the analysis in ways that align with Marxist approaches, while allowing us to recognize and analyze the role of un-commodified labor. On the other hand, most time use data is currently analyzed within theoretical frameworks that do not consider questions of class. The central problematic presented in such analyses is that the burden of unpaid/unwaged/domestic work reduces the well-being of the women (or, more rarely, men) who perform such labor, either because such burdens prevent them from more fully participating in the labor force, or because participating in the labor force prevents them from fully performing or enjoying reproductive labor.

The goal of 'reducing, redistributing and recognizing' reproductive work is thus aimed at improving the well-being of those who perform such work, by emphasizing its widespread benefits (Elson 2008). Increased state subsidies for social reproduction, funded by higher taxes on the wealthy, are usually called for in order to achieve this goal. These demands are clearly consequential, as more extensive subsidies for social reproduction would improve the lives of millions of women, men and children in very concrete ways. But to a large extent these are demands for the redistribution of existing surplus within capitalism, without an explicit critique of the economic system that provides the context for reproductive labor. Feminist political economists looking back at the last four decades may conclude that our difficulties achieving either the redistribution or the reduction of such labor for all but the most privileged women suggests that we have, as Benería et al. (2015) point out, not one problem here, but at least two, a framing that is much more embedded in the genealogy of the term social reproduction.

The residues of those early debates can also be found in the mainstream policy argument that directing social welfare programs toward women will result in the more efficient transformation of welfare/aid money into health or education outcomes (Berik 2017). This latter approach has often had a profoundly conservative bias, reifying both a particular gender division of labor as well as existing capitalist structures of accumulation (Razavi 2009; Benería et al. 2015). In a neoliberal context, this placed the responsibility for economic development upon women, while providing them with very little by way of resources to accomplish these daunting goals (Bakker 2003). As we seek to retheorize social reproduction today, this inadvertent reification of existing structures of inequality remains a danger. One of the most complex acts of navigation for those of us who wish to 'recognize' the role that the labor of social reproduction plays in production, accumulation and politics, is to avoid romanticizing that labor or suggesting that the links between women's work and the labor of social reproduction are anything but historically contingent and entirely mutable (Razavi 2009).

SOCIAL REPRODUCTION IN THE CONTEXT OF WAGE LABOR

Feminist political economy analyses of social reproduction highlight the mutually constitutive articulation between reproductive labor and processes of surplus generation and appropriation, but largely do so in the context of the wage labor–capital relationship (Bhattachary 2017a). The primary link between these processes, as articulated in this literature, is that the labor of social reproduction converts wage income, via the commodity inputs purchased with that wage income, into use values that produce and maintain labor power, which in turn becomes an input back into the production of surplus (Quick 2004; Bhattacharya 2017b). The unresolvable contradiction at the heart of capitalism is then that as capital strives to minimize the wage paid to workers (in order to maximize the rate of exploitation), it can create not just crises of realization, but crises of reproduction as well, as the quality, and at an extreme quantity, of the labor power produced, decreases (Fraser 2013). If we take the dialectical relationship between these processes seriously, changes in 'household relations' – shifts in marriage and childbearing practices, or in household structures – can in turn create crises for capital by setting in motion similar reductions in the quality and quantity of labor power produced and maintained. Unlike some of the early theorizations of reproduction or domestic labor, the diversity of household forms even amongst the professional classes in the Global North, not to mention amongst its working classes, has led to a greater acknowledgement of variations in gender divisions of labor, and less automatic conflation between the work of women and reproductive labor.

The debate over whether or not such labor of social reproduction is itself productive of surplus value appears to have subsided. An examination of advanced capitalist countries today shows that a part of such labor can indeed be subsumed by capital, as the proliferation of home cleaning companies, day care centers and elder care centers would seem to suggest, and thus turn into paid, surplus producing wage labor of the kind performed (mostly by women) in such spaces. Reproductive labor can also be replaced by commodity form substitutes, such as pre-pared food, or by state provisioning such as in the case of state-provided health and education services in at least some parts of the North (Bezanson and Luxton 2006).

But there is also skepticism that capitalism will ever fully subsume the sphere of social reproduction (Fraser 2013; Benería et al. 2015). Most feminist political economists today begin from the observation that forms of capitalism and patriarchy can coexist quite comfort-ably, and while this coexistence can include differing degrees of subsumption of the labor of social reproduction to capital, this subsumption is always incomplete. To the extent that some portion of this labor always remains unpaid and outside the circuits of capital, the literature is interested in examining how, when and why the subsidy to capital provided by this unpaid component of reproductive labor varies, and how that reshapes both capitalism and patriar-chy. The neoliberal revolution in advanced capitalist countries, for example, is thus seen as a successful attempt to shift these processes away from state and capital and back into the household-family (Bakker 2003).

This theorization of social reproduction is explicitly political, in that it aims to reclaim the sphere of social reproduction as a site from which working-class struggles can be launched. Rather than organizing workers only through trade unions, at work sites, and over wages and work days, social reproduction theorists point to successful struggles in the United States and Europe launched from homes and communities and mobilizing protesters around social reproduction issues of education, health care and the social safety net, but this time without the racialized and gendered exclusions of the early twentieth-century movements around these issues (Federici 2012). Social reproduction theorists demand not only the redistribution of surplus towards social reproduction, but also an end to exploitation (read as the capitalist–wage labor relationship), as well as gender- and race-based oppressions (Bhattacharya 2017b).

SOCIAL REPRODUCTION IN THE AGRARIAN SOUTH

Social Reproduction, Production and Accumulation

I would argue that this new formulation of social reproduction remains insufficiently attuned to contexts in the Global South, primarily because it assumes the institutional context of advanced capitalism, which in turn has at its center the wage labor–capital relationship.

As is now widely documented, the livelihood generation strategies of a majority of workers in the developing world do not resemble the 'proper job' of the salaried wage worker (Ferguson and Li 2018). They are instead engaged in non-standard, informal work – a mixture of petty commodity production and spells of wage labor, often requiring intermittent migration both spatially from place to place, but also in terms of industry/occupation, as the same worker moves from agriculture to construction or petty trade (Breman 2010; Scully 2016; Harriss,

Chapter 19 in this volume). While some of these livelihood strategies are directly tied to land, the peasant household that derives most of its income from agriculture is also no longer the dominant empirical reality in the agrarian South.

Thus while the primary link between reproductive labor and surplus production and appropriation in the North may be the conversion of wage income into use values that reproduce the labor force, in the agrarian South there may be a substantial component of reproductive labor that consists of unpaid labor converting 'free' inputs from nature into use values for reproduction. Commodity inputs/substitutes and household technology may play a smaller role (Razavi 2007). These are also contexts in which state provisioning was rarely a viable alternative to family-household-based social reproduction even before the onset of neoliberalism/structural adjustment (Sehgal 2005; Scully 2016).

The relative absence of technology, and of state-provided or commodity form inputs/substitutes, means more time spent on labor-intensive, physically strenuous forms of cooking, cleaning, washing, gathering of fuel, water or firewood, with care work necessarily taking a back seat (Razavi 2007). An important implication is that such reproductive work would also be much more dependent upon land, and upon access to commons of various kinds, making it less mobile and much more rooted in place (Naidu and Ossome 2016). This would also make it much more vulnerable to the threat of climate change. Refusing to give up land, and resisting full proletarianization, may thus be a reproductive rather than an accumulative strategy for rural households (Zhan and Scully 2018).

Last but not least, the labor power thus reproduced has a much more uncertain destiny. It is more likely to be formally rather than really subsumed by capital (Banaji 2013), and more likely to become part of a pool of relative surplus labor than to have a 'proper job' or 'proper business' (Ferguson and Li 2018). To the extent that signals from capital have any effect upon the forms of cultural production that occur as part of social reproduction, these signals are ambiguous at best in such contexts.

The temporal and spatial instability of increasingly diverse livelihood strategies thus creates very sharp contradictions between potentially surplus generating activities and social reproduction (Rao and Vakulabharanam 2018). Reproductive labor may intensify as neither real nor formal subsumption to capital can cover the costs of reproduction. During the Industrial Revolution the working day for children and adults, male and female, was often so long that the reproductive labors of cooking, cleaning or care work were reduced to their barest minimum (Berg 1992). We may find households in the Global South likewise going through phases when the difficulties of temporally and spatially reconciling the labor of reproduction with the demands of petty production/wage reduce the former to a minimum, or force some members of the household to withdraw from the latter (Naidu and Ossome 2017). The same household may go through phases where reproductive work increases, and where it decreases, both in the context of insufficiency.

These spatial and temporal disjunctures can in turn enhance contradictions between class and gender. Gendered and generational divisions of labor may harden as it becomes increasingly impossible to combine productive and reproductive work, and the latter becomes the realm of women, or of the elderly (Jacka 2012); or as dowries or bride-price, are used as a way to access otherwise scarce investible funds (Kapadia 2017). When the promise of male bread-winning cannot be kept, this can generate struggles within household relations that in turn lead to their dissolution and restructuring, and their failure to reproduce themselves (Ferguson 2015). Household relations may be transformed as a consequence of new livelihood strategies, as de facto female-headed households and female farmers emerge as a result of male out-migration, and those relations do not quite return to 'normal' when the spell of migration ends; or as women out-migrate and become primary breadwinners in contexts where this situation strains dominant gender ideologies (O'Laughlin 2008; Ramnarain 2016; Gidwani and Ramamurthy 2018).

There is clearly no telos here, but here is a tentative hypothesis that may be advanced. If Bernstein (1996) is correct in arguing that the agrarian question of capital has largely been bypassed in the age of globalized, financialized capital, then the macro-dynamics of accumulation may play an increasingly small role in explaining or helping us to understand the lives of the majority of those living in the agrarian South. The strategies households adopt to survive may be better understood as struggles against localized and specific forms of surplus extraction, drawing upon household as well as class relations, commodified as well as non-commodified forms of labor, and the commons as much as private property. We may not find significant class differentiation, but rather significant livelihood diversification (O'Laughlin 1996), and from a political perspective it may be that the labors of social reproduction provide the unifying common ground for an otherwise fragmented working class.

Social Reproduction and Politics in the Agrarian South

As with other marginalized groups, peasant struggles have been first and foremost about survival and thus framed in what Marxist feminists would recognize as a language of reproduction first. The empirical realities of this survival have changed with the adoption of more diverse forms of income generation, the continuing if less complete dependence on smaller plots of land, more limited access to the commons and the new threat of climate change. The struggle may no longer be primarily about holding onto land, or for land reforms, although those may remain significant issues (O'Laughlin 2008). Unlike in the North, the struggle may not primarily be over wage labor per se, but rather against the extraction of surplus by capital in a variety of more nebulous and more indirect forms (Banaji 2013). It may be over access to the commons but require fighting against forms of dispossession that involve state and corporate power in new ways (Levien 2018).

As Katz (2001) points out, the realm of social reproduction is tricky terrain for politics. First, the imperative of ensuring the survival of our loved ones may be all-consuming in ways that numb the power and energy to resist. Second, the very fact that social reproduction implicates the intimate sphere of households and families can make it very difficult to organize around the issue of reproductive labor. The difficulties feminist movements have had when they try to organize around issues of intra-household inequality are well documented (Kapadia 2017; Rao 2018). Insofar as social reproduction is about reproducing existing, often problematic, social relations, it can be at odds with a project of radical transformation. These difficulties are compounded by the fact that the labors of social reproduction, as discussed above, are often organized across clear boundaries of family-household. There is no workplace site where workers can be easily found, and reproductive labor may be spatially dispersed across entire neighborhoods or communities. The everywhere of social reproduction can quickly turn into a nowhere from the perspective of organizing (Katz 2001).

But if we believe that livelihood strategies in agrarian societies are driven by the dynamics of social reproduction, a politics that does not understand or respond to those dynamics would not be very fruitful. As pointed out by O'Laughlin (2008) such a politics would have to recognize claims based on class exploitation but also the non-class oppressions that shape household relations, and which are rooted in gender, as well as race or caste. It would have to adjust to a context where exploitation occurs not just through the wage–capital relationship, and where claims can be based upon participation in un-commodified labor. In short, it would have to legitimize 'forms of political agency, however, transient or fragmentary – that have been illegitimized by formal politics' (O'Laughlin 2008, 213).

CONCLUSION

This chapter proposes that feminist social reproduction theory may be a particularly useful way to examine the dynamics of agrarian societies in the Global South. This is not just because it may better explain the unexpected (from the perspective of classical theories both Marxian and Liberal) trajectories of agrarian societies in their survivals, as well as their transformations. But this is also because the realm of social reproduction can provide a model, even if flawed, of mutuality and solidarity that is hard to find elsewhere in capitalist society (Charusheela 2010). This is a realm within which the discursive and material power of productivity, of commodified contributions and of competition are blunted by claim-making based upon belonging. Feminists have extensively documented the ways that these spaces can be suffused with inequality and violence, but, as the Marxist feminist retheorization of social reproduction indicates, feminists have also not given up hope that those spaces can be remade as more inclusive and egalitarian, and that from such spaces can emerge a better vision of a better world.

FURTHER READING

Bhattacharya, T. (ed.) (2017a), *Social Reproduction Theory: Remapping Class, Recentering Oppression*, London: Pluto Press.
Federici, S. (2012), *Revolution at Point Zero*, San Francisco, CA: PM Press.
Deere, C.D. (1990), *Household and Class Relations: Peasants and Landlords in Northern Peru*, Berkeley, CA: University of California Press.
O'Laughlin, B. (2008), Gender justice, land and the agrarian question in southern Africa, in Akram-Lodhi, H.; Kay, C. (eds), *Peasants and Globalization: Political Economy, Rural Transformation and the Agrarian Question*, London: Routledge, 190–213.
Razavi, S. (2009), Engendering the political economy of agrarian change, *Journal of Peasant Studies*, 36(1), 197–226.

REFERENCES

Akram-Lodhi, A.H.; Kay, C. (2010), Surveying the agrarian question (Part 2): Current debates and beyond, *Journal of Peasant Studies*, 37(2), 255–284.
Bakker, I. (2003), Neo-liberal governance and the reprivatization of social reproduction: Social provisioning and shifting gender orders, in Gill, S.; Bakker, I. (eds), *Power, Production and Social Reproduction*, London: Palgrave Macmillan, 66–82.
Banaji, J. (2013), *Theory as History: Essays on Modes of Production and Exploitation*, Delhi: Aakar Books.

Benería, L.; Sen, G. (1981), Accumulation, reproduction and women's role in development: Boserup revisited, in Leacock, E.; Safa, H. (eds), *Women's Work*, South Hadley, MA: Bergin and Garvey, 141–157.

Benería, L.; Berik, G.; Floro, M. (2015), *Gender, Development and Globalization: Economics as if All People Mattered*, London: Routledge.

Berg, M. (1992), Women's work and the Industrial Revolution, in Digby, A.; Feinstein, C.; Jenkins, D. (eds), *New Directions in Economic and Social History*, London: Palgrave, 23–36.

Berik, G. (2017), Making the case for gender equality: Efficiency and social justice arguments – An introduction, *Canadian Journal of Development Studies*, 38(4), 542–546.

Bernstein, H. (1996), Agrarian questions then and now, *Journal of Peasant Studies*, 24(1), 22–59.

Bezanson, K.; Luxton, M. (eds) (2006), *Social Reproduction: Feminist Political Economy Challenges Neo-liberalism*, Montreal: McGill-Queen's Press.

Bhattacharya, T. (ed.) (2017a), *Social Reproduction Theory: Remapping Class, Recentering Oppression*, London: Pluto Press.

Bhattacharya, T. (2017b), Introduction: Mapping social reproduction theory, in *Social Reproduction Theory: Remapping Class, Recentering Oppression*, London: Pluto Press, 1–20.

Breman, J. (2010), *Outcast Labour in Asia: Circulation and Informalization of the Workforce at the Bottom of the Economy*, Oxford: Oxford University Press.

Charusheela, S. (2010), Engendering feudalism: Modes of production revisited, *Rethinking Marxism*, 22(3), 438–445.

Deere, C.D. (1976), Rural women's subsistence production in the capitalist periphery, *Review of Radical Political Economics*, 8(1), 9–17.

Deere, C.D. (1990), *Household and Class Relations: Peasants and Landlords in Northern Peru*, Berkeley, CA: University of California Press.

Deere, C.D. (1995), What difference does gender make? Rethinking peasant studies, *Feminist Economics*, 1(1), 53–72.

Elson, D. (2008), The three Rs of unpaid work: Recognition, reduction and redistribution, Presentation in Expert Group Meeting on Unpaid Work, Economic Development and Human Well-being, UNDP, New York.

Federici, S. (2012), *Revolution at Point Zero*, San Francisco, CA: PM Press.

Ferguson, J. (2015), *Give a Man a Fish: Reflections on the New Politics of Distribution*, Durham, NC: Duke University Press.

Ferguson, J.; Li, T.M. (2018), Beyond the 'proper job': Political-economic analysis after the century of labouring man, Working Paper 51, Cape Town: PLAAS, University of the Western Cape.

Fraser, N. (2013), *Fortunes of Feminism: From State-Managed Capitalism to Neoliberal Crisis*, London: Verso Books.

Fraser, N. (2016), Capitalism's crisis of care, *Dissent*, 63(4), 30–37.

Gidwani, V.; Ramamurthy, P. (2018), Agrarian questions of labour in urban India: Middle migrants, translocal householding and the intersectional politics of social reproduction, *Journal of Peasant Studies*, 45(5–6), 994–1017.

Hart, G. (1995), Gender and household dynamics, in Quibria, M.G. (ed.), *Critical Issues in Asian Development*, New York: Oxford University Press, 39–74.

Hartmann, H. (2010), The unhappy marriage of Marxism and feminism: Towards a more progressive union, in Sitton, J.F. (ed.), *Marx Today: Selected Works and Recent Debates*, New York: Palgrave Macmillan, 201–228.

Jacka, T. (2012), Migration, householding and the well-being of left-behind women in rural Ningxia, *The China Journal*, 67, 1–22.

Kapadia, K. (1995), *Siva and Her Sisters*, Boulder, CO: Westview Press.

Kapadia, K. (2017), Introduction: We ask you to rethink – different Dalit women and their subaltern politics, in Anandhi, S.; Kapadia, K. (eds), *Dalit Women: Vanguard of an Alternative Politics in India*, New York: Taylor and Francis, 1–50.

Katz, C. (2001), Vagabond capitalism and the necessity of social reproduction, *Antipode*, 33(4), 709–728.

Kongar, E.; Connelly, R. (2017), Feminist approaches to time use, in *Gender and Time Use in a Global Context*, New York: Palgrave Macmillan, 1–26.

Levien, M. (2018), *Dispossession without Development: Land Grabs in Neoliberal India*, New Delhi: Oxford University Press.

Luxton, M. (2006), Feminist political economy in Canada and the politics of social reproduction, in Bezanson, K.; Luxton, M. (eds), *Social Reproduction: Feminist Political Economy Challenges Neo-liberalism*, Montreal: McGill-Queen's Press, 11–44.

Marx, K. (1976), *Capital*, vol. 1, translated by B. Fowkes, Harmondsworth: Penguin.

Mies, M. (1982), *The Lace Makers of Narsapur: Indian Housewives Produce for the World Market*, London: Zed Press.

Mohanty, C.T. (2003), 'Under western eyes' revisited: Feminist solidarity through anticapitalist struggles, *Signs: Journal of Women in Culture and Society*, 28(2), 499–535.

Naidu, S.C.; Ossome, L. (2016), Social reproduction and the Agrarian question of women's labour in India, *Agrarian South: Journal of Political Economy*, 5(1), 50–76.

Naidu, S.C.; Ossome, L. (2017), Work, gender, and immiseration in South Africa and India, *Review of Radical Political Economics*, 50(2), 332–348.

O'Laughlin, B. (1996), Through a divided glass: Dualism, class and the agrarian question in Mozambique, *Journal of Peasant Studies*, 23(4), 1–39.

O'Laughlin, B. (2008), Gender justice, land and the agrarian question in Southern Africa, in Akram-Lodhi, H.; Kay, C. (eds), *Peasants and Globalization: Political Economy, Rural Transformation and the Agrarian Question*, London: Routledge, 190–213.

Quick, P. (2004), Subsistence wages and household production: Clearing the way for an analysis of class and gender, *Review of Radical Political Economics*, 36(1), 20–36.

Ramnarain, S. (2016), Unpacking widow headship and agency in post-conflict Nepal, *Feminist Economics*, 22(1), 80–105.

Rao, N. (2018), Global agendas, local norms: Mobilizing around unpaid care and domestic work in Asia, *Development and Change*, 49(3), 735–758.

Rao, S.; Vakulabharanam, V. (2018), Migration, crises and social transformation in India after the 1990s, in Menjívar, C.; Ruiz, M.; Ness, I. (eds), *The Oxford Handbook of Migration Crises*, Oxford: Oxford University Press.

Razavi, S. (2007), The political and social economy of care in a development context: Conceptual issues, research questions and policy options, Working Paper 3, Geneva: United Nations Research Institute for Social Development.

Razavi, S. (2009), Engendering the political economy of agrarian change, *Journal of Peasant Studies*, 36(1), 197–226.

Rowbotham, S. (1981), The trouble with patriarchy, in Samuel, R. (ed.), *People's History and Socialist Theory*, London: Routledge, 364–370.

Ruwanpura, K.N. (2006), *Matrilineal Communities, Patriarchal Realities: A Feminist Nirvana Uncovered*, New Delhi: Zubaan.

Scott, J. (1988), Gender: A useful category of historical analysis, *American Historical Review*, 91(5), 1053–1075.

Scully, B. (2016), Precarity North and South: A Southern critique of Guy Standing, *Global Labour Journal*, 7(2), 160–173.

Sehgal, R. (2005), Social reproduction of third world labour in the era of globalization: State, market and the household, *Economic and Political Weekly*, 40(22), 2286–2294.

Wells, K. (2009), *Childhood in a Global Perspective*, Cambridge: Polity Press.

Zhan, S.; Scully, B. (2018), From South Africa to China: Land, migrant labour and the semi-proletarian thesis revisited, *Journal of Peasant Studies*, 45(5–6), 1018–1038.

13. Peasants

Jan Douwe van der Ploeg[1]

INTRODUCTION

Peasants probably are the *raison d'etre* of critical agrarian studies and certainly one of the most debated, disputed and divisive topics of this intellectual tradition. While there are well-established, but contradictory, views about the role and potential of the peasantry, recent theoretical developments and empirical studies open up the possibility of at least partly reconciling these views and to cast new insights into the present status and future prospects of the world's peasantry. Despite more than a century of people predicting its inevitable demise, the peasantry is more numerous now than at any time in the world's history (Weis 2007; Lattre-Gasquet et al. 2014; Lowder et al. 2016).

The classical works of Marx (1963 [1852]) and Lenin (1964 [1899]) viewed the peasantry as a hindrance to the process of capital accumulation – and therefore as an obstacle to the full development of capitalism and the subsequent transition towards socialism. They saw peasant agriculture as a representation of stagnation and backwardness; a source of chronic underdevelopment. As a consequence, they did not see a place for peasant agriculture (based on small private properties) within a socialist society based on socialized ownership. Lenin seemingly believed that the peasantry would inevitably disappear through processes of class differentiation that would dissolve it into two groups: a small but powerful class of large capitalist farmers and huge masses of peasants who would lose their land and be obliged to engage as wage workers in large farm enterprises or industry (an excellent synthesis of this line of thought is given by Bernstein 2010). There were, at that time, clear indications of such a class differentiation – but this process never came to the assumed end-station: 'the death of the peasantry' (Hobsbawm 1995). Subsequent generations of Marxist scholars such as Kautsky (1974 [1899]) and, more recently, Boltvinik and Mann (2016) have tried to offer explanations for the partial continuity, if not persistence, of peasants and peasant agriculture.

In contrast to this position there is the Chayanovian approach, which follows the views initially developed by Chayanov, a contemporary of Lenin. Chayanov (1966 [1925]) argued that peasant agriculture has a strong capacity to develop and to contribute to the development of society and can be an important ingredient, if not a building block, of socialism, especially when there are vibrant peasant communities and/or effective vertical cooperatives. He also argued that demographic differentiation is more decisive than class differentiation. His thesis of demographic differentiation views changes in the numbers and size of peasant farms as driven by emancipatory and farm-succession aspirations, which make differentiation a cyclical and self-repeating process.

The Leninist and the Chayanovian positions, both of which build on the works of Marx, are integral to critical agrarian studies, even though in many ways they are mutually contradictory. This paradox can be explained by virtue of them addressing different levels of scale. The Leninist analysis seeks to capture historical processes that concern *the peasantry as a whole*;

Chayanovian analysis, by contrast, focuses on *individual peasant farms* and their internal dynamics.

Over recent decades it has increasingly been recognized that the two approaches might well be combined into a more comprehensive analysis of peasant realities (Deere and De Janvry 1979; White 2018). At the same time, ambiguities in the original works of Marx, Lenin and Chayanov have emerged. In his later days Marx, in a letter to 'Dear Citizen' Zasulich, wrote that he had finally become 'convinced ... that the commune is the fulcrum for social regeneration in Russia' (Shanin 2018, 20). Lenin, in turn, not only studied the works of Chayanov but also confirmed that 'every peasant can participate in the construction of socialism', for a 'regime of civilised cooperators ... is a socialist regime' (Shanin 1990, 308). Chayanov readily admitted that there was class differentiation alongside demographic differentiation and that 'literally, before our eyes the world's agriculture ... is being more and more drawn into the circulation of the world economy, and the centres of capitalism are ... subordinating it to their leadership' (Chayanov 1966 [1925], 257). The subsequent harsh suppression of the Chayanovian approach, which resulted in the 'treble death' of Chayanov (Shanin 2009),[2] was probably more due to the authoritarian nature of Stalinism than to any inherent anti-peasant stance within Marxism. This has been subsequently forcefully underlined in the works of several influential authors, including Gramsci (1920, 1992 [1931–1937]), Sereni (1956), Mariátegui (1925), Shanin (1990) and many others.

It should be noted that the Leninist and Chayanovian positions not only represent a theoretical debate but that they have also inspired highly contrasting policies and practices. Diametrically opposed types of land reform – one aiming at collectivization, the other at giving land rights to individual peasant farmers – have their roots in these contrasting positions. In Latin America, in particular, this translated into fierce battles between *campesinistas* (favouring the private peasant farms) and *descampesinistas* (promoting collectivization). A similar difference emerged among peasant organizations and their political positions and strategies. Should peasants regard themselves as allies of the proletariat, or should they organize themselves in independent leagues, equivalent to trade unions? The latter position was defended by Emilio Sereni, a Marxist scholar from Italy, who was greatly influenced by Gramsci and who later became national leader of the *Alleanza Nazionale dei Contadini* (National Peasants' League). Sereni coined the political slogan '*la terra a chi la lavora*' (the land to the tiller). This notion was accepted by the Central Committee of the Italian Communist Party in January 1956 and later accepted by the Party Congress. Sereni clarified that this slogan 'is not only meant for conquering the land and for a general land reform, but is equally the foundation for the right to private ownership of the land within a socialist Italy' (Sereni 1956, 19–20; PCI 1957, 120–130; Zangheri 1981).

The creation, in 1993, of *La Via Campesina* and its subsequent development as a transnational peasant movement is a contemporary and convincing expression of the same position (Edelman and Borras 2016). In short: the 'peasant', understood here as a metaphor for peasant agriculture, peasantries and their potentials, might very well be understood as a central ingredient of radical theory, practices and policies.

SO, WHAT IS A PEASANT?

Until the final decades of the twentieth century peasants were mostly understood as being characterized by the four criteria that, taken together, constitute the foundation of a much used definition (see e.g. Wolf 1955, 1966; Shanin 1971).[3] A peasant:

1. is primarily involved in agricultural production.
2. has effective control of a generally small parcel of land and makes autonomous decisions about its cultivation.
3. is primary subsistence orientated.
4. is subordinate to and dominated by outsiders.[4]

The last 25 years or so have seen an important unfolding of this definition, which has occurred along four axes. First, being *primarily* involved in agriculture turned out to be a complicated and contested notion, because most peasants were *also* involved in extra-agricultural activities. The latter often contribute more to the family income than farming does (Swaminathan and Bakshi 2017). When these non-farming activities consist of wage-labour the peasants involved are sometimes classified as 'disguised proletarians' (Cockcroft 1983). Thus, the specificity of being a peasant fades away into more general notions of 'classes of labour' (Bernstein 2010) forming part of a group of exploited and marginal workers, the 'polibians' (Kearney 1996), who jump, like amphibians, from one job to another.

Yet it has also been argued that such pluri-activity (or multiple jobholding) does not herald a shift away from being a peasant. Rather, peasants engage in 'other gainful activities' (as they are called in French research) in order to safeguard their farm and to continue farming. The remarkable fact is that they do not generally *sell* their farm unless there are very special circumstances. Farms are kept in the family (as security, as a prospect for the future, as a place to live,[5] as an activity to be developed or whatever) and the earnings obtained elsewhere are used to make this possible. For farms and farming can no longer be reproduced solely through the markets for agricultural products and food.[6] This leads farmers, peasants included, to turn to pluri-activity as a mechanism to defend their patrimony.

A second important change regarded the introduction of labour process analysis. 'Being involved in *agriculture*' was considered to be a vague criterion. What matters more is the distinctive way in which *peasants* structure their processes of labour and (re)production. The focus on the specificity of peasant production was partly a response to massive modernization projects such as the Green Revolution in the Global South and the introduction of high-tech entrepreneurial farming in the Global North, which aimed to restructure farming. Methodologically this issue was tackled with an analysis of the labour process (inspired, among others, by the seminal work of Braverman 1974) which highlighted the artisanal nature of peasant production, the skills of peasant producers and the organic unity of mental and manual labour. This showed that while peasants are clearly 'primarily engaged in agricultural activities', this engagement takes a specific form, shaping a distinctive way of farming that differs substantially, and significantly, from both entrepreneurial and capitalist farms.[7] The many differences (that relate to yields, type of cattle, animal/land ratios, cropping schemes, employment levels, irrigation techniques and the like) are rooted in the pursuit of a good 'labour income' (as specified by Chayanov 1966 [1925] and especially 1924). In turn, this exploration of the social and material differences brought an accompanying inquiry into the social relations of production, i.e. 'those relations *that constitute the labour process* and regulate the social distribution of the produced wealth' (Poulantzas 1974, italics added). Agroecology has subsequently further developed this perspective – both practically and theoretically (see for example, Rosset and Altieri 2017). It is important to note that in introducing an analysis of the labour process the issue of 'subsistence' was reconceptualized in a fundamental, and strategically important, way. 'Self-provisioning' not only refers to consumption and the household – today it refers especially to the farm and the process of (re)production. In and through their labour processes, peasants produce and reproduce the resources they need to guarantee their continuation. It is a cyclical process that aims at strengthening the physical and social resource base, rather than maximizing profit. Production and reproduction are intertwined in an organic unity that underpins the autonomy of the peasant farm and helps distance it from circuits controlled by capital and other sources of subordination.

Agency is the third key axis. While peasants are subordinated, at the same time they actively resist this subordination. They do so through a multiplicity of actions that theoretically have been categorized as (1) overt struggles (such as 'peasant wars', milk strikes, land occupations, manifestations, destruction of experimental plots for genetically modified crops, etc.), (2) hidden sabotage (masterfully described by James Scott (1985) as 'weapons of the weak') and (3) altering the material processes of reproduction, production, processing and marketing (I will enlarge on this point later).

The fourth axis derives from feminist studies and brings gender relations in farming to the fore. It starts from the recognition that involvement in the four key features of the peasantry mentioned above might differ greatly between men and women as well as between the old and the young, or different ethnicities. It raises questions such as: who has the titles to the land (point 2)? Who does most of the work and of what kind (point 1)? Who has which responsibilities within the household domain, and under what conditions (point 3)? How do the effects of subordination impact upon different actors (point 4)? This raises questions about how these different positions and roles create and/or maintain gender inequalities, and how they consolidate or undermine patriarchy.

The changes discussed above have resulted in new definitions that adequately synthesize, I think, the wealth of empirical studies from recent decades and help considerably in outlining new perspectives and prospects. Together they have given an enormous impetus to critical agrarian studies.

There are different strands and different points of departure for these new definitions. One centres on the class position of peasants, viewing the peasantry as 'the third class' (Thiemann 2014): distinct from both the ruling classes, which controls the means of production, and from wage workers, who put these means 'into motion'. The peasantry differs from the working class, as workers are separated from the means of production and only have access to their labour that they 'sell' to the owners of the means of production. Peasants, by contrast, are workers who possess and control their own means of production. Classical Marxism saw this combination of the contradictory elements of labour and capital within one unit as highly unstable and doomed to disintegration. Time, however, has shown this combination to be a solid, persistent and omnipresent 'land-labour institution' (Pearse 1975) able to resist harsh conditions.

Another strand centres on the socio-material specificity of the peasant process of production. It argues that peasant production should be understood as 'a struggle for autonomy that takes place in a context characterized by dependency relations, marginalization and deprivation' (van der Ploeg 2018, 28). This struggle materializes in, and as, the building of a self-controlled resource base that is used to engage in co-production. Co-production involves the ongoing interaction, and mutual transformation, of man and living nature. It results in (1) the reproduction of the resource base, (2) the maintenance of the peasant family and (3) the production of a marketable surplus. The interrelations between these three components vary in time and space – with each specific combination creating distinct social and material constellations.

This reworked understanding of the socio-material specificity of the peasant process of production has profound consequences for our understanding of the notion of autonomy, which critically includes the capacity to (re)produce, within the farm itself or in the wider peasant community, most of the resources needed to sustain the process of production. A peasant family seeks to construct an autonomous resource base that it can use according to its needs, prospects, aspirations and experiences, and as a result production does not necessarily follow the 'logic of the market'.

A third strand centres on the peasant household and farm as places where gender-based social relations are located and cultural repertoires are strategically applied and, at least sometimes, transformed. 'Marry whomever you want,' peasant mothers told their daughters in patriarchal and Catholic parts of Spain, 'as long as it isn't a peasant.' This led, in the end, to massive processes of depopulation and the subsequent desertification of many parts of rural Spain, which is still visible today.

These new representations of peasants, peasant agriculture and peasant life have given rise to novel conceptualizations that allow us to transcend previous dichotomies that have restricted the scope of peasant studies. One such concept is 'degrees of peasantness' (coined by Victor Toledo in 1995), which refers to the potential of agriculture to be more peasant-like or less peasant-like; to the capacity of the peasantry to articulate itself as 'a class for itself', as Marx argued; and/or to the potential of peasant life to carry on and renew its own specific cultural repertoires – or not.

The historical trajectory of the peasantry is another issue to consider. In the past, theories about depeasantization and repeasantization appeared to be mutually exclusive. Yet, it is now evident that the two might very well co-exist and interact at different levels and in complex ways, often engendering unexpected outcomes, including newly shaped forms of differentiation, whilst traditional criteria, such as the size of farms, have lost much of their relevance.

NEW QUESTIONS

It is generally accepted that the old 'agrarian question', which put peasantries centre stage as a main barrier to capital accumulation, is now redundant. There are new, burning issues that centre on food. What kind of food? How much? How, where and by whom is it to be produced? How will it be delivered to (urban) consumers? How will the social wealth generated through the production and circulation of food be distributed and used? These are the new, fundamental questions, which have as much relevance for (urban) consumers as rural producers. These questions give rise to the possibility of new coalitions, as Heinisch (2017) has pointed out.

There are further questions. Will capital continue to seek to take direct and increasing control over food production, processing, circulation and consumption?[8] Will different forms of entrepreneurial agriculture, strongly distant from the local ecology, and thus contributing to the artificialization of food, increasingly monopolize food production? Will repeasantization enlarge the degree of peasantness and provide a countervailing force to these tendencies?

Probably all three processes will occur simultaneously, through the interplay of de- and repeasantization, and interact in surprising, and as yet unforeseen, ways. All this will be unveiled in the future. The concept of food sovereignty is likely to provide a powerful intellectual and political tool in these struggles.

This new problematique comes with a series of more specific questions, each of which has a different relevance, according to the specificities of time and place. In many parts of the world, most notably in Africa, agriculture not only renders food and other agricultural products and services but also needs to be able to provide sufficient rural employment opportunities and to contribute significantly to national production and often export earnings (HLPE 2013). Beyond that, there are many places where agriculture plays a vital role in contributing to the protection of biodiversity and scenic landscapes and underpins the rural economy. A new and global challenge is to halt, if not reverse, the processes that contribute to global warming and climate change, the effects of which on patterns of primary production are likely to be massive, if yet poorly understood. Making farming attractive again for young people is another global challenge. Meeting these challenges raises a series of major questions.

Equally important are questions that regard 'peasant workers': the men and women working partly in agriculture and partly in other sectors such as industry, construction, trade and mining. The temporal and spatial variations of this are bewildering. Some of these peasants may travel each day to the next town, while others may become transcontinental migrants. Such migration may be seasonal and pluri-annual. How do these different forms affect peasants' identity and class position? How do they impact on farming? What new skills, ideas and contacts do the migrants return with? Other sets of questions emerge from the construction of new forms of autonomy in an era in which corporate control is seemingly hegemonic, and from the shifting interrelations between autonomy and cooperation (Lucas et al. 2019).

NEW ARENAS

The interlinkages between the production, processing, distribution and consumption of food are increasingly controlled by 'food empires' (van der Ploeg 2018). Peasants are responding to this through constructing new market places where they can directly sell the food that they produce. Such 'peasant markets' are blossoming all over Europe and Latin and North America, whilst in Africa and Asia, traditional 'territorial markets' continue to thrive along the same lines that are being constructed anew in the other continents: delivering fresh, high-quality food to consumers at reasonable prices, making sure that the producers get a fair share of the value added, in market places that are governed by mutually agreed rules. For the peasants involved, such markets ('nested' in coalitions with consumers) are part of a wider struggle to defend and/or reconstruct the autonomy that is central to peasant agriculture. This struggle for autonomy, new markets included, often translates to territorial levels, with 'self-governance' emerging as a slogan that reflects the historical traditions and future aspirations of peasant communities. The emergent 'self-organizing territories' often function as 'economies of opposition' (Pahnke 2015) that, both materially and symbolically, strengthen peasant movements.

The struggle for autonomy also inspires and is driving the turn to agroecology (Rosset and Altieri 2017). Agroecology aims to ground farming, as much as possible, on the use of natural resources, ecological principles and on closing biological cycles at farm or local level. Peasant labour and knowledge play a key role in this. By putting self-controlled natural and social resources centre stage, agroecology also represents a struggle against agribusiness groups that seek to control farming through monopolizing the supply of inputs and technologies. Agroecology is an everyday life struggle. It takes place in the fields, in the stables, in the markets, in the encounters between peasants and consumers and in the exchange of experiences. At the same time, it is becoming an important socio-political force that is changing agriculture, with the resulting transition also significantly contributing to the mitigation of climate change.

A third, and often misunderstood, modality of peasants' struggles is referred to under the umbrella-type names of 'rural development' and 'multifunctionality'. These strategies involve extending the scope of activities of farming: through on-farm processing of food products (Schneider and Niederle 2010) and/or adding economic activities (or 'functions'), such as agro-tourism, energy production, water retention, the maintenance of scenic landscapes or the protection of biodiversity. Such activities generate extra value added (extra 'labour income') on the farm and for the peasant household. At the same time, they help build new circuits for reproduction. As it is becoming increasingly difficult, if not impossible, to reproduce the farm solely through crop and/or livestock production, these new circuits now often support the continuity of the farm and materially sustain its autonomy.

The increased importance of direct marketing through newly constructed or traditional peasant markets, agroecology and the inclusion of new 'functions' has considerably strengthened the role and visibility of rural women. This has not come automatically – but is the fruit of the active struggles of peasant women, who are also extending these struggles into a fourth arena, their fight against patriarchy (La Via Campesina 2017).

Another extremely important arena that needs to be mentioned is the struggle for food sovereignty. This theme, introduced into international socio-political and academic debates by La Via Campesina, refers to the democratic right of people to decide, themselves, on the ways in which they want their food to be produced, processed, distributed and consumed. Food sovereignty has proven to be a forceful new slogan with a strong mobilizing capacity (Edelman 2014). It has already energized scientific debates and strengthened the search for alternatives to the rhetoric of 'food security' favoured by capital and most states; food security being, in the end, the possibility to acquire food in, and through, the 'free market'.

LESSONS TO BE LEARNED

Reviewing the rich tradition of peasant studies leads me to believe that it offers some important guidelines for future research and theory-building in critical agrarian studies. First, the peasantry should be studied as a dialectical process that unfolds over time. It is a complex and contradictory movement through time, shaped by the opposing processes of depeasantization and repeasantization. This implies that time-series and longitudinal analysis are important analytical tools. Special attention needs to be given to the multiple societal forces that regulate and reshift, sometimes slowly and hardly visibly, and at other times abruptly, the balance that ties these processes together. The outcomes are often very different: sometimes the peasantry gains the upper hand, while at other times entrepreneurial or capitalist agriculture establish hegemony. Politico-economic analysis is indispensable for understanding the resultant balances and their differential impacts.

Second, it is important to understand the peasantry as the 'third class' that has its own agency. Peasant struggles and resistance can reset the balance of de- and repeasantization. It is also important to understand peasant farming as an everyday social struggle: a permanent struggle for autonomy, to improve the prospects of the farm and the household and create new opportunities for the next generation. Progress may be made, or setbacks encountered but the desire to move ahead is always there.

Third, it needs to be recognized that peasant struggles (both the seemingly individual and the collective ones) are moving in new, sometimes unexpected and often poorly understood arenas. Currently this includes engagement in various rural development processes: the construction of new markets, agroecology and engagement in temporary labour migration. Undoubtedly, new arenas will emerge in the future.

In the fourth place it is of utmost importance to continue documenting the specificities of peasant agriculture: how it compares with capitalist and entrepreneurial agriculture and how it impacts upon wider society. Special attention needs to be paid to the potentials entailed in peasant agriculture: where might it go in the years to come? In this respect, farming styles research (van der Ploeg 2003) is a useful tool.

Fifth, there is an ongoing need to continue analysing the peasantry's interactions with markets, agribusiness groups, supermarket chains, banks and state apparatuses that, together, operate as a *superstructure* (re. Braudel 1992) that is imposed on and tries to maximize its control and exploitation of peasant agriculture. Special attention needs to be given to new mechanisms that allow for control-at-a-distance, such as new technologies, external prescriptions, regulatory schemes, environmental policies, big data and oligopolistic control over market channels. However, while this superstructure strives, with all means possible, to attain hegemony, the seeds of emancipatory alternatives are germinating everywhere – and again, these need to be carefully documented and theoretically represented.

CONCLUSIONS

There are currently more peasants than ever before in the history of the world and peasant agriculture remains the main source of the world's food. Nonetheless, the modern world – especially the scientific and political communities – finds it extremely difficult to recognize the importance of the world's peasantries, let alone to design enabling policies, technologies and institutional arrangements. Critical agrarian studies, on the other hand, has the potential to unravel the enigmas represented by peasants, peasantries and peasant agriculture. It might also provide insights into the mechanisms and tools needed to help to support and strengthen the multiple and multifaceted struggles for emancipation in which peasants are engaged and upon which much of humanity's food provisioning depends.

NOTES

1.   I am grateful to John Harriss for his thoughtful comments on a previous draft.
2.   'Treble' because (1) Chayanov himself was murdered in the Gulag Archipelago, (2) his work was totally banned in the socialist camp dominated by Stalinism and (3) after the Second World War his work was pushed to the margins in the Western world.

3. An interesting, but seldom noted, consequence of this definition is that it allows for a Leninist reading (following especially point 4) as well as for a Chayanovian interpretation (points 2 and 3 that explain the persistence of the peasantry).
4. 'Peasants, as a rule, have been kept at arm's length from the social sources of power. Their political subjection interlinks with cultural subordination and economic exploitation through tax, corvee, rent, interest and terms of trade unfavourable to the peasant' (Shanin 1971, 15).
5. Kinsella et al. (2000) argue that many rural families engage in pluri-activity as a means to combine the best of two possible worlds (the urban and the rural).
6. In the Netherlands, for example, on 80 per cent of all farms either the man or the wife or both engage in outside jobs. The income obtained from these jobs contributes, on average, 40 per cent of the family income. Without this extra income farming would be de facto impossible.
7. This subsequently raised the question of *why* peasants produce differently – a question that triggered the exploration of different strategies and the implied rationales that govern the organization and development of agricultural production. The Chayanovian specification of the different balances that govern peasant production (and distinguish it from entrepreneurial and capitalist production) turned out to be highly useful here (van der Ploeg 2013).
8. Through, for example, land grabbing, financialization, the imposition of specific technologies, the creation of food empires that operate as obligatory passage points between the production and consumption of food, the prescription of food production regulations and standards by state apparatuses and agro-industries and many, many more.

FURTHER READING

Bernstein, H. (2010), *Class Dynamics of Agrarian Change*, Halifax: Fernwood.
La Via Campesina (2017), Declaration of the 7th Conference: 'We feed our peoples and build the movement to change the world', La Via Campesina, Derio, Basque Country, 16–24 July.
Mariátegui, J.C. (1925), *Siete Ensayos de Interpretación de la Realidad Peruana*, Lima: Amauta.
Shanin, T. (1990), *Defining Peasants: Essays Concerning Rural Societies, Expolary Economies, and Learning from Them in the Contemporary World*, Oxford: Basil Blackwell.
van der Ploeg, J.D. (2013), *Peasants and the Art of Farming: A Chayanovian Manifesto*, Halifax: Fernwood.

REFERENCES

Bernstein, H. (2010), *Class Dynamics of Agrarian Change*, Halifax: Fernwood.
Boltvinik, J.; Mann, S.A. (2016), *Peasant Poverty and Persistence in the Twenty-First Century: Theories, Debates, Realities and Policies*, London: Zed Books.
Braudel, F. (1992), *The Wheels of Commerce: Civilization and Capitalism, 15th–18th Century*, vol. 2, Berkeley, CA: University of California Press.
Braverman, H. (1974), *Labor and Monopoly Capital: The Degradation of Work in the 20th Century*, New York: Monthly Review Press.
Chayanov, A.V. (1924), *Die Sozial Agronomie, ihre Grundgedanke und ihre Arbeitsmethoden*, Berlin: Verlagsbuchhandlung Paul Parey.
Chayanov, A.V. (1966 [1925]), *The Theory of Peasant Economy*, edited by Thorner, D.; Kerblay, B.; Smith, R.E.F., Manchester: Manchester University Press.
Cockcroft, J. (1983), *Mexico: Class Formation, Capital Accumulation and the State*, New York: Monthly Review Press.
Deere, C.D.; De Janvry, A. (1979), A conceptual framework for the empirical analysis of peasants, *American Journal of Agricultural Economics*, 61(4), 601–611.
Edelman, M. (2014), Food sovereignty: Forgotten genealogies and future regulatory challenges, *Journal of Peasant Studies*, 41(6), 959–978.

Edelman, M.; Borras, Jr., S.M. (2016), *Political Dynamics of Transnational Agrarian Movements*, Halifax: Fernwood.

Gramsci, A. (1920), Operai e contadini, in *L'ordine nuovo*, 3 January, Rome.

Gramsci, A. (1992 [1931–1937]), *Prison Notebooks*, vol. 1, New York: Columbia University Press.

Heinisch, C. (2017), Nouveaux circuits alimentaires de proximité dans les Andes: Contribution a la reconnaissance des paysannaries, Tome 1, PhD thesis, Agrocampus Ouest, Université Européenne de Bretagne, Rennes, France.

HLPE (High Level Panel of Experts) (2013), Investing in smallholder agriculture for food security, A report by the High Level Panel of Experts on Food Security and Nutrition of the Committee on World Food Security, Rome: FAO.

Hobsbawm, E. (1995), *The Age of Extremes: The Short Twentieth Century*, London: Penguin Press.

Kautsky, K. (1974 [1899]), *La Cuestion Agraria, Siglo Veintiuno*, Buenos Aires: Argentina Editores.

Kearney, M. (1996), *Reconceptualizing the Peasantry: Anthropology in Global Perspective*, Boulder, CO: Westview Press.

Kinsella, J.; Wilson, S.; de Jong, F.; Renting, H. (2000), Pluriactivity as a livelihood strategy in Irish farm households and its role in rural development, *Sociologia Ruralis*, 40(4), 481–496.

La Via Campesina (2017), Declaration of the 7th Conference: 'We feed our peoples and build the movement to change the world', La Via Campesina, Derio, Basque Country, 16–24 July.

Lattre-Gasquet, M.; Donnars, C.; Marzin, J.; Piet, L. (2014), Quel(s) avenir(s) pour les structures agricoles? *Cahier Demeter*, 15, 169–196.

Lenin, V.I. (1964 [1899]), *The Development of Capitalism in Russia*, Moscow: Progress Publishers.

Lowder, S.K.; Skoet, J.; Raney, T. (2016), The number, size, and distribution of farms, smallholder farms and family farms worldwide, *World Development*, 87, 16–29.

Lucas, V.; Gasselin, P.; van der Ploeg, J.D. (2019), Local inter-farm cooperation: A hidden potential for the agroecological transition in northern agricultures, *Agroecology and Sustainable Food Systems*, 43(2), 145–179.

Mariátegui, J.C. (1925), *Siete Ensayos de Interpretación de la Realidad Peruana*, Lima: Amauta.

Marx, K. (1963 [1852]), *The Eighteenth Brumaire of Louis Bonaparte*, New York: International Publishers.

Pahnke, A. (2015), Institutionalizing economies of opposition: Explaining and evaluating the success of the MST cooperatives and agroecological repeasantization, *Journal of Peasant Studies*, 42(6), 1087–1107.

PCI (Partito Communista Italiano) (1957), Atti e Resoluzioni del VIII Congresso, PCI, Rome.

Pearse, A. (1975), *The Latin American Peasant*, London: Frank Cass.

Poulantzas, N. (1974), *Les classes sociales dans le capitalisme d'aujourd'hui*, Paris: Maspero.

Rosset, P.; Altieri, M.A. (2017), *Agroecology: Science and Politics*, Halifax: Fernwood.

Schneider, S.; Niederle, P. (2010), Resistance strategies and diversification of rural livelihoods: The construction of autonomy among Brazilian family farmers, *Journal of Peasant Studies*, 32(2), 379–405.

Scott, J.C. (1985), *Weapons of the Weak: Everyday Forms of Peasant Resistance*, New Haven, CT: Yale University Press.

Sereni, E. (1956), *Vecchio e Nuovo Nelle campagne Italiane*, Rome: Editori Reuniti.

Shanin, T. (1971), *Peasants and Peasant Societies*, Harmondsworth: Penguin Books.

Shanin, T. (1990), Orthodox Marxism and Lenin's four-and-a-half agrarian programmes: Peasants, Marx's interpreters, Russian revolution, in *Defining Peasants: Essays Concerning Rural Societies, Expolary Economies, and Learning from Them in the Contemporary World*, Oxford: Basil Blackwell, 280–312.

Shanin, T. (2009), Chayanov's treble death and tenuous resurrection: An essay about understanding, about roots of plausibility and about rural Russia, *Journal of Peasant Studies*, 36(1), 83–101.

Shanin, T. (2018), 1881 Letters of Vera Zasulich and Karl Marx, *Journal of Peasant Studies*, 45(7), 1183–1202.

Swaminathan, M.; Bakshi, S. (2017), *How Do Small Farmers Fare? Evidence from Village Studies in India*, Delhi: Tulika Books.

Thiemann, L. (2014), Artisans of the world, unite: The 'peasant way' and alliances for an artisan mode of production, Research paper, The Hague: ISS.

Toledo, V.M. (1995), *Campesinidad, Agroindustrialidad, Sostenibilidad: Los Fundamentos Ecológicos e Históricos del Desarrollo Rural*, Cuadernos de Trabajo 3, Grupo Interamericano para el desarollo sostenible de la Agricultura y los Recursos Naturales, Mexico.

van der Ploeg, J.D. (2003), *The Virtual Farmer: Past, Present and Future of the Dutch Peasantry*, Assen: Royal van Gorcum.

van der Ploeg, J.D. (2013), *Peasants and the Art of Farming: A Chayanovian Manifesto*, Halifax: Fernwood.

van der Ploeg, J.D. (2018), *The New Peasantries: Rural Development in Times of Globalization*, second edition, London: Routledge.

Weis, T. (2007), *The Global Food Economy: The Battle for the Future of Farming*, London: ZED Books.

White, B. (2018), Marx and Chayanov at the margins: Understanding agrarian change in Java, *Journal of Peasant Studies*, 45(5–6), 1108–1126.

Wolf, E. (1955), Types of Latin American peasantry: A preliminary discussion, *American Anthropologist*, 57(3), 452–471.

Wolf, E. (1966), *Peasants*, Englewood Cliffs, NJ: Prentice Hall.

Zangheri, R. (1981), Emilio Sereni e la questione agrarian in Italia, *La Questione Agraria*, 1, 237–262.

14. Gender

Avanti Mukherjee

INTRODUCTION

Critical agrarian studies are concerned with the impact of rural transformation on people dependent on agricultural and allied activities for survival and the potential for improving the lives of such people (Akram-Lodhi 2018). An analytical perspective that takes gender seriously reveals the ways in which agrarian change affect women and men distinctly and also how gender relations are integral to the functioning of agrarian systems.

Gender is linked to the concept of reproduction. Both concepts show us how the unpaid care and subsistence work typically performed by women are vital for household survival and the activities undertaken by household members, and therefore for reproducing class position. Gender also demonstrates systematic disadvantages that women face relative to men within the same class: in the division of labour between women and men, the asymmetric ownership of land and other assets and the ways in which incomes and surpluses are divided and used within agricultural households. A focus on gender can also emphasize the ways in which gender and class are cross-cut by other forms of inequalities such as caste, indigeneity, ethnicity and generation. Such intersectional inequalities in turn motivate the need to unpack both household and class as units of analysis in agrarian change. Incorporating gender thus provides a richer and more intersectional approach to the four central questions of agrarian political economy – 'who owns what? who does what? who gets what? what do they do with it?' (Bernstein 2010). It also reveals the otherwise hidden core of agrarian systems – the reproduction of labour power and gender relations – that make surplus production and accumulation possible.

The chapter is structured as follows. First, gender, reproduction and the gender division of labour are outlined as a key set of ideas for critical agrarian studies. Gender norms along with other structural factors perpetuate women's near exclusive responsibility for labour that is necessary for household survival and maintenance of the labour force. Second, this gender division of labour is a fundamental source of inequality between women and men and serves as an entry point to understanding other intra-household inequalities. In turn, intra-household inequalities within a given class and the ways in which such inequalities vary by class complicates class categories. Nevertheless, the lens of reproduction reinforces the importance of class in understanding the perpetuation of gender inequality. The final section builds on the previous sections to elaborate a number of ways in which placing gender at the heart of agrarian studies makes it critical – from revealing the diverse effects of technology on labour use to the relevance of reproduction for understanding development processes such as proletarianization and crises, as well for goals such as sustainability.

GENDER, REPRODUCTION AND THE GENDER DIVISION OF LABOUR

Gender refers to the social differentiation of people as 'women' or 'men'; categories that are distinct from but projected onto the sex categories of female and male, respectively. The conflation of gender with sex occurs partly through expectations as to how femininity and masculinity are to be embodied by affect, dress, behaviours, roles and the responsibilities that each gender is supposed to take on (West and Zimmerman 1987). Gender differentiation is also inherent in the distinct rights to which each gender is entitled; rights that are asymmetrical and create a hierarchical ordering typically endowing (cis) men with more status and privilege than other genders.[1]

Such social assignment of gender is rooted in and occurs via cultural norms, formal and informal laws and the distribution of wealth and other assets. Cultural norms perpetuate ideas, beliefs and expectations around gender that typically limit women's agency and life possibilities more than that of men (Folbre 1994). For instance, gender expectations in which men are viewed as agricultural household heads and women as responsible for child care and home maintenance places greater constraints on the majority of women who tend to combine child care and home maintenance with agricultural work (Mukherjee 2017). Formal laws and informal rules and practices such as those around marriage and divorce typically shape women's economic dependence on men, and also endow men with more rights than women. Gender inequalities in wealth and asset ownership shape relatively greater vulnerability for women and make it particularly difficult for individual women to advocate for their own interests (Agarwal 2016b). The specific norms and rules in a given context together with wealth and asset inequalities endow men with power over women and also generate a social consensus around appropriate ways of being and doing for women and men.

Gender differentiation is cross-wired with other forms of hierarchical stratification by generation, class, race, caste, ethnicity, etc. such that gender inequality manifests itself in distinct ways for social groups defined by these intersecting axes of hierarchy. Nevertheless, gender is a fundamental source of inequality for women compared to men in the same social group. For example, norms tend to justify sexual harassment and violence against women for perceived transgressions of gender expectations but also endow men with impunity for harassing or violating women's bodily integrity (Mukherjee 2017). Indeed, women who belong to the social groups with least power have gender disadvantages compounded by the limitations and exclusions posed by generation, class, race, caste, ethnicity, etc.

Reproduction refers both to specific forms of labour and the more generalized process of survival and renewal at household and systemic levels. Reproductive labour includes the birthing of human beings and the daily and generational replenishment of their ability to labour and function (Edholm et al. 1977). Such labour ranges from direct care work such as supervisory and hands-on care of children, dependants and family members; indirect care (or domestic work) such as cooking, cleaning and other forms of household maintenance; as well as subsistence tasks such as fetching water and fuel. Such reproductive labour is largely unpaid in rural contexts, where the markets for care work and goods are thinly developed. Agricultural production and reproductive labour also share fuzzy boundaries as some indirect care could be part of the agricultural labour process (e.g. cooking meals for hired labourers) and some agricultural labour such as milking cows, tending to the household vegetable garden or even shelling beans for home consumption are indirect forms of care that are critical for household consumption (Beneria and Sen 1982).

Biological reproduction and the daily and generational reproduction of labour power are necessary and integral to the reproduction of households and societies, or social reproduction per se. Unpaid reproductive labour is a vital component of subsistence at the household level, which allows household members to engage in agricultural and other labour processes (Beneria and Sen 1982). At the societal level, aggregated unpaid reproductive labour along with paid forms of care or reproductive labour are necessary and vital inputs in the formation of a labour force that has diverse skills and which is available for paid work (Razavi 2009). Institutions that organize the reproduction of labour power are therefore as necessary for social reproduction as the institutions that organize the production of goods and services and the distribution of surplus.

The reproduction of labour power has been historically organized in ways that create and perpetuate gender (and class) inequalities (Engels 1902). In particular, *the gender division of labour* is such that women are typically held responsible for reproductive labour and men are not, and in agricultural production per se, several tasks such as sowing, weeding and harvest and post-harvest operations (shelling, threshing) are typically performed by women and categorized as women's work (Mukherjee 2017). The perception of unpaid care work as naturally feminine means that reproductive labour is not recognized as work, leave alone work that entails a significant use of women's time and resources. In turn, women's more burdensome forms of care work such as fetching water and firewood have not been viewed as a burden that needs to be reduced and redistributed by adequate infrastructure, technologies and policies (Elson 2008). Moreover, women tend to be viewed as secondary earners or temporary workers whose primary responsibility is family care, so that the paid work they perform on agricultural fields (and beyond) tends to be remunerated less than that of men. The gender differential in earnings perpetuates women's economically weaker position than men who occupy the same class. The existence of such economic penalties, along with the perceived ignominy for men when they deviate away from expectations of masculinity, makes it difficult to redistribute reproductive labour between women and men (Badgett and Folbre 1999). In general, gender norms are sticky due to their integration with structural factors such as the division of labour, and this dialectic also structures other intra-household inequalities between women and men.

GENDER REVEALS INTRA-HOUSEHOLD INEQUALITIES AND PROBLEMATIZES CLASS

The gender division of labour creates intra-household inequalities in time spent on work because women have to combine reproductive and productive labour, unlike men. Globally, women's total work days are 10 per cent longer than that of men on average (Mukherjee 2018). Studies from rural developing country contexts illustrate how care and income-earning work in these contexts involve longer hours, especially for low-income women (Blackden and Wodon 2006; Razavi and Staab 2012). A review of 20 countries showed that rural women spend almost 45 minutes more a day on unpaid work compared to urban women, and trivial differences between rural and urban men. The gender difference in rural areas was such that women spent on average almost 3.5 hours more in total work per day than men, which was sharper than the gender difference in urban areas (Mukherjee 2018).

Some feminist economists argue that an increase in women's income relative to their husbands' would enable them to either purchase household substitutes or persuade their husbands to do more. However, in rural, agrarian contexts, the largely manual work associated with poor wages makes it difficult to exercise such 'bargaining power' and women's responsibility for care work constrains participation in income-earning work itself. In South Asia, older women are able to delegate domestic chores to younger women such as co-residing daughters-in-law and daughters (Mukherjee 2017). More, in rural, agrarian contexts it is stronger property rights, especially over land, that can give women more power to advocate for their own interests (Agarwal 2016b).

However, another gender asymmetry is that women have weaker rights, access to and control over land and other resources compared to men. Land is the most important asset in agrarian contexts as it helps with earning opportunities even in the non-farm sector, provides insurance in old age and serves as security against erosion of common resources such as forests and during calamities such as drought and famine. Yet, laws governing inheritance, property and marriage have been patrilineal and skewed in favour of men, with daughters, wives and widows having weaker rights. Besides, land reforms have tended to occur in ways where women from landed families receive land titles to circumvent redistribution laws or clauses that place an upper limit on land held so that the men in the family effectively retain control over landed holdings.

Inequalities in ownership and access to land limits women's ability to advocate for their own interests in household decision-making, to respond to life's contingencies and reinforces their economic dependence on men (Agarwal 2016b; Deere and Twyman 2012). Women with weaker property rights *may* not be able to do fewer hours for reproductive labour such as by investing in household technology (Mukherjee 2019). In contrast, women who own immoveable property are at much lower risk of marital violence. When women are more educated and earn higher incomes, they are actually more likely to face marital violence. It is the ownership of immoveable property that reduces the likelihood of marital violence and was a central factor in giving women economic independence (Agarwal 2016b).

A third inequality is around the distribution of surplus within the household. An implicit assumption in peasant studies is that a benevolent male household head oversees family farm production and distributes household production and income in egalitarian ways. The corollary assumption here is that household production and income are pooled and distributed equitably. However, to the extent that household production and income are pooled, it may not occur on democratic terms and it is typically not shared equally. Despite working harder and for longer hours than men, women typically do not have as much decision-making power or control over the family farm's production or household income as men (Deere 1995). In several contexts, women's access to independent income through wage work does not automatically imply control over their earnings. This is because women often have to hand over their earnings to their husbands. Yet, women can be subversive by hiding away some of their income, or by investing in animal assets that are raised in their natal households (Agarwal 2016b). Such subversion counteracts income pooling and is an implicit form of resistance to undemocratic forms of income pooling. There is also the matter of 'patriarchal bargains': in the absence of property rights or access to income, it is a rational strategy for women with seniority to secure a higher share of food or household surplus by using their power over junior women such as daughters-in-law or sisters-in-law (Kandiyoti 1988; Mukherjee 2017).

Typically, the gender of the person controlling household production and income matters for the ways in which these are spent. The benevolence of male household heads cannot be assumed. Evidence shows men tend to spend on their own needs. When women have some control over expenditures, women spend on family needs such as food and children's education (Deere 1995; Agarwal 2016a). Some argue this proves 'feminine' tendencies to care more; others add the necessary nuance that women are more attuned to family needs given their direct responsibility for such needs (Agarwal 2016a). Regardless, the pattern of male control over household expenditure is compounded by the norm of giving preferential treatment to males in food and calorie allocation on the assumption that they work harder. Lower female shares of household consumption lead to significant male–female differentials in health. Studies from around the world demonstrate that there is a male bias in food intake, and South Asian studies show that such bias is related to higher levels of malnourishment, morbidity and mortality among girls and women (Agarwal 2016a).

Intra-household inequalities complicate the concept of class. Women and men from the same class category tend to occupy distinct material positions in terms of their work burden, asset ownership and ability to control or partake of household produce (Akram-Lodhi 1996; Deere 1995). This appears to be true regardless of whether one defines class in terms of income level (poor versus non-poor), source of income (wage labour, cultivation or large-scale farming with hired labour), net labour hired in or the ability to acquire surplus and accumulate (large landowners versus landless or marginal farmers). Whether such gendered material differences constitute 'exploitation' was vigorously debated by western Marxist feminists in the past (see Razavi 2009). Such a question requires disentangling what constitutes the surplus product or not in rural economies that are partially capitalist. Regardless, what is unambiguously clear is that within the same household and class, women contribute more than men in terms of average work hours but tend to receive less either in terms of wages or shares of household product.

At the same time, class distinctions among women and men respectively remain pertinent, and class structures appear to interact with prevalent norms and rules to affect gender differences in time spent on work, work participation and the ability to earn incomes. On the former, Agarwal (2016a) is illustrative for the distinctions among women from landless, marginal, small cultivator and large cultivator households. Women in landless households hire themselves out as labourers in addition to performing unpaid care and subsistence tasks; women in cultivator households that have adequate land for subsistence combine reproductive labour with some manual labour on the family farm, and may or may not engage in wage labour; and in large cultivator households, where much of the farm labour is performed by hired wage labourers, women devote their time largely to reproductive labour (Agarwal 2016a). *Ex ante,* one would assume women in large cultivator households have the least time use burden, and by virtue of being members of upper-class households, may have more to consume, spend or invest in absolute terms despite the lower shares given to women. However, empirical studies demonstrate that this is not necessarily true.

Analysis of 1986 data from northwestern Pakistan demonstrates how the practice of female seclusion and local ideologies of gender worked to create the highest time use burdens for women of richer households compared to other women and all men.[2] While women's exclusive responsibility for domestic labour cut across class, the social consensus on family honour and gender in northwestern Pakistan also translated into strict gender segregation norms that prevented women from participating in wage labour. Gender segregation was relaxed only to mobilize women for on-farm labour. The household reproductive strategy for marginal and small peasants relied on women's on-farm and domestic labour, and men's wage income. Even rich peasant households relied extensively on women's labour given the absence of female wage labour. Not only did women from rich peasant households have the highest absolute total hours worked (20 per cent more than women from small and poor peasant households), they also had the highest absolute and relative hours worked in on-farm labour. Rich peasant women's hours of work were attributed to increased demands for food preparation for hired-in labour, livestock maintenance and possibly higher demands for domestic labour with regard to social entertainment, cleanliness and sanitation. The absence of paid domestic labour thus resulted in increased workload for women of richer classes such that rich peasant women worked the most (Akram-Lodhi 1996).

In contrast, a 2011 study of two villages in central India shows that women from large middle-caste cultivator households have lower work burdens than women in households lower down the social hierarchy, including those from scheduled tribes, because the former do not have to perform on-farm or wage labour and have access to household technology and paid domestic work to reduce their work burden. However, regardless of social group, all women face the threat of violence for gender transgressions (Mukherjee 2017). Gender inequalities in work burdens and other parameters are necessary for the reproduction of household class position (Beneria 1979).

MAKING AGRARIAN STUDIES MORE CRITICAL

Unpacking gender and class highlights how gender disadvantages exist even as their labour time and wage inputs are critical for household survival and reproduction. It also provides a richer analysis of agrarian change. The lens of gender and reproduction unveils and clarifies some of the contradictory processes entailed in agrarian change.

Disaggregating analysis by gender and type of labour per se draws our attention to the diverse effects of technology. For example, mechanization is not always labour-displacing, as assumed in the more mainstream agricultural studies literature. The use of tractors for ploughing in South Asia has tended to shift male permanent labour to different operations rather than reduce demand for casual labour, which is typically not hired for ploughing. However, the use of combine harvesters, threshers and mills in several Asian countries has typically been labour-displacing for women because it is tasks that women are segregated into that have been mechanized. The mechanization of arduous processing may save women labour time but also entails greater dependence on husbands because of their loss of income. There are also the mixed effects of high-yielding varieties of paddy in South Asia for women of small cultivator households. In some places, women face an increase in their work as they have to step up family labour time, sometimes also having to hire themselves out as wage labour to afford inputs related to high-yielding seeds and/or rents from increased land prices. In others, women withdraw from field labour either due to increased income or involuntary unemployment (Agarwal 2016a; Sen 1983).

The diverse effects of technology reveal the necessity of women's labour time for household income even as the women face adverse impacts. In several African countries, agricultural commercialization eroded women's economic independence and their contributions to household nutrition. With cash cropping and irrigation schemes, women lost rights over more fertile tracts of land and/or the use of land for nutritious subsistence crops because men were given greater land rights as well as agricultural extension support services and inputs. Women also had to increase labour time on their husbands' cash crop plots, but with lesser claims to the cash earned and increased dependence on husbands to purchase household necessities. Such transitions entailed less nutritious meals or even a fall in absolute consumption levels such that the subsistence of women and children suffered. Whereas in Africa, commercialization created the counterfactual that demonstrated women's contributions to household nutrition, in Asia, women from labouring households contribute both reproductive labour time and earnings that are critical for household survival, sometimes as *de jure* or even *de facto* household heads (Agarwal 2016a). Such realities problematize the assumption that women are non-earners or secondary earners. Women face systematic disadvantages including in their mobility to the off-farm sector. As outlined earlier, most women have responsibility for reproductive labour which shapes systematically lower female wages. On the one hand, the perceptions of women as primarily mothers and secondary earners reinforces standards of remuneration where tasks (occupations) typically performed by women are valued less than that of men. On the other, women have a lower 'reserve price' for their labour because many tend to have cyclical or even distress-led paid work participation. Women from small cultivator or poor peasant households tend to participate cyclically as ways to manage combining reproductive labour with the earned incomes needed to cover medical expenses, to repay debt or to buy essentials during the lean season (Razavi 2009). Moreover, the Southeast Asian growth experience has amply demonstrated that when women migrate for economic reasons, they face more intense exploitation because gender wage gaps benefit employers (Beneria and Sen 1982; Seguino 2000).

The dynamics of reproduction are relevant for understanding agrarian production and labour mobilization processes. For instance, the process of 'depeasantization' (peasants increasingly rely on wage labour) can be muted when poor peasant or marginal cultivator households rely on women's unpaid labour inputs (Deere 1995). This is because women tend to step up their subsistence labour and reproductive labour inputs, such as by gathering forest produce and relying on kitchen gardening, or by participating in wage labour to ensure household survival and reproduction (Mukherjee 2012). Scholarship on women's work and agrarian change shows that drops in rural women's labour force participation is often a sign of rural distress and household reliance on expenditure-saving activities rather than a process of positive income effects from broader growth processes (Naidu 2016). More, the much touted efficiency of the small farm is often on account of the 'exploitation' of family labour. Specifically, it is the availability of and command over women's domestic and farm labour that allows for greater profitability of small farms (Deere 1995; Akram-Lodhi 1996; Razavi 2009) Analysing the non-linearity of women's participation in agricultural production and/or wage labour offers valuable insights for debates on 'proletarianization' or 'peasantization' versus 'depeasantization'.

The relationship between the dynamics of reproduction and the dynamics of agrarian production is undertheorized and further motivates the need for a more nuanced understanding of class. Such theorization needs to, one, take into account all stocks and flows of labour time regardless of whether these are producing 'surplus value' or not; and two, emphasizes the importance of gender and other forms of social stratification which undergird systems of production and reproduction (Akram-Lodhi 2018). Research from distinct agrarian contexts illustrates the necessity of women's unpaid domestic labour for agricultural production directly or indirectly, with activities that allow households to save limited household cash for agricultural production (Akram-Lodhi 1996; Deere 1990; Agarwal 2016a). Moreover, the ways in which gender and intra-household relations shape the household as a site for the reproduction of labour power needs to be accounted for in critical agrarian studies (Deere 1995; Akram-Lodhi 1996). Thus, the empirical determination of class should account for family structures and hierarchies along with property ownership, and also for net surpluses arising from domestic labour, in addition to multiple sources of income or whether the household has net labour hired in or out.

Viewed through the lens of gender and reproduction, agrarian change reveals tensions that arise between reproduction and surplus accumulation. For instance, in rural, developing country contexts, household fertility decisions are often shaped by the household's capacity to survive and reproduce itself and pro-natalist tendencies can be more pronounced. The more the children, the greater the family labour resources to work on family farms and earn incomes. However, it is women who carry the heaviest burden of child-bearing and child-rearing, and multiple pregnancies negatively affect poor peasant women's health, well-being and capacity for both productive and reproductive labour (Beneria and Sen 1982). Yet, such conflicts are not unique to rural economies subsumed to capitalist markets. Productive and reproductive needs came in conflict with each other in China when collectivization increased demands on peasant households but the state population policy limited each couple to one child (Razavi 2009).

Accounting for gender and reproduction demonstrates that agrarian crises are crises of reproduction at all levels; not just crises of production. Reproductive processes are severely impacted at all levels as the pressure for accumulation in capitalist systems alternatively creates gluts and scarcity, and degrade various ecosystems necessary for livelihoods. Volatility in agricultural production and prices decimates the real incomes of most peasants who tend to be net purchasers of food. Together with the degradation of eco-systems, such processes place relatively greater burdens on poor peasant women to gather fuel, water and food from the commons and homestead plots (Sen and Grown 1987). The increased scale of distress-led migration, internal and transnational, disrupts traditional family structures and arrangements and places heavier demands on women to manage household needs either as migrants or as *de facto* household heads. The rise in xenophobic tendencies over the twentieth and twenty-first centuries have also led to forced family separations, inhumane treatment of migrants and refugees and sexual violation of women and children (Sen and Grown 1987; UN Women 2019). Recurring financial and agrarian crises not only impair the ability of our current economic system to reproduce itself; the accompanying ecological crises are increasingly limiting the ability of human systems to reproduce conditions that make the planet habitable for living beings.

A gender lens gives critical agrarian studies more tools to find creative solutions for urgent problems by drawing attention to intersecting systems and the importance of reproduction. Such a feminist lens exposes the limits to capitalist market-based solutions such as the privatization of land tenure systems to remove inequalities in land access and ownership. These policies show that women, especially women from more marginalized peasant and/or oppressed social groups, lose out disproportionately (Razavi 2009). On the other hand, there are limits to state-based solutions that abolished private ownership of land without taking into account unequal gender relations and prevailing norms. By allocating land to farming families, land reforms can be biased against women and erode polygamous and/or communitarian systems that give women relatively better access to land (Beneria and Sen 1982). A third way could be bottom-up collective solutions. Production collectives for women that pool assets, credit liabilities and risks have been shown to be productive and viable under specific conditions but the viability of expanding such ventures remains an open-ended question (Agarwal 2016a). Feminist analyses of common resource management in South Asia offer some insights on ways to democratize the management of accumulation while enhancing the participation and voice of poor peasants, landless labourers and women and men from oppressed groups (Agarwal 2016c). In this sense, critical agrarian studies can learn much from a gender lens on what it takes to make rural transformation truly democratic.

CONCLUSION

A framework that takes gender seriously leads us to reproduction, and in turn deeper, more realistic analysis of inequality, accumulation and crises. Such an approach goes beyond sex disaggregation by considering structural constraints such as the unequal distribution of assets and resources across and within households, and norms governing the allocation of reproductive labour. Gender and reproduction yield substantive understanding of intra-household and interhousehold inequalities, which can help revise conceptual categories and frameworks around class. They also have the potential to be truly 'intersectional' by accounting for other hierarchical forms of stratification such as by generation, ethnicity, caste, race, etc. The lens of reproduction is a particularly potent tool for critical agrarian studies to understand sustainability and the ways in which accumulation can be tempered and more harmoniously aligned with reproductive needs at the individual, household, local, national and global levels. In short, agrarian studies becomes more critical by incorporating gender and reproduction in its quest to interpret the world and discover the necessary ingredients for positive rural transformation.

NOTES

1. Cisgender refers to people whose gender identity matches their sex identity at birth. The rest of this chapter limits its analysis to cis-women and cis-men because the experiences of people with fluid and/or trans identities have additional layers of differentiation and discrimination that require distinct analysis.
2. Akram-Lodhi (1996) used class categories that were an adaptation of the Patnaik methodology based on net male labour hired in. These categories correlated strongly with the ownership of productive assets and economic surplus.

FURTHER READING

Agarwal, B. (2016), *Gender Challenges, Vol. 1: Agriculture, Technology and Food Security*, New Delhi: Oxford University Press.
Deere, C.D. (1990), *Household and Class Relations: Peasants and Landlords in Northern Peru*, Berkeley, CA: University of California Press.
Deere, C.D. (1995), What difference does gender make? Rethinking peasant studies, *Feminist Economics*, 1(1), 53–72.
Razavi, S. (2009), Engendering the political economy of agrarian change, *Journal of Peasant Studies*, 36(1), 197–226.

Sen, G.; Grown, C. (1987), *Development Crises and Alternative Visions: Third World Women's Perspectives*, Washington, DC: Monthly Review Press.

REFERENCES

Agarwal, B. (2016a), *Gender Challenges, Vol. 1: Agriculture, Technology, and Food Security*, New Delhi: Oxford University Press.

Agarwal, B. (2016b), *Gender Challenges, Vol. 2: Property, Family, and the State*, New Delhi: Oxford University Press.

Agarwal, B. (2016c), *Gender Challenges, Vol. 3: Environmental Change and Collective Action*, New Delhi: Oxford University Press.

Akram-Lodhi, A.H. (1996), 'You are not excused from cooking': Peasants and the gender division of labor in Pakistan, *Feminist Economics*, 2(2), 87–105.

Akram-Lodhi, A.H. (2018), What is critical agrarian studies?, accessed 28 January 2019 at oape.net/2018/03/28/what-is-critical-agrarian-studies/.

Badgett, M.V.L.; Folbre, N. (1999), Assigning care: Gender norms and economic outcomes, *International Labour Review*, 138(3), 311–326.

Beneria, L. (1979), Reproduction, production and the sexual division of labour, *Cambridge Journal of Economics*, 3(3), 203–225.

Beneria, L.; Sen, G. (1982), Class and gender inequalities and women's role in economic development: Theoretical and practical implications, *Feminist Studies*, 8(1), 157–176.

Bernstein, H. (2010), *Class Dynamics of Agrarian Change*, Halifax: Fernwood Books.

Blackden, M.; Wodon, Q. (eds) (2006), *Gender, Time Use and Poverty in Sub-Saharan Africa*, Washington, DC: World Bank.

Deere, C.D. (1990), *Household and Class Relations: Peasants and Landlords in Northern Peru*, Berkeley, CA: University of California Press.

Deere, C.D. (1995), What difference does gender make? Rethinking peasant studies, *Feminist Economics*, 1(1), 53–72.

Deere, C.D.; Twyman, J. (2012), Asset ownership and egalitarian decision-making in dual-headed households in Ecuador, *Review of Radical Political Economics*, 20(10), 1–8.

Edholm, F.; Harris, O.; Young, K. (1977), Conceptualizing women, *Critique of Anthropology*, 9–10, 101–130.

Elson, D. (2008), The three R's of unpaid work: Recognition, reduction and redistribution, Paper presented at the *Expert Group Meeting on Unpaid Work, Economic Development and Human Well-Being*, UNDP, New York, 16–17 November.

Engels, F. (1902), *The Origin of the Family, Private Property and the State*, Chicago, IL: Charles H. Kerr & Co.

Folbre, N. (1994), *Who Pays for the Kids: Gender and the Structures of Constraint*, London: Routledge.

Kandiyoti, D. (1988), Bargaining with patriarchy, *Gender and Society*, Special Issue to Honor Jessie Bernard, 2(3), 274–290.

Mukherjee, A. (2012), Exploring inter-state variations of rural women's paid and unpaid work in India, *Indian Journal of Labour Economics*, 55(3), 371–392.

Mukherjee, A. (2017), *Three Essays: 'Doing Care', Gender Differences in the Work Day, and Women's Care Work in the Household*, Unpublished PhD dissertation, University of Massachusetts, Amherst.

Mukherjee, A. (2018), Global patterns on gender differences in time spent on unpaid and paid work, Background paper to *Turning Promises into Action: Gender Equality in the 2030 Agenda for Sustainable Development Goals*, New York: United Nations Women.

Mukherjee, A. (2019), Gender challenges: A review essay, *Canadian Journal of Development Studies*, 40(3), 440–446.

Naidu, S. (2016), Domestic labour and female labour force participation: Adding a piece to the puzzle, *Economic and Political Weekly*, 51(45–46), 101–108.

Razavi, S. (2009), Engendering the political economy of agrarian change, *Journal of Peasant Studies*, 36(1), 197–226.

Razavi, S.; Staab, S. (2012), *Global Variations in the Political and Social Economy of Care: Worlds Apart*, New York: UNRISD/Routledge.

Seguino, S. (2000), Gender inequality and economic growth: A cross-country analysis, *World Development*, 28(7), 1211–1230.

Sen, G. (1983), Paddy production, processing and women workers in India: The south versus the northeast, in International Rice Research Institute (ed.), *Women in Rice Farming: Proceedings of a Conference on Women in Rice Farming Systems*, Manila, 26–30 September.

Sen, G.; Grown, C. (1987), *Development Crises and Alternative Visions: Third World Women's Perspectives*, Washington, DC: Monthly Review Press.

UN Women (2019), *Progress of the World's Women 2019–2020: Families in a Changing World*, New York: United Nations for Gender Equality and the Empowerment of Women.

West, C.; Zimmerman, D.H. (1987), Doing gender, *Gender and Society*, 1(2), 125–151.

15. Gender, nature, body

Andrea J. Nightingale and Wendy Harcourt

INTRODUCTION: GENDER, NATURE, BODY

The need to link together uneven gender relations with the exploitation of nature and the abuse of bodies deemed 'other' is now well established, yet often overlooked in scholarship about rural economies and extractivism. In this chapter, we examine contemporary thought on gender, nature and body to suggest how these debates can push the boundaries of critical agrarian studies in exciting new directions. We argue that when the co-production of genders, natures and bodies is taken seriously, critical agrarian studies can more readily engage beyond staid debates about sustainability and neoliberalizing economies to think through wider transformations. By expanding concerns for rural economies and extractivism towards the emancipatory politics of life-worlds, research can shift to the more-than-human entanglements that promote justice, equality and alternative forms of knowing and acting in the world (Hall et al. 2015).

Gender is a misused word in agrarian studies, too often associated with 'just' women's issues or confined to intra-household dynamics. In this chapter, we draw from feminist theorists who use gender as an analytical apparatus to capture how the exercise of power differentially subjects men and women, and intersects with other forms of marginalization to produce multiple subjectivities (Butler 1990; Young 2002; Nightingale 2011). As such, we do not associate gender with women, nor feminism with specific social movements. Rather, by examining how intersectional subjectivities circumscribe access to, control over and the distribution of resources and knowledge-making about agrarian change, this kind of analysis illuminates the connections between social injustices and the uneven material conditions of people's lives (Elmhirst 2011; Nightingale 2011, 2014). It demonstrates how power-laden economic and social relations within agrarian and environmental agendas subject diverse bodies, environments and ways of being. Such relations promote an 'othering' of people and nature, and an exclusion of anything that does not fit into a neoliberal model of growth, productivity and efficiency (Laurie and Bondi 2006; Harcourt and Nelson 2015).

We thus argue that uneven gender relations and their entanglements with bodies and natures are of concern for critical agrarian studies at a more fundamental level than simply uneven access to and control over resources. *Gender* is an excellent starting point for analysing the operation of power from the scale of the body to the global political economy. Additionally, too often domination of other humans goes hand in hand with the domination of nature. *Nature* is a term we use to encompass the entangled relations of cultural, social and economic processes, species, and objects that constitute the world. Society is constituted within nature, not separate from it, something captured conceptually in the term 'socionature'. A focus on transformation refers to cultural, social and economic relations, as well as more-than-human relations, to provide a fuller accounting of the costs of extractivism and the neoliberalization of rural economies. As a powerful site of cultural meaning, social experience and political resistance, *the body* is an important scale wherein dimensions of power are played out. Attention to the body has significant implications for critical agrarian studies by allowing research to recognize how corporal and emotional relations shape rural transformations. Feminists conceptualize the body as the first place or scale where exposure to risks and labour demands are experienced, as well as where 'global capitalism writes its script' (Mohanty 2003, 235). Therefore, body politics has looked at how different social, cultural and/or environmental struggles have been fought on the body, making visible the hidden implications of political economies (Harcourt 2016). By taking corporal experiences more seriously, scholars can show how the everyday lived experiences and emotional dimensions of rural transformations are constitutive of resulting political economies.

THINKING THROUGH GENDER, NATURE, BODY

Within agrarian studies, Carmen Diana Deere and others argued decades ago that gender and race need to be considered alongside class when evaluating uneven relations of production and reproduction among peasant households (Deere and Léon de Leal 1981; Radcliffe 1990). Feminist political ecology subsequently added an explicit focus on how uneven social relations resulted in differential access to, distribution of, control over and knowledge of natural resources (Rocheleau et al. 1996). Since the 1990s, this analysis of how the operation of power through intersectional relations of gender, race, class, ethnicity and other social relations of difference shape transformations in nature, societies and economies has been a central contribution of feminist scholarship to agrarian questions (Elmhirst 2002, 2011; Tsing 2005; Nightingale 2006, 2014). In contrast to mainstream agrarian studies therefore, taking gender-nature-body as core concerns places multi-scalar questions of knowledge, neoliberal capitalism, the management of natural resources and sustainability at the forefront of questions of class, agriculture, ecology, politics and economics. These concerns insist that we ask about whose knowledge counts when defining how resources should be managed, and how access to and control over resources produce uneven social and ecological effects. We now turn to a more careful consideration of the concepts – gender, nature, body – to show how these concerns help focus agrarian research on social justice and emancipatory questions.

Gender

Gender is fundamentally a relational concept that helps to explain how social difference based on presumed biological sexual characteristics arises and is perpetuated over time and space (Butler 1990; Young 2002). Following Butler (1990), we advocate for a performative conception of gender. By this we mean that the political, cultural and social meanings and practices of gender are not static, but are rather continually reproduced, challenged and transformed as power is exercised (Nightingale 2006, 2011). This insight is crucial. A narrow focus on the gendered division of labour fails to capture how these relations change over space and time, with significant consequences for the exercise of power.

To take a current example, women in Nepal have started ploughing fields after generations of only men doing such work. This change is the result of the out-migration of men in search of wage labour (Adhikari and Hobley 2015) and other social-cultural changes. Conceptions of gender that begin from a more fixed understanding of gender differences emphasize the extraordinary act of women ploughing and assume that their work burdens must have increased. This has been the focus of the so-called feminization of agriculture discussions in South Asia to date (Bieri 2014). While such issues are important empirical questions for research, a performative conception of gender raises additional questions about the consequences for self-determination, the control over production, the ability to assert needs and desires within the household and other aspects of so-called 'women's empowerment' that a shift in the symbolic meaning of gender opens up (Nightingale 2006). From a critical agrarian studies perspective, therefore, more profound questions need to be asked about how power relations between men and women change because of the pragmatic need for women to plough, and *also* about the implications of such changes in the symbolism of ploughing and gender in terms of access to resources, control over production and transformations in agrarian environments. The most important consequence of women ploughing is not necessarily that their work burdens have changed, but rather how such changes shift the operation of power within agrarian societies.

This approach to gender relations in agrarian contexts insists that power is never refracted through gender alone. Race, class, ethnicity, age, ability, sexuality and other embodied aspects of social difference intersect to shape how power operates to produce inequalities and hierarchies within societies. Conceptions of intersectionality draw from Butler's (1990) performative understanding to think about subjectivities rather than individuals or identities (Nightingale 2011). The subject is an abstract concept that captures how power operates to subject individuals and populations in particular ways, and as such is not reducible to individual identities. These forms of subjection often manifest in the labels we find so convenient (gender, race, etcetera), though they are in fact contested and re-performed in everyday life. Dimensions of social difference continually shape each other, which means that multiple, overlapping subjectivities are the norm. For example, Horvorka (2015) shows how women, chickens, gender relations and class relations all transform together as new forms of production are embraced (poultry rearing) in rural Botswana.

Such studies illuminate not only how gender is inadequate on its own to understand uneven access to and control over resources in agrarian societies, but also how gender itself is always embedded within race, caste and class (Nightingale 2006). Gendered identities make no sense outside of their racialized dimensions, a point which is valid well beyond households and communities (Mollett and Faria 2013). For example, Juanita Sundberg shows how not only are gender and class relations challenged in a women's non-governmental organization associated with a conservation area in Latin America, but also that relations of race and the geopolitics of conservation and development interventions shape how social relations and ecologies transform the rural political economy (Sundberg 2004; see also De La Cadena 2010). Feminists thus argue that the current form of the global economy, and agrarian societies by extension, have been produced by relations of power that are simultaneously racialized, gendered and classed: indeed, they argue that gender-race-class are foundational.

Gender relations must therefore be analysed as operating on different scales (Harris 2008) – from the body to the global – creating specific meanings of femininity and masculinity, affective more-than-human relations, as well as differential access to material resources. As processes of enclosure and dispossession accelerate and extend across the world, taking a performative perspective on gender opens up a broader set of questions for critical agrarian studies. Class, race and gender differences can profoundly affect which crops are planted, who is responsible, the kind of technologies used to prepare fields and conduct harvests and how products reach markets (Carney 1996; Freidberg 2001). While some scholars have taken up these issues, the ways in which these intersectional relations are entangled in changing ecologies has been largely neglected. These more-than-human questions also suggest the need to open up our second concept: nature.

Nature

Current discussions of nature take two related but somewhat separate tacks. First, political ecologists draw attention to the importance for critical agrarian studies of what ends up in the category 'nature'. Claiming something as natural (or unnatural) is a powerful mechanism to deflect attention from the constructed divide between society and nature. This divide is never innocent, as it shapes which people, species, ecosystems and agrarian practices are considered important topics of investigation. Research in conservation, for example, has highlighted how concerns for biodiversity and habitat preservation overprivilege large, charismatic mammals at the expense of worms, insects and microorganisms that are equally important to overall ecosystem health and function (Lorimer 2006).

Second, socionature theorists frame nature as a socially constructed, dynamic domain, both biophysically and in terms of what it is imagined to be (Haraway 1991; Castree and Braun 2001). The concept of 'socionatures' retheorizes nature and society to take both as contingent, dynamic and linked materially and symbolically: in short, co-emergent. By beginning with the intrinsically political character of power and difference, socionatural approaches include equity and justice issues in environmental change processes (Sundberg 2014). Numerous case studies in agrarian contexts have shown how gender, race, class and other intersectional social differences take on meaning, and how they change in importance as environmental and resource conflicts erupt (Nightingale 2006; Harris 2008). Similarly, struggles over intersectional subjectivities and the exercise of power often underpin the emergence of resource conflicts (Peluso 2009). 'Environmental issues, therefore, are not simply about environment, with perhaps some unfortunate social justice implications. They are foundational to how inequality is conceptualized and [reproduced] within societies and across scales' (Nightingale 2014, 10). Society and nature are thus not separate interacting domains, but are rather constituted by, and make sense analytically only in relation to, one another.

Agricultural production always involves substantial realignments of what belongs and what needs to be excluded or even eradicated. How seed selection is done, the types of inputs used, pest and weed control measures are all rooted in particular socionatural relations and carry real consequences. For example, Susanne Freidberg (2004) shows the entanglements of ecologies, colonial histories, plant types, global supply chains and consumer health by looking at the production and consumption of French green beans. She shows how differing consumer choices in Europe shape the kinds of ecologies and production practices that exist in former British and French colonies. Rather than green beans being simply beans, she shows how their emergence as commodities is dependent on socionatural relations that are not easily pried apart. These relations result in food scares and differing perceptions of what good food is. Such insights demand that critical agrarian studies consider more than simply the global circulation of capital, but also the transformation of more-than-human relations through agrarian production.

Body

Understanding the social and material transformations of agrarian environments requires a grasp of race, class, gender and nature, and also embodiment and emotion. Not only is power often exercised on bodies, but the body itself offers a powerful site of resistance and transformation (Harcourt 2009; Mollett and Faria 2013). Of particular relevance for critical agrarian studies, feminist political ecology scholars show how interlinked changes in agrarian economies, environments, production and other rural transformations are often felt first, and most profoundly, on and within the body. The effects of changes in global food chains show up on bodies as work burdens or changes in access to food, and new chemical inputs cause cancers or other health hazards. In understanding the body as a location of resistance and agency, the interconnections of intimate, emotional and embodied relations become important topics of research to understand economic changes in agrarian production.

Bodies are central to the construction of subjectivities, and their 'grammar' are spaces in which peoples' relations to others and nature are reiterated as well as contested, with tangible consequences for emancipatory social movements, resource management, changes in agricultural production (like the Nepal example above) and the circulation of capital in agrarian economies. In search of alternatives to dominant discourses on water governance and neoliberal development more broadly, Leila Harris draws attention to the 'everyday, embodied and emotional relations to resources and natures' (Harris 2015, 158). She looks at the social and emotional tensions produced by water governance based on market-oriented water use, which belie the embodied aspects of everyday hydro-social relations. This focus on everyday, embodied and emotional relations to water opens up political and analytical imaginations for counter-logics. Such insights drive critical agrarian studies research to attend to scale, to link between body, household, community, nation and globe and to show how everyday, intersectional, socionatural relations produce uneven relations of production, exchange and resource management, as well as resistance to extractivism and neoliberal agrarian change.

A focus on body also draws attention to persistent binaries of masculinity and femininity and their roots in heteronormativity. Holding onto binaries of nature-culture or nature-society limits the ability to understand how agrarian political economies entangle life-worlds for humans and non-humans alike. New lines of inquiry open up when agrarian studies analyses go beyond an implicitly heteronormative focus on social reproduction to look instead at how sexual as well as gender and race politics shape rural livelihoods. Drawing from the emerging field of queer ecologies (Sandilands 2016), the complex socionatural linkages between the operation of power through sexuality, race, class and gender, and the problematic conceptual and material framings of (for example) hybrid seeds, and the polluted and exposed bodies of our exploited landscapes, are revealed. Giovanna Di Chiro (2010) analyses how discourses by environmentalists about toxic pollution in the United States use a heterosexist language which appeals to fears about endocrine disruptors disturbing the normal gendered body of humans and non-humans through chemical castration. She points to how otherwise progressive environmentalisms 'mobilize the knowledge/power politics of "normalcy" to enforce a social-environmental order based on a dominant regime of what and who are constructed as normal/natural' (Di Chiro 2010, 199). By analysing how these fears reproduce problematic norms around sexuality and ability, she shows how environmental and political responses are constrained. Scholarship in this vein allows critical agrarian studies to link ecological change and environmental justice politics to agrarian political economies.

GENDER, NATURE, BODY IN CRITICAL AGRARIAN STUDIES

In this chapter, we have shown how gender-nature-body are critical sites for multi-scalar power and politics, which result in uneven access to and control over resources. Rather than externalities or unfortunate social injustices, intersectional socionatural relations are shown to be foundational to key critical agrarian studies' concerns around class formation, resistance, extractivism and land grabs. Understanding agrarian conflicts as the material and emotional outcomes of embodied, differentiated responses to enclosure and the commodification of resources and livelihoods links the global economy to on-the-ground lived realities in rural areas. The formation of subjectivities in socionatures have profound implications for how production, reproduction, extractivism and ecological transformations occur and the possibilities for collective action in response. A feminist political ecology approach is able to account for these material, emotional and corporal threats of neoliberalism and marketization, and show possibilities for emancipatory action.

Nightingale (2013), for example, has explored how the economics and politics of fishing on the west coast of Scotland are embodied, intersectional dynamics that change throughout the socionatural spaces of fishing. Adherence to regulations and desires for collective action shift rather radically from fishing boats, to processing the catch onshore, to meeting rooms with policymakers. These shifts are both products of, and constitutive of, the supply chains and political economy of fishing. As fuel prices rose, fish stocks declined and new management structures were introduced from 2002 to 2015, new associations emerged in Scotland to help advocate for inshore fishers at the national and European levels. Many critical agrarian studies scholars assume that markets in southern Europe overdetermine the class relations and the political economy of fishing in small Scottish coastal communities, but such an analysis misses the power-laden, creative and emotional relations through which fishers decide which companies to sell their catch to, how they interpret regulations and the associations that emerge to represent fishers' geopolitical interests.

Similarly, Harcourt (2016) has explored how agricultural livelihoods are changing in the region of Tuscia around the Lake of Bolsena in Italy, with a study on three different types of eco-tourist enterprises. The cases are attentive to the daily needs, embodied interactions and labours of the women and men adjusting to changes in state provisions and economic possibilities. In analysing their everyday lives and struggles in, for example, ecological soap production, Harcourt traces efforts to build diverse ethical economic and ecological relationships in an economically challenging yet vibrant socionature.

Situating the complex relations of gender-nature-body within analyses of political economic accounts of class relations and agrarian change can be challenging. Not only do they require deep, qualitative investigations into everyday politics and practices, such as those we describe in our work, but they also demand that researchers attend to the geopolitics of race, gender and sexuality (Mollett and Faria 2013; Sundberg 2014). These geopolitics combine with political economic processes to circumscribe who controls agrarian production and who is caught in uneven relations of exchange. The methodological task of linking processes across scales, and recognizing how they serve to constitute these scales (Massey 2005), can be a research agenda within itself. Yet we argue that it is vital that critical agrarian studies scholars embrace these challenges in order to open up new understandings of how agrarian transformations can occur, and by extension, new possibilities for collective action. By attending to the ways in which subjectivities and social differences such as class, race and gender intersect and are produced through changing ecologies and agrarian and environmental transformations (Nightingale 2006, 2011), critical agrarian studies scholarship can push beyond narratives of dispossession and environmental decline within neoliberalizing environments to understand more clearly the spaces of transformation and hope.

FURTHER READING

Collard, R.-C.; Harris, L.M.; Heynen, N.; Mehta, L. (2018), The antinomies of nature and space, *Environment and Planning E: Nature and Space*, 1(1–2), 3–24.

Freidberg, S. (2004), *French Beans and Food Scares: Culture and Commerce in an Anxious Age*, Oxford: Oxford University Press.

Harcourt, W.; Nelson, I. (eds) (2015), *Practising Feminist Political Ecologies: Moving Beyond the 'Green Economy'*, London: Zed books.

Nightingale, A.J. (2018), The socioenvironmental state: Political authority, subjects, and transformative socionatural change in an uncertain world, *Environment and Planning E: Nature and Space*, 1(4), 688–711.

Sundberg, J. (2003), Conservation and democratization: constituting citizenship in the Maya Biosphere Reserve, Guatemala, *Political Geography*, 22(7), 715–740.

REFERENCES

Adhikari, J.; Hobley, M. (2015), 'Everyone is leaving. Who will sow our fields?' The livelihood effects on women of male migration from Khotang and Udaypur districts, Nepal, to the Gulf countries and Malaysia, *HIMALAYA, Journal of the Association for Nepal and Himalayan Studies*, 35(1), 11–23.

Bieri, S. (2014), New ruralities – old gender dynamics? A reflection on high-value crop agriculture in the light of the feminisation debates, *Geographica Helvetica*, 69(4), 281–290.

Butler, J. (1990), *Gender Trouble: Feminism and the Subversion of Identity*, New York: Routledge.

Carney, J. (1996), Converting the wetlands, engendering the environment, in Peet, R.; Watts, M. (eds), *Liberation Ecologies: Environment, Development, Social Movements*, New York: Routledge, 165–186.

Castree, N.; Braun, B. (eds) (2001), *Social Nature: Theory, Practice and Politics*, Oxford: Blackwell.

De La Cadena, M. (2010), Indigenous cosmopolitics in the Andes: Conceptual reflections beyond 'politics', *Cultural Anthropology*, 25(2), 334–370.

Deere, C.D.; Léon de Leal, M. (1981), Peasant production, proletarianization, and the sexual division of labor in the Andes, *Signs*, 7(21), 338–360.

Di Chiro, G. (2010), Polluted politics? Confronting toxic discourse, sex panic, and eco-normativity, in Mortimer-Sandilands, C.; Erickson, B. (eds), *Queer Ecologies: Sex, Nature, Politics, Desire*, Bloomington, IN: Indiana University Press, 199–230.

Elmhirst, R. (2002), Negotiating land and livelihood: Agency and identities in Indonesia's transmigration programme, in Yeoh, B.S.; Teo, P.; Huang, S. (eds), *Gender Politics in the Asia-Pacific Region*, London: Routledge, 79–98.

Elmhirst, R. (2011), Introducing new feminist political ecologies, *Geoforum*, 42(2), 129–132.

Freidberg, S. (2001), To garden, to market: Gendered meanings of work on an African urban periphery, *Gender, Place and Culture*, 8(1), 5–24.

Freidberg, S. (2004), *French Beans and Food Scares: Culture and Commerce in an Anxious Age*, Oxford: Oxford University Press.

Hall, R.; Edelman, M.; Borras, S.M.; Scoones, I.; White, B.; Wolford, W. (2015), Resistance, acquiescence or incorporation? An introduction to land grabbing and political reactions 'from below', *Journal of Peasant Studies*, 42(3–4), 467–488.

Haraway, D.J. (1991), *Simians, Cyborgs and Women: The Reinvention of Nature*, New York: Routledge.

Harcourt, W. (2009), *Body Politics in Development: Critical debates in Gender and Development*, London: Zed Books.

Harcourt, W. (2016), Gender and sustainable livelihoods: Linking gendered experiences of environment, community and self, *Agriculture and Human Values*, 1–13.

Harcourt, W.; Nelson, I. (eds) (2015), *Practising Feminist Political Ecologies: Moving Beyond the 'Green Economy'*, London: Zed books.

Harris, L.M. (2008), Water rich, resource poor: Intersections of gender, poverty, and vulnerability in newly irrigated areas of southeastern Turkey, *World Development*, 36(12), 2643–2662.

Harris, L.M. (2015), Hegemonic waters and rethinking natures otherwise, in Harcourt, W.; Nelson, I.L. (eds), *Practising Feminist Political Ecologies*, London: Zed Book, 157–181.

Hovorka, A.J. (2015), The gender, place and culture Jan Monk distinguished annual lecture: Feminism and animals: exploring interspecies relations through intersectionality, performativity and standpoint, *Gender, Place & Culture*, 22(1), 1–19.

Laurie, N.; Bondi, L. (eds) (2006), *Working the Spaces of Neoliberalism: Activism, Professionalisation and Incorporation*, Malden, MA: Blackwell Publishing.

Lorimer, J. (2006), What about the nematodes? Taxonomic partialities in the scope of UK biodiversity conservation, *Social and Cultural Geography*, 7(4), 539–558.

Massey, D. (2005), *For Space*, London: Sage.

Mohanty, C.T. (2003), *Feminism without Borders: Decolonizing Theory, Practicing Solidarity*, Durham, NC: Duke University Press.

Mollett, S.; Faria, C. (2013), Messing with gender in feminist political ecology, *Geoforum*, 45(1), 116–125.

Nightingale, A.J. (2006), The nature of gender: Work, gender and environment, *Environment and Planning D: Society and Space*, 24(2), 165–185.

Nightingale, A.J. (2011), Bounding difference: Intersectionality and the material production of gender, caste, class and environment in Nepal, *Geoforum*, 42(2), 153–162.

Nightingale, A.J. (2013), Fishing for nature: The politics of subjectivity and emotion in Scottish inshore fisheries management, *Environment and Planning A*, 45(10), 2362–2378.

Nightingale, A.J. (2014), Nature-society, in Lee, R.; Castree, N.; Kitchin, R.; Lawson, V.; Paasi, A.; Philo, C.; Radcliffe, S.; Roberts, S.M.; Withers, C.W.J. (eds), *Sage Handbook of Human Geography*, London: Sage, 120–147.

Peluso, N.L. (2009), Rubber erasures, rubber producing rights: Making racialized territories in West Kalimantan, Indonesia, *Development and Change*, 40(1), 47–80.

Radcliffe, S.A. (1990), Ethnicity, patriarchy, and incorporation into the nation: Female migrants as domestic servants in Peru, *Environment and Planning D: Society and Space*, 8, 379–393.

Rocheleau, D.; Thomas-Slayter, B.; Wangari, E. (1996), *Feminist Political Ecology: Global Issues and Local Experiences*, New York: Routledge.

Sandilands, C. (2016), Queer ecology, in Adamson, J.; Gleason, W.A.; Pellow, D.N. (eds), *Keywords for Environmental Studies*, New York: NYU Press, 53–54.

Sundberg, J. (2004), Identities in the making: Conservation, gender and race in the Maya Biosphere Reserve, Guatemala, *Gender, Place and Culture*, 11(1), 43–66.

Sundberg, J. (2014), Decolonizing posthumanist geographies, *Cultural Geographies*, 21(1), 33–47.

Tsing, A. (2005), *Friction: An Ethnography of Global Connection*, Princeton, NJ: Princeton University Press.

Young, I.M. (2002), Lived body vs gender: Reflections on social structure and subjectivity, *Ratio*, 15(4), 410–428.

16. Kinship

Pauline E. Peters

This chapter urges writers of critical agrarian studies to pay more analytical attention to kinship, which is either ignored or inadequately analysed and theorized. This concern emerges particularly from my immersion in African agrarian issues, which I prioritize here, although I also draw on studies from other regions. Contrary to some expectations, neoliberalism and globalization, associated with increasingly financialized, speculative and highly volatile capital movements, and sharply widening socio-economic and political inequality within and between countries and regions, have shown the need to be more, not less, attuned to the role of kinship in these processes (cf. Yount-André 2018). A recent upsurge in publications from various disciplines highlights the importance of kin relations in a range of contexts and countries.

Many scholars challenge the assumption of a bounded and autonomous domain of the economy and of economic logic, a position surely key to critical agrarian studies, as in other 'critical' approaches to society.

> Our ... approach focuses on the full range of productive powers and practices through which people constitute diverse livelihoods (and from which capitalist inequalities are captured and generated) as they seek to realize the potentialities of resources, money, labor, and investment ... Instead of taking capitalism *a priori*, as an already determining structure, logic, and trajectory, we ask how its social relations are generated out of divergent life projects ... Class does not exist outside of its generation in gender, race, sexuality, and kinship. (Bear et al. 2015, 1–3)

In this chapter, seeking to expand the analytical lens of critical agrarian studies, I concentrate on kinship (relations based on descent and marriage)[1] and its role in the generation of difference and differentiation in a range of contexts, from the most local to the national and beyond. After a brief look at how kinship interacts with other social relations in agrarian life, the chapter considers two specific issues in African agrarian studies where misrepresentations and misconceived conclusions derive from a lack of analysis of kinship and descent relations. There follows a sample of the accumulating evidence beyond Africa of how kinship and descent practices, as they interact with differences based on gender, age/seniority, ethnicity, wealth and class, and with broader political economic processes, are key to understanding agrarian societies, from rural livelihoods to state formation.

Family farms have long been at the heart of agrarian societies, and while there has been a decline over the past century in their significance, especially in richer countries, a recent survey of agricultural census data for 105 countries and territories found that 'family farms constitute 98 per cent of all farms and at least 53 per cent of agricultural land' (Graeub et al. 2016, 1). When comparing other studies with much higher percentages of land controlled by family farms (around 70 per cent), the authors consider their figure to be a 'lower bound estimate' due, in part, to their 'larger and newer dataset and more conservative approach to the definition of family farms' (ibid.). The central feature of such family farms is the use of family labour, defined by the Food and Agriculture Organization (FAO) of the United Nations as:

> A means of organizing agricultural, forestry, fisheries, pastoral and aquaculture production which is managed and operated by a family and predominantly reliant on family labor, including both women's and men's. The family and the farm are linked, co-evolve and combine economic, environmental, social and cultural functions. (FAO in Graeub et al. 2016, 2)

In this, as in other studies, there is a very wide range in terms of the resources, assets and income of family farms, but all involve family labour, while also drawing, again highly variably, on outside labour. In most regions, the majority of family farms, excluding the largest and most specialized, also depend for their livelihoods on non-farm income earned locally or through migration. Research suggests that this has intensified with the globalization of agriculture, especially the role of protectionism in rich countries combined with pressures on poorer agrarian countries to remove subsidies and tax/tariff barriers, and the increased dominance of huge multinational agriculture and food corporations. In turn, increasing instability in income and livelihood sources, rising inequality within and between countries, accelerating demand for land and landed resources from domestic and foreign agents have intensified pressures on all but the rich among rural and urban populations.

While the term 'family' is conventionally used to describe these land-using units, far more specificity is needed to describe and analyse the actual operations. The core unit is usually considered a household, based mostly on a couple and their children, though often with other members of either or both the man's and woman's wider family. Rarely do these households operate independently; rather, they also depend on wider units, collectivities and networks (such as extended family, clans, descent groups, neighbours, patrons, etc.). A huge body of research has been carried out among peasant, smallholder and family farming communities across the world. This cannot be reviewed here, but they all reveal how work, assets, income and expenditure vary by gender, age/generation and other social bases within all these units and networks, which, in interaction with wider social, political and economic processes, generate the kinds of differentiation and inequality mentioned above (among many, see Murray 1981; Netting 1993).

In order to look more closely at the social dynamics relevant to critical agrarian studies, I examine two classic issues in African agrarian studies where a failure to incorporate a rigorous analysis of kinship and descent relations has led to misconceived conclusions. These issues are land tenure and research based on the unit of the household, especially where gender effects form a central focus.

LAND TENURE

The social relations around the use, management and control of land are central to agrarian studies. The currently accelerating appropriation of land across world regions, particularly across Africa, results from a mounting demand for (watered) land by domestic and foreign agents for the production of food and non-food crops, the exploitation of forests, minerals and oil, and speculation (Cotula 2013; Peters 2018a). Land continues to be a critical part of the agrarian question of the present century (Akram-Lodhi and Kay 2010; Hall et al. 2011), and is entailed in struggles over resources and livelihoods at all levels, from the most local to the national and international. It is critical that a full understanding of the dynamics driving modes of land acquisition, management, use and transfer be achieved, especially when land laws and policies proliferate. The failure to examine the critical role of kinship and descent, as these intersect with differences in gender, age, wealth, income and influence, has produced faulty analyses and conclusions, and has misdirected policy actions based on them. Nowhere is this more obvious than with reference to gender relations.

A major theme in the literature on land and land tenure in Africa is the differential ('discriminatory') access to the use and management of land and landed resources by gender. However, the arguments are severely limited by the assumption that the categories of interest are 'men' and 'women'. This is because entitlements to land differ considerably according to specific social relationships based on kinship, descent and marriage: women as daughters and sisters have very different entitlements compared with women as wives and widows.

Vast areas of cultivated or other used land in sub-Saharan Africa remain under 'customary' or 'communal tenure' – colonial terms that refer to land vested in social collectivities based usually on descent. Across most of Africa, people follow patrilineal lines of inheritance and succession, so that land passes from fathers to sons, though occasionally to junior brothers and then to sons. Unmarried daughters may be given temporary access to land by their fathers (or lineage elders or chiefs), while the norm is that upon marriage a woman will gain access to land from her husband's group. On divorce or the death of the husband, she will either lose access if she returns to her natal family, or will maintain access, but only for her lifetime as long as she does not remarry, and/or as the mother of her sons who are their father's heirs.

The logic here is based on descent group or lineage authority over land. In-marrying wives belong to a different lineage[2] and therefore cannot be allowed to hold land of their husband's lineage in their own name or right. The aim is to ensure that the land remains within the husband's lineage. In the woman's natal lineage area, her brothers would hold exactly the same position vis-à-vis their lineage land. Landholding for daughters and sisters, who are members of the lineage of their fathers and brothers, is thus very different from that of in-marrying non-lineal women (wives/widows). One indication is that when husbands and their male agnates refuse wives' or widows' independent rights to land, their sisters and daughters support them, even to the point of chasing the widows away. This, then, should not be understood as simply men versus women but as the differences between lineal descent identities and claims. To posit simply that 'men' are discriminating against 'women' is to completely miss the logic of the landholding system and the motivations of local actors. There is no doubt that when husbands object to efforts made in patrilineal/patrilocal areas by governments or other agencies to extend land rights to wives and widows in their own names, some of their resistance includes a concern for diminished authority over their wives. But to assume that male bias is the *only* cause of resistance is a misrepresentation of the principles and practices of land allocation and of the views of the local actors with reference to the continuing importance of lineal relations.[3]

None of these systems is static. There is an important variation in the implications for women in relation to land *within* patrilineal/patrilocal descent systems, depending critically on whether or not women retain membership and support in their natal clans throughout their lives, including after marriage, as shown in a contrast between Gusii and Luyia groups in Kenya (Hakansson 1994). Adaptations also occur with more daughters (usually divorced or widowed) being given land by different authorities in South Africa (Claassens and Weeks 2009) and Malawi (Alister Munthali, personal communication).

As a final case on land tenure, I consider a minority pattern in Africa, which nevertheless involves millions of people. This is matrilineal descent (where children are members of their mother's lineage and inherit from them). A minority within matrilineal groups practises matrilocal (uxorilocal) residence (where husbands move to their wives' villages). Here, as is typical in much of Malawi and parts of Zambia and Mozambique, only daughters inherit land, while their brothers use the land of their wives' descent groups.[4] The case of Malawi shows how policy that relies on a simplistic 'men versus women' view and that fails to account for the lineage-/kinship-based practices of landholding is misdirected. The latest Land Law in Malawi, passed in 2016, seeks to prevent 'discrimination' against women and proposes that both sons and daughters should inherit land. If implemented, this law will actually disinherit millions of women who are currently the sole inheritors of land (Peters and Kambewa 2007; Peters 2010; Johnson 2012; Berge et al. 2014). Moreover, since descent-based land relations are a lynch-pin in fundamental social interdependence, such radical changes would danger-ously destabilize an entire system of social support.

THE HOUSEHOLD AS A UNIT OF ANALYSIS

Taking 'the household' as the sole unit of analysis is the second major area in African studies (although also relevant for other regions) where a failure to analyse specific social and cultural relations and practices of kinship, descent and marriage leads to mistaken conclusions. During the 1970s, the confluence of critical research on agriculture and land policies with feminist critiques of dominant theories that fail to include gender in their analyses led to significant critique of the convention of taking the household as the only or main unit for the collection and analysis of socio-economic data.

Critics pointed out that the assumptions of a 'unitary' household as unit of analysis and the frequent conflation of the household with a male head render invisible not only the major con-tributions of female members but also, and more fundamentally, the socio-economic dynamics within and outside the household, which produce the data actually being collected. In African societies, men's work patterns, rights to land, authority over labour allocation and management of income usually differ from those of women; work, access to land and other entitlements and obligations vary not only by gender but also according to kinship/descent status, generation and seniority; adults and children move in and out of households for shorter or longer periods for a wide variety of reasons; and households are never autonomous but depend, to varying degrees, on wider social units and networks based on kinship, descent and residence (Guyer and Peters 1987; Russell 1993). The failure to recognize such diversity results in inadequate analysis and in negative outcomes for development projects (O'Laughlin 2013).

The study by economist Christopher Udry (1996), regularly cited by the World Bank and other development agencies, addresses discrimination against women as a key reason for agricultural underperformance. Udry (1996) concluded that the unequal distribution of inputs across women's and men's cultivated plots in Burkina Faso did not maximize yields, and that redistributing resources to women farmers as opposed to men farmers would reduce the poverty of rural households. Critics, however, have convincingly overturned Udry's conclusions, arguing that he had failed to investigate the specific sets of responsibilities and obligations held by *different* categories of 'men' and 'women' within the household, and had separated the household from its surrounding networks and political economic conditions (Whitehead and Kabeer 2001; O'Laughlin 2007).

The error in this type of theorizing is to make gender a binary variable of 'female/woman' versus 'male/man', whether plugged into econometric models, conventional household surveys or analysis. Rather than a static essence, 'gender' is a relationship and not a single variable (Amadiume 1987; Nzegwu 2006; Peters 2018b). Gender relations are *always* cross-cut by (or intersect with) other social (including kinship) and political-economic relations. Thus, the glossing of gender as male versus female erases the many different types of men/women, as we saw in the example of land tenure relations.

A RESURGENCE OF KINSHIP STUDIES

The assertion that 'For the understanding of any aspect of the social life of an African people – economic, political or religious – it is essential to have a thorough knowledge of their system of kinship and marriage' (Radcliffe-Brown and Forde 1950, 1) is as relevant today as it was in 1950, and not just for Africa. From the 1960s on, critics challenged kinship theorists' focus on unilineal descent groups as fixed and corporate structures; their assumed distinction between descent structure as the political domain – associated with men – and kinship as the domestic domain – associated with women; and kinship understood as merely a sexual and biological process. The position now is to see kinship as a socio-culturally specific type of relatedness. One important influence came from feminist studies, which challenged the Western dichotomy of biological/natural/female and social/cultural/male as universal (Collier and Yanagisako 1987). Their insistence on the centrality of gender relations in the constitution and reproduction of social life means that the study of how people variously define and practise descent, marriage and other formulations of kinship remains a key part of the analysis. Cultural conceptions and social practices of kinship concern not only descent, marriage, siblingship and procreation, but also the production and reproduction of sociality, belonging and even good and evil – in short, an entire moral universe and way of living.

BEYOND AFRICA

Current research from other regions also shows how particular elements of kinship and descent practices, interacting with differences of gender, age/seniority, ethnicity, wealth, class and so on, and with broader political economic processes, are key to understanding agrarian societies and their transformations. Similar to the Malawi land reform case mentioned above, Hall and colleagues discuss misguided land reforms in northern Thailand which reveal 'a lack of correspondence between how customary kinship practices structure ownership and inheritance, and the assumptions about families embedded in national land and family law' (Hall et al. 2011, 42). In the Central Highlands of Vietnam, the 1993 Land Law failed to distinguish between 'nuclear families' and 'longhouse extended family units' in the allocation of land, so producing (along with the demands of the newly introduced coffee crop) the rapid splintering of the longhouse units (ibid., 108). The authors emphasize that this is not an issue of disturbing kinship harmony, since 'social intimates' – whether in terms of kinship, residence or friendship – are also divided by 'processes of accumulation and dispossession [taking place] among neighbors and kin who share common histories and social interaction' (ibid., 145). The analytical point is that such 'intimate' relationships, including kinship, are a necessary part of the social (economic and political) circumstances that one is seeking to understand and explain. '[T]he degree of intimacy among villagers – how closely they were related by kinship, and to what extent they shared a common history – stands out as an important variable in access to land and rewards to labour' (ibid., 152). Many studies of agrarian groups in South and Central America also reveal the workings of kinship in relations around land, work and political action (Deere 2001).

The cross-disciplinary literature on post-socialist countries in Europe and Asia provides many examples of the significance of kinship. A major policy effort, funded by Western countries and agencies, was directed towards decollectivization and privatization on the assumption that private and individual ownership are the necessary 'foundations for economic growth, democracy, and sustainable land use' (Sikor et al. 2017, 6). As in Africa, these outcomes have not often been achieved, due in no small part to the discrepancy between the reform's premises and the social realities experienced and represented by the people themselves. Researchers show that for many people in these post-socialist countries, their claims to land frequently had far less to do with achieving an income than 'because property rights to land served as a means for conserving family bonds' (ibid., 8), a strategy related to managing lives in the post-socialist political-economic environment. The rationales for land claims were rarely those posited by the reformers, such as enterprise or liberty, but were related to social values as diverse as historical justice, socially valued identities and kinship ties (Hann 1993, 2008; Verdery 1998).

Kinship and descent are a critical entailment, not only of rural arenas, but also in national and international politics. As in Africa, struggles over classically agrarian resources, particularly land and its products, are never independent of struggles over political authority and power at both the most local level and that of the state (Boone 2014). Collins's (2006) study of regime transition in Central Asia found that over 80 per cent of the parliamentary seats in the Kyrgyz, Tajik and Uzbek elections went not to the new political parties (as theorists of the shift to democracy after socialism expected) but to clan members. Collins concludes that 'kinship is the core foundation of clan relations and identity', including where long-term ties convert a friend or ally into 'kin' (ibid., 25–26). Furthermore, '[o]nly an approach that puts … the organization of clans … at the center of the analysis will get at an understanding and explanation of the real nature of political order and disorder in Central Asia' (ibid., 24).

Several recent studies upend 'one of the tall tales of modernity [namely that as] societies become more complex – more industrial, urban, mass mediated, and public – the importance of kinship as an organizing principle decreases' (CSSH 2018). Rather, 'kinship and modernity in fact constitute one another' (ibid.). Despite the ideological claim in Soviet Russia that kinship should be subordinated to politics, 'kinship ties were profoundly important and durable' (ibid., 2); indeed, in today's Russia under Putin, the exercise of power still also includes kin networks. A study of the United Arab Emirates reveals how kinship is a key idiom of modern Gulf nationalism. The 'glorification of kinship', especially in Saudi Arabia, seeks to bind the kingdom together, even in the face of 'massive in-migration' and a mixed, often non-Arab, population (ibid., 4). In Jordan, the competition, often violent, over land and housing is linked to 'the role of large agnatic kin groups in the communal defense of land' (CSSH 2018, 4). The latter is part of broader processes of 'struggle amongst agnatic kin groups, the Jordanian state, and transnationally situated financiers over the nature and disposition of markets and property' (ibid.). Some Arab scholars have even suggested that the equivalent of 'civil society' in Lebanon is 'kin society' (Longva 2018, 114). In Argentina, labour unions cannot be understood without an analysis of the roles of kinship and 'kinning' in their operation (Lazar 2017).

All of these studies reveal the flexible yet durable role of kinship in social processes. Whereas modernization theories assumed that 'undeveloped' societies were 'characterized by tradition … and a supposed overabundance of kinship [that] prevented … growth and initiative, breeding corruption instead', studies of contemporary societies, fully or partially agrarian, document that kinship continues to be a significant mode of relationship and discourse (CSSH 2018, 7). Consider, too, Piketty (2014) on the crucial role of inheritance in wealth inequality and Hann's conclusion that 'Inheritance … links the sphere of production to that of kinship and marriage [with] far-reaching implications for the development of social institutions' (Hann 2008, 146).

ANALYTICAL POINTS

I doubt that those writing on critical agrarian studies need reminding that any political economy is also social. But they do need reminding that it is simultaneously and necessarily cultural. People are not only farmers and workers, differentiated by gender, wealth/income, class, kinship and descent (and so on), but are also meaning makers, constructing and transforming their lives and worlds as best they can in circumstances not only of their own making. Understanding these efforts and struggles entails not only an analysis of differential power, but also of their interpretive worlds – the concepts, precepts and principles that subjects draw on as their grounds for action. This assumes:

> a culturally inflected political economy, in which the main task is to examine the sets of material and social resources upon which livelihoods are based, track the relations through which they are accessed, and explore how these relations are sustained or changed through struggles that are at once meaningful and material. (Li 2008, 112)

Kinship as a type of relatedness is a critical part of any socio-cultural context, although the particulars (of descent, marriage, residence and so forth) will vary, with significant implications for outcomes, as demonstrated earlier. Across the world and not merely among the vast rural populations, kinship is a critical basis for social, economic and political life, entailed in everyday cooperation and conflict, in the inheritance of resources and status, and in mobilization for various ends.

Kinship is neither totally fixed nor totally contingent. While kinship is everywhere associated with certain ideals, especially solidarity and mutual help, persons inhabiting kinship roles, as with other social roles, often fail to achieve these ideals. To be considered a particular relative does not determine the actual relationship, because kinship requires work to make it effective – that is, the holder of a particular status has to work to act in the expected ways according to the associated ideals or principles. Failure to do so may result in not being considered a proper relative, in being marginalized or sanctioned, or even being denounced as a (potential) witch.[5] Conversely, where two persons enter into a particularly warm, mutually beneficial and satisfying relationship, they may seek to emphasize one strand of the relationship over another; so someone who is genealogically distant may be drawn closer by being called and treated like a brother or sister. Thus, among migrants, workers and urban residents, kinship can be used to reinterpret good friends as relatives (what Lazar (2017) calls 'kinning').

This reinterpretation explicitly draws on the ideals of solidarity and mutual aid associated with kinship, so adding an extra layer of moral imperative. While kinship here acts as a flexible resource, the extension of kin relatedness does not operate merely contingently or strategically, but is based on 'well-established cultural registers' (Bjarnesen and Utas 2018, S3). The invocation of clanship among residents of Khayelitsa, a huge urban settlement outside Cape Town, is not merely a contingent and useful ploy, but is based on 'sets of ideas ... sedimented into consciousness through iterative practice ... a cultural structure underlying people's constructions of kinship links – an enduring yet historically and contingently changing one' (Spiegel 2018, S91, S110). Similarly, analysts of Java do not isolate the 'cultural' from the 'political economic' but see that 'cultural precepts [such as] powers of legitimation, shaped the material outcomes that emerged' and acted 'as grounds for mobilization among differently situated actors engaged in a struggle' over land and livelihoods (Hall et al. 2011, 151).

Kinship is both general and specific: as a general concept defining a type of relatedness, it is an essential part of the analytical toolbox for social (including agrarian) studies; but, like all abstract concepts (including culture), it needs to be deconstructed into the specifics of the relevant context. The implications of kinship particularities for land tenure in Africa made this very clear. This was also emphasized by political scientist Kathleen Collins (2006) in her finding that clan relations are central to politics in Central Asia. She points out that political scientists who worry about using essentialist concepts (such as ethnicity) turned away from the use of clan towards more general terms such as informal institution, social network or clientelism. Her careful study of the politics in the three countries of Central Asia shows, however, that these over-general concepts either ignore or misrepresent the ways in which clanship shapes political life. Similarly, the use of the overly general and culture-specific term 'family' fails to capture the specific dynamics of kinship in places like Africa. Approaches that see kinship as irrelevant or epiphenomenal to contemporary political economy miss an important dynamic, as the above cases attest. Recent contributions to critical agrarian studies emphasize social reproduction – the 'social practices through which people reproduce themselves ... the entire gamut of practical sensuous activity ... and institutions [such as] households, states, markets, communities' (Levien et al. 2018, 872). To this partial list must be added kinship and descent.

NOTES

1. Kinship refers to the social organization and cultural meanings of relatedness through descent and marriage (affinity). Although kinship ideology may evoke blood lines, adoption and other forms of incorporation lead to non-genealogical others being included as kin.
2. There are few exceptions to lineage exogamy in sub-Saharan Africa.
3. An ongoing study in Tanzania has found that when men were told to include wives' names on land titles, 'the vast majority' of the titles were never collected from the offices. Men were worried about their authority over their wives, but also 'that the land would go to the family of the wife if he passed away first and not to his children' (Howard Stein, personal communication; see also Lavers 2018, 470).
4. It is essential to link matrilineality with residence: many to most matrilineal groups follow virilocal post-marital residence, where male heirs (e.g. nephews) inherit land.
5. See Geschiere (1997) on witchcraft in Africa as 'the dark side' of kinship, which turns the ideal of mutual help into harm and the goal of caring for and 'feeding' relatives into 'eating' them.

FURTHER READING

Bear, L.; Ho, K.; Tsing, A.; Yanagisako, S. (2015), Gens: A feminist manifesto for the study of capitalism, *Cultural Anthropology*, accessed 13 June 2019 at https://culanth.org/fieldsights/gens-a-feminist-manifesto-for-the-study-of-capitalism.

Collins, K. (2006), *Clan Politics and Regime Transition in Central Asia*, Cambridge: Cambridge University Press.

Guyer, J.I.; Peters, P.E. (1987), Introduction: Conceptualizing the household: Issues of theory and policy in Africa, *Development and Change*, 18(2), 197–214.

Hall, D.; Hirsch, P.; Li, T.M. (2011), *Powers of Exclusion: Land Dilemmas in Southeast Asia*, Singapore: National University of Singapore Press.

Hann, C. (2008), Reproduction and inheritance: Goody revisited, *Annual Review of Anthropology*, 37, 145–158.

Spiegel, A.D. (2018), Reconfiguring the culture of kinship: Poor people's tactics during South Africa's transition from apartheid, *Africa*, 88(S1), S90–S116.

REFERENCES

Akram-Lodhi, A.H.; Kay, C. (2010), Surveying the agrarian question (Part 2): Current debates and beyond, *Journal of Peasant Studies*, 37(2), 255–284.

Amadiume, I. (1987), *Male Daughters, Female Husbands: Gender and Sex in an African Society*, London: Zed Books.

Bear, L.; Ho, K.; Tsing, A.; Yanagisako, S. (2015), Gens: A feminist manifesto for the study of capitalism, *Cultural Anthropology*, accessed 13 June 2019 at https://culanth.org/fieldsights/gens-a-feminist-manifesto-for-the-study-of-capitalism.

Berge, E.; Kambewa, D.; Munthali, A.; Wiig, H. (2014), Lineage and land reforms in Malawi: Do matrilineal and patrilineal landholding systems represent a problem for land reforms in Malawi?, *Land Use Policy*, 41, 61–69.

Bjarnesen, J.; Utas, M. (2018), Introduction: Urban kinship: The micro-politics of proximity and relatedness in African cities, *Africa*, 88(5), S1–S11.

Boone, C. (2014), *Property and Political Order in Africa: Land Rights and the Structure of Politics*, New York: Cambridge University Press.

Claassens, A.; Weeks, S.M. (2009), Rural women redefining land rights in the context of living customary law, *South African Journal of Human Rights*, 25(4), 491–516.

Collier, J.F.; Yanagisako, S.J. (eds) (1987), *Gender and Kinship: Essays toward a Unified Analysis*, Stanford, CA: Stanford University Press.

Collins, K. (2006), *Clan Politics and Regime Transition in Central Asia*, Cambridge: Cambridge University Press.

Cotula, L. (2013), *The Great African Land Grab? Agricultural Investments and the Global Food System*, London: Zed Books.

CSSH (2018), In dialogue: Making kinship bigger: Andrew Shryock in conversation with Golfo Alexopoulos, Nadav Samin, David Henig, and Gísli Pálsson, *Cambridge Studies in Society and History*, 60(2), 1–9.

Deere, C.D. (2001), *Empowering Women: Land and Property Rights in Latin America*, Pittsburgh, PA: University of Pittsburgh Press.

Geschiere, P. (1997), *The Modernity of Witchcraft*, Charlottesville, VA: University Press of Virginia.

Graeub, B.E.; Chappell, M.J.; Wittman, H.; Ledermann, S.; Kerr, R.B.; Gemmill-Herren, B. (2016), The state of family farms in the world, *World Development*, 87, 1–15.

Guyer, J.I.; Peters, P.E. (1987), Introduction: Conceptualizing the household: Issues of theory and policy in Africa, *Development and Change*, 18(2), 197–214.

Hakansson, N.Y. (1994), The detachability of women: Gender and kinship in processes of socio-economic change among the Gusii of Kenya, *American Ethnologist*, 21(3), 516–538.

Hall, D.; Hirsch, P.; Li, T.M. (2011), *Powers of Exclusion: Land Dilemmas in Southeast Asia*, Singapore: National University of Singapore Press.

Hann, C. (1993), From production to property: Decollectivization and the family–land relationship in contemporary Hungary, *Man*, 28(3), 299–320.

Hann, C. (2008), Reproduction and inheritance: Goody revisited, *Annual Review of Anthropology*, 37, 145–158.

Johnson, J. (2012), Life with HIV: 'Stigma' and hope in Malawi's era of ARVs, *Africa*, 82(4), 632–643.

Lavers, T. (2018), Responding to land-based conflict in Ethiopia: The land rights of ethnic minorities under federalism, *African Affairs*, 117(468), 462–484.

Lazar, S. (2017), *The Social Life of Politics: Ethics, Kinship and Union Activism in Argentina*, Stanford, CA: Stanford University Press.

Levien, M.; Watts, M.; Hairong, Y. (2018), Agrarian Marxism, *Journal of Peasant Studies*, 45(5–6), 853–883.

Li, T.M. (2008), Social reproduction, situated politics, and the will to improve, *Focaal*, 52, 111–118.

Longva, A.N. (2018), The state? What state? State, confessionalism and civil society in Lebanon, in Kapferer, B. (ed.), *State, Resistance, Transformation*, Canon Pyon: Sean Kingston Publishing, 97–118.

Murray, C. (1981), *Families Divided: The Impact of Migrant Labour in Lesotho*, Cambridge: Cambridge University Press.

Netting, R.M. (1993), *Smallholders, Householders: Farm Families and the Ecology of Intensive, Sustainable Agriculture*, Stanford, CA: Stanford University Press.

Nzegwu, N.U. (2006), *Family Matters: Feminist Concepts in African Philosophy of Culture*, Albany, NY: SUNY Press.

O'Laughlin, B. (2007), A bigger piece of a very small pie: Intrahousehold resource allocation and poverty reduction in Africa, *Development and Change*, 38(1), 21–44.

O'Laughlin, B. (2013), Unsettled debates in development thinking: Conceptualizing households in rural Africa, *Development and Change*, accessed 5 July 2021 at www.blackwellpublishing.com/pdf/Virtual _Issue_Papers.pdf.

Peters, P.E. (2010), 'Our daughters inherit our land, but our sons use their wives' fields': Matrilineal-matrilocal land tenure and the New Land Policy in Malawi, *Journal of Eastern African Studies*, 4(1), 179–199.

Peters, P.E. (2018a), Land grabs: The politics of the current land rush across Africa, in Cheeseman, N. et al. (eds), *Oxford Research Encyclopedia of African Politics*, Oxford: Oxford University Press.

Peters, P.E. (2018b), Revisiting the bedrock of kinship and descent in the anthropology of Africa, in Grinker, R.; Lubkemann, S.C.; Steiner, C.B.; Gonçalves, E. (eds), *Companion to the Anthropology of the Africa*, Malden, MA: Wiley-Blackwell, 33–62.

Peters, P.E.; Kambewa, D. (2007), Whose security? Deepening social conflict over 'customary' land in the shadow of land tenure reform in Malawi, *Journal of Modern African Studies*, 45(3), 447–472.

Piketty, T. (2014), *Capital in the Twenty-first century*, Cambridge, MA: Belknap Press of Harvard University.

Radcliffe-Brown, A.R.; Forde, D. (eds) (1950), *African Systems of Kinship and Marriage*, London: Oxford University Press for I.A.I.

Russell, M. (1993), Are households universal? On misunderstanding domestic groups in Swaziland, *Development and Change*, 24(4), 55–85.

Sikor, T.; Dorondel, S.; Stahl, J.; To, P.X. (2017), *When Things Become Property*, New York: Berghahn Press.

Spiegel, A.D. (2018), Reconfiguring the culture of kinship: Poor people's tactics during South Africa's transition from apartheid, *Africa*, 88(S1), S90–S116.

Udry, C. (1996), Gender, agricultural production and the theory of the household, *Journal of Political Economy*, 104(5), 1010–1046.

Verdery, K. (1998), Transnationalism, nationalism, citizenship and property: Eastern Europe since 1989, *American Ethnologist*, 25(2), 291–306.

Whitehead, A.; Kabeer, N. (2001), *Living with Uncertainty: Gender, Livelihoods and Pro-Poor Growth in Rural Sub-Saharan Africa*, IDS Working Paper 134, Brighton: University of Sussex.

Yount-André, C. (2018), New African frontiers: Transnational families in neoliberal capitalism: Introduction, *Africa*, 88(4), 641–644.

17. Generation

Ben White

Despite their obvious relevance, intergenerational relations and related generational inequalities in land rights, decision making and voice have been largely overlooked in studies conducted from a classical agrarian political economy perspective in both the Marxist (Bernstein 2010) and Chayanovian (van der Ploeg 2013) traditions. Although there has been some attention in recent years (Archambault 2014; Berckmoes and White 2016; Cassidy et al. 2019; White 2020), they are still not fully embedded in critical agrarian studies.

We need the concept of generation, alongside gender and class, to understand how agrarian households and communities reproduce themselves from day to day, from season to season and over longer time spans, and the continuities and discontinuities in these processes.[1] Generation thus stands with social reproduction – the material and discursive practices which enable the reproduction of a social formation (including the relations between social groups) and its members over time (Wells 2009, 78)[2] – as key windows on the critical study of continuity and change in agrarian societies.

Generation is used with many different meanings, in both everyday, social science and policy discourse. It may refer to relationships bounded by kinship descent (most often, parent–child relations) in which your generational position – as someone's child or parent – is a permanent location, regardless of your biological age. It may also refer to the life-course phases of (for example) childhood, youth, adulthood and old age and the linear transitions between them. For Karl Mannheim in his landmark essay *The Problem of Generations*, generations were groupings (loosely but not strictly age-based) which besides their similarity in age also shared a particular (social, cultural and particularly political) historical experience and defined themselves in terms of that common experience; not all demographic cohorts emerge as 'generations-for-themselves'[3] in this sense (Huijsmans 2016, 11–18; Mannheim 1952 [1928]).

Each of these understandings of generation is useful. But the key dimension of generation as a tool for understanding agrarian change is of generation as socially (politically, culturally) constructed *relationships* between individuals and groups in society based on their 'social' age or life-course status. Generation, then, is to (biological) age more or less what gender is to (biological) sex: like gender, and class, it is a relationship, not a 'thing', and it is socially constructed. In plain language, you are a 'child', 'youth' or 'adult' – regardless of biological age – if society recognizes, defines and treats you as such. This relational understanding of generation helps us to understand how agrarian changes may restructure 'generational social landscapes' and vice versa (Huijsmans 2016, 4) and how generational relations (like gender relations) are relations of unequal power.

> Generationing ... serves as an exercise of power. This power is not only discursive but also material, shaping people's economic contributions and access to resources ... It shapes people's identities (intersecting with other relationships including gender and class), is lived by individuals and groups and has material effects. Inevitably, generationing is contested: the outcomes of contestations often lead to change. (Ansell 2016, 315)

The generational replacement of agrarian households involves the transmission of land and other agrarian resources, including agricultural knowledge and skills, between generations – or the blockage of such transfers. To explore how young people are included in or excluded from entry into farming, we need to understand the widely differing ways in which access to agrarian resources is structured in different societies, and also the different ways in which the intergenerational transfer of these resources is regulated, with or without contestation.

Traditional agrarian societies are typically sites of patriarchy in both gender and generational relations (Ní Laoire 2002; Stearns 2006, 11–13). In non-mechanized agriculture, the capacity to produce is highly dependent on the labour force at farmers' disposal; hence, the need for parents to control their children's work, which is reflected in patterns of harsh discipline, and cultural emphasis on respect for the older generation, which are commonly seen in peasant societies world-wide.

Within these patriarchal structures, however, young people are not passive victims, but exercise a 'constrained agency'. Ethnographic studies of 'traditional' rural ways of growing up provide many examples in which children who wish to farm negotiate with parents or other adult relatives for a plot of land to farm themselves, or engage in paid work on the farms of others, and control to a greater or lesser extent the product of their farming work. Below are two striking examples from highland Bolivia and from the upland Lauje region of Central Sulawesi (Indonesia) before the cacao boom of the 1990s.[4]

> When Antonio was 13 years old … his father agreed to give him a small plot of land in return for his help in the fields. Antonio chose to sow peanuts and he bought the seed by selling a goat that he had been given on his birthday a few years previously. His younger brother, Javier, helped him plant the seed and Antonio agreed to give him the harvested peanuts from five lines of the crop. (Highland Bolivia; Punch 2011, 156f.)

> We were out on the platform behind the house … when one of the daughters of the house began to pull out bundles of garlic and arrange them in the sun.
> 'Who do they belong to?' I asked casually.
> 'That one belongs to my mother, those belong to my older brother, those belong to my sister, these here are mine, and those belong to my father,' she replied. 'Mother and father work together. Today they are weeding her garlic. When that is finished, they will weed his.'
> This was my introduction to the economic autonomy of household members, each of whom created personal property through his or her work. They also created relations of kinship and care by entering into exchanges with others. (Lauje, Central Sulawesi; Li 2014, 59)

In how many countries and regions is it still possible for young would-be farmers to slip into independent agricultural production and earning in this way?

Among small-scale agriculturalists and pastoralists, the intergenerational transmission of resources plays a key role in perpetuating and strengthening agrarian inequalities (Borgerhoff-Mulder et al. 2009). The transmission of agrarian resources through inheritance (in its narrow sense, of post-mortem transmission) is the last phase in an often longer process of transfer of resources from one generation to the next. The longer process, which includes transfers made before death, is known as 'devolution' (Goody 1976). Devolution takes a bewildering variety of forms around the world. First, the nature of the rights transferred (various kinds of ownership, ownership-like and use rights) varies from place to place and over time. Second, although social reproduction is generally carried out in a vertical rather than lateral direction (looking for one or more heirs in the next descending generation, rather than among siblings or cousins in the same generation), there are multiple ways of regulating who in the next generation is or are eligible as heir(s): patrilineal, matrilineal and ambilineal, partible and impartible and, within the latter, primo- or ultimo-geniture, or simply designating a selected heir regardless of birth order.

In exploring these patterns of inheritance or devolution we must distinguish 'law', 'custom' and actual practice, and be aware that all of these may change over time. This is well illustrated in Cole and Wolf's classic study comparing German- and Romance-speaking communities in Italy's South Tyrol more than half a century ago. Impartible inheritance with male primo-geniture was both ideal and actual practice among the German speakers, as it was among Bavarians across the border (Wolf 1970), while just a short distance away among the Romance speakers, inheritance was partible with sons and daughters inheriting equally (Cole and Wolf 1974). Revisiting the German speakers two decades later, Cole was surprised to find the inheritance system transformed from male primo-geniture to female ultimo-geniture, 'and villagers told the ethnographer this had always been their custom' (Hann 2008, citing Cole 2003).

In some cases, young would-be farmers must first go through a period of tenant farming on their parents' land, as in this example of a 24-year-old young woman rice farmer in the Javanese village of Kaliloro, Indonesia.[5]

> Yaya and her husband have no land in their own right and depend completely on access to her father-in-law's land. Their whole rice-farm is 0.24 ha, but they receive only the harvest from one 1000 m^2 plot (which the father allows them to cultivate free of rent), plus half the harvest from another 700 m^2 plot which he gives them on a share-cropping basis; on the third plot of 700 m^2 they deliver the whole harvest to him. Yaya does not find this arrangement fair: 'we do all the work and pay all the costs ... but what can I do, I can't protest.'[6]

In other situations, rural youth who see possibilities for themselves in a revitalized, modern smallholder agriculture may run up against parental conservatism. In the Saïss plain of Morocco, a region where tubewells and drip irrigation have opened up new opportunities for export production of fruits and vegetables, a 29-year-old agriculture graduate explains his aspirations and frustrations, which encapsulate the experience of many young rural people who aspire to a modern rural farming life:

> Driss doesn't reject farming, but wants to go elsewhere to pursue his life-project, far away from the eyes and the control of his father and family and the community. Driss sees his future self as an independent farmer, responsible for his own farming project and up-to-date with the newest crops and technologies. [But currently] he farms with his brothers on his father's land and under his authority. They cultivate three hectares of irrigated onions and potatoes, and the remaining ten hectares are cropped with rainfed cereals. 'If my father says that we have to cultivate four hectares of onions, I cannot refuse or contradict him ... I'm so fed up with this situation. I just want something for myself, something I can rely on. My own project, my own money.' (Bossenbroek et al. 2015, 344–345, 347)

When access to agrarian resources and independent farming is barred, one mode of young people's agency is open protest, as in the case of these young Abure men in Côte d'Ivoire, who sabotaged the crop when their elders leased land to Burkinabe 'foreigners' for commercial pineapple farming, leaving them without land.

> The young men say they destroyed the foreigners' pineapples because of the old men. For example, if an old man who manages family land leases out most of this land, the children have no land to cultivate to provide for their needs. Don't they have to eat? ... When the old men receive money from

the Burkinabes, they use it for their own needs, they do not give any to the young men and the latter become vagrants who roam the city. (Kouamé 2010, 137)

Another source of the land squeeze on youth is large-scale corporate land acquisitions, which may altogether cut off young people's options for farming futures (Park and White 2018). In her study of Indonesia's extensive oil-palm zones, Tania Li observes that plantation expansion may initially leave the original landholders in place, tucked into enclaves on which they may be able to continue farming; the real squeeze begins a generation later, when land in the enclave proves insufficient for the needs of young (would-be) farmers (Li 2018).

> It is only later, when the enclaves prove too small to accommodate the needs of the new generation, and surrounding forestland is full of plantations, that customary landholders experience the 'grab' as a permanent and complete loss of access to the possibility of farming. As one elder in my research site in Kalimantan explained, 'when the company came we thought our land was as big as the sea'. But more companies came. Now his children and grandchildren are landless. They are marooned in a sea of oil palms in which they have no share, and no means of gaining a share. (Li 2018, 59)

Another common response – which we saw Driss contemplating in the Moroccan example above – is to vote with their feet, to migrate in search of other work and livelihoods, thus withdrawing their labour from the parental farm. Young rural people's mobility now extends to all agrarian classes and (in most countries) genders; the great majority of the world's labour migrants (both domestic and international) are young people. One reason why so many young rural people, almost all over the world, express reluctance to farm may reflect not an aversion to farming as such, but the long period of waiting that they would have to face before they have a chance to engage in independent farming. It is not surprising that so many young rural people migrate, being reluctant to engage in long years of agrarian 'timepass', working for parents or other elder relatives: who wants to wait until they are 40 or 50 years old to be a farmer (White 2012, 14)? What is more important, and still a neglected issue, is whether young people's migration away from rural areas and farming is a permanent, or a part-lifetime process; we need to explore further the phenomenon of cyclical, part-lifetime migration.

In rural Burundi, in a village where one-third of young men and more than half of all young women do not expect to inherit land, three-quarters of all the young men interviewed, and smaller numbers of young women, had made the dangerous and tiring three-day journey to neighbouring Tanzania for work at least once, and half of them more than once, without documents, risking jail, violence from the local population and robbery. These young people looked for non-farm opportunities, not to replace but to complement farming, and indeed to make farming a possible future:

> We want a future as farmers, but if we would have other activities to help, that would be better because farming is not enough.
> … If there was an organization to help us learn a vocation, we could work and have money to buy land before the others do so and there is no more land. (Berckmoes and White 2014, 195f.)

This underlines the importance of a *life-course perspective* in the study of young people's aspirations and their move out of, and perhaps later back into, farming. In many regions today, young people's multi-directional mobility between sectors and places means that rural/urban and farmer/non-farmer dichotomies are increasingly losing their meaning (Rigg et al. 2020). In any case, young people's out-migration not should automatically be assumed to reflect a permanent, lifetime abandonment of rural life, or the possibility of a return to farming; it is a matter for research.

One key distinction among young farmers which needs to be further explored is that between *continuers* (those who take over their parents' or other relative's farm) and *newcomers* (those not from a farm background who find a pathway into farming – thus 'voting with their feet' in the reverse direction). We should also make a distinction between *early continuers* and *late continuers*, the latter being those who first leave the parental farm to engage in other work (whether inside or beyond the village) and return to farming later in life as land becomes available. There is a strong supposition – although it should be noted there is scant evidence on this – that *newcomer* and *late continuer* farmers are likely to be innovators, and more critical of mainstream farming practices.

As a final point, another aspect of generational relationships involving youth is the relationship between young rural people and the (nearly always) adult professional researchers like myself who study and write about them. Young people's 'right to be properly researched' (Beazley et al. 2009) means that critical agrarian study needs to ask: will young people be objects, subjects or participants in our research? Will our ideas about their situation, experiences and relations with the adult world be obtained directly from them, or by proxy from adults? Young people are quite capable of becoming key actors in the process of critical agrarian research if we are willing to do research not 'about' them, but with them.

NOTES

1. The points made in this chapter are explored in greater detail in White (2020), from which this chapter is drawn.
2. See Smriti Rao's chapter in this *Handbook* for discussion of theories of social reproduction.
3. The analogy is to 'class in itself' versus 'class for itself' in Marxist class analysis.
4. For a similar example from Zimbabwe, see Reynolds (1991).
5. For an Ecuadorian example of share-cropping as a phase in intergenerational land transfers, see Lehmann (1986).
6. Quoted with permission from Hanny Wijaya's field notes.

FURTHER READING

Huijsmans, R. (ed.) (2016), *Generationing Development: A Relational Approach to Children, Youth and Development*, London: Palgrave Macmillan.

Li, T.M. (2018), Intergenerational displacement in Indonesia's oil palm plantation zone, in Park, C.M.Y.; White, B. (eds), *Gender and Generation in Southeast Asian Agrarian Transformations*, London: Routledge, 56–74. Also published in (2017), *Journal of Peasant Studies*, 44(6), 1158–1176.

Mannheim, K. (1952 [1928]), The problem of generations, in Kecskemeti, P. (ed.), *Karl Mannheim: Essays on the Sociology of Knowledge*, London: Routledge.

Punch, S. (2011), Generational power relations in rural Bolivia, in Panelli, R.; Punch, S.; Robson, E. (eds), *Global Perspectives on Rural Childhood and Youth: Young Rural Lives*, London: Routledge, 151–164.

White, B. (2020), *Agriculture and the Generation Problem*, Halifax, NS: Fernwood Publishing; Rugby, UK: Practical Action Publishing.

REFERENCES

Ansell, N. (2016), Age and generation in the service of development?, in Huijsmans, R. (ed.), *Generationing Development: A Relational Approach to Children, Youth and Development*, London: Palgrave Macmillan, 315–330.

Archambault, C. (2014), Young perspectives on pastoral rangeland privatization: Intimate exclusions at the intersection of youth identities, *European Journal of Development Research*, 26(2), 204–218.

Beazley, H.; Bessell, S.; Ennew, J.; Waterson, R. (2009), The right to be properly researched: Research with children in a messy, real world, *Children's Geographies*, 7(4), 365–378.

Berckmoes, L.; White, B. (2014), Youth, farming and precarity in rural Burundi, *European Journal of Development Research*, 26(2), 190–203.

Berckmoes, L.; White, B. (2016), Youth, farming and precarity in rural Burundi, in Huijsmans, R. (ed.), *Generationing Development: A Relational Approach to Children, Youth and Development*, London: Palgrave Macmillan, 291–313.

Bernstein, H. (2010), *Class Dynamics of Agrarian Change*, Halifax, NS: Fernwood Publishing.

Borgerhoff-Mulder, M.; Bowles, S.; Hertz, T.; Bell, A.; Beise, J.; Clark, G. et al. (2009), Intergenerational wealth transmission and the dynamics of inequality in small-scale societies, *Science*, 326(30 October), 682–688.

Bossenbroek, L.; van der Ploeg, J.D.; Zwarteveen, M. (2015), Broken dreams? Youth experiences of agrarian change in Morocco's Saïss region, *Cahiers Agricultures*, 24(6), 342–348.

Cassidy, A.; Srinivasan, S.; White, B. (2019), Generational transmission of smallholder farms in late capitalism, *Canadian Journal of Development Studies*, 40(2), 220–237.

Cole, J. (2003), The last becomes first: The rise of ultimogeniture in contemporary South Tyrol, in Grandits, H.; Heady, P. (eds), *Distinct Inheritance: Property, Family and Community in a Changing Europe*, Münster: LIT Verlag, 263–274.

Cole, J.; Wolf, E. (1974), *The Hidden Frontier: Ecology and Ethnicity in an Alpine Valley*, New York: Academic Press.

Goody, J. (1976), *Production and Reproduction: A Comparative Study of the Domestic Domain*, Cambridge: Cambridge University Press.

Hann, C. (2008), Reproduction and inheritance: Goody revisited, *Annual Review of Anthropology*, 37, 145–158.

Huijsmans, R. (2016), Generationing development: An introduction, in Huijsmans, R. (ed.), *Generationing Development: A Relational Approach to Children, Youth and Development*, London: Palgrave Macmillan, 1–31.

Kouamé, G. (2010), Intra-family and socio-political dimensions of land markets and land conflicts: The case of the Abure, Côte d'Ivoire, *Africa*, 80(1), 126–146.

Lehmann, D. (1986), Sharecropping and the capitalist transition in agriculture: Some evidence from the highlands of Ecuador, *Journal of Development Studies*, 23(2), 333–354.

Li, T.M. (2014), *Lands End: Capitalist Relations on an Indigenous Frontier*, Durham, NC: Duke University Press.

Li, T.M. (2018), Intergenerational displacement in Indonesia's oil palm plantation zone, in Park, C.M.Y.; White, B. (eds), *Gender and Generation in Southeast Asian Agrarian Transformations*, London: Routledge, 56–74. Also published in (2017), *Journal of Peasant Studies*, 44(6), 1158–1176.

Mannheim, K. (1952 [1928]), The problem of generations, in Kecskemeti, P. (ed.), *Karl Mannheim: Essays on the Sociology of Knowledge*, London: Routledge.

Ní Laoire, C. (2002), Young farmers, masculinity and change in rural Ireland, *Irish Geography*, 35(1), 16–27.

Park, C.M.Y.; White, B. (2018), Gender and generation in Southeast Asian agrarian transformations, in Park, C.M.Y.; White, B. (eds), *Gender and Generation in Southeast Asian Agrarian Transformations*, London: Routledge, 1–8. Also published in (2017), *Journal of Peasant Studies*, 44(6), 1103–1110.

Punch, S. (2011), Generational power relations in rural Bolivia, in Panelli, R.; Punch, S.; Robson, E. (eds), *Global Perspectives on Rural Childhood and Youth: Young Rural Lives*, London: Routledge, 151–164.

Reynolds, P. (1991), *Dance Civet Cat: Child Labour in the Zambezi Valley*, London: Zed Books.

Rigg, J.; Phongsiri, M.; Promphakping, B.; Salamanca, A.; Sripun, M. (2020), Who will tend the farm? Interrogating the ageing Asian farmer, *Journal of Peasant Studies*, 47(2), 306–325.

Stearns, P. (2006), *Childhood in World History*, London: Routledge.

van der Ploeg, J.D. (2013), *Peasants and the Art of Farming: A Chayanovian Manifesto*, Halifax, NS: Fernwood Publishing.

Wells, K. (2009), *Childhood in a Global Perspective*, Cambridge: Polity Press.

White, B. (2012), Agriculture and the generation problem: Rural youth, employment and the future of farming, *IDS Bulletin*, 43(6), 9–19.

White, B. (2020), *Agriculture and the Generation Problem*, Halifax, NS: Fernwood Publishing; Rugby, UK: Practical Action Publishing.

Wolf, E. (1970), The inheritance of land among Bavarian and Tyrolese peasants, *Anthropologica*, 12(1), 99–114.

18. Intersectionality

Carol J. Pierce Colfer, Markus Ihalainen and Bimbika Sijapati Basnett

INTRODUCTION

The term intersectionality was coined in 1989 by Kimberlé Crenshaw, a civil rights activist and legal scholar at the University of California. However, notions of multiple identities and interacting forms of oppression have been recognized by various ethnographers and other social scientists, writers and civil rights groups long before that. Within feminist and gender studies, intersectionality is now considered by some to be a 'gold standard' for nuanced and relevant research and analyses (Nash 2008) and the term is increasingly percolating outward to influence mainstream gender and development policy debates. This interest reflects growing recognition, especially outside the social sciences, that people are not defined by one characteristic alone, but rather reflect clusters of identities with differing implications in social and political hierarchies.

In this chapter, we begin by unpacking the history and theory behind the concept and present a case study of Nepal which has been pioneering a gender and intersectional approach to policy making and advocacy. Recognizing that much of the literature on intersectionality has been theoretical in nature, we then offer our view of appropriate and more practical lenses through which intersectionality can usefully be viewed in agrarian contexts (elaborated in Colfer et al. 2018).

THE HISTORY AND THEORY OF INTERSECTIONALITY

Ideas about multiple and intersecting forms of oppression are not new and can be traced back long before Crenshaw conceived the concept of intersectionality in the 1980s. Already in 1851, Sojourner Truth, an African-American woman and former slave, pointed out how her own experiences were largely ignored by contemporary notions of femininity:

> That man over there says that women need to be helped into carriages, and lifted over ditches, and to have the best place everywhere. Nobody helps me any best place. And ain't I a woman? Look at me! Look at my arm. I have ploughed and planted and gathered into barns, and no man could head me – and ain't I a woman? (Flexner 1975, 91)

In the 1970s and 1980s in the United States (US), black women within socialist movements drew attention to the triple oppression faced by black, working-class women, while in Europe (and later the US), the International Wages for Housework Campaign spurred debate about the role of working-class women's unrecognized and unpaid reproductive labour in capitalist economies (Federici 2012). Examining western feminist discourses on women in the developing world, postcolonial feminists such as Chandra Mohanty argued that 'contemporary discourses constructed "Third World Women" as a homogeneous "powerless" group often located as implicit victims of particular socio-economic systems' (Mohanty 1988, 57).

In a similar vein, Crenshaw's first conceptualization of intersectionality was born out of a critique of the marginalization of black women's experiences by so called single-axis frameworks, dominant within contemporary anti-discriminatory law as well as feminist and anti-racist politics. In illustration, Crenshaw refers to a court case where five African-American women sued General Motors for discriminatory employment practices against black women. However, the court weighed gender- and race-based discrimination separately, ruling that because the company was hiring white women and black men, there was no case for gender- or race-based discrimination (Crenshaw 1989). Crenshaw argues that anti-discrimination frameworks structured around a single axis of discrimination (e.g. race *or* gender) ignore the compounded race *and* gender discrimination experienced by black women.

Crenshaw refers to the distinct forms of oppression faced by black women as *structural intersectionality*. Importantly, she argues that such oppression cannot be reduced to the sum of race and gender discrimination, or what is often referred to as an additive approach. For instance, as Crenshaw (1989, 1991) illustrates, gender discrimination faced by black women is often qualitatively different from discrimination faced by white women and hence inextricable from race. Regression analyses aimed at identifying the 'most determinant' identity variable in relation to the outcome of interest similarly fail to account for the interaction among identities as well as social power structures (Hankivsky 2014). The idea of mutually constitutive – and often contextually specific – relationships between social categories and power relations is at the core of intersectionality (Hancock 2007). However, Crenshaw argues that the contemporary feminist and anti-racist movements in the US concerned themselves predominantly with the experiences of white women and black men, hence in fact contributing to the political marginalization of the experiences of black women. This is referred to as *political intersectionality* (Crenshaw 1991).

Crenshaw sees structural and political intersectionality as two sides of the same coin: a more disaggregated, nuanced analysis of the 'intersectional experiences' of those most disadvantaged is necessary for building more inclusive movements for social justice and equality (Crenshaw 1989). Born out of liberation struggles, the normative commitment to identify and challenge unequal power relations is central to intersectionality (Hankivsky 2014). Importantly, power is understood as operating at multiple levels, including processes of e.g. socially constructing 'race', 'racializing' certain groups and individuals, as well as enacted and experienced racism (ibid.). Critical power relations include both oppression ('power over') and agency ('power to'), as well as 'power with others'.

Since Crenshaw coined the term in 1989, the concept has continued to be subject to debate among feminist scholars. For instance, as the scope of intersectionality has been broadened beyond the experiences of black women in the US, scholars have discussed how to approach different categories of social differentiation. Indeed, a key tenet of intersectionality holds that every individual is shaped by multiple social identities. These identities (e.g. poor, lower-caste woman) interact with various intersecting social power structures (e.g. class, caste, gender), shaping experiences and viewpoints at each unique social location (Hankivsky 2014). But as the list of pertinent identities or social categories grows with the concept expanding to new fields, so does the number of analytical locations. Tracing the proliferation of 'identities' in social science literature from the 1960s onwards, Brubaker and Cooper (2000, 3) refer to the 'overproduction and consequent devaluation of meaning' as the 'identity crisis'.

To deal with the seemingly illimitable list of social divisions, some scholars have advocated identifying pertinent categories based on contextual and historically situated analyses of relevant macro-level power axes (e.g. patriarchy, capitalism, racism) in relation to the field of interest (e.g. access to resources) (Yuval-Davis 2006). Based on this analysis, researchers would select a set of provisional 'master categories' (e.g. gender, class, race), create a number of social locations based on the categories (e.g. working-class woman of colour) and analyse the relationships among locations (McCall 2005). Others have challenged the idea of master categories with stable, universally shared meanings and non-contested boundaries. Researchers departing from a more deconstructivist point of view may instead prefer in-depth, narrative study, allowing the pertinent social categories and intersections to emanate organically from the lived experiences of the participants (McCall 2005).

According to Hancock, intersectionality is ontologically situated between 'reductionist research that blindly seeks only the generalizable and particularized research so specialized that it cannot contribute to theory' (2007, 74). She sees the intersectional approach as aiming to bridge the structural, macro-level analyses of social power structures with deconstructivist micro analyses of individual experiences in one holistic, multi-level framework. As noted above, the task of translating this into operationalizable methodologies is not easy. To address the rift between the constructivist and deconstructivist approaches discussed above, Walby et al. suggest recognizing the 'historically constructed nature of social inequalities and their sedimentation in social institutions' (2012, 231). While the meanings and boundaries of social categories remain contested and ever changing, the ways in which those categories and inequalities are expressed through social institutions at a given point in time provide a certain degree of stability, in turn allowing for some generalizability and analysis of relations among categories (Walby et al. 2012). However, methodological choices between generalizable populations and in-depth information may still require researchers to weigh theoretical 'purity' with empirical feasibility. As Hancock argued, intersectional analysis is 'the best chance for an effective diagnosis and ultimately an effective prescription' (2007, 73). Exploring methodological options for addressing inter- and intra-categorical complexities (McCall 2005; Hancock 2007) is thus an important task.

To demonstrate this complexity, we turn to Nepal which has been pioneering gender and intersectionality in its approach to policy making and advocacy.

THE NEPAL CASE

There is an emerging consensus within the gender and development policy literature that focusing on 'women' as a group is insufficient to measure progress towards the achievement of gender equality and women's empowerment. After all, many women and girls face multiple forms of discrimination based on aspects of their identities that differentiate them from other advantaged groups. Focusing on averages therefore only serves to mask differences and inequalities in rights, resources and opportunities among 'women' and prevents more meaningful action (Sijapati Basnett 2018). While many countries struggle to highlight attention to inequalities between women and men as a pressing development concern in their own right, the efforts of various actors (government, development partners, civil society) in Nepal are often hailed as going a step beyond by professing to address gender inequalities between women and men and across its highly heterogenous population (Kabeer 2018). Here, we examine how such views are reflected in a variety of depictions of gender issues in the country – including academic scholarship, ongoing social and political struggles, alongside the policy literature – and discuss what kinds of openings and pitfalls they present.

The rich history of ethnographic research in Nepal has demonstrated how 'women's' position in their households and communities is not only variegated but also evolves and shifts across the life-cycle. For instance, Bennett (2002) argued that high-caste Hindu women in Nepal occupy a dual and contradictory position during their life span. Newly married women are often viewed as 'outsiders' and as a 'threat' to the purity of the patriline in their marital homes. Hence, considerable measures are imposed on these women with a view to separating them both physically and ritually from male household members (e.g. fathers-in-law, brothers-in-law). Women's status subsequently changes when they bear a son and thus are viewed as having contributed to the continuity of the patriline. After this stage, women can themselves transition into domineering mothers-in-law or elder sisters-in-law who are able to act as primary persecutors of young wives. In comparison, 'women' when they are in their natal homes are viewed as 'sacred' and of high status, even if they are junior. Even if women are barred from inheriting parental land and other property and marriage serves as a vehicle for transferring women's labour rights from their natal to their marital homes (Moore 1988), bonds of lasting support and affection continue to bind married women with their natal families (and its patriline). Other scholars have pointed out how these bonds serve as safety nets for women in times of marital crisis or other hardships in their lives. It is also one of the reasons there has been such slow progress in reducing the gender gap in land ownership in the country, even though policies restricting women's rights to inherit parental property have been revised, now granting women and men equal rights (Rao 2017). Arable land is not just the most significant form of economic resource in rural Nepal, but it is also strongly associated with hegemonic notions of male identity and entitlement (Jackson 2002). Women are unwilling to stake a claim on parental property for fear of antagonizing their brothers and/or male relatives and jeopardizing their agrarian safety net.

While Bennett discusses the symbolic dimension of women's shifting position, Cameron (1998) highlights the material aspect in her comparative study of high- and low-caste women in a remote village in the far west of Nepal. She points out that low-caste women suffer from inequalities and discrimination that come along with belonging to a low or 'untouchable caste' whereas their high-caste counterparts experience greater financial stability and higher social status by virtue of belonging to their caste. At the same time, low-caste women in her research site did not face the serious restrictions on mobility that their high-caste counterparts did. They were able to assume paid jobs outside their homes and enjoyed greater voice and autonomy in major decisions made at the household level. In comparison, their high-caste counterparts were confined to their households, their contribution to household subsistence and/or commercial farming remained unrecognized and they experienced very little space and influence in decisions made in the household. This study serves to demonstrate that 'low-caste women' are not doubly discriminated against because of their 'gender' and low 'caste', but that 'gender' and 'caste' interact to create particular sets of social relations with differing material and symbolic consequences for women's voice and agency. At the same time, anthropologists studying caste, ethnic and class-based relations in Nepal have long observed the complexity and fluidity of these relations, making it all the more difficult to draw generalizations. The relations among 'caste', 'ethnicity' and 'class' are also often intersected by spatial considerations. Both high and low castes perform more poorly in key socio-economic wellbeing indicators in the far-western and poorer regions of the country than their counterparts who live within closer proximity to urban centres (Thapa et al. 2013).

Trying to fashion practical approaches that incorporate intersectionality has proven a challenge for governments and other implementers. Kabeer (2018) describes Nepal's efforts, which include routinely collecting socio-economic data on men and women at the aggregate level, in ways which in turn can be disaggregated by caste (high and low), ethnicity and geography. Gender and social inclusion concerns, as reflected in the vast majority of national development policies, highlight the importance of focusing on women as a group, but also tending to specific concerns of *Janajati* (or ethnic minority) and *Dalit* (low-caste) women.

Discourses about 'caste' and 'ethnicity' as deployed by politicians, policy makers and activists tend to be interpreted as given (primordial) rather than as a historically negotiated set of social relations that are fluid and in a state of flux. Categories such as 'Dalits', 'Janajati', 'Bahun/Chhetri' (high caste) in turn, conceal considerable variations within, in terms of socio-cultural practices, historical relations with the state and positions of authority and influence in local and national power hierarchies. Uncritical acceptance of these social categories, and the ways in which they are being politicized to pit one group against another, fuel civil unrest, seek rent and other advantages from the state, make it all the more challenging to reach consensus and form coalitions across differences. Hence, while the Nepal case serves to illustrate the possibility of adopting a gender and intersectional approach to policy making and social praxis, it also points to the potential pitfalls of relying on seemingly innocuous categories.

ADDRESSING INTERSECTIONALITY IN CRITICAL AGRARIAN STUDIES

The significance of expanding our purview to include intersectionality should be clear at this point. It allows us to take into account the differences within categories we previously examined in a more undifferentiated manner, such as 'women' or 'a tribal group'. Clearly the differences within categories (e.g. wealthy versus poor women, of this ethnic group or that, in rural versus urban contexts) suggest significant differences in power, in life options and in roles in community decision making about agrarian issues.

The central challenge, however, is that of dealing with such complexity; the literature does not give us much guidance. The focus increasingly has been on dismantling multiple and intersecting identities and not simultaneously examining how intersectional inequalities affect people's freedom to live lives of their choosing (Kabeer 2018). To put it differently, the ways in which intersecting inequalities have a bearing on who is losing, who is not, why and what can be done about it—central questions for agrarian studies as Borras (2009) points out—are inadequately considered. In 2017, we considered how to implement the concept practically in forests (Colfer et al. 2018). We identified five lenses through which intersectionality can be addressed: cognitive, emotional, social, economic and political. One caveat should be mentioned. Whereas our emphasis here, like that of other researchers on intersectionality, has been on those *suffering* from injustices in a given system (the 'marginalized', 'subordinate', 'disadvantaged'), in fact we believe it is equally important to consider those with 'power over' others—a future task for us all.

The cognitive lens involves examining the divergent world views of subgroups within communities. Groups of unequal power are common in agrarian systems. Colfer (1983) examined the interactions between such groups, arguing that those in subordinate positions (particularly those multiply marginalized) had to master both their own systems and those of superordinate groups with whom they interacted, while the latter were able to function well, understanding only their own. This places additional cognitive stress on those less powerful. We argue that the necessity for marginalized groups to straddle and master multiple systems interferes with their ability and willingness to express their wishes, practices and goals; and, therefore, requires explicit efforts by practitioners and researchers to understand such world views in pursuit of more equitable agrarian systems.

The emotional lens is based on a recognition of the difficulties that plague those who are consistently marginalized. Sen (1999) talks about 'psychological capability deprivation', deprivation of people's sense of their own potential and lack of self-confidence. Studies of marginalized groups show a variety of adverse psychological effects of marginalization, including shame and humiliation and feelings of inferiority, vulnerability and lack of transparency. In her studies of divorced women, prostitutes and lesbians, Wieringa (2015, 111) finds that '[b]lame is internalized, while violence and suffering are accepted as "normal"'—perfect examples of what Bourdieu calls 'symbolic violence'.

The social and economic lenses are the most frequently addressed in critical agrarian studies and relate to perceptions and actions of others, with adverse effects on individuals with particular clusters of identities (and on society at large). The social lens emphasizes stereotypes, norms and narratives of inferiority that function to sustain and strengthen inequitable relations among groups. Elmhirst's (2011) intersectional analysis of migration in southern Sumatra captures the power of government narratives and local norms in sustaining and creating inequitable social relations between men and women, married and unmarried, and different ethnic groups (or migrants and natives).

The economic lens identifies access to resources and employment, tenure and rules of inheritance as key features in which clusters of identities play a significant, if understudied, role. Li (2015) studied West Kalimantan palm oil expansion including the roles of gender and ethnicity in determining access to jobs and land. In many areas, a divorced or widowed woman may have greater difficulty retaining land that by custom should have been hers. This is particularly likely to be a problem in matrilineal groups, where governments are prone to assume (and legislate) inheritance through the male line.

The political lens, the distribution of power and resources within a given society, is mediated by formal and informal institutions and organizations, at various levels. Without understanding such institutions and how they function, we fail to address the limited (a) access to political decision making, (b) opportunities to voice aspirations and (c) opportunities to take collection action (beyond capability to vote) of the multiply marginalized.

CONCLUSIONS: BRINGING CRITICAL AGRARIAN STUDIES TOGETHER WITH INTERSECTIONALITY

Addressing intersectionality effectively and critically in agrarian contexts will require holistic approaches and methods, allowing for context-specific and multi-level analyses. One must fully understand the context in which different clusters of identities occur, the interactions that take place and broader social and political relations in which these are inevitably embedded. Attention to intersectionality also points to the importance of 'politicizing' the agrarian context by situating researchers and practitioners within it—social positions in social and institutional hierarchies, assumptions and commitments (Sijapati Basnett et al. 2017). Ultimately, the choice of methods and approaches is influenced by factors such as the scope and scale of the research and epistemological commitments of researchers (McCall 2005). However, there are a number of established approaches available that can help facilitate a more nuanced analysis of intersecting power relations at the local level. These include ethnography, mixed methods and collaboration.

In intersectional analysis, as in critical agrarian studies, there is an explicit recognition of and attention to power differentials and inequities. Much of the scholarship in this field includes significant descriptive analysis, which if linked more self-consciously and systematically with intersectional analysis could better capture the nuances of power relations. This can lead to better understanding, collaboration and policy advice. Explicit recognition of how inequities and power relations map to clusters of identities in specific places can be extremely powerful in helping us figure out how to attack injustice, where leverage points are and how change in what relationships and actions can contribute to overcoming such inequities.

Critical agrarian studies have emphasized economic, social and political issues to the relative exclusion of the cognitive and emotional, both of which can have significant impacts on how rural peoples see and react to the world. Agrarian studies could benefit from more use of these latter lenses. On the other hand, agrarian studies can lend practical, place-based concreteness to intersectionality studies, which have been dominated by theoretical discussions of the concept more than the pragmatics of how to apply it. The five lenses proposed here can also as easily be applied to powerful actors as to the marginalized. Both fields—agrarian studies and intersectionality—would benefit from increased attention to the more powerful clusters of identities, in attempts to find the leverage points mentioned above.

FURTHER READING

Colfer, C.J.P.; Sijapati Basnett, B.; Ihalainen, M. (2018), Making sense of 'intersectionality': A manual for lovers of people and forests, *CIFOR Occasional Paper*, 184.

Elmhirst, R. (2011), Migrant pathways to resource access in Lampung's political forest: Gender, citizenship and creative conjugality, *Geoforum*, 42, 173–183.

Hankivsky, O. (2014), *Intersectionality 101*, Vancouver, BC: Institute for Intersectionality Research and Policy, Simon Fraser University.

McCall, L. (2005), The complexity of intersectionality, *Signs: Journal of Women in Culture and Society*, 30(3), 1771–800.

REFERENCES

Bennett, L. (2002), *Dangerous Wives and Sacred Sisters: Social and Symbolic Roles of High-Caste Women in Nepal*, Kathmandu: Mandala Book Point.

Borras, S.M. (2009), Agrarian change and peasant studies: Changes, continuities and challenges – an introduction, *Journal of Peasant Studies*, 36(1), 5–31.

Brubaker, R.; Cooper, F. (2000), Beyond 'identity', *Theory and Society*, 29(1), 1–47.

Cameron, M. (1998), *On the Edge of Auspicious: Gender and Caste in Nepal*, Urbana, IL: University of Illinois Press.

Colfer, C.J.P. (1983), On communication among 'unequals', *International Journal of Intercultural Communication*, 7, 263–283, republished in Colfer, C.J.P.; Elias, M.; Sijapati Basnett, B.; Hummel, S.S. (eds) (2017), *The Earthscan Reader on Gender and Forests*, London: Routledge, 61–79.

Colfer, C.J.P.; Sijapati Basnett, B.; Ihalainen, M. (2018), Making sense of 'intersectionality': A manual for lovers of people and forests, *CIFOR Occasional Paper*, 184, 40.

Crenshaw, K. (1989), Demarginalizing the intersection of race and sex: A black feminist critique of anti-discrimination doctrine, feminist theory and antiracist politics, *University of Chicago Legal Forum*, 139.

Crenshaw, K. (1991), Mapping the margins: Intersectionality, identity politics, and violence against women of color, *Stanford Law Review*, 43(6), 1241–1299.

Elmhirst, R. (2011), Migrant pathways to resource access in Lampung's political forest: Gender, citizenship and creative conjugality, *Geoforum*, 42, 173–183.

Federici, S. (2012), *Revolution at Point Zero: Housework, Reproduction, and Feminist Struggle*, Oakland, CA: PM Press.

Flexner, E. (1975), *Century of Struggle: The Women's Rights Movement in the United States*, Cambridge, MA: Belknap Press of Harvard University Press.

Hancock, A.M. (2007), Intersectionality as a normative and empirical paradigm, *Politics and Gender*, 3(2), 248–254.

Hankivsky, O. (2014), *Intersectionality 101*, Vancouver, BC: Institute for Intersectionality Research and Policy, Simon Fraser University.

Jackson, C. (2002), Gender analysis of land: Beyond land rights for women?, *Journal of Agrarian Change*, 3(4), 453–480.

Kabeer, N. (2018), Locked out and left behind? Gender, intersecting inequalities and the SDGs, Public Lecture, KIT Royal Tropical Institute and UN Women, accessed 8 November 2018 at www.kit.nl/naila-kabeer-public-lecture-locked-out-and-left-behind-gender-intersecting-inequalities-and-the-sdgs/.

Li, T.M. (2015), Social impacts of oil palm in Indonesia: A gendered perspective from West Kalimantan, *CIFOR Occasional Paper*, 124, 51.

McCall, L. (2005), The complexity of intersectionality, *Signs: Journal of Women in Culture and Society*, 30(3), 1771–1800.

Mohanty, C.T. (1988), Under Western eyes: Feminist scholarship and colonial discourses, *Feminist Review*, 30, 51–80.

Moore, H.L. (1988), *Feminism and Anthropology*, Cambridge, MA: Polity Press.

Nash, J.C. (2008), Rethinking intersectionality, *Feminist Review*, 89, 1–15.

Rao, N. (2017), Assets, agency and legitimacy: Towards a relational understanding of gender equality policy and practice, *World Development*, 95, 43–54.

Sen, A. (1999), *Development as Freedom*, New York: Random House.

Sijapati Basnett, B. (2018), UN Women's evaluation of gender in the SDGs: What's the role for the CGIAR?, *CIFOR Info Brief*, 229.

Sijapati Basnett, B.; Elias, M.; Hummel, S.S.; Colfer, C.J.P. (2017), Concluding reflections for the future, in Colfer, C.; Elias, M.; Sijapati Basnett, B.; Hummel, S.S. (eds), *The Earthscan Reader on Gender and Forests*, London: Routledge.

Thapa, D.; Bennett, L.; Sijapati Basnett, B. (2013), *Gender and Social Exclusion in Nepal Update*, Kathmandu: Social Science Baha.

Walby, S.; Armstrong, J.; Strid, S. (2012), Intersectionality: Multiple inequalities in social theory, *Sociology*, 46(2), 224–240.

Wieringa, S.E. (2015), *Heteronormativity, Passionate Aesthetics and Symbolic Subversion in Asia*, Brighton: Sussex Academic Press.

Yuval-Davis, N. (2006), Intersectionality and feminist politics, *European Journal of Women's Studies*, 13(3), 193–209.

19. Merchant and usurer's capital

John Harriss

The role that the likes of millers, merchants and petty traders, transporters and money-lenders play in agrarian political economy is widely acknowledged, yet relatively little analysed. The roles that some of them play as 'middlemen' have commonly been regarded as unproductive, exploitative and at least partially responsible for the reproduction of the poverty of many rural producers, and for the underdevelopment of rural economies. This has been the claim, for example, of both colonial and post-colonial governments in India, where there have been attempts to eliminate private trade in foodgrains. Significant concepts for the analysis of these roles come from Marx's analysis of capitalism: those of merchant and usurer's capital (the old name for interest-bearing capital), described by Marx as 'twin brothers'. Both belong, he says, 'to the antediluvian forms of capital, which long preceded the capitalist mode of production and are to be found in the most diverse economic formations of society'. He goes on: 'the development of usurer's capital is bound up with the development of merchant capital and especially that of money-dealing capital' (Marx 1967 [1894], 593), the latter being what he elsewhere refers to as a sub-division of merchant's or trading capital, alongside commercial capital (Marx 1967 [1894], 267). This chapter focuses on merchant capital, recognizing its close links conceptually, and in practice, with usurer's capital, as discussed in particular in *Capital* (Vol. III, chapter 36). Following a brief exposition of Marx's arguments, and of those of contemporary commentators upon them, the chapter reviews research findings on the role of merchant capital in agrarian economies. The control of agricultural production by commercial capital can have positive implications for productivity, but it is often responsible for 'paralysing the productive forces', as Marx put it (1967 [1894], 596), and for the reproduction of rural deprivation.

MARX'S ARGUMENTS

The category of merchant capital was actually rather peripheral in Marx's analysis, focused as this was on the dynamics of industrial capitalism. It is discussed especially in Volume III (chapters 16–20) of *Capital*. There, Marx is quite clear that the function of merchant capital is the buying and selling of commodities. It does nothing to change the physical character of these commodities and so it does not alter their use value. It is, in other words, unproductive, though it has a necessary role, nonetheless, in facilitating the circulation of industrial capital because producers do not have to find the consumers for their products. Merchant capital is significant, therefore, essentially as an agent of industrial capital, and is 'always confined to the sphere of circulation of capital' (Marx 1967 [1894], 274). Marx clearly recognized that actually existing commercial capital might well be involved in other activities, such as transport, processing, storage and the final distribution of commodities, but his theoretical definition abstracted from these 'real functions'. For him, too, the role of merchant capital in the development of capitalism is ambivalent. It may be conducive to the development of industrial capital, because of stimulating the production of exchange values and having a 'dissolving influence on the producing organization which it finds at hand ... whose different forms are mainly carried on with a view to use value' (Marx 1967 [1894], 331–332); and it may also enable the formation and concentration of large amounts of money-capital that can be invested in production. On the other hand its influence may be regressive, because of depending upon and conserving pre-capitalist labour processes: this form of capital 'does not directly subordinate labour to itself, and does not, therefore, confront it as industrial capital ... [it] ... impoverishes the mode of production [and] paralyses the productive forces instead of developing them' (Marx 1967 [1894], 595–596). Thus Marx also says that 'The independent development of merchant's capital is inversely proportional to the degree of development of capitalist production' (Marx 1967 [1894], 328).

In the views of scholars who have devoted themselves to the study of the historical role of merchant capital, Marx's formulations mix the complexity (or 'impurities') of history with his theoretical conceptualization in a way that ultimately obscures substantive analysis. Jairus Banaji goes so far as to say that Marx's thinking on the subject was 'inchoate' (n.d., 5). Barbara Harriss-White argues emphatically that 'the actually existing counterpart to merchant capital – commercial capital – needs reformulating, not as an autonomous independent entity floating above production relations and about to be subordinated to industrial capital, but as deeply rooted in productive activity' (Harriss-White 2018, 366). Banaji, on the basis of an extensive review of the historiography of early capitalism, together with a critical analysis of thinking about it among Marxist scholars, aims to 'reinstate a notion of merchant capitalism as a perfectly valid category consistent with Marx's own ideas about capital' (Banaji n.d., 1). Harriss-White has long insisted that trading activity is both necessary and usually involved in productive activities – in practice trade cannot take place without the productive activities of processing, transport and storage. They are inherently interconnected, as Marx acknowledges in *Capital*, Volume II. Beyond this, both she and Banaji emphasize that there can be and there has been *direct control of production by commercial capital*. Marx himself said this, 'in a passing reference to the Dutch East India Company' (Marx 1967 [1894], 329). He also 'allowed for the merchant's domination of craft-labour in the putting out system', while subsequent scholarship has shown that he underestimated 'the degree to which merchants controlled work organisation in [the particular example of] the silk industry of Lyons' (Banaji n.d., 3, 5).

HOW MERCHANT CAPITAL MAY CONSTRAIN THE DEVELOPMENT OF CAPITALISM IN AGRICULTURE

A seminal analysis of the role of the 'antediluvian forms of capital' in the agrarian economy is found in Banaji's earlier study of the peasantry of the Deccan region of western India in the later nineteenth century. He shows how:

> monied capitalists ... came to establish control over (the) reproduction process (of household farms) from one cycle to the next. Elements of the production process would be advanced to the peasant either in money form or directly in material form and the peasant would then surrender the whole of his crop by way of interest payments. (1977, 1387)

Here, although the labour process remains the sphere of the household producer and is thus 'pre-' or 'non-capitalist', the process is nonetheless controlled by the capitalist. Banaji argues that in this case the relations of production are capitalist and that capital extracts surplus value even though the labour process itself remains external to capital and is only 'formally' subsumed. It is on these grounds that Banaji, like Henry Bernstein in his classic 'Notes on capital and peasantry' (1977), argues that so-called 'peasants' may often be considered to be 'disguised proletarians', occupying the structural position of wage labour. However, as Harriss-White, citing Shapan Adnan, argues, so long as the 'labourer' owns assets, 'takes decisions about production, and is accountable for the outcome ... the activity ... must be recognised as petty commodity production' (2018, 61). Indeed, Banaji described the domination of the monied capitalist, based 'on control of *only portions* of the means of subsistence and production of the small producer' as '"a pre-formal" subordination of labour' (1977, 1376, emphasis in original). The point is that commercial capital exercises somewhat varying degrees of control over small-scale commodity production.

This analysis explains how capitalism may often have developed in agrarian economies, and it illuminates much more recent history. In many parts of the world the introduction of modern varieties of the major cereals – what came to be called the 'green revolution' – took off from the later 1960s. The cultivation of these varieties generally required the purchase by cultivators of a whole package of inputs, including chemical fertilizers and pesticides, as well as seeds, and very often machinery for the pumping of irrigation water. This 'new technology' tended, therefore, to intensify the process of commoditization in rural economies, deepening the importance of commodity relations within the reproductive cycle of households. If, with the older technology employed in agriculture, the cycle of reproduction might be almost entirely internal to the household unit of production, this was no longer the case, as cultivators became increasingly dependent upon purchased inputs and so upon commodity production. In this context it seemed altogether likely – and a good deal of empirical evidence supported the point – that somewhat larger and more credit-worthy cultivators would be at an advantage, and that these advantages would be cumulative (a classic source on this is Pearse 1980). Thus it was thought that the green revolution would bring about or would carry much further the process of differentiation among rural producers. It would stimulate the development of capitalism *in* agriculture and bring about, increasingly, polarization between capital and labour in the countryside.

In practice this very often did not happen. In India, for example, the new agricultural technology was introduced into a rural society already characterized by high levels of social inequality, reflecting long-standing inequalities in access to land and a long history of commodity production, some of it the consequence of 'forced commercialisation', as even very small cultivators found themselves compelled to market produce to satisfy the revenue demands of the colonial government. In such circumstances very many small peasants came to depend – exactly as Banaji showed in his study of the Deccan – upon advances from merchants and money-lenders, often the same people, and sometimes also the owners of land that they rented. The poverty and dependency of the mass of poor cultivators thus underpinned, as well as being sustained by, the dominance of 'usurious, speculative and mercantile forms of capital' in the rural economy, and the lack of any incentive to engage in productive investment (Bharadwaj 1985, 15).

These sorts of relationships obtained, as well, in the context of the green revolution in India. As small producers attempted to take advantage of the 'higher-yielding varieties' so they became more 'compulsively involved' in production for the market – seemingly engaged, that is, in free exchange, but in practice compelled to sell their product even in the absence of a real surplus over consumption needs (Bharadwaj 1974). Very many of these small, marginalized, dependent household producers, who constitute the great mass of rural households in most of India, were able, however, to reproduce themselves because of their relationships with merchant-usurers' capital. In studies of the agrarian economy of a part of south India in the 1970s it was found that the new technology had consolidated the more backward forms of capitalist domination by intensifying the dependence on the market of the many farmers who depended on consumption loans and loans of working capital advanced by traders. At the same time,

> large numbers of small traders … are able to maintain themselves from trade and to compete with each other and big traders … (partly by) … lending out money to farmers at rather low interest rates. Thus the marginal trader allows the marginal farmer to reproduce himself and survive. (Harriss 1979, 51–52)

It was found, therefore, that in this case, 'the intensification of capital *in* agricultural production is constrained by the development of merchant, moneylending capital … secured by the persistence of small-scale production and small trading' (Harriss 1982, 85, emphasis added).

PATTERNS IN THE DOMINANCE OF AGRICULTURE BY COMMERCIAL CAPITAL

This process of reproduction of small-scale agricultural production is an instance of the first of the several ways that Banaji distinguishes whereby 'commercial and industrial capitals penetrate, control and/or reshape the countryside' (2016, 419):

1. commercial capitalism of the produce trades;
2. contract farming;
3. stronger forms of vertical integration;
4. industrialized agriculture.

The last two of these are firmly in the realm of industrial capital. In contract farming, too, though production remains in the hands of household farmers, there is intensive management by capital. Still, it is an instance, with the first of these modes of penetration, of those forms of capitalist domination defined by Chayanov as involving a 'purely economic' domination of capital over agriculture. This makes for what he described as 'vertical capitalist concentration', involving the coordination and supervision of the production (in varying degrees) of many individual small producers. This is a point also emphasized by Bernstein, who writes:

> The classic model of capitalist development in agriculture incorporates the expropriation of the peasantry and the *horizontal concentration* of means of production … in units of production equivalent to industrial enterprises in their organisation of production and modes of economic calculation. [But there is also the possibility of '*vertical concentration*' of the producers] … through a central agency, whether this represents productive capital directly (as in outgrower arrangements), forms of merchant's capital which thereby actively intervene in the organization of production, or whether the agency is that of a cooperative or other state managed scheme. (Bernstein 1977, cited in Harriss 1982, 173)

Bernstein goes on to refer to parts of Lenin's *The Development of Capitalism in Russia* and, somewhat ironically given that he is so often identified as the leading theorist of the reproduction of peasant agriculture, to parts also of Chayanov's work on *Peasant Farm Organisation*. Both draw attention to vertical concentration: it may be 'more profitable for productive capital to invest in processing and manufacturing enterprises consuming commodities produced by peasants (production it could find ways of regulating) rather than undertaking production of those commodities itself' (Bernstein 1977, cited in Harriss 1982, 174).

The essential point, says Banaji, speaking of 'commercial capitalism of the produce trades', is 'that capital deals with *household* producers whose aggregate labour power is exploited through price domination'. Three key elements are involved: '(1) households with *some* degree of control of their own means of production; (2) a system of advances (usually in cash, otherwise trade goods); and (3) lead-company reliance on middlemen' (Banaji n.d., 13). He gives a long list of examples of what he is referring to, from West Africa, India, Burma, Indochina and China (Banaji 2016, figure 1). These involved commodity chains with larger commercial capitals at their apex, such as the big merchant firms, like the United Africa Company, that came to dominate West African trade in the twentieth century. However, they were heavily dependent on local dealers – brokers and contractors – in complex systems of advances. Such economic domination of agriculture by commercial capital may involve, exactly as Bernstein puts it, greater or lesser degrees of supervision of the production of small producers – rather little in the south Indian case referred to earlier, but much more where lead companies like those referred to by Banaji are concerned. This domination may have very positive implications for productivity, or in some instances have consequences that correspond with the Marxian characterization of merchant capital as 'antediluvian', with its implications of backwardness, as in the case of the small producers referred to earlier, who are 'compulsively involved' in markets. Commercial capital may also, through the social relations of the marketing system, be very largely responsible for the persistence of rural deprivation, even in circumstances of high rates of agricultural growth, as happened in West Bengal in the later twentieth century (Harriss-White 2013).

Historically, therefore, and in modern agrarian economies, the 'actually existing counterpart to merchant capital – commercial capital' may indeed be 'deeply rooted in productive activity' (Harriss-White, 2018, 366); and it plays a particularly powerful role in agrarian political economy.

FURTHER READING

Banaji, J. (2016), Merchant capitalism, peasant households and industrial accumulation: Integration of a model, *Journal of Agrarian Change*, 16(3), 410–431.

Banaji, J. (n.d.), Marxism and merchant capitalism, in Farris, S.; Toscano, A. (eds), *The Handbook of Marxism*, accessed 21 May 2020 at www.academia.edu/30754308/Marxism_and_Merchant _Capitalism.

Bernstein, H. (1977), 'Notes on capital and peasantry', in Harriss, J. (ed.) (1982), *Rural Development: Theories of Peasant Economy and Agrarian Change*, London: Hutchinson, 160–177.

Harriss, J. (1982), *Capitalism and Peasant Farming*, Bombay: Oxford University Press.

Harriss-White, B. (2018), Awkward classes and India's development, *Review of Political Economy*, 30(3), 355–376.

Marx, K. (1967 [1894]), *Capital: A Critique of Political Economy, Volume III: The Process of Capitalist Production as a Whole*, New York: International Publishers.

REFERENCES

Banaji, J. (1977), Capitalist domination and the small peasantry: Deccan districts in the late nineteenth century, *Economic and Political Weekly*, 12(33–34), 1375–1404.

Banaji, J. (2016), Merchant capitalism, peasant households and industrial accumulation: Integration of a model, *Journal of Agrarian Change*, 16(3), 410–431.

Banaji, J. (n.d.), Marxism and merchant capitalism, in Farris, S.; Toscano, A. (eds), *The Handbook of Marxism*, accessed 21 May 2020 at www.academia.edu/30754308/Marxism_and_Merchant _Capitalism.

Bernstein, H. (1977), 'Notes on capital and peasantry', in Harriss, J. (ed.) (1982), *Rural Development: Theories of Peasant Economy and Agrarian Change*, London: Hutchinson, 160–177.

Bharadwaj, K. (1974), *Production Conditions in Indian Agriculture*, Cambridge: Cambridge University Press.

Bharadwaj, K. (1985), A view on commercialisation in Indian agriculture and the development of capitalism, *Journal of Peasant Studies*, 12(4), 8–24.

Harriss, B. (1979), The role of agro-commercial capital in 'rural development' in south India, *Social Scientist*, 7(7), 42–56.

Harriss, J. (1982), *Capitalism and Peasant Farming*, Bombay: Oxford University Press.

Harriss-White, B. (2013), West Bengal's rural commercial capital, *International Critical Thought*, 3(1), 20–42.

Harriss-White, B. (2018), Awkward classes and India's development, *Review of Political Economy*, 30(3), 355–376.

Marx, K. (1967 [1894]), *Capital: A Critique of Political Economy, Volume III: The Process of Capitalist Production as a Whole*, New York: International Publishers.

Pearse, A. (1980), *Seeds of Plenty, Seeds of Want: Social and Economic Implications of the Green Revolution*, Oxford: Oxford University Press.

20. Agricultural markets

Muhammad Ali Jan and Barbara Harriss-White

Markets lie at the heart of Marxist theory and historiography (Banaji 2020). It is widely accepted that capitalism is fundamentally about the commodification of production and social reproduction, and thus about the spread of market relations, even if markets are not synonymous with capital (Kocka 2016, 21). It is also recognized that the most stubborn resistance to the logic of capital is found in the countryside, where natural and social barriers to its penetration exist (e.g. Mann and Dickinson 1978). So the manner in which capitalist social relations spread to the countryside is considered a barometer for their 'ultimate dominance within a national social formation' (Byres 2003, 55). A long-established body of literature in agrarian political economy has dealt with the complex patterns of rural differentiation and the multiple paths through which capitalist social relations develop in the countryside (Bernstein 2009a; Bernstein and Byres 2001; Byres 1991). However, the significance of the commodification of rural societies transcends this specialist literature: indeed, in many respects the great controversies of the past century among Marxists (and between Marxists and non-Marxists) have in one way or another concerned the relationship between commodification, capitalist social relations and their spread in agrarian societies. This makes these controversies of central importance within critical agrarian studies. Examples include the Russian differentiation debate of the early twentieth century, the transition and World Systems debates of the 1950s, 1970s and 1980s, as well as the post-Green Revolution mode of production debate in India.[1]

If the commodification of the countryside is central to the dominance of capital within a social formation then agricultural commodity markets mediate it. Not only do markets provide price signals to rural producers allowing them to make allocative decisions, but they are also arenas for the exploitation of petty producers and labour and therefore also become sites where the struggles between different classes are fought (Jan and Harriss-White 2012, 39). Markets also act as conduits for the intersectoral flow of resources between agriculture, industry and services (ibid.), playing a central role in rural class formation and technological transformation. They have poignantly been described as the 'midwives of agricultural change' (Harriss 1990, 91). However, despite their importance, agricultural markets remain strangely neglected by scholars and are either ignored altogether or entirely subsumed to production relations.

Against the tendency of taking markets for granted, we argue for casting our analytical gaze upon their inner workings – the means, mechanisms and processes through which systems of provision are generated – in concrete settings. Moreover, while acknowledging the critical Marxist scholarship on merchant capital that has dominated the literature in this terrain, we believe that the focus needs to be broadened from simply observing capital to conceptualizing markets as complex, adaptive systems that exhibit great organizational and institutional diversity: where a number of different capitalist and non-capitalist forms co-exist; where the agency of many individual actors exists alongside the structural constraints of economic concentration; and where conflicts and struggles are precipitated not simply between capital and labour but between a wider array of class and non-class actors (Hodgson 2001, 365).

In our contribution to this volume, we aim to introduce readers to the orthodox Marxist literature on merchant capital and the reified view of markets it engenders; the critical Marxist scholarship that has attempted to salvage the concept from its trappings in orthodoxy but also its limitations and a plea for moving away from merchant capital and supply chains to the scholarship on 'real' markets by historians, anthropologists, economists and other social scientists – both Marxist and non-Marxist. We believe this chimes well with the agenda of critical agrarian studies to broaden the scope of classical 'agrarian questions' and open up pluralist lines of inquiry into the 'political and cultural economy of accumulation' and the diverse links between 'countryside and city, social classes, regions and economic sectors' (Edelman and Wolford 2017, 966).

We begin with the orthodox Marxist conception of 'merchant capital' that has been employed as a substitute for the concrete study of commodity markets. The origin of the orthodoxy is attributable to Marx himself and the ambiguous manner in which he treated the concept. Marx recognized the 'heterogeneous functions' that merchants performed before the advent of industrial capital (productive functions such as transport and unproductive ones such as buying and selling) (Marx 1981 [1894], 395). Marx argued that merchants exerted control over production. In Volume III of *Capital*, he argues that one possible transition from feudalism to capitalism sees the 'merchant taking direct control of production himself' (ibid., 452), referring to the putting-out system, and in the *Grundrisse*, he describes the subsumption of hitherto independent weavers and spinners to the control of the merchant who transforms the property of the former into 'sham property' and reduces them to the status of wage labourers (Marx 1973 [1939–1941], 510).

Other than such scattered observations, however, the thrust of Marx's argument is that merchant capital is not really part of capitalism proper and unable to transform what he terms the 'old mode of production' (Marx 1981 [1894], 452). Merchant capital is an 'antediluvian' form to be suppressed by industrial capital. The former's insubordination to the latter – that is, its independent power – is inversely linked to the general economic development of society (ibid., 445). Merchant capital was at best residual, unconnected to production, and at its worst an active constraint on it. This view of merchant capital gained currency within orthodox Marxist scholarship.

For example, in the 'semi-feudal' literature developed to study rural underdevelopment in India (Bhaduri 1983; Chattopadhyay 1969; Prasad 1974), landlord-trader-cum-moneylenders use 'interlinked contracts' to 'force' peasants into commerce. This results in a siphoning of surplus without productive reinvestment, perpetuating 'agricultural backwardness' in the process. Geoffrey Kay's iconic contribution has argued that merchant capital was a drain from the sphere of production and therefore the principal reason for the third world's underdevelopment (Kay 1975). The unhelpful binary between production and exchange in these orthodox formulations left very little room for realistically conceptualizing processes of agricultural commercialization.

In the 1970s scholars began to question the orthodox conception of merchant capital and its multiple assumptions (e.g. Banaji 1977; Bernstein 1977; Cowen 1981; Roseberry 1983). Against the orthodoxy, critical Marxist scholars emphasized the key role played by merchant capital – both historically and in the contemporary period – in integrating peasant producers within global capitalist circuits. They emphasized the productive character of merchant capital, be it in the form of produce-tying money advances, investments in storage, transport and processing and even direct cultivation. In doing so, they revealed an alternative path to the development of capitalism in agriculture; one where commercial capital takes hold of peasant households, subsumes them to the logic of the market, but does not separate nor differentiate them into classes, as assumed in the Leninist schema (Byres 2003). Instead peasants are transformed into petty commodity producers (PCP) whose 'aggregate labour-power is exploited through price domination' (Banaji 2020).

These scholars showed how merchant capital could exploit PCP even as the latter still retained formal control over some assets and their own family-labour. This was achieved by merchants' gaining strategic command over markets other than labour (i.e. credit, commodities and inputs) in which PCP households reproduced themselves, setting the terms on which PCP participated in markets and profiting from their adverse inclusion (Bernstein 1977). Rejecting the orthodox view that merchant capital and petty producers represented 'survivals' from prior modes of production, they argued that both were thoroughly integrated within contemporary capitalism and constantly reproduced through its circuits (Harriss-White 2012). Merchant capital was rehabilitated from the pre-history of capitalism, as Marx sometimes characterized it, to a category belonging squarely *within* historical and contemporary capitalist societies.

Having said that, these scholarly advances did not extend to a dynamic analysis of accumulation processes. Focusing simply on transactions between cultivators and merchant capital, the wider environment in which they were embedded was ignored. However, the commodification of agriculture seldom takes the simple form of a dyadic relationship, where peasant producers directly confront capital. Instead, the relationship is 'layered' with a range of intermediaries varying in size, function and economic strength, and which is also shaped by the physical and cultural character of the commodity being traded (Thorbecke 1992, 4). All these factors affect the terms on which cultivators are integrated into commercial circuits, the division of surplus value between different players and the trajectory of agrarian change itself (Crow 2001). Thus, a truly materialist theory of merchant capital must include an account of the wider markets in which producers and traders operate.

An important recent attempt at such a formulation has come from Jairus Banaji who argues that household producers in various parts of the nineteenth- and early twentieth-century colonial world were incorporated into networks of 'loose', distended but hierarchically organized 'commodity chains', with large colonial trading houses at the top and various layers of intermediaries underneath (Banaji 2016, 415; 2020). These chains – from sugar, opium and rice in parts of India to groundnuts in West Africa and tea in China – should be viewed as 'combined accumulations of capital' at all levels of the hierarchy. Here Banaji recognizes that markets were more 'involved, complex and full of tensions' than previous theorizations of merchant capital in the critical Marxist framework had recognized and emphasizes the role of 'middle-men' capitalists as intermediaries.

However, in using the commodity chain framework to understand the colonial trading system, Banaji's intervention suffers crucial limitations. The 'supply-chain' literature exhibits an 'absolute, essentialized and over-coordinated understanding' of global markets, without considering the 'often precarious and contested nature of these connections across geographical, material, social and institutional differences and the practical work that sustains them' (Ouma 2015, 7). Scant attention has been paid to what such 'chains' look like 'from below' or even 'within' and, equally importantly, how they are transformed (Bair and Werner 2011).

Moreover, the strategies through which smaller capitals come to entrench themselves in such markets, the manner in which trust is established in the absence of well-developed formal institutions and the organizational differences between colonial and local capitalists are also ignored in this formulation. A framework is needed through which the historical construction of markets in which merchants operated, the range of actors inhabiting them, the relations between them and the conflicts and contradictions arising from such interrelationships can be explored.

This can be developed by creatively combining critical Marxist scholarship on merchant capital with the work of anthropologists, economists and historians who have studied markets as complex, adaptive systems (Braudel 1983; Krishnamurthy 2015; Thorbecke 1992). To date, the framework of agricultural markets as complex systems in critical agrarian studies has been developed and used most extensively in the work of Barbara Harriss-White. Conceptualizing agricultural markets as complex systems helps to understand the processes of accumulation in agriculture in a deeper way than an exclusive focus on merchant capital. Empirical work on real markets has revealed that they consist of many *elements* – firms, farms and a range of other actors – that are internally diverse but interrelated to one another as a whole and not simply as sums of their parts (Garcia 1979, 25). The interrelated elements of a dynamic agricultural marketing system are linked through *flows* of money, commodities and credit, and the elements of real marketing systems exhibit a remarkable ability to configure their component parts in a large number of ways, being complex. Agricultural markets contain an immense diversity of firms according to their function in the system (e.g. broker, processor, cultivator), the sites from which they operate (e.g. peripatetic trader-moneylender, urban trader), technologies (e.g. manual, mechanized) and organizational forms (e.g. family firms, partnerships, corporate capital).

This institutional and technological diversity tends to co-exist and persist rather than converge toward a prototype (Harriss-White 2008, 2016). Furthermore, the same firm or farm can engage in multiple activities, operate from multiple sites and employ multiple technologies, meaning that merchants rarely exist in pure form as mere 'buyers and sellers'. Diverse portfolios do not however result in these markets being egalitarian: on the contrary, markets are internally differentiated in terms of scale and economic power. In fact, a striking feature of agricultural markets is the simultaneous existence of micro-level decentralization, alongside structural concentration of assets and the capacity to appropriate and accumulate resources through various strategies (Barrett 1997).

This means that markets become arenas for socio-economic enrichment, for economic and social competition and for conflict; price-making processes are not simply outcomes of supply and demand but the result of contestation between the interests of capital, labour, PCPs as well as the state. A system of markets is thus at one and the same time a set of prices sending allocative signals to producers and consumers, and a mechanism for the extraction and distribution of resources. This broadens our understanding of exploitation and accumulation by demonstrating how value is being extracted not merely from 'labour' at the point of production but from petty producers, traders, small firms and so on at various points in a web of exchange and rivalry relations (Fourie 1991, 41). Moreover, these processes of accumulation provoke struggles not merely between opposing social classes but also between different factions of the same class (e.g. capitalist farmers and commercial capitalists or corporate and family-owned capital) while being permeated with power relations based on intersectional axes of differentiation beyond class like race, ethnicity and gender (Evers 1994).

Complex agricultural market systems can change in response to 'environmental' stimuli and also develop adaptively. *Relations and flows* between elements take the form not only of commodities (transported, stored, processed – with by-products subject to the same constraints), but also of money, information (especially about prices and contacts) and energy (human, animal, renewable and fossil). Some flows (though not all) are means of appropriating surplus value from petty producers to merchant capitalists by undervaluing the marketed surplus, thereby highlighting the exploitative aspect of marketing systems (Jan and Harriss-White 2012). Environmental stimuli can include both natural and human-made interventions (e.g. episodes of drought and changes in policy, respectively). Mapping these is essential for gaining an understanding of the dynamics of the market system.

Furthermore, despite their dynamism, these systems nonetheless demonstrate recognizable, stable patterns in their configurations while reproducing themselves in a non-equilibrium manner (Foley 2003, 1–2). In agricultural markets both formal and informal institutions regulate transactions and provide order within the system. Formal institutions (market yards and committees) are regulated directly by the state but in large swathes of the agricultural economy in developing countries the state cedes to other 'informal' regulative authority. Agricultural markets are both segmented and ordered by institutions which range from registered business associations and lobbies to social/'cultural' institutions such as kinship, patriarchy, ethnic solidarity, caste and religious authority and the multifarious practices of locality (Harriss-White 2003, 2008).

Finally, markets are also shaped by the nature of the commodity itself; for example, its physical perishability and division into by-products; its character as a staple or cash crop, a raw material requiring processing or a consumption good; and its cultural significance. Taken together, these factors help determine the kind of 'exchange configurations' that will emerge for a particular commodity in a particular society, time and place (Barrett 1997; Thorbecke 1992).

The plea for a study of concrete processes of commodification in particular settings outlined in this chapter is congruous with the broader vision of critical agrarian studies to widen the lens through which classic agrarian questions are viewed. If the aim is to uncover the manifold ways in which urban and rural societies mutually constitute one another, so that we may escape dualistic paradigms of modernization theory (Edelman and Wolford 2017, 966) – paradigms which many strands of Marxism have also been guilty of reproducing – then agricultural markets are a crucial conduit through which such concrete interconnections are forged. In an era where neoliberal ideology encourages us to accept markets as natural, global and inevitable, turning our scholarly attention to the highly contingent, diverse and contested processes through which actual agricultural markets develop allows us to challenge the hegemony of neoliberal capitalism and imagine pathways out of its destructive grip.

NOTE

1.   Bernstein (2009b) and Shanin (1972) for the Russian debate; Tomich (1997) for the transition debate; and Thorner (1982) for a review of the Indian mode of production debate.

FURTHER READING

Bharadwaj, K. (1985), A view on commercialisation in Indian agriculture and the development of capitalism, *Journal of Peasant Studies*, 12(4), 7–25.

Caliskan, C. (2010), *Market Threads: How Cotton Farmers and Traders Create a Global Commodity*, Princeton, NJ: Princeton University Press.
Clough, P. (2014), *Morality and Economic Growth in Rural West Africa: Indigenous Accumulation in Rural Hausaland*, Oxford: Berghahn Books.
Guyer, J. (1997), *An African Niche Economy: Farming to Feed Ibadan 1968–88*, Edinburgh: Edinburgh University Press.
Tsing, A. (2015), *The Mushroom at the End of the World: On the Possibility of Life in Capitalist Ruins*, Princeton, NJ: Princeton University Press.

REFERENCES

Bair, J. and Werner, M. (2011), Commodity chains and the uneven geographies of global capitalism: A disarticulations perspective, *Environment and Planning A*, 43(5), 988–997.
Banaji, J. (1977), Capitalist domination and the small peasantry: Deccan districts in the late nineteenth century, *Economic and Political Weekly*, 12(33/34), 1375–1404.
Banaji, J. (2016), Merchant capitalism, peasant households and industrial accumulation: Integration of a model, *Journal of Agrarian Change*, 16(3), 410–431.
Banaji, J. (2020), *A Brief History of Commercial Capitalism*, Chicago, IL: Haymarket.
Barrett, C.B. (1997), Food marketing liberalization and trader entry: Evidence from Madagascar, *World Development*, 25(5), 763–777.
Bernstein, H. (1977), Notes on capital and the peasantry, *Review of African Political Economy*, 10(2), 60–73.
Bernstein, H. (2009a), Agrarian questions from transition to globalization, in Akram-Lodhi, A.H.; Kay, C. (eds), *Peasants and Globalization: Political Economy, Rural Transformation and the Agrarian Question*, Abingdon: Routledge, 239–261.
Bernstein, H. (2009b), V.I. Lenin and A.V. Chayanov: Looking back, looking forward, *Journal of Peasant Studies*, 36(1), 55–81.
Bernstein, H.; Byres, T.J. (2001), From peasant studies to agrarian change, *Journal of Agrarian Change*, 1(1), 1–56.
Bhaduri, A. (1983), *The Economic Structure of Backward Agriculture*, London: Academic Press.
Braudel, F. (1983), *The Wheels of Commerce: Civilization and Capitalism, 15th–18th Century*, Berkeley, CA: University of California Press.
Byres, T.J. (1991), The agrarian question and differing forms of capitalist transition: An essay with reference to Asia, in Breman, J.; Mundle, S. (eds), *Rural Transformation in Asia*, Oxford: Oxford University Press, 3–76.
Byres, T.J. (2003), Paths of capitalist agrarian transition in the past and in the contemporary world, in Ramachandran, V.K.; Swaminathan, M. (eds), *Agrarian Studies: Essays on Agrarian Relations in Less Developed Countries*, London: Zed Books, 54–83.
Chattopadhyay, B. (1969), Marx and India's crisis, in Joshi, P.C. (ed.), *Homage to Karl Marx*, Delhi: People's Publishing House, 205–260.
Cowen, M. (1981), Commodity production in Kenya's Central Province, in Heyer, J.; Roberts, P.; Williams, G. (eds), *Rural Development in Tropical Africa*, London: Macmillan, 121–142.
Crow, B. (2001), *Markets, Class and Social Change: Trading Networks and Poverty in Rural South Asia*, London: Palgrave.
Edelman, M.; Wolford, W. (2017), Introduction: Critical agrarian studies in theory and practice, *Antipode*, 49(4), 959–976.
Evers, H.-D. (1994), The trader's dilemma: A theory of the social transformation of markets and society, in Evers, H.-D.; Schrader, H. (eds), *The Moral Economy of Trade: Ethnicity and Developing Markets*, London: Routledge, 1–10.
Foley, D.K. (2003), *Unholy Trinity Labor, Capital, and Land in the New Economy*, New York: Routledge.
Fourie, F. (1991), A structural analysis of markets, in Hodgson, G. (ed.), *Rethinking Economics*, Cambridge, Cambridge University Press.

Garcia, R. (1979), *Food Systems and Society: A Conceptual and Methodological Challenge*, Geneva: United Nations Research Institute for Social Development.

Harriss, B. (1990), Another awkward class? Merchants and agrarian change in India, in Bernstein, H.; Crow, B.; Mackintosh, M.; Martin, C. (eds), *The Food Question: Profits versus People*, London: Earthscan Publications, 91–103.

Harriss-White, B. (2003), *India Working: Essays on Society and Economy*, Cambridge: Cambridge University Press.

Harriss-White, B. (2008), *Rural Commercial Capital: Agricultural Markets in West Bengal*, New Delhi: Oxford University Press.

Harriss-White, B. (2012), Capitalism and the common man: Peasants and petty production in Africa and South Asia, *Agrarian South: Journal of Political Economy*, 1(2), 109–160.

Harriss-White, B. (2016), From analysing 'filieres vivrieres' to understanding capital and petty production in rural south India, *Journal of Agrarian Change*, 16(3), 478–500.

Hodgson, G. (2001), *How Economics Forgot History: The Problem of Historical Specificity in Social Science*, London: Routledge.

Jan, M.A.; Harriss-White, B. (2012), The three roles of agricultural markets: A review of ideas about agricultural commodity markets in India, *Economic and Political Weekly*, 52(1), 39–52.

Kay, G. (1975), *Development and Underdevelopment: A Marxist Analysis*, London: Macmillan Press.

Kocka, J. (2016), *Capitalism: A Short History*, Princeton, NJ: Princeton University Press.

Krishnamurthy, M. (2015), The political economy of agricultural markets: Insights from within and across Regions, in IDFC (ed.), *India Rural Development Report 2013/14*, New Delhi: Orient Black Swan.

Mann, S.A.; Dickinson, J. (1978), Obstacles to the development of a capitalist agriculture, *Journal of Peasant Studies*, 5(4), 466–481.

Marx, K. (1973 [1939–1941]), *Grundrisse: Foundations of the Critique of Political Economy*, London: Penguin Books.

Marx, K. (1981 [1894]), *Capital: A Critique of Political Economy*, Volume III, London: Penguin Books.

Ouma, S. (2015), *Assembling Export Markets: The Making and Unmaking of Global Food Connections in West Africa*, Chichester: Wiley.

Prasad, P. (1974), Reactionary role of usurer's capital in rural India, *Economic and Political Weekly*, 9(32–34), 1305–1308.

Roseberry, W. (1983), *Coffee and Capitalism in the Venezuelan Andes*, Austin, TX: University of Texas Press.

Shanin, T. (1972), *The Awkward Class: Political Sociology of Peasantry in a Developing Society: Russia 1910–1925*, Oxford: Clarendon Press.

Thorbecke, E. (1992), *The Anatomy of Agricultural Product Markets and Transactions in Developing Countries*, Institute for Policy Reform No. 43, Washington, DC.

Thorner, A. (1982), Semi-feudalism or capitalism? Contemporary debate on classes and modes of production in India, Part I, *Economic and Political Weekly*, 17(49), 1961–1968.

Tomich, D.W. (1997), World of capital/worlds of labor: A global perspective, in Hall, J.R. (ed.), *Reworking Class*, Ithaca, NY: Cornell University Press, 287–312.

21. Financialization

Jennifer Clapp and S. Ryan Isakson

INTRODUCTION

A growing number of critical agrarian scholars are turning their attention to the ways in which "financialization" is affecting the agrifood sector. Understood as a process in which financial actors and financially driven motivations have taken a larger role in society, across all sectors in the economy (see for example Epstein 2005; Krippner 2011), financialization affects the agrifood sector in myriad ways. While links between food, agriculture and finance date back centuries, at least to early commodity exchanges in the 1600s, the process of financialization in the current era has resulted in a subtle, yet profound reconfiguration of the contours, aims and features of the agrifood order.

In this contribution, we advance the argument that if the traditional agrarian question is about whether and how capitalism is reshaping agricultural production and food systems, a contemporary agrarian question must inevitably consider the modern-day form of financialized capitalism as a driving force in shaping food economies. Our assessment of the literature on the rise and manifestation of modern-day financialization in the agrifood sector reveals that it has three important impacts that must be considered. First, financialization has unfolded in ways that exacerbate inequalities across and within different sets of food system actors, as well as across and within different geographical locations. Second, the rise of financial imperatives in the sector drives a number of socio-economic changes that intensify and exacerbate the fragility of the global food system, including the expansion of an industrial agricultural model, which ultimately undermines the food system's socio-ecological resiliency. Third, financialization in the food system has vastly complicated the work of activists and policymakers in both the global North and the global South who advocate for more just and sustainable food systems. Together, these three broad manifestations of financialization are contributing to the erosion of place-based food economies and weakening the ability of food systems to generate meaningful livelihoods and provide sufficient access to just and sustainably provisioned food.

APPROACHES TO UNDERSTANDING FINANCIALIZATION

What exactly does financialization refer to, and why is it relevant to critical agrarian studies? According to Epstein (2005, 3), financialization refers to "the increasing role of financial motives, financial markets, financial actors and financial institutions in the operation of the domestic and international economies." Krippner adds to this definition with the insight that financialization results in "the tendency for profit making in the economy to occur increasingly through financial channels rather than through productive activities" (2011, 4). Implicit to these definitions is an understanding that one can distinguish financial activities (the investment of funds with the expectation that it will result in interest, dividends or capital gains) from the "real," or "productive" economy (where production, trade and distribution of non-financial goods and services takes place). Although there is some debate about how rigid the boundary is between financial activities and the productive economy, scholars have recognized that finance has become more dominant within the economy, able to generate profits through financial transactions, including speculative investments (Epstein 2005). Financial motives, logics and markets have likewise infused the underlying non-financial economy as well as in the democratic societies in which it resides, and thus has importance for our understanding of the agrifood system.

There are different takes on what is behind the rise of finance as a dominant force in the economy, including in the agrifood sector. As Krippner (2011) suggests, there are three types of explanations, each associated with a different school of thought. Mainstream economists see the growing prominence of financial motives driving economic decision making as the product of an alignment between the interests of corporate chief executive officers with those of the firms' financial shareholders. Whereas corporate managers previously were rewarded for reinvesting profits into the firm to spur innovation and expansion of production and sales, shareholders have increasingly demanded a greater share of the profits to be paid out as financial dividends and stock buybacks (Froud et al. 2000; Krippner 2011). For (post-)Keynesian thinkers, the increased influence of financial markets can be explained by weakened regulation that encourages speculative excesses associated with inherently unstable financial markets that are prone to crashes (Palley 2007; Crotty 2009; Krippner 2011).

Marxist scholars, alternatively, portray financialization as a cyclical feature of capitalism (Arrighi 1994; Kotz 2011). For these thinkers, capitalism is prone to periodic crises, such as those that occur due to falling profits in the face of downward pressure that competition puts on prices, as well as crises of "overaccumulation" that result when the productive capacity of firms greatly exceeds effective demand. During the 1970s, for example, international competition combined with the stagnant profits of United States and British manufacturers led many investors to redirect their surplus capital from productive investments to financial speculation. Channeling surplus capital into financial markets, such as government bonds, stock markets, currency trading and housing mortgages, helps to displace or postpone the full effects of economic crisis by transferring overaccumulated capital to less saturated times and/or places, thereby providing a "spatio-temporal fix" to the contradictions of capitalism (Harvey 2003, 87; cf. Arrighi 1994).

Just as there are different explanations of why finance came to such prominence in the economy more generally, there are also different interpretations of the ways in which key features of financialization unfold in society (for a review, see Krippner 2011; and van der Zwan 2014), which is relevant for the agrifood sector. One approach highlights the ways in which financialization has reshaped economies such that capital is primarily accumulated through financial channels (Krippner 2011). A second strand of literature focuses on the so-called "shareholder revolution" of the 1990s, in which managers for firms of all types reoriented the direction of their enterprises such that their top priority is to satisfy their shareholders' demands for dividends (Froud et al. 2000, 2006; Crotty 2009; Baud and Durand 2012). A third approach many scholars have taken to examine financialization is to reflect on the ways in which finance has become infused in everyday life, wherein quotidian practices are increasingly mediated by financial practices and ordinary citizens have come to respond to financial incentives and adopt financial rationalities in their own lives (Aitken 2007; Langley 2008). Although these three literatures emphasize different dimensions of the phenomenon, each conveys the idea that contemporary capitalism is being transformed by the growing role of finance in the economy, and each is important to understanding how financialization is reshaping the food and agriculture sector.

HOW FINANCIALIZATION RESHAPES FOOD AND AGRICULTURE

Why and in what ways does financialization matter for food systems and agrarian societies? Drawing on the broader literature, we illustrate below the ways in which the agrifood sector has become a new arena for financial accumulation, how shareholder value has become prioritized within the sector and how everyday practices of food provisioning have been reshaped by the growing prominence of financial markets, motives and institutions. While the broader literature tends to focus upon how a single dimension manifests in the broader economy, we argue that these different expressions of financialization overlap and reinforce one another in the agrifood sector.

First, financial investors are increasingly treating the agrifood sector as a new arena for profit accumulation while, at the same time, food and agriculture firms have ramped up their use of financial instruments in order to secure their own profits. In order for the agrifood sector to serve as an hospitable site for financial accumulation, the cultural and physical qualities of food, agriculture and farmland must be transformed and recast into financial values that are of interest to investors, and the regulatory environment needs to be shaped in ways that enable those investments. These dynamics of deregulation and reformatting for financial purposes have played out throughout the food sector. The deregulation of agricultural commodity markets after the 1980s, for example, enabled the proliferation of new complex financial investment tools like commodity index funds and other derivative investment products. They also opened the floodgate to a deluge of speculative activities that have been implicated in the 2007–2008 food price crisis and subsequent volatile commodity prices (Ghosh 2010; Worthy 2011). Similarly, financial deregulation facilitated the engineering of new types of investment funds based on financial exposure to farmland and agribusiness companies, which have been especially attractive to large-scale institutional investors. The rush of capital into these funds has been associated with the global land grab and soaring prices for farmland, which further limits land access for poor and small-scale farmers (Fairbairn 2014; Magnan 2015; Desmarais et al. 2017). In yet another example, financial actors and agribusinesses have devised derivatives based on environmental measures like rainfall that they market to agricultural producers as "insurance" and are often promoted in ways that encourage farmers to borrow more funds, adopt commercial seed varieties and further integrate into globalized value chains. Despite encouraging farmers to take on these new risks, the derivatives-cum-insurance do not actually guarantee compensation to policyholders who suffer agricultural losses (Johnson 2013; Isakson 2015).

Second, reflecting shifts in the broader economy, agrifood businesses have increasingly prioritized financial returns for their shareholders over society's wider interests such as food security and stable livelihoods (Jones and Nisbet 2011; Baud and Durand 2012). Recent decades have seen rising ownership of food and agriculture companies across the supply chain by asset management companies that invest on behalf of others (Clapp 2019). Corporate managers in agrifood firms have increasingly been rewarded based on the value of their firm's shares on the stock market, rather than their investment in innovation and job creation. As such, agrifood firms have increasingly sought growth and profit expansion through mergers and acquisitions, rather than through investment in productive activities (Jones and Nisbet 2011), and have paid out profits in the form of shareholder dividends, rather than reinvesting back into the firm (Rossman 2010; Isakson 2014). Global supply chains have been reshaped by these dynamics, as sourcing and processing are increasingly globalized to locations where wages are lower and environmental standards are weaker. Jobs and wages, as well as environmental conditions, have become more precarious in the sector as a result (Rossman 2010; Baud and Durand 2012; Burch and Lawrence 2013; Clapp 2014).

Third, financialization has infiltrated the everyday activities of food provisioning. The neoliberal rollbacks of state services and protections in most countries during the 1980s resulted in a greater proportion of agricultural research, insurance and credit provision being undertaken by private actors, notably private financial actors (Chang 2009; Martin and Clapp 2015). Following the dismantling of commodity boards, price supports and state crop insurance, for example, farmers have been encouraged to individually manage economic and environmental risks through participation in financial derivatives markets, including markets for commodity futures and derivative-based insurance (Breger Bush 2012; Clapp and Isakson 2018). Similarly, the dismantling of state-sponsored agricultural banks and other supports mean that farmers' access to agricultural inputs and capital is increasingly mediated by private banks, commercial microfinance institutions and specialized agricultural investment products (Boucher et al. 2005; Fairbairn 2014; Sippel et al. 2017). In addition to exacerbating farmers' debt and reducing their control over their agricultural operations, these trends have effectively normalized the idea that investment in stylized financial products is common practice in modern-day farming (Taylor 2011; Johnson 2013). Meanwhile, food retail companies have transformed ordinary shopping trips into financialized exchanges, encouraging their customers to enroll in store-branded financial services, especially credit programs, often seeking their loyalty through points programs (Burch and Lawrence 2013). However, linking food acquisition to the provision of credit by the same provider only heightens consumers' dependence on these firms for both their economic and food security. It is quite possible that normalizing financial activities in such a common and necessary practice as provisioning food has conditioned societal actors to accept the emergence of financial logics and tools elsewhere in their daily lives.

BROADER IMPLICATIONS OF FINANCIALIZATION FOR THE AGRIFOOD SYSTEM

While the specific outcomes associated with the financialized reshaping of the food system are themselves noteworthy, when considered together the broader implications of this financialized reconfiguration of the food system come more clearly into view. We argue that collectively this process has contributed to an intensification of three existing trends in the agrifood system: (1) it exacerbates inequality within the food system; (2) it works to undermine food system resilience; and (3) it creates challenges for political efforts to work toward more just and sustainable food systems.

To begin, financialization has intensified the consolidation of power and wealth in the food system. While inequities have long been present in the agrifood system (Friedmann and McMichael 1989), the changes associated with financialization have aggravated this trend by creating new opportunities for profit accumulation by financial and corporate elites, often at the expense of more vulnerable food system actors. The direct effects of financialization, including food price volatility, threats to land rights, reduced job and livelihood security and corporate concentration, all work to disadvantage less powerful actors in the food system, including poor food consumers, vulnerable agricultural producers and food workers with already precarious employment. The prioritization of shareholder value in the food system has also encouraged more corporate consolidation in the agrifood sector (Howard 2016; Clapp 2019), as corporate executives that have failed to invest in their enterprises seek to boost returns – at least in the short run – by acquiring the assets of other firms. Inequality is further extended when the everyday activities of food provisioning are mediated by a growing array of new financial products that channel incomes from ordinary food system actors to financial elites (for example through new financial products associated with credit, insurance and retirement savings, as noted above).

Financialization also undermines socio-ecological resilience within the food system. The introduction of novel financial instruments designed to enhance investors' opportunities for financial gains, like farmland investment products and commodity index funds, fosters instability within the food system. The extreme food price volatility experienced in the 2007–2012 period was widely associated with increased investment in commodity index funds, and was a key driver of vulnerability and uncertainty for both food producers and consumers. Driven by the need to generate returns on their investments, financial acquisitions of and control over farmland have been widely associated with the promotion of industrial farming methods that have been implicated in climate change, biodiversity loss, and that have exacerbated the economic and environmental vulnerability of agricultural operations (Isakson 2009; Jarosz 2009; Kuns et al. 2016). Compounding these processes, pressure from financial actors to restructure agrifood corporations has reduced the number of commercially available seeds and agrochemicals, thereby contributing to the further homogenization of agricultural systems and farmers' increased dependence upon genetically modified seeds and associated agrochemicals (Deschambault 2016; Clapp 2018).

Finally, financialization complicates political efforts to advocate for policies that encourage more just and sustainable food systems. The complexity of new financial investment tools associated with the agrifood sector works to preclude civil society groups and social movements from participating in policy debates (Clapp 2014; Williams 2015). The lobby power of corporate giants also skews policymaking in favor of large-scale agricultural models that undermine efforts at grassroots level. Moreover, as individuals are encouraged to use financial tools in the food system to manage risk, their attention is constantly directed away from the need for broader systemic change. As farmland and commodity investments become normalized instruments in retirement savings, and as derivatives become normalized as farm insurance, financialization is often not recognized as the cause of insecurities. Instead, it is presented as the solution.

CONCLUSION

If the agrarian question tasks critical agrarian scholars to evaluate whether and how the development of capitalism contours the political economy of food provisioning, then its contemporary relevance necessitates an understanding of whether and how the growing influence of financial actors, markets and motives is reshaping practices and the distribution of wealth and power in the food and agricultural sector. In this chapter, we have argued that the unfolding process of financialization has indeed infiltrated agrifood economies and that the impacts have been profound.

Mirroring developments in the broader economy, financialization in the agrifood sector has taken three interrelated forms. First, financial actors have become more involved in the sector and, enabled by recent deregulations, have reformatted many aspects of food provisioning – including farmland, economic and environmental risk management and the procurement of food – for financial purposes, while conventional agrifood enterprises are earning a greater share of their profits from related financial activities. Second, agrifood enterprises have reoriented their operations, giving greater priority to generating returns to their shareholders over their workers, environmental quality, investment and other social values. Third, as neoliberal restructuring has transferred risks and responsibilities to ordinary individuals, their everyday activities like producing and acquiring food, managing agricultural risk and achieving retirement security are increasingly contingent upon – and mediated by – financial activities in the agrifood sector.

While it is possible to identify specific impacts for each manifestation of financialization in agrifood economies, we maintain that the combined impacts can be categorized into three broad trends that are exacerbating existing problems in the global food economy. Most broadly, phenomena that have been linked to financialization like rising and volatile food prices, the concentration of farmland holdings and the offloading of risk and costs to food workers, consumers and agricultural producers have further entrenched disparities of wealth and power in the food system. Financial processes have also worked to reconfigure land control, agricultural practices and the availability of agricultural technologies in ways that have given greater impetus to the industrialization of agricultural production and attendant ecological problems like climate change, biodiversity loss and depletion of topsoil and water, thereby aggravating food system vulnerabilities. Finally, the complexity of financial interventions and the proliferation of financial products that purport to address problems in the food system (some of which, in fact, are exacerbated by financialization) have worked to diffuse collective action and exclude agricultural producers, food consumers and other civil society actors from discussion about food system change.

Admittedly, the picture that we have painted is bleak. We believe, however, that positive change is possible and can be encouraged by (a) reducing food system actors' dependence upon financial services and delinking them from the dominant financial sector; and (b) fostering the development of an alternative financial sector that is motivated by social justice, environmental sustainability and the broader well-being of society, not speculative profits. To be sure, such changes will not come easily and will likely necessitate the transformation of food economies, including the widespread adoption of agroecological practices that reduce farmers' dependence upon commercial inputs and the corresponding debts and re-embedding food economies in territorial markets that are governed by commitments to social justice and democratic access to healthy and culturally appropriate food. Alternative financial models that support these re-embedded food economies at a more local scale also offer some promise, such as investment cooperatives like FarmWorks, Slow Money and the Fair Finance Fund in North America (Stephens et al. 2019). It is important, however, that such initiatives are supported by public policies that shield them from the kinds of mainstream economic incentives that drive processes of financialization more broadly. We hope that our analysis has contributed to a foundational understanding that will enable critical food and agrarian scholars and activists to investigate these and other potential paths towards the development of more just and environmentally sustainable food economies.

FURTHER READING

Breger Bush, S. (2012), *Derivatives and Development: A Political Economy of Global Finance, Farming, and Poverty*, New York: Palgrave Macmillan.
Burch, D.; Lawrence, G. (2009), Towards a third food regime: Behind the transformation, *Agriculture and Human Values*, 26(4), 267–279.
Clapp, J.; Isakson, S.R. (2018), *Speculative Harvests: Financialization, Food, and Agriculture*, Black Point, Nova Scotia: Fernwood Publishing.
Fairbairn, M. (2014), "Like gold with yield": Evolving intersections between farmland and finance, *Journal of Peasant Studies*, 41(5), 777–795.
Ghosh, J. (2010), The unnatural coupling: Food and global finance, *Journal of Agrarian Change*, 10(1), 72–86.

REFERENCES

Aitken, R. (2007), *Performing Capital: Toward a Cultural Economy of Popular and Global Finance*, New York: Palgrave Macmillan.
Arrighi, G. (1994), *The Long Twentieth Century: Money, Power, and the Origins of Our Times*, London: Verso.
Baud, C.; Durand, C. (2012), Financialization, globalization, and the making of profits by leading retailers, *Socio-Economic Review*, 10(2), 241–266.
Boucher, S.R.; Barham, B.L.; Carter, M.R. (2005), The impact of "market-friendly" reforms on credit and land markets in Honduras and Nicaragua, *World Development*, 33(1), 107–128.
Breger Bush, S. (2012), *Derivatives and Development: A Political Economy of Global Finance, Farming, and Poverty*, New York: Palgrave Macmillan.
Burch, D.; Lawrence, G. (2013), Financialization in agri-food supply chains: Private equity and the transformation of the retail sector, *Agriculture and Human Values*, 30(2), 247–258.
Chang, H.-J. (2009), Rethinking public policy in agriculture: Lessons from history, distant and recent, *Journal of Peasant Studies*, 36(3), 477–515.
Clapp, J. (2014), Financialization, distance and global food politics, *Journal of Peasant Studies*, 41(5), 797–814.
Clapp, J. (2018), Mega-mergers on the menu: Corporate concentration and the politics of sustainability in the global food system, *Global Environmental Politics*, 18(2), 12–33.
Clapp, J. (2019), The rise of financial investment and common ownership in global agrifood firms, *Review of International Political Economy*, 26(4), 604–629.
Clapp, J.; Isakson, S.R. (2018), *Speculative Harvests: Financialization, Food, and Agriculture*, Black Point, Nova Scotia: Fernwood Publishing.
Crotty, J. (2009), Structural causes of the global financial crisis: A critical assessment of the "New Financial Architecture," *Cambridge Journal of Economics*, 33(4), 563–580.
Deschambault, J. (2016), Merge-Santo: New threat to food sovereignty, *ETC Group*, Briefing Note, 23 March, accessed January 22, 2019 at etcgroup.org/content/merge-santo-new-threat-food-sovereignty.
Desmarais, A.A.; Qualman, D.; Magnan, A.; Wiebe, N. (2017), Investor ownership or social investment? Changing farmland ownership in Saskatchewan, Canada, *Agriculture and Human Values*, 34(1), 149–166.
Epstein, G.A. (2005), Introduction: Financialization and the world economy, in Epstein, G.A. (ed.), *Financialization and the World Economy*, Cheltenham, UK and Northampton, MA, USA: Edward Elgar Publishing, 3–16.

Fairbairn, M. (2014), "Like gold with yield": Evolving intersections between farmland and finance, *Journal of Peasant Studies*, 41(5), 777–795.

Friedmann, H.; McMichael, P. (1989), Agriculture and the state system: The rise and decline of national agricultures, 1870 to the present, *Sociologia Ruralis*, 29(2), 93–117.

Froud, J.; Haslam, C.; Johal, S.; Williams, K. (2000), Shareholder value and financialization: Consultancy promises, management moves, *Economy and Society*, 29(1), 80–110.

Froud, J.; Johal, S.; Leaver, A.; Williams, K. (2006), *Financialization and Strategy: Narrative and Numbers*, New York: Routledge.

Ghosh, J. (2010), The unnatural coupling: Food and global finance, *Journal of Agrarian Change*, 10(1), 72–86.

Harvey, D. (2003), *The New Imperialism*, New York: Oxford University Press.

Howard, P.H. (2016), *Concentration and Power in the Food System: Who Controls What We Eat?*, London: Bloomsbury.

Isakson, S.R. (2009), No hay ganancia en la milpa: The agrarian question, food sovereignty, and the on-farm conservation of agrobiodiversity in the Guatemalan Highlands, *Journal of Peasant Studies*, 36(4), 725–759.

Isakson, S.R. (2014), Food and finance: The financial transformation of agro-food supply chains, *Journal of Peasant Studies*, 41(5), 749–775.

Isakson, S.R. (2015), Derivatives for development? Small-farmer vulnerability and the financialization of climate risk management, *Journal of Agrarian Change*, 15(4), 569–580.

Jarosz, L. (2009), Energy, climate change, meat, and markets: Mapping the coordinates of the current world food crisis, *Geography Compass*, 3(6), 2065–2083.

Johnson, L. (2013), Index insurance and the articulation of risk-bearing subjects, *Environment and Planning A*, 45(1), 2663–2681.

Jones, B.; Nisbet, P. (2011), Shareholder value versus stakeholder values: CSR and financialization in global food firms, *Socio-Economic Review*, 9(2), 287–314.

Kotz, D.M. (2011), Financialization and neoliberalism, in Teeple, G. (ed.), *Relations of Global Power: Neoliberal Order and Disorder*, Toronto: University of Toronto Press, 1–18.

Krippner, G. (2011), *Capitalizing on Crisis: The Political Origins of the Rise of Finance*, Cambridge, MA: Harvard University Press.

Kuns, B.; Visser, O.; Wästfelt, A. (2016), The stock market and the steppe: The challenges faced by stock-market financed, Nordic farming ventures in Russia and Ukraine, *Journal of Rural Studies*, 45, 199–217.

Langley, P. (2008), Financialization and the consumer credit boom, *Competition and Change*, 12(2), 133–147.

Magnan, A. (2015), The financialization of agri-food in Canada and Australia: Corporate farmland and farm ownership in the grains and oilseed sector, *Journal of Rural Studies*, 41, 1–12.

Martin, S.J.; Clapp, J. (2015), Finance for agriculture or agriculture for finance?, *Journal of Agrarian Change*, 15(4), 549–559.

Palley, T.I. (2007), Financialization: What it is and why it matters, The Levy Economics Institute Working Paper No. 525, accessed January 22, 2019 at levyinstitute.org/pubs/wp_525.pdf.

Rossman, P. (2010), What "financialization" means for food workers, *Seedling*, 14 January, accessed January 22, 2019 at www.grain.org/article/entries/4078-what-financialisation-means-for-food-workers.

Sippel, S.R.; Larder, N.; Lawrence, G. (2017), Grounding the financialization of farmland: Perspectives on financial actors as new land owners in rural Australia, *Agriculture and Human Values*, 34(2), 251–265.

Stephens, P.; Knezevic, I.; Best, L. (2019), Community financing for sustainable food systems, *Canadian Food Studies/La Revue canadienne des études sur l'alimentation*, 6(3), 60–87.

Taylor, M. (2011), "Freedom from poverty is not for free": Rural development and the microfinance crisis in Andhra Pradesh, India, *Journal of Agrarian Change*, 11(4), 484–504.

van der Zwan, N. (2014), Making sense of financialization, *Socio-Economic Review*, 12(1), 99–129.

Williams, J.W. (2015), Dodging Dodd-Frank: Excessive speculation, commodities markets, and the burden of proof, *Law and Policy*, 37(1–2), 119–152.

Worthy, M. (2011), Broken markets: How financial market regulation can help prevent another global food crisis, World Development Movement, accessed January 22, 2019 at globaljustice.org.uk/sites/default/files/files/resources/broken-markets.pdf.

22. Agrarian law

Sergio Coronado

INTRODUCTION

Law could be broadly defined as a set of norms, procedures and authorities regulating multiple aspects of social life. However, starting from different theoretical perspectives, law can be understood and analysed in multiple and even contradictory ways. On the one hand, it is comprehended as a system that reproduces dominant political and economic interests and power structures based on class, gender or race. On the other hand, it is understood as a field of dispute, on which different social and political actors acquiesce to, challenge or resist law enforcement.

For critical agrarian studies, it is crucial to engage with law and its different branches (such as criminal, administrative or private law) and institutions, because of its importance for analysing agrarian change. Legal rules related to land tenure, agricultural trade agreements and agricultural production and labour shape continuous conflicts and transformations in the countryside. Historically, legal instruments served as tools of class domination by facilitating, legitimizing or regulating capitalist accumulation and transition in the countryside. For instance, the 'Bloody Legislation' from the end of the fifteenth century and the 'Black Act' of 1723 in England fulfilled different roles for the development of capitalist agriculture, whether by forcing the mobilization of labour in the case of the former (Marx 2013), or by privatizing common lands through the suppression of use rights formerly entitled to commoners in the case of the latter (Thompson 1975). Furthermore, large-scale land transfers, both current and previous, are/were frequently undertaken while strictly following a government's legal frameworks (Wily 2012). Law has, however, also played a critical role in terms of confronting and imposing effective inhibitions on the power of dominant groups or classes, and there are both historical and contemporary analyses of how rural labour, peasants, women, indigenous peoples and other dominated groups have engaged with legal means to navigate conflicts that have emerged amid different processes of capitalism's penetration into the countryside (Claeys 2015; Monsalve 2013; Thompson 1975).

This chapter explores the role of agrarian law, specifically its feature of regulating land tenure and tenancy systems, and explores its relevance for critical agrarian studies. The next section provides a discussion of what agrarian law is, and why and how this term is used for the purpose of the chapter. Thereafter, theoretical tensions and disputes between two competing approaches to, and the historical emergence and basic principles of, agrarian law are presented. Furthermore, the section surveys the interrelation of agrarian law and environmental and international human rights frameworks, and discusses how they are challenged and contested by agrarian social movements in the context of the expansion of human rights discourses and instruments. In the conclusion, it is discussed why and how scholars from critical agrarian studies need to engage with agrarian law.

WHY 'AGRARIAN LAW'?

Scholars from critical agrarian studies recurrently engage with the analysis of national and international regulations, legal pluralism, customary law, judiciary rulings and their multiple interpretations for various reasons, including problematizing the interaction between law and space (von Benda-Beckmann and von Benda-Beckmann 2009) or in understanding the role of international regulations regarding the global land rush (Franco et al. 2015). One major challenge here is to decipher and understand the complexity of legal structures and to know what we are all talking about. The delimitation of a specific branch of law dedicated to attending to a particular issue varies from country to country and from one legal tradition to another. Likewise, branches of law are named differently in different countries, although they may refer to the same thing: what in one country is understood as agrarian law or land law, in others is considered agricultural law or civil law.

Legal scholars from the United States, for instance, have defined agricultural law 'as the study of the network of laws and policies that apply to the production, marketing, and sale of agricultural products' (Schneider 2010, 935). Their Mexican counterparts use the notion of agrarian law to define something fairly similar: agrarian law is the sum of norms and institutions allocating property rights over rural land and resolving disputes and conflicts related to what is needed for food production and agriculture, including land, water and labour (Chávez 2004; Vivanco 1962). In addition, each country has developed its own agrarian or agricultural legal framework dependent on the traditions of the legal system in force. In countries with a common law (Anglo-Saxon) system, the issue is generally named land law, while in countries under a continental law (civil law) system, the same legal framework is usually called agrarian law. In many Latin American countries, it is possible to find so-called agrarian law (*Derecho Agrario*) codes and legal doctrines.

The choice of using one notion instead of another remains a major methodological and theoretical challenge. However, for this chapter, the concept of agrarian law is preferred over agricultural or land law. The reason for this relates to the importance of highlighting how such concepts have been significantly influenced by the broader political transformations that took place during the twentieth century, which introduced social justice and redistribution as overarching criteria for governing land tenure systems and allocating land rights. In some countries, peasant rebellions and revolutions shaped entire bodies of what is known today as agrarian law. Thus, in many of these countries, agrarian reform acts, laws or decrees were appointed as pivotal pieces of agrarian reform policies.

During the last decades of the twentieth century and the first decades of the twenty-first century, however, what is known as agrarian law experienced a shift from a redistributive approach to an efficiency approach based on theoretical foundations from new institutional economics. With regard to the latter, agrarian law has once more been subsumed under civil law regulations, eroding the redistributive paradigm. Therefore, despite agrarian law having been shaped in different national contexts throughout the twentieth century as a means for achieving land redistribution, it has been challenged and redefined in recent decades. Currently, there is renewed interest in critical legal scholarship because of the challenges posed by global resource grabbing and climate change, amid the emergence of new human rights instruments pushed by agrarian social movements.

COMPETING APPROACHES TO LAW AND AGRARIAN CHANGE

Throughout history, law has played a crucial role in agrarian change. Law is critical for land privatization, understood as the process through which private property rights over land are allocated by transferring public or uncultivated land to subjects, particularly individuals. Legal procedures legitimize private property rights that are subsequently certified by state authorities (notaries, registers, judges). Entitling private property rights over rural lands could also be a means through which redistributive reforms are enforced, for instance when large-scale landed properties formerly in the hands of only one holder are distributed to many.

Tensions between mainstream (for example, new institutional economics) and critical approaches to agrarian law are centred on the theoretical foundations guiding the rule of law and on the policy implications in terms of the allocation of property rights over rural land. Regarding land rights, these are framed in terms of efficiency versus redistribution. For new institutional economics, the main objective of the formalization of property rights, particularly ownership rights over land, is to trigger a process of commodification. For critical approaches, the formalization of land rights aims primarily for redistribution and the restitution of land rights to people who depend on them to make a livelihood. The contradictions between the efficiency and redistribution approaches are played out in disputes between private and public law. Civil law follows a private law approach, in which private property over rural lands is an absolute right.

Theoretically, for new institutional economics, well-performing land markets require previous processes of privatization and commodification. Law plays a critical role in the making of land markets: civil and land law facilitate land commodification by legalizing private property rights. By following this approach, legal systems aim to facilitate transactions and trade regarding property rights over rural land. For land to be considered a commodity, a process of entitling rights over land to private individuals, rights which are enforced by the legal system, is required.

Scholars such as Deininger and Binswanger (1999) and de Soto and Cheneval (2006) usually see the privatization of property rights over rural lands as the optimal institutional arrangement, because it reduces uncertainties and transaction costs. Moreover, scholars from this theoretical perspective often consider land privatization and the allocation of rights over rural land through the market as the optimal alternative for reaching efficient land use, because they consider that markets can and will allocate land rights to the most efficient users (Vendryes 2014). The process of privatizing rural lands and their further commodification through the consolidation of land markets involves for some (such as stakeholders interested in a well-functioning market) the expectation of a reduction in the transaction costs for property rights over land. Moreover, the individualization and commodification of property rights are both considered necessary for the development of agriculture. This is because ownership rights can operate as collateral for producers in order to access credit and other services, whether offered by the state (as subsidies) or by the market (as loans).

Land privatization and further commodification are thus expected to trigger rural development in an alleged virtuous cycle that begins with the formalization of private ownership rights. However, since land is a finite and extremely coveted asset for agricultural production, the extent to which the individualization, privatization and formalization of land rights is possible for all of those who demand it remains unclear, making the privatization approach insufficient for addressing the issues of land access and concentration. Moreover, commodification processes foster the notion of considering property as an unlimited right.

In contrast, during the twentieth century, different kinds of political transformations shaped a redistributive approach to agrarian law as a means of delivering social justice by addressing issues derived from land concentration. By following such an approach, the goal of different national legislations was to establish effective limitations to private property rights over rural land. The extent of such limitations varies from country to country, and highly depends on the political context and its ideological influence on agrarian law. While in communist regimes private property rights over land were abolished, in other contexts influenced by socialism or egalitarian liberalism, private property rights over land are possible but conditioned towards equity and redistribution (Foster and Bonilla 2011; García 1973).

Redistribution in agrarian law considers power asymmetries among rural actors, mainly determined by the concentration of land, wealth and consequently political power. Different studies demonstrate how the privatization of property rights over rural lands and the establishment of land markets ultimately lead to land transfers from the more impoverished to the wealthiest households, instead of the allocation of land rights to those who are uncritically considered to be the most efficient producers (Vendryes 2014). As a response, the redistributive approach to agrarian law offers an alternative to land privatization, commodification and further concentration, by encouraging the intervention of the state regarding land rights and markets. In this sense, agrarian law seeks material justice among rural dwellers through the constitution of different kinds of property rights over land among those in the population who do not have access to land or do not have enough land to develop a sustainable agricultural livelihood.

Furthermore, it encourages the state to intervene by creating a set of institutions and entities, including judges, special procedures and prosecutors, to promote the implementation of such redistributive legislation and to establish limits to land transfers. Within the redistributive approach to agrarian law, arrangements other than privatization are considered for promoting access to and control over land among rural dwellers, for example the protection of use rights over public or state-owned rural lands, the protection of common property rights and the enforcement of practical barriers for keeping those land rights away from the cycles of land commodification.

The implementation of a redistributive approach to agrarian law has been highly contested by the landed classes and conservative forces within different societies. In many cases, powerful actors seek to bring land conflicts out of the influence of redistributive agrarian law. Neoliberal reforms of agrarian law, as enforced, for example, in different Latin American countries during the late 1980s and early 1990s, diminished critical features of the redistributive approach within agrarian law, such as the proactive role of the state as the principal actor enforcing the social function of property, the redistribution of rural lands and the material justice principle. Consequently, the role of the state was progressively reduced to where it is simply considered an arbiter or facilitator in charge of ensuring a well-functioning land rights market. State-oriented agrarian reform was progressively replaced by market-led agrarian reform, enhancing the dominant position of private property as a near absolute right. Conversely, different actors claim that state intervention in land markets based on agrarian law is still valid in countries in which land concentration and land grabbing have overrun rural landscapes, examples that they argue indicate where the limits of market-led agrarian reform have been proved (De Schutter 2010b; Ziegler 2002).

As much as the tensions between neoliberal and redistributive approaches should be assessed in each specific context, some specific principles of agrarian law that date back to the social justice and redistributive approach are currently being reinvigorated through the emergence of human rights and environmental law.

EMERGENCE AND PRINCIPLES

The development of the redistributive approach to agrarian law is intimately related to political transformations in the countryside that have led to the enactment of different pieces of agrarian reform legislation. Mexico was probably the first country to enact an agrarian law after the revolution of the 1910s. The constitution of 1917 marked a watershed in terms of the evolution of agrarian law. Inspired by the peasants' demands for land throughout the revolutionary struggles, Article 27 of the constitution acknowledged the economic inefficiency of large-scale landholdings (*latifundios*) and obliged the executive authorities to distribute land not being used efficiently among the rural population for agriculture and food production (Mora-Donatto 2016). Other countries followed this experience. In Colombia, the first agrarian law, enacted in 1936 by a liberal government after decades of conservative party supremacy, introduced the institution of the social function of property, setting a different scenario for the resolution of land claims deployed by peasant settlers. Nevertheless, the regulation failed, particularly with regard to the establishment of favourable conditions for peasants' land claims (LeGrand 1988). Other countries where agrarian reforms were enacted after significant political shifts include Bolivia (1953), Ecuador (1964), Peru (1969), Indonesia (1960), Portugal (1975) and the Philippines (1988). Whereas until the 1980s agrarian reform legislation was primarily state-oriented, this changed in the 1990s when market-led agrarian reforms gained momentum.

Pivotal principles of redistributive agrarian law nevertheless remain in force in different legal contexts today, and are the result of the historical evolution of this legal field. Two principles are vital to the social justice approach to agrarian law. The first is the social function of property rights, which in agrarian law refers to the idea of considering property as an absolute right. The social function consequently enables a proactive role of the state for making property rights accountable in terms of social justice and food production. This means that despite the legal character of property rights over land, such rights could be limited and alienated by the state for purposes of equity. Currently, the social function converges with the ecological function of property, when considering environmental limitations to the exercise of property rights.

The second influencing principle in agrarian law is the material justice principle, which is an alternative to the formal justice principle: 'Formal justice is the impartial, consistent and strict application of established rules or laws; material justice concerns the justice or injustice of the contents of rules of law' (Campbell 1974, 445). It could also be defined as the obligation of different state actors to interpret legal frameworks by following a social justice approach. Regarding agrarian law, material justice implies favouring the rural poor, instead of the enforcement of mere formal justice, meaning the impartial enforcement of the law. In pursuing social justice, agrarian law allows the state and its judges to interpret legal frameworks accordingly in order to protect the weakest parties in land conflicts, namely those who depend on land for their livelihood. Consequently, the state must consider and assess each land conflict not only in terms of fulfilling legal commands but also protecting the rights of a specific section of the population. Therefore a set of instruments can be enforced, including, among others, the expiration of ownership rights over uncultivated lands, and the protection against eviction for tenants and occupants who directly till rural lands, particularly in cases where they lack certificates of land ownership (Ramos 2004). This principle has at least two institutional implications: first, the creation of specialized agrarian judges who address land conflicts by following material justice criteria; and second, the empowerment of the executive branches to enforce particular policies to bring about a more egalitarian distribution of agrarian land among the rural population.

Critical nuances must be considered in the enforcement of the redistributive approach to agrarian law. For instance, keeping people on the land by entitling land rights is not always the best option in cases of environmental risk. In other cases, entitling land rights to the rural poor can encompass significant challenges, for instance when this involves displaced persons who have been living in urban areas for years, or where the rural areas in question lack the necessary infrastructure and access to social services. In addition to solving disputes over land, agrarian law also covers a complex web of rights and interactions related to food production and the enforcement of agrarian reform policies. Concerning the latter, agrarian law defines who is entitled to be granted land ownership rights, by defining who is, and who is not, an agrarian reform beneficiary, and under what conditions the state can interfere in the exercise of private ownership rights. Agrarian law is therefore not only concerned with an objective definition of the legal status of the land, but also classifies and differentiates between different subjects that can be considered, or not, landed property rights holders through different rights (use, tenancy, usufruct, ownership), and defines the uses of those lands.

AGRARIAN LAW IN DIALOGUE WITH HUMAN RIGHTS AND ENVIRONMENTAL LAW

Since the end of the twentieth century, not only has a decline in the redistributive approach to agrarian law institutions taken place, but also the enforcement of international environmental and human rights law. For instance, in several Latin American countries, constitutional reforms took place, and one distinct characteristic was the incorporation of international human rights agreements into national legal frameworks. The recognition of instruments such as the International Labour Organization Indigenous and Tribal Peoples Convention Number 169 (1989) reinvigorated social and environmental dimensions of the bill of rights already protected by each country's constitutional framework.

The emergence of environmental and human rights law poses significant challenges for the implementation of agrarian law. On the one hand, global environmental crises raise awareness of the limits of the expansion of agricultural production and the severe deterioration of soils, water sources and forests caused by the expansion of the agrarian frontier worldwide. Conversely, the promotion of agriculture production, particularly subsistence agriculture, as a human right and as a goal to be fostered as soon as possible, comes up against environmental limits. The enforcement of agrarian law today is therefore continuously challenged by the limits of nature, partially imposed by environmental law through legal protections of endangered ecosystems and species. However, both normative frameworks must be harmonized in the pursuit of sustainable food production and agriculture, as proved by different agroecological experiences. Peasant and indigenous movements have constructed alternative approaches to achieving the harmonization of agrarian and environmental legal frameworks. For instance, the struggle of rubber tree trappers or *seringueiros* in the Brazilian Amazon rainforest demonstrates how an initial claim for labour and land rights, amid the pressure exerted by cattle ranchers to enlarge their properties over forested areas, was transformed into demands for the establishment of extractive reserves, spaces created to protect sustainable uses of the forest by the rural poor; a proposal that was articulated within the official system of environmental protection (de Almeida 2002). Such experiences facilitate the articulation of both the social function and the ecological function of property, and contribute to building bridges between environmental and agrarian law.

The emergence and consolidation of an international human rights framework is, furthermore, changing the conditions of action for agrarian movements, at both the national and international levels, invigorating demands for land redistribution in a context of widespread market-led agrarian reform. In recent years, agrarian law has been profoundly influenced by human rights law. The International Covenant on Economic, Social and Cultural Rights (1966), the International Labour Organization Indigenous and Tribal Peoples Convention No. 169 (1989) and the United Nations Declarations on the Rights of Indigenous Peoples (2007) and on the Rights of Peasants and Other People Working in Rural Areas (2018), among other human rights instruments, are influencing current interpretations of existing agrarian legal frameworks at the national level, where such rules are enforced. Other human rights sources also enhance the material justice approach to agrarian law. The United Nations special rapporteur on the right to food has urged national governments to '[p]rioritize the titling of land for those who are dependent on land for their livelihoods and are more vulnerable to land-grabbing, rather than for those who claim to be the formal landowners' (De Schutter 2010a, 21).

The articulation of human rights law with agrarian law permits the introduction of a *pro-homine* principle for the interpretation of legal frameworks to resolve conflicts over land that are overarched by asymmetrical power relations in terms of property, capital and labour. The *pro-homine* or *pro-personae* principle guides the interpretation of legal norms, inviting judicial or administrative authorities to prioritize those interpretations and rules that are more favourable to the protection and realization of individuals' human rights:

> According to this, human rights norms should be interpreted as extensively as possible when recognising individuals' rights and, by contrast, as restrictively as possible when the norm imposes limits on the enjoyment of human rights. At the same time, the principle commands that in case of conflicts between human rights norms, the norm that better protects the individual's rights should prevail. (Rodarte 2017, 9)

Agrarian law is a field of constant development and evolution, highly informed by international human rights instruments. Such instruments envision land as the site of food production and shelter provision, thus bringing a human rights approach to land rather than an economic asset interpretation (Assies 2009). Moreover, such an approach demands the recognition by legal institutions of the special protection of subordinate and non-recognized groups, such as peasants, indigenous peoples and rural women (Edelman and James 2011; Via Campesina 2018).

CONCLUSION

Why should scholars from the field of critical agrarian studies take agrarian law into account? Two overlapping areas of inquiry are crucial for critical agrarian scholars: first, the critical analysis of the historical interactions of legal forms with capitalist advancement in land and agriculture; and second, the interaction between agrarian social movements and legal systems. While the first emphasizes the analysis of institutions and the role fulfilled by them in terms of facilitating or enabling land commodification and dispossession and the penetration of capitalism into the countryside, the latter makes a more considerable effort to understand the multiple reactions of agents facing the consequences and implications of such processes.

Studies addressing the dilemmas of the engagement of agrarian social movements with legal struggles over land and other agricultural inputs have been conducted profusely over the last decades (de Sousa Santos and Rodríguez 2005). The disputes over the legal field are relevant for social movements because the majority of legal debates, including that over property rights over rural land, have direct consequences for the distribution of power and goods in the political field (Garcia Villegas 2006). Houtzager (2005, 218) demonstrates how the peasant movement in Brazil deployed juridical strategies that 'helped to produce watershed precedents [that] contributed to a broader process of constitutionalizing law and made access to land more equitable in parts of Brazil by redefining property rights in practice'. In the Philippines, constitutional changes created unprecedented opportunities for the landless to claim ownership rights to the land they tilled (Franco 2008). These processes could be considered expressions of a counter-hegemonic reinterpretation of human rights, and constitutional and agrarian law. The confrontation between hegemonic and counter-hegemonic interpretations of law and human rights takes place in multiple fields, mainly when the law is put in motion through adjudication.

In practice, however, the interactions between agrarian social movements and the legal field are complex and contradictory. The effects of the use of legal means are not always the same. In some cases, such a process could even lead to the reinforcement of the power of dominant groups over the powerless; this could also be explained by the intrinsic relationship between human rights, constitutional democracies and the development of capitalism (Krever 2018). Understanding the interactions between law and social movements implies an analysis of the material implications for social actors excluded from the distribution of wealth, land and political power, who are engaged with law and social justice struggles. The evolution of agrarian law institutions towards its redefinition through human rights lenses and instruments enhances the idea of this branch of law as a vehicle for material justice and for the protection of the interests of the rural poor.

FURTHER READING

Bourdieu, P. (1987), The force of saw: Toward a sociology of the juridical field, *The Hastings Law Journal*, 38, 805–853.
de Sousa Santos, B.; Rodríguez-Garavito, C.A. (eds) (2005), *Law and Globalization from Below: Towards a Cosmopolitan Legality*, Cambridge: Cambridge University Press.
Franco, J.C. (2011), *Bound by Law: Filipino-Rural Poor and the Search for Justice in a Plural-legal Landscape*, Quezon City: Ateneo de Manila University Press.
Thompson, E.P. (1975), *Whigs and Hunters: The Origin of the Black Act*, London: Penguin Books.

von Benda-Beckmann, P.F.; von Benda-Beckmann, P.K. (eds) (2009), *Spatializing Law: An Anthropological Geography of Law in Society*, Farnham: Ashgate Publishing.

REFERENCES

Assies, W. (2009), Land tenure, land law and development: Some thoughts on recent debates, *Journal of Peasant Studies*, 36(3), 573–589.

Campbell, T.D. (1974), Rights without justice, *Mind*, 83(331), 445–448.

Chávez, M. (2004), *El Derecho Agrario en México*, México, DF: Editorial Porrúa.

Claeys, P. (2015), The right to land and territory: New human right and collective action frame, *Revue interdisciplinaire d'études juridiques*, 75(2), 115–137.

de Almeida, M.B. (2002), The politics of Amazonian conservation: The struggles of rubber tappers, *Journal of Latin American Anthropology*, 7(1), 170–219.

De Schutter, O. (2010a), *Report of the Special Rapporteur on the Right to Food* (No. A/65/281), United Nations.

De Schutter, O. (2010b), The emerging human right to land, *International Community Law Review*, 12(3), 303–334.

de Soto, H.; Cheneval, F. (2006), *Realizing Property Rights*, Zurich: Rüffer & Rub.

de Sousa Santos, B.; Rodríguez-Garavito, C.A. (eds) (2005), *Law and Globalization from Below: Towards a Cosmopolitan Legality*, Cambridge: Cambridge University Press.

Deininger, K.; Binswanger, H. (1999), The evolution of the World Bank's land policy: Principles, experience, and future challenges, *The World Bank Research Observer*, 14(2), 247–276.

Edelman, M.; James, C. (2011), Peasants' rights and the UN system: Quixotic struggle? Or emancipatory idea whose time has come?, *Journal of Peasant Studies*, 38(1), 81–108.

Foster, S.; Bonilla, D. (2011), The social function of property: A comparative law perspective, *Fordham Law Review*, 80, 101–113.

Franco, J.C. (2008), Making land rights accessible: Social movements and political-legal innovation in the rural Philippines, *Journal of Development Studies*, 44(7), 991–1022.

Franco, J.C.; Monsalve, S.; Borras, S.M. (2015), Democratic land control and human rights, *Current Opinion in Environmental Sustainability*, 15, 66–71.

García, A. (1973), *Sociología de la Reforma Agraria en América Latina*, Bogotá: Ediciones Cruz del Sur.

Garcia Villegas, M. (2006), Comparative sociology of law: Legal fields, legal scholarships and social sciences in Europe and the United States, *Law and Social Inquiry*, 31(2), 343–382.

Houtzager, P.P. (2005), The movement of the landless (MST), juridical field and legal change in Brazil, in de Sousa Santos, B.; Rodríguez-Garavito, C.A. (eds), *Law and Globalization from Below: Towards a Cosmopolitan Legality*, Cambridge: Cambridge University Press, 218–240.

Krever, T. (2018), The rule of law and the rise of capitalism, in May, C.; Winchester, A. (eds), *Handbook on the Rule of Law*, Cheltenham, UK and Northampton, MA, USA: Edward Elgar Publishing, 184–200.

LeGrand, C. (1988), *Colonización y Protesta Campesina en Colombia: 1850–1950*, Bogotá: Centro Editorial, Universidad Nacional de Colombia.

Marx, K. (2013), *Capital: A Critique of Political Economy*, Ware: Wordsworth Editions.

Monsalve, S. (2013), The human rights framework in contemporary agrarian struggles, *Journal of Peasant Studies*, 40(1), 239–290.

Mora-Donatto, C.J. (2016), *Derechos y Justicia para el Campo Mexicano*, México, DF: Instituto Nacional de Estudios Históricos de las Revoluciones de México.

Ramos, M. (2004), *La Construcción Histórica de la Jurisdicción Agraria en Colombia*, San José: IICA.

Rodarte, H. (2017), The *pro personae* principle and its application by Mexican courts, *Queen Mary Human Rights Review*, 4(1), 1–27.

Schneider, S.A. (2010), A reconsideration of agricultural law: A call for the law of food, farming, and sustainability, *William and Mary Environmental Law and Policy Review*, 3, 935–964.

Thompson, E.P. (1975), *Whigs and Hunters: The Origin of the Black Act*, London: Penguin Books.

Vendryes, T. (2014), Peasants against private property rights: A review of the literature, *Journal of Economic Surveys*, 28(5), 971–995.

Via Campesina (2018), *UN Human Rights Council Passes a Resolution Adopting the Peasant Rights Declaration in Geneva*, 28 September, accessed 15 May 2019 at https://viacampesina.org/en/un -human-rights-council-passes-a-resolution-adopting-the-peasant-rights-declaration-in-geneva/.

Vivanco, A.C. (1962), Derecho agrario y reforma agraria en América Latina, *Journal of Inter-American Studies*, 4(2), 233–245.

von Benda-Beckmann, P.F.; von Benda-Beckmann, P.K. (eds) (2009), *Spatializing Law: An Anthropological Geography of Law in Society*, Farnham: Ashgate Publishing.

Wily, L.A. (2012), Looking back to see forward: The legal niceties of land theft in land rushes, *Journal of Peasant Studies*, 39(3–4), 751–775.

Ziegler, J. (2002), *Report of the Special Rapporteur of the Commission on Human Rights on the Right to Food*, accessed 20 May 2019 at www.righttofood.org/wp-content/uploads/2012/09/A573561.pdf.

23. Territoriality

Annie Shattuck and Nancy Lee Peluso

The concept of territoriality is a fundamental tool for understanding power. From land rights and land grabs to conceptualizations of what counts as a 'forest' and what spaces should be conserved, from ideas about indigeneity and autonomy to illicit economies, paramilitary actions and migration – many of the biggest issues in agrarian politics navigate territorializing strategies.

The geographic notion of territoriality has been the subject of much discussion and debate; the journal *Territory, Politics, Governance* addresses territory, territoriality and territorialization in many of its dimensions. Based on the founding editor's definition, the two key features of territoriality are (1) the making of material or symbolic boundaries or borders and (2) the deployment of mechanisms of domination or control as a means to enforce them (Agnew 2005). This follows on from another geographer's early definition of territoriality as 'the attempt by an individual or group to affect, influence, or control people, phenomena, and relationships by delimiting and asserting control over a geographic area' (Sack 1986, 19). In practice, however, territoriality has two key aspects. First, it is about claims for the purpose of governance. Territorial classifications of space within boundaries are one way that such claims and related controls manifest. The other key aspect of territoriality is affective and involves attachment to, identification with, belonging to and even the longing for a particular place-cum-territory; these attachments, claims of a sort, are also territorialities. The production of territory through cultural and social practice thus extends beyond spatial classifications and macro processes of, say, state or corporate claims and control of space (Moore 2005), as well as the authority to implement such claims and controls (Sikor and Lund 2009). Territorialization is thus the process by which a specific geographic area comes to be understood, recognized, claimed and controlled (Vandergeest and Peluso 1995).

The practices that produce territory, or the processes of territorialization, are various; they include violence, communication, administration, enclosure, dwelling, movement and imagination. Territorializing practices can be as obvious and visible as the creation of national borders or the posting of military bases or state resource extraction enterprises up against these borders. Territories can also include other, more fractured, claims to space through the zoning of political-economic spaces such as nation states, indigenous autonomous regions, military bases, protected areas and industrial agricultural concessions; or through cultural practices such as naming, the burial of ancestors, rituals meant to render spaces 'safe' and the planting and acknowledgement of ancestral trees that contribute to the production of ethnic identities linked to particular places. Territorialities also mould and are moulded by the ways in which people understand power and belonging. Social and political attributes become ascribed to the territory itself (Murphy 2013). These kinds of social relations are what differentiate territory from space (Peluso and Vandergeest 2011).

Territoriality is an important form of spatiality and its analysis necessarily differs from spatial analysis. Studies of social phenomena in and across space or those that are productive of space, such as economic activities, capital flows or even migration, do not necessarily address the strategies used to classify and control people and things in relation to land or water-based resources (Vandergeest and Peluso 1995). The modern state and most modern economic systems – feudalism, capitalism, communism and socialism – could not work without institutions that produce territory for and within these political-economic systems. For scholars of agrarian studies, perhaps the most important ways of thinking about territory, territorialization and territoriality are those that engage state practices in the name of control-cum-governance, and those that operate in the realm of cultural politics around the control of place and space, such as everyday forms of territory and territoriality. In the following sections, we address these two dimensions of territory and then use a case study from Indonesian Borneo to illustrate how everyday forms of agrarian territoriality are constructed.

STATE TERRITORIALITY AND TERRITORIALIZATION

As a set of processes and practices, territoriality is most often explicitly associated with the workings of state power and authority. The creation of specific territories for social, political and economic goals is a strategy for achieving the impression of undivided authority implied by globally accepted notions of state sovereignty (Agnew 2005). State territorialization generally refers to the deployment of territorial processes by state actors and institutions within the boundaries of a state's sovereign territory (Vandergeest and Peluso 1995); though sometimes this extends to extra-territorial authority and privileges being exerted over constituents by states (Vandergeest and Unno 2012). State authorities territorialize space within their national territories to create internal territories or zones to be governed in specific ways for specific purposes. Most relevant here are the internal territories which states use to govern access to agrarian and environmental resources (Vandergeest and Peluso 1995). Control through territorialization works by limiting, enabling or encouraging specific activities within the boundaries of a particular territory, including the exclusion of people and activities, limiting (human) mobility in and out and dictating the ways in which specific people or groups can access or control natural and agrarian resources and their environments (ibid.). Thus 'internal territorialization' is a common strategy by which states establish control over natural resources and authorize certain users, for example by demarcating land as 'state forest', protected areas, nature reserves or other conservation zones (ibid.). The territorialization of agrarian resources and people can involve the delineation of civil administration units, the mandatory registration of land titles, land surveys and agribusiness concessions, as well as the subjection of urban and rural territories to different kinds of property laws and policies (Woods 2019; Vandergeest and Peluso 1995). In Southeast Asia, states' territorializations of resource access and control have in recent times prioritized the territorial control of land (including coastal and interior land and water bodies), something that constitutes a major shift from both the philosophies and practices of governance and control of labourers, persons and their productions that had long characterized the region (Winichakul 1997). In this way, resource maps and cartographic classification schemes can be seen as formative political and cultural entities, not just representations or documents that make territory; they also become sites of competing territorialities (Bryan and Wood 2015). The specific techniques of state territorialization – classification, registration and mapping – not only structure political perceptions of spatial power, but also influence sociocultural practices, for example what activities or uses of space are allowed within particular territories.

Territorial claims, like all forms of property, have to be recognized in order to be enforceable (Rose 1999); the symbolism of inclusion and exclusion needs to be clear. Territorial symbols such as maps and signs, laws, violence or names are all part of state practices of territorialization. Whether or not such territorial claims are always enforceable is not at issue in trying to understand the strategies of territorialization; nor do states have a monopoly on these tactics. Thus, state territorialities, like other forms of hegemony, are never absolute; they are unstable and subject to social struggles (Ballvé 2012; Escobar 2008; Vandergeest and Peluso 1995).

Control over the diverse social spaces of internal territorializations does not start from a single point. Under certain conditions, such as decentralization, state territorializations are aimed at renationalizing control by central state authorities (Eilenberg 2014). Moreover, territorial authority can be produced by governing institutions beyond the state (Sikor and Lund 2009), including private actors (Agnew 2010, 782). State territoriality can also be reinforced by paramilitary organizations, agribusinesses (Ballvé 2012) and peasant communities (Asher and Ojeda 2009; Bryan 2012; Peluso 1995) when they benefit from state territorial policies. This has been almost universally the case with international conservation institutions, whose territorial strategies for preserving biodiversity nearly always track and produce legitimacy for national state territorial claims (Corson 2011; Woods 2019). Ballvé (2012) draws on Lefebvrian notions of 'abstract space' to show how territory is produced in three ways simultaneously: the material, the ideal and through everyday lived experience. Thus, the notion of 'regimes of territorial legitimation' can be used to analyse 'the [multiplicity of] institutions, practices, and discourses that serve to legitimate specific territorial conceptions of the state' (Murphy 2013, 1217).

We turn now to the ways in which territories are produced through people's everyday lived experiences of them, including through practice and memory, experiences of violence, participation in governmental and cultural institutions, agricultural and resource management and social struggle and suffering (Moore 2005).

ALTERNATIVE AND EVERYDAY TERRITORIALITY

The analysis of territorialities that are imposed or sanctioned by states and their various large-scale collaborators, contesters and 'shadows' – narco and other organized crime figures, corporations, black market businessmen and non-governmental organizations – have become standard parts of the political geography, sociology and political science literatures (Agnew 2005; Jessop 2016; Sassen 2008). However, an alternative understanding of territory, with its own processes of territoriality and logics of territorialization, can be seen as emanating/deriving from everyday practices, that is from 'below'. These territorialities are entangled, as Donald Moore (2005) has called it, or articulated with larger-scale territorializing practices and claims in play within particular contexts. These everyday territorialities are perhaps more diverse than those of states, but are also more intimately connected with the minute dimensions of productive processes that drive – or nudge – agrarian change and its ever shifting power relations embedded in patterns of access to and control over resources or socio-natures. Examining how cultural practices – including agricultural practices – make spaces into territories through labouring – being the first to clear forest, planting certain kinds of long-living trees, travelling through a particular area and making territory through mobility, or digging into the ground to get at subterranean resources – reveals how territory can be made without necessarily seeking out the authority of state institutions, 'big men', charismatic figures or collective actors who derive power from their roles in demarcating and defending territorial claims. However, if state authorities and institutions need not be involved in making territory, then those territories recognized through state territorial practices may be more entangled with on-the-ground practices than any of the contenders are willing to admit. In other words, local territories and territorialities (feelings of belonging to or 'owning' territory) emerge and unfold as a result of competing territorializations at multiple scales (however defined). These articulations are perhaps best illustrated by a few brief examples from different regions.

Indigenous, peasant and Afro-descendent communities have all made explicit claims to territory as part of what scholars call a broader 'territorial turn' in Latin America (Asher and Ojeda 2009; Ballvé 2012; Bryan 2012; Escobar 2008; Haesbaert 2003; Halvorsen et al. 2019). In Latin America, indigenous claims to territory embody broad, sometimes contradictory, demands for equity and autonomy (Bryan 2012). In many countries in the region, these struggles evoke an alternative relation to territory rooted in indigenous cosmovisions and articulated conceptions of Buen Vivir, as a kind of balance between humans and nature. They are not autonomous but articulated with state territorializations, as illustrated by indigenous and marginalized peoples' uses of the 'tools of the master': maps, physical boundary demarcations and oral histories to identify and claim historical settlements and burial sites. In other regions with different colonial and post-colonial histories, specific territorial strategies that do not seek to claim 'autonomy' are also common. And arguably, 'counter'-territorialities are mobilized everywhere by activists working both inside and outside formal government channels through efforts at land and forest reform, social and community forestry, counter-mapping initiatives, indigenous rights struggles and land occupations (Bryan and Wood 2015; Peluso 1995). Conflicting territorialities have also led to no small share of violence. This is at the heart of Moore's 'suffering for (and through) territory' – the often painful struggle for land, belonging and identity (Moore 2005).

Social movements for indigenous or Afro-Latin American autonomy have challenged the notion of territory as simply tracts of land with borders. In Colombia, for example, some movements invoke ideas of territory as 'spaces of life': 'a place-based framework linking history, culture, environment and social life' (Escobar 2008, 62). Like state territoriality, everyday visions, practices and experiences explicitly engage the subject-making dimensions of territorializations, showing how territory is not only about the power to control people and resources, but is fundamental to the making or emergence of subjects – political, agrarian or conservation subjects, for example (Bryan 2012; Escobar 2008). Social movements make claims not only to land, but to the territory necessary to maintain a set of social, economic, cultural and collective relations (Bryan 2012; Halvorsen et al. 2019). As Oaxacan writer Kaido Cruz (2010, 420) elaborates,

> [t]erritory is the foundation of self-determination for our peoples, this natural space of life is the source of wisdom and knowledge, of culture, identity, traditions and rights. Because of this, our vision of our territory is intimately tied to the enactment of our collective rights and our self-determination.

These ontological dimensions of territory motivate struggles against extractive industries, which in Latin America unite under the 'defence of territory' umbrella (Alonso-Fradejas et al. 2015).

Indigenous social movements are not the only ones to use more expansive ideas of territory and territorializing strategies. Building on long-standing demands for land reform, movements for food sovereignty have recently also begun to use territorializing strategies (Copeland 2019; McCune and Sánchez 2018), specifying that 'peasant autonomy' means more than controlling land – it requires a set of ecological, economic and political relationships supportive of such autonomy. Food sovereignty movements have focused on building peasant and indigenous territorialities through education in agroecology and agrarian political organizing, often retracing the histories of popular struggle in their regions as a means to construct a collective peasant identity, reframed in relation to defending and caring for territory through agroecology, as with the Latin American Agroecological Institutes of La Via Campesina (McCune and Sánchez 2018). Even claims to autonomy, self-determination and indigenous sovereignty cannot, however, escape state territorialities: part of the repertoire is to demand state recognition (Asher and Ojeda 2009). Moreover, both 'peasant' and 'indigenous' are themselves relational identity categories.

Changes in everyday practices can be just as effective as formal, state-sanctioned means of laying claim to territories. Indeed, indigenous efforts for state and international recognition of their territories have increased with the rise of conservation and development projects that establish property or territorial rights in the processes of their implementation (Peluso 2005). A case study drawn from one of the authors' work in Borneo provides several examples of how territories are produced by persons or groups other than state actors through practices recognized at local and regional levels – even across international boundaries – and which can remain under the radar of formal law.

LAND, RESOURCES AND EVERYDAY TERRITORIALITIES IN BORNEO

Though it is not possible to provide the full details here, the practices of Salako and Kanayotn Dayaks in western Borneo clearly create territories in practice. Their practices of planting and caring for long-living fruit and nut trees create territories that occupy space *and* time; they create specific rights embedded in individually and commonly held trees and their fruits, as well as their related territories, which change through subsequent generations. Both durian (*Durio zibethanus*) and tengkawang (*Shorea, sp.*) trees are planted in swidden fallows; they represent not only individual rights of access and the claims of descendant groups based on the cognatic kinship of the original planters, but also the mobilities and other practices associated with swidden – also known as 'shifting' – cultivation. Trees are known to last a long time and thus tie up the land. Durian and tengkawang trees live particularly long – through some 11 generations, as recorded in northern Borneo. While the fruits 'belong' to the person or couple who planted the trees during their lifetime, their rightful beneficiaries increase in number across subsequent generations. Among other places, these trees are planted in the spaces left when cultivators move their fields to new sites. They mark territory: the families with rights return annually during the fruiting season, travelling to these older, managed fallows, collecting fruit and recognizing their common ancestors. Friends and family create swiddens adjacent to one another, creating territories in the course of farming. Because of their longevity, the trees create territorial subjects with rights embedded in the fruit (Padoch and Peluso 1996; Peluso 1995).

Clusters of durian trees in forests and agroforests are a common feature of many Salako and Kanayotn landscapes. Those which were planted in the spaces left after the relocation of a longhouse to a new site are called '*tembawang*' in Indonesian, '*timawokn*' in Salako and other cognate words in other Dayak languages. These words mean 'former living spaces' (Padoch and Peters 1993). Tembawang are characterized by their durian or tengkawang trees, and they dominate the agroforested and obviously anthropomorphic landscape. Tembawang are territories, and they evoke territorialities, largely because, before being filled with culturally or economically valuable trees, they were homes, the sites of longhouses. The former owners and residents of the longhouse apartments – both individually and collectively – retain their territorial claims to these multi-scalar spaces in the tembawang when they occupy new longhouses or single-family homes in resettled hamlets. Indeed, standing in a tembawang on a hillside in Borneo, a Salako viewer can 'see' exactly where a longhouse once stood by the straight line of often gigantic durian trees built across the hill, and know who lived where and next to whom. The descendants of the tree planters can remember their ancestors – most of whom would have once waited for durian fruits or tengkawang nuts to fall in their own times. Rights to the spaces where fruit trees grow are territorialized, and trees cannot be cut down to clear access to the land without the permission of the current and ancestral controllers and an expensive ritual to seek that permission; this is particularly important if an ancestor's spirit is occupying the tree. In many places, these practices have declined, as chainsaws and plantations make inroads into the uplands, though this is not the case everywhere.

Before the Indonesian and Malaysian governments claimed forest territories as political forests, the presence of a tembawang represented another scale of territorial belonging that would last through as many generations as the trees did. Other land uses, cultural practices and beliefs render these tembawang spaces territories, including reburial rituals for great men and women in the front or back of their longhouses (or single-family dwellings these days), surrounded by durian trees; this includes the placement within the tembawang of a 'warriors' burial ground', with symbolic trees and plants associated with the resident peoples, and where contenders in more contemporary conflicts often visit for guidance from their strongest ancestors. Both government and green-grabbing activities have generated even greater attachments to these tembawang territories. Local people have faced down or suffered obstacles, such as new formalized structures of access or violent challenges, and have fought to retain or salvage their territories. Yet formally, many of these territories are not recognized: states and corporate land claimants have erased prior claims to the territory – by cutting down ancestral trees, labelling them 'forest species' and rendering the peopled territories 'abstract space'. These local territories resonate with Escobar's 'spaces of life' in Colombia, but are in danger of being permanently lost.

CONCLUSION

Territorialities are not simply tools of the state. People acting under different motivations make recognizable territories on a daily basis. The simple act of planting trees can be a form of territorialization. Without an understanding of territory and territoriality, agrarian studies will miss out on how power works in and through imbrications of land and people, belonging and social practice, violence and historical memory. Understanding these varied forms of territoriality helps to explain how actors beyond the state influence trajectories of agrarian change.

Particular territorialities can shape the ecological conditions for a certain form of living, for particular cultural practices and identities. How they shape the perception and exercise of state power, and how various counter-territorialities resist such efforts at control, all affect social and political life (Bryan 2012). Territorialities affect regimes of natural resource use. They affect strategies for social change in some of today's most powerful agrarian social movements, and they shape how everyday resource users understand and claim space. As such, all manner of territories, territorialities and territorializations deserve careful attention in studies of agrarian change.

FURTHER READING

Elden, S. (2013), *The Birth of Territory*, London: University of Chicago Press.
Haesbaert, R. (2004), *O Mito Da Desterritorialização. Do 'Fin dos Territorios' à Multiterritorialidade*, Rio de Janeiro: Bertrand Brasil.
Moore, D.S. (2005), *Suffering for Territory: Race, Place, and Power in Zimbabwe*, Durham, NC: Duke University Press.
Territory, Politics, Governance, a journal of the Regional Studies Association.
Winichakul, T. (1997), *Siam Mapped: A History of the Geo-Body of a Nation*, Honolulu, HI: University of Hawaii Press.
Yeh, E.T. (2013), *Taming Tibet: Landscape Transformation and the Gift of Chinese Development*, Ithaca, NY: Cornell University Press.

REFERENCES

Agnew, J. (2005), Sovereignty regimes: Territoriality and state authority in contemporary world politics, *Annals of the Association of American Geographers*, 95(2), 437–461.
Agnew, J. (2010), Still trapped in territory?, *Geopolitics*, 15(4), 779–784.
Alonso-Fradejas, A.; Borras, Jr., S.M.; Holmes, T.; Holt-Giménez, E.; Robbins, M.J. (2015), Food sovereignty: Convergence and contradictions, conditions and challenges, *Third World Quarterly*, 36(3), 431–448.
Asher, K.; Ojeda, D. (2009), Producing nature and making the state: Ordenamiento territorial in the Pacific lowlands of Colombia, *Geoforum*, Themed Issue: Gramscian Political Ecologies, 40(3), 292–302.
Ballvé, T. (2012), Everyday state formation: Territory, decentralization, and the narco landgrab in Colombia, *Environment and Planning D: Society and Space*, 30(4), 603–622.
Bryan, J. (2012), Rethinking territory: Social justice and neoliberalism in Latin America's territorial turn, *Geography Compass*, 6(4), 215–226.
Bryan, J.; Wood, D. (2015), *Weaponizing Maps: Indigenous Peoples and Counterinsurgency in the Americas*, New York: Guilford Publications.
Copeland, N. (2019), Linking the defence of territory to food sovereignty: Peasant environmentalisms and extractive neoliberalism in Guatemala, *Journal of Agrarian Change*, 19(1), 21–40.
Corson, C. (2011), Territorialization, enclosure and neoliberalism: Non-state influence in struggles over Madagascar's forests, *Journal of Peasant Studies*, 38(4), 703–726.
Cruz, M.K. (2010), A living space: The relationship between land and property in the community, *Political Geography*, 29(8), 420–421.
Eilenberg, M. (2014), Frontier constellations: Agrarian expansion and sovereignty on the Indonesian-Malaysian border, *Journal of Peasant Studies*, 41(2), 157–182.
Escobar, A. (2008), *Territories of Difference: Place, Movements, Life, Redes*, Durham, NC: Duke University Press.

Haesbaert, R. (2003), Da desterritorialização à multiterritorialidade, *Boletim Gaúcho de Geografia*, 29(1).

Halvorsen, S.; Mançano Fernandes, B.; Torres, F.V. (2019), Mobilizing territory: Socioterritorial movements in comparative perspective, *Annals of the American Association of Geographers*, 109(5), 1454–1470.

Jessop, B. (2016), Territory, politics, governance and multispatial metagovernance, *Territory, Politics, Governance*, 4(1), 8–32.

McCune, N.; Sánchez, M. (2018), Teaching the territory: Agroecological pedagogy and popular movements, *Agriculture and Human Values*, February. https://doi.org/10.1007/s10460-018-9853-9.

Moore, D.S. (2005), *Suffering for Territory: Race, Place, and Power in Zimbabwe*, Durham, NC: Duke University Press.

Murphy, A.B. (2013), Territory's continuing allure, *Annals of the Association of American Geographers*, 103(5), 1212–1226.

Padoch, C.; Peluso, N.L. (1996), *Borneo in Transition: People, Forests, Conservation, and Development*, Oxford: Oxford University Press.

Padoch, C.; Peters, C. (1993), Managed forest gardens in West Kalimantan, Indonesia, in Potter, C.; Cohen, J.; Janczewski, D. (eds), *Perspectives on Biodiversity: Case Studies of Genetic Resource Conservation and Development*, Washington, DC: AAAS Press, 167–176.

Peluso, N.L. (1995), Whose woods are these? Counter-mapping forest territories in Kalimantan, Indonesia, *Antipode*, 27(4), 383–406.

Peluso, N.L. (2005), Seeing property in land use: Local territorializations in West Kalimantan, Indonesia, *Geografisk Tidsskrift-Danish Journal of Geography*, 105(1), 1–15.

Peluso, N.L.; Vandergeest, P. (2011), Political ecologies of war and forests: Counterinsurgencies and the making of national natures, *Annals of the Association of American Geographers*, 101(3), 587–608.

Rose, N. (1999), *Powers of Freedom*, Cambridge: Cambridge University Press.

Sack, R.D. (1986), *Human Territoriality: Its Theory and History*, Cambridge: Cambridge University Press.

Sassen, S. (2008), *Territory, Authority, Rights: From Medieval to Global Assemblages*, Princeton, NJ: Princeton University Press.

Sikor, T.; Lund, C. (2009), Access and property: A question of power and authority, *Development and Change*, 40(1), 1–22.

Vandergeest, P.; Peluso, N.L. (1995), Territorialization and state power in Thailand, *Theory and Society*, 24(3), 385–426.

Vandergeest, P.; Unno, A. (2012), A new extraterritoriality? Aquaculture certification, sovereignty, and empire, *Political Geography*, 31(6), 358–367.

Winichakul, T. (1997), *Siam Mapped: A History of the Geo-Body of a Nation*, Honolulu, HI: University of Hawaii Press.

Woods, K.M. (2019), Green territoriality: Conservation as state territorialization in a resource frontier, *Human Ecology*, 47(2), 217–232.

24. Agrarian/land reform

Ben Cousins

INTRODUCTION

This chapter focuses on contemporary debates on agrarian and land reform, and seeks to clarify the main lines of differences between contending approaches. Four main paradigms are contrasted: neoclassical economics; neoclassical neo-populism; radical populism; and Marxist. These approaches are critically assessed, as is their salience for critical agrarian studies.

The chapter includes a brief survey of reforms launched in the twentieth century, and locates them in different historical periods. It sketches their highly diverse origins, politics and impacts, which suggests that substantive diversity in the experience of such reforms arises because of the very different and dynamic social, economic and political contexts in which they have occurred.

Agrarian/land reforms tend to focus on reconfiguring structural aspects of rural (and national) economies, and for this reason bring together and concentrate a number of different variables. These include land-based social relations, the distribution of different forms of property rights, the structure of agriculture, agro-food systems and value chains and the impacts of reform on wider economic development and growth. Class structure and associated power relations are always relevant, as are gendered inequalities, whether or not these are explicitly addressed within policy. They often generate a range of tensions and contestations – sometimes leading to counter-reforms launched by vested interests.

In recent decades, national and transnational social movements of rural people have contested dominant land and agricultural policies of a neoliberal character. One leading example is Via Campesina ('the way of the peasant'), with strong roots in the Americas and Europe and now representing groups in Asia, Africa and the Caribbean as well. Their advocacy of radical and state-led reforms (with a strong element of popular participation) is in contrast to approaches suggested by mainstream development agencies such as the World Bank that advocate the roll-back of the state, individual land titling and market-oriented agrarian reform. Debates on agrarian/land reform are thus a core concern for critical agrarian studies, which includes scholarship and activist analysis of past reforms and assessments of potential contributions to rural poverty reduction and other objectives.

DEFINING THE TERMS

'Land reform' refers to efforts to change the distribution of property rights in land and natural resources, and is often *redistributive* in character. Much land reform has involved transferring rights of ownership from wealthy landlords to poor, small-scale farmers working the land under various tenancy arrangements. These 'land to the tiller' reforms were common in the twentieth century. Less common are redistributive reforms that resettle small farmers on large estates subdivided into smaller plots.

Land reform also involves a *redefinition of the content and character of land rights*, as when former tenants become landowners, or when collective entities acquire common ownership of what was once individually owned land or the state takes over ownership of land. It can thus include *non-redistributive reform*, as in many programmes of land tenure reform in Africa at present (see Peters 2009). Here the focus is on providing legal recognition of rights derived from customs or other sources, in order to secure them against loss or dispossession and help promote increased agricultural productivity.

When land reform is allied to *structural changes in the organization of agricultural production and a range of complementary socio-economic and political reforms*, as it has been in many countries, it shades into 'agrarian reform'. This might include state policies to provide or enhance the supply of credit to farmers; strengthen their access to farm inputs and markets; invest in infrastructure to help boost productivity (such as irrigation dams, roads, telecommunications and electricity); develop new agricultural technologies; and implement agricultural pricing and trade policies that benefit beneficiaries of reform. It can involve the formation of co-operatives for purposes of input supply, production or marketing and creating new units of production organization such as communes and collectives. It can also involve the dismantling of collectives and co-ops and the promotion of the private sector, as in neoliberal versions of agrarian/land reform that began to be widely promoted from the 1990s, following the collapse of the Soviet Union.

Drawing a clear distinction between land reform and agrarian reform does not always make sense, and historically they have often been closely intertwined. In addition, there is a language problem: in French- and Spanish-speaking countries, the terms for land reform are *reforme agraire* and *reforma agraria*, respectively.

HISTORICAL CONTEXTS AND THE SUBSTANTIVE DIVERSITY OF AGRARIAN/LAND REFORM

Ever since the French Revolution of 1789, deliberate as well as 'organic' changes in the distribution, character and legal status of rights to land and natural resources, and in the class character and productivity of the agrarian economy, have powerfully shaped the making of the modern world. In particular, land reform played a key role in the transition from pre-capitalist forms of economy, in which classes of unproductive landed property dominated the countryside, to capitalism. These transitions became the main focus of debates on the left in the late nineteenth and early twentieth centuries, framed in terms of the 'agrarian question'. Some scholars and activists regard these controversies as still relevant today, while others view them as having been surpassed, or at least in need of a fundamental reformulation, to take account of the vastly changed conditions of contemporary capitalism.

Focusing only on the twentieth century and the first two decades of the current century, the following periods of agrarian/land reform can be distinguished.

1900–1939: Reform and Revolution

Two major revolutionary convulsions took place in the early twentieth century, in Mexico in 1910 and in Russia in 1917. Both saw peasants and the landless play key roles in the overthrow of autocratic states, which were replaced by regimes proclaiming popular democracy in the case of Mexico, and socialism in the case of Russia. In both cases, the mass of the population was engaged in small-scale peasant farming, but power and wealth in the countryside were concentrated in the hands of a small landowning elite. Radical redistributive land reforms were driven 'from below' by peasants and landless workers, supported by their allies within ascendant political forces, and saw large areas of land being transferred to the rural poor.

Subsequent developments in both countries, however, were less beneficial for the rural masses. In Mexico, a new constitution made provisions for agrarian reform based on the principle of 'land to the tiller' and for the creation of a 'social property' sector, with recognition of community-based land tenure (in the *ejidos*), as well as co-operatives and communes. But the redistribution of land took place slowly, and from the 1940s the ruling party supported the rise of large-scale capitalist farming, which dominates the agricultural sector today. From 1992 onward, market-oriented reforms allowed members of *ejidos* to register their land (although this has not led to much individual titling or the emergence of a land market).

In Russia, the revolution was followed by several years of civil war, in which the numerically dominant peasantry was the key social force in alliance with the small but politically powerful industrial proletariat. In the context of a debilitated economy and international isolation, the state initiated a programme of rapid industrialization in which agriculture was subordinated to industry and the needs of the urban population. Ultimately, under the autocratic leadership of Stalin, peasant communes and systems of production were largely destroyed, with massive loss of life, and collectives and state farms were imposed. After the collapse of communism in 1990, private land ownership was reintroduced.

1945–1980: Reform in the Contexts of Decolonization, National Liberation and the Cold War

After the end of World War II (WWII), pressures for decolonization and national liberation increased dramatically in so-called 'underdeveloped' countries. In the 1950s and 1960s many European colonial powers were forced to give up their direct political control of large areas of the world, where access to cheap natural resources and agricultural products had buttressed domestic processes of industrialization. Given that the majority of the population in the colonies was generally rural and engaged in small-scale farming, agrarian/land reform featured strongly in many national liberation struggles. When independence was eventually obtained, new governments in these countries initiated wide-ranging agrarian/land reforms. Another common problem was the dominance of the national agricultural sectors of poor countries by single crops produced for international markets, often under the control of large foreign corporations, as in the case of rubber in Vietnam and sugar in Cuba (Borras et al. 2007; Thiesenhusen 1995).

The post-WWII period also saw the heightening of tensions between the capitalist West (the 'First World'), now under the hegemony of the United States (USA), and the communist bloc led by the Soviet Union (the 'Second World'). Many national liberation movements from poor countries in the 'Third World' embraced socialism or communism and looked to the Soviet Union to lend them support. Wars of national liberation often involved peasants struggling for a radical redistribution of land – thus described by Wolf (1969) as 'peasant wars'. In the majority of cases, these reforms were of the 'land to the tiller' type, but in some cases large estates were collectivized by socialist governments. Examples include Vietnam from 1945 to the mid-1970s, and Algeria and Cuba in the 1950s and 1960s. Similar reforms were implemented by left parties taking power in states within post-independence India (e.g. West Bengal and Kerala).

In Latin America, national independence had been won by almost all countries in the course of the nineteenth century, and agrarian/land reforms were primarily a response to long-standing problems of structural poverty and inequality within the rural economy. With the distribution of land and income being highly skewed, and the modernization of agriculture offering few benefits to the majority of the population, radical reforms became a key focus of many left-wing political movements. The example of Cuba's collectivization of large foreign estates as a key thrust of agrarian/land reform inspired many, and with the prospect of a generalized turn to the left in Latin America, agrarian reform was seen by the USA and its allies as necessary to pre-empt communist revolutions.

The USA-led 'Alliance for Progress' was launched in 1961 and 19 countries initiated programmes of rural reform in the decade that followed (Thiesenhusen 1995). Some were 'minimalist' in character, as in Colombia, Venezuela, Brazil and Paraguay, but others were more ambitious, as in Ecuador, Honduras and the Dominican Republic. In Chile, a somewhat hesitant agrarian reform was initiated by a liberal government in 1967, but its scope and impact were considerably increased under Allende's left-wing government from 1970 to 1973. This led to a right-wing military coup supported by the USA, and the rolling back of reform.

An earlier reform that was driven mainly by widespread discontent amongst the rural poor, including populations of Indigenous people, occurred in Bolivia in 1953, and here too agrarian reform has become central to national politics. In Nicaragua, the 1979 revolution led by the Sandinistas was followed by radical redistributive reforms, that were reversed in the 1990s, and in El Salvador contested versions of reform became central in the decade-long civil war from 1981 to 1992 and the precarious peace that followed.

In Africa, a left-wing military government took power in Egypt and in 1952 initiated a major land reform, redistributing large areas of landlord-owned land to small-scale tenant farmers, agricultural workers and the landless, and securing their tenure rights. These reforms began to be reversed from the 1970s onward, and in the 1990s a decisive return to policies favouring rural elites was realized. In Ethiopia, radical reform followed a military coup in 1972 by left-wing army officers, in the context of a popular uprising that included peasant seizures of landlord property. All land was nationalized and extensive 'land to the tiller' reforms enacted. Peasant associations, state farms and co-operatives were also encouraged.

A revolution in Portugal in 1974 saw the removal of the Salazar dictatorship and the collapse of colonial rule. This allowed the socialist Frelimo party to come to power in Mozambique, where wide-ranging rural reforms included the nationalization of former Portuguese-owned farms and the formation of communal villages. Implementation of reform was slowed by civil war, and in the late 1980s capitalism was embraced. In Tanzania – independent since 1962 – collective agricultural production in communal (*ujamaa*) villages was promoted by the state, but failures led to their abandonment and a new focus on tenure reform to secure family- and community-based systems of property rights.

In China, pre-war support for the struggles of the peasantry by the People's Liberation Army bore fruit in peasant support for the Communist Party of China, which came to power in 1949 after a prolonged civil war. With the mass of poor peasants, tenants and landless labourers under the domination of wealthy landlords, land reform initially took the form of a 'land to the tiller' programme. Later, collectivization occurred through the formation of co-operatives from 1953 to 1958 and large-scale 'people's communes' from 1958. After the poor performance of the Great Leap Forward initiative of the early 1960s, a three-tier system of commune, brigade and production team was established. From 1978, the collective system gave way to family-based production within the Household Responsibility System, but with land ownership remaining in the hands of the collective.

Elsewhere in East Asia, agrarian reform took a very different route, helping to consolidate capitalism and underwriting rapid and successful industrialization. In Japan, South Korea and Taiwan, reforms designed to pre-empt a turn to communism after the end of WWII in 1945 were implemented by authoritarian states backed by occupying US forces under General MacArthur. Again, reforms involved the redistribution of land 'to the tiller', with powerful landlords being expropriated and a large mass of small-scale tenant farmers the main beneficiaries. In all three cases, however, the state was the driving force of reform, rather than peasant rebellion. Agricultural productivity was raised through technological innovation, but administered prices, punitive taxation policies, intersectoral terms of trade biased in favour of industry and supplies of cheap rural labour to emerging industries all meant that capitalist accumulation was subsidized by the appropriation of agricultural surplus.

1980s to the Present: Reform in the Context of Neoliberalism

The 1980s saw something of a hiatus in relation to agrarian/land reform, as the notion of the 'developmental state' gave way to market-oriented reforms driven by neoliberal ideology. International aid agencies insisted that policies of structural adjustment be adopted by poor countries in the Global South. These emphasized 'getting the prices right' rather than providing farmer support through co-operatives and agricultural marketing authorities. In a few countries, populations of poor peasants and landless workers continued to engage in struggles over land and agriculture, and specific political conjunctures created openings for radical agrarian/land reform – as in Nicaragua, El Salvador, Honduras, the Philippines and Zimbabwe, where a history of racialized land dispossession had been a key focus of the liberation war. In the 1990s, these convergences were joined by large-scale peasant mobilizations supporting reform in Indonesia and Honduras.

From 1990, after the collapse of Soviet-style communism in Russia and Eastern Europe, 'new wave' agrarian/land reform was promoted by the USA and the World Bank as a way to consolidate capitalist property relations. In countries such as Nicaragua and Vietnam, where land redistribution had involved the establishment of collective or co-operative forms of property and production, individual land titling formed part of the roll-back of radical reform. At the same time, ongoing shifts in communist countries such as China, Vietnam and in Central Asia towards household-based production systems, rather than collectives and state farming, were welcomed by the World Bank and other donors, and seen as validating neoliberal prescriptions. The new paradigm also emphasized decentralized rather than centralized processes of reform.

In this period, the continued globalization of agricultural markets, often driven by large agri-business corporations, has been accompanied by government, donor and non-governmental organization programmes aimed at 'modernizing' traditional agriculture. This involves increased use of chemical inputs, hybrid and genetically modified organism seed varieties, high-tech irrigation systems, plastic tunnels and, in relation to livestock, the promotion of intensive, industrial-style systems. Modernization packages include individual property rights, access to bank loans, increasing use of hired labour and access to formal value chains – all consistent with neoliberal ideology.

World Bank reports on land policy in 2003, and on agriculture and development in 2008, reflect these shifts of emphasis. The reports appear to acknowledge a degree of nuance (e.g. security of tenure can be achieved by legal recognition of customary rights as well as by individual titling; smallholder farmers can be highly productive) – but overall these messages are drowned out by a dominant narrative shift towards individualization, private property, increasing scale and integration into markets (i.e. fully fledged agrarian capitalism), all seen as inevitable.

In contexts where redistributive land reform is necessary because of historical legacies (e.g. racially inequitable land ownership, as in Southern Africa, or in post-conflict situations), the advocates of 'new wave' land reform argue that policies must be market-friendly rather than 'confiscatory'. Acquisition of land should take place through transactions between willing sellers and willing buyers, and expropriation avoided; in cases where expropriation is required, compensation must be at market prices. This view influenced the outcomes of negotiated transitions to majority black rule in Zimbabwe in 1980, Namibia in 1990 and South Africa in 1994, which all involved constitutional protection of old-order property rights.

In Latin America, many governments have tended to be ambivalent about 'new wave' reform. When countries have moved to the left with the support of rural social movements (as in Venezuela, Bolivia and Ecuador in the 2000s), they have emphasized redistribution of land at scale with the state playing a key role; when they have shifted to the right, market-friendly policies have been adopted. In the case of Brazil, the reform policies of the Lula government were schizophrenic in character, supporting both land occupations by members of the MST (Brazil's Landless Workers Movement) and other social movements of the rural poor, as well as market-oriented land redistribution.

Since the 1980s, most governments across the world have strongly promoted large-scale commercial (and often export-oriented) farming in support of economic growth, even where a degree of support for smallholders has also been on offer. With capitalism becoming hegemonic within the global economy over the past 30 years, these shifts indicate clearly how dramatically changed is the terrain within which agrarian/land reform has to be undertaken.

These shifts have not been uncontested, however. Large social movements have emerged to resist neoliberal-style reforms and urge both redistribution to the poor and smallholders and linked policies to support their production systems and livelihood strategies. At the same time, new issues have become objects of struggle and debate: gender equity, claims to resources by Indigenous peoples, environmental sustainability and the unequal and unsustainable nature of global agro-food systems.

In this brief historical sketch, it is apparent that agrarian/land reform has often been driven 'from below' by insurrectionary forces fuelled by the need to either protect or advance the interests of small farmers, landless labourers and the rural poor. Such reforms have often emerged in the context of wider political crises or struggles. In other cases, land reform has been driven 'from above' by state actors in pursuit of their own political or economic goals. In yet other cases, reform has combined state power and resources 'from above' with the energies of mobilized interest groups 'from below', and can be understood as 'state-and-society-centred reforms' (Borras et al. 2007).

The overview also reveals a great deal of variability in the meaning, thrust and outcomes of land and agrarian reforms. This is true of the post-WWII period as well, encompassing as it does both radical, redistributive reforms in the era of decolonization and struggles for social-ism, *and* programmes of decollectivization and privatization after the collapse of key socialist or communist regimes after 1990, *and* reforms that promote individual land titling and the promotion of capitalist farming at different scales, also strongly evident since 1990.

CONTENDING PARADIGMS AND CORE DEBATES IN RELATION TO AGRARIAN/LAND REFORM

Four main approaches dominate discussion of agrarian/land reform in the academic literature. Their key features are briefly described and assessed.

Neoclassical Economics

In a neoclassical approach to economic analysis, utility-maximizing activities are undertaken by individuals who produce commodities for self-consumption or for sale, operating through a firm (or farm) and in order to maximize profit. Well-functioning markets ensure efficient outcomes, as measured by the relative productivity of land, labour and capital, or factor productivity. Schultz (1964, 37) famously argued that although smallholder farmers are poor, there are 'few inefficiencies in the allocation of factors of production in traditional agriculture'.

In the post-war period, neoclassical development economists accepted that planning and state interventions were necessary in poor countries to create the conditions for market efficiency. This included land reform. Byres (2006) distinguishes these older versions of neoclassical economics from the strongly anti-state views that came to dominate mainstream development economics from the 1970s until the late 1990s, the so-called Washington Consensus. In these, there was no place for land reform of any kind. The beneficiaries of structural adjustment were anticipated as being efficient farmers at any scale, benefitting from economies of scale in relation to capital, farm machinery and purchased inputs. The declining role of the agricultural sector within a successfully developing economy was accepted as necessary and inevitable. Trade liberalization was seen as improving incentives to agriculture through the removal of protections for the urban, import-substituting sector, and agricultural price increases were expected, leading to a switch from subsistence to cash crops, improvements in agricultural productivity and output and hence the incomes of the rural poor. The actual experience of structural adjustment was very different, but neoliberal ideologists continue to blame governments for poor implementation rather than the policies themselves.

More recently, Collier and Dercon (2014) have argued strongly against the view that growth and poverty reduction must begin with smallholder agriculture. They are sceptical of claims for an Inverse Relationship between farm size and productivity, as argued by Lipton (2009), and instead stress three key areas where economies of scale are possible: skills and technology; finance and access to capital; and the logistics of trading, marketing and storage. Increasing the labour productivity of agriculture is critically important for improving incomes, and will lead to fewer people in farming and increased migration to obtain 'secure wage-earning jobs' (Collier and Dercon 2014, 96). This is a vision of market reform rather than agrarian reform, aimed at increasing efficiency and entailing a vast reduction of the number of people in agriculture.

This approach assumes that the historical experience of rich countries and recent experience in fast-growing Asian economies can be replicated, and that secure employment for millions of rural migrants will be available in cities and coastal areas. Massive levels of unemployment across the Global South, as well as the growing inequality within rich capitalist countries in recent decades, are ignored. Neither the specificities of capitalism nor divergent developmental pathways are discussed, and class relations are conspicuously absent, including in relation to 'smallholder farmers' – here viewed as a homogeneous category.

Neoclassical Neo-populism

For some mainstream development economists, including many agricultural economists, the efficiency of smallholder farmers proclaimed by Schultz in the 1960s informs their view of agrarian/land reform. In this view, while both peasants and large landowners are rational decision-makers, real markets are often thin because of inadequate information or high transaction costs (e.g. in supervising hired labour or enforcing contracts). Secure property rights help reduce transaction costs (Lipton 2009).

Power relations and structures are recognized as important, since groups or coalitions seek to use or alter their property rights and resources to their advantage. This is often the case when large landowners prevent land markets from optimizing farm size and thus realizing the strengths of small-scale agriculture. Where an Inverse Relationship exists between farm size and output per hectare, the redistribution of land from large to small, family-operated holdings can 'equalize' the effects of agricultural factor and product markets, technologies and structures of power. Since a highly unequal distribution of land constrains economic growth, effective redistributive land reforms can make large contributions to development, as well as contribute both directly and indirectly to industrial take-off (as in Japan, Taiwan and Korea). Given the strong emphasis on peasants/small-scale farmers and the (undifferentiated) rural poor as key beneficiaries, these economists are characterized as 'neoclassical neo-populists' by Byres (2006).

In his politically conservative version of this approach, Lipton (2009) argues that land reform must be market-oriented and 'incentive compatible'. It must also find a 'power-compatible' path in order for it to be politically feasible. Both criteria are met by 'new wave land reform', which should replace the state-led, land-confiscating approaches of the past that often involved the formation of inefficient collective or co-operative forms of production.

The 2003 World Bank report on land policy presents similar arguments. Redistributive land reform is required where 'the extremely unequal and often inefficient distribution of land ownership' is the result of 'power relationships and distorting policies rather than market forces' (World Bank 2003, 143). Since market forces cannot be expected to lead to land redistribution 'at the rate that would be required to maximize efficiency and welfare outcomes', state interventions are required (ibid.). Complementary and market-friendly policy instruments include progressive land taxation, divestiture of state land, foreclosure of mortgaged land and ensuring the rule of law (ibid., 155–156). The report strongly emphasizes individual land titling, while acknowledging that legally recognized customary land rights can be secure.

In a more radical version, Griffin, Khan and Ickowitz (2002) argue that agrarian/land reform must be state-led and either confiscatory in character or able to acquire land at low cost, emphasizing that reform is a political rather than a technocratic exercise. In other respects, these authors repeat arguments in relation to the Inverse Relationship and the efficiency of smallholder production. Again, questions of class relations, class-based differentiation of small-scale producers and class dynamics over time are absent for the most part.

Radical Populism

Radical populists tend to emphasize the oppression and exploitation of the rural poor by capitalist farmers and agri-business interests, within a global food regime dominated by large corporations. They stress the convergence of the interests of different groups living on the land, including landless labourers and small farm owners (some of them employers), and class, gender and other forms of difference amongst the peasantry are downplayed (hence the 'populist' tag).

Class relations do receive recognition in some strands of radical populism that are influenced by Marxism. In these, redistributive land reforms are seen as a key component of a broader agrarian reform that must seek to radically reconfigure both the agrarian structure and the wider agro-food system (Rosset 2006). Reforms must include policies to support peasant and family farmers and enhance agricultural productivity and rural livelihoods. The Inverse Relationship, and the contribution of equitable distributions of land to economic development more broadly, are sometimes referenced.

Via Campesina, the transnational social movement of small-scale farmers and allied interest groups, is seen as the cutting edge of a global politics that resists neoliberal capitalism and promotes food sovereignty: 'the right of each nation to maintain and develop its own capacity to produce its basic foods, respecting cultural and productive diversity'. This definition has since been updated to include the right of 'peoples' (see Claeys et al., this volume). McMichael (2008) argues that contemporary peasant movements are reframing the classical agrarian question, formulating an alternative version of modernity, and proposing versions of agrarian/land reform appropriate to the conditions of the twenty-first century. Older visions of redistributive agrarian/land reforms are increasingly being combined with more recent concerns such as food quality and environmental sustainability.

Van der Ploeg (2016) endorses many of these views, but has a view of rural class differentiation less influenced by Marxism than Rosset and McMichael and inspired by Chayanov, the early twentieth-century Russian economist. In this view, peasants are motivated primarily by a desire for 'autonomy' from the discipline of (capitalist) markets. They are making a come-back in both the Global South and the North, and agrarian/land reform can strengthen this process of 're-peasantization' (see van der Ploeg, this volume).

Peasants as both beneficiaries and agents of radical reform are thus a key focus of contemporary radical populism. The precise meaning of the term is often unclear. Borras and Edelman (2016) describe the heterogeneity of Via Campesina members, including the landless, peasant farmers, farm workers and artisanal fishers in the global South, middle-income and rich farmers in India, the semi-proletariat in urban and peri-urban settings and small-scale and part-time farmers in Western Europe. Class-based differences and the tensions they produce (e.g. between small-scale capitalist farmers and the landless labourers they employ) are underemphasized in radical populist analyses.

Marxism

Marxist analyses of agrarian/land reform focus on class relations, class structure and the dynamics of capital accumulation. Key concepts include the social relations of production and class power – both economic and political. A core but contentious issue is the (potential) contribution of agriculture to capitalist accumulation and industrialization more broadly (Akram-Lodhi and Kay 2010).

According to Marx (1976), the surplus labour of peasant producers in pre-capitalist societies was appropriated by landed property through rent, and a transition to capitalism involves the formation of new agrarian classes: agrarian capital, capitalist landed property and an agricultural proletariat. The logic of capitalist social property relations establishes conditions of market dependence and drives the growth of agricultural productivity through technical innovation. Primitive accumulation involves the dispossession of peasants 'freed' to work in industry and other non-agricultural enterprises. An enhanced agricultural surplus can be mobilized for industrial accumulation, in part through cheap food lowering the costs of reproducing the urban proletariat (Byres 1996). These processes and their variable pathways and outcomes form the key focus of debates on the 'agrarian question' (see Watts, this volume).

According to Lenin (1974 [1899]), resolution of the agrarian question can be achieved in a variety of ways, including 'from above', as in the case of nineteenth-century Prussia, where a landowning class metamorphosed into an agrarian capitalist class, or 'from below', where peasants differentiate themselves over time into classes of agrarian capital and agrarian labour (the 'American path'). To destroy the power of pre-capitalist landed property and ensure a successful transition to capitalism, a redistributive land reform, typically of the 'land to the tiller' variety, may be required. In this conception, '[o]nce pre-capitalist landed property – with its predatory appropriation of rent (versus productive accumulation) – is destroyed ... *there remains no rationale for redistributive land reform* ... any notion of redistributive land reform that advocates the division of larger, more productive enterprises (capitalist and/or rich peasant farms) is *ipso facto* both reactionary and utopian' (Bernstein 2004, 199). It is utopian because it is unlikely to 'achieve ... increasing agricultural productivity and rural employment and incomes on the basis of an egalitarian structure of 'family' farms' (ibid.).

Bernstein (2004, 202) proposes another interpretation: that in the contemporary world there is '*no longer an agrarian question of capital on a world scale*, even when the agrarian question – as a basis of *national* accumulation and industrialization – has not been resolved in many countries of the "South"'. A new agrarian question of *labour* has come into being, separated from its historic connection to that of capital, and manifested in struggles for land against various forms of capitalist landed property. This is centred on the global crisis of social reproduction experienced by 'fragmented classes of labour' – which can include small-scale farmers (here conceived of as petty commodity producers rather than peasants).

Other Marxists do not agree that the agrarian question of capital has been resolved at a 'world-historical scale', or can be separated from the agrarian question of labour. Akram-Lodhi and Kay (2010) argue that the core of the agrarian question remains the balance of class forces between capital and labour, both nationally and internationally, as well as the nature and trajectory of accumulation within (incomplete) transitions to capitalist agriculture. This is why agrarian/land reform retains its significance.

Some Marxists are critical of smallholder-focused reform as delaying the transition to mature capitalism, while others are more sympathetic and see land struggles as potentially transformative, especially if their class politics can be made more explicit and linked to wider struggles.

ASSESSING THE DEBATES

Paradigms are key to assessments of the performance of agrarian/land reform to date, and to advocacy of particular approaches argued to be most likely to reduce rural poverty.

In relation to the outcomes of agrarian/land reform, it is widely acknowledged that significant poverty reduction has been achieved in certain cases (e.g. China, Taiwan, South Korea, Japan, Cuba and Kerala state in India). This was due to the elimination of parasitic landowning classes by 'land to the tiller' reforms, as well as effective state support for the beneficiaries of reform, that lead to increasing productivity, output and income, and a significant contribution to development more generally. The many disappointing outcomes of reform (e.g. little or no rural poverty reduction; the benefits of reform being captured by a minority of beneficiaries, mostly relatively wealthier ones, etc.), are also acknowledged by many.

Major disagreements exist in the literature, however, in relation to how to *explain* these outcomes. For many neoclassical and neo-populist economists, property rights held in common or by the state (and seen as subject to bureaucratic rent-seeking) are key to explaining the failure of many post-reform production regimes, and individual property key to success. For radical populists, a key explanatory factor is the unequal and untransformed power relations that result in state policies in support of either capitalist farmers and agri-business or the rural poor. The degree and effectiveness of the political mobilization of the latter are often key. For Marxists, class dynamics in both the rural economy and more widely, and the politics that these generate, are key explanatory variables for failures and success.

Issues of scale of production and farm size are also highly contested. Both neoclassical economists and Marxists are sceptical of populist claims for a generalized Inverse Relationship between farm size and yield. For them, real economies of scale exist and larger-scale capitalist ('commercial') farms are often more productive than smaller-scale producers, in relation to yields as well as labour. Marxists see accumulation from below (the 'American path' in Lenin's typology) leading to larger capitalist farms, while neoclassical economists view this as evidence of increased 'efficiency'. Apparent convergence is belied by Marxists pointing to the increasing crisis of social reproduction suffered by the rural poor that accompanies the high productivity of a few capitalist farmers. Populists counter these arguments with empirical evidence that high yields can be achieved by peasant farmers, and point to the hidden costs of damage to the environment, human and animal health, etc. inherent in current systems of large-scale farming.

Another core disagreement across paradigms is in relation to the relative roles of state-led and market-driven processes in agrarian/land reform. For neoclassical economists and neoclassical neo-populists, market-friendly mechanisms are key to effective reform. Some neo-populists acknowledge that market processes by themselves will not redistribute wealth on a significant scale – so the state must initiate and oversee reform. For radical populists, unequal power within capitalist markets means that state power is essential, and the interests of popular classes must inform government interventions. For Marxists, state power has been crucial in enabling 'land to the tiller' reforms that replaced unproductive landowning classes with productive agricultural commodity producers, both small and large scale – but the logic of capital must be acknowledged as a key determinant of outcomes, at least until socialism can be brought into being.

Issues of ecological sustainability in agrarian/land reform have not figured much in debates on agrarian/land reform to date, an exception being the stress on environmental benefits in arguments for 'food sovereignty' advanced by radical populists in recent years. Climate change and the extreme urgency of efforts to address its root causes means that questions of the sustainability of systems of land use and food production will have to become more central in these debates.

CONCLUSION

Debates over agrarian/land reform are crucial for critical agrarian studies because they focus attention on a key question in agrarian politics: *what is to be done* to address fundamental social problems in the contemporary world? As with analysis, advocacy is shaped most powerfully by paradigm.

A central and thorny issue is agency – which social forces are capable of mobilizing the political resources required to ensure effective reform? Candidates include 'the rural poor' (the radical populist view), 'classes of labour' (the Marxists, who might include petty commodity producers in this broad category), successful entrepreneurs in both farming and agri-business (neoclassical and neo-populist economists) and an enlightened state (all schools of thought). Of course, the goals of these social forces are very different. Contestation is thus at the very core of agrarian/land reform, both in society and in the world of ideas and arguments.

FURTHER READING

Bernstein, H. (2004), 'Changing before our very eyes': Agrarian questions and the politics of land in capitalism today, *Journal of Agrarian Change*, 4(1–2), 190–225.
Borras, Jr., S.; Kay, C.; Akram-Lodhi, A.H. (2007), Agrarian reform and rural development: Historical overview and current issues, in Akram-Lodhi, A.H.; Borras, Jr., S.M.; Kay, C. (eds), *Land, Poverty and Livelihoods in an Era of Globalization*, Abingdon: Routledge, 1–40.
Lipton, M. (2009), *Land Reform in Developing Countries: Property Rights and Property Wrongs*, Abingdon: Routledge.
McMichael, P. (2008), Peasants make their own history, but not just as they please ..., *Journal of Agrarian Change*, 8(2–3), 205–228.
World Bank (2003), *Land Policies for Growth and Poverty Reduction*, Washington, DC and Oxford: World Bank and Oxford University Press.

REFERENCES

Akram-Lodhi, A.H.; Kay, C. (2010), Surveying the agrarian question (Part 2): Current debates and beyond, *Journal of Peasant Studies*, 37(2), 255–284.
Bernstein, H. (2004), 'Changing before our very eyes': Agrarian questions and the politics of land in capitalism today, *Journal of Agrarian Change*, 4(1–2), 190–225.
Borras, Jr., S.; Kay, C.; Akram-Lodhi, A.H. (2007), Agrarian reform and rural development: Historical overview and current issues, *Land, Poverty and Livelihoods in an Era of Globalization*, New York: Routledge, 1–40.

Borras, S.M.; Edelman, M. (2016), *Political Dynamics of Transnational Agrarian Movements*, Halifax: Fernwood Publishing.

Byres, T.J. (1996), *Capitalism from Above and Capitalism from Below: An Essay in Comparative Political Economy*, London: Macmillan.

Byres, T.J. (2006), Agriculture and Development: Towards a Critique of the 'New Neoclassical Development Economics' and of 'Neoclassical Neo-populism', in Jomo, K.S.; Fine, B. (eds), *The New Development Economics: After the Washington Consensus*, Delhi and New York: Tulika Books and Zed Books, 222–248.

Collier, P.; Dercon, S. (2014), African agriculture in 50 years: Smallholders in a rapidly changing world?, *World Development*, 63, 92–101.

Griffin, K.; Khan, A.R.; Ickowitz, A. (2002), Poverty and the distribution of land, *Journal of Agrarian Change*, 2(3), 279–330.

Lenin, V.I. (1974 [1899]), *The Development of Capitalism in Russia, Collected Works*, 3, 177.

Lipton, M. (2009), *Land Reform in Developing Countries: Property Rights and Property Wrongs*, New York: Routledge.

Marx, K. (1976), *Capital*, vol. 1, translated by Fowkes, B., London: Penguin.

McMichael, P. (2008), Peasants make their own history, but not just as they please ..., *Journal of Agrarian Change*, 8(2–3), 205–228.

Peters, P.E. (2009), Challenges in land tenure and land reform in Africa: Anthropological contributions, *World Development*, 37(8), 1317–1325.

Rosset, P. (2006), Moving forward: Agrarian reform as a part of food sovereignty, in Rosset, P.; Patel, R.; Courville, M. (eds), *Promised Land: Competing Visions of Agrarian Reform*, Oakland, CA: Food First Books, 301–321.

Schultz, T.W. (1964), *Transforming Traditional Agriculture*, New Haven, CT: Yale University Press.

Thiesenhusen, W.C. (1995), *Broken Promises: Agrarian Reform and the Latin American Campesino*, Boulder, CO: Westview Press.

Van der Ploeg, J.D. (2016), *Peasants and the Art of Farming: A Chayanovian Manifesto*, Halifax: Fernwood Publishing.

Wolf, E. (1969), *Peasant Wars of the 20th Century*, New York: Harper and Row.

World Bank (2003), *Land Policies for Growth and Poverty Reduction*, Washington, DC and Oxford: World Bank and Oxford University Press.

World Bank (2008), *World Development Report: Agriculture for Development*, Washington, DC and Oxford: World Bank and Oxford University Press.

25. Food regimes

Philip McMichael

INTRODUCTION

A 'food regime' lens conceptualizes the evolving geography of food provisioning for the era of industrial capitalism within an asymmetrical state system.[1] Through this it offers perspective on the impacts on domestic farming, land use, ecosystems, social diets and food (in)security across the world. Here, the 'food regime' concept enables critical world-historical analysis of the power relations embedded in cross-scale agrarian transformations. These involve the exercise of, and subordination to, episodic hegemonic political-economic projects within the state system – embodying changing trade, investment and financial strategies in the global food system. Focusing on the contours of world agriculture emphasizes the non-linearity of capitalist development across an unequal state system, offering 'a critique of the nationalist presuppositions that inform the literature on development and dependency' (Friedmann and McMichael 1989, 94).

Food regime analysis is informed in part by the Gramscian concept of 'hegemony', involving a coercion/consent relationship across the interstate system during hegemonic phases.[2] Common to each regime are relations of production and circulation of agricultural commodities within rules of international market participation. Such rules vary across regimes and are either implicit or explicit, depending on power relations within or among participating states.

FOOD REGIME PATTERNING

Food regimes, in the era of industrial capitalism, mark three phases of geo-political ordering of international food production and circulation, governed by world prices. *World* food prices stem from political-economic processes cheapening food supplies to enhance capital accumulation with lowered wage-food costs and/or enlarged profits in successive developments of food processing, global retailing and agro-input supplies. The geo-political orders in question are hegemonic periods: the British, from the 1870s to 1914; the American, from the 1940s to the 1970s; and the neoliberal, from the 1980s to the present (McMichael 2013).

The British-centered imperial food regime combined colonial tropical imports with temperate foods (grains and meat) from settler frontiers to fuel Britain's 'workshop of the world'. Following repeal of (protective) Corn Laws in 1846 by rising industrial classes to reduce labor costs, Britain outsourced its staple food production in the mid-nineteenth century to settler societies (Americas, Australasia and Southern Africa), enclosing and exploiting soil frontiers to provide cheap food supplies for industrializing Europe. From 1859 to 1889, United States (US) grain production almost trebled, forming a single world price for wheat in the late nineteenth century.

In turn, frontier agriculture came to anchor the new settler states, with integrated national farm/manufacturing 'sectors' forming putative national economies. These were represented in an idealized US model of national capitalist development. This model framed the mid-twentieth-century international 'Development Project', through which US hegemonic relations in the Cold War/post-colonial world contributed to nation-building via economic, military and, significantly, food aid via Public Law 480. US food aid was enabled by post-war commodity stabilization programs encouraging surpluses of grains (wheat, corn, soy) for export. These exports, along with sugar and oils, deepened international animal protein and durable foods complexes, intensifying capital accumulation via 'meatification' and food processing. Such transnational supply chains proliferated with financial deregulation and offshore banking in the 1970s, and the 1980s debt crisis opened the door for a neoliberal 'Globalization Project'. This was premised on the dismantling of the development project's economic nationalism. Here states, formerly served by markets within a Keynesian development state structure, now came to serve global markets and capital mobility in a corporate food regime.

The succession of food regimes embodied transforming geo-political and economic relations, with nineteenth-century 'free trade imperialism' yielding to a post-World War II international order with 'economic nationalism' as the organizing principle, followed by a neoliberal global order with capital liberalization as the organizing principle. First, the *British-centered food regime* encouraged imports of cheap wheat and meat from the New World settler frontier (the Americas, Australasia) underwriting European industrialization. Second, the *US-centered food regime* pivoted on American public food aid program sales of food surpluses at concessional prices – reducing wage costs to underwrite industrialization in (Cold War) strategic Third World countries (for example, South Korea, India, Pakistan, Israel, Egypt). Parallel sales of feed grains intensified livestock operations and dietary 'meatification' (Weis 2013), complementing subsidized green revolution technologies producing wage foods for rising urban-industrial classes. Third, a *corporate food regime* intensified the US model of agro-exporting (of food surpluses) via World Trade Organization (WTO) liberalization of global trading in the name of 'feeding the world'. World food prices reached their lowest level in 150 years at the end of the twentieth century. In this era of financialization, agribusiness conglomeration accompanied the universalization of export agriculture with an accelerated displacement of small-scale farming systems.

A corporate-led food regime originated in World Bank/International Monetary Fund-mandated structural adjustment policies in the 1980s, requiring indebted Southern states to reduce farm supports and expand agro-exports to defray debt. In the 1990s, trade agreements (notably the WTO and associated free trade agreements) instituted liberalization measures to universalize 'market rule' via neoliberal agricultural investment and trade freedoms for transnational agribusiness. US and European Union subsidies for agribusiness artificially cheapened foodstuffs for dumping in world markets at the expense of now unprotected Southern farmers. Agribusiness investments expanded Southern agro-exports of high-value fruit, vegetables and seafood for Northern consumers, compounding de-peasantization and food dependency via an international division of agricultural labor. Southern lands in particular have been increasingly converted from local food provisioning to contract farming and agro-industrial estates. Here, the conditions of farm labor have deteriorated as commodification has deepened:

> [O]f the 1.3 billion people employed in agriculture … there are some 450 million waged workers, over half of whom are women. Seventy per cent of child labour globally takes place in agriculture … and agriculture produces over 170,000 work-related deaths annually. Agricultural workers are twice as likely to die at work than in any other sector. Between three to four million pesticide poisonings

occur each year, some 40,000 of them fatal ... chronically high rates of malnutrition occur among agricultural workers. (Rossman 2012, 61)

Agri-food chains have proliferated as global supermarkets responded to agricultural liberalization rules by expanding production contracts across the global South to access cheapened labor and new consumers, sourcing year-round produce. Recent expansion of agro-estates in Southern Europe depends on a migrant labor reserve, increasingly sourced from the Middle East and North Africa (Corrado 2017). Exploitation of such low-cost and flexible migrant labor displaced by agribusiness enclosures in Morocco, Tunisia, Egypt and Turkey enables producers to compress costs as they struggle to survive the withdrawal of Common Agricultural Policy subsidies and new market pressures exerted by powerful Northern European retail chains. Worldwide pressures on small-scale farming systems compel new forms of social reproduction via labor circulation, substantially transforming rural lifestyles. Here, small farming households pursue a 'risk-averse livelihood strategy', by 'maintaining a foothold in agriculture while having varied household members seek income streams from other activities', collapsing the boundaries between urban and rural landscapes (Taylor and Rioux 2018, 111).

Food regime structuring across this long (industrial) century has displaced local food systems via specific forms of enclosure in each episode. This process encompasses annexation of Indigenous lands and capture of colonial food reserves, via taxation and commodification, through the deployment of food aid and green revolution techno-politics, marginalizing post-colonial food producers (Akram-Lodhi 2013, 87–96), to the universalization of export agriculture and dispossession of (Southern and Northern) small farmers by land concentration, land grabbing and extensive food dumping. While the US remains a trade superpower, it no longer sets the world price for wheat, corn and soy – indicative of the rise of rival agro-exporters.

Food regimes have linked imperial, national and transnational moments via successive hegemonic projects. The most recent world ordering deepens corporate hegemony and its 'ability to shape the rules under which [corporations] operate in the middle space that they occupy in the world food economy', between producers and consumers (Clapp 2016, 121). Food regimes are sequential parts of an evolving world-historical conjuncture, namely, the age of industrial agriculture. *Generically*, capital's food regime across these three forms deepens the cumulative planetary ecological crisis.

Each regime embodies a central tension. The British-centered food regime pivoted on the substitution of temperate for tropical food supplies as the imperial age declined; the US-centered food regime pivoted on tension between post-colonial construction of national agricultural sectors and emerging transnational food complexes; and the corporate food regime pivots on escalating socio-ecological tensions between global and local food sourcing.

Regime tensions resolve through crisis and restructuring, emergent relations shaping a successor system. The commercial frontier of the first food regime thus underpinned the subsequent US food aid program provisioning national industrialization in select Third World states alongside green revolution technologies. European adoption of the US agribusiness model elevated agro-exporting as the basis for the third food regime's transnational food complexes, especially animal protein. Thus, in the last quarter century, as global production of maize increased by over 100 per cent and that of soybeans by over 200 per cent, global rice production only increased by 35 per cent and wheat by 25 per cent (Winders 2017, 134) – registering deepening 'meatification' as an expanding profit frontier for surplus absorption of maize and soy (Weis 2013). China is central to this dynamic. Alongside expanding feed crops are sugar and palm oil frontiers for the biofuel industry. Such 'flex-crop' proliferation is symptomatic of a nexus between financialization and land grabbing.

The current food regime pivots on a deepening contradiction between globalizing unsustainable industrial agriculture and smaller-scale, local farming systems represented by indebted mid-sized and local farmers in the global North and networks of peasant and small-scale farmers in the global South (Desmarais 2007; van der Ploeg 2018). Transitions to local food systems and farmer/consumer networking offers a distinct social ethic and ecological sustainability. The struggle between these systems centers on how states may reconfigure at a moment of global uncertainty, with forms of protectionism hedging global trade/supply chains.

ISSUES

Interpretation and Debates

The 'food regime' concept invites different interpretations, stemming from distinct definitional and/or historical understandings. Food regime analysis was an original intervention problematizing a seemingly reified structuring of the 'modern world system' around a single division of labor subdividing the international state system into core, peripheral and semi-peripheral states. The 'food regime' historicized state-building and world agricultural relations as mutually conditioning and non-linear phases of world food provisioning.

Such a macro-historical reinterpretation draws challenges from two related angles. One sees a homogenizing grand narrative, eliding anomalous, local agri-food case studies. However, methodologically food regime analysis enables understanding local agricultures as embodying global relations and processes *in their own way* and/or as constitutive of global developments (Araghi 2003). The initial framework offered perspective on interstate system formation in relation to an agri-food commodification narrative, with lines of inquiry for further analysis of the multiplicity of social, spatial and ecological relations, as complexes of many determinations (McMichael 2013).

A related challenge is that the food regime can encourage 'understandings of the world that exclude subjects and subjectivities … Obscuring diversity and fluidity of the relations, actors, metrics, translations and contexts' (LeHeron and Lewis 2009, 346). Nevertheless, capitalism, or processes of enclosure, present differently in different spaces, with different meanings for various subjects, who respond and resist with their own perspectives and resources – underlining the multiple ways in which commodification takes hold across the world (for example Akram-Lodhi 2013; Lapegna 2016; McMichael 2010). Broader social movements respond, thus: 'food regimes emerge out of contests among social movements and powerful institutions, and reflect a negotiated frame for instituting new rules' (Friedmann 2005, 234). The corporate food regime, by definition, spawns social mobilizations, advocating alternative and democratic, localizing agri-food systems (for example Desmarais 2007; Gaarde 2017; Lapegna 2016). Arguably, global food riots in 2007–2008 (repeated in 2019) marked early transitioning of the corporate food regime, as urban protestors targeted states for policies of food dependency, precipitating a rise in land grabbing for offshore food supplies by predominantly Middle

Eastern and East Asian states among others, via 'agro-security mercantilism' (McMichael 2013), and registering rising national protectionism at the expense of liberal multilateralism.

A further response to food regime 'macro-history' inserts the role of states, in the 'neoliberal' food regime. Thus, Latin American governments fund biotechnological research and promote agro-industrialization via private accumulation initiatives in producing feed and fuel crops (Otero 2012). Bringing the state in seeks to address a perception that a 'corporate' regime presumes state 'retreat', suggesting the concept of 'neoregulation' to underline state agency in promoting agribusiness. While national-level policy initiatives are an important dimension of food regime expression across states, they express world market constraints on states, which are subject to competitive interstate relations and compulsions of heightened capital mobility (McMichael 2020, 123–124). Thus, the WTO's 'investor-state dispute mechanism' has enabled foreign investors to challenge government legal decisions and policies (such as food security, health, environmental protection and workers' rights) if companies can claim such policies affect profits. Here, the post-Keynesian principle of states 'serving' markets does not remove state agency, rather it emphasizes world market conditioning of national policy-making. The difference between states serving markets, and vice versa, is precisely to distinguish the *modus operandi* across the second and third food regimes. Thus, Latin American governments promote corporate feed and fuel crops in the 'new extractivism' – considered a regional form of neoliberal development. As Connell and Dados note: 'These zones of capital accumulation are established through coalitions of state officials, local business elites and international corporate actors' (2014, 127). Here, state power serves agribusiness and agro-exporting, fulfilling the coercion/consent dimensions of neoliberal hegemony.

States *mediate* political, economic and ecological dimensions of food regime structuring. For example, Brazilian and Argentinian state-sponsored soy booms, supplying China's rising demand for industrial pork feed, have combined export revenues with social subsidies. Alternatively, the Indian government's post-food crisis National Food Security Act (2013) consolidated a broad-based food provisioning via the Public Distribution System, which it defended at the Bali WTO Ministerial the following year, appealing to rights-based domestic protections. Here, state food rationing provides a market for grains from small farmers, not unlike Brazil's Zero Hunger Campaign under President Lula in the early 2000s.

Such domestic food initiatives model 'sovereignty' even as they complement domestic footprints of a *global* food regime in the form of large-scale export agriculture and corporate food retailers. Thus, while India courts corporate food retailing at the expense of a multitude of local groceries and producers, it is a substantial beef exporter. Supplying beef to Southeast Asia, Australia and the Middle East, it doubled its maize and soybean feed crops between 2000 and 2015, at a time of serious food insecurity and water shortage (Winders 2017, 101–104).

Definitional Issues

Three definitional perspectives apply here. The *first* reconceptualizes 'capital's food regime' as a 'political regime of global value relations' (Araghi 2003), emphasizing the centrality of global value relations in only two periods: the late nineteenth-century 'imperialism of free trade' era via the international global standard under British hegemony, and recent neoliberal hegemony, or global 'market rule'. Global market rule is not only the institution and protection of private property rights by states, but also the privileging of a capital, over a territorial, logic. It shows in the reduction of land, forests, waterways and ecological relations to uniform price metrics, regardless of their meaning and use-value to inhabitants. Food is thus intrinsic to capitalism's global value relations given its significance for labor costs.

The two periods governed by global value relations were ones in which, first, British and European ruling classes suppressed early industrial wage costs via access to cheap New World grains and meat, and second, (post-welfare state) neoliberal capitalism embodies 'forced under-consumption and under-reproduction strategies [within] *slavish* conditions of employment ... without visible *enslavement*' (Araghi 2003, 60–61). This perspective reinterprets the post-war food aid-based regime, as an 'aid-based food order of an exceptionally reformist period of world capitalism' (ibid., 51). This approach underscores the significance of value relations in the two 'liberal' orders, where markets ruled. But market rule involves managed value relations, paralleled here by US consolidation of a capitalist empire during the Cold War period, including rising transnational capital complexes.

A *second* definitional issue addresses the question whether food regime analysis is at best a 'tool of hindsight. It can help order and organize the messy reality of contemporary global food politics, but its applications are necessarily contingent upon an unfolding and unknowable future' (Pritchard 2007, 8). That is, has a third food regime materialized? How should we 'theorize agriculture's incorporation into the WTO'? Instead of a mechanism for market governance, the WTO is a state-centered 'carryover from the politics of the second food regime, rather than representing any putative successor', wherein WTO protocols 'entrenched world food power in the hands of elite Northern interests' (Pritchard 2009, 301), despite a G20/Southern challenge at the Doha Round, indicating failure to institute 'unfettered market rule' (ibid., 297).[3]

However, since hegemony combines consent with coercion, the General Agreement on Tariffs and Trade Uruguay Round (1986–1994), constituting the WTO (1995), prefigured a hegemonic 'balance' albeit with Northern protectionism, in the name of world market-based food security. Guided by active lobbies of free trader agro-export states (the Cairns Group) and a powerful grouping of agribusiness transnational corporations, the Round promoted services and agricultural liberalization in which the North held a competitive advantage. Northern promise of open markets for Southern products, *including agro-exports*, won consent from Southern states. Given the extent of economic globalization by the mid-1990s, a similar trade-off, so to speak, governed the WTO's Agreement on Agriculture, in which all member states signed on to agri-food liberalization. Finally, one specificity of liberalization was that farmers now *universally* confronted world market prices, so while Northern farm politics carried over, the projection of such power *globally* against smallholder cultures, with artificially cheapened cereal prices, was a *transformed* 'carryover'.[4] A new chapter in 'agriculture's incorporation' into the WTO instituted corporate privilege, enabling a subsidized world price as centerpiece of a cheap food regime deployed against small-scale farmers everywhere.

Returning to Pritchard's notion of the contingency of the present (2007), in interpreting the 'messy reality of contemporary food politics', it is an important observation, especially now. The old is dying, but not without a struggle, as the powerful oligopolistic grip of corporate agriculture is tightening (Mooney 2018), with increasingly acknowledged dangerous social, nutritional, health and ecological effects. In 2018, the Inter-Academy Partnership (involving 130 national academies of science and medicine), identified a 'broken global food system' (*The Guardian*, November 28, 2018).[5] Even as capital liberalization remains the organizing principle of a food regime in transition, 'hindsight' is increasingly significant now in revisionings of the future.

One vision is that a third, 'corporate-environmental food regime' is perhaps immanent, with agribusiness and food companies appropriating environmental activism via 'organic' and 'nutritional' foods (Friedmann 2005). Thus, responding to consumer demand for natural foods, firms 'like General Mills, ADM, Coca-Cola and Unilever have bought up companies that produce natural ingredients and flavours' (*Agrifood Atlas* 2017, 28), often diluting the original intent. These shifts occur in the context of class-based bifurcation of diets across an uneven state system, symbolized in the juxtaposition of Whole Foods and Walmart, dividing the regime 'world'. While powerful Northern corporate oligopolies gain representation in industry associations exerting 'downward pressure on standards', India courts Walmart, and corporate food retailers move offshore to the global South, where obesity and diabetes are ballooning.

Within the food industry, heightened financial and digital-technological[6] competition transforms global foodscapes and centralizes corporate practices: with buyouts of green start-ups undermining sustainability commitments, relaxing nutritional and environmental standards and reducing social responsibility spending (Mooney 2017, 59–61). A corporate-environmental regime vision may include transformed agricultural production methods, reducing chemical inputs, soil decline and carbon release, termed 'sustainable intensification', or now 'climate-smart agriculture' (CSA). Lacking definite criteria, and emphasizing technical rather than political resolution, CSA essentially rebrands agribusiness, excluding farmer knowledges, especially women's seed-sharing practices (cf. Taylor 2018). The World Bank's positive evaluation of 'climate-smart' land-sparing grain monocultures elides, for example, massive soy fields underwriting a global meat complex, with climate change and environmental contamination as additional effects.

Another vision is strengthened by the deepening power of financial-corporate techno-politics in deploying genetic and digital technologies to eliminate farming knowledges in the name of advancing industrial agriculture, without farmers. The increasingly evident poisoning of ecologies – with agro-chemicals and dietary malnutrition contributing to serious public health crises – informs a countermovement in the name of smaller-scale, restorative agricultures. This involves proliferation of alternative, agro-ecological farming methods to restore soil and food health, and associated networks of small-scale producers and consumers, subsumed under the elastic concept of 'food sovereignty' (Da Vià 2012; Patel 2009), and generating analysis of the possibilities of a food commons regime (Vivero-Pol 2017).

The *third* definitional issue concerns regime analytics. The food regime has been defined as a 'rule-governed structure of production and consumption of food on a world scale', where rules are implicit and normalized, reflecting class compromise, and anchored by a stabilizing (hegemonic) international currency (Friedmann 1993, 30–31). This definition questions the existence of a third food regime. However, in a global market 'class compromise' is a translocal inter-elite relation. The corporate food regime has embodied institutional compromise among all member states, adopting liberalized trade rules expressing hegemonic neoliberal principles to which all unevenly consent, albeit under constraint of market participation. This much is clear in how China engages with the global food regime, even as its global infrastructural 'road' and maritime lanes prefigure alternative sourcing patterns (McMichael 2020), in a time of rising defiance of WTO multilateralism.

Food regime analysis emerged to distinguish the temporal and spatial structuring of capitalism and the state system via comparable governing rules. Neither of the first two rather disparate regimes match a formal definition. Nor does a corporate regime fit a standard pattern, even as its agri-food relations have been shaped by universal structural adjustment policies and hegemonic trade rules (both coercive and consensual) alongside a *de facto* dollar system. And internationally, a substantial volume of food now moves within and among transnational corporate subsidiaries, enabled by deregulated global financial flows and interstate deals,[7] with food manufacturers linking large upstream commodity traders and downstream food retailers. Here, 'the focus of competition is shifting: from one firm versus another, to one supply chain versus another' (*Agrifood Atlas* 2017, 29), in multiplex rather than trade-based multipolar relations, where 'interdependence today is denser, consisting of trade, finance and global production networks' (Acharya 2017, 11).

Food regimes express relationships specific to their time/space coordinates. Stability is a relative term across quite different historical periods. Operational convergence can be just as powerfully expressed in market rule, governed by institutions such as the Bank of International Settlements coordinating central banks, the WTO and the International Monetary Fund. Here states are subjected collectively to privatization, structural adjustment, trade agreements and financial maneuvers, with taxpayers as the default. Such structured coercion and consensus is nevertheless unevenly distributed across the state system, exemplified by European Union and US strategic retention of farm subsidies for agro-export power in the world market. Ultimately, regime periods are distinguished by instituted mechanisms in combination that organize the global circulation of food – currency, trade, finance, corporate supply chains and/ or 'food empires' (van der Ploeg 2018).

FOOD REGIME OUTCOMES AND CRITICAL AGRARIAN STUDIES

Most rural and agri-food transformations can be analyzed through the food regime lens. Its historical method allows situating such change across space and time, and perhaps anticipating future developments (McMichael 2013, 2020). Situating change on the ground is more than recognizing broader context, it is also recognizing what may be lost. While food regimes convert land frontiers, commodification undermines and erases Indigenous life-worlds, as ecologies of social reproduction.

A recent book, *Dark Emu, Black Seeds: Agriculture or Accident?* recovers from colonial-settler erasure the sophistication of Australian Aboriginal peoples' socio-economic practices, as a civilization based in landscape and soil management, underlining the ecological rationality of so-called 'pre-historic' people: 'Aboriginal people are born of the earth and individuals within the clan had responsibilities for particular streams, grasslands, trees, crops, animals and even seasons. The life of the clan was devoted to continuance' (Pascoe 2016, 145).

In contrast, food regimes consolidate *dis*continuance: deepening land alienation across Earthly space and time, with overwhelming impacts on Indigenous cultures and ecosystems. Critical agrarian studies has a role to play in reworking food regime histories. That is, rather than a conventional 'accumulation by dispossession' narrative, substituting 'dispossession by accumulation' foregrounds the violent historical process whereby capitalist modernity undermines planetary and species integrity. This narrative includes attention to protective territorial rights struggles[8] by Indigenous and peasant producers on the one hand, and ongoing agro-ecological experimentation and learning – from family farms to peasant cultures – on the other (Gliessman 2018).

While food regime analysis focused on a capital-centric narrative of the making of the industrial world, it spawns contending narratives, whether in policy arenas, in knowledge construction and reconstruction, or in grounded settings. This includes ongoing and diverse forms of resistance: from solidarity alliances in seed-saving practices, agro-ecology schools and gender equity, through opposition to land grabs and demands for land reform, the 'right to *produce* food' (rather than the right to food in the market),[9] to advocacy for National Food Policies and local Food Councils, pressure by the International Planning Committee for Food Sovereignty on the United Nations Committee on World Food Security (CFS) for representation in 2010 in a newly formed Civil Society Mechanism, the CFS High Level Panel of Experts Report, *Agroecology and Other Innovations* (2019), and so on.

The food regime embodies a relational tension between models of agriculture – where large-scale industrial agriculture is privileged over small-scale farming systems, viewed as pre-modern and unable to 'feed the world' (even as small-scale farming feeds up to two-thirds of the world). For its part, the international peasant organization, La Vía Campesina (LVC), views the industrial model as 'agriculture without farmers', underlining its ecological abstractions and vulnerabilities. Under these conditions small and medium-scale producers may withdraw from debt relations and invest in ecological relations – reducing the need for agro-inputs associated with industrial techniques, by instead restoring farming knowledge, biodiversity and soil health (van der Ploeg 2018). This practice is widespread in Europe and Latin America, and in parts of South Asia and Africa. It is also emerging in North America, where farm debt and soil fertility decline threaten farm viability. While these developments signal the possibility of restorative farming with living ecosystems, they must contend with the inordinate power of financialized (and subsidized) agribusiness. How this plays out in locales as well as in states and forms of international governance conditions the landscape of critical agrarian studies.

Internationally, the peasant coalition initiated the critique of food regime capital-centrism, as enshrined in WTO rules. In collectively establishing the WTO, Director-General Renato Ruggiero declared, were 'no longer writing the rules of interaction among separate national economies. [They were] writing the constitution of a single global economy.' Such reconfiguration licensed food corporations to claim 'food security' provisioning via world-scale agricultural liberalization. At the 1996 World Food Summit, LVC challenged this 'mission', advocating 'food sovereignty' – to protect and support domestic food systems rather than surrender sovereignty to private global interests: 'The trade negotiators wanted their farmers to compete: instead, rallying behind the new slogan, the peasants of the world decided to unite' (De Schutter in Gaarde 2017, xvi). As a protective 'countermovement' this response concerned rights of peasants, farmers *and* citizens to sovereign power for and within nation-states – regarding food, economic and ecological security: civilizational goals focusing on organizing social life around ecological principles.

The peasant movement's critique promotes a politics premised on multiclass alliances appealing to 'sovereignty', as strategic essentialism in the first instance – that is, asserting national sovereignty against global rules privileging private interests. Substantively, it advocates democratic, cooperative territorially autonomous rural cultures stewarding ecosystems, as a form of 'agrarian citizenship' underpinning social relations in general (Wittman 2009). While LVC is 'anti-capitalist, it aspires to reimagine a new kind of modernity with the 'middle peasantry' at the center of its alternative vision' (Edelman and Borras 2016, 55). This vision, while not foregrounding orthodox class politics across rural landscapes, is a central oppositional reflex *within* the food regime, envisioning a multifaceted struggle 'on all fronts simultaneously',[10] with broadening implications for longer-term national and global governance impacts.

The unifying issue, certainly beyond simply a peasant solution, is eliminating the subordination of socio-ecological relations to market principles. This issue is routinely misunderstood (and misrepresented) in translating an emphasis on LVC's foundational critique of the neoliberal/corporate solution to global food insecurity into, simply, a 'peasant solution' (cf. Bernstein 2016; Friedmann 2016). The originality of LVC was precisely its recognition that WTO rules promoting monocultural industrial agricultures eliminate farming system knowledges (and farmers' rights to produce domestic foods) across diverse ecosystems to sell agro-inputs, standardized seeds and export nutritionally depleted foodstuffs. In addition, LVC implicated transnational corporations and WTO rules as overriding public sovereignty: a distinguishing characteristic of neoliberal ideology of 'anti-state' politics.

Such institutional privileging of private monopoly power over the terms of humanity's access to healthy and culturally appropriate diets brings us to Polanyi's insight that commodifying land and labor (and money) implies a 'stark utopia', generating protective countermovements (1957). 'Fictitious commodities' are now in runaway mode: 'ecosystem services', labor precarity, swelling migrant labor circuits and uncontrolled financialization – all drive countermovement possibilities for multiclass alliances via counterhegemonic politics (Harvey 2017).[11]

The 'sovereignty' issue is thus central to the contradictory relations of the corporate food regime. It underscores the class-driven override of public protections, at the same time as it has precipitated challenges to 'globalization', not the least being the initial 'peasant'[12] critique of WTO overriding of national as well as farm cultures, livelihoods and ecological 'sovereignty'. Subsequent challenges include food crisis bans on food exporting, reactive 'agro-security mercantilism',[13] trade wars, protectionism, cascading challenges to rising prices and ideologically distinct populisms. Food sovereignty ('food from somewhere' rather than 'food from nowhere') is, for example, highly relevant to resolving the questions of 'corporate capture' versus farmer rights, the ecological questions and the problematic conversion of food crops to feed and fuel crops by global agribusiness, at the expense of global food security, and human health insofar as industrial agricultural 'frontiers' and factory farming encourage pathogens that may pass to humans. The measure of this is Covid-19's world economic impact, revealing the liability of food regime reliance on global food supply chains in deepening food insecurity, and the strategic significance of local infrastructures of care and social reproduction.

CONCLUSION

Such tensions highlight the salience of political territoriality for future resolutions of the (sustainable/healthy) food question, germane to critical agrarian studies. Appeals for 'land sovereignty' anticipate bio-regional formations and/or reformulated rural–urban relations, presaging substantive forms of 'multifunctionality' nurtured by new forms of governance (Ajl 2012).

One formulation is that underway in China, hitherto relatively separate from the food regime, with a huge agrarian sector and largely food self-sufficient since Deng Xiaoping's market reforms in the 1980s. In the twenty-first century, ecological damage and rising levels of consumption have pushed the Chinese, especially under President Xi, to secure access to food offshore and sustain Chinese land, encouraging organic food production in the interests of 'ecological civilization'. Alongside current 'agricultural modernization' via agribusiness expansion, organic or agro-ecological farming is also valued by the state, not necessarily in terms of farmer solidarities, but more pragmatically as a response to soil degradation, and preserving a peasant sector for employment purposes and ensuring grain reserves for food security. This constitutes part of the distinctive multifunctional 'Chinese agricultural paradigm' (van der Ploeg and Ye 2016), in the context of stemming rural–urban migration. It underpins China's technical support for peasant farming cultures abroad, as it engages more directly with the transitioning global food regime (McMichael 2020). Whether China may model domestic retention/support of farming cultures (as opposed to agro-industrialization) and assist consolidation of 'peasant' agriculture elsewhere in the global South remains to be seen. Climate and health emergencies complicate such predictions.

In the meantime, pervasive 'public-private' partnerships are likely to intensify centralized food-provisioning complexes to secure investments and supply chains via strategic multiplex relations – arraigned against world-wide food sovereignty activisms, and localizing responses to domestic food deficits associated with Covid-19. Such world market power struggles (with local expressions) represent a critical nexus for examination in agrarian studies, since they simultaneously precipitate an increasingly vital politics of equity, democracy and ecological resilience.

NOTES

1. I am indebted to Tony Weis for his thoughtful comments on an earlier draft, and to three remarkable copy editors: Bettina Engels, Isabella Pfusterer and Kristina Dietz.
2. Arrighi's formulation of 'world hegemony' (1990) involves a dominant power exercising governmental functions over the system of sovereign states articulating a universally desired direction for a particular historical period, by which state rulers may also consolidate power over willing subjects.
3. The G20 challenged Northern power rather than the WTO's neoliberal paradigm, targeting the hypocrisy of farm sector protection as farm sectors were opened elsewhere. As Hopewell notes: 'the creation of the WTO represented not the realization of the neoliberal project in the realm of trade but only its beginning' (Hopewell 2016, 203). Despite stalemate in 2008, WTO neoliberal rules still apply, alongside proliferating regional and bilateral free trade agreements, which signal increasing 'multipolarity'.
4. Food regimes carry over previous relations, now *reconfigured* in a new complex of institutions and practices, and on a larger geo-political scale, generating emergent relations that, in turn, anticipate a successor regime (McMichael 2020, 120).
5. Holt-Giménez argues: the global food system 'is not broken … It is working precisely as a capitalist food system is supposed to work: it expands constantly, concentrating wealth in a few, powerful monopolies, while transferring all the social and environmental costs onto society' (2019, 89).
6. '"Digital agriculture" will collect massive amounts of geographic and agronomic data and use satellite information systems to direct new, sophisticated farm machinery in the application of synthetic fertilizers and pesticides in the latest iteration of "precision agriculture"' (Holt-Giménez 2019, 83; see also Mooney 2018).
7. Large-scale intertwining of states and firms is prominent in the global South for historical and geo-political reasons, given the substantial network of Northern corporate supply chains already in place (McMichael 2013).
8. In December 2018, the United Nations General Assembly approved the *Declaration on the Rights of Peasants and Other People Working in Rural Areas*, following years of diplomatic work led by La Vía Campesina.

9.   In the 1980s the World Bank redefined 'food security' as the ability to buy food.
10. European LVC member quoted in Gaarde (2017, 136). See also Holt-Giménez (2019).
11. Tilzey (2017), echoing Bernstein (2016), assumes that the peasant mobilization is counterproductive in not conforming to a Marxian class project, therefore inappropriately 'populist' and ineffectual. But as Harvey (2017) points out, Marx's *complete analysis* of capital's movement and pervasive commodification of life broaden the conditions for anti-capitalist political alliances.
12. 'Peasant', here, is not a primordial or analytical category, rather a political category (Edelman 2009). More to the point, the peasant countermovement to WTO rules was itself a product of food regime liberalization at the expense of small-scale/family farming globally, rather than the expression of an obsolete 'class'.
13. Reactive because the liberal market breakdown concentrated efforts by East Asian and Middle Eastern states in particular to acquire land offshore to repatriate food, feed and biofuels, circumventing multilateral food trade (McMichael 2013).

FURTHER READING

Desmarais, A.A.; Claeys, P.; Trauger, A. (eds) (2017), *Public Policies for Food Sovereignty: Social Movements and the State*, London: Routledge.

Hirata, K.A. (2013), *Hidden Hunger: Gender and the Politics of Smarter Food*, Ithaca, NY: Cornell University Press.

Hossain, N.; Scott-Villiers, P. (eds) (2017), *Food Riots, Food Rights and the Politics of Provision*, London and New York: Routledge and Earthscan.

Wilson, M. (ed.) (2017), *Postcolonialism, Indigeneity and Struggles for Food Sovereignty: Alternative Food Networks in Subaltern Spaces*, London: Routledge.

Winders, B.; Ransom, E. (eds) (2019), *Global Meat. Social and Environmental Consequences of the Expanding Meat Industry*, Cambridge, MA: MIT Press.

Wise, T. (2019), *Eating Tomorrow: Agribusiness, Family Farmers, and the Battle for the Future of Food*, New York: The New Press.

REFERENCES

Acharya, A. (2017), After liberal hegemony: The advent of a multiplex world order, *Ethics and International Affairs*, September 8, accessed August 6, 2021 at www.ethicsandinternationalaffairs.org/2017/multiplex-world-order/.

Agrifood Atlas (2017), Heinrich Böll Foundation; Rosa Luxemburg Foundation; Friends of the Earth Europe.

Ajl, M. (2012), Planet of fields, *Jacobin*, 12(Winter), accessed March 5, 2021 at https://jacobinmag.com/2012/01/planet-of-fields.

Akram-Lodhi, H. (2013), *Hungry for Change: Farmers, Food Justice and the Agrarian Question*, Fernwood: Kumarian Press.

Araghi, F. (2003), Food regimes and the production of value: Some methodological issues, *Journal of Peasant Studies*, 30(2), 41–70.

Arrighi, G. (1990), The three hegemonies of historical capitalism, *Review* (Fernand Braudel Center), 13(3), 365–408.

Bernstein, H. (2016), Agrarian political economy and modern world capitalism: The contribution of food regimes analysis, *Journal of Peasant Studies*, 43(3), 611–647.

Clapp, J. (2016), *Food*, second edition, Cambridge: Polity Press.

Connell, R.; Dados, N. (2014), Where in the world does neoliberalism come from? The market agenda in Southern perspective, *Theory and Society*, 43, 117–138.

Corrado, A. (2017), Agrarian change and migrations in the Mediterranean from a food regime perspective, in Corrado, A.; De Castro, C.; Perrotta, D. (eds), *Migration and Agriculture. Mobility and Change in the Mediterranean Area*, London: Routledge, 311–331.

Da Vià, E. (2012), Seed diversity, farmers' rights, and the politics of re-peasantization, *International Journal of Sociology of Agriculture and Food*, 19(2), 229–242.

Desmarais, A.A. (2007), *La Vía Campesina: Globalization and the Power of Peasants*, Halifax and London: Fernwood and Pluto Press.

Edelman, M. (2009), Synergies and tensions between rural social movements and professional researchers, *Journal of Peasant Studies*, 36(1), 245–265.

Edelman, M.; Borras, S.M., Jr. (2016), *Political Dynamics of Transnational Agrarian Movements*, Halifax: Fernwood Press.

Friedmann, H. (1993), The political economy of food: A global crisis, *New Left Review*, 197, 29–57.

Friedmann, H. (2005), From colonialism to green capitalism: Social movements and the emergence of food regimes, in Buttel, F.H.; McMichael, P. (eds), *New Directions in the Sociology of Global Development*, 11, 229–267.

Friedmann, H. (2016), Commentary: Food regime analysis and agrarian questions: Widening the conversation, *Journal of Peasant Studies*, 43(3), 671–692.

Friedmann, H.; McMichael, P. (1989), Agriculture and the state system: The rise and fall of national agricultures, 1870 to the present, *Sociologia Ruralis*, 29(2), 93–117.

Gaarde, I. (2017), *Peasants Negotiating a Global Policy Space: La Vía Campesina in the Committee on World Food Security*, London and New York: Routledge and Earthscan.

Gliessman, S. (2018), Breaking away from industrial food and farming systems: Seven cases of agroecological transition, International Panel of Experts on Sustainable Food Systems, accessed March 5, 2021 at www.ipes-food.org/pages/Seven-Case-Studies-of-Agroecological-Transition.

Harvey, D. (2017), *Marx, Capital and the Madness of Economic Reason*, Oxford: Oxford University Press.

Holt-Giménez, E. (2019), *Can We Feed the World without Destroying It?* Cambridge: Polity Press.

Hopewell, K. (2016), *Breaking the WTO: How Emerging Powers Disrupted the Neoliberal Project*, Stanford, CA: Stanford University Press.

Lapegna, P. (2016), *Soybeans and Power: Genetically Modified Crops, Environmental Politics, and Social Movements in Argentina*, Oxford: Oxford University Press.

LeHeron, R.; Lewis, N. (2009), Theorising food regimes: Intervention as politics, *Agriculture and Human Values*, 26, 345–349.

McMichael, P. (ed.) (2010), *Contesting Development: Critical Struggles for Social Change*, London: Routledge.

McMichael, P. (2013), *Food Regimes and Agrarian Questions*, Halifax: Fernwood.

McMichael, P. (2020), Does China's 'going out' strategy prefigure a new food regime? *Journal of Peasant Studies*, 47(1), 116–154.

Mooney, P. (2017), Too big to feed: Exploring the impacts of mega-mergers, consolidation and concentration of power in the agri-food sector, International Panel of Experts on Sustainable Food Systems, accessed March 5, 2021 at www.ipes-food.org/_img/upload/files/Concentration_FullReport(1).pdf.

Mooney, P. (2018), Blocking the chain: Industrial food chain concentration, big data platforms and food sovereignty solutions, accessed March 5, 2021 at www.etcgroup.org/sites/www.etcgroup.org/files/files/blockingchain2.png.

Otero, G. (2012), The neoliberal food regime in Latin America: State, agribusiness transnational corporations and biotechnology, *Canadian Journal of Development Studies*, 33(3), 282–294.

Pascoe, B. (2016), *Dark Emu, Black Seeds. Agriculture or Accident?* Broome: Magabala Books.

Patel, R. (2009), What does food sovereignty look like?, *Journal of Peasant Studies*, 36(3), 663–706.

Polanyi, K. (1957), *The Great Transformation: The Political and Economic Origins of Our Time*, Boston, MA: Beacon Press.

Pritchard, B. (2007), Food regimes, in Kitchin, R.; Thrift, N. (eds), *The International Encyclopedia of Human Geography*, Amsterdam: Elsevier.

Pritchard, B. (2009), The long hangover from the second food regime: A world historical interpretation of collapse of the WTO Doha Round, *Agriculture and Human Values*, 26, 297–307.

Rossman, P. (2012), Food workers' rights as a path to a low carbon agriculture, in Räthzel, N.; Uzzell, D. (eds), *Trade Unions in the Green Economy*, London: Routledge, 74–79.

Taylor, M. (2018), Climate-smart agriculture: What is it good for? *Journal of Peasant Studies*, 45(1), 89–107.

Taylor, M.; Rioux, S. (2018), *Global Labour Strategies*, Cambridge: Polity Press.

Tilzey, M. (2017), Reintegrating economy, society, and environment for cooperative futures: Polanyi, Marx, and food sovereignty, *Journal of Rural Studies*, 53, 317–334.

Van der Ploeg, J.D. (2018), *The New Peasantries: Rural Development in Times of Globalization*, London: Routledge.

Van der Ploeg, J.D.; Ye, J. (eds) (2016), *China's Peasant Agriculture and Rural Society: Changing Paradigms of Farming*, London: Routledge.

Vivero-Pol, J.L. (2017), Transition towards a food commons regime: Re-commoning food to crowd-feed the world, in Ruivenkamp, G.; Hilton, A. (eds), *Perspectives on Commoning: Autonomist Principles and Practices*, London: Zed Books, 325–379.

Weis, T. (2013), *The Ecological Hoofprint: The Global Burden of Industrial Livestock*, London: Zed Books.

Winders, B. (2017), *Grains*, Cambridge: Polity Press.

Wittman, H. (2009), Reworking the metabolic rift: La Vía Campesina, agrarian citizenship and food sovereignty, *Journal of Peasant Studies*, 36(4), 805–826.

26. Crisis

Robert Chernomas, Ian Hudson and A. Haroon Akram-Lodhi

Critical agrarian studies emerged as a distinct field of study in a time of crisis in the late 2000s.[1] That crisis was four-fold: food, finance, fuel and climate. The four crises were mutually constitutive of each other. Nowhere was this more apparent than in the capitalist world food system. Amidst record harvests, rising food prices drove millions back into a livelihoods crisis. Driving the increase in food prices was the financialization of food (Clapp and Isakson 2018), the diversion of food into agro-fuels (Holt-Giménez and Patel with Shattuck 2009), and spatially specific climate change-driven variability in production and productivity, which itself was largely a consequence of a capitalist world food system predicated upon undermining the biophysical foundations of agriculture (Weis 2013).

More than 10 years on, and in the wake of the COVID-19 pandemic, the crisis continues to shape the operation of the capitalist world food system. Yet critical agrarian studies has not explored what is meant by the concept of crisis. According to *laissez-faire* neoclassical economists crises are caused by external shocks from mother nature (e.g., sunspots, El Nino), human nature (e.g., wars, revolutions) or government policy that disrupts the smooth and efficient class-free capitalist markets ordered by an invisible hand. For mainstream Keynesian economists, capitalist economies require the class-neutral and capable visible hands of the state to enact counter-cyclical stabilization policy to ensure that government compensates when private-sector investment declines. Both thus see crisis as a specific event that is triggered.

Marxist economists adopt a very different perspective. For Marxist economists, capitalism's economic system generates patterns that transcend distinctive historical and regional characteristics, with the force of the profit motive being far more powerful than other factors (Shaikh 2016, 5–6). For economists working in the Marxist tradition the concept of crisis does not mean the breakdown of the capitalist system nor the short-term fluctuations of business cycles, where normal economic activity is sufficient to ensure a return to relative prosperity. Capitalist economies are constantly exposed to a variety of internally and externally generated disturbances and dislocations, but only at certain times do these 'shocks' trigger a general crisis. By way of contrast, periodic crises are driven by internal mechanisms, not by external shocks. When the system is healthy, it rapidly revives from all sorts of setbacks; when it is unhealthy practically anything has the potential to trigger its collapse (Shaikh 1978, 219). Crises are thus much more infrequent, encompassing many business cycles, and much more severe in duration and depth, requiring a transformation in the underlying rules of the capitalist economic structure in order to emerge from the crisis (Gordon 1980, 20–21).

An analysis of capitalist crises (e.g., the Great Depression of the 1930s, the stagflation of the 1970s, the Great Recession of 2007–2009 and the COVID-19 pandemic) requires an examination of the theoretical, historical, empirical and institutional factors that determine why the system periodically becomes unhealthy. This analysis begins by accepting the Marxian premise that capital accumulation – the activity of turning an initial investment into goods and services to be sold for a profit and then reinvested – dominates the structure and dynamics of capitalist society and therefore the requirements of capital accumulation provide the most promising starting point for an examination of the structures shaping concrete life in capitalist societies and the operation of the capitalist world food system (ibid., 13–16).

Corporations, including those operating in the capitalist world food system, are not in the business of producing goods and services, but in the business of making profits. Without enough profits, they shut down their farms, factories, mines, stores and banks. Without profits, they do not invest in new machines or hire more workers. Without profit, there is no production, no labour or property income, no household income on which to base consumption demand and no prospects on which to base investment demand (Shaikh 2016, 615). Maximizing profits is not a matter of morals or ethics for firms, but a condition of survival.

The 'circuit of capital' demands that businesses first must be concerned with acquiring the least expensive inputs. Here, the capitalist world food system has a key role, in that cheap food allows firms to economize on the cost of waged labour. Indeed, starting from the repeal of the Corn Laws in 1846 to the imposition of an income squeeze on the rural petty commodity producers of the outlying regions of the global economy as late as the 1980s, through adverse shifts in the terms of trade, cheap food has been important for capitalism. Second, they must make use of these inputs in a production process that ensures a competitive price in the mar-ketplace. In the capitalist world food system, the capacity to sell at world market prices signals competitiveness. Next, they must be able to sell those products for a profit. In the capitalist world food system, the distribution of aggregate profits is extremely skewed toward down-stream retail firms, most notably supermarkets, with the smallest share of aggregate profits going to farms, whether they be capitalist or petty commodity producers (Akram-Lodhi 2012). Lower-cost capitalists will drive higher-cost capitalists from the market by reducing prices and having more profits to invest for the next round of production and sales. The firm that is able to introduce techniques that lower costs has profits available to invest in new techniques, which enables it to successfully compete with rivals. Without competitive profits, research and development, investment and advertising all become impossible and the fate of the firm is sealed. This also implies that profits are not only crucial for firms, but also for the capitalist world food system and the economy more generally. When profits are low, firms are unwilling to invest or hire, creating economic malaise. Any explanation of economic conditions in the capitalist world food system that fails to place profitability at the centre of the analysis is missing the main story.

Any explanation of crisis, therefore, should involve examining the factors that hinder profits. Samuel Bowles, David Gordon and Thomas Weisskopf (1986) wrote that profits are the spoils of a three-front war that firms must continuously wage with their workforce, the government and other companies (especially those from other countries). The conflict with their workers is over containing wages while at the same time convincing them to increase productivity as much as possible. Cheap food makes wage containment easier. The struggle with the government is over the extent to which the state will impact a firm's bottom line by altering its costs through such things as regulations and taxes, or its revenues, through, for example, government purchases and subsidies. The four dominant powers of the capitalist world food system – the United States, the European Union, Japan and China – all extensively intervene to cut the costs of industrial agriculture, in part by providing extensive state sub-sidies to large-scale farms operating to produce for global markets. However, state support of corporate producers places the firm in conflict with a wide variety of citizens who expect the government to undertake various profit-constraining activities, from those who pressure the state to implement environmental protection, to those who think that the government has a responsibility to provide for the collective good with respect to health, education and welfare. In these dimensions, citizens' activities to constrain profits clearly have implications for food produced in the capitalist world food system. However, while capital requires the state, the state requires economic continuity, and this in turn rests on the proper functioning of capital. 'While the state can modulate the outcomes produced by the profit motive, it cannot set aside the motive itself' (Shaikh 2004, 3). The third and final front is a battle with other firms to reduce any input costs and increase revenues from product sales. On this front, firms may have an important ally in their national governments, which attempt to tilt the rules of the international economy in favour of their own firms. This can be done by changing trade rules, altering exchange rates or using military force (Chernomas and Hudson 2017, 21–22). Forcing adjustments in capitalism's external relations with the 'outlying regions' on the periphery of the global economy, upon which it has always been and continues to be involved, is critical to the profit-seeking firm. In the capitalist world food system, it is trade rules that are the principal means by which governments seek to support industrial agriculture. When business as a class, as opposed to any individual firm, is not successful in this three-front war, crisis is likely, in the capitalist world food system and in the capitalist economy.

Crises are the result of falling profitability. When limits to accumulation (whether political, ecological, cultural or otherwise) appear, the centrality of profits to a healthy economy demands that they be 'overcome'. In the capitalist system, declining profitability is problematic for the economy because firms will reduce their investment, economic growth will fall, unemployment will increase and income growth will stagnate. This is particularly true of those capitalist countries in which there is a greater reliance on the private sector for investment, and where industrial agriculture governed by the profit motive is the norm. When profits fall, firms' efforts to alter the broader policy framework in a manner more conducive to profits often generate considerable support among the general population suffering through an economic downturn. However, the centrality of profits does not mean that the capitalist system is a blank cheque for business. Often policies that increase the profitability of firms have detrimental impacts on the rest of the society and so various opposing groups in society will resist, or even reverse, the expansion of profit-enhancing rules if they perceive that particular aspects of life should remain buffered from this influence.

It has long been recognized that capitalist economies go through 'long waves' of boom and bust cycles. The bust periods of these cycles are periods of crisis. One explanation for the cause of these inevitable severe downturns is the Regulation Approach (RA), which links these long swings of capitalist economies with institutional structures, and which is the basis of the analysis of the capitalist world food system that uses food regimes as its central conceptual apparatus (Friedmann and McMichael 1989). RA scholars argue that institutions emerge to govern and stabilize the conflicts and crises that inevitably emerge in a capitalist economy. A coherent institutional structure will emerge and persist when it can, at least temporarily, create stability and legitimacy in the process of generating profits. It is the crucial role of 'regularizing' or normalizing the process of making profits that gives the regulation school its name, not merely the study of regulation, narrowly defined (Jessop and Sum 2006, 4). While the RA is far from a homogeneous single entity, and has been adopted for a wide variety of political stripes, from the more radical historical materialist to more reformist theories, the

RA does focus on a set of social institutions that come together to facilitate a specific kind of context in which firms generate profits, both domestically and globally (ibid., 8).

An offshoot of the RA, Social Structure of Accumulation (SSA) theory explains long waves through the ability of the broad economic policy environment to facilitate or hinder firms' pursuit of profits. The SSA is defined as the set of formal and informal rules and institutions that influence firms' profits but are outside of the direct decision-making discretion of the individual firm. This theory claims that the SSA forms a coherent policy environment and will be backed by an accompanying ideology. In the boom period, in the first part of the cycle, the SSA will abet profits. However, inevitably the cycle will tip into crisis during the bust period, often because the same institutional rules that aided profits in the boom period hinder them either because of changed conditions or the internal contradictions in the rules of the SSA. In SSA theory, an economic crisis can be defined as a period of economic instability in capitalist economies, whose resolution depends upon the construction of a new SSA. Often, the resolution of an economic crisis will take place beyond the boundaries of the state, by a rewriting of the institutional rules that govern international economic relations in a way that rebuilds corporate profitability. In an economic system that relies on private investment, low profits are problematic not just for firms and their owners, but for all of society, so the bust period will instigate a quest for a new SSA that will restore profits. The specific form that the new SSA takes will depend on the relative strength of different classes or groups in society. Once a set of rules is found that restore profits, these create the conditions for the long-term boom that marks the beginning of the next SSA (Bowles et al. 1986). In short, a new SSA does not fall from the sky but will be generated, to a substantial degree, by forces endogenous to the general process of capital accumulation (Gordon 1980, 25).

In SSA theory, there is predictability to both the general institutional structure and its inevitable crisis. An SSA generally comes in two types, depending on the balance of class forces during its formative years. In the first, capital is strong. In this type of SSA, firms' greater relative political clout results in an institutional structure that benefits firms at the expense of their workers and other citizens. In this type of SSA, workers' wages will tend to stagnate relative to productivity, generating a favourable profit per unit of production. Government will be unwilling or unable to impose taxes and regulations that increase costs on firms, like environmental or safety regulation. It could be argued that this describes the contemporary capitalist world food system. While this will generate a profit-enhancing environment in the boom part of the long swing, it creates the seeds of its own destruction because firms needing to sell their products will run up against the barrier of an income-constrained population. This is referred to as an underconsumption crisis in the Marxist tradition. The Great Depression, the 2008 crisis and the 2020 crisis caused by COVID-19 can be seen in this light. The crisis of a strong capital SSA is not the result of declining profit per unit produced or a profit squeeze, but of its inability to realize profit through the sale of its commodities (Foster and McChesney 2009).

The second type of SSA features relatively weak capital. Although profits must always be ensured in any SSA, in this type, citizens or workers have relatively greater power in influencing the institutions of the SSA. In this SSA wages tend to grow more rapidly and the profit-seeking behaviour of firms is moderated by government constraints. The crisis of a weak capital SSA is caused by profits being squeezed by increased costs (referred to as profit squeeze theory in the Marxist literature), as was the case, according to many SSA analysts, in the 1970s (Kotz 2015; Chernomas et al. 2019, 8–10). For Marx in Volume 3 of *Capital* and the 'orthodox' Marxists who follow in this tradition, operating beneath both the strong and the weak SSA is the tendency of the rate of profit to fall as a gravitational force when the conflicted economy is buffeted from the strong and weak forms of relative capitalist power (Shaikh 1978).

The clearest and most coherent account of crisis is thus that of Marxist political economy. The Marxist conceptualization of crisis offers keen insights into the contradictions of the capitalist world food system, and indeed the four-fold crisis of food, finance, fuel and climate should be seen as mutually constitutive because each is a response to the need to sustain profitability in a capitalist economy. Thus, scholars of critical agrarian studies should not be shocked when crises occur or argue that they are the result of surprising exogenous events, outside the normal, smooth functioning of the economic system. Rather, they should follow the advice of Anwar Shaikh (1978, 240), who suggests that they might take a more careful look at the theory that they use to explain the economic realities of the capitalist world food system. 'It has often been said that those who ignore history are condemned to repeat it. To this it should perhaps be added that those who ignore theory are condemned to reconstruct it.'

NOTE

1.   The authors thank Prabhat Patnaik for comments on the original draft of this chapter.

FURTHER READING

Bowles, S.; Gordon, D.; Weisskopf, T. (1986), Power and profits: The social structure of accumulation and the profitability of the postwar US economy, *Review of Radical Political Economics*, 18(1–2), 132–167.
Friedmann, H.; McMichael, P. (1989), Agriculture and the state system: The rise and decline of national agricultures, 1870 to the present, *Sociologia Ruralis*, 29(2), 93–117.
Gordon, D.M. (1980), Stages of accumulation and long economic cycles, in Hopkins, T., Wallerstein, I. (eds), *Processes of the World System*, Beverly Hills, CA: Sage, 9–45.
Shaikh, A. (2016), *Capitalism: Competition, Conflict, Crises*, Oxford: Oxford University Press.

REFERENCES

Akram-Lodhi, A.H. (2012), Contextualizing land grabbing: Contemporary land deals, the global subsistence crisis and the world food system, *Canadian Journal of Development Studies*, 33(2), 119–142.
Bowles, S.; Gordon, D.; Weisskopf, T. (1986), Power and profits: The social structure of accumulation and the profitability of the postwar US economy, *Review of Radical Political Economics*, 18(1–2), 132–167.
Chernomas, R.; Hudson, I. (2017), *The Profit Doctrine: The Economists of the Neoliberal Era*, London: Pluto Press.
Chernomas, R.; Hudson, I.; Hudson, M. (2019), *Neoliberal Lives: Work, Politics, Nature and Health in Contemporary America*, Manchester: Manchester University Press.
Clapp, J.; Isakson, S.R. (2018), *Speculative Harvests: Financialization, Food and Agriculture*, Winnipeg: Fernwood Publishing.
Foster, J.; McChesney, R. (2009), Monopoly-finance capital and the paradox of accumulation, *Monthly Review*, 61(5), 1–20.
Friedmann, H.; McMichael, P. (1989), Agriculture and the state system: The rise and decline of national agricultures, 1870 to the present, *Sociologia Ruralis*, 29(2), 93–117.

Gordon, D.M. (1980), Stages of accumulation and long economic cycles, in Hopkins, T.; Wallerstein, I. (eds), *Processes of the World System*, Beverly Hills, CA: Sage, 9–45.

Holt-Giménez, E.; Patel, R. with Shattuck, A. (2009), *Food Rebellions: Crisis and the Hunger for Justice*, Berkeley, CA: Food First Books.

Jessop, B.; Sum, N. (2006), *Beyond the Regulation Approach: Putting Capitalist Economies in Their Place*, Cheltenham, UK and Northampton, MA, USA: Edward Elgar Publishing.

Kotz, D. (2015), *The Rise and Fall of Neoliberal Capitalism*, Cambridge, MA: Harvard University Press.

Shaikh, A. (1978), An introduction to the history of crisis theories, in Union for Radical Political Economics (ed.), *US Capitalism in Crisis*, New York: Economics Education Project of Union for Radical Political Economics, 219–241.

Shaikh, A. (2004), The power of profit, *Social Research*, 71(2), 371–382.

Shaikh, A. (2016), *Capitalism: Competition, Conflict, Crises*, Oxford: Oxford University Press.

Weis, T. (2013), *The Ecological Hoofprint: The Global Burden of Industrial Agriculture*, London: Zed Press.

27. Food sovereignty, food security and the right to food

Priscilla Claeys, Annette Aurélie Desmarais and Jasber Singh

INTRODUCTION

In 1996, representatives of the transnational agrarian movement La Via Campesina (LVC) introduced its peasant notion of food sovereignty at the World Food Summit and accompanying events in Rome.[1] In doing so, rural people, including peasants, farm workers, women and Indigenous communities from the Global North and Global South, declared their collective agency. In their struggles not to be disappeared by a capitalist model of rural development, LVC argued that another agriculture was possible as evidenced by the fact that peasant farming persisted in many places. In effect, food sovereignty aimed to 'turn the global food system upside down' (GRAIN 2005) as it sought to build models of agriculture that prioritized 'social justice, ecological sustainability and respect for peasant knowledge, cultures and economies' (Desmarais 2007, 200).

Subsequently, LVC's notion of food sovereignty gained traction as local, national and transnational social movements, non-governmental organizations and some governments adopted the discourse of food sovereignty.[2] As 'an ontological alternative' to the neoliberal food regime (McMichael 2014), food sovereignty contributed to a paradigm shift in thinking about food and agriculture in people's lives, cultures and politics. Through food sovereignty, peasants and other food providers became key protagonists in defining what food systems should look like.

Debates held at the 2007 Nyéléni Food Sovereignty Forum between LVC and wider groups of food providers and urban-based movements led to a consensus that food sovereignty rests on six pillars: it 'focuses on food for people, values food providers, localizes food systems, puts control locally, builds knowledge and skills, and works with nature' (Nyéléni 2007). While these pillars might appear like a wish list, they were the result of decades of social movement struggles to work together in solidarity to define new pathways to a 'future without hunger' (La Via Campesina 1996). The Nyéléni process subsequently inspired and strengthened food sovereignty demands among broader national and regional coalitions (see among others, Desmarais and Wittman 2014; Brent et al. 2015). Building on the earlier work of the International Planning Committee for Food Sovereignty, it facilitated the convergence of various constituencies (such as pastoralists, smallholder farmers, fishers, Indigenous peoples, agricultural workers, women and youth) and their engagement in global food security policy-making (Claeys and Duncan 2018). Eventually, academics entered the scene to examine the potential, politics and limitations of food sovereignty.

The momentum achieved through civil society mobilization, international deliberations, academic research and legislation means that, for many, food sovereignty now constitutes a powerful anti-capitalist vision for food system transformation. Food sovereignty is distinct from food security, the right to food, food justice and food democracy, although the relationship between these concepts is contested and constantly evolving. We examine food security and the right to food below, and leave out of this contribution the concepts of food democracy[3] and food justice,[4] which have gained prominence in specific geographical areas, rather than globally. Our analysis focuses on food sovereignty because its place-based yet global dimensions and radical agenda make it unique and important for those interested in critical agrarian studies.

WHAT IS FOOD SOVEREIGNTY?

[S]ome academics and analysts were concerned that La Via Campesina seems to have a new and different definition of Food Sovereignty after every meeting and forum. Maybe they think this reflects a lack of seriousness on our part. But that would be a misunderstanding. We are not trying to create the perfect definition, for a dictionary or for a history book. We are trying to build a movement to change the food system, and the world. To build a powerful movement, you need to add more allies. And as you add more allies, you have more voices. More contributions. More issues to take into account. So your concept grows, it evolves, it broadens ... Food Sovereignty is ... a vision of the food system we are fighting for, but, above all, it is ... an ever evolving banner of struggle. (Mpofu 2014, General Coordinator of La Via Campesina)

Food sovereignty 'is the right of peoples and nations to control their own food and agricultural systems including their own markets, production modes, food cultures and environments' (Wittman et al. 2010, 2). This concise definition only hints at the complex ideas, theories and practices that are at the heart of food sovereignty. Food sovereignty, as a political project and social movement, is about much more than agriculture and food, and therein lies its potential. It is about social change writ large as it seeks 'a transformation of societies that can be achieved through the vehicle of food, agriculture, [and food provisioning]' (Desmarais and Wittman 2014, 1156). Trauger's analysis of place-specific resistance strategies reveals just how profound food sovereignty can be since it entails cultural transformation:

Food sovereignty is as much about changing systems of production as it is about something more fundamental and perhaps more ontologically threatening to capitalist modernity: the transformation of meaning, primarily around land, labour and exchange. (2017, 30)

Food sovereignty then is about changing people's ways of thinking and being, and their relations to food, agriculture, nature and one another; it is about transforming who we are, how we relate to one another and nature and how we live in this world. And social change is always messy; it rarely, if ever, follows a singular unidirectional path. As Desmarais and Wittman (2014, 1156–1157) argue:

To better understand food sovereignty as an organizing frame for transformative social change, it is useful to conceptualize it as a *process* involving persistent, diverse and interconnected struggles ... [T]o understand this diversity of struggles there is a need to pay attention to the multiplicity of sites and multifaceted nature of resistance to dispossession and inequality ... A range of factors, including history, social relations (class, race, gender, age), ecology, politics and culture, shapes the particular nature of each food sovereignty struggle in any given place ... Food sovereignty is very much situated; it occurs in particular places and how it is expressed is determined largely by local dynamics, but also in response to changing global dynamics.

Food sovereignty is complex because it is multi-dimensional, multi-sited and multi-scale. Food sovereignty struggles to build community and regain access to and control over land, seeds, water and other resources, and the power dynamics therein are in constant flux, as Elizabeth Mpofu stressed above. Moreover, food sovereignty centres on the local and the daily, as food providers engage in transformative everyday practices to refine and expand agroecology in their fields and gardens, link to local and territorial markets and fight gender violence.

HOW IS FOOD SOVEREIGNTY DIFFERENT FROM FOOD SECURITY AND THE RIGHT TO FOOD?

Food sovereignty surfaced in a particular context in which the discourse of food security, trade liberalization and neoliberal globalization dominated discussions on hunger, poverty and rural development. Food security, as defined by the United Nations (UN) Food and Agriculture Organization, 'exists when all people, at all times, have physical, social and economic access to sufficient, safe and nutritious food that meets their dietary needs and food preferences for an active and healthy life' (FAO 2001). It is understood as resting on four pillars: availability, access, utilization and stability (FAO 2008). The roots of food security lie in the post-war era that emphasized national food self-sufficiency, especially the production of grains. Throughout the 1970s, it emerged in institutional development circles and was aimed at governments with a view to stabilize international grain prices. The 1986 World Bank Report 'Poverty and hunger' induced an important shift in the deployment of food security. In addition to national food production, food security was now linked to individual purchasing power (Jarosz 2014, 171). Since then, food security has become increasingly embedded in neoliberal development with international trade identified as *the* key instrument that would lead to global food security.[5] In this global discourse, hunger is seen as a technical problem that is best addressed by productivist-, market- and trade-focused solutions (Hopma and Woods 2014, 777). Global food security effectively reinforces the new corporate food regime (Patel 2009) since it focuses on intensifying production and productivity, notably through agro-biotech solutions. In this narrative, nation states are seen as obstacles and must be compelled to remove trade restrictions and deregulate controls on biotech, intellectual property rights and foreign capital investment.

By introducing food sovereignty, LVC rejected this distorted vision of food security to emphasize power relations and the politics of food systems. Food sovereignty activists argued that 'issues related to *what* food is produced/harvested, *who* produces/harvests the food, *where and how* it is produced/gathered, and at what *scale*' are as important as ensuring adequate and accessible amounts of food (Desmarais 2015, emphasis added). LVC envisioned food sovereignty as 'a precondition to genuine food security' that also required realizing the right to food, implementing genuine agrarian reform, protecting natural resources, reorganizing global food trade, ending global hunger, securing social peace and democratizing control of the food system (La Via Campesina 1996).

Food sovereignty emphasized small-scale farmers' and peasants' 'right to produce their own food in own territory, and the right of consumers to be able to decide what they consume and how and by whom it is produced' (La Via Campesina 2003, 1). In so doing, it emerged as a holistic rights-based framework that both contested and expanded the UN defined human right to adequate food (Claeys 2015a). Protected under international human rights and humanitarian law, the right to food is defined as:

> the right to have regular, permanent and unrestricted access, either directly or by means of financial purchases, to quantitatively and qualitatively adequate and sufficient food corresponding to the cultural traditions of the people to which the consumer belongs, and which ensures a physical and mental, individual and collective, fulfilling and dignified life free of fear. (Ziegler et al. 2011, 1)

The right to food pays specific attention to categories of people that are marginalized, such as the landless, the unemployed, the elderly, Indigenous peoples, women, children, lower castes, religious and ethnic minorities and people with disabilities. It is a state-centric approach that highlights states' accountability and judicial remedies along with specific obligations to respect, protect and fulfil human rights through laws, policies and programmes. The right to food approach to food insecurity is based on the premise that tackling world hunger requires improving not the availability of food, but access to food for the marginalized and deprived. Indeed, lack of access to food is almost never the result of a general scarcity of food. Instead, people are deprived of food because they have no opportunity to produce it, cannot earn a sufficient income to buy the food they need or are unable to work at all (Künnemann and Ratjen 2004, 1).

Initially, the right to food had limited appeal for agrarian movements since their radical agenda was at odds with the right to food's emphasis on the intervention of the liberal state to curb the inequalities generated by the capitalist market economy, for example through compensatory policies such as social programmes or food aid (Claeys 2012, 849). Yet in the last decade, food sovereignty proponents have strategically used the right to food to advance their agenda, notably in global governance processes like the UN Committee on World Food Security. In such arenas where food sovereignty is perceived as too controversial, agrarian activists have leveraged the UN-recognized right to food to defend their claims, for example to achieve the recognition of legitimate land tenure rights through the adoption of the Voluntary Guidelines on the Responsible Governance of Tenure (Claeys and Duncan 2018). Engaging in institutional processes can be both empowering and disempowering for social movements, as it can lead to cooptation, professionalization and demobilization. Food sovereignty activists thus constantly assess the advantages and limitations of deploying human rights arguments, and try to maintain the right balance between institutional and disruptive tactics.

In the last two decades, food sovereignty activists have defined, demanded and defended their own versions of human rights, successfully pushing the human rights regime to address their collective claims (Claeys 2015b). This struggle led to getting the UN General Assembly to recognize a new set of group rights, now compiled in the UN Declaration on the Rights of Peasants and Other People Working in Rural Areas (UNDROP).[6] This new legal instrument recognizes new human rights including the right to land, seeds and other natural resources, and the right to food sovereignty (Claeys 2015b). Initially drafted by LVC and amended during a six year intergovernmental negotiation process, the UNDROP points to agroecology, relocalized markets and participatory decision-making as key pathways to realizing the rights of peasants and food sovereignty.

ACADEMIC DEBATES ON FOOD SOVEREIGNTY

Food sovereignty has spurred important debates in academic circles where the evolving and malleable nature of food sovereignty has been both praised and criticized. For example, some have argued that food sovereignty lacks conceptual clarity (Edelman et al. 2014), is incoherent and associated with a closed epistemic community (Hospes 2014, 121). Others have argued that food sovereignty is difficult to operationalize and inevitably coopted in practice (Hopma and Woods 2014; Kelly 2018). We provide only a glimpse into some of these debates here, and direct the reader to four special issues of key journals for more details (*Journal of Peasant Studies*, 2014; *Third World Quarterly*, 2015; *Globalizations*, 2015; *Dialogues in Human Geography*, 2014).

One of the most cited debates is the 'for or against' position on food sovereignty and the peasantry. Bernstein (2014), among others, argues that neither the social actor of the peasantry nor the concept of food sovereignty are possible. In his view, the food sovereignty discourse fails to adequately differentiate between and within various agrarian classes and tends to homogenize peasants into a single category that no longer exists. Bernstein rejects a unitary 'peasant way' (2014, 1056) and what he sees as a misplaced veneration of peasants who are supposedly all engaged in virtuous farming and wrongly constituted in food sovereignty discourse as 'capital's other' (2014, 1057). So-called peasants are located within the structure of agrarian capitalism, he argues, rather than outside of it. McMichael (2014), in historicizing food sovereignty, counters this view by arguing that 'it is precisely the peasant experience and presence that is able to articulate not only the problem, but a solution to food regime contradictions' (2014, 10). Pérez-Vitoria (2005) and Van der Ploeg (2008) provide ample empirical evidence of a twenty-first-century resurgence of the peasantry, or repeasantization. Meanwhile, Jansen (2015) insists that the food sovereignty movement focuses too much on dispossession and enclosure at the expense of state power and labour organization, and over-states the potential of agroecology as an alternative.

Others question the applicability and desirability of food sovereignty, or point to the vision of food sovereignty itself as misguided. Agarwal (2014) argues the food sovereignty project is unrealistic, and its localization agenda is neither achievable nor desirable. She says there is a 'critical contradiction' inherent in food sovereignty because many small-scale farmers, if given the choice, would actually not opt for (re)localized, low-input, self-sufficient types of agriculture. She further argues that food sovereignty's focus on family farming is not compatible with, nor supportive of, gender equality, and fails to address women's unpaid labour. Li (2015) questions whether or not food sovereignty is even possible in places where small-scale farmers are already part of global supply chains and few other options exist. In a similar vein, Burnett and Murphy (2014) criticize what they see as the food sovereignty movement's unclear stance on international trade, which fails to acknowledge that many smallholders depend on or seek opportunities that international markets can provide.

Still others criticize the way some academics and movement activists have positioned food sovereignty as opposed to food security, obscuring the fact that food sovereignty is necessarily also about food security. Clapp (2014) argues that issues of access, nutrition and stability are often overlooked by the producer rights-driven food sovereignty agenda. In research terms, it is thus useful to understand food security as a descriptive (and not necessarily normative) concept. Hopma and Woods (2014) contend that both food sovereignty and food security discourses are fluid and interrelated and that there are real limits to seeing them as oppositional.

Yet they recognize that, at the global level, food sovereignty is an 'anti-hegemonic discourse' which food security is not. Similarly, Jarosz (2014, 170) sees food security as embedded in technocratic neoliberal development discourse while food sovereignty reflects a Marxist political economic analysis of power relations and capitalist development. Although the opposition between the two approaches has blurred since the global food crisis of 2007–2008, they remain at odds on the role of genetically modified organisms, science and technology (Jarosz 2014).

Also much debated by academics and activists alike are questions related to the meaning of 'sovereignty' in food sovereignty (Edelman et al. 2014; Hospes 2014; Grey and Patel 2015; Schiavoni 2015; Daigle 2019), the role of the state and limits of state-led food sovereignty and the interactions of social movements with the state (Araújo 2014; Trauger 2014; Peña 2016; among others). Patel (2009) argues the food sovereignty discourse is contradictory because it is anti-statist and anarchist, while at the same time calling on the state to act as guarantor of rights. In his view, 'the language of rights … might not be well suited to the idea of food sovereignty' because 'to demand a space of food sovereignty is to demand specific arrangements to govern territory and space' and displace the state as sovereign (Patel 2009, 668). Noting the same tension, Trauger (2014) stresses that the food sovereignty movements' appeals to the liberal state for rights are not viable. These enquiries highlight the need to better understand the multi-scale dimensions and relations of food sovereignty (Iles and Montenegro de Wit 2015), that in reality help shape multiple and competing sovereignties (Schiavoni 2015) and the complexities involved in developing and implementing public policies for food sovereignty (Giunta 2014; Roman Alcalá 2016; Desmarais et al. 2017). Here, Schiavoni's (2017) historical, relational and interactive approach offers a framework to analyse the *processes* of 'food sovereignty construction'. That is, 'how it [food sovereignty] is articulated and attempted, as well as contested – including resisted, refracted or reversed, in a given setting' (Schiavoni 2017).

In countries with a colonial past and present colonial-settler context, this means understanding the affinities and tensions between Indigenous sovereignty (self-determination and decolonization) and food sovereignty (Grey and Patel 2015; Mayes 2018; Daigle 2019). Indigenous food sovereignty makes explicit the colonial-settler state as a major source of violence and oppression (Grey and Patel 2015; Bradley and Herrera 2016). In these landscapes, Indigenous food sovereignty is a 'day-to-day mode of resistance' that entails decolonizing social relations and food systems (Grey and Patel 2015) and engaging in a 'resurgent politics' (Daigle 2019, 301) that includes repatriation of lands (Tuck and Wayne Yang 2012). It also means shifting away from an ag-centric vision of food sovereignty (Morrison 2011) to include and foster Indigenous food pathways (Coté 2016; Daigle 2019). Indigenous food sovereignty also demands the decolonization of non-Indigenous food sovereignty movements to build powerful Indigenous–settler alliances (Kepkiewicz 2017) thereby contributing to 'unsettling food politics' (Mayes 2018).

ISSUES FOR FUTURE RESEARCH

In our view, four critical issues are crucial for the future of food sovereignty as a vision, political project and movement. First, the development of new knowledge to support the transition to decentralized and locally controlled circular socio-ecological systems that mimic natural ecosystems at different scales (such as agroecology), with a view that contests, neutralizes and replaces the modernist capitalist agenda (Pimbert 2018, 786).

Second, a better understanding of the kinds of alternative spaces and practices food sovereignty helps to create (Desmarais 2014, 9). In the economic realm, while some authors have documented the impacts of 'mediated markets' (Wittman and Blesh 2017), or 'nested markets' (Van der Ploeg 2008), more research is needed on the economic models that can advance radical social change. Possibilities do exist in the ways food sovereignty contributes to decommodification of food and how it is inherently anti-capitalist. Decommodification does not require, nor even suggest, that food is not marketed. Rather, it means that the value of food is not reduced simply to its exchange value in the marketplace. Concerns about nutrition and healthfulness of food, the environmental sustainability of food production and the social costs and benefits of particular models of food production all play important roles in the desirability of the particular ways food is produced. Some of this can be captured by the market and represented in exchange values, but food as a commodity can never adequately represent the totality of these concerns. In a similar manner, as food sovereignty seeks to protect and strengthen culturally and socially appropriate means for producing food, and posits a defence of peasant agriculture, it challenges the very nature of agrarian capitalism, which is based on the freedom of capital to control the means of production, accumulate land and dispossess small farmers through the concentration of capital and technology. Increasingly, complex technology and the domination of nature have helped capital overcome the natural advantages enjoyed by peasants when producing food in diverse, and occasionally unpredictable environments. More research is needed on how food sovereignty strengthens peasant production models that work with nature and how it can help build economies based on the 'rich possibilities of solidarity economics, de-growth thinking, anarchist economics, feminist economics, and other alternatives' (Pimbert 2018, 788).

Third, investigation into how communities create, strengthen and expand political spaces for the kind of inclusive participatory decision-making that food sovereignty demands (Menser 2008; Patel 2005, 2009). What kinds of mechanisms, processes and institutional innovations can help reconcile class interests and balance power dynamics to ensure that the demands of the marginalized take centre stage (Patel 2006, 2007)? Linked to this, how can food sovereignty contribute to transforming gender, racialized, class and colonial power relations?

Gender equity is a critical element of the theory, discourse and practice of food sovereignty. Early on, LVC put in place governance mechanisms to achieve gender equality and emphasized the representation and participation of women in determining organizational strategies and policies (Desmarais 2007). It also launched an international campaign to stop violence against women by declaring: 'If we do not eradicate violence towards women within our movement, we will not advance in our struggles, and if we do not create new gender relations, we will not be able to build a new society' (La Via Campesina 2008). More recently, some in LVC have denounced discrimination towards LGBTIQ+ in the countryside (Gioia 2016). These are, of course, all critical steps.

There remains, however, considerable gender gaps in food sovereignty movements and research (Masson et al. 2017).[7] Researchers have documented the specific contributions of women's leadership and agroecological knowledge (Oliver 2016; Bezner-Kerr et al. 2019), the relationship between everyday practice and gendered economies (Turner et al. 2020), evolving feminist politics in the discourse of food sovereignty (Masson et al. 2017; Conway 2018) and the importance of critically analysing the gendered nature of food sovereignty struggles (Park et al. 2015). Yet several key questions remain underexplored: How does food sovereignty address deeply entrenched social relations and structural barriers to women's equality and equity in specific locales? How does women's agency shape food sovereignty approaches, strategies and actions? How are gendered struggles around food sovereignty locally, nationally or internationally constructed, and why does this matter?

Gender, though, is heterogenous and oppression operates in intersectional ways. Women can face discrimination for their gender, in addition to their class, race and other differences (Crenshaw 1989). Work around intersectionality – that addresses class, race and colonial power relations – is critical, both in food sovereignty research and within food sovereignty movements themselves (Grey and Patel 2015; Bradley and Herrera 2016). Indeed, collective identities have emancipatory potential only when they challenge power relations (Calvávio et al. 2019). This includes understanding that while a collective identity of being a 'peasant' serves the social and political objective of consolidating commonalities and collectivizing claims, it can also obfuscate power relations based on various forms of intersectionality (Grey and Patel 2015; Bradley and Herrera 2016). Concealing power relations delays the process of transforming privilege and abolishing oppressions thus highlighting the importance of understanding how identities are linked to structures of power (Dahl et al. 2004).

The key question is, how can food sovereignty – as an ongoing *process* of food system transformation (Schiavoni 2017) – help create a 'deep egalitarianism' (Menser 2008)? Developing a political anti-capitalist praxis that actively fosters radical inclusivity and decolonization is a critical challenge for the future of food sovereignty.

NOTES

1. We indicate here a peasant notion of food sovereignty to clearly distinguish it from what had been proposed by other political actors earlier on (Edelman 2014).
2. We focus on LVC's efforts to advance food sovereignty since it has been the most important driver of this alternative vision.
3. Food democracy is about organizing the food system so that communities participate in decision-making (Lang 1999). Mostly used in the United States (and the United Kingdom), food democracy includes farmers' markets, community-supported agriculture, food policy councils and urban agriculture (Carlson and Chappel 2015, 7).
4. Food justice argues the elimination of racial hierarchies and class divisions is central to restructuring food systems (Jarosz 2014). The approach is criticized for leaving out the issues of loss of control over food and food-producing resources (Alkon and Mares 2012), and for being too embedded in market mechanisms (Clendenning et al. 2016).
5. Hopma and Woods (2014) establish a useful distinction between national food security and global food security. A number of nations adopted a national food security approach in response to the 2007–2008 global food crisis that led, in some cases, to closing their borders to food imports, and in other cases to land grabbing in other countries.
6. The UNDROP was approved by the UN General Assembly in December 2018. It is available at http://ap.ohchr.org/documents/dpage_e.aspx?si=A/HRC/39/L.16.
7. There is, however, an emerging literature on this. See, among others, Portman (2018), Ngcoya and Kumarakulasingam (2017), Hammelman (2018) and Schwendler and Thompson (2017).

FURTHER READING

Claeys, P. (2015), *Human Rights and the Food Sovereignty Movement: Reclaiming Control*, London: Routledge.
Desmarais, A.A. (2007), *La Vía Campesina: Globalization and the Power of Peasants*, Winnipeg and London: Fernwood Publishing and Pluto Press.
Globalizations (2015), Food sovereignty: Concept, practice and social movements, Special issue, 12(4).
Journal of Peasant Studies (2014), Global agrarian transformations, vol. 2: Critical perspectives on food sovereignty, Special issue, 41(6).
Third World Quarterly (2015), Food sovereignty: Convergence and contradictions, condition and challenges, Special issue, 36(3).

REFERENCES

Agarwal, B. (2014), Food sovereignty, food security and democratic choice: Critical contradictions, difficult conciliations, *Journal of Peasant Studies*, 41(6), 1247–1268.
Alkon, A.H.; Mares, T.M. (2012), Food sovereignty in US food movements: Radical visions and neoliberal constraints, *Agriculture and Human Values*, 29(3), 347–359.
Araújo, S. (2014), The promise and challenges of food sovereignty policies in Latin America, *Yale Human Rights and Development Law Journal*, 13, 493–506.
Bernstein, H. (2014), Food sovereignty via the 'peasant way': A sceptical view, *Journal of Peasant Studies*, 41(6), 1031–1063.
Bezner-Kerr, R.; Hickey, C.; Lupafya, E.; Dakishoni, L. (2019), Repairing rifts or reproducing inequalities? Agroecology, food sovereignty, and gender justice in Malawi, *Journal of Peasant Studies*, 46(7), 1499–1518.
Bradley, K.; Herrera, H. (2016), Decolonising food justice: Naming, resisting, and researching colonizing forces in the movement, *Antipode*, 48(1), 97–114.
Brent, Z.W.; Schiavoni, C.M.; Alonso-Fradejas, A. (2015), Contextualising food sovereignty: The politics of convergence among movements in the USA, *Third World Quarterly*, 36(3), 618–635.
Burnett, K.; Murphy, S. (2014), What place for international trade in food sovereignty?, *Journal of Peasant Studies*, 41(6), 1065–1084.
Calvávio, R.M.O.; Desmarais, A.A.; Azkarraga, J. (2019), Solidarities from below in the making of emancipatory rural politics: Insights from food sovereignty struggles in the Basque Country, *Sociologia Ruralis*, https://doi.org/10.1111/soru.12264.
Carlson, J.; Chappel, J. (2015), Deepening food democracy: The tools to create a sustainable, food secure and food sovereign future are already here – deep democratic approaches can show us how, *IATP*, accessed 9 July 2021 at www.iatp.org/sites/default/files/2015_01_06_Agrodemocracy_JC_JC_f_0 .pdf.
Claeys, P. (2012), The creation of new rights by the food sovereignty movement: The challenge of institutionalizing subversion, *Sociology*, 46(5), 844–860.
Claeys, P. (2015a), Food sovereignty and the recognition of new rights for peasants at the UN: A critical overview of La Via Campesina's rights claims over the last 20 years, *Globalizations*, 12(4), 452–465.
Claeys, P. (2015b), *Human Rights and the Food Sovereignty Movement: Reclaiming Control*, New York: Routledge.
Claeys, P.; Duncan, J. (2018), Do we need to categorize it? Reflections on constituencies and quotas as tools for negotiating difference in the global food sovereignty convergence space, *Journal of Peasant Studies*, 46(7), 1477–1498.
Clapp, J. (2014), Food security and food sovereignty: Getting past the binary, *Dialogues in Human Geography*, 4(2), 206–211.
Clendenning, J.; Dressler, W.; Richards, C. (2016), Food justice or food sovereignty? Understanding the rise of urban food movements in the USA, *Agriculture and Human Values*, 33(1), 165–177.
Conway, J. (2018), When food becomes a feminist issue: Popular feminism and subaltern agency in the World March of Women, *International Feminist Journal of Politics*, 20(2), 188–203.

Coté, C. (2016), 'Indigenizing' food sovereignty: Revitalizing Indigenous food practices and ecological knowledges in Canada and the United States, *Humanities*, 5(3), 57–71.

Crenshaw, K. (1989), Demarginalizing the intersection of race and sex: A Black feminist critique of anti-discrimination doctrine, feminist theory and antiracist politics, *University of Chicago Legal Forum*, 1(8), 139, 167.

Dahl, H.M.; Stoltz, P.; Rasmus, W. (2004), Recognition, redistribution and representation in capitalist global society: An interview with Nancy Fraser, *Acta Sociologica*, 47, 374.

Daigle, M. (2019), Tracing the terrain of Indigenous food sovereignties, *Journal of Peasant Studies*, 46(2), 297–315.

Desmarais, A.A. (2007), *La Via Campesina: Globalization and the Power of Peasants*, Halifax and London: Fernwood Publishing and Pluto Books.

Desmarais, A.A. (2014), Food sovereignty: Some initial thoughts and questions for research, in Schanbacher, W.D. (ed.), *The Global Food System*, Santa Barbara, CA: Praeger, 1–12.

Desmarais, A.A. (2015), The gift of food sovereignty, *Canadian Food Studies*, 2(2), 154–163.

Desmarais, A.A.; Wittman, H. (2014), Farmers, foodies and First Nations: Getting to food sovereignty in Canada, *Journal of Peasant Studies*, 41(6), 1153–1173.

Desmarais, A.A.; Claeys, P.; Trauger, A. (eds) (2017), *Public Policies for Food Sovereignty: Social Movements and the State*, London: Routledge.

Edelman, M. (2014), Food sovereignty: Forgotten genealogies and future regulatory challenges, *Journal of Peasant Studies*, 41(6), 959–978.

Edelman, M.; Weis, T.; Baviskar, A.; Borras, Jr., S.M.; Holt-Giménez, E.; Kandiyoti, D.; Wolford, W. (2014), Introduction: Critical perspectives on food sovereignty, *Journal of Peasant Studies*, 41(6), 911–931.

FAO (2001), *State of Food Insecurity in the World 2001*, Rome; FAO, accessed 26 January 2019 at www.fao.org/docrep/003/y1500e/y1500e00.htm.

FAO (2008), *An Introduction to the Basic Concepts of Food Security*, Rome; FAO, accessed 26 January 2019 at www.fao.org/docrep/013/al936e/al936e00.pdf.

Gioia, P. (2016), Gender diversity in the peasant movement, La Via Campesina, accessed 26 January 2019 at https://viacampesina.org/en/gender-diversity-in-the-peasant-mov.

Giunta, I. (2014), Food sovereignty in Ecuador: Peasant struggles and the challenge of institutionalization, *Journal of Peasant Studies*, 41(6), 1201–1224.

GRAIN (2005), Food sovereignty: Turning the global food system upside down, *Seedling*, April, accessed 26 January 2019 at www.grain.org/seedling/?id=329.

Grey, S.; Patel, R. (2015), Food sovereignty as decolonization: Some contributions from Indigenous movements to food system and development politics, *Agriculture and Human Values*, 32(3), 431–444.

Hammelman, C. (2018), Urban migrant women's everyday food insecurity coping strategies foster alternative urban imaginaries of a more democratic food system, *Urban Geography*, 39(5), 706–725.

Hopma, J.; Woods, M. (2014), Political geographies of 'food security' and 'food sovereignty', *Geography Compass*, 8(11), 773–784.

Hospes, O. (2014), Food sovereignty: The debate, the deadlock, and a suggested detour, *Agriculture and Human Values*, 31(1), 119–130.

Iles, A.; Montenegro de Wit, A. (2015), Sovereignty at what scale? An inquiry into multiple dimensions of food sovereignty, *Globalizations*, 12(4), 481–497.

Jansen, K. (2015), The debate on food sovereignty theory: Agrarian capitalism, dispossession and agro-ecology, *Journal of Peasant Studies*, 42(1), 213–232.

Jarosz, L. (2014), Comparing food security and food sovereignty discourses, *Dialogues in Human Geography*, 4(2), 168–181.

Kelly, M. (2018), Food sovereignty, in Zeunert, J.; Waterman, T. (eds), *Routledge Handbook of Landscape and Food*, Abingdon: Routledge, 475–486.

Kepkiewicz, L. (2017), Understanding food sovereignty in Canada: Settler colonialism and Indigenous–settler alliances, in Desmarais, A.A.; Claeys, P.; Trauger, A. (eds), *Public Policies for Food Sovereignty: Social Movements and the State*, Abingdon: Routledge, 164–180.

Künnemann, R.; Ratjen, S. (2004), The right to food: A resource manual for NGOs, Huridocs, accessed 26 January 2019 at www.fuhem.es/media/ecosocial/file/Boletin%20ECOS/ECOS%20CDV/Bolet%C3%ADn%204/Right_to_food.pdf.

La Via Campesina (1996), The right to produce and access to land, position of La Via Campesina on food sovereignty presented at the World Food Summit, 13–17 November, Rome, accessed 26 January 2019 at www.viacampesina.org.

La Via Campesina (2003), What is food sovereignty?, Jakarta: Operational Secretariat of La Via Campesina, accessed 26 January 2019 at www.viacampesina.org.

La Via Campesina (2008), Declaration of Maputo: V International Conference of La Via Campesina, Maputo, Mozambique, 19–22 October, accessed 26 January 2019 at www.viacampesina.org.

Lang, T. (1999), Food policy for the 21st century: Can it be both radical and reasonable?, in Koc, M.; MacRae, R.; Mougeot, L.J.A.; Welsh, J. (eds), *For Hunger-Proof Cities: Sustainable Urban Food Systems*, Ottawa: International Development Research Centre, 216–24.

Li, T.M. (2015), Can there be food sovereignty here?, *Journal of Peasant Studies*, 42(1), 205–211.

Masson, D.; Paulos, A.; Bastien, E.B. (2017), Struggling for food sovereignty in the World March of Women, *Journal of Peasant Studies*, 44(1), 56–77.

Mayes, C. (2018), *Unsettling Food Politics: Agriculture, Dispossession and Sovereignty in Australia*, London: Rowman and Littlefield: London.

Menser, M. (2008), Transnational participatory democracy in action: The case of La Via Campesina, *Journal of Social Philosophy*, 39(1), 20–41.

McMichael, P. (2014), Historicizing food sovereignty, *Journal of Peasant Studies*, 41(6), 933–957.

Morrison, D. (2011), Indigenous food sovereignty: A model for social learning, in Wittman, H.; Desmarais, A.A.; Wiebe, E. (eds), *Food Sovereignty in Canada: Creating Just and Sustainable Food Systems*, Halifax: Fernwood Publishers.

Mpofu, E. (2014), Keynote address at Food Sovereignty: A Critical Dialogue, International Institute of Social Studies, The Hague, 24 January.

Ngcoya, M.; Kumarakulasingam, N. (2017), The lived experience of food sovereignty: Gender, Indigenous crops and small-scale farming in Mtubatuba, South Africa: The lived experience of food sovereignty, *Journal of Agrarian Change*, 17(3), 480–496.

Nyéléni Food Sovereignty Forum (2007), Synthesis report. Nyéléni Forum for Food Sovereignty (2007), Selingué, 23–27 February, accessed 9 July 2021 at www.viacampesina.org.

Oliver, B. (2016), 'The Earth gives us so much': Agroecology and rural women's leadership in Uruguay, *Culture, Agriculture, Food and Environment*, 38(1), 38–47.

Park, C.M.Y.; White, B.; Julia (2015), We are not all the same: Taking gender seriously in food sovereignty discourse, *Third World Quarterly*, 36(3), 584–599.

Patel, R. (2005), Global fascism, revolutionary humanism and the ethics of food sovereignty, *Development*, 48(2), 79–83.

Patel, R. (2006), International agrarian restructuring and the practical ethics of peasant movement solidarity, *Journal of Asian and African Studies*, 41, 71–93.

Patel, R. (2007), Transgressing rights: La Vía Campesina's call for food sovereignty, *Feminist Economics*, 13(1), 87–116.

Patel, R. (2009), What does food sovereignty look like?, *Journal of Peasant Studies*, 36(3), 663–706.

Peña, K. (2016), Social movements, the state, and the making of food sovereignty in Ecuador, *Latin American Perspectives*, 43(1), 221–237.

Pérez-Vitoria, S. (2005), *Les Paysans sont de Retour*, Paris: Actes Sud.

Pimbert, M. (2018), Food sovereignty and the regeneration of terraced landscapes, *Annales. Series Historia and Sociologia*, 28(4), 779–794.

Portman, A. (2018), Food sovereignty and gender justice, *Journal of Agricultural and Environmental Ethics*, 31(4), 455–466.

Roman-Alcalá, A. (2016), Conceptualising components, conditions and trajectories of food sovereignty's 'sovereignty', *Third World Quarterly*, 37(8), 1388–1407.

Schiavoni, C.M. (2015), Competing sovereignties, contested processes: Insights from the Venezuelan food sovereignty experiment, *Globalizations*, 12(4), 466–480.

Schiavoni, C.M. (2017), The contested terrain of food sovereignty construction: Toward a historical, relational and interactive approach, *Journal of Peasant Studies*, 44(1), 1–32.

Schwendler, S.F.; Thompson, L.A. (2017), An education in gender and agroecology in Brazil's Landless Rural Workers' Movement, *Gender and Education*, 29(1), 100–114.

Trauger, A. (2014), Toward a political geography of food sovereignty: Transforming territory, exchange and power in the liberal sovereign state, *Journal of Peasant Studies*, 41(6), 1131–1152.

Trauger, A. (2017), *We Want Land to Live! Making Political Space for Food Sovereignty*, Athens, GA: University of Georgia Press.

Tuck, E.; Wayne Yang, K. (2012), Decolonization is not a metaphor, *Decolonization Indigeneity, Education and Society*, 1(1), 1–40.

Turner, K.L.; Idrobo, C.J.; Desmarais, A.A.; Peredo, A.M. (2020), Food sovereignty, gender and everyday practice: The role of Afro-Colombian women in sustaining localised food systems, *Journal of Peasant Studies*, 12 August.

Van der Ploeg, J.D. (2008), *The New Peasantries: Struggles for Autonomy and Sustainability in an Era of Empire and Globalization*, London: Earthscan.

Wittman, H.; Blesh, J. (2017), Food sovereignty and Fome Zero: Connecting public food procurement programmes to sustainable rural development in Brazil, *Journal of Agrarian Change*, 17(1), 81–105.

Wittman, H.; Desmarais, A.A.; Wiebe, N. (2010), The origins and potential of food sovereignty, in Wittman, H.; Desmarais, A.A.; Wiebe, N. (eds), *Food Sovereignty: Reconnecting Food, Nature and Community*, Halifax and Oakland, CA: Fernwood Publishing and Foodfirst Books.

World Bank (1986), *Poverty and Hunger: Issues and Options for Food Security in Developing Countries*, accessed 26 January 2019 at http://documents.worldbank.org/curated/en/166331467990005748/pdf/multi-page.pdf.

Ziegler, J.; Golay, C.; Mahon, C.; Way, S.-A. (2011), The definition of the right to food in international law, in Ziegler, J.; Golay, C.; Mahon, C.; Way, S.-A. (eds), *The Fight for the Right to Food: Lessons Learned*. International Relations and Development Series, London: Palgrave Macmillan, 15–22.

PART III

METHODOLOGIES

28. Qualitative research

Elisa Greco

If eight hours seem too few
You should try to work yourself
So you'll realise what the difference is
Between giving orders and doing the work.
(Protest song by women working on rice farms, northern Italy, 1930s)

Defining the use of qualitative methodologies in an eclectic field such as critical agrarian studies is like shooting a moving target. For those landing in critical agrarian studies from a farming background, the importance of qualitative research is rooted in the awareness that agrarian realities are often hidden and that agrarian statistics hide at least as much as they reveal. While very often there is little sense of surprise when approaching fieldwork in a field that is reminiscent of one's own family history – evictions, landlessness and the indebtedness and tribulations of family farms – there is also an awareness of the uneasy place of academic researchers in a rural society, of the challenges of (often politically conservative) rural anti-intellectualism and of the persistent yet hidden passive resistance based on a deep mistrust towards all institutions of power, but especially bureaucracy, surveyors and university researchers with their obsession for quantification.

To clarify, this is far from a glorification of the lived experience. Direct experience is no shortcut for analysis. It is, rather, a defence of the type of slow-paced primary research that allows for participant observation and its emotional labour at a time when, alongside the acceleration of the pace of research, this work is increasingly being substituted by delegation to research assistants and remote technologies.

This applies particularly when critical agrarian studies sees Northern researchers collecting data in the Global South, but also – and increasingly – when Southern researchers do 'quick and dirty' extractive research in the countryside. Within Global North universities, the neoliberal ideological project has turned the Global South into a place of danger and risk, from which Western scholars need to be shielded (Duffield 2014). Since the mid-1990s, the rise of remote technologies – the internet, remote communications, sensing and mapping – has contributed to the decrease of long-term immersive fieldwork research in favour of remoteness. Critical agrarian studies has partly resisted this trend, having suffered less from the existential distancing from the Global South than other fields of enquiry. However, the increased pressure in critical agrarian studies to deliver findings fast – in a way similar to that witnessed in development studies (Thomas and Mohan 2007) – has tended to shorten research times towards a 'consultancy mode' of research, giving priority to 'finding out fast' through 'quick and dirty' fieldwork efforts. In the last decade, the literature on land grabs showed that this can take place at the expense of the depth and quality of data, be it qualitative or quantitative (Oya 2013).

Theoretically a deeply diverse field, critical agrarian studies pushes against the theoretical and disciplinary boundaries of rural sociology and agricultural economics to examine the complexity of agrarian change through an interdisciplinary perspective that is the mark of both peasant studies (JPS 1973–1974; Shanin 1972) and agrarian political economy (Bernstein and Byres 2001). Works that have become classic readings in critical agrarian studies are truly interdisciplinary; as such, they rely on a wide range of mixed methods originating in different disciplines. Historically grounded, interdisciplinary anthropological works by Eric Wolf (1982) and Sidney Mintz (1985) show the importance of painstaking archival research beyond fieldwork. Polly Hill's ethnographic enquiry into 'field economics' in farming (Hill 1963; Serra 2018) questions the methods of development economics while challenging Marxist anthropologists. Sociological surveys applied to nutrition and food studies (De Castro 1952) show the power of mixing qualitative and quantitative methods in the study of famine, as do historically situated geography and political economy (Watts 1983). Qualitative observation of agronomic practices and their social and political aspects has inspired the 'farmers first' approach (Chambers et al. 1989) and agroecological knowledge (Altieri 1987).

This chapter refers to qualitative methods as a whole, acknowledging that those most frequently used in critical agrarian studies are open-ended and semi-structured interviews, archival resources, participant observation, life histories and focus groups. Participant observation is of prime importance in critical agrarian studies, not least for shaping the class consciousness of the researcher through the shared lived experience of farm and agrarian work.

AGRARIAN FIELDWORK: THE 'HAUNTED' RESEARCHER

> After my fieldwork I, too, was not the person I was before. I was a haunted being – haunted by the people among whom I had lived and of whose joys and suffering I had had direct experience. When I think of my villages, I am both hopeful and fearful of change, because change has now ceased to be an impersonal process for me. It has assumed a personal meaning as a source of joy and suffering, hope and despair, for persons whom I had known intimately. (Joshi 1981, 475)

Qualitative research has the unique ability to capture features of social, political, economic and ecological rural life that can go undetected in quantitative research. Rural politics, both organized and spontaneous, is mostly a qualitative effort; as examined within political sociology in terms of 'village studies' on the 'politics of the poor' and rural labour relations. Such works include the politicization of the 'untouchables' in Uttar Pradesh in the 1990s (Lerche 1999). Where there are organized agrarian social movements (Borras et al. 2008), political ethnography has proved central to shedding light on the contradictions of mobilization and demobilization, and the ways in which common sense mediates such social movements in times of demobilization (Wolford 2006). By comparing and contrasting cases, comparative ethnography can shed light not only on why mobilization does or does not occur, but also why and how it ends (Lapegna 2016). Studies on spontaneous rural politics, 'weapons of the weak' and everyday hidden rural resistance are based on immersive fieldwork (Scott 1985). Life histories, participant observation and semi-structured interviews can detect resistance acts that would be missed in a quantitative survey: from night harvesting in palm oil plantations as a form of resistance to land dispossession in Ghana (Amanor 2005), to burning sisal plants to reclaim land on sisal plantations in Tanzania (Greco 2017). Qualitative methods can also uncover agroecological practices that can go unnoticed in standard agronomic research, such as the practice of anthropogenic dark earth (terra preta) in Africa (Leach and Fairhead 1995; Leach et al. 2012), as well as slash-and-burn, shifting cultivation and agroforestry systems (Netting 1974).

Regarding politically sensitive extreme events in rural areas – such as famines, droughts and floods – qualitative research based on lived social experience can be vital in order to counter the official narratives of governments and donors, which revolve around the (often instrumental) support of quantitative data. A village-level study of the 2001/2002 Malawi famine revealed the true extent of the famine, in contrast to the government's and donors' refusal to recognize it as a fully fledged national 'food crisis', based on aggregate food balance sheet data and estimates on the production of tubers and roots (Tiba 2011).

Finally, qualitative research is key to producing meaningful data on marginalized groups within rural societies. Given the interconnected, multiple ways in which class, gender, age and race oppression manifest themselves, many vulnerable and marginalized groups tend to be less visible and are often unreachable through quantitative, large sample research surveys in rural areas. From nomadic and highly mobile pastoralist groups (Randall 2015) to migrant, seasonal workers (Breman 1996), marginalized group include 'hard to reach' groups (Singer 2012), like those farming illegal crops or stigmatized HIV-positive people. For these reasons, rigorous quantitative research in critical agrarian studies should be always based on, and preceded by, in-depth qualitative research, to avoid the invisibilization of marginalized and vulnerable groups in rural societies, especially during sampling and informant selection (Cramer et al. 2008, 2014).

'Hard to reach' groups are, however, not always and not necessarily vulnerable. Notably, the landlord class can refuse to collaborate in quantitative surveys in order to avoid disclosing data on property, as in the case of Pakistan's North-West Frontier Province in the mid-1980s, where powerful groups from the landlord class refused to collaborate in large-scale quantitative surveys (Akram-Lodhi 2001).

Qualitative methods can uncover the agrarian aspects of conflicts that might at first sight appear unrelated to agrarian issues, such as Paul Richard's work on the rural youth in the guerrilla war in Sierra Leone (Richards 1996). To sum up, qualitative methods are crucial for uncovering hidden transcripts, for mapping rapid processes of change and for understanding political struggles, resistance and agrarian social movements. Qualitative methods capture well the interconnected layers of class oppression, often working through the overlapping levers of gender, race and generation.

THE PITFALL OF LOCALISM

> The microlevel studies that focus on the peasantry of a country without attempting to conceptualize the global connection number in the thousands. (Araghi 1995, 337)

The challenge of localism arises, as very often qualitative research operates on a small scale. This is not necessarily a limitation if the choice of scale is based on a comprehensive, multi-scalar analysis. Weaving the threads between the different geographical scales of analysis – connecting a rural village to the dynamics of global political economy – is an analytical strength of the Marxist tradition in critical agrarian studies. Dialectical thinking requires starting from deductive analysis, which necessarily precedes fieldwork and the collection of qualitative data. The explicit identification of an analytical approach and multiple hypotheses is thus not put to the test, but rather constantly challenged through fieldwork and the practice of dialectical thinking, whereby the synthesis systematically overcomes the initial thesis/

antithesis theorizing in order to analyse the real and lift the veil of appearances. In Ilyenkov's words, 'dialectics is the area where conscious, intentional coincidence of the inductive and the deductive moments takes place, the two constituting indissolubly linked, and mutually assuming moments of inquiry' (Ilyenkov 1960, ch. 3). Post-fieldwork elaboration and interpretation of qualitative data brings us to a 'big picture' analysis. The dialectical method allows for an empirically grounded, non-deterministic analysis of the local, national, regional and global levels of the processes under study through a multi-scalar approach.

THE TIME FACTOR AND THE QUALITY OF QUALITATIVE DATA

The collection of good-quality qualitative data depends on the wider social experience of the researcher, which can be only guaranteed by immersion. Extrapolating qualitative techniques from immersion and using them for 'quick and dirty' research runs the risk of producing low-quality data with the possibility of unseen multiple biases. As trivial as it may sound, qualitative research should not be rushed. The qualitative processes of interpreting the local reality that lies behind effective participant observation represent a time-consuming and often excruciatingly slow process. It involves negotiating the researcher's access to the field, an awareness of her positioning and a mapping of the multiple biases, which then leads to the establishment of correction mechanisms to avoid biases in sampling and to the formulation of questions. Because of these aspects, qualitative data collection cannot generally be delegated to research assistants, who (if present at all) act as gatekeepers and brokers for research activities, but do not collect qualitative data on their own.

Given the nature of qualitative data, their quality can be seriously compromised when researchers act under time constraints. Time is certainly a key factor in research design and the selection of methods. A crucial practice in qualitative research is triangulation – the verification of the consistency and veracity of information on one fact, argument, aspect or theme, requiring the cross-examination of collected data through (at least) three different sources. Triangulation can occur through the same type of source, or across different types of sources; it is particularly useful in the study of contentious or sensitive issues, when different groups of informants tend to offer diverging information on the same set of events or processes. Discrepancies, when not caused by the poor quality of the data, are often revealing of contentious social fields and can thus inform the next steps to take in the process of qualitative research. As a slow, time-consuming practice, qualitative research runs counter to the pressures of neoliberal academia with its push to accelerate the pace of intellectual processes, putting pressure on researchers to publish at an increasingly fast pace.

REIFICATION OF THE QUALITATIVE, DESCRIPTIVISM AND EMPIRICISM

To conclude with a word of caution, there are perils in relying exclusively on qualitative data, and in taking a 'data speak for themselves' attitude, which reifies the empirical. More specifically, qualitative research in critical agrarian studies is exposed to two potential pitfalls: descriptivism and empiricism. Descriptivism entails the rejection of analysis and is thus based on the delusion that it is possible to produce a 'mere description' of reality independent of a specific theoretical interpretation. Empiricism is an approach that refuses to admit any analytical statement which is not strictly based on empirical evidence. This is sometimes a reaction to the opposite tendency to theoretically override evidence.

We need to counterbalance the importance of immersion. Immersion in a local setting runs the risk of offering limited analytical insight, if its findings are not located within a theoretical analysis that makes sense of the specific modalities of integration of that local setting in the global economy and the world market. In this regard, Marx's dialectical method shows that induction and deduction are complementary rather than antagonistic. Dialectics helps to avoid empiricism and descriptivism – two potential pitfalls of qualitative research – as it imposes a back-and-forth, pendulum-like swing of the research process between induction and deduction. Mixed methods are especially conducive to dialectical analysis when the quantitative helps to locate the qualitative data in a broader picture.

An exemplary piece of historically grounded, mixed-methods research is the collection on contract farming by Little and Watts (1994), which offers a dialectical analysis of the evolution of contract farming through a historically grounded, mixed-methods, political economic analysis.

CONCLUSIONS

Critical agrarian studies is 'not a consensus field' (Edelman and Wolford 2017) and is at its core theoretically eclectic and methodologically highly diverse. Based since its very inception on interdisciplinary research, and including extremely varied and sometimes contradictory epistemologies, critical agrarian studies employs a very wide range of methodological choices. Partly because of this, within the field, reflections on methods have been relatively sparse. Within this diversity, the unifying tract of critical agrarian studies is critical theory; note, however, that not all critical agrarian studies approaches are radical. Similar to what happened in geography (Castree 2000), critical theory in critical agrarian studies has been professionalized, besides having been unduly influenced by 'critical post-Marxism' (Shanin 1972). Marxist analysis is crucial to radical agrarian studies, as it entails an application of both dialectics and the historical materialist method, combining qualitative and quantitative data by grounding them in the historical process of analysing the relation between structures and superstructures. Here, qualitative data integrates a 'big picture' analysis, to unearth the 'hidden scripts' of oppression and let the voice of the voiceless emerge.

To conclude, mixed methods can help overcome the difficulties of a joint analysis of locality-specific features and general patterns. Developing the dialectical relation between critical agrarian studies in advanced capitalist countries and critical agrarian studies in poor, non-industrialized countries is key both to avoiding the 'us and them' analysis that underlies much fieldwork, and to rendering more explicit the class relations within and outside research. Immersive qualitative research is especially necessary at a time when the politics of research are engendering neo-colonial patterns of knowledge extraction, where 'fieldwork' often becomes a box-ticking exercise for academic and professional success. To counter this trend, radical scholarship commits to methods that engage the society under study on an equal level, in a shared process of knowledge production that works at its best in a constant dialogue with activism (Nabudere 2008). Slow, long and immersive fieldwork efforts are existentially engaging and emotionally challenging for the researcher. With Joshi, becoming a 'haunted researcher' constitutes a central part of the emotional and intellectual life of radical scholarship, based on shared humanness and the belief in the fundamental unity of humankind that is at the basis of the necessity for the abolition of class relations.

FURTHER READING

Burawoy, M. (2009), *The Extended Case Method: Four Countries, Four Methods, Four Great Transformations and one Theoretical Tradition*, Berkley, CA: University of California Press.
Engels, F. (1969 [1884]), *The Condition of the Working Class in England*, London: Penguin Books.
Little, P.; Watts, M. (1994), *Living under Contract: Contract Farming and Agrarian Transformation in Sub-Saharan Africa*, Madison, WI: University of Wisconsin Press.

REFERENCES

Akram-Lodhi, A.H. (2001), 'We earn only for you': Peasants and 'real' markets in northern Pakistan, *Capital and Class*, 25(2), 79–108.
Altieri, M.A. (1987), *Agroecology: The Scientific Base of Alternative Agriculture*, London: IT Publications.
Amanor, K. (2005), Night harvesters, forest hoods and saboteurs: Struggles over land expropriation in Ghana, in: Moyo, S.; Yeros, P. (eds), *Reclaiming the Land: The Resurgence of Rural Movements in Africa, Asia and Latin America*, London: Zed Books, 112–117.
Araghi, F. (1995), Global depeasantization, 1945–1990, *The Sociological Quarterly*, 36(2), 337–368.
Bernstein, H.; Byres, T. (2001), From peasant studies to agrarian change, *Journal of Agrarian Change*, 1(1), 1–56.
Borras, J.; Edelman, M.; Kay, C. (2008), *Transnational Agrarian Movements Confronting Globalization*, Wiley: Chichester.
Breman, J. (1996), *Footloose Labour: Working in India's Informal Economy*, Cambridge: Cambridge University Press.
Castree, N. (2000), Professionalisation, activism, and the university: Whither 'critical geography'?, *Environment and Planning A*, 32, 955–970.
Chambers, R.; Pacey, A.; Thrupp, L.A. (1989), *Farmer First: Farmer Innovation and Agricultural Research*, London: IT Publications.
Cramer, C.; Oya, C.; Sender, J. (2008), Lifting the blinkers: A new view of power, diversity and poverty in Mozambican rural labour markets, *Journal of Modern African Studies*, 46(3), 361–392.
Cramer, C.; Johnston, D.; Mueller, B.; Oya, C.; Sender, J. (2014), How to do (and how not to do) fieldwork on fair trade and rural poverty, *Canadian Journal of Development Studies*, 35(1), 170–185.
De Castro, J. (1952), *The Geography of Hunger*, Boston, MA: Little and Brown.
Duffield, M. (2014), From immersion to simulation: Remote methodologies and the decline of area studies, *Review of African Political Economy*, 41(1), 75–94.
Edelman, M.; Wolford, W. (2017), Introduction: Critical agrarian studies in theory and practice, *Antipode*, 49(4), 959–976.
Greco, E. (2017), Farmers or squatters? Collective land claims in sisal estates, Tanzania (1980s–2000s), *Journal of Agrarian Change*, 17(1), 166–187.
Hill, P. (1963), *Migrant Cocoa Farmers of Southern Ghana: A Study in Rural Capitalism*, Cambridge: Cambridge University Press.
Ilyenkov, E. (1960), *The Dialectics of the Abstract and the Concrete in Marx's Capital*, accessed 12 February 2019 at www.marxists.org/archive/ilyenkov/works/abstract/index.htm.
Joshi, P.C. (1981), Fieldwork experience: Relived and reconsidered: The Agrarian society of Uttar Pradesh, *Journal of Peasant Studies*, 8(4), 455–484.
JPS (*Journal of Peasant Studies*) (1973–1974), Editorial statement, 1(1).

Lapegna, P. (2016), *Soybeans and Power: Genetically Modified Crops, Environmental Politics, and Social Movements in Argentina*, Oxford: Oxford University Press.

Leach, M.; Fairhead, J. (1995), Ruined settlements and new gardens: Gender and soil ripening among Kuranko farmers in the forest-savanna transition zone, *IDS Bulletin*, 26(1), 24–32.

Leach, M.; Fairhead, J.; Fraser, J. (2012), Green grabs and biochar: Revaluing African soils and farming in the new carbon economy, *Journal of Peasant Studies*, 39(2), 285–307.

Lerche, J. (1999), Politics of the poor: Agricultural labourers and political transformations in Uttar Pradesh, *Journal of Peasant Studies*, 26(2–3), 182–241.

Little, P.; Watts, M. (1994), *Living under Contract: Contract Farming and Agrarian Transformation in Sub-Saharan Africa*, Madison, WI: University of Wisconsin Press.

Mintz, S.W. (1985), *Sweetness and Power: The Place of Sugar in Modern History*, New York: Penguin.

Nabudere, D.W. (2008), Research, activism and knowledge production, in Haley, C. (ed.), *Engaging Contradictions: Theory, Politics and Methods of Activist Scholarship*, Berkeley, CA: University of California Press, 62–87.

Netting, R. (1974), Agrarian ecology, *Annual Review of Anthropology*, 3, 21–56.

Oya, C. (2013), Methodological reflections on 'land grab' databases and the 'land grab' literature 'rush', *Journal of Peasant Studies*, 40(3), 503–520.

Randall, S. (2015), Where have all the nomads gone? Fifty years of statistical and demographic invisibilities of African mobile pastoralists, *Pastoralism*, 5(1), 1–22.

Richards, P. (1996), *Fighting for the Rain Forest: War, Youth and Resources in Sierra Leone*, Portsmouth: Heinemann.

Serra, G. (2018), Pleas for fieldwork: Polly Hill on observation and induction, 1966–1982, *Research in the History of Economic Thought and Methodology*, 36B, 93–108.

Scott, J. (1985), *Weapons of the Weak: Everyday Forms of Peasant Resistance*, New Haven, CT: Yale University Press.

Shanin, T. (1972), Comment, in *The Rules of the Game*, London: Tavistock Publications, 145–147.

Singer, M. (2012), 'Studying hidden and hard-to-reach populations', in Lecompte, J. (ed.), *Specialized Ethnographic Methods: A Mixed Methods Approach Ethnographer's Toolkit 4*, Lanham, MD: Altamira Press.

Thomas, A.; Mohan, G. (eds) (2007), *Research Skills for Policy and Development: How to Find out Fast*, London: Sage.

Tiba, Z. (2011), 'Maize is life, but rice is money!' A village case study of the 2001/02 famine in Malawi, *Journal of Agrarian Change*, 11(1), 3–28.

Watts, M. (1983), *Silent Violence: Food, Famine and Peasantry in Northern Nigeria*, Berkley, CA: University of California Press.

Wolf, E. (1982), *Europe and the People without History*, Berkeley, CA: University of California Press.

Wolford, W. (2006), The difference ethnography can make: Understanding social mobilization and development in the Brazilian northeast, *Qualitative Sociology*, 29, 335–352.

29. Quantitative analysis

J. Paul Dunne

INTRODUCTION

Unlike critical agrarian studies, its predecessor peasant studies relied heavily on quantitative analysis. This is a lacunae in the field, for quantitative analysis is a very important means of investigating data. It is widely used to establish patterns in the data that suggest what is going on, either over time or in units such as individuals, households or countries. It is of course important to have confidence in the data and to be sure that the strengths and weaknesses of the data are well understood. There are an awful lot of bad-quality data available, especially in many of the countries of the global South, where critical agrarian studies undertakes a disproportionate share of its research, and undertaking good, sophisticated quantitative analysis on the basis of bad data does not make the bad data any better. Indeed, there is the risk that it obscures the poor quality of the data and the existence of alternative information that might challenge any findings.

There are different types of data-based empirical work. Firstly, there is the historical, institutional and spatial systematic observation and collection of qualitative and quantitative information within a consistent organizing framework. Secondly, there is the descriptive empirical analysis of the quantitative data that have been collected. Both of these are widely accepted and used by scholars engaged in critical agrarian studies. However, there is a third type, which is more controversial: statistical analysis using formal probability-based techniques of inference. One central issue, which acts as a significant deterrent to the use of statistical analysis by many social scientists working in critical agrarian studies, is that the most suitable methods may appear to be technically sophisticated and so involve a lot of work for researchers wanting to gain specialized knowledge. However, this is deceptive; a great deal of solid quantitative analysis can be carried out using fairly elementary tools when those tools are suitable to the research that is being undertaken.

Political economists use these methods, but with less enthusiasm for statistical analysis than disciplinary-based economists, political scientists and sociologists. Quantitatively minded social scientists are likely to consider the available techniques and consider what might be the most useful, both to illustrate the patterns observed in the data and to provide forms of statistical analysis. However, quantitatively focused social scientists have a reputation for too often using the most sophisticated techniques to hide the limitations of their analysis. This reputation is not wholly undeserved, especially among economists, although it is actually often inexperienced researchers who simply take techniques and apply them without concern for their suitability and unquestioningly report the results as a demonstration of causality when in fact misspecification means that they are not even demonstrating correlation. For non-economists there are many lessons to be learned in observing the experience of economists in the uses and misuses of statistical analysis.

THE MISUSES OF QUANTITATIVE ANALYSIS

The misuses of statistical analysis have been amply demonstrated in economics. In the 1980s Dewald et al. (1986) published an article in a high-profile economics journal that attempted to replicate the results produced in published articles and found that they could only replicate 40 per cent of the results. This was a bit of a wake-up call for the profession, a call that was reinforced by a high-profile article by influential economists Reinhart and Rogoff (2009). Their technical analysis determined that as the share of debt in gross domestic product rose the rate of growth of gross domestic product declined, and indeed at very high levels of debt could become negative. This result was used as evidence to justify austerity policies to reduce debt levels. However, when a research student tried to replicate their findings, he found a mistake in a spreadsheet that was used for the technical analysis; when corrected, the result was no longer apparent (Herndon et al. 2014). A revised version of the analysis by the authors that took the error into account further undermined the original findings.[1] It is because of issues like these that many journals, and not just economics journals, now ask for data sets and technical analysis to be made available online for both referees and for other researchers.[2]

These examples show how difficult quantitative empirical research is, from collecting consistent data to processing them and using the tools correctly. With the increasing complication of empirical analysis can come an increased problem of mistakes that are not noticed and influential. Errors can be made and can remain hidden in complex methods, questionable data transformations and erroneous data choices. Complexity can result in disagreements over minor differences in the modelling of data, obscuring the deeper issue of whether the modelling strategy is appropriate. The complications of the techniques can also be used to obscure the focus of the analysis onto the available data, which can limit the scope of the analysis. After all, statistical analysis can only address issues for which quantifiable data are available and in much of critical agrarian studies this severely restricts the scope of the analysis. This can result in research questions being chosen not because they are relevant socially, politically and theoretically, but simply due to data availability.

In addition to the quality of the data, the data used in any quantitative analysis can be criticized as to whether they truly represent a theoretical process. However, this is not something that is very much considered in economics or in other quantitative social sciences. For example, it is common to see neoclassical economic theory used to specify a model, which is then calibrated using data that were collected using a Keynesian theoretical construct and not neoclassical theoretical underpinnings. In this way, data can positively misrepresent theory, and as a field of critical social enquiry critical agrarian studies must be cognizant of this. Radical statistics groups have played an important role in questioning any attempts to treat data in a neutral manner.[3] Such groups have also pointed to the non-neutral basis of some quantitative techniques; for example, regression analysis, which is very widely used, emerged from eugenics research (McKenzie 1999).

THE USES OF QUANTITATIVE ANALYSIS

Having said that, quantitative methods do provide a consistent and potentially transparent framework of analysis for critical agrarian studies and, when the data used are made available, the opportunity to check the results independently. At the same time, statistics and mathematics do provide a means of communication, in the form of a language that limits confusion and provides consistent concepts. This can mean that it is difficult to the uninitiated and this can be off-putting, but often it is unfamiliarity with notation and terms rather than conceptual difficulty that is involved. In this light, it might be better to consider a benefit-cost evaluation for quantitative work in critical agrarian studies. This requires asking whether better and more difficult methods make much of a difference in the statistical results. This can be answered by considering the mean squared error of different approaches or the power of different tests.

Indeed, many quantitative economists – and fewer political scientists and sociologists – who do careful empirical research warn of the dangers of taking a too-technical approach. Here, there are important lessons for the use of quantitative analysis in critical agrarian studies. The Duhem-Quine thesis states that it is impossible to test a hypothesis because the test requires a set of auxiliary assumptions that shape the findings of the test. So, if a hypothesis from a theory is rejected it is not clear whether the theory is wrong or one or more of the auxiliary assumptions made in constructing the empirical test do not hold. For this reason, there are careful empirical analysts who will first consider the nature of the data and how well they work to represent a theory. They then consider the patterns in the data, either over time and or in cross-section, before deciding how to approach it to investigate what seems to be taking place. This is sensible advice for researchers in critical agrarian studies; high-profile econometricians, such as David Hendry and Hashem Pesaran, have always advised plotting data and looking at simple descriptive statistics to understand the data before deciding to do any more advanced statistical analysis.[4] Indeed, in many instances careful tabular analysis can reveal important patterns in the data.

This demonstrates that it is important for quantitative analysis to move away from 'cookbook' econometrics and the tendency to move straight toward more complicated methods when something simpler will do because it is analytically better suited and will certainly be better understood. Too many political scientists, sociologists and economists will simply put data into a programme such as Stata and run a regression. They may have theory, but it is one that they have picked up from a textbook or from an earlier paper and have not really thought about whether the theory really explains the model specification that they estimate.

QUANTITATIVE MARXIST ECONOMICS AND CRITICAL AGRARIAN STUDIES

One area that illustrates both the concerns and opportunities of quantitative analysis for critical agrarian studies has been its use within Marxist political economy. The debates presented in Dunne (1991) considered whether one could and should do quantitative Marxism and raised concerns that reflected more generally upon political economy, and now upon critical agrarian studies. While Marx was not an empiricist, in the sense of arguing that one could only understand by empirical observation, he was certainly an empirical analyst. The revival of Marxist economics in the 1970s focused on debates over theory, but within this revival there were some influential theoretical critiques and empirical analyses of the post-war boom in the advanced capitalist economies. There was also, following the empirical analysis of Lenin, Kautsky and Chayanov, extensive use of quantitative analysis in peasant studies, as exemplified by the Indian 'mode of production' debate. However, there was a much broader strand that proclaimed anti-quantitative views, both in terms of subject matter and methodology, which led to a rather inward-looking attitude. In the 1980s Marxist economics became marginalized, partly a result of the general malaise of the left and a series of political defeats, but also, it can be argued, because the inward-looking attitude of the 1970s produced a failure to become involved in debates with the prevailing neoclassical economics orthodoxy. Marxist economists tended to dismiss their analysis, the tools and the data they used as having little value or interest. Indeed, some Marxist economists argued that the very attempt to capture the dynamics of capitalist accumulation with statistical analysis and the available data was a complete waste of time, being focused on outward appearances rather than underlying forces, and with data being merely phenomenological forms that gave little insight into what was happening within the structures of the capitalist economy (see Dunne 1991). The contributions in Dunne (1991) argued that this was not only misplaced but was positively damaging because it understated the importance of empirical analysis to Marx.

Certainly, Marx's method of distinguishing between appearance and essence, treating economic processes as historical and social and using a materialist dialectical form of analysis, in no way precludes an empirical analysis and his work is extensively empirical, moving from the abstract to the concrete through the illustrative use of data. This methodology underpins much of the use of quantifiable analysis in critical agrarian studies. Granted, while variables from theory may be non-quantifiable and non-operational in any absolute sense, they are the products of underlying real processes and so do reflect them. If definitions are consistent over time then movements and patterns can be identified that give information on the processes at work. For example, important empirical analyses of crisis have been undertaken since the early work of Kondratief. These have offered alternative perspectives to the orthodox explanations of capitalist boom and bust, which are explained as the result of exogenous shocks to a well-behaved system, of which the Covid-19 pandemic is but the most recent.

There is a now a well-established stream of quantitative Marxist economics that has developed the empirical side of the analysis and it is in developing this work that statistical analysis using formal probability-based techniques of inference have been used to assist in analysis. Indeed, this analysis has seeped into critical agrarian studies, particularly but not exclusively in the analysis of the financialization of food that came to be understood in the wake of the 2007/2008 food, financial, fuel and climate crises (Field 2016). This has been important, because orthodox perspectives tend to use quantitative analysis for support as though it is unproblematic, which it is not. For critical agrarian studies failing to engage in quantitative analysis is likely to mean not engaging with the mainstream analysis of rural issues and leaving the terrain to the orthodoxy, meaning debates may stay within pockets of relatively like-minded individuals. Quantitative analysis also has the potential to provide students coming from orthodox rural development programmes an alternative perspective that uses familiar tools to undertake investigations in critical agrarian studies.

GUIDELINES FOR UNDERTAKING QUANTITATIVE ANALYSIS

If quantitative analysis is worth doing, it is worth doing well. Fortunately, there is an excellent guide, provided by Ron Smith in an influential piece for political scientists, which is equally applicable to scholars of critical agrarian studies (Smith 1998). He provides a set of questions to help guide the researcher, which are now briefly summarized.

Why Are You Doing This?

Often the method can be determined by the purpose of the critical agrarian studies research and the use of statistical analysis is justified because of the purpose of the research. However, far too often, especially in economics, statistical analysis is undertaken because the author has just come across some techniques and feels the need to apply them to make the work look more 'advanced'. It is important to understand that models that are employed to describe the kinds of processes of interest in critical agrarian studies are very different than the kinds of model used to undertake forecasting, which are of little interest to scholars in critical agrarian studies. Having said that, for the understanding of processes there is no single 'best' model. Large structural models, small structural systems, small atheoretical systems, single equation structural models: all have advantages and disadvantages and can be used for different purposes. The researcher really should be able to convince the reader that s/he has chosen the right model for the purpose.

What Are the Data?

As has been made clear, how good and useful the results are will depend on how good the data are. As the adage goes, 'rubbish in, rubbish out', and this is very much the case in settings where research in critical agrarian studies is carried out. It is useful to know how data are collected and constructed, and whether the measured data actually reflect the theoretical categories. Not looking at the data to see if they look sensible can lead to many problems, particularly with large data sets where mistakes, such as survey errors, miscoding and misplaced decimal points are more common.

Is the Model Plausible?

It is advisable to consider whether the theoretical model being used for the analysis and estimation is a reasonable representation of the processes at work. Statistical models can be developed for specific purposes and it is often quite inadvisable to apply them generally. In other words, theory and data should drive the model, rather than the convenience of the model. Issues of structural stability, exogeneity and stochastic structure also need to be considered. Moreover, it is advisable to ask whether what is observable should be interpreted using a different theoretical construct, because there could be observational equivalence.

Does the Model Fit the Data?

How well the model fits the data is often the focus of the empirical analysis, with tests to see if the auxiliary assumptions embodied in the model hold in the data. In regression this means using various diagnostic tests and they are important to stop systematic errors influencing results. It is also advisable to ask how well the model performs relative to alternative models. This can be done by allowing for a general model and testing for models nested within the more general model. This may be restricted by the problem of overparameterization, where there is not enough information in the data to get sensible estimates of the general model.[5]

Can You Tell the Difference between Statistical and Substantive Significance?

Statistical significance provides a measure of the strength of the fit between the model and the data. However, the presence of statistical significance need not produce analytically important results. Some statistically significant results may be trivial, such as the finding that as the temperature rises the consumption of beer in beer-consuming places also rises. Statistical significance is also usually present if the sample is large enough, in which case the result may not be of much analytical relevance. Statistical significance may be present but may be so small as to be unimportant. Finally, statistical significance can only be estimated using the available data, and if the data omit important analytical variables statistical significance may be present but may be quite misleading as to the underlying processes at work. It is therefore necessary to distinguish between statistical and substantive significance because findings can be statistically significant but not of substantive significance because they are of little relevance.[6]

Can Your Results Be Reproduced?

Many journals ask for data sets and technical details in order to allow the reproduction of the results by making these available on the website. This is an important development, coming in economics after the recognition that it was difficult to replicate published works. It remains a valuable means of checking the validity of research as well as assisting in the development of research and teaching by making data more readily available.

Can Your Results Be Triangulated?

In addition to Ron Smith's questions, for critical agrarian studies it is worth asking if there is other evidence that verifies the results. This comes from the critical realist dismissal of econometric analysis because of the closed nature of the systems required for quantitative analysis. Downward and Mearman (2002, 405–412) have, however, argued that critical realism and empirical analysis can be productively synthesized. Both require an appeal to qualitative invariance that may not be justified; and both measure things at different times and places and assume they are the same thing, which in dynamic social processes they may not be. Recognizing this means that the use of statistical analysis can be justified but that it is important to see it as one bit of information and use other forms of analysis to triangulate the results and thus strengthen the overall findings. Making an attempt to check if the results hold with other forms of theoretical and observational/empirical analysis and qualitative analysis is, therefore, an important means of validating the analytical results that are produced in critical agrarian studies research.

CONCLUSIONS

Quantitative analysis is important in the social sciences and the lack of enthusiasm in its use in critical agrarian studies, relative to its precursor peasant studies, is unjustified. This is certainly true of attempts to understand data through investigative and descriptive analysis and this chapter has argued it is also true of statistical analysis. This is not to say that quantitative and statistical analysis has not been misused, but it has also been well used to great effect. The confusing nature of some quantitative analysis can reflect the use of statistics as a language, to provide clarity in terms, concepts and methods. While it can always be used to obscure or impress, good empirical work will always be justifiable and understandable and clear about its limitations. Many of the objections to quantitative analysis in critical agrarian studies reflect those put forward in Marxist political economy and the chapter has shown how there are good reasons why they should not convince.

Of course if quantitative analysis is worth doing it should be done properly. Researchers should attempt to ask and answer the questions provided by Smith (1998) and be willing to attempt to triangulate any results, seeing the quantitative analysis as just a part of the overall analysis. If this sort of careful work is done it will only be to the benefit of critical agrarian studies.

ACKNOWLEDGEMENTS

I am grateful to Haroon Akram-Lodhi and to Jurgen Brauer and Ron Smith for comments and suggestions.

NOTES

1. See Alexander (2013) and Cassidy (2013) for summaries of the debate. The original working paper is Herndon et al. (2013).
2. Indeed, there is now a replication network in economics: https://replicationnetwork.com/.
3. See www.radstats.org.uk.
4. See for example Hendry (2000) and Pesaran and Pesaran (2009).
5. For example, a general model may contain 10 variables and the data may only have 11 observations, meaning that even though the model can be estimated the results do not tell us much.
6. In medical research we may know the causes of a disease relatively well. We may still be able to add another variable to an equation and it may be significant, but it might add very little to our understanding.

FURTHER READING

Dorling, D.; Simpson, L. (eds) (1999), *Statistics in Society*, London: Arnold.
Dunne, P. (ed.) (1991), *Quantitative Marxism*, Cambridge: Polity Press.
Smith, R.P. (1998), Quantitative methods in peace research, *Journal of Peace Research*, 35(4), 419–427.

REFERENCES

Alexander, R. (2013), Reinhart, Rogoff ... and Herndon: The student who caught out the profs. *BBC News Magazine*, April, accessed 10 March 2021 at www.bbc.co.uk/news/magazine-22223190.
Cassidy, J. (2013), The Reinhart and Rogoff controversy: A summing up. *The New Yorker*, April, accessed 10 March 2021 at www.newyorker.com/news/john-cassidy/the-reinhart-and-rogoff-controversy-a -summing-up.
Dewald, W.G.; Thursby, J.G.; Anderson, R.G. (1986), Replication in empirical economics, *American Economic Review*, 76(4), 587–603.

Downward, P.; Mearman, A. (2002), Critical realism and econometrics: Constructive dialogue with post Keynesian economics, *Metroeconomica*, 53(4), 391–415.

Dunne, P. (ed.) (1991), *Quantitative Marxism*, Cambridge: Polity Press.

Field, S. (2016), The financialization of food and the 2008–2011 food price spikes, *Environment and Planning A: Economy and Space*, 48(11), 2272–2290.

Hendry, D.F. (2000), *Econometrics: Alchemy or Science? Essays in Econometric Methodology*, Oxford: Oxford University Press.

Herndon, T.; Ash, M.; Pollin, R. (2013), Does high public debt consistently stifle economic growth? A critique of Reinhart and Rogoff. Political Economy Research Institute Working Paper 322, accessed 10 March 2021 at www.peri.umass.edu/images/WP322.pdf.

Herndon, T.; Ash, M.; Pollin, R. (2014), Does high public debt consistently stifle economic growth? A critique of Reinhart and Rogoff, *Cambridge Journal of Economics*, 38(2), 257–279.

McKenzie, D. (1999), Eugenics and the rise of mathematical statistics in Britain, in Dorling, D.; Simpson, L. (eds), *Statistics in Society*, London: Arnold, 53–61.

Pesaran, B.; Pesaran, M.H. (2009), *Microfit 5.0*, Oxford: Oxford University Press.

Reinhart, C.M.; Rogoff, K. (2009), *This Time Is Different: Eight Centuries of Financial Folly*, Princeton, NJ: Princeton University Press.

Smith, R.P. (1998), Quantitative methods in peace research, *Journal of Peace Research*, 35(4), 419–427.

30. Geographical research
Oliver Pye

INTRODUCTION

Critical agrarian studies has always been a discussion of spatial-temporal dynamics, as in the question of how capitalist relations of production expand into and transform rural areas or the 'periphery'. In this way, it has always been embedded within a particular way of seeing the world and the spatial relations between different geographical parts of this world – usually within a Global North versus Global South framework. A large part of contemporary critical agrarian research is therefore situated in the Global South. The challenge for critical agrarian studies is how to develop research methodologies that are open for and do justice to the spatial dynamics of a globalized world that connects particular places in different ways.

A CRITICAL GEOGRAPHICAL APPROACH: FOUNDATIONAL UNDERPINNINGS

Critical agrarian studies research is implicitly geographical, but (at least) since the 'spatial turn' in the social sciences it has become (or should be) explicitly so. Researchers should consciously think through spatial dimensions when designing their research, rather than rushing straight to the list of questions for the ubiquitous semi-structured interview.

Critical geographical research starts from Lefebvre's (2011 [1974]) idea that space is socially produced; that is, it is not simply physically there. It follows that space is not just a quantitative dimension (small versus large, near versus far) but a qualitative one: different things happen at different scales (Herod 2011) and different spatial logics have different social implications (Taylor 1982). Capitalism is constantly reworking the spatial manifestation of global 'unequal development' (Smith 1984), as capital and production shift across the globe. In his influential book *The Rise of the Network Society*, Castells (1996) argues that changes in information technology have transformed the basic spatial structure of our economy into a 'space of flows', leading to new configurations between the concrete place and the global economy. In her equally influential *Space, Place and Gender*, Massey (1994) shows how industrial development is a highly political and gendered process, in which global linkages and cultural formations of particular gender relations interact in specific places, shaping production and reproduction.

A good starting point for thinking through the geographical dynamics of your research is to spatialize Henry Bernstein's four famous research questions – Who owns what? Who does what? Who gets what? What do they do with it? – by adding: And where? To systematize the where-question, it is also useful to follow the so-called TPSN approach forwarded by Bob Jessop, Neil Brenner and Martin Jones (2008, 389), who argue that different spatial dimensions – territories (T), places (P), scales (S) and networks (N) – 'must be viewed as mutually constitutive and relationally intertwined dimensions of sociospatial relations'.

Critical agrarian studies often starts out from the perspective of 'accumulation by dispossession' (Harvey 2003); a 'spatial fix' by which capitalism prolongs itself by privatizing the commons and expanding into 'pre-capitalist' spaces, feeding upon 'cheap nature' and 'cheap labour' (Moore 2015). This is the territorial dynamic, and much of contemporary critical agrarian studies focuses on the social and environmental problems this creates and the corresponding processes of social differentiation and 'adverse incorporation' (McCarthy 2010). In juxtaposition to place, which refers to the specific social and cultural history and embeddedness of a particular part of a physical landscape (such as a village and its geographical embeddedness), territoriality explains many of the conflicts and politicizations around agrarian change. As Haesbaert (2013) argues, the supposed deterritorialization of globalized capital creates an unequal reterritorialization, leading to struggles over contested, multiple territorialities. Much critical agrarian studies research, particularly land-grabbing studies, selects a place and then uncovers the dynamics of this territorial incursion by non-place-based actors such as corporations and various state entities.

These territorial dynamics are, however, connected to other spatial processes. Each territorial expansion and each place is embedded within networks. New studies on the financialization of agriculture (Clapp 2014) acknowledge that the global 'meta-network' of finance shapes the temporal and geographical pattern of territorializing waves of investment (and de-investment). Production itself is increasingly organized in global production and distribution networks. Each specific locality (or place) is thereby connected via networks to the global 'corporate food regime' (McMichael 2009). This also applies to the 'scale of experience' – peasants and the landless rural proletariat have become 'footloose' (Breman and Wiradi 2002; see Pattenden in this volume), mobile and networked, looking for work in various geographical locations, both rural and urban.

Geographical research draws on the instruments of empirical research in general, be it quantitative or qualitative or a combination of both. The point about geographically informed research is to tailor the research design to the spatial dynamics of the research question, rather than simply adopting the usual instruments (such as a household survey, questionnaire, in-depth interview). This leads to the research question itself, which should also be geographically informed.

To qualify as critical, geographical research needs to be useful in some way in terms of changing the status quo. Usefulness is, of course, debatable. Researchers should think seriously about adopting a transdisciplinary (Fam et al. 2017) or action research approach that explicitly incorporates a change agenda into the research design. Furthermore, the research itself does not necessarily have to be connected to or reflect a praxis of change; rather, in providing an enhanced understanding of the causes and dynamics of the current situation, it could be useful for those trying to change it. Understanding the local situation, or the cultural embeddedness or history of a struggle in a particular place might be interesting for a social anthropologist or a political scientist, but this can be rather irrelevant for the people being interviewed – after all, they know this already. Locating the issue within different TPSN spatial dynamics could lead to a different research question and geographical design; perhaps a research on power structures (of the rice trade) or a network analysis (of sugar cane players) would be more useful to the actors whom critical agrarian studies aims to support.

RESEARCHING THE POLITICAL ECOLOGY OF THE KAPUAS RIVER IN WEST KALIMANTAN IN INDONESIA: A CASE FOR ILLUSTRATION

A research project that I was involved in on the political ecology of the Kapuas River in West Kalimantan in Indonesia (Pye et al. 2017) can serve to illustrate how a spatially informed research design can shape research methodology. It can also illustrate the many problems and blunders that can arise when doing so.

West Kalimantan, a province on the island of Borneo, has experienced a wave of land grabs over the last couple of decades. So much so, in fact, that the area covered by concessions and conservation areas is now larger (because of overlaps) than the total area of the whole province. The research project wanted to uncover the dynamics behind these land grabs, their social-ecological impact and what could be done about it. To do so, in the research design we rejected a sole focus on the territorial dynamics of the land grabs, and instead examined the river as an eco-social system that connects different places at a landscape scale. We selected different rural places that represented key transformation dynamics (such as palm oil, bauxite mining, conservation projects, gold mining) and tried to uncover the networks that connected them to urban places (Pontianak at the river mouth, Singapore, New York and so on).

Our research method adapted a participatory action research approach (Kindon et al. 2007) to identify spatial intervention points in order to change dynamics that local inhabitants and broader civil society networks found problematic. Rather than simply critiquing various case studies of outside investors moving in on local communities and appropriating their resources, this method enabled us to locate a particular place within specific 'urban-rural transformation loops' that connected the place, via networks, with other places functioning at different scales. In one bauxite mining area, for example, we helped local activists use drones to map the territorial conflict with the mining company, showing that the latter had intruded into areas not covered by the concession. The map was used in a legal intervention at the national scale, which eventually led to the mine being shut down. While this counter-mapping action was framed by the 'locals' as defending indigenous territory, it also unearthed how the conflict was situated within a gendered political economy network of regional and national politicians, including indigenous leaders.

This success was, nevertheless, the exception to the rule. By the time we had conducted our series of action research exercises that we termed 'participatory hydro-political appraisals', the project lifetime had nearly finished. We had mainly concentrated on what our research groups already knew, rather than on what they needed to find out in order to change their situation. The 'transformation loops' remained rough sketches, and action strategies could not be scaled up. Furthermore, starting out from exemplary places rather than mobile groups of workers, for example, led to a 'community' bias which emphasized territorial dynamics over mobile networks, gendered social relations and the class differentiation dynamics of agrarian change.

WHY APPLY CRITICAL GEOGRAPHICAL RESEARCH WITHIN CRITICAL AGRARIAN STUDIES?

Critical agrarian studies often does not reflect enough on the geographical underpinnings and assumptions of its research. Commonsense spatial units such as households, communities or nation states are not questioned but are taken at face value. The spatial assumptions we make about social dynamics shape and constrain the geography of our research design. One such pitfall has been criticized as 'methodological nationalism' (Wimmer and Glick Schiller 2002; Goswami 2004); that is, taking the 'national container state' as a natural spatial entity, such as in discussing the agrarian question in India or Mexico. This is problematic, because many of the political decisions relevant to agrarian change are no longer (and never were) made exclusively at the national scale (for instance, structural adjustment programmes, World Trade Organization regulations).

Methodological nationalism becomes even more problematic when discussing the spatial dimensions of the global economy, including global inequality, which are often analysed as relationships between countries; as in the terms 'developed' and 'developing' countries or the Global North and Global South. While there are clear (yet changing) geographical patterns of global inequality, it is unlikely that using a territorial concept can explain how these social relations play out in space. Too often, a territorial concept is substituted for a spatially differentiated class analysis (for instance, 'We in the Global North consume X-Y-Z agrarian product or have a per capita footprint of ...').

Many case studies looking at agrarian change and land grabs in particular show a similar pattern: a large investor moves into a particular area; the investor gains a large concession – through persuasion, deceit and/or force; this changes the ecology, political economy and social structure of the area; some of the local inhabitants become richer and most become poorer, losing the basis of their livelihoods; a gendered process of social differentiation takes place, leading to patterns of migration and proletarianization. This can be called 'methodological localism': external global forces impact a unique – traditional – locality. This leads to an endless repetition: the same processes happen again and again, in ever new locations. When the resistance of the local indigenous community is included, this becomes 'Avatar research': the destruction of the mother tree (insert the resource pertaining to your case study) by an alien mining corporation (insert bad corporation of your choice) is resisted by the blue-skinned indigenous population, with the help of their supernatural connection to Mother Earth (your 'locals' and their 'non-capitalist ontology').

Whilst this does undoubtedly describe what is happening 'on the ground' in many places, it is unclear how further research of this kind will help us to understand the interconnected whole and what to do about it. As Hart (2006, 996) argues, we need to develop relational comparative research methods that conceive of 'place as nodal points of connection in socially produced space'. While engaged scholars can (and should) take the side of indigenous struggles resisting corporate land grabbing, the analytical task is to uncover how localized power structures and class dynamics are entwined with networks that play out at the national level and which also reach up to the global scale. Localized resistance, in order to win, also needs to be scaled up. Arguably, corporate and authoritarian forces are on the offensive, because they operate globally and/or nationally. Rather than using spatial concepts as a cypher for strategies of resistance (as in the local autonomy and territoriality of many indigenous movements), or deglobalization and renationalization processes (Bello 2002), social movements need to recast the social content of emancipatory politics in spatial terms (including but not limited to territoriality) that can also shape and transform the global. In the critical agrarian studies context, food sovereignty, as an alternative vision and practice, also needs a global strategy regarding what to do with the corporate food regime, which is not simply about ignoring it and only celebrating the local.

CONCLUSION

Critical agrarian studies should draw on geographical research to make sense of the relational connections that shape rural lives and struggles today. Going beyond naturalized categories of the local, national and global, critical agrarian studies needs to understand spatial structures as socially produced. Systematically exploring relations between places, territory, scale and networks can help to sharpen our analysis of agrarian class dynamics, the everyday mobile lives of rural populations and their political struggles and how these are shaped by and can change globalized power structures.

FURTHER READING

Glasberg, D.S. (1989), Bank hegemony research and its implications for power structure theory, *Critical Sociology*, 16(2), 27–49.
Jessop, B.; Brenner, N.; Jones, M. (2008), Theorizing sociospatial relations, *Environment and Planning D: Society and Space*, 26, 389–401.
Marcus, G.E. (1995), Ethnography in/of the world system: The emergence of multi-sited ethnography, *Annual Review of Anthropology*, 24, 95–117.
Sassen, S. (2010), The global inside the national: A research agenda for sociology, *Sociopedia. isa*, accessed 20 November 2019 at www.saskiasassen.com/PDFs/publications/the-global-inside-the -national.pdf.
Tsing, A.L. (2005), *Friction: An Ethnography of Global Connection*, Princeton, NJ: Princeton University Press.

REFERENCES

Bello, W. (2002), *Deglobalization, Ideas for a New World Economy*, London: Zed Books.
Breman, J.; Wiradi, G. (2002), *Good Times and Bad Times in Rural Java*, Leiden: KITLV Press.
Castells, M. (1996), *The Rise of the Network Society, the Information Age: Economy, Society and Culture*, vol. 1, Malden, MA: Blackwell.
Clapp, J. (2014), Financialization, distance and global food politics, *Journal of Peasant Studies*, 41(5), 797–814.
Fam, D.; Palmer, J.; Riedy, C.; Mitchell, C. (eds) (2017), *Transdisciplinary Research and Practice for Sustainability Outcomes*, London: Routledge.
Goswami, M. (2004), *Producing India: From Colonial Economy to National Space*, Chicago, IL: University of Chicago Press.
Haesbaert, R. (2013), Del mito de la desterritorialización a la multiterritorialidad, *Cultura y Representaciones Sociales*, 8(15), 9–42.
Hart, G. (2006), Denaturalizing dispossession: Critical ethnography in the age of resurgent imperialism, *Antipode*, 38(5), 977–1004.
Harvey, D. (2003), *The New Imperialism*, Oxford: Oxford University Press.
Herod, A. (2011), *Scale*, London: Routledge.
Jessop, B.; Brenner, N.; Jones, M. (2008), Theorizing sociospatial relations, *Environment and Planning D: Society and Space*, 26, 389–401.
Kindon, S.; Pain, R.; Kesby, M. (eds) (2007), *Participatory Action Research Approaches and Methods*, London: Routledge.
Lefebvre, H. (2011 [1974]), *The Production of Space*, Malden, MA: Blackwell.
Massey, D. (1994), *Space, Place, and Gender*, Minneapolis, MN: University of Minnesota Press.
McCarthy, J.F. (2010), Processes of inclusion and adverse incorporation: Oil palm and agrarian change in Sumatra, Indonesia, *Journal of Peasant Studies*, 37(4), 821–850.

McMichael, P. (2009), A food regime genealogy, *Journal of Peasant Studies*, 36(1), 139–169.

Moore, J. (2015), *Capitalism in the Web of Life: Ecology and the Accumulation of Capital*, London: Verso Books.

Pye, O.; Radjawali, I.; Julia (2017), Land grabs and the river: Eco-social transformations along the Kapuas, Indonesia, *Canadian Journal of Development Studies*, 38(3), 378–394.

Smith, N. (1984), *Uneven Development, Capitalism, Nature and the Production of Space*, Oxford: Blackwell.

Taylor, P.J. (1982), A materialist framework for political geography, *Transactions of the Institute of British Geographers*, 7(1), 15–34.

Wimmer, A.; Glick Schiller, N. (2002), Methodological nationalism and beyond, nation-state building, migration and the social sciences, *Global Networks*, 2(4), 301–334.

31. Questions and answers

A. Haroon Akram-Lodhi

ARGUMENTS VERSUS OPINIONS

The purpose of critical agrarian studies is to construct 'alternative forms of knowing and of acting in the world' (Edelman and Wolford 2017, 4) that are a better reflection of the lived realities of people in contemporary ruralities. This however begs a key question: how do we know something, alternative or otherwise? This is the purpose of undertaking scientific research: to uncover new knowledge that addresses an issue that has been identified because the new knowledge answers an important, well-articulated and significant research question. However, new knowledge is not self-evident; it is constructed through the generation and assembly of evidence and the interpretation of that evidence. In this way, knowledge differs from an opinion. An opinion is an assertion that is not substantiated by evidence; scholars and advocates in critical agrarian studies are not interested in assertions. Again, though, the generation and assembly of evidence is not self-evident. The generation of evidence is a function of the questions that the researcher asks. Similarly, the assembly of evidence does not take place in a vacuum; it is guided by the key concepts the researcher uses to make sense of the issue through the research question that the new knowledge is meant to address. Thus, research questions shape the generation and assembly of evidence that supports new knowledge that addresses an issue. However, in formulating questions and constructing evidence the researcher makes a series of choices. Because these choices matter for the new knowledge that is developed in order to provide an answer to the research question, they must all be justified as being appropriate for the issue at hand. Within the community that comprises critical agrarian studies, the justification of choices is important because it makes the research process, and hence the research findings, accountable, in part because they can be replicated; such is the objective of all rigorous social science research.

Research in critical agrarian studies requires the development of solid arguments that address key research questions that are demonstrably worth answering for the field. A research question is an inquisitive statement that narrowly defines a researchable investigation within an issue that has been identified as being of importance, provides boundaries to that investigation and gives it direction (O'Leary 2004, 28). An argument consists of a claim that is substantiated by reasons that explain and justify the connection of the reasons to the claim and which are in turn supported by evidence (Booth et al. 2003, 115). In so doing, arguments supply substantiated answers to the research question. Moreover, a solid argument must acknowledge alternative ways of substantiating the claim and clearly explain why the proposed argument is assessed as being the best explanation of the evidence.

LINKING RESEARCH QUESTIONS, ANALYTICAL FRAMEWORKS AND METHODOLOGY

If research questions are answered through arguments it is important to clearly understand how each contributes to the generation of new knowledge that addresses an issue. Starting with the former, the research question guides the investigation. From the research question, the overarching objective of the research can be identified, in terms of the issue, the general approach to the research can usually be inferred and the terminal point of the research can be identified because the research question must be capable of being answered. In so doing, the research question provides a pathway toward the completion of the research.

Clearly, then, the research question drives the research, which means it needs to be clear, focused, concise, complex and arguable. A well-articulated research question provides critical information about the research by not only defining its focus and scope but also making clearer the motivation of the researcher undertaking the investigation. Having said that, the research question is not static; because research itself is an iterative process, the research question will evolve and change during the course of the actual research as the new and the unexpected emerge. For this reason, researchers must be open in their thinking to alternative ways of evaluating issues. Indeed, the final research question often only emerges upon the completion of the research.

The research question assists in the development of the analytical framework, but before exploring the role of an analytical framework an aside is in order. Generally speaking, it is usually held that research can be inductive or deductive. Inductive research begins with evidence and establishes a framework by which that evidence can be analysed. Deductive research begins with a framework and uses the framework to collect and analyse evidence. However, within critical agrarian studies the inductive/deductive distinction is considered to be somewhat misleading. This is because in inductive research, evidence must be collected and organized and this requires making choices that are theoretically embedded, and which are thus deductive. In other words, critical agrarian studies is predicated upon the methodological proposition that everyone thinks theoretically and that solid arguments require explicitly confronting, justifying and, where necessary, abandoning one's theoretical orientation. While this should hold true for all rigorous social science research, it is unfortunately the case that in many instances this standard is not met. But it must be, because this helps ensure that research is not confirmatory in character but rather more openly exploratory, which is important in critical agrarian studies because confirmatory research closes off avenues of exploration and explanation and in so doing can serve to mitigate against the development of new knowledge that more accurately reflects the lived realities of rural peoples.

Analytical frameworks link the theoretical underpinnings of the research question to the empirical analysis by critically evaluating what is theoretically known about the issue that motivates the research question. The critical evaluation should identify the key concepts within theory that can assist in answering the research question, clearly explain why and how they assist in answering the research question and explain how the key theoretical concepts may be connected. As part of this, assumptions about presumed relationships between key theoretical concepts must be explicitly confronted and justified. In so doing, the analytical framework is not simply assumed to address the research question; rather, the claim that the analytical framework addresses the research question is substantiated through the development of an argument. At the same time, as the research question evolves, so too will the analytical framework. Like the research question, the development of the analytical framework is an iterative process in which choices must be substantiated at all stages of the iteration.

The analytical framework must itself be operationalized in order for the research question to be empirically investigated. This means that the methodology and methods that are to be used to gather the empirical phenomena to answer the question must be derived from and consistent with the analytical framework. Again, it is not adequate to simply present a methodology; methodological choices must be justified as being the best means by which the evidence necessary to answer the research question in a way that is consistent with the analytical framework can be obtained. From the methodology will come the specific methods that will gather information about a list of agents and their properties, activities, the conditions, affects and effects of their activities, as well as possible relationships between agents. Once more, as the research question evolves, so too will the analytical framework, and therefore so too will the methodology. The key point to emphasize about an iterative and interactive research process is that at all steps and stages choices must be justified.

The research questions of critical agrarian studies remain firmly rooted in the 'agrarian question': whether, and if so, how, the transformation of rural society is taking place in ways that are socially, economically and ecologically detrimental to small-scale farming households (Akram-Lodhi 2018). Thus, how agrarian classes are historically and contemporarily formed, reproduced, transformed and cease to be is a central arena of investigation. At the same time, however, class analysis in critical agrarian studies should be multidimensional and intersectional. Intersectionality explores how multiple inequalities are constructed in ways that are mutually reinforcing; inequalities of class, gender, generation, ethnicity, ability and other markers of social status. Thus, intersectionality makes it possible to identify and explore the cultural, ecological, social, political and economic factors and forces that facilitate or impede class formation, from the local to the global. Underpinning these research questions should be a broader understanding of structure and agency in which power is asymmetrical and relational, and thus critical agrarian studies should seek to uncover the sources of social power and subordination. As has been nicely stated by Henry Bernstein (2010), empirically evaluating sources of rural social power and subordination requires focusing upon four central questions of agrarian political economy: 1. Who owns what? 2. Who does what? 3. Who gets what? 4. What do they do with it? These four questions align with changes in: farm production, most notably the distribution of assets, the capture of the benefits of technical change by social forces and processes of commodification; the accumulation that emerges out of changing technical coefficients of production; and the political implications, across a myriad variety of forms, of changing patterns of production and growth. However, while assets and their distribution along with processes of commodification and accumulation may be an important determinant of power, critical agrarian studies should stress the dialectics of structure and agency, and in so doing, not exclusively focus upon the material as the sole basis or expression of power. Indeed, critical agrarian studies takes seriously the role of cultural forms and constructs. Here, cultural forms and constructs refer to a wide variety of socially constructed identities, meanings, norms and values that are expressed in local institutions of authority and subservience, religion, food, art and everyday politics, among others. The political expression of cultural forms and constructs intersect with and interact through the material and cumulatively are how agency is expressed within overarching structures that are themselves capable of being transformed.

CLAIMS, REASONS AND EVIDENCE WHEN THINKING METHODOLOGICALLY

The research question is intimately connected to the argument because it *is* a claim and an argument is a claim that has been substantiated. A claim states a specific position by an individual on something that can be considered debatable and so will not be universally agreed by an audience. It is thus a statement of what the researcher is trying to convince the audience. There are four different primary types of claims: claims of fact, which assert that something is true or not true; claims of effect, which assert that something will lead to something else; claims of value, which assert that something is good or bad, or more or less desirable; and claims of policy, which assert that one course of action is superior to another. Claims must be specific, logical and significant. At the same time though claims should not be definitive because the researcher has to demonstrate a willingness to be open, and hence to be corrected, because this acknowledges the limitations of the research. Forms of words should therefore be constructed in a way that limits certainty; these are called hedges, and result in a disinclination to use 'is' and a preference to use variations of 'may be'. In critical agrarian studies, claims focus upon interrogating sources of social power, from the local to the global, emphasizing the dialectics of structure and agency, and in so doing can go beyond a focus upon the material as the sole basis or expression of power, as, for example, when claims are developed around the socio-cultural bases of political agency.

Claims must be substantiated if they are going to be part of an argument, which requires two forms of support. The first is a reason or a set of reasons and sub-reasons, which explains why the claim should be accepted. For example, if the claim is that peasant class differentiation is present, the reason could be because it can be inferred from the distribution of machinery. There are three different kinds of reason. The first is a normative reason, because the claim is supported by reference to what the audience should do or should believe. Explanatory reasons explain why something happened or how an observed situation can be explained. Finally, motivating reasons explain why individuals undertake actions that bring themselves benefits. In critical agrarian studies, normative reasons might be used to support claims that are used in conclusions and which are derived from complex arguments. However, the use of explanatory and motivating reasons are widely used at all stages of an argument.

Reasons on their own do not substantiate a claim unless they are based on the second form of support, evidence. Indeed, when researchers use evidence as the basis of a reason they are using reasons to organize the presentation of their evidence, and in so doing the structure of their argument. Evidence comes in many forms: it may be primary, secondary or tertiary; and it may be quantitative, qualitative or use a set of mixed methods. A primary source provides direct first-hand evidence about an event, place, object, person or process, offering a direct account of what was witnessed in a particular place at a particular time. Primary sources reflect the individual viewpoint of either a participant or an observer. Secondary sources describe, discuss, interpret, comment upon, analyse, evaluate, summarize and process primary sources. As such, secondary sources such as research reports or research articles are generally one or more steps removed from the event, individual or place, and are written or produced after the fact with the benefit of hindsight. Their value emerges from their role in collecting, organizing and repackaging primary source information to increase usability. A secondary source does not have to be written. A tertiary source is a textual consolidation of primary and secondary sources. Quantitative evidence consists of numerical or statistical information that comes from direct measurement, surveys, surveillance or from administrative records. Qualitative evidence is descriptive information, which often comes from interviews, focus groups, observations or artistic depictions such as photographs. Mixed methods combine elements of the quantitative with elements of the qualitative.

Critical agrarian studies relies heavily upon primary evidence as it is seeking to understand rural realities. Secondary sources are widely used, but are often critically interrogated and indeed subverted, bringing into arguments support for claims that are often not self-evident in the secondary source but which require excavation. This is because in secondary sources the evidence has been shaped by someone else, who has decided what will be investigated, how it will be recorded and how it will be presented. Quantitative evidence is used, but is rarely used for explanatory purposes and as such is not used to support the reasons that substantiate claims. Rather, quantitative evidence is used to describe a circumstance or a process that can be witnessed. As such, quantitative evidence is used to provide a 'what'; to paint a picture of what is happening and to which a claim may be addressed. Qualitative evidence is used to explain why what is happening can be observed; in other words, qualitative evidence is what is normally used as the basis of a reason substantiating a claim and in so doing provide a 'why' as to what is being witnessed. Indeed, in that qualitative evidence can be used to explore quantitative findings, it is often the case that superior examples of research in critical agrarian studies place a heavy reliance on the use of mixed methods that rely on primary sources to understand rural lives and livelihoods.

When evidence is presented as the basis of a reason, it is not directly presented but is usually reported in summary form. As just noted, secondary evidence is shaped by the researcher responsible for it. However, primary evidence is also shaped, being rendered more clearly and coherently than when it was collected. This means that when reporting evidence it is important to be accurate and precise as well as providing sufficient evidence that is explained; reported evidence must be methodically explained by the researcher if the choice to use that evidence as the basis of a reason is to be justified.

The final part of constructing an argument is in some ways the most challenging. Specific claims are supported by specific reasons based upon specific evidence. However, part of the purpose in undertaking research is to be able to move from the specific to the general; in other words, to make productive generalizations out of the specifics of a piece of research. A warrant is a general principle that allows a specific claim to be supported by a specific reason. In other words, a warrant embeds the specific within the general: that when it is broadly agreed that general circumstances lead to general consequences then specific reasons can be inferred to substantiate specific claims. Thus, the specific reason is consistent with more general circumstances and the specific claim is consistent with more general consequences (Booth et al. 2003, 167). This means, of course, that a warrant has to apply to a reason and a claim. In critical agrarian studies the analytical framework is usually used to provide the basis of a warrant, and so the strength of a warrant will reflect the extent to which the choices that have been made in developing the analytical framework have been adequately justified. A warrant need not necessarily be presented as part of an argument, but has to be presented when a specific claim and its supporting reason is broadly agreed but where the link between the specific claim and its supporting reason and the more general circumstances and consequences might be contentious. Warrants are therefore used to explain that which is not self-evident within a field of investigation to a broader community of scholars.

Constructing solid arguments in critical agrarian studies is of course more demanding than the stylizations depicted here. Claims can be supported by multiple reasons, each of which must be based upon evidence. Reasons may require sub-reasons in order to support a claim, and these sub-reasons must too be based upon evidence. More fundamentally, answering research questions often involves making multiple claims. Each has to be substantiated by an argument, which results in a set of interlocking arguments that cumulatively come together to generate the new knowledge that answers the research question and addresses the issue. It is this process by which answers to questions can be found, and powerful explanations of social change in contemporary rural societies around the world have been established in the critical agrarian studies literature.

REFERENCES

Akram-Lodhi, A.H. (2018), What is critical agrarian studies?, accessed 8 February 2019 at http://roape .net/2018/03/28/what-is-critical-agrarian-studies/.

Bernstein, H. (2010), *Class Dynamics of Agrarian Change*, Halifax: Fernwood Publishing.

Booth, W.C.; Colomb, G.G.; Williams, J.M. (2003), *The Craft of Research*, second edition, Chicago, IL: University of Chicago Press.

Edelman, M.; Wolford, W. (2017), Introduction: Critical agrarian studies in theory and practice, *Antipode*, 49(4), 959–976.

O'Leary, Z. (2004), *The Essential Guide to Doing Research*, London: Sage.

PART IV

REGIONAL PERSPECTIVES

32. The agrarian question in Africa: Past, present and future

Samir Amin

Peasant agriculture in Africa, Asia and Latin America has been integrated into global capitalism for a long time, even if the forms of that integration have been shaped differently, in keeping with the specific functions assigned to the various peripheries of the capitalist system. Sub-Saharan Africa was reshaped through the slave trade and became the periphery of the new American colonial periphery (1500–1800). Then, after the colonial conquest, the continent was assigned the lowest position in the international division of labour: that of an exclusive exporter of agricultural and mineral resources. This political economy of colonization was not radically challenged following the independence of the nations of the African continent beginning in 1960. This is why the subtitle of the original French version of my book *Assessing Changes in Post-Independence West Africa* is *The Political Economy of Colonisation 1880–1970* (Amin 1970). (This subtitle does not, however, appear in the English translation: *Neo Colonialism in West Africa*.) In this book, I defined three patterns carried out in different regions of the continent: (1) the 'trade economy' (in French: *l'économie de traite*) in the regions of West and East Africa, assigned basically to agricultural exports; (2) the 'reserve economy' for Southern Africa, assigned basically to mineral exports; and (3) the 'plunder economy' in Central Africa.

Yet in spite of these peculiarities inherited from history, contemporary Africa is facing a major challenge similar to Asia, Latin America and the Caribbean, all of which are being submitted to a violent systemic imperialist project aimed at the dismantling of rural/peasant societies to the exclusive benefit of the expansion of industrial/capitalist patterns of agriculture. What follows focuses on this new agrarian question.

CAPITALISM'S CONTINUED EXPANSION INTO SOUTHERN AGRICULTURES

All societies before modern times were peasant societies, whose production was ruled by various systems, none of which were like the system that rules capitalism. Modern capitalist agriculture is now looking forward to a massive attack on Third World peasant production. Capitalist agriculture, which governs by the principle of return on capital, localized almost exclusively in North America, Europe, the southern cone of Latin America and Australia, employs only a few tens of millions of farmers who are no longer 'peasants'. Their productivity, which depends on mechanization, ranges from between 10 000 and 20 000 quintals of equivalent cereals per worker annually. On the other hand, peasant farming systems still constitute nearly 3 billion human beings. The ratio of productivity of the most advanced segment of world agriculture to the poorest is now approaching 100:1 (Mazoyer and Roudard 2006, 24). The new agrarian question is the result of this unequal development.

One can imagine some 20 million additional modern farmers producing whatever the 3 billion present peasants can offer on the market beyond their own subsistence. The success of such an alternative necessitates the transfer of important pieces of good land to these new agricultural producers, as well as access to capital and consumer markets. Such agriculturalists would indeed 'compete' successfully with the billions of existing peasants. Under the circumstances, this means accepting that billions of 'non-competitive' producers would be eliminated within a few decades. What would become of these billions of human beings, the majority of whom are already the poorest of the poor, and who feed themselves with great difficulty? Within 50 years, no relatively competitive industrial development, even in the fanciful hypothesis of a continued growth of 7 per cent annually for three-quarters of humanity, could absorb even one-third of this reserve.

The major argument presented to legitimate the competition doctrine is that such development occurred in nineteenth-century Europe, and ultimately produced a wealthy urban society, as well as modern agriculture able to feed the nation and even to export. Why should this pattern not be repeated in the contemporary Third World? The argument fails to consider several major factors that make the reproduction of the pattern in Third World countries today almost impossible. The first is that the European model developed, over the course of a century and a half, along with industrial technologies that were labour-intensive; modern technologies, by comparison, are far less labour-intensive. Therefore, in order for the newcomers of the Third World to be competitive with their exports on global markets, they will have to adopt labour-saving technologies. The second factor is that Europe benefited during its long transition from the possibility of a massive out-migration of its 'surplus' population to the Americas.

An alternative framework would imply that peasant agriculture should be maintained throughout the foreseeable future of the twenty-first century, but it should simultaneously be engaged in a process of continuous technological/social change and progress at a rate that would allow for a progressive shift towards non-rural, non-agricultural employment. This alternative proceeds from the recognition that land is not a tradable commodity but a common wealth that belongs to the community and the people, the use of which is entrusted to peasant communities, thus guaranteeing the right to access for all on an equal footing, reinforced by actual access to the means that permit its efficient use.

Such a strategic set of targets involves a complex mix of policy. At the national level, this implies macro-policies protecting peasant food production from the unequal competition of modernized agricultural producers, with a view to guaranteeing acceptable internal food prices, and the eventual disconnection from so-called international market prices (prices that are, in fact, also biased by subsidies handed out by the wealthy North, namely the United States, Canada and Europe). Such policy targets also question the patterns of industrial-urban development, which should be based less on export-oriented priorities, which themselves take advantage of low wages (implying, in turn, low prices for food), and should rather be more attentive to socially balanced internal market expansion. At the regional and global levels, this implies the development of international agreements and policies that would move away from doctrinaire liberal principles.

FAMILY FARMING IN THE NORTH AND THE PEASANTRY IN THE SOUTH

Modern family agriculture in Western Europe and the United States, which produces 1000 to 2000 tons of cereal equivalents annually per worker, has no equal, and has enabled less than 5 per cent of the population to supply whole countries abundantly and to produce exportable surpluses. Modern family farming has an exceptional capacity to absorb innovation and adapt to both environmental conditions and market demand. Yet, family agriculture in the Global North does not share that specific characteristic of industrial organized labour that was at the origin of the modern leap in productivity, namely that in the factory, the higher number of workers enables an advanced division of labour. On family farms, labour supply is reduced to the farming couple, sometimes helped by a few permanent labourers, but also, in certain cases, a larger number of seasonal workers. Generally speaking, there is not a fixed division of labour, the tasks being complex, polyvalent and variable. Nevertheless, modern family agriculture in the Global North is an inseparable, integrated part of the capitalist economy. Yet despite its efficiency, the agricultural family unit is only a sub-contractor, caught between upstream and downstream activities: on the one hand, the agro-industry, which imposes genetically modified organisms and supplies the equipment, chemical products and finance (such as the necessary credits); on the other hand, the traders, processors and commercial supermarkets. Self-consumption has become practically irrelevant to the business of family farming; the family economy depends entirely on its market production.

The Third World counterparts of Northern family farmers are the peasants who constitute nearly half of humanity. The types of agriculture here vary, from those who benefited from the Green Revolution, whose production has risen to 100–500 quintals per labourer, to those others whose production hardly goes beyond 10 quintals per labourer (Mazoyer and Roudard 2006, 12). There are huge differences between the North and South, one of which is the importance of subsistence food for survival in the peasant economies and vast poverty; indeed, three-quarters of the victims of global undernourishment are rural. In spite of these differences, peasant agriculture in the Global South is part of the dominant global capitalist system. Peasants depend on purchased inputs and are increasingly preyed upon by the oligopolies that sell them. Furthermore, these farmers feed nearly two-thirds of the world's population (including themselves).

THE IMPERIALIST THREAT TO PEASANT AND FAMILY FOOD SYSTEMS

In response to the global food regime, Northern governments, multilateral institutions, agro-food oligopolies and big philanthropic capital propose to modernize areas in the Global South considered to have high agricultural potential ('breadbasket' regions) and to integrate them into global markets. This, we are invited to believe, will eradicate rural poverty. This strategy is supported by the so-called 'absolute and superior rationale' of economic management, based on private ownership of the means of production. According to this principle, land and labour become merchandized in order to guarantee best use of the land for its owner and for society as a whole. This is nothing but mere tautology. The global system of private land ownership required for the free movement (and concentration) of capital is justified in social terms by the argument that private property alone guarantees that the farmer will not suddenly be dispossessed of the fruit of his or her labour. Obviously, for most of the world's farmers, this is not the case. Other forms of land use can ensure that farmers as well as workers and consumers benefit equitably from production. To subjugate land, labour and consumption everywhere to private property is to spread the policy of monopoly 'enclosures' the world over, to hasten the dispossession of peasants and to ensure the food insecurity of vast numbers of poor communities. The aim is clear: to create the conditions that would allow modern islands of agribusiness to take possession of the land they need in order to expand. Such a policy simply accelerates the process of accumulation-by-dispossession which necessarily generates poverty. Supporting this principle and then looking for means to 'reduce poverty' – the approach prescribed by the World Bank – is an oxymoron.

Is the North's capitalist modernization of Southern agricultures really desirable? Although capitalism did accomplish this transition for the industrial societies of the Global North, this proposition does not hold true for the 85 per cent of the world's population in the Global South. Capitalist modernization has now reached a stage where its continued expansion requires the implementation of enclosure policies on a worldwide scale, which will be nothing less than synonymous with genocide: on the one hand, the destruction of the peasant societies of Asia, Africa and Latin America; on the other, billions in windfall profits for global capital, derived from socially useless production that is unable to cover the needs of billions of hungry people in the South, even as it increases the number of obese people in the North. Capitalism has entered into its phase of senility, because the logic of the system is no longer able to ensure the simple survival of humanity. Capitalism's continued expansion into Southern agricultures will result in a planet full of hungry slums. Once a creative force sweeping away the bonds of feudalism, capitalism has now become barbaric. It is necessary to replace it – now more than ever before – by other development logics, which would be more rational and more humane.

NO ALTERNATIVE TO FOOD SOVEREIGNTY

Resistance by peasants and poor consumers is essential in order to build a real and genuinely humane alternative. We must ensure the functionality and resilience of family and peasant agriculture for the foreseeable future, quite simply because it would allow us to resolve the agrarian question underlying world hunger and poverty.

Current food consumption worldwide is basically realized through local production. Nevertheless, this production corresponds to very different levels of satisfaction of food needs: generally good for North America and Europe, acceptable for China, mediocre for the rest of Asia and Latin America, disastrous for Africa. The United States and Europe understand the importance of national food sovereignty very well and have successfully implemented it through systematic economic policies. But, apparently, what is good for them is not good for others. Accordingly, Third World countries do not need food sovereignty and should rely on industrial agriculture and international trade to cover the deficit – however large – in their food requirements. This may seem easy for countries that are large exporters of natural resources. For others, the advice of the Western powers is maximum specialization of agricultural commodities for export, such as cotton, tropical fruits, oils and, more recently, agro-fuels. The defenders of 'food security' for others – not for themselves – do not consider the fact that this specialization, which has been practised since colonization, has not improved the miserable food rations of the peoples concerned and has resulted in a global epidemic of diet-related diseases. There is no alternative to food sovereignty, and its efficient implementation does in fact require a commitment to the construction of deeply diversified economies in terms of production, processing, manufacturing and distribution.

THE STRUGGLE FOR AN ALTERNATIVE

Whether it is growing pauperization, inequality, unemployment or precariousness, it is normal that people will start to resist and organize around the world. New peasant organizations exist in Asia, Africa and Latin America that support the current struggles. In Europe and the United States, farmer, worker and consumer organizations are forming alliances for more equitable and sustainable food systems. Where they do exist, these actions and programmes must be more closely examined. What social forces do they represent, and whose interests do they defend? We should be wary of hasty replies to these complex and difficult questions. Neither should we subscribe to the discourse of 'naive alter-globalism' that often sets the tone of forums and fuels the illusion that the world could be set on the right track through the work of dispersed social movements alone. Social movements are, by and large, still on the defensive: they are facing the offensive of capital to dismantle whatever they had conquered in the previous decades, and are trying to maintain whatever can be maintained; furthermore, they remain extremely fragmented. What is needed is a move beyond a defensive position towards building a wide progressive alliance emboldened by the force of a positive alternative.

The balance of forces cannot be changed unless these fragmented movements forge a common platform based on some common grounds. I call this 'convergence with diversity', for which there is no blueprint. Forms of organization and action are always invented by those in struggle; they are not preconceived by a handful of intellectuals, to then be put into practice by the people. To move from this fragmented and defensive position towards some kind of unity, and to build convergence with strategic targets and a respect for diversity, requires the repoliticization of social movements.

EDITORS' NOTE

Samir Amin was, without a doubt, amongst the most distinguished writers, not just in the field of critical agrarian studies but in political economy, global history and development studies in general. His critiques of imperialism and neo-colonialism have influenced more than a generation of scholars and activists. He drafted his chapter for this handbook not even three months before he passed away, at the age of 86, in August 2018. Unfortunately, he was therefore unable to revise his contribution himself. We are grateful to publish, with minor editorial revision, the original version, in remembrance of the author.

FURTHER READING

Amin, S. (2006), Globalization and the agrarian question: Peasants' conflicts in Africa and Asia, in Ghosh, B.C.; Guven, H.M. (eds), *Globalization and the Third World*, London: Palgrave Macmillan, 165–181.

Amin, S. (2011), *Global History: A View from the South, Cape Town, Dakar, Nairobi*, Oxford: Pambazuka.
Amin, S. (2017), The agrarian question a century after October 1917: Capitalist agriculture and agricultures in capitalism, *Agrarian South: Journal of Political Economy*, 6(2), 149–174.
Amin, S.; Bush, R. (2014), An interview with Samir Amin, *Review of African Political Economy*, 41(supl. 1), 108–114.

REFERENCES

Amin, S. (1970), *L'Afrique de l'Ouest bloquée, l'économie politique de la colonisation 1880–1970*, Paris: Minuit.
Mazoyer, M.; Roudart, L. (eds) (2006), *A History of World Agriculture: From the Neolithic Age to the Current Crisis*, New York: Monthly Review.

33. Social movements in times of extractivism: The ecoterritorial turn in Latin America

Maristella Svampa

INTRODUCTION

In this chapter,[1] I propose to make a synthesis of the expansion of neo-extractivism in Latin America, to give an account of the dynamics of socio-environmental conflicts, as well as of the emergence of new languages of valuation associated with the defence of land and territory. I argue that recent struggles over land and resources have given rise to what can be called an *ecoterritorial turn* in social mobilization. This turn is characterized by the convergence of different indigenous, environmental and peasant movements, their struggles and the emergence of an autonomous environmentalist narrative. The chapter is structured as follows. I will first highlight the emergence of new movement networks and intercultural assembly experiences at the local, national and regional levels in the context of the commodity boom. I will also emphasize the relevance of popular feminisms for the struggles against extractivism, particularly towards the end of the political left-wing cycle and the conservative return in Latin America around 2014. Finally, I will outline the growing threats, not only in terms of the judicialization and criminalization of social struggles, but also regarding the increasing rates of intimidation and murder of environmental activists.

NEO-EXTRACTIVISM

Extractivism has a long, albeit not linear, history in Latin America. It has been intersected by successive economic cycles, changing world market demands and processes of national state affirmation. The latter are marked by the control of non-ordinary revenues, especially from the mining and oil sectors, by the state. The likelihood of rent capture by the state through resource extraction has reinforced a particular social imaginary about Latin America. In the course of successive commodity booms over the last centuries, an *el doradista* vision emerged, founded on the idea that the convergence between natural wealth and international market opportunities would lead to development.

What is new then about the current cycle of neo-extractivism? Several global, regional and territorial factors need to be considered. The consolidation of neoliberal capitalism at the global scale since the 1970s has triggered a further expansion of commodity frontiers at the regional scale (Moore 2011; Svampa 2015). Associated with rising international prices in metals and the liberalization of national regulatory frameworks during the 1990s, this has led to an unprecedented boom in the mining sector from 2002 onwards, which came along with tax exemptions and high profits for large mining companies.

Given the exhaustion of conventional and easily extractable hydrocarbon resources, the eagerness to maintain an energy matrix based on fossil fuels has led to the extraction of non-conventional gas and oil deposits via fracking (hydraulic fracturing), despite the facts that the economic cost of their extraction is higher, their energy yield is much lower than conventional fuels and that the environmental and socio-health impacts are serious and burdensome. The United States has actively promoted fracking, which has not only reshaped the energy agenda at the global level, but has also generated a new cartography of conflicts, which has been transferred to Latin America, notably to Argentina, Brazil, Mexico and Colombia (see Delgado 2018).

Another factor that has pushed the neo-extractivist agenda since the beginning of the 2000s are large infrastructure projects. In 2002, the infrastructure project portfolio the Initiative for the Integration of Infrastructure in the South American Region (IIRSA) was signed (it was later called the South American Council for Infrastructure and Planning (COSIPLAN), which covers transport (waterways, ports, bi-oceanic corridors, among others), energy (large hydroelectric dams) and communications projects. Between 2004 and 2014, this portfolio grew rapidly from 335 to 579 projects (Carpio 2017, 130). In this context, the fever for mega-dams increased, placing the Latin American region, along with Southeast Asia, at the epicentre of investments in this sector (Vidal 2017).

Moreover, capitalist, large-scale, intensive and mono-cultural agricultural production has expanded, leading to land hoarding and environmental degradation. In several South American countries, for instance, the expansion of the soybean frontier has led to a reconfiguration of the rural world. Between 2000 and 2014, soybean plantations in South America expanded by 29 million hectares, comparable to the size of Ecuador. Although Brazil and Argentina account for nearly 90 per cent of regional production, in Paraguay soybeans occupy the largest area in relation to other crops: 67 per cent of the total agricultural area (Oxfam 2016, 30). All of this has redefined the dispute over land due to increasing land concentration: 'overall in the region, one percent of the largest farms concentrate more than half of the agricultural area. In other words, 1% of the farms take up more land than the remaining 99%' (ibid.).

Industrial mining, agriculture and mega infrastructure projects are capital-intensive, thus most of the investors in these sectors are transnational corporations, including national mega-companies such as Petrobras, the Venezuelan PDVSA and the Argentinean YPF, among others. Alongside this is the fact that mega-projects are not labour-intensive, as they generate few direct jobs. In the case of large-scale mining, for every $1 million invested, only 0.5 to two direct jobs are created (Machado Aráoz et al. 2011). In Peru, the country of transnational mega-mining *par excellence*, this sector represents barely 2 per cent of total employment, against 23 per cent for agriculture, 16 per cent for trade and almost 10 per cent for manufacturing.

Another relevant factor that characterizes the neo-extractivist era is the increase in social conflicts. Throughout Latin America, as the number of extractive projects and involved land areas has increased, socio-environmental conflicts have grown steadily, particularly in relation to large-scale mining. Currently, there is no single Latin American country that is developing mining projects that does not also have social conflicts, which pit communities against mining companies and the government. According to the Observatory of Mining Conflicts in Latin America, in January 2019 there were 256 conflicts, six of them cross-border, involving 274 projects, 192 cases of criminalization and 37 popular consultations.[2] The countries with the highest number of mining conflicts in the region are Peru, Mexico, Chile, Argentina, Brazil, Colombia and Ecuador (see also Villegas 2014, 10–11).

In short, extractivism runs through the long memory of the continent and its struggles, defining a mode of appropriation of nature and a pattern of colonial accumulation associated with the birth of modern capitalism. Its updating in the twenty-first century brings with it new dimensions at different levels: at the global level, with the expansion of commodity frontiers, the exhaustion of non-renewable natural goods and intensified socio-ecological crises of planetary scope; at the regional and national levels, regarding the relationship between the extractive-export model, the nation state and the capture of resource rents; at the territorial level, with intensive occupation of the territory through mining and land grabbing; and finally at the political level, in terms of social conflicts, the emergence of a new contentious political grammar, and an increase in state and para-state violence.

THE ECOTERRITORIAL TURN IN SOCIAL STRUGGLES

Since the beginning of the recent commodity boom in the early 2000s, socio-environmental conflicts have intensified throughout the Global South. In Latin America, in the heat of the emergence of new social resistances, the bases for a common language of valuation of the territory were established. In theoretical and practical terms, this involved an innovative crossing between the indigenous–communitarian matrix, an environmentalist discourse and, more recently, a feminist narrative. This common language not only challenges hegemonic conceptions of development, but also seeks to place the right to citizen participation on the public and political agenda by demanding the democratization of decision-making. This convergence of matrices and demands illustrates the way in which current rural struggles, which are centred on the defence of land and territory, are thought of and represented from the perspective of collective resistance. This is what I call the ecoterritorial turn (Svampa 2011, 2018).

The ecoterritorial turn refers to the construction of new collective action frames, which function as structures of meaning and schemes of interpretation that challenge dominant views, and which produce a new collective subjectivity. The most novel aspect of these frames is that they are founded on an articulation between different actors: indigenous-peasant movements, socio-environmental movements, environmental non-governmental organizations (NGOs), networks of intellectuals and experts and cultural collectives. This translates into a dialogue of knowledges and disciplines, and develops an important mobilizing capacity, installs new themes, languages and slogans and orients interactive dynamics towards the production of a common subjectivity. Out of this dialogue, knowledge that is independent of the dominant discourses emerges, and alternative forms of local knowledge, many of them rooted in peasant and indigenous life, are valorised. Another result of this cross-sector dialogue is the diversification of strategies of struggle, that is the combination of grassroots mobilizations with the articulation of social networks at the national scale, and the generation and application of different technical and legal instruments such as collective protections, demands for public consultations, stricter environmental laws and the recognition of cultural and political rights of indigenous groups.

In the context of the ecoterritorial turn of social mobilization against extractivism, other languages of valuation of territory are affirmed, other modes of relating with nature are foregrounded and other narratives of Mother Earth based on reciprocity, complementarity and care have emerged. These other languages aim for alternative approaches to appropriation and to engage in a dialogue of knowledges, and for other ways of organizing social life. The languages are nourished by different political-ideological matrices, for example anti-capitalist, environmentalist, indigenous, feminist and anti-patriarchal perspectives, which come from the heterogeneous world of the subordinate classes. The ecoterritorial turn also shows significant links with the environmental justice movements that originated in the 1980s in urban Black communities in the United States, and which are at the origin of several environmental justice networks in Latin America today. Environmental justice 'implies the right to a safe, healthy and productive environment for all, where the environment is considered in its totality, including its ecological, physical, built, social, political, aesthetic and economic dimensions' (Acselard 2004, 16).

The different topics of the ecoterritorial turn account for the emergence of a new grammar of struggle, and this has a strong resonance with the struggles against extractivism. This grammar consists of a common framework of meanings, which articulates indigenous struggles, territorial-ecological issues, peasants' concerns and feminist militancies. It contributes to the expansion of the boundaries of law, in opposition to the dominant model of accumulation and exploitation. Whether in a language of defence of the land, territory and common goods (water, land), of human rights, of the rights of Nature or of *buen vivir* (good living), these claims point to a democratization of decision-making regarding projects that could seriously affect the living conditions of the most vulnerable sectors of rural society and compromise future generations.

Given the heterogeneity of the involved organizations and struggle traditions, it would be a mistake to interpret these collective frames as univocal. Instead, it is necessary to read the ecoterritorial turn as a tendency that runs through the struggles and configures a general framework of intelligibility. The ecoterritorial turn evidences the emergence of a new political subjectivity, insofar as it expresses the way in which collective resistances against neo-extractivism are conceived and represented, focused on the defence of land and territory, from a multi-scale perspective that contemplates both local and territorial, regional and global anchoring.

The language of a new territoriality is far from being exclusive to those geographies where indigenous people live, even if they had an important role in its making. The ecoterritorial turn extends to socio-environmental, rural, urban and intercultural movements and spaces. Moreover, the crossings and articulations between different movement sectors have given rise to numerous (transnational) networks of activism, thematic forums (for example, in defence of water, rivers and natural goods), platforms for joint actions against the Free Trade Area of the Americas, the IIRSA/COSIPLAN mega-projects, agro-ecology networks and more recently national and regional networks against fracking. In the following, I will illustrate the articulation between socio-environmental struggles and new narratives, languages of valuation and protest strategies, using cases from Peru, Ecuador, Colombia and Argentina. The selected cases give an account of the variety of organizations and the scale of the struggles.

Peru has been a pioneer in terms of organizing networks against large-scale mining. Among the different networks and organizations that have emerged, the role of National Confederation of Communities Affected by Mining (CONACAMI), born in 1999, was crucial. CONACAMI maintained an important territorial presence and a capacity for local and national articulation until 2009. Later, other organizational structures – particularly those of peasants – emerged. One such example is the peasant patrols created in Cajamarca in 1976 with the aim of fighting crime and cattle theft. Another is the so-called *rondas campesinas* (peasant patrols), which are organized into committees at the district, provincial and regional levels (Damonte et al.

2016). At the national level, they are grouped under the *Central Única Nacional de Rondas Campesinas*. An emblematic case of the peasant patrols mobilizing against mining relates to the Conga project in Cajamarca, an industrial gold and copper mine whose construction would have threatened important water sources. Peasants from the affected communities, who called themselves the Guardians of the Lagoons, managed to get the company involved to halt the project, despite constant police repression, by holding vigils in front of the lagoons (see Paredes Peñafiel and Li 2019).

Another country in Latin America with a high level of socio-environmental conflict is Ecuador, where the response of the government of Rafael Correa (2007–2017) to mobilizations against extractivism was the criminalization and judicialization of protest. In addition to resistance against mining, one of the most original movements in Ecuador was that of the *Yasunidos*, which emerged after the Correa government unilaterally decided to put an end to the extraction moratorium in Yasuni National Park and gave the green light to oil exploitation (Acosta 2014). In 2013, the *Yasunidos* collective took up the matter and collected signatures to enable a popular consultation to be held in order to stop this. The movement, which is primarily made up of urban youth, promotes a strong critique of extractivism. Although the necessary number of signatures were collected to warrant holding a referendum on whether the oil in Yasuni National Park should be exploited or not, the government used various legal mechanisms to invalidate the consultation. The protest of the *Yasunidos* nevertheless succeeded in placing several issues on the public agenda, for example the defence of the rights of nature (introduced by the new constitution of 2008), the defence of indigenous rights, especially those in a state of isolation, and the demand for participatory democracy. What makes the *Yasunidos* movement unique is its autonomy, and the fact that the collective achieved an articulation among different social classes (though it is dominated by middle sectors), bringing together environmental and human rights groups, NGOs such as *Acción Ecológica* and Pachamama, artists' collectives and student organizations, as well as indigenous organizations such as the Confederation of Peoples of the Kichwa Nationality of Ecuador, the Confederation of Indigenous Nationalities of Ecuador and the Federation of Indigenous and Peasant Organizations of Azuay.

In Colombia, the ecoterritorial turn is articulated through demands for participation in mobilizations against industrial mining, the expansion of the oil frontier, several IIRSA/COSIPLAN projects and in defence of water. As for mining, one project that has prompted a significant mobilization is the La Colosa gold mining project, run by the South African company AngloGold Ashanti. The construction of the La Colosa mine would have affected several locations in the department of Tolima, which is considered the bread basket of Colombia due to the high productivity of its small-scale agriculture. In order to halt the project, local and regional Environmental Committees in Defence of Life (*Comités Ambientales en Defensa de la Vida*) were created, promoting popular consultations on La Colosa at the municipal level. The committees consisted of a cross-class and cross-sector alliance, bringing together both individual peasants and peasant organizations, landlords, youth and student groups, as well as environmental and human rights organizations. After a first successful consultation in the municipality of Piedras, in July 2013 the environmental committees mobilized for consultations in Cajamarca and Ibagué, though they encountered serious legal and business obstacles. In March 2017, a popular consultation was held in Cajamarca, which resulted in a rejection of the La Colosa mining project. In the absence of a social license, AngloGold Ashanti has decided thus far to suspend all activities related to the project (Dietz 2019).

With regard to infrastructure projects in Colombia, a key subject of conflict is the master plan for the use of the Magdalena River. The river crosses Colombia over a length of nearly 1,500 km and represents an important source of livelihood for residents and a habitat for flora and fauna. The plan aims to transform the river into a large waterway for container ships and an energy generator through the construction of several dams, for which the government will grant concessions to private companies. With the foundation of the movement Living Rivers (*Ríos Vivos*), a platform could be created to articulate the protest of grassroots organizations against the privatization of the river at a broader scale.[3] The movement consists of environmental NGOs and local organizations of fishermen and women, peasants and artisanal miners, all of whose livelihoods are threatened by the dams and the proposed transformation of the river.

Finally, a historic ruling made by the Colombian Constitutional Court in 2016 stresses the ecoterritorial turn in protests against extractivism in the country. The court, in its judgment T-622 of 2016, recognized a basin of the River Atrato, located on the Pacific coast of Colombia and heavily affected by mining exploitation, as a 'subject of rights'. In order to represent these rights, the court also ordered the creation of a commission of Guardians of the Atrato River, consisting of a representative of the national Ministry of the Environment and members of seven community councils. It was the first time in the Colombian jurisdiction that a river was declared a rights holder. This ruling was the result of a joint protective action filed by the Chocó Solidarity Inter-Ethnic Forum, different community councils of the Atrato River and peasant organizations (see Tierra Digna 2017).

In Argentina, the first anti-extractivist assembly collectives were forged in the struggle against industrial mining. The most important national network is the Union of Citizens Assemblies (*Unión de Asambleas Ciudadanas*, UAC), created in 2006. Later, the UAC extended its platform of protest, both in relation to criticism of the agribusiness model (transgenic soy) and, more recently, the exploitation of non-conventional hydrocarbons (fracking). The UAC fosters common strategies of resistance to the expansion of mining and against the cancellation of provincial laws that prohibit industrial mining. Another fundamental milestone of joint and multi-scalar action between diverse organizations (NGOs, political parties, intellectuals and academics, citizens' assemblies) was the approval of the National Glacier Law in 2010, which protects glaciers and peri-glaciers from mining and oil exploitation. In this context, the role of grassroots organizations (local and citizens' assemblies) with regard to the emergence of a new, transformative language of protest needs to be emphasized. It was community assemblies and grassroots organizations that, in their struggles against mining, oil and gas exploitation, started to turn their frames from 'no to mining' in the defence of water and common goods to the development of economic alternatives in order to strengthen the regional economy as well as regional solidarity.

Currently, one of the most dynamic struggles in Latin America is against fracking. At the regional level, the Latin American Alliance against Fracking (*Alianza Latinoamericana Contra el Fracking*) was created. It is a network of organizations that seeks to promote public debate related to fracking by analysing the energy sectors of each country and the implementation of public policies that promote and regulate fracking. It also tries to identify the territorial, socio-sanitary, environmental and economic impacts caused by fracking for the entire population, and documents the strategies for advocacy, mobilization and resistance deployed in each context. A country where a controversial political debate on the question of fracking has emerged is Colombia, where as of mid-2017, the government had taken no unanimous position. In addition, a moratorium was proposed, backed by a powerful network of scholars, peasant and environmental organizations as well as trade unions (including the Workers Union, *Unión Sindical Obrera*) (Jiménez 2020).

TOPICS OF THE ECOTERRITORIAL TURN AND FEMALE PROTAGONISTS

The topics covered within the ecoterritorial turn are varied: *buen vivir*, food sovereignty, environmental justice, common goods, the rights of nature, communality and an ethics of care, among others. These topics and concepts allow for an opening up of thought to other horizons of life and society (Svampa 2016). They illustrate the emergence of a new grammar of struggle, of an alternative language with a strong resonance throughout the region and of a common framework of meanings that relates indigenous struggles to territorial-ecological and feminist militancies in order to expand social, political and cultural rights in relation to the dominant model of exploitation, extraction and development.

One of the transversal themes of the ecoterritorial turn is the conception of natural goods as common goods, which, in the first instance, refers to demercantilization – that is, the need to keep out of the market those resources and goods that, due to their natural, social and cultural heritage, belong to the community and have a value that exceeds any price. To conceptualize natural goods as common goods refers, second, to the need to link production and reproduction processes to each other. This poses a different view of social relations, based on the configuration or emergence of spaces and forms of social cooperation, of common use and enjoyment. In recent years, popular feminisms in Latin America have opened up other possible avenues related to *commons*: indigenous women, peasant women, afro-descendants, poor rural and urban women, lesbians and trans people are all coming out of their silence, mobilizing and recreating relationships of solidarity and new forms of collective self-management. To account for this empowerment, there is increasing talk of 'popular feminisms', which represent the most marginalized sectors of society beyond their differences, and question the individualistic and contemporary Western way of life while promoting a greater appreciation of the collective and community experience (Korol 2016). Among the possible figures that popular feminisms acquire, 'community feminisms' stand out, which underline the existence of other forms of modernity (than the dominant Western form), and link decolonization with depatriarchalization (Gargallo Celentani 2015; Svampa 2017).

Popular feminisms are increasingly reflected in socio-environmental struggles throughout the region. A case in point is the Argentinean movement against the use of the herbicide glyphosate in soy production, known as the Mothers of the Ituzaingó Neighbourhood (*Las Madres del Barrio Ituzaingó*). The movement pioneered the denouncement of the health impacts of using glyphosate in soy cultivation, which led to the first criminal trial on the issue in Argentina (Svampa and Viale 2014). Another example is seen in the persistence of the women who formed the citizens' assemblies of the self-organized neighbourhoods of Chilecito, Famatina and La Rioja in Argentina, who successfully resisted the determined actions of various mining corporations – expelling four companies between 2009 and 2015 – to extract gold from the mountain of Famatina.[4]

Popular feminisms, in terms of ecology and care, challenge the reductionist ideas of autonomy and individualism, and instead emphasize the notion of interdependence. The language of popular feminisms that emphasizes, on the one hand, the relationship between body, territory and nature, and on the other, the revaluation and universalization of an ethics of care – seen as a relational faculty that the patriarchy has essentialized (for women) or detached (from men) – opens up a process of significant liberation (see Nightingale and Harcourt in this volume).

SCOPE AND THREATS

With the expansion of socio-environmental struggles, other languages of land and territory have been affirmed, and other modes of social relations with nature and other narratives of Mother Earth have emerged. Altogether, these new constructions exhilarate a relational paradigm based on reciprocity, complementarity and care, pointing toward other modes of appropriation, other dialogues of knowledge and other forms of organizing social life. The peasant rounds in Peru, the experience of the *Yasunidos* movement in Ecuador, the Guardians of the Atrato River, the environmental committees in Colombia, the assemblies in defence of water in Argentina and more generally the resistance to the expansion of unconventional technologies to exploit oil and gas (fracking, offshore exploitation), all constitute examples of the ecoterritorial turn in Latin American (Roa Avendaño and Scandizzo 2017). They consist of different actors with a common narrative nourished by different political-ideological matrices and indigenous, ecological, peasant, feminist and anti-patriarchal perspectives, all of them rooted in the heterogeneous world of the subordinate classes.

It is necessary to read the ecoterritorial turn as a trend that runs through all of the abovementioned struggles and which shapes a more general intelligibility framework, whilst weaving new social solidarities and collective subjectivities. It would nevertheless be a mistake to interpret these collective frameworks as if they were univocal or cut across all experiences, taking into consideration the heterogeneity of the organizations and the traditions of struggle. Thus, in spite of the fact that socio-environmental conflicts have contributed to giving visibility to this new language, most governments and a significant number of social sectors and urban unions tend to understand the environmental problem in a limited way, as a single dimension, without noticing the multiple implications that neo-extractivism brings. Finally, it is important to note that the ecoterritorial turn has not become the dominant counter-hegemonic narrative within the field of subaltern sectors. Rather, its ties to other struggles remain weak and problematic. A significant proportion within the urban trade unions and the various territorial organizations continues to conceive of development from a productive and worker perspective. There are also those who openly minimize or deny the legitimacy of the new ecoterritorial languages, and rather support a positive correlation between economic growth, development and environmental protection.

Certainly, despite having made fertile crossovers and advances, a great part of the left as well as the populist progressive force still retains a conception of development based on production. This is nourished by a tendency to privilege exclusively a reading of social conflict in terms of the dichotomy between capital and labour. As a consequence, it minimizes or places little attention on the relation between capital and nature, and on the related social struggles. In this context, especially during the so-called 'progressive cycle' in Latin America – which ran from the end of the 1990s to around 2013, when centre-left parties and movements won presidential elections in many countries of the region – the neo-extractivist dynamic and its effects of dispossession were a blind spot lacking conceptualization. In consequence, socio-environmental issues were considered a secondary concern, or simply issues to be sacrificed, when facing the persistent structural problems of poverty, inequality and exclusion in Latin America.

In other words, although there is an unmistakable trend to reject neo-extractivist projects and develop counter-hegemonic narratives in an ecoterritorial way, it is also true that many social sectors in Latin American societies gratefully receive the economic compensations from, or even expect the 'economic spillover' promised by, governments and mining and oil companies. Likewise, it is necessary to recognize that the process of constructing territoriality is carried out in a complex space, in which the logic of actions and rationalities intersect with different valuations. Let us bear in mind that an important number of the organizations involved in socio-environmental struggles are based in rural territories, inhabited by peasants and indigenous groups, whose power to exercise pressure is weaker than that of many urban actors. In any case, the geographical distance from the big cities strengthens the disconnection between rural and urban areas, particularly as mining, oil exploitation, agribusiness and dams seem far away from the cities and affect urban dwellers only indirectly. As a result, in many cases there is a poor connection between the organizations and movements fighting extractive logics and the trade unions and socio-territorial organizations that operate in urban centres. This does not mean that there are no alliances – both horizontal and vertical – between rural and urban movements, and between rural movements and powerful social and political actors; yet it is also the case that such alliances are tactical and volatile, and might be more strongly influenced by the timing of political opportunities rather than by the commitment to a cultural or strategic transformative project.

Alongside the increase in protests against extractivism, state and para-state violence, as well as the criminalization of socio-environmental struggles, have also increased. Latin America is the world region with the highest murder rate of human rights defenders and environmental activists; women are amongst the most affected (Front Line Defenders 2018). Most of the attacks are carried out in contexts of forced eviction, where women are physically and sexually assaulted by the police or paramilitary groups (FAU-AL 2016). In March 2016, the well-known leader Berta Cáceres was murdered in Honduras by the national repressive forces for opposing a hydroelectric dam. In January 2017, Laura Vasquez Pineda, a feminist and anti-mining activist in Guatemala, was murdered. She was a member of the Network of Ancestral Healers of Community Feminism. Thus, the beginning of a new cycle of human rights violations highlights both the limitations of democracy and the retraction and violation of political, territorial and environmental rights, all of which are enshrined in constitutions and national and international laws.

CONCLUSION

Nothing indicates that the high number of attacks and murders against human rights defenders and environmental activists in Latin America will go down; quite the contrary, especially if we take into account the current political turn to the right in the region. As in former times, the *el doradista* illusion has been transformed into a renewed dialectic of dispossession and dependence, which is accompanied by more extractivism, more violence and therefore less democracy. From the point of view of alternatives, however, it is impossible to ignore the fact that an ecoterritorial perspective of a communitarian, indigenist and ecofeminist nature has been created in Latin America. Through this perspective, decolonization, *buen vivir*, an ethics of care, the depatriarchalization of body and territory and the affirmation of interdependence are highlighted.

NOTES

1. Translated from Spanish by Rita Bitar Deeb.
2. https://mapa.conflictosmineros.net/ocmal_db-v2/.
3. https://riosvivoscolombia.org/, accessed 17 October 2020.
4. https://ejatlas.org/print/famatina-gold-mining-argentina, accessed 17 October 2020.

FURTHER READING

Svampa, M. (2017), *Del Cambio de Época al Fin de ciclo. Gobiernos Progresistas, Extractivismo, Movimientos Sociales en América Latina*, Buenos Aires: Edhasa.
Svampa, M. (2019), *Neo-extractivism in Latin America: Socio-environmental Conflicts, the Territorial Turn, and New Political Narratives*, Cambridge: Cambridge University Press.
Vergara-Camus, L. (2013), Rural social movements in Latin America: In the eye of the storm, *Journal of Agrarian Change*, 13(4), 590–606.

REFERENCES

Acosta, A. (2014), Iniciativa Yasuni-ITT: The difficult construction of utopia, *Línea de Fuego*, 4 February, accessed 14 October 2020 at https://lalineadefuego.info/2014/02/04/iniciativa-yasuni-itt-la-dificil-construccion-de-la-utopia-por-alberto-acosta/.
Acselard, H. (2004), *Conflitos Ambientais no Brasil*, Rio de Janeiro: Relume Dumará.
Carpio, S.M. (2017), Integración energética sudamericana: entre la realidad, perspectivas e incertidumbres, in Guzmán Salinas, J.C.; Carpio, S.M. (eds), *Discursos y Realidades. Matriz Energética, Políticas e Integración*, La Paz: CEDLA, 91–138.
Damonte, G.; Glave, M.; Cabrera, A. (2016), *Las Rondas Campesinas y el Desarrollo Minero: El Caso del Proyecto Minero La Granja*, accessed 14 October 2020 at https://core.ac.uk/download/pdf/79478868.pdftulo.
Delgado, E. (2018), Fracking Vaca Muerta: Socioeconomic implications of shale gas extraction in Northern Patagonia, Argentina, *Journal of Latin American Geography*, 17(3), 102–131.
Dietz, K. (2019), Direct democracy in mining conflicts in Latin America: Mobilising against the La Colosa project in Colombia, *Canadian Journal of Development Studies/Revue canadienne d'etudes du développement*, 40(2), 145–162.
FAU-AL (2016), Extractivism in Latin America: Impacts on women's lives and proposals for the defense of territory. Bogotá: Urgent Action Fund for Latin America, accessed 17 October 2020 at https://fondoaccionurgente.org.co/site/assets/files/1175/b81245_6cc6d3d7edd447d0ab461860ae1ae64f.pdf.
Front Line Defenders (2018), *Front Line Defenders Global Analysis 2018*, Dublin: Front Line Defenders, International Foundation for the Protection of Human Rights Defenders.
Gargallo Celentani, F. (2015), *Feminisms from Abya Yala: Ideas and Proposals of the Women of 607 Towns in Our America*, Bogotá: Ediciones Desde abajo.
Jiménez, I. (2020), *'Fracking ni Hoy, ni Nunca'. Entrevista a Tatiana Roa*, Quito: Fundación Rosa Luxemburg Oficina Andina, accessed 22 October 2020 at www.rosalux.org.ec/pdfs/FrackingNiHoyNiNunca.pdf.
Korol, C. (ed.) (2016), *Feminismos Populares. Pedagogy and Policy*, Buenos Aires: América Libre-El Colectivo.

Machado Aráoz, H.; Svampa, M.; Viale, E.; Giraud, M.; Wagner, L.; Antonelli, M.; Giarraca, N.; Teubal, M. (2011), *15 Mitos y Realidades de la Minería Transnacional en Argentina*, Buenos Aires: El Colectivo, Ediciones Herramienta.

Moore, J.W. (2011), Ecology, capital, and the nature of our times: Accumulation and crisis in the capitalist world-ecology, *Journal of World-Systems Research*, 17(1), 107–146.

Oxfam (2016), Unearthed: Land, power and inequality in Latin America, accessed 14 October 2020 at www.oxfam.org/sites/www.oxfam.org/files/file_attachments/bp-land-power-inequality-latin-america -301116-en.pdf.

Paredes Peñafiel, A.P.; Li, F. (2019), Nourishing relations: Controversy over the Conga mining project in northern Peru, *Ethnos*, 84(2), 301–322.

Roa Avendaño, T.; Scandizzo, H. (2017), What do we understand by extreme energy? In *Extreme: The New Frontiers of Energy Extractivism in Latin America*, Vitoria: Oilwatch Latin America, 5–9.

Svampa, M. (2011), Extractivismo neodesarrollista y movimientos sociales. Un giro ecoterritorial hacia nuevas alternativas?, in Lang, M.; Mokrani, D. (eds), *Más Allá del Desarrollo*, Quito: Ediciones Abya Yala, 185–216.

Svampa, M. (2015), Commodities consensus: Neoextractivism and enclosure of the commons in Latin America, *South Atlantic Quarterly*, 114(1), 65–82.

Svampa, M. (2016), *Latin American Debates. Indianism, Development, Dependence and Populism*, Buenos Aires: Edhasa.

Svampa, M. (2017), *From the Change of Era to the End of Cycle: Progressive Governments, Extractivism and Social Movements*, Buenos Aires: Edhasa.

Svampa, M. (2018), *Las Fronteras del Neoextractivismo en América Latina*, Buenos Aires: Calas-Unsam.

Svampa, M.; Viale, E. (2014), *Maldesarrollo: The Argentina of Extractivism and Dispossession*, Buenos Aires: Editorial Katz.

Tierra Digna (2017), *Todas y Todos Somos Guardianes del Atrato*, accessed 22 September 2020 at http:// guardianesdelatrato.tierradigna.org/.

Vidal, J. (2017), Why is Latin America so obsessed with Mega Dams? *The Guardian*, 27 May, accessed 10 March 2021 at www.theguardian.com/global-development-professionals-network/2017/may/23/ why-latin-america-obsessed-mega-dams.

Villegas, P.N. (2014), Notas sobre movimientos sociales y gobiernos progresistas, in CEDIB (eds), *Extractivismo: Nuevos Contextos de Dominación y Resistencias*, Cochabamba: CEDIB, 9–66.

34. Agrarian change in China: Historical origins and competing perspectives

Qian Forrest Zhang

HISTORICAL ORIGINS AND CONTEMPORARY DEVELOPMENTS

The agrarian society of late Imperial China during the seventeenth to nineteenth centuries had been deeply mired in political and economic crises, which were in no small part caused by the country's confrontation with global capitalism and Western imperialism (Huang 1990). However, the first serious intellectual and political movement that was both a response to the agrarian crisis and an effort to steer agrarian change toward more desirable outcomes only emerged about a hundred years ago in the 1920s. Led by either intellectuals such as James Yen and Liang Shumin or industrialists such as Zhang Jian and Lu Zuofu, the so-called Rural Reconstruction movement promoted self-organization and self-government within grassroots rural society in a context of national crises. Depending on the availability of financial support from either the leader himself or his political patron, these locally based experiments had varying degrees of success. But, without the support of a competent and committed state, these experiments all inevitably failed to extend beyond their original localities or sustain over a long period. Their impact on the national scale and in shaping the trajectory of agrarian change had been negligible.

Serious rural reform only took place in the 1940s when a major political force – in this case, the Chinese Communist Party (CCP) – adopted some of the principles of the Rural Reconstruction movement and implemented the reforms in the base areas under its control. These reform measures included rent and interest reduction, land redistribution, mass education, women's liberation and provision of public health (Hinton 1966). The success of these rural reforms in Yan'an and other base areas provided strong economic and political support to the CCP's war efforts against first the Japanese and then the Nationalist government; it also gave the CCP great confidence and urgency to extend the reforms nationwide after founding the new People's Republic. The nationwide rural reform after 1949 was implemented in a more radical fashion, spearheaded by a land reform that aimed at the total destruction of the landlord class. The land reform soon gave way to the socialist transformation of the entire agrarian economy and rural society, which culminated in the collectivization of all agricultural land and farming production in the late 1950s (Li 2009).

Initially, the hasty expansion of communal farming and excessive extraction of rural surplus to finance industrialization during the Great Leap Forward resulted in a disastrous famine. Corrections were soon made. In the two ensuing decades, the collectivization of the rural society enabled the socialist state to mobilize the masses in building agricultural infrastructure, raising productivity and transforming local governance and social structures. Although it was too often underappreciated or even intentionally obscured in both the academic literature and the government's official historical narrative, China's collective rural economy delivered great progress in both human development and agricultural growth (Bramall 2009).

During the collective era of the 1960s and 1970s, China followed the Soviet model of agrarian transition (Bernstein 2015). Through monopolizing the procurement and distribution of agricultural products, the state became the agent that extracted rural surplus to provide the capital accumulation for industrialization. A key difference from the Soviet experience is that in China the capital accumulation for industries also took place in the countryside in the form of collectively owned Commune and Brigade Enterprises, which provided the foundation for successful rural industrialization in the 1980s.

In the late 1970s, China's economic reform started in rural areas with a gradual decollectivization of agriculture – rural households were given more and more autonomy in making production decisions and selling their outputs for profits. The increased surplus and freed-up labour supply from agriculture then provided the necessary conditions for the rapid growth of rural industries in coastal provinces. These were led by collectively owned Commune and Brigade Enterprises – now called Township and Village Enterprises (TVEs) – and joined by a large number of small household businesses. For the entire 1980s, while urban reforms faltered, rural China enjoyed a decade of unprecedented growth, massive reduction of poverty and political stability.

The most notable development during this period was the TVE-led rural industrialization, not least because it was so rarely accomplished in other developing countries. The success of the rural industry shaped the trajectory of agrarian change in China in important ways. It unleashed the transfer of surplus agricultural labour into non-farm employment, where they not only received higher income but also underwent the training for industrial wage work. Multiple job holdings across economic sectors gradually became a common livelihood strategy for many rural households. China's rural industrialization also followed a path that has been called "accumulation without dispossession" (Arrighi 2007), where the collective ownership shielded peasants from land dispossession by expanding industries while at the same time providing industrial job opportunities for many, creating a more equitable outcome.

The period of "triumphant industrialization" came to an end in the mid-1990s. Economic and political challenges began to mount in rural China. The once vibrant TVE sector in coastal areas lost its lustre under both increasing competition from urban firms and the burden of its own institutional constraints. Bankruptcy of TVEs and massive privatization soon followed, weakening a key revenue source of local rural governments and reducing the demand for surplus rural labour. The fiscal recentralization reform in 1994 concentrated more revenue sources in the central coffer while shifting more expenditure to local governments. This added another impetus that drove local governments, especially in inland provinces, into imposing excessive and arbitrary fees and taxes on the rural population, giving rise to the "peasant burden" problem. This became a lightning rod that triggered widespread resentment among the rural population and rising incidences of political contention (Bernstein and Lu 2003).

The stagnation in rural areas increasingly drove rural residents into searching for migratory wage jobs in cities, where market reform and urbanization had accelerated. By the turn of the century, the magnitude of this exodus of the rural labour force had reached the order of hundreds of millions. Earlier, the TVE-led rural industrialization had allowed many rural households to shift from a sole dependence on agriculture to pluriactivity that combined family farming with *in situ* industrial employment. But now that wage jobs were mostly found in urban areas and required migration, many rural households had to coordinate their social reproduction not only across multiple jobs, but also over distant geographical space and the rural–urban social divide. While their wage incomes had mostly increased and even become the dominant income source, this multiple boundary-crossing had put increasing strains on both the rural families and rural society.

The exodus of the most able-bodied and educated portion of the labour force drained rural areas and agriculture of its vitality. It created a "left-behind" population that disproportionately consisted of children, women and the elderly (Ye and Pan 2011; Ye et al. 2013). Abandoned farmland became widespread and agricultural output stagnated.

If the first 15 years of rural reform can be characterized by the triumphant success of rural industrialization, the following decade from the mid-1990s onwards formed a sharp contrast. The multitude of problems mentioned above – the political contention between local states and rural residents, the plight experienced by rural migrant workers in cities and the hardship faced by the left-behind populations – have been known and discussed within China as the "three rural problems" (*sannong wenti*, or the problems of countryside, agriculture and peasantry).

The aggravation of rural problems led the central government to introduce a slate of policy reforms in the early 2000s aiming to rejuvenate the countryside. These new reforms started with the rural tax-for-fee reform in 2000, which culminated in the nationwide abolition of agricultural tax from 2004 to 2006. The reforms later expanded to the streamlining of township-level government, the launch of the Constructing a New Socialist Countryside program around 2005, the building of a rural social welfare system and the provision of an increasingly wide range of agriculture-related subsidies.

While these reform policies target a wide range of issues, the central government's programme of "rural rejuvenation" is built around a central agenda – agricultural modernization. The central government's hope is that a modernized agriculture that is larger in scale, uses more technology and greater capital investment and integrates deeper into markets will enable agricultural producers who are either "left behind" in rural areas or driven back from their precarious urban sojourn to achieve higher incomes and productivity. The revitalized agriculture would then become the new pillar of the rural economy and a ballast for stability.

The conditions for the "modernization of agriculture" have also become ripe in rural China. The exodus of rural labour into urban wage jobs and the declining rural fertility rate have left more farmland available in the countryside, while the rapidly rising urban consumer demand for fruits, vegetables, dairy products, meat and poultry and processed foods also present new opportunities for the accumulation of the surplus capital that has started to plague China's urban sector in recent years (Huang and Peng 2007).

The convergence of these new developments has ushered in a new phase in China's agrarian transition. While both the Soviet model pursued during the collective era and the rural industrialization "from below" of the 1980s and 1990s transferred surplus from agriculture to fuel industrial growth, in this new phase, capital – from the state, urban industries and rural households alike – is going into agriculture and changing the social organization of agricultural production.

COMPETING PERSPECTIVES ON CHINA'S NEW AGRARIAN TRANSITION

The entry of capital into agriculture – from diverse origins via different paths, and in uneven processes – has introduced fundamental changes to agricultural production and transformed rural politics and society in important ways. A direct result of these changes is the rise of scaled-up agriculture, made possible by land transfers and the entry of capital. An intellectual debate, deploying competing perspectives from critical agrarian studies, about the nature and implications of this development soon emerged. One side, with a strong pro-peasant populist bend, argues that Chinese agriculture is still – and should continue to be – based on a "small peasant economy," because of a host of advantages it enjoys, which range from economic productivity to social equitability, ecological viability and cultural significance (Huang et al. 2012; He 2013; van der Ploeg and Ye 2016). The other side characterizes this process as the rise of agrarian capitalism, documents the widespread subsumption of smallholding family producers to capital and predicts a dissolution of the Chinese peasantry (Zhang and Donaldson 2008, 2010; Webber 2012; Huang 2015; Yan and Chen 2015).

The debates between these two perspectives mainly revolve around three key questions: (1) how to characterize the peasantry, peasant farming and the peasant way of life in China; (2) how to understand the changes that are taking place in Chinese agricultural and rural society today; and (3) how to conceptualize the Chinese experience in a global context.

Proponents of the "peasant persistence" view see China's peasant agriculture as a closely integrated organic whole of land, labour and household (van der Ploeg and Ye 2016). This integration gives peasant households greater flexibility with labour use and a deep bond with the land that enables them to adapt to external changes, remain competitive in productivity and hold commodification at bay. The new forms of production we find in Chinese agriculture today are but various ways in which the peasant household reinvents itself. For example, the migration of rural residents will remain circulatory, and wage work is merely used to supplement the farming operation of an autonomous family economy that remains unshakably rooted in land, the countryside and the peasant culture. On the other hand, capitalized, non-family-based farms – to the extent that they have emerged – are seen as mainly an artificial creation of misinformed state interventions and expected to be transient, losing ground to peasant family farms once state subsidies and the labour supply dry out. China's agrarian transition, therefore, offers a distinctive alternative to the Western model based on large-scale corporatized farms and hired labour – a unique Chinese paradigm that can be emulated in other developing countries.

The opposing camp, informed by the Marxist materialist theory, contends that the traditional peasant household economy in China comprises a set of malleable livelihood strategies adapted to the socioeconomic environment and thus can evolve when challenges of social reproduction demand new responses. Chinese peasants had a long history of participating in commodity production; many also had experiences in wage work in Commune and Brigade Enterprises and TVEs. Starting in the 1990s, when a booming urban economy began to generate a seemingly insatiable demand for labour, hundreds of millions of former peasants responded to this "market enrolment" (Webber 2012). Rather than trapping their labour in unproductive family farming on a miniscule scale and suffering "self-exploitation", they chose instead to commodify their labour power. If anything made China's experience unique, it is not peasants' resistance to commodification, but rather their acceptance of it, even when they had not been forced off their land. In other words, it was primarily not land dispossession, but the economic needs of social reproduction that compelled Chinese farmers to commodify their labour.

These scholars also see the new types of agricultural producers that have emerged with land transfer and labour hiring not as a continuation or reinvention of the peasantry, but as its dissolution. Rural households' different degrees of participation in various types of markets

– capital, labour, products and land – differentiate them into new class positions and create drastically different relationships with capital, land and agriculture (Zhang 2015) – a far cry from the image of a homogenous, land-bound peasantry. To put this in the global context, this perspective also finds, in China's transition to agrarian capitalism, the manifestations of global trends such as land grabbing, boom and flex crops and agro-extractivism, albeit with significant Chinese characteristics (Schneider 2014; Bernstein 2015; Xu 2018).

PLACING CHINA IN CRITICAL AGRARIAN STUDIES: THE QUESTIONS OF LAND, CAPITAL AND LABOUR

Agrarian change in China today provides a fertile ground for investigating key issues in critical agrarian studies, such as the questions of land, labour and capital. One unique characteristic of China's agrarian transition, as mentioned earlier, has been the relative low degree of land dispossession to make way for large-scale farms or industrial uses. Proponents of the "peasant persistence" thesis have used this as evidence of the persistence of smallholding peasant agriculture. The collective land ownership in rural China, which allocated usufruct rights of land to rural residents as an economically inalienable entitlement, helped to provide farmers some protection from land dispossession. Instead of dispossessing farmers of their land, capital accumulation came from either collective contribution and state investment in the case of rural industrialization during the 1980s and 1990s, described as "accumulation without dispossession" (Arrighi 2007), or from rural households' savings in the case of the rise of capitalized family farming since the 2000s. For the latter case, Philip Huang and his co-authors (2012) describe it as "capitalization without proletarianization", in which rural families used the "blood-and-sweat capital" that they saved from either industrial wage incomes or family business incomes to invest in the scaling-up and technological upgrading of their family farming operations. These capitalized family farms may have increased their scales through renting land from those who have shifted out agriculture, but mostly eschewed from hiring long-term wage labour – hence the term "capitalization without proletarianization".

This capitalization made the small-scale family farming of many households economically viable in producing new crops to meet market demands, allowing them to resist the pressure to rent out their land to large-scale producers. At the same time, rural labour either was channelled into higher-paying urban wage jobs or stayed in family farming. As a result, both the supply of land and labour available to large-scale capitalist farms were restricted, stunting their growth. It is from this analysis that proponents of the "peasant persistence" thesis gain the confidence that smallholding family farming will continue to dominate Chinese agriculture and keep large-scale capitalist farming at bay (van der Ploeg and Ye 2016).

Although it correctly identified one key process in the rise of agrarian capitalism in China, the above analysis has nevertheless missed at least four other developments. First, conceptually, the capitalized family farmers are surely different from the traditional subsistence peasants due to their different relationships with commodification and markets, and thus should not be seen as just a reinvented version of peasant farming. These family farms have become capitalist enterprises that operate and reproduce through a host of commodity relationships: if they fail to use the family land and labour efficiently to make a profit, it becomes economically more rational to shift the labour to wage jobs and transfer out land to collect a rent, as many indeed have done.

Second, besides the blood-and-sweat capital from rural households, there are other mechanisms of capital accumulation and paths of entry into agriculture. Both Yan and Chen (2015) and Zhang (2015), for example, discussed capital accumulation *from above* (politically assisted accumulation by local office-holders) and *from without* (investment by urban and foreign capital), in addition to accumulation *from below*. The use of wage labour emerged together with the rise of scaled-up, capitalized farming and has been growing steadily (Zhang and Donaldson 2008). Even the capitalized household farmers use wage labour frequently, albeit mostly short term. The large-scale agriculture created by the other forms of capital relies heavily on wage labour, which is mainly provided by migrants from poorer rural areas and local casual labourers.

Third, a narrow focus on dispossession of land as the only form of "proletarianization" is inadequate in capturing the complex labouring experiences of Chinese farmers/migrant workers and their relationships with capital. The miniscule size of many rural households' landholding and the decline of agricultural productivity means that even though their land rights remain intact, they are still compelled to sell their labour power for wages to meet the needs of social reproduction. Furthermore, household farmers can be subsumed into the domination of capital in various ways (Huang 2015; Yan and Chen 2015).

Last, since the 2010s, there has been a turn of the tide. The scaling-up of agriculture must begin with a consolidation of farmland, which in China's case has been allocated across rural households in an egalitarian way and fragmented pattern. In the early years of this new phase of agrarian transition, transfers of land use rights emerged spontaneously among rural households through informal arrangements. Later institutional changes imposed by the central government – first, the prohibition of administrative land reallocation across households within villages, and then regulatory changes to support transfers of land rights – aided its growth. By now, formal institutions have been established across the country to handle the increasing volumes of transfer of land rights from households to large-scale producers (Trappel 2016).

In recent years, governments at all levels have become increasingly supportive of large-scale capitalist farms and have been actively or even coercively wresting land from rural households to make way for large-scale farming (Andreas and Zhan 2016; Gong and Zhang 2017; Luo et al. 2017). The collective land system that once provided a protection against dispossession by either market or political coercion has been weakened by both the institutional changes and the local states' increasing commitment to land consolidation. Various national estimates have put the proportion of transferred farmland in total farmland between 20 to 30 per cent. How much of such land transfers can be considered land dispossession and thus resulting in the proletarianization of farmers may still be debatable, but the trend of farmland consolidation in the hands of large-scale producers is unmistakable. In this new phase of China's agrarian transition, rural land – both farmland and construction land – is being rapidly separated from the original owners and turned into capital.

CONCLUSION: LESSONS FROM CHINA

As the summary above shows, the common themes in critical agrarian studies are also salient in China's agrarian change: the diverse dynamics of accumulation, the commodification of subsistence and expansion of wage work, the social differentiation and class formation, rural–

urban interconnection through migration and capital flow and the role of gender and age in intermediating commodification and differentiation.

In China, these processes unfold in unique historical and political-economic contexts. Most of the unique characteristics of China's agrarian change since the second half of the twentieth century are rooted in the prolonged but eventually successful peasant revolution led by the CCP. The revolution owed much of its success to the rural reforms that the CCP championed while a rebel force. The revolution then enabled the CCP to first carry out the largest-scale and one of the most egalitarian land reforms in history and to then shift to collectivization within a short period. These revolutionary changes put Chinese agriculture and rural society on a drastically different platform than other developing countries, characterized by a far lower degree of socioeconomic differentiation, a much higher degree of human development, a greater integration of agriculture and industry and a much weakened traditional culture. It is from this unique starting point that the ensuing agrarian change since the 1980s then embarked on a different path.

Furthermore, in the recent four decades when China has been on a course of converging toward capitalism, important distinctions remain. First, the socialist state of China was in effect built from years of peasant mobilization and rural transformation. At the central level, the state remains bound by the revolutionary tradition of sourcing its legitimacy from improving the welfare of the rural masses. This mission continues to drive the central state to constantly devising new programmes aimed at transforming the countryside – from the agricultural modernization in the Deng Xiaoping era, to building a new socialist countryside under Hu Jintao and to rural rejuvenation and poverty eradication under Xi. At the local level, even after more than a decade of hollowing out, the local states in China remain more effective than its counterparts in other developing countries in implementing the central programmes and intervening in agrarian change. Second, the sustained economic growth in China has also been far more capable both of shifting labour out of agriculture into urban employment and settlement and of pumping capital into agriculture.

If there ever is a Chinese paradigm of agrarian change, as some contend (van der Ploeg and Ye 2016), then the unique features of this paradigm can only develop from the material conditions in the politics and economy that are shaped by history, as outlined here. The Chinese culture may inform peasants' relationship with the land and perception of the family, but it does not create an ahistorical essence of peasantness that is impervious to the evolving political-economic context.

ACKNOWLEDGEMENTS

This research was supported by the Singapore Ministry of Education Academic Research Fund Tier 1 grant (C242/MSS17S003).

FURTHER READING

Day, A.F. (2013), *The Peasant in Postsocialist China: History, Politics, and Capitalism*, Cambridge: Cambridge University Press.

Huang, P.C.C.; Gao, Y.; Peng, Y. (2012), Capitalization without proletarianization in China's agricultural development, *Modern China*, 38(2), 139–173.

van der Ploeg, J.D.; Ye, J. (2016), *China's Peasant Agriculture and Rural Society: Changing Paradigms of Farming*, London: Routledge.
Zhang, Q.F.; Donaldson, J.A. (2010), From peasants to farmers: Peasant differentiation, labor regimes, and land-rights institutions in China's agrarian transition, *Politics and Society*, 38(4), 458–489.
Zhang, Q.F. (2015), Class differentiation in rural China: Dynamics of accumulation, commodification and state intervention, *Journal of Agrarian Change*, 15(3), 338–365.

REFERENCES

Andreas, J.; Zhan, S. (2016), Hukou and land: Market reform and rural displacement in China, *Journal of Peasant Studies*, 43(4), 798–827.
Arrighi, G. (2007), *Adam Smith in Beijing*, London: Verso.
Bernstein, H. (2015), Some reflections on agrarian change in China, *Journal of Agrarian Change*, 15(3), 454–477.
Bernstein, T.P.; Lu, X. (2003), *Taxation without Representation in Rural China: State Capacity, Peasant Resistance, and Democratization*, Cambridge: Cambridge University Press.
Bramall, C. (2009), *Chinese Economic Development*, Abingdon: Routledge.
Gong, W.; Zhang, Q.F. (2017), Betting on the big: State-brokered land transfers, large-scale agricultural producers, and rural policy implementation, *The China Journal*, 77, 126.
He, X. (2013), *Xiaonong Lichang (From the Small Peasants' Point of View)*, Beijing: The China University of Political Science and Law Press.
Hinton, W. (1966), *Fanshen: A documentary of revolution in a Chinese village*, New York, NY: Monthly Review Press.
Huang, P.C.C. (1990), *The Peasant Family and Rural Development in the Yangzi Delta, 1350–1988*, Stanford, CA: Stanford University Press.
Huang, P.C.C.; Gao, Y.; Peng, Y. (2012), Capitalization without proletarianization in China's agricultural development, *Modern China*, 38(2), 139–173.
Huang, P.C.C.; Peng, Y. (2007), The confluence of three historical trends and the prospects for small-scale agriculture in China [J], *Social Sciences in China*, 2007(4), 74–88.
Huang, Y. (2015), Can capitalist farms defeat family farms? The dynamics of capitalist accumulation in shrimp aquaculture in South China, *Journal of Agrarian Change*, 15(3), 392–412.
Li, H. (2009), *Village China under Socialism and Reform: A Micro-history, 1948–2008*, Stanford, CA: Stanford University Press.
Luo, Q.; Andreas, J.; Li, Y. (2017), Grapes of wrath: Twisting arms to get villagers to cooperate with agribusiness in China, *The China Journal*, 77, 27–50.
Schneider, M. (2014), Developing the meat grab, *Journal of Peasant Studies*, 41(4), 613–633.
Trappel, R. (2016), *China's Agrarian Transition: Peasants, Property, and Politics*, Lanham, MD: Lexington Books.
van der Ploeg, J.D.; Ye, J. (2016), *China's Peasant Agriculture and Rural Society: Changing Paradigms of Farming*, London: Routledge.
Webber, M.J. (2012), *Making Capitalism in Rural China*, Edward Elgar Publishing.
Xu, Y. (2018), Politics of inclusion and exclusion in the Chinese industrial tree plantation sector: The global resource rush seen from inside China, *The Journal of Peasant Studies*, 1–25.
Yan, H.; Chen, Y. (2015), Agrarian capitalization without capitalism? Capitalist dynamics from above and below in China, *Journal of Agrarian Change*, 15(3), 366–391.
Ye, J.; Pan, L. (2011), Differentiated childhoods: impacts of rural labor migration on left-behind children in China, *The Journal of Peasant Studies*, 38(2), 355–377.
Ye, J.; Wang, C.; Wu, H.; He, C.; Liu, J. (2013), Internal migration and left-behind populations in China, *Journal of Peasant Studies*, 40(6), 1119–1146.
Zhang, Q.F. (2015), Class differentiation in rural China: Dynamics of accumulation, commodification and state intervention, *Journal of Agrarian Change*, 15(3), 338–365.
Zhang, Q.F.; Donaldson, J.A. (2008), The rise of agrarian capitalism with Chinese characteristics: Agricultural modernization, agribusiness and collective land rights, *The China Journal*, 60, 25–47.

Zhang, Q.F.; Donaldson, J.A. (2010), From peasants to farmers: Peasant differentiation, labor regimes, and land-rights institutions in China's agrarian transition, *Politics & Society*, 38(4), 458–489.

35. Beyond confrontation: Silent growers, symbiosis and subtle peasantness in post-socialist Eurasia

Oane Visser, Brian Kuns and Petr Jehlička

INTRODUCTION

The vast expanses of post-socialist Eurasia, spanning from the territory just outside of Berlin to Russia's sparsely inhabited Far East, have experienced arguably the most dramatic and large-scale agrarian transformations of the past century. These include the shift to socialist agriculture with – often violent – collectivization sweeping through the countryside following the Russian October revolution and then an unprecedented wave of market-oriented land reforms taking place in over 25 countries following the fall of the Berlin Wall in 1989 and the demise of the Soviet Union in 1991. The large number of countries starting market-based land reform almost simultaneously from a roughly similar (socialist) background, yet with different outcomes, makes the region a unique 'laboratory of land reform' (Spoor 2012) and agrarian transformation. Yet insights generated by research on this region tend not to make it into wider agrarian studies.[1] During the socialist era, difficulties in conducting independent fieldwork in the countryside hampered agrarian research, although a few excellent ethnographies were produced (see for example Humphrey 1983 and Kideckel 1993). Following the demise of socialism, most rural research was framed in terms of transitions from socialism to capitalism or accession to the European Union (EU), rather than as (agrarian) development more broadly.

This chapter ventures into the largely uncharted territory of research on socialist and post-socialist Eurasian agrarian issues, with the aim to uncover some key concepts that have sprouted out of this region and that might be of wider relevance. It will discuss three major sets of insights (and/or research agendas) emerging from the region. First, we argue that the region constitutes fertile ground for nuancing and interrogating the concept of the peasant, and ideas of predictable trajectories of either the disappearance or re-emergence of peasants. This is largely due to the region's uneasy fit in development studies' classifications (Global North versus South) and agrarian studies' influential theories. In terms of food regime theory (McMichael, this volume), for instance, during the Cold War the region was the alien – largely blank – 'other' in the second food regime. Meanwhile Russia, as the Soviet Union's largest post-socialist successor, sits somewhat awkwardly within the global corporate food regime, given the Russian government's growing protectionism in the agricultural sector in general and pressure on multinational food traders and foreign large-scale farmland investors (Lander and Kuns 2020) in particular. This protectionism and pressure is in line with Russia's recent push for food sovereignty, not along the lines of La Via Campesina, but *via Kremlina* style (Visser et al. 2015, 14), i.e. top-down, state-controlled and oligarch-led.

Second, research from/about the region unsettles the idea of smallholders versus corporate farms as separate worlds, instead stressing co-existence, symbiosis, overlap and fuzzy boundaries. It directs attention to how farms might not easily be pinpointed as belonging to either alternative or conventional food networks, with some post-socialist rural dwellers pragmatically having a leg in both worlds.

Third, this chapter argues that it is crucial to go beyond ideological and discursive aspects of food systems and movements, to pay more serious attention to the theoretical implications of everyday experiences and their – sometimes striking and underestimated – cumulative impact. So far, within agrarian studies, the study of local micro-encounters and their cumulative influence is still overshadowed by protests and large-scale mobilizations as research angles. International scholars in East European studies – and particularly Soviet studies – also have long focused predominantly on large-scale mobilizations, with much research devoted to the period just before and after the socialist revolution (including the resistance against collectivization), while the decades of socialist agriculture following it have received sparse treatment by critical social science scholars. We will highlight the unappreciated resilience of weakly organized, and muted, yet culturally rich smallholder food provisioning with food practices that cross class boundaries and are largely environmentally friendly.

POST-SOCIALIST REPEASANTIZATION?

Views on the 'agrarian question' in the post-socialist region are quite divergent, even if most studies have not explicitly framed research in terms of the agrarian question. While some authors have argued that there has been a return of the peasant (Dorondel and Serban 2014; van der Ploeg, this volume), and a continuation or reinvigoration of a peasant moral economy, others have vigorously criticized the idea of a moral economy driving post-socialist producers, arguing that rural dwellers have behaved as rational economic actors, either by remaining farm workers or trying to become commercial farmers.[2] Still others have argued, more matter of fact, that the label of peasant is not easily applicable considering the hybrid character of rural producers, as well as the huge variety in smallholder farming across a country like Russia (Pallot and Nefedova 2007).

While peasants have repeatedly been declared to be a thing of the past or on the verge of extinction, peasants stubbornly refuse to wither away. Today, after often violent and harsh collectivization, and many decades (up to seven in the Soviet Union) of varying denunciation and repression of peasants, post-socialist villagers are still not devoid of peasant characteristics. At the same time, while numerous observers and non-governmental organizations (NGOs) have celebrated widespread repeasantization in other parts of the world, there is insufficient evidence that rural dwellers across Eurasia have turned into full-blown peasants, or widely identify as such.

Expressions such as 'hybrid' or 'partial' as adjectives for peasants are clearly not exclusive to (post-)socialist Eurasia (van der Ploeg, this volume), but it is almost impossible to proceed without them in this region (Kaneff and Leonard 2002). Even terms like 'hybrid' or 'partial' might understate the manifold contradictions and complexities that surround characterizing small agrarian producers in the region, such as the blurred distinctions between rural and the numerous (peri-)urban 'peasants'/smallholders (Kaneff and Leonard 2002), or the co-existence and/or symbiosis with large farms, all discussed further on.[3]

A strong post-socialist repeasantization has only taken place in the agriculturally marginal pockets, mostly the mountainous areas. In the socialist era, in isolated, marginal areas such as

Table 35.1   *Smallholders' share in land and food production, 2013*

Country	Utilized agricultural area as percentage of total agricultural land	Smallholders' agricultural output as percentage of total output
Hungary	2.5	8.1
Poland	3.0	4.0
Romania	12.1	25.1
Russia	4.4	42.6
Tajikistan	23.3	63.4 (2014)

Note: Only household plots with less than 2 hectares are included.
Source: Wegren and O'Brien (2018) based on Eurostat and Rosstat, and statistical reports for 2015 and 2019 from the Statistical Agency of Tajikistan (Tajstat).

swamps and highlands far away from the centres of power, collectivization occurred cosmetically or not at all, with peasant farms persisting. As a result, mountainous countries, such as Georgia, Armenia (see Spoor 2012) and Albania, or regions, such as Romania's Transylvania or Tajikistan's Pamir (see Hofman and Visser 2014), saw a widespread re-emergence of peasants (cf. Hann and 'Property Relations' Group 2003).[4] Steppe regions of Ukraine and Russia (Allina-Pisano 2008), and areas of Russia and Kazakhstan with roughly similar agro-climatic conditions, had remarkably similar agrarian transformations, despite different national land reform policies, with a patchy repeasantization, occurring mostly in outlying districts. The difference in the level of repeasantization in post-socialist countries, as indicated by the agricultural area utilized by smallholders and their economic contribution, is illustrated in Table 35.1.

Three decades after the fall of the Berlin Wall, it is still observable that geography (e.g. topography and the landscape) often has had a more lasting influence on agrarian structures than post-socialist land reforms (cf. Hofman and Visser 2014). Human-made physical infrastructure in the form of farm fields and irrigation works (Kuns 2018; Sikor et al. 2017), rather than land reform policies, seem to have had an equally profound effect on agrarian structures.

For the majority of the post-socialist rural population inhabiting the vast tracts of fertile land in the agrarian heartland of the former Soviet Union (Russia, Ukraine, Kazakhstan) and Central and Eastern Europe (CEE) (Romania's southern plains, Hungary, Czechia), it is difficult to speak of widespread (let alone voluntary) repeasantization. Instead, collective and state farms were privatized, but stayed largely intact as large-scale enterprises (as in most of the former Soviet Union) or were quickly rebuilt through leaseholds (as in various CEE countries). What is more, in most post-socialist countries large-scale farms have grown even bigger, and the corporate farms ('agroholdings') in Russia, Ukraine and Kazakhstan are currently among the largest in the world (Spoor 2012). As a result, rural dwellers have mostly remained farm workers or out-migrated to the cities (or abroad), while many urban dwellers have maintained – and often intensified – food production on their small 'subsidiary' plots (usually located on the outskirts of cities) after the demise of the socialist regime (Kaneff and Leonard 2002; Pallot and Nefedova 2007; Spoor 2012; Visser et al 2015), or after the shift to more market-oriented socialism as in China[5] and Vietnam. In countries where the dissolution of collective farms was enforced by the post-socialist state, such as, for instance, Romania, many villagers were unable to work all the land they were allocated, and 'stopped working four out of five hectares' (Sikor et al. 2017, 200) ending up with an effective size similar to the subsidiary plots of farm workers in countries with less drastic privatization, such as Russia and Ukraine.

SYMBIOSIS AND CO-EXISTENCE

The manifold complexities and contradictions, mentioned above, surrounding small agrarian producers in the region can be traced, in part, to what is usually referred to in the literature as 'symbiotic' relations between communist-era peasants and the industrial farming complex of the collective farms (Allina-Pisano 2008; Kitching 1998; Kuns 2017; Pallot and Nefedova 2007; Visser et al. 2015, 2019a). More specifically, symbiosis refers to a state of mutual dependence, which arose in the late communist period between, on the one hand, farm workers, many of whom spent considerable time working privately on small garden plots to produce food (for their own consumption and for surplus sales), and collective farm management, on the other hand, who in theory were focused on delivering production quotas. According to this arrangement, farm workers received a salary under urban norms, but could avail themselves of collective farm resources for use in their small plots. Such resources could include, among other things, fertilizer, antibiotics for animals or ploughing services from collective farm tractors, and these inputs were obtained in some cases legitimately and openly and in some cases through informal channels in ways that legally speaking could be considered squandering of state/collective resources (and for which the perpetrators were occasionally prosecuted). These resources were one important reason why small garden production in communist countries could be so productive; private plot production was in essence subsidized by the industrial farming complex (Ioffe et al 2006).

Particularly in the Soviet Union, household plot production proved remarkably persistent, among other reasons because collective farm workers would not have had enough food were it not for the produce from their own gardens and because the broader Eastern European public was reliant on the surplus produce from these gardens. Thus collective farms were constituted by two, interwoven food production systems (Small 2007): a large-scale, 'modern' industrial system focusing on bulk production of grains, oilseeds, dairy and meat that required a large and cheap labour reserve to help with labour-intensive seasonal operations, and a small-scale, supposedly 'primitive' system that produced food that in Soviet conditions was less amenable to scaled-up industrial operations, such as fruits and vegetables, but also produced important staples such as dairy, meat and eggs. This small garden production then allowed farm workers to both feed their families and sell surplus on collective farm markets to meet the broader public's demand for food (Ioffe et al 2006; Pallot and Nefedova 2007).

Official attitudes towards widespread garden production on collective farms ranged from hostile to indifferent and there were various, mostly unsuccessful, attempts following World War II to curtail garden production – Wegren and O'Brien (2018) refer to this as 'regime bias'. Only in the 1980s did the Soviet regime express appreciation and seek to increase the possibilities for garden production.

This duality of the 'actually existing' *kolkhoz* is a microcosm of communist rule in general that helps to understand the contradictions of late communist political economy. Thus, the establishment of collective farms was achieved through communist domination of the countryside, a domination backed by extreme violence, particularly in the Soviet grain-belt of Ukraine, southern Russia and Kazakhstan. But the collective farm is also emblematic of the late communist failure to establish basic control over production. Kitching (1998, 63) refers to this late communist state of affairs as a 'balance of power', with peasants deploying various weapons of the weak to affect that balance (see e.g. Mincyte 2009). Peasants were forced to join collective farms, and most did so reluctantly under force of arms, but this did not prevent 'subsequent generations of rural dwellers from cultivating affective ties with the land and farm where they worked and lived' (Allina-Pisano 2009, 194). Collective farms were production units, but they also became 'living spheres' (Wädekin 1971, 160) providing a variety of different welfare services (in addition to farm inputs), and they were regulated by a powerful but ultimately uncodified 'social contract' (Pallot and Nefedova 2007). Collective farm members were workers, drawing a salary, which was 'progress' according to communist ideology, but still dependent on their garden plots for their livelihoods, thus not losing all features of a peasant. This state of affairs occasioned a complex mix of attitudes ranging from recognition of some material progress to disappointment and bitterness that the standard of living had not improved more, particularly in relation to communist promises (Kitching 1998). That being said, if we compare the late communist period to today's situation, 'strong arguments can be made that land grabbing, social and economic exclusion, and rural poverty are worse than the regime bias during the communist period' (Wegren and O'Brien 2018, 6).

These late communist, collective farm dualities[6] can help to account for contemporary attitudes in many rural areas that are somewhat more forgiving and, in some cases, even supportive of today's emerging corporate farms,[7] in contrast with less ambiguous rural fault-lines in other parts of the world. Despite the fact that they were the notional beneficiaries, many former collective farm workers in the post-Soviet grain-belt opposed post-Soviet land reforms because, among other things, these reforms are seen as facilitating land grabbing. However, they did not oppose the idea of being farm workers in large-scale corporate farms, and promises of employment to former collective farm workers have helped agroholdings acquire land in the region. Furthermore, research on the above-discussed symbiosis has been used to speak to international debates on (varieties of) inclusion of smallholders in large-scale farmland investment (Mamonova 2015), particularly with respect to the investors' corporate social responsibility (Visser et al. 2019a) and debates on food sovereignty (see below).

QUIET ALTERNATIVE AGRARIAN PRACTICES

Many of the more well-known studies on Eurasian agrarian relations were framed by debates on the degree of revolutionary potential of the peasantry, and on their appetite (or lack thereof) for mobilization and resistance (see Tauger 2010 for a discussion). While studies on the former died out after the different countries became socialist, some debate on rural resistance – but then against socialism, and more specifically collectivization – was continued by Western researchers. These debates, we contend, have mostly focused on resistance against the socio-economic aspects of socialist industrial farming (loss of autonomy, livelihoods), whereas environmental causes and motivations have received scant treatment.

The theoretical apparatus of concepts around resistance and mobilization (and even to some extent everyday resistance), currently so widely, and often fruitfully, applied to agrarian studies, faces major limitations when applied to the (post)-socialist agrarian context. The limitations are largely due to: (1) the ambivalent status of the smallholders as peasants and, related, their symbiosis with large-scale farms (as discussed above), as well as (2) the historical experience of post-socialist societies reflected in specific forms of political (dis)engagements. Regarding the latter point, the concept of 'anti-politics' (Gille 2010) inherited from the socialist era is relevant. In the socialist era, political critique and resistance often took the form of scepticism of state power and civil organizations (which were mostly tightly controlled by the state) and an ethical stance of distancing oneself from the public sphere with its constant political mobilizations and imposed activism (Gille 2010). The fall of the socialist bloc, and its ideology, further reinforced ideological disillusionment. As a result, even in post-socialist countries that experienced a stable trajectory of democratization and integration in EU structures, a 'model of resistance as unobtrusiveness, nonshowiness, and refusal to enter into overt political debates' (Aistara 2018, 40) has been prevalent.[8]

Whereas research on societal initiatives in post-socialist Eurasia has often featured an exclusively negative interpretation of such anti-politics (Petrova and Tarrow 2007; Telešienė and Balžekienė 2015), recent agrarian studies in the sphere of food provisioning have offered a different reading of these ostensibly non-political behaviours. The widespread self-provisioning of the (post-)socialist population should not be interpreted in narrow economic terms, as just a survival strategy (Alber and Kohler 2008) or even backward practice (Rose and Tikhomirov 1993), as is mostly done in policy and scholarly debates (see Smith and Jehlička 2013 for a critique). Instead, as several observers have claimed, producing food for own subsistence, and selling and/or exchanging through informal food chains or networks – rather than through supply chains dominated by the state (socialism) or corporations (post-socialism) – can be seen as a form of autonomy and political agency (Mincyte 2009). Yet while providing rich descriptive and analytic examples, the literature has faced difficulties with conceptualizing these post-socialist self-provisioning practices in generalizable terms that, first, fundamentally depart from the negative (or even demeaning) views that have haunted the debate on post-socialist smallholders, and, second, build fruitful connections with other – international – debates.

The introduction of the concept 'quiet sustainability' (Smith and Jehlička 2013) substantially contributed to reconfiguring these debates. Based on research on self-provisioning in CEE countries (Czechia and Poland), the concept highlights the remarkable nature of such post-socialist practices, which are not motivated by activism or political engagement. At the same time, however, these small but widespread practices, silently aggregated, have far-reaching, positive implications in terms of sustainability (for instance, short food supply chains, limited or no use of inorganic pesticides, etc.) (Smith and Jehlička 2013), as well as in terms of social and ecological resilience of these practices (Jehlička et al. 2019). Socialist and post-socialist food self-provisioning has also proven to be remarkably resilient, by offering a refuge from the communist regime's political mobilizations, the introduction of market economy and the arrival of 'supermarketization' and consumerism, the 2008 financial crisis, and for CEE countries the EU accession and the adoption of CAP directives. Social resilience and the relevance of these practices is also illustrated by the finding that food self-provisioning remains a socially diverse and remarkably evenly spread practice regardless of class, age, income and educational attainment. It is also practised by both rural and urban dwellers (Smith and Jehlička 2013). While high percentages of rural populations in Poland and Czechia producing food in their households are perhaps to be expected, 21 per cent of Prague dwellers are also involved in these practices. Forty-three per cent of Czech middle-class people and 37 per cent of the working class produce food in their households; in Poland these figures are 55 and 51 per cent (Smith et al. 2015).

Although post-socialist smallholders often occupy a minority (and sometimes even tiny) share of total agricultural land, they manage to produce large volumes of food (see Table 35.1).[9] All across post-socialist Eurasia, their share in production is substantially larger than their share in agricultural land.

Even people who do not grow food themselves are often involved in informal, non-market food-sharing networks as recipients of home-grown food. Forty per cent of Czechs grow some of the food consumed in their households. Home production combined with food received as a gift accounts for 35–40 per cent of their consumption of vegetables, fruits, potatoes and eggs (Jehlička et al. 2019). Importantly, the motivations for these practices are manifold and in some CEE countries can be primarily non-economic – it is an enjoyable hobby practised with the objective of obtaining fresh and healthy food – and financial savings are only a secondary consideration (ibid). Further east in countries like Russia, Belarus and Ukraine, and even more so in the more rural societies of Central Asia like Kyrgyzstan and Tajikistan, economic motivations (reducing costs of food consumption and/or gaining some income from limited sales) are relatively more predominant (Hofman and Visser 2014; Pallot and Nefedova 2007; Veldwisch 2008; Visser et al. 2015).

The concept of 'quiet sustainability' (sustainability by outcome rather than intention) has stimulated further conceptualization of the deeply interlinked political and environmental dimensions of post-socialist agrarian practices. Visser et al. (2015) speak of 'quiet food sovereignty' to denote how practices of quiet sustainability in the former Soviet Russia embody the key notions of food sovereignty without the existence of the organizational structure and outspoken ideologies of a food sovereignty movement. Aistara (2018) innovatively compares organic and/or alternative farmers in post-socialist Latvia and post-colonial Costa Rica and sees quiet sustainability (with a longing for quiet food sovereignty) as a key element of what she calls the local 'organic sovereignties' in Latvia.

While the concept of 'quiet sustainability' and its offshoots emerged from the post-socialist context, its imperative of taking everyday, silent forms of environmentalism seriously, combined with hidden forms of rural autonomy and resilience, arguably has an unrecognized relevance in food debates that often privilege the global and discursive, within a hyper-connected world 'that can't stop talking' (as Susan Cain phrased it in her book *Quiet: The Power of Introverts in a World That Can't Stop Talking*). Quiet sustainability has recently been used to highlight silent resilience through self-provisioning in Greece, during its sharp economic downturn following the global financial crisis and austerity policies enforced by the EU. In Western Europe, the concept has been expanded to capture, for instance, grass-roots community gardening, characterized as a 'quietly radical' form of food justice (Kneafsy et al. 2017, 624) and the 'quiet activism' of seed-sharing initiatives.

The concept of 'quiet food sovereignty' has been taken up beyond the CEE region, especially in research on groups which tend to be somewhat at the margins of the food sovereignty movement, such as youth or urban gardeners in the Global South (Siebert 2019). The concept was applied, for instance, in the study of food self-provisioning in urban South Africa, where food sovereignty was not shouldered by organizations but appeared to be grounded in everyday life, inherent in their local food practices (Siebert 2019).

CONCLUSIONS

Until recently, research conducted on the vast land masses of post-socialist Eurasia has remained largely under the radar within agrarian studies. The region remains virtually invisible in influential global treatments of agrarian issues, such as food regime theory (McMichael, this volume), debates on cheap nature(s) (Moore 2015) and the global meat complex (Weis, this volume). This observation is particularly striking when the rising importance of the region within the global food system is considered.

From a net food importer during the Socialist era, the region's agrarian heartland (Russia, Ukraine, Kazakhstan) rapidly turned into a net exporter of staple crops over the past decade. In 2018, Russia overtook the United States as the world's largest exporter of wheat, the staple that was so central in the earlier United States domination of the global food system. The region is also a 'frontrunner' in farm enlargement, corporatization and financialization of agriculture (Spoor 2012). Only two decades after the fall of socialism, the region accounted for some of the largest corporate farms on Earth (Lander and Kuns 2020; Spoor 2012; Visser et al. 2019a) and half of the world's publicly traded farm companies.

In contrast to the region's headline-making export-oriented mega-farms, it is its almost invisible multitude of smallholders – or 'ambivalent peasants' – who, operating in the shadow of these mega-farms, provide a substantial proportion of the non-grain staples on the household table such as potatoes, fruit and vegetables (Hofman and Visser 2014; Pallot and Nefedova 2007; Veldwisch 2008). Voicing neither major anti-corporate nor environmental claims, these smallholders nevertheless manage to silently provide culturally appropriate food in considerable magnitude. Moreover, food provisioning by post-socialist smallholders is conducted in, for the most part, an environmentally friendly way, compared to corporate farms. The large share of people producing part of their food themselves in post-socialist Eurasia is unmatched in the Global North, and in terms of the urban population involved, even rarely encountered in the Global South.

The actually existing combination of widespread, localized and socially embedded Eurasian food alternatives such as food self-provisioning and sharing, side by side with strongly corporatized market-based food supply chains, invite us to think about the food system's resilience and sustainability in novel ways. Studying interactions and mutual dependencies in everyday lives in post-socialist countries between binaries usually seen in opposition (formal versus informal, mainstream versus alternative, market versus non-market, local versus global) provides a fertile ground for creativity and offers opportunities for rethinking future developments of the food system in uncommon but important ways.

NOTES

1. Only very recently, more sustained efforts in this direction seem to be developing, with special issues or joint articles that aim to distil more general and/or theoretical insights from the post-socialist world and bring them to agrarian studies audiences (see Jehlička et al. 2020; Visser et al. 2019b; Wegren and O'Brien 2018).
2. Wegren (2005) argued against a moral economy amongst rural dwellers in CEE, whereas Chris Hann and the 'Property Relations' Group (2003) – and other authors linked to the Max Planck Institute for Social Anthropology – widely applied a moral economy lens.
3. For discussions on often ambivalent and complex (self)-perceptions see Kaneff and Leonard (2002).
4. Poland is unique in the post-socialist world with the persistence of smallholders in most of the country.
5   *South China Morning Post* (2012), www.scmp.com/business/china-business/article/1018114/urban-farming-growing-trend-china.
6. Now a tripartite agrarian structure has emerged in many parts of post-Soviet Central Asia as household plot production tends to co-exist with substantial private (commercial) farming and with large farm enterprises (Veldwisch 2008).

7. While there is nostalgia in much of the post-Soviet grain-belt for the period of 'high collective farming' (the 1970s and 1980s), the collective farm is also seen as a symbol of oppression in other parts of Eastern Europe (Mincyte 2009).
8. Out-migration, which is especially widespread in South-Eastern Europe and the periphery of the former Soviet Union, e.g. Tajikistan (see Hofman and Visser 2014), can be interpreted as a form of unobtrusiveness or 'exit'.
9. In the Baltic countries, the share of smallholders in food production is smaller (up to 2.5 per cent), yet also here, as in the rest of Eastern Europe, their share in production is substantially larger than their share in agricultural land (Wegren and O'Brien 2018, 875).

FURTHER READING

Jehlička, P.; Balázs, B.; Grīviņš, M.; Visser, O. (2020), Thinking food like an East European: A critical reflection on the framing of food systems, *Journal of Rural Studies*, 76, 286–295.
Kaneff, D.; Leonard, P. (eds) (2002), *The Post-Socialist Peasant? Rural and Urban Constructions of Identity in Eastern Europe, East Africa and the Former Soviet Union*, New York: Palgrave Macmillan.
Kuns, B. (2017), Beyond coping: Smallholder intensification in southern Ukraine, *Sociologia Ruralis*, 57(4), 481–506.
Smith, J.; Jehlička, P. (2013), Quiet sustainability: Fertile lessons from Europe's productive gardeners, *Journal of Rural Studies*, 32, 148–157.
Visser, O.; Mamonova, N.; Spoor, M.; Nikulin, A. (2015), 'Quiet food sovereignty' as food sovereignty without movements? Understanding food sovereignty in post-socialist Russia, *Globalizations*, 12(4), 513–528.

REFERENCES

Aistara, G.A. (2018), *Organic Sovereignties: Struggles over Farming in an Age of Free Trade*, Seattle, WA: University of Washington Press.
Alber, J.; Kohler, U. (2008), Informal food production in the enlarged European Union, *Social Indicators Research*, 89(1), 113–127.
Allina-Pisano, J. (2008), *The Post-Soviet Potemkin Village: Politics and Property Rights in the Black Earth*, Cambridge: Cambridge University Press.
Allina-Pisano, J. (2009), Property: What is it good for?, *Social Research*, 76(1), 175–202.
Cain, S. (2012), *Quiet: The Power of Introverts in a World That Can't Stop Talking*, London: Penguin.
Dorondel, S.; Serban, S. (2014), *At the Margins: The Agrarian Question in South-East Europe*, Bucharest: MARTOR.
Gille, Z. (2010), Is there a global postsocialist condition? *Global Society*, 24(1), 9–30.
Hann, C.; 'Property Relations' Group (2003), *The Post-Socialist Agrarian Question: Property Rights and the Rural Condition*, Münster: LIT Verlag.
Hofman, I.; Visser, O. (2014), Geographies of transition: The political and ecological factors of agrarian change in Tajikistan, IAMO Discussion Paper 151, Halle: Leibniz Institute of Agricultural Development in Transition Economies.
Humphrey, C. (1983), *Karl Marx Collective: Economy, Society and Religion in a Siberian Collective Farm*, Cambridge: Cambridge University Press.
Ioffe, G.V.; Nefedova, T.G.; Zaslavsky, I. (2006), *The End of Peasantry? The Disintegration of Rural Russia*, Pittsburgh, PA: University of Pittsburgh Press.
Jehlička, P.; Daněk, P.; Vávra, J. (2019), Rethinking resilience: Home gardening, food sharing and everyday resistance, *Canadian Journal of Development Studies*, 40(4), 511–527.
Jehlička, P.; Balázs, B.; Grīviņš, M.; Visser, O. (2020), Thinking food like an East European: A critical reflection on the framing of food systems, *Journal of Rural Studies*, 76, 286–295.
Kaneff, D.; Leonard, P. (eds) (2002), *The Post-Socialist Peasant? Rural and Urban Constructions of Identity in Eastern Europe, East Africa and the Former Soviet Union*, New York: Palgrave Macmillan.

Kideckel, M. (1993), *The Solitude of Collectivism: Romanian Villagers to the Revolution and Beyond*, Ithaca, NY: Cornell University Press.

Kitching, G. (1998), The revenge of the peasant? The collapse of Russian agriculture and the role of the peasant 'private plot' in that collapse, 1991–1997, *Journal of Peasant Studies*, 26(1), 43–81.

Kneafsy, M.; Owen, L.; Bos, E.; Broughton, K.; Lennartsson, M. (2017), Capacity building for food justice in England: the contribution of charity-led community food initiatives, *Local Environment*, 22(5), 621–634.

Kuns, B. (2017), Beyond coping: Smallholder intensification in southern Ukraine, *Sociologia Ruralis*, 57(4), 481–506.

Kuns, B. (2018), 'In these complicated times': An environmental history of irrigated agriculture in post-communist Ukraine, *Water Alternatives*, 11(3), accessed 6 December 2018 at www.water-alternatives.org/index.php/alldoc/articles/vol11/v11issue3/468-a11-3-21.

Lander, C.; Kuns, B. (2020), The sinking of the Armada: Problems for the three 'flagship' foreign investment agroholdings in Russia and Ukraine, *Europe-Asia-Studies*, https://doi.org/10.1080/09668136.2020.1842330.

Mamonova, N. (2015), Resistance or adaptation? Ukrainian peasants' responses to large-scale land acquisitions, *Journal of Peasant Studies*, 42(3–4), 491–516.

Mincyte, D. (2009), Everyday environmentalism: The practice, politics, and nature of subsidiary farming in Stalin's Lithuania, *Slavic Review*, 68(1), 31–49.

Moore, J. (2015), *Capitalism in the Web of Life: Ecology and the Accumulation of Capital*, London: Verso Books.

Pallot, J.; Nefedova, T. (2007), *Russia's Unknown Agriculture: Household Production in Post-Socialist Rural Russia*, Oxford: Oxford University Press.

Petrova, T.; Tarrow, S. (2007), Transactional and participatory activism in the emerging European polity: The puzzle of East-Central Europe, *Comparative Political Studies*, 40(1), 74–94.

Rose, R.; Tikhomirov, Y. (1993), Who grows food in Russia and Eastern Europe?, *Post-Soviet Geography*, 34(2), 111–126.

Siebert, A. (2019), Transforming urban food systems in South Africa: Unfolding food sovereignty in the city, *Journal of Peasant Studies*, 47(2), 401–419.

Sikor, T.; Dorondel, S.; Stahl, J.; To, P.X. (2017), *When Things Become Property: Land Reform, Authority, and Value in Postsocialist Europe and Asia*, New York: Berghahn.

Small, L. (2007), East meets West: Utilising Western literature to conceptualise post-Soviet agrarian change, *Journal of Peasant Studies*, 34(1), 29–50.

Smith, J.; Jehlička, P. (2013), Quiet sustainability: Fertile lessons from Europe's productive gardeners, *Journal of Rural Studies*, 32, 148–157.

Smith, J.; Kostelecký, T.; Jehlička, P. (2015), Quietly does it: Questioning assumptions about class, consumption and sustainability, *Geoforum*, 67, 223–232.

Spoor, M. (2012), Agrarian reform and transition: what can we learn from 'the east'? *Journal of Peasant Studies*, 39(1), 175–194.

Tauger, M. (2010), Soviet peasants and collectivisation, 1930–39: Resistance and adaptation, *Journal of Peasant Studies*, 31(3–4), 427–426.

Telešienė, A.; Balžekienė, A. (2015), The influence of biographical situational factors upon environmental activist behaviour: Empirical evidence from CEE countries, *Sociální Studia*, 12(3), 159–178.

Veldwisch, G.J.A. (2008), *Cotton, Rice and Water: The Transformation of Agrarian Relations, Irrigation Technology and Water Distribution in Khorezm, Uzbekistan*, PhD Dissertation, Rheinische Friedrich-Wilhelm's University of Bonn.

Visser, O.; Mamonova, N.; Spoor, M.; Nikulin, A. (2015), 'Quiet food sovereignty' as food sovereignty without movements? Understanding food sovereignty in post-socialist Russia, *Globalizations*, 12(4), 513–528.

Visser, O.; Kurakin, A.; Nikulin, A. (2019a), Corporate social responsibility, co-existence and contention: Large farms' changing responsibility towards rural households in post-Soviet Russia, *Canadian Journal of Development Studies*, 40(4), 580–599.

Visser, O.; Dorondel, S.; Jehlička, P.; Spoor, M. (2019b), Post-socialist smallholders: Silence, resistance and alternatives, *Canadian Journal of Development Studies*, 40(4), 499–510.

Wädekin, K.-E. (1971), The nonagricultural rural sector, in Millar, J.R. (ed.), *The Soviet Rural Community*, Urbana, IL: University of Illinois Press, 159–179.

Wegren, S.K. (2005), *The Moral Economy Reconsidered: Russia's Search for Agrarian Capitalism*, New York: Palgrave Macmillan.

Wegren, S.K.; O'Brien, D.J. (2018), Introduction to a symposium: Smallholders in communist and postcommunist societies, *Journal of Agrarian Change*, 32, 148–157.

36. BRICS and global agrarian transformations

Gustavo de L.T. Oliveira and Ben M. McKay

INTRODUCTION

There is no doubt that Euro-American imperialism and colonialism were powerful forces shaping agrarian dynamics worldwide in the past few centuries. Imperial and colonial metropoles placed themselves at the center of a global regime of capitalist agrarian accumulation, dispossessing indigenous peoples of their land and resources, enslaving some and subjecting others to adverse incorporation into export-oriented production of cash crops, expelling landless peasants to settler colonies and establishing uneven terms of trade between (post-)colonies and metropoles in increasingly complex global markets. After World Wars I and II, the United States (US) and the Soviet Union emerged as competing leaders of a seemingly bipolar world order. Both Cold War hegemons promoted 'agricultural modernization' worldwide, interlinking development assistance, technological transfer and geopolitical realignment in these efforts. With the collapse of the Soviet Union, the US and its model of neoliberal globalization appeared to become hegemonic worldwide, simplifying even further the terms of agrarian studies to a technocratic discussion of neoliberal rural development towards a US-modeled idea of modernity.

After almost two decades of supposed hegemony, US-led neoliberal globalization failed to end food insecurity, rural poverty and economic instability, and came to a head with the global financial and food price crisis of 2007–2008. Meanwhile, new agroindustrial powerhouses were emerging in Brazil and China with strong state support, while India led resistance to further neoliberalization of global agriculture markets at the World Trade Organization, and a resurgent Russia began to challenge the geopolitical dominance of the US. In 2009, the presidents of these countries came together to formally establish the BRIC group, soon joined by South Africa in 2010, and declared the need 'for a more democratic and just multipolar world order'. Global agribusinesses, agroindustrial technologies, rural development practices and global food markets could no longer be understood or defined simply from the perspective of the US and Europe alone, nor simply reduced to a North–South dynamic of post-colonial relations. The rise of emerging economies is changing the fundamental dynamics of global agrarian transformations (Cousins et al. 2018). Thus, the purpose of our chapter is to examine how the field of critical agrarian studies is now fully engaged in the effort to grasp the transformations occurring within these countries, and through new transnational relations they establish among themselves and with other regions of the world. Furthermore, the field must itself transform with the incorporation of scholars from these countries, and their own endogenous theories, concepts, epistemologies, methodologies and debates. One such effort to do just this is the Brazil, Russia, India, China and South Africa (BRICS) Initiative for Critical Agrarian Studies (BICAS) which is a collective of largely BRICS-based or connected academic researchers and scholar-activists concerned with understanding the BRICS countries and their implications for global agrarian transformations. Specifically, BICAS sets out to produce cutting-edge research around four key themes: (1) agrarian transformations in the

BRICS countries, (2) agrarian transformations in the BRICS regions, (3) new dynamics in the agrofood system and (4) BRICS and middle-income countries in relation to the old hubs of global capital (McKay et al. 2016b). BICAS has held numerous international conferences in the BRICS countries, produces a Working Paper Series and has released several Special Issues in peer-reviewed academic journals.[1]

The chapter is structured as follows: the next section discusses some of the new dynamics of agrarian change in relation to the rise of BRICS. The third section provides an overview of three broad competing perspectives regarding the implications of the rise of BRICS for global agrarian transformations. The fourth and final section concludes and points to the importance of understanding the rise of BRICS for global agrarian transformations, not just in terms of the new elites, but also the scholars and activists pushing for new alternatives.

THE RISE OF BRICS: NEW DYNAMICS OF AGRARIAN CHANGE

'BRICS' as a concept first emerged during the 2000s in discussions of Brazil, Russia, India and China as 'emergent economies' that were projected to become increasingly important targets for investment and drivers of global economic growth. After its institutionalization, the explicit purpose of the bloc was to reform global financial institutions, establish a global reserve currency (as alternative to the US dollar) and better coordinate development among emerging economies, having the global financial crisis (centered in the US and western Europe) as a backdrop (Cooper 2016).

Beyond their creation of the New Development Bank, which has already taken a backseat to the China-led establishment of the much larger Asian Infrastructure Investment Bank, there is little evidence of significant achievements of those goals. This is generally credited to the imbalances within the group, with China far outpacing all the others in all economic categories, Russia holding disproportionate geopolitical influence with its nuclear arsenal, Brazil sliding from a moment of strong economic growth to its deepest recession in modern history, India turning inwards with a strong nationalist movement and South Africa becoming entangled in domestic crises (Cooper 2016).

Consequently, most debates have turned on whether the category of BRICS is meaningful at all, given drastic differences in the sizes, character and prospects of their economies, insufficient ability to (or even interest in) coordinating structural transformations to multilateral governance institutions and lack of cohesion in major geopolitical and geoeconomic contentions. Debates have focused on whether, how and to what extent the BRICS (either as a bloc or more generically as key actors among a broader set of emerging economies) may drive a 'global convergence' between the Global North and the Global South, cultivate a 'new development paradigm' and construct a 'new multipolar world order' (Bond and Garcia 2015; Gray and Gills 2016).

Within the field of critical agrarian studies, these debates have taken place in parallel with a high-profile discussion of renewed interests in farmland and agribusiness investments worldwide. Often called a 'global land grab' (Borras et al. 2011), this process has unfolded as investors sought safer havens for financial capital than the crisis-torn financial centers of the Global North, high returns from commodity speculation and valuable assets for the long term. All of this is underpinned by the conviction that a growing global population, rising incomes and declining environmental conditions for food production will ensure rising prices and profits for agribusinesses, as well as the strategic importance of the sector for state actors. Unlike previous eras, however, the post-2008 moment was marked by the prominent partici-pation of state and agribusiness investors from the BRICS alongside the usual actors from the Global North (Margulis and Porter 2013).

Attempted, perceived or even imagined 'land grabs' by Chinese investors have been particu-larly prominent in discussions of this phenomenon, even while several scholars demonstrated that Chinese and other 'emerging' investors remain dwarfed by US, European and Japanese investors in transnational land and agribusiness deals worldwide (Yan and Sautman 2010; Hofman and Ho 2012; Oliveira 2018). Nonetheless, the role of Brazilian, Indian and Chinese state and private endeavors in African agriculture became a central concern to critical agrarian studies, as well as cross-border deals by these and other emerging economies in their regions, such as Thai companies expanding their influence across Southeast Asia, and Argentinian agribusinesses operating across Latin America (see Craviotti 2016; Oliveira and Hecht 2016; Scoones et al. 2016; Schoenberger et al. 2017).

Accusations of land grabs as neo-colonial incursions are balanced in the literature not only with demonstrations that actors from the Global North remain far more prominent in such endeavors, but also with arguments that the BRICS and other emerging economies are in fact developing new forms of 'South–South cooperation' that may transfer agroindustrial technol-ogies and successful agrarian development paradigms to less developed countries around the world (Li et al. 2013).

Debates about the rise of emerging economies encompass various forms of rural develop-ment assistance, policy and technology transfer and new terms for investment and trade across 'South–South' relations. Going beyond simplistic narratives of either mutually beneficial emerging partnerships or a new imperialism, scholars have pointed to the politics of resource control which underpins and remains the driving force behind both the Washington and Beijing Consensus, led by new and old classes of political and economic elites (see McKay et al. 2016a). Critical agrarian studies tend to question the highly optimistic and technocratic nar-ratives that Brazilian public and private actors may transplant the 'success story' of soy, maize, cotton and sugarcane agribusiness expansion over the Brazilian cerrado to the savannahs of Africa, the highlands of Colombia or the plains of Southeast Asia (Monjane 2015; Wolford and Nehring 2015), including its world-leading biofuel programs (McKay et al. 2016c; Oliveira et al. 2017). Instead, critical agrarian scholars highlight the dramatic socio-ecological damages and opportunity costs of this agroindustrial development paradigm that consolidated Brazil's historically imbalanced land concentration in the hands of a minute class of large-scale land-owners, financiers and agribusiness corporations (Oliveira 2016). Moreover, many point to India to show how both neoliberal capitalism and modern state-making alike plunge emerging countries into agrarian crises, even despite government efforts to sustain public procurement and price assistance for (larger-scale) farmers (Lerche 2013), ultimately sacrificing its peas-antry to ethnic and caste conflict (Ramakumar 2017) and landlessness in order to advance urban and industrial development (Vijayabaskar and Menon 2018).

Similarly, critical agrarian studies have emphasized the negative aspects of China's rapid industrial and urban development, particularly the challenges of sustaining labor-intensive agroecological production (Wen 2007), the plight of 'left-behind' elders, women and children in 'hollow villages' (Ye et al. 2013; Zhang 2020), growing social inequality and elite capture of cooperatives (Yan and Chen 2013; Zhang 2015) and the dramatic food safety crisis the country is now facing (Zhang and Qi 2019). And even when challenging simplistic narratives about the 'neo-imperialism' or 'neo-colonialism' of Chinese foreign investments in farmland and agribusiness, they also question optimistic views that China's agricultural demonstration centers in Africa and contract-farming schemes across Southeast Asia may produce positive socio-ecological results (Yan and Sautman 2010; Lu 2017).

In addition, South Africa's apparent achievements in modernizing agri-food distribution through supermarket chains and capital-intensive investments in agricultural production are frequently promoted as a model and mechanism for similar developments across southern Africa (Campbell 2016; Hall and Cousins 2018). Yet the reemergence of intense land conflicts in South Africa belies any sanguine technocratic narratives in that direction. Critical scholars debate in turn how radical land redistribution and agrarian reform may unfold in South Africa, avoiding elite capture on the one hand, as well as the breakdown of agricultural production if smallholders are not provided with effective means to succeed on redistributed land on the other hand (Cousins 2017).

Debates about the rise of these emerging economies extend from examination of their domestic agrarian transformations, transnational investments and development cooperation efforts to their role in reshaping geopolitics and global agroindustrial markets. Illustrative cases include the denouement of sanctions and counter-sanctions imposed on and by Russia in the aftermath of its annexation of Crimea in 2014. The European Union, US and some allied countries imposed sanctions and restricted imports from Russia, which in turn restricted its own purchases of agri-food products from those countries. While in previous decades Russia would have been isolated to markets in its immediate periphery (that is the former Soviet Union), which would not be able to satisfy the volume and diversity of agri-food products restricted, now a wide array of countries across Asia, Africa and Latin America quickly seized the opportunity to replace US and European exports. Brazilian grains, Chilean fruits and nuts, Argentinian cheeses, Nigerian vegetables, Tanzanian flowers, Vietnamese seafood and Chinese processed foods fulfilled Russian demand and essentially turned the economic pressure from Russia back on Europe and the US (Wegren and Elvestad 2018). Not only does Crimea remain under Russia's control, but the latter became emboldened to reassert its geopolitical influence even further.

Another notable example regards the US–China trade war. Ostensibly focused on the trade imbalance that favors China, China responded to US tariffs on Chinese imports with its own tariffs on US exports. Before 2000, it was unimaginable that China – a net soybean exporter – would become the largest market for US soybeans. And hand in hand with that massive transformation in global demand there, has also been a fundamental transformation to global soybean supplies, as Brazil quickly matched and now surpassed the US as the world's leading exporter (Oliveira and Schneider 2016). Consequently, when Trump initiated tariffs in March 2018, US soy exports had already been largely depleted but global markets were flush with a bumper crop from Brazil. Brazilian soy exports were further redirected from Europe, Japan and other markets to attend Chinese demand well into 2019, when the new US soy harvest was seeking markets but finding insufficient buyers to substitute China's demand, which amounts to about two-thirds of global trade. As Brazilian agribusinesses and soy farmers rake in windfall profits, China stood its ground in the trade war and US soybean prices collapsed, forcing the Trump administration to scrounge for 12 billion dollars in subsidies to protect its soy farmers from bankruptcy. Meanwhile, China's leading agribusiness companies consolidate their mergers and acquisitions of some of the world's leading trading, agrochemical, seed and biotechnology companies, placing COFCO and ChemChina shoulder to shoulder with the likes of Cargill, Bunge, Monsanto-Bayer and Dow-Dupont. In places like Bolivia, these Chinese agribusinesses already control more market share of agroindustrial inputs and trading than their US and European counterparts (McKay 2018).

COMPETING PERSPECTIVES IN CRITICAL AGRARIAN STUDIES

The debates in critical agrarian studies about the rise of emerging economies and its consequences for global agrarian transformations can be roughly synthesized into three camps. First, there are those who celebrate the rise of post-colonial economies as a counter-balance to the hegemony of European, US and other industrialized and imperialist nations (Moyo et al. 2013; West 2014). In their view, the fact that Brazil emerged as a global agroindustrial leader, Russia regained its power to confront US and western European geopolitical ambitions, India was able to coordinate a halt to agricultural neoliberalization in the World Trade Organization, poverty reduced most dramatically in China, and South Africa can represent an independent model for development of the continent, are all positive aspects that should be further advanced. Second, there are others who argue all these developments amount simply to the reproduction of neo-colonial dynamics between these emerging powers and an impoverished and underdeveloped global periphery (Langan 2018; Reeves 2018). Brazilian land grabs in Paraguay and Bolivia, Chinese efforts to steer infrastructure developments around the world to satisfy its natural resource demands, India's pressure on neighboring countries to resist China's infrastructure construction priorities and Russia's opportunistic defense or sacrifice of geopolitical partners worldwide are often invoked to sustain such skeptical views. Both views have merit and can draw upon significant empirical evidence to sustain their arguments.

Nonetheless, we argue a third approach to these debates holds a far stronger position and provides the most fruitful implications for critical agrarian studies. That is the view that we should not examine the rise of the BRICS and middle-income countries primarily in geopolitical and macroeconomic terms, naturalizing nation-states as actors with precedence over the multiple class and other socio-environmental struggles that take place within these countries, and amidst their global interactions. This means that the so-called 'rise of the BRICS' is nothing to be celebrated in its own right, if it ultimately amounts merely to the inclusion of new elites from the Global South into an unjust and unsustainable system of global capitalist exploitation. On the other hand, it is important to recognize that this shifting global political economy does create new opportunities for class struggle all around the world, and the global challenge to the US-led neoliberal development paradigm results in fractures within a hegemonic project that may be exploited by rural social movements for food sovereignty, agroecological sustainability and anti-capitalist mobilization.

According to this third point of view, it is not only Brazilian-based multinational agribusiness corporations that are reshaping global agrarian transformations, but also the Brazilian Landless Rural Workers' Movement through its collaborations with rural movements worldwide for the establishment of La Via Campesina as a peasant international for the advancement of food sovereignty. What matters is not simply that Russia can confront US geopolitical hegemony, but that discourses of food sovereignty and agroecology make gains within Russia despite the post-socialist absence of organized mass social movements (Visser et al. 2015). Similarly, India's power at the World Trade Organization should not be attributed simply to the acumen and authority of its national leadership, but fundamentally to the power of its peasant social movements and even the intractability of its Maoist insurrection (Ramakumar 2017). On the other hand, China's spectacular urbanization and industrialization are not to be celebrated uncritically, without acknowledging their foundation in socialist redistribution and collective social infrastructures, condemning the socio-ecological contradictions of capitalist restoration and recognizing the rise of 'quiet' social movements for agroecology, feminism and food sovereignty (Zhang 2020). Finally, if South Africa is to be described as a model for the rest of its continent, it is not because of its capitalist agribusinesses but rather because of the militancy of its youth who put the demand for land expropriation without compensation on the national agenda once again (Cousins 2017; Hall and Cousins 2018).

CONCLUSION

Understanding the rise of emerging economies like the BRICS is central to our analyses of contemporary global agrarian transformations. Yet it is not simply their associated geopolitical transformations that call attention from and provide new insights for critical agrarian studies. The point is not to debate whether new agribusiness companies and development models from the BRICS are a success of resistance to the Global North, or a new sub-imperialist project against middle-income and the least developed countries. Instead, these global agrarian transformations must be rooted in the conflicts and contradictions within emerging economies themselves, as subaltern actors struggle for food sovereignty and agroecology in a protracted struggle against neoliberal elites, populist authoritarianism and conservative nationalist movements. Our goal here is not to fully describe and analyze these struggles and their repercussions for global agrarian change, but rather to emphasize that such conflicts and heterogeneities are the most fruitful springboard for new insights in critical agrarian studies. Debates that focus upon 'global convergence', 'multipolarity' and 'new development paradigms' but understate grounded socio-ecological struggles and transformations (cf. West 2014; Reeves 2018) are misguided and misplaced in the social sciences in general, and critical agrarian studies in particular. As climate change advances further and the socio-ecological foundations of human life become increasingly more unstable and vulnerable, new theories, methodologies and debates are required. The dramatic transformation of the global political economy of food and farming due to the rise of the BRICS is fertile ground for the cultivation of such new ways of thinking, and critical agrarian scholars from these regions are stepping up to the task at hand, inviting colleagues who remain snagged in the provincial terms of bygone scholarship rooted in fallen and decaying empires.

NOTE

1. See McKay et al. (2016b); Cousins et al. (2018); Oliveira et al. (2021); McKay et al. (2020). More information can be found at www.iss.nl/bicas.

FURTHER READING

Cousins, B.; Borras, Jr., S.M.; Sauer, S.; Ye, J. (eds) (2018), BRICS and MICS: Implications for global agrarian transformation, Special Issue, *Globalizations*, 15(1).

Gray, K.; Gills, B.K. (eds) (2016), Rising powers and south-south cooperation, Special Issue, *Third World Quarterly*, 37(4).

McKay, B.M.; Hall, R.; Liu, J. (eds) (2016), BRICS and global agrarian change, Special Issue, *Third World Thematics: A TWQ Journal*, 1(5).

Oliveira, G. de L.T.; McKay, B.M.; Liu, J. (eds) (2021), New insights on land grabs in the BRICS and Global South, Special Issue, *Globalizations*, 18(3).

Scoones, I.; Kojo, A.; Arilson, F.; Qi, G. (eds) (2016), China and Brazil in African agriculture, Special Section, *World Development*, 81.

REFERENCES

Bond, P.; Garcia, A. (2015), *BRICS: An Anti-capitalist Critique*, London: Pluto Press.

Borras, Jr., S.M.; Hall, R.; Scoones, I.; White, B.; Wolford, W. (2011), Towards a better understanding of global land grabbing: An editorial introduction, *Journal of Peasant Studies*, 38(2), 209–216.

Campbell, M. (2016), South African supermarket expansion in sub-Saharan Africa, *Third World Thematics: A TWQ Journal*, 5(1), 709–725.

Cooper, A. (2016), *The BRICS: A Very short Introduction*, Oxford: Oxford University Press.

Cousins, B. (2017), Land reform in South Africa is failing: Can it be saved?, *Transformation*, 92, 135–157.

Cousins, B.; Borras, Jr., S.M.; Sauer, S.; Ye, J. (2018), BRICS, Middle-income countries (MICs) and global agrarian transformations: Internal dynamics, regional trends and international implications, *Globalizations*, 15(1), 1–11.

Craviotti, C. (2016), Which territorial embeddedness? Territorial relationships of recently internationalized firms of the soybean chain, *Journal of Peasant Studies*, 43(2), 331–347.

Gray, K.; Gills, B.K. (2016), South–South cooperation and the rise of the Global South, *Third World Quarterly*, 37(4), 557–574.

Hall, R.; Cousins, B. (2018), Exporting contradictions: The expansion of South African agrarian capital within Africa, *Globalizations*, 15(1), 12–31.

Hofman, I.; Ho, P. (2012), China's 'developmental outsourcing': A critical examination of Chinese global 'land grabs' discourse, *Journal of Peasant Studies*, 39(1), 1–48.

Langan, M. (2018), Emerging powers and neo-colonialism in Africa, in *Neo-Colonialism and the Poverty of 'Development' in Africa*, London: Springer, 89–117.

Lerche, J. (2013), The agrarian question in neoliberal India: Agrarian transition bypassed?, *Journal of Agrarian Change*, 13(3), 382–404.

Li, X.; Tang, L.; Xu, X.; Qi, G.; Wang, H. (2013), What can Africa learn from China's experience in agricultural development?, *IDS Bulletin*, 44(4), 31–41.

Lu, J. (2017), Tapping into rubber: China's opium replacement program and rubber production in Laos, *Journal of Peasant Studies*, 44(4), 726–747.

Margulis, M.; Porter, T. (2013), Governing the global land grab: Multipolarity, ideas, and complexity in transnational governance, *Globalizations*, 10(1), 65–86.

McKay, B.M. (2018), Control grabbing and value-chain agriculture: BRICS, MICs and Bolivia's soy complex, *Globalizations*, 15(1), 74–91.

McKay, B.M.; Alonso-Fradejas, A.; Brent, Z.W.; Sauer, S.; Xu, Y. (2016a), China and Latin America: Towards a new consensus of resource control?, *Third World Thematics: A TWQ Journal*, 1(5), 592–611.

McKay, B.M.; Hall, R.; Liu, J. (2016b), The rise of BRICS: Implications for global agrarian transformation, *Third World Thematics: A TWQ Journal*, 1(5), 581–591.

McKay, B.M.; Sauer, S.; Richardson, B.; Herre, R. (2016c), The political economy of sugarcane flexing: Initial insights from Brazil, Southern Africa and Cambodia, *Journal of Peasant Studies*, 43(1), 195–223.

McKay, B.M.; Liu, J.; Oliveira, G. de L.T. (2020), Authoritarianism, populism, nationalism and resistance in the agrarian South, *Canadian Journal of Development Studies/Revue Canadienne D'études du Développement*, 41(3), 347–362.

Monjane, B. (2015), Resistance to an erroneous 'development' model: A critique of ProSAVANA in Mozambique, *Pambazuka News*, September 3, 740.

Moyo, S.; Yeros, P.; Jha, P. (2013), The classical agrarian question: Myth, reality and relevance today, *Agrarian South: Journal of Political Economy*, 2(1), 93–119.

Oliveira, G. de L.T. (2016), The geopolitics of Brazilian soybeans, *Journal of Peasant Studies*, 43(2), 348–372.

Oliveira, G. de L.T. (2018), Chinese land grabs in Brazil? Sinophobia and foreign investments in Brazilian soybean agribusiness, *Globalizations*, 15(1), 114–133.

Oliveira, G. de L.T.; Hecht, S. (2016), Sacred groves, sacrifice zones and soy production: Globalization, intensification and neo-nature in South America, *Journal of Peasant Studies*, 43(2), 251–285.

Oliveira, G. de L.T.; Schneider, M. (2016), The politics of flexing soybeans: China, Brazil and global agroindustrial restructuring, *Journal of Peasant Studies*, 43(1), 167–194.

Oliveira, G. de L.T.; McKay, B.M.; Plank, C. (2017), How biofuel policies backfire: Misguided goals, inefficient mechanisms, and political-ecological blind spots, *Energy Policy*, 108, 765–775.

Oliveira, G. de L.T.; McKay, B.M.; Liu, J. (2021), Beyond land grabs: New insights on land struggles and global agrarian change, *Globalizations*, 18(3), 321–338.

Ramakumar, R. (2017), Jats, khaps and riots: Communal politics and the Bharatiya Kisan Union in northern India, *Journal of Agrarian Change*, 17(1), 22–42.

Reeves, J. (2018), Imperialism and the middle kingdom: The Xi Jinping administration's peripheral diplomacy with developing states, *Third World Quarterly*, 39(5), 976–998.

Schoenberger, L.; Hall, D.; Vandergeest, P. (2017), What happened when the land grab came to Southeast Asia?, *Journal of Peasant Studies*, 44(4), 697–725.

Scoones, I.; Kojo, A.; Arilson, F.; Qi, G. (2016), A new politics of development cooperation? Chinese and Brazilian engagements in African agriculture, *World Development*, 81, 1–12.

Vijayabaskar, M.; Menon, A. (2018), Dispossession by neglect: Agricultural land sales in southern India, *Journal of Agrarian Change*, 18(3), 571–587.

Visser, O.; Mamonova, N.; Spoor, M.; Nikulin, A. (2015), 'Quiet food sovereignty' as food sovereignty without a movement? Insights from post-socialist Russia, *Globalizations*, 12(4), 513–528.

Wegren, S.; Elvestad, C. (2018), Russia's food self-sufficiency and food security: An assessment, *Post-Communist Economies*, 30(5), 565–587.

Wen, T. (2007), Deconstructing modernization, *Chinese Sociology and Anthropology*, 39(4), 10–25.

West, M. (2014), China, Africa and the Bandung idea, then and now, *Agrarian South: Journal of Political Economy*, 3(1), 111–123.

Wolford, W.; Nehring, R. (2015), Constructing parallels: Brazilian expertise and the commodification of land, labour and money in Mozambique, *Canadian Journal of Development Studies/Revue Canadienne D'études du Développement*, 36(2), 208–223.

Yan, H.; Chen, Y. (2013), Debating the rural cooperative movement in China, the past and the present, *Journal of Peasant Studies*, 40(6), 955–981.

Yan, H.; Sautman, B. (2010), Chinese farms in Zambia: from socialist to 'agro-imperialist' engagement?, *African and Asian Studies*, 9(3), 307–333.

Ye, J.; Wang, C.; Wu, H.; He, C.; Liu, J. (2013), Internal migration and left-behind population in China, *Journal of Peasant Studies*, 40(6), 1119–1146.

Zhang, L. (2020), From left behind to leader: Gender, agency, and food sovereignty in China, *Agriculture and Human Values*, 31, 1111–1123.

Zhang, L.; Qi, G. (2019), Bottom-up self-protection responses to China's food safety crisis, *Canadian Journal of Development Studies*, 40(1), 113–130.

Zhang, Q.F. (2015), Class differentiation in rural China: Dynamics of accumulation, commodification and state intervention, *Journal of Agrarian Change*, 15(3), 338–365.

37. Neoliberalism and the crisis in India's countryside

Prabhat Patnaik

There is a pervasive impression that neoliberalism means "leaving things to the market", and that this entails a retreat of the State from its earlier role of intervening in the economy. This is erroneous. Neoliberalism entails not a cessation of State intervention, but a change in the nature of State intervention compared to the previous *dirigiste regime*. This change consists in the fact that the State now directly promotes the interests of a domestic corporate-financial oligarchy that is integrated with international capital, ostensibly for bringing about "development", while withdrawing from its earlier role of supporting the traditional petty production sector, including peasant agriculture. Such withdrawal allows this oligarchy, and international capital, to encroach upon the latter. This encroachment upon peasant agriculture by big capital, leading to a squeeze on the assets and incomes of peasants and agricultural labourers, is a general phenomenon across the third world under the neoliberal regime, and therefore provides a central frame of reference for any empirical investigation within critical agrarian studies; the Indian case is of interest because it illustrates this phenomenon most vividly.

DIRIGISME AND NEOLIBERALISM VIS-À-VIS INDIAN AGRICULTURE

The post-colonial *dirigiste regime*'s support for peasant agriculture in India, from which there is now a retreat, had itself been a legacy of the anti-colonial struggle. India's anti-colonial struggle had really taken off in the 1930s when the peasantry, suffering from the impact of the Great Depression, had joined it in large numbers. The anti-colonial struggle on its part had held out the promise that when the country became independent of colonial rule, the peasantry would never again face a situation like it had in the 1930s. The post-colonial *regime* had to redeem that promise.

Accordingly, it adopted a number of measures to protect and promote peasant agriculture (Patnaik 2003; Ghosh 2011). It imposed tariffs and quantitative trade restrictions to insulate the peasantry from world price fluctuations; it subsidized inputs, including credit after bank nationalization in 1966, when norms with regard to the minimum ratio of agricultural to total credit by banks and the differential interest rates they were to charge upon it, were imposed; a system of procurement prices for food crops, which were supposed to be remunerative and at which the government actually procured these crops, came into being; various commodity boards were set up (such as the Tea Board, the Coffee Board and the Coir Board), which had a marketing function and intervened to prevent price crashes in a range of cash crops; research and development on seed varieties and agricultural practices was carried out in government institutions and their results disseminated through a massive extension programme that the government set up; investment in irrigation and rural infrastructure, long neglected under colonial rule, was hugely stepped up; and so on.

To be sure not all peasants were equal beneficiaries of these measures; the better-off segments of the peasantry, and the landlords who had been goaded into capitalist farming by the land reform legislation that took away non-*khudkasht* (non-own-cultivated) land from the erstwhile non-cultivating landlords, reaped the lion's share of these benefits. Capitalism in agriculture, an admixture of both peasant and landlord capitalism, got no doubt a fillip through these government measures, but their benefits were certainly not confined only to the capitalist or proto-capitalist segments.

Two implications of these measures must be noted. First, even while they promoted capitalism in agriculture, they kept the *corporate capitalist world* from encroaching upon agriculture. The capitalism that developed in agriculture under the *dirigiste regime* in other words was from *within the sector*, not through any encroachment of the capitalist sector existing outside of it upon agriculture. In fact, the agricultural sector was kept out of bounds both for the domestic private corporate sector and for international agribusiness, with the State interposing itself between this sector and these outside actors.

There was no doubt primitive accumulation of capital, as tenants and sharecroppers were evicted and converted into agricultural labourers by the emerging "junker" capitalists, but it occurred within a context where there was no unambiguous tendency for a reduction in labour demand arising from agriculture. It was certainly not primitive accumulation in the more usual sense, of the corporate capitalist sector, whether domestic or foreign, squeezing peasant agriculture and dispossessing peasants, as was to happen later, within the context of an unambiguous tendency toward a reduction in labour demand arising from agriculture.

The second implication was a substantial increase in per capita agricultural, and especially food grain, output. The significance of this should be judged in the context of the sharp decline that had occurred in the last half-century of colonial rule in the per capita output and availability of food grains.[1] The annual average net per capita output of food grains for "British India" for the quinquennium 1897–1902 had been 201.1 kg. It fell to 146.7 kg for the quinquennium 1939–1944. In fact, in 1945–1946, it was as low as 134.8 kg. The *dirigiste regime* however reversed this declining trend. By the end of the *dirigiste* period, when liberalization was introduced in India in 1991, the annual average net per capita food grain output for the Indian Union had increased to 178.77 kg for the triennium ending 1991–1992. It was still lower than the figure for "British India" at the beginning of the century, but considerably higher than at independence.

These output trends were matched by similar trends in availability. The average annual per capita food grain availability for "British India" was 199.9 kg at the beginning of the century, 148.5 kg for 1939–1944 and 136.8 kg for 1945–1946. For the triennium ending 1991–1992, the figure for the Indian Union had increased to 177 kg.

Since the scope for any further increase in net sown area was exhausted by the mid-1950s, the increase in per capita output over the *dirigiste* period came about largely through "land augmentation"; that is, through increases in cropping intensity and in yields per unit of gross sown area, which is what the high-yielding varieties of seeds caused during the so-called "Green Revolution". While labour-displacing mechanization in agriculture, on capitalist farms in particular, occurred aplenty, the increase in output through land augmentation had a *ceteris paribus* positive effect on employment, which is why the primitive accumulation that occurred within this sector, associated with the growth of *kulak*-cum-landlord capitalism internal to it, was not necessarily accompanied by shrinking employment opportunities.

With neoliberalism, however, this support by the State to peasant agriculture, and petty production in general, was withdrawn, as part of the immanent logic of such a regime (Patnaik 2003; Ghosh 2011). The need for "fiscal responsibility" by controlling the fiscal deficit, and that too in a situation where taxing capitalists must be eschewed since they have to be enticed to undertake investment for ushering in "development", resulted in a reduction in input subsidies for agriculture. The growing private presence in the banking sector, and the pressure on public-sector banks to become more "commercially-oriented", led to an open flouting of "priority-sector" lending norms, which was covered up by the government by conveniently widening the definition of the "priority sector". A reduction occurred accordingly in institutional credit to agriculture, which pushed peasants into borrowing at exorbitant rates from a new class of private moneylenders that came into being. Quantitative trade restrictions were eliminated and tariffs reduced, so that domestic prices were aligned to world prices, especially for cash crops where the commodity boards were made to shed their marketing function. For food grains, while the earlier system of procurement and public distribution continued, a question mark arose over it because of the pressure to dismantle it under the Doha round of World Trade Organization negotiations. The privatization of essential services like education and health, which raised their prices inordinately, increased the cost of living of the agricultural producers, and, since they were not compensated for such increases through higher procurement prices (as these did not count as cost-of-living increases), their real income shrank. The funding crunch affected research and development in public institutions, and the public extension network was wound up. Global agribusiness entered the agricultural sector as a supplier of seeds, pesticides and credit, while multinational companies, alongside domestic corporations, entered as buyers of agricultural produce. Public investment in irrigation and in capital formation in general, including in rural infrastructure, dwindled greatly.

The net result of these developments ushered in by neoliberalism is: a decline in the real profitability of agriculture (profits deflated by cost of living); a growing mass indebtedness of the peasants, arising both because of this decline in profitability and because of sharp price drops occasionally being visited upon them, as well as medical emergencies; and a slowing down in the growth rate of agriculture, involving especially a complete stagnation in per capita food grain production.

The agricultural capitalists, including in particular the landlord-capitalists, have coped with this strain experienced by the sector as a whole by diversifying their activities into other areas, such as building contracts and the provision of local services; but the peasants, and of course the agricultural labourers, who are confined to this sector, have borne the brunt of this strain, which is why more than 300 000 of them have committed suicide over the last two decades, a phenomenon totally unprecedented in post-independence India.[2]

The stagnation in per capita food grain production in the neoliberal period provides a sharp contrast to the increase that had been witnessed during the *dirigiste* period. If we simply take the annual average gross food grain output for triennia 1989–1992, 1999–2002 and 2014–2017, and divide it by the population of the middle year in each case (at the end of that particular year), we get per capita figures of 201.4 kg, 199.9 kg and 200.5 kg, respectively.[3] The fact that over a period of almost three decades per capita food grain output has remained virtually unchanged is highly significant.

Matters are no better with regard to per capita food grain availability. This, we have seen, had been increasing over the *dirigiste* period, reversing the experience of the last half-century of colonial rule. Over the neoliberal period however it has ceased to increase. The annual net per capita food grain availability was 177 kg for the triennium ending 1991–1992 (or 485 grammes per day); the figure for the triennium ending 2016–2017 was virtually the same, 178.2 kg (or 488 grammes per day).

GROWING NUTRITIONAL POVERTY

This stagnation in per capita net food grain availability has occurred in a period when the growth rate of per capita gross domestic product has been substantial, at between 7 to 8 per cent per annum, so much so that India has been talked of as an "emerging economic super-power". At the same time there has been an enormous increase in income inequality: indeed, Chancel and Piketty (2017, 19) have argued that the share of the top 1 per cent of households in total national income has, since the introduction of income tax in 1922, never been as high as it has been of late. This share has increased from 6.2 per cent in 1982–1983 to 21.3 per cent in 2014–2015 (the terminal year of the study). Alongside the top 1 per cent, however, there has been a sizeable upper middle class that has also been a major beneficiary of growth under the neoliberal regime.

Now, while the income elasticity of demand for food grains of these beneficiaries of neo-liberal growth is likely to be lower than that of the poorer segments of the population (even though their per capita consumption, both directly and indirectly, the latter through animal products and processed food, is higher than of the poorer segments), it certainly is not nega-tive. It follows therefore that since the per capita availability of food grains for the population as a whole has been constant during the neoliberal era, *it must have declined for the majority of the population, as a larger amount of this constant figure must have been taken by the well-off segments*. This means that nutritional poverty must have increased.

In fact, this is exactly what we find. Poverty in India has been traditionally defined with regard to a nutritional norm (though a lot of *ad hoc* changes have been made in this definition of late): the "poverty line" was that particular level of per capita expenditure at which a person just accessed 2100 calories per day in urban India and 2200 calories in rural India; and if we look at the proportion of the population below these norms then the figures are 58 per cent for 1993–1994 and 68 per cent for 2011–2012 in rural India and 57 and 65 per cent respectively in urban India.[4] The increase in the proportion of the absolutely poor, defined by these nutritional norms, during the neoliberal period is thus in conformity with the trend of per capita food grain availability discussed earlier.

What is striking is the *manner* of this impoverishment. It has not occurred, as one would have expected, through a rise in food grain prices relative to money incomes of the working population, i.e. through an inflation caused by an excess demand for food grains; rather it has occurred through a reduction in real purchasing power in the hands of the people *that is effected by means other than food price inflation per se*.

Since the income elasticity of demand for food grains is supposed to be positive for all segments of population, the fact that per capita food grain availability has not increased should have caused substantial excess demand in the food grain market and inflation in food grain prices. This, however, has not been the case. Indeed, barring a handful of occasions, the quarter-end food grain stocks with the government throughout this period have been larger than the levels that are officially considered "normal".

The inflationary episodes of this period have been of the cost-push variety, including cost-push arising from higher import costs, and especially of oil, owing to exchange rate depreciation, rather than of the demand-pull variety that is associated with a shortage of domestic availability. There certainly has been no demand-pull in the food grains market, in the sense of a *scarcity* of domestic availability of food grains.

The absence of any excess demand pressures in the food grain market, despite stagnant per capita food grain availability in the face of substantial per capita growth in gross domestic product, appears paradoxical on the face of it. While it is a reflection not just of growing income inequality but of growing absolute poverty (by the conventional official definition), the poor have been the victims not of food price inflation but of real income deflation occurring via a rise in the administered prices they face in *other* markets.

A very important reason for such real income deflation is the rise in the cost of essential services like education and healthcare, owing to their privatization. The exorbitantly higher prices that the working population has to pay for such services after their privatization do not get reflected in any cost-of-living index, since all such indices are Laspeyre indices and the base-year bundles of goods thus do not include the private provision of these services. They do not get reflected in the procurement prices of the agricultural producers, both because procurement prices are supposed to take account only of the cost of *production* and not of the cost of *living*, and also because the cost-of-living indices do not, as just mentioned, reflect increases in the prices of these essential services. They are also not reflected in the usual terms of trade movements between agriculture and manufacturing, since the prices of services do not enter these terms of trade at all. Their impact in short gets invariably missed when we look at the standard variables that figure in economic discussions.

This of course is not the only factor behind real income deflation. Since the workforce engaged in agriculture constitutes a significant part (almost half) of the total workforce, income deflation must also encompass the agriculture-dependent population. In other words, the strain on agriculture that we discussed earlier affects not just the supply side, but also the demand for food grains arising from within agriculture itself.

These demand-side effects from within agriculture have two components. One is the deceleration in agricultural output growth, including of food grains, whose growth has barely kept pace with the rate of population growth; in the *dirigiste* period, by contrast, per capita food grain output growth was well above 0.5 per cent per annum.

When agricultural output is less, there is less purchasing power in the hands of the peasants and agricultural workers; hence, if there is less production, there will be less demand from the producers. However, any reduction in output necessarily leads to a reduction in demand by the producers by a lesser amount. If for instance there is a reduction in food grain output by one unit, then the demand for food grains by the producers, i.e. peasants and labourers, would certainly go down, both directly (as they consume less food grains) and also indirectly through their reduced demand for other commodities, whose producers in turn are therefore forced to demand less food grains. But a *one unit* fall in food grain output cannot realistically reduce food grain demand in this manner by *more than one unit*; for if this was the case then the converse too would be true, and a one unit increase in food grain output would lead to a more than one unit increase in the demand for food grains, causing uncontrollable inflation in the economy. It follows therefore that if output falls, say, from 100 to 99, that is by one unit, then demand must fall by less than one unit, say 99.5, in which case there would be excess demand of 0.5, if this was the only factor to consider.

However, something else is clearly involved, which is the second component on the demand side. The real purchasing power in the hands of the agriculture-dependent population depends not just on the output it produces, but also the real purchasing power *per unit of the output it produces*. Even if the same physical output is produced, the real purchasing power, or the real income, in the hands of the producers can differ, depending upon the input costs they have to incur, the net revenue from output they obtain and the amounts they have to pay out for the bundle of goods they purchase.

What we have had in India during the neoliberal period is that the real income in the hands of the agricultural producers (peasants and agricultural labourers) has been squeezed *both* because of the decline in agricultural (especially food grain) output growth *and* because the real income per unit of output has also declined. The latter decline has occurred because of: the rise in input prices, including of credit, with greater indebtedness arising because of being exposed *inter alia* to world market price fluctuations, at least for cash crop producers; the fact that procurement prices in food crops have remained relatively restrained even as there has been a withdrawal of price support from cash crop producers; and the rise in the prices of the bundle of goods that they purchase, especially essential services like education and healthcare that we have already discussed.

This decline in real income per unit of output has been a result of the change in the institutional arrangement that has occurred under neoliberalism, a change involving the withdrawal of State support from peasant agriculture; and it is this which also underlies the decline in agricultural growth. Hence, the crisis in India's countryside, which gets manifested through greater hunger, increased peasant indebtedness, reduced income growth and mass suicides, can be traced essentially to the change in the class orientation of the State under neoliberalism, and the fact that the State, while promoting the interests of globalized capital and the corporate-financial oligarchy aligned to it, withdraws itself from supporting peasant agriculture and other forms of petty production.

This reduction in real income growth has become particularly acute in the period when international primary commodity prices have slumped. Between 2013–2014 and 2017–2018, for instance, both good harvest years but spanning a period of declining world commodity prices, per capita gross value added in "agriculture and allied activities" in current prices, when deflated by the consumer price index for rural India, shows a *total* increase by 1.4 per cent, which is almost absolute stagnation. Since within such a short period the ratio between the agriculture-dependent population and total population could hardly have changed much, the real per capita income of the *entire agriculture-dependent population* must have remained stagnant over this period, which ironically had seen nearly 7 per cent growth in gross domestic product per annum.

Considering the fact that the consumer price index does not capture fully the impact of the privatization of essential services, and also that the better-off segments of the agriculture-dependent population would certainly have witnessed an increase in their living standards, it follows that the vast bulk of the agriculture-dependent population must have experienced an absolute decline in their real per capita income over these years. The squeeze on peasant agriculture thus became particularly heightened in the period when world commodity prices were on a declining trajectory.

PEASANT AGRICULTURE AND PRIMITIVE ACCUMULATION

The *dirigiste* period witnessed, we have noted, a process of primitive accumulation of capital in the sense of a loss of rights over land by small peasants: tenants and sharecroppers were evicted by the landlords turning capitalist, and pushed into the ranks of agricultural labourers. However, since there was "land augmentation" occurring simultaneously, even though labour-displacing mechanization also accompanied the growth of capitalist agriculture overall, employment opportunities did not necessarily shrink in agriculture, so that the loss of rights over land did not mean loss of employment.

Some may say that this is true of all primitive accumulation of capital anyway; that while primitive accumulation entails the eviction of peasants from land and their conversion into free wage labourers, the growth of capitalism generally means that, barring a small reserve army of labour, these newly created free wage labourers get absorbed into capitalist production, if not immediately, then at least over time.

This conception however is erroneous. The fact that primitive accumulation in Europe did not create a vast permanent mass of unemployed workers was not because this is what necessarily happens under capitalism, but because of large-scale emigration from Europe to the temperate regions of settlement such as Canada, the United States, Australia, New Zealand and South Africa. William Arthur Lewis (1978, 14) suggested that during the "long nineteenth century", as many as 50 million Europeans emigrated to the temperate regions of the world (to which tropical migration was strictly restricted, and still is). From Britain alone, between 1820 and 1913 the number of persons emigrating annually was about half the annual increase in population (Patnaik 2012, 8). These migrants, in their new habitats, drove the original inhabitants off the land and occupied that land to set themselves up as farmers with relatively high per capita incomes; and it is this rather than any so-called "agricultural revolution" in England or elsewhere in Europe which had the effect of raising the "reservation wage" for workers back home in the capitalist metropolis.

There is nothing to suggest therefore that the petty producers displaced by primitive accumulation of capital necessarily get absorbed by capitalism. If there was no such creation of fresh mass unemployment in India through the process of primitive accumulation under *dirigisme*, then that was because of the special circumstance we have noted, namely the substantial "land augmentation" that occurred. We must distinguish therefore between primitive accumulation accompanied by land augmentation and primitive accumulation unaccompanied by land augmentation. The primitive accumulation that has been occurring under neoliberalism, which also constitutes an enriching of the capitalist sector at the expense of the petty production sector, is unaccompanied by any land augmentation; and this is the cause for growing destitution and distress.

There are two distinct aspects of primitive accumulation, a flow and a stock aspect; and both are occurring under neoliberalism. The flow aspect refers to a squeeze on the real incomes of the petty producers in order to enrich the capitalist sector, while the stock aspect refers to the taking over of the assets of the petty production sector by the capitalist sector *gratis* or at throwaway prices.

We seen that there has been a squeeze on peasant agriculture in the neoliberal period, in the sense of a reduction in the real purchasing power per unit of output produced by it. The question may be asked: even though there is intrusion by the capitalist sector, especially international agribusiness and the domestic corporate-financial oligarchy, upon peasant agriculture, in what sense can the squeeze itself be attributed to such intrusion *per se*? Moreover, if not, how can the squeeze be called an instance of primitive accumulation, since the term refers to the capitalist sector enriching itself at the expense of the pre-capitalist sector? This, however, is a narrow view of primitive accumulation. The State, whose actions we have seen primarily underlie the squeeze imposed upon peasant agriculture, has simultaneously made substantial transfers to international and domestic corporate capital in the name of causing larger corporate investment and hence "development". The State has thus become an instrument for bringing about a redistribution of resources by imposing a squeeze on the peasant agricultural sector and transferring resources to the capitalist sector. The neoliberal State is a means of imposing primitive accumulation of capital, in the *flow* sense, upon peasant agriculture.

Primitive accumulation of capital in the *stock* sense has attracted far greater notice in India in this period, and this is because the takeover of peasant land for "development projects" being undertaken by corporate capital has caused much peasant resistance. In fact, peasant agitations against such takeovers have been a prominent feature of the neoliberal era. It may be suggested that such takeovers have usually been compensated at "market prices", while agitations have been launched either because some peasants were unwilling to hand over land even at market prices or because they were denied the substantial capital gains that accrued from the appreciation in land price that occurred as the project got started; there has been no question therefore of land being expropriated, and hence of any primitive accumulation of capital.

This is based on a misconception.[5] Pre-capitalist societies, unlike capitalism, did not have a single integral notion of ownership: different persons had customary rights to different parts of the produce, including even agricultural labourers who had a certain customary right to employment. Even though colonialism in India sought to introduce ownership rights in the bourgeois sense, customary rights to the produce on land (including payment for the customary right to employment) continued to exist. The takeover of land in the present context therefore must entail compensation, and not just for the legal "owners", of an amount that corresponds to the discounted present value of the *surplus* from the land that they would have obtained (which is what the "market value" is supposed to reflect), but for *all* claimants on the produce of the land (including tenants and agricultural labourers), of an amount that corresponds to the discounted value of the *total produce* of the land.

Payment of compensation for land taken over at the so-called "market value" therefore still amounts to primitive accumulation of capital, for it still entails snatching away without payment the customary rights (and hence the customary claims to output) of tenants and agricultural labourers. It is not surprising that peasant agitations occur even when the so-called "market value" is paid for the land taken over.

Primitive accumulation, both in its flow and stock aspects, has led to a reduction in the number of "cultivators", as defined by the Indian Census, by about 15 million between 1991 and 2011 (Government of India, Office of the Registrar General, various years). Some of them may have lingered in the agricultural sector itself as "labourers", while others would have migrated to cities in search of employment, and, because of the limited growth in employment opportunities there, swollen the labour reserves.

Since in India the bulk of employment takes the form of casual, intermittent or part-time employment, a swelling of labour reserves implies a reduction in average employment per worker, which lowers not only the average income of this vast army of workers but also the bargaining strength of the small percentage of workers who have "full-time" employment. Altogether it adversely affects the average material conditions of all the workers outside agriculture. Within agriculture itself primitive accumulation leads to a glutting of the labour market and a worsening of the workers' conditions. It follows therefore that primitive accumulation hurts the entire working class in the economy. Starting with a worsening of the conditions of the peasantry, it has the effect of worsening the conditions of the working class as well.

This overall worsening, and the fact of limited growth of employment opportunities in the economy, is in conformity with, and can be inferred from, what has been said above about food availability. Since the incidence of open unemployment is limited, a measure of the extent of employment in the economy is the proportion of the workforce earning above a certain benchmark level of real income. A reduction in unemployment in the economy would therefore mean a larger proportion of workers above this benchmark, and hence, normally, an increase in the average real income per worker; but if this happened then per capita food grain consumption by the working people should have increased, which, we saw earlier, it has not. Primitive accumulation in short has led to a swelling of labour reserves and increased general distress among the workers and peasants.

CONCLUDING OBSERVATIONS

A common theme in development economics, ever since the work of Yevgeny Preobrazhensky (1965 [1926]), has been that "development" requires the squeezing out of a surplus from the agricultural sector so that workers outside of agriculture can be employed. Some form of primitive accumulation of capital is therefore considered essential for "development".

This as a general conception is erroneous. "Development" in countries like India that are saddled with mass poverty because of their colonial past must mean above all an alleviation of poverty. This requires not any process of primitive accumulation of capital, which can only aggravate mass poverty (and that too not just transitionally), but a process of "land augmentation". The *dirigiste regime* achieved "land augmentation" but within a context of developing capitalism, including landlord capitalism, for which it desisted from breaking land concentration and even accepted a certain primitive accumulation. This prevented the benefit of "land augmentation" from being widely shared. What is required for "development" in countries like India is "land augmentation" *alongside* land redistribution, or the breaking up of land concentration. Neoliberalism prevents both.

NOTES

1. The food grains output and availability figures used here for "British India" were computed by George Blyn (1966) and are reproduced in Patnaik (2007, 127), who also provides output and availability estimates for independent India for the *dirigiste* period (2007, 129).
2. Based on updating figures given in Nagaraj et al. (2014), using the same sources.
3. The population figures for the mid-years of the first two triennia are taken from Censuses (Government of India, Office of the Registrar General, various years) and for the last triennium by extrapolating on the basis of the growth rate for the 2001–2011 period. All other data are from the *Economic Surveys* (Government of India, Ministry of Finance, various years).
4. For the 1993–1994 figures see Patnaik (2013). She has kindly made available to me the figures for 2011–2012.
5. The argument that follows is based on Patnaik (2017).

FURTHER READING

Ghosh, J. (2011), Growth and exclusion: The Indian economy in the phase of globalization, in Shireern Moosvi (ed.), *Capitalism, Colonialism and Globalization*, Delhi: Tulika Books, 126–162.

Nagaraj, K.; Sainath, P.; Rukmani, R.; Gopinath, R. (2014), Farmers' suicides in India: Magnitudes, trends, and spatial patterns, 1997–2012, *Review of Agrarian Studies*, 4(2), 53–83.

Patnaik, P. (2018), Globalization and the peasantry in the South, *Agrarian South: Journal of Political Economy*, 7(2), 234–248.

Patnaik, U. (2003), Global capitalism, deflation and agrarian crisis in developing countries, *Journal of Agrarian Change*, 3(1–2), 33–66.

REFERENCES

Blyn, G. (1966), *Agricultural Trends in India 1891–1947*, Philadelphia, PA: University of Pennsylvania Press.

Chancel, L.; Piketty, T. (2017), Indian income inequality 1922–2015: British Raj to billionaire Raj?, WID.world Working Paper Series No. 2017/11.

Ghosh, J. (2011), Growth and exclusion: The Indian economy in the phase of globalization, in Shireern Moosvi (ed.), *Capitalism, Colonialism and Globalization*, Delhi: Tulika Books, 126–162.

Government of India, Ministry of Finance (various years), *Economic Survey*, accessed 22 April 2020 at www.indiabudget.gov.in.

Government of India, Office of the Registrar General (various years), *Population Census*, accessed 22 April 2020 at www.censusindia.gov.in.

Lewis, W.A. (1978), *The Evolution of the International Economic Order*, Princeton, NJ: Princeton University Press.

Patnaik, P. (2017), The concept of primitive accumulation of capital, *The Marxist*, 34(4), 1–9.

Patnaik, U. (2003), Global capitalism, deflation and agrarian crisis in developing countries, *Journal of Agrarian Change*, 3(1–2), 33–66.

Patnaik, U. (2007), *The Republic of Hunger and Other Essays*, Delhi: Three Essays Collective.

Patnaik, U. (2012), Capitalism and the production of poverty, *Social Scientist*, 40(1), 3–20.

Patnaik, U. (2013), Poverty trends in India 2004–2005 to 2009–2010, *Economic and Political Weekly*, 48(40), 43–58.

Preobrazhensky, Y. (1965 [1926]), *The New Economics*, Oxford: Oxford University Press.

38. Crises of capitalism in the countryside: Debates from the South

Praveen Jha and Paris Yeros

INTRODUCTION

Let us state a couple of caveats at the outset. The field of critical agrarian studies is necessarily a dynamic one as it confronts theoretical and empirical challenges that are organically connected with the evolution of the global capitalist system. In other words, there are no fixed boundaries as we grapple with the relevant conceptual canvas, frameworks and analytical categories. Nonetheless, there would possibly be near consensus amongst the practitioners of critical agrarian studies that the agrarian question and its multiple dimensions are at the centre of relevant debates and discourses; furthermore, it may not be an exaggeration to take the view that, methodologically, political economy approaches offer appropriate scaffolding and tools to engage with the core concerns of critical agrarian studies. This is the point of departure in this chapter for engaging with the broad conspectus of 'capitalism and the countryside' and specifically to investigate the debates on crises from a Southern perspective. However, given the contending approaches and multiple lines of enquiry with respect to the agrarian question, even within the political economy tradition, it is obviously important to interrogate, even if very briefly, the relevant contested terrain. In fact, it would be hardly inappropriate to claim that the understanding of crises itself, in large measure, is contingent on framing contending conceptions of the agrarian question.

We are referring to a large and complex canvass, entwining several themes. For instance, from the *longue durée*, the historical-structural, to the short-term, policy-driven and conjunctural, we can have several kinds, and typologies, of crises. In fact, to take a step back, 'crises of capitalism' itself can be interpreted in two fundamentally different, almost diametrically opposed, ways: (1) it could mean crisis for the elemental driving force and primary logic of capitalism; that is, the accumulation process hitting road blocks and the challenges of addressing the same; or (2) it may refer to, precisely because of the logic of capitalism, the thwarting of the prospects for a better world, with respect to economic, social, political, cultural and ecological dimensions. In other words, the latter essentially refers to a diminution or even loss of emancipatory goals in the project of human progress (Yeros and Jha 2020). It is such a view that our discussion here is tilted toward. Likewise, if we need to engage seriously with 'debates in the South', it is extremely important to begin with the acknowledgement that there are varieties of 'South', shaped by long historical trajectories and their specificities, and one obviously needs to be sensitive to these (ibid.). In light of this, one obvious challenge is to think in terms of lowest common denominators to conceptualize the notion of 'South' that is theoretically and empirically worthwhile and provides considerable mileage.

There is a large and growing literature on the above-noted themes which, taken together, provide a very rich terrain to the relevant critical issues. In our treatment of the subject chosen here, we proceed at the most general level, and our effort is best viewed as sketching a perspective to flag some of the most significant markers of debates, contentions and, hopefully, in the classic radical spirit, some suggestions for the way forward. In the next section, we provide an overview of the conceptual thrusts associated with the agrarian question, in particular within Marxist political economy. For the relevant Marxist literature, Akram-Lodhi and Kay (2010a, 2010b) provide very useful surveys.

Our arguments here draw upon some of our earlier publications (Moyo and Yeros 2005; Moyo et al. 2012, 2013, 2015, 2016). The central claim advanced is the following: the evolution of the literature, since the late nineteenth century, on the agrarian question was largely dominated by Eurocentric discourses and got trapped in privileging a narrow conception of 'industrialization-driven modernization' as the presumed resolution of the agrarian question. Such a construction of the 'classical agrarian question', which became the conventional wisdom, is fundamentally misleading in our view. The subsequent section, building on our understanding of the debates on the agrarian question, provides an overview of the arguments on 'crises of capitalism in the countryside of the South', in the sense hinted above.

THE AGRARIAN QUESTION: QUESTIONING THE 'CONVENTIONAL WISDOM'

In some of our earlier work we have tried to engage with critical issues in the relevant debates in detail (e.g., Moyo and Yeros 2005; Moyo et al. 2012, 2013, 2015, 2016). Here we state very briefly two very different, almost dramatically so, conceptions of the agrarian question, simply to counterpose the crux of parallel visions and tracks within the Marxist political economy. We first summarize the essence of what seems to have been the 'received conventional wisdom', which has also been the dominant one. Then we outline the alternative view. We begin with the 'conventional wisdom', of which Terry Byres has been among the most eminent and sophisticated scholars.

In a well-known formulation, Byres (1991a, 9), summarizing the essence of the discourses on the agrarian question in Marxist political economy since the late nineteenth century, suggested that: '[t]hree distinct senses of the agrarian question may be distinguished: (a) the Engels sense, (b) the Kautsky-Lenin sense, and (c) the Preobrazhensky sense'. It is not necessary to dwell on the details and usefulness of this classification here, except to highlight that the three senses were supposed to capture the crux of the political, social and economic dimensions of 'backwardness', respectively. However, these three converged in their core understanding of the resolution of the agrarian question with achieving industrialization, which meant transcending backwardness, whether by capitalist or socialist routes and means, and which England had achieved earlier, ahead of her European rivals. The subsequent evolution of much of the Marxist discourse on the agrarian question, largely framed within a Eurocentric 'imagination', using the binary of backwardness/industrialization, became the conventional wisdom on the subject. To quote Byres (1991a, 9) again:

> An unresolved agrarian question is a central characteristic of economic backwardness. In its broadest meaning, the agrarian question may be defined as the continuing existence in the countryside of a poor country of substantive obstacles to an unleashing of the forces capable of generating economic development, both inside and outside agriculture. Originally formulated with respect to incomplete capitalist transition, and certain political consequences of that incompleteness, the agrarian question is now part, also, of the debate on possible socialist transition in poor countries.

Sure enough, such a discourse on the agrarian question could accommodate a variety of views on the economics and politics of industrialization and was quite open to the possibility of a spectrum of historical trajectories of transition. For instance, building on the earlier generations of Marxist scholars who had focused largely on the turn-of-the-century Europe and later North America, Byres (1991b) discusses six different trajectories of capitalist agrarian transition in Asia. However, the point worth emphasizing is that in all such diverse trajectories of transition, industrialization was viewed as the benchmark, or sheet anchor, of the resolution of the agrarian question. Thus if the 'capitalist industrialisation is permitted to proceed' and 'the social transformation comes to be dominated by industry and by the urban bourgeoisie, there ceases to be an agrarian question with any serious implications. There is no longer an agrarian question in any substantive sense' (1991b, 12). In short, it is precisely such a view of the agrarian question, largely trapped in Eurocentric heritage, which has been quite influential, almost assuming a 'cult' status, within the Marxist political economy.

As it happens, such a perspective gelled quite well with the dominant paradigms in the newly emerging fields of 'development economics', 'development studies' and so on after the Second World War. With 'modernization' theories ruling the roost, which essentialized the meaning of development as transition from the 'traditional' to 'modern' activities and processes, the challenge of development was a simple one: to get over, as fast as possible, the drag of the 'traditional' and 'move to the modern' through adequate resource mobilization, building appropriate institutions and so on. For agriculture such a transition meant a transformation of the 'small-scale', 'inefficient' and 'subsistence-oriented' production system to 'efficient', 'market-oriented', 'large-scale' and 'capital-intensive' production systems. Models of 'dualism' and 'stages of growth' abounded in the literature and the high priests of development economics preached the virtues of industry-led economic transformation, which was presumed to be predicated on, *inter alia*, appropriate technocratic and institutional changes in 'backward' agriculture. The presumed experience of the 'West', constructed superficially, became the 'beacon of hope' and 'mirror of its own future' for the 'Rest'.

Thus, during the period after the Second World War visions of 'modernity' or 'modern economic growth' (to borrow the expression used by Simon Kuznets) were profoundly shaped by the tales of industrialization, even though these tales evolved in different directions, ranging from conservative to radical, and were often framed with considerable sophistication. Yet the core of it, or its minimalist formulation, is very simple and may be stated as follows: a significant spurt in the growth of agriculture is a prerequisite and/or accompanies early to middle stages of modern economic transformation; a stage is reached when the share of agriculture in total output as well as workforce starts declining; the faster the process of such a decline, the more successful is the trajectory of economic transformation. Such a minimalist scaffolding version is padded up, in multiple and sophisticated ways, with a whole range of economic and social prerequisites.

In the language of what we have designated as 'conventional wisdom' within Marxist political economy, the minimalist version amounts to the identification and specification of a set of changes that result in the firming up of the logic of capitalist relations in agriculture, with the unfolding of several important concomitant consequences. These include enhanced surplus generation, which gets used in agriculture and elsewhere for further accumulation, and technological developments. Should this happen, it is assumed that a robust process of industrialization-led economic transformation gets underway and the agrarian question is presumed to be resolved. In fact, such a view of the agrarian question has been extremely powerful for more than a century. It continues to be influential and has acquired an even more minimalist rendering – a 'lean and mean' version of backwardness/industrialization binary – in the writings of eminent scholars such as Henry Bernstein (2004, 200, emphasis in original):

> The 'classic' agrarian question, I would suggest, is the agrarian question of capital. To the extent that its logic of agrarian transition succeeded (and may still succeed?) in accomplishing the social transformation and technical development of agriculture ... and in ways that contribute to industrialization ... then the agrarian question of capital is *also* that of labour as the two definitive classes of a new mode of production, representing historical progress.

Thus, Bernstein's agrarian question is predicated on the requisite resources (in particular economic) as a springboard for the launch of capitalist development in agriculture and industry, and the 'agrarian question of labour' is subsumed in the 'agrarian question of capital'. Further, if 'agrarian capital' has sources beyond its local context and has access to 'the range of non-agrarian capital', then clearly there is an easing of constraints for the capitalist transformation of agriculture and its contribution towards industrialization. The essence of such a conception of the agrarian question is best summed up in Bernstein's own words (2004, 202, emphasis in original):

> with contemporary 'globalization' and the massive development of the productive forces in (advanced) capitalist agriculture, the centrality of the 'classic' agrarian question to industrialization is no longer significant for international capital. In this sense, then, there is *no longer an agrarian question of capital on a world scale*, even when the agrarian question – as a basis of national accumulation and industrialization – has not been resolved in many countries of the 'South'.

To put it bluntly, contemporary neoliberal globalization, in particular the fluidity of capital mobility on a large scale associated with such a regime, implies that the 'classical agrarian question' is dead, or has become irrelevant, on a global scale.

The above-noted formulation by Bernstein almost negates the rich heritage of Marxist scholarship at one stroke. More centrally, however, in general the narrow rendering of the agrarian question, as a backwardness/industrialization binary, suffers from several profound problems. First of all, linking the agrarian question to the backwardness/industrialization axiom and its 'internal resolution' completely misses the powerful contribution of global primitive accumulation in the transition to industrial capitalism, and thus the colonial/imperialist roots of the structural transformation of metropolitan countries. It hardly needs emphasis that global primitive accumulation was foundational to the industrial transition in England and Europe, and treating it as 'incidental' is deeply problematic. Second, it also displaces the debates over politics and policy from North to South, absolving the former from its blood-stained past, and of any transformative obligation in the present, except by the provision of 'aid and charity'. Third, there is an utter banalization of the prospects, possibilities and processes of industrial transition in the South, as all these are abstracted from the hegemony of global monopoly finance capital and its deleterious economic, social, political and ecological consequences. Fourth, the analytical rupture between the so-called agrarian question of capital and labour for the contemporary South, evading questions relating to nature and quality of industrial transition and so on, are not only misleading, but are also a serious misreading of the 'classics' (e.g. contributions by Marx and some of his most important immediate successors), where such questions and issues were handled in a dialectical manner.

In sharp contrast to the above-noted 'conventional wisdom' of the agrarian question, with industrialization as its cornerstone, there is a long history of alternative discourses within Marxist political economy (as also in the Chayanovian tradition), running almost along parallel tracks, the crux of which is equitable, democratic and sustainable autonomous development, with national liberation at its core. The most profound difference between the 'agrarian question of industrialization' and what we call the 'agrarian question of liberation' is that the latter articulates the conviction of sovereign industrialization and economic transformation with remarkable clarity, insisting on safeguarding the capacity and autonomy to determine one's own external relations and internal balances. We submit that the agrarian question of liberation has been central to this alternative conception of the agrarian question in Marxist political economy and continues to be at the heart of the contemporary agrarian question.

Although, Marx, his important comrades and fellow travellers, as well as his immediate successors, did not engage in any systematic manner with the agrarian question of liberation, and much of their writing on the subject may appear closer to the agrarian question of industrialization, it is, arguably, worth noting that there may be interesting hints and clues in their contributions (particularly in Lenin's writings) towards the agrarian question of liberation and some of the very important issues relevant for our times. Further, we also need to note the obvious point that the agrarian question of liberation matured over a period of time, through continuous restructuring and clarifications, and the intellectual ground for this process was largely the South, through seminal contributions by Mao (2004 [1926]) and Fanon (1968 [1961]), among others. In this alternative tradition, the peasantry emerges as the 'subject in history', the 'revolutionary class', not only in practice, but also in theory, to take forward the project of national revolution for political and economic sovereignty. Arguably, China's experiment of building socialism in the immediate aftermath of the 1949 revolution remains the most outstanding engagement, in practice, with the agrarian question of liberation, which included, *inter alia*, land reforms and collectivization and a vision of industrialization organically connected with agriculture and the countryside.

Essentially, the agrarian question of liberation, in our view, ought to have the mantle of 'classical agrarian question'. This would: restore the centrality of the national sovereignty; acknowledge the land and peasant components of the national question; and reiterate the importance of sovereign industrialization and other critical dimensions of autonomous, democratic, sustainable and equitable socio-economic transformation. There is a large and growing literature, especially of Marxist persuasion, on the diversity of transitions in the South, which is testimony to our claim that the neglect of the national liberation project generally has implied transition to perilous passages, although along diverse trajectories, depending on the nature of the State, contingent agrarian structures or the insertion of a country in the world economy. Similarly, for societies where national sovereignty was embedded in transition projects, there have been modicums of success, in some instances quite substantive, depending on a number of structural and conjunctural correlates. Interested readers may benefit considerably on these issues through the large corpus of established research; for instance, on transitions in Asia (Amin 1981; Patnaik 1986, 2006, 2011; Patnaik 2012, 2018) and in Africa and Latin America (Amin 1972; Cardoso and Falleto 1979; Mafeje 1991; Moyo 2008; Moyo and Yeros 2011). The two extremes in the spectrum of long transitions in the peripheries have been: (1) a handful of East Asian countries, such as Japan, South Korea and Taiwan, often referred to as 'miracle' cases, which managed to pursue structural reforms and protected economic transformation; and (2) an overwhelming number of developing countries which have remained trapped in limited, if not failed, economic transformation trajectories, with large masses of precarious, vulnerable and semi-proletarianized peasants in an ongoing crisis of social reproduction.

CRISIS IN THE COUNTRYSIDE

The crisis of capitalism in the countrysides of the South can be visualized along a whole range of axes, of which we highlight three important ones. The first of these, in a *longue durée* perspective, is the nature and intensity of primitive accumulation inflicted on the South to feed and facilitate the transition to industrial capitalism in the North. To be sure, inherent hostility of 'spontaneous' capitalism (i.e. driven by its own immanent tendencies) vis-à-vis almost every dimension of the countryside, such as its inhabitants, its ecology and so on, through ceaseless primitive accumulation, is a universal feature; however, through colonialism and imperialism, the adverse impacts of primitive accumulation were distributed dramatically unevenly between the North and the South, contributing in large measure to the possibility of a permanent state of crisis in agriculture and the countryside in the South. The specific trajectories of incorporation of the different parts of the South, in the rise and ascendency of global capitalism, left indelible marks on their future prospects and the nature of structural crises. For instance, at a high level of generality, we can distinguish between the extreme cases of 'colonies of conquest' (also known as 'colonies of exploitation'), such as South Asia, and contrast it with Southern Africa and Latin America, where 'colonies of settlement' and 'enclave capitalism' prevailed. The overwhelming majority of the population in the countryside in both these areas were subjected to brutal colonial machinations and primitive accumulation, yet the nature of the long-term structural crises in the countryside in both these regions were quite different, along a wide spectrum of divide-and-rule and settlement-cum-genocide experiences. The nature and structure of 'combined and uneven' global capitalism during the last five centuries, and the texture of economic-structural crises in different countries of the South have been shaped, in substantial measure, through ways in which metropolitan centres have fed off the peripheries in consecutive rounds of primitive accumulation, which have been a permanent feature of global capitalism.

Second, the nature and quality of long-run structural transformations and crises are organically connected with, *inter alia*, competing perspectives on the agrarian question and their operational counterparts on the ground. In a nutshell, after their respective decolonizations, most countries across the South embarked on the projects of capitalist economic transformation, in contexts of varying degrees of regulated/autonomous capitalism (with respect to global capitalism and especially erstwhile colonial/imperialist powers). However, more often than not, in spite of important politico-ideological differences, these were trapped in what we have labelled the 'agrarian question of industrialization'. The shared policy paradigm was one of traditional peasant agriculture being backward; the way out was presumed to be fast-track, often capital-intensive industrialization, along with the modernization of agriculture, in the mould of industry itself, through a barrage of technocratic interventions, in particular chemicalization. It was presumed that the proletarianized peasantry would be automatically accommodated through an expansion of employment in the secondary and tertiary sectors.

The dominant discourses on modernization pushed the view that this is how developed countries in Europe, and elsewhere, were modernized; in other words, the eminently desirable, if not paramount, project of modernity had to be capitalist modernity and the Clark-Kuznets strait-jacket of structural transformation in the North would also be the model for successful socio-economic transformation in the South. Sure enough, the experiences of the countries in the South, with respect to their trajectories of economic transformation, are highly differentiated. However, for the overwhelming majority of these countries, the projected future with respect to structural transformation and livelihoods remained a myth, and continues to be so. In other words, one kind of crisis in the countrysides and urban areas of the capitalist modernization projects in the countries of the South is that of a crisis of labour absorption for the overwhelming majority of workers – or what in Marxist discourse constitutes the growing labour reserves or the relative surplus population. This results in a crisis of social reproduction which is organically linked to capitalism not only by its effects on wages, but also by the unpaid labour, especially of women, that is appropriated outside the market ever more intensively as labour reserves expand (Naidu and Ossome 2016; Prasad 2016; Tsikata 2016). The long process of unsettling peasant agriculture and degrading formal employment, sometimes through shock and awe, has created masses of new nomads hunting for livelihoods across large swathes of uncertain and hostile terrains, contributing to what Mike Davis (2007) has designated the 'planet of slums'. In addition to the crisis of labour absorption and social reproduction, policy paradigms adopted in the countries of the South have contributed to crises on multiple fronts, both within agriculture and outside, some of which we briefly flag in our remarks pertaining to the contemporary neoliberal era; the point worth highlighting is that the roots of some of these lie in the earlier 'regulated' phase itself. Of course, depending on the long-term structural-historical legacy, and the nature of post-colonial regimes, the nature of crises in the countryside in different countries and regions of the South show significant differences.

Third, the ascendency of neoliberal capitalist order since the 1970s has had profound economic and social implications across the globe. With respect to agriculture, apart from the strengthening of quite a few tendencies that were contributing to different kinds of crisis in the countryside, several powerful forces have been unleashed which impact on the ongoing dynamics of agriculture in the South. For the population dependent on agriculture, almost all the major correlates relating to their well-being, whether livelihoods, assets, incomes, food security or public health, have received serious setbacks, almost everywhere. In particular, for peasant agriculture in the South, which directly and indirectly accounts for almost half of humanity – approximately 3 billion human beings – overall stress levels have increased in multidimensional ways. Many of these are organically connected with the rise and domination of neoliberal capitalism. Essentially, contemporary capitalism, in its monopoly-finance form and the multitude of the *laissez-faire* devices at its service, courtesy of the hegemony of neoliberalism, has accelerated the degradation of the peasantries everywhere in the South. Large segments of these constitute semi- or proto-lumpen-proletariats and growing labour reserves. Further, such a system has aggravated all major crises of our times – economic, ecological, climate, energy and public health – which then in complex, dialectical ways, reinforce the crisis of peasant agriculture.

There is an important literature that documents the increasing salience of adversities during the last half century or so, such as the stranglehold of agro-industrial capital and corporate food regimes; the growing financialization of food and agriculture; the scramble for land and other natural resources, such as forests, fisheries and water, and 'commons' of various kinds, including the global environmental commons; and the destruction of bio-diversity and exposure to new pathogens. The architecture of contemporary neoliberalism, through its trade, investment and financial flows, has succeeded in the remarkable and multifaceted domination of peasant agriculture and nature, which constitutes the crux of the crises in the countryside of the South. To illustrate the thrust of widely shared thinking on these themes, see for example the surveys of the major developments during the neoliberal era impacting on peasantries and food production (Patnaik and Moyo 2011; Herrera and Kin Chi Lau 2015; Jha et al. 2020); the transitions in gender relations (Naidu and Ossome 2016; Prasad 2016; Tsikata 2016); and the new scramble for land and natural resources (Moyo et al. 2019). There are also important new possibilities for global dialogue on a range of issues on the food question generally and ecological disequilibria (Wallace 2016; Wise 2019).

In their domestic settings, due to the ascendency of neoliberalism, peasant cultivators have been subjected to a variety of policy-driven adversities, and given that they are part of what Samir Amin (1976) characterized as 'dominated peripheral capitalism', their integration into the dominant global capitalist system has made things much worse for them: in essence, they are subjected to a 'double burden'. Most countries in recent decades have been subjected to low and declining levels of public investment in every area that impacts on agriculture, particularly for small cultivators, through backward and forward linkages, which include: the compression, if not the disappearance, of publicly funded support for basic infrastructure, both physical, such as irrigation, and social, such as in research, extension, health and education; sharp curtailments in the public provisioning and regulation of a variety of inputs, thus leaving smallholder agriculture to the mercy of large domestic and global corporations; and the reduction of a whole range of subsidies, such as for credit, irrigation and electricity, which pushes up cultivation costs. Along with this, increasing openness to global capitalism has resulted in several important changes in overall production systems which include: a decline in food output for domestic markets and their replacement by a variety of 'cash crops', such as from horticulture and floriculture; an increasing dependence on imports for domestic food requirements; an increasing share of crops in total agricultural production that are directed to industrial uses such as bio-fuels; shifts in input regimes and technologies which have resulted in a transition toward higher-energy and environmentally more damaging production packages; and a growing financialization of agriculture, including through speculation in agricultural commodities.

The above-noted constitute some of the important correlates, indicators and symptoms of crises in the countryside, which can be easily connected with shifts in the basic contours of the overall macroeconomic landscape. The ascendency of market-oriented and so-called liberalization policies have exposed countries in the South to extremely unfair import competition from highly subsidized and protected developed countries, apart from making them ever more vulnerable on several fronts, including increased volatility in global agricultural prices. In recent years, one of the most dramatic manifestations of such vulnerability was the global food crisis of 2007, which contributed to food riots in several developing countries, and the currently unfolding Covid-19 pandemic.

CONCLUDING REMARKS

Based on our discussions in the foregoing, if we choose a grand canvas to answer the question central to this chapter, *viz.* the root cause of crises in the countryside, in a simple, telegraphic manner, we may of course conclude that it is due to the immanent tendencies of capitalism.

It is these tendencies of the system that have created, over the *longue durée* of capitalism, a polarized, racialized, structurally hierarchical world – as 'core and periphery', 'North and South', 'developed and underdeveloped' – stitching them together in an international division of tasks, responsibilities, gains and losses. The 'comparative advantage in violence' (Findlay 1992) has often been at the centre, at different stages, in the evolution of 'combined and uneven' global capitalism. However, to get into the nitty-gritty of different stages and transitions, we need a fulsome engagement with the details of the immanent tendencies – and this is a politically crucial task.

To the extent that the inherent logic and laws of motion of capitalism can be regulated and kept in check, relatively favourable, or at least less damaging, outcomes for the countryside are indeed feasible, as we know very well from our historical experiences. However, whether such outcomes can be durable or can be sustained beyond particular conjunctures, within capitalism, or necessarily require transcending capitalism, may be difficult to answer. Of course, the task at hand is not to theorize in 'ivory towers'; theory must burst into practice. There has to be a dialectical unity between theory and progressive politics: as Lenin (1902) said, 'without revolutionary theory there can be no revolutionary movement'.

It seems to us that addressing the challenges of crisis in the countryside of the South requires, first and foremost, a clear 'no' to neoliberal globalization, which has to be the necessary condition for an alternative trajectory of development, and for liberating the peasantry from the stranglehold of capital. In other words, the 'peasant path' needs to be taken seriously, which is feasible in a context of an autonomous and regulated economic framework, with supportive macropolicy regimes. To address the shortcomings of peasant production, institutional frameworks for cooperatives and collective actions have to be prioritized; such trajectories, potentially, are well placed in terms of labour absorption, ecological balance, low energy requirements, popular participation, gender relations, food sovereignty and so on. Of course, there is no reason to believe that the peasant path implies the abandonment of industrialization or the expansion of non-agricultural economic activities. It is worth emphasizing that gender equity and ecological sustainability have to be the mainstay of an alternative vision of economic development, which has the potential of, at least, containing and managing the major causal correlates of the crises in the countryside of the South. It may be worth recalling the very perceptive remarks by Marx (2010, 83) that 'the capitalist system works against a rational agriculture, or that a rational agriculture is incompatible with the capitalist system ... and needs either the hand of the small farmer living by his own labour or the control of associated producers'.

FURTHER READING

Moyo, S.; Yeros, P. (2005), *Reclaiming the Land: The Resurgence of Rural Movements in Africa, Asia and Latin America*, London: Zed Books.

Moyo, S.; Yeros, P. (2011), *Reclaiming the Nation: The Return of the National Question in Africa, Asia and Latin America*, London: Pluto Press.

Moyo, S.; Jha, P.; Yeros, P. (2013), The classical agrarian question: Myth, reality and relevance today, *Agrarian South: Journal of Political Economy*, 2(1), 93–119.

Moyo, S.; Jha, P.; Yeros, P. (eds) (2019), *Reclaiming Africa: Scramble and Resistance in the 21st Century*, Singapore: Springer.

Patnaik, U.; Moyo, S. (2011), *The Agrarian Question in the Neoliberal Era: Primitive Accumulation and the Peasantry*, Cape Town: Pambazuka Press.

REFERENCES

Akram-Lodhi, A.H.; Kay, C. (2010a), Surveying the agrarian question (Part 1): Unearthing foundations, exploring diversity, *Journal of Peasant Studies*, 37(1), 177–202.

Akram-Lodhi, A.H.; Kay, C. (2010b), Surveying the agrarian question (Part 2): Current debates and beyond, *Journal of Peasant Studies*, 37(2), 255–284.

Amin, S. (1972), Underdevelopment and dependence in Black Africa: Origins and contemporary forms, *Journal of Modern African Studies*, 10(4), 503–524.

Amin, S. (1976), *Unequal Development*, New York: Monthly Review Press.

Amin, S. (1981), *The Future of Maoism*, translated by Finkelstein, N., New York: Monthly Review Press.

Bernstein, Henry (2004), Changing before our very eyes: Agrarian questions and the politics of land in capitalism today, *Journal of Agrarian Change*, 4(1–2), 190–225.

Byres, T. (1991a), Agrarian question, in Bottomore, T.; Harris, L.; Kiernan, V.G.; Miliband, R. (eds), *A Dictionary of Marxist Thought*, second edition, Oxford: Basil Blackwell, 9–11.

Byres, T. (1991b), The agrarian question and differing forms of capitalist agrarian transition: An essay with reference to Asia, in Berman, J.; Mundle, S. (eds), *Rural Transformation in Asia*, Oxford: Oxford University Press, 3–76.

Cardoso, F.H.; Falleto, E. (1979), *Dependency and Development in Latin America*, translated by Urquidi, M.M., Berkeley, CA: University of California Press.

Davis, M. (2007), *Planet of Slums*, London: Verso.

Fanon, F. (1968 [1961]), *The Wretched of the Earth*, New York: Grove Press.

Findlay, R. (1992), The roots of divergence: Western economic history in comparative perspective, *American Economic Review*, 82(2), 158–161.

Herrera, R.; Kin Chi Lau (eds) (2015), *The Struggle for Food Sovereignty: Alternative Development and the Renewal of Peasant Societies Today*, London: Pluto Press.

Jha, P.; Yeros, P.; Chambati, W. (2020), *Rethinking the Social Sciences with Sam Moyo*, New Delhi: Tulika Books.

Lenin, V. (1902), What Is to Be Done?, accessed 7 May 2020 at www.marxists.org/archive/lenin/works/1901/witbd/i.htm.

Mafeje, A. (1991), *The Theory and Ethnography of African Social Formations: The Case of the Interlacustrine Kingdoms*, Dakar: CODESRIA.

Mao Zedong (Tse-tung) (2004 [1926]), Analysis of the classes in Chinese society, in *Selected Works*, vol. 1, accessed 30 December 2019 at www.marxists.org/reference/archive/mao/selected-works/volume-1/mswv1_1.htm.

Marx, K. (2010), *Capital: A Critique of Political Economy, Vol. 3: The Process of Capitalist Production as a Whole*, accessed 7 May 2020 at https://libcom.org/files/Capital-Volume-III.pdf.

Moyo, S. (2008), *African Land Questions, Agrarian Transitions and the State: Contradictions of Neoliberal Land Reforms*, Dakar: CODESRIA.

Moyo, S.; Yeros, P. (2005), *Reclaiming the Land: The Resurgence of Rural Movements in Africa, Asia and Latin America*, London: Zed Books.

Moyo, S.; Yeros, P. (2011), *Reclaiming the Nation: The Return of the National Question in Africa, Asia and Latin America*, London: Pluto Press.

Moyo, S.; Yeros, P.; Jha, P. (2012), Imperialism and primitive accumulation: Notes on the new scramble for Africa, *Agrarian South: Journal of Political Economy*, 1(2), 181–203.

Moyo, S.; Jha, P.; Yeros, P. (2013), The classical agrarian question: Myth, reality and relevance today, *Agrarian South: Journal of Political Economy*, 2(1), 93–119.

Moyo, S.; Jha, P.; Yeros, P. (2015), The agrarian question in the 21st century, *Economic and Political Weekly*, 50(37), 35–41.

Moyo, S.; Jha, P.; Yeros, P. (2016), The agrarian question and trajectories of economic transformation: Perspective from the South, in Reinert, E.S.; Ghosh, J.; Kattel, R. (eds), *Handbook of Alternative Theories of Economic Development*, Cheltenham, UK and Northampton, MA, USA: Edward Elgar Publishing, 487–503.

Moyo, S.; Jha, P.; Yeros, P. (eds) (2019), *Reclaiming Africa: Scramble and Resistance in the 21st Century*, Singapore: Springer.

Naidu, S.C.; Ossome, L. (2016), Social reproduction and the agrarian question of women's labour in India, *Agrarian South: Journal of Political Economy*, 5(1), 50–76.

Patnaik, P. (2012), The peasant question and contemporary capitalism: Some reflections with reference to India, *Agrarian South: Journal of Political Economy*, 1(2), 27–42.

Patnaik, P. (2018), Capitalism, socialism and petty production, Nyerere Dialogue Lecture, Dar es Salaam, 8 November.

Patnaik, U. (1986), The agrarian question and development of capitalism in India, *Economic and Political Weekly*, 21(18), 781–793.

Patnaik, U. (2006), The free lunch: Transfers from the tropical colonies and their role in capital formation in Britain during the Industrial Revolution, in Jomo, K.S. (ed.), *Globalization Under Hegemony*, New Delhi: Oxford University Press, 30–70.

Patnaik, U. (2011), The 'agricultural revolution' in England: Its cost for the English working class and the colonies, in Moosvi, S. (ed.), *Capitalism, Colonialism and Globalization*, New Delhi: Aligarh Historian's Society and Tulika Books, 17–27.

Patnaik, U.; Moyo, S. (2011), *The Agrarian Question in the Neoliberal Era: Primitive Accumulation and the Peasantry*, Cape Town: Pambazuka Press.

Prasad, A. (2016), Adivasi women, agrarian change and forms of labour in neoliberal India, *Agrarian South: Journal of Political Economy*, 5(1), 20–49.

Tsikata, D. (2016), Gender, land tenure and agrarian production systems in Sub-Saharan Africa, *Agrarian South: Journal of Political Economy*, 5(1), 1–19.

Wallace, R. (2016), *Big Farms Make Big Flu: Dispatches on Infectious Disease, Agribusiness and the Nature of Science*, New York: Monthly Review Press.

Wise, T.A. (2019), *Eating Tomorrow: Agribusiness, Family Farmers, and the Battle for the Future of Food*, New York: New Press.

Yeros, P.; Jha, P. (2020), Late neo-colonialism: Monopoly capitalism in permanent crisis, *Agrarian South: Journal of Political Economy*, 9(1), 78–93.

PART V

DEBATES

39. Land grabs

Ariane Goetz

INTRODUCTION

The debate over land grabbing is characterized by a rich and growing body of interdisciplinary research on present-day agrarian-environmental transformations. It has brought land struggles back on the international policy agenda, together with the search for new forms of governance.

At the core, the 'land grab' framing challenges orthodox economic theories and neoliberal institutions that assume self-regulatory markets and neutrality of money, and promote privatization, economic liberalization and attraction of foreign capital as a primary source of growth and development. Coined by the civil society organization GRAIN in response to foreign land acquisitions in Latin America in 2008, the framing and related themes transpired to a range of epistemic communities[1] and policy-oriented discourse coalitions,[2] including international finance and development institutions, journalists, government agencies, scholars and activists. It has been argued that 'land grab studies' emerged 'as a field co-produced by activists, policy-oriented researchers, academics and others' (Schoenberger et al. 2017, 2–5). The plurality of perspectives and the high degree of politicization have contributed to the continuous contestation of terminology (for example, 'investments in land', 'land acquisitions', 'land deals'), analytical categories, methods and policy (Edelman et al. 2013; Scoones et al. 2013; Oya 2013b). This chapter focuses primarily on the scholarly debate in critical agrarian studies over 'land grabs' and 'land grabbing'.

What is a 'land grab'? In addition to the complexity of struggles over land, research on 'land grabbing' is confronted with the problem of terminological ambiguity, namely the lack of any clear definition of what a land grab is – and what it is not. The vagueness of conceptual boundaries makes it difficult to distinguish land grabs and analyse them in the broader development contexts of agrarian change and economic restructuring of which they form a part. Several studies synthesize the scholarly debate as a way to come to terms with 'land grabbing' terminology the way it is being applied. Central within critical agrarian studies is Borras et al.'s (2011) neo-Marxist argument that '[t]he phrase "global land grab" has become a catch-all to describe and analyze the current explosion of large scale (trans)national commercial land transactions', and the description by Borras and Franco (2010), according to whom land grabbing refers to land conflicts as a result of large-scale (trans)national commercial land transactions, land speculation and/or control grabbing. Schoenberger et al. (2017, 2) identify a 'standardized package' of what they call 'land grab studies', including 'the global land grab story [that] provides the umbrella and the global scope'; land grab case studies that provide the basis for the global land grab story; and largely inconclusive conceptual work on 'land grabbing' that emerged in the context of interdisciplinary and policy-oriented conferences. More broadly, two analytical approaches prevail in the debate: treating 'land grabs' and 'land grabbing' as stable concepts with distinguishable characteristics (see GRAIN 2008; McMichael 2013), or scrutinizing the initial 'land grab' terminology and related claims (regarding timing, scale, location, actors, drivers, novelty), however, without negating the existence of struggles over land altogether.[3] Many studies apply a mix of both.

Whether 'land grabs' are a category or a subfield of critical agrarian studies remains an open question, as well as whether it makes sense to speak of 'a' debate over land grabbing, as long as many contributions co-exist next to, rather than engage with each other. It appears that critical agrarian studies emerged together with the debate over 'land grabs' or 'land grabbing' (Schoenberger et al. 2017). Considering the issues raised in critical agrarian studies, land grabbing intersects with long-standing as well as more recent issues of agrarian change, such as accumulation by dispossession (Hall 2013), depeasantization and (semi-)proletarianization of the countryside (see Hiraldo 2018; McMichael 2012a, 2012b), financialization of food and agriculture (Clapp 2014; Fuchs et al. 2013), ecological degradation (Dauvergne and Neville 2010), neoliberalization of nature (Fairhead et al. 2012; Green and Adams 2015; Ojeda 2012) or processes of transnationalization of agro-industrial capital (Akram-Lodhi 2018; Borras 2009; Borras and Franco 2012; Levien et al. 2018). Research confronts predominant policy paradigms of 'agriculture (f)or development' (World Bank 2007) with empirical evidence about rural realities and social formations. Case studies assess the institutions, properties and outcomes of commercial land transactions, and highlight the heterogeneity and complexity of rural livelihoods and agency. Analyses comprise (sub)national and global, urban and rural, material and ideational, structural and actor-specific dimensions of local agrarian crises. However, long-term case studies (post-grab); agrarian political economy questions;[4] and historical antecedents should be included in the assessment of present-day changes in land use and property relations, to move beyond the up-to-date focus on 'snapshot accounts' of land grabs (see Borras and Franco 2012; Edelman et al. 2013; Hall 2011; Oya 2013a).

The chapter proceeds as follows: the next section provides an overview of key definitions and explanations of 'land grabbing'. It also discusses central viewpoints and controversies of the debate as a way to navigate the plurality of perspectives involved. The focus is on the scholarly debate of 'land grabbing'. The chapter then outlines unresolved challenges, as well as implications from the viewpoint of critical agrarian studies, before summarizing central issues.

LAND GRABBING: FROM META-NARRATIVE TO PLURALITY OF PERSPECTIVES

In the midst of the crises of food and finance in 2007–2008, the international non-governmental organization GRAIN raised worldwide attention to what it called land grabbing. The report 'Seized: The 2008 landgrab for food and financial security' described the grabbing of large areas of land by foreign states, or corporations, especially illegally, deceitfully or unfairly, through foreign investments in agriculture. Referencing more than 100 case studies, it showed how such instances of 'foreign private corporations getting new forms of control over farmland to produce food [and financial returns] not for the local communities but for someone else' led to 'the brutal expulsion of Indigenous communities', dispossession and displacement of customary land users, and the eradication of previous advances in food sovereignty[5] (GRAIN 2008, 1–2). Importantly, GRAIN provided a framing and established a meta-narrative about how and why land grabbing occurs that prevails in policy-oriented research and media outlets. Accordingly, foreign investors from food-insecure countries (particularly emerging economies) were grabbing arable land overseas to produce food for consumption back home, as a way to ease their food crisis; and private investors were involved due to the search for profitable investment opportunities at a time of economic crisis (GRAIN 2008). In a nutshell, this narrative postulated resource scarcity and related security concerns and/or speculative interests as a driver of land grabbing; and it focused on food sovereignty and peasant farming as the future of farming threatened by foreign investments.

The initial debate was largely policy-oriented, involving activists as well as researchers of international finance and development cooperation. The former contested the neoliberal development paradigm embedded in policies and institutions at the national and international levels via the meta-narrative. The latter attempted to distinguish the policy prescriptions of their neoliberal institutions from the phenomenon of 'land grabbing', asking whether and in which ways the 'global interest in farmland' (Deininger and Byerlee 2011) and other commercial land transactions constitute a 'land grab or development opportunity' (Cotula et al. 2009). The policy-oriented debate tends to treat 'the global land grab' as a stable concept, holding onto GRAIN's meta-narrative as a point of reference (see Peters 2018). Governance emerged as a central issue in the debate, based on the presumption that land grabs are the result of weak, poor or opaque (national and international) governance of foreign investment. This position has led different institutions to promote principled guidelines for a more ethical governance of investment in land or natural resources as a way to prevent land grabs.[6]

In response to the activist/policy debate on 'the global land grab', a scholarly debate on 'land grabbing' developed. The scholarly debate tries to reconfigure what 'the global land grab' is about (or whether it is relevant at all). However, the scholarly debate should not be seen as totally unrelated to policy-oriented assessments, due to the overlap in personnel, principles, presumptions or analytical categories (Goetz 2019).

The subsequent 'making sense period' (Edelman et al. 2013) in critical agrarian studies (and to a lesser degree, policy-oriented publications) scrutinized the meta-narrative with its focus on large-scale *foreign* investments in *farm*land for *food security* and *financial returns* at a time of *global crisis*, and its emphasis on food sovereignty and smallholder farming. Empirical evidence of individual 'land grabs' discloses that government-backed deals were linked to commercial interests (rather than food security). This understanding applies even to Chinese investments in Africa, a central reference point of the initial narrative about state-driven investments serving the food security of home countries (Bräutigam 2011; Cotula et al. 2009). Empirical evidence also suggests that only a minor share of large-scale foreign investments in agriculture are actually producing food (see Anseeuw et al. 2012; Bräutigam 2011). Correspondingly, the 'foreignization of space', that is the 'radical changes in the use and ownership of land', includes foreign investment in multiple sectors other than food and agriculture, including tourism, infrastructure, mining or industry (Zoomers 2010). Critical agrarian studies also relates the neoliberalization and seizing of water and forest resources to individual land grabs, by legal or illegal means, 'with little regard for how this will impact the millions of other users' (Skinner and Cotula 2011, 1; see also Barbesgaard 2018; Bizikova et al. 2013). Other significant themes that were introduced under 'the global land grab' umbrella are the financialization of land (Fairbairn 2015; McMichael 2012b; Ouma 2014); the role of host country states and local elites in promoting (transnational) agro-industrial farming and food systems and other land-intensive modernization projects (Boamah 2014; Kay 2015; Lavers 2012; Wolford et al. 2013); and 'green grabbing', for example in the case of biofuels projects, 'where "green" credentials are called upon to justify appropriations of land' (Fairhead et al. 2012, 237; see also

Green and Adams 2015). Some studies refer to the role of peasants and 'smallholders as poten-tial *agents* of land grabbing' (Hall 2011, 838; see also Cotula et al. 2009), as well as domestic investors (Anseeuw et al. 2012), albeit these issues remain understudied. Research also queries the presumption that peasants are necessarily opposed to large-scale farming models. Instead, empirical evidence from (post-)transitional countries suggests that large-scale investments in farming are often met with a relatively positive anticipation of production (Mamonova 2015; Soper 2019; Steggerda and Visser 2012). Finally, empirical evidence about the investor side undermines widespread perceptions of land grabbing. Contrary to policy-driven expectations of a win (investor) – win (peasant, host country) scenario, and different from the win (investor) – loss (peasant) scenario of critical research, many projects fail, and it is often blurred as to who actually benefits.

In addition, the analytical utility of the concept land grabbing has been interrogated. While it is well suited for activist purposes, the framing tends to neglect the context-specificity of dynamics and processes in the host and home countries (Baird 2014; Hall 2011). Critical agrarian studies and policy-oriented research point to the difference of political economies and capital origin involved in land grabbing. Take regions as an example: the largest share of foreign investments (involved in land transactions) in Africa allegedly emanates from outside the continent, while intra-regional land grabs prevail in other regions, namely Europe, Latin America ('translatino' capital, see Borras et al. 2012) and Asia (until 2012, see Anseeuw et al. 2012).[7] Also, the variety of land-based social relations involved in land grabbing have been highlighted, ranging from property rights to customary regimes (Borras and Franco 2012).

Further, the general assumption of absolute or relative scarcity as a driver of 'land grabs' underpinning the meta-narrative has been reviewed, and the importance to recognize the political construction of scarcity stressed. Research shows many land grabs that are not resource-seeking, but control- and market-seeking in their behaviour. This observation is based on cases where more indirect forms of accessing land are practised; such as projects using contract farming to establish monopsony markets and lasting control over what is being produced and how (Borras et al. 2012; Vicol 2017). Correspondingly, studies about investor and home country rationalizations of 'land grabs' identify a variety of considerations at play, including geopolitical interests and/or attempts to restructure business operations and the home country's economy, in addition to the search for new markets and resources (see Bräutigam 2009; Goetz 2019; Woertz 2013).

Finally, the policy debate on governance has been critiqued by some authors of the schol-arly debate. Being an intermediate between investor and community, states and states, states and communities, and states and corporations, governance is inherently political (Margulis et al. 2013; Otsuki et al. 2017a; von Braun and Meinzen-Dick 2009; Wolford et al. 2013). Therefore, policy attempts at a 'formalization fix' (Dwyer 2015) for land grabbing via govern-ance (treated as technicality) are being disapproved: they discount how legal systems or the governance of land reform and land titling can be a means, or at least a contributing factor, for grabbing (rather than prevention) (Dwyer 2015; Kay 2015; Tura 2018). The argument of poor governance being the cause of land grabbing is also scrutinized for its strategic component: it allows neoliberal institutions to separate land struggles from their ideological foundations and related policy advice, turning the problem into a technical question of improved imple-mentation instead (Akram-Lodhi 2018). Kenney-Lazar (2018) emphasizes the necessity to pay attention to capital–state relations, socio-environmental relations, community–state relations and internal community relations that are governing struggles over land in the form of dispossession (rather than assuming the absence of governance being the cause).

UNRESOLVED CHALLENGES AND IMPLICATIONS FOR CRITICAL AGRARIAN STUDIES

From the viewpoint of critical agrarian studies, the debate provides important impulses to (critically) revisit the theories and research approaches in explaining contemporary agrarian changes (e.g. the agrarian question reaches beyond the nation state, Borras 2009; land grabs as 'new enclosures' by corporate actors, White et al. 2012). At the same time, land grabbing still affords additional effort. This applies to the clarification of terminology and conceptual underpinnings, advancements of epistemology and methodology, comparison of contemporary land grabbing with historical antecedents, historical baselines or the integration of longstanding issues of agrarian political economy (Akram-Lodhi and Kay 2010; Borras and Franco 2012; Edelman et al. 2013; Hall 2011; Kay 2015).

To date, any research on and debate over land grabbing suffers from unreliable data, unclear epistemologies and (in many cases) insufficient methodologies. Even the most comprehensive of the existing non-government organization-led databases, the Land Matrix, cannot solve the lack of transparency of governments and corporations with regard to land use, conflicts or investment. More profoundly, it has not resolved the conceptual problems involved. Additional data problems concern, for instance, the a-historicity of databases that ignore land seized prior to the year 2000; the impossibility to stay up to date in the face of constantly changing project details; the opaqueness about epistemological presumptions informing the database (e.g. uncertainty); as well as methodological problems in the form of biased reporting as a result of crowdsourcing of data. Zoomers (2010) warns that Big Data will not solve the underpinning problem that what is being reported is not necessarily what is important. The Land Matrix, specifically, has also played an important role in accentuating the empirical dimensions of commercial land transactions with regards to land use and project scales (rather than other categories), and the perception of land grabs as a stable concept. Edelman (2013) has criticized the epistemologically and methodologically unsubstantiated focus on scale as a selection criterion for what is considered a land grab, as well as the postulation of 'pre-grab' stability. Moreover, Oya (2013b) has shown that many publications fail to meet basic scientific standards: they do not lay open (nor test) their assumptions and simulate the precision of facts ('false precision').

Several other issues deserve attention as the debate is continuing. The initial focus on smallholder farming and food sovereignty does not pay sufficient attention to the transnational character of many institutional contexts and processes of depeasantization. Moreover, the politics of change in land use and property relations (Borras and Franco 2012) and the history of institutions that are part of the phenomenon deserve greater attention (Edelman et al. 2013). Studying historical antecedents might uncover unintended dynamics. Kay (2015, 75), for instance, shows how commercial land transactions and related land and capital concentration in Latin America have been the unintended outcome of land reform processes: these 'weakened the hold of the traditional landed class over land and thereby facilitated later with the neoliberal turn the development of an active land market'. From a postcolonial perspective, the study of the history of power influencing land and territorial control in a region is vital for understanding whether and in which ways land grabbing is an 'old routine practice' (such as racial thinking embedded in land control) rather than a new phenomenon (Mollett 2016). Accordingly, historical accounts would need to include aspects of social differentiation (gender, class, lineage) and recognize that even consensus-based solutions are not neutral (Behrman et al. 2012; Hall et al. 2015; Mollett 2016; Otsuki et al. 2017a, 2017b; Ryan 2018). Largely unknown are also the effects of such land transactions on the power of the state (Lavers 2012); or the mediating roles of social capital, social institutions and communal reciprocity. However, these are necessary to comprehend the livelihood effects of individual land grabs for different persons of the same community and for social cohesion (Akram-Lodhi and Kay 2012; Boamah and Overå 2016; Nyantakyi-Frimpong and Bezner Kerr 2017). Another neglected issue area is the processes, forms and effects of land grabs in the 'Global North' (Magnan 2015). Research on land grabbing has also been called upon to advance the understanding of global capitalism(s) in view of traditional agrarian political economy issues, such as grassroots resistance, labour or capital development (Borras and Franco 2012; Edelman et al. 2013; Hall 2011; Li 2011).

What's more, land grabbing offers an interesting field to study the challenges of research-activist interrelations in critical agrarian studies. One point is to advance the understanding of research ethical questions, as well as ontological and methodological issues involved in the critical (co-)production of knowledge about the complexity of contemporary rural realities of land grabbing. How is conflict dealt with in co-production, how are incommensurable ontologies brought together, how much diversity of viewpoints is allowed, how are critical inquiry and analysis upheld in the process and what does critical mean in this context? A related point is how to reconcile the scientific approach of critically co-producing knowledge with the strategic imperative for offensive meta-narratives and *a priori* knowledge in the struggle and resistance against modernization theory-induced policy orthodoxies (see Akram-Lodhi 2018; Borras 2009; Edelman and Wolford 2017; Hall et al. 2015; Hunsberger et al. 2017). While research on strategic change has its place in critical agrarian studies research, the recent role of the meta-narrative in the formation of a shared understanding and foundation for joint action deserves greater attention. On the one hand, it seems worthwhile to study the tension this might create with regards to the critical co-production of knowledge. On the other hand, the transformative potential is of interest. 'Grand narratives' (Lyotard 1979) such as 'neoliberal development' or the offensive 'land grab' meta-narrative justify and legitimize particular cultural practices. While these forms of institutional or ideological knowledge have been critiqued by post-modern theorists for their hegemonial implications, it is equally interesting to note the transformative potential of the 'land grab' meta-narrative; for instance, the ways in which it served as a 'vehicle for strategic change', by way of sensemaking and as a 'means of co-orientation' (Kajamaa 2015). At least to a certain degree, this explains the two approaches in the literature: the activist-driven debate uses the 'land grab' narrative as a stable concept for strategic purposes, creating significant impact and attention for the problems raised; and the scholarly debate revolves around deconstruction and decentring of the meta-narrative, being less influenced by strategic considerations.

CONCLUSION

The original framing and meta-narrative by GRAIN has provoked an interdisciplinary debate on contemporary land struggles that has yet to fully integrate traditional agrarian questions with those from contemporary political economy, aside from defining what it is about. During the early phase, activist and policy research stressed questions of whether and in which ways large-scale (foreign) investments constituted a land grab or development. At the heart of the debate was the contestation of neoliberal institutions and policies, and the capitalist development of agriculture and natural resources. The scholarly debate has then engaged in scrutinizing and questioning the terms, frames and perspectives of the initial narrative and has produced a rich and nuanced body of empirical-analytical assessments of contemporary agrarian changes. For the debate to mature, research has to advance critical agrarian debates, including issues of scale, peasant differentiation, socio-ecological relations, food sovereignty, urban–rural interlinkages or the agency of small-scale farmers in transformation. This might occur under 'the global land grab' umbrella, or as part of a more decentred revisiting of ongoing land struggles in different contexts. Regardless how the debate(s) evolve(s), challenges of terminological ambiguity, and the neglect of methodological and epistemological issues, should be addressed in either case, and presumptions of 'pre-grab stability' critically reviewed. Moreover, medium- to long-term studies of what occurs after the implementation of land grab projects are required. Ultimately, the dialectic between the different approaches of treating 'land grabbing' as a stable concept or as something to be questioned (in its alleged novelty, or in view of core categories) offers the opportunity for studies of agrarian change and peasant studies to revisit their own 'grand narratives', as well as to debate land-related agrarian struggles with a wider audience of different disciplinary and professional backgrounds.

NOTES

1. The term epistemic community, a term applied by Haas, describes the role that 'networks of knowledge-based experts – epistemic communities – play in articulating the cause-and-effect relationships of complex problems, helping states identify their interests, framing the issues for collective debate, proposing specific policies, and identifying salient points for negotiation' (Haas 1992).
2. Discourse coalitions refers to 'ensemble[s] of a set of story lines, the actors that utter these story lines, and the practices that conform to these story lines, all organized around a discourse' (Hajer 1993), such as agriculture for development. In the policy debate over land grabbing, various discourse coalitions can be identified that differ in view of their core principles, presumptions, categories, embraced practices and story lines regarding the future of agriculture and farming in general, and rural development in particular (Goetz 2019, 53–76).
3. I would like to thank Derek Hall for sharing this observation.
4. For a discussion of agrarian political economy and critical agrarian studies, see Akram-Lodhi and Kay (2010); Borras (2009); Bernstein (2009); Edelman et al. (2013); and Akram-Lodhi (2018). Also see the discussion by Hall (2011) and Edelman and Wolford (2017) on the challenges of explaining land grabbing through the lens of traditional theories of agrarian change.
5. The political concept of food sovereignty describes the right of countries, producers and consumers 'to determine ... own food producing systems and policies' (Nyéléni 2007). See Claeys et al. (this volume) on food sovereignty for more details.
6. Three guidelines have been central in the land grab debate: 'Responsible agricultural investments' (RAI) established and promoted by the World Bank; 'Voluntary guidelines on the responsible governance of tenure of land, fisheries and forests in the context of national food security', established

and promoted by the Food and Agriculture Organization; and 'Voluntary guidelines to support the progressive realization of the right to adequate food in the context of national food security' (RtAF Guidelines), established by FAO (2004) and promoted by the Special Rapporteur on the Right to Food. For more information, see the RAI (www.worldbank.org/en/topic/agriculture/publication/responsible-agricultural-investment, accessed 20 December 2018); RtAF Guidelines (www.fao.org/3/a-y7937e.pdf, accessed 20 December 2018); and Voluntary Guidelines (www.fao.org/docrep/016/i2801e/i2801e.pdf, accessed 20 December 2018).

7. Due to data problems confronting research on land grabbing, the quantitative regional differentiation of capital flows can at best (if at all) serve as rough orientation. In the absence of clear definitions and data, these numbers remain speculative. Nevertheless, this information is referenced to highlight the need to critically engage with the meta-narrative, including its focus on foreign investors. For a discussion of data problems, see the third section of this chapter.

FURTHER READING

Borras, Jr., S.M.; Franco, J.C. (2012), Global land grabbing and trajectories of agrarian change: A preliminary analysis, *Journal of Agrarian Change*, 12(1), 34–59.
Edelman, M.; Oya, C.; Borras, Jr., S.M. (2013), Global land grabs: Historical processes, theoretical and methodological implications and current trajectories, *Third World Quarterly*, 34(9), 1517–1531.
GRAIN (2008), *Seized: The 2008 Land Grab for Food and Financial Security*, Barcelona: GRAIN.
Li, T.M. (2011), Centering labor in the land grab debate, *Journal of Peasant Studies*, 38(2), 281–298.
Zoomers, A. (2010), Globalisation and the foreignisation of space: Seven processes driving the current global land grab, *Journal of Peasant Studies*, 37(2), 429–447.

REFERENCES

Akram-Lodhi, A.H. (2018), 'What is critical agrarian studies?', ROAPE, accessed 20 December 2018 at http://roape.net/2018/03/28/what-is-critical-agrarian-studies/.
Akram-Lodhi, A.H.; Kay, C. (2010), Surveying the agrarian question (Part 2): Current debates and beyond, *Journal of Peasant Studies*, 37(2), 255–284.
Akram-Lodhi, A.H.; Kay, C. (2012), The agrarian question: Peasants and rural change, in Akram-Lodhi, A.H.; Kay, C. (eds), *Peasants and Globalization*, Abingdon: Routledge, 15–46.
Anseeuw, W.; Alden Wily, L.; Cotula, L.; Taylor, M. (2012), *Land Rights and the Rush for Land: Findings of the Global Commercial Pressures on Land Research Project*, Rome: International Land Coalition.
Baird, I.G. (2014), The global land grab meta-narrative, Asian money laundering and elite capture: Reconsidering the Cambodian context, *Geopolitics*, 19(2), 431–453.
Barbesgaard, M. (2018), Blue growth: Savior or ocean grabbing?, *Journal of Peasant Studies*, 45(1), 130–149.
Behrman, J.; Meinzen-Dick, R.; Quisumbing, A. (2012), The gender implications of large-scale land deals, *Journal of Peasant Studies*, 39(1), 49–79.
Bernstein, H. (2009), Agrarian questions from transition to globalization, in Akram-Lodhi, A.H.; Kay, C. (eds), *Peasants and Globalization: Political Economy, Rural Transformation and the Agrarian Question*, London: Routledge, 239–261.
Bizikova, L.; Roy, D.; Swanson, D.; Venema, H.; McCandless, M. (2013), *The Water-Energy Food Security Nexus: Towards a Practical Planning and Decision Support Framework for Landscape Investment and Risk Management*, Manitoba: International Institute of Sustainable Development.
Boamah, F. (2014), How and why chiefs formalise land use in recent times: The politics of land dispossession through biofuels investments in Ghana, *Review of African Political Economy*, 41(141), 406–423.
Boamah, F.; Overå, R. (2016), Rethinking livelihood impacts of biofuel land deals in Ghana, *Development and Change*, 47(1), 98–129.

Borras, Jr., S.M. (2009), Agrarian change and peasant studies: Changes, continuities and challenges – an introduction, *Journal of Peasant Studies*, 36(1), 5–31.

Borras, Jr., S.M.; Franco, J.C. (2010), Towards a broader view of the politics of global land grab: Rethinking land issues, reframing resistance, *Initiatives in Critical Agrarian Studies Working Paper Series*, 1, 1–39.

Borras, Jr., S.M.; Franco, J.C. (2012), Global land grabbing and trajectories of agrarian change: A preliminary analysis, *Journal of Agrarian Change*, 12(1), 34–59.

Borras, Jr., S.M.; Hall, R.; Scoones, I.; White, B.; Wolford, W. (2011), Towards a better understanding of global land grabbing: An editorial introduction, *Journal of Peasant Studies*, 38(2), 209–216.

Borras, Jr., S.M.; Kay, C.; Gómez, S.; Wilkinson, J. (eds) (2012), Land grabbing and global capitalist accumulation: Key features in Latin America, Special Issue, *Canadian Journal of Development Studies*, 33(4), 399–551.

Bräutigam, D. (2009), *The Dragon's Gift: The Real Story of China in Africa*, Oxford: Oxford University Press.

Bräutigam, D. (2011), Testimony on China's growing role in Africa before the United States Senate Committee on Foreign Relations Subcommittee on African Affairs, Washington, DC: United States Senate.

Clapp, J. (2014), Financialization, distance and global food politics, *Journal of Peasant Studies*, 41(5), 797–814.

Cotula, L.; Vermeulen, S.; Leonard, R.; Keeley, J. (2009), *Land Grab or Development Opportunity? Agricultural Investment and International Land Deals in Africa*, London and Rome: IIED/FAO/IFAD.

Deininger, K.; Byerlee, D. (2011), *Rising Global Interest in Farmland: Can It Yield Sustainable and Equitable Benefits?*, Washington, DC: World Bank.

Dwyer, M.B. (2015), The formalization fix? Land titling, land concessions and the politics of spatial transparency in Cambodia, *Journal of Peasant Studies*, 42(5), 903–928.

Edelman, M. (2013), Messy hectares: Questions about the epistemology of land grabbing data, *Journal of Peasant Studies*, 40(3), 485–501.

Edelman, M.; Wolford, W. (2017), Introduction: Critical agrarian studies in theory and practice: Symposium: agrarianism in theory and practice, *Antipode*, 49(4), 959–976.

Edelman, M.; Oya, C.; Borras, Jr., S.M. (2013), Global land grabs: Historical processes, theoretical and methodological implications and current trajectories, *Third World Quarterly*, 34(9), 1517–1531.

Fairbairn, M. (2015), Foreignization, financialization and land grab regulation, *Journal of Agrarian Change*, 15(4), 581–591.

Fairhead, J.; Leach, M.; Scoones, I. (2012), Green grabbing: A new appropriation of nature?, *Journal of Peasant Studies*, 39(2), 237–261.

Fuchs, D.; Meyer-Eppler, R.; Hamenstädt, U. (2013), Food for thought: The politics of financialization in the agrifood system, *Competition and Change*, 17(3), 219–233.

Goetz, A. (2019), *Land Grabbing and Home Country Development: Chinese and British Land Acquisitions in Comparative Perspective*, Berlin: Verlag.

GRAIN (2008), *Seized: The 2008 Land Grab for Food and Financial Security*, Barcelona: GRAIN, accessed 20 December 2018 at www.grain.org/article/entries/93-seized-the-2008-landgrab-for-food-and-financial-security.

Green, K.E.; Adams, W.M. (2015), Green grabbing and the dynamics of local-level engagement with neoliberalization in Tanzania's wildlife management areas, *Journal of Peasant Studies*, 42(1), 97–117.

Haas, P.M. (1992), Introduction: Epistemic communities and international policy coordination, *International Organization*, 46(1), 1–35.

Hajer, M. (1993), Discourse coalitions and the institutionalisation of practice: The case of acid rain in Great Britain, in Fischer, F.; Forester, J. (eds), *The Argumentative Turn in Policy Analysis and Planning*, Durham, NC: Duke University Press, 43–67.

Hall, D. (2011), Land grabs, land control, and Southeast Asian crop booms, *Journal of Peasant Studies*, 38(4), 837–857.

Hall, D. (2013), Primitive accumulation, accumulation by dispossession and the global land grab, *Third World Quarterly*, 34(9), 1582–1604.

Hall, R.; Edelman, M.; Borras, Jr., S.M.; Scoones, I.; White, B.; Wolford, W. (2015), Resistance, acquiescence or incorporation? An introduction to land grabbing and political reactions 'from below', *Journal of Peasant Studies*, 42(3–4), 467–488.

Hiraldo, R. (2018), Experiencing primitive accumulation as alienation: Mangrove forest privatization, enclosures and the everyday adaptation of bodies to capital in rural Senegal, *Journal of Agrarian Change*, 18(3), 517–535.

Hunsberger, C.; Corbera, W.; Borras, Jr., S.M.; Franco, J.C.; Woods, K.; Work, C.; Rosa de la, R.; Eang, V.; Herre, R.; Kham, S.S.; Parl, C.; Sokheng, S.; Spoor, M.; Thein, S.; Aung, K.T.; Thuon, R.; Vaddhanaphuti, C. (2017), Climate change mitigation, land grabbing and conflict: Towards a landscape-based and collaborative action research agenda, *Canadian Journal of Development Studies/Revue canadienne d'études du développement*, 38(3), 305–324.

Kajamaa, A. (2015), Transformative metanarrative as a vehicle for strategic change, *Academy of Management Proceedings*, 1, 18614.

Kay, C. (2015), The agrarian question and the neoliberal rural transformation in Latin America, *European Review of Latin American and Caribbean Studies/Revista Europea de Estudios Latinoamericanos y del Caribe*, 73–83.

Kenney-Lazar, M. (2018), Governing dispossession: relational land grabbing in Laos, *American Association of Geographers*, 108(3), 679–694.

Lavers, T. (2012), Land grab as development strategy? The political economy of agricultural investment in Ethiopia, *Journal of Peasant Studies*, 39(1), 105–132.

Levien, M.; Watts, M.; Hairong, Y. (2018), Agrarian Marxism, *Journal of Peasant Studies*, 45(5–6), 853–883.

Li, T.M. (2011), Centering labor in the land grab debate, *Journal of Peasant Studies*, 38(2), 281–298.

Lyotard, J.-F. (1979), *The Postmodern Condition: A Report on Knowledge*, Manchester: Manchester University Press.

Magnan, A. (2015), The financialization of agri-food in Canada and Australia: Corporate farmland and farm ownership in the grains and oilseed sector, *Journal of Rural Studies*, 41, 1–12.

Mamonova, N. (2015), Resistance or adaptation? Ukrainian peasants' responses to large-scale land acquisitions, *Journal of Peasant Studies*, 42(3–4), 607–634.

Margulis, M.E.; McKeon, N.; Borras, Jr., S.M. (2013), Land grabbing and global governance, *Globalizations*, 10(1), Special Issue.

McMichael, P. (2012a), Depeasantization, *The Wiley-Blackwell Encyclopedia of Globalization*, Chichester: Wiley.

McMichael, P. (2012b), The land grab and corporate food regime restructuring, *Journal of Peasant Studies*, 39(3–4), 681–701.

McMichael, P. (2013), Land grabbing as security mercantilism in international relations, *Globalizations*, 10(1), 47–64.

Mollett, S. (2016), The power to plunder: Rethinking land grabbing in Latin America, *Antipode*, 48(2), 412–432.

Nyantakyi-Frimpong, H.; Bezner Kerr, R. (2017), Land grabbing, social differentiation, intensified migration and food security in northern Ghana, *Journal of Peasant Studies*, 44(2), 421–444.

Nyéléni (2007), Declaration of the forum for food sovereignty, 27 February, Sélingué, Mali, accessed 20 December 2018 at https://nyeleni.org/spip.php?article290.

Ojeda, D. (2012), Green pretexts: Ecotourism, neoliberal conservation and land grabbing in Tayrona National Natural Park, Colombia, *Journal of Peasant Studies*, 39(2), 357–375.

Otsuki, K.; Schoneveld, G.C.; Zoomers, A. (2017a), From land grabs to inclusive development?, *Geoforum*, 83.

Otsuki, K.; Achá, D.; Wijnhoud, J.D. (2017b), After the consent: Re-imagining participatory land governance in Massingir, Mozambique, *Geoforum*, 83, 153–163.

Ouma, S. (2014), Situating global finance in the land rush debate: A critical review, *Geoforum*, 57, 162–166.

Oya, C. (2013a), The land rush and classic agrarian questions of capital and labour: A systematic scoping review of the socioeconomic impact of land grabs in Africa, *Third World Quarterly*, 34(9), 1532–1557.

Oya, C. (2013b), Methodological reflections on 'land grab' databases and the 'land grab' literature 'rush', *Journal of Peasant Studies*, 40(3), 503–520.

Peters, P. (2018), Land grabs: The politics of the land rush across Africa, in *Oxford Research Encyclopedia of Politics*, Oxford: Oxford University Press.

Ryan, C. (2018), Large-scale land deals in Sierra Leone at the intersection of gender and lineage, *Third World Quarterly*, 39(1), 189–206.

Schoenberger, L.; Hall, D.; Vandergeest, P. (2017), What happened when the land grab came to Southeast Asia?, *Journal of Peasant Studies*, 44(4), 697–725.

Scoones, I.; Hall, R.; Borras, Jr., S.M.; White, B.; Wolford, W. (2013), The politics of evidence: Methodologies for understanding the global land rush, *Journal of Peasant Studies*, 40(3), 469–483.

Skinner, J.; Cotula, L. (2011), Are land deals driving 'water grabs'? *Briefing: The Global Land Rush*, London: IIED.

Soper, R. (2019), From protecting peasant livelihoods to essentializing peasant agriculture: Problematic trends in food sovereignty discourse, *Journal of Peasant Studies*, 1–21.

Steggerda, M.; Visser, O. (2012), A farm manager should get his hands dirty: global land acquisitions and the export of western farm models to Russia, *International Conference on Global Land Grabbing II*.

Tura, H.A. (2018), Land rights and land grabbing in Oromia, Ethiopia, *Land Use Policy*, 70, 247–255.

Vicol, M. (2017), Is contract farming an inclusive alternative to land grabbing? The case of potato contract farming in Maharashtra, India, *Geoforum*, 85, 157–166.

von Braun, J.; Meinzen-Dick, R.S. (2009), *Land Grabbing by Foreign Investors in Developing Countries: Risks and Opportunities*, Washington, DC: International Food Policy Research Institute.

White, B.; Borras, Jr., S.M.; Hall, R.; Scoones, I.; Wolford, W. (2012), The new enclosures: Critical perspectives on corporate land deals, *Journal of Peasant Studies*, 39(3–4), 619–647.

Woertz, E. (2013), The governance of Gulf agro-investments, *Globalizations*, 10(1), 87–104.

Wolford, W.; Borras, Jr., S.M.; Hall, R.; Scoones, I.; White, B. (eds) (2013), Governing global land deals: The role of the state in the rush for land, *Development and Change*, 44(2), Special Issue.

World Bank (2007), *World Development Report 2008: Agriculture for Development*, Washington, DC: World Bank.

Zoomers, A. (2010), Globalisation and the foreignisation of space: Seven processes driving the current global land grab, *Journal of Peasant Studies*, 37(2), 429–447.

40. Water for agriculture
Larry A. Swatuk

INTRODUCTION

Water sustains all living organisms. As the saying goes: without water there is no life. How it falls and where it flows shapes ecosystems and the biodiversity contained therein. With regard to human communities, variation in the hydrological cycle across time and space constitutes the foundation for the existence of and variations in social forms (Linton and Budds 2014). Historically, humans had very little control over these natural processes, so shaped their societies in relation to the natural environment (Solomon 2010). As Hulme (2015) trenchantly put it, climate is culture. With time, humanity's increasing ability to manipulate the environment, in particular to alter the natural flow of water across the landscape, dramatically changed the relationship between human communities and the natural world. Such efforts at control gave rise to ideologies of 'man over nature'. No longer were humans regarded as part of nature; rather they came to define themselves as apart from it. Technological innovation facilitated the spread and establishment of human communities well beyond the limits defined by the natural resource base. Over the long course of the Neolithic revolution came not only the rise of agrarian-based civilizations but social differentiation and hierarchy within and between societies (Ponting 1991). Put differently, water came to be at the very heart of social power.

While the attempt to dominate nature, including developing the capacity to 'push rivers around' (Conca 2006), is a millennia-old project, it has gained speed over the last century during the high-modern era, a period Tony Allen (2003) says is characterized by the 'hydraulic mission': capturing water for state power. At the heart of this mission is water for energy, industry and agriculture (ICOLD n.d.; Molden 2007). Of all of the freshwater withdrawn for human use, on average 70 per cent is directed to irrigation (WWAP 2015, 25). A significant amount of this water is impounded behind the walls of large dams. According to the International Commission on Large Dams (ICOLD n.d.), as of September 2019 there were 57 985 large dams registered in the world.[1] Almost 50 per cent of all single-purpose large dams have been constructed for irrigation; overall, irrigation constitutes a key purpose in 33 per cent of all large dams (ibid.). China (23 841 registered large dams) and the United States (9263 registered large dams) are by far the greatest dam-building countries in the world. They are followed by India (4408), Japan (3130) and then Brazil, Republic of Korea, Canada, South Africa and Spain (all with more than 1000 large dams registered with ICOLD) (ibid.). Clearly, the list of major large dam builders reflects state capacity to martial the financial, technical and political resources necessary to undertake large-scale infrastructure. In addition, Chinese state-owned enterprises are at the heart of the dam-building renaissance currently underway across the Global South (Fearnside 2017; Perry and Praskiewicz 2017; Swatuk 2018a). Without doubt, influential studies such as the World Bank's and the Food and Agriculture Organization's (FAO) (2009) *Awakening Africa's Sleeping Giant* have helped to drive this late-modern hydraulic mission in service of a new green revolution for China, India and large swaths of Africa and South America. At the same time, the findings of the World Commission on Dams (WCD 2000), mustered to investigate the socio-economic and environmental impacts of large dam-building projects over time, helped raise important questions regarding the beneficiaries of these enterprises; by the end of the first decade of the twenty-first century powerful coalitions of political and economic actors came together to drive a new era in large dam-building (Swatuk 2018a; Swatuk and Wirkus 2018).

In addition to irrigation's central role in motivating dam construction of all sizes, in many parts of the world groundwater's role in irrigation is increasing in importance. This is especially so across the arid and semi-arid savanna regions. According to Shah (2014), groundwater now accounts for one-third of all water used in irrigation. Hirji et al. (2017, 11) state that 'India, Pakistan and Bangladesh combined, pump almost half of the world's groundwater used for irrigation, supporting the livelihoods of 60–80 per cent of the population'. In 2012, the World Bank estimated India to be using approximately 230 km^3 of groundwater of which 90 per cent was used in irrigation (quoted in Chindarkar and Grafton 2019). Chindarkar and Grafton (2019, 109) state that 'approximately 90 million households are directly dependent on groundwater irrigation'.

There are numerous problems linked to treating water – which constitutes a fundamental element of a socio-natural system – primarily as an input into industrial or agricultural production. Large-scale infrastructure projects fundamentally alter natural system dynamics, often pushing ecosystems into unsustainable directions, with the Aral Sea being the prime example (Gleick and Palaniappan 2010). In addition to environmental impacts, treating water as an ordinary economic good, subject to market forces, often results in what Homer-Dixon (1994) identified as ecological marginalization of the poor and resource capture by the wealthy or simply slightly better-off. For example, as groundwater becomes scarcer, only those with the economic means to drill deeper will continue to have access to the water they 'need' (Hirji et al. 2017). Moreover, water is a public good; is location-bound; has high mobilization costs; generates a heterogeneous market among stakeholders with dissimilar needs; is subject to macro-economic interdependencies; is prone to market failure; and has high merit (non-use) value (Savenije 2002).

In the context of critical agrarian studies, not only is it important to understand the biophysical nature of water, but it is equally important to understand the ways it is embedded in society and how the interaction between society and the natural world alters the lived reality (Linton and Budds 2014; Swyngedouw 2015). Thus, how water is used reflects society back to itself. While water in its natural form flows along the hydraulic gradient, more often than not, in its social form, it flows toward power (Swatuk 2018b).

In the balance of this chapter, water is briefly described biophysically, then discussed largely in relation to human needs. The chapter argues that dominant approaches to water security are invested in the capture of available surface and groundwater through large-scale infrastructure. In the words of Falkenmark and Rockstrom (2004), they are 'blue water biased'. It is argued here that those centrally invested in livelihood security need to challenge this bias through better articulation of such a perspective's negative consequences. The chapter argues that critical agrarian studies should adopt a green water preference; that is, concentrating on assisting farmers to make better use of the rainfall available to them, while simultaneously challenging and exposing the uneven outcomes deriving from state, private-sector and financial capital biases toward large-scale infrastructure projects. The chapter concludes that strategies for sustainability and equity in agrarian transformation must include new ways of seeing and thinking about water. Extant orthodoxies regarding resource capture and the control of nature not only harm the many but exacerbate vulnerabilities in a climate-changing world.

PERSPECTIVES AND DEBATES

There is a vast amount of water in the world. Indeed, earth is the 'blue planet'. According to L'vovich (1979), 525 100 km³ of precipitation falls on the earth each year, with most of that falling over the oceans (411 600 km³). Approximately 113 500 km³ of precipitation falls over land, so constituting the bulk of freshwater available to humans. Precipitation partitions in two ways. As it lands on the ground, it either runs off as surface flow or soaks into the soil (i.e., a first partitioning point). Once it soaks into the soil, water either evaporates back to the atmosphere or transpires through plants (together often described as 'evapo-transpiration') or infiltrates into the land to constitute groundwater (i.e., a second partitioning point). There is much made about the so-called 'freshwater lens', wherein of all water on earth only 2.5 per cent is freshwater of which an estimated 0.3 per cent is readily available to humans as either surface flow or groundwater flow. This perspective of global limits fuels a scarcity narrative. This narrative is unhelpful partly because 0.3 per cent of 525 100 km³ is a large amount of water; and partly because water is a highly localized resource. Aggregate data obscure this variability. It is more important to know that water ceaselessly cycles through the atmosphere. It is equally important to know how precipitation falls – continuously over the whole year; in great amounts for short periods of time; in the winter or the summer or both; and so on – and how it partitions. For example, the same amount of water may fall over temperate and savanna zones during the course of a year. However, evaporative demand is much lower in temperate zones than in savanna zones. Moreover, water generally falls year round in temperate zones, whereas across the world's tropics it tends to be highly seasonal. These conditions create very different challenges for harnessing water for human needs without compromising the health of ecosystems despite the fact that a similar amount of precipitation falls over both areas.

There is enough water for all human needs. There is especially enough water for domestic purposes, given that this is 'small water' in relation to the huge amount of 'big water' used in agriculture (Savenije 2002). It is important to understand, however, that where planning for water resources access, use and management is concerned, there is a significant blue water bias. This bias extends to discussions concerning food security, into modelling water availability and so on to discussions and characterizations of various forms of temporal and spatial 'scarcity' (Lautze and Hanjira 2014; Mehta 2018). Combined with an obsession with yield – versus, say, nutrition of crops grown or types of crops relative to water productivity and crop water requirements – organizations such as the World Bank and the FAO focus on aggregate data to make their claims about suitable policy regarding both the possibility and need to develop infrastructure on a massive scale. In contrast, there is a wide array of scholars and activists who argue that food security must begin with the localized specificities of the hydrological cycle and with the existing needs of the millions of smallholder farmers in the world (Zeitoun et al. 2016). Let us now unpack this debate.

Blue Water Bias

To get beyond the blue water bias, it is useful to think of different types of water in terms of their color. In addition to blue (that is readily available surface and groundwater), there is grey water (non-potable domestic water that may be recycled for other purposes; storm-water runoff), black water (industrial and household water that contains a variety of toxins, pathogens and heavy metals that are not easily reintroduced to the system without significant technological intervention) and, most importantly, green water (that which soaks into the soil and either evaporates back to the atmosphere or transpires through plants creating biomass). Through history, the most successful and durable human communities have settled in what Keegan (1994) calls 'zones of first choice', that is areas where land and water combine to create highly arable land. Seeking certainty, farmers have long endeavored to create stocks of water (that is stored blue water through simple impoundments) to supplement the green water – rainfall that nourishes the plants directly – that may or may not be sufficient in any one planting season. Humans have long exploited blue water, practicing flood recession agriculture, digging wells and canals, constructing impoundments and barriers of every size and type and settling around rivers, streams and deltas (Solomon 2010). As technologies have improved so has the capacity of human communities to extend their reach across the natural world, settling in the most unlikely places. Multi-billion dollar projects such as the Central Arizona Project make it possible for not only urban settlement but extensive agriculture to take place in arid environments (Molle 2008). 'Successes' such as these lead others to imagine new hydraulic futures, giving rise to the current dam-building bonanza across Latin America and Sub-Saharan Africa as well as providing inspiration for India's long-standing river-linking project. As stated earlier, mastering blue water is at the heart of state power (Swyngedouw 2015). This is understandable. With few exceptions, there is a direct correlation between gross domestic product (GDP) per capita and water use per capita (Hoekstra and Chapagain 2006; Shiklomanov 2000). The countries with the lowest GDP per capita are those with the highest percentage of their GDP derived from agriculture (that is cash crop production for export) and the highest percentage of their population engaged in primarily rainfed agriculture. Facts like these lead organizations such as the FAO and the World Bank to argue that these countries are poor because of their inability to exploit blue water on a large scale. The International Water Management Institute states that many countries located across the tropics suffer not physical water scarcity but economic water scarcity; that is, they have failed in their hydraulic mission to capture and deploy blue water for economic growth and social development (Molden 2007).

Perspectives such as these privilege policy making that focuses on techno-economic approaches to increased scale and yield. Rare is the farmer who is not interested in either expanding their land under cultivation or improving yield. Policy makers, however, continue to envision the 'big win'. China's Three Gorges Dam, Turkey's Ilisu Dam and Ethiopia's Grand Renaissance Dam are three examples of multi-purpose construction projects designed to bring energy and food security to entire countries and regions (Swatuk and Wirkus 2018). There are similar projects underway in Latin America, Southeast and Central Asia. What World Bank and FAO advisors are modelling and counselling is a flattened hydrograph: to make a desired quantity and quality of water available throughout the year in places where it is generally only available seasonally and often in extremes. Grey et al. (2013) describe such places as 'hydrologically complex' where, moving forward, only a type of fragile water security is thought to be possible at very high cost. Moreover, the hypothesized impacts of climate change on global hydrological cycles has introduced both a sense of urgency in decision-making and a recognition that climate actions will require trade-offs to ensure water, energy, food and ecosystem security (Allouche et al. 2015; WEF 2011).

The consequences of this discursive framing for agrarian transformation are significant. Influential sets of state and private-sector actors are engaged in cash crop – for example biofuel and food – production through the dramatic expansion of agricultural land and surface and groundwater exploitation. The land-grabbing literature has articulated this phenomenon very clearly (Akram-Lodhi 2012; Borras and Franco 2013; Cotula et al. 2009). The point being made here is that harnessing blue water through large-scale infrastructure often leads to the marginalization of the very people in whose interest states claim to be acting. Somewhat paradoxically, food security through big infrastructure is a conversation too often undertaken by the already food secure: representatives of governments, banks and large-scale commercial enterprises.

Green Water Opportunities

Access to capital and technology allows powerful actors to push into formerly marginal lands to engage in large-scale production. Rice and sugar cane production along the Senegal River is a good example. Smallholder farmers find it difficult to benefit from such an approach to agricultural production. States are generally not interested in the marginal gains to be made among 1 ton per hectare farmers. Yet, with erratic rainfall, unpredictable growing seasons and more frequent extreme events (drought/flood) those without access to irrigation stand to suffer most under climate change. Falkenmark and Rockstrom (2004, 2006) argue that rainfed farming is exactly where planning and policy making should focus to enhance local, regional and global food security. They argue that policy should focus on 'vapor shift' – that is focusing on land management to encourage less evaporation and more infiltration of rainfall into the soil (so encouraging biomass production through transpiration), especially across the savanna zones.

The world's savanna zones have seen the greatest expansion of agriculture over the last several decades, particularly as groundwater technology has advanced. Such technological innovations are at the heart of land grabbing, as those with capital are best able to take advantage not only of new technologies but government policies regarding expanded yields. For Falkenmark and Rockstrom (2004), the majority of the world's food is produced through rainfed farming. While irrigation commands roughly 60 per cent of freshwater withdrawals, it contributes roughly 40 per cent of world food production (Falkenmark and Rockstrom 2004). Given the millions of smallholder farmers across the savanna zones, small innovations in land management will yield great gains in crop production (Recha et al. 2015).

The blue water bias makes policy makers blind to the importance of green water. Indeed, global freshwater per capita availability models completely ignore the contribution of green water to individual water needs. For example, it is suggested that each individual requires approximately 1760 m^3 of water per year (Recha et al. 2015). Influential organizations such as the FAO calculate these needs relative to freshwater availability, that is in relation to measurable annual runoff. However, if 60 per cent of human food requirements are derived from rainfed agriculture, then the amount of freshwater needed for humans should be adjusted accordingly.[2] The current model paints an often alarmist picture of water availability, so encouraging resource capture by influential actors in pursuit of their own water, energy and food security; or in pursuit of the huge profit to be made by trading on inaccurate conceptualizations of scarcity. As techno-economic efforts increase in number and scale, there is an urgent need to reflect on the ends to which new irrigation is put: cash crops for export that benefit the few, or a mix of cash and food crops that benefit the many? The concept 'virtual water', pioneered by Allen (2011), helps illustrate the global flows of water and capital through agricultural commodity trade.

Scarcity for most peasant farmers is seasonal and increasingly tied to their diminished land holdings on increasingly marginal lands. This socially constructed water scarcity (Mehta 2001) makes green water approaches to crop production all the more important. Green water approaches focus on where the rainfall hits the soil. Unlike attempts to flatten the hydrograph, such an approach locates sustainable water (and land) management within the context of local geography. Rather than work against nature through the introduction of expensive technologies, green water management works with the long experience of those on the land in relation to rainfall-based land management and crop choice. For example, farmers in savanna regions would be wise to plant drought-resistant crops such as millet and sorghum which are native to semi-arid regions instead of crops such as barley and wheat which perform better in temperate zones. Improved soil management through the use of minimum tillage, and inter- and rotational-cropping systems combined with micro-scale rainwater harvesting systems (such as zaï pits in the Sahel or micro-dams and high earth bunds in Eastern Africa), are forms of locally appropriate technology generally long known to, but increasingly disused by, smallholder farmers (Ibraimo and Munguambe 2007). This is not to say that smallholder farmers should not have access to irrigation. To the contrary, they must, but this irrigation can be supplemental and less expensive when combined with green water perspectives on sustainable resource management (Falkenmark and Rockstrom 2008). In addition, water is not the only limiting factor to smallholder production. Research shows that soil health is equally if not more important (Van der Zaag 2010). Achieving water and food security among the millions of peasant farmers across the tropics and in the savanna zones is a labor-intensive exercise, requiring appropriate extension services and government support. The important point here, however, is to recognize that even in 'drylands' there is much more water for agriculture than one might think. So, before rushing off to foreign investors for big infrastructure, locking governments into long-term loans in support of dubious projects in the name of the water-energy-food nexus, policy makers would do well to engage smallholder farmers, through cooperatives, and ask them about what happens when the rainfall hits the soil. Van der Zaag (2010) labels this a 'farmer-centered approach'.

CONCLUSION

The value of a green water perspective for critical agrarian studies is twofold. One, by helping the analyst to see beyond their blue water bias, such an approach provides a better means to understanding how much water is available seasonally. Two, it helps smallholder farmers and all those interested in their welfare and enhanced livelihoods to make better arguments regarding appropriately embedded approaches to water for food security. While this does not ensure that governments will be persuaded by such arguments, nevertheless it provides a better basis for the empirical analysis necessary to show policy makers the folly of their ways and to support farmers, activists and activist-academics in pressing for meaningful social change, including land reform, extension services and appropriate technology.

NOTES

1. A large dam is defined by ICOLD as having 'a height of 15 metres or greater from lowest foundation to crest or a dam between 5 metres and 15 metres impounding more than 3 million cubic metres [of water]' (ICOLD n.d.).
2. According to Falkenmark and Rockstrom (2004), people in developed countries require approximately 1760 m^3/cap/year of which 1600 m^3/cap/year is derived from food, 130 m^3 in industry and only 30 m^3 for domestic use. Sixty per cent (that is, food from green water) of 1600 m^3 is 960 m^3, so the FAO misrepresents water needs per capita (all water) by not factoring out green water use from the calculation. Thus actual blue water requirements are not 1760 m^3 but are $130m^3 + 30m^3 + 740m^3 = 900m^3$ (see www.fao.org/nr/water/aquastat/didyouknow/index2.stm).

FURTHER READING

Allen, T. (2011), *Virtual Water*, London: I.B. Taurus.

Falkenmark, M.; Rockstrom, J. (2004), *Water for Humans and Nature*, London: Earthscan.

Falkenmark, M.; Rockstrom, J. (2006), The new blue and green water paradigm: Breaking new ground for water resources planning and management, *Journal of Water Resources Planning and Management*, May/June, 129–132.

Savenije, H.H.G. (2002), Why water is not an ordinary economic good, or why the girl is special, *Physics and Chemistry of the Earth*, 27, 741–744.

Van der Zaag, P. (2010), Viewpoint: Water variability, soil nutrient heterogeneity and market volatility – why Sub-Saharan Africa's Green Revolution will be location-specific and knowledge-intensive, *Water Alternatives*, 3(1), 154–160.

REFERENCES

Akram-Lodhi, A.H. (2012), Contextualizing land grabbing: Contemporary land deals, the global subsistence crisis and the world food system, *Canadian Journal of Development Studies*, 33(2), 119–142.

Allen, J.A. (2003), IWRM/IWRAM: A new sanctioned discourse? Occasional paper 50, SOAS Water Issues Study Group, London: School of Oriental and African Studies/King's College London, April.

Allen, T. (2011), *Virtual Water*, London: I.B. Taurus.

Allouche, J.; Middleton, C.D.; Gyawali, D. (2015), Technical veil, hidden politics: Interrogating the power linkages behind the nexus, *Water Alternatives*, 8(1), 610–626.

Borras, Jr., S.M.; Franco, J.C. (2013), Global land grabbing and political reactions 'from below', *Third World Quarterly*, 34(9), 1723–1747.

Chindarkar, N.; Grafton, R.Q. (2019), India's depleting groundwater: When science meets policy, *Asia and Pacific Policy Studies*, 6, 108–124.

Conca, K. (2006), *Governing Water*, Cambridge, MA: MIT Press.

Cotula, L.; Vermeulen, S.; Leonard, R.; Keely, J. (2009), *Land Grab or Development Opportunity? Agricultural Investment and International Land Deals in Africa*, London and Rome: IIED, FAO and IFAD.

Falkenmark, M.; Rockstrom, J. (2004), *Water for Humans and Nature*, London: Earthscan.

Falkenmark, M.; Rockstrom, J. (2006), The new blue and green water paradigm: Breaking new ground for water resources planning and management, *Journal of Water Resources Planning and Management*, May/June, 129–132.

Falkenmark, M.; Rockstrom, J. (2008), Building resilience to drought in desertification-prone savannas in Sub-Saharan Africa: The water perspective, *Natural Resources Forum*, 32(2), 93–102.

Fearnside, P.M. (2017), How a dam building boom is transforming the Brazilian Amazon, *Yale Environment 360*, 26 September, accessed 10 March 2021 at https://e360.yale.edu/features/how-a-dam-building-boom-is-transforming-the-brazilian-amazon.

Gleick, P.; Palaniappan, M. (2010), Peak water limits to freshwater withdrawal and use, *Proceedings of the National Academy of Science of the United States of America*, 107(25), 11155–11162.

Grey, D.; Garrick, D.E.; Muller, M.; Sadoff, C.W. (2013), Water security in one blue planet: Twenty-first century policy challenges for science, *Philosophical Transactions of the Royal Society A: Mathematical, Physical and Engineering Science*, September, 371, 1–10.

Hirji, R.; Mandal, S.; Pangare, G. (eds) (2017), *South Asia Groundwater Forum: Regional Challenges and Opportunities for Building Drought and Climate Resilience for Farmers, Cities, and Villages*, New Delhi: Academic Foundation.

Hoekstra, A.Y.; Chapagain, A.K. (2006), Water footprints of nations: Water use by people as a function of their consumption pattern, in Craswell, E.; Bonnell, M.; Bossio, D.; Demuth, S.; Van De Giesen, N. (eds), *Integrated Assessment of Water Resources and Global Change*, Dordrecht: Springer, 35–48.

Homer-Dixon, T. (1994), Environmental scarcities and violent conflict: Evidence from cases, *International Security*, 19(1), 5–40.

Hulme, M. (2015), Climate and its changes: A cultural appraisal, *Geo: Geography and Environment*, 2, 1–11.

Ibraimo, N.; Munguambe, P. (2007), *Rainwater Harvesting Technologies for Small Scale Rainfed Agriculture in Arid and Semi-Arid Areas*, Colombo and Harare: CGIAR and Waternet.

ICOLD (International Commission on Large Dams) (n.d.), *World Register of Dams: General Synthesis*, accessed 22 April 2020 at www.icold-cigb.org/GB/world_register/general_synthesis.asp.

Keegan, J. (1994), *A History of Warfare*, Toronto: Vintage.

Lautze, J.; Hanjira, M.A. (2014), Water scarcity, in Lautze, J. (ed.), *Key Concepts in Water Resource Management: A Review and Critical Evaluation*, London and New York: Routledge and Earthscan, 7–24.

Linton, J.; Budds, J. (2014), The hydrosocial cycle: Defining and mobilizing a relational-dialectical approach to water, *Geoforum*, 57, 170–180.

L'vovich, M.I. (1979), *World Water Resources and Their Future*, translated by American Geophysical Union, Chelsea: LithoCrafters.

Mehta, L. (2001), The manufacture of popular perceptions of scarcity: Dams and water-related narratives in Gujarat, India, *World Development*, 29(12), 2025–2041.

Mehta, L. (2018), Taking the scare out of scarcity: The case of water, in Dawson, M.C.; Rosin, C.; Wald, N. (eds), *Global Resource Scarcity: Catalyst for Conflict or Cooperation?*, London: Routledge, 21–38.

Molden, D. (ed.) (2007), *Water for Food, Water for Life: A Comprehensive Assessment of Water Management in Agriculture*, London: Earthscan for IWMI.

Molle, F. (2008). Why enough is never enough: The societal determinants of river basin closure, *International Journal of Water Resources Development*, 24(2), 217–226.

Perry, D.; Praskievicz, S.J. (2017), A new era of big infrastructure? (Re)developing water storage in the US west in the context of climate change and environmental regulation, *Water Alternatives*, 10(2), 437–454.

Ponting, C. (1991), *A Green History of the World*, Harmondsworth: Penguin.

Recha, C.W.; Mukopi, M.N.; Otieno, J.O. (2015), Socio-economic determinants of adoption of rainwater harvesting and conservation techniques in semi-arid Tharaka Sub-County, Kenya, *Land Degradation and Development*, 26, 765–773.

Savenije, H.H.G. (2002), Why water is not an ordinary economic good, or why the girl is special, *Physics and Chemistry of the Earth*, Parts A/B/C, 27(11–22), 741–744.

Shah, T. (2014), Groundwater governance and irrigated agriculture, TEC Background Papers, No. 19. Stockholm: Global Water Partnership.

Shiklomanov, I.A. (2000), Appraisal and assessment of world water resources, *Water International*, 25(1), 11–32.

Solomon, S. (2010), *Water: The Epic Struggle for Wealth, Power and Civilization*, New York: HarperCollins.

Swatuk, L.A. (2018a), The land-water-food-energy nexus: Green and blue water dynamics in contemporary Africa-Asia relations, in Raposo, P.A.; Arase, D.; Cornelissen, S. (eds), *Routledge Handbook of Africa–Asia Relations*, Oxford: Routledge, 386–405.

Swatuk, L.A. (2018b), *Water in Southern Africa*, Pietermaritzburg: UKZN Press.

Swatuk, L.A.; Wirkus, L. (eds) (2018), *Water, Climate Change and the Boomerang Effect: Unintentional Consequences for Resource Insecurity*, London: Earthscan.

Swyngedouw, E. (2015), *Liquid Power: Contested Hydro-Modernities in Twentieth Century Spain*, Cambridge, MA: MIT Press.

Van der Zaag, P. (2010), Viewpoint: Water variability, soil nutrient heterogeneity and market volatility – why Sub-Saharan Africa's Green Revolution will be location-specific and knowledge-intensive, *Water Alternatives*, 3(1), 154–160.

WCD (World Commission on Dams) (2000), *Dams and Development: A New Framework for Decision Making – The Report of the World Commission on Dams*, London: Earthscan.

WEF (World Economic Forum) (2011), *Water Security: The Water-Food-Energy-Climate Nexus*, Washington, DC: Island Press.

World Bank; FAO (2009), *Awakening Africa's Sleeping Giant: Prospects for Commercial Agriculture in the Guinea Savannah Zone and Beyond*, Washington, DC: World Bank.

WWAP (United Nations World Water Assessment Programme) (2015), *The United Nations World Water Development Report 2015: Water for a Sustainable World*, Paris: UNESCO.

Zeitoun, M.; Lankford, B.; Krueger, T.; Forsyth, T.; Carter, R.; Hoekstra, A.Y.; Taylor, R.; Varis, O.; Cleaver, F.; Boelens, R.; Swatuk, L.A.; Tickner, D.; Scott, C.A.; Mirumachi, N.; Matthews, N. (2016), Reductionist and integrative research approaches to complex water security policy challenges, *Global Environmental Change*, 39, 143–154.

41. Biofuels

Carol Hunsberger

INTRODUCTION

Biofuels represent a polarized and fast-moving topic that links competing visions of agriculture with issues of energy and climate change. In the early 2000s, demand for liquid fuels derived from plants rose dramatically, driven by policies that claimed to promote climate change mitigation, energy security and rural development. The production of energy crops expanded rapidly in response – with repercussions for land use and land control around the world. More than a decade of evidence now makes it possible to ask: what have been the impacts of this recent biofuel 'boom', socially and ecologically, where and for whom? What values and assumptions about agriculture guided the biofuel project? And, is it possible to produce biofuels in ways that are socially and environmentally just? This chapter explores these questions.

A BRIEF HISTORY OF BIOFUELS

Bioenergy includes three categories: liquid biofuels (ethanol and biodiesel), solid biomass (firewood, charcoal and briquettes) and biogas (methane). This chapter focuses on liquid biofuels because they attracted widespread recent interest as a 'drop-in' alternative to fossil fuels, especially for transportation. Biofuels have two main forms. Ethanol, made from sugary or starchy plants such as sugarcane and corn, can be blended with gasoline. Biodiesel, made from oilseeds such as oil palm, soy and canola, can be blended with fossil fuel diesel. Many of the plants used to make biofuels are 'flex crops': they have multiple uses such as food, fuel and animal feed (Borras et al. 2016), making it more complicated to trace their demand and use.

Using biofuels for transport is not new. The first automobiles of the early 1900s were designed to run on a combination of gasoline and ethanol, and many countries initiated biofuel programmes during wartime or in response to the Organization of the Petroleum Exporting Countries crisis of the early 1970s (Worldwatch Institute 2007). Brazil, which introduced a 5 per cent fuel blending requirement in 1931 and expanded its ethanol programme in the 1970s, provides an example of long-term investment in biofuels as well as associated technologies such as flex-fuel cars (Bennertz and Rip 2018).

In the early 2000s another surge of interest in biofuels saw dozens of countries introduce production or fuel-blending targets (Bailis and Baka 2011). These policies reflected a convergence of agendas: concerns over energy security and climate change combined with a desire for growth in the agriculture sector (Bailis and Baka 2011; Franco et al. 2010; Hunsberger et al. 2017). Biofuels served geopolitical interests such as reducing dependence on foreign oil supplies (e.g. European Union (EU) use of Russian fossil fuels), offered a tempting energy return on investment and acted as a sink for surplus crop production (e.g. corn in the United States) – all while fitting into timely narratives about 'clean', 'green' and 'renewable' energy.

Crops that can be used to make liquid fuels expanded rapidly, including corn, soy, oil palm and sugarcane, while experimental crops such as jatropha proliferated across the Global South.

A backlash soon followed. Intensified by rising commodity prices and food riots during the 2007–2008 financial crisis, critics attacked biofuels for trading off 'food versus fuel'. News stories blamed biofuels for rising food prices, while political cartoons portrayed rich Westerners filling gas tanks at the expense of stereotypically depicted hungry children in the Global South (Einsiedel et al. 2017). Critics also questioned official rationales for biofuel policies by pointing to problems with carbon balance, labour practices and land control (White and Dasgupta 2010).

In response, some governments reduced their biofuel targets or added conditions to try to make biofuel production 'sustainable'. For example, the EU included environmental sustainability criteria in its 2009 Renewable Energy Directive (RED), while Brazil introduced a short-lived social certification programme (Labruto 2014). Certification schemes emerged, including the Roundtable for Sustainable Palm Oil and Roundtable for Responsible Soy, involving a combination of non-governmental organization and private actors – discussed further below.

Were early critics right about the impacts of biofuels on food prices, carbon emissions, workers and land rights? And have 'sustainable biofuel' initiatives succeeded in reducing such harms? The following sections review evidence of the social and environmental outcomes of expanded biofuel production and the extent to which sustainability measures have mitigated these impacts to date.

BIOFUEL OUTCOMES: ASSESSING THE EVIDENCE

Has demand for biofuels reduced access to food? Most studies on the relationship between biofuels and food rely on models rather than observations (Goetz et al. 2017). These models find that biofuel crop expansion likely reduces food production and consumption: for example, that 20–50 per cent of calories used for ethanol from corn or wheat come out of food or feed supplies that are not replaced through increased production elsewhere (Searchinger et al. 2015). Investors reportedly shifted assets into agricultural commodities after the 2007–2008 real estate crash, increasing demand for food crops and pushing up prices, particularly affecting urban consumers (Salter et al. 2018). Evidence from biofuel producing areas in the Global South shows that in most cases, biofuel plantations have decreased local food security by reducing the land available for small-scale farming while providing low and unstable wages, and/or competing for labour (Goetz et al. 2017). However, some outgrower schemes managed to improve food security by increasing the productivity of both food and biofuel crops while providing some income (Goetz et al. 2017).

What about biofuels' environmental credentials? While they were often promoted as 'clean' energy, and biofuel policies explicitly referred to climate change (e.g. climate change is the first issue raised in the preamble of the 2009 EU RED), research on land use change challenges this narrative. Seminal studies documented the 'carbon debt' associated with converting other land uses to produce biofuels, especially on peatlands and tropical forests (Fargione et al. 2008; Gibbs et al. 2008; Searchinger et al. 2008). Nitrous oxide emissions from fertilizer use also emerged as a concern (Melillo et al. 2009). More recent work affirms that the carbon savings of plant-based fuels have been regularly overestimated (Searchinger et al. 2017).

Biofuel production has also been implicated in biodiversity and habitat loss, deforestation, pollution and aquatic nutrient enrichment (Goetz et al. 2017). Since different biofuel sources have very different land, water and nutrient requirements, replace different kinds of vegetation and have different impacts on biodiversity, much depends on which crops are chosen as well as where and how they are grown (Elshout et al. 2015).

What have been the social outcomes in places where biofuel crops are grown? While initially research on the social outcomes of biofuel production was limited (Blaber-Wegg et al. 2015; Robledo-Abad et al. 2017), this literature has grown quickly. Expectations of widespread employment have largely disappointed: fewer jobs were created than anticipated, especially where harvests could be mechanized and where experimental ventures failed; jobs were unequally distributed, as migrant workers filled many more plantation jobs than local residents; and job quality frequently remained low, with temporary, low-paid positions on plantations vastly outnumbering more stable, higher-paying factory jobs (Hunsberger et al. 2017). Plantations have faced scrutiny for exploitative working conditions. For example, sugarcane harvesters in Brazil have experienced serious health risks and slave-like conditions (Labruto 2014; McGrath 2013). However, some oil palm plantation workers in Indonesia reported improvements to their livelihoods due to improved regularity of income (Obidzinski et al. 2012).

Smallholder experiences with biofuels have been mixed. In Brazil, despite efforts to compel biodiesel processors to buy part of their crop from smallholders, only 1 per cent of the country's biodiesel in 2014 came from crops considered well suited to smallholder production such as sunflower and castor, while soy production tended to aggregate small plots into larger ones (Hunsberger et al. 2017; Lima et al. 2011; USDA Foreign Agricultural Service 2015). In Indonesia, smallholder outcomes have varied widely: some farmers were able to generate significant income from oil palm, while others lost land when they were unable to repay debts (McCarthy 2010). Despite policy claims in several countries that biofuel production would alleviate poverty, better-off farmers (such as those with larger landholdings or a well) have managed to capture the majority of incentives for biofuel production (Hunsberger et al. 2017). Barriers to entry are high considering that farmers must wait several years for some crops, such as oil palm and jatropha, to mature.

What about impacts on land rights? By replicating the pattern of large-scale, intensive agriculture, the biofuel 'boom' has in many places contributed to the consolidation of land control (Hall et al. 2009; Oliveira et al. 2017). Displacement of local people to establish plantations – known as land grabbing – has been widely documented in relation to biofuels, particularly where protection for customary land tenure is weak (Goetz et al. 2017; Vermeulen and Cotula 2010; Zoomers 2010). In many cases, local consultation over biofuel projects fell short of a meaningful interpretation of free, prior and informed consent – and at times local land users were left out of negotiations entirely (Goetz et al. 2017). Labelling land as 'available', 'idle' or 'wasteland' has helped investors gain access to lands that are in reality sites of active, customary use (Borras et al. 2010; Goetz et al. 2017). Such 'green grabs' – land grabs undertaken in the name of environmental ends (Fairhead et al. 2012) – have led to dispossession and increased conflicts.

Writing about biofuels' impacts on food security, poverty and emissions, Searchinger et al. (2015, 1420) conclude: 'much of the uncertainty is only over which adverse effects predominate, not whether adverse effects occur at all'. These negative outcomes are not automatically linked to biofuels per se, or to particular crops; they depend on decisions made about how to produce them. A capitalist approach to biofuels focused on maximizing energy return on investment has generally led to large-scale, mechanized production on plantations rather than decentralized production by empowered smallholders – with attendant consequences for ecologies, workers and land rights.

ASSESSING SUSTAINABILITY INITIATIVES

Have measures aimed at making biofuels 'sustainable' succeeded in reducing social and environmental harms? Many such measures are market-based certification schemes: some developed by the private sector, others styled as multi-stakeholder roundtables involving civil society as well as industry actors. Policies like the 2009 EU RED rely on third-party certification to verify compliance with sustainability criteria. To meet EU requirements, biofuel producers must be certified by one of the schemes approved by the European Commission – meaning that private-sector instruments have become integral to public policy (de Man and German 2017).

Research points out significant weaknesses in the scope, effectiveness, transparency and reach of biofuel certification initiatives (de Man and German 2017; Fortin and Richardson 2013; German and Schoneveld 2012; Pols 2015; Ponte 2014). In terms of the issues covered, environmental criteria predominate while social criteria are both less prevalent and less binding (de Man and German 2017). Even so, de Man and German (2017) found that none of the standards they reviewed included indirect land use change and associated greenhouse gas emissions, while loopholes and exclusions weakened requirements related to biodiversity and water quality.

Criteria on food security, land competition and rights were found to be weak across the board (de Man and German 2017). For example, a standard requiring proof of legal land ownership or lease to protect local land rights (ISCC) allowed producers to displace small-scale farmers if those farmers were not legal owners – for instance, if they rented from landlords (Tomei 2015). Schemes vary widely in how rigorous and comprehensive they are, leaving producers free to choose between more and less demanding sets of requirements (German and Schoneveld 2012; Pols 2015; Ponte 2014). For example, the Roundtable on Sustainable Biomaterials (RSB) has a relatively comprehensive list of requirements, while ISCC requires compliance with a list of 'major musts' but lets producers choose from a list of 'minor musts'. Further scrutiny has focused on the industry-dominated character of certification schemes, their focus on global goals rather than the priorities of affected communities, their inability to track cumulative impacts, flawed auditing and enforcement processes, and absent or ineffective grievance mechanisms (German and Schoneveld 2012; Ponte 2014).

Despite these weaknesses, the global share of certified biofuel crops remains small. Palm oil has the highest certified market share at 21 per cent while sugarcane and soy remain at less than 5 per cent each (de Man and German 2017) – largely going to industrialized markets. There is a clear and inverse relationship between the strictness of a standard and its uptake: in March 2019, the more stringent RSB listed only one valid certificate on its website (RSB 2019) while ISCC listed 3226 (ISCC 2019).

Complicating the picture, the fact that most biofuel crops are 'flex crops' makes it difficult to trace what portion of a given crop is used for biofuel, and to enforce production standards for one end use of a crop but not others.

VISIONS OF AGRICULTURE

Biofuel policies across the Global North and South express the goal of stimulating rural development but attach widely different meanings to the term. Some focus on promoting economic growth, modernization, international investment and trade; others on alleviating poverty and creating opportunities for disadvantaged farmers (Hunsberger et al. 2017). As an example of the first type, the United States Renewable Fuels Standard of 2007 set ethanol production targets intended to support midwestern corn farmers practicing large-scale, high-input agriculture and to stimulate biorefineries in the region (Gillon 2010). South Africa's policy includes features of the second type: by connecting biofuel production to its Black Empowerment Plan (Hunsberger et al. 2017), this strategy engages with socially inclusive visions of decentralized, smallholder biofuel production (Milder et al. 2008; Tilman et al. 2009). This dual vision – of large-scale production and global integration on one hand, and locally oriented, 'pro-poor' initiatives on the other – produces many contradictions.

Producing enough biofuel to fulfil national targets has proven largely incompatible with smallholder production models, as experiences in Brazil suggest (Hall et al. 2009; Lima et al. 2011). Meanwhile, claims that biofuel crops can provide multiple benefits obscure the fact that each benefit may be specific to a particular scale or mode of production; not all can occur at once. For example, jatropha has been promoted as a plant that provides aesthetic and medicinal benefits, shade, erosion control, live fencing and seeds useful for biofuel as well as soap – but shade depends on letting trees grow wide and leafy; fencing and erosion control depend on closely spaced plants; seeds yields are highest in a plantation format; and one must choose between soap or fuel production since they use the same part of the plant (Hunsberger 2016; van der Horst et al. 2014). As van der Horst et al. (2014, 8) conclude: 'win-win situations are assumed to be generic, whereas real world trade-offs and conflicts are overlooked' – a statement that aptly summarizes the optimistic promotion of biofuels.

SUSTAINABLE BIOFUELS: OXYMORON OR REALISTIC GOAL?

Some question why so much scrutiny has focused on biofuels without evaluating other energy sources in the same conversation. Biofuels may be bad, this argument goes, but are the alternatives better? Fossil fuels are highly polluting; nuclear energy is risky; hydroelectricity can destroy livelihoods and ecosystems; wind power is plagued by siting controversies; solar is intermittent; and so on. Given that even drastic improvements in efficiency will not eliminate demand for energy, can biofuels, in some form, be part of a responsible energy mix? Community projects using biofuels for cookstoves, electrification or transport (FAO and PISCES 2009; Maroun and La Rouere 2014) reflect this line of reasoning.

Others question why more scrutiny has focused on biofuels than on other crops, or other uses of flex crops. If land use change, working conditions, ecological damage and smallholder displacement are crucial issues for biofuels, then why not take action to address these problems across agriculture as a whole rather than only for biofuels? Efforts to promote certification standards based on crops rather than their end uses, as well as activism that seeks to leverage the Voluntary Guidelines on the Responsible Governance of Tenure of Land, Fisheries and Forests (Franco and Monsalve Suárez 2018), fall into this category.

In conclusion, some see biofuels as an outright maladaptation – an example of climate change action gone wrong – while others remain optimistic that under certain conditions, biofuels can be part of a just energy system. Moving forward, research must continue to probe whether biofuels and other land-based energy projects enhance or undermine environmental protection, farmer autonomy, fair working conditions and Indigenous rights. If critical agrarian scholars reject biofuels outright, as it is tempting to do, then their ideas about how to pursue energy strategies with more sustainable and fair rural outcomes will be crucial to defining alternative pathways.

FURTHER READING

Bailis, R.; Baka, J. (2011), Constructing sustainable biofuels: Governance of the emerging biofuel economy, *Annals of the Association of American Geographers*, 101(4), 827–838.

Borras, S.M.; McMichael, P.; Scoones, I. (eds) (2010), Special issue on biofuels, land and agrarian change, *Journal of Peasant Studies*, 37(4).

Goetz, A.; German, L.; Weigelt, J. (eds) (2017), Virtual special issue: Scaling up biofuels? A critical look at expectations, performance and governance, *Energy Policy*, 110, 719–723.

Hall, J.; Matos, S.; Severino, L.; Beltrao, N. (2009), Brazilian biofuels and social exclusion: Established and concentrated ethanol versus emerging and dispersed biodiesel, *Journal of Cleaner Production*, 17, S77–S85.

Ponte, S. (2014), 'Roundtabling' sustainability: Lessons from the biofuel industry, *Geoforum*, 54, 261–271.

REFERENCES

Bailis, R.; Baka, J. (2011), Constructing sustainable biofuels: Governance of the emerging biofuel economy, *Annals of the Association of American Geographers*, 101(4), 827–838.

Bennertz, R.; Rip, A. (2018), The evolving Brazilian automotive-energy infrastructure: Entanglements of national developmentalism, sugar and ethanol production, automobility and gasoline, *Energy Research and Social Science*, 41, 109–117.

Blaber-Wegg, T.; Hodbod, J.; Tomei, J. (2015), Incorporating equity into sustainability assessments of biofuels, *Current Opinion in Environmental Sustainability*, 14, 180–186.

Borras, S.M.; McMichael, P.; Scoones, I. (2010), The politics of biofuels, land and agrarian change: Editors' introduction, *Journal of Peasant Studies*, 37(4), 575–592.

Borras, S.M.; Franco, J.C.; Isakson, S.R.; Levidow, L.; Vervest, P. (2016), The rise of flex crops and commodities: Implications for research, *Journal of Peasant Studies*, 43(1), 93–115.

de Man, R.; German, L. (2017), Certifying the sustainability of biofuels: Promise and reality, *Energy Policy*, 109, 871–883.

Einsiedel, E.F.; Remillard, C.; Gomaa, M.; Zeaiter, E. (2017), The representation of biofuels in political cartoons: Ironies, contradictions and moral dilemmas, *Environmental Communication*, 11(1), 41–62.

Elshout, P.M.F.; van Zelm, R.; Balkovic, J.; Obersteiner, M.; Schmid, E.; Skalsky, R.; van der Velde, M.; Huijbregts, M.A.J. (2015), Greenhouse-gas payback times for crop-based biofuels, *Nature Climate Change*, 5(6), 604–610.

Fairhead, J.; Leach, M.; Scoones, I. (2012), Green grabbing: A new appropriation of nature?, *Journal of Peasant Studies*, 39(2), 237–261.

FAO; PISCES (2009), *Small-Scale Bioenergy Initiatives: Brief Description and Preliminary Lessons on Livelihood Impacts from Case Studies in Asia, Latin America and Africa*, accessed 13 July 2021 at www.fao.org/bioenergy/17019-0277c3709ec15e8ae298d528de2c4c098.pdf.

Fargione, J.; Hill, J.; Tilman, D.; Polasky, S.; Hawthorne, P. (2008), Land clearing and the biofuel carbon debt, *Science*, 319(5867), 1235–1238.

Fortin, E.; Richardson, B. (2013), Certification schemes and the governance of land: Enforcing standards or enabling scrutiny?, *Globalizations*, 10(1), 141–159.

Franco, J.; Monsalve Suárez, S. (2018), Why wait for the state? Using the CFS Tenure Guidelines to recalibrate political-legal struggles for democratic land control, *Third World Quarterly*, 39(7), 1386–1402.

Franco, J.; Levidow, L.; Fig, D.; Goldfarb, L.; Hönicke, M.; Luisa Mendonça, M. (2010), Assumptions in the European Union biofuels policy: Frictions with experiences in Germany, Brazil and Mozambique, *Journal of Peasant Studies*, 37(4), 661–698.

German, L.; Schoneveld, G. (2012), A review of social sustainability considerations among EU-approved voluntary schemes for biofuels, with implications for rural livelihoods, *Energy Policy*, 51, 765–778.

Gibbs, H.K.; Johnston, M.; Foley, J.A.; Holloway, T.; Monfreda, C.; Ramankutty, N.; Zaks, D. (2008), Carbon payback times for crop-based biofuel expansion in the tropics: The effects of changing yield and technology, *Environmental Research Letters*, 3(3), 034001.

Gillon, S. (2010), Fields of dreams: Negotiating an ethanol agenda in the Midwest United States, *Journal of Peasant Studies*, 37(4), 723–748.

Goetz, A.; German, L.; Hunsberger, C.; Schmidt, O. (2017), Do no harm? Risk perceptions in national bioenergy policies and actual mitigation performance, *Energy Policy*, 108, 776–790.

Hall, J.; Matos, S.; Severino, L.; Beltrao, N. (2009), Brazilian biofuels and social exclusion: Established and concentrated ethanol versus emerging and dispersed biodiesel, *Journal of Cleaner Production*, 17, S77–S85.

Hunsberger, C. (2016), Explaining bioenergy: Representations of jatropha in Kenya before and after disappointing results, *SpringerPlus*, 5(1), 2000.

Hunsberger, C.; German, L.; Goetz, A. (2017), 'Unbundling' the biofuel promise: Querying the ability of liquid biofuels to deliver on socio-economic policy expectations, *Energy Policy*, 108, 791–805.

ISCC (2019), *Valid Certificates*, accessed 14 March 2019 at www.iscc-system.org/certificates/valid -certificates/.

Labruto, N. (2014), Experimental biofuel governance: Historicizing social certification in Brazilian ethanol production, *Geoforum*, 54, 272–281.

Lima, M.; Skutsch, M.; de Medeiros Costa, G. (2011), Deforestation and the social impacts of soy for biodiesel: Perspectives of farmers in the south Brazilian Amazon, *Ecology and Society*, 16(4), 4.

Maroun, M.R.; La Rouere, E.L. (2014), Ethanol and food production by family smallholdings in rural Brazil: Economic and socio-environmental analysis of micro distilleries in the State of Rio Grande do Sul, *Biomass and Bioenergy*, 63, 140–155.

McCarthy, J.F. (2010), Processes of inclusion and adverse incorporation: Oil palm and agrarian change in Sumatra, Indonesia, *Journal of Peasant Studies*, 37(4), 821–850.

McGrath, S. (2013), Fuelling global production networks with slave labour? Migrant sugar cane workers in the Brazilian ethanol GPN, *Geoforum*, 44, 32–43.

Melillo, J.M.; Reilly, J.M.; Kicklighter, D.W.; Gurgel, A.C.; Cronin, T.W.; Paltsev, S.; Felzer, B.S.; Wang, D.; Sokolov, A.P.; Adam Schlosser, C. (2009), Indirect emissions from biofuels: How important?, *Science*, 326(5958), 1397–1399.

Milder, J.C.; McNeely, J.A.; Shames, S.A.; Scherr, S.J. (2008), Biofuels and ecoagriculture: Can bioenergy production enhance landscape-scale ecosystem conservation and rural livelihoods?, *International Journal of Agricultural Sustainability*, 6(2), 105–121.

Obidzinski, K.; Andriani, R.; Komarudin, H.; Andrianto, A. (2012), Environmental and social impacts of oil palm plantations and their implications for biofuel production in Indonesia, *Ecology and Society*, 17(1), 25.

Oliveira, G. de L.T.; McKay, B.; Plank, C. (2017), How biofuel policies backfire: Misguided goals, inefficient mechanisms, and political-ecological blind spots, *Energy Policy*, 108, 765–775.

Pols, A.J.K. (2015), The rationality of biofuel certification: A critical examination of EU biofuel policy, *Journal of Agricultural and Environmental Ethics*, 28(4), 667–681.

Ponte, S. (2014), 'Roundtabling' sustainability: Lessons from the biofuel industry, *Geoforum*, 54, 261–271.

Robledo-Abad, C.; Althaus, H.J.; Berndes, G.; Bolwig, S.; Corbera, E.; Creutzig, F.; Garcia-Ulloa, J.; Geddes, A.; Gregg, J.S.; Haberl, H.; Hanger, S.; Harper, R.J.; Hunsberger, C.; Larsen, R.K.; Lauk, C.; Leitner, S.; Lilliestam, J.; Lotze-Campen, H.; Muys, B.; Nordborg, M.; Ölund, M.; Orlowsky, B.;

Popp, A.; Portugal-Pereira, J.; Reinhard, J.; Scheiffle, L.; and Smith, P. (2017), Bioenergy production and sustainable development: Science base for policymaking remains limited, *GCB Bioenergy*, 9(3), 541–556.

RSB (2019), *Participating Operators*, accessed 14 March 2019 at http://rsb.org/certification/participating -operators/.

Salter, R.; Gonzalez, C.; Kronk Warner, E.; Gonzalez, C.G. (2018), An environmental justice critique of biofuels, in Salter, R.; Gonzalez, C.C.; Kronk Warner, E.A. (eds), *Energy Justice*, Cheltenham, UK and Northampton, MA, USA: Edward Elgar Publishing, pp. 41–72.

Searchinger, T.; Heimlich, R.; Houghton, R.A.; Dong, F.; Elobeid, A.; Fabiosa, J.; Tokgoz, S.; Hayes, D.; Yu, T.-H. (2008), Use of US croplands for biofuels increases greenhouse gases through emissions from land-use change, *Science*, 319(5867), 1238–1240.

Searchinger, T.; Edwards, R.; Mulligan, D.; Heimlich, R.; Plevin, R. (2015), Do biofuel policies seek to cut emissions by cutting food?, *Science*, 347(6229), 1420–1422.

Searchinger, T.; Beringer, T.; Strong, A. (2017), Does the world have low-carbon bioenergy potential from the dedicated use of land?, *Energy Policy*, 110, 434–446.

Tilman, D.; Socolow, R.; Foley, J.A.; Hill, J.; Larson, E.; Lynd, L.; Pacala, S.; Reilly, J.; Searchinger, T.; Somerville, C.; Williams, R. (2009), Beneficial biofuels: The food, energy, and environment trilemma, *Science*, 325(5938), 270 LP–271.

Tomei, J. (2015), The sustainability of sugarcane-ethanol systems in Guatemala: Land, labour and law, *Biomass and Bioenergy*, 82, 94–100.

USDA Foreign Agricultural Service (2015), Brazil biofuels annual – ethanol and biodiesel. GAIN Report Number BR15006.

van der Horst, D.; Vermeylen, S.; Kuntashula, E. (2014), The hedgification of maizescapes? Scalability and multifunctionality of Jatropha curcas hedges in a mixed farming landscape in Zambia, *Ecology and Society*, 19(2), 48.

Vermeulen, S.; Cotula, L. (2010), Over the heads of local people: Consultation, consent, and recompense in large-scale land deals for biofuels projects in Africa, *Journal of Peasant Studies*, 37(4), 899–916.

White, B.; Dasgupta, A. (2010), Agrofuels capitalism: A view from political economy, *Journal of Peasant Studies*, 37(4), 593–607.

Worldwatch Institute (2007), *Biofuels for Transport: Global Potential and Implications for Sustainable Energy and Agriculture*, London: Earthscan.

Zoomers, A. (2010), Globalisation and the foreignisation of space: Seven processes driving the current global land grab, *Journal of Peasant Studies*, 37(2), 429–447.

42. Industrial fisheries and oceanic accumulation
Elizabeth Havice and Liam Campling[1]

INTRODUCTION

Three-fourths of the world's marine capture fisheries are at or beyond 'full exploitation', indicating the likelihood that many fish populations, and the ecosystem of which they are a part, will decline (if they are not already) with current and expanded levels of competitive extraction, though the geographies of fisheries decline and recovery are uneven. Fish, whether saltwater or freshwater, farmed or captured, are an important source of animal protein, micro-nutrients and fatty acids crucial to alleviating malnutrition, hundreds of millions of people are employed as fish workers and in fisheries-related activities, and fish exports from developing countries generate a higher export value than coffee, bananas, cocoa, tea, sugar and tobacco combined (Campling et al. 2012). State and market pressures from outside fishing industries also shape the ecological resources that fisheries depend upon. For example, the 'deadly trio' of oceanic warming, acidification and deoxygenation – all driven by terrestrial capitalism – threatens in particular larger-bodied animals living at the top of trophic levels in the oceans' ecosystems (Payne et al. 2016). These changes and declines are a likely oceanic outcome of 'business as usual' for global capitalism.

Mainstream social science fisheries research has largely been underattentive to fisheries systems in general and particularly in relation to questions of how they are shaped through capitalism. Historically, the prevailing treatment of fisheries in the social sciences has been biologically and economically reductionist, and policy thinking is 'subsumed under the goals of economic growth and wealth creation' (Symes and Phillipson 2009, 1). Fisheries have been treated as 'a technicality, an exercise of narrow, instrumental rationality ruled by universal theory' (Jentoft 2007, 435), and 'the individual producer [is theorized] as an autonomous isolate engaged in the technical act of catching fish' (Pálsson 1991, 21). However, over the last 10 years, this has begun to change rapidly (for a recent review, see Bavnick et al. 2018).

With Penny McCall Howard, in 2012 we edited a special double issue of *Journal of Agrarian Change* that sought to examine the political economy and ecology of capture fisheries, drawing explicitly from the analytical tools available to critical agrarian studies and enriching these tools with cases from the water. In our introduction to that special issue (Campling et al. 2012), we charted three themes that we saw then as pertinent to critical agrarian studies and the political economy of capture fisheries: market dynamics and competition in fisheries production-consumption systems; labour, forms of exploitation and resistance; and resource access and the state. In the years since, there has been a flourish of attention to fisheries specifically, and of extractive relations in aquatic spaces more broadly. Here we advance two main objectives: (1) to introduce the study of industrial fisheries to a critical agrarian studies audience and indicate relevant intersections between the two, and (2) to highlight new advances, emergent research themes and exciting scholars working in the field of 'oceanic accumulation' (Sibilia 2019).

Given space limitations, we focus on industrial marine capture fisheries and raise questions about ocean accumulation more generally. We recognize the profound socio-economic and ecological importance of artisanal and small-scale coastal fisheries, and inland or riverine fisheries, as well as booming aquaculture and mariculture industries. These are essential areas for critical agrarian studies and each presents important analytical similarities and differences and we encourage scholars working in the critical agrarian studies tradition to research these and their articulations; our hope is that the discussion here offers foundations for ongoing and expanding attention to critical agrarian studies beyond the terrestrial.

MARKET DYNAMICS AND COMPETITION IN FISHERIES PRODUCTION-CONSUMPTION SYSTEMS

Capitalism works through nature at sea in the particular geographies where fish are present, in the techniques developed to capture them and in the organizational strategies of firms that operate fishing vessels. Capitalist production has a tendency to undermine the environmental conditions for its own reproduction. The drive to create profit often leads firms to widen and deepen extraction, which can create tensions between resource management and capitalist firms extracting fish.

In the mainstream fisheries management literature, boats are abstract units of production. Fishing vessels are differentiated (if at all) by vessel size, fishing gear and country of registry (also referred to as 'flag', the country to which the vessel is legally responsible). This relatively simplistic framing obscures who owns and controls fishing vessels and their relations with each other and with other firms in fisheries commodity chains. Further, it hides that many vessel owners purposely obscure ownership, separating ownership and registration to evade regulation and reduce costs. In contrast, Campling (2012) defines an industrial fishery as a geographical area of operation of a complex of capitals whose form of organization is the firm and whose medium of operation is fishing vessels.

There is a diversity of types of fishing firms and accumulation strategies in fisheries, ranging from multinational corporations through to household producers and individual owner-operators. Scholarship now reveals varying levels of concentration and control, ownership structure and models of industrial organization in fisheries ranging from industrial to artisanal scale (Havice and Campling 2017; Havice et al. 2021; Österblom et al. 2015; Steenbergen et al. 2019). This includes relationships between fishing firms and interests in other functional activities in the commodity chain, particularly processing (the manufacturing node of fisheries production) and trading companies.

Plainly, the 'business of fishing' is not to be understood as an isolate. As with agriculture, any political economy of fisheries must incorporate analytically the challenges of extracting fish and bringing them, profitably, to market. Here we are signalling our underlying concern with fish as commodities (in Marx's sense) that are extracted in and through relation to their ecological properties. That fish move, for instance, intimately shapes the techniques and politics of capitalist extraction, as hunters (capitalist enterprises) must chase them through the water. Recent research traces fisheries commodity chains from fisheries to retail, identifying and examining the power dynamics running through interfirm relations (Havice and Campling 2017; Longo et al. 2015). As in other contemporary food systems, world market cost structures and emergent standards shape power relations in fisheries production systems (Foley 2012;

Longo and Clark 2012; Marks 2012). But there are also distinctive ecological features specific to fisheries that shape the business strategies of firms as they transform nature into commodities (Campling 2012; Howard 2016; Howse et al. 2012).

The development of specific techniques of fisheries production used in particular fisheries is shaped by a range of variables, including, for instance: existing environmental conditions, available boats and gear, market pressures (and opportunities), transport infrastructure and social relations in and around fisheries systems. Constant change and innovation in all aspects of fishing, transportation, processing and marketing techniques is a feature of industrial fisheries, as boat owners and processors seek to catch fish and get them to market in the most economically efficient manner. Markets are often distant from the location of extraction. As a result, firms have to overcome the social and technical constraints of geographical distance to market and the organic durability of highly perishable fish products (Freidberg 2009; Friedmann 1992). Firms deploy specific techniques to meet different market demands and cultures of consumption.

International organizations concerned with fisheries-related development collate statistics on fisheries consumption trends, yet generalized data obscure the highly variable political and social processes by which fish are connected to (and/or disconnected from) local socio-economies in coastal communities and in fish-processing hubs. Conflicts between fishers and fishing firms using different gear and techniques are common. Such 'gear conflicts' have a social and/or economic basis and impact (Leroy et al. 2016). For instance, in Kerala, 'small-scale' fishers organized politically to improve the efficiency of their own techniques and to strengthen their position vis-à-vis industrial, more capital-intensive fishing gears (Sinha 2012). In Ghana, long-term industrial fishing by foreign fleets and the resulting dwindling of fish populations is pushing local fishers to extract unsustainably, further eroding livelihoods (Nolan 2019).

Conflicts between gear types are only one aspect in the social conflict over fisheries, food security and livelihoods the world over, including in developing countries. While '80 per cent of world production of fish and fishery products takes place in developing countries' (Committee on Fisheries 2010, 2), there are concerns that growth of fish exports from the Global South to markets in the North can undermine food security in the former (Alder and Sumaila 2004; Béné et al. 2007; Le Manach et al. 2013). Further, coastal communities where industrial fishing and processing take place often lack access to these products, and/or have access only to inferior products rejected for export markets (Bell et al. 2019; HLPE 2014; Isaacs 2016). In general, the politics of unequal fisheries development and resource use are not well understood (Béné et al. 2015, 187).

Attention to firm strategy and industry structure offers the opportunity to examine socio-economic outcomes in fisheries systems (that is, who gets what). It is also increasingly clear that nuanced understanding of firm structure is essential for understanding ecological outcomes and potentials. For instance, recent work in sustainability science has argued that increasingly concentrated firms that engage in fishing as part of their business strategies can function as 'keystone' actors in marine ecosystems, usefully drawing attention to the corporate form in fisheries management that usually focuses on the state and interstate politics (Österblom et al. 2015). However, without a theory of capitalism to inform the analysis, scholars risk idealizing the potential for highly concentrated firms to use their corporate power to introduce measures that will enhance sustainability. We suggest that conceptualization of real competition in highly competitive global seafood commodity chains (a hallmark of critical agrarian studies) enables researchers to explain *why* firms take such measures, and identify the kinds of measures that are consistent with economic imperatives for those firms' survival.

'Sustainable seafood' as a tool of market-led governance is now a permanent fixture in many industrial fisheries and in some cases is essential for market access (Foley and Havice 2016). Critical agrarian studies approaches to this private ordering offers a prime opportunity to examine the intersection between sustainability and corporate logics. Debate revolves over what ecological impacts (if any) these forms of private ordering deliver (Hadjimichael and Hegland 2016; Ponte 2012), and the restructuring of power relationships along seafood commodity chains and in resource access dynamics that eco-labelling produces (Foley 2012; Miller and Bush 2015).

There is much potential for future work in critical agrarian studies-related literature that can capture the heterogenous market dynamics and competitive relations in fisheries production-consumption systems. Constance and Bonanno (2000) were the first to apply food regimes analysis (see McMichael in this volume) to fisheries and it has subsequently been developed by Campling and Havice (2018), who emphasize that a political economy of seafood systems bridges *state-led* fisheries management and *market-led* reform of 'sustainable' seafood commodity chains. Through a sketch of industrial fisheries through the twentieth century, they argue that the two must be understood in articulation. That is, the present moment of privatized seafood governance is firmly embedded in, and dependent upon, the historical institutions of *national* seafood production systems. Foley and Mather (2018) similarly map food regimes in fisheries, identifying the coexistence of different models of the third food regime – corporate, neoliberal globalization *and* corporate-environmental – but importantly, they also show resistance against them, and other, more ambiguous existing social relations and networks in fisheries systems. Further work linking the dynamics of fisheries commodity chains across species and product types and articulating these with/within seafood regimes would provide a powerful research project for critical agrarian studies scholars; however, as Foley and Mather (2018) make clear, this must also incorporate differentiated forms of exploitation and the politics of resistance, to which we now turn.

LABOUR, FORMS OF EXPLOITATION AND RESISTANCE

Any political economy of fisheries must include an understanding of the labour process that underpins the creation of value across all sectors of the fishing industry. The labour process forms the basis for how fishers and fish-processing workers experience and understand the industries in which they work. Creating value from seafood while competing in global or regional markets has generated a diversity of social relations to production, and these can and do evolve over time. For instance, individuals may begin work in the fishing industry as hired or kin-based fishing crew (Howard 2016). If they earn enough to buy their own vessel (or inherit one), they shift to owner-operator, probably still actively working the vessel with either hired hands or kin as crew. Eventually, a boat owner may cease working on the boat and hire skippers and crew, and if very (economically) successful, buy multiple boats; of course, crew are more often excluded from any possibility of buying industrial vessels (see Hara 2009).

Fishing share systems are a common method for distributing surplus among boat owners and crew, and have some significant parallels to sharecropping in agriculture. A major difference between the two is that share systems in fisheries are organized around access to a boat, rather than land. In a fishing share system, crew are remunerated with an agreed portion of the value of the catch, which some have argued is non-capitalist on the assumption that the share system is not exploitative of labour, but instead 'crew or team production' (St Martin 2007, 538). While these types of relationships may be found on some boats, the pressures of operating commercially and selling seafood commodities in the marketplace can mean that 'the relations between skipper and crew at sea become a key site of struggle' (Menzies 2002, 20). Owners may try to increase power over labour processes on board as they try to produce maximum value with their operations and appropriate a greater portion of the surplus, or they may self-exploit (Marks 2012). Boat owners can also use fishing share systems to appropriate surplus value produced by crew, transforming the share system to function more like a budget for crew wages, which over time can become more casual and variable wages (Howard 2012).

Labour in most industrial fisheries operations is contract- rather than share-based, and has gained much recent attention as a result of exposés of labour abuses, slavery or slave-like conditions on board fishing vessels and in fish-processing work around the world, including: Thai vessels and processing plants, Taiwanese vessels, New Zealand-flagged vessels and Philippines processing plants, among others (McDowell et al. 2015; Richardson et al. 2017; Stringer et al. 2015). These cases, initially hidden from public view beneath the glisten of cheap seafood, garnered attention precisely because media reporting linked labour abuses around the world to consumer markets in the Global North, implicating the North American and European consumer in the scandal. Unfree labour practices on fishing boats remain widespread, and critical agrarian studies scholarship has an important role to play in nuancing understanding of labour conditions at sea. Scholars have begun to contest the simplistic and populist tropes around slave labour that can obscure worker voice and agency in fisheries systems (Vandergeest 2018; Vandergeest and Marshke 2020), even as working conditions present challenges around state- and market-based monitoring and enforcement tools, and legal contracts for fish work can formally introduce discriminatory practices between national and migrant workers on board vessels (Greenpeace 2020; Howard 2012).

Competitive market pressures do not just have the potential to change social relations, they can result in the disease, injury and even death of fishers and processing workers. Work on fishing boats is dangerous and regulating worker safety on vessels is challenging (Couper et al. 2015; Howard 2016). Examining labour requires attention to the 'exceptional' nature of fisheries work that cannot be easily monitored or regulated nor confined easily to structured work hours. For instance, the International Labour Organization's (ILO) general standard is an eight-hour working day, a 48-hour working week and a minimum weekly rest of 24 hours without work. In contrast, the ILO Work in Fishing Convention (ILO 188) requires 10 hours of rest per 24 hours, which translates into a 14-hour working day and does not specify any minimum period of continuous rest, meaning that a worker can acceptably be required to work day and night, interspersed by periods of rest adding up to 10 hours. Reliable statistics on deaths and injuries on fishing boats do not exist because most countries fail to systematically report them, which is partly a symptom of open vessel registries or 'flags of convenience' (Couper et al. 2015).

In contrast to factories, fields and mines, fishing circumscribes the labour process to floating platforms of production that can transcend legal jurisdictions in various ways (for example, legally through flag-of-convenience vessels and/or geographically following the fish between exclusive economic zones (EEZs) and the legal grey zone of the high seas). This makes fishing one of the world's most dangerous jobs and also among the most poorly regulated, in both policy and practice (Campling and Colás 2021). As these conditions are being made increasingly visible, labour regulation and social accounting are emerging as a new site of struggle in the regulation of capitalist enterprise at sea through state and private-sector moves to audit and certify vessels and processing plants for fair labour conditions. A critical agrarian studies approach provides tools through which to examine differentiated forms of exploitation at sea and to critically assess efforts to reform labour conditions on boats as part and parcel of processes of 'unequal ecological exchange' (Clark et al. 2019).

The tensions that generate social differentiation within societies and fisheries systems can result in new forms of social organization and resistance. For instance, Maori in New Zealand have organized around their Indigenous identity and waged large-scale political protests, in part to reclaim access to coastal fisheries resources that their ancestors extracted before and during the colonial era (De Alessi 2012). Yet this development of capitalist fishery has produced several axes of antagonism by 'increasing wealth consolidation by [a] few economically and/or politically significant entities and the persistence of the barriers that preclude small-scale fishers from securing fishing access' (Song et al. 2018, 8). Keralan fishers' transnational contacts were (and continue to be) constitutive of the diversity of forms of fisheries and worker organization in multiple historical periods. Today, the formal international networks of fishworkers that emerged in part from the Keralan movement remain influential in international fisheries politics (Sinha 2012). 'Fisheries justice' movements exist at local, national and international scales, including the two global fisher movements – the World Forum of Fisher Peoples and the World Forum of Fish Harvesters and Fish Workers. Fisheries justice movements continue to highlight intersecting propositions: the right to food, food sovereignty, resource access and conflict, climate change resilience and mitigation (see De Schutter 2012). These convergences highlight fisheries sector and fishers' movements in food and climate politics and transnational social movements (Mills 2018). Yet these movements are rarely framed around the capital relation, making any blueprint overlay of class dynamics difficult.

Class antagonisms have long been a feature of work at sea. The term 'strike' originated with seafarers in the eighteenth century, who realized that the captain was powerless to sail the ship if they 'struck' the top sails (Rediker 1989, 110). And 'the deep-sea proletariat' was among the largest and most prominent workforce in Britain's era of commercial capitalism (Linebaugh 2003). Yet seafarers working on oceangoing vessels and industrial fishing crew have long been considered separate and only very rarely cooperate. Strikes and union organization tend to be more common in industrial fisheries where some processing is done on board, such as in Alaska, Argentina and Norway. Many of these unions are part of the Fisheries section of the International Transport Workers' Federation, or the International Union of Foodworkers, which includes unions representing workers in fish-processing factories. Yet union penetration in the fisheries sector is notoriously low at under 1 per cent through the supply chain – fishing and processing.

Meanwhile, owners and managers of boats and fishing companies – 'classes of capital' (Baglioni 2015) – continue to organize to improve their positions in the commodity chains of which they are a part. Industry associations enable firms to co-operate and use their collective bargaining power in relations with national and regional governments, including in fisheries access negotiations (Havice and Campling 2010). Foley (2012) describes efforts by processing firms to collaboratively resist attempts by organized inshore fishers to push up the prices that processors will pay for catch, while Sinha (2012) shows how local employers/boat owners have been shown to make alliances with fishers' unions to exclude more capitalized foreign fishing vessels.

In sum, producing value from seafood in the context of world market competition has generated a diversity of social relations to production that evolve over time. Many of these are familiar to debates in agrarian political economy, such as gendered and racialized labour relations, class politics, exploitative working conditions and modes of resistance. We point to the need for more research in these areas using the conceptual tools available to agrarian political economy (see Barclay 2008; Muszynski 1996; Neis et al. 2005).

RESOURCE ACCESS AND THE STATE

Resource access and control is a central concern in academic and policy work on fisheries. Outside of critical agrarian studies scholarship, access relations are often reduced to fisheries management and its failure to control fishing pressures, but this too has changed quite dramatically in recent years with a significant broadening of scholarly attention to contests over territory and control as they work on and through not only fish, but ocean spaces and resources more broadly. We review foundational research on resource access in fisheries systems, noting that access relations have long been subject to state-based management and related contestation and signalling the utility of critical agrarian studies approaches to the flourishing of questions of access and control over ocean spaces (e.g. ports and logistics hubs, the high seas, the melting poles) and resources (e.g. seabed minerals, genetic resources, the common heritage of humanity) that are now a central preoccupation in a wide array of sub-disciplines.

Much fisheries-specific research focuses on resource access, and its environmental outcomes. Property rights regimes and distorted market signals – technical components of fisheries systems that can be controlled by centralized regulatory policy frames – continue to be fetishized as positivist rule-making and models of efficient modes of resource extraction; a trend worth noting because the 'academic' and 'applied' intersect around fisheries management practices.

Whether conceptualized around capturing 'maximum sustainable yield', ecosystem-based management or using fisheries resources for socio-economic development, fisheries management (and related social–property relations) is a political process that is inextricably bound up with processes of capitalist accumulation (Austen et al. 2016; Hubbard 2014; Ramesh and Namboothri 2018). As in other natural resource industries, resource access in fisheries involves bundles of rights as well as bundles of powers (Ribot and Peluso 2003). 'Access' is not only a site of political contestation narrowly organized around management, but defined by a combination of social relations such as geopolitics, access to capital, Indigenous identity or market access, all of which can dictate fisheries use patterns and their socio-economic and ecological outcomes. This bundle of powers is also intimately related to the materiality of fish: the simple fact that they move and must be chased through the seas to be extracted matters tremendously for questions of resource access and control.

Efforts to define property in the sea must be understood as projects associated with territory making and unmaking. The oceans and the resources in them have long been sites of struggle over property and geopolitical control. The ascendency of sea tenure between the thirteenth and seventeenth centuries demonstrates that access relations in the sea reflect the power that certain social classes have to influence others' ability to extract fish. In the context of the transition to capitalism in Sicily in the 1600s, merchant bankers took private control of bluefin tuna fisheries that were historically organized around feudal ownership and property structures (Longo and Clark 2012). Along the Scottish coast in the 1700s, entire fishing towns were built by landlords (modern landed property) and peopled by displaced crofters (Howard 2012). Throughout the seventeenth century, major fishing nations – England, France, Spain, Portugal and the Netherlands – were propelled into marine boundary contests that have left lasting geopolitical legacies (Cordell 1989).

Grotius' (1916) work in the early seventeenth century is most commonly marked as the beginning of the struggle over property relations in the sea. His proposal in *The Free Sea* to ensure open access conditions across the oceans was developed to support the Dutch capitalist trading regime and prevent rival European states from gaining control of shipping lanes and increasing English appropriation of herring fishing grounds. As part of this effort, Grotius maintained that fisheries were inexhaustible and should be open to all peoples. By the time Grotius was developing his treatise on property in the sea, pressures to define ocean use rights, territory and ownership were deeply entangled with the development of emerging fishing interests, trade patterns, shipping lanes and geopolitics in the world market of early capitalism. These further advanced throughout the colonial era as Europeans continued to develop fishing presence throughout Africa and the Japanese expanded their so-called 'Pelagic Empire' (Campling 2012; Tsutsui 2013). In the post-World War II era, Nazi jurist Carl Schmitt (2015), in his world-historical meditation, identifies the oceanic turn of the European powers in colonialism as the most important spatial revolution in human history. This process continued after World War II. For example, the United States fishing fleet was decimated during the war, and post-war demand for profitable convenience foods in light of growing labour costs drove a government programme of subsidies and state-sponsored science oriented towards an expansive, extractivist logic in the Pacific Ocean (Campling and Havice 2018; Finley 2011).

The long process of creating property relations in the sea is marked by the largest single enclosure in history: state sovereignty over EEZs. In the 1970s, multiple individual states declared their EEZs (others had done so significantly earlier). Later this customary law was institutionalized when most states ratified the 1982 United Nations Convention on the Law of the Sea which instils state sovereignty over national EEZs and the resources in them by recognizing a series of rights that individual states have over fishing activities including, inter alia, the right to: charge access and fishing fees (ground rent) to fishing firms, define the conditions of production (i.e. resource management) and prohibit or exclude fishers. Since property is a bundle of rights implemented and conferred by social relations and reflected in juridical practices (MacPherson 1983), these sovereign rights mean that EEZ fish are state property. Importantly, and following Schmitt's pronouncement, it was the colonial powers that gained a disproportionate expanse of the global ocean in the EEZ enclosures. In particular Britain, France and the United States were major beneficiaries because their control over a large number of overseas territories (the 'confetti of empire') delivers large oceanic territories (Campling and Colás 2021).

Overall, then, marine fisheries have been moving towards the enclosure of open access regimes for hundreds of years. This has been far more significant in ocean management than the polemic that 'open access' is rampant and the driver of problems in fisheries systems, though several have noted that historical property relations in fisheries have been designed as strong, weak, private or open access according to the interests of the group doing the defining (Cordell 1989; McCay 1981). Policy makers, though aware that fisheries are state property, often do not treat them as a part of any property relation until private property regimes are applied in the sector (Mansfield 2008). State property is not ignored, but is at best seen as a step toward private property rights – and the related individual incentive for profit, steward-ship and improved management – and at worst as a cover for open access (Mansfield 2004).

Turning attention to the role of the state as landlord in the EEZ enables analysis of state–firm relations through which struggles over industrial fishing unfold. Campling and Havice (2014) argue that whether retaining control over fisheries property relations or using them to create and deploy private property regimes, states do not act solely as functional rent-maximizing agents as mainstream fisheries economics and institutions such as the World Bank assume. Instead, states are active players in struggles over the creation and distribution of surplus value from the production of fisheries commodities, and are involved in mediating domestic and foreign interests and the multiscalar fisheries relations among them, including the 'socio-political substance of access dynamics' such as local ethnic and class relations (Fabinyi et al. 2019, 93). As state-landed property, coastal states sit at the nexus of rent appropriation and other distributional struggles around surplus value, (perceived) 'national interest', geopolitics, resource management and industry regulation in EEZs. As such, there is a historical and political naiveté in imploring states to promote 'good governance' by instating and enforcing idealized private property relations. Thus, policy proposals for 'equilibrium' conditions and 'rent maximization' in EEZ fisheries will always face serious problems in practice – particu-larly in transboundary and industrial fisheries (Andriamahefazafy et al. 2019; Havice 2018).

Questions of resource access and control are now a central concern across the oceans as marine spaces and resources that are presently beyond full incorporation into capitalist circuits are increasingly in their sights. These transformations are manifest in critical scholarship that is in part a response to the mainstream 'blue economy' paradigm (Barbesgaard 2018); the field includes fisheries, but also incorporates and sometimes analytically integrates conservation (e.g. marine protected areas), maritime logistics, coastal tourism, deep sea mining and the capitalist relations that underwrite them (see Havice and Zalik 2019).

One connected area of focus here has been on 'ocean grabbing', a debate that is starting to take sharper analytical and political shape, in part influenced by the contributions of agrarian political economy work on 'land grabbing' (see Goetz, this volume). As a whole, the language of 'grabbing' and the blue economy moment is 'more adequately investigated and understood as part of a longue durée transformation of capitalist relations with the sea' (Mallin and Barbesgaard 2020, 2). Critical agrarian studies-inspired ocean-grabbing literature is driven by an underlying concern with capitalist social relations of production and reproduction, and their articulations with geopolitics (e.g. China's maritime silk road), local labour politics (Barbesgaard 2019) and powerful private interests such as philanthropic organizations (Mallin et al. 2019). The concern with geopolitics illuminates the distinctive ways in which the appro-priation of oceanic resources is framed by domestic and interstate power struggles throughout history (see Campling and Colás 2021; Finley 2011; Gorostiza and Cerda 2016; Tsutsui 2013).

CONCLUSION

Industrial fisheries systems articulate with the hallmarks of critical agrarian studies. Here we have reviewed foundational and emergent work that develops these articulations to turn attention to understanding capitalist relations in fisheries systems and the seas at large.

However, these examinations are in their infancy. Critical agrarian studies scholarship is urgently needed alongside the emergent processes of capitalist expansion – and resistance to it – in the seas. These areas of concern also offer advancements for critical agrarian studies as a more-than-terrestrial field of study.

Rather than a recapitulation, we use this conclusion to draw attention to areas of potential interest for future critical agrarian studies work in the realms of fisheries and oceans. For instance, more research is needed on the articulations of particular fish commodity chains with historical shifts in seafood regimes, including whether and how they shape and/or are shaped by broader dynamics, such as corporate concentration and state regulation, in food regimes. What are the accumulation strategies of capitalists in the oceans and how do they differ from those with terrestrial origins? What are the articulations between land and sea in systems of food provisioning? We have noted how working on fishing boats is among the most dangerous jobs in the world, yet very little remains known of this world of work. For example, why is it that seafarers are relatively well organized but fishing crew are not? How can we think about industrial fisheries and other kinds of work at sea from a lens that differentiates among 'labouring classes'?

The biggest area of development in the critical agrarian studies literature on fisheries over the last 10 years has been fisheries and resource access and control in the oceans more generally. However, this work is most commonly undertaken from a geopolitical or political geography lens, often to the exclusion of nuanced attention to capitalism in questions of access and control. Our review of critical agrarian studies work on industrial fisheries reveals that breaking down land/sea binaries will enable better understanding of the maritime factor in the development of global capitalism (Foley and Mather 2019). It is capitalism – particularly in its industrial form – which has most intensified the relationship between land and sea, incorporating the oceans into the law of value, extending maritime commodity frontiers and attempting in the process to 'flatten' the geophysical and geopolitical division between solid ground and fluid water (Campling and Colás 2021). Drawing on this line of reasoning, perhaps critical agrarian studies researchers and activists who tend to the terrestrial can learn analytical lessons and build solidarities with those working on sea, and, of course, vice versa.

NOTE

1.   Authorship of this chapter is equal and fully collaborative.

FURTHER READING

Campling, L.; Havice, E.; Howard, P.M. (eds) (2012), The political economy and ecology of capture fisheries, Special Double Issue, *Journal of Agrarian Change*, 12(2–3), 177–457.

Havice, E.; Zalik, A. (2019), Ocean frontiers, Special Issue, *International Social Science Journal*, 68(229–230), 213–368.

Howard, P.M. (2016), *Environment, Labour and Capitalism at Sea: 'Working the Ground' in Scotland*, Manchester: Manchester University Press.

Longo, S.B.; Clausen, R.; Clark, B. (2015), *The Tragedy of the Commodity: Oceans, Fisheries, and Aquaculture*, New Brunswick, NJ: Rutgers University Press.

Muszynski, A. (1996), *Cheap Wage Labour: Race and Gender in the Fisheries of British Columbia*, Montreal: McGill-Queens's University Press.

REFERENCES

Alder, J.; Sumaila, U.R. (2004), Western Africa: A fish basket of Europe past and present, *Journal of Environment and Development*, 13(2), 156–178.

Andriamahefazafy, M.; Kull, C.A.; Campling, L. (2019), Connected by sea, disconnected by tuna?, *Journal of the Indian Ocean Region*, 15(1), 58–77.

Austen, G.; Jennings, S.M.; Dambacher, J.M. (2016), Species commodification, *Review of Radical Political Economics*, 48(1), 20–35.

Baglioni, E. (2015), Straddling contract and estate farming, *Journal of Agrarian Change*, 15, 17–42.

Barbesgaard, M. (2018), Blue growth, *Journal of Peasant Studies*, 45(1), 130–149.

Barbesgaard, M. (2019), Ocean and land control-grabbing, *Journal of Rural Studies*, 69, 195–203.

Barclay, K. (2008), *A Japanese Joint Venture in the Pacific*, London: Routledge.

Bavinck, M.; Jentoft, S.; Scholtens, J. (2018), Fisheries as social struggle: A reinvigorated social science research agenda, *Marine Policy*, 94, 46–52.

Bell, J.D.; Sharp, M.K.; Havice, E.; Batty, M.; Charlton, K.E.; Russell, J.; Adams, W.; Azmi, K.; Romeo, A.; Wabnitz, C.C. (2019), Realising the food security benefits of canned fish for Pacific Island countries, *Marine Policy*, 100, 183–191.

Béné, C.; Macfadyen, G.; Allison, E.H. (2007), *Increasing the Contribution of Small-Scale Fisheries to Poverty Alleviation and Food Security*, Rome: FAO.

Béné, C.; Arthur, R.; Norbury, H.; Allison, E.H.; Beveridge, M.; Bush, S. et al. (2015), Contribution of fisheries and aquaculture to food security and poverty reduction, *World Development*, 79, 177–196.

Campling, L. (2012), The tuna 'commodity frontier': Business strategies and environment in the industrial tuna fisheries of the western Indian Ocean, *Journal of Agrarian Change*, 12(2–3), 252–278.

Campling, L.; Cólas, A. (2021), *Capitalism and the Sea*, London: Verso.

Campling, L.; Havice, E. (2014), The problem of property in industrial fisheries, *Journal of Peasant Studies*, 41(5), 707–727.

Campling, L.; Havice, E. (2018), The global environmental politics and political economy of seafood systems, *Global Environmental Politics*, 18(2), 72–92.

Campling, L.; Havice, E.; Howard, P.M. (2012), The political economy and ecology of capture fisheries, *Journal of Agrarian Change*, 12(2–3), 177–203.

Clark, B.; Longo, S.B.; Clausen, R.; Auerbach, D. (2019), From sea slaves to slime lines, in Frey, R.; Gellert, P.; Dahns, H. (eds), *Ecologically Unequal Exchange*, London: Palgrave Macmillan, 195–219.

Committee on Fisheries (2010), Recent developments in fish trade, Sub-Committee on Fish Trade, Argentina, 26–30 April, Rome: FAO.

Constance, D.; Bonanno, A. (2000), Regulating the global fisheries, *Agriculture and Human Values*, 12, 125–139.

Cordell, J. (ed.) (1989), *A Sea of Small Boats*, Cambridge: Cultural Survival.

Couper, A.; Smith, H.D.; Ciceri, B. (2015), *Fishers and Plunderers*, London: Pluto.

De Alessi, M. (2012), The political economy of fishing rights and claims, *Journal of Agrarian Change*, 12(2–3), 390–412.

De Schutter, O. (2012), Fisheries and the right to food, Report of the Special Rapporteur on the Right to Food, United Nations General Assembly (A/67/268).

Fabinyi, M.; Dressler, W.; Pido, M. (2019), Access to fisheries in the maritime frontier of Palawan Province, Philippines, *Singapore Journal of Tropical Geography*, 40, 92–110.

Finley, C. (2011), *All the Fish in the Sea*, Chicago, IL: University of Chicago Press.

Foley, P. (2012), The political economy of Marine Stewardship Council certification, *Journal of Agrarian Change*, 12(2–3), 436–457.

Foley, P.; Havice, E. (2016), The rise of territorial eco-certifications: New politics of transnational sustainability governance in the fishery sector, *Geoforum*, 69, 24–33.

Foley, P.; Mather, C. (2018), Bringing seafood into food regime analysis, in Keske, C. (ed.), *Food Futures*, St John's: ISER Books.

Foley, P.; Mather, C. (2019), Ocean grabbing, terraqueous territoriality and social development, *Territory, Politics, Governance*, 7(3), 297–315.

Freidberg, S. (2009), *Fresh*, Cambridge, MA: Harvard University Press.

Friedmann, H. (1992), Distance and durability, *Third World Quarterly*, 13(2), 371–383.

Gorostiza, S.; Cerda, M.C. (2016), The unclaimed latifundium, *Journal of Historical Geography*, 52, 26–35.

Greenpeace (2020), Forced labour and illegal fishing in Taiwan's distant water fisheries, *Greenpeace East Asia*, 19 March, accessed 29 June 2020 at www.greenpeace.org/southeastasia/publication/3690/choppy-waters-forced-labour-and-illegal-fishing-in-taiwans-distant-water-fisheries/.

Grotius, H. (1916), *Mare Liberum (The Free Sea)*, New York: Oxford University Press.

Hadjimichael, M.; Hegland, T.J. (2016), Really sustainable? Inherent risks of eco-labeling in fisheries, *Fisheries Research*, 174, 129–135.

Hara, M. (2009), Crew members in South Africa's squid industry, *Marine Policy*, 33(3), 513–519.

Havice, E. (2018), Unsettled sovereignty and the sea, *Annals of the American Association of Geographers*, 108(5), 1280–1297.

Havice, E.; Campling, L. (2010), Shifting tides in the western central Pacific Ocean tuna fishery, *Global Environmental Politics*, 10(1), 89–114.

Havice, E.; Campling, L. (2017), Where chain governance and environmental governance meet, *Economic Geography*, 93(3), 292–313.

Havice, E.; Zalick, A. (2019), Ocean frontiers, Special Issue, *International Social Science Journal*, 68(229–230), 213–368.

Havice, E.; Campbell, L.M.; Campling, L.; Smith, M.D. (2021), Making sense of firms for ocean governance, *One Earth*, 4(5), 602–604.

HLPE (2014), Sustainable fisheries and aquaculture for food security and nutrition, High Level Panel of Experts on Food Security and Nutrition of the Committee on World Food Security, Rome.

Howard, P.M. (2012), Sharing or appropriation?, *Journal of Agrarian Change*, 12(2–3), 316–343.

Howard, P.M. (2016), *Environment, Labour and Capitalism at Sea: 'Working the Ground' in Scotland*, Manchester: Manchester University Press.

Howse, D.; Jeebhay, M.F.; Neis, B. (2012), The changing political economy of occupational health and safety in fisheries, *Journal of Agrarian Change*, 12(2–3), 344–363.

Hubbard, J. (2014), In the wake of politics, *History of Science Society*, 105(2), 364–378.

Isaacs, M. (2016), The humble sardine, *Agriculture and Food Security*, 5, Art. 27.

Jentoft, S. (2007), In the power of power, *Human Organization*, 66(4), 426–437.

Le Manach, F.; Chaboud, C.; Copeland, D.; Cury, P.; Gascuel, D.; Kleisner, K.M.; Standing, A.; Sumaila, U.R.; Zeller, D.; Pauly, D. (2013), European Union's public fishing access agreements in developing countries, *PLoS One*, 8(11), e79899.

Leroy, B.; Peatman, T.; Usu, T.; Caillot, S.; Moore, B.; Williams, A.; Nicol, S. (2016), Interactions between artisanal and industrial tuna fisheries, *Marine Policy*, 65, 11–19.

Linebaugh, P. (2003), *The London Hanged*, London: Verso.

Longo, S.B.; Clark, B. (2012), The commodification of bluefin tuna, *Journal of Agrarian Change*, 12(2–3), 204–226.

Longo, S.B.; Clausen, R.; Clark, B. (2015), *The Tragedy of the Commodity: Oceans, Fisheries, and Aquaculture*, New Brunswick, NJ: Rutgers University Press.

MacPherson, C.B. (1983), *Property*, Toronto: University of Toronto Press.

Mallin, F.; Barbesgaard, M. (2020), Awash with contradiction, *Geoforum*, 113, 121–132.

Mallin, M.A.F.; Stolz, D.; Thompson, B.S.; Barbesgaard, M. (2019), In oceans we trust, *Marine Policy*, 107, 103421.

Mansfield, B. (2004), Neoliberalism in the oceans, *Geoforum*, 35(3), 313–326.

Mansfield, B. (2008), Comments on Daniel Bromley's paper, *Maritime Studies*, 6(2), 23–26.

Marks, B. (2012), The political economy of household commodity production in the Louisiana shrimp fishery, *Journal of Agrarian Change*, 12(2–3), 227–251.

McCay, B.J. (1981), Development issues in fisheries as agrarian systems, *Culture and Agriculture*, 11, 1–8.

McDowell, R.; Mason, M.; Mendoza, M. (2015), Are slaves catching the fish you buy?, *Associated Press*, 25 March, accessed 29 June 2020 at www.ap.org/explore/seafood-from-slaves/ap-investigation-slaves-may-have-caught-the-fish-you-bought.html.

Menzies, C. (2002), Work first, then eat!, *Anthropology of Work Review*, 23(1–2), 19–24.

Miller, A.M.M.; Bush, S.R. (2015), Authority without credibility?, *Journal of Cleaner Production*, 107, 137–145.

Mills, E.N. (2018), Implicating 'fisheries justice' movements in food and climate politics, *Third World Quarterly*, 39(7), 1270–1289.

Muszynski, A. (1996), *Cheap Wage Labour: Race and Gender in the Fisheries of British Columbia*, Montreal: McGill-Queens's University Press.

Neis, B.; Binkley, M.; Gerrard, S.; Maneschy, M.C. (eds) (2005), *Changing Tides: Gender, Fisheries and Globalization*, Halifax: Fernwood.

Nolan, C. (2019), Power and access issues in Ghana's coastal fisheries, *Marine Policy*, 108, 103621.

Österblom, H.; Jouffray, J.-B.; Folke, C.; Crona, B.; Troell, M.; Merrie, A.; Rockström, J. (2015), Transnational corporations as 'keystone actors' in marine ecosystems, *PLoS One*, 10(5), e0127533.

Pálsson, G. (1991), *Coastal Economies, Cultural Accounts*, Manchester: Manchester University Press.

Payne, J.L.; Bush, A.M.; Heim, N.A.; Knope, M.L.; McCauley, D.J. (2016), Ecological selectivity of the emerging mass extinction in the oceans, *Science*, 353(6305), 1284–1286.

Ponte, S. (2012), The Marine Stewardship Council (MSC) and the making of a market for 'sustainable fish', *Journal of Agrarian Change*, 12(2–3), 300–315.

Ramesh, M.; Namboothri, N. (2018), Maximum sustainable yield, *Economic and Political Weekly*, 53(41), 58–63.

Rediker, M. (1989), *Between the Devil and the Deep Blue Sea*, Cambridge: Cambridge University Press.

Ribot, J.C.; Peluso, N.L. (2003), A theory of access, *Rural Sociology*, 68(2), 153–181.

Richardson, B.; Harrison, J.; Campling, L. (2017), Labour rights in export processing zones with a focus on GSP+ beneficiary countries, Brussels: European Parliament's Subcommittee on Human Rights.

Schmitt, C. (2015), *Land and Sea*, translated by Zeitlin, S.G., Candor: Telos Press.

Sibilia, E.A. (2019), Oceanic accumulation, *Environment and Planning A*, 51(2), 467–486.

Sinha, S. (2012), Transnationality and the Indian Fishworkers' Movement, 1960s–2000, *Journal of Agrarian Change*, 12(2–3), 364–89.

Song, A.M.; Bodwitch, H.; Scholtens, J. (2018), Why marginality persists in a governable fishery, *Maritime Studies*, 17, 285–293.

St Martin, K. (2007), The difference that class makes, *Antipode*, 39, 527–549.

Steenbergen, D.J.; Fabinyi, M.; Barclay, K.; Song, A.M.; Cohen, P.J.; Eriksson, H.; Mills, D.J. (2019), Governance interactions in small-scale fisheries market chains, *Fish and Fisheries*, 20(4), 697–714.

Stringer, C.; Whittaker, D.H.; Simmons, G. (2015), New Zealand's turbulent waters: The use of forced labour in the fishing industry, *Global Networks*, 16(1), 3–24.

Symes, D.; Phillipson, J. (2009), Whatever became of social objectives in fisheries policy?, *Fisheries Research*, 95(1), 1–5.

Tsutsui, W.M. (2013), The Pelagic Empire: Reconsidering Japanese expansion, in Miller, I.J.; Thomas, J.A.; Walker, B.L. (eds), *Japan at Nature's Edge*, Honolulu, HI: University of Hawaii Press, 21–38.

Vandergeest, P. (2018), Law and lawlessness in industrial fishing, *International Social Science Journal*, 68(229–230), 325–342.

Vandergeest, P.; Marschke, M. (2020), Modern slavery and freedom, *Antipode*, 52, 291–315.

43. Forests and current transitions

Markus Kröger

THE IMPORTANCE OF FORESTS AND THEIR TRANSITIONS FOR CRITICAL AGRARIAN STUDIES

The topic of forests and their current transitions – for example, deforestation within rural transformations, tree plantations and regenerating pastures as tree-covered areas – is at the core of understanding several overarching themes in critical agrarian studies. There is often an inherent schism between agriculture and retaining forest cover, but such a schism is not inevitable. People maintain a substantial variety of forest activities, including different types of agroforestry, swiddens, hunting and gathering and non-wood- and wood-based forest product usage (González and Kröger 2020). Modernity and capitalism (Moore 2010) – as well as many prior "civilizations", such as the Roman and other ancient empires (Perlin 2005) – have largely seen forests as sources of wood essential to the growth and expansion of their power, and have consequently erased most of the world's old-growth forests (Radkau 2012).

Critical agrarian studies has and can continue to contribute to these and other closely related forest debates in different disciplines and topics by adding a deeper analysis of power relations, agrarian political economy and political ecology. For example, analyses have challenged the claim that swidden practices or forest commons are unsustainable or unviable practices, highlighting how modernizing states and the expansion of corporate profit-seeking have labelled the common lands of peasants and Indigenous populations "empty" or "unproductive" (Fox et al. 2009; Toivanen and Kröger 2018). Such barring of customary rights and legal access to common ancestral forests have pushed peasants towards illegal uses of forests and hostile attitudes towards these areas that they formerly held as commonly governed (Peluso 1992). Modern industrial forestry has often cast prior practices that sustained natural forest cover as "unsustainable" to delegitimize competing land uses and control by traditional populations and to legitimize the sector's own deforestation and tree plantation practices (Shiva and Bandyopadhyay 1985; Carrere and Lohmann 1996; Hall 2002; McCarthy 2010). In these forest transitions, the very concept of "forest" is at the core of the debate: whether there actually is a forest in a place does not matter if powerholders manage to label an area a forest (Vandergeest and Peluso 2006, 2015). Transforming the *Cerrado* forests in inland Brazil into monoculture plantations (Oliveira and Hecht 2016) or the worldwide labelling of any areas by would-be "development" inducers as shrubland, savannah, already degraded forest or other non-natural forests – or as simply nothing – (see Scott 1998) is a key discursive tactic that shapes the understanding of what forests are and whether they are transformed or not. Therefore, in addition to providing an analysis of the actual forest practices of different social groups (see Schroeder and González 2019), definitional issues (see Kröger 2014) and forest discourses (see Pülzl et al. 2014) are at the core of critical agrarian studies of forest transitions. Other scholars and theorists have also studied forest transitions for different purposes, such as trying to generalize the broad changes that, for example, urbanization and industrialization bring to tree cover.[1]

The discussion on forest transitions in this chapter will reveal that we urgently need a better definition of forests, or understandings of forests that are based on Indigenous ontologies, not only on western conceptualizations. I will showcase the different positions within critical agrarian studies regarding the debate around monocultures (including tree plantations) and forest transitions in different parts of the globe, including the important forest transitions occurring in the Global South as well as the Global North. I canvas the current major forest transitions globally, examining the changes in forests due to the development of pastures, soybeans, oil palm and/or mining and other extractive capitalist expansions that are currently expanding at an increasing rate despite dire global and regional climate disruptions. Particular attention is focused on Brazil, where contemporary forest transitions are used to illustrate what critical agrarian studies has already contributed and what should be studied.

The key debates around how to provide answers to pressing sustainability issues, such as the clean development mechanism (CDM), REDD+[2] and other "carbon capture" issues, are addressed. These debates are likely to become ever more influential in policies impacting the "lived environments" of forest-dwelling populations and other peasant and rural peoples (see Taylor 2015). Currently, most of the focus on battling climate change has focused on curbing carbon emissions without giving due importance to biodiversity; tree mass and carbon capture are prioritized at the cost of rich forest ecosystems inhabited by people. This chapter also identifies several research gaps and provides ideas for deepening the criticality of agrarian studies on forests – including suggesting world-ecological, political ontological and other post-cartesian and post-extractivist analyses of forests and forest transitions. I will also provide a list for further reading on this fascinating topic, which (for abovementioned reasons) should be studied more deeply and broadly by critical agrarian studies.

FORESTS: CONTEMPORARY DEBATES AND CONCEPTUAL ISSUES

What are forests? Lund (2018) found that there are more than 1700 different definitions of forests and wooded areas in the academic literature and official reports. How should we define forests? What is the difference between an area with trees and a forest? Who has and who should have the power to define forests? These questions have risen to a prominent position since the spread of industrial tree plantations started to drastically shape rural landscapes in the Global South and the Global North, often under the guise of expanding forests. The different Food and Agriculture Organization (FAO) definitions of these tree plantations, which are typically large-scale, continuous monoculture plantations consisting of the industrial forestry and charcoal sectors of eucalyptus, pine or acacia and are produced for the purposes of pulp-making or charcoal, still call these plantations "forests".[3] The former definition, "industrial forest plantations", was at least somewhat better than the current "planted forests" definition, which unites all kinds of semi-natural, semi-planted forests with monoculture tree plantations (Kröger 2014), making it difficult to know what specific data are referring to or for researchers to follow what a fellow researcher is arguing (but see Jackson et al. 2005; Hua et al. 2018). International and national organizations' forest definitions have also been the victim of "forestry imperialism", where powerful nations have steered the definition towards their own interests and stripped away many of the signifiers that are crucial for forest-dwelling traditional populations' livelihoods and understandings of what forests are (Kröger 2013b, 2014).

Uruguay and Chile provide examples of industrial forestry expansions that have been argued to have colonial-type power relations (Groglopo 2012) and both visibly violent and hidden conflicts (Ehrnström-Fuentes and Kröger 2017). The battles around defining and conceptualizing forests and areas consisting of planted trees are constantly gaining more importance. In addition to critical agrarian studies, many other fields such as ecology are joining the criticism on existing forest definitions used by powerful institutions (Sasaki and Putz 2009).

Critical agrarian studies on forests is particularly appropriate for assessing the dilemmas related to these endeavours due to its focus on power relations, especially those issues left unexamined by more technically minded or natural scientific forest and forestry researchers, those who focus on conservation without people, or even many political economists of forestry. There are crucial dimensions to these debates that readily escape the analysis of even radical political economics. Forests are often home to many Indigenous and traditional populations who still retain some of the longest-lasting commoning practices (McElwee 2009) but are also typically ethnic minorities and targets of land grabs (Ferreira 2009). An example could be swidden cultivation (Fox et al. 2009), which can be considered sustainable in comparison to modern consumption and production patterns (Nepstad et al. 2006; Hecht 2011). Forests and trees also have an "agency" or spiritual side to them that political ontology, ethnographies of non-modernist forest dwellers (Kohn 2013), analyses of Indigenous forest-based cultivation practices (Schroeder and González 2019) and even some biologists/foresters examining the deeper nature of trees and forests are starting to discover (Wohlleben 2016). Forest knowledge of Amazon Indigenous groups has been found to offer untapped potential for challenging and contributing to the current definitions in global forest governance, offering onto-epistemological openings and practical tools to address the climate crisis (González and Kröger 2020). These post-Cartesian analyses offer a new viewpoint to question the modern notion of "sustainable forestry", where sustainability has come to signify sustained yields. "Sustainability" emerged from the concept of sustainable forestry in German forestry in the nineteenth century (Scott 1998). Such anthropocentric notions of forests and trees as (primarily or even only) wood resources are and have been challenged by many of those populations studied by critical agrarian studies, such as those who are heavily pressed by the advance of land grabs, deforestation, industrial plantation expansions and extractivism.

Forests should thus be defined as areas with multiple tree species that grow together with other vegetation, in natural or semi-natural formations, and allow for the co-existence of multiple forms of life, that is, a web of life that only a forest can sustain. On the other hand, tree monocultures or tree plantations with very few species should not be called forests or planted forests but should be referred to as plantations, which are more akin to agricultural crop production.

There is a long history of the physical and symbolic degradation of forests and the conflicts these transitions have caused (Perlin 2005; Miller 2007; Moore 2010; Radkau 2012; Ghazoul 2015). The worst damage to millennial forests and trees has been accomplished through the past centuries' unprecedented advances in western deforestation practices and means. Timber and logging frontiers have been essential for building the core regions of empires for 5000 years (Perlin 2005), and later the capitalist world-system and providing fuel for the production of sugar and other early industrial mills that were essential for the system (Moore 2015). The historical frontiers of the deforestation of capitalism were defined by the decimation of forests and valuable trees in regions such as coastal Brazil (especially Brazilwood and later araucarias) and in countries such as Poland, Norway (logging for building materials for Amsterdam and other cities) (Moore 2010), Burma (teak for construction) and Finland (potash, tar, and paper) (Kröger 2013b).

In many political economies – such as Brazil and Argentina – whose "agrohegemonies" were built upon agribusiness and latifundio (large historic landholders') lobby groups (Miller 2007; Campbell 2015), forests are cast by these agrohegemonies as non-possibilities for development and as impediments to economic growth through pasture expansion, monocultures, mining, dams, infrastructure and cities. It is important to note that the motives of forest policy are intersectoral (Kröger 2017) and vary strongly across different world-ecologies; their constellations depend on the regionally dominant political economies and ecologies. However, it is not common to construct alternative forest policies due to the pressure of the capitalist world-ecology, which could be said to have an inherent bias against forest-based livelihoods, as well as forest commons (Toivanen and Kröger 2018).

Natural forests have been both useful for and impediments to different varieties of capitalism. Standing forests have played a major role in the capitalist world-system, for example, during the rubber boom of the Amazon, which left the forest standing while exploiting the rubber tappers, illustrating the importance of studying the situated histories of social relations taking place in forests and behind the creation of forest-based commodities (Peluso 2012). Recently, Amazon cooperatives harvesting non-tree-based forest products have thrived and managed to increase the wealth of those living close to cities rich with collectable fruits, nuts, medicinal extracts and oils and other products (Hecht 2007). In addition to these value creations, natural and semi-natural forests continue to be crucially important for many peasant livelihoods.

CURRENT FOREST TRANSITIONS: MONOCULTURES AND DEFORESTATION

The past decades have seen massive deforestation, especially in the tropics but also in other parts of the globe. Perversely, this deforestation is often promoted in the name of expanding "forests", which actually means replacing native forests with "forest plantations" or tree plantations (Marchak 1995; Carrere and Lohmann 1996; Hua et al. 2018). This problem is rapidly increasing due to climate mitigation initiatives (Scheidel and Work 2018). Studies of tree plantations have shown that states have major roles in these modernizing ventures (Scott 1998; Kröger 2013a). State subsidies (Bull et al. 2006), ideological support and the creation of neoliberal policies to promote corporate power at the cost of regulatory capacities are keys in birthing extractivism (Ehrnström-Fuentes and Kröger 2018). The socio-economic impacts of tree plantations depend on whether they are corporate, smallholder, community or state-owned/controlled ventures; for instance, whether popular, pro-poor agrarian reform has been carried out and forestry holdings divided more equally (Kröger 2014). There remains, however, a debate among scholars and a need for further research on the precise socio-economic impacts of tree plantations (Malkamäki et al. 2018), as well as on their socio-environmental impacts (see Kröger 2014; Ehrnström-Fuentes 2016). Climate mitigation and speculation cause tree plantations to displace forests and other areas at an increasing pace (Lohmann 1999; Lyons and Westoby 2014), both materially and discursively. This change is visible in the discussion around flex crops, including flex trees, which revolves around the rapidly changing multiple-ness and flexible-ness (or their absence or lessening) in different tree- and wood-based production systems (Kröger 2016) and represents an important and underdeveloped area of research.

In addition to the replacement of natural or other forests of greater biodiversity with oil palm, rubber, eucalyptus, acacia, pine, teak and other tree monocultures to produce agrofuels, fibre and so forth (Overbeek et al. 2012), there is an important and partially interlinked process of deforestation for the purposes of cattle ranching and feed production for the global meat industry (Oliveira and Hecht 2016; Fearnside 2017; Hoelle 2017). Logging valuable timber accompanies these deforestation initiatives (Kröger 2017, 2018) and is linked to the expansion of corn, soybean, sugarcane and rice plantations. There is also an important capital–labour division component in these expansions that needs to be studied in order to understand it; one important difference, for example, is that soybean and eucalyptus plantations require much less manual labour than oil palm plantations (Alonso-Fradejas et al. 2016). The production boom of biodiesel and food-based oil palm has had direct impacts to forest annihilation in Southeast Asia, and to some extent Central America, Colombia and Africa, possibly due to the presence of a larger labour force (see Gerber 2010; Alonso-Fradejas et al. 2016). Regionally dominant political economies need to be studied to understand how, when, where and what kind of forest transitions these activities are pushing and by whom. In South America, for example, deforestation has been largely caused by those involved in the "value web" (see Borras et al. 2015) of meat production, such as soybean and beef producers (see Weis 2013). The process of forestland transitions has become increasingly internationalized and institutionalized, with pension and other funds enabling expansions.

Forest and forestry politics need to be further studied to explain the causes and outcomes of forest transitions; in particular, different types of resistance and conflict. Tree plantations have been mired in myriad national- and international-level conflicts, which have already been studied from many perspectives around the world (see Hellström 2001; Hall 2002; Prudham 2008; Gerber 2010; Pakkasvirta 2010). The study of tree plantation conflicts is likely to merge more closely with the study of "natural forest" conflicts, which thus far have been mostly separate study focuses (Kröger 2020a), as plantations increasingly supplant natural forests.

Tropical deforestation gained ground globally during the 1980s and 1990s, becoming a much-studied topic in political ecology (see Schmink and Wood 1984; Hecht and Cockburn 1989; Hecht 2007, 2011) and forest politics (see Marchak 1995; Dauvergne and Lister 2011). Brazil and particularly the Amazon have been central in these discussions, and their study has opened up the dynamics of forest transitions in several ways. The initial concerns about Amazon deforestation included pasture expansion as a direct result of the wasteful practices of antiquated rural elites, who often burned and razed large forest areas (Fearnside 2017). The field has evolved much since then. The "modern monocultures" of agribusiness, whether they consist of trees or crops, can be contrasted with the old, less productive large estates, such as latifundios in Latin America, which can be seen as speculative ventures that seek to make money on expected future land valuation rather than production per se (Campbell 2015). In latifundio-type speculative landholdings, deforested areas contain very few cows; by contrast, "modern cattle capitalism" is characterized by intensively managed pasture areas, where the focus is actually on producing the maximum amount of beef (and other animal-derivative products). The latifundio speculative holdings typically hold cattle solely to ward off possible farmland productivity inspectors from land authorities seeking distributable or unproductive land, such as in Brazil. This "primitive cattle capitalism" remains the greatest threat to the Brazilian Amazon forests.

Since the 2000s, the rapid development of increasingly precise satellites and remote sensing technologies has dramatically improved the capacity to monitor events in forests. Satellites are currently used by some non-governmental organizations (NGOs) and state entities to uncover patches of deforestation as small as 10 metres. However, this is not to say that curbing deforestation is easy: would-be deforesters constantly adapt to monitoring by, for example, covering open-pit iron mines with very large blue-green plastic canvasses to prevent objectors from spotting them with open-access satellite data, as happened in Goa (Kröger 2020b), or degrading and polluting forests rather than clear-cutting them. These dynamics between deforestation and production oscillate between high demands from global markets and developments in regulation capacities (Hecht 2011; Fearnside 2017). A perverse outcome of this situation is the large-scale aerial poisoning of forests with Tordon and other agrotoxics, which can only be detected after a few weeks. This practice started in Brazil in spring/summer 2018 as a response to authorities' and researchers' newly refined skill in rapidly detecting, even under cloudy conditions, initiated clear-cuts and major degradations by loggers. Areas as large as 70 000 hectares have been sprayed from airplanes, and although NGOs such as the Brazilian *Instituto Socioambiental* notified the environmental authorities, who were able to end at least some of these practices, the damage had already been done (author's interview, 20 November 2018).

The current push by the Brazilian Bolsonaro government to allow the use of many pesticides that are banned elsewhere in the world is of concern. Brazil is already the world's largest pesticide importer, and the compound effects of aerial spraying new soybean plantations deep in the Amazon may impact delicate ecosystems and species (Pedlowski et al. 2012). A similarly worrying and wanton process of polluting deforestation is occurring in the Peruvian Amazon province of Madre de Dios, where illegal medium-size gold miners spilling mercury into waters that they muddy are the key proximate agents causing most deforestation (Swenson et al. 2011). In this process, miners spread mercury into rivers, which are brought by fish into distant Indigenous communities and may potentially represent lethal impacts to human life. Examples of long-term forest changes can be found within the oil industries in Nigeria, Ecuador and the Arctic, among others. Some troubling features of contemporary deforestation are its intersectoriality (Kröger 2017), the expansion of overlapping deforested land claimed by various industries (which together and wantonly destroy forests in an ungoverned ultraliberal, globalized process) (Käkönen and Thuon 2018) and the spread of forest transitions (to worse living conditions) to populations far away from the initial cleared sites (Swenson et al. 2011). These issues are particularly problematic because the phenomenon of deforestation and other major forest transitions, such as pollution and degradation, become harder to detect and track and thus govern.

Several processes in different parts of the globe highlight these dynamics. For example, in Finland, harvesting rates have increased sharply since 2015, while the area of protected forests has remained very low especially in Southern Finland (Kröger and Raitio 2017), and China's ambitious policies to "protect" and "restore" forests have actually meant a transformation of both native forests and croplands into tree plantations (Hua et al. 2018). Such qualitative worsening of tree-covered areas from forests to tree plantations has not, however, been noted by the global community (or state authorities) as much as the clear-cut deforestation brought by the multiple "flex crop" expansions in Latin America (see Borras et al. 2015) and by oil palm and pulpwood expansion in Southeast Asia (particularly in Indonesia and Malaysia) (McCarthy 2010). When deforestation is carried out mostly by large landholders, who are often linked to corporations and export markets, these transitions can be more easily detected by would-be regulators (be they research entities, government agencies, NGOs or others). The massive losses in the Brazilian *Cerrado*, for example, where soybean plantations have quickly wiped out vast areas of forestland, have been noted (Oliveira and Hecht 2016). When deforestation takes place in a patchwork fashion, however, it usually remains less visible (as in the Nordic countries) (Kröger and Raitio 2017). Nonetheless, the phenomenon is the same; forests and all that lives and comes to life with them are disappearing. The tree line is travelling north due to climate warming, but forests are being degraded by the expansion of logging, fires, pests and other interlinked climatic and productivist expansions into the Arctic (Kröger 2019a).

In this sense, deforesting resource frontiers (see Kröger and Nygren 2020) should be understood not merely in political economic terms but in terms of major changes in what exists and can exist in a given piece of land: they should be understood as "frontiers of existence" (Kröger 2022). An analysis with a central focus on existences and the value of life itself (be this the lives of peasants, other humans, animals, insects, trees or other forms of life) – which takes as a starting point the fact that different forms of life do exist and should be valued as existences – is still lacking in critical agrarian studies. The discipline typically continues unreflectively using (in the vein of existing vocabulary) terms such as "volume of meat produced" instead of, for example, focusing on the numbers of lives lost. This type of vocabulary is at odds with the conceptions of life and the web of life of many Indigenous forest dwellers, who see trees as entities that have lives.[4] Future critical agrarian studies should be careful not to unreflectively engage in the modernist project of making the world commensurable and consumable through Cartesian analysis (see Moore 2015), which hides lives and assumes an anthropocentric or peasant-centric posture (if these peasants are studied at the cost of everything else that exists in the web of life).

CONTEMPORARY FOREST TRANSITIONS AND POLICY DEBATES

In this section, I will provide some examples of the debates around contemporary forest policies. I will first address the financialization of forest (non-)transitions through the debates on REDD+ and *yasunization*. Second, I will discuss how progressive governments have tried to develop social welfare policies and monetary handouts to people for not deforesting and the debate around this through a discussion of Brazil's *Bolsa Verde* and other initiatives. The third subsection discusses different conservation policies, including "fortress conservation" and biocultural conservation areas, and their current relation to deforestation. Finally, before the conclusion, I will briefly introduce the large debate around certification schemes and their (questioned) importance in governing forest transitions.

Yasunization of Forests

In the existing literature, some of the above concerns on the commercialization and westernization of nature are visible in the debate around REDD+ (Schroeder and González 2019; González and Kröger 2020), "yasunization" (Temper et al. 2013) and other environmental economics-promoted initiatives. These initiatives try to protect forests and offer higher returns for forest stewardship by forest dwellers and governments that protect forests through financial compensation for such acts. Critiques of the aforementioned initiatives are mostly found in critical agrarian studies, where the World Rainforest Movement, Corner House and Chris Lang's writings have been highly influential. These studies argue that the CDM, REDD+ and other carbon market initiatives have major obstacles to overcome before they can be launched or calculated (Lohmann 1999; Kröger 2016) and often have negative consequences. These initiatives may even result in replacing native forests with tree plantations and dispossessing forest dwellers (Lyons and Westoby 2014). These and other conservation ventures that bar traditional forest uses by peasants and Indigenous groups have been criticized as green grabs (Fairhead et al. 2012). Other fields, such as ecological economics, have also criticized ecosystem services as commodity fetishism (Kosoy and Corbera 2010).

Targeted Social Policies for Curbing Deforestation

While the global commercialization of forests has been severely criticized, under some circumstances national- and regional-level policies similar to REDD+ ideas seem to have had positive impacts on forest-based "lived environments". According to Adriana Margutti, who worked for Brazil's Workers' Party (interview, 21 November 2018) as a key person in developing and launching Brazil's *Bolsa Verde* programme, *Bolsa Verde* was a success. The policy gave approximately R$100.00 to forest-dwelling people in extreme poverty (earning less than R$70.00 per month, according to *Bolsa Familia* statistics) as compensation for not deforesting, which was verified by increasingly sophisticated remote sensing and geoinformatics by state institutions and researchers. However, the policy of Green Municipalities (*municípios verdes*), developed during the same era by the country's Ministry of the Environment, was not a success according to many of my informants. Many (or possibly even most) of the Amazon-located municipalities' secretaries of the environment have not received the federal funds allocated to each municipality to tackle deforestation. No funds came to the Belterra secretary of the environment, for example, according to the secretary himself, and the funds may have actually been used in advancing soybean and logging expansions into forests. These examples illustrate the importance of sound systems that ensure the functioning of finance-based deforestation-curbing activities and how difficult this is given the existing politics and power relations, according to which those in power usually benefit from deforestation.

Conservation Policies and Deforestation

The western idea of conservation requiring pristine forests emptied of people has been heavily criticized by political ecologists and others with field research experience. Brockington (2002) offers a fruitful critique on this "fortress conservation". This continues to be one of the biggest political forces affecting forests and their dwellers in, for example, several parts of Africa but also elsewhere, as the literature on "green grabbing" has illustrated (Fairhead et al. 2012). The more inclusive biocultural conservation parks, such as the multiple-use conservation areas found in South America, where peasants can continue to live in forests, have been applauded as policy innovations. However, recent developments in many of these multiple-use conservation areas, such as the expansion of ranching, authoritarian populism that sees no problem with deforestation and the decline of rubber prices, have placed severe political pressure on this more socially inclusive and often more politically feasible conservation model (Kröger 2019b). The fall of the rubber subsidies/markets has meant that rubber tappers are turning to cattle ranching and logging unless key activists resisting deforestation activities retain and build contentious agency in the forests (Kröger 2013a). This approach is increasingly difficult due to intergenerational dynamics in which the old rubber holdings of rubber tappers cannot be viably divided equally among their children on which to base their families' livelihoods. Ranching offers an easily available short-term means of obtaining funds for many families in the Chico Mendes Extractive Reserve, for example (Kröger 2019b). While extractive reserves and other multiple-use conservation areas developed by Chico Mendes and others in Brazil during and after the 1980s have had major impacts on the institutionalization of Latin American conservation and successfully created barrier zones against deforestation and offered forest rights to inhabitants (Hecht 2011), this model also poses intrinsic problems. One such problem is the high amount of labour required to collect and process non-wood-based forest products, which is often borne disproportionally by women; for this and other reasons, the most successful multiple-use conservation areas are located closer to urban centres. The successful areas have managed to thrive in the current superfoods booms of açai, nuts and other products (Hecht 2007). States should offer much greater assistance for developing and launching these sustainable forest-based markets and livelihoods. The way to ensure such an approach is to build international and national coalitions that are based on globally attuned contentious agency for forest-based livelihoods. Civil society must simultaneously use multiple strategies, including both contentious and routine acts. Resistance should be embedded in state and multilateral institutions, such as the United Nations and FAO, in addition to influencing crucial financial sectors to globally expand a forest conservation agenda that is socially and environmentally just. Actions by forest dwellers themselves are essential. The push to deforest is relentless. The mere creation of conservation areas as barrier zones is not enough, as for example the rapidly risen deforestation in conservation areas during the Bolsonaro era proves (Kröger 2020c). The international system still de facto treats forests as something that can be lost to maintain the international flow of commodities, even in the face of global climate and ecological crises.

Certification Schemes

In the weak presence of markets for non-wood-based forest products, the push for logging inside conservation areas is currently severe. This result is due to the adoption of Forest Stewardship Council (FSC) certification schemes for would-be "sustainable communitarian logging" (Kröger 2018). These dynamics show how certification schemes that aim to support forest dwellers typically function as a veil to hide and legitimize the bulk of the wood trade, which is illegal (in approximately 80 per cent of the Brazilian Amazon), as the sawmills use FSC export openings to place illegal wood within the piles of "certified" logs for which no chain of custody can be guaranteed in practice. FSC and other forest certifications are currently heavily challenged, and NGOs such as Greenpeace have left the scheme, as it cannot establish a chain of custody in practice.

CONCLUSION

This chapter has offered some glimpses into current forest transitions, a vast topic for which an exhaustive account or comprehensive review is beyond the scope of this brief analysis.

Forests are in transition due to expanding monocultures. The key reasons for deforestation, forest degradation and pollution are the value web of meat production, which drives the expansion of meat consumption; existing practices of (illegal) land grabbing and deforestation for speculative purposes; the expansion of the wood-based bioeconomy based on flex tree plantations; and mining, hydrocarbon, dam and other industrial and urbanizing ventures. Indigenous people and other traditional forest dwellers have largely managed to retain forest cover in areas where they have gained de jure and/or de facto land control (Garnett et al. 2018). Critical agrarian studies should delve more deeply into the analysis of both tree plantations and natural forests and all types of wooded landscapes between these two. This analysis should be critical in the sense of conducting political economic analyses of power relations and control, with a focus on who are the winners and losers of different forest transitions. Forest politics, including conflicts and their absence, should be studied to explain the causalities in forest transitions. Such analyses should also include an understanding of the multiple forms of life that are present in forests and are lost to deforestation.

Critical agrarian studies should continue to go beyond remote sensing, rational choice theory and other explanations of forest transitions that lump all human actions together without distinguishing who is doing what; without considering the systemic, structural and contingent impacts; and/or assuming that all humans or groups would act in a similar fashion. There should be an analysis of both the proximate agents (who actually cuts the trees, for example, and all the steps in the "value web") and the ultimate causes of forest transitions (which economic sectors and varieties of capitalism are behind the push, and what local contextual issues enable such transitions?) (Geist and Lambin 2002; Kröger 2019b). This approach can help in highlighting who is responsible for what and thus avoid the "flat anthropocentrisms" so common in the more popular bestselling books of global history that also touch upon the issue of forest transitions (such as Weisman 2008). The study of different strategies by which contentious agency and other forms of resistance are created can elaborate the local varieties of forest politics and how these possibly affect forest transitions (Kröger 2013a, 2020b).

The ongoing push for polluting deforestation in the forms of mining using mercury, oil exploration and the use of agrotoxics to kill vegetation, which influence not only the targeted forest areas but also very distant communities and inhabited environments, is a dire concern. There are many authoritarian populist governments currently in power for whom forests are considered an impediment to growth. The development of sustainable forest-based alternatives to global extractivism is an urgent topic for which critical agrarian studies should provide answers. The ways in which forest communities and forest advocates could preserve and develop forest-based livelihoods through resistance and scaling up successful state–society policies should be studied in more detail. The current frontiers of deforestation also require more analysis in terms of their global linkages. The issue of who is responsible for what has occurred and is occurring in past and contemporary forest transitions is also a topic requiring more analysis, which should cover the different commodity and deforestation sectors and their linkages to reveal who are the key actors and what is their responsibility and power in forest transitions.

NOTES

1. For example, the generalizing theory on "forest transitions" (FTT) by Mather (1990) argues that deforestation first increases with urbanization and industrialization over a long period, followed by reforestation (see also Rudel et al. 2010). Hecht (2010) offers a useful critique of FTT and a similar theory of "deforestation", the Environmental Kuznets Curve, both of which have underlying Malthusian frameworks, and for example do not differentiate between tree plantations and forests.
2. Reducing emissions from deforestation and forest degradation, sustainable management of forests and the conservation and enhancement of forest carbon stocks (REDD+) is the key global programme through which the United Nations and FAO try to combat deforestation (www.fao.org/redd/en/).
3. See the latest FAO definitions of natural forests and "planted forests" with their new subcategories, which show some improvement in comparison to the definition before the latest version, here: www.fao.org/forestry/plantedforests/67504/en/ (accessed 28 January 2019).
4. Many Indigenous people and other animists do not see trees as "things" as a flat or Latourian-inspired ontology would see them (see Kohn 2013; Schroeder and González 2019) but rather as beings or entities that escape Cartesian dualisms; some trees "consist", for example, of multiple visible and invisible (to most people) beings that share the "tree". Similar non-modernist understandings of what trees are can be found in folklore in traditional forest-dweller locations, such as Finland (Kröger 2022).

FURTHER READING

Ehrnström-Fuentes, M. (2016), *Legitimacy in the Pluriverse: Towards an Expanded View on Corporate–Community Relations in the Global Forestry Industry*, Doctoral dissertation, Hanken School of Economics, Helsinki.
Kröger, M. (2013), *Contentious Agency and Natural Resource Politics*, London: Routledge.
Kröger, M. (2016), The political economy of "flex trees": A preliminary analysis, *Journal of Peasant Studies*, 43(4), 886–909.
Perlin, J. (2005), *A Forest Journey: The Story of Wood and Civilization*, New York: Countryman Press.
Vandergeest, P.; Peluso, N.L. (2015), *Political Forests*, in Bryant, R. (ed.), *International Handbook of Political Ecology*, Cheltenham, UK and Northampton, MA, USA: Edward Elgar Publishing, 162–175.

REFERENCES

Alonso-Fradejas, A.; Liu, J.; Salerno, T.; Xu, Y. (2016), Inquiring into the political economy of oil palm as a global flex crop, *Journal of Peasant Studies*, 43(1), 141–165.
Borras, Jr., S.M.; Franco, J.; Isakson, R.; Levidow, L.; Vervest, P. (2015), The rise of flex crops and commodities: Implications for research, *Journal of Peasant Studies*, 43(1), 93–115.
Brockington, D. (2002), *Fortress Conservation: The Preservation of the Mkomazi Game Reserve, Tanzania*, Bloomington, IN: Indiana University Press.
Bull, G.; Bazett, M.; Schwab, O.; Nilsson, S.; White, A.; Maginnis, S. (2006), Industrial forest plantation subsidies: Impacts and implications, *Forest Policy and Economics*, 9(1), 13–31.
Campbell, J. (2015), *Conjuring Property: Speculation and Environmental Futures in the Brazilian Amazon*, Seattle, WA: University of Washington Press.
Carrere, R.; Lohmann, L. (1996), *Pulping the South*, London: Zed Books.
Dauvergne, P.; Lister, J. (2011), *Timber*, Cambridge: Polity.
Ehrnström-Fuentes, M. (2016), *Legitimacy in the Pluriverse: Towards an Expanded View on Corporate–Community Relations in the Global Forestry Industry*, Doctoral dissertation, Hanken School of Economics, Helsinki.

Ehrnström-Fuentes, M.; Kröger, M. (2017), In the shadows of social license to operate: Untold investment grievances in Latin America, *Journal of Cleaner Production*, 141, 346–358.

Ehrnström-Fuentes, M.; Kröger, M. (2018), Birthing extractivism: The role of the state in forestry politics and development in Uruguay, *Journal of Rural Studies*, 57, 197–208.

Fairhead, J.; Leach, M.; Scoones, I. (2012), Green grabbing: A new appropriation of nature?, *Journal of Peasant Studies*, 39(2), 237–261.

Fearnside, P. (2017), Deforestation of the Brazilian Amazon, in Shugart, H. (ed.), *Oxford Research Encyclopedia of Environmental Science*, New York: Oxford University Press.

Ferreira, S. (2009), *"Donos do lugar": a territorialidade quilombola do Sâpe do Norte – ES*, Doctoral dissertation, Universidade Federal Fluminense, Niterói.

Fox, J.; Fujita, Y.; Ngidang, D.; Peluso, N.; Potter, L.; Sakuntaladewi, N.; Sturgeon, J.; Thomas, D. (2009), Policies, political-economy, and swidden in Southeast Asia, *Human Ecology*, 37(3), 305–322.

Garnett, S.; Burgess, N.D.; Fa, J.E.; Fernández-Llamazares, A.; Molnár, Z.; Robinson, C.J.; Watson, J.E.M.; Zander, K.K.; Austin, B.; Brondizio, E.S.; French Collier, N.; Duncan, T.; Ellis, E.; Geyle, H.; Jackson, M.V.; Jonas, H.; Malmer, P.; McGowan, B.; Sivongxay, A.; Leiper, I. (2018), A spatial overview of the global importance of Indigenous lands for conservation, *Nature Sustainability*, 1, 369–374.

Geist, H.; Lambin, E. (2002), Proximate causes and underlying driving forces of tropical deforestation, *BioScience*, 52, 143–150.

Gerber, J. (2010), Conflicts over industrial tree plantations in the South: Who, how and why?, *Global Environmental Change*, 21(1), 165–176.

Ghazoul, J. (2015), *Forests: A Very Short Introduction*, Oxford: Oxford University Press.

González, N.; Kröger, M. (2020), The potential of Amazon indigenous agroforestry practices and ontologies for rethinking global forest governance, *Forest Policy and Economics*, 118, 102257.

Groglopo, A. (2012), *Appropriation by Coloniality: TNCs, Land, Hegemony and Resistance: The Case of Botnia/UPM in Uruguay*, Doctoral thesis, Umeå University, Umeå.

Hall, D. (2002), Environmental change, protest, and havens of environmental degradation: Evidence from Asia, *Global Environmental Politics*, 2(2), 20–28.

Hecht, S. (2007), Factories, forests, fields and family: Gender and neoliberalism in extractive reserves, *Journal of Agrarian Change*, 7(3), 316–347.

Hecht, S. (2010), The new rurality: Globalization, peasants and the paradoxes of landscapes, *Land Use Policy*, 27(2), 161–169.

Hecht, S. (2011), From eco-catastrophe to zero deforestation? Interdisciplinarities, politics, environmentalisms and reduced clearing in Amazonia, *Environmental Conservation*, 39(1), 4–19.

Hecht, S.; Cockburn, A. (1989), *The Fate of the Forest*, London: Verso.

Hellström, E. (2001), Conflict cultures: Qualitative comparative analysis of environmental conflicts in forestry, *Silva Fennica Monographs*, 2, 109.

Hoelle, J. (2017), Jungle beef: Consumption, production and destruction, and the development process in the Brazilian Amazon, *Journal of Political Ecology*, 24(1), 743–762.

Hua, F.; Wang, L.; Fisher, B.; Zheng, X.; Wang, X.; Yu, D.W.; Tang, Y.; Zhu, J.; Wilcove, D.S. (2018), Tree plantations displacing native forests: The nature and drivers of apparent forest recovery on former croplands in Southwestern China from 2000 to 2015, *Biological Conservation*, 222, 113–124.

Jackson, R.; Jobbágy, E.; Avissar, R.; Roy, S.; Barrett, D.; Cook, C.; Farley, K.; le Maitre, D.; McCarl, B.; Murray, B. (2005), Trading water for carbon with biological carbon sequestration, *Science*, 310(5756), 1944–1947.

Käkönen, M.; Thuon, T. (2018), Overlapping zones of exclusion: Carbon markets, corporate hydropower enclaves and timber extraction in Cambodia, *Journal of Peasant Studies*, 1–27.

Kohn, E. (2013), *How Forests Think*, Berkeley, CA: UCB.

Kosoy, N.; Corbera, E. (2010), Payments for ecosystem services as commodity fetishism, *Ecological Economics*, 69, 1228–1236.

Kröger, M. (2013a), *Contentious Agency and Natural Resource Politics*, London: Routledge.

Kröger, M. (2013b), Globalization as the "pulping" of landscapes: Forestry capitalism's North–South territorial accumulation, *Globalizations*, 10(6), 837–853.

Kröger, M. (2014), The political economy of global tree plantation expansion: A review, *Journal of Peasant Studies*, 41(2), 235–261.

Kröger, M. (2016), The political economy of "flex trees": A preliminary analysis, *Journal of Peasant Studies*, 43(4), 886–909.

Kröger, M. (2017), Inter-sectoral determinants of forest policy: The power of deforesting actors in post-2012 Brazil, *Forest Policy and Economics*, 77, 24–32.

Kröger, M. (2018), The new "sustainable communitarian" logging schemes and their critique inside multiple-use conservation areas in the Brazilian Amazon: Preliminary notes, *Globalizations*, 15(5), 1–12.

Kröger, M. (2019a), The global land rush and the Arctic, in Finger, M.; Heininen, L. (eds), *The Global Arctic Handbook*, New York: Springer International Publishing, 27–43.

Kröger, M. (2019b), Deforestation, cattle capitalism and neodevelopmentalism in the Chico Mendes Extractive Reserve, Brazil, *Journal of Peasant Studies*, 47(3), 464–482.

Kröger, M. (2020a), *Natural Resources, Energy Politics, and Environmental Consequences*, Oxford: Oxford University Press.

Kröger, M. (2020b), *Iron Will: Global Extractivism and Mining Resistance in Brazil and India*, Ann Arbor, MI: University of Michigan Press.

Kröger, M. (2020c), Field research notes on Amazon deforestation during the Bolsonaro era, *Globalizations*, 17(6), 1080–1083.

Kröger, M. (2022), *Extractivisms, Existences and Extinctions: Monoculture Plantations and Amazon Deforestation*, London: Routledge.

Kröger, M.; Nygren, A. (2020), Shifting frontier dynamics in Latin America, *Journal of Agrarian Change*, 20(3), 364–386.

Kröger, M.; Raitio, K. (2017), Finnish forest policy in the era of bioeconomy: A pathway to sustainability?, *Forest Policy and Economics*, 77, 6–15.

Lohmann, L. (1999), *The Carbon Shop: Planting New Problems*, Montevideo: WRM.

Lund, H. (2018), Definitions of forest, deforestation, afforestation, and reforestation, Gainesville, VA: Forest Information Services. DOI: 10.13140/RG.2.1.2364.9760.

Lyons, K.; Westoby, P. (2014), Carbon colonialism and the new land grab: Plantation forestry in Uganda and its livelihood impacts, *Journal of Rural Studies*, 36, 13–21.

Malkamäki, A.; D'Amato, D.; Hogarth, N.; Kanninen, M.; Pirard, R.; Toppinen, A.; Zhou, W. (2018), A systematic review of the socio-economic impacts of large-scale tree plantations, worldwide, *Global Environmental Change*, 53, 90–103.

Marchak, P. (1995), *Logging the Globe*, Montreal: McGill-Queen's University Press.

Mather, A. (1990), *Global Forest Resources*, London: Bellhaven Press.

McCarthy, J. (2010), Processes of inclusion and adverse incorporation: Oil palm and agrarian change in Sumatra, Indonesia, *Journal of Peasant Studies*, 37(4), 821–850.

McElwee, P. (2009), Reforesting "bare hills" in Vietnam: Social and environmental consequences of the 5 million hectare reforestation program, *AMBIO: A Journal of the Human Environment*, 38(6), 325–333.

Miller, S. (2007), *Environmental History of Latin America*, Cambridge: Cambridge University Press.

Moore, J.W. (2010), "Amsterdam is standing on Norway" (Part 2): The global North Atlantic in the ecological revolution of the long seventeenth century, *Journal of Agrarian Change*, 10(2), 188–227.

Moore, J.W. (2015), *Capitalism in the Web of Life*, London: Verso Books.

Nepstad, D.; Schwartzman, S.; Bamberger, B.; Santilli, M.; Ray, D.; Scheslinger, P.; Lefebvre, P.; Alencar, A.; Prinz, E.; Fiske, G.; Rolla, A. (2006), Inhibition of Amazon deforestation and fire by parks and indigenous lands, *Conservation Biology*, 20(1), 65–73.

Oliveira, G.; Hecht, S. (2016), Sacred groves, sacrifice zones and soy production: Globalization, intensification and neonature in South America, *Journal of Peasant Studies*, 43(2), 251–285.

Overbeek, W.; Kröger, M.; Gerber, J. (2012), An overview of industrial tree plantations in the global South: Conflicts, trends and resistance struggles, *Ejolt Report*, 3.

Pakkasvirta, J. (2010), *Fábricas de celulosa: historias de la globalización*, Buenos Aires: La Colmena.

Pedlowski, M.A.; Canela, M.; da Costa Terra, M.; Ramos de Faria, R. (2012), Modes of pesticides utilization by Brazilian smallholders and their implications for human health and the environment, *Crop Protection*, 31(1), 113–118.

Peluso, N.L. (1992), *Rich Forests, Poor People: Resource Control and Resistance in Java*, Oakland, CA: University of California Press.

Peluso, N.L. (2012), What's nature got to do with it? A situated historical perspective on socio-natural commodities, *Development and Change*, 43(1), 79–104.

Perlin, J. (2005), A *Forest Journey: The Story of Wood and Civilization*, New York: Countryman Press.

Prudham, S. (2008), Tall among the trees: Organizing against globalist forestry in rural British Columbia, *Journal of Rural Studies*, 24(2), 182–196.

Pülzl, H.; Kleinschmit, D.; Arts, B. (2014), Bioeconomy: An emerging meta-discourse affecting forest discourses?, *Scandinavian Journal of Forest Research*, 29(4), 386–393.

Radkau, J. (2012), *Wood: A History*, Cambridge: Polity.

Rudel, T.; Schneider, L.; Uriarte, M. (2010), Forest transitions: An introduction, *Land Use Policy*, 27(2), 95–97.

Sasaki, N.; Putz, F. (2009), Critical need for new definitions of "forest" and "forest degradation" in global climate change agreements, *Conservation Letters*, 2, 226–232.

Scheidel, A.; Work, C. (2018), Forest plantations and climate change discourses: New powers of "green" grabbing in Cambodia, *Land Use Policy*, 77, 9–18.

Schmink, M.; Wood, C. (1984), *Frontier Expansion in Amazonia*, Miami, FL: University Press of Florida.

Schroeder, H.; González, N. (2019), Bridging knowledge divides: The case of Indigenous ontologies of territoriality and REDD+, *Forest Policy and Economics*, 100, 198–206.

Scott, J. (1998), *Seeing Like a State: How Certain Schemes to Improve the Human Condition Have Failed*, London: Yale University Press.

Shiva, V.; Bandyopadhyay, J. (1985), *Ecological Audit of Eucalyptus Cultivation*, Dehra Dun: English Book Depot.

Swenson, J.; Carter, C.; Domec, J.; Delgado, C.I. (2011), Gold mining in the Peruvian Amazon: Global prices, deforestation, and mercury imports, *PloS ONE*, 6(4), e18875.

Taylor, M. (2015), *The Political Ecology of Climate Change Adaptation*, London: Routledge.

Temper, L.; Yánez, I.; Sharife, K.; Ojo, G.; Martinez-Alier, J. (2013), Towards a post-oil civilization: Yasunization and other initiatives to leave fossil fuels in the soil, Environmental Justice Organizations, Liabilities and Trade Report 6.

Toivanen, T.; Kröger, M. (2018), The role of debt, death and dispossession in world-ecological transformations: Swidden commons and tar capitalism in nineteenth-century Finland, *Journal of Peasant Studies*, 1–21.

Vandergeest, P.; Peluso, N.L. (2006), Empires of forestry: Professional forestry and state power in Southeast Asia, Part 2, *Environment and History*, 12(4), 359–393.

Vandergeest, P.; Peluso, N.L. (2015), *Political Forests*, in Bryant, R. (ed.), *International Handbook of Political Ecology*, Cheltenham, UK and Northampton, MA, USA: Edward Elgar Publishing, 162–175.

Weis, T. (2013), *The Ecological Hoofprint: The Global Burden of Industrial Livestock*, London: Zed Books.

Weisman, A. (2008), *The World Without Us*, New York: Macmillan.

Wohlleben, P. (2016), *The Hidden Life of Trees: What They Feel, How They Communicate – Discoveries from a Secret World*, Vancouver: Greystone Books.

44. Artisanal and small-scale mining

Boris Verbrugge and Robin Thiers

INTRODUCTION

The Global South has witnessed a veritable mining boom in recent decades. While the expansion of large-scale industrial mining has undoubtedly attracted the most attention, there has also been a massive expansion of more small-scale, low-tech and labour-intensive mining activities, which mostly take place outside the regulatory control of the state. This latter type of mining is now widely referred to as artisanal and small-scale mining (ASM). Available estimates – which should be taken with a grain of salt – suggest that more than 40 million people in over 80 countries are directly involved in ASM. They extract and process a variety of minerals, including gold, diamonds, cobalt and gemstones (IGF 2018). The unrelenting expansion of ASM has attracted growing attention in development studies. So far, this growing body of research on ASM has developed largely in isolation from critical agrarian studies.

Despite the differences between agriculture and mining, there are at least two good reasons to engage in a dialogue between ASM and critical agrarian studies. First, agricultural activities and ASM often take place in the same rural environments, so the dynamics that are described in both fields of study tend to be interconnected as well. Second, while agriculture and ASM are distinct activities with their own dynamics of extraction, production and processing, they are subject to similar processes of social differentiation, capital accumulation and exploitation, which play out against the background of the broader rural political economy. Yet these processes have been described and debated in much more detail in critical agrarian studies than in the literature on ASM.

This chapter provides an introduction to the ASM phenomenon from a critical agrarian studies perspective. It is divided into three parts. First, we zoom in on the empirical realities of ASM, upsetting homogenizing views that see it as a purely subsistence-oriented and informal activity. Second, we assess how existing research evaluates the linkages between ASM and agriculture. Third, we suggest two lines of inquiry derived from classic theoretical debates within critical agrarian studies that we believe would enhance our understanding of the complex dynamics of ASM.

EMPIRICAL REALITIES IN ARTISANAL AND SMALL-SCALE MINING

By mining, we refer to the wide range of activities related to the exploration, extraction and processing of a wide range of minerals. These activities can be undertaken by individuals, families or communities, but also by state-owned or private corporations. They can entail a diverse range of methods and technologies. Within social sciences and in policy circles, it has become commonplace to distinguish between artisanal and small-scale mining and large-scale industrial mining.

ASM is commonly defined as low-tech, labour-intensive mineral extraction and processing. Its expansion is widely seen as a consequence of (agricultural) poverty that 'pushes' people into mining (Hilson and Garforth 2012), though aspirations for social mobility undoubtedly play a role as well (Bryceson and Jønsson 2010). It is further claimed that 'barriers to entry remain low enough that anybody with a strong back and the need for income can enter the labour force' (Siegel and Veiga 2010, 277), either as an independent miner or under some sort of revenue-sharing arrangement. Another defining characteristic of ASM is its pervasive informality, which is embodied by a complete lack of formal mining rights and government regulation. This image of ASM as a poverty-driven and informal activity is contrasted with large-scale industrial mining, which is seen as the realm of big (private) mining companies which monopolize mining rights to the detriment of marginalized ASM operators (Hilson 2013).

Yet in a growing number of cases, this dominant image of ASM as a poverty-driven and informal activity does not – or no longer does – correspond with empirical realities on the ground. Instead, ASM has become a catch-all term for a wide variety of mining practices that involve a heterogeneous range of actors, including not just different types of workers (alongside those doing the actual digging or panning there are also people involved in carrying, grinding, processing ores and so on), but also mineral traders, financiers, local politicians, landowners and many others. In most cases, a select group of elite actors driven by a desire for accumulation benefits disproportionately from the presence of ASM (see for example Cortés-McPherson 2019). Depending on the type of mineral that is being targeted, the geophysical characteristics of particular ore deposits and the availability of capital and technology, ASM activities may range from rudimentary mining practices to sizeable open-pit and underground mining systems (Ferring et al. 2016). There is also growing evidence that ASM relies on more sophisticated processing methods (think only of the increased use of cyanidation) that are more commonly associated with large-scale mining. In short, the intensity of capital and labour, the available technical expertise, the social division of labour and the entry barriers for employment now vary widely within ASM (Peluso 2018). Finally, while the lion's share of ASM activities continues to take place without the necessary permits or licenses, in a growing number of countries, efforts to formalize ASM are having at least some effect, so that an increasing number of activities operates with some degree of government recognition – although this recognition rarely if ever extends to the workforce (Verbrugge and Besmanos 2016).

While these empirical realities are increasingly being acknowledged at an empirical level, research on ASM lacks the conceptual, analytical and theoretical tools to make sense of this growing complexity. It is here that an engagement with critical agrarian studies could prove very fruitful. First, however, we turn to a brief description of the linkages between ASM and agriculture.

LINKAGES BETWEEN AGRICULTURE AND ARTISANAL AND SMALL-SCALE MINING

The major (perceived) differences in the temporal, spatial and social dynamics of mining and agriculture primarily stem from their different material characteristics. Mining is understood as a predominantly extractive activity, in which humans get hold of mineral deposits which are the product of age-old geophysical processes. These mineral deposits are both fixed and scarce: they are located in particular places and are non-renewable; that is, the human-induced process of extracting and processing these deposits occurs at a speed beyond the earth's reproductive capacity. As a result, mining is characterized by a repeated and mobile dynamic of discovery, extraction and depletion. Agriculture, on the other hand, is considered to be a largely (re)productive activity in which humans engage, as they manipulate the soil, plants, animals, water and so on in a specific place to produce a variety of crops. While some places are arguably more suitable for agricultural activities than others, humans can engage in a variety of forms of agriculture in most places on earth. Moreover, the more rapid biophysical processes involved in agriculture (think of photosynthesis, and different agro-environmental metabolisms) could theoretically allow for agricultural (re)production to continue virtually endlessly.

Such differences matter. Yet they should not lead to an overly categorical distinction between the two types of activities. Indeed, the spread and intensification of modern agricultural methods over the past centuries has engendered dynamics of deforestation and soil depletion, arguably turning capitalist agriculture into an extractive industry in its own right. Moreover, both minerals and crops demand a range of productive activities to transform them (extract, produce, process, sort, label and so on) into a commodity that is ready to be sold on the market. Whether we dig up gold, plant wheat, sift for alluvial diamonds or harvest grapes, the material (biological, physical, chemical, geological and so on) characteristics, as well as the specific ways in which consumers and traders have come to appreciate them as commodities (packaged, processed, rough, clean, fresh, pure), matter for minerals as well as for crops (Selwyn 2007).

Zooming in on the 'small-scale' segments of agriculture and mining, another apparent difference revolves around the social organization of its core productive units. While small-scale agriculture is typically understood as a sedentary activity undertaken by household-based economic units, ASM is commonly understood as an individual activity undertaken by highly mobile and young men (De Boeck 2001). While these individuals may well develop working arrangements between themselves, none of these arrangements is expected to have the same durability as the social ties that bind the land- and family-based agricultural endeavour. We do not intend to dispute the significant differences between the social organization of productive forces in these sectors, but we warn against any type of categorical depiction of either or both. There is empirical evidence of the existence of vibrant rural labour markets, including among small-scale and family-based farms, that engage in patterns of hiring in and out labour (Cramer et al. 2008; Sender and Johnston 2004). Often, this rural workforce is highly mobile and segmented along gendered, racial, caste, age and ethnic lines. Small-scale agricultural production in many parts of the world may depend upon the mobilization of both 'footloose labour' (Breman 1996) as well as sedentary (possibly but not necessarily) family-based economic units. At the same time, while ASM – particularly 'rush-type' mining – indeed does involve mobile individualized labour, sedentary family-based economic units may also play a role. Entire communities may even emerge around more durable ASM sites, involving particular types of social organization, labour mobilization and land access (Bryceson and Yankson 2010; Verbrugge et al. 2015).

As noted above, the main causal explanations for the expansion of ASM treat it as the product of a pervasive crisis in agriculture. This agricultural crisis is in turn explained by a combination of demographic growth, climate change, structural adjustment and in some cases armed conflict (Hilson and Garforth 2012). In this context, a growing number of rural poor are finding their way into ASM. With this 'poverty-driven' argument, the literature on ASM dovetails with a broader debate on rural livelihood diversification. Gaining clout in the 1990s, livelihood scholars have drawn attention to a widespread transition away from a rural economy that revolves primarily around agriculture, towards more diverse rural livelihood systems marked by an increased importance of off-farm livelihoods (see for example Rigg 2006). The expansion of ASM lends further credence to this 'de-agrarianization thesis', as rural areas in countries like Ghana and Tanzania are witnessing the emergence of a group of professional 'gold rush miners' (Hilson 2010) or 'career miners' (Bryceson and Jønsson 2010) that are involved in ASM on a permanent basis, and that maintain no (more) direct ties to agriculture (Lahiri-Dutt 2018).

Others focus more explicitly on the direct and indirect linkages that connect ASM to agriculture. Intuitively, one would expect mining and agriculture to compete over the same resources. For instance, Schueler et al. (2011) draw attention to how gold mining in Ghana leads to widespread soil erosion and the loss of valuable farmland, while Fanthorpe and Maconachie (2010) suggest that the expansion of small-scale diamond mining in Sierra Leone absorbs vital labour power that would otherwise be available for agriculture. However, a growing body of empirical evidence suggests that the interaction between ASM and (smallholder) agriculture can also be mutually beneficial (Pijpers 2014). One argument focuses on seasonality: individuals or households can combine mining and farming, depending on the demands of the agricultural cycle. One example is Godoy's (1988) description of the Jukumani Indians in Bolivia, where young and 'agriculturally secure' men engage in mining activities when the demand for agricultural labour is low. Other empirical accounts demonstrate that income from mining may be reinvested in agriculture, with the potential of lifting it beyond subsistence level (Maconachie 2011). Others (Verbrugge et al. 2015) identify reciprocal arrangements between miners and landowners, whereby the latter provide the former with access to mineral-bearing land in exchange for royalties or other types of benefits. Finally, the presence of ASM may rejuvenate the rural economy through increased demand for agricultural produce (to feed the workforce).

CRITICAL AGRARIAN STUDIES-INSPIRED LINES OF INQUIRY INTO ARTISANAL AND SMALL-SCALE MINING

Research on ASM is slowly starting to grapple with how the activity is inserted into the rural political economy. For instance, different scholars have recently described how ASM becomes embedded in complex and dynamic local governance constellations that involve a wide variety of actors, including local politicians, junior and major mining companies, landowners, local (indigenous) communities and/or non-state armed actors (see Geenen and Verweijen 2017; Côte and Korf 2018). At the same time, while several studies have taken a Marxist approach to understanding dynamics between capital and labour in large-scale mining (a key example is the work of Burawoy 1976 in southern Africa), research on ASM still leaves many of the basic questions driving Marxist agrarian political economy unanswered, including Bernstein's (2010) four key questions: 'Who owns what? Who does what? Who gets what? And what do they do with it?'. A more systematic focus on the dynamics of capital and labour could push the inquiry into ASM forward in two important ways. First, it can provide new and more systematic insights into intricate processes of social differentiation in ASM, and consequently into who stands (not) to benefit from its presence. Second, it can shed new light on the myriad interactions between ASM and large-scale mining, which include, but are by no means limited to, instances of conflict.

Capital, Labour and Social Differentiation

Analysing the dynamics of rural social differentiation has long been the core business of Marxist political economy. Particular attention has been paid to what happens to small-scale, agrarian or 'peasant' farming under the pressures of capitalization. Most likely, the spread of capitalism engenders dynamics of social differentiation in which small-scale farmers are forced to sell their means of production to capitalists. Yet this process does not inevitably lead to the complete disappearance of small-scale agricultural production. Instead, in many cases, small or 'petty' capital is found to maintain a competitive edge over ordinary capital, because it has access to cheap informal labour through socially regulated labour relations.

It is worthwhile asking whether a similar logic of socially regulated and cheap labour partly explains not only the persistence, but possibly even the further expansion, of ASM. One of the defining features of ASM activities across the globe is precisely its reliance on cheap and flexible informal labour (Verbrugge 2015). Moreover, labour relations in ASM are regulated by social institutions such as kinship, patronage, gender, age and ethnicity (Fisher 2007). In many cases, these social institutions serve to disguise blatant instances of exploitation, and the opposing class interests of those doing the actual work of extraction and processing on the one hand and of the smaller group of elite actors that owns the means of production (including mineral-rich land, tunnels, mining and processing technology and capital) on the other. A more systematic and critical focus on the diverse and dynamic relationship between capital and labour, as it evolves over time and in specific mining sites and operations, could greatly further our understanding of how these class distinctions emerged and how they are maintained.

From Conflicts and Land Grabs to Configurations of Mining Capitalism

In nearly all countries with a significant presence of ASM, it has expanded alongside large-scale mining. While the expansion of ASM has mostly taken place outside the regulatory ambit of the state, large-scale industrial mining is in many countries actively promoted by governments that seek to attract foreign direct investment. For a long time, researchers have focused on documenting and analysing instances of conflict between ASM and large-scale industrial mining. In many cases, these empirical accounts draw attention to acts of 'land grabbing' or 'dispossession' by mining companies, which generate resentment and resistance on the part of ASM operators (Bush 2009; Geenen 2014). Yet in recent years, case studies have documented more complex and multi-layered sets of relations and linkages that connect ASM to large-scale mining (see Geenen and Verweijen 2017; Luning and Pijpers 2017). For instance, Bansah et al. (2018) note how in Ghana, there exists an elaborate tailings (mine waste) trade between ASM and large-scale mining companies. In one mining area in the Philippines, ASM operators and a Manila-based mining company have entered into a 'contract mining' scheme. Under this arrangement, teams of informal workers using rudimentary mining methods are hired by contractors, who are responsible for extracting gold-bearing material for the company, which in turn processes and sells the gold before redistributing the revenues through a complex revenue-sharing scheme (Verbrugge 2017). In both cases, mining companies benefit dispro-portionately from these arrangements, to the detriment of informal ASM operators. This is an important observation, because similar arrangements are emerging across the globe and are promoted by influential actors like the World Bank, for whom 'mining together' is a key solution for conflicts between ASM and large-scale mining (World Bank 2009).

Critical agrarian studies is similarly preoccupied with instances of land grabbing and accumulation by dispossession, in this case by corporate agribusinesses, to the detriment of small-scale farmers. Yet rather than simply focusing on how small-scale producers are being dispossessed in spectacular, rapid or violent ways, Marxist political economy also attempts to understand how small-scale producers become (often adversely) incorporated into the global circuits of corporate capital. In practice, this incorporation occurs through a range of forward and backward linkages, for example through the procurement of agricultural inputs, the selling of crops on the market or by obtaining loans and money advances. Scholars in the field of critical agrarian studies have long argued that this incorporation into the capitalist economy is one of the primary drivers of rural social differentiation, which often has negative consequences for the farmers involved (see for example McMichael 2013).

In line with the World Bank's efforts to promote negotiated solutions to conflicts between ASM and large-scale mining, contract farming is often portrayed as a potential win-win solution by neo-institutional economists and policymakers. Under a contract farming arrangement, a farmer and a corporate buyer sign a formal agreement that covers the production of a certain product for a given period of time, and the price at which it is to be sold on the market. In many cases, it also entails agreements about the provision of agricultural inputs, technical advice and so on. However, critical agrarian scholars have stressed that contract farming arrangements are often unbalanced, and in many cases lead to a disproportionate appropriation of profit by large agribusinesses (Oya 2021). More broadly, it has been suggested that the growing popularity of contract farming arrangements forms part of a wider tendency towards post-Fordist strategies of flexible accumulation (Starosta 2010). It would be extremely interesting to analyse both the expansion of ASM and the growing number of linkages that connect it to large-scale mining, through the prism of shifting strategies of accumulation in the global capitalist economy (Verbrugge and Geenen 2019).

CONCLUSION

The swift expansion of ASM is rapidly transforming the global countryside, where it provides an urgently needed source of cash income for millions of poor rural individuals and households and ample opportunities for accumulation for local elites. It is therefore attracting increased attention from development scholars and policymakers. With notable exceptions, the latter seem to be gradually moving away from a 'prohibitionist' stance regarding ASM, towards one that attempts to unlock its development potential (notably through formalization efforts). Scholars, meanwhile, have demonstrated that the expansion of ASM is at least partly the product of a pervasive crisis in smallholder agriculture, and have identified a range of positive and negative linkages between mining and agriculture. In short, they are gradually coming to terms with how the expansion of ASM intertwines with broader dynamics of agrarian change.

At the same time, earlier research on ASM has failed to engage with some of the key questions and debates that inform critical agrarian studies. A more systematic engagement with these questions and debates could significantly improve our understanding of ASM – and by extension, of dynamics in the global countryside – both at an analytical and a theoretical level.

First, a critical focus on capital–labour dynamics in ASM, and how these intersect with similar dynamics in agriculture, can provide new insights into the dynamics of social differentiation in the countryside. Second, an inquiry inspired by critical agrarian studies can help us to not only understand how ASM functions as a repository of cheap and flexible labour, but can also help us to make sense of the myriad ways in which it is functionally integrated into the global capitalist economy.

FURTHER READING

Bryceson, D.F.; Fisher, E.; Jønsson, J.B.; Mwaipopo, R. (eds) (2013), *Mining and Social Transformation in Africa: Mineralizing and Democratizing Trends in Artisanal Production*, London: Routledge.
Hilson, G. (2011), Artisanal mining, smallholder farming and livelihood diversification in rural sub-Saharan Africa: An introduction, *Journal of International Development*, 23(8), 1031–1041.
Lahiri-Dutt, K. (2018), Extractive peasants: Reframing informal artisanal and small-scale mining debates, *Third World Quarterly*, 39(8), 1561–1582.
Verbrugge, B. (2016), Voices from below: Artisanal and small-scale mining as a product and catalyst of rural transformation, *Journal of Rural Studies*, 47, 108–116.
Verbrugge, B.; Geenen, S. (eds) (2020), *Global Gold Production Touching Ground: Expansion, Informalization, and Technological Innovation*, London: Palgrave Macmillan.

REFERENCES

Bansah, K.J.; Dumakor-Dupey, N.K.; Stemn, E.; Galecki, G. (2018), Mutualism, commensalism or parasitism? Perspectives on tailings trade between large-scale and artisanal and small-scale gold mining in Ghana, *Resources Policy*, 57, 246–254.
Bernstein, H. (2010), *Class Dynamics of Agrarian Change*, Halifax: Fernwood Publishing.
Breman, J. (1996), *Footloose Labour: Working in India's Informal Economy*, Cambridge: Cambridge University Press.
Bryceson, D.F.; Jønsson, J.B. (2010), Gold digging careers in rural East Africa: Small-scale miners' livelihood choices, *World Development*, 38(3), 379–392.
Bryceson, D.F.; Yankson, P.W. (2010), Frontier mining settlements, in Agergaard, J.; Fold, N.; Gough, K. (eds), *Rural–Urban Dynamics: Livelihoods, Mobility and Markets in African and Asian Frontiers*, London: Routledge, 158–174.
Burawoy, M. (1976), The functions and reproduction of migrant labor: Comparative material from Southern Africa and the United States, *American Journal of Sociology*, 81(5), 1050–1087.
Bush, R. (2009), 'Soon there will be no-one left to take the corpses to the morgue': Accumulation and abjection in Ghana's mining communities, *Resources Policy*, 34(1–2), 57–63.
Cortés-McPherson, D. (2019), Expansion of small-scale gold mining in Madre de Dios: 'Capital interests' and the emergence of a new elite of entrepreneurs in the Peruvian Amazon, *The Extractive Industries and Society*, 6(2), 382–389.
Côte, M.; Korf, B. (2018), Making concessions: Extractive enclaves, entangled capitalism and regulative pluralism at the gold mining frontier in Burkina Faso, *World Development*, 101, 466–476.
Cramer, C.; Oya, C.; Sender, J. (2008), Lifting the blinkers: A new view of power, diversity and poverty in Mozambican rural labour markets, *Journal of Modern African Studies*, 46(3), 361–392.
De Boeck, F. (2001), Garimpeiro worlds: Digging, dying and 'hunting' for diamonds in Angola, *Review of African Political Economy*, 28(90), 549–562.
Fanthorpe, R.; Maconachie, R. (2010), Beyond the 'crisis of youth'? Mining, farming, and civil society in post-war Sierra Leone, *African Affairs*, 109(435), 251–272.
Ferring, D.; Hausermann, H.; Effah, E. (2016), Site specific: Heterogeneity of small-scale gold mining in Ghana, *The Extractive Industries and Society*, 3(1), 171–184.

Fisher, E. (2007), Occupying the margins: Labour integration and social exclusion in artisanal mining in Tanzania, *Development and Change*, 38(4), 735–760.

Geenen, S. (2014), Dispossession, displacement and resistance: Artisanal miners in a gold concession in South-Kivu, Democratic Republic of Congo, *Resources Policy*, 40, 90–99.

Geenen, S.; Verweijen, J. (2017), Explaining fragmented and fluid mobilization in gold mining concessions in eastern Democratic Republic of the Congo, *The Extractive Industries and Society*, 4(4), 758–765.

Godoy, R.A. (1988), Small-scale mining and agriculture among the Jukumani Indians, northern Potosi, Bolivia, *Journal of Development Studies*, 24(2), 177–196.

Hilson, G. (2010), 'Once a miner, always a miner': Poverty and livelihood diversification in Akwatia, Ghana, *Journal of Rural Studies*, 26(3), 296–307.

Hilson, G. (2013), 'Creating' rural informality: The case of artisanal gold mining in Sub-Saharan Africa, *SAIS Review of International Affairs*, 33(1), 51–64.

Hilson, G.; Garforth, C. (2012), 'Agricultural poverty' and the expansion of artisanal mining in Sub-Saharan Africa: Experiences from southwest Mali and southeast Ghana, *Population Research and Policy Review*, 31(3), 435–464.

IGF (2018), Global trends in artisanal and small-scale mining (ASM): A review of key numbers and issues, accessed 5 October 2018 at www.iisd.org/sites/default/files/publications/igf-asm-global-trends .pdf.

Lahiri-Dutt, K. (2018), Extractive peasants: Reframing informal artisanal and small-scale mining debates, *Third World Quarterly*, 39(8), 1561–1582.

Luning, S.; Pijpers, R.J. (2017), Governing access to gold in Ghana: In-depth geopolitics on mining concessions, *Africa*, 87(4), 758–779.

Maconachie, R. (2011), Re-agrarianising livelihoods in post-conflict Sierra Leone? Mineral wealth and rural change in artisanal and small-scale mining communities, *Journal of International Development*, 1067, 1054–1067.

McMichael, P. (2013), Value-chain agriculture and debt relations: Contradictory outcomes, *Third World Quarterly*, 34(4), 671–690.

Oya, C. (2021), Contract farming, in Akram-Lodhi, A.H.; Dietz, K.; Engels, B.; McKay, B.M. (eds), *Handbook of Critical Agrarian Studies*, Cheltenham, UK and Northampton, MA, USA: Edward Elgar Publishing.

Peluso, N.L. (2018), Entangled territories in small-scale gold mining frontiers: Labor practices, property, and secrets in Indonesian gold country, *World Development*, 101, 400–416.

Pijpers, R. (2014), Crops and carats: Exploring the interconnectedness of mining and agriculture in Sub-Saharan Africa, *Futures*, 62, 32–39.

Rigg, J. (2006), Land, farming, livelihoods, and poverty: Rethinking the links in the rural South, *World Development*, 34(1), 180–202.

Schueler, V.; Kuemmerle, T.; Schröder, H. (2011), Impacts of surface gold mining on land use systems in Western Ghana, *Ambio*, 40(5), 528–539.

Selwyn, B. (2007), Labour process and workers? Bargaining power in export grape production, north east Brazil, *Journal of Agrarian Change*, 7(4), 526–553.

Sender, J.; Johnston, D. (2004), Searching for a weapon of mass production in rural Africa: Unconvincing arguments for land reform, *Journal of Agrarian Change*, 4(1–2), 142–164.

Siegel, S.; Veiga, M.M. (2010), The myth of alternative livelihoods: Artisanal mining, gold and poverty, *International Journal on Environment and Pollution*, 41(3/4), 272–288.

Starosta, G. (2010), Global commodity chains and the Marxian law of value, *Antipode*, 42(2), 433–465.

Verbrugge, B. (2015), The economic logic of persistent informality: Artisanal and small-scale mining in the southern Philippines, *Development and Change*, 46(5), 1023–1046.

Verbrugge, B. (2017), Towards a negotiated solution to conflicts between large-scale and small-scale miners? The Acupan contract mining project in the Philippines, *The Extractive Industries and Society*, 4(2), 352–360.

Verbrugge, B.; Besmanos, B. (2016), Formalizing artisanal and small-scale mining: Whither the workforce?, *Resources Policy*, 47, 134–141.

Verbrugge, B.; Geenen, S. (2019), The gold commodity frontier: A fresh perspective on change and diversity in the global gold mining economy, *The Extractive Industries and Society*, 6(2), 413–423.

Verbrugge, B.; Cuvelier, J.; Van Bockstael, S. (2015), Min(d)ing the land: The relationship between artisanal and small-scale mining and surface land arrangements in the southern Philippines, eastern DRC and Liberia, *Journal of Rural Studies*, 37, 50–60.

World Bank (2009), *Mining Together: Large-Scale Mining Meets Artisanal Mining – a Guide for Action*, Washington, DC: World Bank.

45. Footloose labour

John Harriss

WHAT IS 'FOOTLOOSE LABOUR'?

Following the declaration by the Government of India, on 24 March 2020, with just four hours notice, of what was to be the most stringent lock-down in the world in the Covid-19 pandemic, there came about a massive movement of people. It seemed that the government did not recognize the vast numbers of temporary migrant workers in Indian cities, very many of whom, confronting the loss of their precarious urban livelihoods, set out to return to their native villages. Pictures of men and women and their children trudging along the highways, or along railway lines, carrying their small bundles of possessions, flashed across the world. Perhaps as many as 30 million people were on the move – a number dwarfing even that of those who moved as a result of the partition of India in 1947 (Harriss 2020a).

This great movement of people was of those described by the sociologist Jan Breman as 'footloose labour'. The term appears in the title of a book of his, *Footloose Labour: Working in India's Informal Economy* (1996), based on many years of ethnographic research in south Gujarat, in western India – though he actually uses it rather little in the text.[1] The book is about the lives of those who, pushed out of the agrarian labour market, depend for their livelihoods on a variety of temporary jobs, both in the countryside and in the cities. '(This) footloose proletariat,' Breman (1996, 23) writes, 'is detached from its place of origin, but does not strike roots in the workplaces to which it temporarily finds its way.' More recently he has written of it as, 'A new class of nowhere people … forced to drift between what passes for "home" and a place of "work" [and who] in their marginality … seem to pose no threat to the vested interests of capital and its agents' (Breman 2019, xi–xii). The final point in this quotation was tragically confirmed during the Covid-19 pandemic, when the 'nowhere people' seemed of such little real concern, either to employers or to the state.

WHAT CAUSES IT?

The circumstances of the formation of footloose labour are those of what has been described in India as 'stunted structural transformation' (Binswanger-Mkhize 2013). Influenced by the theories about the process of economic development that were current in the mid-twentieth century – and in particular the two-sector models of Arthur Lewis and Simon Kuznets, which were, in turn, based on the experience of the first industrialized countries – the expectation in India was that development would bring about a shift from an agrarian to an industrial society. Labour would gradually shift out of agriculture into industry, and come 'to enjoy the comfort of regularity, security and protection of a standard labour contract'. But by the later twentieth century, 'it was clear that the long-awaited transformation from a rural-agrarian to an urban-industrial economy and society would not take place' (Breman 2019, xi). The Indian economy, and others such as those of China (even though it has industrialized so much more extensively) or Indonesia, have not gone through the same structural transformation that was experienced in the first generation of industrializing economies, when 'the process of industrialization enabled the dismissed agrarian workforce to leave the countryside and settle down with their families in the rapidly growing urban economy for regular and better jobs in industry' (ibid., 158, referring to observations of Max Weber's on nineteenth-century Germany). Though India did industrialize after independence, and the share of agriculture in gross domestic product dropped to around 15 per cent by 2011, having accounted for almost 50 per cent in 1961, the share of employment in agriculture still remained at about 55 per cent. These figures conceal the fact that, as careful research in the rural economy has shown, a majority of households depend upon several different activities, as well as cultivation or agricultural labour – they depend on pluriactivity, in other words, usually in different sectors and locations – often contributing to the numbers of footloose labour. At the same time India, though it has several of the biggest cities in the world, has not urbanized in the way that was anticipated. The population remains about two-thirds rural, at least in terms of primary residence, and the structural transformation of the economy has remained 'stunted'.

HOW IS IT EXPERIENCED?

For most village households, in large parts of India, agriculture is no longer the mainstay of their work and income (Himanshu et al. 2016). The substantial landowners have invested in education, and have increasingly sought 'service' occupations. For most of them farming is no longer their main occupation. They have turned away from the village – though they have consolidated their control at local levels and reinforced their hold over wider regions. Their erstwhile farm servants, with whom they formerly often shared what were, in a sense, intimate social relations of patronage, but with whom they now practise mutual distancing, have also turned away from the village. For many of them, as in Breman's (2019, 165) research area in south Gujarat, 'the lack of sufficient and somewhat regular alternative employment means that they depend upon labour contractors to take them away to remote destinations for many months of the year' – to construction sites, or brick kilns, for example, or to sugar cane fields. And whereas it used to make good sense for landowners to employ local labour, including farm servants tied to them in relations of patronage, latterly in some parts of the country – like south Gujarat – they have been able to rely on employing workers from outside the locality, benefiting from their greater pliability and the possibility of paying lower wages. Contrary to what is usually assumed, Breman has shown, the use of migrant labour has not come about because of labour shortages locally, but rather for reasons of labour control and reducing labour costs. Work by a team of anthropologists, in villages spread across the country (Shah et al. 2018), has shown how widespread this is, and how it involves, disproportionately, people from the Scheduled Castes and Scheduled Tribes of India. These are people who are subject to conjugated oppression (the intertwined multiple oppressions based on caste, tribe, class, gender and region). Alpa Shah and Jens Lerche (2020a; see also 2020b) have also drawn attention to what they describe as 'the invisible economies of care' that are crucial to the exploitation of migrant labour. Seasonal migrants, they point out, 'can only be workers because of all the work undertaken across generations at home, including care provided by the spouse, children, siblings and elderly parents', though they may be widely separated spatially.

It is now a matter of public record in India, following the belated publication (in 2015) of the findings of the Socio-Economic Caste Census of 2011, that half of all rural households are landless, have to survive on casual wage labour that is often not available locally and live in circumstances of severe deprivation. There is, therefore, a massive amount of labour migration, from one rural area to another (agriculture in Punjab, for example, has long depended on migrant workers coming from Bihar and Uttar Pradesh), and from villages to cities. But whereas industrialization and urbanization in the West saw workers moving on a permanent basis to the cities, a high proportion of workers in Indian cities are temporary, *circular* migrants, moving between village homes and the urban centres. Exactly what the total numbers of footloose labour are in India is uncertain, but when the Government of India at last made some niggardly provision for supporting the livelihoods of temporary migrants during the pandemic, it was for 80 million people, so at least one-fifth of the labour force as a whole.

FOOTLOOSE LABOUR, CAPITALISM AND FREEDOM

To be 'footloose', then, is to move between sites of production and between these and sites of reproduction (the significance of the latter movement is emphasized by Shah and Lerche (2020a, 2020b)); and as the title of Breman's book suggests, the state of being 'footloose' goes hand in hand with informal and casual work. It 'facilitates the informalization of economic activity; at the same time the informal economy puts a premium on labour mobility' (Breman 2019, 179). It is the outcome, he clearly shows, of the commodification of agriculture, which changes labour relations, and of the way in which the development of the industrial, urban economy has taken place. In India this has been in such a way, it has been suggested by Sanyal (2007), as to have 'excluded' labour, certainly from the most dynamic and productive sectors of the capitalist economy. The argument recalls earlier writings by Latin American economists (e.g. Quijano 1974). Analytically, therefore, the idea of 'footloose labour' locates labour migration in the context of the dynamics of capitalist development.

It is also an evocative descriptive term, suggesting the contradictory character of the circumstances of very large numbers of workers under capitalism, not only in India, but across the world. Describing someone as being 'footloose' implies that they enjoy freedom (as in 'footloose and fancy-free' – the state of not having commitments and responsibilities) but there is also a hint that this is not necessarily chosen. A person is 'footloose' perhaps because of having nothing better to do. Those employed, for instance, in the 'gig economy' might perhaps be described as 'footloose'. They do enjoy a kind of freedom, but many would certainly prefer the commitments and responsibilities entailed in holding more secure employment (see Parry 2019, on the class divisions within the working class in India, and elsewhere – he refers particularly to studies from Indonesia and from Egypt – that hinge around the security, or not, of employment). The idea of footloose labour thus brings to the fore the inherently contradictory relationship of capitalism and freedom.

In practice footloose labour is subject to varying degrees of 'unfreedom'. Rather than the dichotomy of free/unfree labour, however, Breman (2019, 239) observes 'a continuum ranging from greater to lesser ability to choose when, where and for whom to work'. Workers are often subject to the conditions that he describes as those of 'neo-bondage' – the prefix reflecting the fact that these are no longer master–servant relationships moderated by patronage. In the past in the rural economy, Breman (ibid., 3) shows, landowners' interest in the subordination of client labour was not only economic 'but driven by ambition to gain political power and social status'. They were interested therefore in maintaining retinues of clients, who in return gained at least a degree of livelihood security, perhaps a place to live and various perquisites. But as the commercialization and monetization of the rural economy have taken place, labour relations have become thoroughly commodified and characterized by 'naked exploitation'. Now, '[e]mployers use the payment of advance wages ("earnest money") as a mechanism of attachment' (ibid., 184) – subsequently often delaying or undercutting wage payments. This is 'neo-bondage'. The relationship is stripped of any sense of a morality of mutual dependence and intimacy. Breman's overarching argument is that 'capitalism and bondage are not mutually incompatible but coexist' (ibid., 264): capital accumulation benefits from unfree labour (as Jairus Banaji (2003) has also argued, and Philip Corrigan (1977), years ago, in an essay entitled 'Feudal relics or capitalist monuments?').

We should note, however, that people may want to move for reasons other than those that are entirely economic – perhaps, indeed, to escape from the constraints of patronage, or patriarchal family relations. The anthropologist Alpa Shah (2006) has shown, for instance, how migrants from rural Jharkhand went to work in brick kilns in West Bengal in order to find a temporary space of freedom to escape problems at home or pursue love affairs. This is not to say that they were not also ruthlessly exploited.

THE POLITICAL IMPLICATIONS OF FOOTLOOSE LABOUR

In India, therefore, there is a vast segment of the working population that is impoverished and has become footloose, and that is – of necessity – dependent upon the 'deeply problematic type of urban living' (Breman 2019, 213) characteristic of Indian cities. Part of the reason why urban living is so problematic for so many people living in the vast slums of India's cities is that they are effectively disenfranchised and are thus of little account politically (see e.g. Routray 2014). Woven through Breman's studies of footloose labour is an argument about the ways in which politicians and policy makers have neglected and disregarded working people, deliberately, as well as because of the development policies that they have pursued. He contends that the footloose workers do have a proletarian identity, but they have little sense of class solidarity. The upshot is that, remarkably, 'the interests of the largest working class in India – the huge mass of agricultural-to-rural labour – have remained by and large unrepresented in the political and economic arena' (Breman 2019, 172). It is a great irony that, as Irene Pang (2020) has shown in research on 'footloose' construction workers in Beijing and Delhi, democracy notwithstanding, the Indian workers should be less able to exercise rights of citizenship than their peers in authoritarian China.

NOT IN INDIA ALONE

I have focused on India because the idea of footloose labour, and analysis of its implications in relation to the development of capitalism and for politics, are due so much to Jan Breman and his many years of field research in western India. But the idea is undoubtedly of relevance much more widely. The extent of the flow of surplus labour out of agriculture in China, into the cities, has long been recognized, and was reckoned to account for 145 million people in

2009, the great majority of them being circular migrants, without permanent homes in the cities (Hu et al. 2011). Vietnam, like China, has a household registration system – *ho kau* – that puts the social safety net out of reach of most migrants to the cities from rural areas. For this reason alone, many are circular migrants (Liu and Meng 2019). Scholars working on Indonesia recognized the importance of circular migration at about the same time that Breman began to write about it in western India – and there too the numbers involved are large (Hugo 1982). There is also evidence of footloose labour in many parts of Africa. A study that reflects Breman's themes and his concern with the dynamics of capitalism is that by Maxim Bolt (2015) on Zimbabwean workers across the border in South Africa.

The idea of footloose labour is thus a powerful one for the analysis of contemporary capitalist development and agrarian political economy.

NOTE

1. This chapter draws mainly on Jan Breman's (2019) most recent exposition of his argument, and I have made use of my own account of this book (Harriss 2020b). I also acknowledge the extremely helpful comments of Jonathan Pattenden on a draft of this chapter, many of which I have incorporated almost verbatim.

FURTHER READING

Binswanger-Mkhize, H. (2013), The stunted structural transformation of the Indian economy: Agriculture, manufacturing and the rural non-farm sector, *Economic and Political Weekly*, 48(26–27), 5–13.

Breman, J. (1996), *Footloose Labour: Working in India's Informal Economy*, Cambridge: Cambridge University Press.

Breman, J. (2019), *Capitalism, Inequality and Labour in India*, Cambridge: Cambridge University Press.

Shah, A.; Lerche, J. (2020), Migration and the invisible economies of care: Production, social reproduction, and seasonal migrant labour in India, *Transactions of the Institute of British Geographers*, 45(4), 719–734.

Shah, A.; Lerche, J.; Axelby, R.; Benbabali, D.; Donegan, B.; Raj, J.; Thakur, V. (2018), *Ground Down by Growth: Tribe, Caste, Class and Inequality in Twenty-First Century India*, London: Pluto Press.

REFERENCES

Banaji, J. (2003), The fictions of free labour: Contract, coercion and so-called unfree labour, *Historical Materialism*, 11(3), 69–95.

Binswanger-Mkhize, H. (2013), The stunted structural transformation of the Indian economy: Agriculture, manufacturing and the rural non-farm sector, *Economic and Political Weekly*, 48(26–27), 5–13.

Bolt, M. (2015), *Zimbabwean Migrants and South Africa's Border Farms*, Cambridge: Cambridge University Press.

Breman, J. (1996), *Footloose Labour: Working in India's Informal Economy*, Cambridge: Cambridge University Press.

Breman, J. (2019), *Capitalism, Inequality and Labour in India*, Cambridge: Cambridge University Press.

Corrigan, P. (1977), Feudal relics or capitalist monuments? Notes on the sociology of unfree labour, *Sociology*, 11(3), 435–463.

Harriss, J. (2020a), 'Responding to an epidemic requires a compassionate state': How has the Indian state been doing in the time of Covid-19?, *Journal of Asian Studies*, 79(3), 609–620.

Harriss, J. (2020b), Review article: The implications of 'stunted structural transformation' for rural India, *Canadian Journal of Development Studies*, https://doi.org/10.1080/02255189.2020.1805302.

Himanshu, H.; Jha, P.; Rodgers, G. (eds) (2016), *The Changing Village in India: Insights from Longitudinal Research*, Delhi: Oxford University Press.

Hu, F.; Xu, Z.; Chen, Y. (2011), Circular migration or permanent stay? Evidence from China's rural–urban migration, *China Economic Review*, 22(1), 64–74.

Hugo, G. (1982), Circular migration in Indonesia, *Population and Development Review*, 8(1), 59–82.

Liu, S.; Meng, X. (eds) (2019), *Rural-Urban Migration in Vietnam*, Berlin: Springer.

Pang, I. (2020), Rethinking civil society and democracy: Lessons from construction workers in Beijing and Delhi, Unpublished manuscript, School for International Studies, Simon Fraser University.

Parry, J. (2019), *Classes of Labour: Work and Life in a Central Indian Steel Town*, Delhi: Social Science Press.

Quijano, A. (1974), The marginal pole of the economy and the marginalized labour force, *Economy and Society*, 3(4), 393–428.

Routray, S. (2014), The post-colonial city and its displaced poor: Rethinking 'political society' in Delhi, *International Journal of Urban and Regional Research*, 38(6), 2292–2308.

Sanyal, K. (2007), *Rethinking Capitalist Development: Primitive Accumulation, Governmentality and Post-Colonial Capitalism*, Abingdon: Routledge.

Shah, A. (2006), The labour of love: Seasonal migration from Jharkhand to the brick kilns of other states of India, *Contributions to Indian Sociology*, 40(1), 91–118.

Shah, A.; Lerche, J. (2020a), The five truths about the migrant workers crisis, *Hindustan Times*, 13 July, accessed 7 August 2020 at www.hindustantimes.com/analysis/the-five-truths-about-the-migrant-workers-crisis-opinion/story-awTQUm2gnJx72UWbdPa5OM.html.

Shah, A.; Lerche, J. (2020b), Migration and the invisible economies of care: Production, social reproduction, and seasonal migrant labour in India, *Transactions of the Institute of British Geographers*, 45(4), 719–734.

Shah, A.; Lerche, J.; Axelby, R.; Benbabali, D.; Donegan, B.; Raj, J.; Thakur, V. (2018), *Ground Down by Growth: Tribe, Caste, Class and Inequality in Twenty-First Century India*, London: Pluto Press.

46. Contract farming

Helena Pérez Niño and Carlos Oya

INTRODUCTION

Contract farming, also known as agricultural production through 'outgrower schemes', is generally understood as an institutional arrangement in agriculture whereby buyers and processors contract farmers to provide agricultural goods under certain specifications, as opposed to procuring these in open spot markets. More broadly, the vast literature on contract farming engages with key questions in agrarian studies, namely: the conditions under which rural producers and workers reproduce themselves in land-based activities; the prospects of smallholder farming within contemporary global agro-food systems; the institutional changes necessary to make 'markets work'; the penetration of global value chains in contemporary agriculture; the implications for farming of trends toward vertical integration and the expansion of buyer-driven chains; and, more recently, the connections between large-scale land deals and contract farming 'solutions' (Li 2011; Vicol 2017). Contract farming is a contested field and different questions and analytical frameworks have been deployed to make sense of it, as this chapter will show. However, mainstream agricultural economics seems to dominate the literature both in terms of the volume of publications and of the empirical evidence collected.

Agricultural economics treats contract farming as an institutional arrangement designed to address market failures by smoothing out the uncertainties and shocks characteristic of agricultural production, which are often amplified by market dynamics (Eaton and Shepherd 2001; Masakure and Henson 2005; Minot 2007). In low-income countries, contract farming is presented as an arrangement that allows for commodity production to take place in settings characterized by 'missing markets', that is, contexts with underdeveloped financial services, poor access to remunerative markets, deficient input distribution systems or poorly specified property rights.

In orthodox accounts, power relations and historical change, the two central concerns of critical agrarian studies, are conspicuously missing. However, as the critical agrarian literature has shown, at stake is an arrangement that attracts producers by guaranteeing a market outlet and access to inputs on credit in exchange for giving buyers/processors the ability to exert more control over production than they could in open markets, without the need to engage in risky land acquisition and direct production. Contract farming is thus an arrangement characterized by (1) a reduction of marketing-related uncertainty for buyers and producers; (2) increased vertical integration (more intervention of the buyers in productive decision-making); and (3) a shifting of production costs and risks onto direct producers, compared with estate (plantation) production. Contract farming is a different form of incorporation into capitalist relations of production whereby labour and land are exploited through an indirect contractual arrangement that seemingly preserves the property rights of smallholders and thus avoids direct dispossession.

The degree of buyers' control and their ability to push risk and costs onto producers is an empirical question that depends on the power relations and bargaining between (different classes of) producers and buyers in specific periods and specific regions. The market outlet guarantee that attracts producers to contract farming comes at the expense of a loss of control and greater exposure to production risks, as another form of 'adverse incorporation' (McCarthy 2010; Hickey and du Toit, 2013; Martiniello 2016; Vicol 2017). But it is the combination of greater control and the shedding of risks that lies at the basis of the profitability of this business model for buyers and processors. In fact, contract farming provides an outlet for a tension that is characteristic of the process of the capitalist penetration of the countryside: as demand increases, so does the pressure on the factors of production such as land and labour that in many instances have not been fully commodified, i.e. cannot be always procured in the market. In contrast with the estate and plantation model, non-equity production arrangements such as contract farming allow capital (agribusiness, buyers, processors) to set in motion the production process without requiring their ownership of the means of production or their direct hiring of labour by contracting with direct producers (UNCTAD 2009; Vrousalis 2018). Hence, different currents of critical agrarian studies concur that both in regions fully integrated into global commodity markets as well as in agrarian frontiers, the specific character of contract farming arrangements is indicative of the balance of forces between direct producers on one hand and agribusiness, processors and traders on the other; of the ways in which direct producers resist buyers' attempts to appropriate surplus value and of the ways in which capital attempts to erode such resistance.

This chapter aims to provide a selective overview of basic questions about contract farming: What is it? Why did it emerge? Does it matter for critical agrarian studies? What are the main debates and questions? How have different approaches debated contract farming? What is the empirical evidence on key issues such as the scale of this arrangement in contemporary agriculture, its effects on producers and the power dynamics in contract farming relations? The chapter is therefore organized as follows. After having defined the core attributes of contract farming in this introduction, the next section addresses the question of the rise of it in contemporary agriculture, with a focus on developing countries, and the drivers of this trend. Second, we explore the variety of contract farming arrangements and what this means for relations between buyers/processors and agricultural producers and broader market dynamics. Third, we critically examine the main contributions and questions in mainstream agricultural economics approaches and in critical agrarian studies, including agrarian political economy, emphasizing the different research questions asked and the unevenness of empirical evidence provided in these camps.

CONTEMPORARY DYNAMICS IN CONTRACT FARMING

The expansion in the literature on contract farming does not only indicate a rising interest in this form of organization of production and marketing but also reflects dynamics of change in agricultural production on a global scale. Particularly significant is the fact that the rise of contract farming is a reflection of the growing importance of global value chains in trade, a phenomenon that affects most sectors. As a form of production and marketing, contract farming has been expanding globally in connection to three significant dynamics. First is the continuous growth in global agricultural trade and the share of global value chains in the trade of agricultural commodities (Maertens and Swinnen 2014; World Bank 2020). This has been particularly facilitated by dramatic improvements in the logistics for agricultural trade, and especially the container revolution. Second, the processes of market liberalization and deregulation and the demise of parastatal marketing boards in developing countries since the 1980s left a vacuum in access to export output as well as domestic input markets that could be (partly) filled by new institutional arrangements such as contract farming (Oya 2012). There is thus some evidence to suggest that contract farming has been rapidly expanding in the era of agricultural liberalization both geographically and as a share of total output (Sautier et al. 2006; Prowse 2012). In this context, the rise of contract farming can be seen as analogous to the expansion in services and manufacturing of forms of outsourcing where 'owner-operators' mobilize the factors of production (in the case of agriculture, their land and their labour) and alone absorb the risks and costs of the process of production, while using intermediaries to reach final consumers.

The challenge is to know the real extent of participation of producers in formal contract farming schemes and how sustained or contingent it is, depending on the context. Global data on contract farming is fragmentary and the variety of contract farming arrangements is daunting (see below), making quantitative assessments of scale almost impossible. Contract farming is present in all farming geographies of the world, although its share of the total volume and value of production, of agricultural trade, employment and acreage may vary considerably in different value chains, and is extremely difficult to determine. A recent systematic review suggests that the rapid expansion of the midstream and downstream actors in output value chains (e.g. processors, traders and cooperatives), which buy crops and livestock products from smallholders, *without* formal contracts, has made these types of informal relations more widespread than conventional forms of contract farming (Liverpool-Tasie et al. 2020).

Given the dearth of systematic panel and cross-country data on contract farming, evaluations and case studies, often focused on particular commodities and specific locations, play an important role in the analysis and theorization of contract farming (Oya 2012; Bellemare and Bloem 2018). From this literature it is hard to ascertain the true scale of these arrangements globally and within countries. Therefore, it is also difficult to assess the real contribution that these schemes have made to the processes of structural transformation and agrarian change, at least with any quantitative precision. The task is also made harder by the fact that similar forms of contracting have existed in the past, linking agricultural producers to both private and state agencies, as in the cotton and opium contracts in Calcutta (Banaji 2016) and the parastatal marketing boards in many African countries in the 1960s and 1970s (Oya 2012). So, while the conventional contract farming scheme linking private buyers with smallholder producers may have grown rapidly since the 1980s, the overall incidence of any kind of contract farming arrangement (including through state marketing boards) may not have changed that much.

A VARIETY OF CONTRACT FARMING ARRANGEMENTS

Evidence on the scale and effects of contract farming arrangements in both developed and developing countries is clouded by the existence of multiple varieties of contract farming. The precise characteristics of a contract farming arrangement do have substantial implications for production conditions, risk, prices, market access and labour relations. Generally, the variety of conditions tends to be related to the relative degree of vertical integration, i.e., how much direct control the buyer or processor has over production conditions and farmers' decisions. In turn, the relative flexibility or rigidity of contracts is associated with a range of factors, from crop characteristics, property rights, to the prevailing institutional frameworks governing specific markets. It has been argued that contract farming, as one of the forms in which capital can control production, or alternatively, as a tool of vertical integration in agriculture, would be more prevalent in the case of crops that are more labour intensive or that demand more coordination, for example in the production of highly perishable produce or high-value crops with a quality premium (Kirsten and Sartorius 2002; Minot 2007; Bijman 2008). However, the sheer variety of crops and productive practices in contract farming arrangements prevents the formulation of sweeping generalizations (Smalley 2013; Otsuka et al. 2016; Bellemare and Lim 2018; Ton et al. 2018). For purposes of simple illustration, a contract farmer may just agree to deliver a given volume of output at the end of the season, without particular specifications and at a verbally agreed price; or may be subject to strict requirements in terms of volume, quality, timeliness and agronomic practices, all stipulated in a contract, that may involve the provision of inputs, seasonal credit, extension services and access to more secure and remunerative markets by buyers. There are many variations along a continuum between these two examples.

The drivers of contract farming expansion are particularly difficult to account for using a single set of criteria and definitions. This is the case because contract farming encompasses a considerable variety of practices, types of producers and examples of arrangements. A large range of agricultural and livestock commodities are produced in contract farming agreements; contract farming may also involve considerable state participation, although it has become predominantly private-led (with some important exceptions e.g. China and Zimbabwe); contract farming is used in highly integrated agro-industrial production as well as in farms with low levels of labour productivity, and may involve rich capitalist farmers and resource-poor and land-scarce smallholders, depending on the crop, location and buyer (Oya 2012).

The relation between processors/buyers and producers/contracted farmers can take many forms: a simple distinction is that between buyers that are themselves producers and buyers that are not directly engaged in production. The prevalent model in the first case is that of the 'nucleus estate' model in which buyers contract with outgrowers to increase or smooth out supply. This is in contrast with the 'centralized' model, which characterizes schemes where buyers procure all output from contracted farmers operating in large numbers in a given area. Instances in which producers are not involved in production, typically in the contract farming outgrower model with a core estate, may be best understood as forms of land lease where the land rental fee is a function of the farm output. This is most prominently the case in sugarcane farming in Southern Africa, where contract farmers (i.e. the owners of the land) do not necessarily take part in production either as coordinators or workers (Dubb et al. 2017). Both in the 'nucleus estate' model and in the 'centralized' model, buyers could be primary and secondary processors of the commodities contracted and these sourcing schemes may have been created as a mechanism to source the necessary throughput that utilizes processing capacity optimally. In both of these models large buyers/processors engage directly with contract farmers and the corresponding contracts tend to be formal. A different model, often called 'informal', is less centralized and is prevalent in regions where small traders and small processors contract production with farmers. These schemes typically involve a larger number of buyers and are characterized by more informal contracts and less vertical integration, as described in Liverpool-Tasie (2020). Lastly, an 'intermediary' model lies somewhere between the 'centralized' and 'informal' models of contract farming and describes schemes in which large-scale buyers or processors outsource the management of the contracts to intermediary and smaller traders. However useful this schema of four models of contract farming ('nucleus estate', 'centralized', 'informal' and 'intermediary') may be (Eaton and Shepherd 2001; Bellemare and Lim 2018), it has been criticized because the boundaries between these four models are in practice frequently blurred, with contract farming schemes that do not neatly fit any of the categories or that display characteristics from across different models. One way of avoiding conflation is to distinguish varieties of contract farming from other forms of buyer–producer relations by defining contract farming varieties only for arrangements that include some service-providing clauses (for material or financial services), which denote an 'intervention' of buyers in the production process (Ton et al. 2018).

Variation can also be found in terms of the nature and specificities of each contract. Whereas contract farming production typologies (as described above) focus on the character of the contracting parties, the contract typologies largely describe differences in the roles and obligations of the parties as stipulated by the contract (Bellemare and Lim 2018). For instance, 'market specification' contracts include agreements about the deliverables of the contract (quantity, quality, timing) but leave the producers to manage the production process. In contrast, 'production management' contracts allow buyers to stipulate specific methods of production, to make critical productive decisions – including on highly sensitive issues such as the use of inputs or machinery and the timing of irrigation or harvesting – and frequently involve them more closely in monitoring the production process. Lastly, there are 'resource-providing' contracts that although may include elements of the other two types, are distinctive in that they bind producers to use inputs provided by buyers as part of the contract, usually on credit (Kirsten and Sartorius 2002; Bijman 2008). The degree of vertical integration can therefore be evaluated from the perspective of these contract typologies. Contract variations are also linked to the length of the contract (only seasonal or several years-long) and the degree of formality in the arrangements (from verbal agreements to notarized contracts). Contracts make provisions with substantial effects on the profitability of the arrangement for both parties and are therefore frequently contested. This includes the terms and timing of price setting and purchasing, which can be a key driver of profits or losses for producers. In some contract farming schemes prices are set in reference to open market prices, whereas in other cases the prices are fixed. These variations may be related to a host of factors, including the type of commodity, nature of buyer, location, alternative market options, credit availability and technology, among other issues. Classifications of contract farming arrangements are however only relevant if other questions are addressed at the same time, namely: what effects does contract farming have on farmers' welfare? What determines participation and exit? What are the main power dynamics in contract farming relations? Does contract farming effectively solve market failures? At whose expense? The answer to these questions (in fact, even their formulation) depends on the conceptual framework and methodological preferences of researchers studying contract farming. The next two sections draw a contrast between two traditions offering very different analysis of contract farming.

MAINSTREAM APPROACHES TO CONTRACT FARMING

By and large, mainstream agricultural economics' analysis of contract farming is theoretically grounded in New Institutional Economics. Contract farming is understood as an institutional arrangement that helps redress market failures and asymmetrical information. Market failure arises for instance in the absence of factor markets; where productive assets and inputs like farmland or irrigation services cannot simply be acquired in the market, where banks are reluctant to provide finance because of the high transaction costs of engaging with small credits and the limitations that prevent the use of land deeds as collateral (Barrett et al. 2012). In contexts where barriers to output markets are substantial, due to quality, phytosanitary or scale requirements, contract farming may provide a route to overcome those obstacles by letting buyers/ processors take some control over the production process in exchange for guaranteed supplies of product with the required specifications.

The intermediation of supply and demand by the contract may contribute to ease the coordination of the productive process: producers know in advance the volume and quality requirements demanded by buyers instead of taking their product to spot markets, hoping to find buyers. Conversely, buyers ensure that the output they need to source is available on time and in their preferred conditions. The gist of the argument is that contractual arrangements contribute to lowering the transaction costs in the system: a win-win solution (Bijman 2008; Wang et al. 2014).

Agricultural economics has also devoted considerable attention to the conceptual construction of typologies and the empirical association of different contract farming schemes to diverse groups, using the terms of the contract as the key parameters for the construction of contract farming varieties, in order to analyse farmers' and buyers' preferences for different types of arrangements (Minot 2007; Bellemare and Lim 2018).

Similarly, in the fields of business studies, management and commodity studies, contract farming is characterized as a form of vertical integration where buyers or lead firms use production contracts to secure the supply of commodities (Minot 2007; Bellemare and Lim 2018). Specifically, contract farming would be a case of backward integration or 'vertical coordination' whereby commodity buyers can modulate supply and thus lower transaction costs (Swinnen 2007). Unlike primary vertical integration, in contract farming lead firms do not acquire the commodity-producing firms they source from, but contract them. Both cases result in lead firms exerting more control over the referred segments of the supply chain. Institutionalist and value chain analyses are concerned with similar problems, but whereas the former looks horizontally at transaction costs; the latter focuses on vertical linkages along commodity chains.

It is not surprising that contract farming, seen here as a solution to market imperfections, as a risk management mechanism and as a form of vertical coordination, has been enthusiastically endorsed by development practitioners. It has been promoted in agricultural-based, low-income countries as an avenue for farmers, especially smallholder farmers, to be able to participate in the production of high value-added agricultural commodities and to overcome the credit, technological, coordination, inputs and marketing barriers that often exclude small-scale producers from remunerative value chains (Maertens and Swinnen 2014). Contract farming has also been extolled as a kind of capacity incubator in which agricultural sectors in low-income countries can learn to produce commodities that require tighter coordination and with higher quality demands (Eaton and Shepherd 2001).

A large share of the mainstream empirical research on contract farming is devoted to answering two main empirical questions: what are the drivers of participation and what is the income effect of participating in contract farming schemes (Minot 2007; Barrett et al. 2012; Bellemare 2012; Otsuka et al. 2016; Bellemare and Bloem 2018; Ton et al. 2018)? The majority of empirical studies tend to reveal a positive effect on farmers' incomes but also find evidence of selection bias in participation, with richer producers (also among smallholders) generally being over-represented among outgrowers. Bellemare (2018) also qualifies the effect on farm income with evidence on trade-offs and loss of other income sources (wage and off-farm activities). Much of this empirical literature on welfare effects suffers from a combination of internal and external validity problems (Bellemare and Bloem 2018) and a recent systematic review also suggested potential publication and survival biases, meaning that the finding that contract farming has a positive effect on farmers' incomes may be misleading (Ton et al. 2018). Given the multiple observed and unobserved effects of a contract farming intervention, it is hard to attribute causality to mere participation in a contract farming scheme.

Apart from these methodological challenges, acknowledged by some agricultural economists, positive accounts of the social and economic impact of contract farming have been criticized from other angles. Contract farming involves a purchasing promise that bypasses spot markets, but by suppressing the market mechanism it can prevent producers from profiting from competition among buyers. Conversely, for buyers to profit it is critical to stamp out side-selling: the possibility that producers renege on their contract to sell to a third party offering a better price (Kirsten and Sartorius 2002). Despite the potential agency of contract farmers in the form of side-selling (Thiers 2017), there are different ways in which buyers press for contract enforcement, for instance by providing inputs on credit as a condition of the contract and locking producers into debt or by setting up schemes that operate as monopsonies or oligopsonies, curtailing the very availability of alternative outlets. This, compounded with price-setting mechanisms in which producers frequently have limited or insignificant bargaining power, means that contract farming – far from the beneficial encounter between buyers and producers – can instead be characterized by highly skewed distribution of benefits and costs and provide the conditions for the 'adverse incorporation' of direct producers into commodity markets. As price takers who bear most of the risk, producers cease to be able to benefit from price spikes, and on the contrary end up absorbing the cost of harvest failures and other productive shocks. Regulating oligopsonistic rents, price-setting collusion between buyers and the dumping of risk and costs onto producers would all require strong regulation by the state, but in many cases states are unwilling or unable to intervene in the regulation of contracts (Oya 2012). Many of these issues are under-researched in mainstream approaches that are driven by methodological individualism and a tendency to focus only on mathematically and statistically tractable problems. Still, there is a wealth of accumulated evidence for the narrow set of questions addressed by mainstream agricultural economics.

CONTRACT FARMING IN CRITICAL AGRARIAN STUDIES

Critical agrarian studies is an umbrella term for a heterogeneous collection of disciplinary and theoretical perspectives broadly grounded in critical social sciences. Authors in critical agrarian studies share an interest in revealing and problematizing the uneven power relations among different groups of participants in contract farming. Such 'baseline' power relations are either altogether ignored or translated into the rather more restrictive rubrics of 'bargaining power differentials' or 'information asymmetries' in mainstream analysis of contract farming. Agrarian studies are interested in the social, economic and political context in which contract farming takes place and not merely in the individual income effect of farmers' participation in contract farming schemes. A different set of questions emerges in the critical literature: How do contract farming schemes interact with the prevailing dynamics of production and property in the regions where it is in operation? What do the terms of the contract, its negotiation and regulation say about the power relations between producers and buyers? What is the role of the state or other authorities in the regulation of this form of production and marketing? How does contract farming shape and influence processes of agrarian change (Little and Watts 1994; Zhang 2012; Hall et al. 2017; Kuzilwa et al. 2017; Thiers 2017; Dubb 2018; Martiniello 2021)? Finally, common to most approaches in critical agrarian studies is a square rejection of methodological individualism. Contract farming operates in a field of social relations and cannot be accounted for in terms of the relation between individual buyers and individual producers alone. Not only does this conceal the social relations of power, production and property at village, region and global scales, but it obscures the class, gendered and generational conflicts and tensions that characterize commodity production whether through contract farming or other forms of incorporation into capitalist markets (Carney 1988; Clapp 1988; Raynolds 2002; Li 2011; Pérez Niño 2016).

While the dynamics of contract farming provide an insight into some of the most pressing questions in contemporary agrarian change, the study of contract farming also reveals key fault lines within critical agrarian studies. Crucially, one condition of production taking place under contract arrangements is that direct producers, regardless of their scale of production or the character of their involvement, retain access to, or property over, the land under cultivation.[1] In this way, the very prevalence of contract farming interrogates the idea in agrarian studies that the expansion of capitalist relations of production occurs mainly as a result of processes of 'accumulation by dispossession', a premise that gave way to the so-called 'land grab' literature rush of the 2010s. The diverse interpretation of this core feature of contract farming lends itself to debate within critical agrarian studies: those analytically invested in 'accumulation by dispossession' as the core rubric of agrarian analysis tend to ascribe the retention of access to the means of production in contract farming as spurious, contending that contract farming implies ultimately a loss in control and autonomy over the production process that is functionally akin to outright dispossession; whereas those interested in the diverse historical trajectories of capital–labour relations focus on the transformation of property relations and the labour process brought about by contract farming and the extent to which it results in deepening the processes of commodification (including of labour) and socioeconomic differentiation, with different consequences for outgrowers and their workers depending on the arrangement. In this view, contract farming has the potential to raise agricultural productivity and surplus appropriation, thus opening new frontiers of accumulation and dismantling old forms of production. Contract farming ultimately forges more complex sets of (class) contradictions and interests in the countryside (Oya 2012). While in the first case, contract farming is seen as yet another manifestation of the onslaught of peasants and direct producers by corporate, and frequently transnational, capital, in the second case, contract farming may be seen as a catalyst for class differentiation and capitalist development in agriculture with considerable implications for local and global struggles (Little and Watts 1994; Bernstein 2010). Many of these questions require a leap forward in terms of a more systematic observation of the scale and trends of the phenomenon, as well as more external validity to ascertain the real impact on capitalist development and social differentiation over time. Thus, these questions remain largely unanswered because critical agrarian studies research on contract farming is not always based on rigorous field-based quantitative and mixed-methods studies and is comparatively more limited in volume than research in mainstream agricultural economics.

CONCLUSION

This chapter has explored the meaning, dynamics and implications of contract farming in contemporary capitalism while contrasting mainstream and critical approaches to this institutional arrangement. The chapter has shown why focusing on the formal organization of contract farming and narrowly on the interaction between buyers and producers as parties to a discretionary agreement misses some fundamental relations that are transformed by contract farming, besides marginal quantitative effects on incomes and food security. Notably, while mainstream approaches miss key aspects of contract farming, critical agrarian approaches to contract farming (can) focus instead on a range of different questions, namely: the tapestry of tenure relations that alternatively give and deny access to land and land tenure changes over time; the actual labour process that enables commodity production and that frequently entails the mobilization of household labour or hired workers and the attendant tensions of such mobilization; the barriers of entry into contract farming and its effect as an accelerator of capital accumulation; how contract farming modulates socio-economic differentiation and reshapes social relations with consequences for structural transformation; the role of contract farming in opening up frontier regions or uncaptured parts of the economy to processes of surplus appropriation; problems of ownership and state intervention that frustrate the promises of upgrading and structural transformation – the very grounds for agricultural economics' enthusiastic support for the adoption of contract farming in developing countries to begin with. The challenge for critical agrarian studies is to significantly expand and improve the evidence base to address all these important questions.

NOTE

1.   This land can be collectively or individually owned. There are examples of contract farming schemes operating on communal land, land under customary rights, state-owned and freehold land.

FURTHER READING

Kuzilwa, J.A.; Fold, N.; Henningsen, A.; Larsen, M.N. (eds) (2017), *Contract Farming and the Development of Smallholder Agricultural Businesses: Improving Markets and Value Chains in Tanzania*, London: Routledge.
Little, P.D.; Watts, M. (eds) (1994), *Living under Contract: Contract Farming and Agrarian Transformation in Sub-Saharan Africa*, Madison, WI: University of Wisconsin Press.
Oya, C. (2012), Contract farming in sub-Saharan Africa: A survey of approaches, debates and issues, *Journal of Agrarian Change*, 12(1), 1–33.
Prowse, M. (2012), *Contract Farming in Developing Countries: A Review*, Paris: Agence française de développement.
Ton, G.; Vellema, W.; Desiere, S.; Weituschat, S.; D'Haese, M. (2018), Contract farming for improving smallholder incomes: What can we learn from effectiveness studies?, *World Development*, 104, 46–64.

REFERENCES

Banaji, J. (2016), Merchant capitalism, peasant households and industrial accumulation: Integration of a model, *Journal of Agrarian Change*, 16(3), 410–431.

Barrett, C.B.; Bachke, M.E.; Bellemare, M.F.; Michelson, H.C.; Narayanan, S.; Walker, T.F. (2012), Smallholder participation in contract farming: Comparative evidence from five countries, *World Development*, 40(4), 715–730.

Bellemare, M.F. (2012), As you sow, so shall you reap: The welfare impacts of contract farming, *World Development*, 40(7), 1418–1434.

Bellemare, M.F. (2018), Contract farming: opportunity cost and trade-offs, *Agricultural Economics*, 49(3), 279–288.

Bellemare, M.F.; Bloem, J.R. (2018), Does contract farming improve welfare? A review, *World Development*, 112, 259–271.

Bellemare, M.F.; Lim, S. (2018), In all shapes and colors: Varieties of contract farming, *Applied Economic Perspectives and Policy*, 40(3), 379–401.

Bernstein, H. (2010), *Class Dynamics of Agrarian Change*, Blackpoint: Fernwood.

Bijman, J. (2008), *Contract Farming in Developing Countries: An Overview*, Working Paper, Wageningen: Wageningen University.

Carney, J.A. (1988), Struggles over crop rights and labour within contract farming households in a Gambian irrigated rice project, *Journal of Peasant Studies*, 15(3), 334–349.

Clapp, R.A. (1988), Representing reciprocity, reproducing domination: ideology and the labour process in Latin American contract farming, *Journal of Peasant Studies*, 16(1), 5–39.

Dubb, A. (2018), The value components of contract farming in contemporary capitalism, *Journal of Agrarian Change*, 18(4), 722–748.

Dubb, A.; Scoones, I.; Woodhouse, P. (2017), The political economy of sugar in Southern Africa, *Journal of Southern African Studies*, 43(3), 447–641.

Eaton, C.; Shepherd, A. (2001), *Contract Farming: Partnerships for Growth*, Rome: Food and Agriculture Organization.

Hall, R.; Scoones, I.; Tsikata, D. (2017), Plantations, outgrowers and commercial farming in Africa: Agricultural commercialisation and implications for agrarian change, *Journal of Peasant Studies*, 44(3), 515–537.

Hickey, S.; du Toit, A. (2013), Adverse incorporation, social exclusion and chronic poverty, in Shepherd, A.; Brunt, J. (eds), *Chronic Poverty: Rethinking International Development Series*, London: Palgrave Macmillan.

Kirsten, J.; Sartorius, K. (2002), Linking agribusiness and small-scale farmers in developing countries: Is there a new role for contract farming?, *Development Southern Africa*, 19(4), 503–529.

Kuzilwa, J.A.; Fold, N.; Henningsen, A.; Larsen, M.N. (eds) (2017), *Contract Farming and the Development of Smallholder Agricultural Businesses: Improving Markets and Value Chains in Tanzania*, London: Routledge.

Li, T.M. (2011), Centering labor in the land grab debate, *Journal of Peasant Studies*, 38(2), 281–298.

Little, P.D.; Watts, M. (eds) (1994), *Living under Contract: Contract Farming and Agrarian Transformation in Sub-Saharan Africa*, Madison, WI: University of Wisconsin Press.

Liverpool-Tasie, L.S.O.; Wineman, A.; Young, S.; Tambo, J.; Vargas, C.; Reardon, T.; Galiè, A. (2020), A scoping review of market links between value chain actors and small-scale producers in developing regions, *Nature Sustainability*, 3, 799–808.

Maertens, M.; Swinnen, J. (2014), *Agricultural Trade and Development: A Value Chain Perspective*, WTO Working Paper No. 2015/04, Geneva: WTO.

Martiniello, G. (2016), 'Don't stop the mill': South African capital and agrarian change in Tanzania, *Third World Thematics: A TWQ Journal*, 1(5), 633–652.

Martiniello, G. (2021), Bitter sugarification: Sugar frontier and contract farming in Uganda, *Globalizations*, 18(3), 355–371.

Masakure, O.; Henson, S. (2005), Why do small-scale producers choose to produce under contract? Lessons from nontraditional vegetable exports from Zimbabwe, *World Development*, 33(10), 1721–1733.

McCarthy, J.F. (2010), Processes of inclusion and adverse incorporation: Oil palm and agrarian change in Sumatra, Indonesia, *Journal of Peasant Studies*, 37(4), 821–850.

Minot, N. (2007), Contract farming in developing countries: Patterns, impact and policy implications, Ithaca, NY: Cornell University Library.

Otsuka, K.; Yuko, N.; Kazushi, T. (2016), Contract farming in developed and developing countries, *Annual Review of Resource Economics*, 8, 353–376.

Oya, C. (2012), Contract farming in Sub-Saharan Africa: A survey of approaches, debates and issues, *Journal of Agrarian Change*, 12(1), 1–33.

Pérez Niño, H. (2016), Class dynamics in contract farming: The case of tobacco production in Mozambique, *Third World Quarterly*, 37(10), 1787–1808.

Prowse, M. (2012), *Contract Farming in Developing Countries: A Review*, Paris: Agence française de développement.

Raynolds, L.T. (2002), Wages for wives: Renegotiating gender and production relations in contract farming in the Dominican Republic, *World Development*, 30(5), 783–798.

Sautier, D.; Vermeulen, H.; Fok, M.; Biénabe, E. (2006), *Case Studies of Agri-Processing and Contract Agriculture in Africa*, Washington, DC: World Bank.

Smalley, R. (2013), Plantations, contract farming and commercial farming areas in Africa: A comparative review, land and agricultural commercialisation in Africa (LACA), *Future Agricultures Consortium Working Paper no. 55*.

Swinnen, J.F.M. (2007), *Global Supply Chains: Standards and the Poor*, Oxford: CABI Publishing.

Thiers, R. (2017), Flying bananas: Small producer tactics and the (un)making of Philippine banana export chains, *Journal of Peasant Studies*, 46(2), 337–357.

Ton, G.; Vellema, W.; Desiere, S.; Weituschat, S.; D'Haese, M. (2018), Contract farming for improving smallholder incomes: What can we learn from effectiveness studies?, *World Development*, 104, 46–64.

UNCTAD (2009), *World Investment Report 2009*, Geneva: United Nations Conference on Trade and Development.

Vicol, M. (2017), Is contract farming an inclusive alternative to land grabbing? The case of potato contract farming in Maharashtra, India, *Geoforum*, 85, 157–166.

Vrousalis, N. (2018), Capital without wage-labour: Marx's modes of subsumption revisited, *Economics and Philosophy*, 34(3), 411–438.

Wang, H.H.; Wang, Y.; Delgado, M.S. (2014), The transition to modern agriculture: Contract farming in developing economies, *American Journal of Agricultural Economics*, 96(5), 1257–1271.

World Bank (2020), *World Development Report 2020: Trading for Development in the Age of Global Value Chains*, Washington, DC: World Bank.

Zhang, Q.F. (2012), The political economy of contract farming in China's agrarian transition, *Journal of Agrarian Change*, 12(4), 460–483.

47. Biotechnology

Matthew A. Schnurr and Lincoln Addison

Agricultural biotechnology comprises a spectrum of breeding tools that manipulate a plant's genome in order to improve performance and productivity. This specific targeting of genomic sequences ushered in a new era of plant breeding that moved beyond phenotypic selection (the sorting and ranking of beneficial traits visible to the naked eye) towards genotypic selection (the sorting and ranking of beneficial traits inscribed in the plant genome). Agricultural biotechnology is being heralded as a core component of the dominant paradigm of sustainable intensification, a 'pro-poor' technology capable of enhancing yields, alleviating poverty and improving rural development.

In this chapter, we argue that critical agrarian studies should move beyond the critique of agricultural biotechnology as an instrument of industrial agriculture and engage in more empirical analysis of its diverse implications for agrarian change. Specifically, we call for more attention to: (1) the constraints and opportunities presented to smallholders by the emerging partnership models that structure recent efforts to disseminate biotechnology in the Global South; (2) the localized agricultural systems into which new technologies are introduced, in order to assess the economic and environmental interactions both upstream and downstream; and (3) the differentiated impacts adoption of the technology is likely to have on class, labor and gender dynamics, both within and across production systems.[1]

In order to critically evaluate agricultural biotechnology, one must first understand the specific mechanisms and capacity of the technologies themselves. We distinguish three waves of biotechnology. The first wave emerged in the 1970s and was founded upon scientists being able to identify and target specific areas of a plant's genome in order to improve their ability to respond to biotic and abiotic stressors. The two most established biotechnology techniques are marker-assisted breeding, which utilizes identifiable DNA sequences to target specific genes that code for desired traits, and tissue culture, which involves the regeneration of plant cells from an excised section that enables the propagation of disease-free planting material.

Genetic engineering (GE) constitutes the second and much more controversial wave of biotechnology. This series of technologies is defined by its reliance on laboratory methods of genetic recombination, which enables the collation of genetic material from multiple sources. The most common combination for GE crops involves the insertion of genetic material coding for a beneficial trait such as increased yield, larger fruit or pest resistance into a high-performing host. This mode of breeding, known as transgenesis, requires a vector to transplant the foreign DNA: the two most common mechanisms are the physical bombardment of heavy metal particles using a gene gun and a soil bacterium that transfers the recipient sequence to the target genetic material. The resultant progeny are identical to their parent in every way except that they now have the beneficial trait embedded in their genomic sequence.

The third and most recent wave of biotechnology moves beyond some of GE's most persistent limitations by allowing scientists to alter, remove or turn off genes that code for particular traits, without the insertion of foreign DNA. Three techniques are worth noting here. The first is genome editing, exemplified by the CRISPR[2] technique, which makes use of an enzyme to identify and edit specific genes of interest, leading to insertions, deletions or inversions to modify phenotypic expression without the use of transgenic materials. Genome editing has revolutionized the process of GE by making it more precise, more affordable and more available. Second are gene drives, mechanisms of biased inheritance that perpetuate the transmission of a gene from parent to offspring at an accelerated rate. The result is that this gene will increase in frequency in a population over multiple generations. In agriculture, gene drives are especially promising as tools for genetic pest management, which can eliminate harmful pests via population suppression or replacement. Third is synthetic biology, which utilizes an engineering-based approach to genomics to develop novel components, organisms or products. Most applications focus either on the design and construction of new biological parts or devices or the redesign of existing biological systems to maximize utility.

The adoption of biotechnology around the world has major consequences for agricultural productivity, patterns of rural poverty and struggles to achieve food sovereignty, and is thus of intrinsic interest to critical agrarian studies. Yet, critical agrarian studies has paid little attention to the actual implications for rural development, allowing perspectives from agricultural economics and crop science to predominate in empirical analysis. A recent review of agrarian Marxism identified biotechnology as a crucial blind spot for critical scholars:

> At the risk of pointing fingers, the question of biotechnology both upstream and downstream is an arena which requires more careful Marxian analysis whether focused on the laboratories and the bench science, the question of financialization and corporate control, or how the technologies themselves might stimulate new debates over work and the labor process, how capital is taking hold of the point of production, and challenging the ways in which we think about surplus extraction or relations of domination and control. (Levien et al. 2018, 877)

Much of the scholarship within critical agrarian studies has tended to dismiss agricultural biotechnology as a tool of the neoliberal food regime that serves to restructure agrarian relations to the detriment of the rural poor (Ezquerro-Cañete 2016; Leguizamón 2016). Three strands of scholarship feature most prominently within this overarching critique. The first seeks to unravel the confluence of powerful interests that come together to privilege biotech over other possibilities in agricultural development. Separate analyses undertaken in Argentina (Newell 2009), Canada (Andrée 2007) and Uganda (Schnurr 2013) mobilized Gramscian insights to unpack the network of corporations, policy officials and research scientists that support the unquestioned dominance of GE in their respective contexts, shining a light on the tactics employed by this consensus in order to maintain its position of dominance. This analytical emphasis on unraveling the social relations that underpin biotech's expansion exposes how a coalition of supporters were able to create institutions, norms and narratives that facilitate the social approval of biotechnology (Schnurr and Gore 2015).

The second strand of scholarship shines a light on the role that philanthropic capital plays in shaping the imperative for biotechnology. A political economy perspective has been employed to zero in on the specific alignment, interests and behaviors of the new philanthropic model, which emerged to fill the gap left by neoliberal policies that had gradually dismantled the capacity of developing countries to redress pressing issues in agricultural production (Thompson 2014). Philanthropic initiatives embedded with the logic of venture capitalism promoted a narrative of science, growth and technology as the solution to increasing the productivity of smallholder farming in the Global South. Biotechnology's position as a cutting-edge technology embedded within a strict corporate ownership model, stringent Intellectual Property and mandated farm management practices fit neatly within this ideal. Studies within critical agrarian studies have sought to expose the specific tools used by philanthropic capital to advance biotechnology's penetration into new markets, including public–private partnerships (P3s), which have been accused of depoliticizing questions of agrarian poverty and advancing the interests of multinational corporations within an overarching commitment to agricultural modernization (Morvaridi 2012; Morvaridi 2016; Ignatova 2017; Schurman 2017), and agricultural value chains, which uncritically assume that integrating small producers within global markets will create benefits that are universal and uniform (McMichael 2013; Gengenbach et al. 2018). Others have synthesized these attempts to subsume small-scale producers to global markets as evidence that philanthropic capital utilizes biotechnology as a tool of accumulation by dispossession in order to monetize genetic wealth (Thompson 2014).

The third strand of scholarship examines the social resistance that has mobilized to oppose the encroachment of agricultural biotechnology. Much of the existing scholarship has focused on uncovering the strategies employed to contest dominant framings linking biotechnology with broader notions of economic growth and agrarian change (Newell 2009; Motta 2016a, 2016b). This research has stressed the interplay of global and local scales, showing how resistance tends to coalesce around global concerns—implications of restrictive Intellectual Property regimes for subsistence farmers, linkages between biotech and export-oriented agribusiness, objections to knowledge monopolization—while the character of the social movements themselves are shaped by domestic dynamics (Kinchy 2012; Klepek 2012). This work also seeks to promote alternatives to corporate controlled biotechnology, such as open source plant breeding (Montenegro De Wit 2019). Proponents view open source initiatives as restoring farmer control over genetic material, particularly when their access has been curtailed through bioprospecting or the Trade Related Intellectual Property agreement of the World Trade Organization (Kloppenburg 2010). Moreover, by releasing seeds from propriety control, such initiatives can also revitalize public breeding programs long underfunded and constrained by Intellectual Property law. Advocates argue that public breeders are better placed to develop varieties that meet the needs of poorer, small-scale farmers than for profit entities (Kloppenburg 2014). Finally, this emphasis on resistance has also sparked important questions around the 'dynamics of mobilization' (Lapegna 2015, 206) and the legitimacy of these movements that purport to speak for rural voices, but tend to be dominated by leaders that are urban-based, well educated and middle class (Scoones 2008).

The propensity to critique biotechnology as a tool of industrial agriculture has tended to obscure other dynamics crucial to understanding contemporary debates around the potential for biotechnology to enhance rural livelihoods. Critical research on agricultural biotechnology tends to remain mired in the same tropes: biotechnology is a tool designed to extend the penetration of multinational corporations, restrictive Intellectual Property regimes mean that control over seed will shift from producers to corporations, contamination with neighboring non-biotech crops is inevitable and so on. In many cases these refrains are justified—particularly when dealing with genetically engineered versions of commodity crops owned by corporations that restrict the replanting, recycling or sharing of seed. But more recent biotechnological innovations evade these well-entrenched critiques. The P3s that underpin the renewed investment in a uniquely African Green Revolution, for instance, are dedicated to carbohydrate staple crops overlooked by innovation and investment. P3s including bacteria-resistant cooking banana and virus-resistant cassava are designed to minimize pests and diseases that matter to poor farmers, and will be distributed license-free for humanitarian purposes. Further, both of the above examples include crops that reproduce clonally, making them effectively sterile, negating the risk of genetic contamination.

In our view, this interplay of new technological innovations and institutional arrangements requires a more nuanced scholarly analysis, one that zeroes in on the specific interplay between crop and context. As Lapegna argues 'attention to their localized and tangible effects can help us to avoid broad generalizations about global capitalism, as well as keep us from overlooking its spatial manifestations and uneven geographies' (2015, 205). Below we sketch out the three arenas where critical agrarian studies can offer particular value to the study of biotechnology as a 'pro-poor' technology.

THE LOGIC, ORGANIZATION AND FUNDING OF THE PARTNERSHIP MODEL

Much of the enthusiasm for agricultural biotechnology's potential to improve rural livelihoods is premised on the delivery mechanism of P3s, whereby private corporations donate licensed technology to national government agencies for use in specific applications, facilitated by a third party such as a philanthropic foundation (see Schurman 2017 for the important role African Agricultural Technology Foundation plays in this process). Critical agrarian studies needs to delve deeper into the P3s guiding each biotechnological innovation, which have become the standard mechanism governing technology-for-development programming. Critical agrarian studies is well positioned to uncover the power and politics that determine how these innovations are 'designed, championed and promoted' (Taylor 2020, 484), and the tendency for such ventures to manage up to donors as opposed to managing down to the technology's intended beneficiary (Schurman 2018). There is a need to learn more about the role played by public agricultural research institutions within these partnerships. Such institutions are often seen as more connected with the needs of local farmers, as compared with philanthropic donors or private-sector investors (Kloppenburg 2010). To what extent are local public-sector agencies able to shape the agenda of P3s?

The long-term implications of these P3s also deserve more consideration. For example, Ignatova (2017, 2267) asked multiple stakeholders about the Intellectual Property ownership regimes accompanying a genetically engineered insect-resistant cowpea partnership and received answers that were confused and conflicting. This syncs with our own experience studying the genetically engineered versions of cooking bananas in Uganda, where questions over long-term implications of licensing remain ambiguous, particularly the role of the private seed companies who will be needed to multiply planting materials in order to reach small-scale producers (Schnurr et al. 2020). Such questions will help to reveal how biotechnology fits within the broader model of development-oriented agronomy, and its preoccupation with utilizing private capital as a vehicle for modernizing rural agricultural production (Andersson and Sumberg 2017).

UNDERSTANDING AGRICULTURAL SYSTEMS

There are two dimensions to this emphasis on agricultural systems. First, critical agrarian studies needs to pay more attention to the specific agro-ecological system that a particular biotechnology is designed to enhance. Scholarly analyses need to integrate biological mechanisms of pests and diseases, farmer growing regimes, secondary pests and differences in host varieties in order to comprehensively assess the implications of any new agricultural technology. For example, issues with host variety performance was the key factor undercutting early successes with genetically engineered cotton in Burkina Faso (Dowd-Uribe and Schnurr 2016), while issues around implementing proper buffer zones have undermined efforts to grow GE maize in South Africa (Fischer and Hadju 2015).

Second, we need studies that foreground dynamics of production and consumption. Attention to scale is crucial here: much of the current hype surrounding biotech revolves around its potential to enhance small-scale farming systems, yet there is little research that examines the 'fit' between a particular biotechnological innovation and the production system it is designed to enhance (Schnurr 2019). This necessitates a focus on economies of scale, purchasing power of inputs and farmer-based preferences for planting materials. The in-depth, grounded studies that have been undertaken reveal important insights regarding farmer preferences for value-based preferences such as color, taste and texture (Soleri et al. 2008), the complications of scaling up biotechnological interventions, especially as they pertain to the multiplication of planting materials (Rao and Huggins 2017) and how biotechnology creates a treadmill effect that undermines farmer autonomy by leaving them 'locked in' within a particular technological pathway (Flachs and Stone 2018).

DIFFERENTIATED IMPACTS

The final area requiring emphasis relates to the differentiated impacts of agricultural biotechnology (Dowd-Uribe 2017; Schnurr 2019). With its historic focus on understanding the relationship between forms of rural stratification and wider processes of development, critical agrarian studies can offer much needed insight into how agricultural biotechnology reconfigures patterns of rural inequality. Any new technology produces differentiated benefits refracted by categories of power including class, gender, race, age, land size, access to information and so forth. And yet there exist few studies that engage explicitly with these questions of uneven distribution. The dynamics of labor and gender are particularly relevant here. Existing scholarship is largely split on the labor implications of agricultural biotechnology: studies in India (Subramanian and Qaim 2010) and Uganda (Addison and Schnurr 2016) found that the introduction of GE crops intensified the time and labor burdens for (particularly women) farmers, while research in Colombia (Zambrano et al. 2011), Burkina Faso (Falck-Zapeda and Zambrano 2013) and South Africa (Gouse et al. 2016) found that GE technology lessened women's work of land preparation and weeding and, in the case of Paraguay (Ezquerro-Cañete 2016), led to an increase in rural–urban migration. Our own work in Uganda exposed how a genetically engineered bacteria-resistant banana would likely increase yields while simultaneously intensifying agricultural labor burdens of women in the central and eastern growing regions (Addison and Schnurr 2016). A study of the orange fleshed sweet potato in Tanzania similarly found commercialization efforts skewed to benefit male over female farmers (Rao and Huggins 2017). More broadly, the very decision by farming households to adopt biotechnology can represent a terrain of gendered struggle and negotiation that requires empirical investigation.

The case study of Bt brinjal[3] showcases how a critical agrarian studies lens can serve to foreground some of these overlooked considerations. This genetically modified variety was developed by India-based Maharasthra Hybrid Seed Company (Mahyco) by introducing the Cry1Ac gene—a crystal protein sourced from *Bacillus thuringiengis*, which confers resistance to insects belonging to the genus Lepitoptera—into brinjal as a single-trait product to control the fruit and shoot borer, a major pest for eggplant farmers (Shelton et al. 2018). Mahyco sourced the Cry1Ac gene from Monsanto, who owns 26 per cent of the Indian company (Kulkarni 2013; Abdelgawad 2015). In 2005, a tripartite agreement was signed between Mahyco, Sathguru Management Consultants and Bangladesh Agricultural Research Institute (BARI), in which Mahyco donated the technology to BARI license-free. At this point the genetic construct was introgressed into nine local Bangladeshi varieties of eggplant (Shelton et al. 2018). Through this P3, Mahyco retains ownership of the technology itself while granting BARI license to test, produce and distribute the seeds (Hammadi 2014). The major donors for the project are the United States Agency for International Development and Cornell University.

Laboratory trials of Bt brinjal were initiated in 2005, followed by confined field trials in 2009. In June 2013, BARI applied to the National Technical Committee for Crop Biotechnology requesting that it recommend commercial release to the National Committee of Biosafety. Approval was granted in October 2013 for the conditional release of four Bt brinjal varieties (Akhter 2016). In January 2014, 20 farmers from across four districts received seedlings from BARI. These numbers swelled in subsequent growing seasons: from 108 farmers in 2014–2015 to 250 in 2015–2016. In 2016–2017, the Department of Agricultural Extension began providing seeds to farmers directly, and adoption rates spiked to over 6000 farmers. This rapid growth continued into the 2017–2018 growing season: a 2018 update written by the project scientists estimates that 27 012 farmers have adopted Bt brinjal, representing approximately 17 per cent of all brinjal farmers in Bangladesh (Shelton et al. 2018).

Recent research undertaken by the technology developer outline the plethora of benefits farmers derive from this biotechnology, including cost savings from reduced pesticide applications, increased incomes and lower health and environmental risks (Meherunnahar and Paul 2009; Shelton et al. 2018). A comparison of pesticide applications between Bt and non-Bt farmers reported that the former sprayed at 25 per cent of the latter's rate, which reduced both the expense on inputs as well as on human labor (Rashid and Hasan 2018). This translated into higher profits for Bt adopters, who reported average net returns of USD $2151/hectare compared to $357/hectare for non-adopters in the 2016–2017 growing season (Shelton et al. 2018). Bt brinjal has been hailed as a success story showcasing how genetically engineered crops can help poor, rural farmers.

Analyzing this case study through the lens of critical agrarian studies reveals the flimsiness of this story of success. First, consider the partnership model underpinning the dissemination of this particular biotechnology. Unlike more traditional GE varieties like Bt cotton or Bt maize that are covered by more restrictive Intellectual Property agreements, farmers who choose to adopt Bt brinjal do not pay a supplemental technology fee to cover Intellectual Property, nor do they sign a stewardship agreement that limits their growing regime (though they are discouraged from replanting by the technology developer; see Shelton et al. 2018). But the arrangements that govern this partnership remain murky: opponents argue that the program's success hinges on hidden subsidies that enable farmers to obtain planting materials and other inputs for free, claiming that the vast majority of farmers would abandon Bt brinjal if they were forced to pay for these (UBINIG 2015; Robinson 2018). Studies elsewhere have shown that sky-high early adoption rates tend to reflect beneficial adoption regimes, and that once these disappear farmer adoption rates plummet (Schnurr 2012). Longitudinal studies are needed to reveal how much of this early success is due to this partnership's incentives and whether this support can be sustained over the long term. Furthermore, Bangladesh's initial approval of Bt brinjal in 2013 stipulated that all GE produce brought to market must be labeled (Akhter 2016). However, in practice farmers and retailers rarely label the Bt brinjal (Roy 2018), preventing consumers from knowing what they are buying.

From an agro-ecological standpoint, while Bt brinjal's resistance to the fruit and shoot borer remains strong, farmers have reported that this biotechnology is more vulnerable to secondary pests and diseases, including whitefly and bacterial wilt, which may undermine much of Bt's competitive advantage (Roy 2018). Additionally, the Bt event donated by Mahyco is a single-trait product, which makes it particularly vulnerable to evolved resistance on the part of its target pest, the fruit and shoot borer. In order to stave off resistance, farmers must plant refuge crops that serve as buffers—generally between 20 and 30 per cent of the entire acreage under the crop. But brinjal producers in Bangladesh are smallholders with an average farm size under a quarter hectare (FAO 2016), and may not have sufficient land to implement this control strategy (similar issues were encountered by smallholders growing Bt cotton in India and Bt maize in South Africa; see Dutta et al. 2014; Fischer and Hajdu 2015).

Finally, a critical agrarian studies lens reveals that the benefits associated with Bt brinjal remain skewed towards larger, wealthier farmers. The only farm-level study that has currently been undertaken classifies all of the Bt adopters as slightly, somewhat or moderately knowledgeable about Bt brinjal, compared to only 30 per cent of non-adopters (Roy 2018). Over 90 per cent of Bt farmers reported frequent or very frequent visits from BARI extension officers, and adopters reported a higher reliance on hybrid seeds than did non-adopters (Roy 2018). These results suggest that biotech adopters have better access to information and enjoy regular visits from extension officers, and have more experience with improved varieties than non-adopters. This corroborates results from elsewhere that suggest that early adopters of biotech varieties tend to be farmers with greater influence and affluence (Schnurr and Addison 2017), reinforcing Glenn Stone's claim about selection bias; that is, that the sample of farmers who adopt early adoption of biotech crops tend to be elite within the broader population (Stone 2012). Another report suggests that farmers who adopted Bt brinjal were regularly supervised by BARI extension officers and that failing plants were replaced—some farmers even stated that the officers essentially controlled the fields and they were not actually aware of the cultivation requirements of the Bt brinjal (UBINIG 2015). This raises questions about cultivation bias; that is, that biotech varieties are prioritized relative to their conventional counterparts, which could further serve to inflate early positive assessments (Stone 2012). In these ways, the case study of Bt brinjal underscores how critical agrarian studies can serve as a useful entry point for nuanced assessments of whether agricultural biotechnology serves the needs of the rural poor.

While the technological capacity of agricultural biotechnology is novel, the process of plant breeding for beneficial traits has a long history that provides a useful lens for evaluating the potential for new technologies to enhance rural development. Scholars within critical agrarian studies have detailed the historical continuities connecting colonial efforts of breeding for yield enhancement, the original Green Revolution and the current commitment to agronomy for development, in which biotechnology features prominently (McCann 2005). Scholars such as Raj Patel (2013) and Jack Kloppenburg (2005) have chronicled how capital accumulation drove previous efforts to extract value from agricultural production, arguing that these efforts privileged wealthier, larger farmers at the expense of smallholders. Currently, critical agrarian studies has tended to dismiss biotechnology as an instrument of industrial agriculture, one that expands the influence of private capital and undermines peasant livelihoods. Biotechnology cannot be reduced to this frame alone. New biotechnologies including genome editing, gene drives and synthetic biology carry enormous potential for remaking agricultural systems. Any new agricultural technology presents opportunities and risks. Yet, most empirical work regarding the farm-level impacts of biotechnology has been carried out by agricultural economists and crop scientists who present arguments that largely support adoption. These perspectives tend to ignore the political economic context of adoption, the complexity of local agricultural systems and the nuanced impacts on class, labor and gender relations, leaving us with a very narrow understanding of how these technologies affect rural development. There is a clear need therefore for critical agrarian studies to engage in a more empirically grounded study of agricultural biotechnology in order to reveal these vital areas of concern.

NOTES

1. Our focus in this chapter is agricultural biotechnology as it applies to plants and crops. However, it is important to mention that biotechnology is also widely used in livestock and aquaculture.
2. Clustered Regularly Interspaced Short Palindromic Repeats.
3. Brinjal is more commonly referred to as eggplant in North America and aubergine in Europe.

FURTHER READING

Kloppenburg, J.R. (2005), *First the Seed: The Political Economy of Plant Biotechnology*, second edition, Madison, WI: University Wisconsin Press.
Lapegna, P. (2015), Popular demobilization, agribusiness mobilization, and the agrarian boom in a post-neoliberal Argentina, *Journal of World Systems Research*, 21(1), 69–87.
Newell, P. (2009), Bio-hegemony: The political economy of agricultural biotechnology in Argentina, *Journal of Latin American Studies*, 41(1), 27–57.
Schnurr, M.A. (2019), *Africa's Gene Revolution: Genetically Modified Crops and the Future of African Agriculture*, Montreal: McGill-Queen's University Press.
Stone, G.D. (2012), Constructing facts: By cotton narratives in India, *Economic and Political Weekly*, 47(38), 62–70.

REFERENCES

Abdelgawad, W. (2015), The Bt brinjal case: The first legal action against Monsanto and its Indian collaborators for biopiracy, *Biotechnology Law Report*, 31(2), 136–139.
Addison, L.; Schnurr, M. (2016), Growing burdens? Disease-resistant genetically modified bananas and the potential gendered implications for labor in Uganda, *Agriculture and Human Values*, 33(4), 967–978.
Akhter, F. (2016), Seed freedom and seed sovereignty: Bangladesh today, in Shiva, V. (ed.), *Seed Sovereignty, Food Security: Women in the Vanguard of the Fight against GMOs and Corporate Agriculture*, Berkeley, CA: North Atlantic Books.

Andersson, J.A.; Sumberg, J. (2017), Knowledge politics in development-oriented agronomy, in Sumberg, J. (ed.), *Agronomy for Development: The Politics of Knowledge in Agricultural Research*, London: Routledge.

Andrée, P. (2007), *Genetically Modified Diplomacy the Global Politics of Agricultural Biotechnology and the Environment*, Vancouver: UBC Press.

Dowd-Uribe, B. (2017), GMOs and poverty: Definitions, methods and the silver bullet paradox, *Canadian Journal of Development Studies*, 38(1), 129–138.

Dowd-Uribe, B.; Schnurr, M.A. (2016), Briefing: Burkina Faso's reversal on genetically modified cotton and the implications for Africa, *African Affairs*, 115(458), 161–172.

Dutta, M.J.; Thaker, J.; Abid, A. (2014), *Bt Brinjal: A Review of Key Debates*, Singapore: National University of Singapore.

Ezquerro-Cañete, A. (2016), Poisoned, dispossessed, and excluded: A critique of the neoliberal soy regime in Paraguay, *Journal of Agrarian Change*, 16(4), 702–710.

Falck-Zapeda, J.; Zambrano, P. (2013), *Gender Impacts of Genetically Engineered Crops in Developing Countries: Final Technical Paper*, Washington, DC: International Development Research Centre.

FAO (2016), *Agricultural Development Economics*, Rome: Food and Agriculture Organization of United Nations.

Fischer, K.; Hajdu, F. (2015), Does raising maize yields lead to poverty reduction? A case study of the massive food production programme in South Africa, *Land Use Policy*, 46c, 304–313.

Flachs, A.; Stone, G.D. (2018), Farmer knowledge across the commodification spectrum: Rice, cotton, and vegetables in Telangana, India, *Journal of Agrarian Change*, 39, 1272–1296.

Gengenbach, H.; Schurman, R.A.; Bassett, T.J.; Munro, W.A.; Moseley, W.G. (2018), Limits of the new green revolution for Africa: Reconceptualising gendered agricultural value chains, *Geographical Journal*, 184(2), 208–214.

Gouse, S.; Sengupta, D.; Zambrano, P.; Zepeda, J.F. (2016), Genetically modified maize: Less drudgery for her, more maize for him? Evidence from smallholder maize farmers in South Africa, *World Development*, 83.C, 27–38.

Hammadi, S. (2014), Bangladeshi farmers caught in row over $600 000 GM aubergine trial, *The Guardian*, accessed 24 September 2018 at www.theguardian.com/environment/2014/jun/05/gm-crop-bangladesh-bt-brinjal.

Ignatova, J.A. (2017), The 'philanthropic' gene: Biocapital and the new green revolution in Africa, *Third World Quarterly*, 38(10), 2258–2275.

Kinchy, A.J. (2012), *Seeds, Science, and Struggle: The Global Politics of Transgenic Crops*, Cambridge, MA: MIT Press.

Klepek, J. (2012), Against the grain: Knowledge alliances and resistance to agricultural biotechnology in Guatemala, *Canadian Journal of Development Studies*, 33(3), 310–325.

Kloppenburg, J.R. (2005), *First the Seed: The Political Economy of Plant Biotechnology*, second edition, Madison, WI: University of Wisconsin Press.

Kloppenburg, J.R. (2010), Impeding dispossession, enabling repossession: Biological open source and the recovery of seed sovereignty, *Journal of Agrarian Change*, 10(3), 367–388.

Kloppenburg, J.R. (2014), Re-purposing the master's tools: The open source seed initiative and the struggle for seed sovereignty, *Journal of Peasant Studies*, 41(6), 1225–1246.

Kulkarni, V. (2013), Bt brinjal: Stunted in India, to grow in Bangladesh, *The Hindu Business Line*, accessed 12 October 2019 at www.thehindubusinessline.com/economy/agri-business/bt-brinjal-stunted-in-india-to-grow-in-bangladesh/article20683306.ece1.

Lapegna, P. (2015), Popular demobilization, agribusiness mobilization, and the agrarian boom in a post-neoliberal Argentina, *Journal of World Systems Research*, 21(1), 69–87.

Leguizamón, A. (2016), Disappearing nature? Agribusiness, biotechnology, and distance in Argentine soybean production, *Journal of Peasant Studies*, 43(2), 313–330.

Levien, M.; Watt, M.; Hairong, Y. (2018), Agrarian Marxism, *Journal of Peasant Studies*, 45(5–6), 853–883.

McCann, J. (2005), *Maize and Grace: Africa's Encounter with a New World Crop, 1500–2000*, Cambridge, MA: Harvard University Press.

McMichael, P. (2013), Value-chain agriculture and debt relations: Contradictory outcomes, *Third World Quarterly*, 34(4), 671–690.

Meherunnahar, M.; Paul, D.N.R. (2009), *Bt Brinjal: Introducing Genetically Modified Brinjal (Eggplant/Aubergine) in Bangladesh*, Falls Church, VA: Bangladesh Development Research Center.

Montenegro de Wit, M. (2019), Beating the bounds: How does 'open source' become a seed commons?, *Journal of Peasant Studies*, 46(1), 44–79.

Morvaridi, B. (2012), Capitalist philanthropy and hegemonic partnerships, *Third World Quarterly*, 33(7) 1191–1210.

Morvaridi, B. (2016), Does sub-Saharan Africa need capitalist philanthropy to reduce poverty and achieve food security?, *Review of African Political Economy*, 43(147) 151–159.

Motta, R. (2016a), *Social Mobilization, Global Capitalism and Struggles over Food: A Comparative Study of Social Movements*, New York: Routledge.

Motta, R. (2016b), Global capitalism and the nation state in the struggles over GM crops in Brazil, *Journal of Agrarian Change*, 16(4), 720–727.

Newell, P. (2009), Bio-hegemony: The political economy of agricultural biotechnology in Argentina, *Journal of Latin American Studies*, 41(1), 27–57.

Patel, R. (2013), The long green revolution, *Journal of Peasant Studies*, 40(1), 1–63.

Rao, S.; Huggins, C. (2017), Sweet 'success': Contesting biofortification strategies to address malnutrition in Tanzania, in Sumberg, J. (ed.), *Agronomy for Development: The Politics of Knowledge in Agricultural Research*, London: Routledge, 104–120.

Rashid, A.; Hasan, K. (2018), Socio-economic performance of Bt eggplant cultivation in Bangladesh, *Bangladesh Journal of Agriculture*, 43(2), 187–203.

Robinson, C. (2018), GM Bt brinjal in Bangladesh: GMO win or smoke and mirrors? *GM Watch*, accessed 24 September 2018 at https://gmwatch.org/en/news/latest-news/18447-gm-bt-brinjal-in-bangladesh-gmo-win-or-smoke-and-mirrors.

Roy, A. (2018), *Understanding the Status of Social License: Adoption of Bt Brinjal in Bangladesh*, Master's thesis, accessed 26 September 2018 at https://harvest.usask.ca/bitstream/handle/10388/8572/ROY-THESIS-2018.pdf?sequence=1&isAllowed=y.

Schnurr, M.A. (2012), Inventing makhathini: Creating a prototype for the dissemination of genetically modified crops into Africa, *Geoforum* 43(4), 784–792.

Schnurr, M.A. (2013), Biotechnology and bio-hegemony in Uganda: Unraveling the social relations underpinning the promotion of genetically modified crops into new African markets, *Journal of Peasant Studies*, 40(4), 639–658.

Schnurr, M.A. (2019), *Africa's Gene Revolution: Genetically Modified Crops and the Future of African Agriculture*, Montreal: McGill-Queen's University Press.

Schnurr, M.A.; Addison, L. (2017), Which variables influence farmer adoption of genetically modified orphan crops? Measuring attitudes and intentions to adopt gm matooke banana in Uganda, *AgBioForum*, 20(2), 133–147.

Schnurr, M.A.; Gore, C. (2015), Getting to 'yes': Governing genetically modified crops in Uganda, *Journal of International Development*, 27(1), 55–72.

Schnurr, M.A.; Addison, L.; Mujabi-Mujuzi, S. (2020), Limits to biofortification: Farmer perspectives on a Vitamin-A enriched banana in Uganda, *Journal of Peasant Studies*, 47(2), 326–345.

Schurman, R. (2017), Building an alliance for biotechnology in Africa, *Journal of Agrarian Change*, 17(3), 441–458.

Schurman, R. (2018), Micro(soft) managing a 'green revolution' for Africa: The new donor culture and international agricultural development, *World Development*, 112, 180–192.

Scoones, I. (2008), Mobilizing against GM crops in India, South Africa and Brazil, *Journal of Agrarian Change*, 8(2), 315–344.

Shelton, A.M.; Hossain, M.; Paranjape, V.; Azad, A.; Rahman, M.; Khan, A.; Prodhan, M.; Rashid, M.; Majumder, R.; Hossain, M.; Hussain, S.; Huesing, J.; McCandless, L. (2018), Bt eggplant project in Bangladesh: History, present status, and future direction, *Frontiers in Bioengineering and Biotechnology*, 6, 1–6.

Soleri, D.; Cleveland, D.A.; Glasgow, G.; Sweeney, S.H.; Cuevas, F.A.; Fuentes, M.R.; Humberto, R.L. (2008), Testing assumptions underlying economic research on transgenic food crops for third world farmers: Evidence from Cuba, Guatemala and Mexico, *Ecological Economics*, 67(4), 667–682.

Stone, G.D. (2012), Constructing facts: By cotton narratives in India, *Economic and Political Weekly*, 47(38), 62–70.

Subramanian, A.; Qaim, M. (2010), The impact of Bt cotton on poor households in rural India, *Journal of Development Studies*, 46(2), 295–311.

Taylor, M. (2020), Hybrid realities: Making a new green revolution for rice in south India, *Journal of Peasant Studies*, 47(3), 483–502.

Thompson, C.B. (2014), Philanthrocapitalism: Appropriation of Africa's genetic wealth, *Review of African Political Economy*, 41(141), 389–405.

UBINIG (Unnayan Bikalper Nitinirdharoni Gobeshona) (2015), *Bt Brinjal Is under 'Life Support': Experiences of Farmers in Second Round Field Cultivation*, Dhaka: UBINIG.

Zambrano, P.; Maldonado, J.H.; Mendoza, S.L.; Ruiz, L.; Fonseca, L.A.; Cardona, I. (2011), *Women Cotton Farmers Their Perceptions and Experiences with Transgenic Varieties: A Case Study for Colombia*, Washington, DC: International Food Policy Research Institute.

48. Agroecology

Nils McCune and Peter Rosset

Popular pressure has caused many multilateral institutions, governments, universities and research centers, some NGOs, corporations and others to finally recognize "agroecology." However, they have tried to redefine it as a narrow set of technologies, to offer some tools that appear to ease the sustainability crisis of industrial food production, while the existing structures of power remain unchallenged. This co-optation of agroecology to fine-tune the industrial food system, while paying lip service to the environmental discourse, has various names, including "climate smart agriculture," "sustainable-" or "ecological-intensification," industrial monoculture production of "organic" food, etc. For us, these are not agroecology: we reject them, and we will fight to expose and block this insidious appropriation of agroecology. The real solutions to the crises of the climate, malnutrition, etc. will not come from conforming to the industrial model. We must transform it and build our own local food systems that create new rural–urban links, based on truly agroecological food production by peasants, artisanal fishers, pastoralists, indigenous peoples, urban farmers, etc. We cannot allow agroecology to be a tool of the industrial food production model: we see it as the essential alternative to that model, and as the means of transforming how we produce and consume food into something better for humanity and our Mother Earth.
(Declaration of the International Forum for Agroecology at Nyéléni, LVC 2015)

INTRODUCTION

Agroecology is simultaneously critical thought, agricultural practice and a social movement that applies ecological and social principles in the organization of sustainable, healthy and fair agri-food systems (Wezel et al. 2009; Gliessman 2014). Also known as low external input sustainable agriculture, agroecology has been practiced for thousands of years in Indigenous and peasant food systems, which have proven capable of feeding populations without exhausting resource bases. The interactive, dialectical relationship between peasant communities and living nature formed a cultural basis for ecological land stewardship that people and social movements across the planet—such as the peasants, family farmers, Indigenous peoples, landless workers, urban agriculturalists, traditional herders and forest dwellers gathered at the Nyéléni International Forum for Agroecology and quoted above—are working to recover, study and spread, within the broader framework of food sovereignty (Altieri and Toledo 2011; Rosset et al. 2011). Due to its unique role within a vast global social movement that represents the unity of peoples, movements and organizations with highly distinct historical experiences, agroecology can also be understood as the result of an emerging decolonizing dialogue between traditional non-Western knowledge systems and modern, transdisciplinary academic ways of understanding the world. The agroecological "dialogue of ways of knowing" also includes the interactions among concepts from distinct social subjects in the rural world, such as rural proletarians, peasants and Indigenous peoples (Martínez-Torres and Rosset 2014).

After passing decades marginalized by mainstream Green Revolution thinking, agroecology is rapidly coming to be included in discussions and debates in international scientific and policy circles. However, considerable contention over the meaning and significance of agroecology is shedding light on already existing tensions between class and social forces that reflect opposing models for food systems and society as a whole, in a context of catastrophic environmental change (Giraldo and Rosset 2018; Giraldo and McCune 2019).

Across the planet, grassroots agrarian movements increasingly adopt agroecology into their historical praxis—and discourse—as an on-the-ground alternative to corporate-dominated industrial agriculture (Martínez-Torres and Rosset 2014), and academic programs are including agroecology as an emerging discipline that combines ecology with agronomy, anthropology and rural sociology, as well as action-based, socially committed methods (Dalgaard et al. 2003; Méndez et al. 2013). For movements, agroecology has a very important political character—it is feminist, anti-colonial and anti-capitalist (LVC 2017).

At the same time, agribusiness corporations are busy developing their own version of agroecology, as a technical approach that integrates some ecological principles into conventional management practices (see CropLife 2018). In this way, transnational capital is attempting to co-opt the language of agroecology and limit its emancipatory potential (Giraldo and Rosset 2018). Global institutions such as the United Nations' Food and Agriculture Organization (FAO) have developed processes to stimulate public policy in favor of agroecology, but these policies also tend to use a very narrow understanding of agroecology—often confusing it with the substitution of synthetic inputs by organic inputs without challenging the structures of monoculture (Rosset and Altieri 1997).

The scramble to define and contain agroecology is mirrored in the debate over agroecology's future. If transnational agricultural input corporations have their way, agroecology will ultimately provide a set of ecologically sound technologies and organic inputs sourced from across the globe that will be incorporated into the toolset of conventional, capitalist agriculture. In this sense, the discourse of sustainable intensification, climate-smart agriculture and even the scale-neutral organic model largely serves to disperse the social pressure for transforming food systems and confuse the debate by presenting green-washed, corporate-friendly "sustainable" agriculture.

On the other hand, if the diverse global movements that have emerged to fight neoliberal hegemony continue to grow, mobilize and train people using agroecological thought (McCune et al. 2014), then agroecology may be a fundamental pillar of a popular and comprehensive agrarian reform (LVC 2017) and the rebuilt peasant sector may be the critical social actor that, along with popular subjects from the cities, reconstructs local and regional economies and sustainable food systems. Doing so would require the consolidation of a counter-hegemonic historical bloc capable of disarticulating the corporations that represent the unsustainable dominant agri-food system, and would involve simultaneously replacing resource-dependent industrial techniques with agroecological management and radically transforming the agrarian and political structures of inequality that currently sustain the corporate food regime (Levidow et al. 2014; Giraldo and Rosset 2018). La Via Campesina's 7th International Conference, held in Euskal Herria in 2017, employed the slogan, "We feed our peoples and build the movement to change the world." Rural social movements work at local, national and international levels to build momentum for the recovery of food systems using agroecology.

This chapter will examine the multiple meanings of agroecology as science, practice and movement. Then, it will summarize some of the key current debates around agroecology, both in terms of politics and as a transdisciplinary realm of science. Throughout, the chapter uses tables to clarify key concepts in agroecology. The chapter will end citing the five main reasons

Table 48.1   Key concepts in debates on food and agriculture

Food system
The entire, scale-dependent process that includes interacting components and activities related to production, distribution, processing and consumption of food, including the manufacture of farming inputs, the management of genetic diversity, energy and water, as well as the impact of this process on people and the environment.
Monoculture
A type of agricultural production focused on single crops in large areas, where economies of scale and capital-intensive technologies can be applied to diminish the labor required per unit of production.
Polyculture
Found in all Indigenous food systems, a type of agricultural production based on spatial (intercropping) and/or temporal (crop rotation) diversity, emphasizing the complementarity of distinct plant and animal components, diminishing the amount of area required per unit of production.

that agrarian movements across the globe are coming to embrace and lay claim to agroecology. Agroecology is immersed in peasant questions, territorial reconfigurations and the tensions between institutional politics and social mobilization. Looking forward, the relevance of these tensions is likely to grow as agroecology represents one of the most available, accessible and decentralized solutions to cataclysmic global climate change.

WHAT IS AGROECOLOGY?

Agroecology stems from the accumulation of knowledge about nature through Indigenous and traditional farming and food production systems over centuries. Using their intricate local knowledge, traditional peasant farmers have maintained high levels of biodiversity associated with their farming systems, developing agroecosystems that cycle nutrients through closed systems, maintain soil fertility and need very few external inputs (Gliessman 2014). In its contemporary usage (following Wezel et al. 2009), agroecology is variously known as:

- the science that studies and attempts to explain the functioning of agroecosystems, primarily concerned with biological, biophysical, ecological, social, cultural, economic and political mechanisms, functions, relationships and design;
- a set of practices that permit farming in a more sustainable way, without using dangerous chemicals; and
- a movement that seeks to make farming more ecologically sustainable and more socially just.

Agroecology as a science and a movement has been built upon the rejection of the main tenets of the Green Revolution, namely that crop genetics and the application of purchased synthetic chemicals to monoculture plantations is the most efficient way to produce food (see Table 48.1). The basic assumptions of high-input, industrial agriculture have led to enormous negative externalities, in terms of resource depletion, air, land and water pollution, and greenhouse gas (GHG) emissions, at the same time as they have concentrated power over food systems in the hands of a few large corporations, and contributed to the deterioration of the health of farm workers and consumers (Lappé et al. 1998).

Agroecology is the science that considers the ecology of food systems (Francis et al. 2003). At the same time, however, agroecology has emerged globally since the 1980s as a response to the devastating impacts of agricultural modernization—a sort of counter-proposal to industrial agriculture (Holt-Gimenez and Shattuck 2011; Gliessman 2013). As such, it encompasses a science that understands farms as ecosystems, a set of productive practices that incorporate ecological principles into farming and a global social process of people becoming engaged with farming and food systems (Wezel et al. 2009). Agroecology as a science combines peasant and Indigenous knowledge with agronomy and systems ecology, in a scaled, systemic approach that recognizes biological, social, cultural and economic factors of complexity. As a set of productive principles, agroecology emphasizes nutrient cycling, energy and water efficiency, enhanced above- and below-ground biological diversity and a fundamental reliance on locally available resources and knowledge, such as that found in Indigenous polycultures the world over (Gliessman 2014). The United Nations Special Rapporteur on the Right to Food recognized in 2010 that agroecological farming could double food production in many parts of the world, and with lower usage of water and energy resources (De Schutter 2010).

The industrial agribusiness model is currently the world's largest contributor of GHG emissions. In 2011, the research organization GRAIN added together the combined impact of conventional agriculture, including the advancing agricultural frontier's responsibility for 70–90 per cent of global deforestation (this portion of global land use changes add up to 15–18 per cent of total GHG emissions), on-farm emissions (11–15 per cent of global total), food processing, transport, packaging and retail (15–20 per cent of GHG emissions) and decomposition of organic waste (3–4 per cent of emissions) to find that 44–57 per cent of all global GHG emissions are directly related to the industrial food system. The alternative—a model based upon relatively small, diversified farms that use only local resources and create mixed, complementary systems of crops, livestock and trees to produce healthy food with an emphasis on local and regional markets—could potentially slow, stop and even reverse global climate change through widespread and diverse agroforestry systems, but this would require radical reversals in the forms and tendencies of land purchases, agricultural subsidies and global trade (GRAIN 2009).

As a science, agroecology developed the concept of an agroecosystem, which is any type of farm unit, seen and analyzed as an ecosystem (Gliessman 2014). Agroecosystems are themselves comprised of various subsystems, or components, which interact with one another to produce outputs (see Table 48.2). In more sustainable agroecosystems, these outputs include both food products for harvest, as well as ecological services that contribute to maintaining and enhancing the productive capacity of the system, such as soil fertility, water retention capacity, biodiversity and favorable microclimates.

One of the guiding principles of agroecology is that the more the interactions between agroecosystem components resemble those that occur in natural ecosystems, the more likely the agroecosystem is to be sustainable over time (Altieri 1999). In natural ecosystems, components such as plants (primary producers), herbivores (primary consumers), predators (secondary consumers) and soil fungi (decomposers) engage in highly complex, reciprocal interactions. The complexity of these interactions helps ensure that energy (which enters the ecosystem as sunlight), nutrients (which generally enter by tree root uptake) and water (entering as precipitation) are recycled over and over within an ecosystem. This is called ecological efficiency. Agroecological design refers to the creation of agroecosystems with complex, circular flows of energy, nutrients and water, in order to maximize total system productivity (food products + ecological services) using a minimum of external inputs like fertilizer or irrigation water. By following nature's lead, agroecologists look to produce a sustainable yield that can be

Table 48.2   Key concepts within agroecology as a science

Agroecosystem
The basic unit of analysis. Any type of farm unit, understood as an ecosystem with inputs, outputs and internal subsystems or components.
Inputs
These include everything that enters the agroecosystem, including both purchased farm inputs, such as fertilizers, electricity and pesticides, as well as unpurchased inputs like sunshine and rain.
Outputs
In an agroecosystem, these include yields which are removed from the systems, as well as waste products, and mineral losses in runoff, erosion or leaching. Outputs also include ecological services such as water quality, biodiversity, pollination and carbon sequestration, among others.
Components
Parts of the overall agroecosystem that interact with inputs and other components. For example, the soil component interacts with the seed component and the water component. Each component is in turn made up of subcomponents (in the case of soil, this includes minerals, organic matter, ecological decomposers and roots).

ecologically maintained over time and prove resilient even in challenging conditions, such as droughts, hurricanes or economic crises.

One of the most important aspects of agroecology is the crucial role of human beings, who both manage the system and benefit from the outputs of the system. In Indigenous agricultural systems, land produces many goods: diverse, year-round nutritious food, several types of fuel, fodder, medicines and materials for building shelter and clothing. Ecological land management also produces clean water, moderate temperatures, resistance to natural and human-made disasters and conditions favorable to community function. This is important because it leads to the next meaning of agroecology: less as science and more as sustainable practices implemented by people in harmony with the land.

Agroecology as a practice should be ecologically sound, socially just and economically viable. In agroecological farming, a set of productive, ecological and ethical principles are applied, not as a "technical package" but as guiding principles, to be creatively adapted to each biophysical, climatic, social, cultural and political context (Rosset and Altieri 2017). A fundamental difference exists between agroecological principles and the practices that people carry out in agroecosystems (see Table 48.3). Agroecological principles are universal, because they are pillars necessary for ecosystems to function. In contrast to principles, agroecological practices are context-specific and depend on local conditions. For example, oxen ploughs may be appropriate in one agroecosystem that is largely flat or lightly undulated, but inappropriate for applying to a neighbor's sloped agroecosystem. Research in agroecology treats agricultural problems as symptoms of underlying structural problems caused by imbalances among agroecosystem components. As such, agroecological management generally focuses on prevention, rather than treatment, of pests, weeds and low soil fertility, through cropping patterns, recycling of manures and crop residues, as well as maintenance of farm agrobiodiversity (Morales and Perfecto 2000; Gliessman 2014).

Indigenous and traditional peasant agricultures provide crucial examples and knowledge systems for agroecological practice (Gliessman et al. 1981; see Table 48.4). The relationship between people and the land is more complex in Indigenous and peasant culture than in the modern, market-based real estate model of land relations. Many Indigenous peoples and nations understand the concept of Mother Earth as being more accurate than simply saying land, because Mother Earth implies a relationship of belonging, rather than ownership.

Table 48.3   Key principles for applying agroecology as practice

Agrobiodiversity
The use, management and conservation of both planned and unplanned biodiversity in farms, including crops and animals as well as tree and bird species, arthropods and soil organisms. Practices may incorporate agrobiodiversity over time (as rotations, relay crops and/or succession) and in space (as intercropping, hedgerows, contour strips, home gardens, etc.), in either case, resulting in facilitation, or one component's creation of better conditions for another component.
Nutrient cycling
The flows, captures and exchanges of nutrients among agroecosystem components. This takes place fundamentally through the decomposition of organic matter and nutrient intake through roots, but it also can include the use of on-farm sources of animal feed, composts and legume species.
Energy efficiency
The ability of an agroecosystem to effectively harness solar energy through photosynthesis, and then manage biomass in order to maximize ecological processes and nutrient cycling. Also refers to the minimum use of fossil fuels, and their replacement by renewable, animal or human energy.
Water efficiency
The ability of an agroecosystem to harness and cycle water among components. This may have to do with managing shade and temperature, as well as capturing rainwater, improving soil water retention capacity and switching to drought-resistant varieties.
Conservation of genetic resources
The activities that people do in order to maintain available stock of the seeds, stalks, bulbs and/or animal races that are adapted to local conditions, especially those conserved for generations. This includes seed saving, local plant and animal breeding, seed exchanges among farmers and active protection of local varieties from genetic contamination or replacement.

Agroecological practice, then, becomes a long-term relationship between Mother Earth and human beings who belong to Earth. In this sense, agroecological production implies reciprocity, care, nurture, stewardship and protection of nature.

In highly industrialized countries, where there are many approaches to alternative agriculture, such as permaculture, organic agriculture, biodynamic and biointensive systems, among others, agroecology may arguably encompass all of these tendencies (De Schutter 2010), or none. While all shifts toward new and more sustainable relationships with nature are part of an agroecological transition, agroecology has specifically political dimensions that often are lacking in other forms of alternative agriculture. For example, agroecology has an emphasis on recovering "invisible" forms of knowledge; rather than simply implementing a productive system on a "new" piece of land, an agroecological approach would seek to recover the agrarian knowledge of the place and find native seeds and traditional rotations and tools, while integrating external knowledge or technologies in a dialogical manner. This interest in sociocultural recovery sets agroecology apart from other approaches. In colonized lands such as the current United States, agroecology involves the recognition of the Indigenous peoples who have been dispossessed, as well as the historical experience of African diaspora people, for whom centuries of farming were carried out in bondage, as well as the contemporary exploitation of migrant workers in agriculture, including organics (Ramírez and Taylor 2018). The concept of restorative justice is particularly relevant for agroecology as a practice and movement.

Just as the notion of agroecosystems includes agronomic, ecological and cultural criteria to broaden the ideas around land, agroecology also broadens the thinking about people who take care of the land, including such notions as biocultural resistance (Toledo and Barrera-Bassols 2008) and food justice (Sbicca 2018). A simplified way of understanding this is by thinking about squeezing value out of things, or exploitation. Rather than the classic argument for land

Table 48.4   Examples of agroecological production systems

Name	Description	Agroecological principles at work
Milpa intercropped with fruit trees	Milpa is a traditional Mesoamerican polyculture usually including maize, bean, squash, tomato, chili peppers, melons and various flavorful herbs.	Facilitation = beans fix nitrogen, benefiting maize; maize provides structure for climbing bean; squash prevents weeds and reduces soil temperature. Soil conservation = root systems of fruit trees prevent erosion.
Fish-duck-rice paddy systems	Traditional Chinese rice paddies include fish, ducks and diverse vegetables planted on borders of terrace fields.	Facilitation = fish eliminate weeds and pests, benefiting rice; rice leaf shade cools water. Nutrient cycling = ducks and fish oxygenate water and provide nutrients for rice.
Quesungal	Mesoamerican system of accommodating forest species and annual crops by applying heavy pruning of trees before planting annuals.	Nutrient cycling = heavy pruning provides a thick layer of organic matter. Energy efficiency = allows more light to reach soil during peak seasonal need. Water efficiency = organic matter layer cools and shades soil, improving water retention.
Shade coffee	Agroforestry system in which coffee bushes are underneath a canopy of diverse tree species, providing habitat for forest species, especially birds.	Facilitation = trees reduce weeds by reducing sunlight and adding leaf litter. Nutrient cycling = deep roots extract nutrients from subsoil, then cycles them into system. Energy efficiency = coffee plants receive needed sunlight, and trees pick up enough to provide ecosystem services.
Diversified home gardens	Ubiquitous ancient system of herb, spice and medicine gardens under shade near the home.	Water efficiency = shade trees cool soil temperature, intercropped plants share water. Conservation of genetic resources = seeds, culinary and medicinal knowledge are saved.
Dehesa	Mediterranean agrosilvopastoral system producing cattle, goats, sheep, pigs and forest products on communal land forested with oaks that also provide cork.	Nutrient cycling = grazing animals fertilize grasses and trees. Conservation of genetic resources = wild game, honey bees, mushrooms and other traditional food sources are maintained.

reform, "exploit land, not people," agroecology proposes to "exploit neither land nor people" in opposition to monoculture agribusiness, which "exploits both land and people." The vastly different stance of agroecology signifies that it has a strong ethical-political component. To practice agroecology is to take a stance against all forms of exploitation. The global agroecology movement has very clear political dimensions, because it is based on popular control over seeds and genetic resources, water, land and territory (see Table 48.5).

For global movements that advocate agroecology, such as La Vía Campesina, agroecology without food sovereignty runs the risk of being a purely technical solution, as were the Green Revolution technologies that preceded it (LVC 2015). At the same time, food sovereignty without agroecology is an abstract framework that provides working people with little in terms of tangible strategies for developing alternatives. This is why both agroecology and food sovereignty are best together, as a combined approach of theory and practice that includes both daily actions (building composts, planting hedgerows, holding workshops for local consumers) as well as global, historical solutions (peasant and farm worker united movements, including food sovereignty in national constitutions) to the hunger-amidst-plenty model of corporate, chemical agriculture and food. Rather than seeing hunger as an excuse for more resource-intensive production of food commodities, the food sovereignty-through-agroecology approach sees

Table 48.5   *Key concepts for the movement form of agroecology*

Redistributive land reform
A political process that facilitates access to physical spaces where agroecology can occur, based on the criteria of social justice and ecological sustainability. An urgent need for the agroecology movement, since land grabbing has limited availability of farm land for local food systems.
Territory
Area of land or place pertaining to, or combined with, a specific people, history, culture, language, knowledge, agriculture, food, sovereignty, tradition and the sense of belonging. Often legally recognized for Indigenous peoples but rarely respected in practice.
Peasant and Indigenous knowledge
Accumulated experience, practice, philosophy, cosmovision and know-how applied to agroecological production. Agroecological knowledges are diverse and they can be shared but are not for packaging and selling as "climate-smart agriculture" or "sustainable intensification."
Food sovereignty
The collective right or authority of peoples to govern, protect or defend food systems, recovering knowledge, promoting local economies and preventing corporations from controlling food systems. A political-historical model of popular participation to replace capitalist agribusiness with democratic assembly-style governance of food systems, comprehensive and popular agrarian reform, complete rights for women and agroecological production.
Equality for non-men
The right of women, youth, elders and, in general, non-men to be full subjects of food system transformation. In large part, this means recognizing women's unique historical contribution to creating agriculture and their sustained, monumental labor in guaranteeing food sovereignty, health and well-being, and peasant agricultural systems, as well as their role in agroecological movements and organizations for social and political change.

hunger as a violation of the right of peoples to produce their own food, through access to land, seeds, water and agroecological knowledge. This challenges the conventional consumer/producer dichotomy, and encourages creative organizational forms such as community-supported agriculture, urban agriculture and food cooperatives (Chappell 2018; Sbicca 2018).

Two of the world's most significant agroecological transitions have taken place since 1990. The liberalization of the global coffee market, beginning with the dismantling of the International Coffee Agreement in 1989, led to an overproduction crisis and a drastic fall in coffee prices over the next decade and a half. In response, millions of coffee farmers around the world adopted agroecological methods, and the production of organic coffee soared (Raynolds et al. 2007). Rather than shift from purchased conventional inputs to purchased organic inputs, as imagined by most theories of agroecological transition, many coffee farmers simply stopped using purchased inputs of any kind, while others began incorporating shade trees in order to recreate ecological processes of fertility and pest management (Martínez-Torres 2006). However, the high price of organic certification, a drop in the prices of organic coffee and the eventual (and partial) recovery of conventional coffee prices have led to stagnation in the agroecological transition of global coffee farms (Bacon 2005).

In Cuba, the possibility of importing conventional farm inputs and petroleum disappeared with the destruction of the socialist bloc and the tightening of the United States embargo in the early 1990s. In the absence of industrial inputs, Cuba began a widespread transition toward agroecological techniques, implementing a combination of traditional peasant practices and technical knowledge from Cuban researchers who had been warning for years of the need to transition to sustainable agriculture. The development of a horizontal social movement methodology, Campesino-a-Campesino (peasant-to-peasant), for spreading agroecology in the Cuban context and through the leadership of the National Association of Small Farmers (*Asociación Nacional de Agricultores Pequeños*), led to an agroecological transition that had reached over 200,000 farmers by 2010 and continues to grow (Machín et al. 2010; Rosset et al. 2011). The examples of coffee and Cuba, which go beyond individual farm-level transitions mediated by the market, point to the need to transcend conventional neoclassical economics in order to plan, organize and implement agroecological transitions at landscape, national and international levels (van der Ploeg 2009).

AGROECOLOGY TO CONFORM VERSUS AGROECOLOGY TO TRANSFORM

Agroecology has been defined in very different terms by the distinct food system actors. As climate variability increasingly puts the profit margin of industrial monoculture at risk, and market-based mechanisms continue to dominate institutional approaches to handling environmental destruction, a new sort of "agroecology" is appearing on the agenda of international institutions, including "climate-smart agriculture" and "sustainable intensification," as options to be folded into conventional agribusiness value chains (LVC 2015). The purely technical version of agroecology, and its incorporation into the vacuous, dominant "win–win" discourse, has been denounced as a case of co-optation and domestication of the emancipatory demands of popular sectors (Giraldo and Rosset 2018; Copeland 2019).

In Rome, on September 18–19, 2014, the FAO held its first ever official event on agroecology. At the International Symposium on Agroecology for Food Security and Nutrition some 400 participants heard from more than 50 experts, including academic professors, researchers, the private sector, government officials and leaders of civil society organizations and social movements. "Today a window was opened in what for 30 years has been the cathedral of the Green Revolution," said FAO Director-General José Graziano da Silva in his closing remarks to the symposium. "Agroecology continues to grow, both in science and in policies. It is an approach that will help to address the challenge of ending hunger and malnutrition in all its forms, in the context of the climate change adaptation needed." He added that the problems facing the world are so great that we must pursue all approaches, affirming that "agroecology represents a promising option and is one possibility among others, such as genetically modified organisms (GMOs) and reducing the use of chemicals" (FAO 2015), thus echoing the position of the World Bank and Monsanto. This view is diametrically opposed by agroecologists, who typically argue that GMOs and agroecology are incompatible and cannot coexist (Rosset and Altieri 1997).

AGROECOLOGY, LAND REFORM AND FOOD SOVEREIGNTY

Van der Ploeg (2014, 48) notes that to qualitatively transform the global food system, agroecology needs a social carrier: a group whose "own emancipation (the struggle for its own interests and prospects) strongly *coincides* with the defense and further development of agro-ecological practices" (emphasis in original). He further concludes that the peasantry is the only possible such social driver of the agroecological transition (Calle-Collado and Gallar 2010; Sevilla-Guzman and Woodgate 2013) on a sociohistorical scale. Agroecological thinking posits a critical interpretation of capitalist development and global inequality, disputing the "neoliberal ecological rationality" (Wittman 2010) that guides agribusiness and the consolidation of the global food system by corporations under the guise of efficiency (Altieri and Toledo 2011). As an offspring of the classical agrarian question, agroecological social theory sees small farmers and the peasantry as part of the working classes, rather than petty bourgeois commodity producers (Moyo et al. 2013; Sevilla-Guzmán and Woodgate 2013). Global resistance to the corporate food regime (Friedmann and McMichael 1989) is growing, in the form of agroecological labor-based intensification (Van der Ploeg 2009), as communities reorder natural and social resources to meet local needs into the future (McCune et al. 2016).

AGROECOLOGY AND THE PEASANTRY

The relevance of peasant studies to contemporary agroecology is significant. Eduardo Sevilla-Guzmán and other rural sociologists have traced the origins of agroecological thought in social science and social theory to neo-Narodnism and libertarian heterodox Marxism (Sevilla-Guzmán and Woodgate 2013). Marx (1991 [1894], 949) noted that capitalist property relations "provoke an irreparable rift in the interdependent process of social metabolism, a metabolism described by the natural laws of life itself." Primitive accumulation associated with the European invasion of the Americas and slave economies became the primordial means for de-peasantization, on one hand, and the development of imperialist and industrial powers on the other. Subsequent development of agricultural capitalism and proletarianization, in each specific context, were by no means endogenous transitions, but rather related to the expansion of a global capitalist economic system (Wallerstein 1979).

Peasants are often defined by their deep connection with and control over the farming activities occurring in a specific place, self-organization of labor at the family level and emergence as a social class whose economic activity is subordinated to capital, yet not capitalist (Bryceson 2000). Jan Douwe van der Ploeg (2009) puts forth a theoretical proposition about the peasantries of today. Rather than defining "peasant," he chooses to define what he calls "the peasant condition," or the "peasant principle," characterized by the constant struggle to build autonomy: central to the peasant condition, then, is the struggle for autonomy that takes place in a context characterized by dependency relations, marginalization and deprivation. The peasant principle materializes as the creation and development of a self-controlled and self-managed resource base through permanent interactions between cultural and biological processes. The territorial systems of peasant agroecology demonstrate a capacity to strategically engage or disengage with the market, based upon the internal decision-making and logic of families and communities whose goal is to remain on the land. This relative autonomy from market forces combines with the conversion of present production into the factors of future production, which may manifest as seed saving, animal breeding, soil improvement, toolmaking, or other activities that connect farming with itself over time, to limit dependencies upon external capital.

Political agroecology has its foundations in agrarian social thought and movements that emerged in opposition to early processes of agricultural industrialization and has developed in an ongoing dialectic between capitalist modernization and resistance to it. Thus, agroecology is viewed as an applied science embedded in a social context, problematizing capitalist relations of production and allying itself with agrarian social movements. In this regard, agroecology was greatly influenced in Latin America by the ongoing debates between *descampesinistas* (de-peasantizers), who predicted the eventual disappearance of the peasantry (*campesinado*), and the *campesinistas* (peasantists), who believed that the peasantry could continue to reproduce itself at the margins of the capitalist economy (Rosset and Altieri 2017).

According to van der Ploeg (2010), peasants may pursue agroecology to the extent that it permits them to strengthen their resource base and become more autonomous of input and credit markets (and thus indebtedness) while improving their conditions. This use of agroecology to move along a continuum from dependency toward relative autonomy—from being the entrepreneurial farmers they in some cases had become, toward being peasants again—is one axis of what he calls "re-peasantization" (2009). Another axis of re-peasantization is the conquest of land and territory from agribusiness and other large landowners, whether by land reform, land occupations or other mechanisms (Rosset and Martínez-Torres 2012). When farmers undergo a transition from input-dependent farming to agroecology based on local resources, they are becoming "more peasant," as found in cases in the Caribbean, Central America and Europe (van der Ploeg 2009; Steckley and Weis 2016; McCune et al. 2019). Agroecological practices are similar to, and frequently based upon, traditional peasant practices, so in this transition re-peasantization takes place.

In marking the difference between the ecological and social wasteland of agribusiness-controlled land and land recovered through ecological farming, peasants are reconfiguring territories as peasant, peasant-worker and peasant-Indigenous territories, as they re-peasantize them through agroecology (McCune and Sánchez 2018). Conversely, when peasants are drawn into greater dependence, use of industrial agricultural technologies, market relations and the debt cycle, this is one axis of "de-peasantization." Another axis of de-peasantization is when land-grabbing corporations or states displace peasants from their land and territories and reconfigure these as territories for agribusiness, mining, tourism or infrastructure development (Rosset and Martínez-Torres 2012). The twin processes of re- and de-peasantization move back and forth over time as circumstances change (van der Ploeg 2009). During the heyday of the Green Revolution in the 1960s and 1970s, the peasantry was incorporated en masse into the system, many of them becoming entrepreneurial family farmers. But today, faced with growing debt and market-driven exclusion, the net tendency is the reverse, according to van der Ploeg (2009, 2010). He presents convincing data to show that even those farmers in Northern countries most integrated into the market are in fact taking (at least small) steps toward becoming "more peasant" through relatively greater autonomy from banks, input and machinery suppliers and corporate intermediaries. Some even become organic farmers. In other words, there is a net retreat from some or many elements of the market (Rosset and Martínez-Torres 2012).

CONCLUSIONS

We are increasingly witnessing a global territorial conflict, material and immaterial, between agribusiness and diverse resistances (Rosset and Martínez-Torres 2012), including by peasants, organized urban communities and Indigenous peoples. In this context we see the post-1992 emergence of La Vía Campesina, arguably the world's largest transnational social movement (Desmarais 2007; Martinez-Torres and Rosset 2010), promoting agroecologically diversified farming, as a key element in resistance, re-peasantization and the reconfiguration of territories (Sevilla-Guzmán 2006; Sevilla-Guzmán and Alier 2006). Of course, this somewhat stylized dichotomy should in no way be taken to imply that there is no longer a significant number of medium-scale farmers who still maintain both agribusiness and peasant identities. Many organized peasant- and Indigenous-based agrarian movements, such as La Vía Campesina, consider that only by changing the export-led, free trade-based, industrial agriculture model of large farms can the downward spiral of poverty, low wages, rural–urban migration, hunger and environmental degradation be halted (LVC 2013).

These movements embrace the concept of agroecology as a pillar of food sovereignty which focuses on local autonomy, local markets and community action for access and control of land, water, agrobiodiversity, etc., which are of central importance for communities to be able to produce food locally. Many peasant and Indigenous organizations have adopted agroecology as the technological basis of small-scale farming and actively promote it among its thousands of members via farmer-to-farmer networks and grassroots educational processes (Rosset and Martínez-Torres 2012; LVC 2013; McCune and Sánchez 2018; McCune et al. 2017). Agroecology also holds enormous potential in urban settings and is increasingly taken on as a pillar of food justice struggles (Chappell 2018; Sbicca 2018).

The following are the five main reasons why agroecology has been embraced by many social rural movements (Rosset and Altieri 2017):

1. Agroecology is a socially activating tool for the transformation of rural realities through collective action and is a key building block in the construction of food sovereignty, meaning healthy food for peasant and farm families and for local markets.
2. Agroecology is a culturally acceptable approach as it builds upon traditional and popular knowledge and promotes a dialogue of wisdoms with more Western scientific approaches.
3. Agroecology allows human beings to live in harmony with, and take care of, our Mother Earth.
4. Agroecology provides economically viable techniques by emphasizing the use of Indigenous knowledge, agrobiodiversity and local resources, avoiding dependence on external inputs, thus helping to build relative autonomy.
5. Agroecology helps peasant families and communities adapt to and resist the effects of climate change.

FURTHER READING

Gliessman, S.R. (2014), *Agroecology: The Ecology of Sustainable Food Systems*, Boca Raton, FL: CRC Press.

La Via Campesina (2015), Agroecology for food sovereignty and Mother Earth, *Notebook No. 7*, Harare: Via Campesina.

Patel, R. (2012), *Stuffed and Starved: The Hidden Battle for the World Food System*, Brooklyn, NY: Melville House Publishing.

Perfecto, I.; Vandermeer, J.H.; Wright, A.L. (2009), *Nature's Matrix: Linking Agriculture, Conservation and Food Sovereignty*, London: Routledge.

Shiva, V. (2016), *Who Really Feeds the World? The Failures of Agribusiness and the Promise of Agroecology*, Berkeley, CA: North Atlantic Books.

REFERENCES

Altieri, M.A. (1999), The ecological role of biodiversity in agroecosystems, *Agriculture, Ecosystems and Environment*, 74, 19–31.

Altieri, M.A.; Toledo, V.M. (2011), The agroecological revolution in Latin America: Rescuing nature, ensuring food sovereignty and empowering peasants, *Journal of Peasant Studies*, 38(3), 587–612.

Bacon, C. (2005), Confronting the coffee crisis: Can fair trade, organic, and specialty coffees reduce small-scale farmer vulnerability in northern Nicaragua?, *World Development*, 33(3), 497–511.

Bryceson, D.F. (2000), Peasant theories and smallholder policies: Past and present, in Bryceson, D.F.; Kay, C.; Mooij, J. (eds), *Disappearing Peasantries*, London: Intermediate Technology Publications, 1–36.

Calle-Collado, Á.; Gallar, D. (2010), Agroecología Política: transición social y campesinado, Paper presented at the VII Congreso Latinoamericano de Sociologia Rural, November 15–19.

Chappell, J. (2018), *Beginning to End Hunger: Food and the Environment in Belo Horizonte, Brazil and Beyond*, Berkeley, CA: University of California Press.

Copeland, N. (2019), Meeting peasants where they are: Cultivating agroecological alternatives in neoliberal Guatemala, *Journal of Peasant Studies*, 46(4), 831–852.

CropLife (2018), How much do you know about agroecology? *Plant Science Post*, accessed May 5, 2019 at www.croplife.org/news/agroecology-quiz/.

Dalgaard, T.; Hutchings, N.J.; Porter, J.R. (2003), Agroecology, scaling and interdisciplinarity, *Agriculture, Ecosystems and Environment*, 100(1), 39–51.

De Schutter, O. (2010), Report submitted by the Special Rapporteur on the right to food, Olivier De Schutter, United Nations Human Rights Council, 16th session, agenda item 3.

Desmarais, A.A. (2007), *La Vía Campesina: Globalization and the Power of Peasants*, Halifax: Fernwood Publishing; London: Pluto Press.

FAO (2015), Final Report for the International Symposium on Agroecology for Food Security and Nutrition 18 and 19 September 2014, Rome.

Francis, C.; Lieblein, G.; Gliessman, S.R.; Breland, T.A.; Creamer, N.; Harwood Salomonsson, L. et al. (2003), Agroecology: The ecology of food systems, *Journal of Sustainable Agriculture*, 22(3), 99–118.

Friedmann, H.; McMichael, P. (1989), Agriculture and the state system: The rise and decline of national agricultures, 1870 to the present, *Sociologia Ruralis*, 29(2), 93–117.

Giraldo, O.F.; McCune, N. (2019), Can the state take agroecology to scale? Public policy experiences in agroecological territorialization from Latin America, *Agroecology and Sustainable Food Systems*, 43(7–8), 785–809.

Giraldo, O.F.; Rosset, P.M. (2018), Agroecology as a territory in dispute: Between institutionality and social movements, *Journal of Peasant Studies*, 45(3), 545–564.

Gliessman, S.R. (2013), Agroecology: Growing the roots of resistance, *Agroecology and Sustainable Food Systems*, 37(1), 19–31.

Gliessman, S.R. (2014), *Agroecology: The ecology of sustainable food systems*, Boca Raton, CO: CRC Press.

Gliessman, S.R.; Garcia, R.E.; Amador, M.A. (1981), The ecological basis for the application of traditional agricultural technology in the management of tropical agro-ecosystems, *Agro-ecosystems*, 7(3), 173–185.

GRAIN (2009), The climate crisis is a food crisis. Small farmers can cool the planet. A way out of the *mayhem* caused by the industrial food system, PowerPoint slides, accessed July 19, 2021 at www.grain.org/article/entries/4168-smallfarmers-can-cool-the-planet-presentation.

GRAIN (2011), *Food and Climate Change: The Forgotten Link*, accessed May 17, 2019 at www.grain.org/e/4357-food-and-climate-change-the-forgotten-link.

Holt-Giménez, E.; Shattuck, A. (2011), Food crises, food regimes and food movements: rumblings of reform or tides of transformation?, *Journal of Peasant Studies*, 38(1), 109–144.

Lappé, F.M.; Collins, J.; Esparza, L.; Rosset, P.; Esparza, L. (1998), *World Hunger: 12 Myths*, New York: Grove Press.

Levidow, L.; Pimbert, M.; Vanloqueren, G. (2014), Agroecological research: Conforming—or transforming the dominant agro-food regime?, *Agroecology and Sustainable Food Systems*, 38(10), 1127–1155.

LVC (La Vía Campesina) (2013), From Maputo to Jakarta: 5 years of agroecology in La Vía Campesina, Jakarta: La Vía Campesina, accessed May 5, 2019 at http://viacampesina.org/ downloads/pdf/en/ De-Maputo-a-Yakarta-EN-web.pdf.

LVC (La Vía Campesina) (2015), Declaration of the International Forum for Agroecology, accessed May 5, 2019 at https://viacampesina.org/en/index.php/main-issues-mainmenu-27/sustainable-peasants -agriculturemainmenu-42/1749-declaration-of-the-international-forum-for-agroecology.

LVC (La Vía Campesina) (2017), Declaración de Euskal Herria, accessed May 5, 2019 at https:// viacampesina.org/en/viith-international-conference-la-via-campesina-euskal-herria-declaration/.

Machín, B.; Roque Jaime, A.M.; Rocío, D.; Lozano, Á.; Rosset, P.M. (2010), *Revolución agroecológica: el movimiento campesino a campesino de la ANAP en Cuba*, La Habana: Asociación Nacional de Agricultores Pequeños and La Vía Campesina.

Martínez-Torres, M.E. (2006), *Organic Coffee: Sustainable Development by Mayan Farmers*, Athens, OH: Ohio University Press.

Martínez-Torres, M.E.; Rosset, P.M. (2010), La Vía Campesina: The birth and evolution of a transnational social movement, *Journal of Peasant Studies*, 37(1), 149–175.

Martínez-Torres, M.E.; Rosset, P.M. (2014), Diálogo de saberes in La Vía Campesina: Food sovereignty and agroecology, *Journal of Peasant Studies*, 41(6), 979–997.

Marx, K. (1991 [1894]), *Capital: A Critique of Political Economy*, vol. 3, New York: Penguin Classics.

McCune, N.; Sánchez, M. (2018), Teaching the territory: Agroecological pedagogy and popular movements, *Agriculture and Human Values*, 36, 595–610.

McCune, N.; Reardon, J.; Rosset, P. (2014), Agroecological formación in rural social movements, *Radical Teacher*, 98, 31–37.

McCune, N.; Rosset, P.M.; Salazar, T.C.; Saldívar Moreno, A.; Morales, H. (2016), Mediated territoriality: Rural workers and the efforts to scale out agroecology in Nicaragua, *Journal of Peasant Studies*, 44(2), 354–376.

McCune, N.; Rosset, P.M.; Cruz Salazar, T.; Morales, H.; Saldívar Moreno, A. (2017), The long road: Rural youth, farming and agroecological formación in Central America, *Mind, Culture, and Activity*, 24(3), 183–198.

McCune, N.; Perfecto, I.; Avilés-Vázquez, K.; Vázquez-Negrón, J.; Vandermeer, J. (2019), Peasant balances and agroecological scaling in Puerto Rican coffee farming, *Agroecology and Sustainable Food Systems*, 43(7–8), 810–826.

Méndez, V.E.; Bacon, C.M.; Cohen, R. (2013), Agroecology as a transdisciplinary, participatory, and action-oriented approach, *Agroecology and Sustainable Food Systems*, 37(1), 3–18.

Morales, H.; Perfecto, I. (2000), Traditional knowledge and pest management in the Guatemalan highlands, *Agriculture and Human Values*, 17(1), 49–63.

Moyo, S.; Jha, P.; Yeros, P. (2013), The classical agrarian question: Myth, reality and relevance today, *Agrarian South: Journal of Political Economy*, 2(1), 93–119.

Ramírez, K.; Taylor, G. (2018), The People's Agroecology Process: Implementing farmer-to-farmer methodology to scale out agroecology in the United States, Presentation at the 2018 Young Farmers Conference, Stone Barns Center for Food and Agriculture, New York, December 6.

Raynolds, L.T.; Murray, D.; Heller, A. (2007), Regulating sustainability in the coffee sector: A comparative analysis of third-party environmental and social certification initiatives, *Agriculture and Human Values*, 24(2), 147–163.

Rosset, P.M.; Altieri, M.A. (1997), Agroecology versus input substitution: A fundamental contradiction of sustainable agriculture, *Society and Natural Resources*, 10(3), 283–295.

Rosset, P.M.; Altieri, M.A. (2017), *Agroecology: Science and Politics*, Winnipeg: Fernwood Publishing.

Rosset, P.M.; Martínez-Torres, M.E. (2012), Rural social movements and agroecology: Context, theory, and process, *Ecology and Society*, 17(3).

Rosset, P.M.; Sosa, B.M.; Roque Jaime, A.M.R.; Ávila Lozano, D.A. (2011), The Campesino-to-Campesino agroecology movement of ANAP in Cuba: Social process methodology in the construction of sustainable peasant agriculture and food sovereignty, *Journal of Peasant Studies*, 38(1), 161–191.

Sbicca, J. (2018), *Food Justice Now!*, Minneapolis, MN: University of Minnesota.

Sevilla-Guzmán, E. (2006), Agroecología y agricultura ecológica: Hacia una "re"construcción de la soberanía alimentaria, *Revista Agroecología*, 1, 7–18.

Sevilla-Guzmán, E.; Woodgate, G. (2013), Agroecology: Foundations in agrarian social thought and sociological theory, *Agroecology and Sustainable Food Systems*, 37(1), 32–44.

Sevilla-Guzmán, E.; Martinez-Alier, J. (2006), New rural social movements and agroecology, in Cloke, P.; Marsden, T.; Mooney, P. (eds), *The Handbook of Rural Studies*, London: Sage, 472–484.

Steckley, M.; Weis, T. (2016), Peasant balances, neoliberalism, and the stunted growth of non-traditional agro-exports in Haiti, *Canadian Journal of Latin American and Caribbean Studies/Revue Canadienne Des Études Latino-Américaines Et Caraïbes*, 41(1), 1–22.

Toledo, V.; Barrera-Bassols, N. (2008), *La memoria biocultural: la importancia ecológica de las sabidurías tradicionales*, Barcelona: Icaria Editorial.

van der Ploeg, J.D. (2009), *The New Peasantries: New Struggles for Autonomy and Sustainability in an Era of Empire and Globalization*, London: Earthscan.

van der Ploeg, J.D. (2010), The peasantries of the twenty-first century: The commoditization debate revisited, *Journal of Peasant Studies*, 37(1), 1–30.

van der Ploeg, J.D. (2014), Peasant-driven agricultural growth and food sovereignty, *Journal of Peasant Studies*, 41(6), 999–1030.

Wallerstein, I. (1979), *The Capitalist World-Economy*, vol. 2, Cambridge: Cambridge University Press.

Wezel, A.; Bellon, S.; Doré, T.; Francis, C.; Vallod, D.; David, C. (2009), Agroecology as a science, a movement and a practice: A review, *Agronomy for Sustainable Development*, 29(4), 503–515.

Wittman, H. (2010), Reconnecting agriculture and the environment: Food sovereignty and the agrarian basis of ecological citizenship, in Desmarais, A.A.; Wiebe, N.; Wittman, H. (eds), *Food Sovereignty: Reconnecting Food, Nature and Community*, Halifax: Fernwood Publishing, 91–105.

49. Identities and culture in the rural world

Nicholas Copeland

INTRODUCTION

Rural *identity* refers to the ways in which rural people identify themselves, their wants and needs, and their location in relation to others in the social landscape. Rural *culture* refers to shared patterns of knowledge and affect (feelings and somatic states) that open and close spaces for action, encompassing identification as well as conceptions of justice, nature, gender, well being, the future and power. Identity and culture are constitutive of heterogeneous forms of life configured and reconfigured in shifting fields of power and conditions of possibility. Political parties, state agents, international organizations, religious sects, peasant organizations, mining companies, non-governmental organizations, social movements, labour unions, development workers, anthropologists, historians and communal authorities themselves stake out a range of positions regarding rural and indigenous identities, habits, interests and communities. Such assertions frequently reproduce a modernity/tradition binary, and conceive of rural cultures and identities as homogenous, bounded, unchanging and non-modern. Truths about rural culture and identity are routinely deployed to justify a range of interventions and modes of extraction and to weave together assemblages aimed at improving and developing human groups by transforming their productive relations, settlement patterns, outlooks, values and capacities (for example, their cultures and identities). Often, these interventions aim to bring rural culture and identity into alignment with modern social, economic and political life, while at other times they challenge prevailing structures.

Rural people draw on variegated reservoirs of knowledge and experience as they confront problems and seek to expand the range of individual or collective agency, often with contradictory and unforeseen effects. Discourses about culture and identity should not be seen as neutral representations of a separate reality, but as material forces that are part and parcel of efforts to shape rural identity, culture and conduct, enabling and constraining certain kinds of action, or influencing policies that affect rural people directly. Often, these are political and social positions staked out by rural people themselves. Efforts to reform culture and identity routinely fail in their stated aims even as they transform thought, practice and livelihoods – often extending the effects of rule and modes of capital accumulation. Rural identities and culture are shaped in relation to social and environmental forces, are the target of various projects of rule and in turn greatly influence processes of agrarian change, making these dynamics a central concern for critical agrarian studies, which aims to understand how power works in these processes.

In the sections that follow, I first describe the dominant approaches to rural identity and culture, then argue that critical agrarian studies would benefit from adopting a dialectical approach informed by critical anthropology. In the next sections, I explain what it means to study culture from a dialectical perspective, provide an extended example of this approach drawing on my own work in Guatemala and finally discuss what this analytical approach brings to light.

CONSERVATIVE, LIBERAL AND MULTICULTURAL APPROACHES TO RURAL IDENTITY AND CULTURE

Despite their vast diversity, rural identities and cultures are the subjects of a number of common disputes: Are rural cultures backwards, pathological and in need of replacement? Or are they disappearing and in need of preservation? Do they wish to continue their subsistence practices, preserve their languages and remain in their territories? Or do they want to leave their communities and integrate into modern economies and society? These binaries echo competing stances in the literature on rural, peasant and indigenous societies. All too often, such assertions pay little attention to the complexities of experience or the voices of rural people themselves.

Perspectives on rural identity and culture, which influence the answers to the questions above, can be roughly organized into three distinct approaches: conservative, liberal/progressive and multicultural. Each of these approaches holds some ground in the repertoire of common sense assumptions about rural identity and culture, and informs policy towards rural areas. For centuries, with its fullest expression through colonization, a conservative frame has guided the way in which states perceive and act upon rural populations: as inherently, irretrievably inferior, ignorant and even dangerous, plagued with a backwards communal culture and mindset, stuck in the past and incapable of improvement (Morgan 1877; Galton 1889). Girded by evolutionary theory after the mid-nineteenth century, this frame disparagingly essentializes (treats as homogeneous) rural cultures, and has justified all manner of dispossession, enslavement and violence, as well as contemporary inequalities between urban and rural, North and South.

The liberal or progressive frame similarly regards rural identity and culture as degraded, but sees hope in overcoming the tyranny of tradition. It calls for directed assimilation to remove pathological cultural practices and identities, and to fashion backwards people into modern subjects in the name of progress or development, such as through Native American boarding schools (Pratt 1892). Some Marxists have also viewed rural peoples and their cultures as regressive impediments to class consciousness, and thus sought to produce revolutionary subjects through assimilative development, often limiting the resonance of left movements (Saldaña-Portillo 2003).

Indigenous activism in the twentieth century challenged the hegemony of conservative and liberal frames, eventually gaining international recognition for indigenous peoples, broad acceptance of indigenous rights and a shift to multicultural discourses away from monocultural nationalisms and assimilationist narratives. The multicultural approach celebrates distinctive cultures and identities, whose variety is seen as valuable (Kymlicka 2001). It also recognizes certain rural groups as 'indigenous', who are presumed to follow millennia-old ways of life, for instance through subsistence practices, rituals, medicine, gender systems and food habits that exhibit a close connection with the natural world; a system of inter-relationships that sustains them against the disarticulating forces of modernity. This frame is enshrined in official definitions of the term indigenous and in the United Nations (UN) Declaration on the Rights of Indigenous Peoples (United Nations General Assembly 2007). The multicultural approach also tends to essentialize indigenous cultures and identities, but informs a range of policies and programmes aimed at protecting and preserving them.

Beginning in the 1970s, a recognition of shared histories of colonization among dispersed groups led to international alliances for indigenous recognition and rights (Niezen 2003). This sparked an uneven reimagining of rural populations as indigenous, alongside a reshaping of normative legal structures to recognize distinct peoples who have experienced historical exclusion and to validate to varying degrees their demands for cultural revitalization and territorial self-determination (Anaya 2004). Claiming indigenous identity has been more complicated in Africa and South Asia, where now dominant social groups were also colonized and can claim local ancestry. These processes paralleled the end of the Cold War, which saw the global defeat of Marxism and the decline of class as a viable political identity. Aided by new technologies of communication and transportation, indigenous identification and recognition have expanded globally in the interstices of the political, economic and social systems that were founded through colonialism and which continue to systematically exclude rural peoples.

These competing approaches are ideal types that oversimplify the nuances of any actual situation and obscure shared assumptions between seemingly opposing positions; each pole reduces the complexity of the texture of rural life and the forces shaping it. All perspectives share the assumption that modernity and tradition are opposite and essential categories, rather than dialectical and interpenetrating; they disagree on which is better. None of the categories holds the potential to resolve the structural exclusion of rural peoples or the continued legacies of colonialism.

All three perspectives contain risks, the conservative only the most obvious. It remains common for states and corporations to refuse to recognize indigenous groups, and to argue that rural people have adopted indigenous identities opportunistically or have been misled by international organizations. The liberal and multicultural approaches present rural subjects with double binds (Cattelino 2008): the liberal approach offers development in exchange for relinquishing claims to authenticity, identity or tradition; the multicultural approach offers to protect tradition but only for certain subjects, and in exchange for forfeiting claims to modernity and resources. Furthermore, claiming rights obliges subjects to hold fast to rigid conceptions of tradition that enshrine colonial assumptions and limit rural agency, especially for indigenous women.

Conservative, liberal and multicultural approaches often work in tandem, with violence awaiting groups that resist assimilation or which challenge dominant political economic orders (Hale 2002). An enduring concern expressed by Tania Li (2000) is that the category of indigenous and the related legal protections exclude vast rural populations which, for whatever reasons, do not understand themselves in these terms, reducing the possibility for broad alliances.

A CRITIQUE: TOWARDS A DIALECTICAL UNDERSTANDING

Critical agrarian studies may benefit from engaging with the dialectical, non-essentialist, non-teleological conception of identity and culture that is prevalent in critical anthropology, and which moves beyond the modern/primitive binary. The dialectical approach consists of the critical examination of the relationship between, on the one hand, the forces transforming the conditions of rural life, and on the other, the agency of rural peoples. It regards culture and identity simultaneously as products of social, environmental and political forces, and as shapers of historical processes. The dialectical approach does not reify or demonize tradition, limit rural people to tradition or attempt to 'liberate' them from it, nor does it regard only indigenous-identified rural people as possessing valuable knowledge or as deserving of rights and protections.

In order to understand, for example, how rural villagers relate to an agricultural development programme, this approach examines how development is framed and implemented, and how development knowledge, practices and technologies mesh with local practices and understandings of the problems that development aims to resolve. It looks at the structural determinants of the identified problems, the effects and unintended consequences of similar programmes in the past, the strings attached and local perceptions of the actors and institutions involved. It also examines the effects of these programmes on rural identity, cultural understandings, social and productive relations and so on, even when they fall short of their stated intentions. Significant here is the attention to how governance – efforts to shape conduct – operates through agency rather than simply repression, and how it connects to existing struggles, but also how spaces of agency may simultaneously be shaped by violence.

Central to the dialectical approach is a conception of identity as articulation – enunciations and positionings within specific conjunctures and relations – rather than as fixed or false consciousness (Li 2000). This dialectical approach recognizes that rural cultures and identities are not self-enclosed, but interconnected and mutually determined. They are in a dynamic, asymmetrical relationship to urban centres and modern economies, as well as to dominant cultures and projects of rule. Likewise, this approach understands the imperial coproduction of the Global North and South, with emphasis on structural transformations in the global food regime and resource extraction, which impinge directly on rural territories and livelihoods. A dialectical approach asks how certain articulations of culture and identity came about, the possibilities they open and close and how they might be otherwise.

WHAT DOES IT MEAN TO STUDY CULTURE AND IDENTITY FROM A DIALECTICAL PERSPECTIVE?

I will now illustrate this approach drawing on historical and ethnographic research into the political, economic and cultural transformations in a Mayan town in rural Guatemala that I conducted between 2004 and 2014. When Guatemala's second social democratic president began implementing land reform in 1952, the United States interpreted it as communism and sponsored a coup in 1954, installing military rule. Repression spawned revolutionary movements, leading to decades of armed conflict that culminated in genocide in indigenous communities in the 1980s. With the counterinsurgency in full swing, Guatemala began a transition to democracy in 1985. Peace agreements signed in 1996 called for moderate reforms, recognized indigenous rights and streamlined free market reforms. How were these processes experienced in rural indigenous communities? What did market democracy mean after decades of armed conflict?

My research explored these processes since the mid-twentieth century in the Maya Mam-majority town of San Pedro Necta, Huehuetenango, Guatemala. I examined how conditions of life have been transformed in relation to shifting processes of state formation and encounters with religious organizations, development programmes, nationalist projects, social movements, an armed insurgency and an intensive counterinsurgency campaign, many of which have attempted to define villager identity and culture for their own purposes. I asked how indigenous *Sampedranos* resisted, avoided, accommodated, embraced and resignified the imperatives of these external forces for their own ends, sometimes playing them against one another, sometimes incorporating elements as their own, but never entirely under conditions of their choosing. I studied how these interactions altered livelihoods, organizational forms, conceptions of self and community, gender and class relations, notions of tradition, perceptions of the state and corporations, and ethnic and political identities. I also mapped out the forces shaping how *Sampedranos* narrate the past and imagine their own agency.

Motivated by a desire to overcome discrimination as '*indios*' and to avoid forced plantation labour, indigenous *Sampedranos* supported the governments of the Democratic Revolution in the 1940s and 1950s, finding hope in its promise of democracy, equality and land reform. After the coup, some rural villagers sought development through conversion to new forms of Catholicism and Evangelical religion that supported indigenous advancement through individual training. Developmentalism, which emphasized villager identities as poor peasants in need of improvement, found further support in the new agricultural inputs of the Green Revolution – chemical fertilizers, herbicides, pesticides and hybrid seeds – and rising coffee prices. Several notable indigenous leaders spearheaded an attack on traditional religion, known as *costumbre*, in the name of development. Local *Ladinos* (Guatemalan mestizos) opposed such efforts out of fear of losing control over local government and thereby access to a low-wage workforce. In the 1970s, many villagers backed developmentalist indigenous candidates representing moderate reformist parties in local elections. A few won, but were blocked by the *Ladino* establishment. Development and education also opened limited space for individual indigenous women to assume positions of authority in their homes and communities.

Greg Grandin (2011) describes an 'insurgent individuality' in indigenous communities at this time, in which individual and collective aspirations were conjoined. The clash between this improvement-oriented political culture and local and national obstacles to individual and collective advancement created the conditions for widespread sympathy for the guerrilla movement, whose critiques of capitalism and promise of land reform and equality resonated with local experiences of discrimination, poverty and the desire for a better life. The revolution framed villagers as poor peasants and the victims of racial discrimination, emphasizing both indigenous and peasant identities.

At the peak of revolutionary ferment, the scorched earth campaign of 1981–1983 tore through the highlands, followed by the militarization of the countryside, sowing terror and crushing the revolutionary movement. Villagers turned inward and recriminated themselves for believing in the first place. As extreme violence closed down political space, the army blamed the guerrillas and insisted that villagers were trapped 'between two armies', rather than being active agents in the revolution. Anthropologists have laboured to understand how decades of 'militarism wraps and warps through institutions, life forms, conditions of possibility, meaning systems, and abilities to affect and be affected' (Nelson 2019, 124). The violence infused both post-war democracy and development, altering their meanings and effects.

Indigenous political organizations reorganized after 1983, led by developmentalist leaders who were deeply influenced by the guerrillas, but denied ever supporting them. These leaders looked to education, market-oriented development promoted by the state and electoral politics as alternative paths to advancement that appeared similar to, but safer than, the guerrilla movement (Copeland 2015). These programmes provided a way to escape the trap of 'Indian' identity and also made gender hierarchies more malleable. Market-oriented capacity development had been promoted by the United States Agency for International Development and the Guatemalan state as a non-land reform pathway to solving poverty and inequality and the threat to 'stability' that they represented, but these strategies were opaque to rural communities. Alongside the peace accords, indigenous political organizations took political power across the highlands and pursued economic security with new skills, framed simultaneously as individual and collective advancement, first as *de-Indianization*, and by the mid-1990s as *indigenous* empowerment.

Organization leaders now identified as Mayas, a new articulation of identity made possible through global discourses on indigenous rights, non-governmental organization programmes, state multiculturalism, the UN Accord on Identity and Rights of Indigenous Peoples and the Pan Mayan movement, which had pushed for these reforms. The peace process also advanced the cause of women's rights. Indigenous identification was further reinforced by the UN truth commission reports that accused the army of committing genocide and found that over 80 per cent of the victims of the armed conflict were Mayan (CEH 1999). The UN truth commission and another organized by the Catholic Church opened space for thinking of the political past outside of the 'two army' frame.

By the mid-2000s, rural communities maintained radical worldviews, consistent with many elements of the revolutionary narrative, such as critique of the violence and injustices imposed by states and corporations and the need for far-reaching reform. But such beliefs were now conjoined with the sense that meaningful change was impossible. Such radical pessimism, reinforced through targeted 'democratic' violence, was further mixed with the notion that individual capacity development and market activity were sufficient alternatives. New discourses on human, women's and indigenous rights generally ignored historic political struggles, as did anti-political Evangelical discourses, more popular after the violence, which framed the war and post-war chaos as proof of the imminent arrival of the Biblical apocalypse. As a small number of developmentalist villagers had gotten ahead, villagers increasingly blamed poverty on individual irresponsibility, rationalizing deepening class divisions even as the majority languished in poverty.

Additionally, although leaders narrated electoral politics as collective empowerment, it was a cesspool of personal interest dominated by development-minded men who monopolized projects and the windfalls of corruption, fuelling resentment. Exclusion and corruption were structural, but discussed locally as the result of the self-interested behaviours of certain individuals. Neoliberal democracy was a governing assemblage composed of various forms of development alongside violence during an ongoing counterinsurgency that reformatted local struggles into market-oriented and electoral spaces that undermined capacities for collective action (Copeland 2019a).

Distrust, pessimism and resentment were the dominant affects of neoliberal democracy, which operated as an extension of the counterinsurgency by channelling radical desires into limited and self-defeating forms of agency, particularly internecine competition for projects. The failure and violence of dominant forms of development drove support for right-wing populist parties that tapped into local resentments, divisions and grinding poverty. In 2003, many disaffected villagers supported the presidential campaign of Ríos Montt, a former dictator who was the primary intellectual author of the genocidal scorched earth campaign, rebranded as a populist. Local supporters I spoke with rationalized their affiliation on the basis that all parties were corrupt, change was impossible, that Ríos Montt may be a murderer but that war was unlikely to return and that the party had offered them a gift or a job and had helped them to even the score against their developmentalist rivals. Authoritarian populism inflamed divisions and left the conditions driving them unchanged, further undermining possibilities for collective action.

Even as they joined right-wing parties, Guatemalan Mayan communities, including those in San Pedro Necta, resisted the extractive industries. Mining operations, hydroelectric dams, monocrop expansion and other forms expanded throughout the 2000s in response to growing international demand for land-based commodities, and were streamlined by neoliberal policies (de León and Bastos 2014). Indigenous communities wielded the right to consultation – as recognized in national and international law, especially the International Labour Organization Treaty 169 – in order to resist extractivism, which the overwhelming majority view as a threat to their livelihoods, territories, water, health and identities. The defence of territory, as this resistance is known, has strengthened indigenous identifications and environmentalism, foregrounding place-based identities and cosmological concepts such as *buen vivir* (living well) that are rooted in a reciprocity with nature (Alonso-Fradejas 2017). Territorial defenders face punitive incarceration, intimidation and outright violence and states of siege, while communities receive gifts from the extractive industries.

The defence of territory represents a new articulation of indigenous identity and community mobilization that questions the foundational assumptions of settler-colonial modernity, particularly its inevitability, and overlaps significantly with food sovereignty movements that emphasize traditional and ecological agriculture, native seeds and resource access (Copeland 2019b). The growing threat of climate change, whose effects are already visible in disrupted rainfall patterns, lost harvests and forced migration, adds force to these peasant environmentalist movements. Economic misery and the environmental fallout and health effects of extractivism and ecological collapse, alongside the increasing illegitimacy of corrupt authoritarian governments which do nothing to solve the crisis, open new possibilities. These possibilities include revisiting the historic demands of the revolutionary left, such as land reform, reimagined now through indigenous cosmologies, environmentalism and feminism. The right to water is a uniquely promising focal point of resistance, because all extractive industries overuse or contaminate water systems, threatening access, health and food security and provoking conflict with surrounding communities. Meanwhile, the government sides with industry and global warming raises the stakes. Defending water as a public and common good and as a human right, as required by the Guatemalan Constitution, would significantly limit the extractive economy, increase food security and sovereignty and protect poor communities from some of the worst effects of climate change.

The systemic and intertwined failures of extractive development and neoliberal democracy propel new political imaginaries and alliances with the potential to undo the suffocating effects of the histories of racial violence, but they also foreshadow a new wave of the criminalization of resistance. Critical agrarian studies must endeavour to illuminate how rural communities perceive, somaticize and position themselves amid this atmosphere of frustration, uncertainty, exposure and abandonment; as well as with unexpected forms of optimism, such as agroecology, water rights networks and the decolonizing cultures of peasant and youth environmentalism.

WHAT CAN CRITICAL AGRARIAN STUDIES LEARN FROM APPLYING A DIALECTICAL PERSPECTIVE?

The anthropological conception of culture highlights the conceptual lenses, narrative frames and affective dispositions through which rural populations apprehend and somaticize their experience, fashion identities and act in the world. A dialectical imagination reveals culture and identity as charged processes that shift in relation to changing conditions of possibility in complex fields of power. It shows consciousness, affect and behaviour to be products of changing historical, political and environmental conjunctures, and reveals identifications as positionings within unfolding relations. It also foregrounds the contouring, open-endedness and messiness of historical processes.

Adopting a dialectical approach to culture would attune critical agrarian studies to a wide range of embodied sensibilities and understandings that rural communities bring to bear on development programmes, state initiatives, environmental changes and political movements, unburdening analysis from the prejudicial and deadening frames through which rural behaviour is commonly enclosed. This approach provides a far better understanding of behaviours such as voting for corrupt politicians, avoiding certain forms of development or joining a social movement than hastily applied notions of ignorance, resistance, conservatism or populism. Attention to the webs of meaning, affect and power which rural communities create and inhabit and through which they grasp the world, promises a nuanced and politically useful understanding. Rural Guatemalans sometimes ignore development initiatives due to lacklustre experiences with similar programmes, pessimism about development in general and mistrust of the organizations, or because of an unwillingness to engage in hard work for minimal gains, not to mention having their own understandings of the problems called into question. None of this is to suggest that rural Guatemalans are against development in general; understanding such orientations and the forces shaping them is the analytical payoff.

Such a fluid conception informs Franz Fanon's (1964) vision of 'national culture', which he saw not as a static thing to be resurrected from a pre-colonial past, but an active force developed in the heat of de-colonial struggle, with the potential to forge a revolutionary 'national consciousness' that transcends rural and urban divisions and international borders. A central question for critical agrarian studies is how to bring Fanonian futures into being in response to neoliberalism and, conversely, how to disrupt the rise of authoritarian populism.

Critical agrarian studies examines how rural peoples respond to the ways in which neoliberalism transforms the conditions for collective action by creating avenues for individual market advancement at the expense of group solidarity. The state as a site for redistributive politics is thereby diminished, opening limited space for indigenous rights; environmental destruction is normalized in the name of 'development'; poverty is framed incessantly as an individual rather than a structural problem; and alternatives are violently repressed. Critical agrarian studies also examines rural responses to the slow-moving violence of ecological collapse that primarily affects peasant and indigenous peoples in the Global South.

Although right-wing politics predominate in the reconfigured political field, emergent movement paradigms incorporate indigenous rights with peasant demands to combat the logic of an emerging ecological apartheid – the culmination of settler colonialism and capitalism – and representing alternative possibilities for rural political culture and identity. A dialectical approach focuses attention towards the possibilities and obstacles for building alliances among rural communities around common concerns, such as sustainable ecological production, challenging extractive development, access to land-based resources, regenerating spoiled landscapes and reclaiming hollowed-out democracies and public-sector institutions.

CONCLUSION

Critical agrarian studies could find much value in adopting a dialectical approach to culture and identity, informed by critical anthropological perspectives on culture as shared meaning and affect, in order to break away from the rigid orthodoxies of understanding and acting upon rural peoples, and to foreground how rural peoples both shape and are shaped by historical processes. This begins with recognizing that rural peoples reproduce culture and identities in dynamic encounters with an array of sovereigns on an evolving and increasingly hostile terrain. Cultural dynamics are best studied through qualitative methods such as ethnography, which reveal conceptual frames and lived experience in relation to institutional processes and external forces, with attention to history and environmental transitions. The move towards critical anthropology could form an important part of interdisciplinary collaborations with the environmental sciences and humanities, grounded in the dilemmas facing rural communities. A dialectical perspective on rural identity and culture could transcend the romanticism and reflexive anti-developmentalism of many indigenous studies framings, and the developmentalist and state-centric tendencies of traditional peasant studies. It could demonstrate how rural subjects live the structural and physical violence of capitalist order. And it could inform the work of building durable political alliances and more just economies and societies that are in harmony with human needs and natural cycles, and which make room for other ways of being human and relating to nature, alternatives that remain within collective reach.

FURTHER READING

Andolina, R.; Laurie, N.; Radcliffe, S.A. (2009), *Indigenous Development in the Andes: Culture, Power, and Transnationalism*, Durham, NC: Duke University Press.
Hodgson, D.L. (2011), *Being Maasai, Becoming Indigenous: Postcolonial Politics in a Neoliberal World*, Bloomington, IN: Indiana University Press.
Li, T.M. (2007), *The Will to Improve: Governmentality, Development, and the Practice of Politics*, Durham, NC: Duke University Press.
Postero, N. (2017), *The Indigenous State: Race, Politics, and Performance in Plurinational Bolivia*, Berkeley, CA: University of California Press.
Wolford, W. (2010), *This Land Is Ours Now: Social Mobilization and the Meanings of Land in Brazil*, Durham, NC: Duke University Press.

REFERENCES

Alonso-Fradejas, A. (2017), Anything but a story foretold: Multiple politics of resistance to the agrarian extractivist project in Guatemala, in Edelman, M.; Hall, R.; Borras, S.M.; Scoones, I.; White, B.; Wolford, W. (eds), *Global Land Grabbing and Political Reactions 'from Below'*, London: Routledge, 23–50.
Anaya, J. (2004), *Indigenous Peoples in International Law*, Oxford: Oxford University Press.
Cattelino, J. (2008), *High Stakes: Florida Seminole Gaming and Sovereignty*, Durham, NC: Duke University Press.

CEH (Comisión para el Esclaramiento Histórico) (1999), *Guatemala: Memoria del Silencio*, Guatemala City: UNOPS.

Copeland, N. (2015), Regarding development: Governing Indian advancement in revolutionary Guatemala, *Economy and Society*, 44(3), 418–444.

Copeland, N. (2019a), *The Democracy Development Machine: Neoliberalism, Radical Pessimism, and Authoritarian Populism in Mayan Guatemala*, Ithaca, NY: Cornell University Press.

Copeland, N. (2019b), Linking the defense of territory to food sovereignty: Peasant environmentalisms and extractive neoliberalism in Guatemala, *Journal of Agrarian Change*, 19(1), 21–40.

de León, Q.; Bastos, S. (2014), *Dinámicas de Despojo y Resistencia en Guatemala: Comunidades, Estado, empresas*, Guatemala: Diakonía/Colibrí Zurdo.

Fanon, F. (1964), *The Wretched of the Earth*, New York: Grove/Atlantic.

Galton, F. (1889), *Natural Inheritance*, London: Macmillan.

Grandin, G. (2011), *The Last Colonial Massacre: Latin America in the Cold War*, second edition, Chicago, IL: University of Chicago Press.

Hale, C.R. (2002), Does multiculturalism menace? Governance, cultural rights and the politics of identity in Guatemala, *Journal of Latin American Studies*, 34(3), 485–524.

Kymlicka, W. (2001), *Politics in the Vernacular: Nationalism, Multiculturalism and Citizenship*, Oxford: Oxford University Press.

Li, T.M. (2000), Articulating indigenous identity in Indonesia: Resource politics and the tribal slot, *Comparative Studies in Society and History*, 42(1), 149–179.

Morgan, L.H. (1877), *Ancient Society; or, Researches in the Lines of Human Progress from Savagery, through Barbarism to Civilization*, New York: Henry Holt.

Nelson, D. (2019), Low intensity, *Current Anthropology*, 60(19), 122–133.

Niezen, R. (2003), *The Origins of Indigenism: Human Rights and the Politics of Identity*, Berkeley, CA: University of California Press.

Pratt, R.H. (1892), *The Advantages of Mingling Indians with Whites*, Official Report of the Nineteenth Annual Conference of Charities and Correction, accessed 26 February 2020 at http://carlisleindian .dickinson.edu/sites/all/files/docs-resources/CIS-Resources_PrattSpeechExcerptShort.pdf.

Saldaña-Portillo, M.J. (2003), *The Revolutionary Imagination in the Americas and the Age of Development*, Durham, NC: Duke University Press.

United Nations General Assembly (2007), *UN Declaration on the Rights of Indigenous Peoples*, accessed 26 February 2020 at www.un.org/development/desa/indigenouspeoples/wp-content/uploads/sites/19/ 2019/01/UNDRIP_E_web.pdf.

50. Everyday politics in agrarian societies

Benedict J. Tria Kerkvliet

Politics, according to one pithy definition, is about who gets what, when and how (Lasswell 1958). To elaborate a bit, politics is about the control, allocation, production and use of resources, and the values and ideas underlying those activities. Resources include land, water, money, power and education, among other tangible and intangible things. Behaviour regarding producing, distributing and using resources can range from cooperation and collaboration to discussions and debates to bargains and compromises to conflicts and violence. Participants in such behaviour can include individuals, groups, organizations and governments.

Understood this way, politics occurs in many forms and settings, not just in governments, during elections, in protest marches, by rebellions and other such activity, but also in everyday life. And politics is done not just by government officials, politicians, lobbyists, revolutionaries and other such people but also by everyone else. Taking seriously this broad understanding of politics alerts us to the presence of everyday politics. And analyses of everyday politics reveal its variety and importance.

TYPES OF POLITICS

To recognize everyday politics, it helps to distinguish it from two other broad types of politics. One is official politics, which involves authorities in organizations making, implementing, changing, contesting and evading policies regarding resource allocations. The key words here are authorities and organizations. Authorities in organizations are the primary actors. The organizations include governments and states, but are not limited to those forms. Official politics also occurs, for example, in churches, universities, corporations, political parties, non-government organizations, labour unions, peasant associations and revolutionary organizations. The people involved in official politics hold positions authorizing them to make decisions or have a substantial hand in an organization's decision-making and implementation processes. Official political activities can range from public to private (even secret) spheres. For instance, government authorities might make budget decisions in an open, transparent manner, behind closed doors or gradations in between. Official political activities also can range from formal to informal to illegal activities. For example, authorities following the rules for collecting and spending membership dues is official politics; but so is authorities embezzling money belonging to the organization.

Advocacy politics is another type of politics. It involves direct and concerted efforts to support, criticize and oppose authorities, their policies and programmes, or the entire way in which resources are produced and distributed within an organization or a system of organizations. Also included is openly advocating alternative programmes, procedures and political systems. The key words here are direct and concerted. Advocates are straightforwardly, outwardly and deliberately aiming their actions and views about political matters at authorities in governments, states and other organizations. Advocacy behaviour can extend from friendly, civil and peaceful to hostile, rebellious and violent. Advocates may be individuals, groups or associations. Usually advocacy politics is public, but some advocacy politics, such as that of a revolutionary organization, may have clandestine features.

Everyday politics involves people embracing, complying with, adjusting and contesting norms and rules regarding authority over, production of or allocation of resources and doing so in quiet, mundane and subtle expressions and acts that are rarely organized or direct. Key to everyday politics' differences from official and advocacy politics is that it involves little or no organization, is usually low-profile and private behaviour and is done by people who probably do not regard their actions as political. It can occur in organizations, but everyday politics itself is not organized. It can occur where people live and work. Often it is entwined with individuals and small groups' activities while making a living, raising their families, wrestling with daily problems and interacting with others like themselves and with superiors and subordinates. Everyday politics also includes resource production and distribution practices within households and families and within small communities in ways that rely primarily on local people's own resources with little involvement from formal organizations.

As with most efforts in the social sciences to make distinctions among similar social phenomena, the lines between these three types of politics may not be stark and bold. Overlapping and blurred boundaries are unavoidable. Such lack of precision, however, does not negate the value of drawing attention to the political significance of everyday practices.

TYPES OF EVERYDAY POLITICS

Analyses of everyday politics in agrarian societies identify various forms, which can be clustered under four headings: support, compliance, modifications and evasions, and resistance.

Like society generally, agrarian societies are rife with relationships between people in unequal social, status and class positions and between citizens and government or state authorities. Village life has everyday forms of support for and compliance with those relationships and their roles in the production, distribution and use of resources. Village societies also teem with everyday forms of support and compliance with government authorities and the prevailing political systems. Support involves deliberate, perhaps even enthusiastic endorsement of the system. Compliance is more a matter of going through the motions of support without much thought about it. Everyday forms of support and/or compliance in rural societies of Asia, Africa and Latin America can include daily practices of people in superordinate positions, such as landlords and employers, as well as subordinates, such as tenants and labourers.

One large realm of everyday political support and compliance in agrarian societies involves interpersonal relations within households and families, among neighbours and others in rural communities, between employers and employees, landowners and their labourers and tenants and so forth. Creating and maintaining networks in order to have access to land, labour, money and emergency assistance is a big part of many rural people's everyday politics. Families with little or no land, employment or income regularly seek and cultivate favourable relations with people in the village or elsewhere who have land, businesses, money and connections to still other individuals with these resources. And vice versa; people with means typically like to have a network of villagers on whom they can depend to provide services – plough and harvest their fields, tend their gardens, wash and iron their clothes, cook their meals, serve their guests during parties and holiday feasts, drive their vehicles, labour in their shops – without needing to pay them much or even regularly employ them. These exchange networks and patron–client relationships are primarily private matters, unorganized, and go on pretty much day in and day out.[1] Because they involve the production, distribution and use of resources, they are political. And they reinforce class and status differences and help to perpetuate a political system in which inequalities, personal relationships and dependencies are endemic.

Everyday support and compliance in a political system can also involve behaviour that is perhaps less about personal relationships and more about particular authorities, governments and regimes. In a village in northern Thailand, discourses about government policies, elections, candidates for public office and political party campaigns have been a regular feature of day-to-day life. Electoral contests are embedded in local social relationships, and values that relate to the day-to-day politics of the village readily spill over into the electoral arena (A. Walker 2008, 87). In central Thailand during the 1990s and early 2000s, peasants, labourers, shopkeepers, truck drivers and other ordinary people regularly talked with relatives, friends, neighbours, customers and others about local officials, government policies, public projects and other such matters. Particularly important was the pride people had for their province, Suphanburi, which possessed roads, schools, hospitals and other facilities that were envied by Thais living in other provinces. Much of the credit for these improvements, Suphanburi residents said, went to an official who, according to many scholars and journalists, was a corrupt, dirty, 'godfather'-type politician. But a large proportion of Suphanburi people privately praised him because of what he had done to improve their province. Their positive view of him often fed into advocacy politics, such as when residents openly campaigned for him during elections and publicly defended him against his critics (Nishizaki 2011).

More in the realm of compliance than support are daily activities that help to sustain authority and political systems. Václav Havel (1985) writes eloquently about this in his analysis of power and politics in communist-ruled Czechoslovakia. Using the example of a greengrocer who day after day 'places in his window, among the onions and carrots, the slogan, "Workers of the World, Unite!"', Havel talks about citizens complying with authorities and rules, often without much thought let alone conviction, 'because these things must be done if one is to get along in life. It is one of the thousands of details' to help have a 'relatively tranquil life "in harmony with society"' (ibid., 27–28). Such actions, Havel argues, are signs of obedience, however modest or low level that may be. In Czechoslovakia and other countries with similar political systems aimed at maximizing conformity, uniformity and discipline, any behaviour that is exceptional – out of line with what authorities expect – is a transgression, a 'genuine denial of the system' (ibid., 30). So, lest individuals be seen as transgressors and thereby risk punishment, they must 'behave as though' they believe, or at least 'tolerate … in silence' (ibid., 31) what the system expects of them. In such behaviour, the greengrocer and others doing the routine, daily things expected of them by the system become players in the game, 'thus making it possible for the game to go on, for it to exist in the first place' (ibid., 36). Much the same can be said about virtually every other political system and set of authority–follower relationships.

A third realm of everyday politics involves people modifying and evading what society condones, authorities expect or the political system presumes. These actions usually convey indifference to the rules and processes regarding production, distribution and use of resources. They are typically things people do while trying to 'cut corners', not to oppose superiors or advance claims at odds with superiors' interests, but so as to get by. Labourers paid a specific amount to plough or weed a landowner's field, for instance, might do less than a thorough job in order to complete the tasks quickly. Modifications and evasions can also include behaviour done at the expense of neighbours and other people in similar conditions as those acting or speaking. Examples are people privately bad-mouthing fellow peasants and co-workers for their different ethnicities and religious beliefs, men putting down women and vice versa, or poor persons stealing from other impoverished individuals.

The fourth form of everyday politics is everyday resistance. Resistance refers to what people do that shows disgust, anger, indignation or opposition to what they regard as unjust, unfair or illegal claims on them by people in higher, more powerful class and status positions or institutions. Stated positively, through their resistance, subordinated people struggle to affirm their claims to what they believe they are entitled to based on values and rights recognized by a significant proportion of other people similar to them. Some scholars of agrarian politics argue that resistance need not be intentional; others insist, however, that resistance involves intentionally contesting the claims made by people in superordinate positions or intentionally advancing the claims at odds with what superiors want. In any event, acts at the expense of other people who are in the same or similar boat is not resistance. And behaviour by people in higher class or status positions to counter the actions of subordinates is not resistance; that is often repression or coercion. How subordinates resist can vary from organized and confrontational forms, such as demonstrations and rebellions, to less elaborate but still direct and confrontational action, such as peasants boldly taking over land they claim belongs to them or petitioning authorities or other superiors to meet their demands. Resistance can also be subtle, indirect and non-confrontational; and that is where everyday forms of resistance are found.

Everyday resistance has little or no organization; and the persons or institutions targeted by the resistance typically do not know, at least not immediately, what has been done at their expense. The nasty, derogatory things peasants say or the jokes they crack about their landlords, employers, government officials or the like behind their backs can be forms of everyday resistance. Other examples are villagers pilfering grain or tools from egregious landowners and employers; harvesting in the dead of night fruit or grain belonging to abusive officials; and surreptitiously setting fire to tractors, combines and other equipment that displace people who are desperate for employment. A highly influential analysis of such everyday speech and activities in a village in Malaysia shows that daily life is rife with class struggle that only occasionally bursts into the open (Scott 1985).

WHY STUDY EVERYDAY POLITICS

Literature on everyday resistance in agrarian societies has contributed to debates about hegemony. A pronounced finding is that outward signs by poor and other lower-class villagers of quiescence or acceptance of impoverishment, exploitation and the like cannot be taken at face value. Researchers find that often such appearances are facades hiding different, often contrary views and actions that grow from peasants' discontent and antipathy to how higher status or more powerful people and institutions treat them. Rather than accepting the status quo, villagers often harbour alternative visions, values and beliefs for how resources should be produced, distributed and used.

Everyday resistance studies also help to understand better the emergence of peasant organizations, movements and rebellions. Stated generally, peasants' everyday forms of resistance and the thinking underlying their hidden criticisms of prevailing political conditions can feed into confrontational forms of advocacy politics. For instance, everyday resistance in rural societies has been an important precursor to open, confrontational, advocacy forms of politics, such as land take-overs (Kerkvliet 1993). In China, villagers' covert everyday resistance against corrupt local officials, taxes, government confiscation of land and other adverse conditions in the mid-1980s developed into overt collective action in the late 1980s and 1990s (K.L.M. Walker 2008).

Scholars have investigated the conditions under which everyday resistance might feed into open, organized and confrontational resistance. One important reason appears to be changing political circumstances that favour peasants and disfavour individuals and agencies peasants have been surreptitiously resisting. Such altered circumstances help subordinates to overcome their fears. In Bangladesh, a growing appreciation of their collective strength in numbers encouraged peasants to express their real views openly and support the candidates running for parliament whom they preferred rather than the ones favoured by people to whom they were beholden (Adnan 2007). Another condition is the emergence of leaders and groups who are able to 'frame' discontent and resistance in ways that enable peasants and agrarian workers to overcome or set aside reluctance and fear so as to begin to band together and confront collectively authorities and other powerful entities. Such framing typically involves joining people's everyday ideas and experiences regarding oppression and resistance with broader ones. The importance of this condition has been shown in studies of how peasant-based revolts and revolutions have developed.[2]

Examining what rural people say and do among themselves, how they treat each other, their views of folks different from them and their assessments of social-economic conditions helps to understand changes and continuities in governance regimes. Probing everyday politics in societies enhances the possibilities of revealing degrees to which people endorse or not authoritarian, populist, democratic, militaristic and other political systems. Such research also helps to assess what people's public behaviour – speech, votes, participation in the rallies and the like – on behalf of a regime or politician means to themselves. Public displays of support may well hide people's far more complex and telling reasoning and aspirations.[3]

CONCLUSION

Studying everyday politics leads to deeper analysis and comprehension of agrarian societies. Taking seriously politics in everyday life broadens 'politics' and what is 'political' beyond the narrow corridors to which most contemporary mass media and academia relegate them. It also broadens the scope of political science to encompass much more of human experience, comparable to the range of study common in sociology, economics and other social sciences.

NOTES

1. A valuable compendium of influential early research on exchange networks and patron–client relations in agrarian societies is Schmidt et al. (1977).
2. For examples of studies in which this and other conditions are important explanations, see Mason (2004); Rutten (1996); Wood (2003).
3. See, for instance, Wedeen (1999) and Mamonova (2019).

FURTHER READING

Bayat, A. (2010), *Life as Politics: How Ordinary People Change the Middle East*, Stanford, CA: Stanford University Press.
Kelliher, D. (1992), *Peasant Power in China: The Era of Rural Reform, 1979–1989*, New Haven, CT: Yale University Press.
Kerkvliet, B.J.T. (2005), *The Power of Everyday Politics: How Vietnamese Peasants Transformed National Policy*, Ithaca, NY: Cornell University Press.
Leftwich, A. (1984), On the politics of politics, in Leftwich, A. (ed.), *What Is Politics?*, Oxford: Basil Blackwell, 1–18.
Scott, J.C. (2009), *The Art of Not Being Governed: An Anarchist History of Upland Southeast Asia*. New Haven, CT: Yale University Press.

REFERENCES

Adnan, S. (2007), Departures from everyday resistance and flexible strategies of domination: The making and unmaking of a poor peasant mobilization in Bangladesh, *Journal of Agrarian Change*, 7(2), 183–224.
Havel, V. (1985), The power of the powerless, in Havel, V. et al. (eds), *The Power of the Powerless: Citizens against the State in Central-Eastern Europe*, Armonk, NY: M.W. Sharpe, 23–96.
Kerkvliet, B.J.T. (1993), Claiming the land: Take-overs by villagers in the Philippines with comparisons to Indonesia, Peru, Portugal, and Russia, *Journal of Peasant Studies*, 20(3), 459–493.
Lasswell, H. (1958), *Politics: Who Gets What, When, How*, Cleveland, OH: World Publishers.
Mamonova, N. (2019), Understanding the silent majority in authoritarian populism: What can we learn from popular support for Putin in rural Russia?, *Journal of Peasant Studies*, 46(3), 561–585.
Mason, D.T. (2004), *Caught in the Crossfire: Revolutions, Repression, and the Rational Peasant*, Boulder, CO: Rowman and Littlefield.
Nishizaki, Y. (2011), *Political Authority and Provincial Identity in Thailand*, Ithaca, NY: Cornell Southeast Asia Program Publications.
Rutten, R. (1996), Popular support for the revolutionary movement CPP-NPA: Experiences in a hacienda in Negros Occidental, 1978–1995, in Abinales, P.N. (ed.), *The Revolution Falters: The Left in Philippine Politics after 1986*, Ithaca, NY: Cornell Southeast Asia Program Publications, 110–153.
Schmidt, S.W.; Guasti, L.; Landé, C.H.; Scott, J.C. (eds) (1977), *Friends, Followers, and Factions: A Reader in Political Clientelism*, Berkeley, CA: University of California Press.
Scott, J.C. (1985), *Weapons of the Weak: Everyday Forms of Peasant Resistance*, New Haven, CT: Yale University Press.
Walker, A. (2008), The rural constitution and the everyday politics of elections in northern Thailand, *Journal of Contemporary Asia*, 38(1), 84–105.
Walker, K.L.M. (2008), From covert to overt: Everyday peasant politics in China and the implications for transnational agrarian movements, *Journal of Agrarian Change*, 8(2–3), 462–488.
Wedeen, L. (1999), *Ambiguities of Domination: Politics, Rhetoric, and Symbols in Contemporary Syria*, Chicago, IL: University of Chicago Press.
Wood, E.L. (2003), *Insurgent Collective Action and Civil War in El Salvador*, Cambridge: Cambridge University Press.

51. The state and rural politics

Leandro Vergara-Camus

INTRODUCTION

Rural politics is fundamentally about control of land, labour, nature, territory and ultimately life. The state is at the centre of these struggles for control. The form of agriculture practised on a specific territory, the way the allocation of (and access to) natural resources and the division of labour are organized, the decision of implementing a redistributive agrarian reform or privatizing land and natural resources, all directly or indirectly involve the state.

This entry will begin by attempting to define the term state and explore the ways in which it is associated with the term power, understood either as *power over* or *power to*. This will be followed by an overview of some of the foundational approaches to the state (Liberal, Marxist and Weberian) and a basic presentation of a few contributions to the theory of the state in the 1970s and 1980s, notably the "discovery" of Antonio Gramsci and the contribution of Michel Foucault. I will then move on to a discussion on the role of the state in the countryside through a commentary on the work of James Scott. In the last section, I will present a sample of recent studies within critical agrarian studies that explicitly deal with the state in the South and show how these studies build on the different foundational approaches.

My central argument is that the different conceptualizations of the state in critical agrarian studies continue to build on the classical foundational approaches and reproduce some of their assumptions about the role of the state in social conflict and capitalist development. Although the conception of state power developed by James Scott, which emphasizes its *power over* rural communities and the reliance of the latter on a moral economy, remains influential, critical agrarian studies seem to be moving toward a minimal consensus on the state and rural politics. This consensus recognizes the diffused nature of power and the need to understand the state and the rural community less as unitary actors and more as contradictory spaces, partly rejecting the more "structuralist" understanding of the state, and moving away from a romantic idea of the rural community. However, remnants of the classical approaches continue to influence contemporary scholarship, especially in respect to whether the state can represent and mediate the different interests within rural society or not, and thus be a vehicle for progressive politics or not.

DEFINING THE STATE AND UNDERSTANDING ITS ROLE AND NATURE

Descriptively, the conventional use of the term "state" refers to the legal institutions where formal political power lies (the crown, the government, the legislative, provincial/district/municipal governments) and the institutions in charge of protecting, overseeing, administering and implementing the social and political order (the judiciary, the army, the police, ministries, specific regulatory bodies, as well as state enterprises and economic agencies). The state hence appears in our lives under different concrete or abstract disguises: the police officer, the border agent, the unemployment officer, a law, a public regulation or a symbol like a flag. The state is thus perceived by many as a body of institutions that produces decisions, policies and norms that have effects on the population of a territory and that has the power or the legitimacy, as well as the personnel, to impose it upon (or have it accepted by) the population of a territory. Critical scholars have, however, either contested the transhistorical validity of the nation-state, called for a rethinking of the concept to account for the power and influence of transnational capital within the nation-state, or for the extension of the concept of the state to include supra-state institutions. To complicate matters further, within the Liberal tradition the term state is used conceptually in contrast to the market and civil society, while Marxist-influenced scholars do not recognize this distinction because it is the bourgeois social order that artificially separates social life into spheres, including the private and the public.

Although the state is arguably one of the terms most commonly used in political discussions and the social sciences, it is one of the most difficult concepts to define because it is intricately fused with the equally elusive term power. Power is often associated with the ability to impose or influence someone into doing something that s/he would not do otherwise. For the individual or group of individuals on the receiving end of this relationship, power appears negatively as someone having "power over" oneself. But the term power is also used to refer to the ability to act collectively toward a determinate end that can improve a group's status, position or situation. Power in the latter meaning is understood as "power for" (Holloway 2002, 52–56). As we will see, these two conceptions of power are often in the background of the way different scholars approach state power.

THE CLASSICAL FOUNDATIONS

Broadly speaking, three traditions can be said to have set the contours of the discussion on the state: the Liberal social contract one, the Marxist class power one and the Weberian rational-bureaucratic one. Within the Liberal tradition, the state is understood as an entity— Hobbes (2016 [1651]) called it the *Leviathan*—that is created by individuals to tame their destructive self-interested instincts and establish order. The modern pluralist school (Dahl 1972) builds on this and, although it recognizes the power of elites, sees the state as an arbiter of the conflicts and demands of society. Following the writings of Marx and Engels, Marxists have always underlined that the state is a form of alienated power, ultimately based on coercion. The state presents itself as being neutral but is fundamentally the instrument of the dominant class. Marx (1990, 873–940) traces the origin of capitalism itself to the actions of the state in his famous chapter on "The so-called primitive accumulation" in *Capital* Volume I. In this chapter he shows how the separation of the labourers from their means of production, through the expropriation of the land of the peasantry, the establishment of private property, market dependence and discipline, was imposed violently by the English ruling classes through a series of laws over the course of more than 300 years. He also shows how the conquest and pillage of the colonies and transatlantic slavery were key features of the emergence of capitalism. This means that state and market for Marxists cannot be understood separately. For Marx and Engels (1978, 33), in the capitalist society, "the executive of the modern state is but a committee for managing the common affairs of the whole bourgeoisie". Concurrently, the politics of different politicians can be read through the interests of the class from which they emerge and/or represent. This is the foundation of the long tradition that we could call the "instrumentalist view" of the state, upon which different types of Marxists have built further theorizations (Brenner et al. 2003). Some Marxists consider that the state can become the instrument through which the labouring classes can establish a different social order. But we should remember that Marx called for the abolition of the state and its replacement by a self-governed community of equals—including the equality between men and women—which in his lifetime was epitomized by the experience of the Paris Commune. We hence find within the Marxist tradition "statist" and "anti-state" Marxists.

The third tradition builds on the work of Max Weber (1968a), whose well-known definition of the state also recognizes its coercive nature but adds the element of legitimacy. A political organization is a state when it has successfully claimed the "monopoly of the legitimate use of violence" over the population of a determinate territory (Weber 1994, 311). Weber's other contribution to the theorization of the state comes through his preoccupations to further develop the Liberal tradition by explaining the distinctive Modern tendency toward the rationalization of life. His defence of the market and his argument about certain cultural traits being exemplary of Modern capitalist economic rationality is well known. But for Weber the other distinctive element of Western Modernity was the emergence of the bureaucracy as the form of organizing collective rationality within organizations and the state. Its internal division of labour, its professionalization, its expert knowledge and its obedience of procedures and hierarchy make the bureaucracy the ultimate rational entity in the achievement of the optimal use of means to an end. Weber distrusts politicians, not because they are class representatives, but because the inherent logic of modern politics leads them to take decisions that are guided by their self-interest of maintaining their status and power. Weber (1968b) sees the professionalized, technocratic and apolitical state bureaucracy as the institution capable of rationalizing societal decisions and reigning in self-interested politicians. For Weber, the degree of state autonomy from societal vested interests will depend on the nature of the bureaucracy, the division of powers and the hierarchical order between different institutions of the state. Though Weber was a strong believer in Modernity, he did recognize the danger of the rationalization of life under Modernity, seeing it as an "iron cage" that could gradually trap individuals into growing encompassing and impersonal forms of control.

For the advanced capitalist world, the debate about the state had a high point in the debate between Ralph Miliband (1969) and Nicos Poulantzas (1974, 1978). Both recognized the class nature of the state, but Miliband demonstrated it empirically through the class origin of the ruling class, state officials and bureaucrats. Poulantzas, following Louis Althusser (1970), adopted a more structural-functionalist explanation where the predominance of economic relations pushed the state to take decisions that guaranteed the reproduction of capitalist relations, sometimes even against the interests of specific sectors of the dominant classes. He also pointed to tensions and conflicts within the state and the structural presence of transnational capital within the nation-state but relied on a Weberian-like explanation in which the hierarchical organization between the different state ministries worked to produce results that privileged the more advanced fractions of the bourgeoisie.

Hamza Alavi (1982) is arguably one of the scholars from the South who went the furthest in attempting to grasp the specificity of the state in the Third World through his concept of the "overdeveloped state". For him, the peripheral state was not the capitalist state of the core, because of the type of articulation of peripheral countries to the capitalist core, the survival of pre-capitalist forms of production on its territory and the contradictory nature of the dominant classes. Alavi argued that in the South the dominant classes were the landowning classes, the domestic bourgeoisie and foreign capital. He argued that their interests were not complementary but mutually exclusive; landowning classes having a heavy responsibility for the inability of dominant classes to find a common interest. Moreover, the state apparatus was not in their hands, but it was controlled by members of the middle classes, who had an interest in overextending the size of the state. The state was thus neither an instrument of the dominant classes nor a rationalizing agent or a general capitalist, but a locus of power and income.

The changes in fashion within the Western academia influenced by the rise of postmodernism, post-structuralist and post-Marxist approaches saw the eclipse of the state as a research and analytical focus.[1] Two authors stand out during this period of "crisis of Marxism": Antonio Gramsci and Michel Foucault. Gramsci's understanding of hegemony as coercion and consent and its respective "extended state" that includes political society and civil society are built on a diffused notion of power (Gramsci 1971, 12–13, 260–264). The class power of the bourgeoisie is not concentrated in the institutions of the state but spread throughout society. It does not depend only on its control of the apparatus of the state but also on its ability to have other classes, including subaltern classes, accept its leading role and see the interest of the bourgeoisie as the interest of the whole society. This acceptance is acquired through the cultural diffusion and reproduction of bourgeois worldviews, values, institutions and aesthetics that make up the common sense. Strategically, radical change must come through the long-term development of a counter-hegemony of subaltern classes and the emergence of "organic intellectuals" that can collectively challenge the bourgeois order and culture, as well as develop their ability to mobilize a different form of *power for* their liberation. This learning process happens through the active participation of individuals in a new type of political party, the Modern Prince (Gramsci 1971, 123–205).

Foucault's diffused understanding of power is similar to Gramsci's in the sense that power for him also does not reside (or is not even) concentrated in any place (Foucault 2001 [1977], 379). They draw their inspiration, however, from very different sources. Gramsci builds on the work of Marx, Lenin and Italian political theorists and remains firmly within the class power tradition, while Foucault builds on the clearly Weberian *problematic* of the iron cage metaphor, which he pushes to its ultimate consequence into a radical critique of Modernity. Foucault's dislocation of power away from the state is operationalized through his concept of "governmentality". In his famous text, Foucault (1991) traces the genealogy of the distinctive form of governing that emerges and develops with Western Modernity. Foucault calls it "governmentality" to refer to the fact that, although it emerges as a form of organizing populations for the needs of the Sovereign, such as in the state, it quickly generalized as a form of rule and *power over* others throughout society. Governmentality is thus in the strong Weberian sense a rationality or more specifically a Modern form of rationalization of society. Foucault goes further than any other theorist before him, however, and argues that governmentality—or this will to normalize, control and punish—props up in any attempt by an individual or a collective subject to elaborate an emancipatory project in the name of the common good (Foucault 1982). This leads him to a radically encompassing and negative conception of power where power has its own logic that imposes itself on subjects regardless of their will. In some sense, governmentality is a form of power that operates without subjects but through them.

THE STATE AND RURAL POLITICS

Critical agrarian political economists examine the social organization of agrarian communities through the lenses of land, labour, class, ethnicity, gender, livelihoods, incomes, rents, wages, prices and profits. The focus is on understanding how different classes and ethnic groups, as well as women and men, gain access to the essential elements that allow them to carve out a living through farming and the appropriation of nature, and how they make sense of this through cultural and spiritual beliefs and practices. This means finding out what accounts for social cohesion, collective identities, subjectivities and agencies, what accounts for inequalities, hierarchies and domination. Power, violence and laws, as well as norms, values and traditions, are what determine what an individual (man or woman) or a household (from a particular racial or ethnic group) is entitled to, what they can (or cannot) do and with which other individual or group they can interact. As is well known, gaining access to land, water, forest and animals can be achieved in many ways. However, two entities have traditionally been the subject granting this access: the community or the state. In critical agrarian studies, the pre-modern state is very often represented as an instrument of a central dynasty and/or the local landlord class, which they use against each other or local communities who strive to maintain the basis of their livelihoods. The focus is on how different groups use or challenge the state to organize and/or modify land rights, subsistence margins, customs, rents, taxes, labour obligations and population mobility. In studies of societies that are organized along (or transitioning to) modern or capitalist relations, the focus moves to how the above categories are transformed and/or commodified through the state and begin to take a monetary form, but also on how new categories like private property, wages, profits and economic compulsion slowly transform the way rural subjects reproduce themselves. For authors working from a Liberal or Weberian tradition this shift does not radically transform how the market and the state are conceived. For Marxists, this shift establishes a fundamentally different form of society in which the state form guarantees that the fundamental institutions that organize economic life are isolated from political scrutiny (Wood 1995).

No scholar in agrarian studies has written as much on the state and its relation to different forms of peasant politics (and as little on the market!) than James Scott (1976, 1998, 2009). Throughout his prolific career, Scott has remained consistent in his view of the state and the peasant community. He began with the state as claimant in *The Moral Economy of the Peasant* (1976), where the state is an entity that extracts a portion of the peasant revenue in the form of taxes, to the state as an entity whose reach peasant populations actively seek to escape because of this same appetite in *The Art of Not Being Governed* (2009). On the opposite end, Scott has consistently conceived peasant communities as seeking autonomy from the state to protect their forms of land allocation, rights to the territory, cultural customs and languages and forms of taking decisions. Although Scott recognizes that peasant communities are internally socially differentiated and hierarchical, he highlights that peasant communities strive to maintain a certain social equilibrium through a "moral economy". The moral economy consists of a set of principles enforced culturally by a community that delineate the rights, duties and responsibilities that different strata of the community have toward natural resources and each other (Scott 1976). The poor have a right to subsistence and a share of the natural resources. The rich can exploit them, but they have the duty of doing it in a way that will permit the former to have a livelihood within the margins of subsistence. These opposed logics lead Scott to speak of the existence of "state spaces" and "non-state spaces" throughout human history. There is, however, for him a difference between the pre-modern and the modern state.

Following a Foucauldian perspective, Scott (2009, 2) argues that the principal problem of statecraft in the countryside is legibility. The state is akin to a machine that requires making nature and society legible through simplification and standardization. It requires maps, cadastres, measurements and experts to produce them. Like Weber's iron cage of rationalization, the difference between the pre-modern and modern state—whether capitalist or socialist—seems to be the ability of the latter (especially in its socialist version) to take high modernist ideology to the ultimate possible consequences: ecological collapse, famine, extermination. For Scott, then, the modern state is more an expansion and sophistication of pre-modern instincts, which culminates in the arrogance of its bureaucracy that has nothing but disdain for local popular knowledge about the ecosystem.

NEOLIBERAL GLOBALIZATION, THE STATE AND CONTEMPORARY RURAL POLITICS

There are three important challenges for critical agrarian studies concerning the state and rural politics: (1) how to account for the new articulation between the state and capital under neoliberal globalization, notably the increased importance of transnational processes and actors; (2) how to overcome the overly structuralist conceptualization of the state; and (3) how to avoid juxtaposing an encompassing understanding of the power of the state and capital onto an over-romanticized idea of peasant communities and movements.

There seems to be a consensus across different perspectives that the state should be conceptualized as a contradictory space, where different subjects deploy their strategies across different scales. There is also a consensus around rejecting a unitary/monolithic understanding of the state by highlighting the tensions and conflicts between the different institutions, scales and actors within the state. There is also a growing consensus around acknowledging internal class differentiation within the peasantry, which makes class unity much more difficult but not impossible.

Following Marx's insights about primitive accumulation, many have highlighted the role of the state in facilitating capital accumulation in agriculture and furthering the interests of transnational corporations and large-scale capitalist farmers (Borras et al. 2011; Fairhead et al. 2012). Others, following Poulantzas, have pointed to the role of the state in facilitating the appropriation of natural resources by capital at the national level and transnational level (Görg and Brand 2006; Brand and Wissen 2012). In these studies, the state ultimately is the instrument of capitalist classes or economic and political elites, but many also point to the presence of allied (reformist) officials within the state (Akram-Lodhi et al. 2007; Edelman and Borras 2016) that can implement policies in favour of peasants and rural workers.

Some scholars use the term "state–society relations" or "state–society interactions" to express the idea that the state and society are two distinctive albeit inter-related or intertwined entities. Sometimes, this term following the pluralist tradition also implies that the state is a relatively neutral actor responsive to the needs, demands and pressures of society, and eventually a rationalizing entity. For instance, Dauvergne and Neville (2010) in their analysis of the prospects for biofuel development in the South shy away from acknowledging that the state is an instrument of class rule, although their article is replete with passages where the state is in the background of population displacement in favour of national and/or transnational capital. When assessing the prospects of a country to see the emergence of an economically successful biofuel sector, Dauvergne and Neville (ibid., 643–646) rely on a neo-Weberian conception of the state (Evans 1995): a predatory state will benefit transnational capital and a small elite, while a developmental state will create conditions for the participation of a broader array of actors. However, the distinction lays not as with Weber on how much the state is autonomous from society, but on just how embedded enough the bureaucracy is in industry to be able to know what is required for it to contribute to national competitiveness and inclusive growth.

McKay et al. (2014), using this same terminology but more committed to class analysis, sought to determine how state and civil society actors negotiated power and how this led to different variations of food sovereignty in Bolivia, Ecuador and Venezuela. The state is more consistently conceptualized as a contradictory space, in which different institutions and scales can be controlled by different and even opposing groups. The state is also understood as being constrained by global forces and not necessarily having the capacity or the will to push through food sovereignty. Adopting a Gramscian perspective, the ideological and political project of politicians and peasant movements matter because it can lead to the decision to centralize or decentralize power, which in turn can respectively inhibit progressive change, as in Bolivia and Ecuador, or empower social movements as agents of it, as in Venezuela under Chavez. McKay et al. avoid falling into the facile argument that the state inevitably co-opts peasant and indigenous movements but show that the type of relationship between the state and civil society will depend on the ideology and relative power of the different actors within the state and civil society.

In their framework to study the role of the state in land grabbing, Wolford et al. (2013) adopted Jessop's strategic relational approach that combines Poulantzas's structuralism with Foucault's governmentality (Jessop 2007). They sought to "unbundle the state to see government and governance as processes, people, and relationships [by focusing on] territory, sovereignty, authority and subjects ... as relationships produced in and through place, property, power and production" (Wolford et al. 2013, 189). The image that is conveyed in this article is one of extreme complexity and fluidity. The objective is to challenge the conventional representation of the state as having a coherent agenda and the capacity and legitimacy to control decisions regarding the allocation of resources over a territory. The target is also some Marxist representations of the state as subservient to the needs of capital. The authors, following Foucault more than Gramsci, put a special emphasis on discourse and cultural representation/contestation, to highlight that the state attempts to create subjects whose conduct is not in line with the needs of development with a view at marginalizing them more than to exploit them. To account for the contingency of outcomes in the process of land grabbing—including successful resistance where different levels of the state were mobilized by different local, national and transnational actors—the authors highlight that determining which individual and institution has authority and legitimacy over the resources of a territory is not a given. This can be challenged and depends more on the actors' strategic choices and alliances than on the structural constraints on the state or the perceived power of different actors. Although this approach clearly delivers on its promise to "unbundle the state", by adopting an overly diffused conception of power it underestimates that the control of core institutions of the state come with an increased capacity to mobilize the different technologies of *power over others*.

I also conceptualize the state as a contradictory space. It is however not a neutral space. Following the work of Ellen Wood (1995) on the separation of the economic from the political and Fernando Coronil (1997), I have sought to develop an understanding of the state that builds on Marx's concept of ground rent, which he mobilized to understand the place and role of landownership in capitalist agriculture (Vergara-Camus 2014; Vergara-Camus and Kay 2017). Drawing inspiration from Alavi, my approach stresses that in the South capital accumulation in the countryside, and possibly in many sectors of the economy, relies more on access to the state than in core capitalist countries.[2] The centrality of rent in the process of accumulation of wealth places the state at the centre of the struggle over resources and shapes the strategies of the different actors. Gaining access to the rent that the state extracts from extractive industries (oil, gas, mining, public land leases) is an obvious mechanism of wealth accumulation, but so is the access to state officials that grant monopoly rights and regulate the economy. Transnational agribusiness, for instance, uses its monopoly position in the trading of several commodity chains or over the private property rights over seeds, both allowed or enforced by the state, to extract rent. Large landlords extract rent from large-scale producers or agribusiness by renting them their land, which is protected by the state. This option is also open to medium or small-scale producers that do not have the funds to enter globalized capital-intensive agriculture, fracturing the already difficult alliance of rural subaltern classes. The state *appears* as all powerful not only because it has the cultural symbols to make its rule accepted by society, but also because the individuals speaking through the state often have the ability and the means to make it so. The state (or specific institutions of the state) can thus be an instrument of class power. Subaltern classes know this and often strategize to challenge the right and legitimacy of the different state agents to act on behalf of the state and monopolize the right of granting access to land and other natural resources and later protecting it through private property rights. As Scott has pointed out, the protection or creation of commons or moral economies, often through the reinvention of tradition or the *de facto* territorial control over a geographic (non-state) space, *can be* strategies of rural subaltern classes to mobilize their collective *power for* contesting the appropriation of resources by private individuals acting through the state. However, these are not the most commonly adopted strategies, to a great extent because of the class differentiation within the peasantry. These tend to require a long process of politicization of subaltern rural subjects in which class unity is politically created and sustained. As was the case under left-wing governments in Latin America, subaltern classes tend to take the chance of seeking state power to push their interest further in order to influence policy making or to seek to reform the state from within to increase their class or ethnic autonomy. The capitalist state, however, since it stands on—and is the guarantor of—the separation of the labourers from the means of production, can never really cease to be an alienated form of power for subaltern classes. Its form ultimately serves the interests of capitalists and rentiers, as long as this separation is not challenged and the exercise of power throughout society, including within the market, is not radically democratized.

CONCLUSION

The state, whether one is statist or anti-state, is unavoidable in any discussion about rural politics and progressive social change because it is inextricably tied to the issue of power, either understood negatively as *power over* or positively *as power for*. It is also unavoidable because it is arguably the modern form of power around which societies have and continue to organize the exercise of power and the allocation of resources. Rural subaltern subjects when they seek to challenge their marginalization, even if this marginalization is due to the "free functioning" of the market or the culturally enforced gender division of labour within the household, will eventually confront (or appeal to) the state. Any analysis of the form that peasant struggles take, what or who they struggle against, what their utopian horizon is, and which concrete institutions and practices they create, ends up being carried out under the shadow of the state. However, this entry has shown that there are different ways of conceiving and theorizing the state that can be linked to three different "classical foundational" approaches, namely Liberalism, Marxism and Weberianism. These have, in turn, been further developed and modified away from more "structuralist" understandings of the state, conceived as either the instrument of capital and the dominant class or as an autonomous agent able to rationalize and balance out the different interests within society. Gramsci and Foucault stand out for having partially moved away from these conceptions by expanding the traditional way of thinking about power as resting in the state.

The sample of recent studies of the state in critical agrarian studies presented in the previous section shows how the different understandings of the state that are explicitly or implicitly adopted by different scholars draw on classical foundations as well as more contemporary conceptualizations of power. This sample signals the emergence of a minimal consensus that seeks to avoid reifying the state and the rural community. Most have also moved away from monolithic understandings of the state as a unitary actor. They tend to adopt conceptions that conceive the state as a contradictory space made of a multiplicity of social relations, institutions and actors. The rural community is also understood in this fashion. Most recognize the importance of the fragmented nature of rural politics, but not all believe in the possibility (or even desirability) of class unity within the peasantry. This has led critical agrarian scholars to highlight the contingency of the outcomes of rural politics and the importance of understanding and assessing the different strategies adopted by rural subjects to explain these outcomes. However, ultimately different scholars can be distinguished on the basis of whether they think that progressive change can happen through, within, or against the state. By analysing what the state is and does, whether any group can control and use its institutions and technologies and what can/should be done with it, they intervene differently in the debate about the possibility of progressive or radical social change in the South.

NOTES

1. There are two important exceptions to this, like the debate around the edited book *Bringing the State Back In* (Evans et al. 1985) and the Marxist derivation debate, but space does not allow us to tackle them in this entry.
2. An argument could be made that given the monopolistic nature of global capitalism today and its reliance on exclusive property rights and patents that this is becoming also true of advanced capitalism (for a similar perspective see Andreucci et al. 2017).

FURTHER READING

Brenner, N.; Jessop, B.; Jones, M.; Macleod, G. (2003), *State/Space, A Reader*, Oxford: Blackwell.
Foucault, M. (1991), Governmentality, in Burchell, G.; Gordon, C.; Miller, P. (eds), *The Foucault Effect: Studies in Governmentality: With Two Lectures by and Interviews with Michel Foucault*, Chicago, IL: University of Chicago Press, 87–104.

Gramsci, A. (1971), *Selections from the Prison Notebooks*, edited and translated by Quentin Hoare and Geoffrey Nowell Smith, London: Lawrence and Wishart.
Marx, K. (1990), *Capital: A Critique of Political Economy*, vol. 1, London: Penguin.
Scott, J. (1998), *Seeing Like a State: How Certain Schemes to Improve the Human Condition Have Failed*, New Haven, CT: Yale University Press.
Weber, M. (1968a), *Economy and Society: An Outline of Interpretative Sociology*, vol. 1, New York: Bedminster Press.

REFERENCES

Akram-Lodhi, A.H.; Borras, Jr., S.M.; Kay, C.; McKinley, T. (2007), Neoliberal globalisation, land and poverty: Implications for public action, in Akram-Lodhi, H.A.; Borras, Jr., S.M.; Kay, C. (eds), *Land, Poverty and Livelihoods in an Era of Globalization*, London: Routledge, 383–398.
Alavi, H. (1982), State and class under peripheral capitalism, in Alavi, H.; Shanin, T. (eds), *Introduction to the Sociology of "Developing Societies"*, London: Macmillan, 289–307.
Althusser, L. (1970), Les appareils idéologiques d'Etat, *La Pensée*, 151, 3–39.
Andreucci, D.; García-Lamarca, M.; Wedekind, J.; Swyngedouw, E. (2017), "Value grabbing": A political ecology of rent, *Capitalism Nature Socialism*, 28(3), 28–47.
Borras, Jr., S.M.; Hall, R.; Scoones, I.; White, B.; Wolford, W. (2011), Towards a better understanding of global land grabbing: An editorial introduction, *Journal of Peasant Studies*, 38(2), 209–216.
Brand, U.; Wissen, M. (2012), Global environmental politics and the imperial mode of living: Articulations of state–capital relations in the multiple crisis, *Globalizations*, 9(4), 547–560.
Brenner, N.; Jessop, B.; Jones, M.; Macleod, G. (2003), *State/Space, A Reader*, Oxford: Blackwell.
Coronil, F. (1997), *The Magical State: Nature, Money and Modernity in Venezuela*, Chicago, IL: University of Chicago Press.
Dahl, R. (1972), *Polyarchy: Participation and Opposition*, New Haven, CT: Yale University Press.
Dauvergne, P.; Neville, K.J. (2010), Forests, food, and fuel in the tropics: The uneven social and ecological consequences of the emerging political economy of biofuels, *Journal of Peasant Studies*, 37(4), 631–660.
Edelman, M.; Borras, Jr, S.M. (2016), *Political Dynamics of Transnational Agrarian Movements*, Rugby: Practical Action Publishing.
Evans, P.B. (1995), *Embedded Autonomy: States and Industrial Transformation*, Princeton, NJ: Princeton University Press.
Evans, P.B.; Rueschemeyer, D.; Skocpol, T. (1985), *Bringing the State Back In*, Cambridge: Cambridge University Press.
Fairhead, J.; Leach, M.; Scoones, I. (2012), Green grabbing: A new appropriation of nature? *Journal of Peasant Studies*, 39(2), 237–261.
Foucault, M. (1982), The Subject and Power, *Critical Enquiry*, 8(4), 777–795.
Foucault, M. (1991), Governmentality, in Burchell, G.; Gordon, C.; Miller, P. (eds), *The Foucault Effect: Studies in Governmentality: With Two Lectures by and Interviews with Michel Foucault*, Chicago, IL: University of Chicago Press, 87–104.
Foucault, M. (2001 [1977]), Le Pouvoir, Une Bête Magnifique, in *Dits et Écrits II, 1976–1988*, Paris: Gallimar, 368–382.
Görg, C.; Brand, U. (2006), Contested regimes in the international political economy: Global regulation of genetic resources and the internationalization of the state, *Global Environmental Politics*, 6(4), 101–123.
Gramsci, A. (1971), *Selections from the Prison Notebooks*, edited and translated by Quentin Hoare and Geoffrey Nowell Smith, London: Lawrence and Wishart.
Hobbes, T. (2016 [1651]), *Leviathan*, London: Penguin.
Holloway, J. (2002), *Cambiar El Mundo Sin Tomar El Poder*, Buenos Aires: Herramienta.
Jessop, B. (2007), From micro-powers to governmentality: Foucault's work on statehood, state formation, statecraft and state power, *Political Geography*, 26(1), 34–40.
Marx, K. (1990), *Capital: A Critique of Political Economy*, vol. 1, London: Penguin.

Marx, K.; Engels, F. (1978), Manifeste Du Parti Communiste, in *Karl Marx et Friedrich Engels Œuvres Choisies*, Moscow: Editions du progrès, 31–59.

McKay, B.; Nehring, R.; Walsh-Dilley, M. (2014), The "state" of food sovereignty in Latin America: Political projects and alternative pathways in Venezuela, Ecuador and Bolivia, *Journal of Peasant Studies*, 41(6), 1175–1200.

Miliband, R. (1969), *The State in Capitalist Society*, London: Quartet Books.

Poulantzas, N. (1974), *Les classes sociales dans le capitalisme aujourd'hui*, Paris: Editions du Seuil.

Poulantzas, N. (1978), *State, Power, Socialism*, London: Verso.

Scott, J.C. (1976), *The Moral Economy of the Peasant: Rebellion and Subsistence in Southeast Asia*, New Haven, CT: Yale University Press.

Scott, J.C. (1998), *Seeing Like a State: How Certain Schemes to Improve the Human Condition Have Failed*, New Haven, CT: Yale University Press.

Scott, J.C. (2009), *The Art of Not Being Governed: An Anarchist History of Upland Southeast Asia*, New Haven, CT: Yale University Press.

Vergara-Camus, L. (2014), Sugarcane ethanol: The hen of the golden eggs? Agribusiness and the state in Lula's Brazil, in Webber, J.R.; Spronk, S. (eds), *Crisis and Contradiction*, Leiden: Brill, 211–235.

Vergara-Camus, L.; Kay, C. (2017), Agribusiness, peasants, left-wing governments, and the state in Latin America: An overview and theoretical reflections, *Journal of Agrarian Change*, 17(2), 239–257.

Weber, M. (1968a), *Economy and Society: An Outline of Interpretative Sociology*, vol. 1, New York: Bedminster Press.

Weber, M. (1968b), The types of legitimate domination, in *Economy and Society: An Outline of Interpretative Sociology*, vol. 1, New York: Bedminster Press, 212–235.

Weber, M. (1994), *The Profession and Vocation of Politics*, in *Political Writings*, Cambridge: Cambridge University Press, 309–341.

Wolford, W.; Borras, Jr., S.M.; Hall, R.; Scoones, I.; White, B. (2013), Governing global land deals: The role of the state in the rush for land, *Development and Change*, 44(2), 189–210.

Wood, E.M. (1995), *Democracy against Capitalism: Renewing Historical Materialism*, Cambridge: Cambridge University Press.

52. Experts, land regimes and the politics of mapping

Facundo Martín

INTRODUCTION

The notion of agrarian progress, based on ideas of the rationalization, bureaucratization and professionalization of the countryside, remains one of the most relevant issues in rural politics. It operates in multiple domains, from the ideological foundations of Western societies, to global institutions, national development policies and specific processes and actors. As Mitchell (2002, 15) argues, national development and economic growth have been materialized in a 'politics of techno-science, which claimed to bring the expertise of modern engineering, technology, and social science to improve the defects of nature, to transform peasant agriculture, to repair the ills of society, and to fix the economy'. In the course of these processes, agrarian experts have emerged and expanded in the workforce as engineers, administrators, lawyers, surveyors, anthropologists and economists, as well as scientists and rural development practitioners. These heterogeneous actors are united by their use of scientific knowledge and technologies to bring about political, ideological, social, economic, agricultural and environmental changes in rural areas. More often than not, these experts occupy a position of privilege and power based on their knowledge, training and institutional affiliations. They are involved in multiple processes of agrarian change, and shape the rural development programmes and policies that influence rural social structures. Their daily practices – near or far from farms and rural communities – affect the agency of those who live on those farms and in those communities.

Dominant paradigms regarding the rural world, such as modernization theory, are profoundly ideological, yet they are disseminated as scientific knowledge through, for example, neoclassical economics, quantitative sociology, technological research and innovation. Experts have plausibly been the privileged 'conveyor belt' of agrarian modernization politics (Mosse 2014; Pritchard et al. 2015; Teisch 2011). In looking for 'alternative forms of knowing and of acting in the world' (Edelman and Wolford 2017, 962), as critical agrarian studies strives to do, it is worth critically scrutinizing the roles that experts play in the transformation of rural worlds. In doing so, the field would have better tools to understand the ambivalences and possibilities of expertise and its practice.

This text analyses the role of agrarian experts in rural social transformation and agrarian change, with a focus on land management and land regime transformation. By land regime, I mean the stabilization, over a period of time, of rules about who controls land, how land is accessed and for what purposes land is controlled. With respect to recent land-grabbing debates, one aspect that has often been overlooked is how expert knowledge and land surveyors' practices, particularly the use and institutionalization of geospatial technologies (GPS and GIS), have fostered the transformation of regimes of land control, access and ownership (Li 2017; Nalepa et al. 2017; Spiegel et al. 2012). Therefore, in this chapter, the impact of contemporary mapping politics on the commodification of land by corporate and state actors is analysed. Cadastral mapping refers to the broad set of spatial practices aimed at producing official and registered documents that define the precise locations, boundaries, ownership and tenure of property rights. Contemporary mapping politics involves technological and cartographic actions which seek to (re)make cadastral maps of land from a physically distant point. In contrast to peasants, who tend to use land regardless of its legal status, agribusiness companies seek to own land as private property and are consequently dependent on procuring cadastral maps as a legal precondition for market operations. Cadastral mapping thus contributes to rendering land investible (Li 2017). Central questions that guide the text are how surveyors' knowledge is constructed, asserted and conditioned by technology and how remote mapping practices influence the transformation of land regimes. I argue that land surveyors and their cadastral mapping practices facilitate and legitimate market-led land commodification, contributing to the de jure and de facto alienation of peasants from land.

The chapter is structured as follows. It begins with an explanation of agrarian experts' place within a broader historical and geographical context, and a review of key aspects that have structured scholarly debates, especially in the fields of the history of science, and science and technology studies. Second, the field of critical cartography is introduced in order to build a theoretical framework that articulates land-related mapping knowledge and practices. Third, the role of cadastral mapping is analysed in a case study of a land dispute in northern Mendoza, Argentina, which began in 2004 and is still ongoing. The chapter concludes with a call for more in-depth critical research on the role of agrarian experts within critical agrarian studies.

THE HISTORY OF KNOWLEDGE AND EXPERTISE IN AGRARIAN TRANSFORMATION

Since the colonial period and propelled by imperialism and globalization, agrarian experts have travelled to all corners of the world. They certainly have not travelled alone, but have been supported by powerful and influential international institutions and networks of so-called cooperation and development. Agrarian experts have been engaged to 'solve problems' such as poverty, famine, worker resistance, pests, low productivity and ecological constraints. However, their interventions have not simply been technical or scientific; these experts have also been involved in spreading the ideology of modernization and progress by fostering the transformation of existing cultures and social orders. And although thoroughly planned, expert interventions have often resulted in unexpected effects; the dissemination of knowledge, practices and technologies may fail or be transformed based on the local context. What works in one place may fail in another. Irrigation schemes, for example, require more than mere infrastructure; they are influenced by context-specific social uses and customs, social inequalities and institutions (Teisch 2011; Wolfe 2017).

Heroic stories of humans dominating nature have strengthened confidence in the ability to master diverse places and peoples and extend 'progress' to the whole world (Pratt 1992). In this regard, agrarian experts became bearers of the spirit of progress. In this long journey, they have acted as more than simple messengers; supported by the development of specific and powerful initiatives, the number of agrarian experts and the diversity of tasks they deal with have markedly increased (Tilley 2011). In the process, they have become core and ubiquitous agents in rural policies.

I argue that in order to fully understand the role of experts and their modernizationist bias, critical agrarian studies needs first to 'move back to go forward'; in other words, it needs to first internalize significant lessons from the past regarding the power of scientific knowledge and rural politics. To this end, I briefly recap the scholarly debates and evidence from the fields of the history of science, environmental history and science and technology studies that involve experts playing a key role in the attempt to modernize rural areas (Fogelman and Bassett 2017; Jørgensen et al. 2013; Li 2017).

Edelman and Wolford (2017, 960) argue that despite the considerable amount of critical literature on modern epistemology, reductionist and binary views of rural life still operate (from agriculture to industry, primitive to modern, rural to urban, feudal to market-oriented). In my view, this lack of comprehension is probably due to an insufficient understanding of how technical-rational control has expanded to include practically all areas of rural life. At the same time, there are continuities and overlappings that may take the form of coloniality (cultural, economic and political patterns that remain after formal colonialism ends), building a complex picture of the cultural and political background in rural worlds.

James Scott's book *Seeing Like a State* (1998) is a radical critique of the 'technocratic optimism' of rural development projects. It focuses on modernization failures due to legibility and simplification. Legibility, according to Scott, was the perennial 'state's attempt to make a society legible, to arrange the population in ways that simplified the classic state functions of taxation, conscription, and prevention of rebellion' (ibid., 2). Both legibility and simplification were seen as a central problem of statecraft, especially regarding the ordering of nature and rural areas. At the same time, the apparent reduction in the complexity of systems, Scott argues, is the central explanation for failed attempts at development. Here, the idea of state maps of legibility emerged as the key device capable of condensing and simplifying these hard-to-pin-down fugitive landscapes (Craib 2004). In fact, attempts to fix the land to the state appear to be more complex than the simple creation of a perfect map.

The process of state (and corporate) simplification demanded the dramatic development of expert knowledge and the formation of a myriad of experts. These experts and their expertise began to circulate worldwide, influencing distant and heterogeneous places. Agrarian progress is, furthermore, often assimilated into infrastructure projects. California-based mining and irrigation engineers constitute one of the paradigmatic examples of the nodal role played by experts in rural transformation (Teisch 2011). Since the beginning of the twentieth century to the present, California engineers were part of the worldwide elite of water experts, exerting power and influencing land and infrastructural projects all over the world. Through an analysis of the uneven outcomes of their initiatives and of the various deviations in practice from the engineers' initial motivations that occurred, Teisch (2011) offers a clear picture of the complexities involved in the application of expertise and technology.

Hodge (2007) focuses on the practices of advisers, scientific researchers and technical experts as a particular group of actors operating within the late-imperial state involved in colonial policy and project planning – the agrarian development doctrine – between 1895 and 1960. He demonstrates that despite power asymmetries, imperial plans were often considerably challenged by local actors and communities and changed (ibid., 4–6). By examining the concerns of the agrarian development practitioners operating in the British colonies, Hodge shows how 'colonial knowledge' was produced and institutionalized. Particularly relevant is the idea that experts on the ground had, in this case, considerable space to negotiate the official policy goals considering the local conditions and livelihoods. On several occasions, they had to understand and make visible traditional and local practices.

The role played by experts in agrarian transformations has been traditionally considered by scholars in disciplines such as the history of science, environmental history and science and technology studies. In their practices, experts condense and articulate the overlapping cultural, technical and political legacies. Understandably, these disciplines have a clear interest in the past, and pose stimulating questions around how the relation between expertise and agrarian transformation has recently been reconfigured in the context of increasing pressure on land resources and the massification of geospatial technologies. As the literature has shown, expert knowledge and its putting in place has been developed and challenged through specific devices, technological objects and institutions. Experts' knowledge and practices constitute an unbeatable lens through which to examine the complexity of the transformation of land regimes. Cartography, understood as a contentious process of mapping and codifying land, as well as land ownership, rights and use, is a paradigmatic case, where critical dimensions linking expertise and agrarian issues emerge.

CRITICAL CARTOGRAPHY, THE POLITICS OF MAPPING AND CADASTRAL MAPS

How experts work through maps and mapping alongside agrarian transformations is the central question of this chapter. A map is the key device through which experts – surveyors – influence the transformation of land regimes. They use the map as their work tool and weapon. It is through maps that their practice is materialized: they simplify the complex, they create and erase uses and rights, they legalize appropriations and expropriations of land rights and they create and destroy social-natural relations.

Critical cartography is a vigorous field of inquiry devoted to scrutinizing what maps are, how they are constructed and the political effects derived from their creation and circulation. In what follows, I analyse the debates within the field of critical cartography, giving an account of the epistemological and political commitments of the various currents that make up the field. This allows me to critically review various possible relationships between surveying and land politics. Afterwards, I assume a combined understanding of two of them in order to analyse a concrete case study.

In his book *Cartographic Mexico*, Craib (2004) describes the unsuccessful efforts to achieve a comprehensive and definitive registry of Mexican rural lands. The main obstacle, he shows, was the difference between official records and the reality on the ground. Throughout the twentieth century, public and private lands were legally and illegally sold, rented, divided and occupied. Different users claimed the same lands, new occupants arrived on abandoned properties and lands belonging to municipalities or states were transferred to others as jurisdictions shifted (ibid., 1). The author meticulously examines how experts dealt with the terrain, maps and people they met in the field. He describes surveyors as active agents in rural politics, as opposed to being passive or objective 'land officers'. In many rural areas, they appear as the human face and body of corporations and the state (ibid., 9–10).

Other scholars have discussed the various dimensions of property regimes, comprising not only the legal aspects of land control but also the social, political and territorial processes that commodification and capital accumulation are based on (Goldstein and Yates 2017; Pritchard

et al. 2015). Debates on land ontology and epistemology have contributed to a more sophisticated understanding of the connections between expert knowledge and land politics, drawing
upon insights from the field of critical cartography, particularly the idea of the 'power of maps'
(Crampton 2001; Harley 1989; Kitchin and Dodge 2007).

Contrary to positivistic cartography, critical cartography argues that maps do not only represent the territory but also produce it (Fogelman and Bassett 2017). The idea of 'map effectiveness' was coined by Robinson et al. (1995) to highlight the fact that maps need to capture
and (re)present relevant information. Critical cartography, then, asks what is relevant and from
what point of view, for whom maps are made and what are the political effects.

Fogelman and Bassett (2017) describe varying views of maps within critical cartography.
The three main perspectives see maps as representational, inscriptional or processual. Scholars
advocating a representational perspective emphasize the accuracy of maps and argue that maps
always demonstrate a certain truth about reality (Harley 1989; Robinson 1952). Scholars with
an inscriptional view focus on the effects that maps produce (e.g. commodification, taxation
and dispossession), and argue that maps have inherently powerful effects. Scott (1998), for
example, sees maps as having a prescriptive role in both simplifying and altering the world
around us. He argues that government cadastral maps are created to designate taxable property
holders. Such a map 'does not merely describe a system of land tenure; it creates such a system
through its ability to give its categories the force of law' (ibid., 3). Another influential work
that seeks to go beyond the representational view towards a more inscriptional perspective is
John Pickles' (1995) book *Ground Truth*, in which he discusses the work that maps do, how
they act to shape people's understandings of the world and how they code the world. Pickles
characterizes maps as 'inscription devices' that not only represent the world but create it.
Furthermore, a created world is not neutral, but responds to the map-makers' interests. This is
particularly evident in cadastral maps, which essentially transform land into an economic asset
– governed by the state, and which is transferable through the market – thereby negating prior
social rules and the social control of land. Finally, proponents of the processual perspective
understand maps as processes rather than final products. From this perspective, maps have
no ontological security or stability. They are constantly being remade – by surveyors – based
on changing contexts. Proponents of a processual perspective call for a focus on the 'spatial
practices enacted to solve relational problems' (Kitchin and Dodge 2007, 342).

In sum, there are mapping practices and then there are uses of maps, and regardless of the
specific perspective and context, the surveyor is the principal actor. Cartography needs to
be understood as a contingent and relational process (Crampton 2003). Maps are historical
products that operate within 'a certain horizon of possibilities' (ibid., 51), and not finite
representations of land. Thus, analyses of remote mapping practices and their territorial and
political effects become feasible by understanding cadastral maps as both inscription devices
and processes. Land surveyors with power and access to the state operate between maps and
mapping. They literally (re)make cadastral maps as much as they need to in order to increase
the effectiveness of the maps. This dialectic relationship between map and mapping takes
the form of a meta-process, in the sense that it is a process that encompasses several discrete
and overlapping processes (e.g. mapping and remapping, buying land, assigning titles and
negotiating revisions to cadastral maps). A processual comprehension of cadastral mapping
focuses on surveyors' recursive practices and the specific effects of cadastral maps as effective
inscription devices.

The next section presents a case study in which both inscriptional and processual perspectives are considered in order to understand the role of surveyors in land regime transformation through an intricate process of cadastral mapping.

LAND SURVEYORS, CADASTRAL MAPPING AND LAND POLITICS: A CASE STUDY FROM MENDOZA, ARGENTINA

This case study follows land surveyors and public officers during a land dispute between an agribusiness company and a peasant family in the northern border province of Mendoza, Argentina. It illustrates how the use of remote sensing technologies in land surveying and cadastral mapping has enabled the acceleration of legal and illegal land control and ownership by agribusiness companies in the province. It is based on my own ethnographic research undertaken between 2016 and 2018 on the sites of the land dispute, as well as in governmental institutions and archives such as the Land Registry Office and the Irrigation Department. I interviewed peasants, surveyors, public officers and other land-related experts such as lawyers and agronomists. I also reviewed in detail a key lawsuit pertaining to the dispute, including the judicial records.

The analysis reveals that contemporary conflicts over land use are dependent on remote mapping technologies, which elevate the surveyor-as-expert to a central role. I trace the importance of cadastral mapping in a particular conflict in Mendoza, and reveal how the practices of surveyors, in conjunction with agribusiness and the Land Registry Office, made peasant claims invisible and led to violent conflict. I reveal two main operations in the mapping practice: technicity and (in)visibility. The first refers to the power of technology to 'solve' field mapping problems, which results in techno-dependent working methodologies and auto-justification (it is a 'good' map because it is made with 'advanced' technology), in opposition to the traditional 'accuracy' mapping principle (as per the representational perspective described in the previous section). The second operation, (in)visibility, occurs when land surveyors – wittingly or unwittingly, due to their physical distance from the terrain to be mapped – neither perceive nor record the actual land users and the ways they are using the land. Meanwhile, due to the use of remote technologies and the physical absence of the surveyors themselves, peasants are not even aware that they and their lands are being measured, surveyed and formally expropriated.

The actors involved in the case study conflict are an agribusiness company, *Agropecuaria Elaia*, a resistant peasant family, the Domínguez family and the state, through the local Land Registry Office. *Agropecuaria Elaia* is a branch of a Spanish holding whose agroindustrial production represents one sector of a wide range of activities. The contested land has been irrigated since the nineteenth century, and the arrival of irrigation initiated a process of land and water commodification that dispossessed native and peasant groups from their traditional land and water rights. The land was mainly appropriated by European migrants, who rapidly made it 'productive' by planting wine grapes as part of an expansive agroindustrial business model. This model had collapsed by 1970 due to shifts in the economy, market restrictions and wine overproduction. As a consequence, most of the land was abandoned and peasants returned to it to breed and herd goats, sheep, cows and horses. In the early twenty-first century, these 'marginal lands' again came into investors' sights, who saw the area as potentially profitable.

In Mendoza, buying or selling land requires a surveyor to make a new cadastral map of the land, which has to be approved by and registered at the Land Registry Office. According to the law, surveyors act as public officials in land market transactions. In other words, cadastral mapping is born as a private action between the surveyor and the land claimant, but it becomes a public document when the state becomes involved, through the Land Registry Office, at the moment of registering the cadastral map. Thus, land surveyors play a critical role in facilitating and accelerating the commodification of land in Mendoza in the service of the agroindustry. The extent and velocity of this process has been possible due to the versatility of land survey- ors' mapping work. One core issue in this story is that the traditional fieldwork – legally oblig- atory, according to the local Civil Code – done by surveyors has become redundant in modern mapping practices, due to the increasing use of remote sensing technologies over the past 15 years. In fact, building cadastral maps exclusively through remote technologies is not legal.

The Domínguez family is a well-known ranching family with cattle, goats and horses, who lived outside Jocolí, a rural village in northern Mendoza, at the time of my fieldwork. They were living on a farm that had been abandoned by its previous owner since 1944. In 2004, their livelihood and routine work were disrupted when *Agropecuaria Elaia* started an ambi- tious project in the olive oil industry in Mendoza, buying from another private owner around 32 000 hectares of land in Jocolí, including part of the Domínguez family's grazing lands. In 2007, the company began to build wire fences sectioning off surrounding grazing areas of the family farm. In this process the family retained access to some areas but lost it to others. In May 2011, peasants from the local area who shared breeding lands, which included the Domínguez family, gathered together on a neighbouring farm to vaccinate and trade animals. The company took advantage of the family's absence from their own farm to build more fences, thereby enforcing their claim over part of the family's grazing lands they had bought in 2004. The fences, however, extended 5 kilometres beyond the boundaries of the company's property. On the same day they also destroyed – without prior notice or a court order – one of the family's barns that had been standing since 1944.

This act of destruction and illegal land appropriation via physical demarcation attracted public attention and marked a turning point in the conflict (La Nación 2011). The company was formally denounced in court and publicly condemned in the national media. The family recovered its land and rebuilt the buildings that had been destroyed. The company removed the fences and replaced them back along the previous boundary line. In 2015, the courts ruled in favour of the Domínguez family and recognized their property title for part of the grazing lands they had lost. The conflict over the Domínguez family farm brought to light the chaotic history of mapping this land and resulted in a request by the judge of the lawsuit for an expert's cadastral report. This report concluded that the company had indeed illegally appropriated the Domínguez family's land in its action in May 2011.

The crucial role in the conflict of remote mapping conducted by private surveyors becomes evident when the actions of the public officers – not always professional surveyors – at the provincial Land Registry Office are scrutinized. Cadastral maps are a key inscription device used to register and secure private property rights over land, and can therefore lead to the com- modification of communal lands. As mentioned above, land surveyors define precise locations and boundaries on cadastral maps and thus create the foundation for property rights. The state formally enforces the process of maintaining the publication and updating of cadastral maps in order to guarantee a working land market. But in the process of mapping, other histories and practices can be invisibilized and – intentionally or unintentionally – errors in the practices of surveyors can have far-reaching consequences.

The first misappropriation, for instance, was carried out in 1971, when a cadastral map of the land was registered at the Land Registry Office without recognizing existing properties. The owner of the land specified that there were no previous properties or registered owners. The land mapped in 1971 was validated by the Land Registry Office as a supposedly 'empty' space without a legal history. In fact, it was not only being used by peasants, but there were other registered maps and titles already existing. The Land Registry Office ignored these previous property records, however, not to mention the peasants' actual physical presence. This action effectively nullified the previous land titles. Furthermore, with this new cadastral map registered at the Land Registry Office, future operations could take advantage of this now legally validated 'cleansed' history of the land. Here, both the private surveyor and public officers failed, in favour of land misappropriation. According to the law, this 1971 cadastral map and its property title should not have been valid because of the existence of previous and overlapping registered titles; legally, it is possible to register cadastral maps with overlapping titles, but this must be designated on the official maps. What this case demonstrates, however, is how in a single legal operation, with nothing more than the creation of a new map, multiple properties can be erased from the cadastral registry. This was the 'cleansed' title procured by *Agropecuaria Elaia* in 2004.

According to the expert's cadastral report, as requested by the court in 2011, the surveyor for *Agropecuaria Elaia* had also intentionally omitted and falsified information in order to erase the land's history and extend the boundaries of its new title beyond those established in prior registered maps in 2006. Officers in the Land Registry Office had approved this new cadastral map without reviewing any previous records. Typically, mapping a property of this size would require about six months of intensive fieldwork. The property is divided into two sections, one of which includes mountainous terrain 3000 meters above sea level in an area with no roads. According to the court expert's report, *Agropecuaria Elaia*'s survey was performed in only 15 days. This could be grounds for arguing that the surveyors did not fulfil their legal obligation to make the cadastral map based on fieldwork; a claim that, if proven correct, would invalidate the map. But the map was approved and registered. The case also clearly makes evident the role of geospatial technologies used by the private surveyor, not just in terms of how they 'assisted' the surveyor's work, but also replaced it, inasmuch as he did not perform the required fieldwork with all its complexities, but rather satellites, software and computers did the work for him.

In 2008, another survey was carried out by *Agropecuaria Elaia* due to a property split of the land. When the company presented its new cadastral map to the Land Registry Office to be validated, the officers this time requested that it be reviewed due to inconsistencies and overlaps with other property titles. The company's surveyor rejected these critical remarks and insisted on the map's veracity. The Land Registry Office requested revisions for a second time and the surveyor presented a completely new map, without justifying the changes, in which he marked some of the overlaps with other existing titles. This new map was formally approved and registered by the Land Registry Office. This is a clear case of cadastral mapping as both an inscriptional and processual operation: the kind of knowledge and expertise that a private surveyor must have in order to achieve the goal – getting the cadastral map registered by the state – has changed. This new cadastral map was carried out because it is mandatory in each land market transaction. In this case *Agropecuaria Elaia* sold off a part of the land to a sister company. This time, the surveyor shifted the property boundaries to include 500 hectares of land beyond the existing lands in the previous registered map. Again, in a single stroke, a large piece of land was incorporated into the company's property. This new piece of appropriated land was, as in the case of the fences laid out in 2007, part of the Domínguez family's grazing lands.

In 2017, with the cadastral map approved by the Land Registry Office, the company started to build a new wire fence, which naturally led to resistance by the local peasants. This new episode took a serious turn, when one young peasant was seriously wounded by the police due to his refusal to move from the fence line during its construction. A trial over this incident is currently underway, and therefore the company has momentarily stopped the construction of the fence.

The land dispute has, thus far, had mixed results regarding the transformation of the land regime. On the one hand, the company has established direct control over the majority of the lands, including several areas that were previously being used by the Domínguez family as grazing lands. On the other hand, even though the Domínguez family did lose control over some key areas within their previous grazing lands, they did manage to consolidate control over other parts when the court ruled in their favour in 2011. In both cases, however, the process of transformation was clearly and dramatically dependent on cartographic development, which in turn relied on the surveyors' mapping practices and the involvement of the state. The surveyors' mistakes and omissions in mapping and remapping seem to be oriented not towards the goal of achieving a faithful representation of the land, but rather towards fulfilling the desires of *Agropecuaria Elaia* to expand their land holdings, and towards fulfilling the administrative requirements necessary for the map to be registered by the state. This demands the development of new and specific expertise that is more linked to the idea of maps as instrumental and processual devices than of maps as representational.

CONCLUSION

The goal of this chapter was to address the role of experts within contemporary agrarian transformations, exploring the ways in which land regimes and expert knowledge are produced and interrelated. In doing so, I first framed the place of science and expert knowledge both historically and geographically in the literature, illuminating the remaining linkages between the roles of colonial, modernizationist and contemporary experts. Recent trends in land grabbing have fostered a new wave of conflicts and disputes over land, and more generally around natural resource politics. In this context, this chapter investigated the extent to which we are witnessing a transformation of the land regime, where the commodification of land is highly influenced by surveyors' knowledge and practices. Maps and cartography thus remain centre stage, but with renovated characteristics due to the massification of geospatial technologies in land surveying.

Throughout the analysis of the case study of a land dispute in northern Mendoza, mapping practices had significant effects on land policies. As inscription devices, these maps were effective in completing economic transactions and making them official and formal through registration at the Land Registry Office. At the same time, through this formal registration, powerful agents were able to claim and occupy the mapped piece of land, and in this case, to effectively displace and disenfranchise the peasants who had previously occupied and controlled the land. Furthermore, the map of the land went through several versions throughout the course of the dispute. This confirms that cadastral mapping is highly processual and relies on mapping practices that are dramatically mediated by geospatial technologies, which at the same time demand a specific expertise linked to technicity and invisibility.

This brings to light some differences from previous land control and access regimes. Remote mapping produces mutual invisibility. On the one hand, the surveyor cannot see the people who actually use and dwell on the land. Thus they can be easily erased from the map and formally disenfranchised. On the other hand, peasants are unaware that the mapping is even taking place, and therefore often have no chance to resist the appropriation of their lands. New maps that disregard local peasants become legal before these peasants even become aware of the process. This impacts how land conflicts unfold and how land control and access are negotiated and contested. Peasants practise direct, daily and collective control over their lands, and they react to the presence of strangers or activities on their lands. The presence and visibility of land surveyors used to be necessary prior to the use of geospatial technologies. However, now that maps are drawn in offices far from the actual land itself, the possibilities for land control and resistance by peasants have changed considerably.

Expert knowledge and technologies will continue to play a significant role in land commodification. The field of critical agrarian studies has typically scrutinized land questions and land politics by focusing mainly on the macro and public dimensions that involve protests, conflicts, rebellions, disasters and migration, to name just a few. The intersection between these visible issues and more surreptitious ones – such as the mapping practices analysed in this chapter – opens up a promising critical research agenda around the role of agrarian experts in the conflictive transformation of the countryside. How expertise is challenged and altered according to the political and technological context deserves more attention. This critical research field could draw advantages by going deep into conversation with disciplines such as science and technology studies, and environmental history. This would involve not only epistemological and theoretical issues, but also methodological challenges, considering that critical agrarian studies is in its early stages. In contemporary land struggles and changing land regimes, a renewed critical research agenda is needed. It must take into account the tensions inherent in unveiling the biased narratives and practices of modernizationist experts, and in recreating forms of alternative expertise.

FURTHER READING

Craib, R.B. (2004), *Cartographic Mexico: A History of State Fixations and Fugitive Landscapes*, Durham, NC: Duke University Press.

Hodge, J.M. (2007), *The Triumph of the Expert: Agrarian Doctrines of Development and the Legacies of British Colonialism*, Athens, OH: Ohio University Press.

Saraiva, T. (2016), *Fascist Pigs: Technoscientific Organism and the History of Fascism*, Cambridge, MA: MIT Press.

Teisch, J.B. (2011), *Engineering Nature: Water, Development, and the Global Spread of American Environmental Expertise*, Chapel Hill, NC: University of North Carolina Press.

Tilley, H. (2011), *Africa as a Living Laboratory: Empire, Development and the Problem of Scientific Knowledge, 1870–1950*, Chicago, IL: University of Chicago Press.

REFERENCES

Craib, R.B. (2004), *Cartographic Mexico: A History of State Fixations and Fugitive Landscapes*, Durham, NC: Duke University Press.

Crampton, J.W. (2001), Maps as social constructions: Power, communication and visualization, *Progress in Human Geography*, 25(2), 235–252.

Crampton, J.W. (2003), *The Political Mapping of Cyberspace*, Edinburgh: Edinburgh University Press.

Edelman, M.; Wolford, W. (2017), Introduction: Critical agrarian studies in theory and practice, *Antipode*, 49, 959–976.

Fogelman, C.; Bassett, T.J. (2017), Mapping for investability: Remaking land and maps in Lesotho, *Geoforum*, 82(Supplement C), 252–258.

Goldstein, J.E.; Yates, J.S. (2017), Introduction: Rendering land investable, *Geoforum*, 82, 209–211.

Harley, J.B. (1989), Deconstructing the map, *Cartographica*, 26, 1–20.

Hodge, J.M. (2007), *The Triumph of the Expert: Agrarian Doctrines of Development and the Legacies of British Colonialism*, Athens, OH: Ohio University Press.

Jørgensen, D.; Jørgensen, F.A.; Pritchard, S.B. (2013), *New Natures: Joining Environmental History with Science and Technology Studies*, Pittsburgh, PA: University of Pittsburgh Press.

Kitchin, R.; Dodge, M. (2007), Rethinking maps, *Progress in Human Geography*, 31(3), 331–344.

La Nación (2011), La Posesión de la Tierra, Eje de un Conflicto en Mendoza, *La Nación*, 11 June, accessed 3 October 2019 at www.lanacion.com.ar/1380472-la-posesion-de-la-tierra-eje-de-un-conflictoen-mendoza.

Li, T.M. (2017), Rendering land investible: Five notes on time, *Geoforum*, 82(Supplement C), 276–278.

Mitchell, T. (2002), *Rule of Experts: Egypt, Techno-Politics, Modernity*, Berkeley, CA: University of California Press.

Mosse, D. (2014), *Cultivating Development: An Ethnography of Aid Policy and Practice*, London: Pluto Press.

Nalepa, R.A.; Short Gianotti, A.G.; Bauer, D.M. (2017), Marginal land and the global land rush: A spatial exploration of contested lands and state-directed development in contemporary Ethiopia. *Geoforum*, 82(Supplement C), 237–251.

Pickles, J. (1995), *Ground Truth: The Social Implications of Geographic Information Systems*, New York: Guilford.

Pratt, M.L. (1992), *Imperial Eyes: Travel Writings and Transculturation*, London: Routledge.

Pritchard, S.B.; Wolf, S.A.; Wolford, W. (2015), Knowledge and the politics of land, *Environment and Planning A*, 48(4), 616–625.

Robinson, A.H. (1952), *The Look of Maps: An Examination of Cartographic Design*, Madison, WI: University of Wisconsin Press.

Robinson, A.H.; Morrison, J.L.; Muehrcke, P.C.; Kimmerling, A.J.; Guptil, S.C. (1995), *Elements of Cartography*, sixth edition, New York: Wiley.

Scott, J.C. (1998), *Seeing Like a State: How Certain Schemes to Improve the Human Condition Have Failed*, New York: Yale University Press.

Spiegel, S.J.; Ribeiro, C.A.A.S.; Sousa, R.; Veiga, M.M. (2012), Mapping spaces of environmental dispute: GIS, mining, and surveillance in the Amazon, *Annals of the Association of American Geographers*, 102(2), 320–349.

Teisch, J.B. (2011), *Engineering Nature: Water, Development and the Global Spread of American Environmental Expertise*, Chapel Hill, NC: University of North Carolina Press.

Tilley, H. (2011), *Africa as a Living Laboratory: Empire, Development, and the Problem of Scientific Knowledge, 1870–1950*, Chicago, IL: University of Chicago Press.

Wolfe, M.D. (2017), *Watering the Revolution: An Environmental and Technological History of Agrarian Reform in Mexico*, Durham, NC: Duke University Press.

53. Rural social movements/transnational agrarian movements

Giuliano Martiniello

INTRODUCTION: RURAL SOCIAL MOVEMENTS AND CRITICAL AGRARIAN STUDIES

On 29 November 2018, 35 000 farmers and agricultural workers from all over India organized under various umbrella groups, among which was the All-India Kisan Sabha, and marched to Parliament in Delhi in a two-day protest against soaring operating costs and plunging produce prices. In one of the largest farmers' mobilizations that Delhi has ever seen, demonstrators chanted slogans against Narendra Modi's right-wing government's false assurances and unfulfilled promises, demanding a special parliament session to discuss the persistent agrarian crisis in India. The social reproduction crisis manifested into generalized levels of poverty fuelling vast levels of indebtedness – a dynamic that many consider behind the suicide crisis, which has claimed the lives of 3 million farmers in the last 20 years (Nilsen and Roy 2016).

Far from being epiphenomenal, these mobilizations represent the culmination of a decade of agrarian struggles between farmers' organizations and the Indian state around issues of farmers' rights, livelihoods and voices, especially in Rajasthan and Maharashtra state – the latter known as the 'graveyard of farmers'. Rural discontent generated by agricultural stagnation, unemployment and state-sponsored elite-driven land grabs manifested into various forms of large-scale protests. These grievances culminated in a 200 km long march on 6–12 March 2018 which began in Nashik with 25 000 people and concluded in Mumbai with over 50 000 protesters, and a mass demonstration of 100 000 people (Dhawale 2018, 261). The vigorous, democratic and unprecedented Long Kisan March, which saw hundreds of women marching barefoot, with bruised and bleeding feet, succeeded in putting the agrarian crisis at the core of the political debate, capturing the imagination of many and symbolically stirring the consciousness of the nation. To the astonishment of those who have been espousing grand narratives of modernity and industrialization, and theorized the demise of peasants, the resurgence of rural social movements had shaken the edifice of consensus of Modi's government at its foundations. By providing opposition leaders and other civil society organizations, who joined the farmers in protest, with a common ground and rallying point, rural social movements significantly contributed to opposing Modi's neoliberal and authoritarian political project.

These dramatic events and symbolic protests point to the resurrection and lasting relevance of rural social movements and peasants' collective action both as terrain of analysis and as an alternative political project to authoritarian populism in the Global South. Agrarian struggles occurring in India are not an isolated phenomenon; there exist, in fact, a myriad of instances of contestation in the countryside of the Global South which do not necessarily take the shape of organized collective action that reaches the public sphere. In some cases, localized episodes of resistance do not automatically translate into broader social movements at the national and regional levels. Studying rural social movements and transnational agrarian movements

(TAMs) allows us to understand the character of contemporary rural social struggles and the responses from below to processes of neoliberal agri-food restructuring. For critical agrarian studies, understanding the politics, class composition, praxis and ideology of rural social movements represents a fundamental task. Analysing rural social movements involves asking questions about the existing material and political conditions as well as the levels of political, class and collective consciousness that spearheaded the emergence of these networks, coalitions and mobilizations. It allows identifying the key elements that contribute to the rise of peasants' agency, including questions of class composition, organization and communication, ideology, the praxis of struggle and so on. It also helps to understand the internal dynamics of any given movement, the critical role in advocating change played by peasant organizations and the content of social struggles to gain greater access and control over productive resources.

Rural social movements analysis helps us in highlighting and informing the continuing centrality of the agrarian question to development studies and policies (Edelman and Borras 2016, 3). Studying rural social movements also allows framing the emergence of these movements in the context of the impact of neoliberal capitalist restructuring in the countryside, and the obstacles that pre-existing land-based social relations pose to fully fledged development of capitalist relations. Inquiries into the role of rural social movements also allow understanding the linkages between changes in the political economy of a specific country and the implications for the birth and development of agrarian movements. There is, in fact, a trend within social sciences to situate the rise of social movements in the context of the growth of civil society activism, often at the expense of an analysis of capitalism, the political economy, class struggle and conflict (Hetland and Goodwin 2013). And indeed, the global political and economic context that, in some way, shaped the emergence of rural social mobilizations is a crucial element in the analysis of social movements. Yet there is also a need to analyse how global forces impact the local since it is at the local level that rural social movements are most often engaged in concrete struggles. It is impossible to understand the politics of rural social movements in the absence of an in-depth analysis of the class-based division of labour in the countryside (large commercial farmers, rich peasants, small peasants or landless labourers). Understanding the class composition and differences among rural social movements also allows to plan alliances between various social constituencies which compose rural social movements, but also to underscore some contradictions and differences among them.

Yet an analysis that considers only class relationships alone is no longer a sufficient toolbox to explore the diverse terrains of the unfolding rural politics in the Global South. In this regard, French philosopher Etienne Balibar argued that: in a capitalist world, class relations are '*one determining* structure, covering *all* social practices, without being the only one' (quoted in Therborn 2007, 88). According to Henry Bernstein, 'class relations are *universal but not exclusive* determinations of social practices in capitalism' (2010, 115). They intersect and combine with other forms of social difference and division, among which gender and other oppressive relations such as race, ethnicity, age, religion and caste are among the most important (ibid.). These sources of social contradiction, which predate the spread of capitalism, contribute to the complex and contradictory nature of capitalist social relations. Deepening social differentiation and intensifying competition over land, which result from the penetration of capitalism in petty commodity production, take many forms including generational, gender, ethnic and religious confrontations. Yet as Pauline Peters has argued: 'proliferating tensions and struggles between generations and genders, or between groups labelled by region, ethnicity or religion are intimately tied up with the dynamics of division and exclusion, alliance and inclusion that constitute class formation' (2004, 305). In what follows, the chapter will provide an overview of critical debates around the origins, emergence and development of rural social movements. It will later discuss two selected case studies – the Movimiento dos Trabahadores Rurais Siem Terra (MST) and the Korean Peasant League (KPL). Finally, it will explore the political and economic dynamics of change in the neoliberal era that have pushed them to coalesce into TAMs.

DEBATING RURAL SOCIAL MOVEMENTS

Rural social movements are networks, coalitions, assemblages of peasant and other popular organizations, community-based and human rights organizations, women and youth associations and trade unions, struggling for a radical transformation (or reform) of the existing structures of political, social and economic power (Desmarais 2007). Their main objective is to produce political mobilizations, advocacy campaigns and social struggles that aim at democratizing the political space and radically contesting state policies (Moyo and Yeros 2005). They have developed diffused and elaborated repertoires of collective action and contention (Tilly 1978) though mobilizations and public protests remain the most important strategies of struggle that radical agrarian movements use in their battle for greater access and control over productive resources. Some of them claim to be representative of the disenfranchised, dispossessed and excluded by global capitalism. At the same time, their vision takes inspiration from principles of economic and social justice, which include gender and ethnic equality.

Rural social movements do not represent newness. Massive peasant-based insurrections have informed revolutions in China (1949), Bolivia (1952) and Cuba (1959) (see Wolf 1969); the anti-colonial, liberation and anti-imperial movements in Vietnam, Algeria, Portuguese Africa and Rhodesia (see Cabral 1965; Fanon 1967); and the rise of guerrilla movements in Malaysia, the Philippines and Colombia (Edelman and Borras 2016, 28). These events also coincided with the emergence of a new field of enquiry, 'peasant studies', which aimed at understanding the role of the peasantry as an important historical actor and protagonist of social and political change (Shanin 1990). Over the last 15 years, there has been a resurgence of interest in peasant studies as evidenced by the growing importance of the *Journal of Peasant Studies* and the *Journal of Agrarian Change*.

In the last couple of decades, there has been a renewed interest in social movements and civil society activism. The emergence of multiple and diversified sets of collective practices and networks, such as those coalescing in the World Social Forums and the 'altermondialiste' movement, contributed to the articulation of demands about the environment, human rights, Indigenous populations, women's rights and structures of governance (Della Porta and Tarrow 2005; Della Porta et al. 2006). This school of thought mostly saw new social movements emerging out of the weakening and fragmentation of the state and the ensuing growth of civil society networks and activism. Most of the contemporary scholarship heavily focused on urban social movements (Edelman and Borras 2016). Scholarly work on rural social movements in the Global South also increased in part because some of the social organizations that spearheaded these mobilizations had a rural character and were among the largest in the world.

Critical agrarian scholarship significantly contributed to the study and mapping of the resurgence of rural social movements across the world as a response from below to the profound socio-economic and political changes brought about by neoliberal globalization in the

1980s and onwards. Studies from around the globe have shown how agrarian restructuring, structural adjustment programmes and growing state authoritarianism contributed to the dramatic deterioration of the conditions of social reproduction for millions of peasants and rural workers pushing them to the desperate search for political and economic alternatives (Borras et al. 2008b; Edelman 2008; Moyo and Yeros 2005; Peluso et al. 2008). This scholarship contributed to squarely situating the question of rural social movements within the frame of the political economy of agrarian change, reintegrating debates over capitalism and class conflict as crucial elements in the analysis of their origins, class composition, ideology and praxis. Such reintroduction is particularly welcome given the not-so-surprising absence of notions such as capitalism, political economy and class struggle from most of the studies of social movements (Hetland and Goodwin 2013), with priority given to concepts such as global networks and global civil society, which may obscure hierarchies and power relations within civil society itself (Desmarais 2007).

However, not every corner of the world where economic and social conditions have worsened has witnessed growing contestation. It would be therefore erroneous to link protest mechanically to the worsening of socio-economic conditions; so how do we explain thus these cycles of protest (Tarrow 1988)? How do we understand the recrudescence of these forms of social mobilization and collective action? A good starting point is to distinguish between objective conditions and their subjective perceptions. It is only when rural subjects collectively define the actual terms of exploitation and oppression as unjust and subject to change, and a translation from objective to subjective interests occur, that the process of becoming a class for itself begins, as Marx would have put it (Shin 1994). Class, collective or other social forms of consciousness do not depend strictly on one's position in the division of labour of the capitalist economy, but are historically and collectively constructed through struggles (see Thompson 1978). Yet consciousness alone without the mobilization of material, symbolic and cultural resources cannot succeed in sustaining long-term mobilizations. There is, therefore, a relationship between past protests, processes of consciousness formation, the mobilization of material and symbolic resources and the current phase of rural protest which needs to be identified if we intend to grapple with the complexities shaping peasants' collective action.

And yet, the objective position occupied in the capital/labour relationship does not facilitate, for example, grappling with the multiple forms of informal, non-monetary, social reproductive labour undertaken within rural households (Razavi 2009). Nor does it help us disentangle the work and power differentials in control, access and use of land within rural households and the implications for the political agency (Bezner-Kerr 2017). Recent studies on large-scale land acquisitions have highlighted their gendered effects and how they differentially affect men and women, exasperating gender inequalities in control, access and use of land (Julia and White 2012). In other words, gender shapes how women respond to large-scale land acquisitions and their politics (Park 2019). By the same token, how do we explain the character of specific rural mobilizations such as those led by Dalits and Adivasi in India without incorporating caste and ethnicity in the analysis? It is therefore of paramount importance to integrate class, gender, ethnicity, age, caste, religion and other social cleavages to unpack the dynamics of agrarian change and rural political agency.

Critical agrarian scholarship on agrarian movements allowed to capture the dynamics, origins and forms of a new wave of peasant activism, intersecting at local, national and transnational levels (Borras 2008; Desmarais 2007; Edelman 2008; Peluso et al. 2008). In what follows, I will provide a discussion of some of the critical elements (origins, class, ideology and praxis) of some of the most influential rural social movements such as the MST and KPL. These organizations have been vital promoters in the making of broad coalitions of TAMs such as Vía Campesina, an umbrella organization which gathers together more than 170 peasant organizations around the world (Borras 2008; Desmarais 2007; Desmarais 2007). I locate their emergence in the context of variegated national and regional experiences, mixed political cultures and historical memories whose convergence shaped the making of a genuinely transnational peasant movement.

MOVIMIENTO DOS TRABAHADORES RURAIS SIEM TERRA AND KOREAN PEASANT LEAGUE: CASE STUDIES

In the 1960s, the massive peasant agitations which erupted in Central and South America against uneven landholding patterns inherited from colonialism and plantation society spurred several left-wing governments to implement a variety of redistributive agrarian reforms (De Janvry 1981). However, under pressures from the US government, land reforms were also embraced by more conservative and authoritarian governments as instruments to quell rural unrest, pacify the countryside and remove support for armed rebellions (McMichael 2006). In Brazil – a country with one of the most uneven landholding patterns in the world (along with South Africa) – land reforms and struggles have threatened the interests of large latifundio (large-scale estates) proprietors and landed elites whose interests triggered a coup d'état and the instauration of a military dictatorship (1964–1985). In such a context, the agrarian reform then became a highly strategic and security issue to both promote capitalist development and industrialization through large-scale schemes in order to reduce the dependency on smallholder production and undermine class struggle in the countryside, transforming potentially revolutionary peasants into conservative, individual-minded small-scale farmers (Baletti et al. 2008, 125; Martins 2006).

With the restoration of democracy, the MST, founded in 1984 with the support of grassroots religious organizations, the Confederation of Workers and the Workers Party, started challenging the classical agrarian reform model and legislation of the Brazilian state, campaigning more vigorously for redistributive land reforms and the rights of smallholder peasants and landless workers to (re)productive resources. The MST first became popular on the national and international scene through land occupations in the state of Rio Grande do Sul, denouncing the problem of land concentration and latifundios, and successfully forcing on the political agenda of the country the question of redistributive land reforms and cooperative settlements. Exploiting legal caveats and taking advantage of constitutional provisions, which permit the confiscation of unused land in cases of labour and environmental violations, the MST increased the number of land occupations from 119 in 1990 to 2210 in 2005 (Martins 2006). Despite repressive measures, and the incarceration of MST activists, defamatory campaigns and attempts at co-opting the leaders of the mobilizations, the MST campaigns and struggle contributed to putting into question the sanctity of property rights: a core value in the capitalist and neoliberal ideology.

According to Baletti et al. (2008), the reasons for this spectacular rise and success include leadership, occupations and autonomy. In terms of leadership, the movement has been able to maintain an essential base of peasant leadership. Nourished in various cooperative settlements resulting from land occupations and agrarian reform, young peasants and tenants of these settlements have progressively become the base of the leadership of the movement. The *acampamentos*, the sites where 2 million people settled in government-funded land reform settlement schemes, have become the focus of cooperation and the centre of a new radical praxis which contributed to mould new social relations based on the social ownership of the means of production (Martins 2006). Others such as Martins have emphasized the role of settlements as pedagogic units based on the work-and-study methodology and the intense process of political and ideological formation through study groups on radical theories (Martins 2006, 265). In the political language of the MST, land redistribution is not a means to incorporate smallholders within the circuits of the capitalist economy; it instead involves a radical shift in the production and power relations embedded in the agrarian social structure of the country.

According to João Pedro Stédile, leader of the MST, agrarian reforms are a means:

> to take land and other productive resources off the market and to practice the principle of social ownership of land, whereby families who work on it have usufruct right ... We want an agricultural practice that transforms farmers into guardians of the land, and a different way of farming that ensures cultural heritage, genetic diversity, ecological equilibrium and also guarantees that land is not seen as private property. (Stédile 2002, 100)

Rather than strive for inclusion into existing political structures, radical social movements struggle to transform the institutions in which they operate (Alvarez et al. 1998). In doing so, they engage with the broader cultural politics, striving to create alternative political identities and solidarities and new spaces of social interaction (Eschle 2001).

Capitalist restructuring of agriculture and the trade liberalization of agricultural commodities at other latitudes spearheaded the emergence of another influential farmers' organization in South Korea, the Korean Peasant League (KPL). Established in a period of agrarian distress in the 1980s by the current president Lee Gwangsuk, the organization has grown into an intricate network of village, city, country and provincial-level organizations. Since then, it has fought to create farmer-controlled food systems and promote farmer-to-farmer practices of knowledge sharing. The organization has grown in visibility due to its radical opposition to the liberalization of the rice market after South Korea, the third largest Asian economy, joined the World Trade Organization (WTO) in 1995, and implemented a series of bilateral Free Trade Agreements (FTAs). With cheap food imports (especially rice) flowing into the country in increasing quantities due to continuous rounds of liberalization, agricultural prices have plummeted, generating a four-fold increase in indebtedness and an exodus of smallholders from the countryside, decreasing from 6 to 3.5 million (Korean Peasants League 2005).

In a context of corporate control of agriculture and food dumping, Korean farmers have been lobbying the government to include food sovereignty into law, guarantee fair prices for farmers (through public provisions) and compensation for their losses. Yet as the political and economic forces they confronted went beyond national borders, they simultaneously 'globalized' their struggle by addressing their grievances against a series of WTO interministerial meetings and negotiations. Meeting the challenges emerging from the international domain demanded forging new alliances, links and networks among peasant, worker and civil society organizations around the world. On 10 September 2003, a delegation of Korean peasants joined the protests at the Fifth Ministerial Conference of the WTO held in Cancun, Mexico, to discuss a new set of agreements about agriculture, access to non-agricultural markets, services and so on. In one of the most tragic and symbolic episodes of protests ever seen, Korean farmer Lee Kyung Hae stabbed a knife into his heart on the top of barricades and fences raised by police shouting, 'WTO kills farmers'. This extreme act of protest went to the heart of many farmers around the world, not only in Korea, and galvanized attention and support worldwide. His sacrifice highlighted the catastrophic social implications inscribed in the process of *tout court* liberalization of agricultural commodities, healthcare, education, culture, energy and other essential services. It called into cause not only the mechanics of the WTO's operation but also the conniving role of the Korean state and its ruling class.

The KPL's struggle against trade liberalization and the resultant lowering of rural incomes and price-cost squeeze has continued unabated, despite ongoing FTAs being ratified, such as that between South Korea and the United States in 2011. In an interview at the margins of the mobilizations that ensued in 2012, Lee Gwangsuk reiterated the KPL's adversity to industrial modes of farming: 'Agriculture is perceived to be part of the industry. It is important for us to understand and raise awareness about the value of agriculture and food sovereignty to farming and non-farming people globally' (Gwangsuk 2012). Neoliberal restructuring of agriculture, its integration within the circuits of industrial production and globalized trade, pushed peasants' organizations to continuously mobilize in order to reaffirm its centrality in the strategies of social reproduction of farmers. As a food-related activity, peasant agriculture has therefore to be reimagined and reframed as a pillar in the strategies of food sovereignty at national and global levels, reconnecting farmers and urban consumers, city and the countryside, through a series of horizontal interlinkages and short value chains (Van der Ploeg et al. 2012). And yet, the emergence of new global food empires, with their new norms and rules, has not gone uncontested. Social movements have in fact become key agents in shaping the emergence, formation and functioning, tensions and crises of various international food regimes (Friedmann 2005).

TRANSNATIONAL AGRARIAN MOVEMENTS: LA VÍA CAMPESINA

The changing global political economy shaped by the power of corporate-driven industrialization of agriculture has posed peasants and rural workers around the world with a series of similar political and economic challenges. The growing concentration of power by TNCs in the international food regime and the liberalization of agricultural exchanges generated immiseration and marginalization for the majority of people in the countryside of the Global South. These global dynamics of pauperization of, and exodus from, the countryside have been furthermore accentuated by the contemporary wave of land dispossession, the appropriation of genetic agro-biodiversity and the phenomenon of climate change especially, but not only, in Africa, triggering new responses from below (Martiniello 2013).

Neoliberalism has enormously altered the dynamics of agrarian (re)production providing even higher power to transnational and domestic capital to dictate the terms of agricultural production and exchange (Borras et al. 2008a, 170). As the political and economic forces driving the capitalist transformation and restructuring of agriculture during the neoliberal era 'globalized', peasant and farmer organizations around the world started to 'internationalize' their struggles (Desmarais 2007). The aim was to develop a political subjectivity and unified voice that would raise the visibility of peasant struggles around the world and help to consolidate the power base of rural social movements within their countries. This scenario had profound implications on how the rural poor understand their conditions of social existence, assess the framework of political opportunities and respond to existing economic and political challenges (Martiniello and Nyamasenda 2018, 147). In this sense neoliberal globalization produced both new challenges but also new opportunities for interexchange, communication and alliance making (Edelman and Borras 2016).

In such a context, in April 1993 a global peasant movement was created: La Vía Campesina (LVC). Its emergence coincided temporally with the Uruguay Round of the General Agreement on Tariffs and Trade, spurring representatives of rural organizations from North, South, East and West to coalesce into a single global peasant movement. At the moment, it includes more than 170 rural social movement organizations from Latin America, Caribbean, North America, Eastern and Western Europe, Asia and Africa. LVC situated itself in the struggle against the corporate takeover of agriculture and food, denouncing the increasing rural poverty and growing hunger, and providing peasants in the South and farmers in the North with a common platform. Since its creation, LVC has been at the forefront of the global justice movement participating in anti-capitalist globalization marches held at various WTO ministerial conferences in Geneva (1998), Seattle (1999), Cancun (2003) and Hong Kong (2005). It was also involved in massive demonstrations against international financial institutions and G8 countries in Prague (2000), Genova (2001), Washington (2002) and Quito (2002), among others. In its effort to promote global solidarity, widen the inclusivity of the movement and support existing struggles for land, LVC moved its operative secretariat from Honduras to Indonesia in 2004, and more recently to Zimbabwe.

In world-historical terms, today's global peasant movement stands on the shoulders of previous movements for rights to self-determination (McMichael 2008). From a world-systems perspective, we could define it as a genuinely anti-systemic movement (see Arrighi et al. 1989) challenging the capitalist systems at its foundations. TAMs are thus movements, organizations, solidarity links, coalition networks of national peasant and farmer groups and their allies that cross national boundaries and seek to influence national and global policies. LVC is the most well known of all the contemporary TAMs, networks and coalitions, and has gained a considerable political reputation (Borras 2004; Desmarais 2007). There are, however, numerous other transnational movements and alliances that are based among rural sectors or advocate for rural people; some are engaged in left-wing politics, while others are less radical (Borras et al. 2008a, 170–171). According to Edelman and Borras (2016, 4), transnational alliances and actions often facilitate the mobilization of material, intellectual and symbolic resources and the identification of political opportunities. In a way, 'it is a particular part of civil society that "intervenes" in the development of agriculture, pulling it away from the route determined by the economy only' (Van der Ploeg 2013, 10). TAMs represent an arena of action (Borras 2008b, 93), a space of interactions between an array of different organizations.

Yet TAMs are hardly new. Early transnational farmers' organizations sometimes manifested eclectic amalgams of agrarian populism, communism, elite-led reformism and noblesse oblige, pacifism and feminism (Borras et al. 2008a, 173). Some movements and networks have been in existence for decades, for example, the Campesino a Campesino (Peasant to Peasant) movement, which generated a horizontal process of knowledge exchange in Central America and Mexico in the 1960s (Boyer 2010; Holt-Giménez 2006).

LVC claims to be fighting against transnational companies and agribusiness, capitalism and free trade, but also against patriarchy (Vía Campesina 2006). Its vision for a twenty-first-century agriculture is pivoted on notions of food sovereignty, land redistribution, agro-ecology and peasants' seeds, climate and environmental justice and dignity for migrant and waged workers while trying to galvanize international solidarity (Vía Campesina 2019). In the last years, LVC has been more vigorously recognizing the central role played by women in food production and social reproduction, promoting gender diversity in the peasant movement. Its most significant international advocacy activities include the global campaign for agrarian reform (GCAR) (Borras 2006, 2008; Rosset et al. 2006), the anti-genetically modified organisms campaign (Scoones 2008) and the campaign for peasant agro-ecology (Rosset and Altieri 2017; Wittman et al. 2010). In doing so, LVC has defied the traditional forms of organizing and mobilizing the countryside, bringing in new innovative visions about agriculture and rural development.

Though LVC's main political motto has been the attempt to prioritize unity within diversity, it doesn't mean that internal differences do not exist as it pulls together a wide array of organizations. These differences range in terms of representation and agenda, political strategies and forms of action, class basis and ideological and political differences. LVC's main effect has been to significantly contribute to reframing the terms of critical debates and practices in the field of international development with a thematic focus on issues such as environmental sustainability, climate change, food sovereignty, land rights and redistributive agrarian reforms, neoliberal trade policies, corporate control of genetic material and intellectual property rights. However, LVC is absent from Russia, Central Asia, the Middle East (with the exception of Palestine) and North Africa region, and most notably China, which, together, host most of the world's rural poor (Borras et al. 2008a, 183). And yet, while according to some scholars LVC provides an ontological detour that rejects the grand narrative of modernity (McMichael 2008) and has the potential of challenging the dominance of capital in the Global South (Akram-Lodhi and Kay 2009), others have adopted a more sceptical position. Bernstein (2009), for example, highlights their defensive, erratic, fragmentary and contradictory character. In a similar vein, Baletti et al. (2008) point to the internal contradictions and differences among various players within LVC showing how stronger players tend to influence weaker organizations and impose their visions and practices of struggle.

CONCLUSION

The chapter explored the political economy and politics of rural social movements and their coalescence into TAMs. It situated their emergence in the context of changing political economies and agrarian social relations at local, national and global levels. The study analysed their origins, the social constituencies behind them, the ideologies inspiring their actions and the visions driving their practices of contestation of often authoritarian regimes. It identified the political dynamics that have led to the emergence of LVC, highlighting the dialectic between efforts towards localization and globalization of agrarian struggles. It pointed to elements of virtuosity exposed in their innovative praxis but also some of their internal differences, contradictions, failures and challenges. The chapter focused on two large and influential agrarian movements, such as the MST and KPL, leaving little space to the discussion of less powerful and relatively younger rural organizations emerging out of more recent social struggles, especially in Africa (see Martiniello and Nyamasenda 2018).

Studying rural social movements from a critical agrarian studies perspective is fundamental to unpack the emergence of various forms of contestation to state-led and capital-orchestrated agrarian restructuring. While these mobilizations do not exhaust the spectrum of the forms of resistance and the responses from below, they represent important entry points in the study of agrarian contestations. Rural social movements (and their transnational articulations) represent important actors in shaping the trajectories of agrarian change and the agrarian politics in the countryside of the Global South, at local, national and global scales. Their coalescence into TAMs represents an historical tipping point in the making of truly anti-systemic social forces confronting global corporate and national capital, and the state for equitable access to land, social justice and climate change.

FURTHER READING

Borras, Jr., S.M.; Edelman, M.; Kay, C. (eds) (2008), *Transnational Agrarian Movements: Confronting Globalization*, Chichester: Wiley-Blackwell.
Desmarais, A. (2007), *La Vía Campesina: Globalization and the Power of Peasants*, Halifax: Pluto.
Edelman, M.; Borras, Jr., S.M. (2016), *Political Dynamics of Transnational Agrarian Movements*, Halifax: Fernwood Publishing.
Holt-Giménez, E. (2006), *Campesino a Campesino: Voices from Latin America's Farmer to Farmer Movement for Sustainable Agriculture*, Oakland, CA: Food First Books.
Moyo, S.; Yeros, P. (eds) (2005), *Reclaiming the Land: The Resurgence of Rural Movements in Africa, Asia and Latin America*, London: Zed Books.

REFERENCES

Akram-Lodhi, H.; Kay, C. (eds) (2009), *Peasants and Globalization: Political Economy, Rural Transformation and the Agrarian Question*, London: Routledge.
Alvarez, S.E.; Dagnino, E.; Escobar, A. (eds) (1998), *Culture of Politics: Politics of Culture, Re-visioning Latina American Social Movements*, Boulder, CO: Westview Press.
Arrighi, G.; Hopkins, T.K.; Wallerstein, I. (1989), *Anti-Systemic Movements*, London: Verso.
Baletti, B.; Johnson, T.M.; Wolford, W. (2008), 'Late mobilization': Transnational peasant networks and grassroots organizing in Brazil and South Africa, in Borras, Jr., S.M.; Edelman, M.; Kay, C. (eds), *Transnational Agrarian Movements: Confronting Globalization*, Chichester: Wiley-Blackwell, 123–146.
Bernstein, H. (2009), Agrarian questions from transition to globalization, in Akram-Lodhi, A.H.; Kay, C. (eds), *Peasants and Globalization: Political Economy, Rural Transformation and the Agrarian Question*, London: Routledge, 239–261.
Bernstein, H. (2010), *Class Dynamics of Agrarian Change*, Halifax: Fernwood Publishing.
Bezner-Kerr, R. (2017), Gender and agrarian inequities, in Sieglinde, S.; Pound, B. (eds), *Agricultural Systems: Agro-ecology and Rural Innovation for Development*, London: Academic Press, 330–373.
Borras, Jr., S.M. (2004), La Vía Campesina: An evolving transnational social movement, Transnational Institute Briefing Paper, October.
Borras, Jr., S.M. (2006), The underlying assumptions, theory and practice of neoliberal land policies, in Rosset, P.; Patel, R.; Courville, M. (eds), *Promised Land: Competing Visions of Agrarian Reform*, Oakland, CA: Food First Books, 99–128.
Borras, Jr., S.M. (2008), La Vía Campesina and its global campaign for agrarian reform, in Borras, Jr., S.M.; Edelman, M.; Kay, C. (eds) (2008), *Transnational Agrarian Movements: Confronting Globalization*, Chichester: Wiley-Blackwell, 91–122.
Borras, Jr., S.M.; Edelman, M.; Kay, C. (2008a), *Transnational Agrarian Movements: Confronting Globalization*, Chichester: Wiley-Blackwell.
Borras, Jr., S.M.; Edelman, M.; Kay, C. (2008b), Transnational agrarian movements: Origins and politics, campaigns and impact, *Journal of Agrarian Change*, 8, 169–204.

Boyer, J. (2010), Food security, food sovereignty, and local challenges for transnational agrarian movements: The Honduras case, *Journal of Peasant Studies*, 37(2), 319–351.

Cabral, A. (1965), *Lutte nationale dans le colonies*, Algiers: CONCP.

De Janvry, A. (1981), *The Agrarian Question and Reformism in Latin America*, Baltimore, MD: Johns Hopkins University Press.

Della Porta, D.; Tarrow, S. (2005), Transnational processes and social activism, in Della Porta, D.; Tarrow, S. (eds), *Transnational Protest and Global Activism*, Boulder, CO: Rowman and Littlefield, 1–20.

Della Porta, D.; Andretta, M.; Mosca, L.; Reiter, H. (2006), *Globalization from Below: Transnational Activism and Protest Networks*, Minneapolis, MN: University of Minnesota Press.

Desmarais, A. (2007), *La Vía Campesina: Globalization and the Power of Peasants*, Halifax: Pluto.

Dhawale, A. (2018), Remarkable farmers struggles in India: Some notes from Maharashtra and Rajastan, *Agrarian South: A Journal of Political Economy*, 7(2), 257–274.

Edelman, M. (2008), Transnational organizing in agrarian Central America: Histories, challenges, prospects, in Borras, Jr., S.M.; Edelman, M.; Kay, C. (eds), *Transnational Agrarian Movements: Confronting Globalization*, Chichester: Wiley-Blackwell, 61–90.

Edelman, M.; Borras, Jr., S.M. (2016), *Political Dynamics of Transnational Agrarian Movements*, Halifax: Fernwood Publishing.

Eschle, C. (2001), *Global Democracy, Social Movements and Feminism*, Boulder, CO: Westview Press.

Fanon, F. (1967), *The Wretched of the Earth*, London: Penguin Books.

Friedmann, H. (2005). From colonialism to green capitalism: Social movements and emergence of food regimes, in Buttel, F.H.; McMichael, P. (eds), *New Directions in the Sociology of Global Development*, Amsterdam: Elsevier, 227–264.

Gwangsuk, L. (2012), Lee, Gwangsuk, President of the Korean Peasant League, accessed 4 March 2019 at www.youtube.com/watch?v=4MK8WXG4DbQ.

Hetland, G.; Goodwin, J. (2013), The strange disappearance of capitalism from social movement studies, in Barker, C.; Cox, L.; Krinsky, J.; Gunvald Nilsen, A. (eds), *Marxism and Social Movements*, Leiden: BRILL.

Holt-Giménez, E. (2006), *Campesino a Campesino: Voices from Latin America's Farmer to Farmer Movement for Sustainable Agriculture*, Oakland, CA: Food First Books.

Julia; White, B. (2012), Gendered experiences of dispossession: Palm oil expansion in a Dayak Hibun community in West Kalimantan, *Journal of Peasant Studies*, 39(3–4), 995–1016.

Korean Peasants League (2005), Launching resolution, accessed 4 March 2019 at www.ijunnong.net/en/article/.

Martiniello, G. (2013), Land dispossession and rural social movements: The 2011 conference in Mali, *Review of African Political Economy*, 40(136), 309–320.

Martiniello, G.; Nyamsenda, S. (2018), Agrarian movements in the neoliberal era: The case of MVIWATA in Tanzania, *Agrarian South: Journal of Political Economy*, 7(2), 145–172.

Martins, M.D. (2006), Learning to participate: The MST experience in Brazil, in Rosset, P.; Patel, R.; Courville, M. (eds), *Promised Land: Competing Visions of Agrarian Reform*, Oakland, CA: Food First Books, 265–276.

McMichael, P. (2006), *Development and Social Change: A Global Perspective*, Thousand Oaks, CA: Pine Forge.

McMichael, P. (2008), Peasants make their own history, but not just as they please ..., in Borras, Jr., S.M.; Edelman, M.; Kay, C. (eds), *Transnational Agrarian Movements: Confronting Globalization*, Chichester: Wiley-Blackwell, 37–60.

Moyo, S.; Yeros, P. (2005), The resurgence of rural movements under neoliberalism, in Moyo, S.; Yeros, P. (eds), *Reclaiming the Land: The Resurgence of Rural Movements in Africa, Asia and Latin America*, London: Zed Books, 8–64.

Nilsen, A.; Roy, S. (eds) (2016), *New Subaltern Politics: Reconceptualizing Hegemony and Resistance in Contemporary India*, New Delhi: Oxford University Press.

Park, C.M.Y. (2019), 'Our lands are our lives': Gendered experiences of resistance to land grabbing in rural Cambodia, *Feminist Economics*, 25(4), 21–44.

Peluso, N.L.; Afiff, S.; Rachman, N.F. (2008), Claiming the grounds for reform: Agrarian and environmental movements in Indonesia, in Borras, Jr., S.M.; Edelman, M.; Kay, C. (eds), *Transnational Agrarian Movements: Confronting Globalization*, Chichester: Wiley-Blackwell, 209–238.

Peters, P.E. (2004), Inequality and social conflict over land in Africa, *Journal of Agrarian Change*, 4(3), 269–314.

Razavi, S. (2009), Engendering the political economy of agrarian change, *Journal of Peasant Studies*, 36(1), 197–226.

Rosset, P.; Altieri, M. (2017), *Agro-ecology: Science and Politics*, Winnipeg: Fernwood Publishers.

Rosset, P.; Patel, R.; Courville, M. (2006), *Promised Land: Competing Visions of Agrarian Reform*, Oakland, CA: Food First Books.

Scoones, I. (2008), Mobilizing against GM crops in India, South Africa and Brazil, in Borras, Jr., S.M.; Edelman, M.; Kay, C. (eds), *Transnational Agrarian Movements: Confronting Globalization*, Chichester: Wiley-Blackwell, 147–175.

Shanin, T. (1990), *Defining Peasants: Essays Concerning Rural Societies, Expolary Economies, and Learning from Them in the Contemporary World*, Oxford: Basil Blackwell.

Shin, G. (1994), The historical making of collective action: The Korean peasant uprisings of 1946, *American Journal of Sociology*, 99(6), 1596–1624.

Stedile, J.P. (2002), Landless battalions: The Sem Terra movement of Brazil, *New Left Review*, 15, 77–104.

Tarrow, S. (1988), National politics and collective action: Recent theory and research in Western Europe and the United States, *Annual Review of Sociology*, 14, 421–440.

Therborn, G. (2007), After dialectics: Radical social theory in a post-communist world, *New Left Review*, 43, 63–114.

Thompson, E.P. (1978), Eighteenth-century English society: Class struggle without class?, *Social History*, 3(2), 133–165.

Tilly, C. (1978), *From Mobilization to Revolution*, Reading, MA: Addison-Wesley.

Van der Ploeg, J.D. (2013), *Peasants and the Art of Farming: A Chayanovia Manifesto*, Halifax: Fernwood Publishing.

Van der Ploeg, J.D.; Jingzhong, J.; Schneider, S. (2012), Rural development through the construction of new, nested, markets: Comparative perspectives from China, Brazil and the European Union, *Journal of Peasant Studies*, 39(1), 133–173.

Vía Campesina (2006), Gender diversity in the peasant movement, accessed 2 March 2019 at https://viacampesina.org/en/gender-diversity-in-the-peasant-movement/.

Vía Campesina (2019), What are we fighting for?, accessed 2 March 2019 at https://viacampesina.org/en/what-are-we-fighting-for/.

Wittman, H.; Desmarais, A.A.; Wiebe, N. (eds) (2010), *Food Sovereignty: Reconnecting Food, Nature and Community*, Oakland, CA: Food First.

Wolf, E.R. (1969), *Peasant Wars of the Twentieth Century*, New York: Harper and Row.

54. Industrial agriculture and agrarian extractivism
Ben M. McKay and Henry Veltmeyer

INTRODUCTION

The evolution of capitalism as theorized by Marx entails the productive and social transforma-tion of an agrarian society characterized by a traditional communalist culture and precapitalist production relations into a modern industrial system based on the capital–labour relation. As Marx theorized it, capitalism in this context is based on a process of 'primitive accumulation' (the separation of the direct producers from the land and their means of production) and an associated process of agrarian change involving the conversion of the peasantry into an industrial proletariat and the exploitation of the unlimited supply of surplus agricultural labour released in the capitalist development process. However, notwithstanding the centrality of the capital–labour relation in this development process, the evolution of capitalism was to some extent predicated on the advance of resource-seeking extractive capital—capital accumulated by means of extracting the wealth of society's natural resources—and the way in which these two modalities of accumulation in different regional and historical contexts are combined in the capitalist production process.

The aim of this chapter is to clarify these dynamics in the current context of the capitalist development process as they are playing out in the agricultural sector. Agriculture, as it turned out, played a crucial role in the development of industrial capitalism. But it was also a critical factor in the evolution of capitalism on the periphery of the system—in shaping the geoeconomics of capital in diverse regional contexts. Our argument in this regard is constructed as follows. First, we review the debate on the agrarian question posed by the capitalist development of agriculture—so-called industrial agriculture. Here we point towards the extractive character of corporate-controlled plantation agriculture, or agro-industry, with reference to a literature in which these dynamics of agrarian change are understood as agro- or agrarian extractivism We then establish the contemporary dynamics of industrial agriculture as presented in the literature on agrarian change that point to a fundamental tendency towards the concentration and centralization of capital in agriculture. We then discuss the extractive features of corporate-controlled plantation agriculture, challenging the notion that the capi-talist development of agriculture results in industrial agriculture—that capitalism is actually industrializing the countryside. Building on the literature on extractivism as a distinct modality of capital accumulation, we emphasize the importance of specifying the extractive nature of the capitalist development process in the agricultural sector. We end this discussion with ref-erence to some of the recent advances made in applying the concept of agrarian extractivism.

AGRARIAN CHANGE AND CAPITALIST DEVELOPMENT

Central to critical agrarian studies is understanding the ways in which agriculture is trans-formed under capitalism. The classic agrarian question posed by Kautsky (1988) interrogated the extent and ways in which capital takes hold of agriculture, revolutionizes it and establishes new forces and relations of production (Banaji 1980). Other classic texts by Marx (1976 [1867]), Engels (1950 [1894]) and Lenin (1964 [1899]) contributed to what is now referred to as the classic agrarian question formulated by Byres (1991, 1996) as a problematic of politics, production and accumulation; and further revised by Bernstein (1996, 2004) as the agrarian questions of capital and labour, of which only the latter remains relevant in the current context of capitalism in the era of neoliberal globalization. Writing in 1899, Kautsky (1988, 297) asserted that:

> [a]gricultural production has already been transformed into industrial production in a large number of fields, and ... others can be expected to undergo this transformation in the immediate future. No field of agriculture is completely safe. Every advance in this direction must inevitably multiply the pressures on farmers, increase their dependence on industry and undermine their security.

As for the contemporary period, there is no doubt that capital has indeed penetrated and is taking hold of agriculture, transformed it at the level of both the forces and relations of production, albeit in variegated ways in a process of uneven development.

Indeed, industrial agriculture based on the global operations of agribusiness corporations has become the dominant model of agricultural development, a primary means of combatting global rural poverty as promoted by the most influential development agencies and international financial institutions (World Bank 2007). For critical agrarian studies, this has generated diverse debates concerning the socioeconomic, political and ecological implications of the agro-industrial model vis-à-vis alternative models based on cooperative, smallholder or peasant farming and agro-ecological methods. This includes both old and new debates pertaining to the role and viability of peasant farming in generating a surplus and for feeding the world (McMichael 2009); the persistence or disappearance of the peasantry based on socioeconomic or demographic factors of differentiation (van der Ploeg 2018); of productivity related to farm size (Woodhouse 2010); and the biophysical contradictions of the agro-industrial model (O'Connor 1998; Weis 2010). While many of these debates in critical agrarian studies are addressed in this *Handbook* (also see Akram-Lodhi and Kay 2010), this chapter examines the nature and character of industrial agriculture today, pointing to the ways and extent to which both extractive capital and industrial capital have penetrated and transformed agriculture. This process, we argue, points towards the need to analytically distinguish the production operations and development dynamics of agro-extraction and agro-industry, and the need to study the form and dynamics of their interaction.

Before delving into the nature and character of industrial agriculture, it is necessary to briefly discuss industrial and extractive capital as two related yet distinct modalities of accumulation. While both modalities depend on the exploitation of labour and nature, the latter requires increasingly *less* labour as it is based on various combinations of financialized, high-technology, resource-seeking extractive capital and the appropriation of resource rents. Rather than unlimited supplies of labour (keeping wages low) being transferred to the industrial sector for a productive and social transformation, the current period of extractive capitalism is generating surplus populations whereby 'labour is surplus *in relation to* its utility for capital' (Li 2009, 68; emphasis in the original). In other words, rather than having a labour reserve which could keep wages depressed and whereby capital accumulation is largely dependent on labour exploitation, the current conjuncture is characterized by 'one in which places (or their resources) are useful, but the people are not, so that dispossession is detached from any prospect of labour absorption' (Li 2009, 69).

Extractive capital is most prominent in developing countries, although the United States and Europe are also undergoing a process of deindustrialization and the erosion of the middle class as manufacturing industries move to regions, such as China, with lower production costs, i.e. cheaper labour. Since the advent of neoliberal globalization in the 1980s, developing countries have experienced falling manufacturing shares in both employment and real value added, eroding the gains they made from import-substitution policies in the 1950s and 1960s—referred to as 'premature deindustrialization' (Dasgupta and Singh 2006; Rodrik 2016). This coincided with the expansion of activities associated with the extractive sector, and a process of export primarization facilitated by neoliberal policies of privatization, deregulation and trade liberalization, and further fuelled by several forces of change and conditions that converged to increase the weight of extractive capital in the development process. They included a commodity price boom that was 'unprecedented in … magnitude and duration', with the price of energy and metals doubling from 2003 to 2008, and the price of food on capitalist markets increasing by 75 per cent (Erten and Ocampo 2013, 14). They also included the growing demand for raw materials in 'emerging markets' (Brazil, Russia, India, China and South Africa); the financialization of land and the agro-food sector (Fairbairn 2014; Isakson 2014); and the increased demand for flex crops such as soybeans, sugarcane, maize and oil palm that have multiple and flexible uses as food, feed, fuel and industrial inputs—which, as argued by Borras et al. (2012) and White et al. (2012), should be understood in the context of a global land grab. This rush for natural resources, and the forces of change in the global political economy, signals a shift from industrial capitalism based on the exploitation of labour to extractive capitalism based predominantly on the pillage of natural resource wealth, or, it could be argued, the exploitation of nature (Veltmeyer 2016). With the exportation of these resources predominantly in primary commodity form with little to no processing or added value, the diverse agents and agencies, or 'actors' and 'economic interests' located along what amounts to a global exploitation chain, are able to appropriate both the surplus value generated by agricultural labour and the marketed value of nature's bounty (natural capital), resulting in superprofits for capital (windfall gains on investments) and additional fiscal resources derived from resource rents that are appropriated by the state in the form of royalty payments and taxes. It is close to impossible to precisely calculate the magnitude of the economic benefits associated with the export of agro-food and biofuel commodities in the midst of a primary commodities boom and expanding markets. But, given that in the agricultural sector neither industrial nor extractive capital has to share appropriated rents with the state, rents that in other extractive sectors (fossil fuels, minerals and metals) in the form of royalty payments are substantial, indications are that the profits associated with commodity exports in the agricultural sector are as high as in other extractive sectors. See, for example, the *Financial Times* report on 18 April 2013, which documented the fact that traders in agricultural commodities, who are at or near the top of the surplus value extraction chain, have accumulated large reserves of capital in the context of the primary commodities boom (2002–2012). As the author of this report (Blas 2013) observed: 'The world's top commodities traders have pocketed nearly US$250 billion over the last decade', making the big commodity traders, together with the corporations that have managed to achieve virtual monopoly control over export sales in the agricultural sector, 'the [main] beneficiaries of the rise of China and other emerging countries'—and, we might add, beneficiaries of the turn, or return, towards extractivism and export primarization. In 2000, the corporations and traders in the sector had made US$2.1 billion in profits, but by 2012 these profits had climbed to US$33.5 billion.

And while some capitalists (investors, corporations and traders) enjoyed returns up to and even in excess of 50 per cent or 60 per cent in the mid-2000s—comparable to or even higher than profit rates in the highly profitable mining sector, where, according to Eduardo Gudynas (cited by Cisnero 2011) the average profit rate in this period was 37 per cent—today, in the context of a downturn in some commodity markets and the sway of monopoly capital in the agricultural sector, profits on investments and operations are still averaging 20 per cent to 30 per cent. Not bad by any business standard. This development is the result of prevailing conditions of agro-extraction, which allows agricultural capital to not only benefit from the boom in export prices for agricultural commodities associated with the periodic food crises but also to benefit from relatively low ground and resource rents, the low cost of agricultural labour and the appropriation of product and technology rents under conditions of monopoly capital in the agricultural sector. On this see the pathbreaking studies by Delgado Wise (2017; Delgado Wise and Chávez 2016) on the 'imperialist innovation agenda' in agriculture, as well the discussion below on the development dynamics of industrial agriculture.

It is within this context that we must understand the ways in which capitalism is transforming agriculture, as well as its extractive character and the social, economic and ecological implications of the model used to advance the capitalist development process in this sector.

THE DEVELOPMENT DYNAMICS OF INDUSTRIAL AGRICULTURE

The International Assessment of Agricultural Knowledge, Science and Technology for Development (IAASTD) report (2009, 563–564) defines industrial agriculture as a 'form of agriculture that is capital-intensive, substituting machinery and purchased inputs for human and animal labour'. It is highly mechanized and specialized, often based on monocrop cultivation, large in scale, dependent on industrialized external inputs and controlled under private-sector production in capitalist contexts. The industrial transformation of agriculture— first via mechanization which reduced the need for labour, then through the dissemination of hybrid and genetically modified seeds and finally the dependence on agro-chemicals—has led to 'a series of partial, discontinuous appropriations of the rural labour and biological production processes' (Goodman et al. 1987, 2). This is what Goodman et al. refer to as 'appropriationism', 'constituted by the action of industrial capitals to reduce the importance of nature in rural production, and specifically as a force beyond their direction and control' (ibid., 3). With farmers increasingly dependent on genetically modified seeds, agro-chemicals and machinery, industrial capital has penetrated agriculture by partially eliminating its material base and part of the natural production process incompatible with capital accumulation (ibid., 156).

Not only has industry transformed agricultural production in its technical form, it has also changed the particular configurations of productive relations and forms of appropriation of the productive process. This has emerged through new forms of land use and value-chain control that exclude the rural majority and in the production process extract value (the wealth of natural resources) embodied in 'nature'. One of the principal forms of control has been through market concentration and consolidation of seed and chemical companies which has led to a market oligopoly largely controlled globally by just four corporations (the 'Big Four'):

BASF, Bayer (Monsanto), ChemChina (Syngenta) and DowDuPont (Clapp 2018). Together, these companies control 75 per cent of the global agro-chemical market, 63 per cent of the commercial seed market and over 75 per cent of private-sector research in seeds and pesticides (ETC Group 2015, 4).

As recently as the 1970s, these markets were controlled by thousands of small-scale, mostly family-owned businesses (Howard 2015). The massive increase in intellectual property protection for living organisms in the 1970s and 1980s, including the full patent protection on transgenic seeds, attracted large firms which rapidly acquired 'hundreds of formerly independent biotechnology and seed companies' that eventually led to these mega-mergers (Howard 2015). The commodification and patenting of seeds—what Kloppenburg calls the 'biological nexus of farm-level production'—was the most important component of private industry's accumulation interests (Kloppenburg 2004, 37).

Without technological innovation based on the advance of scientific knowledge and the introduction of new legislation, this level of concentration and monopoly control over both the production process and the appropriation of its rich harvest would have never been possible. Since the seed reproduces itself as grain and can be replanted infinitely, legislation was required in order to separate the farmer from the reproduction of the seed—that is, from the agricultural means of production. Shared mutual interests between the biotech industry and government agencies, 'revolving door' politics and powerful lobbyists from multinationals such as Monsanto are major reasons why such legislation gets passed (Newell and Glover 2003).

As seeds became commodified and monopolized, so too did agricultural research. In the 1990s, private industry began to both recruit the leading scientific faculty and form strategic partnerships with public universities. In 1998, for example, Novartis (which would later become part of a merger which formed Syngenta) signed a partnership with the University of California Berkeley's Department of Plant and Microbial Biology which 'gave Berkeley $25 million and access to Novartis' genomic database in return for a seat on departmental committees and first right to negotiate a license to patents from selected discoveries' (Kloppenburg 2004, 329). The seed market consolidated even more as transgenic crops became commercialized and more and more countries legalized genetically modified varieties. For example, from 1996 to 2013, the top ten seed firms acquired almost 200 seed companies (Howard 2015). With this agro-chemical-seed market concentration, the Big Four now engage in cross-licensing agreements for transgenic seed traits, which has resulted in 'the formation of a shared monopoly or cartel to exclude other potential competitors' (Howard 2015).

More than the material commodification and control of agro-inputs, the Big Four also control access to information and innovations. Combined, their budgets for agriculture research and development (R&D) is some 20 times larger than that of the Consortium of International Agricultural Research Centres and 15 times that of the United States Department of Agriculture's Agricultural Research Service budget for crop science research, giving them significant control over the agricultural R&D industry (ETC Group 2015). As Kloppenburg argues, agricultural research has been 'an important means of eliminating the barriers to the penetration of agriculture by capital' by commodifying agro-inputs and displacing productive activities off the farm and into an industrial setting (Kloppenburg 2004, 10). But while agricultural innovations are certainly important, it becomes problematic when a small, self-interested group dictates the research agenda and the interlinked technologies and products which are available in the market (see Miller and Conko 2001). With significant influence and control over the agricultural research agenda, the Big Four can invest in shaping agriculture's technical form through continued innovations which require their technological packages complete with patented seeds, agro-chemical inputs and access to advanced mechanization. This control over information and knowledge production represents the power agro-industry has over patented ideas and technological innovation, and ultimately authority over the terms of modern agricultural production (Delgado Wise and Chávez 2016).

The industrialization of agriculture has been further intensified through the financialization of land and agriculture as both new and old actors increasingly engage in speculation and hedging (see Clapp and Isakson, this volume). This has not only reinforced existing unequal relations of power among farmers, agribusiness and new financial actors far removed from production but has led to increasing food price volatility on international markets (Isakson 2014).

This market concentration and control has important implications for rural populations—especially small-scale, capital-poor peasant farmers who are further displaced from the production process and forced to migrate—and the environment. Agro-industry integrates farmers into their production processes and value chains, requiring the use (and purchase) of certain seeds and chemical inputs (upstream) in order to comply with standardized market requirements (downstream) controlled by the same agro-industrial market oligopoly. These new institutional arrangements bind farmers into cycles of debt and dependency, altering their relationship and access to land and other factors of production in subtler ways than physical dispossession or displacement (McKay 2018; see McMichael 2013).

All of this raises important questions concerning the degree to which industrial agriculture actually leads to a form of value-added industrial development in the countryside and where and by whom the surplus value and rents are appropriated. Rather than a process of industrialization, industrial agriculture proves to be extractive in character as the industrial process takes place in the upstream and downstream components of the value chain in faraway places and is controlled by corporate oligopolies. Referring to this type of agricultural development as industrial agriculture is misleading both analytically and politically and thus requires a new conceptualization which emphasizes these extractive characteristics.

AGRARIAN EXTRACTIVISM

The concept of agrarian extractivism brings the extractive character of corporate-controlled plantation agriculture to the fore. The concept directly challenges the notion that plantation agriculture is actually industrializing the countryside—developing industries which generate quality employment opportunities, develop forward and backward linkages and value-added processing in the places where production takes place. In fact, as the preceding section demonstrates, industrial agriculture is characterized by industrialized external inputs controlled by market oligopolies upstream and processing, distribution and 'flexing' downstream similarly controlled by a few multinational corporations. Industrial capitals therefore control both ends of the value chain, extracting natural and surplus value by circulating through the soil, contaminating the ecological material base and exploiting or outright displacing labour. This type of agricultural model parallels the dynamics of extractive sectors and should be conceptualized as such.

More than just removing or extracting natural resources from the land,[1] extractivism refers to the broad complex of social relations and production processes found on the frontier of extractive capital in the countryside and associated enclave economies and communities. It includes both the operations of resource-seeking capital, the modality of accumulation and the social relations of production (i.e. extraction), as well as the exportation of natural resources in primary commodity form and the sale of these resources on capitalist markets.

Gudynas (2015) refers to extractivism as a 'mode of appropriation' which refers to the different forms of organizing the appropriation of distinct natural resources (physical materials, energy and ecological processes) for human purposes in specific social and environmental contexts. Since we do not 'produce' natural resources but rather appropriate or extract them from nature, Gudynas rejects the notion of 'mode of production' when referring to extractivism (ibid., 188). From this perspective, extractivism is not analogous to an industry since the industrial, value-added processes usually occur in places far away from the extraction. This builds on Bunker's argument that the 'internal dynamics of extractive economies differ significantly from those of productive economies in their effects on the natural environment, on the distribution of human populations, on the construction of economic infrastructure, and therefore on the subsequent development potential of the affected regions' (1984, 1019). Bunker goes on to say that 'when natural resources are extracted from one regional ecosystem to be consumed or transformed in another, the socioeconomic and ecological linkages to the extracted commodity tend to a loss of value in the region of origin and to accretion of value in the region of consumption or transformation' (ibid.).

Extractivism not only leads to uneven economic and ecological exchange but can also have devastating social consequences. Incomes often rise and fall rapidly, populations are displaced, ecosystems destroyed and political elites become susceptible to forms of corruption. For Bunker, these processes represent 'modes of extraction' which he introduced to characterize the systemic connections between changes in 'the class structures; the organization of labour; systems of property and exchange; the activities of the state; the distribution of populations; the development of physical infrastructure; and the kinds of information, beliefs, and ideologies which shape social organization and behaviour' (1984, 1020). In other words, extractivism encompasses particular exploitative social relations combined with unequal ecological and economic exchange. It is therefore important to consider both the social relations of production (the commodification of labour) and the predatory and exploitative relation of extractive capital to the wealth of natural resources that constitute the common heritage of humankind (the commodification of nature).

In addition to hydrocarbons or fossil fuels, and minerals and metals, agriculture has been included as a form of extractivism in the literature on neoextractivism. Gudynas (2010b, 2) for example, has used the term agricultural extractivism to refer to agriculture oriented toward monoculture, the use of transgenics, machinery, chemical herbicides, with 'little or no processing and exportation of the produce as a commodity'. Gudynas suggests that this is not an 'industry' and using the term industry implies some kind of industrialization or value added—not primary production for export (ibid.). For Gudynas, agricultural activity which is characterized by a high volume/intensity of extraction, semi-processed and destined for export is considered extractivism, with particular reference to soybean plantations in Latin America (Gudynas 2010a, 2013). Giarracca and Teubal (2014, 48) suggest the term 'also applies to a certain type of agriculture in which essential resources such as water and fertile land, and biodiversity, are degraded by extractivism'. Petras and Veltmeyer (2016, 64) use the term agro-extractivism in the context of the agrarian question of the twenty-first century, arguing that what governments such as China and other international investors 'primarily seek are lands to meet their security need for agro-food products and energy, while multinational corporations in the extractive sector of the global economy are primarily concerned to feed the lucrative biofuel market by producing oil palm, sugarcane (for ethanol) and soya' or what we might refer to as 'flex crops'. Petras and Veltmeyer go on to say that 'agricultural extractivism takes a number of forms, but in the current context that has dominated the debate—apart from the dynamics of land grabbing—has been what we might term the political economy of biofuels capitalism: the conversion of farmland and agriculture for food production into the production of biofuels' (2016, 70). And Maristella Svampa includes agribusiness and biofuels production in her understanding of the new extractivism in Latin America, 'due to the fact that they consolidate a model that tends to follow a monoculture, the destruction of biodiversity, a concentration of land ownership and a destructive re-configuration of vast territories' and driven by what she calls the Commodities Consensus[2] (Svampa 2013, 118–119).

Agrarian extractivism has therefore been introduced under the umbrella of extractivism to refer broadly to large-scale, intensive monocrop production for export. But what is the 'extractive' character of agrarian extractivism? Are all types of large-scale chemical-intensive monocrop plantations extractive? Evidently, this type of agricultural production can take diverse forms in terms of land control and use, labour relations, surplus distribution, as well as the social relations of production and consumption. Some large-scale plantations may require a large labour force, or be cooperatively owned by the workers, reinvesting the surplus in the domestic economy creating forward and backward linkages, exploit dynamic intersectoral synergies and produce value-added consumer goods for the domestic market. Yet this type of large-scale industrial agriculture is distinct from that which is highly mechanized requiring minimal wage labour, export-oriented with little or no processing, corporate-controlled in a monopolized market and highly dependent on external chemical-based inputs. Agro-industry may not be inherently extractive as such, which is why it is important to specify the extractive character of the process. Agrarian extractivism as conceptualized here builds from the literature on extractivism as a mode of accumulation (Acosta 2013) and appropriation (Gudynas 2015) and a mode of extraction (Bunker 1984). As a mode of accumulation, agrarian extractivism involves particular exploitative social relations combined with unequal ecological and economic exchange in which the surplus value is extracted and labour opportunities and conditions deteriorate via new forms of value chain control and mechanization. It is therefore important to consider the relations of production (or extraction), of property, of divisions of labour, of income distribution and of consumption, reproduction and accumulation in extractive economies.

As an emerging concept in the literature, agrarian extractivism has rarely been rigorously defined. Evidently, simply using the term synonymously with agro-industry is neither analytically nor politically useful. An exception is the work of Alonso-Fradejas (2018) on the agro-extractive capitalist project in Guatemala. Using an approach grounded in agrarian political economy and ecology, Alonso-Fradejas (2018) defines the extractive character of the sugarcane and oil palm complex with reference to the economic, social and environmental extractive dynamics of sugarcane and oil palm production in Guatemala. They include: (1) the extraction and appropriation of the surplus value, rents and state revenues, including by means of financialization; (2) the appropriation of productive and reproductive labour; and (3) the contamination and exhaustion of external nature's energy and materials as well as damaging workers' health and vitality. Building on an earlier conceptualization of agrarian extractivism by Alonso-Fradejas (2015), as well as the classic work of Bunker (1984) and Gudynas (2015), McKay (2018, 2020) characterizes the agro-industrial soy complex in Bolivia as a type of agrarian extractivism defined by four interlinked features: (1) significant volumes of raw material exports; (2) value chain concentration and sectoral disarticulation; (3) high intensity of environmental degradation; and (4) deterioration of labour opportunities, labour conditions or both. Rather than seek an all-encompassing definition, these works highlight some of the key interlinked features which characterize the degree of extractiveness of the dominant 'agro-industrial' model. While the degree of extractiveness will certainly vary, we can identify at least seven key aspects which should be considered when analysing the extractive features of agrarian change. These include: (1) sectoral and commodity particularities; (2) flows of capital; (3) labour dynamics; (4) resource access and property dynamics; (5) flows of knowledge; (6) flows of non-human nature's energy and materials; and (7) territorial restructuring and developmental effects (see McKay et al. 2021). Despite these advances, the concept of agrarian extractivism remains in its infant stages. More case studies and critical analyses into agriculture's extractive features across various crop complexes, modalities, spaces, geographies and political economies will undoubtedly contribute to its analytical and political utility.

CONCLUSION

Extractivism has predominantly been used to characterize mining and hydrocarbons, although more recently it has come to characterize certain forms and modes of agricultural production in the context of the wave of literature on extractivism. Dominant forms of agricultural expansion which extract large volumes of raw materials with little to no processing, lack sectoral linkages and remain controlled by a market oligopoly contribute to widespread environmental degradation and destruction, and deteriorate labour opportunities and/or conditions are not leading to any form of industrial development, nor contributing to inclusive rural development. It is a mode of extraction, appropriating the economic and ecological value from the regions in which it operates, while exploiting or excluding the rural as they become surplus to the needs of capital accumulation. As a concept, agrarian extractivism exposes the extractive character of this dominant model, challenging the use of 'industrialization' as a form of discursive legitimation used by governments and corporations alike. We need to go beyond the debates of large- versus small-scale and genetically modified organisms versus agro-ecology to a more encompassing framework of agrarian extractivism to reveal the socioeconomic and socioecological implications of various forms and modes of agricultural activity. This chapter has attempted to shed light on the nature and character of industrial agriculture in the contemporary period, calling for a critical engagement with the dominant model of agricultural development and putting forth an emerging concept which may offer analytical and political utility in the debates regarding agrarian change and rural transformations.

NOTES

1. Modalities or mechanisms of extraction include mining (for minerals and metals), drilling (for gas and petroleum), as well as fishing and harvesting of agro-foods.

2.   For Svampa, the 'Commodities Consensus' refers to 'the beginning of a new economic and political order sustained by the boom in international prices for raw materials and consumer goods, which are increasingly demanded by industrialised and emerging countries' (Svampa 2013, 117).

FURTHER READING

Alonso-Fradejas, A. (2021), 'Leaving no one unscathed' in sustainable transitions: The life purging agro-extractivism of corporate renewables, *Journal of Rural Studies*, 81, 127–138.

Gudynas, E. (2015), *Extractivismos: Ecología, Economía y Política de un Modo de Entender el Desarrollo y la Naturaleza*, Cochabamba: CEDIB.

McKay, B.M. (2020), *The Political Economy of Agrarian Extractivism: Lessons from Bolivia*, Blackpoint: Fernwood Publishing.

McKay, B.M.; Alonso-Fradejas, A.; Ezquerro-Cañete, A. (2021), *Agrarian Extractivism in Latin America*, Abingdon: Routledge.

Veltmeyer, H.; Petras, J. (2014), *The New Extractivism: A Post-Neoliberal Development Model or Imperialism of the Twenty-First Century?*, London: Zed Books.

REFERENCES

Acosta, A. (2013), Extractivism and neoextractivism: Two sides of the same curse, in Lang, M.; Mokrani, D. (eds), *Beyond Development: Alternative Visions from Latin America*, Quito: Fundación Rosa Luxemburg, 87–104.

Akram-Lodhi, A.H.; Kay, C. (2010), Surveying the agrarian question (Part 1): Unearthing foundations, exploring diversity, *Journal of Peasant Studies*, 37(1), 177–202.

Alonso-Fradejas, A. (2015), Anything but a story foretold: Multiple politics of resistance to the agrarian extractivist project in Guatemala, *Journal of Peasant Studies*, 42(3–4), 489–515.

Alonso-Fradejas, A. (2018), *The Rise of Agro-Extractive Capitalism: Insights from Guatemala in the Early 21st Century*, The Hague: International Institute of Social Studies.

Banaji, J. (1980), Summary of agrarian question, in Wolpe, H. (ed.), *The Articulation of Modes of Production: Essays from Economy and Society*, London: Routledge and Kegan Paul.

Bernstein, H. (1996), Agrarian questions then and now, *Journal of Peasant Studies*, 24(1/2), 22–59.

Bernstein, H. (2004), 'Changing before our very eyes': Agrarian questions and the politics of land in capitalism today, *Journal of Agrarian Change*, 1–2, 190–225.

Blas, Javier (2013) Financial Times Commodities Report, 18 April.

Borras, S.M.J.; Kay, C.; Gomez, S.; Wilkinson, J. (2012), Land grabbing and global capitalist accumulation: Key features in Latin America, *Canadian Journal of Development Studies/Revue Canadienne d'Études du Développement*, 33(4), 402–416.

Bunker, S.G. (1984), Modes of extraction, unequal exchange, and the progressive underdevelopment of an extreme periphery: The Brazilian Amazon, 1600–1980, *American Journal of Sociology*, 89(5), 1017.

Byres, T.J. (1991), The agrarian question and differing forms of capitalist agrarian transition: An essay with reference to Asia, in *Rural Transformation in Asia*, Delhi: Oxford University Press.

Byres, T.J. (1996), *Capitalism from Above and Capitalism from Below: An Essay in Comparative Political Economy*, Basingstoke: Palgrave Macmillan.

Cisnero, F. (2011), Los pa ses mineros quieren dejar de serlo, Interview with Eduardo Gudynas, *Qué Pasa*, 9 April, accessed at www.elpais.com.uy/suplemento/quepasa/-lospaises-mineros-quieren-dejar-deserlo-/quepasa_558586_110409.html.

Clapp, J. (2018), Mega-Mergers on the menu: Corporate concentration and the politics of sustainability in the global food system, *Global Environmental Politics*, 18(2), 12–33.

Dasgupta, S.; Singh, A. (2006), *Manufacturing, Services and Premature Deindustrialization in Developing Countries: A Kaldorian Analysis*, Research Paper N.2006/49, accessed 11 March at www.wider.unu.edu/sites/default/files/rp2006-49.pdf.

Delgado Wise, R. (2017), El capital en la era de los monopolios generalizados: Apuntes sobre el capital monopolista, *Observatorio del Desarrollo*, 6(18), 48–58.

Delgado Wise, R.; Chávez, M.G. (2016), ¡Patentad, patentad!: Apuntes sobre la apropiación del trabajo científico por las grandes corporaciones multinacionales, *Observatorio del Desarrollo*, 4(15), 22–30.

Engels, F. (1950 [1894]), The peasant question in France and Germany, in Marx, K.; Engels, F. (eds), *Selected Works*, vol. 2, London: Lawrence and Wishart.

Erten, B.; Ocampo, J.A. (2013), Super cycles of commodity prices since the mid-nineteenth century, *World Development*, 44, 14–30.

ETC Group (2015), *Breaking Bad: Big Ag Mega-Mergers in Play Dow + DuPont in the Pocket? Next: Demonsanto?*, accessed 11 March 2021 at www.etcgroup.org/sites/www.etcgroup.org/files/files/etc_breakbad_cover4web.jpg.

Fairbairn, M. (2014), 'Like gold with yield': Evolving intersections between farmland and finance, *Journal of Peasant Studies*, 41(5), 777–795.

Giarracca, N.; Teubal, M. (2014), Argentina: Extractivist dynamics of soy production and open-pit mining, in Veltmeyer, H.; Petras, J. (eds), *The New Extractivism: A Post-Neoliberal Development Model or Imperialism of the Twenty-First Century?*, London: Zed Books, 47–79.

Goodman, D.; Sorj, B.; Wilkinson, J. (1987), *From Farming to Biotechnology: A Theory of Agro-Industrial Development*, Oxford: Basil Blackwell.

Gudynas, E. (2010a), Agropecuaria y nuevo extractivismo bajo los gobiernos progresistas de América del Sur, *Territorios*, 5, 37–54.

Gudynas, E. (2010b), The new extractivism of the 21st century: Ten urgent theses about extractivism in relation to current South American progressivism, *Americas Program Report*, January, 1–14.

Gudynas, E. (2013), Extracciones, extractivismos y extrahecciones, *Observatorio del Desarrollo*, 18, 1–18.

Gudynas, E. (2015), *Extractivismos: Ecología, Economía y Política de Un Modo de Entender El Desarrollo y La Naturaleza*, Cochabamba: CEDIB.

Howard, P.H. (2015), Intellectual property and consolidation in the seed industry, *Crop Science*, 55(6), 1–7.

IAASTD (2009), *Agriculture at a Crossroads: Global Report*, Washington, DC: International Assessment of Agricultural Knowledge, Science and Technology for Development and Island Press, accessed at www.agassessment.org/reports/IAASTD/EN/Agriculture%20at%20a%20Crossroads_Global%20Report%20(English).pdf.

Isakson, S.R. (2014), Food and finance: The financial transformation of agro-food supply chains, *Journal of Peasant Studies*, 41(5), 749–775.

Kautsky, K. (1988), *The Agrarian Question*, London: Zwan Publications.

Kloppenburg, J.R. (2004), *First the Seed: The Political Economy of Plant Biotechnology*, second edition, Madison, WI: University of Wisconsin Press.

Lenin, V.I. (1964 [1899]), *The Development of Capitalism in Russia*, Moscow: Progress Publishers.

Li, T.M. (2009), To make live or let die? Rural dispossession and the protection of surplus populations, *Antipode*, 41(S1), 66–93.

Marx, K. (1976 [1867]), *Capital: A Critique of Political Economy*, vol. 1, Middlesex: Penguin Books.

McKay, B.M. (2018), Control grabbing and value-chain agriculture: BRICS, MICs and Bolivia's soy complex, *Globalizations*, 15(1), 74–91.

McKay, B.M. (2020), *The Political Economy of Agrarian Extractivism: Lessons from Bolivia*, Blackpoint: Fernwood Publishing.

McKay, B.M.; Alonso-Fradejas, A.; Ezquerro-Cañete, A. (2021), *Agrarian Extractivism in Latin America*, Abingdon: Routledge.

McMichael, P. (2009), Feeding the world: Agriculture, development, and ecology, in Panitch, L.; Leys, C. (eds), *Coming to Terms with Nature: Socialist Register*, vol. 43, London: Merlin Press, 170–194.

McMichael, P. (2013), Value-chain agriculture and debt relations: Contradictory outcomes, *Third World Quarterly*, 34(4), 671–690.

Miller, H.I.; Conko, G. (2001), Precaution without principle, *Nature Biotechnology*, 19(4), 302–303.

Newell, P.; Glover, D. (2003), *Business and Biotechnology: Regulation and the Politics of Influence*, IDS Working Paper 192, Brighton.

O'Connor, J. (1998), *Natural Causes: Essays in Ecological Marxism*, New York: Guilford Press.

Petras, J.; Veltmeyer, H. (2016), *Power and Resistance: US Imperialism in Latin America*, Leiden: Koninklijke Brill.

Rodrik, D. (2016), Premature deindustrialization, *Journal of Economic Growth*, 21(1), 1–33.

Svampa, M. (2013), Resource extractivism and alternatives: Latin American perspectives on development, in Lang, M.; Mokrani, D. (eds), *Beyond Development: Alternative Visions from Latin America*, Amsterdam and Quito: Transnational Institute and Rosa Luxemburg Foundation.

van der Ploeg, J.D. (2018), Differentiation: Old controversies, new insights, *Journal of Peasant Studies*, 45(3), 489–524.

Veltmeyer, H. (2016), Extractive capital, the state and the resistance in Latin America, *Sociology and Anthropology*, 4(8), 774–84.

Weis, T. (2010), The accelerating biophysical contradictions of industrial capitalist agriculture, *Journal of Agrarian Change*, 10(3), 315–41.

White, B.; Borras, Jr., S.M.; Hall, R.; Scoones, I.; Wolford, W. (2012), The new enclosures: Critical perspectives on corporate land deals, *Journal of Peasant Studies*, 39(3–4), 619–647.

Woodhouse, P. (2010), Beyond industrial agriculture? Some questions about farm size, productivity and sustainability, *Journal of Agrarian Change*, 10(3), 437–453.

World Bank (2007), *World Development Report 2008: Agriculture for Development*, Washington, DC: World Bank, accessed 11 March 2021 at https://doi.org/10.1596/978-0-8213-7233-3.

55. Rural dispossession and capital accumulation
Derek Hall

INTRODUCTION

Dispossession is one of the most important topics in contemporary critical agrarian studies. An enormous literature has inquired into the ways in which people living in rural areas (and especially small farmers, pastoralists, fisherfolk and Indigenous peoples) have been deprived of some of the most basic affordances of life, particularly their land (understood both as property and territory) and access to water for drinking, farming, irrigation and fishing. These dispossessions have seen the new holders or controllers of land and water put them to diverse uses, including plantations, protected areas, mines, industrial zones, dam reservoirs, energy generation, small-scale farms, housing complexes, airports, roads and speculation. Dispossession's consequences for the livelihoods of vast numbers of people, for local, national and global political economies and for the politics of resistance have been immense.

Rural dispossession has been understood and theorized in diverse ways in critical agrarian studies and related fields like political ecology and geography. Concepts including dispossession itself, enclosure, privatization, exclusion, alienation, expulsion, displacement, grabs and grabbing, appropriation, (neo)colonialism, deprivation and (fictitious) commodification have featured prominently in the debate. Many scholars, too, have employed the foundational critical agrarian studies concept of primitive accumulation and David Harvey's (2003) reconceptualization of it as accumulation by dispossession (ABD). Both terms highlight the indispensable role that dispossession plays in capitalism. Marx (1976 [1867]) used primitive accumulation to theorize the origins of capitalist social relations. His analysis in Volume 1 of *Capital* emphasized the violent processes through which direct producers were separated from their means of production and subsistence (primarily land) and turned into proletarians who needed to sell their labour for a wage to survive, while ownership of the means of production was concentrated in capitalist hands. Long-standing debates over primitive accumulation and its relationship to transitions to and the expansion of capitalism were rejuvenated in the early 2000s by a number of efforts to rethink the concept and to theorize its ongoing applicability in 'advanced' capitalism (Perelman 2000; De Angelis 2001; Federici 2004; Glassman 2006). In agrarian studies, Jack Kloppenburg's *First the Seed* (2004 [1988]) anticipated many of these moves and extended the analysis of primitive accumulation to seed understood as a means of production. Perhaps the most influential approach, however, has been Harvey's use of ABD to understand how capitalist crisis leads to new rounds of dispossession, privatization and financialized and fraudulent accumulation (2003).

Analyses of primitive accumulation, ABD and related terms have made essential contributions to critical agrarian studies by grappling with what Tor Benjaminsen and Ian Bryceson call, in an appropriately broad framing, 'the combination of dispossession and capital accumulation' (2012, 336). This scholarship has some common ground. It is very widely agreed that dispossession for capital accumulation plays a central role in contemporary agrarian relations, and that these dispossessory projects aim much more at appropriating land and resources than they do at shaking loose new sources of waged labour; as Tania Li put it in a widely quoted phrase describing plantation development in Southeast Asia, the 'locals' discover that 'their land is needed, but their labor is not' (Li 2011, 286). Debates over primitive accumulation and ABD have also, however, been marked by ambiguous use of key terms and by disagreement over the processes at work and what they mean (Hall 2012, 2013; Levien 2012). This is in part because many new conceptualizations of primitive accumulation have expanded the range of processes the concept covers (for recent examples in critical agrarian studies see Adnan 2015; Hiraldo 2018). It also reflects differing positions on the extent to which these terms denote the enclosure of non-capitalist spheres of social life (and what such spheres might be) and thus the expansion of, or transitions to, capitalist social relations; the role of 'extra-economic' as opposed to 'economic' force (and the viability of that dichotomy); and the question of whether the main drivers of contemporary dispossessions are to be found at the global level (as responses to capitalist crisis) or have more national or local origins. Many attempts at conceptual reformulation and definitional precision have been made in critical agrarian studies and beyond (see especially Levien 2012; Adnan 2013; Ince 2014), but the quite different stances on primitive accumulation and ABD taken in these works may, ironically, lead to more rather than less divergence in the ways the terms are used.

This short chapter cannot cover the empirical scope of the processes that critical agrarian studies has explored under the heading of 'dispossession' or the theoretical variety of current debates over capitalism, primitive accumulation and ABD. What I seek to do instead is to discuss the roles played by the obviously central, but rarely defined, concept of 'dispossession'. I begin by outlining Michael Levien's approach to studying rural land dispossession in *Dispossession without Development* (2018). Levien's (2018, 7) unusually systematic effort to clear 'a path through the terminological thicket' both sharply delineates his own object of study and highlights some of the literature's key areas of divergence and disagreement. I then briefly survey work that uses primitive accumulation and/or ABD to address a wider terrain than does Levien with respect to dispossession's objects, mechanisms and relationship to capitalism. The final section poses a series of questions about the meaning of dispossession that are designed to help focus the scope of critical agrarian studies research on dispossession and capitalism.

REGIMES OF DISPOSSESSION

Michael Levien has argued that an appropriately redefined version of Harvey's ABD could serve as the basis for studying 'the role of dispossession under advanced capitalism' (Levien 2012, 936). He began this work of reconstruction by outlining ambiguities in the ways in which primitive accumulation has been used in agrarian studies, ambiguities which go all the way back to Marx. The most important for our purposes is 'whether primitive accumulation is defined above all by its *function* for capitalism or by the *means* specific to it' (Levien 2012, 937). The function in *Capital* was the combined processes of separating direct producers from the means of production and subsistence, concentrating those means in the hands of capitalists and turning former direct producers into wage labourers, while the means Marx emphasized above all was the use of what are often called 'extra-economic' forces (such as violence and law) as opposed to 'economic' or market ones. The ambiguity here is that market pressures can also lead to direct producers losing their land, particularly as they struggle to reproduce themselves, fall into debt and eventually have to sell up. Levien (2012, 938; 2018, 12–14) argues that in much research on the agrarian question, 'primitive accumulation came to mean any process that separated peasants from their means of production'. Rather than trying to solve this problem, Levien took Harvey's ABD on board as a way of breaking away from debates over transitions to capitalism and grappling instead with dispossession's place in already-existing capitalism (Levien 2012, 936; 2018, 15). He argued that while Harvey's own accounts were too underspecified and self-contradictory to be fit for purpose, a new definition of ABD as involving 'the use of extra-economic coercion to expropriate means of production, subsistence or common social wealth for capital accumulation' (Levien 2012, 940) could serve as a basis for studying and explaining many contemporary 'land grabs'.

While Levien's analytical framework in *Dispossession without Development* does not rely as centrally on the term ABD as did his earlier article, it builds on the arguments developed in that work. The book's object of study is the *coercive dispossession* of *rural land* by the *state*, and a good start on understanding his approach can be made by unpacking the three italicized terms. First, Levien (2018, 8) focuses on the dispossession of rural land specifically. He is careful to emphasize (against many takes on primitive accumulation and ABD) that land subject to dispossession is not necessarily held in common or by peasants or small farmers. Rather, it can be in the initial possession of 'heterogeneous agrarian classes'; held under various property forms, including private property; and is '*often already held within capitalist social relations*' (Levien 2018, 17, 16fn68, 14, emphasis in original; see also 159). Second, Levien makes a move that is less common than one might expect by explicitly stating what he takes 'dispossession' to mean for the purposes of his study. He treats it as a relationship of directly coercive redistribution, and excludes both 'market-induced dispossession' and 'land loss through forces that are proximately natural, if ultimately human-induced' (Levien 2018, 5f.). While he seems to remain open to the treatment of land loss through these latter mechanisms as 'dispossession' (see below), the process as he understands it in the book is carried out by an agent and is involuntary from the point of view of the dispossessed. 'Land dispossession' thus denotes a situation in which 'those who control means of coercion ... transfer portions of the earth from one set of people to another' (Levien 2018, 6). Third, while he recognizes that the agents of coercive land dispossession can include non-state actors, the book restricts itself to dispossession carried out by the state. His substantive reason for doing this is that states are 'the predominant owners of the means of coercion in the contemporary world'; his methodological reason is that isolating state-driven dispossession allows its nature and drivers to be analysed more precisely (Levien 2018, 7f., 18).

With this understanding of what dispossession is, who is being dispossessed of what and who is doing the dispossessing in hand, Levien argues that the 'grabbing' of rural land in India that he studies relates to capitalism not in forming part of a transition to or expansion of capitalist social relations *qua* primitive accumulation, but rather because of the role land dispossession plays within already-existing Indian capitalism. This role has changed with time, and Levien (2018, 17) states that historical 'regimes of dispossession' 'can be differentiated by the specific economic purposes and associated class interests they serve'. Levien insists against many Harvey-inspired analyses of ABD that these regimes operate primarily at the national and sub-national levels rather than emanating from the vagaries and crises of global capitalism (Levien 2018, 16–18; see also Hall 2013, 1587–1590). The shift to the current regime in India took place in the 1990s as state governments moved from dispossessing land for public-sector infrastructure and industry to doing so for, especially, private-sector real estate projects (Levien 2018, 5). The ability of states to acquire land through these 'regimes' and the consequences of such acquisitions, meanwhile, can be explained through the interactions between the regimes and varying 'agrarian milieux' (Levien 2018, 17). Much of Levien's book is devoted to an ethnographic account of the mechanisms, politics and consequences of land dispossession for a special economic zone in the village of Rajpura (in Rajasthan) from the mid-2000s, with particular and fine-grained concern for what happened to dispossessed farmers; the book also makes the broader case that land grabs in neoliberal India involve 'dispossession without development'.

WIDENING THE LENS

Levien's work presents a carefully elaborated and valuable framework for comparative study of an important but explicitly limited aspect of dispossession and its relationship to capitalism, and other scholars have drawn on and modified the 'regimes of dispossession' framework in studying dispossession elsewhere (Kenney-Lazar 2018; Woods forthcoming). In what follows, however, I focus on work that uses primitive accumulation and ABD to take a broader, or at least different, view of the what, how and why of dispossession and its relationship to capitalism.

A first set of issues relates to the 'objects' of dispossession – that is, *what* people are being dispossessed of. Much recent work on primitive accumulation, ABD and dispossession more broadly in critical agrarian studies and related fields has focused on land, notably through debates over 'land grabbing' or 'the land rush' (for a review see Hall 2013; see also Vorbrugg 2019; Goetz, this volume). Water, however, has also featured prominently and in diverse ways. Lyla Mehta, Gert Jan Veldwisch and Jennifer Franco (2012) draw on ABD to analyse 'water grabbing' in relation to land deals/grabs and to explore the role of this process in the agricultural, energy, mining and water sectors. Other scholars have used primitive accumulation and/ or ABD to understand dispossessions related to fisheries and other uses of lakes and coastal areas. Chris Sneddon (2007) discusses the complex roles of these processes in the dispossession of small-scale fishers around Cambodia's Tonle Sap lake as the state assigned fishing lot licenses to well-connected people. Benjaminsen and Bryceson (2012) employ primitive accumulation and ABD to theorize the conservation-driven and multi-faceted dispossession of small-scale fishers and villagers, and the new opportunities for capital accumulation opened up by marine and coastal conservation, as 'blue grabbing'. An emerging literature, too, discusses the forms, mechanisms, drivers, legitimations and protagonists of 'ocean grabbing', which Nathan Bennett and his co-authors (2015, 62f.) define as 'dispossession or appropriation of use, control or access to ocean space or resources from prior resource users, rights holders or inhabitants' and as occurring when an 'initiative' is characterized by poor governance, undermines human security or livelihoods and negatively affects 'social-ecological well-being'. AlShehabi and Suroor (2016, 835, 838, 843f.), finally, take up land reclamation in Bahrain as a 'limit case' for 'ABD involving land' in that it involved the production of new land from the sea as, in Polanyian terms, a 'real' rather than a 'fictitious' commodity, and discuss the dispossessions that occurred as once-coastal villages became inland ones.

The two main drivers that Levien excludes from his approach to dispossession – 'proximately natural, if ultimately human-induced' forces and markets – have also been widely studied. On the former, Tom Perreault's (2013, 1051) nuanced account of 'the complex relationship between the accumulation of toxic sediments and the dispossessionary effects of capital accumulation' shows that water can itself become a mechanism of dispossession. Perreault examined a mining operation along Bolivia's Huanuni River that was using enormous amounts of the river's water and discharging it loaded with heavy metals and other pollutants. Indigenous *campesino* communities living downstream suffered the consequences, including the contamination of the water sources on which they and their livestock relied and the deposition of toxic silt on agricultural lands in the river's widening floodplain. People have been pushed away from the river, and in some cases out of the community, through this 'livelihood dispossession' (Perreault 2013, 1063). Perreault (2013, 1051) argues that while what he calls 'dispossession by accumulation' is not ABD in Harvey's terms, it is primitive accumulation in Marx's: 'the residents of the Huanuni Valley are steadily being separated from their means of production and social reproduction'. Nature has thus become 'enrolled in' extra-economic means of dispossession (Perreault 2013, 1054f.). In this case the source of the pollution is proximate and clear, but climate change will surely be a massive driver of this kind of dispossession in the twenty-first century while being less easily attributed to a specific agent or project.

Land markets as mechanisms of dispossession have also received ongoing attention in the current debate (Li 2010; Akram-Lodhi 2012). In a recent paper on land dispossession in India (particularly Tamil Nadu), M. Vijayabaskar and Ajit Menon (2018, 572) critique Levien's focus on coercive land redistribution by the state, and call for much greater attention to 'small-scale market-based transactions'. Empirically, they argue that farmers in post-reform India may more often be dispossessed of their land by such transactions than by direct state coercion (Vijayabaskar and Menon 2018, 574). They also make the case that land sales on the market are shaped by state policies that privilege non-agricultural sectors and undermine farming. Lack of investment in and upkeep of irrigation facilities, among other state acts of omission, generate 'dispossession by neglect', and mean that 'dispossession seemingly driven by the "silent compulsion of economic relations" is actually mediated by shifts in state policies and less visible forms of non-economic coercion' (Vijayabaskar and Menon 2018, 583; see also Hall 2013, 1593f.; Hiraldo 2018, 520). On the basis of this argument that Levien's distinction between voluntary/market and coercive/state processes is difficult to maintain, they suggest incorporating the former into the study of 'regimes of dispossession' (Vijayabaskar and Menon 2018, 584). There may be some scope for this in Levien's framework: he recognizes some blurriness with respect to the distinction (Levien 2018, 6fn10), and while his broadest definition of 'dispossession' as 'a social relation of coercive redistribution' should exclude 'voluntary' transfers of land on the market, he also seems to accept the concept of 'market-induced dispossession' (Levien 2018, 6, 17).

WHAT IS DISPOSSESSION?

The objects and mechanisms of dispossession covered in the previous section, while enormously important in themselves, can only point toward the range of themes a full study of 'the combination of dispossession and capital accumulation' in agrarian settings may need to grapple with. Rather than continue to expand that range, I would like in this section to consider how its boundaries might be established. As Levien points out, it is unusual for analysts of dispossession to state explicitly what they mean by it. I would thus like here to think through the ways the term tends to get used in practice and their implications. I focus on land dispossession, but also incorporate other forms.

One basic issue is whether being dispossessed of land means that the dispossessed have lost it entirely – that they no longer have any rights or access to it (see Ribot and Peluso 2003) – or whether dispossession can take place through transformations in access short of such a complete shift. My sense is that the implicit definition of dispossession in most of the literature is close to the idea of expulsion/full exclusion. Borras et al. (2012, 850), for instance, treat 'expulsion of peasants from their lands' and 'dispossession' as equivalents in their influential definition of land grabbing as control grabbing. Shelley Feldman and Charles Geisler (2012, 974), on the other hand, argue that their theorization of '*in situ* displacement' (which uses 'displacement' and 'dispossession' as synonyms) 'helps to reveal land grabs as both physical appropriations and, perhaps most crucially, as diminishments in the capacity to socially reproduce everyday lives and livelihoods'. Several recent papers, too, have reformulated the concept of primitive accumulation to incorporate widespread processes of alienation and of articulation with capitalism that can take place while producers retain possession of land (Ince 2014; Hiraldo 2018; Sugden 2019).

By focusing on what has changed in people's relationships to their labour and land, some of these works connect to a broader (and often Harvey-inspired) expansion of the range of 'things' of which people can be dispossessed. These have included earnings from existing arrangements (Benjaminsen and Bryceson 2012, 341), 'supportive institutions and infrastructures' (Vorbrugg 2019, 1011f.; see also Hiraldo 2018) and perhaps even the possibility of future entitlements (AlShehabi and Suroor 2016, 844). These expansions raise questions about whether, to be 'dispossessed' of something, one must first have 'possessed' it, and what such 'possession' should be taken to mean, that are barely raised in the literature reviewed here. Adnan (2013, 96, emphasis in original) proposes a contrast between the 'dispossession' of resources 'initially owned or held by the dispossessed groups' and 'deprivation' as the '*denial of entitlements that have not yet been realized*'. The concept of 'possession' also requires care when applied to water, which is often not 'possessed' in the way that other 'things' are. One way to pose the theoretical question involved here would be to ask whether any negative change in people's situations should be categorized as 'dispossession' and, if not, how the scope of 'things' that can be dispossessed might be limited. It is striking, finally, that work on dispossession in critical agrarian studies has so little to say about taxation, one of the preeminent ways in which states forcibly expropriate people's assets; this topic is surely worth further attention.

A second overarching question asks *who* can be dispossessed. Harvey's understanding of ABD has been so influential in part because of its extension of the range of people affected by capital's dispossessions to include the broad citizenry of 'advanced' capitalist countries. As ABD has been brought into critical agrarian studies and the field has incorporated and developed new ways of thinking about primitive accumulation, however, the focus on the 'who' of dispossession has continued to be on 'peasants', or at least small farmers, fishers and pastoralists. Some authors make this kind of focus clear, as in James Fairhead, Melissa Leach and Ian Scoones' (2012, 238) definition of 'appropriation' (a term that is 'central to the dual, related processes of accumulation and dispossession') as implying 'the transfer of ownership, use rights and control over resources that were once publicly or privately owned – or not even the subject of ownership – from the poor (or everyone including the poor) into the hands of the powerful. Levien, on the other hand, critiques the assumption that people being dispossessed are necessarily 'peasants' operating outside of capitalism and engaged with the 'commons', arguing rather (and demonstrating empirically for Rajpura) that they are 'heterogeneous agrarian classes that often have different interests vis-à-vis large capital projects' (Levien 2018, 17; see also Hall et al. 2011, 14; Hall 2013, 1596–1598). While a focus on the poor and marginalized will usually be appropriate both empirically and normatively, students of dispossession should, in defining their terms and structuring their research, consider the possibility that richer and more powerful people can be dispossessed, and if they want to exclude such people from their understanding of 'dispossession' they should be clear about why they are doing so.

These issues connect to a third: the extent to which and ways in which dispossession is a normative concept. Definitions of dispossession (and, indeed, of primitive accumulation and ABD) can be presented in a value-neutral way, as referring to certain observable criteria. Attention to dispossession in critical agrarian studies and related fields, however, is not just an analytical but a political matter; it arises out of deep concern over the huge numbers of people being deprived of core aspects of their livelihoods and identities. Fairhead et al. (2012, 238) continue the definition quoted above by stating that appropriation 'is an emotive term because it involves injustice; it is what Robin Hood objected to'. Just as the term 'land grab' carries a clearer normative judgement than does 'land acquisition', so the use of 'dispossession' has a more critical edge than would, say, 'transfer of assets'. What it is that's wrong about dispossession, however, is not usually spelled out in detail. The reasons for this seem obvious: the literature contains both an enormous number of straightforwardly appalling cases and many analyses of why it is that capitalism requires or thrives on the more or less forcible seizure of land and other resources by the rich and powerful from the poor and the marginalized.

While I do not want to diminish the power of those analyses, I do argue that one way of clarifying one's sense of what dispossession is would be to ask whether dispossession is always unjust – or, alternatively, whether people can lose access to 'things' without being dispossessed of them. Levien, as noted above, calls attention to the tendency in some work to treat any process that 'separates' producers from the means of production as primitive accumulation. The same tendency can be seen in most uses of 'dispossession' and closely related terms, which see such separation (or 'divorcing'), or processes by which small farmers 'lose' their lands, or 'land markets for rural land that transfer land from small and marginal farmers to private firms and urban elites' (Vijayabaskar and Menon 2018, 579, 584) as clearly involving dispossession. One reason is that land markets, as noted above, are so often shot through with power and biased against smallholders. Another is that even land markets closer to liberal visions of fairness would see so many sales that, while 'voluntary', would be undertaken with a heavy heart, by people overwhelmed by debt or illness or their efforts to maintain status. Any effort to map the contours of Benjaminsen and Bryceson's 'combination of dispossession and capital accumulation' must emphasize these sales, though grappling with their extent will be a formidable undertaking. Yet it is also worth asking whether transfers of land (or other resources) from rural people could happen in a way that is not unjust. In a situation in which a poor family sold (some of) its farmland to a rich speculator and still felt 10 years later that they had made a good deal, would they have been 'dispossessed'? Might small farmers, pastoralists or fisherfolk sometimes be willing to see the state involve itself in establishing a conservation zone on some of their land or waters? I am not saying that such scenarios are common, but to exclude them from the range of the possible may be to impose normative judgements on farmers that they would not share, and to seek to prevent them from doing things that they want to do.

A 2019 article by Shaohua Zhan takes up some of these issues in an original way in the context of land relations in post-1978 China. Zhan (2019, 449) defines dispossession not as an act (see Levien 2018, 5f.) but as an outcome close to the 'full expulsion' approach discussed above, one 'in which peasants lose land, assets, or entitlements and become full proletarians without access to income-generating assets, and as a result, suffer a loss of livelihood'. Zhan emphasizes that by this definition China has in recent decades seen enormous amounts of ABD, but the paper also draws on work by Gillian Hart and Giovanni Arrighi to claim that China has seen several varieties of 'accumulation without dispossession' with respect to land. Three aspects of his approach are of particular interest here. Zhan makes the striking case that if peasants receive sufficient compensation of appropriate kinds (especially new, secure sources of livelihood), they can be expropriated without being dispossessed (Zhan 2019, 452, 460); argues that peasants sometimes consent to giving up land (Zhan 2019, 447); and makes the normative argument that different forms of AWD, including expropriation with sufficient compensation, can serve as an 'effective counterbalance' to the 'injustice' of ABD (Zhan 2019, 460).

A final question for the study of the relationship between capital accumulation and dispossession to consider is the extent to which dispossession continues to be driven by motives and dynamics other than capital accumulation (and what that might mean). While some of the literature on primitive accumulation presents dispossession as deriving overwhelmingly from capital's general logic and imperatives (De Angelis 2001; Moore 2015), other work leaves things more open. Shapan Adnan's (2013, 94) analysis of primitive accumulation in particular highlights the 'non-capitalist' motivations that continue to underlie some 'land grabs', including conflicts over race, ethnicity, caste, religion, status and power, and states that 'the expropriation of land can be regarded as corresponding to primitive accumulation only when it feeds into the expansionary dynamic of capitalist production'. Other analyses of primitive accumulation and ABD highlight the ways land dispossession can forward goals related to political power, elite factional balance and state territorial control (Sneddon 2007, 179, 184–187; Woods 2011; AlShehabi and Suroor 2016, 840). Hall, Hirsch and Li (2011), too, explicitly distinguish their concept of 'exclusion' from primitive accumulation, ABD and enclosure in order to try to bring in a broader range of processes, drivers and agents. None of this is to suggest, of course, that these other motivations should be studied in isolation from capital and capitalism; the point is rather that there is more to land dispossession than 'capital's enclosures'.

ACKNOWLEDGEMENTS

I am grateful to the participants of a July 2019 workshop at the Balsillie School of International Affairs for their comments.

FURTHER READING

Adnan, S. (2013), Land grabs and primitive accumulation in deltaic Bangladesh: Interactions between neoliberal globalization, state interventions, power relations and peasant resistance, *Journal of Peasant Studies*, 40(1), 87–128.

Hall, D. (2013), Primitive accumulation, accumulation by dispossession and the global land grab, *Third World Quarterly*, 34(9), 1582–1604.

Kloppenburg, Jr., J.R. (2004 [1988]), *First the Seed: The Political Economy of Plant Biotechnology*, second edition, Madison, WI: University of Wisconsin Press.

Levien, M. (2018), *Dispossession without Development: Land Grabs in Neoliberal India*, New York: Oxford University Press.

Perreault, T. (2013), Dispossession by accumulation? Mining, water and the nature of enclosure on the Bolivian Altiplano, *Antipode*, 45(5), 1050–1069.

REFERENCES

Adnan, S. (2013), Land grabs and primitive accumulation in deltaic Bangladesh: Interactions between neoliberal globalization, state interventions, power relations and peasant resistance, *Journal of Peasant Studies*, 40(1), 87–128.

Adnan, S. (2015), Primitive accumulation and the 'transition to capitalism' in neoliberal India: Mechanisms, resistance, and the persistence of self-employed labour, in Harriss-White, B.; Heyer, J. (eds), *Indian Capitalism in Development*, London: Routledge, 23–45.

Akram-Lodhi, A.H. (2012), Contextualising land grabbing: Contemporary land deals, the global subsistence crisis and the world food system, *Canadian Journal of Development Studies*, 33(2), 119–142.

AlShehabi, O.H.; Suroor, S. (2016), Unpacking 'accumulation by dispossession', 'fictitious commodification', and 'fictitious capital formation': Tracing the dynamics of Bahrain's land reclamation, *Antipode*, 48(4), 835–856.

Benjaminsen, T.A.; Bryceson, I. (2012), Conservation, green/blue grabbing and accumulation by dispossession in Tanzania, *Journal of Peasant Studies*, 39(2), 335–355.

Bennett, N.J.; Govan, H.; Satterfield, T. (2015), Ocean grabbing, *Marine Policy*, 57, 61–68.

Borras, Jr., S.M.; Franco, J.C.; Gómez, S.; Kay, C.; Spoor, M. (2012), Land grabbing in Latin America and the Caribbean, *Journal of Peasant Studies*, 39(3–4), 845–872.

De Angelis, M. (2001), Marx and primitive accumulation: The continuous character of capital's 'enclosures', *The Commoner*, 2(1), 1–22.

Fairhead, J.; Leach, M.; Scoones, I. (2012), Green grabbing: A new appropriation of nature?, *Journal of Peasant Studies*, 39(2), 237–261.

Federici, S. (2004), *Caliban and the Witch: Women, the Body and Primitive Accumulation*, Brooklyn, NY: Autonomedia.

Feldman, S.; Geisler, C. (2012), Land expropriation and displacement in Bangladesh, *Journal of Peasant Studies*, 39(3–4), 971–993.

Glassman, J. (2006), Primitive accumulation, accumulation by dispossession, accumulation by 'extra-economic' means, *Progress in Human Geography*, 30(5), 608–625.

Hall, D. (2012), Rethinking primitive accumulation: Theoretical tensions and rural Southeast Asian complexities, *Antipode*, 44(4), 1188–1208.

Hall, D. (2013), Primitive accumulation, accumulation by dispossession and the global land grab, *Third World Quarterly*, 34(9), 1582–1604.

Hall, D.; Hirsch, P.; Li, T.M. (2011), *Powers of Exclusion: Land Dilemmas in Southeast Asia*, Singapore and Honolulu: National University of Singapore Press and University of Hawai'i Press.

Harvey, D. (2003), *The New Imperialism*, Oxford: Oxford University Press.

Hiraldo, R. (2018), Experiencing primitive accumulation as alienation: Mangrove forest privatization, enclosures and the everyday adaptation of bodies to capital in rural Senegal, *Journal of Agrarian Change*, 18(3), 517–535.

Ince, O.U. (2014), Primitive accumulation, new enclosures, and global land grabs: A theoretical intervention, *Rural Sociology*, 79(1), 104–131.

Kenney-Lazar, M. (2018), Governing dispossession: Relational land grabbing in Laos, *Annals of the American Association of Geographers*, 108(3), 679–694.

Kloppenburg, Jr., J.R. (2004 [1988]), *First the Seed: The Political Economy of Plant Biotechnology*, second edition, Madison, WI: University of Wisconsin Press.

Levien, M. (2012), The land question: Special economic zones and the political economy of disposses-sion in India, *Journal of Peasant Studies*, 39(3–4), 933–969.

Levien, M. (2018), *Dispossession without Development: Land Grabs in Neoliberal India*, New York: Oxford University Press.

Li, T.M. (2010), Indigeneity, capitalism, and the management of dispossession, *Current Anthropology*, 51(3), 385–414.

Li, T.M. (2011), Centering labor in the land grab debate, *Journal of Peasant Studies*, 38(2), 281–298.

Marx, K. (1976 [1867]), *Capital*, vol. 1, Harmondsworth: Penguin Books.

Mehta, L.; Veldwisch, G.J.; Franco, J. (2012), Introduction to the special issue: Water grabbing? Focus on the (re)appropriation of finite water resources, *Water Alternatives*, 5(2), 193–207.

Moore, J.W. (2015), *Capitalism in the Web of Life: Ecology and the Accumulation of Capital*, New York: Verso.

Perelman, M. (2000), *The Invention of Capitalism: Classical Political Economy and the Secret History of Primitive Accumulation*, Durham, NC: Duke University Press.

Perreault, T. (2013), Dispossession by accumulation? Mining, water and the nature of enclosure on the Bolivian Altiplano, *Antipode*, 45(5), 1050–1069.

Ribot, J.C.; Peluso, N.L. (2003), A theory of access, *Rural Sociology*, 68(2), 153–181.

Sneddon, C. (2007), Nature's materiality and the circuitous paths of accumulation: Dispossession of freshwater fisheries in Cambodia, *Antipode*, 39(1), 167–193.

Sugden, F. (2019), Labour migration, capitalist accumulation, and feudal reproduction: A historical analysis from the Eastern Gangetic Plains, *Antipode* 51(5), 1600–1639.

Vijayabaskar, M.; Menon, A. (2018), Dispossession by neglect: Agricultural land sales in Southern India, *Journal of Agrarian Change*, 18(3), 571–587.

Vorbrugg, A. (2019), Not about land, not quite a grab: Dispersed dispossession in rural Russia, *Antipode*, 51(3), 1011–1031.

Woods, K. (2011), Ceasefire capitalism: Military-private partnerships, resource concessions and military-state building in the Burma–China borderlands, *Journal of Peasant Studies*, 38(4), 747–770.

Woods, K. (forthcoming), Smaller-scale land grabs and accumulation from below: Violence, coercion and consent in spatially uneven agrarian change in Shan State, Myanmar, *World Development*, 1–16.

Zhan, S. (2019), Accumulation by and without dispossession: Rural land use, land expropriation, and livelihood implications in China, *Journal of Agrarian Change*, 19(3), 447–464.

56. Ecological crises in the rural world

Marcus Taylor

Barely a month goes by without the release of another high-level report warning of the heightening tensions between global agriculture and its foundational ecological premises. From soil erosion to biodiversity loss to chemical runoff to greenhouse gas emissions, there is increasing cognisance across governmental levels that agricultural production is both the cause of substantial environmental degradation while simultaneously being highly vulnerable to its impacts. Typically, such reports are accompanied by calls to move towards new and more sustainable forms of practising agriculture. Yet there exist competing visions of the normative goals that sustainable agriculture should entail, how it should be realised and who should drive it forward. While the Food and Agriculture Organization (FAO), CGIAR and World Bank have promoted varied rubrics such as sustainable intensification, climate-smart agriculture and precision agriculture, agrarian social movements such as *La Vía Campesina* have countered with alternative concepts such as agroecology and regenerative farming. To complicate matters, the FAO and other international institutions now incorporate some of the lexicon and practices of agroecology into their policy prescriptions, yet elsewhere retain a strong emphasis on conventional practices of agricultural intensification (FAO 2018).

As a result of this fast evolving discourse, addressing questions of sustainability is a pressing political issue for those working in critical agrarian studies. In particular, the field has sought to understand the synergies and trade-offs inherent to interlacing sustainability goals with those of social justice. At one level, contributions have scrutinised existing practices and projects labelled as sustainable agriculture, therein critically assessing their intended and unintended impacts in terms of both equity and sustainability. At another, work from within critical agrarian studies has sought to draw out marginalised histories, perspectives and practices that are all too often sidelined within dominant rubrics at national and international levels. While the ensuing debates are complex, the primary strength of the field has been to emphasise how contrasting ideas and practices of sustainable agriculture rest upon diverging imaginaries of how rural regions should be organised socially, culturally and politically.

FOUNDATIONS OF A CRITICAL AGRARIAN STUDIES ANALYSIS

Mainstream perspectives on agricultural sustainability betray a notable tension. On the one hand, they are typically framed within a neo-Malthusian perspective that emphasises the enduring need to raise productivity systematically in order to feed a growing population. This sentiment is aptly captured in the oft-repeated refrain of feeding a global population of 9 billion people by 2050 (World Bank 2015). At the same time, however, there is widespread acknowledgement that existing agricultural intensification trends have driven a range of debilitating ecological transformations including land degradation, toxicity, declining water resources, energy inefficiency, unrelenting biodiversity loss and greenhouse gas emissions (UNEP 2014; United Nations Convention to Combat Desertification 2017). The latter are rightly recognised as posing simultaneous threats to human welfare alongside undermining the potential for future food production.

Recognition of these potential crises typically leads to declarations of the need to fundamentally transform agriculture and food production (World Bank 2015; FAO et al. 2018). The rubric of sustainable intensification, for example, typically calls for a transformative approach that can 'produce more outputs with more efficient use of all inputs ... while reducing environmental damage and building resilience, natural capital and the flow of environmental services' (Montpellier Panel 2013). Within this discourse, however, there is a clear tendency to represent sustainability transformations as a question of technical fixes at the level of production and surrounding institutions (Loos et al. 2014). This urge to improve the efficiency of intensification is explicit in current discourses of 'Agriculture 4.0' which advocate for the systematic incorporation of digital technologies into crop design, agricultural management and food production as the cutting edge of sustainability (De Clercq et al. 2018; cf. Rotz et al. 2019; Clapp and Ruder 2020).

For critical agrarian studies, the danger of viewing environmental crises as a series of technical problems is that it obscures the ways in which the production of environmental degradation is not simply an unfortunate side effect of otherwise rational processes of agricultural intensification. Rather, the field highlights how environmental degradation is a systematic feature of capitalist agricultural intensification that subordinates environmental integrity to the pursuit of profit (Foster et al. 2010; Moore 2015). In so doing, critical agrarian studies foregrounds questions of power and inequality that are typically excluded from the mainstream lens yet are indispensable for understanding why degrading forms of agricultural production are perpetuated over time and who bears the brunt of their social and environmental costs. In this manner, critical agrarian studies seeks to provide analytical weight to the study of environmental justice in rural regions (Sikor and Newell 2014).

While there are different emphases within the field, it is possible to identify four common elements that provide a foundation for critical analysis. First, in contrast to the mainstream literature, agriculture is not an activity that has 'environmental impacts'. Rather, agriculture is better understood as a process of environment-making in a far more encompassing sense. As David Ludden put it, farming is a critical point of contact between human powers and the changing natural environment, a process by which humanity 'sculpts the earth' (Ludden 1999, 19). This sculpting is evident in the landscape transformations by which farmers work to organise the distribution of species over the landscape: attempting – only ever partially successfully – to manage what grows where and when in order to provide a stream of food, fuel and fibre from the land. Alongside transforming the spatial arrangements of plant and animal life, agricultural production also depends on the construction of elaborate infrastructures, from terraces to irrigation systems, storage structures to transportation networks. By practising agriculture, humanity works in and through nature to create malleable and dynamic agrarian environments that are constantly evolving (van der Ploeg 2013). For agrarian studies, therefore, analysis starts by asking how specific agricultural landscapes have been produced over time (Ingold 1993; Gidwani 2000).

Second, these produced agricultural landscapes represent complex amalgamations of social forces and ecological processes that defy any clear division into neat categories of 'social' and 'natural' (Moore 2015). Arun Agrawal and K. Sivaramakrishnan (2000) usefully advanced the term 'agrarian environments' to capture how the biophysical characteristics, social relations and cultural representations of landscapes co-evolve. For example, in a south Indian paddy field we might encounter a process of seed germination, development, ripening and harvesting that takes form through the human reshaping of water flows to channel and flood specific areas of land; the social patterns of seeding and weeding and their associated divisions of labour and embedded knowledge; the historical engineering of seeds through genetic manipulation via selective breeding or biotechnology; the frequent additions of natural or synthetic chemicals that alter the nutrient and biotic balance of the paddy; the networks of credit provision, land tenure and labouring bodies that shape where and when agricultural production can commence; the cultural forms and practices that give meaning to agricultural activities; and the circuits of capital accumulation, market shifts and governmental policies within which rice production is integrally assimilated (Taylor 2015). This entanglement of social and ecological forces makes it evident that there is no such thing as an ecological crisis per se. Rather we must think in terms of how social and ecological processes are wrought together in ways that cause moments of tension, degradation and stress across an agrarian environment.

Third, the production of agrarian environments necessarily involves the correlate production of knowledge and subjectivities. The original term agriculture expresses the synthesis of cultivation techniques and collective ways of knowing by which humans work busily alongside nature to produce plants and animals and, in so doing, co-produce various knowledge systems for this purpose (Pretty 2002). Distinct social groups, however, come to 'know nature' in distinct ways owing to their divergent roles within the production of the agrarian environment (Gupta 1998; Goldman et al. 2012). Differences of embodied experience on the basis of gender, class and ethnicity, for example, lead to the formation of contrasting subjectivities and associated bodies of knowledge about agricultural production and ecological change (Nightingale 2006; Li 2007; Kerr 2014; Flachs 2019). In particular, much attention has focused on discrepancies and potential conflicts between indigenous ecological knowledges, on one hand, and scientific knowledge, on the other (Jansen 1998; Agrawal 2005). This has led to an enduring focus on how different knowledges about agriculture and sustainability are formed, hierarchicalised and mobilised for the purpose of making political claims (Scoones and Thompson 1994; Sumberg and Thompson 2012; Luna and Dowd-Uribe 2020).

This leads us to our fourth essential framing point of critical agrarian studies: agrarian environments are inescapably landscapes of power in which the socio-ecological organisation of producing food, fuel and fibre is interlaced with hierarchies between social groups that determine what is produced, for whom, by whom and under what conditions (Bernstein 2010). The core political-economic questions of critical agrarian studies are extremely relevant here: tenure and labour relations, the production and distribution of surpluses, the role of agricultural commercialisation and market forces, social differentiation, the construction of labour forces, patterns of migration, government policies and the cycles of credit and debt that shape the seasonal rhythms of farming from Canada to Cambodia. What recent contributions to critical agrarian studies have sought to do is better connect those dynamics to the biophysical processes of ecological transformation and landscape change (Montefrio 2017; Jakobsen 2020).

Two elements are particularly salient in the current literature. First has been to examine how the experience of ecological crises can serve to recalibrate relations of class, gender and ethnicity in ways that unequally distribute benefits and risks involved between social actors. A classic example is the provocatively titled book by renowned Indian journalist P. Sainath – *Everybody Loves a Good Drought* (1996). Sainath showed how the experience of drought was closely written into the reproduction of power relations across the agrarian environment in northern India. The seeming 'ecological crisis' of failed rains was consistently harnessed by privileged households who used their control over key assets at a time of hardship to re-establish hierarchical and extractive relationships with other producer households. In this way, an ecological crisis for some can be an accumulation strategy for others (Taylor 2015). A more contemporary example is provided by de la Cruz and Jansen (2018) in their examination of Panama disease outbreaks in the Philippine banana industry. Through an analysis of the social dynamics of contract farming, they uncovered a distinctly uneven distribution of risks in which corporate buyers insulated themselves from the costs of management by displacing the burdens of managing the disease upon smallholder producers. While fostering a narrative of blame that placed smallholders as the vectors of disease transmission, corporate buyers occluded their role in driving down prices to a level that undermined the ability of direct producers to stem the disease therein reproducing the crisis over time.

Relatedly, the second aspect of these studies has been to establish how patterns of landscape formation and degradation are interlaced within circuits of capital that operate across scales (cf. Jackson 2008; Clapp 2015). These contributions ask how the scaled organisation of surplus extraction can produce an agrarian environment that systematically degrades soil, biodiversity, water resources and other key elements. In the words of Don Mitchell, agrarian studies analyses the processes by which 'the violent destruction of landscape (and livelihood) in one place can redound very much to the benefit of landscapes (and people) in other places' (Mitchell 2003, 791). For example, consider the externalisation of environmental costs occurring on the agricultural frontier region of San Luis, some 800 kilometres west of Buenos Aires in Argentina where the plains start to gradually arch upwards towards the eastern fringes of the Andes range. Here we encounter an agrarian environment transformed by the expansion of soy, wheat, maize and sunflower production that has all but obliterated the previous agrarian environment predicated upon extensive cattle ranching and small-scale food production within a largely forested environment (Romá and Garro 2016). Often declared a success story of export-orientated agricultural development – one that was strongly promoted by an Argentinean government desperate to raise foreign revenues in the wake of repeated debt crises – the ecological shifts that underpinned agricultural intensification have unleashed a series of consequences most dramatically evident in the abrupt appearance of large rivers where none previously existed.

This phenomenon – first noted in the mid-1980s – has escalated with some of the new rivers reaching 50 meters in width and cutting canyons 25 meters deep into the land. When powerful summer storms occur, new torrents can appear overnight while existing ones can shift course markedly and unpredictably, carving through farmland, destroying built infrastructure and threatening ranches and towns (El Semiárido 2015). Superficially, it would be possible to analyse this phenomenon as a localised 'environmental' crisis in need of technical fixes at the point of production. Indeed, the Argentinean government did precisely this when it declared an environmental emergency in the region in 2016 and mandated landowners to maintain a minimum of 5 per cent wooded area on landholdings.

From a critical agrarian studies perspective, however, it is first necessary to analyse how multiscalar forces repositioned the agrarian environment in this region as an epicentre in the production of soy, corn and other 'flex crops' aimed at global markets (Leguizamón 2020). This reworking of the Argentine landscape is inextricably linked to the export of soy on a vast scale to the United States, Europe and China, where it is used to sustain the industrial production of pigs, cattle and chickens required to satisfy increasingly meat-centric diets in those locations (Weis 2013; Oliveira and Schneider 2016). This extractivist agriculture was achieved through a steady process of consolidation of landholdings in which large corporate enterprises bought out smaller farmers as a means to expand economies of scale (Otero and Lapegna 2016; Leguizamón 2020). As corporate farming entities expanded, local environmental management predicated on embedded ecological knowledges collapsed (Cáceres et al. 2009). Tree cover was reduced from 50 per cent to less than 10 per cent of total land area (Contreras et al. 2012). Replacing forests with short duration crops such as soy that have shallow roots disrupted evapotranspiration processes and has led to the accumulation of groundwater levels at an unprecedented rate, therein creating the conditions for rampant soil erosion, formation of new rivers, increased prevalence of flooding and the accelerated salinization of the soil as pockets of minerals deposited over millennia are carried upwards to the surface level (Jayawickreme et al. 2011). Far from a localised crisis, these processes are scaled manifestations of a global agro-industrial metabolism that is unfolding across the region (Correia 2019; McKay 2020).

THE TENSIONS OF SUSTAINABLE INTENSIFICATION

These foundational points of a critical agrarian studies perspective – the emphasis on produced landscapes within which processes of accumulation and extraction unequally distribute benefits and risks across the agrarian environment – provides a useful gateway into the analysis of policies and projects designed to promote agricultural sustainability. It is presently rare to find any agricultural development project that does not make claims on behalf of sustainability, whether it is in terms of resilient rural development (Engström and Hajdu 2019), biodiversity conservation (Idrobo et al. 2016) climate-smart agriculture (Newell et al. 2019), climate-resilient villages (Taylor and Bhasme 2020) or carbon finance for development projects (Cavanagh et al. 2020). Critical agrarian studies perspectives, however, have been central to deconstructing the differentiated impacts of these programmes.

As an example, consider the case of a government-sponsored project in south India to promote the system of rice intensification (SRI) among smallholder farmers. The latter has been promoted across many parts of Asia as an alternative method of cultivating rice that has the potential to simultaneously increase yields, reduce water requirements and lower methane emissions (Glover 2011). For advocates, a compelling feature of SRI is that it requires primarily a managerial change in cultivation practices rather than the use of substantial new inputs or technologies. Specifically, it is the synergistic interaction of four combined alterations to cultivation practices – (1) the transplantation of very young seedlings in (2) a widely spaced grid formation combined with (3) alternate wetting and drying (AWD) irrigation and (4) the use of a basic mechanical weeder that aerates the soil – that is argued to provide the conditions for sustained yield increases while also reducing aggregate water requirements and methane emissions (Thakur et al. 2016).

Given this 'triple-win' potential that aligns closely with discourses of both sustainable intensification and climate-smart agriculture, many southern Indian state governments have actively promoted the method through agricultural extension networks across the region (Johnson and Vijayaragavan 2011; Basu and Leeuwis 2012). SRI emerged as a governmental solution to livelihood and sustainability problems of rice cultivation in the context of semi-arid agrarian environments that had been remade through a disruptive process of agricultural liberalisation in combination with the growing subdivision of landholdings, a proliferation of household indebtedness and the uncertainties wrought by climatic variability (Harriss-White

2008; Swaminathan and Baksi 2017). The promise of being able to produce more through solely a change in cultivation practices therein appeared to address longstanding state goals to narrow yield gaps in rice production while boosting smallholder incomes. That this could work while saving water appeared to be something of a silver bullet for distressed inland areas facing increased climatic variability owing to climate change and where groundwater abstraction repeatedly reached crisis levels in many areas (Taylor 2015).

Notwithstanding such expectations, however, in a study of the uptake of SRI in six villages in Telangana, Taylor and Bhasme (2019) showed how the ability to work effectively with the cultivation method was strongly shaped along the lines of class, caste and gender. Indeed, despite the widespread recognition among all classes of farmers that the technique increased yields and decreased aggregate water usage as promised, only a minority of relatively well-resourced farmers persisted with the method. The reasons for this abandonment of an apparently 'successful' sustainable intensification technique demonstrate the importance of using a critical agrarian studies perspective to understand how the diffusion of new technologies is shaped by inequities in resource access and the mobilisation of labour.

First, to work effectively, SRI requires a more precise timing of agricultural tasks: transplanting, weeding and irrigation follow a demanding timeline. This in turn assumes that farmers can ensure the presence of labour at those specific moments. Control over labour, however, is established through a mix of market and extra-market mechanisms and is strongly shaped by gender, class and caste relations (Pattenden 2016). While affluent farmers were able to employ greater resources and social prestige to ensure the presence of female labour groups, small landholders found exercising this control over labour a far more difficult task. As a result, they regularly missed the optimal transplantation timings for SRI leading to negative impacts upon yields.

Second, as the above point highlights, rice cultivation in southern India is predicated upon strictly gendered divisions of labour. The adoption of SRI, however, appeared to overturn established norms that unequally apportioned drudgery between men and women. This was because the use of the mechanical weeder – often an arduous task – was considered to be masculine work because it involved the use of technology. This raised complaints by numerous male farmers that SRI transferred the burden of agricultural drudgery associated with weeding from women to them, a social shift that many were unwilling to accept despite the yield benefits (see also Resurreccion et al. 2008). More affluent farmers who used hired labour throughout their operations could circumvent this social impediment.

Finally, the SRI technique was widely cited as saving aggregate water owing to the AWD method. Problematically, however, using AWD required a precise choreography of irrigation that was beyond the means of many smallholders who relied upon fickle groundwater pumps plagued by inconsistent electricity supply and frequent absences of water. As a result, despite it breaking with SRI recommendations, most small landholders modified SRI to maintain a steady supply of water (about 1 inch) in the field throughout cultivation. This practice reduced risks, but had a negative impact on yields and water conservation. Large landholding farmers, in contrast, were mostly able to implement the full AWD technique because access to formal credit allowed them to invest in more and deeper bore-wells in ways that consolidated their ability to operate within an increasingly water-scarce agrarian environment.

ECOLOGICAL CRISES AND THE POLITICS OF TRANSFORMATION

The above short case study demonstrated how sustainable intensification strategies that operate as technical solutions outside of a wider political economic context can have socially polarising outcomes that mitigate or undermine perceived ecological benefits (see also Taylor and Bhasme 2020). This reinforces a broader emphasis within critical agrarian studies that a sustainable transformation of agriculture can only be realised through the wider transformation of food systems (Duncan et al. 2020). In this respect, contributions to critical agrarian studies have tended to be solidly supportive of agroecological initiatives, not least because the surrounding discourses of agroecology explicitly cast the approach as grassroots driven and orientated towards the empowerment of local producer groups (Warner 2007; Brescia 2017). Indeed, contrary to the piecemeal approach of integrating agroecological practices as technical solutions to environmental problems as witnessed in institutions such as the FAO and CGIAR, many advocates emphasise the socially transformative agenda of agroecology, noting that its social mission is essential to its renovation of agricultural practices (Gonzalez de Molina 2013; Rosset and Altieri 2017). By replacing chemical-intensive agricultural techniques with ones founded on the harnessing of biodiversity, agroecology promises to increase producer autonomy from extractive value chains and debt relations.

The rise of the zero-budget natural farming movement in southern India, for example, has specifically targeted the liberation of smallholders from crippling debts (Khadse et al. 2018; Bharucha et al. 2020). On the other hand, by embedding the production of ecological values alongside yield considerations ('multifunctionality') into agricultural systems, agroecological strategies seek to provide socio-ecological benefits at wide scale, including erosion control, water flow regulation and purification, biodiversity conservation and carbon sequestration (Garbach et al. 2017).

There is, however, a need to retain a productive yet critical engagement with agroecology that avoids representing it as a ready-made silver bullet solution to the social and ecological contradictions of agrarian environments both in the north and the south (Woodhouse 2010). Agroecological production systems are inherently knowledge intensive because they deliberately increase the complexity of the agroecosystem to harness biodiversity as a productive tool within the agrarian environment (Tittonell 2020). This necessarily results in a high degree of complexity and uncertainty at a landscape level, with farmers needing to adopt a more adaptive style leading to significant management challenges (Duru et al. 2015). Similar to the SRI example above, it is therefore important to recognise the barriers in the pursuit of agroecological practices for resource-poor households, particularly where dependence on input-intensive methods has led to a process of relative de-skilling with respect to ecological management (Stone 2011).

Given these risks and uncertainties, it is important to avoid essentialisations that represent smallholders as inherently predisposed to agroecology (Luna 2020; Soper 2020). In the absence of enabling political economic contexts, many smallholders will strive to better position themselves within global industrial commodity chains as a means towards livelihood preservation (Castellanos-Navarrete and Jansen 2018). As Andrew Flachs (2019) notes in his detailed study of organic cotton farming in Telangana, farmers who rejected the model of input-intensive cotton farming typically required non-governmental organisation provision of subsidised seeds and bio-inputs, access to specialist markets for marketing, technical support and social legitimation within village structures. On this basis, the pursuit of agroecological approaches will require its own enabling political economy that supports a wider transformation of food systems across scales (Akram-Lodhi 2015). To such ends, there is much ground to be made in reversing international institutional biases that direct research priorities and flows of financing towards input-intensive models of agriculture (IPES-Food 2020). Such a transformation, however, requires the difficult work of coalition building to address the power imbalances highlighted within the critical agrarian studies tradition (Leach et al. 2020).

FURTHER READING

Agrawal, B. (2013), *Gender and Green Governance: The Political Economy of Women's Presence within and beyond Community Forestry*, Oxford: Oxford University Press.
Dunlap, A.; Jakobsen, J. (2019), *The Violent Technologies of Extraction: Political Ecology, Critical Agrarian Studies and the Capitalist Worldeater*, London: Palgrave Press.
Formation en Agroecologie Paysanne Nyeleni de Selingué (2017), *The Nyéléni Peasant Agroecology Manifesto*, accessed 19 July 20202 at https://africaconvergence.net/The-Nyeleni-Peasant-Agroecology-Manifesto.
Martinez-Alier, J. (2002), *The Environmentalism of the Poor: A Study of Ecological Conflicts and Valuation*, Cheltenham, UK and Northampton, MA, USA: Edward Elgar Publishing.
Rosset, P.; Altieri, M. (2017), *Agroecology: Science and Politics*, Nova Scotia: Fernwood Press.

REFERENCES

Agrawal, A. (2005), *Environmentality: Technologies of Government and the Making of Subjects*, Durham, NC: Duke University Press.
Agrawal, A.; Sivaramakrishnan, K. (2000), Introduction: Agrarian environments, in Agrawal, A.; Sivaramakrishnan, K. (eds), *Agrarian Environments: Resources, Representation and Rule in India*, Durham, NC: Duke University Press, 1–22.
Akram-Lodhi, A.H. (2015), Accelerating towards food sovereignty, *Third World Quarterly*, 36(3), 563–583.
Basu, S.; Leeuwis, C. (2012), Understanding the rapid spread of system of rice intensification (SRI) in Andhra Pradesh: Exploring the building of support networks and media representation, *Agricultural Systems*, 111(1), 34–44.
Bernstein, H. (2010), *Class Dynamics of Agrarian Change*, Halifax: Fernwood.
Bharucha, Z.P.; Mitjans, S.B.; Pretty, J. (2020), Towards redesign at scale through zero budget natural farming in Andhra Pradesh, India, *International Journal of Agricultural Sustainability*, 18(1), 1–20.
Brescia, S. (ed.) (2017), *Fertile Ground: Scaling Agroecology from the Ground Up*, Oakland, CA: Food First Books.
Cáceres, D.; Silvetti, F.; Díaz, S. et al. (2009), Environmental winners and losers in Argentina's soybean boom, in Tiessen, H.; Stewart, J. (eds), *Applying Ecological Knowledge to Landuse Decisions*, São Paulo: Inter-Anerican Institute for Global Change Research, 65–72.
Castellanos-Navarrete, A.; Jansen, K. (2018), Is oil palm expansion a challenge to agroecology? Smallholders practising industrial farming in Mexico, *Journal of Agrarian Change*, 18(1), 132–155.
Cavanagh, C.J.; Vedeld, P.O.; Petursson, J.G.; Chemarum, A.K. (2020), Agency, inequality, and additionality: Contested assemblages of agricultural carbon finance in western Kenya, *Journal of Peasant Studies*, 1–21, https://doi.org/10.1080/03066150.2019.1707812.
Clapp, J. (2015), Distant agricultural landscapes, *Sustainability Science*, 10(2), 305–316.
Clapp, J.; Ruder, S.-L. (2020), Precision technologies for agriculture: Digital farming, gene-edited crops, and the politics of sustainability, *Global Environmental Politics*, 20(3), 49–70.

Contreras, S.; Santoni, C.S.; Jobbágy, E.G. (2012), Abrupt watercourse formation in a semiarid sedimentary landscape of central Argentina: The roles of forest clearing, rainfall variability and seismic activity, *Ecohydrology*, 6(5), 794.

Correia, J.E. (2019), Soy states: Resource politics, violent environments and soybean territorialization in Paraguay, *Journal of Peasant Studies*, 46(2), 316–336.

De Clercq, M.; Vats, A.; Biel, A. (2018), *Agriculture 4.0: The Future of Farming Technology*, Dubai: World Government Summit.

de la Cruz, J.; Jansen, K. (2018), Panama disease and contract farming in the Philippines: Towards a political ecology of risk, *Journal of Agrarian Change*, 18(2), 249–266.

Duncan, J.; Carolan, M.; Wiskerke, J. (2020), Regenerating food systems: A socio-ecological approach, in Duncan, J.; Carolan, M.; Wiskerke, J. (eds), *Routledge Handbook of Sustainable and Regenerative Food Systems*, London: Routledge, 1–10.

Duru, M.; Therond, O.; Fares, M.H. (2015), Designing agroecological transitions: A review, *Agronomy for Sustainable Development*, 35(8), 1237–1257.

El Semiárido (2015), Jobbágy: la solución para el Río Nuevo es un drástico cambio en el uso de la tierra, in *El Semiárido*, San Luis: Información Agropecuaria de San Luis y la Región, 8 May, accessed 11 March 2021 at www.elsemiarido.com/jobbagy-la-solucion-para-el-rio-nuevo-es-un-drastico-cambio-en-el-uso-de-la-tierra/.

Engström, L.; Hajdu, F. (2019), Conjuring 'win-world': Resilient development narratives in a large-scale agro-investment in Tanzania, *Journal of Development Studies*, 55(6), 1201–1220.

FAO (2018), *FAO's Work on Agroecology: A Pathway to Achieving the SDGs*, Rome: FAO.

FAO; IFAD; UNICEF; WFP; WHO (2018), *The State of Food Security and Nutrition in the World 2018: Building Climate Resilience for Food Security and Nutrition*, Rome: FAO.

Flachs, A. (2019), *Cultivating Knowledge*, Tucson, AZ: University of Arizona Press.

Foster, J.B.; Clark, B.; York, R. (2010), *The Ecological Rift: Capitalism's War on the Earth*, New York: Monthly Review Press.

Garbach, K.; Milder, F.; DeClerck, F.; Montenegro de Wit, M.; Driscoll, L.; Gemmill-Herren, B. (2017), Examining multi-functionality for crop yield and ecosystem services in five systems of agroecological intensification, *International Journal of Agricultural Sustainability*, 15(1), 11–28.

Gidwani, V. (2000), Labored landscapes: Agro-ecological change in central Gujarat, India, in Agrawal, A.; Sivaramakrishnan, K. (eds), *Agrarian Environments: Resources, Representation and Rule in India*, Durham, NC: Duke University Press, 216–249.

Glover, D. (2011), The system of rice intensification: Time for an empirical turn, *NJAS – Wageningen Journal of Life Sciences*, 57(2), 217–224.

Goldman, M.; Nadasdy, P.; Turner, M. (eds) (2012), *Knowing Nature: Conversations at the Intersection of Political Ecology and Science Studies*, Chicago, IL: University of Chicago Press.

Gonzalez de Molina, M. (2013), Agroecology and politics: How to get sustainability? The necessity for a political agroecology, *Agroecology and Sustainable Food Systems*, 37(1), 45–59.

Gupta, A. (1998), *Postcolonial Developments: Agriculture in the Making of Modern India*, Durham, NC: Duke University Press.

Harriss-White, B. (2008), India's rainfed agricultural dystopia, *European Journal of Development Research*, 20(4), 549–561.

Idrobo, C.J.; Davidson-Hunt, I.J.; Seixas, C.S. (2016), Produced natures through the lens of biodiversity conservation and tourism: The Ponta Negra Caiçara in the Atlantic Forest Coast of Brazil, *Local Environment*, 21(9), 1132–1150.

Ingold, T. (1993), The temporality of the landscape, *World Archaeology*, 25(2), 152–174.

IPES-Food (2020), *Money Flows: What Is Holding Back Investment in Agroecological Research for Africa?*, Geneva: Biovision Foundation for Ecological Development and International Panel of Experts on Sustainable Food Systems.

Jackson, L. (2008), Who 'designs' the agricultural landscape?, *Landscape Journal*, 27(1), 23–42.

Jakobsen, J. (2020), The maize frontier in rural south India: Exploring the everyday dynamics of the contemporary food regime, *Journal of Agrarian Change*, 20(1), 137–162.

Jansen, K. (1998), *Political Ecology, Mountain Agriculture, and Knowledge in Honduras*, Amsterdam: Thela Publishers.

Jayawickreme, D.H.; Santoni, C.S.; Kim, J.H.; Jobbágy, E.G.; Jackson, R.B. (2011), Changes in hydrology and salinity accompanying a century of agricultural conversion in Argentina, *Ecological Applications*, 21(7), 2367–2379.

Johnson, B.; Vijayaragavan, K. (2011), Diffusion of system of rice intensification (SRI) across Tamil Nadu and Andhra Pradesh in India, *Indian Research Journal of Extension Education*, 11(3), 72–80.

Kerr, R.B. (2014), Lost and found crops: Agrobiodiversity, indigenous knowledge, and a feminist political ecology of sorghum and finger millet in northern Malawi, *Annals of the Association of American Geographers*, 104(3), 577–593.

Khadse, A.; Rosset, P.; Morales, H.; Ferguson, B. (2018), Taking agroecology to scale: The zero budget natural farming peasant movement in Karnataka, India, *Journal of Peasant Studies*, 45(1), 192–219.

Leach, M.; Nisbett, N.; Cabral, L.; Harris, J.; Hossain, N.; Thompson, J. (2020), Food politics and development, *World Development*, 134, 105024.

Leguizamón, A. (2020), *Seeds of Power: Environmental Injustice and Genetically Modified Soybeans in Argentina*, Durham, NC: Duke University Press.

Li, T. (2007), *The Will to Improve: Governmentality, Development, and the Practice of Politics*, Durham, NC: Duke University Press.

Loos, J.; Abson, D.; Chappell, M.J.; Hanspach, J.; Mikulcak, F.; Tichit, M.; Fischer, J. (2014), Putting meaning back into 'sustainable intensification', *Frontiers in Ecology and the Environment*, 12(6), 356–361.

Ludden, D. (1999), *An Agrarian History of South Asia*, Cambridge: Cambridge University Press.

Luna, J.K. (2020), Peasant essentialism in GMO debates: Bt cotton in Burkina Faso, *Journal of Agrarian Change*, 20(4), 579–597.

Luna, J.K.; Dowd-Uribe, B. (2020), Knowledge politics and the Bt cotton success narrative in Burkina Faso, *World Development*, 136, 105–127.

McKay, B. (2020), *The Political Economy of Agrarian Extractivism: Lessons from Bolivia*, Halifax: Fernwood Press.

Mitchell, D. (2003), Cultural landscapes: Just landscapes or landscapes of justice?, *Progress in Human Geography*, 27(6), 787–798.

Montefrio, M.J.F. (2017), Land control dynamics and social-ecological transformations in upland Philippines, *Journal of Peasant Studies*, 44(4), 796–816.

Montpellier Panel (2013), *Sustainable Intensification: A New Paradigm for African Agriculture*, Bonn: Montpellier Panel.

Moore, J. (2015), *Capitalism in the Web of Life*, London: Verso.

Newell, P.; Olivia, T.; Naess, L.O.; Thompson, J.; Mahmoud, H.; Ndaki, P.; Rurangwa, R.; Teshome, A. (2019), Climate smart agriculture? Governing the sustainable development goals in Sub-Saharan Africa, *Frontiers in Sustainable Food Systems*, 3(55), 1–15.

Nightingale, A. (2006), The nature of fender: Work, gender, and environment, *Environment and Planning D: Society and Space*, 24(2), 165–185.

Oliveira, G.d.L.T.; Schneider, M. (2016), The politics of flexing soybeans: China, Brazil and global agroindustrial restructuring, *Journal of Peasant Studies*, 43(1), 167–194.

Otero, G.; Lapegna, P. (2016), Transgenic crops in Latin America: Expropriation, negative value and the state, *Journal of Agrarian Change*, 16(4), 665–674.

Pattenden, J. (2016), *Labour, State and Society in Rural India: A Class-Relational Approach*, Manchester: Manchester University Press.

Pretty, J. (2002), *Agri-Culture: Reconnecting People, Land and Nature*, London: Earthscan.

Resurreccion, B.; Sajor, E.; Sophea, H. (2008), *Gender Dimensions of the Adoption of the System of Rice Intensification (SRI) in Cambodia*, Phnom Penh: Report for Oxfam America.

Romá, M.C.; Garro, B.F. (2016), Agriculturalización e impacto ambiental en San Luis (Argentina). Un relevamiento de estudios científicos en la provincia, *Jornadas de Sociología de la UNLP*, 9(December), 1–19.

Rosset, P.; Altieri, M. (2017), *Agroecology: Science and Politics*, Halifax: Fernwood.

Rotz, S.; Duncan, E.; Small, M.; Botschner, J.; Dara, R.; Mosby, I.; Reed, M.; Fraser, E.D.G. (2019), The politics of digital agricultural technologies: A preliminary review, *Sociologia Ruralis*, 59(2), 203–229.

Sainath, P. (1996), *Everybody Loves a Good Drought*, Delhi: Penguin.

Scoones, I.; Thompson, J. (1994), Knowledge, power and agriculture: Towards a theoretical understanding, in Scoones, I.; Thompson, J. (eds), *Beyond Farmer First: Rural People's Knowledge, Agricultural Research, and Extension Practice*, London: Intermediate Technology Publications, 16–30.

Sikor, T.; Newell, P. (2014), Globalizing environmental justice?, *Geoforum*, 54, 151–157.

Soper, R. (2020), From protecting peasant livelihoods to essentializing peasant agriculture: Problematic trends in food sovereignty discourse, *Journal of Peasant Studies*, 47(2), 265–285.

Stone, G.D. (2011), Contradictions in the last mile: Suicide, culture and e-agriculture in rural India, *Science, Technology and Human Values*, 36(6), 759–790.

Sumberg, J.; Thompson, J. (eds) (2012), *Contested Agronomy: Agricultural Research in a Changing World*, London: Easthscan.

Swaminathan, M.; Baksi, S. (2017), *How Do Small Farmers Fare? Evidence from Village Studies in India*, New Delhi: Tulika Books.

Taylor, M. (2015), *The Political Ecology of Climate Change Adaptation: Livelihoods, Agrarian Change and the Conflicts of Development*, London: Routledge.

Taylor, M.; Bhasme, S. (2019), The political ecology of rice intensification in south India: Putting SRI in its places, *Journal of Agrarian Change*, 19(1), 3–20.

Taylor, M.; Bhasme, S. (2020), Between deficit rains and surplus populations: The political ecology of a climate-resilient village in south India, *Geoforum*, https://doi.org/10.1016/j.geoforum.2020.01.007.

Thakur, A.; Uphoff, N.; Stoop, W. (2016), Scientific underpinnings of the system of rice intensification (SRI): What is known so far?, *Advances in Agronomy*, 135(1), 147–179.

Tittonell, P. (2020), Assessing resilience and adaptability in agroecological transitions, *Agricultural Systems*, 184, 102862.

UNEP (2014), *Assessing Global Land Use: Balancing Consumption with Sustainable Supply*, Geneva: United Nations Environment Programme.

United Nations Convention to Combat Desertification (2017), *The Global Land Outlook*, Bonn: UNCCD.

van der Ploeg, J. (2013), *Peasants and the Art of Farming: A Chaynovian Manifesto*, Halifax: Fernwood.

Warner, K.D. (2007), *Agroecology in Action: Extending Alternative Agriculture through Social Networks*, Cambridge, MA: MIT Press.

Weis, T. (2013), *The Global Hoofprint: The Global Burden of Industrial Livestock*, London: Zed Books.

Woodhouse, P. (2010), Beyond industrial agriculture? Some questions about farm size, productivity and sustainability, *Journal of Agrarian Change*, 10(3), 437–453.

World Bank (2015), *Future of Food: Shaping a Climate-Smart Global Food System*, Washington, DC: World Bank.

57. Microfinance and rural financial inclusion

Marcus Taylor

In 2005 the United Nations launched its 'International Year of Microcredit' with a staged display of award-winning microfinance clients ringing the opening bells at 10 international stock markets including, most prominently, the NASDAQ in New York. The symbolism of having small-scale rural entrepreneurs summon the epicentres of global finance into action marked the high point of what seemed the irresistible rise of microfinance as the preeminent tool of rural development. José Antonio Ocampo – Under-Secretary-General of the United Nations Department of Economic and Social Affairs – captured the missionary zeitgeist when he enthusiastically claimed that microfinance 'has the potential to unleash a new wave of microentrepreneurship, giving poor and low-income people a chance to build better lives'.[1] By providing financial services directly to households excluded from the formal banking system, the argument ran, microfinance could trigger a wave of entrepreneurship to lift households above the poverty line.[2] Moreover, by directing small disbursements of credit directly into the hands of women borrowers, microfinance was simultaneously heralded as a mechanism of social empowerment. On this basis the microfinance revolution was anticipated to transform rural spaces in both their material and cultural dimensions.

Despite such audacious predictions, the projected big bang of microfinance has since turned into something of a whimper. Claims regarding the transformative impacts of microfinance have been dampened by a lack of compelling evidence to show discernibly positive welfare outcomes. This absence has been compounded by concerns that microfinance has the potential to encourage household indebtedness through overlending practices leading to local debt traps and sectoral crises. Although the initial enthusiasm over microcredit as a silver bullet solution to rural poverty has waned, advocates have nonetheless responded by recasting microfinance under the banner of financial inclusion. While downplaying the poverty alleviation angle, microfinance is now enthusiastically presented as offering rural households a range of valued services that allow them to better manage their livelihood portfolios, meet unexpected financial obligations and improve capacity for risk management. This renovated agenda typically includes a greater emphasis on microinsurance and microsavings products to accompany the established goal of credit provision (World Bank 2013). On this foundation, microfinance initiatives persist as a common component of many rural development strategies. As Philip Mader notes, access to financial services features in at least five of the 17 Sustainable Development Goals established by the United Nations in 2015 (Mader 2017).

In response, this chapter draws upon multifaceted work within the agrarian studies tradition to demonstrate the complexity and multifaceted nature of microfinance programmes at a local level. As this work attests, microfinance-in-practice typically operates with a range of unanticipated outcomes that are far removed from the sanitised stories common to the mainstream literature (Shakya and Rankin 2008; Guérin 2014). This stems from an underlying tension in which microfinance programmes seek to align profitable financial operations with a client base composed of marginal households that have irregular sources of income and are often struggling to manage a range of active debt relations. With reference to both microcredit and microinsurance programmes, work within critical agrarian studies demonstrates the paramount importance of situating microfinance in its context-specific settings to uncover how it interfaces with existing debt relationships, how it impacts upon individual and collective subjectivities and how it reorganises local power relations.

THE SHIFTING NARRATIVES OF MICROFINANCE

The idea of using credit facilities as a tool of rural development was not new to the 1990s microfinance fad. Through the 1970s and 1980s, many non-governmental organisations (NGOs) and state programmes introduced forms of credit provision to poor households as one tool within integrated rural development planning across Asia, Latin America and Africa. Within the NGO sector specifically, many such initiatives tended to be small scale, heavily subsidised and often focused on the economic empowerment of rural women above and beyond wider anti-poverty goals. These often started by establishing and fortifying self-help groups for rural women in which collective savings programmes, rather than credit provision, formed the central component of activities (Mayoux 1999; Edward and Olsen 2006).

This emphasis on microfinance as one component of a broader empowerment mission began to shift in the 1990s in the context of an era dominated by neoliberal thinking around the virtues of the market and the inefficiencies of the state (Weber 2004). As C.K. Pralahad – promoter of the 'bottom of the pyramid' thesis – provocatively demanded, state agencies and the corporate sector alike needed to stop thinking of the poor as a burden and 'start recognizing them as resilient and creative entrepreneurs and value-conscious consumers' (Pralahad 2004, 1). The genius of microfinance, its advocates proclaimed, was that it could harness such latent entrepreneurial energies by providing much needed capital to poor households while circumventing overbearing state interventions and unnecessary bureaucracy. This argument was based on a simple underlying theoretical basis. In the absence of access to formal credit – 'financial disenfranchisement' as it is termed in the literature – poor households are deprived of the ability to invest in new income-generating activities. This trapped them in short-term, low-return activities that perpetuated their poverty. In response, creating new institutions to facilitate the provision of credit to such households would allow them to avail themselves of market opportunities that held better rates of return. Collectively, this could foster an entrepreneurial revolution in the countryside in which the rapid expansion of commercial activities would multiply off-farm income generation and employment (Smith and Thurman 2007). In short, microfinance was expected to propel a Smithian growth cycle by unleashing increased specialisation leading to an expanded division of labour, market growth and increased output (Kelly 1997).

At the same time, microfinance was simultaneously pitched as a vehicle for cultural transformation. Proponents identified that male control over household finances frequently limited the ability of women to partake in livelihood planning or to pursue commercial ventures outside the household. By placing control over finances directly in the hands of women, programmes were envisaged to empower them financially, fracturing the bedrock of patriarchal relationships while also undermining cultural mores that restrained the rise of women as entrepreneurs within rural society. As Cull et al. (2009, 170) put it:

> [M]icrofinance institutions have proven particularly able to reach poor women, providing the hope of breaking gender-based barriers. In most places men dominate farming decisions, but women play larger roles in running household side-businesses, and women have quickly become the main microfinance clients, even in countries where gender equality is far from the norm.

On these grounds microfinance was frequently put forward as a transformative tool to help undermine regressive cultural practices that blocked women's economic empowerment, limiting their ability to interact with markets on equal terms. This reinforced prevailing ideas that it was traditional culture that restrained women's empowerment and – in so doing – frustrated the development of a vibrant rural economy (Bergeron 2002).

For international institutions keen to champion microfinance as a development intervention in the 1990s, the key constraint was the relatively small scale of existing microfinance operations that typically relied on either state subsidisation or limited NGO operational funds (Cull et al. 2009). In response, a new institutional model was heavily promoted by financial institutions such as the World Bank and its subsidiary organisation the Consultative Group to Assist the Poorest, in which NGOs would transform themselves into commercial microfinance institutions (MFIs), accessing credit from national or international financial markets and extending it to households on a for-profit basis (Weber 2004). In contrast to most development interventions, the underlying profitability of the model would make subsidisation irrelevant, allowing the roll out of microfinance to become a self-sustaining and infinitely scalable form of anti-poverty policy. The Reserve Bank of India exemplified this new orthodoxy:

> [P]ast experience shows that dollops of sympathy in the form of subsidy and reduced rate of interest have not helped matters much. Micro-credit has to be commercialized where all patrons – microfinance providers, intermediaries, NGOs, facilitators and the ultimate clients – must get compensated appropriately … [We] believe that freedom from poverty is not for free. The poor are willing and capable to pay the cost. (Cited in Chavan and Ramakumar, 2005)

This commercialisation of microfinance – known as the 'financial sustainability' model – was founded on the idea that profitability could foster a more rapid expansion of operations by attracting capital into the sector. It invariably had a strong impact upon operational practices in which MFIs would encounter market pressures to continually expand their lending portfolios and to ensure high repayment rates among borrowing clientele. For proponents, these pressures would help ensure efficiency and ultimately ensure that the paradigm would meet the demand for credit within the rural world. Critics, however, pointed to tensions – often termed 'mission drift' – in which market imperatives subordinated the original empowerment goals that animated the original microfinance genre (Edward and Olsen 2006). With the imperative to ensure financial sustainability, MFIs had a built-in imperative to target more the reliable and profitable segments of rural populations and to go to great lengths to ensure uninterrupted cycles of loan disbursement and repayment (Bastiaensen et al. 2013). These pressures, moreover, typically fell heavily on the local-level staff of MFIs for whom job advancement was often closely tied to expanding loan portfolios and ensuring client compliance, even if this meant cutting regulatory corners in practice (Maîtrot 2018).

CRITICAL AGRARIAN STUDIES AND THE MICROFINANCE REVOLUTION

Through detailed empirical cases, analysts within the field of critical agrarian studies were at the forefront of highlighting how these tensions emerged in practice. Perhaps the most immediate contribution was the rapid unsettling of the trope of female empowerment that underpinned official microfinance discourse. Analysts showed how lending to groups of women was a profoundly double-edged process, creating a tension between the rhetoric of collective empowerment and its role as an operational tactic by lending agencies to instil financial discipline among borrowers and ensure high repayment rates that were the prerequisite for profitability (Shakya and Rankin 2008; Bee 2011; Karim 2011). Making a borrower group as a whole liable for repayments addressed three key operational problems for credit providers. First, the model decentralised the task of selecting participants because women were assumed to self-select only reliable group members and screen out credit risks. Second, the group dynamics were expected to help ensure good conduct and instil financial discipline for fear of social stigma and shame attached to those who might default. Third, the joint-liability model ensured that the group members themselves had a keen interest in self-policing and enforcing repayment, often resorting to quite drastic disciplinary measures as discussed below (Kalpana 2005; Rao 2005). While unquestionably helping to lower operating costs for MFIs, these social dynamics also tended to consolidate rural hierarchies in which women recruited group members that they considered least likely to default from within established social networks (Cons and Paprocki 2010).

At the same time, agrarian studies authors soon pointed out that the expectations placed on women to engage in entrepreneurial activities to lift themselves out of poverty clashed with the marginal opportunities afforded by rural markets and their associated power relations (Rankin 2008; Guérin and Servet 2015). Drawn from poor households, most female microcredit clients had no specialised skills, few tangible assets and therefore faced extremely competitive markets with insufficient capital to increase low levels of productivity (Kalpana 2005). They also remained tied to household incomes strongly reliant on the risks of agricultural production (Heales 2017). In such circumstances, providing small doses of credit to promote inclusion in rural markets, it turned out, was no guarantee of generating adequate incomes to lift households out of poverty. As Banerjee and Duflo explained:

> Microcredit and other ways to help tiny businesses still have an important role to play in the lives of the poor, because these tiny businesses will remain, perhaps for the foreseeable future, the only way many of the poor can manage to survive. But we are kidding ourselves if we think that they can pave the way for a mass exit from poverty. (Banerjee and Duflo 2011)

Banerjee and Duflo's argument effectively suggested that, rather than a linear process of Smithian growth that would transform the countryside from the inside out, microfinance-powered entrepreneurialism would likely end up bottlenecked in an involutionary trajectory predicated on marginal occupations with low rates of productivity increase. As Morgan and Olsen pointed out with reference to south India, the types of commercial activities promoted by microfinance can serve to consolidate labour market segmentation keeping women trapped in low-paying areas of the off-farm economy (Morgan and Olsen 2011; also Karim 2011). Such conclusions resonated with surveys of microcredit outcomes that strongly challenged the evidentiary basis for the claims that microcredit led to widespread welfare improvements. Perhaps most notable for its impact at the time, the synthesis survey conducted by Martha Duvendack and others controlled for inbuilt selection biases and other methodological problems and found that microcredit impacts on welfare variables ranged between negligible to – at best – extremely modest (see Duvendack et al. 2011; also Cull and Morduch 2017).

When placed within the political economy of agrarian change, the expansion of microfinance in rural areas can be interpreted not necessarily as evidence of its inherent success but rather a result of the pressing need for households to access new forms of liquidity in the context of an increasing commercialisation of rural social relations (Taylor 2011). What many MFIs knew, yet had silenced in their official discourses, was that households often tended not to use credit productively – as both microfinance theory and the requirements of implementing authorities stated – but rather for a variety of consumption purposes (Rankin 2008; Cons and Paprocki 2010). At the same time, cross-borrowing practices became common within many rural regions. Households would take on accounts from multiple lenders, including different MFIs and informal sources, using new infusions of credit to pay off old loans, and juggling sources of credit accordingly. Microfinance programmes therein elicited a self-sustaining process of financial penetration of rural regions, yet without any necessarily positive transformative outcomes (Shakya and Rankin 2008).

These tendencies closely matched the expectations of agrarian studies authors who had long emphasised how credit – whether formal or informal – serves as an essential bridging tool for households attempting to knit together the diverging temporalities of income and expenditures stemming from distinct growing seasons, the uncertain availability of local agricultural labouring, the rhythms of demand for casual labour in rural and urban centres and the dynamics of petty commerce and production. Maryann Bylander's work on rural Cambodia, for example, showed how microfinance loans became integral to the circuits of informal labour migration across borders. In theory, microfinance initiatives were intended to slow undocumented migration by promoting local entrepreneurship. Using microcredit for migratory purposes was strictly prohibited. In practice, however, households simply folded the microfinance loans into existing debt relations as one more source of credit. Informal sources certainly had higher rates of interest than the MFIs, yet MFIs had more stringent repayment schedules and – in theory – more restrictive regulations on what borrowed money could be used for. As a result, households juggled these different debts and relied heavily on remittances from cross-border migrants to pay back loans. In short, the penetration of microfinance consolidated, rather than undermined, migratory trends (Bylander 2014).

Other studies showed how microfinance transformed existing power relationships within localities, creating new trajectories of enrichment and political clientelism that could reinforce class polarisation and gendered inequalities in the countryside. Lamia Karim's (2011) study of major Bangladeshi microfinance lenders offers perhaps the most penetrating close-up examinations of these dynamics. With deep ethnographic detail, it shows how lending NGOs placed extreme pressures upon local communities to ensure inscrutable rates of repayment. Defaulters within borrowing groups were often subject to ritual shaming and community ostracization. At its most perverse, local actors directly stripped defaulting borrowers of key assets – including the roofs from their houses – as a strident punishment for bringing the community into disrepute.

In a similar vein, David Picherit's examination of the expansion and crisis of microfinance in the Chittoor district of Andhra Pradesh (now Telangana) highlights how MFIs became embedded within pre-existing local power structures based on class, caste and gendered divides (Picherit 2015). With the landed upper class seeking to move out of agriculture and diversify income-generating opportunities into less risky ventures, the boom of microfinance in Andhra Pradesh across the mid-1990s into the 2000s appeared to be an ideal vehicle for a reconsolidation of rural power relations. Local powerbrokers set themselves up as gate-keepers for microfinance initiatives, offering the ability to keep expanding debt portfolios and ensuring high repayment rates in return for new enrichment opportunities. As a result, positions of power within local NGOs went to those already established within the rural hier-archy and forms of intimidatory violence – including sexual violence against women – were routinely transferred from the political sphere into the realm of microloan collection (see also Arunachalam 2011). Ultimately, however, the escalating saturation of this impoverished agrarian region with microfinance debt led to a collapse in repayment despite the coercive tactics used to ensure repayment. As it spiralled outwards, the collapse of multiple MFIs resulted in a crisis of immense proportions that shook the integrity of the sector nationwide and resulted in a host of new and profoundly restrictive regulatory measures (Taylor 2017).

MICROFINANCE 2.0: THE RISK-MANAGEMENT PARADIGM

Given the significant public financing placed into its global propagation, the recognition that microfinance was not the dependable anti-poverty tool promised by advocates raised considerable alarm. Activists and scholars challenged the founding legitimacy of microcredit as a development intervention. They pointedly asked whether the propagation of microcredit was driven first and foremost by its ideological function within a broader scheme of neoliberal policy making or to sustain the large and increasingly corporate technocracy that had built up around it (Bateman 2010; Roy 2010; Weber 2014). Such concerns were compounded by a series of recurrent microfinance crises in which private microfinance lenders saturated target populations, predicating collapsing rates of repayment (see Regehr et al. 2015; Taylor 2017).

In response, the industry that had grown up around microfinance changed tack and sought to make a virtue out of necessity (Taylor 2012; Mader 2017). If studies showed that microcredit gave households not a direct ladder upwards out of poverty but rather a tool to manage the symptoms of poverty, then this would become the new rallying call of the sector. Two aspects of this renovated financial inclusion discourse were strongly emphasised. First, microfinance provided poor households with access to services that advocates argued were strongly in demand yet otherwise out of reach, therein resolving a vital equity gap (Cull et al. 2009; Rosenberg 2010). On the other hand, in facilitating what was termed 'consumption smooth-ing', these services provided the basis for effective risk management that allowed households to plan activities and adjust to unexpected shocks in ways that facilitated a more resilient future. As the World Bank put it:

> With these tools, people can smooth consumption, finance their own or their children's education, deal with health and income shocks, improve nutrition, and plan for a better future, among other socially useful activities. In this way, the financial system can advance overall development and help create an environment of equal opportunity and a level playing field, including for the poor. (World Bank 2013, 194)

This line of argument was buttressed by a new emphasis on further financial services including microsavings and microinsurance. Proponents increasingly stress how credit facilities should be accompanied with microsavings and microinsurance products to create a synthesis of financial tools that help households manage risk and seize productive opportunities. On this basis, microsavings accounts are argued to provide a degree of security for formalised saving that avoid the need for households to seek out complicated and costly strategies for households without formal bank accounts (Banerjee and Duflo 2011, 188). In the Indian rural context, for example, the National Bank for Agriculture and Rural Development emphasised how microsavings accounts for rural women allow them to safely save money outside the house, thereby preventing concentration of economic power within the household, and – in creating a small pool of saved capital – helps to mitigate the risks that the poor face as a result of economic shocks (National Bank for Agriculture and Rural Development 2009).

While microsavings products are regarded as minor additions to commercial microfinance initiatives, microinsurance is seen as potentially the next major extension of the paradigm and much of the accompanying rhetoric reflects a similar 'win-win' mentality that accompanied the first expansion of microfinance. In rural areas specifically, many international institutions view microinsurance provision to farmers as a mutually beneficial institutional arrangement in which household risks can be reduced while opening up a growth area for the financial sector. For such international institutions, microinsurance is highly coveted as it is projected to allow smallholder farmers to escape from longstanding risk-averse cultivation strategies and embrace a more entrepreneurial approach through the cultivation of higher-value crops using more input-intensive approaches. On this basis, some have heralded insurance as a transformative tool that can help refashion smallholder agriculture to be simultaneously more resilient and more dynamic. Notably, in the CGIAR's portfolio of 'climate smart agriculture' success stories, index-based weather insurance is featured as the first example (CGIAR 2013, 20). It is in this context that the 2015 G7 InsuResilience initiative, for example, mobilised a financial commitment of USD 550 million to help insure an additional 400 million vulnerable individuals against climate risks by 2020.

This projected expansion of agricultural microinsurance is predicated on a shift away from standard, indemnity models of insurance that, in the absence of heavy subsidisation, typically result in heavy premiums that place formal insurance firmly out of the reach of the rural poor (Greatrex et al. 2015). In contrast, new forms of index-based microinsurance are argued to represent a breakthrough that can allow the inclusion of smallholders into formal insurance markets. Rather than insuring individual losses, index-based products use proxy indicators to estimate the impacts of harmful events across a given area. For example, index-based weather insurance schemes may use an index composed of indicators of rainfall patterns, maximum and minimum temperatures or peak wind speeds that are seen to be an objective and scientific measure of risk. If one or more of these proxies is judged to have passed a given threshold that indicates the likelihood of substantial crop losses in a district, then payments will be made to all policyholders regardless of the individual losses they experience. Other forms of index-based insurance can use an independent estimation of average crop or herd losses in an area and make payments according to that threshold, regardless of the actual losses incurred.

The advantages of indexing in this fashion are argued to be threefold (CGIAR 2013; Greatrex et al. 2015). First, by circumventing the arduous process of detailing and compensating for losses on an individual basis, index-based insurance reduces operation costs making it more feasible to roll out on a micro scale for smallholders. Second, with payments triggered by a seemingly objective index passing a pre-determined threshold, there is a strong reduction of moral hazard. Farmers have no incentive to allow a crop to fail because the payment is not tied to their individual losses but to a seemingly neutral index measured according to objective factors. Indeed, should farmers be able to secure a crop despite adverse weather, they could receive both the insurance payment and revenues from crop sales. Index-based insurance is therein argued to be a positive reinforcement for good farming techniques. Third, index-based insurance is argued to overcome adverse selection problems in which those farmers facing the strongest risks would be most likely to select insurance, therein raising premiums for all. By separating individual losses from payments, this problem is circumvented because farmers will benefit from payments when thresholds are passed even if they did not suffer actual harm. Low-risk farmers therefore have as much incentive to join the programme as those with high risk.

Notwithstanding such high expectations, there is an emerging agrarian studies literature that is charting a number of core tensions within microinsurance programmes (Peterson 2012; Da Costa 2013; Isakson 2015; Taylor 2016). Three key concerns have been put forward. First, despite the bullish rhetoric of proponents, index-based insurance initiatives often remain tenuous in implementation and effectiveness, requiring extensive public subsidisation and guarantees to ensure profitability (Sheth 2017). Indeed, CGIAR's own write up of its supposedly model climate-smart insurance programme in Bihar indicates that there are significant issues with design and implementation including high premiums, insufficient payouts and tenuous consumer demand (CGIAR 2013). Second, despite the assumption that poor agricultural households would be natural consumers of microinsurance, uptake of index-based insurance has often been disappointing and frequently requires the mobilisation of an extensive institutional apparatus to inculcate the appropriate rationalities of risk management among a clientele that was assumed to be in desperate need of the product (Binswanger-Mkhize 2012; Da Costa 2013; Taylor 2016). Third, the entry of insurance in agrarian environments has been argued to facilitate a financialization of risk management that can compromise existing social and environmental risk-mitigation practices intrinsic to agrarian livelihoods (Peterson 2012; Isakson 2015). In their place, existing forms of community cohesion are weakened and replaced by individual purchased insurance contracts that – requiring scarce cash at the start of the agricultural season – can be exclusionary of the most marginal households who most need effective protection.

It is on this basis that the scholarship has begun to highlight how microinsurance raises strong equity concerns wherein, outside of strong subsidisation, the profitability motive pushes up premiums making it inaccessible to poorer households (Fisher et al. 2019). In the case of a Mongolian livestock microinsurance scheme, for example, Taylor (2016) notes how more affluent herders were better positioned to take on the insurance premiums despite having better resources to avoid weather-related losses. Many smaller herders, in contrast, shied away from the high insurance premiums that needed to be paid at the start of the season when liquidity was lowest. Instead, they often become clients of larger herders in order to gain a degree of risk protection but at the cost of dependency relationships predicated upon transfers of labour and resources to the benefactor (see Murphy 2018). On this basis, contrary to its stated goals, microinsurance played a role in the restructuring of class relations within the herding economy, facilitating a consolidation of livestock holdings under the control of larger herders and the parallel reduction of small herders to the status of waged labourers. As with the original microfinance paradigm, it is these social dynamics that agrarian studies is uniquely placed to uncover.

CONCLUSION

Research conducted within the paradigm of agrarian studies has been foundational in developing a critical perspective on the role of microfinance in rural areas. In contrast to prevailing narratives of microfinance as a simple risk-mitigation tool that empowers households to pull themselves out of poverty, these works have shown how microfinance is extremely complex and uneven in its day-to-day operations and impacts. In particular, the foundational idea of 'financial inclusion' has been challenged by work that shows how rural households routinely engage in complex financial transactions with a range of formal and informal actors. Rural households therein tend to view MFIs as one further source of credit among others, each with their own peculiar assemblage of interest rates, repayment schedules, social obligations and collection tactics. In this respect, the key role of critical agrarian studies has been to situate microfinance initiatives within their broader social contexts as a way to examine their complex interactions with rural power dynamics. Such an approach facilitates a finely graded examination of how different forms of microfinance impact household livelihoods, labour market dynamics, local social hierarchies, patterns of capital accumulation and rural indebtedness.

NOTES

1. www.un.org/press/en/2004/dev2492.doc.htm, accessed 2 February 2019.
2. Microfinance is typically defined as the provision of financial services – including credit, insurance and savings accounts – to households that cannot access the formal, private financial system owing to a lack of income, collateral or access.

FURTHER READING

Bateman, M.; Maclean, K. (eds) (2017), *Seduced and Betrayed: Exposing the Contemporary Microfinance Phenomenon*, Santa Fe, NM: SAR Press.
Clapp, J.; Isakson, S.R. (2018), *Speculative Harvests: Financialization, Food and Agriculture*, Halifax: Fernwood Press.
Guérin, I.; Labie, M.; Servet, J.-M. (eds) (2015), *The Crises of Microcredit*, London: Zed Books.
Karim, L. (2011), *Microfinance and Its Discontents: Women in Debt in Bangladesh*, Minneapolis, MN: University of Minnesota Press.
Yunus, M. (2008), *Banker to the Poor: Micro-Lending and the Battle against World Poverty*, New York: PublicAffairs Press.

REFERENCES

Arunachalam, R. (2011), *The Journey of Indian Micro-Finance*, Chennai: AAPTI Press.
Banerjee, A.V.; Duflo, E. (2011), *Poor Economics: A Radical Rethinking of the Way to Fight Global Poverty*, New York: PublicAffairs.
Bastiaensen, J., Marchetti, P., Mendoza, R.; Pérez, F. (2013), After the Nicaraguan non-payment crisis: Alternatives to microfinance narcissism, *Development and Change*, 44(4), 861–885.
Bateman, M. (2010), *Why Doesn't Microfinance Work? The Destructive Rise of Local Neoliberalism*, London: Zed Books.
Bee, B. (2011), Gender, solidarity and the paradox of microfinance: Reflections from Bolivia, *Gender, Place and Culture*, 18(1), 23–43.

Bergeron, S. (2002), The post-Washington consensus and economic representations of women in development at the World Bank, *International Feminist Journal of Politics*, 5(3), 397–421.

Binswanger-Mkhize, H. (2012), Is there too much hype about index-based agricultural insurance? *Journal of Development Studies*, 48(2), 187–200.

Bylander, M. (2014), Borrowing across borders: Migration and microcredit in rural Cambodia, *Development and Change*, 45(2), 284–307.

CGIAR (2013), *Climate-Smart Agriculture Success Stories from Farming Communities around the World*, Montpellier: CGIAR.

Chavan, P.; Ramakumar, R. (2005), Interest rates on micro-credit, in Ramachandran, V.K.; Swaminathan, M. (eds), *Financial Liberalization and Rural Credit in India*, New Delhi: Tulika Books, 145–162.

Cons, J.; Paprocki, K. (2010), Contested credit landscapes: Microcredit, self-help and self-determination in rural Bangladesh, *Third World Quarterly*, 31(4), 637–654.

Cull, R.; Morduch, J. (2017), Microfinance and economic development, *World Bank Policy Research Working Papers*, 8252, 1–45.

Cull, R.; Demirgüç-Knut, A.; Morduch, J. (2009), Microfinance meets the market, *Journal of Economic Perspectives*, 23(1), 167–192.

Da Costa, D. (2013), The 'rule of experts' in making a dynamic micro-insurance industry in India, *Journal of Peasant Studies*, 40(5), 845–865.

Duvendack, M.; Palmer-Jones, R.; Copestake, J.; Hooper, L.; Loke, Y.; Rao, N. (2011), *What Is the Evidence of the Impact of Microfinance on the Well-Being of Poor People?*, accessed 10 March 2021 at www.givedirectly.org/wp-content/uploads/2019/06/DFID_microfinance_evidence_review.pdf.

Edward, P.; Olsen, W. (2006), Paradigms and reality in micro-finance: The Indian case, *Perspectives on Global Development and Technology*, 5(1–2), 31–56.

Fisher, E.; Hellin, J.; Greatrex, H.; Jensen, N. (2019), Index insurance and climate risk management: Addressing social equity, *Development Policy Review*, 37(5), 581–602.

Greatrex, H.; Hansen, J.; Garvin, S.; Diro, R.; Blakeley, S.; Le Guen, M.; Osgood, D. (2015), *Scaling Up Index Insurance for Smallholder Farmers: Recent Evidence and Insights*, Copenhagen: CGIAR Research Program on Climate Change, Agriculture and Food Security.

Guérin, I. (2014), Juggling with debt, social ties, and values: The everyday use of microcredit in rural south India, *Current Anthropology*, 55(S9), S40–S50.

Guérin, I.; Servet, J.-M. (2015), Microcredit crises and the absorption capacity of local economies, in Regehr, E.; Guérin, I.; Labie, M.; Servet, J.-M. (eds), *The Crises of Microcredit*, London: Zed Books.

Heales, C. (2017), Agricultural microfinance and risk saturation, in Bateman, M.; Maclean, K. (eds), *Seduced and Betrayed: Exposing the Contemporary Microfinance Phenomenon*, Santa Fe, NM: SAR Press, 219–236.

Isakson, R. (2015), Derivatives for development? Small-farmer vulnerability and the financialization of climate risk management, *Journal of Agrarian Change*, 15(4), 569–580.

Kalpana, K. (2005), Shifting trajectories in microfinance discourse, *Economic and Political Weekly*, 40(51), 5400–5410.

Karim, L. (2011), *Microfinance and Its Discontents: Women in Debt in Bangladesh*, Minneapolis, MN: University of Minnesota Press.

Kelly, M. (1997), The dynamics of Smithian growth, *Quarterly Journal of Economics*, 112(3), 939–965.

Mader, P. (2017), Contesting financial inclusion, *Development and Change*, 49(2), 461–483.

Maîtrot, M. (2018), Understanding social performance: A 'practice drift' at the frontline of microfinance institutions in Bangladesh, *Development and Change*, 50(3), 623–654.

Mayoux, L. (1999), Questioning virtuous spirals: Micro-finance and women's empowerment in Africa, *Journal of International Development*, 11(7), 957–984.

Morgan, J.; Olsen, W.K. (2011), Aspiration problems for the Indian rural poor: Research on self-help groups and micro-finance, *Capital and Class*, 35(2), 189–212.

Murphy, D. (2018), 'We're living from loan-to-loan': Pastoral vulnerability and the cashmere-debt cycle in Mongolia, *Research in Economic Anthropology*, 38(1), 7–30.

National Bank for Agriculture and Rural Development (2009), *Financial Inclusion: An Overview*, Mumbai: NBARD.

Peterson, N. (2012), Developing climate adaptation: The intersection of climate research and development programmes in index insurance, *Development and Change*, 43(2), 557–584.

Picherit, D. (2015), When microfinance collapses: Development and politics in Andhra Pradesh, in Regehr, E.; Guérin, I.; Labie, M.; Servet, J.-M. (eds), *The Crises of Microcredit*, London: Zed Books, 170–188.

Pralahad, C.K. (2004), *The Fortune at the Bottom of the Pyramid*, Philadelphia, PA: Wharton School Press.

Rankin, C. (2008), Manufacturing rural finance in Asia: Institutional assemblages, market societies, entrepreneurial subjects, *Geoforum*, 39(4), 1965–1977.

Rao, S. (2005), Women's self-help groups and credit for the poor: A case study from Andhra Pradesh, in Ramachandran, V.K.; Swaminathan, M. (eds), *Financial Liberalization and Rural Credit in India*, New Delhi: Tulika Books, 204–237.

Regehr, E.; Guérin, I.; Labie, M.; Servet, J.-M. (eds) (2015), *The Crises of Microcredit*, London: Zed Books.

Rosenberg, R. (2010), *Does Microcredit Really Help Poor People?*, Washington, DC: CGAP.

Roy, A. (2010), *Poverty Capital: Microfinance and the Making of Development*, London: Routledge.

Shakya, Y.; Rankin, K. (2008), The politics of subversion in development practice: An exploration of microfinance in Nepal and Vietnam, *Journal of Development Studies*, 44(8), 1214–1235.

Sheth, A.S. (2017), Cultivating risk: Weather insurance, technology and financialization in India, Unpublished PhD dissertation, Massachusetts Institute of Technology.

Smith, P.B.; Thurman, E. (2007), *A Billion Bootstraps: Microcredit, Barefoot Banking, and the Business Solution for Ending Poverty*, New York: McGraw-Hill.

Taylor, M. (2011), 'Freedom from poverty is not for free': Rural development and the microfinance crisis in Andhra Pradesh, India, *Journal of Agrarian Change*, 11(4), 484–504.

Taylor, M. (2012), The antinomies of 'financial inclusion': Debt, distress and the workings of Indian microfinance, *Journal of Agrarian Change*, 12(4), 601–610.

Taylor, M. (2016), Risky ventures: Financial inclusion, risk management and the uncertain rise of index-based insurance, *Research in Political Economy*, 31(1), 267–295.

Taylor, M. (2017), From tigers to cats: The rise and crisis of microfinance in rural India, in Bateman, M.; MacLean, K. (eds), *Seduced and Betrayed*, Sacramento, CA: SAR Press.

Weber, H. (2004), The 'new economy' and social risk: Banking on the poor?, *Review of International Political Economy*, 11(2), 356–386.

Weber, H. (2014), Global politics of microfinancing poverty in Asia: The case of Bangladesh unpacked, *Asian Studies Review*, 38(4), 544–563.

World Bank (2013), *World Development Report 2014: Risk and Opportunity – Managing Risk for Development*, Oxford: Oxford University Press.

58. Rural indebtedness

Julien-François Gerber

INTRODUCTION

Rural indebtedness is an old-new question in critical agrarian studies. On one hand, the phenomenon has been discussed for more than a century by Marxist political economists. On the other hand, however, rural indebtedness has never occupied a central position in the field – even if it has reached unparalleled levels worldwide and placed at the core of many rural movements, as for example in India where massive anti-debt protests have taken place almost uninterruptedly over the past three years (as I write these lines in December 2018).

Perhaps because Marx's general emphasis was on the employer/employees relation, the credit/debt couple has not received the full theoretical attention it deserved in critical agrarian studies. Many case studies have focused on debt as an instrument of domination and as a factor of economic inertia, thereby neglecting other important aspects of this multidimensional phenomenon called 'rural indebtedness'. In this chapter, summarizing my previous work on the topic, I will try to broaden the understanding of the issue, and especially its implications (Gerber 2013, 2014, 2015; Gerber et al. 2021). I hope to show that the consequences of rural indebtedness, taken as a whole, can be seen as a crucial factor shaping the evolution of capitalism at different levels.

BRIEF BACKGROUND

Rural indebtedness is certainly not a new phenomenon. It is in fact concomitant to the appearance of money and probably even paved the way for its creation (Graeber 2011). The phenomenon was widespread in Ancient Near Eastern civilizations, Greece and the Roman Empire, as well as China and India. It was also present in medieval Europe.

But by the second half of the sixteenth century, after much politico-ethical controversy, a new factor entered the post-medieval picture of most of Western Europe: interest-bearing loans started to be legalized and enforced. The morality of charging an interest was relegated to individual conscience and the state largely ceased to hamper 'usury' (Jones 1989). Although much variation existed between the different regions, the use of credit became routine throughout society (Muldrew 1998; Fontaine 2008). The general context was favourable, characterized by new emerging property relations, rapid urbanization and increases in population size. Generalized indebtedness – both rural and urban – thus seems to correlate with the birth and spread of capitalism.

As consolidating nation-states and colonial authorities quickly moved from taxes in kind and labour to taxes in cash, the tax system played a key role in pushing peasants into indebtedness (up until now, as debts may allow farmers, ironically, to pay today *less* tax). In parallel, debts were also incurred for investment purposes. As soon as the seventeenth century, French peasants borrowed to improve their production, and apparently not only rich farmers (Hoffman

1996; Postel-Vinay 1998). This observation is consistent with the assumption that capitalism had already taken root in rural Western Europe. Through credit, middle peasants had to invest productively in order to preserve the independence of the family farm under the conditions of emerging market competition (Kriedte et al. 1981).

Continuing on these older trends, farmers' dependency on credit increased dramatically with the generalization of cash crop monocultures generating income only intermittently. Many peasants became obliged to borrow during the unproductive seasons. Subsistence-oriented peasants, in contrast, had elaborated complex polycultures supplying food all through the year. But even in these cases, a bad harvest could make creditors indispensable again. The 'green revolution' of the 1960s typically exacerbated the dependency on credit to buy seeds and inputs.

Today, indebtedness has spread to virtually every corner of the world, and credit is still often regarded as *the* major instrument of rural development. Different forms of credit policies have been favoured according to the changing ideological contexts. Since the 1980s, there has been a general shift from state-sponsored rural subsidies towards the financial market approach, including through rural 'microfinance'. Under this 'new paradigm', the attention has shifted from the borrower's production to the lender's returns, and the goal has often been to 'modernize' agriculture via agribusiness involvement and new (bio)technologies.

While credit may allow, without previous savings, to project one's imagination into future improvements – a powerful potential that explains why credit is still attractive to many (Steppacher 2008) – it simply represents for most the possibility to sustain a 'normal life' within a given institutional setting with specific values and unequal power relations. This 'normal life' consists in being able to eat, produce, pay taxes and cover the basic life-cycle events such as weddings, funerals, housing, health care and education. But whatever the circumstances, credit has a debt side which has consequences.

CLASSIC VIEWS ON THE CONSEQUENCES OF RURAL INDEBTEDNESS

The relatively small number of studies that address – usually in passing – the implications of rural indebtedness can broadly be divided into four camps. The 'stagnationists' emphasize the poverty-generating and stagnation effects of rural indebtedness (e.g. Kriedte et al. 1981), while the 'entrepreneurialists' stress the credit-based improvement of production and associated business acumen (e.g. Hoffman 1996). The 'culturalists' have highlighted the gradual shift from an embedded 'moral economy' of local lending practices to an impersonal large-scale system of formal credit (e.g. Muldrew 1998; Fontaine 2008; Graeber 2011). And finally, while acknowledging a shift, the Marxist camp has emphasized exploitation and the social differentiation effect of credit/debt (Kautsky 1900 [1899]; Lenin 1967 [1899]).

While Marx largely concentrated on the employer/employees relationship, he clearly pointed out that the surplus value is appropriated by both the owners of capital who receive profit of enterprise and those who collect interest (Marx 1992 [1894], ch. 23). For him, circulating capital (including credit) and production capital represent the two constitutive pillars of capitalism. In his unfinished analysis of the credit system, Marx mainly focused on intercapitalist relations within a (relatively) modern banking system, but he also studied (albeit sketchily) rural indebtedness (that he called 'usury').

Very briefly, Marx saw 'usury' as one factor – among others – 'assisting in establishment of the new mode of production by ruining the feudal lord and small-scale producer, on the one hand, and centralizing the conditions of labour into capital, on the other' (1992 [1894], 732). In this 'centralizing' phenomenon, the producer pays the capitalist his surplus labour in the form of interest and this exploitative process prevents the producer, Marx thought, from improving productivity and technological conditions.

Subsequently, some Marxist analysts of the rural world expanded on these observations. Kautsky (1900 [1899]) identified rural indebtedness as *the* key mechanism alienating peasants from their means of production, stressing, like Marx, the counter-productive effect of debt on the development of productive forces. Both Lenin and Chayanov agreed that one of the main consequences of modern credit is the social differentiation induced within pre-capitalist communities. Importantly, Lenin (1967 [1899]) stressed both potentials of credit: not only the stagnation effect of debt but also the economic growth associated with credit. The emergence of agrarian capitalism, he argued, gave rise to two different types of debt: one was a sign of precariousness, the other of increasing consolidation and capitalization.

Among more recent authors, Banaji (1977) and Roseberry (1978) mainly updated these observations with additional fieldwork data. They illustrate the idea that usury capital is the strategic form of circulating capital in many rural areas – arguably representing a distinctive form of 'production relation' – because peasants are increasingly dependent on credit to reproduce their households. Bernstein's (1979) notion of 'simple reproduction squeeze' elaborates on similar ideas. Extremely vulnerable to external demands and ecological conditions, poor peasants become ever more dependent on credit, frequently mortgaging their land. They may eventually become full proletarians if they fail to generate sufficient income by supplying (cheap) labour and/or commodities.

In this context often characterized by 'contractual interlocking', Bhaduri (1983) showed that rural indebtedness gives rise to an exploitative system of 'forced commerce'. More recently, Brass (1999) argued that unfree labour – typically made possible through debt – is not only compatible with capitalism but that it is capitalism's production relation of choice when the class struggle allows it. Debt thus leads, he wrote, to a 'deproletarianization' of the workforce (i.e. its shift from the status of free to unfree labour).

Building on these interventions, I will try below to systematize their implications, also including elements taken from studies of rural credit/debt that could be classified as either 'stagnationist', 'entrepreneuralist' or 'culturalist'.

RURAL INDEBTEDNESS AND THE EVOLUTION OF CAPITALISM

Indebtedness and the Reconfiguration of Ownership and Labour

Indebtedness represents, together with (legal or extra-legal) expropriation and purchase, the third main mechanism of 'primitive accumulation' and labour control.

The debt-driven reconfiguration of land ownership, especially its concentration, is a well-known consequence of rural indebtedness. The decline of the smallholder and the rise of the landless labourer has been one of the most important themes in the historiography of early modern Western Europe. While a great majority of studies acknowledge the role of debt in land concentration, few actually address the issue in detail. Those that do focus on this question tend to reveal the vast extent of the phenomenon. The effects of these debt-driven processes seem comparable – and even more powerful in many regions – to those of the different 'enclosure movements'.

Overall, however, these processes remain difficult to evaluate – both historically and in the present – because they often leave the written trace of standard 'voluntary' land sales, glossing over the fact that the owner was forced to sell in order to repay creditors. But it is fair to say that debt-driven ownership reconfiguration is one of the key mechanisms behind social differentiation.

Of course, instead of being reimbursed or accumulating assets, creditors may prefer to remain interest collectors. This was, for instance, true in early modern France, where long-term debts formed the major source of credit in much of the rural world (Postel-Vinay 1998). These long-term debts consisted of perpetual and life annuities (*rentes*) that lenders with extra funds 'bought' from individuals needing money. The debtors then paid interest on the capital, either 'in perpetuity' or until the death of the creditor – a phenomenon that is also applicable to modern banks.

In the same way, creditors may seek to control as long as possible the labour of the debtor. Such mechanisms may take different forms and have been observed virtually everywhere. In rural Asia, Li (2010, 387) found that:

> the principal mechanism through which owners of capital have been able to profit from rural peoples' labour and the principal vector of dispossession long before the introduction of high-input agriculture has been debt ... Debt makes nominally independent landholders in effect their tenants, disciplined by the need for further loans and the threat of foreclosure.

Some scholars have called this situation 'concealed', 'partial' or 'disguised' proletarianization (Banaji 1977; Little and Watts 1994).

One classical form of labour control is through advances on sales, but many variants of debt bondage have been described, including numerous mechanisms for keeping workers in perpetual debt to their creditors, sometimes over generations (Brass 1999). Subcontracting credit can be seen as a modern form of debt-based labour control (Little and Watts 1994). The companies-cum-creditors usually provide technical and management advice in order to increase productivity and ensure payments. The main advantage for them is the minimization of costs by removing the need to purchase land and hire labour. Unlike banks, such companies can extract interest directly from the crop prices and make sure the credit will be spent on production by distributing loans in kind or in the form of vouchers.

However, the effects of rural indebtedness should not simply be understood as a process whereby the poor debtor gets expelled/exploited by rich creditors. In reality, indebtedness also concerns the élites and the capitalists. Their own debts have crucially modified ownership relations in order to maintain their solvency, notably through land expansion (including imperialism) and by selecting the most cost-efficient tenants. Debts have pushed many landlords to enclose with the aim of generating extra income to reimburse their creditors (Habakkuk 1994). In other words, credit/debt relations may generate social differentiation in every rural class, not only among the poor or middle strata.

Although credit/debt relations predate capitalism, the latter offered them a particularly flourishing ground, amplifying their impacts both quantitatively and qualitatively. Credit and debt became in fact a central element of the 'capitalist social-property relations' defined by Brenner (1982) as the particular class relations generating capitalism's relentless drive to accumulate through market dependence. Credit/debt relations, in this sense, are clearly more than a mere 'assistant' to the birth of capitalism (Marx). They were an essential lever in the transition from market as opportunity to market as compulsion, as we will see next.

Indebtedness and Behavioural Reconfigurations

Once an economic actor – whether rich or poor – has entered an interest-bearing and guarantee-based credit contract, he/she is compelled (to different degrees) to think and to behave in a particular way in order to secure timely repayments (Steppacher 2008). The typical debtor must fundamentally focus on the potential demand of moneyholders. He/she is forced to produce commodities that, from the very beginning, are not designed for personal consumption but for the purpose of obtaining money. Moreover, the interest rate forces upon the debtor a value of production which must be greater than the principal, and hence requires economic growth (Heinsohn and Steiger 2013).

The expansion of credit in early modern England remarkably correlates with the rise of a more commercial mentality. Habakkuk (1994, 315) wrote that 'there is a strong case for supposing that debt was a stimulus to development' ('development' meaning here productivity increase, commercial activities and industrialization). Muldrew (1998, 95) wrote that 'it was credit, above all, which dominated the way in which the market was structured and interpreted'. According to him, credit imposed upon everyone in the society new and similar constraints. Initially, in the absence of a fully functioning legal enforcement system, people had to trust that those with whom they dealt would honour their word and possessed the means to repay their loans. Since credit was an imperative, people lived always with an eye to reputation, monitoring conduct so as to avoid a bad name (Finn 2003). There was a torrent of moral literature warning against the perils of the 'prodigal' indebted life and fostering people to discipline in order to ensure payments. In the early eighteenth century, Daniel Defoe wrote that a government, a businessman, a farmer or a labourer could properly handle credit only if they endorsed a specific pattern of 'good behaviours' notably characterized by a calculating and industrious attitude (Hoppit 1990).

Defaulting is no minor matter for most borrowers. Until the nineteenth century, imprisonment was not rare, and slavery and prostitution remain classic outcomes of indebtedness (Graeber 2011). Today, property selling or foreclosures are the most frequent means to recover an unpaid debt, which has led to countless suicides worldwide – not only in India. There is little doubt that such pressures make debtors work hard and do everything they can to repay loans on time. The first thing indebted farmers do is to implement a 'structural adjustment programme' in their exploitation through intensifying production, engaging in commercial activities and enrolling in temporary wage labour (Gerber 2013). Rural indebtedness is therefore not just a factor of stagnation.

From this perspective, economic growth does not simply result from 'unlimited wants' or an innate 'drive for profits' made possible via investment credit; it also results from the obligation to take out loans and from the subsequent constant threat of defaulting in a competitive context. The threat of bankruptcy is the key component of the familiar 'whip of market competition'.

This threat defines the entire hierarchy of economic decision-making and the valuation process associated with it (Steppacher 2008). Above everything else, the debtor must focus on a monetary cost/benefit valuation of all economic transactions and resources, based on the current market prices. He/she must think in individual terms and prioritize short-term benefits.

Accordingly, land, labour and natural resources are monetarily evaluated while surrounding socio-cultural and ecological considerations remain secondary. A researcher studying the African plantation sector reported that 'every [indebted] household is thus little by little brought to prioritize its needs and to make painful choices, to choose between ... social expenditures and productive investments' (Janin 1995, 126).

Cost/benefit calculations, personal discipline, cost-cutting innovations and intensification are all elements that acquire a particular meaning in the mind of many debtors. Taken as a whole, all these small and big pressures (depending on the actors) contributed to shape mental representations and priorities. Of course, these mental reconfigurations have very material consequences. The need to improve cost-cutting technological innovations is a prime example of this. In early modern rural economies, there is evidence that indebtedness led to increased land productivity and cost-cutting techniques as well as many productive innovations (Habakkuk 1994; Hoffman 1996; Watt 2006). Exemplifying this for the United States, Post (2011, 152) describes how, after 1840, indebtedness and taxes forced family farmers to compete in the market, a process that 'unleashed a dynamic of productive specialisation, technical innovation and accumulation'. These dynamics, as anyone can guess, are not necessarily good news for the community and the environment.

Indebtedness and Socio-ecological Reconfigurations

Rural indebtedness has played a role in eroding community-based ways of life. Very directly, debt undermines community by dispossessing defaulting debtors and fostering social differentiation. It is also an important factor behind temporary, permanent and circular migrations outside of the community. In addition, credit destabilizes customary commons because it frequently requires that alienable portions of the community's land are provided as collateral, a phenomenon already noticeable in early modern Europe (see Pichard 2001). In twentieth-century Latin America, commons were dissolved as peasants turned to coffee production and therefore to collateral-based credit (Roseberry 1978).

More indirectly, credit dissolves traditional bonds between community members by individualizing economic responsibilities within dyadic relations. With the initial sixteenth-century credit boom, indebtedness exacerbated tensions in rural communities and led to an explosion of debt litigations in local courts. 'The culture of credit was generated through a process whereby the nature of the community was redefined as a conglomeration of competing but interdependent households' (Muldrew 1998, 4). In modern Southeast Asia, a study on credit reported that village conversations 'rarely failed to raise statements bemoaning the decreasing cooperation between villagers', stressing 'the fact that people in the village are becoming increasingly "calculating" (*berkira*) in their approach to money matters' (quoted in Scott 1985, 188).

Rural indebtedness also creates adverse pressures on the environment as a result of the new priorities it generates. Ecologically damaging growth may for instance represent a response to prior levels of indebtedness. This has already been reported in early modern France where commercial agriculture expanded because of mounting communal debts (Pichard 2001) as well as in early modern Scotland where the aristocracy's indebtedness stimulated extractivism and deforestation (Watt 2006).

More recently, Canada's National Farmers Union (2010, 19–20) observed that 'Debt repayment deadlines push farmers to make choices based on short-term cash flow, rather than on the needs of the soil or of the next generation ... Debt forces farmers to adopt the short-term thinking common to corporate boardrooms, with predictable results for the environment, fertility, and the future.' In Central America, a study reported that 'if peasants have access to credit, particularly at high interest rates, increasing annual productivity becomes vital to their ability to repay their loans' (Wilson 2010, 88), a situation that leads to an increased risk of pollution and ecosystem damage.

Policy and Political Implications

What kinds of lending organizations could alleviate some of the negative effects of rural indebtedness? Credit unions could be a candidate. Named differently across the world, they pool their members' savings to finance their own loan portfolios. F.W. Raiffeisen (1818–1888) is considered one of the fathers of the modern credit union. As nineteenth-century Germany was characterized by the progressive decline of small farmers and the rise of agribusiness, Raiffeisen's goal was to free smallholders from indebtedness to outside capital. His goal was thus to finance them, at reasonable rates and usually without collateral, relying on solidarity and Christian values. The essential rule was to stay local, thereby allowing interpersonal relationships, and democratic as the cooperative was governed by a general assembly.

Socialists have been critical of credit unions, fearing the 'embourgeoisement' of subordinate classes and emphasizing production cooperatives rather than financial cooperatives that are accommodating capitalism. Yet specific worker- or state-run credit unions could be compatible with some models of socialism. Among more radical options, forms of (planned) 'social credit' and (unplanned) 'mutual credit' have been proposed by various authors (Gerber 2015). In the short run, however, debt cancellation and the (re)building of public services are crucial reforms to be pursued against rural indebtedness (Graeber 2011). These policies will only be possible if the anti-debt movements increase their pressure, which does not seem to be unlikely.

Gerber et al. (2021) provide a preliminary global overview of mobilizations against private debts. Our database shows that the rural world is at the forefront of such struggles. These movements have contested various aspects of the creditor–debtor relation and involved different social classes with various political objectives, ranging from populist-opportunistic to radical-revolutionary. The majority of the cases come from members of rural lower classes, for whom credit is a fundamental albeit dangerous 'last resort' (or 'safety net') when the compulsory payments are no longer immediately possible. This is observable in ancient agrarian economies as well as in contemporary America.

Indebtedness – and the struggles that go with it – must always be placed within their broader politico-institutional context. In the United Kingdom, for instance, Davies et al. (2015, 5) found that 'there is a clear link between a lack of social safety net and borrowing in times of personal/family crisis. This ... poses a direct challenge to policy narratives which seek to individualise debt as a personal problem.' The simultaneous necessity and burden of the credit/debt couple explains why it is politically inflammable, and probably increasingly so as economies continue to financialize. At the same time, the frequent harsh repression of anti-debt protests – seen as a threat to the very foundation of capitalism – and the particular subjectivity associated with debt have also deterred mobilizations.

CONCLUSION

Capitalism has witnessed the dramatic expansion of credit – and therefore debt – both quantitatively and qualitatively. Together with the employer/employee relations, there is little doubt that the creditor/debtor relations should figure at the core of the capitalist social-property relations.

The present chapter shows that rural indebtedness is not only a factor of stagnation and subjugation, as several agrarian analysts have argued. Debt is also a multifarious phenomenon that cannot be dissociated from credit and that has had far-reaching consequences at different levels. At the micro level, these consequences take the form of new pressures on debtors: pressures to remain solvent, to respect time constraints and to make a profit. These pressures vary, of course, along class and other lines, but they retain these fundamental features. At the macro level, all these pressures – small and large – represent a powerful evolutionary force influencing the trajectory of capitalism. As we have seen, credit and debt have not only played an important role in reconfiguring land ownership and labour relations; they have also contributed to shape capitalist rationality and culture according to the strategic principle of creditworthiness.

In a nutshell, the threat of bankruptcy and its disciplining effect have contributed to generate some of the typical productive features of capitalism (i.e. innovations, productivity, growth) but also some of its most emblematic impacts – exploitation, social differentiation, economic crises, and the degradation of the environment. With the worsening of the multiple debt crises, debt-centred organizing may reinvigorate radical movements in the rural world.

FURTHER READING

Gerber, J.-F. (2014), The role of rural indebtedness in the evolution of capitalism, *Journal of Peasant Studies*, 41(5), 729–747.

Graeber, D. (2011), *Debt: The First 5,000 Years*, New York: Melville House.

Lazzarato, M. (2012), *The Making of the Indebted Man: An Essay on the Neoliberal Condition*, Cambridge, MA: MIT Press.

Muldrew, C. (1998), *The Economy of Obligation: The Culture of Credit and Social Relations in Early Modern England*, London: Macmillan.

Taylor, M. (2011), 'Freedom from poverty is not for free': Rural development and the microfinance crisis in Andhra Pradesh, India, *Journal of Agrarian Change*, 11(4), 484–504.

REFERENCES

Banaji, J. (1977), Modes of production in a materialist conception of history, *Capital and Class*, 6, 1–44.

Bernstein, H. (1979), African peasantries: A theoretical framework, *Journal of Peasant Studies*, 6(4), 421–443.

Bhaduri, A. (1983), *The Economic Structure of Backward Agriculture*, London: Academic Press.

Brass, T. (1999), *Towards a Comparative Political Economy of Unfree Labour*, London: Frank Cass.

Brenner, R. (1982), The agrarian roots of European capitalism, *Past and Present*, 97(1), 16–113.

Davies, W.; Montgomerie, J.; Wallin, S. (2015), 'Financial melancholia: Mental health and indebtedness', ESRC report, Political Economy Research Centre, Goldsmiths, London.

Finn, M.C. (2003), *The Character of Credit: Personal Debt in English Culture, 1740–1914*, Cambridge: Cambridge University Press.

Fontaine, L. (2008), *L'Economie Morale: Pauvreté, Crédit et Confiance dans l'Europe Préindustrielle*, Paris: Gallimard.

Gerber, J.-F. (2013), The hidden consequences of credit: An illustration from rural Indonesia, *Development and Change*, 44(4), 839–860.

Gerber, J.-F. (2014), The role of rural indebtedness in the evolution of capitalism, *Journal of Peasant Studies*, 41(5), 729–747.

Gerber, J.-F. (2015), An overview of local credit systems and their implications for post-growth, *Sustainability Science*, 10(3), 413–423.

Gerber, J.-F.; Moreda, T.; Sathyamala, C. (2021), The awkward struggle: A global overview of social conflicts against private debts, *Journal of Rural Studies*, 86, 651–662.

Graeber, D. (2011), *Debt: The First 5,000 Years*, New York: Melville House.

Habakkuk, J. (1994), *Marriage, Debt, and the Estates System: English Landownership, 1650–1950*, Oxford: Oxford University Press.

Heinsohn, G.; Steiger, O. (2013), *Ownership Economics*, London: Routledge.

Hoffman, P. (1996), *Growth in a Traditional Society: The French Countryside, 1450–1815*, Princeton, NJ: Princeton University Press.

Hoppit, J. (1990), Attitudes to credit in Britain, 1680–1790, *Historical Journal*, 33(2), 305–322.

Janin, P. (1995), 'L'immuable, le changeant et l'imprévu: les économies de plantation Bamiléké et Béti du Cameroun confrontées aux chocs extérieurs', PhD dissertation, University of Paris IV.

Jones, N.L. (1989), *God and the Moneylenders: Usury and Law in Early Modern England*, Cambridge, MA: Basil Blackwell.

Kautsky, K. (1900 [1899]), *La Question Agraire*, Paris: Giard et Brière.

Kriedte, P.; Medick, H.; Schlumbohm, J. (1981), *Industrialization before Industrialization: Rural Industry in the Genesis of Capitalism*, Cambridge: Cambridge University Press.

Lenin, V.I. (1967 [1899]), *The Development of Capitalism in Russia: Collected Works*, vol. 3, Moscow: Progress Publishers.

Li, T.M. (2010), Indigeneity, capitalism, and the management of dispossession, *Current Anthropology*, 51(3), 385–414.

Little, P.; Watts, M. (eds) (1994), *Living under Contract: Contract Farming and Agrarian Transformation in Sub-Saharan Africa*, Madison, WI: University of Wisconsin Press.

Marx, K. (1992 [1894]), *Capital*, vol. 3, New York: Penguin Classics.

Muldrew, C. (1998), *The Economy of Obligation: The Culture of Credit and Social Relations in Early Modern England*, London: Macmillan.

National Farmers Union (2010), Losing our grip: How a corporate farmland buy-up, rising farm debt, and agribusiness financing of inputs threaten family farms and food sovereignty, Report, 7 June.

Pichard, G. (2001), L'espace absorbé par l'économique? Endettement communautaire et pression sur l'environnement en Provence (1640–1730), *Histoire et Sociétés Rurales*, 16, 81–115.

Post, C. (2011), *The American Road to Capitalism: Studies in Class-Structure, Economic Development and Political Conflict, 1620–1877*, Leiden: Brill.

Postel-Vinay, G. (1998), *La Terre et l'Argent: L'Agriculture et le Crédit en France du XVIIIe au Début du XXe Siècle*, Paris: Albin Michel.

Roseberry, W. (1978), Peasants as proletarians, *Critique of Anthropology*, 3(11), 3–18.

Scott, J.C. (1985), *Weapons of the Weak: Everyday Forms of Peasant Resistance*, New Haven, CT: Yale University Press.

Steppacher, R. (2008), Property, mineral resources and 'sustainable development', in Steiger, O. (ed.), *Property Economics: Property Rights, Creditor's Money and the Foundations of the Economy*, Marburg: Metropolis-Verlag, 217–241.

Watt, D. (2006), 'The laberinth of thir difficulties': The influence of debt on the Highland élite c.1550–1700, *The Scottish Historical Review*, 85(219), 28–51.

Wilson, B.R. (2010), Indebted to fair trade? Coffee and crisis in Nicaragua, *Geoforum*, 41(1), 84–92.

59. The neoliberal diet

Gerardo Otero

Food and diets are the end products of agricultural production, which is why they have not figured so prominently in critical agrarian studies. The latter have been top heavy on peasant studies, agrarian reforms, agricultural modernization, agribusiness corporations and so on. Food is an intimate commodity that most people ingest up to three or more times a day. We should thus be very aware of the extent to which us individuals actually have a choice in what we eat. This is especially the case when our world has become mostly urban, since 2007, so that less than half of the population is able to produce its own food. We have become almost entirely dependent on others to produce the main ingredients that go into our daily diets, many of which are increasingly processed industrially. A growing proportion of people make fewer meals at home and instead buy their food at restaurants or elsewhere.

In this chapter, I analyze food and diets as resulting from larger structures that have been studied within the 'food regime' framework to understand the strategic role of agriculture in the world capitalist economy. A food regime refers to the set of explicit and implicit rules and regulations that account for capital accumulation in agriculture and the food industry (see McMichael, this volume). Harriet Friedmann and Philip McMichael (1989) identified two food regimes in the world economy since 1870. The first emerged under the hegemony of Great Britain until World War I, predicated on extending agricultural frontiers, including in its settler colonies. Following a transition period which lasted until the end of World War II, the second food regime emerged under the leadership of the United States. This was an intensive food regime based on new agricultural technologies like machinery, hybrid seeds, fertilizers, irrigation and so on. It also produced surpluses beyond what the United States could consume, so the state developed policies to dispose of such surpluses via trade. Other countries like Australia and Canada also became agro-exporting powerhouses. A third food regime started in the 1980s which was labeled the 'corporate food regime' by Philip McMichael (2009), who highlights 'deregulation' as the key state response. I opted for naming this the 'neoliberal' food regime (Otero 2018) instead. This label allows us to highlight that this food regime is the product of state policies, 'neoregulation', that enable corporations to become the key economic actors, for instance through strengthening intellectual property rights. For me, therefore, the state continues to play a central if different role in food production.

State neoregulation is one of four key dynamic factors of the neoliberal food regime. These dynamics are the state, which provides the political, legislative and policy context via neoregulation; agribusiness multinational corporations, which constitute the driving economic actors; biotechnology as the main technological form chosen to expand profitability; and supermarkets, which have become the dominant food buyers and distributors across the globe. Biotechnology is the continuation of the modern agricultural paradigm, which started with the petrochemical, mechanical and hybrid seeds revolution of the 1930s in the United States and is dominated by agribusiness multinationals (Otero 2018).

So, what is the *neoliberal diet* emerging from the third food regime? I see the neoliberal diet as the globalized version of the industrial diet that first emerged in the United States in the

1940s (Winson 2013). This energy-dense, industrial, Western, ultra-processed and cheap diet, popularly known as junk food, is directly or indirectly implicated in making working-class humans most vulnerable to obesity and being overweight. In some places like Mexico City processed foods already make up about 58 per cent of food caloric consumption, compared with 30 per cent in China (Popkin 2014). The fundamental issue is that eating energy-dense food is much less about individual choice than about having more or less economic access to healthy and nutritious food, which tends to be more expensive. People with middle to low incomes thus have a greater exposure to the energy-dense, economically accessible diets that are also engineered to be tasty (Moss 2013). Mainstream explanations have been blaming individuals – the victims. Consequently, most policy and commentary on how to stem obesity and being overweight focus on interventions at the individual level (for example, Popkin 2009; Vallgårda 2015). This focus must shift toward structural, systemic solutions.

My goal in this chapter is to establish the neoliberal diet's causal connections to obesity. This liaison became tragically relevant in 2020, when obesity became one of the major co-morbidity factors accounting for severe or fatal cases of COVID-19. 'Co-morbidities' such as diabetes, heart disease, hypertension and other maladies are enhanced by obesity and being overweight. There is ample consensus in many medical journals about this fact (for example, Hernández-Garduño 2020). This strong consensus highlights the tremendous relevance of discussing the neoliberal diet, what it consists of, whether individuals can modify it or what is the role for the state in shaping food choices – or reshaping the system of agricultural production and income inequality. My focus here is thus on the socioeconomic determinants of obesity via the neoliberal diet.

OBESITY AND THE NEOLIBERAL DIET

Close to 1 billion people continue to face the challenge of not having access to sufficient quantities of food; they are food insecure in its quantitative modality. But a larger and growing number now face the prospect of accessing mostly energy-dense foods that are nutritionally compromised. This is a new form of food insecurity that has less to do with quantity and more with quality. Alas, not all calories are made equal. Energy-dense foods or pseudo-foods are rich in fats and sugars that the human body may turn into adipose tissue or cholesterol. Michael Pollan (2006, 91) calls energy-dense foods the Western diet, or purchased, store-bought food. Such edibles are particularly high in refined flour, saturated fat, sugars and processed foods low in fiber (Moss 2013). Western diseases closely follow this diet: obesity, type 2 diabetes, hypertension, stroke and heart disease (Popkin 2009).

In 2000, the World Health Organization (WHO) set off alarm bells about the 'obesity epidemic'. It was following a United states official who had used this label a year earlier (Moss 2013). The scholarly and popular literature on food and weight has proliferated massively in the intervening period, with many observers giving advice to eaters on what are the healthier food fares. The WHO found that obesity has tripled worldwide since 1975. In 2016, there were 1.9 billion overweight adults and 650 million obese adults. Already, obesity kills more people than being underweight. Ominously, 340 million children and adolescents, aged 5–19, are overweight or obese (WHO 2020).

FROM INDIVIDUAL CHOICE TO SOCIAL STRUCTURES

The WHO suggests that obesity is preventable, but how? For most analysts, even many critical ones, obesity and being overweight could be modified if people only paid attention to their good advice and made the right food choices – 'voting with forks' (Nestle 2013 [2002], 372). The assumption is that what we eat is simply a matter of personal or individual choice, part of a given lifestyle that may or may not include routinely engaging in physical activity and exercise.

The individual consumption focus was causally articulated by the United Nations Special Rapporteur on the Right to Food as follows: 'The food we eat determines how we produce food' (De Schutter 2009). Many observers in critical food studies have followed the same view of taking the individual as the main agent or point of intervention: to modify eating, 'one meal at a time' or 'voting with your fork' (Nestle 2013 [2002]). This is an illusion. If there are larger social-structural and political forces at work, including inequality and agricultural subsidies, then the point of intervention would be quite different from the individual consumer: it takes a societal actor like the state to modify income inequality and which agricultural products become the raw materials that shape food choices in the first place. I argue that social structure and not individuals is the locus where state interventions should be made. The main foci should be on amending social inequality within and between nations and reshaping the system of agrifood production.

Sociologist Anthony Winson (2013) is particularly critical of what Julie Guthman (2011), also critically, calls the energy-balance model of explanation: 'Too many nutrients going in and not enough energy expended' (Winson 2013, 6). The proposed solution, says Winson, was both 'remarkably simplistic and entirely focused on individual responsibility: eat less and/or move more' (ibid.). The individual focus raises the state policy dilemma of whether 'to govern or not to govern', that is, to let individuals choose food for themselves or steer populations to eat as their governments see fit (Vallgårda 2015). If it were merely an issue of individual choice, then perhaps educational efforts and some regulation (for example, labeling or taxes) geared to shape such choice ('the conduct of conduct') would be in order. But studies have confirmed that increased education and knowledge of food are not enough to counter inequality (Nestle 2013 [2002], 392–393). You still need to be able to afford healthy comestibles.

Julie Guthman also critiques the energy balance explanation of obesity being overweight for its individualistic approach. She addresses systemic causes so that solutions can be better focused on the social structure (Guthman 2011, 1–23). Labeling obesity as an epidemic is a big problem for her, as this would assume that being fat is a disease rather than, more likely, a condition associated with a disease (ibid., 32). She asks, for instance, if your neighborhood makes you fat: is it a matter of obesogenic environments at large? While the correlation of such spaces with the prevalence of fat people is established, the causality is inverted: people live in obesogenic places because their class status does not allow them to do otherwise. Class and race are the key factors determining where one can live. Guthman rightly critiques the attempt to elevate genetic predisposition to explain obesity, as this may amount to 'reinscribe the idea that race is biological' (Guthman 2011, 97). That is to say, most associations in the United States between 'race' and obesity harken back to prior class or socioeconomic conditions like slavery, not biology.

CONCLUSION: THE STATE AND REGULATION

Among the four dynamic elements of the food regime and its diet – state, agribusiness multinationals, biotechnology and supermarkets –the state is the societal factor that could reshape them all. The roots of social inequality are varied and include class, gender and 'race'/ethnic constructions of difference. Income inequality, in particular, has been growing in the United States and other nations since the 1980s, which coincides with the neoliberal turn in the development model (Otero 2018). Both income inequality and food production and distribution are in turn shaped or facilitated by neoliberal state intervention. There is an intrinsic hypocrisy in states of the wealthy nations, especially the United States, in preaching free trade and keeping the state from intervening in the economy, while practicing agricultural subsidies that benefit primarily large farmers and agribusiness multinationals. The United States agribusiness lobby has spent well over $100 million since 2008; hence their interests remain highly represented. On the other hand, many states in developing nations have been pressured to adopt the policy recommendations of the International Monetary Fund, geared to keep state intervention from subsidizing agriculture, while the World Bank promotes so-called non-traditional agricultural exports – at the expense of food for the domestic market – so that the foreign debt can be paid.

Because food regimes are very entrenched structures, it will take social movements to change the character of state intervention in pursuit of public interest in healthier food and equitable income. Society's big challenge is thus to push for changes in state policies in a progressive direction. Whereas neoliberal policies have primarily promoted the interests of large agribusiness corporations, the point now is to steer state intervention toward promoting healthier agricultural and food production and engage in income and wealth redistribution policies. Such a shift requires nothing short of a strong social movement from below, of the type that seems to be building to convince governments to fight climate change.

Reforming these structures could allow people to have affordable nutritional choices that are ecologically sustainable. Transcending individualistic and consumption-focused approaches will help us appreciate that, with bottom-up pressure from social movements, the state, not the individual, is best positioned to implement change when it comes to food 'choices' and food production. I use 'the state' in a strict sense, as the sphere of domination or the institutions of government. But an expanded notion of the state includes civil society, the sphere of hegemony or consent, made up of private associations, unions, social movements, the family, churches and so on. It is the progressive sectors of civil society which must mobilize to exert pressure on the state for it to become a societal actor in the wider public interest regarding broad access to healthy food.

ACKNOWLEDGEMENTS

This chapter draws on sections from the introduction to *The Neoliberal Diet* (Otero 2018). Thanks very much to Haroon Akram-Lodhi, Bettina Engels and Ben McKay for useful comments on an earlier draft. Any remaining limitations are my own.

FURTHER READING

Clapp, J. (2020), *Food*, Cambridge: Polity Press.
Howard, P.H. (2016), *Concentration and Power in the Food System: Who Controls What We Eat?* London: Bloomsbury.
Nestle, M. (2018), *Unsavory Truth: How Food Companies Skew the Science of What We Eat*, New York: Hachette Books.
Winders, B. (2017), *Grains*, Cambridge: Polity Press.
Wise, T.A. (2019), *Eating Tomorrow: Agribusiness, Family Farmers, and the Battle for the Future of Food*, New York: The New Press.

REFERENCES

De Schutter, O. (2009), The meatification of diets and global food security, UN Special Rapporteur on the Right to Food Speech to the European Parliament, accessed 18 July 2016 at www.europarl.europa.eu/climatechange/doc/speeche_Mr_de_schutter.pdf.
Friedmann, H.; McMichael, P. (1989), Agriculture and the state system: The rise and decline of national agricultures, 1870 to the present, *Sociologia Ruralis*, 29(2), 93–117.
Guthman, J. (2011), *Weighing In: Obesity, Food Justice, and the Limits of Capitalism*, Berkeley, CA: University of California Press.
Hernández-Garduño, E. (2020), Obesity is the comorbidity more strongly associated for COVID-19 in Mexico: A case-control study, *Obesity Research and Clinical Practice*, 14(4), 375–379.
McMichael, P. (2009), A food regime analysis of the 'world food crisis', *Agriculture and Human Values*, 26(4), 281–295.
Moss, M. (2013), *Salt, Sugar, Fat: How the Food Giants Hooked Us*, New York: Random House.
Nestle, M. (2013 [2002]), *Food Politics: How the Food Industry Influences Nutrition and Health*, Berkeley, CA: University of California Press.
Pollan, M. (2006), *The Omnivore's Dilemma: A Natural History of Four Meals*, New York: Penguin.
Popkin, B. (2009), *The World Is Fat: The Fads, Trends, Policies and Products That Are Fattening the Human Race*, New York: Avery.
Popkin, B. (2014), Nutrition, agriculture, and the global food system in low and middle income countries, *Food Policy*, 47(August), 91–96.
Otero, G. (2018), *The Neoliberal Diet: Healthy Profits, Unhealthy People*, Austin, TX: University of Texas Press.
Vallgårda, S. (2015), Governing obesity policies from England, France, Germany and Scotland, *Social Science and Medicine*, 147(December), 317–323.
WHO (World Health Organization) (2020), Overweight and obesity, accessed 1 April 2020 at www.who.int/en/news-room/fact-sheets/detail/obesity-and-overweight.
Winson, A. (2013), *The Industrial Diet: The Degradation of Food and the Struggle for Healthy Eating*, Vancouver: University of British Columbia Press.

60. Meatification

Tony Weis

INTRODUCTION

Meatification is a term given to identify the momentous shift in meat from the periphery to the centre of human diets, which is interwoven with important aspects of agrarian change on a world scale, namely the rapid expansion of industrial grain, oilseed and livestock production (Weis 2013). The meatification of diets has been a powerful yet underappreciated aspiration of development and modernity. One reflection of this is the steady growth in per capita meat consumption in the context of a fast-rising human population: whereas 3 billion people consumed an average of 23 kg of meat in 1961, in 2018 over 7.6 billion people consumed an average of 45 kg of meat (FAOSTAT 2020). This translates into a rough quadrupling in the total annual volume of meat produced and consumed, in just a few generations, and an eight-fold increase in the annual population of slaughtered animals on a world scale, from around 8 billion to over 70 billion (ibid.). The importance of meatification in conceptions of development and modernity is also evident in consumption disparities between rich and poor.

There is a growing consensus that the dramatic increase in livestock production and consumption on a world scale bear heavily, and unequally, on a range of environmental, social and ethical problems, including climate change, biodiversity loss, food insecurity, rising levels of non-communicable diseases, intensifying zoonotic disease risks, declining antibiotic effectiveness and animal suffering (IPCC 2019; Godfray et al. 2018; Poore and Nemecek 2018; Crist et al. 2017; Springmann et al. 2016; Wallace 2016; Machovina et al. 2015; Weis 2013). Yet despite this recognition, it is widely assumed that per capita meat consumption is bound to continue rising on a world scale as the world population grows towards 10 billion (OECD and FAO 2019), an expectation that is often wrapped up in ambiguous language about dietary change linked to increasing affluence. This is a significant aspect of claims-making about the need for continuing technological innovation geared to enhancing productivity and thus meeting future demand for food.

Meatification is a term that is meant to cut through abstractions about the trajectory of dietary change, marking the gravity of rising meat consumption as a basis for problematizing it. This chapter stresses the importance of understanding meatification through a political economic lens and placing the exploding scale and changing nature of livestock production in the context of the relentless pursuit of profits, capital accumulation and growth in the agro-food sector and capitalism more generally. It begins by stressing how patterns of meatification do not stem from physiological necessity or improved health but rather reflect socioeconomic inequalities. It then indicates the crucial role that rising demand for meat has had in enabling the continuing growth of industrial grain and oilseed production in the face of chronic surpluses, and highlights some of the basic ways that capitalist imperatives shape the organization of livestock production, before suggesting how critical attention to meatification can contribute to anti-systemic thinking. In exploring the structural dimensions of meatification, it seeks to challenge radical scholars and activists who might be inclined to see this as a marginal concern, following in strong intellectual and political currents on the left that have associated concerns about animals with bourgeois inclinations (Sanbonmatsu 2005). The overarching message is that the need to challenge and ultimately reverse meatification is much bigger than a 'single-issue' moral campaign: it is fundamental to the prospect of transforming contemporary agro-food systems and building more sustainable, equitable and humane alternatives.

MEATIFICATION AS EFFECTIVE DEMAND

Rising demand for meat and animal products obviously relates to a range of factors, some of which have very long roots and nothing to do with capitalism, from simple palate pleasure, to beliefs about the necessity of animal protein, to cultural venerations, including strong associations with masculinity (Adams 2010 [1990]). The attitudes about meat that developed over the 10,000 year history of agriculture arose out of fundamentally different sorts of relations with animals and food than those that prevail across much of the world today. On the production side, small populations of a variety of animal species fed mostly on fallowed farmland, crop stubble and household food wastes, and by scavenging on organized pastures and unorganized grasslands and forests. This meant that encounters with animals on and around farms and pastures were a regular part of life for most people, and that livestock did not compete for the product of arable land. Well into the twentieth century, planted crops were overwhelmingly consumed directly by humans, save for the overwintering needs of livestock in temperate regions. On the food and nutrition side, farming cultures tended to prize meat, milk and eggs as sources of protein, though relatively small animal populations meant that consumption tended to be sporadic, and often around particular celebrations, contributing to an elevated status in many cultural cuisines.

Whatever nutritional value milk, eggs and meat once had or still have in contexts of protein scarcity cannot begin to explain or morally justify contemporary global patterns of meatification. Patterns of meatification do not reflect the desire to improve human health or reduce malnutrition (or what might be seen as real, material demand) but rather pivot on uneven *effective demand*, which essentially means the monetary capacity to act on consumer preferences.[1] Three basic elements of meatification make this clear. First, meatification strongly mirrors global disparities. People in high-income countries consume over twice as much meat per year as the world average, and far more protein than their bodies actually need, while people in low-income countries consume less than half as much meat per year as the world average. Further, most growth in the coming decades is expected to unfold not in food-insecure regions but among the surging upper and middle classes in rapidly industrializing economies (OECD and FAO 2019; Godfray et al. 2018). Second, patterns of meatification involve highly regressive dynamics for food availability, as disparities in meat consumption are entwined with disparities in grain and oilseed consumption, with large shares of protein and other useable nutrition in crops being lost before it is converted into flesh, eggs and dairy. The pressure this exerts on world markets reverberates on the cost of key staples in many of the world's poorest countries in contexts where food security has been significantly tied to grain imports, with vulnerability that grows worse in light of the especially severe and proximate threats to agricultural productivity in many poor countries. Third, there is compelling evidence that the heavy consumption of animal foods is a major contributing factor in rising rates of obesity and many non-communicable diseases (e.g. cardiovascular disease, type-2 diabetes, hypertension, fatty liver disease and some cancers) while, conversely, diverse plant-based diets contribute to improved health outcomes on the whole (Willett et al. 2019; Springmann et al. 2016; Lim et al. 2012).

MEATIFICATION AS PROFITABLE SURPLUS ABSORPTION

In capitalist economies, demand and supply are dialectically related, meaning that neither causes the other in simple, unidirectional ways. Thus, while meatification reflects the uneven effective demand exerted by wealthier populations, in part, it cannot be understood only as a response to consumer preferences. A fuller picture emerges when increasing meat production is connected to the pursuit of profits, accumulation and incessant growth in agro-food systems, which requires attention to the consistently large agricultural surpluses in many industrialized countries.

As McMichael argues in this volume, the rise of chronic agricultural surpluses was a pivotal aspect in the development of the global food economy in the twentieth century, emerging from a series of interlocking technological innovations including the development of combustion engines, synthetic fertilizers, high-yielding seeds, pesticides and greatly expanded irrigation capacity, which drove soaring yields of output per farmer. While this had a major part in population growth on a world scale (along with an array of public health improvements) and might appear on the surface like a categorically good outcome for human development, chronic surpluses pose intractable economic challenges for farmers, states and corporations. For farmers, chronic surpluses deflate unit prices and contribute to the competitive pressure to grow in scale and continually reinvest in labour-saving technology to cope with smaller margins, a treadmill that inevitably expunges many farming livelihoods – the famous 'get big or get out' refrain issued by the former United States Secretary of Agriculture (Cochrane 2003). For states and corporations, the deflationary price pressures associated with chronic surpluses threatens the prospect of continual growth in the agro-food system as a whole. This necessitates government intervention, which has taken a range of forms, but ultimately depends upon finding durable economic ways of converting surpluses into ongoing sources of profits (Weis 2013; Berlan 1991).

The United States government began to wrestle with the challenges posed by soaring productivity in the mid-twentieth century, soon followed by the European Community. One route for the state to stabilize prices for farmers was to buy and hold back a portion of annual crop production, though this presents a serious fiscal burden and largely defers structural pressures into swelling reserves. Another notable response in the 1950s and 1960s was to establish aid and subsidized trade programmes, 'dumping' surpluses in the name of humanitarian impulses (and Cold War alliances), which had a major impact in transforming diets in many low-income countries, in particular towards wheat. But these programmes were also a fiscal burden and increasingly gave way to commercial exports, leaving a legacy – food security hinged to world grain markets – that remains especially problematic for many low-income countries. While state-sponsored surplus dumping and the ensuing export sales did enhance growth prospects for high-yielding monoculture production, the bigger mechanism for profitably absorbing grain surpluses that emerged in the twentieth century was to cycle them through fast-rising populations of concentrated livestock, starting with chickens and followed by pigs (Winders and Nibert 2004; Berlan 1991).

Lappé (1991 [1971]) first drew attention to the socially inequitable and environmentally damaging impacts of 'burning' rising amounts of usable nutrition by cycling it into the metabolic processes of animals. This systematic nutritional wastage has been a crucial mechanism for transforming chronic crop surpluses into low-margin sources of profits, because the perceptual values attached to meat, milk and eggs – along with many externalized costs – allow them to sell for slightly higher prices than the feed used to produce them. In other words, meatification provided a durable way to increase effective demand for the booming productivity of industrial monocultures, or to profitably absorb chronic surpluses, while also opening a range of other value-added opportunities in animal genetics, processing and retailing (Weis 2013). This absorptive capacity is clearly reflected in the fact that nearly one-third of the world's cropland is now devoted to producing livestock feed, which includes a much greater share of arable land in the temperate world. It is also evident in the explosive growth of soybean production on a world scale, with soybean acreage having quadrupled since 1961 (FAOSTAT 2020), led by the United States and the southern cone of South America.

While the surplus absorptive capacity of meatification rests upon nutritional inefficiencies, there is still a competitive discipline to reduce feed inputs per unit of livestock production. The pressure to optimize feed together with the omnipresent pressure to reduce labour costs are central to the nature of technological innovation and industrial design, including the nature of genetic enhancement; specialization of breeding sites; reliance on artificial insemination; intensity of bodily confinement; ubiquity of physical mutilations; proliferation of antibiotics; automation of feeding, watering, monitoring and ventilation systems; and mechanisms to remove and store great concentrations of feces and urine (Weis 2013). These compulsions are also at the heart of why meatification has centred upon chickens and pigs (witnessed in the volume of production exceeding population growth) and why these species – which now account for 70 per cent of the total annual volume of global meat production (FAOSTAT 2020) – are expected to account for nearly all further increases, as they convert feed to flesh less inefficiently than ruminants and can be produced at greater densities with faster turnover time.

MEATIFICATION AS A STRUCTURAL PROBLEM

Industrial livestock production resembles a spatially disaggregated assembly line that is marked by the growing scale and shrinking number of operations and driven by consolidating corporate power in animal genetics and breeding, grain and oilseed processing, slaughter and packing and various retailer sectors. The ways that animal lives and deaths are organized and accelerated across this assembly line not only greatly reduces the relative human labour involved in livestock production, but fundamentally alters it from the complex interspecies relations that prevailed through the long history of animal husbandry in mixed farming and herding. The nature of these industrial labour processes, from breeding and growing to live transport and slaughter, are filled with emotional anguish and a range of health risks. This also relates to a broader perceptual change: whereas the interspecies relations with livestock animals were a familiar part of everyday life for most people over many millennia, they have increasingly been cast out of sight in modern societies (Weis 2013).

However, it is incontrovertible that diets heavy in animal products tend to require much more land and other resources than plant-based diets and, as indicated at the outset, there is mounting evidence that the rising scale of livestock production and consumption is contributing to a series of urgent problems. This recognition can be a valuable starting point into wider conversations about the course of world agriculture and food systems, such as the narrowing of power, the transformation of agrarian livelihoods, the pathology of pursuing endless growth and the immeasurable interspecies violence unfolding. In this, it is important to be clear that while dietary change may be implicated in problems, responses cannot be left at the scale of individual choices. As Guthman (2011) has stressed, 'voting with your fork' can only do so much, and there is a need to appreciate the structural dimensions of dietary change.

CONCLUSION

This chapter has made the case that the meatification of diets is deeply entangled with the course of agrarian change under capitalism, and that the exploding scale and changing nature of livestock consumption and production are vital subjects in the field of critical agrarian studies. Central to this is the dialectic relation between uneven effective demand (where wealthier consumers command much more meat, grains and oilseeds than do poor ones) and the profitable absorption of chronic surpluses (as the wastage of useable nutrition helps enable the continuing growth of grain and oilseed production), which expand the scope for capital accumulation in a range of sectors. Thus, just as struggles to confront meatification cannot be separated from broader anti-systemic political movements, struggles to rebuild more ecologically rational and equitable agro-food systems cannot ignore the need to question and reverse meatification.

Moving forward, it is important for scholars in the field of critical agrarian studies to consider the sociocultural dimensions of meatification, especially in contexts where growth is unfolding quickly (e.g. Hansen and Jakobsen 2020), and how changing consumption relates to transnational commodity flows – meat, feed, breeding stock, antibiotics, etc. – and established and newly emerging constellations of corporate power (e.g. Schneider 2017). It is also essential to examine the specific ways that livestock production is being transformed, including both technological innovations and the social relations of production, along with the range of costs this entails for the environment, public health, workers in this sector and the animals in industrial systems. Wallace (2016) provides one brilliant example of this with respect to rapid disease evolution and attempts to contain it in industrial livestock production, making it clear that capital accumulation in this sector is underpinned by the externalization of incalculable risks.

NOTE

1. Discussions of food insecurity should always foreground this distinction, because there are large numbers of people around the world who have a real but *in*effective demand for food, in that they are hungry or malnourished but lack the money to meet basic needs.

FURTHER READING

Godfray, H.C.J.; Aveyard, P.; Garnett, T.; Hall, J.W.; Key, T.J.; Lorimer, J.; Pierrehumbert, R.T.; Scarborough, P.; Springmann, M.; Jebb, S.A. (2018), Meat consumption, health, and the environment, *Science*, 361(6399), https://doi.org/10.1126/science.aam5324.

Imhoff, D. (ed.) (2011), *The CAFO Reader: The Tragedy of Industrial Animal Factories*, Berkeley, CA: University of California Press.

Weis, T. (2013), *The Ecological Hoofprint: The Global Burden of Industrial Livestock*, London: Zed Books.

Willett, W., Rockström, J., Loken, B., Springmann, M., Lang, T., Vermeulen, S. et al. (2019), Food in the Anthropocene: The EAT–Lancet commission on healthy diets from sustainable food systems, *The Lancet*, 393(10170), 447–492.

REFERENCES

Adams, C. (2010 [1990]), *The Sexual Politics of Meat: A Feminist-Vegetarian Critical Theory*, New York: Bloomsbury.

Berlan, J.-P. (1991), The historical roots of the present agricultural crisis, in Friedland, W.H.; Busch, L.; Buttel, F.H.; Rudy, A.P. (eds), *Towards a New Political Economy of Agriculture*, Boulder, CO: Westview Press, 115–136.

Cochrane, W.W. (2003), *The Curse of American Agricultural Abundance: A Sustainable Solution*, Lincoln, NE: University of Nebraska Press.

Crist, E.; Mora, C.; Engelman, R. (2017), The interaction of human population, food production, and biodiversity protection, *Science*, 356(6335), 260–264.

FAOSTAT (Food and Agriculture Organization Statistics Division) (2020), *Production and Resource STAT Calculators*, accessed 15 June 2020 at www.fao.org/faostat/en/.

Godfray, H.C.J.; Aveyard, P.; Garnett, T.; Hall, J.W.; Key, T.J.; Lorimer, J.; Pierrehumbert, R.T.; Scarborough, P.; Springmann, M.; Jebb, S.A. (2018), Meat consumption, health, and the environment, *Science*, 361(6399), https://doi.org/10.1126/science.aam5324.

Guthman, J. (2011), *Weighing In: Obesity, Food Justice, and the Limits of Capitalism*, Berkeley, CA: University of California Press.

Hansen, A.; Jakobsen, J. (2020), Meatification and everyday geographies of consumption in Vietnam and China, *Geografiska Annaler: Series B, Human Geography*, 102(1), 21–39.

IPCC (2019), *Climate Change and Land: IPCC Special Report on Climate Change, Desertification, Land Degradation, Sustainable Land Management, Food Security, and Greenhouse Gas Fluxes in Terrestrial Ecosystems. Summary for Policymakers*, accessed 15 May 2020 at www.ipcc.ch/report/srccl/.

Lappé, F.M. (1991 [1971]), *Diet for a Small Planet*, New York: Ballantine.

Lim, S.S., Vos, T., Flaxman, A.D., Danaei, G., Shibuya, K., Adair-Rohani, H. et al. (2012), A comparative risk assessment of burden of disease and injury attributable to 67 risk factors and risk factor clusters in 21 regions, 1990–2010: A systematic analysis for the Global Burden of Disease Study 2010, *The Lancet*, 380(9859), 2224–2260.

Machovina, B.; Feeley, K.J.; Ripple, W.J. (2015), Biodiversity conservation: The key is reducing meat consumption, *Science of the Total Environment*, 536, 419–431.

OECD; FAO (2019), *OECD-FAO Agricultural Outlook 2019–2028*, Paris: OECD Publishing, accessed 10 May 2020 at doi.org/10.1787/agr_outlook-2019-en.

Poore, J.; Nemecek, T. (2018), Reducing food's environmental impacts through producers and consumers, *Science*, 360(6392), 987–992.

Sanbonmatsu, J. (2005), Listen, ecological Marxist! (Yes, I said animals!), *Capitalism, Nature, Socialism*, 16(2), 107–114.

Schneider, M. (2017), Dragon head enterprises and the state of agribusiness in China, *Journal of Agrarian Change*, 17(1), 3–21.

Springmann, M.; Godfray, H.C.J.; Rayner, M.; Scarborough, P. (2016), Analysis and valuation of the health and climate cobenefits of dietary change, *PNAS*, 113(15), 4146–4151.

Wallace, R. (2016), *Big Farms Make Big Flu: Dispatches on Infectious Disease, Agribusiness, and the Nature of Science*, New York: Monthly Review Press.

Weis, T. (2013), *The Ecological Hoofprint: The Global Burden of Industrial Livestock*, London: Zed Books.

Willett, W., Rockström, J., Loken, B., Springmann, M., Lang, T., Vermeulen, S. et al. (2019), Food in the Anthropocene: The EAT–Lancet commission on healthy diets from sustainable food systems, *The Lancet*, 393(10170), 447–492.

Winders, B.; Nibert, D. (2004), Consuming the surplus: Expanding 'meat' consumption and animal oppression, *International Journal of Sociology and Social Policy*, 24(9), 76–96.

61. Digital agriculture

Kristina Dietz and Franza Drechsel

INTRODUCTION

The Brain controls everything: how much fertilizer or water is needed by which lettuce head and when; at what time and into which container it should be re-potted; where each robot is currently located and where it is needed more urgently; as well as when the lettuce should be packaged and how long it will be edible for. The Brain – a nickname given to the computer program that oversees all of this – was put to use in 2018 at an indoor farm in California run by agritech start-up Iron Ox. It renders human labour almost redundant, ensures the economical use of water, energy and nutrients, guarantees efficient production in a small area and provides a fresh daily supply of healthy heads of lettuce (Winik 2018).

Iron Ox's Brain ties in with initiatives and discourses around the digitalization of agriculture. In struggles over the transformation of the global agri-food system in the era of global warming, soil depletion, population growth, increasing urbanization and enduring hunger, digitalization is gaining ever more importance. The agri-food system ranges from the production and circulation of agricultural commodities to the consumption of food items. Digitalization of agriculture means the introduction of digital technological innovations into all areas of the agri-food system: agricultural inputs (seeds, insurance and finances), on-farm operations, food processing, transport, storage, retail and consumption. Examples of such technologies are automatic and data-intensive precision technologies, cloud computing, artificial intelligence and robotics. Proponents of digital agriculture argue that data-based digital technologies help to increase efficiency and productivity on fields and in stables, foster resource-efficient, sustainable and climate-smart agricultural production and increase income and prosperity in rural areas (see Newell and Taylor 2018; Trendov et al. 2019). Hence, digital agriculture promises 'triple win' solutions to the global food crisis, the ecological and climate crisis and the social crisis of reproduction in rural areas. It is also argued that digitalization can enhance transparency and democratic control, as producers and consumers can use digital devices to trace the production process, transport routes and quality standards (Trendov et al. 2019; see also Thomasson 2019).

The Food and Agriculture Organization of the United Nations (FAO) expects that over the next 10 years, the global agri-food system will undergo 'dramatic changes' driven by 'advanced digital technologies' such as robotics, blockchains and artificial intelligence (Trendov et al. 2019, 1). However, beyond promises, narratives and expectations, still not much is known about the state-of-the-art of activities in digital agriculture. Many publications and initiatives on the topic come from policy circles and focus on pathways, potentials, future outlooks and the setting up of new institutions (for an overview, see Klerkx et al. 2019). The European Union (EU) has commissioned a series of reviews on digital agriculture (Pesce et al. 2019; Poppe et al. 2013), and in 2019, 25 EU member states signed a declaration called 'A smart and sustainable digital future for European agriculture and rural areas' (European Commission 2020). The FAO has published a status report and is about to establish an international digital council for food and agriculture (FAO 2020; Trendov et al. 2019). The World Bank has produced a future outlook (2017) and a source book (2019), and the Organisation for Economic Co-operation and Development has published a policy-oriented publication on digital opportunities for trade in the agri-food system (Jouanjean 2019).

Most journal articles published on the topic either focus uncritically on the technical aspects of the implementation of digital technologies in farming, on the role and management of Big Data in smart farming, or on human–technology interactions, or they discuss the transformative potential of digital technologies for the agri-food system. Many of these publications are authored by agricultural scientists or engineers, and are not (yet) based on original empirical data but rather review existing publications or newly available technologies (for an overview, see Fielke et al. 2020; Friedrichs et al. 2019; Klerkx et al. 2019; Panetto et al. 2020; Vanderroost et al. 2017; Wolfert et al. 2017). Critical scholars, in contrast, have asked to what extent digitalization and smart automation technologies are shaping labour and social relations in the countryside, lead to job losses (Carolan 2020; Rotz et al. 2019b), or impact power relations through data development, control and ownership (Rotz et al. 2019a), or to what extent the decision to invest in automated technologies is linked to overall political and structural transformations in the sector (Vik et al. 2019). Starting from these studies, we argue that critical agrarian studies has a lot to contribute to an academic scrutiny of the impacts of digital agriculture on agrarian change.

In this chapter, we aim to identify entry points for such an endeavour by providing an overview of what is already taking place with regard to digital transformations beyond policy debates and future outlooks. Based on a literature and media review, we identify different areas of and activities in digital agriculture, which range from farm robotics, autonomous systems, remote sensing and precision technologies at the farm level, to genome editing at the input level, to the integration and coordination of transport and investments via blockchains and platform technologies. We illustrate our descriptions with examples taken from the media, policy and grey literature, and a growing number of critical scholarly publications (Klerkx et al. 2019; Lioutas and Charatsari 2020; Mooney 2018; Prause et al. 2020; Rotz et al. 2019a, 2019b). Departing from a critical agrarian studies perspective and the general observation that technology is never socially neutral (Strate 2012), we discuss who will benefit from digitalization, who are the corporate actors behind the digital revolution, what they do and to what extent digitalization will have an impact on power relations in the global agri-food system through the penetration of non-sector-specific companies such as Google.

The chapter is structured as follows. In the next section, we introduce the areas of agriculture where digitalization is taking place and describe the status of implementation. This is followed by an analysis of the expected implications for labour, social structures and power relations in the agri-food system. In the conclusion, we summarize our findings and identify starting points for future research on digital agriculture from the field of critical agrarian studies.

THE AREAS OF DIGITAL AGRICULTURE

Current developments point to three central areas of digital transformation in agriculture: precision and remote sensing technologies and intelligent systems (robotics, autonomous systems, machine learning) at the farm level; genetic engineering and modification methods (genome editing) at the input level for farming; and integration and coordination along the agri-food production chain (platform technologies).

At the farm level, precision and remote sensing technologies and intelligent systems include autonomous machines, drones and robots. Autonomous machines are still operated by humans, despite automated propulsion technologies. Drones are remote-controlled aircraft (or watercraft) without passengers. If they are able to move autonomously, they are classified as robots, which are characterized by the fact that they are computer-controlled, or programmed, which means that they act without any direct human operation. Some are equipped with artificial intelligence and are thus capable of learning. The deployment of machines at the farm level is, of course, nothing new. Wherever machines are in use, they are usually controlled by humans. With digitalization, this is set to change. More and more of the newest machinery has sensors and cameras to collect data, with the aim of supporting human decision-making regarding sowing, watering and harvesting. World market-leading agricultural machinery manufacturers John Deere (United States (US)), CNH (Netherlands and United Kingdom), AGCO (US) and Kubota (Japan) are all developing autonomous, driverless tractors (Mooney 2018, 13). Case IH and New Holland (both brands of CNH) introduced autonomous tractors in 2016. The New Holland tractor can be controlled from a computer or tablet from home, while other tractors can be programmed to autonomously do the driving and input applications.

Though some of these driverless tractors are already in use (Bennett 2019), it still remains a challenge to fully replicate the farmer's role in this area (Jurgens 2020). However, developers envision that the driverless vehicles will soon be able to plough by themselves, decide independently which seed should be sown and when, which fertilizer and pesticide a plant should be treated with, how much irrigation it needs and when it will be harvested. Already in 2014, the French company Naio Technologies brought into operation an autonomous tractor called Oz for weeding and hoeing. Oz uses laser and camera technology to navigate through the fields and sensors to distinguish crops from weeds (Carolan 2020). For vineyards, the weeding Oz is called TED and for vegetables DINO. This machinery – driverless or not – requires a corresponding infrastructure (large surface areas of farmland, monocultures, roads, workshops, petrol stations) as well as suitable crops that are compatible with automated sowing, planting, weeding, hoeing and harvesting; for example, wheat, corn, vines, vegetables and soy. The more complicated harvesting, for example of coffee, bananas and cocoa, will likely continue to be performed by hand.

Drones in agriculture are deployed in and on water and in the air. They monitor farmed plants for pest or fungus infestation, produce aerial photos for mapping purposes or conduct plant pollination as roboticized bees. The main advantages lie in crop dusting and the management of small and large farms alike for rice and other crops (Ipsos 2017, 10). Viticulturists in the US use drones to monitor the growth and activity of plants (Karpovicz 2018). In Malaysia, drones have replaced manual labour not only to monitor oil palm plantations but also to spray pesticides (Avtar et al. 2019; Ismail 2020). Drones are used for the surveillance of workers on these plantations, too (Mooney 2018, 15). In Australia, cattle farmers are experimenting with drones to herd their livestock and to direct them to greener pasture (Sheehan 2019). Aquatic drones appear particularly promising in deep-sea fishing, where they drive fish into the nets autonomously or repair and monitor mobile fish cages (Mooney 2018, 15f.). Drones are a growth industry. They are most common in the US and Canada, but the market for drones is growing rapidly in Japan, Australia and the EU, as well as in Brazil, India and China (Trendov et al. 2019).

Robots are already in use at all stages in the supply chain. They substitute human labour in produce cultivation, as the example of the Brain shows, assist in the processing, inspecting and palletizing of beer barrels, as in the Belgian Haacht Brewery (FANUC n.d.), package and label vegetable produce, such as for Amazon's distribution centres, mix cocktails (BBC 2018), fry burgers (Vincent 2020) and milk cows (Carolan 2020). Robotics in dairy farming is a growth industry already worth US$1.6 billion. More than 80 per cent of the world's robotic milking systems are located in north-western Europe (the Netherlands, Germany, Denmark, Norway) (Walsh 2016). This will continue to grow in the coming future, particularly in the US, where less than 5 per cent of dairy farms utilize robots or automated milking systems (Mulvany 2018).

The essential aspect of said machinery is that it is equipped with global positioning system and sensor technologies, through which it not only receives programmed instructions but also translates all work processes and other relevant information into data. Data on soil conditions and photosynthesis, climate and weather conditions and on workers' travel and break times are linked up with satellite information, combined to create key indicators and stored on data platforms. They are available to both the producers and the manufacturing companies. To the former, they allow for a timely and targeted intervention – say, in the case of infestation, drought or nutrient deficits – and the surveillance of work. The latter receive constant feedback on the performance of their systems and learn how they can optimize them.

At the input level, genome editing in particular is emerging as the latest innovation in the toolbox of genetic engineering, modification methods and synthetic biology (SynBio). Genome editing refers to techniques in which specialized enzymes that have been modified can insert, replace or remove DNA from a genome 'with a high degree of specificity' (Friedrichs et al. 2019, 208). Particularly the genome editing system CRISPR/Cas9 (Clustered Regularly Interspaced Short Palindromic Repeats, using the CRISPR-associated protein 9) is being used widely, as it enables the development of easily deployable, low-cost tools for innovation in agriculture, industrial biotechnology and other sectors relating to the bioeconomy (ibid.). While the production of genetically modified seeds in the past required the complicated insertion – with a high error rate – of the genetic sequence of one plant into the genome of another, today genomes can be split up into sequences, cut up and recomposed in a targeted manner in what is called computer-based genome editing. That is, new plant varieties can be created at the click of a mouse. Proponents argue that these are more resistant to pests, aridity or heat, produce more fruit, contain more oil or develop specific flavours. Genome editing allows for more than the breeding of plants; disease-resistant pigs or cattle that develop more muscle mass can also be genetically designed. In July 2018, the European Court of Justice decided that these new procedures would be grouped together with conventional methods of genetic engineering. Genetically modified meat or fish products are therefore not yet approved in the EU, but in Canada and the US the sale of genetically modified salmon is already permitted (eurofins n.d.).

SynBio techniques make it possible to artificially produce food, tissue, scents and flavourings using yeast and algae (TAB 2015). This in turn allows for a reduction of both climate-related risks and dependency on labour-intensive production processes, as, for example, in the production of vanilla. The extraction of natural vanilla is based on a labour- and time-intensive process of growing and fermenting the pods of the vanilla orchid. The global demand for natural vanillin, mainly produced in Indonesia and Madagascar, is increasing steadily and prices on world markets have skyrocketed. Farmers that have specialized in vanilla production thus generate stable and increasing incomes. However, food makers such as Nestlé, in order to keep their costs low and guarantee a constant supply, have started to produce synthetic vanillin. In comparison to natural vanilla, synthetic vanilla flavouring – that is almost identical to the original – can be produced in a lab using yeast DNA at very little cost. Here, the engineered yeast cells provide a new source of 'cheap nature' (Moore 2015) through their ability to convert one substance into another, thus replacing the cost of labour that until now was required to produce natural vanilla. Artificial vanilla is being applied in the food, beverage, perfume and pharmaceutical industries. The majority of the most common products such as chocolate or breakfast cereals are now made using artificial vanilla, although US regulations for ice cream imply that most of it be made using natural vanilla (Bomgardner 2016; Vijayalakshmi et al. 2019). Synthetic food production is not, however, limited to flavourings. The US agribusiness Cargill is investing in the development and marketing of meat cell cultures for burgers. The so-called 'Impossible Burger' – which contains legume haemoglobin or heme, produced using genetically modified yeast and which makes the burger seem to bleed – is already available in US restaurants as well as Burger King and supermarkets, also beyond the US (Piper 2019).

A third area of digitalization that is significant for the entire supply chain is that of platform and financial technologies, such as cryptocurrencies and blockchains. Blockchains are technical procedures for the network-based, swift handling of trade and financial transactions. They consist of chronologically organized chains of data units, the so-called 'blocks'. Blockchains can be used in multiple ways in agriculture; contracts, seed databases and land registries can all be managed digitally via blockchains (Mooney 2018, 23–26; Sanghera 2018). Companies along the agricultural supply chain can use blockchains in order to accelerate the production, processing and transport of certain foods through direct, digital access to consumer data. For example, if a supermarket is running low on soy yoghurt, it can input this information into a blockchain, which then leads, without any further human communication, to the soy producer increasing production. The blockchain will ensure that the transport vehicles are available at the right moment to take the soy to the already informed processing plant. As soon as the yoghurt is produced, the trucks are once again on standby to take the product to the respective supermarket. At no point is there any need for direct contact, as quantities, prices and deadlines are all digitally communicated via the blockchains.

Blockchains do not only link up companies, producers and farmers. Consumers can be integrated, too, which makes it much easier for them to trace the products they buy. In our fictive example, a consumer buying said soy yoghurt could be dissatisfied with the quality. Due to the supply via blockchain, it would not only be possible for the consumer to find out which factory had processed the soy into yoghurt, but it might also be possible to trace the soy back to the farm on which it had been grown. In Peru, an initiative between various companies is developing a blockchain to ensure better meat quality. When cattle producers vaccinate their animals, this information will be entered into the blockchain. This will enable the consumer who buys a beef steak to scan a code on the packaging to be assured that the cow was vaccinated (Jimenez 2019; New India Express 2019).

Blockchains are supposed to lower transaction costs and reduce delivery times and food waste. Such procedures are also interesting for small-scale producers. Using blockchains, subsidies can be directly transferred, products can be marketed without intermediaries and inputs can prove their authenticity, as long as there is internet and an adequate technical device available (Cornish 2018; Sanghera 2018). Another advantage of blockchains is the improved traceability of processed food in particular. This is becoming more relevant in times where stricter safety regulations are being put in place and food allergies are on the rise (Prause et al. 2020; Sanghera 2018).

DIGITAL AGRICULTURE FROM A CRITICAL AGRARIAN STUDIES PERSPECTIVE

Beyond the promises in terms of increased productivity, efficiency, climate protection and prosperity, another set of questions emerges when studying digital agriculture from a critical agrarian studies perspective. How does the introduction of digital technologies shape and influence processes of agrarian change? Who wins and who loses from the digital revolution in agriculture? How do automation and drones transform labour relations and working conditions in agriculture? What effects does digitalization have on the social structure in agriculture? To what extent does digitalization impact power relations in the global agri-food system, for example through the emergence of new start-up companies and the penetration of non-sector-specific companies, such as Google, into agriculture?

These and other questions have been raised by critical scholars in recent years. With regard to labour, scholars argue that digitalization and smart automation will most likely lead to job losses in particular areas, for example in the dairy industry, in the plantation cultivation of fruit and vegetables and in monocultural sugar cane production, where masses of seasonal migrant workers will be displaced by automation or the reduction of labour to a few higher-skilled jobs (Carolan 2020; Rotz et al. 2019b). Throughout the twentieth century, one of the reasons for the increase in productivity in agriculture was the mechanization and automation of labour; that is, the replacement of human labour by machines. This trend will continue and will accelerate under conditions of digitalization, with the effects of an increase in rural unemployment and a continued pauperization of the so-called 'labouring poor' or 'classes of labour' (Bernstein 2010); that is, those mostly low-skilled male and female workers who already today have to pursue their social reproduction through a range of insecure, seasonal and often informal jobs. This transformation in employment opportunities will hit rural dwellers in the Global South the most, as human labour in agriculture in the Global North has already been tremendously reduced through mechanization since the mid-twentieth century. Instead of the promised increase in income and prosperity for rural societies, digitalization will make reproduction conditions more difficult for those who depend on selling their labour power. On the contrary, automation offers few, but mostly well-paid, highly skilled jobs. For those family farmers who can afford automation devices, it can additionally displace family labour, which could contribute to the survival of the farm, especially when the freed-up family labour can secure additional income from off-farm work (Carolan 2020, 194).

It is not only jobs that will be lost and requirements that will be changed through digitalization; work processes as such are being altered. Those who control the machines are in turn monitored and controlled by them. Drones monitor workers on oil palm plantations, harvesting machines in the sugarcane sector record how much each worker has harvested over which period of time (and how many workers there were) and when (and how often) they took a break or were slower than others (Brunner 2017). Digitalization serves, above all, the surveillance, standardization and acceleration of work, resulting in a reduction of the autonomous action scope of workers worldwide. In other words, digital technologies are a tool to control labour processes in order to extract greater surplus value.

Digitalization also affects the labour of self-employed small-scale farmers, especially when labour-intensive small-scale production becomes redundant as a result of genetic modification and synthetic production methods. During the 1990s and 2000s, genetic research into rice triggered major protests (AFP 2000). Thai jasmine rice accounted for a large share of the fragrant rice imported to the US. Patented genetic modification would make it possible for this type of rice to be cultivated in the US. These plans have not been implemented thus far, but could potentially cause small-scale farmers in Thailand to lose their livelihood if rice cultivation is no longer a worthwhile activity (Winn 2011).

The discussion about the labour effects of digital agriculture points out that digitalization in agriculture will change and/or deepen rural social structures. Whereas low-skilled rural (migrant) workers will lose income opportunities, which will lead to an increase in the rural 'surplus population', in theory, small-scale peasants could profit from digital technologies. Apps with precise weather forecasts, digital tools that help to recognize fungal infestations or robots which replace dangerous human labour such as pesticide spraying – these developments could make a farmer's life easier. However, against the backdrop of a still existing digital divide – unequal access to information and communication technologies – there will be winners and losers of such technologies, not only between small farmers and agribusiness companies, but also within the group of peasants. Although many do use smartphones for daily communication and the organization of farming processes, not all have the material means to frequently update their hardware and software in order to use new apps. Others live in remote rural areas where broadband internet is not the norm. Gaining from new digital devices in agriculture is thus a question of class (and certainly of gender) and geographical location. Thus, digital technologies are not automatically equalizers; instead, they can deepen class and rural–urban differences.

Besides labour and social differentiation, a key issue of digital agriculture is its impacts on power relations in the global agri-food system, particularly through data development, control and ownership. Rotz et al. (2019a, 208) argue that digitalization represents the most significant change in the food system since the Green Revolution of the 1950s and 1960s and the neoliberalization of agriculture in the 1970s and 1980s, which resulted in a growth in and concentration of corporate power. The global agri-food system is today dominated by a small number of 'food empires': transnational firms that control all parts of the food chain, from agricultural inputs and food packaging to transport and retailing (Howard 2016; van der Ploeg 2020). In 2017, 70 per cent of worldwide trade in agricultural commodities was dominated by four corporations (Archer Daniels Midland, Bunge, Cargill and Louis Dreyfus Company); four companies (ChemChina Syngenta, Bayer, BASF and Corteva Agriscience) dominated 70 per cent of agrochemicals; and John Deere, Kubota, CNH Industrial and AGCO held more than 38 per cent of the world's land machinery market shares (Heinrich Böll Foundation et al. 2017, 26; Mooney 2018, 8f.). Concentration and centralization are likely to continue; therefore, according to Alistair Fraser (2019), so-called 'data grabs' accompany today's restructuring of agriculture.

The main beneficiaries from digital technologies and the 'sharecropping of agricultural data' (Rotz et al. 2019b, 117) are, above all, financially strong enterprises and corporations. This is due, on the one hand, to the technologies being capital-intensive and, on the other, to the growing competition for cultivation and consumer data. Agricultural machines with digital technology are expensive and their use is only profitable over a sufficiently large area. Consequently, they are acquired mainly by enterprises and capitalist agriculturalists with access to capital and land. Indeed, there are all kinds of assurances that digitalization will make genetic engineering procedures cheaper and thereby offer small start-ups the possibility to invest in them as well. However, start-ups are frequently bought out by large corporations, for often enormous sums. In 2017, for instance, John Deere invested US$305 million to acquire the start-up Blue River Technology that makes 'see-and-spray' robots that affix to tractors (Kolodny 2017; Mooney 2018, 12–13). This apparent competition thus leads to further monopolization.

Furthermore, the competition for access to and control of data does not only increase the rivalry among companies and the tendencies towards concentration within a single sector, but across sectors as well. The agri-food system is, thus far, characterized by corporate concentration; however, this concentration has occurred horizontally, or within each sector of seeds, fertilizers, agrochemicals, machinery and food and beverage processing (Mooney 2018, 4f.). Current concentration processes are, by contrast, marked by vertical integration; that is, companies are merging with corporations from other sectors. The recent merger in 2017 between Bayer and Monsanto, both amongst the top seven companies of global seed and pesticide producers (Heinrich Böll Foundation et al. 2017, 20), implies that today's Bayer has even more control over which seed variety should be sprayed with which pesticide in order to grow best. Monopolization will therefore be accelerated by digitalization and players from other sectors will join the competition, as the data acquired today become the capital for making profits tomorrow.

Internet corporations like Google, Amazon and Alibaba are particularly interested in the cultivation and consumer data gathered by agricultural machines. This makes the machinery sector also appealing for producers of pesticides and fertilizers, who adjust their products based on the cultivation data. Mooney (2018, 35) suggests that the three nodes along the agricultural supply chain – inputs, agricultural machinery and food processing – will be controlled by only one or two companies in the future. In line with the case of Bayer today, vertical integration and centralization will, under the conditions of digital agriculture, mean that the company producing agricultural machine X will decide which of its own seeds will be sown when, and which of its own fertilizers and pesticides will be used and at what time. The machine is simply incompatible with the products of other companies, securing the market position of the company that manufactured it. The farmers, then, are increasingly unable to make their own decisions, as they are forced to use the products from the same company as a complete package.

Finally, blockchains promise decentralized and transparent, tamper-proof dealings in networks because, at least theoretically, all computers in a network – that is, all those involved, from farmers and agriculturalists, agribusinesses and banks, to supermarket chains, etc. – can form blocks (Sanghera 2018). But this promise is based on the assumption that all actors within a network are equally powerful; as is also the assumption under 'ideal' market conditions. Yet, the power across the network is in effect distributed highly unequally: the more computing power an actor has, the more influence they can exert.

Regarding the benefits in terms of a transformation towards sustainability in agriculture, digitalization raises the hopes of increasing efficiency on the fields, thereby guaranteeing more resource-conserving, sustainable and climate-neutral production (Lioutas and Charatsari 2020). If, in the future, measuring probes report nutrient levels in the soil, this will allow for a more demand-based use of fertilizer. Regular information on fungus or pest infestation levels provided by drones can facilitate the more targeted and selective use of pesticides and herbicides, replacing the blanket spraying that is common today. Consequently, agribusiness and digitalization proponents argue, soils will be less overfertilized and fewer insects as well as people will die from pesticides or herbicides (Ismail 2020). A second argument is that digital technologies will raise yields and productivity, as a natural world that is monitored 'around the clock' can be exploited more efficiently in terms of profit maximization (Trendov et al. 2019). What both arguments ignore, however, are the social relations and ecological contradictions associated with an agriculture geared towards surplus value production and the domination of nature. After all, in capitalism, even a system of digitalized agriculture must grow. The expansion of machine-readable production processes in monocultures will displace not only locally adjusted modes of production focused on biodiversity, but will also cause rebound effects. Driven by the compulsion to continue growing, more and more farmland will be needed so that it can be worked by the digitally enhanced machines. The development of this land will only be possible through the displacement of other forms of use, the transformation of green spaces and wetlands and deforestation. Given the coupling of machinery and genome editing – genetically modified seeds, fertilizers and pesticides – the increase of cultivated land will also increase the overall input of nutrients and pesticides, despite any potential reduction thereof per individual land unit.

Up until the 1960s and 1970s, capitalist agriculture was marked by enormous productivity increases. The reasons for this were the reduction of production costs through high-yielding seed varieties, judicious water application, the use of synthetic fertilizers and pesticides and mechanization. Since the 1980s, crop yields have begun to decline in proportion to the use of fertilizer, and the same is true for the ratio between harvest yields and chemical inputs. Increasingly, heavier tractors and harvesting machines increase the compaction of the soil, resulting in lower soil fertility (Weis 2010). This shows that even technologically advanced agricultural production relies on nature's capacity to regenerate. Ignoring this fact and instead assuming that a technologically enhanced domination of nature will solve the ecological crisis is precisely what will lead to its intensification.

CONCLUSION

In this chapter, we have explored the state of the art of activities in digital agriculture in different areas, ranging from farm robotics, autonomous systems, remote sensing and precision technologies at the farm level, to genome editing at the input level, to the integration and coordination of transport and investments via blockchains and platform technologies. While many of the existing contributions on digitalization uncritically focus on the technical aspects of the implementation of digital technologies and the transformative potentials of digital technologies for the agri-food system with regard to increasing productivity, efficiency and sustainability, critical approaches focus on different questions. These questions include: How do digital technologies shape and influence processes of agrarian transformation? Who will be the winners and losers of the revolution 4.0 in agriculture? How will intensified automation transform labour and labour relations? What effects will the introduction of digital technologies have on social differentiation in rural areas? And to what extent will digitalization impact power relations in the global agri-food system? The challenge for critical agrarian studies is to significantly expand the engagement with digital agriculture and to improve the evidence base to address all of these important questions.

FURTHER READING

Carolan, M. (2020), Automated agrifood futures: Robotics, labor and the distributive politics of digital agriculture, *Journal of Peasant Studies*, 47(1), 184–207.

Fraser, A. (2019), Land grab/data grab: Precision agriculture and its new horizons, *Journal of Peasant Studies*, 46(5), 893–912.

Klerkx, L.; Jakku, E.; Labarthe, P. (2019), A review of social science on digital agriculture, smart farming and agriculture 4.0: New contributions and a future research agenda, *NJAS – Wageningen Journal of Life Sciences*, 90–91, 1–16.

Mooney, P. (2018), Blocking the chain: Industrial food chain concentration, Big Data platforms and food sovereignty solutions, accessed 31 July 2020 at www.land-conflicts.fu-berlin.de/_media_design/ Policy-Paper-Reihe/BlockingTheChain_Englisch_web.pdf.

Rotz, S.; Duncan, E.; Small, M.; Botschner, J.; Dara, R.; Mosby, I.; Fraser, E.D.G. (2019), The politics of digital agricultural technologies: A preliminary review, *Sociologia Ruralis*, 59(2), 203–229.

REFERENCES

AFP (2000), Thai farmers protest against GM rice, accessed 21 October 2020 at www.iatp.org/news/thai -farmers-protest-against-gm-rice.

Avtar, R.; Snak Suab, S.; Yunus, A.P.; Kumar, P.; Srivastava, P.K.; Ramaiah, M.; Juan, C.A. (2019), Applications of UAVs in plantation health and area management in Malaysia, in Avtar, R.; Watanabe, T. (eds), *Unmanned Aerial Vehicle: Applications in Agriculture and Environment*, New York: Springer, 85–100.

BBC (2018), Robot bartender: The bar where machines mix drinks, accessed 20 October 2020 at www .bbc.com/news/av/technology-42737844.

Bennett, C. (2019), Driverless goes big in farming 2019, accessed 19 October 2020 at www .agprofessional.com/article/driverless-goes-big-farming-2019.

Bernstein, H. (2010), Rural livelihoods and agrarian change: Bringing class back in, in Long, N.; Jingzhong, Y.; Yihuan, W. (eds), *Rural Transformations and Development: China in Context*, Cheltenham, UK and Northampton, MA, USA: Edward Elgar Publishing, 79–109.

Bomgardner, M.M. (2016), The problem with vanilla: After vowing to go natural, food brands face a shortage of the favored flavor, accessed 20 October 2020 at https://cen.acs.org/articles/94/i36/ problem-vanilla.html.

Brunner, J. (2017), Die Verhandlungsmacht von Arbeiter*innen und Gewerkschaften in landwirtschaft-lichen Transformationsprozessen: Eine Analyse des Zuckerrohrsektors im Bundesstaat São Paulo, GLOCON Working Paper No. 6.

Carolan, M. (2020), Automated agrifood futures: Robotics, labor and the distributive politics of digital agriculture, *Journal of Peasant Studies*, 47(1), 184–207.

Cornish, C. (2018), Ag tech fundraising doubles as farmers seek disruptive solutions, *Financial Times*, 8 January, accessed 31 July 2020 at www.ft.com/content/02950380-d6f2-11e7-a303-9060cb1e5f44.

eurofins (n.d.), Genetically modified salmon, accessed 31 July 2020 at www.eurofins.de/food-analysis/ food-news/food-testing-news/genetically-modified-salmon/.

European Commission (2020), EU member states join forces on digitalisation for European agriculture and rural areas, accessed 20 October 2020 at https://ec.europa.eu/digital-single-market/en/news/eu -member-states-join-forces-digitalisation-european-agriculture-and-rural-areas.

FANUC (n.d.), Palletising kegs of beer: Robotic handling solutions drive efficiency in beverage industry, accessed 20 October 2020 at www.fanuc.eu/uk/en/customer-cases/palletising-beer-kegs.

FAO (2020), Realizing the potential of digitalization to improve the agri-food system: Proposing a new international digital council for food and agriculture: A concept note, accessed 20 October 2020 at www.fao.org/3/ca7485en/ca7485en.pdf.

Fielke, S.; Taylor, B.; Jakku, E. (2020), Digitalisation of agricultural knowledge and advice networks: A state-of-the-art review, *Agricultural Systems*, 180, 1–11.

Fraser, A. (2019), Land grab/data grab: Precision agriculture and its new horizons, *Journal of Peasant Studies*, 46(5), 893–912.

Friedrichs, S.; Takasu, Y.; Kearns, P.; Dagallier, B.; Oshima, R.; Schofield, J.; Moreddu, C. (2019), An overview of regulatory approaches to genome editing in agriculture, *Biotechnology Research and Innovation*, 3(2), 208–220.

Heinrich Böll Foundation; Rosa Luxemburg Foundation; Friends of the Earth Europe (eds) (2017), Agrifood atlas: Facts and figures about the corporations that control what we eat, accessed 20 October 2020 at www.boell.de/sites/default/files/agrifoodatlas2017_facts-and-figures-about-the-corporations-that-control-what-we-eat.pdf?dimension1=ds_konzernatlas.

Howard, P.H. (2016), *Concentration and Power in the Food System: Who Controls What We Eat?*, London: Bloomsbury.

Ipsos (2017), Commercial drone adoption in agribusiness: Disruption and opportunity, accessed 1 October 2021 at www.ipsos.com/sites/default/files/ct/publication/documents/2017-09/Commercial-Drone-Adoption-in-Asia-Pacific-Agribusiness.pdf.

Ismail, I. (2020), #Tech: Dawn of the drones, accessed 20 October 2020 at www.nst.com.my/lifestyle/bots/2020/09/624371/tech-dawn-drones.

Jimenez, D. (2019), Peru implementa tecnología blockchain para trazabilidad de productos cárnicos, accessed 20 October 2020 at https://es.cointelegraph.com/news/peru-implements-blockchain-technology-for-traceability-of-meat-products.

Jouanjean, M.-A. (2019), Digital opportunities for trade in the agriculture and food sectors, OECD Food, Agriculture and Fisheries Papers, No. 122.

Jurgens, J. (2020), Autonomous tractors, excavators and more: Examining the path toward a driverless tomorrow, accessed 19 October 2020 at www.aem.org/news/autonomous-tractors-excavators-and-more-examining-the-path-toward-a-driverless-tomorrow.

Karpowicz, J. (2018), How are drones making a difference in viticulture?, accessed 23 November 2021 at https://www.commercialuavnews.com/forestry/drones-viticulture.

Klerkx, L.; Jakku, E.; Labarthe, P. (2019), A review of social science on digital agriculture, smart farming and agriculture 4.0: New contributions and a future research agenda, *NJAS – Wageningen Journal of Life Sciences*, 90–91, 1–16.

Kolodny, L. (2017), Deere is paying over $300 million for a start-up that makes 'see-and-spray' robots, accessed 1 October 2021 at https://finance.yahoo.com/news/deere-paying-over-300-million-000807879.html.

Lioutas, E.D.; Charatsari, C. (2020), Big Data in agriculture: Does the new oil lead to sustainability?, *Geoforum*, 109, 1–3.

Mooney, P. (2018), Blocking the chain: Industrial food chain concentration, Big Data platforms and food sovereignty solutions, accessed 31 July 2020 at www.land-conflicts.fu-berlin.de/_media_design/Policy-Paper-Reihe/BlockingTheChain_Englisch_web.pdf.

Moore, J.W. (2015), Nature in the limits to capital (and vice versa), *Radical Philosophy*, 193(September/October), 9–19.

Mulvany, L. (2018), Robots coming to a dairy farm near you, accessed 23 November 2020 at www.farmprogress.com/dairy/robots-coming-dairy-farm-near-you.

New India Express (2019), Andhra government to adopt blockchain tech to end land record tampering, accessed 20 October 2020 at www.newindianexpress.com/states/andhra-pradesh/2019/dec/15/andhra-government-to-adopt-blockchain-tech-to-end-land-record-tampering-2076359.html.

Newell, P.; Taylor, O. (2018), Contested landscapes: The global political economy of climate-smart agriculture, *Journal of Peasant Studies*, 45(1), 108–129.

Panetto, H.; Lezoche, M.; Hernandez Hormazabal, J.E.; del Mar Eva Alemany Diaz, M.; Kacprzyk, J. (2020), Special issue on Agri-Food 4.0 and digitalization in agriculture supply chains: New directions, challenges and applications, *Computers in Industry*, 116, 1–3.

Pesce, M.; Kirova, M.; Soma, K.; Bogaardt, M.-J.; Poppe, K.; Thurston, C.; Monfort Belles, C.; Wolfert, S.; Beers, G.; Urdu, D. (2019), Research for AGRI committee: Impacts of the digital economy on the food-chain and the CAP, accessed 23 November 2020 at www.europarl.europa.eu/RegData/etudes/STUD/2019/629192/IPOL_STU(2019)629192_EN.pdf.

Piper, K. (2019), Meatless meat is becoming mainstream – and it's sparking a backlash: The growing pushback against Impossible and Beyond burgers in fast-food chains, explained, accessed 20 October 2020 at www.vox.com/future-perfect/2019/10/7/20880318/meatless-meat-mainstream-backlash-impossible-burger.

Poppe, K.J.; Wolfert, S.; Verdouw, C.; Verwaart, T. (2013), Information and Communication Technology as a driver for change in agri-food chains, *EuroChoices*, 12(1), 60–65.

Prause, L.; Hackfort, S.; Lindgren, M. (2020), Digitalization and the third food regime, *Agriculture and Human Values*, 38, 641–655.

Rotz, S.; Duncan, E.; Small, M.; Botschner, J.; Dara, R.; Mosby, I.; Reed, M.; Fraser, E.D.G. (2019a), The politics of digital agricultural technologies: A preliminary review, *Sociologia Ruralis*, 59(2), 203–229.

Rotz, S.; Gravely, E.; Mosby, I.; Duncan, E.; Finnis, E.; Horgan, M.; Horgan, M.; LeBlanc, J.; Martin, R.; Neufeld, H.T.; Nixon, A.; Pant, L.; Shalla, V.; Fraser, E.D.G. (2019b), Automated pastures and the digital divide: How agricultural technologies are shaping labour and rural communities, *Journal of Rural Studies*, 68, 112–122.

Sanghera, A. (2018), How adoption of blockchain technology will disrupt agriculture: Understanding the implications of blockchain technology in agriculture, accessed 20 October 2020 at https://inc42.com/resources/blockchain-technology-agriculture/.

Sheehan, M. (2019), How drones are being used in Australia to make farming more efficient, accessed 1 October 2021 at https://foresttech.events/how-drones-are-being-used-in-australia-to-make-farming-more-efficient/.

Strate, L. (2012), If it's neutral, it's not technology, *Educational Technology*, 52(1), 6–9.

TAB (Office of Technology Assessment at the German Bundestag) (2015), Synthetic biology – the next phase of biotechnology and genetic engineering, Working Report No. 164, accessed 31 July 2020 at www.tab-beim-bundestag.de/en/pdf/publications/summarys/TAB-Arbeitsbericht-ab164_Z.pdf.

Thomasson, E. (2019), Carrefour says blockchain tracking boosting sales of some products, accessed 20 November 2020 at https://de.reuters.com/article/us-carrefour-blockchain-idUKKCN1T42A5.

Trendov, N.M.; Varas, S.; Zeng, M. (2019), Digital technologies in agriculture and rural areas: Status report, accessed 23 November 2020 at www.fao.org/3/ca4985en/CA4985EN.pdf.

van der Ploeg, J.D. (2020), From biomedical to politico-economic crisis: The food system in times of Covid-19, *Journal of Peasant Studies*, 47(5), 944–972.

Vanderroost, M.; Ragaert, P.; Verwaeren, J.; De Meulenaer, B.; De Baets, B.; Devlieghere, F. (2017), The digitization of a food package's life cycle: Existing and emerging computer systems in the logistics and post-logistics phase, *Computers in Industry*, 87, 15–30.

Vijayalakshmi, S.; Disalva, X.; Srivastava, C.; Arun, A. (2019), Vanilla-natural vs artificial: A review, *Research Journal of Pharmacy and Technology*, 12(6), 3068–3072.

Vik, J.; Stræte, E.P.; Hansen, B.G.; Nærland, T. (2019), The political robot: The structural consequences of automated milking systems (AMS) in Norway, *NJAS – Wageningen Journal of Life Sciences*, 90–91, 1–9.

Vincent, J. (2020), This robot fry chef on rails can be yours for $30,000, accessed 20 October 2020 at www.theverge.com/2020/10/6/21503892/miso-robotics-flippy-roar-robotic-fry-chef-on-sale-price.

Walsh, J. (2016), The development of a next generation robotic milking parlour: Final summary ROTABOT, accessed 23 November 2020 at https://cordis.europa.eu/project/id/315407/reporting.

Weis, T. (2010), The accelerating biophysical contradictions of industrial capitalist agriculture, *Journal of Agrarian Change*, 10(3), 315–341.

Winik, E. (2018), New autonomous farm wants to produce food without human workers, *MIT Technology Review*, 3 October, accessed 31 July 2020 at www.technologyreview.com/2018/10/03/139937/new-autonomous-farm-wants-to-produce-food-without-human-workers/.

Winn, P. (2011), Rice wars: Has the US pirated Thailand's finest rice?, accessed 21 October 2020 at www.pri.org/stories/2011-01-24/rice-wars-has-us-pirated-thailands-finest-rice.

Wolfert, S.; Ge, L.; Verdouw, C.; Bogaardt, M.-J. (2017), Big Data in smart farming: A review, *Agricultural Systems*, 153, 69–80.
World Bank (2017), ICT in agriculture: Connecting smallholders to knowledge, networks, and institutions, accessed 23 November 2020 at https://openknowledge.worldbank.org/handle/10986/27526.
World Bank (2019), Future of food: Harnessing digital technologies to improve food system outcomes, accessed 23 November 2020 at https://openknowledge.worldbank.org/handle/10986/31565.

62. COVID-19

A. Haroon Akram-Lodhi

ZOONOTIC DISEASES

Zoonotic diseases are human bacterial and viral infections that originate in animals and which cross the species barrier. While something on the order of 60 per cent of emerging new diseases cross from animals to humans (Farm Animal Investment Risk and Return 2020), over the course of the last three decades the process of transiting across the species barrier appears to have accelerated as 'over 30 new human pathogens have been detected in the last three decades, 75 per cent of which have originated in animals' (World Health Organization 2014). Since 2000 there have been three pandemics: severe acute respiratory syndrome, or SARS, in 2003; H1N1, commonly known as swine flu, in 2009; and now COVID-19, from which people can directly die, as they have in huge numbers, or from which people can be made vulnerable to other conditions from which they die. There have also been major regional outbreaks of zoonotics. The success of these diseases lie in them entering human immune systems that do not have the antibodies to resist infection precisely because they have recently crossed from animals to humans.

Zoonotic transmission from animal to human is as old as settled agriculture. The question that therefore needs to be asked is why has zoonotic transmission seemingly accelerated. The answer lies in the structural characteristics of the capitalist world food system which, as Eric Holt-Giménez (2019, 89) reminds us, 'is working precisely as a capitalist food system is supposed to work: it expands constantly, concentrating wealth in a few, powerful monopolies, while transferring all the social and environmental costs onto society'. The capitalist world food system produces ever cheaper food that moderates the need for real wage increases and facilitates the redistribution of income from wages to profits, creating the inequality well documented by Piketty (2020) and many others. Since the first emergence of a global food economy in the latter quarter of the nineteenth century (see McMichael, this volume) cheap food has been and remains integral to the logic of capitalism because it lowers the cost of reproducing labour, increases the rate of exploitation and in so doing increases the rate of surplus value (Akram-Lodhi 2012). Yet the capitalist world food system requires massive quantities of unpaid care and domestic reproductive work. It also requires both capitalism's capacity to work through nature and nature's capacity to work through capitalism, as new agricultural frontiers, in terms of space, in terms of nature, in terms of labour and in terms of commodification, are enclosed and as the unpaid work of nature provides the energy upon which the capitalist world food system operates. It is this very logic that has created a food system that operates 'as both propulsion for and nexus through which pathogens of diverse origins migrate from the most remote reservoirs to the most international of population centers' (Wallace 2020).

THE CAPITALIST WORLD FOOD SYSTEM

To understand this process, it is of central importance to understand the character of the food system. In 2018 the total value of global food sales was around US$8.7 trillion (Clapp 2020, 10). However, it must be stressed that the contemporary capitalist food system is not concerned with the production of food *per se*. Rather, it is concerned with the production of commodities whose value can be realized through market sales that generate profits for the producer of the commodities. In this light, the contemporary capitalist world food system is dominated by global agro-food transnational capital, which are driven by world market prices and the financial imperatives of short-run profitability (Akram-Lodhi 2019). It is characterized by the relentless food commodification processes that underpin broadening and deepening 'supermarketization' as well as the increasing oligopolization of agro-chemicals, food trading and food processing and manufacturing (Clapp 2020). Agro-food transnational capital source, store, ship and sell food on a global scale, off-loading risk and other costs and reaping economies of scale that produce profitability despite the narrow margins that have driven the concentration and centralization of agro-food transnational capital during the twenty-first century. Indeed, times of crisis increase the profitability of the global supermarkets that structure the operation of the capitalist world food system (Akram-Lodhi 2012). At the point of production, the dominant model of the capitalist world food system is the fossil fuel-driven, large-scale, linear-flow-through capital-intensive industrial agriculture megafarm (Qualman et al. 2018). This produces, through enclosures of land and multiple other resources as well as the market imperative of cost competitiveness, an agrarian crisis for many small-scale petty commodity-producing peasant farmers around the developing world. As Harriet Friedmann so cogently reminds us,

> transnational agrifood capitals disconnect production from consumption and relink them through buying and selling ... Suppress[ing] ... particularities of time and place in both agriculture and diets ... [t]hey have created an integrated productive sector of the world economy, and peoples of the Third World have been incorporated or marginalized—often both simultaneously—as consumers and producers. (Quoted in Bello and Baviera 2010, 45)

The result is that peasant farmers face a 'simple reproduction squeeze' because world market prices fail to cover the costs of production at the farmgate (Akram-Lodhi and Kay 2010). A core market for agro-food transnational capital are relatively affluent global consumers in the developed and the developing world whose food preferences have shifted toward 'healthier', 'organic', 'green' and 'safer' products that have significantly larger profit margins. At the same time, for the global middle class the capitalist world food system sustains the mass production of very durable highly processed food manufactures that are heavily reliant on bad fats, high fructose corn syrup and sodium. The lower profit margins of highly processed food mean that significantly higher volumes of products must be shifted. For both segments, the capitalist world food system fosters 'meatification': 'the increasing and highly uneven global consumption of meat' that is 'highly skewed toward wealthier consumers' (Weis 2013, 4; and this volume). The capitalist world food system is thus predicated upon global human inequality. The capitalist world food system is sustained by states, and most notably the huge farm subsidies allocated by the United States and the European Union to industrial agriculture (Clapp 2020), by the international financial and development institutions that govern the global economy in their support of supermarketization (World Bank 2007) and by the big philanthropy that finances research that deepens the capital intensity of the system (Fridell and Konings 2013).

The COVID-19 pandemic has thrown the capitalist world food system onto the precipice of a crisis, if crisis is understood as an interruption in the process of capital accumulation (see Chernomas et al., this volume). The networks of interconnected global food supply chains that run from farm to fork are designed to foster enhanced specialization across countries that is based upon the lowest unit labour costs and hence the highest rates of exploitation. While meeting the market imperative has as its correlate the increasing monopolization of key segments in global food supply chains, low prices are sustained, real wage increases can be dampened and value can be extracted from the food system in the form of corporate profits. However, a less understood by-product of increasingly monopolistic control of a highly specialized food system is its vulnerability.

VULNERABILITIES IN THE DEVELOPED COUNTRIES

In particular, the COVID-19 pandemic has demonstrated a vulnerability of the capitalist world food system that was perhaps less readily apparent: that an economic system that produces social marginalization, particularly among gendered and racialized peoples, but which is based upon the extraction of surplus labour from those very same gendered and racialized workers, requires gendered and racialized workers from whom to extract surplus labour. The lockdowns across the developed countries in the wake of the pandemic led to the wholesale withdrawal of workers from the food system, with critical implications for food supplies in the developed countries: supplies of farm labour, often migrant, commonly low paid and lacking in social protection withdrew, particularly as borders closed; transportation and logistical systems contracted as trucks, trains and planes stopped moving because they are vectors of human-to-human transmission; and the meatpacking industry around the world, where workers work in frequently dangerous conditions, in not enough places, temporarily shut down because of concentrated outbreaks of COVID-19 among a workforce that works both in poor sanitary conditions and in close proximity to each other. The lack of resilience in the capitalist world food system has been recognized by agro-food transnational capital itself, which lamented that 'the food supply chain is breaking' (Tyson 2020), with the monopolization of meatpacking by four key companies in the United States being a specific vulnerability. Clearly, the gendered and racialized workers that keep global food supply chains operating in the developed countries are both essential and insecure, and this creates a central contradictory vulnerability at the heart of the capitalist world food system. As industrialized agricultural megafarms do not have the storage space or resources needed to retain crops and to keep animals alive the result has been rotting vegetables and euthanized farm animals, a massive increase in the food waste regime that while integral to the operation of the capitalist world food system has now become a site of overproduction (Gille 2012).

Moreover, there is another dimension to the vulnerability of the capitalist world food system. Women in both the United States and the United Kingdom were more likely to have lost their jobs and/or suffered a fall in earnings after the pandemic took hold (Adams-Prassl et al. 2020). This was particularly the case in low-income households, where women were disproportionately employed in food service, cleaning and maintenance, and personal care, among other occupations; many 'essential services' have a food dimension.[1] Women workers in such positions were also far more likely to be racialized. Yet it is precisely these low-income, gendered and racialized households that disproportionately relied upon women's incomes to sustain food provisioning. At the same time, in addition to the loss of income, the food system relies upon unpaid care and domestic reproductive work to put food on the plate and reproduce biologically and socially the members of the household. Here, the COVID-19 pandemic appears to have exacerbated the gender division of labour. Whether still working or not, women in the United Kingdom were typically spending at least an extra 1.5 hours on childcare and home schooling every day, for a total of around six hours. The extent of the deterioration in the intrahousehold gender division of labour was positively associated with income (Adams-Prassl et al. 2020). This took place even as women in households that had lost income had to strategize as to how to best maintain food consumption for their households, from which emerged worries about food security that women in particular faced within those developed countries that lacked adequate social protection systems. The COVID-19 pandemic is a gendered care crisis of proportions that have not been witnessed for 75 years wrapped up in 'the worst human and economic crisis of our lifetimes' (United Nations Economic and Social Research Council 2020).

VULNERABILITIES IN THE DEVELOPING COUNTRIES

With specific respect to the operation of the food system in developing countries, the pandemic has been equally severe to that witnessed in the developed countries but is likely to become far worse over time. As in the developed countries, the path from farm to fork also involves lengthy supply chains that very frequently cross borders. Parts of these food supply chains are global. Just as in the developed countries, the impact of the pandemic was to clog these food supply chains with unforeseen bottlenecks, with critical implication for food security; even in Sub-Saharan Africa it is estimated that in many countries only a fifth of food is eaten by the household that grows the food (Tschirley et al. 2015), suggesting that widespread exposure to lengthy food supply chains has the possibility of enhancing vulnerability to food insecurity when bottlenecks emerge.

However, the principal driver of deteriorating access to food was falling incomes in circumstances where many households allocate at least half of their income to food purchases. The majority of workers in developing countries work in the informal economy, where wages are low, the terms and conditions of employment are poor and indeed where work can be both infrequent and unsafe.[2] Workers in the informal economy, of whom 52 per cent are men and 48 per cent are women (International Labour Organization (ILO) 2018a), need their jobs in order to be able to access food, but the impact of the pandemic was to either close informal businesses or dramatically reduce their turnover, both of which increased unemployment, constrained access to food and in the process presented a new threat to the food security of hundreds of millions (Anthem 2020). The ILO estimated that hundreds of millions lost their jobs in early 2020, and that half the global workforce, or 1.6 billion people, as a result faced a threat to their livelihoods as a result of the COVID-19 pandemic (ILO 2020). Certainly, in 2014, when the outbreak of Ebola in Sierra Leone led to the institution of a strict lockdown, food insecurity quickly emerged as a major threat (Elston et al. 2017). Recent evidence from Senegal indicates that the pandemic is having an impact on incomes and food security (Le Nestour and Moscoviz 2020). Similar evidence has been found in Bangladesh, where people reliant on daily wages have reported dramatic income declines and have had to cut spending and hence food consumption (Ali et al. 2020). Globally, the World Food Programme (2020) expected the numbers facing acute hunger to rise by 130 million in 2020, doubling the world-wide total, as a result of the pandemic.

In developing country rural economies the pandemic was acutely felt, in myriad ways. In many developing countries it is well established that lockdowns forced hundreds of millions of newly unemployed urban workers to migrate back to the villages from which they originated so that they could attempt to resume farming. This has been anecdotally recounted to me from contacts in Latin America, Africa and Asia, and substantiated for Senegal (Le Nestour and Moscoviz 2020), Bangladesh (Ali et al. 2020) and India (Foundation for Agrarian Studies 2020). This created the preconditions for significantly increased competition over land and other scarce resources in the countryside, which had important gender dimensions as the bulk of returning migrants were men while farming has become an increasingly female activity. At the same time, urban–rural migration established a transmission vector that could spread the SARS-CoV-2 virus into rural populations that were particularly vulnerable because of extraor-dinarily weak health-care systems.

Producers of non-traditional agricultural exports for global food supply chains saw their markets shrivel as transport restrictions made exports impossible. Lacking the ability to store highly perishable products, which often have very limited domestic markets, had implications for producer incomes and the operation of the rural labour market as employment and wages were cut at the same time on those farms that relied on hired labour. Similar impacts were wit-nessed for rural waged labour working outside the non-traditional agricultural export sector. In rural China, while small-scale farmers continued working at the onset of the pandemic, employment of rural waged labour was reduced to essentially zero from early January through February 2020. Not surprisingly, in a survey of seven villages, 92 per cent of village inform-ants reported that their income levels had been reduced as a result of COVID-19 (Rozelle et al. 2020). In India, while rain-fed farming was largely unaffected because the pandemic struck during the off season, in irrigated areas the pandemic corresponded to a peak work period for agricultural labour employed by farmers who were harvesting, and who were largely unaffected by the pandemic (Foundation for Agrarian Studies 2020). In rapid surveys rural waged workers reported a dramatic drop in the availability of work, whether on the fields or in non-agricultural activities. This was caused by a marked reduction in labour hiring, with hired labour being replaced by family labour or by farm machinery. Moreover, for those able to get work rural wages dramatically dropped. In this light, it is not surprising that rural households reliant on waged labour reported eating less, and less healthily. Income-poor households reported a widespread rise in indebtedness, mainly to meet expenses on basic needs such as food (ibid.). It is a reasonable hypothesis that these impacts were also witnessed in rural Latin America and Sub-Saharan Africa, where rural labour markets are critical components of livelihood strategies. Thus, in many rural settings, the impact of the pandemic was felt, as it was in urban areas, through the labour market, with significant rises in unemployment, lower wages and lower incomes.

In the developing countries it is also very important to reflect upon the impact of the COVID-19 pandemic on the provision of care. Across Asia, Africa and Latin America when workers fall ill women within the home take principal responsibility for caring for them; health-care provision within the household attempts to offset inadequacies in health-care systems in the wider economy. In order to do so, women have to withdraw at least some of their labour from their income-generating activities, which are very often in food and agricultural production, which has implications for production and productivity. The HIV/AIDS crisis in Sub-Saharan Africa demonstrated the extent to which the need for caring labour within the home during a medical emergency resulted in reduced access to food as a consequence of less time being available to work in farming (Johnston 2013). Thus, even though the pandemic was generating unemployment and lower wages for those that relied on rural waged work to construct a livelihood, for low-income farming families afflicted by the SARS-CoV-2 virus, and in the absence of adequately functioning systems of health-care provision, the possibility of labour shortages emerging within small-scale petty commodity-producing peasant farms as people fell ill came to the fore. The lack of adequate family labour to work these farms lay behind some suggestions that agricultural production might fall in Sub-Saharan Africa as a result of COVID-19 (World Bank 2020).

Finally, in the developing countries the pandemic had macroeconomic consequences that were quite different from those in the developed countries and which were both especially severe and structural. The loss of income from non-traditional agricultural and commodity exports had multiplier effects because many countries relied on those earnings to finance imported food, and particularly staples such as wheat and rice, and the loss of these earnings was likely to have had three macroeconomic impacts. The first was an effect on local food prices, which in the continuing aftermath of the 2007 global food price crisis still remained some 35 per cent above those that were seen in 2006. Given that in many developing countries food prices are the principal drivers of inflation, inflation might result from the pandemic. The second was that trade imbalances put pressure on exchange rates, which had implications for countries that have witnessed significant increases in public-sector debt over the course of the last 20 years (Onyekwena and Ekeruche 2019); the debt burden will worsen as a result of the pandemic. The third is that the fiscal position of governments deteriorated as they had to increase spending on securing access to food supplies. The development implications of these processes were quite pernicious. World Bank President David Malpass (2020) publicly said that the Bank would increase lending to developing countries to deal with the consequences of the pandemic but that the condition of such lending was that after the immediate impact of the crisis had subsided countries would need to implement 'structural reforms' to 'foster markets, choice and faster growth prospects' by eliminating regulations and subsidies that restricted the operation of markets. Malpass' comments demonstrate the extent to which, at a time of crisis, the international development institutions were prepared to use the crisis as an opportunity to promote the further entrenchment of the capitalist world food system despite the fact that the system had demonstrated a marked incapacity to accommodate the pandemic because of the structural contradictions within which it is enmeshed.

INDUSTRIAL AGRICULTURE, SMALL-SCALE FARMERS AND COVID-19

The capitalist world food system has also laid the foundations to facilitate the expanded spread of zoonotics. This operates through two dimensions: the ongoing marginalization of small-scale petty commodity producers; and the ever expanding remit of industrial agriculture. As to the first dimension, the global expansion of industrial agriculture has marginalized hundreds of millions of small-scale farmers around the world. Worldwide, there are more than

570 million farms, most of which are small and family-operated. Small farms of 2 hectares or less operate about 12 per cent of the world's agricultural land, and family farms more generally operate about 75 per cent of the world's agricultural land (Lowder et al. 2016). Faced with farmgate prices that far too often do not cover local costs of production, small-scale farms have faced the aforementioned simple reproduction squeeze. To cope, some small-scale farmers have had to move: to less cultivable, often forested, areas, where they encroach on wilder habitats, putting in place a possible channel through which animal viruses can be transmitted to humans as 'forest disease dynamics' (Wallace 2020) enter peri-urban settings.

Alternatively, some small-scale farmers have diversified production in more lucrative higher-value products that when commodified can be easily sold in nearby markets. For livestock farmers marginalized by industrial livestock production, one group of these higher-value products are animals that were once caught and eaten for subsistence and which have not been traditionally bred in captivity to be sold as food—snakes, turtles, baby crocodiles and mallard ducks, among others. For these small-scale livestock farmers, economic marginalization has forced them to produce such commodities for niche markets in which they can realize more value; such commodities can be supplemented by higher-value domesticated animals that are not traditionally eaten as food but for which a food market exists—dogs and cats, to name two. In some instances the commodification of so-called 'wild' animals raised in captivity can create the opportunity for pathogens to cross from non-traditional farmed animals to livestock and from there into humans. Indeed, when farmers raising non-traditional farmed animals are successful in exploiting the opportunities afforded by markets, this creates incentives to increase the scale of their activity, which amplifies the possibility of zoonotic transmission. This has been a well-established route by which small-scale farmers unable to compete with Chinese industrial livestock production have crafted livelihood strategies (Lynteris and Fearnley 2020). In a commodity economy two ways of dealing with market imperatives is to expand the commodity frontier or to deepen the commodification of that which was not previously widely commodified. This has been the route of some small-scale petty commodity producers marginalized by industrial agriculture, and this can create pathways through which new pathogens emerge.

In the second dimension, as industrial agriculture has grown across the developing countries, including China, its expanded control and operation of better farming land has not only forced the exit of many small-scale farmers but has also created fertile breeding grounds for new infections as industrial livestock production increases. Industrial livestock breeds its own diseases, like swine flu and avian flu, in concentrated animal feeding operations and on factory farms because:

> the entirety of the production line is organized around practices that accelerate the evolution of pathogen virulence and subsequent transmission. Growing genetic monocultures … removes immune firebreaks … Pathogens … quickly evolve around the commonplace host immune genotypes … (C) rowded conditions depress immune response … (and) facilitate greater transmission and recurrent infection. High throughput … provides a continually renewed supply of susceptibles … Housing a lot of animals … rewards those strains that can burn through them best. Decreasing the age of slaughter … is likely to select for pathogens able to survive more robust immune systems. (Wallace 2020, 51)

These 'modern' industrial farming methods thus significantly enhance the virulence of those viruses that do emerge from farmed pigs and poultry, among others, before they cross from animal to human because modern animal farming significantly weakens the resistance of animals to pathogens even as the massive application of antibiotics to combat pathogens contributes to antibiotic resistance, cumulatively exacerbating the problem of new pathogens. As Rob Wallace (2016) cogently puts it, 'big farms make big flu'. The asset management companies that effectively control agro-food transnational capital already recognize this: its Farm Animal Investment Risk and Return Initiative is predicated on the understanding that industrialized animal production poses material risks to the global financial and economic system and suggests that 70 per cent of the biggest meat, fish and dairy producers are in danger of fostering future zoonotic pandemics because of lax safety standards, closely confined animals and the overuse of antibiotics (Farm Animal Investment Risk and Return 2020). This is why enhanced virulence has been documented in the United States, Canada, Europe and Australia rather than developing countries: these are the heartlands of industrial agriculture, and the principal driver of contemporary zoonotic disease has been industrial livestock production, most notably pig production. COVID-19 may not have emerged in industrial agriculture; but the market imperatives of industrial agriculture were imposed on small-scale farms, which responded by producing commodities with which industrial agriculture could not compete: non-traditional farmed animals for niche markets. The central issue at the source of the COVID-19 pandemic is not some people's taste for seemingly strange or exotic food, which in any event is culturally constructed, but rather the globalized, profit-driven, meat-centred capitalist world food system.

THE GLOBAL SUBSISTENCE CRISIS, COVID-19 AND SOCIAL MURDER

The capitalist world food system is clearly awash with a host of contradictions, the most glaringly obvious of which is the ongoing global subsistence crisis (Akram-Lodhi 2012). The global subsistence crisis reflects the fact that missing from the profit-driven logic of the capitalist world food system are those that lack the money needed to access commodified food in markets and who are thus bypassed. They are denied entitlements to food as a result of the normal working of the food markets of the capitalist world food system (Akram-Lodhi and Kay 2010). Officially, these numbered 690 million in 2020 (FAO 2020), using as a benchmark caloric intakes that meet 'minimum dietary energy requirements ... [for] ... a sedentary lifestyle' (FAO 2012, 55), or around 1800 calories per day. However, if the caloric intake is based upon that needed for 'normal' activity the numbers of hungry people nearly double, and if the caloric intake is based upon that needed for 'intense' activity the numbers of hungry people triple (FAO 2012, 55).[3] Overlapping with this figure, it is estimated that 2 billion people suffer from one or more micronutrient deficiencies (FAO 2013). Finally, of course, a consequence of the consumption pattern of the capitalist world food system has been the emergence of a global obesity crisis among the middle class (Akram-Lodhi 2013); in 2016 1.9 billion adults and 380 million children were overweight or obese (World Health Organization 2020). The capitalist world food system creates a planet of 'stuffed and starved' (Patel 2007), in which at least 60 per cent of the global population is in some way malnourished, the inequalities of which have a well-established co-morbidity with the SARS-CoV-2 virus.

The food insecurities and malnutrition created by the food system thus render large swathes of the global population more susceptible to new diseases, while inequalities in work and care place stresses on gendered and racialized populations, most notably those that rely on rural labour markets as the principal source of their income. The capitalist world food system thus creates: the structural foundations of overproduction and underconsumption; the social conditions within which virulent pathogens can thrive; and inequalities that 'can also prolong the pandemic and worsen its severity' (Nassif-Pires et al. 2020), creating negative self-reinforcing feedback loops. Clearly, the terms and conditions by which the capitalist world food system operates serves to simultaneously multiply and deepen threats to global health.

The COVID-19 pandemic has exposed a central pathology of contemporary capitalism: its reliance on what Friedrich Engels called 'social murder' (Engels 1969 [1845]; Chernomas and Hudson 2007). Engels' understanding of social murder rested on three conditions that he witnessed in Manchester in the early 1840s (Seim 2020). The first was that those that died were those at the bottom of a highly unequal society. The second was that those that died did so because of the terms and conditions by which capitalism operated. The third was that those that died did so because of the lax indifference of those in positions of economic, political and social power. In other words, it was 'the ruling power of society, the class which at present holds social and political control … the bourgeoisie' (Engels 1969 [1845], fn. 35) that fostered social murder. Social murder has always been integral to the operation of contemporary capitalism, but with all three conditions being demonstrated in the 2020 pandemic nowhere has this been more starkly revealed than in the morbidities arising out of the capitalist world food system and embodied in COVID-19.

NOTES

1. Women are of course also disproportionately represented in frontline health care.
2. Sixty per cent of the world's workforce works in the informal economy, of which more than 90 per cent is in the developing countries (ILO 2018b).
3. Thus, in 2012 852 million were hungry at a calorie intake needed for a sedentary life, 1.52 billion were hungry at a calorie intake needed for a normal life and 2.57 billion were hungry at a calorie intake needed for an intense life (FAO 2012, 55). I have never met a hungry person that lived a sedentary life.

FURTHER READING

Wallace, R. (2016), *Big Farms Make Big Flu: Dispatches on Infectious Disease, Agribusiness and the Nature of Science*, New York: Monthly Review Press.
Wallace, R. (2020), *Dead Epidemiologists: On the Origins of COVID-19*, New York: Monthly Review Press.
Weis, T. (2013), *The Ecological Hoofprint: The Global Burden of Industrial Livestock*, London: Zed Books.

REFERENCES

Adams-Prassl, A.; Boneva, T.; Golin, M.; Rauh, C. (2020), Inequality in the impact of the coronavirus shock: Evidence from real time surveys, University of Cambridge Faculty of Economics/Institute for New Economic Thinking *Cambridge-INET Working paper series*, no. 2020/18/*Cambridge Working Papers in Economics*, 2032, accessed 11 May 2020 at www.inet.econ.cam.ac.uk/working-paper-pdfs/wp2018.pdf.

Akram-Lodhi, A.H. (2012), Contextualising land grabbing: Contemporary land deals, the global subsistence crisis and the world food system, *Canadian Journal of Development Studies/Revue canadienne d'études du développement*, 33(2), 119–142.

Akram-Lodhi, A.H. (2013), *Hungry for Change: Farmers, Food Justice and the Agrarian Question*, Halifax: Fernwood Books.

Akram-Lodhi, A.H. (2019), Food regime, in Brunner, J.; Dobelmann, A.; Kirst, S.; Prause, L. (eds), *Wörterbuch der Land- und Rohstoffkonflikte*, Bielefeld: Transcript, 79–87.

Akram-Lodhi, A.H.; Kay, C. (2010), Surveying the agrarian question (Part 2): Current debates and beyond, *Journal of Peasant Studies*, 37(2), 255–284.

Ali, T.O.; Hassan, M.; Hossain, N.; Ul Hoque, Md.M.; Mamun-Ur-Rashid, Md.; Matin, I.; Rabbani, M. (2020), *Trust, Institutions, and Collective Action: How Are Communities Responding to COVID-19 in Bangladesh?*, BRAC Institute of Governance and Development Webinar, 22 April, accessed 11 May at https://bigd.bracu.ac.bd/publications/trust-institutions-and-collective-action/.

Anthem, P. (2020), Risk of hunger pandemic as COVID-19 set to almost double acute hunger by end of 2020, *World Food Programme Insight*, accessed 9 May 2020 at https://insight.wfp.org/covid-19-will-almost-double-people-in-acute-hunger-by-end-of-2020-59df0c4a8072.

Bello, W.; Baviera, M. (2010), Food wars, in Magdoff, F.; Tokar, B. (eds), *Agriculture and Food in Crisis: Conflict, Resistance and Renewal*, New York: Monthly Review Press, 33–50.

Chernomas, R.; Hudson, I. (2007), *Social Murder, and Other Shortcomings of Conservative Economics*, Winnipeg: Arbeiter Ring Publishing.

Clapp, J. (2020), *Food*, third edition, Cambridge: Polity Press.

Elston, J.W.T.; Cartwright, C.; Ndumbi, P.; Wright, J. (2017), The health impact of the 2014–2015 Ebola outbreak, *Public Health*, 143(February), 60–70.

Engels, F. (1969 [1845]), *The Condition of the Working Class in England*, accessed 11 May 2020 at www.marxists.org/archive/marx/works/1845/condition-working-class/.

FAO (Food and Agriculture Organization) (2012), *The State of Food Insecurity in the World 2012*, Rome: Food and Agriculture Organization, accessed 8 May 2020 at www.fao.org/3/i3027e/i3027e.pdf.

FAO (Food and Agriculture Organization) (2013), *The State of Food Insecurity in the World 2013*, Rome: Food and Agriculture Organization, accessed 8 May 2020 at www.fao.org/3/i3300e/i3300e.pdf.

FAO (Food and Agriculture Organization) (2020), *The State of Food Insecurity in the World 2020*, Rome: Food and Agriculture Organization, accessed 24 September 2020 at www.fao.org/publications/sofi/2020/en/.

Farm Animal Investment Risk and Return (2020), An industry infected: Animal agriculture in a post-COVID world, accessed 3 June 2020 at www.fairr.org/article/industry-infected/.

Foundation for Agrarian Studies (2020), Rural distress, *Frontline*, 22 May, accessed 11 May 2020 at http://fas.org.in/blog/wp-content/uploads/2020/04/Rural-Distress-FL-May-8.pdf.

Fridell, G.; Konings, M. (eds) (2013), *Age of Econs: Exploring Philanthrocapitalism in the Contemporary World*, Toronto: University of Toronto Press.

Gille, Z. (2012), From risk to waste: Global food waste regimes, *The Sociological Review*, 60(2 supplement), 27–46.

Holt-Giménez, E. (2019), *Can We Feed the World Without Destroying It?*, Cambridge: Polity Press.

ILO (International Labour Organization) (2018a), Empowering women working in the informal economy, ILO, *Issue Brief*, no. 4, accessed 23 September at www.ilo.org/wcmsp5/groups/public/---dgreports/---cabinet/documents/publication/wcms_618166.pdf.

ILO (International Labour Organization) (2018b), *Women and Men in the Informal Economy: A Statistical Picture*, Geneva: International Labour Organization, accessed 9 May 2020 at www.ilo.org/global/publications/books/WCMS_626831/lang--en/index.htm.

ILO (International Labour Organization) (2020), *ILO Monitor: COVID-19 and the World of Work, Third Edition: Updated Estimates and Analysis*, 29 April, accessed 11 May 2020 at www.ilo.org/wcmsp5/groups/public/---dgreports/---dcomm/documents/briefingnote/wcms_743146.pdf.

Johnston, D. (2013), *Economics and HIV: The Sickness of Economics*, Abingdon: Routledge.

Le Nestour, A.; Moscoviz, L. (2020), Five findings from a new phone survey in Senegal, *Center for Global Development*, 24 April, accessed 9 May at www.cgdev.org/blog/five-findings-new-phone -survey-senegal?utm_source=200428&utm_medium=cgd_email&utm_campaign=cgd_weekly.

Lowder, S.K.; Skoet, J.; Raney, T. (2016), The number, size, and distribution of farms, smallholder farms, and family farms worldwide, *World Development*, 87(November), 16–29.

Lynteris, C.; Fearnley, L. (2020), Why shutting down Chinese 'wet markets' could be a terrible mistake, *The Conversation*, 31 January, accessed 8 May 2020 at https://theconversation.com/why-shutting -down-chinese-wet-markets-could-be-a-terrible-mistake-130625.

Malpass, D. (2020), Remarks by World Bank Group President David Malpass on G20 Finance Ministers conference call on COVID-19, World Bank, *Speeches and Transcripts*, 23 March, accessed 9 May at www.worldbank.org/en/news/speech/2020/03/23/remarks-by-world-bank-group-president-david -malpass-on-g20-finance-ministers-conference-call-on-covid-19.

Nassif-Pires, L.; de Lima Xavier, L.; Masterson, T.; Nikiforos, M.; Rios-Avila, F. (2020), Pandemics of inequality, Levy Economics Institute of Bard College, *Public Policy Brief*, no. 149, accessed 25 May 2020 at www.levyinstitute.org/publications/pandemic-of-inequality.

Onyekwena, C.; Ekeruche, M.A. (2019), Is a debt crisis looming in Africa, *Brookings*, 10 April, accessed 9 May 2020 at www.brookings.edu/blog/africa-in-focus/2019/04/10/is-a-debt-crisis-looming-in -africa/.

Patel, R. (2007), *Stuffed and Starved: Markets, Power and the Hidden Battle for the World's Food System*, London: Portobello Books.

Piketty, T. (2020), *Capital and Ideology*, translated by A. Goldhammer, Cambridge, MA: Belknap Press.

Qualman, D.; Akram-Lodhi, A.H.; Desmarais, A.A.; Srinivasan, S. (2018), Forever young? The crisis of generational renewal on Canada's farms, *Canadian Food Studies*, 5(3), 100–127.

Rozelle, S.; Rahimi, H.; Huan, W.; Dill, E. (2020), Lockdowns are protecting China's rural families from COVID-19, but the economic burden is heavy, International Food Policy Research Institute, *IFPRI Blog*, 30 March, accessed 11 March 2020 at www.ifpri.org/blog/lockdowns-are-protecting-chinas -rural-families-covid-19-economic-burden-heavy.

Seim, J. (2020), COVID-19 as social murder: Putting capitalism on trial, *Spectre*, 22 April, accessed 9 May 2002 at https://spectrejournal.com/covid-19-as-social-murder/?fbclid=IwAR1PE46Q4RZNl7K -5Rbw5EyrCBkOSw9mnsjO61g2tdlxlFrf8pmzPUCgi0g.

Tschirley, D.; Minten, B.; Haggblade, S.; Livepool-Tasie, S.; Dolislager, M.; Snyder, J.L.; Ijumba, C. (2015), *Transformation of African Agrifood Systems in the New Era of Rapid Urbanization and the Emergence of a Middle Class*, accessed 11 May 2020 at https://pdfs.semanticscholar.org/bf74/6eb469 4e8a99fba1013e2d7519022173e4e0.pdf.

Tyson, J.H. (2020), A delicate balance: Feeding the nation and keeping our employees healthy, *Washington Post*, 26 April, accessed 11 May at www.washingtonpost.com/context/tyson-ad/ 86b9290d-115b-4628-ad80-0e679dcd2669/?itid=lk_inline_manual_2.

United Nations Economic and Social Research Council (2020), *Progress Towards the Sustainable Development Goals: Report of the Secretary-General*, accessed 9 July at https://sustainabled evelopment.un.org/content/documents/26158Final_SG_SDG_Progress_Report_14052020.pdf.

Wallace, R. (2016), *Big Farms Make Big Flu: Dispatches on Infectious Disease, Agribusiness and the Nature of Science*, New York: Monthly Review Press.

Wallace, R. (2020), *Dead Epidemiologists: On the Origins of COVID-19*, New York: Monthly Review Press.

Weis, T. (2013), *The Ecological Hoofprint: The Global Burden of Industrial Livestock*, London: Zed Books.

World Bank (2007), *World Development Report 2008: Agriculture for Development*, Washington, DC: World Bank, accessed 9 May at https://openknowledge.worldbank.org/handle/10986/5990.

World Bank (2020), *COVID-19 (Coronavirus) Drives Sub-Saharan Africa Toward First Recession in 25 Years*, World Bank, Press release, 9 April, accessed 11 May 2020 at www.worldbank.org/en/news/ press-release/2020/04/09/covid-19-coronavirus-drives-sub-saharan-africa-toward-first-recession -in-25-years.

World Food Programme (2020), *COVID-19 Will Double Number of People Facing Food Crises Unless Swift Action Is Taken*, accessed 9 July 2020 at www.wfp.org/news/covid-19-will-double-number -people-facing-food-crises-unless-swift-action-taken.

World Health Organization (2014), Zoonotic disease: Emerging public health threats in the region, *Report to the 61st session of the WHO Regional Committee of the Regional Office for the Eastern Mediterranean*, accessed 8 September 2020 at www.emro.who.int/about-who/rc61/zoonotic-diseases .html.
World Health Organization (2020), *Obesity and Overweight*, accessed 8 May 2020 at www.who.int/news -room/fact-sheets/detail/obesity-and-overweight.

PART VI

TRAJECTORIES

63. The interface of critical development studies and critical agrarian studies

Henry Veltmeyer

THE ORIGINS AND MEANING OF CRITICAL DEVELOPMENT STUDIES

As noted in the Introduction to this *Handbook*, in 2017 Marc Edelman and Wendy Wolford wrote a piece called 'Introduction: Critical agrarian studies in theory and practice', raising questions as to what the parameters of this apparently new field of study might entail and what issues it might encompass. However, at the time this article was written it was already possible to identify a seemingly similar yet somewhat older notion of critical development studies, which departed from the idea of development as an academic pursuit embodied within the rapidly growing interdisciplinary field of international development studies. Critical development studies as it began to coalesce in the late 1980s was an effort to give international development studies, as a field of academic enquiry, a 'critical edge'. This was done by shifting the focus from policy reform and institutional development toward the underlying operating system, and in so doing focusing on the workings of what some theorists have described as the 'world capitalist system'. It was the project of a network of activist-scholars who were concerned with a broad array of development issues. This is evident, for instance, from publications such as *The Critical Development Studies Handbook: Tools for Change* (Veltmeyer 2011). When Taylor & Francis bought out Ashgate a few years later the series was taken over by Routledge. As of 2019 seven books have been published in this series, including *Postdevelopment in Practice* (Klein and Morreo 2019), *The Rise and Fall of Global Microcredit* (Bateman et al. 2018), *Neoextractivism and Capitalist Development* (Canterbury 2018), *Reframing Latin American Development* (Munck and Delgado Wise 2019), *The Class Struggle in Latin America* (Petras and Veltmeyer 2017) and *The Essential Guide to Critical Development Studies* (Veltmeyer and Bowles 2017).

In this chapter, the origins, overlappings and divergencies of critical development studies and critical agrarian studies are assessed. Whereas critical development studies is broader in its thematic range, both fields of research share common theoretical grounds, namely (agrarian) Marxism, but in their concrete analyses assume a sort of division of labour, therefore being complementary. A main intersection is the interest in cycles of development and resistance.

CRITICAL DEVELOPMENT STUDIES AND THE AGRARIAN QUESTION

Although the issues addressed in critical development studies networks are wide-ranging they are fundamentally focused on the workings of the capitalist system in diverse temporal and spatial contexts. That is to say the focus is on complex dynamics of capitalist development and the associated process of productive and social transformation. Because this process has historically been rooted in the dispossession of an agrarian precapitalist society of small-scale peasant farmers and agricultural producers, converting this peasantry into a proletariat (a class-owning nothing except for their capacity to labour, which they are therefore compelled to exchange against capital for a living wage), a central concern of critical development studies has been to analyse the complex, diverse and shifting dynamics of what has been conceptualized by political economists of agrarian change as the 'agrarian question' (see Watts, this volume). This question has taken diverse forms in different historical and regional contexts. In the current context of capitalist development in the so-called 'neoliberal era' the agrarian question is associated with the advance of resource-seeking 'extractive' capital (investments in the acquisition of land and the extraction of natural resources for the purpose of exporting them in primary commodity form). As in earlier phases of capitalist development the advance of capital in the development process can be traced out in the form of an evolution in the development of the forces of production, the corresponding changes in the social relations of production and in the resulting form taken by the resistance to the forces of capitalist development. For practitioners within critical development studies, then, the point is that each advance of capital in the development process generates new forces of change and resistance.

A closer look at *The Essential Guide to Critical Development Studies* (Veltmeyer and Bowles 2017, 2021) reveals that the political economy of agrarian change practised within critical development studies clearly fits within the purview of what Edelman and Wolford describe as critical agrarian studies. The same diversity of critical perspectives that underpins critical development studies can be found in the *Journal of Peasant Studies* and the *Journal of Agrarian Change*, the major publication outlets for scholars concerned with the political economy of agrarian change and with critical agrarian studies. So, from this perspective there would seem to be little difference between the political economy of agrarian change within critical development studies and critical agrarian studies, except for a change of terminology— renaming a now well-established field of research and academic studies. Perhaps, as in the case of scholars and researchers concerned to differentiate international development studies in the mainstream from an explicitly critical perspective focused on the capitalist system, the aim of critical agrarian studies is to make the central focus on the underlying operating capitalist system explicit, and thus differentiate it from empirical or theoretical studies that do not share this critical perspective. If so, the term could be seen as having some descriptive and analytical utility.

But is this the aim? Is there a substantive difference between the field of studies previously branded as the political economy of agrarian change, and what Edelman and Wolford denote as critical agrarian studies? Is critical agrarian studies distinct from or a field within critical development studies? This can be examined by firstly looking at the origins of critical agrarian studies, and by secondly looking at the shared theoretical concerns of critical development and critical agrarian studies.

THE NOTION OF CRITICAL AGRARIAN STUDIES

The notion of critical agrarian studies was introduced, it could be argued, in the context of a conversation held between Jun Borras, editor of the *Journal of Peasant Studies*; Errol Sharpe, publisher of Halifax-based Fernwood Publishing; and myself in 2009, and then a broader discussion with a group of agrarian studies activist-scholars at the Institute of Social Studies (ISS) in The Hague on 20 January 2011. At issue in these discussions was the idea—voiced by Jun Borras—to create a series of small state-of-the-art books on the big questions in the field of agrarian change and peasant studies. From the 2009 conversation was born the Initiatives in Critical Agrarian Studies (ICAS), a project to produce at least two small books a year, each translated from English into a minimum of three languages (Spanish, Portuguese and Chinese), with the responsibility for translation falling on individuals at a consortium of institutions represented at the 2011 meeting held at ISS, where the project was 'institutionalized', as it were, with the foundation of an international editorial committee and advisory board. In addition to the ISS, the institutions represented at this meeting of what would emerge as an extensive network of activist-scholars and researchers in the field of agrarian change and peasant studies included the Universidad Autónoma de Zacatecas (Mexico), the College of Humanities and Development Studies at the China Agriculture University in Beijing; and the Universidade Estadual Paulista (Presidente Prudente, Brazil). The first book in the ICAS series, *Class Dynamics of Agrarian Change* (Bernstein 2010), was a direct outcome of the 2009 meeting.

From this auspicious beginning the ICAS network expanded from the project of publishing to holding international conferences. The first of these conferences, hosted and organized by Sergio Sauer at the Universidade de Brasilia, was held in Brasilia in 2014. This was followed by Beijing (2016), Moscow (2017) and then again Brasilia (2018). The Beijing conference was notable not only for the size of the event but for the creation of a supplementary project—and network (the BRICS Initiative in Critical Agrarian Studies, BICAS)—focused on critical agrarian studies in the BRICS (Brazil, Russia, India, China and South Africa) cluster of newly 'emerging markets' as well as the emergence of China as a world economic power (see Oliveira and McKay, this volume). In fact, the subsequent series of international conferences was organized by members of the BICAS network.

As for the theoretical framework reflected in both these small books and the *Journal of Peasant Studies*, which remains the main publication outlet for scholars engaged in the project of critical agrarian studies, it is evident that the change from Terence Byres and Henry Bernstein to Jun Borras as editor-in-chief has brought about a broadening of theoretical perspectives on agrarian change. Under the editorship of Bernstein and Byres the journal had a pronounced bias toward agrarian Marxism, but as A. Haroon Akram-Lodhi (2018) has observed Jun Borras has promoted a broader perspective on the dynamics of rural development and agrarian change, suggesting that there may even be a 'fundamental break' between critical agrarian studies and agrarian Marxism. Critical agrarian studies involves a substantive interest in issues going beyond those that are of concern to political economists—issues such as the agency of change and the social dimensions of rural identities and power relations. What this means, however, for the underlying theory and practice of critical agrarian studies is not clear. The wider critical development studies network from which ICAS emerged has not undergone such a reorientation. This is undoubtedly because critical development studies from the outset was concerned to promote a broad and diverse range of 'critical perspectives'—for example, by welcoming postdevelopment, postcolonial and other forms of critical theory, as well as studies on the sociology of development, along with research into the political economy of development that was grounded in Marxism. What is not always clear is whether critical agrarian studies has a lesser concern with the issue of system dynamics, which is a major feature of critical development studies.

THE INTERFACE: TOWARD A COMMON THEORETICAL FRAMEWORK

Within the broader framework and mainstream of international development studies, 'development' is conceived of as a theoretical-political 'project', and as such actions taken to advance one idea or the other as to what actions or strategy, and what institutional and policy framework, are needed or appropriate for improving the social condition of a targeted or identified population. The range of alternative ideas as to how to promote development, to bring about these defined improvements, is broad-ranging from economic growth and poverty reduction to social inclusion and sustainable development of the environment and rural livelihoods. But what they all have in common is a concern with and focus on the best policy or institutional mix for bringing about 'development' so defined.

Critical development studies does not share this perspective, and in this it diverges from international development studies and converges with critical agrarian studies. Both fields of activist thought—activist in the shared concern for bringing about transformative systemic change rather than merely institutional development—view 'development' rather differently: as a *process*, rather than a *project*. That is to say, they view systemic change as a complex of dynamics generated by the evolution of the capitalist system in the development of the forces of production. Such development generates conditions that are, as Marx stated as a matter of principle (for the sake of analysis), *objective* in their effects on individuals or nation-states, according to their location in the system—in the class structure of social relations or the centre-periphery structure of the world capitalist system (Veltmeyer and Delgado Wise 2018). Thus, critical development and critical agrarian studies converge in the understanding of the fundamental dynamics of capitalist development as being about the development of the forces of production within the capitalist system, a mode of commodity production based on the exploitation of labour. Granted, the analyses of many researchers in critical agrarian studies do not delve into an assessment of the fundamental dynamics; but this does nonetheless underpin their research.

This is one dimension of the theoretical framework shared by critical development and critical agrarian studies as a guide to social scientific and political class analysis. Another is the assumption that capitalist development in diverse historical and regional contexts is invariably accompanied by a process of productive and social transformation—the transformation of an agrarian society of precapitalist production relations and a traditional communalist culture into a capitalist system based on the capital–labour relation. In regard to this process, critical development and critical agrarian studies scholars have assumed a sort of division of labour, or complementary analysis. The former theorizes and analyses the structural and political dynamics of this development process, with reference to what Marx described as the general law of capital accumulation; that is to say, the concentration and centralization of capital, and corresponding to this the 'multiplication of the proletariat'. The latter theorizes and analyses the associated dynamics of agrarian change: the conversion of a society of small-scale agricultural producers and 'peasants' into an industrial proletariat, a reserve army of labour, a relative surplus population, or some combination thereof. In this division of intellectual labour critical development studies scholars have established the fundamental role of agriculture in the development process to be the production of a seemingly unlimited supply of surplus labour to fuel and advance the accumulation of industrial capital. Critical agrarian studies scholars, on the other hand, have explored the dynamics of agrarian change associated with this development—the 'agrarian question' in its diverse permutations.

A third theoretical presupposition shared by both critical development and critical agrarian studies scholars is that each phase of capitalist development generates new forces of resistance, leading to a series of development-resistance cycles. The first cycle corresponded to the first three decades of the process set in motion by the idea of development that was constructed in the immediate aftermath of the Second World War in order to assure that the 'economically backward' countries in the global South (at that time the so-called 'Third World'), seeking to break away from European colonialism and British imperialism, would take the capitalist rather than socialist path toward national development (Sachs 1992). The idea of development, constructed for this purpose, was advanced as a project of international cooperation, understood by some (Hayter 1971; Veltmeyer and Petras 2005) as a form of imperialism—a means of realizing the foreign policy objectives of the imperial state, now led by the United States, including the project of international cooperation. In the 1960s, in the wake of the Cuban revolution, this development idea was reconstructed toward the notion of 'integrated rural development', a project designed with the purpose of integrating the 'rural poor' (to use the World Bank's term used to describe the mass of 'peasants' dispossessed from the land and their means of production) into the process of capitalist development (Moyo and Yeros 2005).

In the analysis advanced by both critical development and critical agrarian studies scholars the advent of the neoliberal era was of critical importance, leading as it has to an entirely new development and resistance dynamic. The neoliberal era was inaugurated with the implementation of a series of structural 'reforms' in macroeconomic policy—globalization, privatization, deregulation and the liberalization of capital flows and trade (Petras and Veltmeyer 2001). These reforms were designed to liberate the 'forces of economic freedom' (private enterprise, capital, the market, the multinational corporation, free trade) from the regulatory constraints of the welfare development state. However, what they did instead was to generate new forces of capitalist development and agrarian change, the dynamics of which—in the form of a development-resistance cycle—have been the main object of both critical development and critical agrarian studies.

Thus, it can be argued that the critical point through which critical development studies converges with critical agrarian studies is the analysis of cycles of development and resistance. Within this shared theoretical framework, critical development and critical agrarian studies scholars in recent years have confirmed the validity and analytical utility of the ideas used to analyse the complex dynamics of capitalist development and agrarian change. And they have also confirmed the importance of investigating and analysing the dynamics of this process in diverse theoretical and regional contexts. For example, Latin American scholars in the critical development studies tradition in their accounts of the capitalist development process have established an important divergence of the actual development process from Marxist theory: rather than a transformation of the peasantry into an industrial proletariat on the (Latin American) periphery of the system the outcome (in the context of the 'new world order' and associated 'structural reforms') was the formation of a semiproletariat of rural landless workers and periurban 'on their own account' workers in the informal sector of the cities. As a corollary of this 'development' critical development studies scholars have argued that rather than the 'disappearance of the peasantry'—the expectation derived from Marxist theory—what we have seen instead is the disappearance of a nascent industrial proletariat as well as the persistence of both the peasantry and rural poverty (Boltvinik and Mann 2016).

CONCLUSION

Critical agrarian studies could be viewed as being within the domain of critical development studies; both share the project of viewing and analysing the dynamics of both the development process and agrarian change from critical perspective. Whereas critical development studies is focused on the broad field of international development, including in its purview a broad range of issues and sub-fields, critical agrarian studies is sharply focused on issues arising out of the capitalist development of agriculture—the agrarian question, we might say; a question that is reformulated with every advance of capital in the development process. In this regard, whether or not critical agrarian studies represents something different or new in relation to the more established fields of academic study, such as the political economy of capitalist development and agrarian change, it has served as a valuable tool in building various networks and analyses dedicated to moving beyond capitalism—to viewing capitalism from a critical perspective in the search for alternative, more people-centred forms of development oriented toward systemic transformation and 'another world' of social and environmental justice and inclusion. This is clearly demonstrated in this *Handbook*.

FURTHER READING

Bernstein, H. (2010), *Class Dynamics of Agrarian Change*, Halifax: Fernwood Publishing.
Bernstein, H.; Byres, T.J. (2001), From peasant studies to agrarian change, *Journal of Agrarian Change*, 1(1), 1–56.
Boltvinik, L.; Mann, S. (eds) (2016), *Peasant Poverty and Persistence in the 21st Century*, London: Zed Books.
Borras, Jr., S.M. (2009), Agrarian change and peasant studies: Changes, continuities and challenges—an introduction, *Journal of Peasant Studies*, 36(1), 5–31.
Veltmeyer, H.; Bowles, P. (2017), *The Essential Guide to Critical Development Studies* (2021 2nd edition), London: Routledge.

REFERENCES

Akram-Lodhi, A.H. (2018), What is critical agrarian studies?, accessed 19 October 2020 at http://roape .net/2018/03/28/what-is-critical-agrarian-studies/.
Bateman, M.; Blankenburg, S.; Kozul-Wright, R. (2018), *The Rise and Fall of Global Microcredit: Development, Debt and Delusion*, London: Routledge.
Bernstein, H. (2010), *Class Dynamics of Agrarian Change*, Halifax: Fernwood Publishing.
Boltvinik, L.; Mann, S. (eds) (2016), *Peasant Poverty and Persistence in the 21st Century*, London: Zed Books.
Canterbury, D. (2018), *Neoextractivism and Capitalist Development*, London: Routledge.
Edelman, M.; Wolford, W. (2017), Introduction: Critical agrarian studies in theory and practice, *Antipode*, 49(4), 959–976.
Hayter, Teresa (1971), *Aid as Imperialism*, Harmondsworth: Penguin Books.
Klein, E.; Morreo, C.E. (2019), *Postdevelopment in Practice: Alternatives, Economies, Ontologies*, London: Routledge.
Moyo, S.; Yeros, P. (eds) (2005), *Reclaiming the Land: The Resurgence of Rural Movements in Africa, Asia, and Latin America*, London: Zed Books.
Munck, R.; Delgado Wise, R. (2019), *Reframing Latin American Development*, London: Routledge.

Petras, J.; Veltmeyer, H. (2001), *Globalization Unmasked: Imperialism in the 21st Century*, London: ZED Press/Halifax: Fernwood Publishing.

Petras, J.; Veltmeyer, H. (2017), *The Class Struggle in Latin America: Making History Today*, London: Routledge.

Sachs, W. (ed.) (1992), *The Development Dictionary*, London: Zed Books.

Veltmeyer, H. (2011), *The Critical Development Studies Handbook: Tools for Change*, Halifax: Fernwood Publishing/London: Pluto Press.

Veltmeyer, H.; Bowles, P. (2017), *The Essential Guide to Critical Development Studies* (2021 2nd edition), London: Routledge.

Veltmeyer, H.; Delgado Wise, R. (2018), *Critical Development Studies: An Introduction*, Halifax: Fernwood Publishing.

Veltmeyer, H.; Petras, J. (2005), Foreign aid, neoliberalism and imperialism, in Saad-Filho, A.; Johnston, D. (eds), *Neoliberalism: A Critical Reader*, London: Pluto Press.

64. Political ecology

Kristina Dietz

INTRODUCTION

Ecological questions related to agricultural production, social reproduction and social power relations in the countryside have long been absent from critical agrarian studies.[1] For many years, neither the ecological contradictions of industrialized capitalist agriculture, nor the vulnerability of peasants towards environmental threats and changes, were placed prominently on the research agenda. However, in the 1980s scholars from critical geography and agrarian political economy began to study the relationship between capitalism, agriculture and ecological crises in the Global South, for instance regarding soil erosion, land degradation, deforestation, famine and drought (Blaikie and Brookfield 1987; Watts 2013 [1983]). In their analyses, they pointed to the social relations of production, power and property relations as the root causes of ecological degradation.

Since the early 2000s, the attention paid to ecological questions in critical agrarian studies and politics in general has increased. The manifold adverse effects of ecological crises – including severe droughts and heavy rains, the loss of agro-biodiversity, soil erosion and degradation, deforestation, water and air pollution – impact rural social relations and rural life to a degree that cannot be ignored. Both the aggravation of ecological crises and the increasing importance given to them within global politics have led to a growing engagement in recent years with the contradictions between ecology and capitalist agriculture (Taylor 2015; Weis 2010). To address ecological questions of agricultural production and rural social relations, many scholars link critical agrarian studies to another study field: political ecology.

In what follows, political ecology will be brought into dialogue with critical agrarian studies. Such an encounter is promising, as the emergence of both fields was influenced by the resurgence of Marxism in the 1960s and 1970s. In fact, there are many authors that can be associated with both fields, including Bina Agarwal, Susanna Hecht, Nancy Peluso, Marcus Taylor, Michael Watts and Tony Weis. Both fields share a common concern with social power relations and social structures and how they change over time. Whereas scholars within critical agrarian studies are mainly concerned with the relationship between capital and agriculture, political ecologists point to the power relations inherent in ecological crises and in the ways in which nature is managed, appropriated, known, destroyed and represented.

This chapter is structured as follows: in the next section, the field of political ecology will be introduced, with a focus on its origins and theoretical and analytical common grounds. Subsequently, different research strands will be presented, which have evolved since its emergence in the 1970s; these strands are closely related to the theoretical and epistemological turns within the social sciences. Thereafter, the question of what critical agrarian studies can learn from political ecology will be discussed. In the conclusion, the main arguments outlining why a dialogue with political ecology would be fruitful and productive for critical agrarian studies will be summarized.

WHAT IS POLITICAL ECOLOGY?

Political ecology is a normative research field that seeks both to explain the power relations inherent to environmental problems and to transform them. Hence, political ecologists position themselves against the dehistoricization of both society and of nature. However, there is no single definition of what political ecology is. Eric Wolf (1972) was among the first to mention the term in an article on the relationship between landed property relations and the politics of resource management, though he did not elaborate on it. Since then, political ecology has been defined in various ways: as combining the 'concerns of ecology and a broadly defined political economy' (Blaikie and Brookfield 1987, 17), as a study field which 'seeks to understand the complex relations between nature and society through a careful analysis of ... the forms of access and control over resources' (Watts 2000, 257), as 'the study of power relations and political conflict over ecological distribution and the social struggles for the appropriation of nature' (Leff 2015, 33) and as an approach that 'deals with the complex context in which gender interacts with class, race, culture and national identity to shape our experience of and interest in "the environment"' (Rocheleau et al. 1996, 5).

These definitions show that political ecology is many things at the same time: a study field, a normative political commitment, a critique of positivist and apolitical explanations of environmental degradation, a feminist perspective on the relationship between power, nature and gender and a set of conceptual and analytical tools for studying the power relations inherent in defining, knowing, appropriating, representing, altering and managing nature. It is, in any case, not a comprehensive theory. It can best be understood as a cross-disciplinary study field, nourished by various critical theories, such as Marxist political economy, poststructuralism, feminist and postcolonial theory, and social movements emerging from conflicts over access to, and control and rights over, natural resources. The different theoretical streams and movements bring together scholars and activists from a wide range of disciplines such as geography, anthropology, sociology, (agrarian) political economy and political sciences, and from different world regions.

As a study field, political ecology emerged in the 1970s as an answer to apolitical explanations of rising environmental degradation in the Global South. Problems such as soil erosion, deforestation, water pollution and resource scarcity in general were prevailingly conceptualized in neo-Malthusian and positivist terms as resulting from poverty and overpopulation. These approaches referred to the general human tendency to overexploit common resources and lands that are not protected by private property rights or state regulations. In these explanations, social power relations and hierarchies (class, gender, race, caste and ethnicity, unequal North–South relations and epistemological hierarchies), as influencing factors in environmental degradation, are hidden. In contrast, and influenced by Marxist thinking in agrarian political economy as well as dependency and world system approaches within development theory, scholars from political ecology studied problems of degradation, deforestation and famine first and foremost in political economic terms, as grounded in the social relations of capitalist production and distribution and the international division of labour.

In order to grasp the relations between land degradation and social relations of capitalist production in a globalized world, Piers Blaikie and Harold Brookfield (1987, 27) applied a 'chain of explanation' approach, which can also be understood as a multi-scalar approach. It starts with the land managers and their relation with the land, with each other and other land users, and with other social groups that affect them in any way, and ends by examining relations to the state and the world economy. Such a view offered a new way of conceptualizing the relationship between society and nature by linking environmental changes to the expansion of capitalism. Herewith, these scholars opened up a way of making sense of the power of global forces (transnational corporations, instruments and functions of the global market) over particular activities (such as peasant farming). Since then, research topics, disciplines and analytical scales have widened greatly, leading from rural to urban contexts, from global environmental politics to the scale of the body, from knowledge production to the formation of subjectivities in relation to nature, from geography to anthropology, from the Global South to the Global North.

Despite the variety of topics and theoretical diversity, political ecologists nevertheless share common grounds and premises. This includes, first of all, a non-dualistic, dialectical understanding of nature–society relations based on a feminist critique of the nature–culture divide in modern science (Plumwood 1993), as well as Marx's ontological principle that humans need to transform (metabolize) nature in order to meet their existential needs. By transforming nature for the satisfaction of human needs, however, not only is nature altered but also society itself (Marx 1976 [1867], 283). The dialectical transformation of nature and society is not arbitrary, but occurs within a socially and historically specific context; that is, under specific social relations of production. From this perspective, social structures, social relations of power and subject positions are deeply interwoven in the way in which nature is and has been appropriated, managed and represented. In turn, ecological crises such as climate change, biodiversity loss and soil erosion do not occur outside of society; they are inextricably linked to social relations of production and power. From this ontological standpoint, political ecologists underline the co-constitution of nature and society. They view social relations of power and domination as constitutive of environmental degradation; and in turn, they see the way in which nature is appropriated, transformed and represented as constitutive of the (re) production of social relations of power, domination and inequality.

A second common ground of political ecology is its commitment to critical social theory, which aims to denaturalize social relations of power by highlighting their historical, human-made and dynamic character, and thus the possibility for social change. In this sense, political ecology intends to denaturalize prevailing society–nature relations by showing how they are historically and socially produced, and that they can and should be transformed. Thus, political ecologists insist on the '*inherently political character of environmental problems*' (Wissen 2015, 17, original emphasis). Studying environmental problems and society–nature relations as 'politicized' (Bryant and Bailey 1997, 27) means to question how environmental changes are politically produced, how access to, control over and use of natural resources are influenced by social relations of power and how the impacts of environmental degradation are distributed unequally in society.

These theoretical commitments enable a consensus on methodological approaches. Political ecology research is mainly based on qualitative research designs. Depending on the research questions and the disciplinary backgrounds of the researchers, qualitative methods and field research are combined with quantitative data such as surveys and remote sensing, as well as biophysical methods in some cases. Empirical analyses are mostly historically contextualized, and research is increasingly multi-scalar in its perspective and action-oriented, as it mainly draws on the struggles, rights, claims, interests, perceptions, subjectivities and everyday social practices of marginalized social groups (the rural poor, peasants, indigenous movements and others).

RESEARCH STRANDS WITHIN POLITICAL ECOLOGY

Within the field of political ecology, the most prominent research traditions since the 1970s have been Marxist, feminist, poststructuralist, Gramscian and postcolonial approaches to political ecology and critical science studies (see Forsyth 2003). Sharing the common grounds outlined in the previous section, these traditions highlight the importance of relations of production, the divisions of labour and social structures and the meanings and representations of identity constructions and epistemological hierarchies.

Marxist Approaches to Political Ecology

Marxist approaches to political ecology study environmental changes and the uneven distribution of environmental damages within society in relation to social structures and power relations. Based on a political economy perspective, the core concepts are class relations and a structural concept of power. To exert power means to control access to, the distribution of and the decisions over the use of natural resources. A person's, group's, state's or company's ability to exert power in this sense depends on its position within the social relations of production, distribution and reproduction; that is, within class structures and – from a global perspective – within the capitalist world market (Wissen 2015). The contributions to the field of Blaikie and Brookfield (1987) and Watts (2013 [1983]) are good examples of a Marxist political economic approach.

From such a perspective, scholars also underline capitalism's inherent ecological contradictions. The point of departure here is Marx's concept of the double character of labour: capitalist production is both a labour process – here in terms of labour producing use value – and a valorisation process – in terms of abstract labour and the production of exchange value (Marx 1976 [1867], 283). The purpose of capitalist production is not the production of use values but the production and realization of surplus value. Use values of commodities are only of interest for capital since commodities need to satisfy human needs in order to be demanded and to realize the reified surplus value. It is this double character that explains the contradiction between the capitalist mode of production and the qualities of nature (Altvater 1993). The main argument is that capitalism transforms nature (land, water, primary forests, the atmosphere and so on) to an extent and degree like no other mode of production has done before. In material terms, capitalism is highly dependent on nature, but at the same time it abstracts itself from this dependency; it is indifferent to the spatio-temporal qualities of nature and frames environmental problems as externalities. Thus, capitalist production constantly undermines the socio-ecological conditions on which it depends in the labour process; a process that sooner or later leads to crises, such as climate crises. According to people's social positions, these crises are felt earlier by some than by others, and they negatively impact some people's lives whereas others might benefit. Political ecology therefore does not only point to the inherent contradictions between nature and capitalism, but also stresses that there is no global ecological crisis that means the same to all: there are always winners and losers.

Feminist Political Ecology

Feminist political ecology aims to bridge both the initial gender gap in political economy analyses and the gendered binary codifications that link nature and emotions to femininity, and culture and reason to masculinity. Bina Agarwal (1992) emphasized the need to consider society–nature relations through the lenses of gender *and* class. She argues that poor women in rural areas in the Global South are more often exposed to environmental changes and hazards, not because they are women but because of socially produced (international) gendered divisions of labour and gendered environmental roles. Recent poststructuralist approaches to feminist theory have inspired new thoughts in feminist political ecology. Beyond class–gender relations, scholars place an emphasis on intersectionality. They explore how gender and gendered subjectivities are constituted alongside other identities and markers of difference (class, caste, race, ethnicity) through the material interaction with and the symbolic understandings of nature, as well as changes in and knowledge of the environment (Elmhirst 2015; see Nightingale and Harcourt, this volume).

Poststructuralist Political Ecology

In the 1990s, the 'macro-structural' framework of Marxian political ecology was contested by pointing to two omissions: the micro-politics of peasant struggles over access to productive resources and the symbolic contestations that constitute these struggles. This critique underlies a poststructuralist political ecology. Analysis focuses on the micro-dynamics of socio-nature transformation: everyday resistance and social struggles, subject constructions, cultural and discursive articulations, practices and symbolic meanings. The main assumption is that an appreciation of everyday processes that shape people's lives in relation to nature requires a discourse analysis, since questions of nature and lived reality are inseparable from the ways in which nature and reality are represented (Escobar 1996). A pivotal analytical entry point is the recognition of different notions, cultural visions and situated forms of knowledge about the material world. There is no singular, unique or universal concept of nature; rather, there are multiple natures. Concepts, visions and notions of nature are not static but result from historical situations and cultural experiences. They coexist, overlap and are constantly contested, especially in times of ecological crises. Drawing on discourse analysis, knowledge–power relations are central to poststructuralist accounts in political ecology. Scholars from this epistemological standpoint ask how nature is socially constructed and how certain ideas and knowledge about nature, ecology, society and political economy shape and have shaped the ways in which people perceive and use nature, as well as how this perception shapes and has shaped subjects and power positions. To analyse these interrelations, scholars have introduced the concept of 'environmentality', which is used to examine how power in environmental management systems becomes productive; that is, how certain knowledge systems are normalized or certain subject positions are elicited that work to the ends of a governing authority (Harris 2006; Ulloa 2010).

Gramscian Political Ecology

Since the 2000s, a Gramscian perspective has emerged within political ecology. Highlighting both cultural and structural dimensions of power, scholars use Gramsci's concepts of 'hegemony' and 'philosophy of praxis' to investigate the implementation of both environmental politics and struggles over nature with regard to power relations and domination. Hegemony is a form of stable domination characterized by a combination of force and consent. A social group or class is hegemonic when it achieves consent from members of other social classes

(Gramsci 1992). With the notion of 'philosophy of praxis', Gramsci links structure and agency. He stresses on the one hand that social relations are ultimately based on capitalist relations of production. On the other hand, he develops a non-deterministic, actor-centred understanding of social change. Using Gramsci's concept of hegemony within political ecology means to study how certain notions of nature or explanations of ecological crises are generalized and gain consent; that is, how they become 'commonsense', how they are institutionalized and what other explanations and social actors are thereby marginalized. Scholars thus refer to Gramsci to study the role of the environment in the exercise and consolidation of ruling class hegemony, or to understand subaltern mobilizations and their effects on existing power relations (Ekers et al. 2009).

Postcolonial Political Ecology

Postcolonial political ecology expands upon postcolonial and subalternity studies by focusing on society–nature relations. It departs from the crises of modernity, articulated in the failing promise to provide sustainable worlds for everybody and the concept of global coloniality. The latter conceptualizes places, bodies, subjects and natures as intricately entangled in historical processes of accumulation that create social hierarchies, marginalization, subordination and destruction, but therewith also yield resistance and alternative practices. The notion of the 'coloniality of nature' (Alimonda 2011) refers, for example, to the continuity of colonial power relations that have shaped and shape society–nature relations until today. The notion refers to the concept of the 'coloniality of power', which understands coloniality as a pattern of power organized around the idea of race. Postcolonial political ecology extends this understanding by focusing on patterns of power organized around nature. In this regard, Juanita Sundberg (2008) argues for understanding human–environment relations as sites in which racial hierarchies are constituted: historically under colonial rule and contemporarily under capitalist rule. Hector Alimonda (2011) suggests studying the recent expansion of large-scale industrial mining as a continuity of a colonized nature, where nature is conceptualized as an inferior quasi-subject that needs to be controlled, dominated and ultimately exploited. Postcolonial political ecology aims to give voice to marginalized subjects and to nature, and to decolonize knowledge production; that is, to question the centrality of Western knowledge, also within political ecology.

WHAT CRITICAL AGRARIAN STUDIES CAN LEARN FROM POLITICAL ECOLOGY

Recently, scholars from critical agrarian studies have emphasized that in order to understand contemporary rural social life and changes, one of the major challenges for future research is to address the ecological dimensions of agricultural production, accumulation and politics, and the relationships between ecology, social reproduction and power relations (see Watts, this volume). To this endeavour, political ecology can contribute a lot.

From a Marxist political economy perspective, the transnational relationships between the changes in global agrarian production and environmental degradation can be fruitfully examined. Furthermore, a structural concept of power visualizes the asymmetrical distribution of the responsibilities for and impacts of environmental damages among different social classes, as well as political means of action. For example, scholars have convincingly identified industrial agriculture, and particularly increasing meat production, as one of the key drivers of greenhouse gas emissions, deforestation and biodiversity loss in the Global South (see Weis, this volume). Pointing to the inherent ecological contradictions of capitalism provides a starting point for criticizing concepts of the ecological crisis of the Earth system that see the crisis as disconnected from social relations (this includes, for instance, the concept of 'planetary boundaries', Rockström et al. 2009). Another powerful notion in this regard is the Anthropocene, the claim that the Earth has entered a new geological epoch. The idea behind this is that humans have altered natural systems to such an extent that they are no longer 'natural'. Proponents of this concept focus primarily on the relation between the Earth system and humanity as a whole, thereby hiding social relations and structures. In contrast to this, scholars with links to political ecology and critical agrarian studies have fruitfully engaged with these debates in order to bring capitalism, social structures and political economy back into the picture (Moore 2017).

Feminist political ecology in particular provides tools for studying how rural social relations are shaped not only by political-economic forces, but also by dominant forms of knowing and doing that are permeated by social relations of power in its intersecting expressions: class, caste, gender, ethnicity and race. Scholars show, for example, how and why men and women are differently affected by the expansion of agro-industrial production patterns such as palm oil plantations. Using a performative feminist theoretical approach, Andrea Nightingale (2011) examines how symbolic ideas of gender differences are continuously reproduced and expressed through everyday embodied (materialized) practices within agro-forestry production schemes in Nepal.

Examining the process of the normalization of certain forms of knowledge of nature and the environmental crisis from a poststructuralist perspective is useful for critical agrarian studies for two reasons. First, it helps us to understand how new subjectivities in rural settings are constituted in relation to the environment. Second, it reveals how powerful notions of nature become politically effective across national borders, through the way in which local knowledge and practices in rural settings are reinterpreted, marginalized and/or transformed in the name of the environment. Knowledge production based on modern socio-environmental rationalities and epistemology is also questioned from a postcolonial political ecology perspective which demands the decolonization of that knowledge. Decolonizing environmental and agrarian knowledge means inquiring into how Western and Euro-centric ideas of agrarian production and nature appropriation have been introduced to non-Western societies, how modern scientific, technological and economic rationalities have been institutionalized and with what cultural, social and ecological effects. Decolonizing is thereby not an end in itself but a condition for a cultural-political emancipation, and for constructing alternative paths to rural sustainability (Leff 2015).

From a Gramscian political ecology perspective, one can study how powerful social interests around nature appropriation emerge and materialize in agrarian settings, not in the form of an external constraint which subordinates other social classes' interests and relations to nature, but as they are strengthened through the 'active consensus' of the subaltern. At the same time, a Gramscian approach to political ecology helps us to understand how and to what extent rural social movements become an agent for change through organization building, political education and alliances and the application of alternative agro-ecological production strategies. Calvário et al. (2017) use Gramscian political ecology to comprehend how alternative ideas and practices related to the environment have been mobilized by subaltern actors during the Greek financial crisis, and to what extent these alternatives lead to a transformation of existing power relations.

CONCLUSION

The increasingly obvious ecological contradictions of the capitalist appropriation of nature in the agricultural sector – for instance, in the form of the climate crisis, agro-biodiversity loss, deforestation, (ground) water pollution and the nitrate overload of soils – call for an 'ecological turn' within critical agrarian studies. In order to do this, a dialogue with political ecology would be fruitful and productive, as it provides an appropriate analytical framework for understanding the politics *and* ecology of agriculture. Both critical agrarian studies and political ecology are part of a critical political economy and social theory. Although both fields share the same general intentions, political ecology goes beyond them by explicitly addressing the nature–society relations that are fundamental to agricultural production and reproduction, but which in critical agrarian studies often remain implicit or have only recently been highlighted. The different research strands that have evolved within political ecology since its emergence in the 1970s, and their respective theoretical underpinnings, provide a comprehensive set of analytical tools for studying ecology-related research questions within agrarian studies.

NOTE

1.   I am grateful to Andrea J. Nightingale and Bettina Engels for their comprehensive suggestions and advice on an earlier version of this text.

FURTHER READING

Peet, R.; Watts, M. (eds) (2004), *Liberation Ecologies. Environment, Development, Social Movements*, London: Routledge.
Perreault, T.; Bridge, G.; McCarthy, J. (eds) (2015), *The Routledge Handbook of Political Ecology*, London: Routledge.
Robbins, P. (2012), *Political Ecology: A Critical Introduction*, second edition, Malden: Wiley-Blackwell.
Rocheleau, D.; Thomas-Slayter, B.; Wangari, E. (eds) (1996), *Feminist Political Ecology: Global Issues and Local Experiences*, London: Routledge.

REFERENCES

Agarwal, B. (1992), The gender and environment debate: Lessons from India, *Feminist Studies*, 18, 119–158.
Alimonda, H. (ed.) (2011), *La Naturaleza Colonizada. Ecología política y minería en América Latina*, Buenos Aires: CLACSO.
Altvater, E. (1993), *The Future of the Market*, London: Verso.
Blaikie, P.; Brookfield, H. (1987), *Land Degradation and Society*, London: Methuen.
Bryant, R.L.; Bailey, S. (1997), *Third World Political Ecology*, London: Routledge.

Calvário, R.; Velegrakis, G.; Kaika, M. (2017), The political ecology of austerity: An analysis of socio-environmental conflict under crisis in Greece, *Capitalism Nature Socialism*, 28(3), 69–87.

Ekers, M.; Loftus, A.; Mann, G. (2009), Gramsci lives!, *Geoforum*, 40(3), 287–291.

Elmhirst, R. (2015), Feminist political ecology, in Perreault, T.; Bridge, G.; McCarthy, J. (eds), *The Routledge Handbook of Political Ecology*, London: Routledge, 519–530.

Escobar, A. (1996), Construction nature: Elements for a post-structuralist political ecology, *Futures*, 28(4), 325–343.

Forsyth, T. (2003), *Critical Political Ecology: The Politics of environmental Science*, London: Routledge.

Gramsci, A. (1992), *Prison Notebooks*, vol. 1, edited by Buttigieg, J.A., New York: Columbia University Press.

Harris, L. (2006), Irrigation, gender, and social geographies of the changing waterscape in southeastern Anatolia, *Environment and Planning D: Society and Space*, 24(2), 187–213.

Leff, E. (2015), Political ecology: A Latin American perspective, *Desenvolvimento e Meio Ambiente*, 35(1), 29–64.

Marx, K. (1976 [1867]), *Capital*, vol. 1, Harmondsworth: Penguin Books.

Moore, J.W. (2017), The capitalocene, Part 1: On the nature and origins of our ecological crisis, *Journal of Peasant Studies*, 44(3), 594–630.

Nightingale, A. (2011), Bounding difference: Intersectionality and the material production of gender, caste, class and environment in Nepal, *Geoforum*, 42, 153–162.

Plumwood, V. (1993), Nature, self, and gender: Feminism, environmental philosophy and the critique of rationalism, in Zimmermann, M. (ed.), *Environmental Philosophy: From Animal Rights to Radical Ecology*, Englewood Cliffs, NJ: Prentice-Hall, 284–309.

Rocheleau, D.; Thomas-Slayter, B.; Wangari, E. (1996), Gender and environment: A feminist political ecology perspective, in Rocheleau, D; Thomas-Slayter, B.; Wangari, E. (eds), *Feminist Political Ecology: Global Issues and Local Experiences*, London: Routledge, 1–23.

Rockström, J., Steffen, W., Noone, K., Persson, A., Chapin III, F.S., Lambin, E.F. et al. (2009), A safe operating space for humanity, *Nature*, 461, 472–475.

Sundberg, J. (2008), Placing race in environmental justice research in Latin America, *Society and Natural Resources*, 21(7), 569–582.

Taylor, M. (2015), *The Political Ecology of Climate Change Adaptation: Livelihoods, Agrarian Change and the Conflicts of Development*, London: Earthscan/Routledge.

Ulloa, A. (2010), *The Ecological Native: Indigenous Movements and Eco-governmentality in Colombia*, New York: Routledge.

Watts, M.J. (2000), Political ecology, in Sheppard, E.; Barnes, T.J. (eds), *A Companion to Economic Geography*, Malden, MA: Blackwell, 257–274.

Watts, M.J. (2013 [1983]), *Silent Violence. Food, Famine, and Peasantry in Northern Nigeria*, Athens, GA: University of Georgia Press.

Weis, T. (2010), The accelerating biophysical contradictions of industrial capitalist agriculture, *Journal of Agrarian Change*, 10(3), 315–341.

Wissen, M. (2015), The political ecology of agrofuels: Conceptual remarks, in Dietz, K.; Engels, B.; Pye, O.; Brunnengräber, A. (eds), *The Political Ecology of Agrofuels*, Abingdon: Routledge, 16–33.

Wolf, E.R. (1972), Ownership and political ecology, *Anthropological Quarterly*, 45(3), 201–205.

65. Pluriloguing postcolonial studies and critical agrarian studies

Johanna Leinius

INTRODUCTION

Postcolonial approaches are concerned with critically analysing how European colonialisms have shaped past and present societies' 'modes of seeing, being, and knowing' (Go 2016, 8), and with striving towards decolonizing colonial mindsets, relations and structures. They combine the Marxist interest in the material bases of power with the poststructuralist concern for the discursive and cultural forms that constitute subjectivities, establish truths and naturalize unequal power relations. Such approaches look at both the 'form and content of prevailing knowledge' (McLeod 2007, 9), politicizing how we come to make sense of the world and what becomes a matter of concern (see Young 2001, 57). The main argument of postcolonial scholars is that colonial constellations of power and authority did not end with the independence of colonized territories, but in fact persist until today.

In this contribution, I bring critical agrarian studies and postcolonial approaches into a plurilogue. According to Ella Schohat (2001, 5), a plurilogue constitutes a polyphonic space 'where many critical voices engage in a dialogue in which no one voice hopefully muffles the other'. Tensions can remain unresolved and no perspective needs to claim the last word; rather, the blind spots and silences in the respective perspectives are elucidated.

At first glance, both approaches share the aim of challenging hierarchizations and of contributing to social justice through a politics of knowledge that starts from the views and practices of those who have been marginalized in modern capitalist societies. It is surprising, therefore, that in the article by Marc Edelman and Wendy Wolford (2017), postcolonial approaches are not referenced explicitly, even though several postcolonial authors are cited and some of the contributions to the symposium that the article introduces explicitly draw on postcolonial studies (see, for example, Jakes 2017). I argue that more than citational politics, this silence signals some key epistemological and methodological divergences; divergences which nevertheless do not inhibit a mutually enriching dialogue. My argument is that if the aim of critical agrarian studies is to go beyond rural class formation, the insights of postcolonial approaches would certainly merit deeper engagement.

To explicate my argument, I follow the already existing and potential intersections between postcolonial approaches and critical agrarian studies, rather than giving a general assessment of the scope of postcolonial approaches (for an introduction, see Loomba 2015; Young 2001). I firstly provide a genealogy of postcolonial approaches, from anti-colonial writings to post-colonial studies and beyond. Secondly, I focus on the topics and debates relevant for critical agrarian studies. Thereafter I bring the latter into a plurilogue with postcolonial approaches, and conclude by making a case for a postcolonially informed critical agrarian studies.

TRAJECTORIES AND THEMES IN POSTCOLONIAL APPROACHES

Postcolonial approaches can be found in a variety of disciplines and under a multitude of names. They share the common concern of critically studying the legacies of colonial conquest and imperialism, and are often rooted in the work of anti-colonial scholars like W.E.B. Du Bois, Frantz Fanon, Aimé Césaire, Amilcar Cabral and others. These scholars did not only write illuminating analyses of colonial exploitation, domination, violence and the psychological and cultural costs of colonization on both colonizer and colonized, but were also engaged in anti-colonial struggles. More than merely critiquing unequal power relations, they envisioned possibilities for transforming colonizing ways of relating to one another. As Julian Go (2016, 9) notes, the 'post' in postcolonial consequently invokes a body of thought that seeks to transcend colonial legacies from a positionality that is emphatically anti-colonial and does not seek to imply that colonialism is over.

Postcolonial studies rose to prominence in the 1980s, mainly in English literature departments in universities in the Global North. As a discipline, it strives to identify the specific logics of colonial rule that have endured even beyond official decolonization; an aim that has been largely achieved quite early on. In this context, Stuart Hall underlines the productive tension between the focus on a particular chronological period – the history of European colonialism, imperialism and decolonization – and an epistemological project – the challenge to the order of knowledge that has its basis in European colonization and continues to subjugate other peoples and their knowledges (Hall 1996, 254). Edward Said, Gayatri Spivak and Homi Bhabha, though differing in their disciplinary and personal backgrounds, theoretical reference points and political outlooks, are usually perceived as central scholars of the postcolonial project. Their perspectives developed in part in critical dialogue with the South Asia Subaltern Studies Group, a group of South Asian and Indian scholars who combine the epistemological challenge within the discipline of history related to its universalizing tendencies with a specific empirical project: reading colonial archives against the grain, striving to uncover modes of subaltern peasant consciousness (Guha 1988) and proving the inadequacy of European concepts to explain peasant uprisings in colonial India.

Nowadays, postcolonial approaches have made a home in most university departments and disciplines – though the primary locus of enunciation, especially of postcolonial studies, continues to be the humanities (Go 2016, 12). As postcolonial interventions have addressed different contexts and constituencies, postcolonial approaches are a heterogeneous field that encompasses a plethora of perspectives, projects and analyses. Some scholars identify as postcolonial, while others actively resist the term and claim to articulate their analyses from contexts and histories that are not and have never been postcolonial. The modernity/coloniality/decoloniality project, for example, is a 'community of argumentation' (Escobar 2010, 45) consisting of scholar activists who see the colonization of the Americas in 1492 as the starting point of the modern colonial world system. They argue that modernity and capitalism are inextricably intertwined with coloniality, racism and Eurocentrism, and see themselves as part of a larger debate on global coloniality in which postcolonial studies are but one strand grounded in 'the experience of British India and Orientalism' (Tlostanova and Mignolo 2012, 25). Native and indigenous scholars underline the uninterrupted colonization of native peoples, criticizing postcolonial studies for neglecting the continuing violent occupation of native lands (Tuck and Yang 2012). Critically scrutinizing settler colonialism, they point to the fact that 'both Marxists and capitalists view land and natural resources as commodities to be exploited' (Grande 2004, 27).

These heterogeneous concepts and perspectives have influenced social movements and politics in both the Global North and South, just as they are transformed by and intersect with emancipatory struggles. The Zapatista rebellion for a 'world in which many worlds fit', as well as indigenous, afro-Latin and other place-based communities and movements, have spearheaded a debate on the global 'civilizational crisis' (Lander 2005). They take the colonial character of contemporary societies as a starting point for carrying out a scathing critique of capitalist modernity, proposing other ways of being that put the sustainability of life centre-stage (Lang et al. 2018). They challenge academic knowledge practices and strive to put into practice other ways of producing knowledge collectively and in community (Tuhiwai Smith 1999; Levya et al. 2015).

While internally heterogeneous and sometimes competing, postcolonial approaches converge in several themes that provide intersections with critical agrarian studies.

The Legacies of Colonialism and the Politics of Resistance

A common denominator of postcolonial approaches has been the focus on both the effects of colonization and the politics of decolonization. Contemporary and historical inequalities are examined concerning their entanglement with empire and with a view towards challenging them in their multiple dimensions.

Modernity is seen as having naturalized a view of the world that rests on hierarchized and hierarchizing binaries such as man-woman, public-private, nature-culture. Orientalism is exemplary of this logic, giving authority for knowing the world to the colonizers, who identify and internally homogenize regions in a way that sets the affluent, modern and progressive West against the deficient and degenerate rest (McEwan 2001, 93; Said 1978). Economically, postcolonial approaches trace how production and reproduction are based on unequal exchanges on a global scale (Hoogvelt 2001). They hold that a linear model of development prevails which locates capitalist modernity as the endpoint of progress, without a concern for the interrelated modes of subjugation and exploitation that historically enabled the industrialization of the Global North. Scrutinizing development as an idea that has material consequences, Orientalist scholars analyse how it commodifies and destroys other forms of life (Ziai 2007).

Postcolonial feminist work has shown how the distinction between a public and a private realm has devalued the work of social reproduction, which is mainly seen as the responsibility of women, revealing repercussions for women's economic, political and familial position (de la Cadena 1992). Political institutions are examined concerning the ways in which power and authority are formed, exercised and distributed, and how liberal democratic modes of decision-making continue to be shaped by colonial logics that result in unequal access (Mamdani 1996). Anti-colonial resistance movements have been criticized for how they have hierarchized emancipatory struggles, relegating for example women's and minorities' struggles to the margins by proclaiming the need for unity (Spivak 1988). They have also shown how in feminist movements, the concerns of middle-class urban women have come to stand for feminist concerns, while the concerns of peasant women for clean water, food and adequate medical care have been read as pre-feminist 'practical gender interests' (McEwan 2001, 98).

Postcolonial scholars have pointed to the devastating impact of colonization on the living world but have also discussed the appropriation of indigenous knowledges by both environmental movements and transnational companies. Work on indigenous communities' relations to land and territory has traced how indigenous ontologies have historically been violently suppressed by colonizers, and continue to be invisibilized in contemporary struggles for land rights and territorial sovereignty (de la Cadena 2010). They have critiqued the notion that women are closer to nature than men and have undertaken decolonizing and anti-racist ecofeminist work (Sandilands 1999). More recently, the debate on climate change (Chakrabarty 2009) has been examined concerning its embeddedness in colonial relations of power and knowledge.

The Critique of Universal Reason

Postcolonial interventions have been oriented towards producing knowledge about colonization and its effects, while at the same time expressing an uneasiness about the truth claims of knowledge production. Scholars have discussed European knowledge production as a provincial mode of representing the world and Others (Chakrabarty 2000). Human rights (Grovogui 2006), for example, have been examined in relation to the underlying practices of hierarchization and silencing. The politics of representation has been central. Within feminism, Chandra Talpede Mohanty has traced how Western feminism has constructed an essentialized image of the 'Third World woman' as the victim of a timeless, universal patriarchal culture, ignoring the enormous diversity of women's experiences and positing shared oppression as common for all women (Mohanty 2003 [1991]). By Othering women in the Global South, she argues, the authority of Western feminists to define the parameters and subjects of a universally applicable feminism is stabilized.

In the field of history, the Subaltern Studies Group has challenged the practice of applying concepts derived from European historical processes to postcolonial territories. They reframe subalternity, for example, to describe the positionality and consciousness of peasants in colonial India. Spivak comments on the ambivalences of this endeavour in her essay 'Can the subaltern speak?' (1988). Subalternity, according to Spivak, is a 'position without identity', characterized by its lack of access to the state, citizenship and to upward mobility (Spivak 2014a, 10). Scholars identifying with or close to the modernity/coloniality/decoloniality project have argued for the need to trace how exploitation, but also resistance, have their roots in specific places (Escobar 2008). Seeing place as 'a conjunction of many histories and many spaces' (Massey 1995, 191), the multiperspectival character of how place is constructed and employed is underlined. Notions of hybridity and diaspora have counteracted a romanticizing notion of belonging and have been applied for thinking through the ambivalences of subject constitution under conditions of global coloniality (Bhabha 1994).

The Politics of Knowledge Production

Postcolonial approaches have, since their beginning, straddled the uneasy line between theory and practice. One of their foremost aims, for instance, has been to decolonize the canon of knowledge. One of the first central volumes in postcolonial studies, *The Empire Writes Back* (Ashcroft et al. 2004 [1989]), challenged the canon of English literature departments. The colonizing aspects of education and the historical injustices that have accompanied projects of modern education, especially for colonized and indigenous peoples worldwide, have also come under scrutiny (Bristol 2010).

At the core of these projects have been the questions of who can legitimately produce knowledge about the world, and how this can be done (Harding 2011). These questions have motivated both historical accounts of colonial writings and contemporary analyses of postcolonial encounters, in academia and beyond. The critical gaze is also turned towards postcolonial scholars themselves (Coronil 2013). As Dipesh Chakrabarty holds, 'as intellectuals operating in academia, we are not neutral to these struggles and cannot pretend to situate ourselves outside of the knowledge procedures of our institutions' (Chakrabarty 2000, 43).

These debates have resulted in a great sensitivity for the constitution and distribution of power and privilege among those who claim to represent the struggles and knowledges of the marginalized as well as between the latter and the marginalized themselves (Grewal and Kaplan 2000). Intertwined with this has been the question of how the production and dissemination of knowledge is shared between postcolonial intellectuals and marginalized and racialized communities. More than merely acknowledging the situatedness of all knowledge, postcolonial approaches have striven to develop representational practices based on explicating positionality in a way that makes visible and enables the agency and subjectivity of all those involved in knowledge production (Harding 2008). Postcolonial methodologies refuse easy dichotomies and the ideologically chosen high ground, critically approaching postcolonial problematics instead (Go 2016, 194). Against all forms of essentialism, Said (1993, 52) argues for the critical analysis of how things come into existence through their connections, oppositions and embeddedness. Postcolonial feminists practise a politics of location that understands struggles as context-specific but not context-bound, seeking to establish critical practices of solidarity that allow for mutual dialogue, learning and transformation (Mohanty 2003).

Debating the Materialist Critique

One of the attacks most commonly led against postcolonial approaches has been the charge that they pay insufficient attention to the material realities of people on the ground (Sylvester 1999). Postcolonial theory, the argument goes, is fine for literary scholars, but cannot adequately address social and political processes (Chibber 2013, 293). By diluting Marxism with poststructuralism, these critics argue, postcolonial scholars fail to address the problems that actually matter, as 'all we need is a recognition that people need to eat – and capitalism prevents them [from] doing so' (Go 2016, 199).

Vivek Chibber, in a recent version of this critique, has argued that subaltern studies – which he sees as representative of postcolonial approaches (Chibber 2014, 617–618) – has ontologized the Orient by arguing that capitalism developed differently in the Global North and Global South. By denying the existence of objectively existing structures of capitalism that transcend local particularities, the possibility of solidarity based on the shared fight for 'physical well-being' (Chibber 2013, 200–202) is inhibited. Beyond reflecting on the effects of academic debates on contemporary politics, not only in India (see also Nanda 2001), the subsequent critiques by postcolonial scholars have also helped to clarify their take on political economy: Spivak, in a reply to Chibber's arguments, holds that the question is not whether Marxism or postcolonialism are able to explain empirical reality, but how analytical categories such as class travel to postcolonial contexts; contexts which were formed by potentially other modes of production, cultural practices and political institutions. Tracing the entanglement between racialized, classed, gendered and other 'cultural' refractions of the purportedly 'universal' desire for physical well-being is indispensable for emancipatory politics (Spivak 2014b, 189). Chakrabarty's study of industrial workers in colonial Calcutta (1989) exemplifies Spivak's point well: he shows that the specific form that capitalism took in colonial India led neither to a split between industrialized and agrarian processes of production, nor to a divide between the public and private spheres. Industrial workers retained their connections to their peasant communities in terms of both social reproduction and production, which meant that their struggles followed other logics and trajectories to those of the European proletariat. He argues that global capitalism has consequently resulted in the reproduction of the small peasantry in the Global South, a fact that has been invisible to those using Eurocentric theories.

PLURILOGUING CRITICAL AGRARIAN STUDIES AND POSTCOLONIAL STUDIES

In linking cultural analysis and political economy, critical agrarian studies examines how the 'expansion into and exploitation of agrarian life … gives rise to conquest and colonization, vesting modernity with violence, dispossession and racial prejudice' (Edelman and Wolford 2017, 961). It examines how the rural has been constituted as lacking and backwards, and strives to combine this analysis with the examination of extractivist capitalism. Edelman and Wolford enumerate three analytical assumptions shared by scholars of critical agrarian studies. The first is that dualisms shape how the world is made sense of. Critical agrarian studies focuses in particular on the duality between city and countryside, and strives to reveal the interdependent and mutual constitution of the urban and the rural. Second, the cultural and political economy is the centre of analysis, which third, also entails the:

> analysis of the experiences and political culture of agrarian classes and communities, of generations of women and men, and of the urban groups and institutions – nearby and distant – that interact with and affect the countryside. (Edelman and Wolford 2017, 966)

From this short overview alone, it seems unquestionable that critical agrarian studies and postcolonial approaches deeply resonate with each other. Many of the topics that critical agrarian studies posits as central have been discussed in postcolonial approaches, with some strands – the Subaltern Studies Group and the modernity/coloniality/decoloniality project come immediately to mind – examining the experiences and struggles of those living on the land. Both apply materialist approaches to make sense of agrarian life, but while in postcolonial approaches they are refracted by a concern for the particularities of the postcolonial setting, critical agrarian studies continues to perceive the agrarian question primarily through the lens of class dynamics. Rooted in peasant studies, which has primarily focused on uncovering the contradictory dynamics of class formation at the periphery (Bernstein and Byres 2001, 8), critical agrarian studies has just begun to go beyond the confines of political economy. In short, postcolonial approaches see colonialism in all its dimensions as foundational for contemporary relations, while for critical agrarian studies, labour relations continue to be at the heart of critical analysis.

Postcolonial approaches are especially sensitive to the ways in which markers of differentiation that can provide the basis for identity formations – such as race, gender, sexuality and others – intersect with class in the lived experiences of the marginalized to shape specific forms of exploitation that cannot be addressed by singling out one dimension of oppression alone (Lorde 1984, 138). These debates provide a fruitful point of engagement for critical agrarian studies' concern with taking into account the 'intersectionality of structure and agency, in terms of gender, generation, ecology, space and landscapes' (Akram-Lodhi 2019). Postcolonial approaches have made great strides in terms of scrutinizing the mutual con-stitution of structure and agency, looking at hegemony and subject formation (Stoler 1995) to trouble dichotomous and essentializing readings. When Akram-Lodhi argues that critical agrarian studies 'seeks to uncover the sources of social power' (Akram-Lodhi 2019), postco-lonial approaches can offer a way to take into account the specific setting of the postcolonial world. Postcolonial approaches, in turn, have been hesitant to abandon humanity as their main concern, even when critically intervening in debates on environmental racism and climate change (Álvarez and Coolsaet 2018; Chakrabarty 2009). Critical agrarian studies' interest in going beyond human-nature dichotomies (see, for example, Fleischman 2017), as well as its grounding in the material worlds of agrarian life, can inspire mutually enriching dialogues.

The subject matter of postcolonial approaches and critical agrarian studies, I have argued, overlap, not only concerning their general critical outlook but also their interest in the life worlds of those living at the relative exteriority of modernity. Looking at the *how* of critical analysis, both disciplines orient knowledge production towards revealing and challenging injustices and inequalities. Postcolonial approaches have, in this context, debated both the powerful constitution of the epistemologies and ontologies of knowledge production, as well as the power and privileges shaping the minutiae of scholarly research. They see (academic) knowledge production as part of the problem. Critical agrarian studies, in turn, identifies engaged scholar activism as one of its identifying markers of distinction (Akram-Lodhi 2019). A. Haroon Akram-Lodhi (2019), in this context, underlines the necessity of 'empirically eval-uating actually-existing agrarian questions'. Postcolonial approaches can provide examples of how 'nuanced and granular ethnographic and sociological investigations' (ibid.) can be under-taken that are conscious of the power effects of knowledge production as well as of the impact of coloniality on social relations. Studies such as Janet Conway's (2018) analysis of food sov-ereignty as a mobilizing discourse in the World March of Women or Marisol de la Cadena's (2015) ethnography of the role of Earth Beings in Andean life worlds are recent examples of such postcolonial research that can productively dialogue with critical agrarian studies.

CONCLUSION

Critical agrarian studies, though recent in its disciplinary formation, does not hesitate to for-mulate far-reaching claims. According to Edelman and Wolford,

> the field of Critical Agrarian Studies provides a lens for understanding everything from state for-mation to modern subjectivities; shifting politics, policies and practices; the production of forms of knowledge and ignorance, as well as popular beliefs, rituals, and norms; informal and formal practices of collective action, within and across borders; and the ways in which the past can foreclose certain taken-for-granted futures. (Edelman and Wolford 2017, 966)

Maybe more specifically, critical agrarian studies examines the rural from a relational perspec-tive that centres on 'the mutual constitution of and ongoing interactions between the rural and urban not only concerning political economy, but also political, cultural, and other formations' (ibid.).

Postcolonial approaches, as I have shown above, can contribute – and already have contributed much – to this critical endeavour. Taking the wealth of knowledge of postcolonial approaches into account can therefore only strengthen the critical impetus and work of critical agrarian studies. Postcolonial approaches, in turn, would profit from engaging with how critical agrarian studies rephrases the agrarian question in a way that takes land, non-human subjects and the environment seriously as interlocutors of socio-economic, cultural and political processes. Deepening the dialogue would undoubtedly enrich both perspectives.

FURTHER READING

Chakrabarty, D. (2000), *Provincializing Europe: Postcolonial Thought and Historical Difference*, Princeton, NJ: Princeton University Press.
de la Cadena, M. (2015), *Earth Beings: Ecologies of Practice across Andean Worlds*, Durham, NC: Duke University Press.
Grewal, I.; Kaplan, C. (2000), Postcolonial studies and transnational feminist practices, *Jouvert: A Journal of Postcolonial Studies*, 5(1), accessed 6 February 2020 at https://legacy.chass.ncsu.edu/jouvert/v5i1/grewal.htm.
Tuhiwai Smith, L. (1999), *Decolonizing Methodologies: Research and Indigenous Peoples*, London: Zed Books.

REFERENCES

Akram-Lodhi, A.H. (2019), What is critical agrarian studies?, *Review of African Political Economy*, accessed 20 August 2019 at www.roape.net/2018/03/28/what-is-critical-agrarian-studies/.
Álvarez, L.; Coolsaet, B. (2018), Decolonizing environmental justice studies: A Latin American perspective, *Capitalism Nature Socialism*, 10.1080/10455752.2018.1558272, 1–20.
Ashcroft, B.; Griffiths, G.; Tiffin, H. (2004 [1989]), *The Empire Writes Back: Theory and Practice in Post-Colonial Literatures*, London: Routledge.
Bernstein, H.; Byres, T.J. (2001), From peasant studies to agrarian change, *Journal of Agrarian Change*, 1(1), 1–56.
Bhabha, H.K. (1994), *The Location of Culture*, New York: Routledge.
Bristol, L. (2010), Practising in betwixt oppression and subversion: Plantation pedagogy as a legacy of plantation economy in Trinidad and Tobago, *Power and Education*, 2(2), 167–182.
Chakrabarty, D. (1989), *Rethinking Working-Class History: Bengal 1890–1940*, Princeton, NJ: Princeton University Press.
Chakrabarty, D. (2000), *Provincializing Europe: Postcolonial Thought and Historical Difference*, Princeton, NJ: Princeton University Press.
Chakrabarty, D. (2009), The climate of history: Four theses, *Critical Inquiry*, 35(2), 197–222.
Chibber, V. (2013), *Postcolonial Theory and the Specter of Capital*, London: Verso.
Chibber, V. (2014), Making sense of postcolonial theory: A response to Gayatri Chakravorty Spivak, *Cambridge Review of International Affairs*, 27(3), 617–624.
Conway, J.M. (2018), When food becomes a feminist issue: Popular feminism and subaltern agency in the World March of Women, *International Feminist Journal of Politics*, 20(2), 188–203.
Coronil, F. (2013), Latin American postcolonial studies and global decolonization, *Worlds and Knowledges Otherwise*, 3(3), accessed 6 February 2020 at https://globalstudies.trinity.duke.edu/sites/globalstudies.trinity.duke.edu/files/file-attachments/v3d3_Coronil%20.pdf.

de la Cadena, M. (1992), Las mujeres son más indias: etnicidad y género en una comunidad del Cuzco, *Revista Isis Internacional, Ediciones de las Mujeres*, accessed 9 October 2014 at http://red.pucp.edu.pe/ridei/files/2011/08/104.pdf.

de la Cadena, M. (2010), Indigenous cosmopolitics in the Andes: Conceptual reflections beyond 'politics', *Cultural Anthropology*, 25(2), 334–370.

de la Cadena, M. (2015), *Earth Beings: Ecologies of Practice across Andean Worlds*, Durham, NC: Duke University Press.

Edelman, M.; Wolford, W. (2017), Introduction: Critical agrarian studies in theory and practice, *Antipode*, 49(4), 959–976.

Escobar, A. (2008), *Territories of Difference: Place, Movements, Life, Redes*, Durham, NC: Duke University Press.

Escobar, A. (2010), World and knowledges otherwise: The Latin American modernity/coloniality research program, in Mignolo, W.; Escobar, A. (eds), *Globalization and the Decolonial Option*, London: Routledge, 33–64.

Fleischman, T. (2017), 'A plague of wild boars': A new history of pigs and people in late 20th century Europe, *Antipode*, 49(4), 1015–1034.

Go, J. (2016), *Postcolonial Thought and Social Theory*, New York: Oxford University Press.

Grande, S. (2004), *Red Pedagogy: Native American Social and Political Thought*, Lanham, MD: Rowman and Littlefield.

Grewal, I.; Kaplan, C. (2000), Postcolonial studies and transnational feminist practices, *Jouvert: A Journal of Postcolonial Studies*, 5(1), accessed 6 February 2020 at https://legacy.chass.ncsu.edu/jouvert/v5i1/grewal.htm.

Grovogui, S.N'Z. (2006), Mind, body, and gut! Elements of a postcolonial human rights discourse, in Jones, B.G. (ed.), *Decolonizing International Relations*, Lanham, MD: Rowman and Littlefield, 179–196.

Guha, R. (1988), The prose of counter-insurgency, in Guha, R.; Spivak, G.C. (eds), *Selected Subaltern Studies*, New York: Oxford University Press, 45–84.

Hall, S. (1996), When was the 'postcolonial'? Thinking at the limit, in Chambers, I.; Curti, L. (eds), *The Post-Colonial Question: Common Skies, Divided Horizons*, London: Routledge, 242–260.

Harding, S. (2008), *Sciences from Below: Feminisms, Postcolonialities, and Modernities*, Durham, NC: Duke University Press.

Harding, S. (ed.) (2011), *The Postcolonial Science and Technology Studies Reader*, Durham, NC: Duke University Press.

Hoogvelt, A. (2001), *Globalization and the Postcolonial World: The New Political Economy of Development*, Houndmills: Palgrave.

Jakes, A. (2017), Boom, bugs, bust: Egypt's ecology of interest, 1882–1914, *Antipode*, 49(4), 1035–1059.

Lander, E. (2005), La ciencia neoliberal, *Revista Venezolana de Economía y Ciencias Sociales*, 11(2), 35–69.

Lang, M.; König, C.-D.; Regelmann, A.-C. (eds) (2018), *Alternatives in a World of Crisis*, Brussels: Rosa-Luxemburg Stiftung and Universidad Andina Simón Bolívar.

Levya, X., Alonso, J., Hernández, R.A., Escobar, A., Köhler, A., Cumes, A. et al. (eds) (2015), *Prácticas Otras de Conocimiento: Entre Crisis, Entre Guerras*, San Cristóbal de las Casas: Cooperativa Editorial Retos.

Loomba, A. (2015), *Colonialism/Postcolonialism*, third edition, London: Routledge.

Lorde, A. (1984), *Sister Outsider: Essays and Speeches*, New York: Crossing Press.

Mamdani, M. (1996), *Citizen and Subject: Contemporary Africa and the Legacy of Late Colonialism*, Princeton, NC: Princeton University Press.

Massey, D. (1995), Places and their pasts, *History Workshop Journal*, 39(1), 182–192.

McEwan, C. (2001), Postcolonialism, feminism and development: Intersections and dilemmas, *Progress in Development Studies*, 1(2), 93–111.

McLeod, J. (2007), Introduction, in McLeod, J. (ed.), *The Routledge Companion to Postcolonial Studies*, London: Routledge, 1–18.

Mohanty, C.T. (2003), *Feminism Without Borders: Decolonizing Theory, Practicing Solidarity*, Durham, NC: Duke University Press.

Mohanty, C.T. (2003 [1991]), Under Western eyes: Feminist scholarship and colonial discourses, in Lewis, R.; Mills, S. (eds), *Feminist Postcolonial Theory: A Reader*, Edinburgh: Edinburgh University Press, 49–74.

Nanda, M. (2001), We are all hybrids now: The dangerous epistemology of post-colonial populism, *Journal of Peasant Studies*, 28(2), 162–186.

Said, E. (1978), *Orientalism*, New York: Vintage Books.

Said, E. (1993), *Culture and Imperialism*, New York: Vintage Books.

Sandilands, C. (1999), *The Good-Natured Feminist: Ecofeminism and the Quest for Democracy*, Minneapolis, MN: University of Minnesota Press.

Schohat, E. (2001), Introduction, in *Talking Visions: Multicultural Feminism in a Transnational Age*, Cambridge, MA: MIT Press, 1–13.

Spivak, G.C. (1988), Can the subaltern speak?, in Nelson, C. and Grossberg, L. (eds), *Marxism and the Interpretation of Culture*, London: Macmillan, 271–313.

Spivak, G.C. (2014a), The 2012 Antipode AAG lecture: Scattered speculations on geography, *Antipode*, 46(1), 1–12.

Spivak, G.C. (2014b), Review: Postcolonial theory and the specter of capital, *Cambridge Review of International Affairs*, 27(1), 184–198.

Stoler, A.L. (1995), *Race and the Education of Desire: Foucault's History of Sexuality and the Colonial Order of Things*, Durham, NC: Duke University Press.

Sylvester, C. (1999), Development studies and postcolonial studies: Disparate tales of the 'Third World', *Third World Quarterly*, 20(4), 703–721.

Tlostanova, M.V.; Mignolo, W. (2012), *Learning to Unlearn: Decolonial Reflections from Eurasia and the Americas*, Columbus, OH: Ohio State University Press.

Tuck, E.; Yang, K.W. (2012), Decolonization is not a metaphor, *Decolonization: Indigeneity, Education and Society*, 1(1), 1–40.

Tuhiwai Smith, L. (1999), *Decolonizing Methodologies: Research and Indigenous Peoples*, London: Zed Books.

Young, R.C. (2001), *Postcolonialism: An Historical Introduction*, Malden, MA: Blackwell.

Ziai, A. (ed.) (2007), *Exploring Post-Development: Theory and Practice, Problems and Perspectives*, London: Routledge.

66. Agrarian justice: Land, human rights and democratization

Jennifer C. Franco and Sofía Monsalve Suárez

INTRODUCTION

Agrarian justice is a social movement framework (Snow and Benford 1992) that starts with an overarching idea of social justice as the measure of a good society and guide for corrective social and political action (e.g. identifying unjust conditions that should be changed). It then focuses attention on issues around the meaning and control of land and related natural resources. Social struggles to (re)gain control of land, increasingly framed in terms of a human right to land, link the concepts of agrarian justice and rural democratization.

Working peoples' struggles for land control are neither new nor simply random accidents of history. Instead, they are part and parcel of the 'double movement' (Polanyi and MacIver 1944) involving the extension of a market-controlled economy and related efforts to organize things that are 'obviously not commodities', namely, land, labor and money, into markets (see Polanyi's notion of 'fictitious commodities') – which in turn provokes resistance. Often marked by high social and political conflict, rural democratization is another way to conceptualize historical struggles by 'working people' (Shivji 2017). Inspired by visions of agrarian justice, it resists the ongoing extension of market economies by (re)gaining control of the meaning and use of land and related resources.

Nearly 30 years ago Fox (1990) highlighted rural democratization (unfolding within and in relation to rural political arenas) as a process – inseparable from democratization more generally – involving struggles within society and the state 'to rollback authoritarian political practices' and 'to extend effective access to democratic governance to the entire citizenry'. The character and pace of these struggles was seen to vary from one particular historical and institutional setting to another, to exhibit variable degrees of uncertainty and contingency (e.g. human agency and political strategies matter), stalemate and setback (e.g. movement forward is not inevitable) and to spark movement in multiple directions (e.g. not just moving back and forth along a unilinear continuum). The emphasis on *rural* democratization invited attention to social struggles taking place 'system-wide' (and not just in more populous urban centers and national capitals), and to the possibility that what happens even in remote rural spaces can matter for the democratic-ness of authoritative decision making at the national level, and vice versa.

In the last 30 years, human rights, including assertions of a human right to land as a social movement frame (Claeys 2016), have increasingly shaped the action repertoires, advocacy campaigns and struggles of the rural working class, Indigenous, ethnic, rural women and other marginalized groups (Monsalve Suárez 2013). This trend reflects, in part, defensive reactions to a new round of capitalist encroachment and enclosures ('global land grab') and to the ways in which powerful state and non-state actors use law to capture control of land to facilitate capitalist accumulation. Both global and national land policy making have become key battlegrounds. Recent decades rekindled debate over land tenure/land reform and land law in relation to 'development', with competing perspectives and conceptual framings initially revolving broadly around two main poles of vision: 'a marketability-based vision and a security and rights-based vision of land tenure legalization and how to go about doing it' (Assies 2009, 575). Marketability-based visions conceptualized a 'right to land' based on a narrow view of land as 'property': an economic asset to be exploited through private ownership.

Popular resistance to this view often invokes a deep social justice interpretation of human rights. While potentially increasing the legibility of agrarian justice movements and the legitimacy of their land claim making, a human rights framing of land and land struggles also involves strategic assertion of human rights as law/legal instruments that can be used in courts to engage/face state actors as 'duty bearers' given that law has been essential to defining and organizing statehood. Working people's assertion of their human right to land has resulted, at times, in positive gains for movement participants in terms of discrete claim making, and at times in movement toward more democratic land control and agrarian justice.

What a human right to land looks like to the working people participating in these mobilizations is situational, shaped by subaltern experiences, imaginaries, moral economies *and* calculated responses to 'circumstances not of their own choosing but directly encountered, given and transmitted from the past' (Marx 1968). In this sense, a human right to land can and does vary, in terms of broad contours as well as specific contents, both over historical time and across geographical spaces. This point will be discussed in more detail below.

DEFINITION OF THE PERSPECTIVE: WHAT DOES A HUMAN RIGHT TO LAND LOOK LIKE?

A human right is a right that is inherent to human beings without any discrimination based on sex, origin, race, place of residence, religion or any other status (Monsalve Suárez 2013). Human rights constitute an ethical code that seeks to promote and protect the human dignity of all and is derived from the needs and aspirations of ordinary people, and therefore express universal ethical and moral values. They are necessarily interdependent, indivisible and inter-related, and serve to empower each human being, their communities and peoples with entitlements and enforceable claims vis-à-vis their own governments as well as other governments and international organizations. In this view, to resist oppression is at the very core of the human rights idea. Human rights explicitly address power imbalances and raise the question of the legitimacy of the powerful (UDHR 1948; WCHR 1993).

Human rights are not the same as rights without the epitome 'human', which by contrast, generally speaking, refer to specific, exclusive, non-universal entitlements that persons, legal or natural, can have with respect to different matters (e.g. property, labor, an economic activity) according to respective law regimes (e.g. commercial, civil, customary, environmental law). The distinction between a 'human right to land' and 'land rights' is significant in light of rising interest globally in land and related ascendency of technical-legal 'land rights' approaches in contemporary land policy making (see White et al. 2012; Claeys and Vanloqueren 2013; Golay and Biglino 2013). In many parts of the world, the challenge of democratizing political arenas is related to the distribution of access and control of land, since land is a source of wealth and power. Land governance in many societies tends to be undemocratic, favoring elites within the state and in society (HLPE 2011). Democratizing land control means deliberately addressing inequalities in land ownership, control and use, in favor of excluded and marginalized social classes and groups (Franco et al. 2015). This kind of intervention operationalizes the notion of a human right to land: as with any other human right, the change needed involves 'putting the last first' in the sense of prioritizing access and control of land for those who have been deprived of it.

The United Nations Declaration on the Rights of Peasants and Other People Working in Rural Areas (UNDROP) recognizes their rights to land, individually or collectively, including the right to have access to, sustainably use and manage land and water bodies, coastal seas, fisheries, pastures and forests therein, to achieve an adequate standard of living, to have a place to live in security, peace and dignity and to sustain cultural practices tied to identity and livelihoods (Article 17.1). As the *travaux préparatoires* on the negotiations of UNDROP show (OHCHR n.d.; FIAN 2015), the way the right to land in Article 17 was drafted covers three distinct but interrelated tasks, each representing dimensions of agrarian justice.

The first task is to ensure authoritative recognition and protection of relatively democratic land access/control against erosion through processes of land accumulation and land concentration. Here the focus is on settings where a good degree of democratic land control by rural working people exists, including for instance many areas under customary tenure systems, or Indigenous territories or pastoralist routes and grazing areas, but especially where such control is under threat from state and/or corporate enclosures (Wily 2012). This category can include diverse modalities of customary arrangements based on ideals of moral economy or subsistence/social insurance for land users – all of which can be recognized by law without necessarily assuming that they are egalitarian (Peters 2004, 2013). Sometimes, the imperative to protect human rights may require explicitly recognizing *individual private property* rights by law, such as in cases where statutory law recognizes household claims via the 'head of household' while remaining silent on the rights of all the individuals in a household, e.g. spouses, siblings, children. Or, it may require recognizing *individual usufruct* rights, such as in the Chinese household responsibility system.

Ensuring recognition and protection of democratic land control where it already exists differs from Hernando de Soto's (2000) formula of 'formalization' of land rights interpreted as individual private property rights (for a critique of de Soto, see Cousins 2009), and from more recent efforts to formalize customary tenure in the face of the global land rush (Krantz 2015). Rather than redistribute power, formalization schemes tend to ratify and consolidate existing power distributions. Unlike a human right to land, formalization does not by definition try to detect land inequality or other kinds of land injustice (such as land grabbing); is not designed to question the dominant model of development; and typically is rolled out in lieu of public debate over the social function of land and the social purpose of land policy (Nyamu 2007; Dwyer 2015). Formalization schemes at best ignore, but at worst undermine, a human right to land.

The second task of a human right to land is to ensure promotion of democratic distribution of access/control where it does not exist. In settings marked by unequal distribution of land control, technical-oriented land rights formalization initiatives are likely to formalize unequal land access and consolidate inequality (Borras and Franco 2010a; see Borras et al. 2007 for the case of the Philippines). In such settings, if agrarian justice is the aspiration, then land redistribution is needed. The type of redistributive land program needed can vary depending on the specific socioeconomic and historical-institutional context at hand (De Schutter 2010a; Ziegler 2002). Where unequal land control is embedded in a private property regime (large latifundia in Brazil – see Wolford 2010), redistributive land reform must be coupled with a general agricultural policy that does not disadvantage the farming sector, while providing state support such as credit, irrigation and post-harvest facilities. Where unequal land relations exist in a state/public ownership regime, such as in Myanmar, redistributive land reallocation must target agrarian working-class households and not corporate and other landed elites. Where unequal land control exists in the context of relatively smaller plots controlled by non-working elite owners, such as in some parts of South Africa or parts of India (e.g. Kerala), the challenge is to ensure effective tenure and lease arrangements guaranteeing the rights of those who actually work the land.

The third task is to restore prior democratic land control that was lost due to historical expulsion, theft, violence and armed conflict or civil war resulting in working people's loss of land control (OHCHR 2007). In settings where rural working-class households and other social groups were thrown off the land in such circumstances, as in South Africa, Colombia or Myanmar, the task is to combine meaningful land restitution with land redistribution to prevent restitution processes from ushering in a new cycle of land concentration. This differs from monetized forms of restitution; monetization of one's land claim as a form of restitution risks reducing remedial justice to a technical 'quit claim' procedure, as happened in South Africa (Walker 2008). Rather, the task is to realize the wider frame of restorative justice for displaced people, where land restitution is intrinsically linked to voluntary return and resettlement, in safety and with dignity, and whenever appropriate, to their places of origin.

This three-fold notion of a human right to land must be understood in a wider context that is itself deeply rooted in capitalism: not only in relation to the global land rush, but also in the context of the profound ecological climate crisis confronting humanity, largely caused by capitalism, and the growing rush to implement climate change adaptation/mitigation schemes that implicate land and related natural resources. These processes – combined with policy-making processes that fall short of a minimum democratic threshold – are 'recasting the political economy of land, water, fisheries and forests in the rural world today, and reconfiguring how capital penetrates agriculture and the countryside', and negatively (re)framing rural working people, Indigenous groups, rural women and others as either 'economically inefficient' or 'environmentally destructive' or both (Borras and Franco 2018, 12). This suggests the need to address two additional challenges – ecological regeneration and democratizing representation – alongside the three described above (recognition, redistribution, restitution) (ibid.). Completing the picture is an across-the-board minimum land size floor, coupled with a maximum land size ceiling, to 'sandwich' these five tasks, reinforcing this framing of a human right to land as anti-capitalist (ibid.).

This view of a human right to land contrasts sharply with the neoclassical economics view of land governance. The latter reduces land to 'property' in the sense of a commodity with only economic use value, while privileging those who can mobilize the strongest legal basis for individual private property rights claims in the name of economic efficiency (De Schutter 2010b). Throughout the world, the biggest threat to a human right to land – and thus to initiatives to democratize land control as a necessary step toward agrarian justice – is the imposition of this very 'particular conception of property and the associated practices through which property is secured', which Hornby et al. (2017, 10) have aptly described as 'an 'edifice', connoting both an imposing structure and a 'complex system of beliefs'.

LOOKING BACK, MOVING FORWARD

Land and agrarian reform have factored in human rights research and advocacy since at least the early 1990s, when FIAN International, the organization for the human right to food and nutrition, for instance, began conceptualizing agrarian reform as a human rights obligation with the right to adequate food. Human rights and land reform have been part of radical rural activism since that time, if not before (e.g. in the era of national liberation struggles). Many activists 'cut their teeth' and became connected by participating in human rights fact-finding missions to investigate and inform the public about summary killings and disappearances of peasants by state and non-state armed forces, mass evictions and displacements of entire villages and customary systems to make way for 'mega development' projects and industrial plantations, for example. In this earlier period, influenced by Latin American peasant organizations, the emerging transnational movement framed food sovereignty in relation to poor peasants' struggles for land redistribution against large private landholdings (latifundia) and backed by a public support system (e.g. policy, programs, etc.) to create a mass of farmers with sufficient land for economically viable full-time farming.

Over time, as the movement grew, this conception of 'land reform' came to be seen as unable to capture the circumstances and contexts of a wider range of subaltern social classes and groups who were also in urgent need of land (Rosset 2013; La Via Campesina 2017). In large parts of Africa, the main target of the recent wave of enclosures has been non-private (e.g. state or public and community) land. Defending community lands and strengthening and democratizing customary systems in terms of gender, generation and ethnic dimensions are key issues for food sovereignty and agrarian justice activism in much of Africa and Asia. Land restitution is a key issue in societies marked by violent conflict such as Colombia (Cramer and Wood 2017), South Africa (Walker 2008) and Myanmar (TNI 2019). Inaccessibility of land for young people, whether young farmers or young people from non-agricultural backgrounds, is a pressing issue across Europe, where market forces and existing institutional architecture create barriers to new entrants to farming (Borras et al. 2013). Indigenous peoples and other ethnic groups everywhere are losing territorial access and control due to encroachment by extractive industries (Bebbington et al. 2018).

Once a powerful policy and political platform, land reform had initially evolved in response to historically conditioned demands for redistribution of large private landholdings as a step towards social justice. But this framing lacked relevance and power as a remedy for other kinds of unjust land situations that existed elsewhere in the world. This realization led to a revised concept and framing that built upon ongoing dialogue and collective construction of a land and natural resource perspective on food sovereignty. This process was facilitated especially by the International Planning Committee for Food Sovereignty – a platform aggregating diverse constituencies of social movements representing and defending the rights of hundreds of millions of small food producers (Edelman and Borras 2016). As discussed above, the concept of 'democratic land control' emerged with the notion of a human right to land at its core. The concept continues to evolve, shaping and shaped by discussion and debate, both within and beyond the movements, countries and regions.

Yet the notion of a human right to land remains contested; and two recent steps towards legal recognition both resulted from fraught negotiation processes. First was the adoption of the Voluntary Guidelines on the Responsible Governance of Tenure of Land, Fisheries and Forests in the Context of National Food Security (or 'CFS-TGs'), by the United Nations

Committee on World Food Security in May 2012 (Seufert 2013; CSM 2016; Hall et al. 2016; FAO 2017). Development of these guidelines occurred in parallel with several contrasting attempts to shape global land regulation (e.g. the International Food Policy Research Institute Code of Conduct; World Bank Responsible Investment in Agriculture and Food Principles; for the differences see Kunnemann and Monsalve 2013; Franco et al. 2017). The CFS-TGs were the first 'soft law' instrument to apply economic, social and cultural rights to the governance of land, fisheries and forests. Anchored in human rights values and in existing international human rights law, they address, among others, formal and informal, individual and collective and unequal tenure situations (Franco and Monsalve 2018). Second was the adoption of UNDROP by the United Nations General Assembly in December 2018. This declaration recognizes the right to land of peasants and other working-class groups (Article 17). Together with the right to land and territory of Indigenous peoples enshrined in International Labour Organization Convention N° 169 and the United Nations Declaration of the Rights of Indigenous Peoples (UNDRIP), UNDROP strengthens the international legal basis for rural working people to demand a right to land.

Both developments have increased momentum toward formal recognition of a human right to land. How they will be used and where, by whom and for what purposes, and to what effect are questions that warrant deeper investigation. Are human rights (whether legal or not) in the end 'just a piece of paper', or can they be a tool for social change toward agrarian justice? Studying the significance of the UNDRIP for Indigenous struggles, Sawyer and Gomez (2008, 3) found that 'seeking and acquiring Indigenous rights is not, in and of itself, emancipatory. Rather, it recalibrates the arena of struggle.' Adoption of the UNDRIP alters the institutional field on which battles for control of land now take place, potentially causing actors to alter their strategies. Marginalized social actors may be emboldened to take actions they considered too risky before or to join campaigns they earlier eschewed. Powerful economic actors may find popular resistance to mega-projects harder to ignore; state actors may try to use new means to increase their political legitimacy. Whether this happens and what difference it makes is an empirical question; the facts on the ground cannot be deduced from abstract theory alone. But ideas on using new human rights instruments can be tested in practice (Franco et al. 2017; Franco and Monsalve 2018; see also TNI and FIAN n.d.).

CONCLUSION

A major recasting of the rural political economy is underway, along with a major reconfiguration of capitalist penetration of the countryside, with many rural areas being targeted for either acquisition or conservation (Borras and Franco 2018). Such areas are often populated, productive and governed through customary regulatory orders that allocate and enforce rights and obligations, and value and protect environmental biodiversity. When introduced, new economic production (or extraction) and environmental protection arrangements involve either expulsion or adverse incorporation of people.[1] As a result, people are displaced when the deemed land (or biodiversity) is needed but their labor is not (Li 2011). Or, when their land (or biodiversity) and labor are both needed, the people are incorporated into the emerging enterprises as laborers, environmental protection guards or contract growers, frequently under unfavorable and onerous terms. In the process, human rights are being violated and/or undermined (GRAIN 2008; Von Braun and Meinzen-Dick 2009; Borras and Franco 2010b; Zagema 2011, 114–164; Mehta et al. 2012, 193; White et al. 2012, 619–647; Monsalve Suárez 2013).

At the same time, human rights rhetoric appears to be making deep inroads into the edifice of global regulatory and financial institutions, even as these same institutions are playing a bigger role than ever before in transforming 'land' into 'property' and 'nature' into 'commodity', alongside turning 'corporations' into 'persons' in juridical terms. Seen in this light, rejection of human rights and criticism of social movement calls for a human right to land may seem relevant (see for example D'Souza 2018). Yet rural working people *are* framing their efforts to claim land, democratize land control and construct 'land sovereignty' in the face of capitalist expansion, whether these efforts are explicitly anti-capitalist or not, in terms of human rights, democratization and agrarian justice. Surely the perceptions and calculations of those whose lands, villages or territories have been lost or are under threat of being grabbed exist independently of the observer's standpoint and can be taken seriously. Meanwhile, the political significance of a perceived human right to land may lie less in its 'statutoriness' or likelihood of achieving formal-legal status, and more in its ability to inspire, mobilize and sustain rural working class-based movements in favor of democratic land and control and towards their vision of agrarian justice.

In the end, the relationship between how intentions or claims are framed and organized and what outcomes they produce in terms of social transformation is not so clear-cut empirically or predetermined analytically. There are competing logics and interpretations of human rights, including those that arise from anti-capitalist aspirations. There are political strategies based on alternative readings of context, of what counts as meaningful action and of what matters as an outcome in terms of emancipatory social change. And there are intervening and contingent factors that can knock any intended scenario off-course unexpectedly, can lead to unanticipated outcomes and still matter in radical emancipatory terms. Rather than be ignored or dismissed, all these aspects and factors (and more) can be perceived and investigated further.

NOTE

1. See research linked to the Land Deals Politics Initiative and several academic journal special issues on the topic, such as *Journal of Peasant Studies*, *Development and Change*, *Globalizations*, *Canadian Journal of Development Studies*, *Third World Quarterly* and *Water Alternatives*, among others.

FURTHER READING

De Schutter, O. (2010b), The emerging human right to land, *International Community Law Review*, 12, 303–334.

Nuila, A.; Seufert, P. (2019), A view from the countryside: Contesting and constructing human rights in an age of converging crises, *Issue Brief*, December, TNI, ERPI and FIAN, accessed July 24, 2021 at www.tni.org/files/publication-downloads/web_countryside.pdf.

Razavi, S. (2003), Introduction: Agrarian change, gender and land rights, *Journal of Agrarian Change*, 3(1–2), 2–32.

Sandwell, C.; Casteneda Flores, A.; Fernanda Forero, L.; Franco, J.; Monsalve Suarez, S.; Nulia, A.; Seufert, P. (2019), A view from the countryside: Contesting and constructing human rights in an age of converging crises, *Research Paper*, Amsterdam: TNI.

REFERENCES

Assies, W. (2009), Land tenure, land law and development: Some thoughts on recent debates, *Journal of Peasant Studies*, 36(3), 573–589.

Bebbington, A., Humphreys Bebbington, D., Sauls, L.A., Rogan, J., Agrawal, S., Gamboa, C. et al. (2018), Resource extraction and infrastructure threaten forest cover and community rights, *PNAS*, 115(52), 13164–13173.

Borras, S.M.; Franco, J.C. (2010a), Contemporary discourses and contestations around pro-poor land policies and land governance, *Journal of Agrarian Change*, 10, 1–32.

Borras, S.M.; Franco, J. (2010b), From threat to opportunity? Problems with the idea of a 'code of conduct' for land-grabbing, *Yale Human Rights and Development Journal*, 13(2), 507–523.

Borras, S.M.; Franco, J. (2018), The challenge of locating land-based climate change mitigation and adaptation politics within a social justice perspective: Towards an idea of agrarian climate justice, *Third World Quarterly*, 39(7), 1308–1325.

Borras, S.; Carranza, D.; Franco, J. (2007), Anti-poverty or anti-poor? The World Bank's market-led agrarian reform experiment in the Philippines, *Third World Quarterly*, 28(8), 1557–1576.

Borras, S.M.; Franco, J.; van der Ploeg, J.D. (2013), Introduction, *Land Concentration, Land Grabbing and People's Struggles in Europe*, Amsterdam: TNI, accessed July 24, 2021 at www.tni.org/files/download/land_in_europe-jun2013.pdf.

Claeys, P. (2016), The right to land and territory: New human right and collective action frame, FMSH-WP-2016-109, March.

Claeys, P.; Vanloqueren, G. (2013), The minimum human rights principles applicable to large-scale land acquisitions or leases, *Globalizations*, 10, 193–198.

Cousins, B. (2009), Capitalism obscured: The limits of law and rights-based approaches to poverty reduction and development, *Journal of Peasant Studies*, 36(4), 893–908.

Cramer, C.; Wood, E.J. (2017), Introduction: Land rights, restitution, politics, and war in Colombia, *Journal of Agrarian Change*, 17(4), 733–738.

CSM (2016), Synthesis report on civil society experiences regarding use and implementation of the tenure guidelines and the challenge to monitoring CFS decisions. A contribution of civil society to the Global Thematic Event during the 43rd session of the United Nations Committee on World Food Security and to developing an innovative mechanism to monitor CFS decisions and recommendations. Rome, accessed July 24, 2021 at www.csm4cfs.org/wp-content/uploads/2016/09/CSM-Monitoring-Report-VGGT-final1_EN-1.pdf.

De Schutter, O. (2010a), Access to land and the right to food, report of the Special Rapporteur on the right to food presented at the 65th General Assembly of the United Nations [A/65/281], October 21.

De Schutter, O. (2010b), The emerging human right to land, *International Community Law Review*, 12, 303–334.

De Soto, H. (2000), *The Mystery of Capital: Why Capitalism Triumphs in the West and Fails Everywhere Else*, New York: Basic Books.

D'Souza, R. (2018), *What's Wrong with Rights? Social Movements, Law and Liberal Imaginations*, London: Pluto Press.

Dwyer, M. (2015), The formalization fix? Land titling, land concessions and the politics of spatial transparency in Cambodia, *Journal of Peasant Studies*, 42(5), 903–928.

Edelman, M.; Borras, S. (2016), *Political Dynamics of Transnational Agrarian Movements*, Halifax: Fernwood Publishing.

FAO (2017), Final evaluation of the global programme to support the implementation of the voluntary guidelines on the responsible governance of tenure of land, fisheries and forests (2012–2016), Office of Evaluation, Project Evaluation Series, November, Rome, accessed July 24, 2021 at http://www.fao.org/3/BD722/bd722.pdf.

FIAN (2015), The right to land and other natural resources in the UN Declaration on the rights of peasants and other people working in rural areas, FIAN International Briefing, Heidelberg.

Fox, J. (ed.) (1990), *The Challenge of Rural Democratization: Perspectives from Latin America and the Philippines*, London: Franck Cass.

Franco, J.; Monsalve, S. (2018), Why wait for the state? Using the CFS tenure guidelines to recalibrate political-legal struggles for democratic land control, *Third World Quarterly*, 39(7), 1386–1402.

Franco, J.; Monsalve, S.; Borras, S. (2015), Democratic land control and human rights, *Current Opinion in Environmental Sustainability*, 15, 66–71.

Franco, J.; Park, C.; Herre, R. (2017), Just standards: International regulatory instruments and social justice in complex resource conflicts, *Canadian Journal of Development Studies*, 38(3), 341–359.

Golay, C.; Biglino, I. (2013), Human rights responses to land grabbing: A right to food perspective, *Third World Quarterly*, 34, 1630–1650.

GRAIN (2008), *Seized: The 2008 Land Grab for Food and Financial Security*, Barcelona: GRAIN.

Hall, R.; Scoones, I.; Henley, G. (2016), Strengthening land governance: Lessons from implementing the voluntary guidelines, LEGEND State of the Debate Report, May, accessed July 24, 2021 at: www.researchgate.net/publication/303340553_Strengthening_Land_Governance_Lessons _from_implementing_the_Voluntary_Guidelines_on_the_Responsible_Governance_of_Tenure_of _Land_Fisheries_and_Forests_in_the_Context_of_National_Food_Security.

HLPE (2011), Land tenure and international investments in agriculture, Report by the High Level Panel of Experts on Food Security and Nutrition of the Committee on World Food Security, Rome, July, accessed July 24, 2021 at www.fao.org/3/a-mb766e.pdf.

Hornby, D.; Kingwill, R.; Royston, L.; Cousins, B. (eds) (2017), *Untitled: Securing Land Tenure in Urban and Rural South Africa*, Pietermaritzburg: University of KwaZulu-Natal Press.

Krantz, L. (2015), Securing customary land rights in Sub-Saharan Africa: Learning from new approaches to land tenure reform, Working Papers in Human Geography 1, Department of Economy and Society, Goteborgs Universitet, Handelshogskolan, accessed July 24, 2021 at https://gupea.ub.gu.se/bitstream/ 2077/38215/1/gupea_2077_38215_1.pdf.

Kunnemann, R.; Monsalve, S. (2013), International human rights and governing land grabbing: A view from global civil society, *Globalizations*, 10(1), 123–139.

La Via Campesina (2017), Struggles of La Via Campesina for agrarian reform and the defense of life, land and territories, Harare.

Li, T. (2011), Forum on Global Land Grabbing: Centering labor in the land grab debate, *Journal of Peasant Studies*, 38(2), 281–298.

Marx, K. (1968), *The Eighteenth Brumaire of Louis Bonaparte*, in *Marx/Engels Selected Works in One Volume*, London: Lawrence and Wishart.

Mehta, L.; Veldwisch, G.J.; Franco, J. (2012), Introduction to the special issue: Water grabbing? Focus on the (re)appropriation of finite water resources, *Water Alternatives*, 5(2), 193–207.

Monsalve Suarez, S. (2013), The human rights framework in contemporary agrarian struggles, *Journal of Peasant Studies*, 40(1), 239–290.

Nyamu Musembi, C. (2007), De Soto and land relations in rural Africa: Breathing life into dead theories about property rights, *Third World Quarterly*, 28(8), 1457–1478.

OHCHR (2007), *Handbook on Housing and Property Restitution for Refugees and Displaced Persons. Implementing the 'Pinheiro Principles'*, Geneva: OHCHR.

OHCHR (n.d.), Records of open-ended intergovernmental working group on a United Nations declaration on the rights of peasants and other people working in rural areas, accessed July 24, 2021 at www .ohchr.org/EN/HRBodies/HRC/RuralAreas/Pages/WGRuralAreasIndex.aspx.

Peters, P. (2004), Inequality and social conflict over land in Africa, *Journal of Agrarian Change*, 4, 269–314.

Peters, P. (2013), Land appropriation, surplus people and a battle over visions of agrarian futures in Africa, *Journal of Peasant Studies*, 40, 537–562.

Polanyi, K.; MacIver, R.M. (1944), *The Great Transformation*, Boston, MA: Beacon Press.

Rosset, P. (2013), Re-thinking agrarian reform, land and territory in La Via Campesina, *Journal of Peasant Studies*, 40(4), 721–775.

Sawyer, S.; Gomez, E.T. (2008), Transnational governmentality and resource extraction: Indigenous peoples, multinational corporations, multilateral institutions and the state, Identities, Conflict and Cohesion Programme Paper Number 13, United Nations Research Institute for Social Development, September, accessed July 24, 2021 at: www.unrisd.org/80256B3C005BCCF9/httpNetITFramePDF ?ReadForm&parentunid=DD4690C7DCC1A303C1257512003066D6&parentdoctype=paper& netitpath=80256B3C005BCCF9/(httpAuxPages)/DD4690C7DCC1A303C1257512003066D6/$file/ SawGomez-paper.pdf.

Seufert, P. (2013), The FAO voluntary guidelines on the responsible governance of tenure of land, fisheries and forests, *Globalizations*, 10, 181–186.

Shivji, I.G. (2017), The concept of 'working people', *Agrarian South: Journal of Political Economy*, 6(1), 1–13.

Snow, D.; Benford, R. (1992), Master frames and cycles of protest, *Frontiers in Social Movement Theory*, New Haven, CT: Yale University Press.

TNI (2019), First they grabbed our lands with guns; now they are using the law: A Commentary by TNI on the right to land of people displaced by war and militarization, accessed July 24, 2021 at www.tni .org/en/article/first-they-grabbed-our-land-with-guns-now-they-are-using-the-law.

TNI; FIAN (n.d.), Using the tenure guidelines for action research: A primer. Funded by IDRC, accessed July 24, 2021 at www.tni.org/files/publication-downloads/web_tenure_guidelines.pdf.

UDHR (1948), Universal Declaration of Human Rights, New York, accessed July 24, 2021 at www.un .org/en/about-us/universal-declaration-of-human-rights.

Von Braun, J.; Meinzen-Dick, R. (2009), 'Land grabbing' by foreign investors in developing countries: Risks and opportunities, *IFPRI Policy Brief 13*, April, Washington, DC: IFPRI.

Walker, C. (2008), *Landmarked: Land Claims and Land Restitution in South Africa*, Johannesburg: Jacana Media.

WCHR (1993), World Conference on Human Rights, Vienna Declaration and Programme of Action.

White, B.; Borras, S.; Hall, R.; Scoones, I.; Wolford, W. (2012), The new enclosures: Critical perspectives on corporate land deals, *Journal of Peasant Studies*, 39, 619–647.

Wily, L.A. (2012), Looking back to see forward: The legal niceties of land theft in land rushes, *Journal of Peasant Studies*, 39, 751–775.

Wolford, W. (2010), *This Land Is Ours Now: Social Mobilization and the Meanings of Land in Brazil*, Durham, NC: Duke University Press.

Zagema, B. (2011), Land and power: The growing scandal surrounding the new wave of investments in land, 151 Oxfam Briefing Paper, September.

Ziegler, J. (2002), Access to land, agrarian reform and the right to food, Report of the Special Rapporteur on the right to food presented at the 65th General Assembly of the United Nations [A/57/356], August 27.

67. Strategic linkages between STS and critical agrarian studies

Ryan Nehring

INTRODUCTION

Work in critical agrarian studies has ranged from the theoretical to the grounded or empirical and has been enriched with methods that present "the lived experience of the peoples making up those [agrarian] societies" (Scott and Bhatt 2001, 2). Part of the lived experiences of agrarian life is the skills and knowledge acquired and used to work, and ultimately transform, the land and resources for social needs and change. By adding "critical" to agrarian studies, it is implied that a critical framework is being embraced by the field. Edelman and Wolford (2017, 962) claim this means to "identify, analyze and combat the biases and forms and values of representing and legitimizing knowledge that characterize conventional wisdom" or, in other words, "working from and for the margins."

Critical frameworks were also foundational to the establishment of science and technology studies (STS) as an academic discipline (Hackett et al. 2008). Political agendas were and continue to be at the center of both fields. Almost from the field's inception, STS scholars were crudely understood by critics to be relativizing science, its "facts" and authority.[1] This is where (the West) and when (the 1970s) the Cold War was in full swing and, at the same time, the growth of the environmentalist and anti-colonial movements pitted socialism against capitalism. Such context matters a great deal in shaping the agenda and politics of an academic field or discipline as particular lines of inquiry are rooted in ideological battles on the ground.

The broadly Marxist roots of critical agrarian studies emerged out of anti-colonial movements and intense interest in the role of agrarian classes – primarily the peasantry – as a potentially revolutionary force (Bernstein and Byers 2001). These "real world" and materialist politics formed much of the agrarian insurgency movements around the world and were deeply intertwined with the ideological interests of agrarian studies scholars. As the applicability of the "agrarian question" was interrogated from Australia to Zimbabwe, materialist frameworks have dominated the field. Struggles over and against the commodification of land and labor make agrarian issues central to broader questions of state formation, development and social change. These struggles demonstrate the ways in which commodification is never totalizing. The control over land and territory is contingent on mechanisms and technologies to make enforceable claims through coercion and consent (Peluso and Lund 2011). In other words, land claims go hand in glove with knowledge claims (Pritchard et al. 2016). This chapter intends to chart strategic linkages between the fields of STS and critical agrarian studies by concomitantly "working from and for the margins" while centering the importance of science and technology for agrarian issues.

CIRCULATION AND CRITIQUE IN AND OF STS

Prior to the establishment of STS as a field, the social study of science of scientific knowledge was relatively autonomous from the social, political and cultural context. This "internalist" account was one of the first critiques from emerging STS scholars who analyzed the ways in which social, cultural and political factors were not only part of the context but also the content of scientific "discoveries" and technological development. Thomas Kuhn's *The Structure of Scientific Revolutions* (1962) is a common starting point for the founding of STS as he provided one of the earliest critiques of knowledge as an accumulative and progressive[2] endeavor. An early focus on laboratory studies was common as that was commonly held as the key location where scientific knowledge is produced as a contingent process (Latour and Woolgar 1979). The question of contingency, or how and why specific forms of knowledge and technology emerge and are considered true, is a running theme among STS scholarship. Contingency also aligns with a key focus of the discipline to question the epistemological authority of science as objective, and politically and socially neutral. Scientific facts were no longer understood to be external to scientists and observers, but rather, the emergence of facts was integral to the social and political conditions from which knowledge claims were made.

Bruno Latour (1999) famously outlined such an encounter by observing three scientists in different disciplines – a botanist, a geographer and a soil scientist – as they tried to understand why a border between forest and savannah was shifting in the Amazonian region of Brazil. As they collected samples to identify the reasons for the shifting vegetation, it was an opportunity to watch science in action. His explanation is that as the scientists created references of the material world, they interacted with the non-human in the circulation of these references. Science then becomes *thingified* as scientific texts, samples and other material references are circulated as "immutable mobiles" (Latour 1987). Soil samples were taken by the scientists from the ground and placed in reference with other, different samples on a grid. Scientific understandings of the soil took on new meaning in reference to its material existence and in relation to both other non-material objects and humans. This process of circulating reference renders important relationships visible in otherwise innumerable natural relationships in reality. It is a real-world example of Latour's version of Actor-Network Theory (see de Vries 2016).

Many scholars in STS have increasingly become aware of Eurocentrism and micro theorizing (such as lab studies) in the field. A critique of the discipline as being primarily Western in its focus and politics has only been a more recent contribution by postcolonial STS scholarship (c.f. Mitchell 1991; Ong and Collier 2005; Anderson 2009; Harding 2011). Postcolonial STS is potentially much closer to critical agrarian studies in that the study of science and technology is situated within broader structural questions of development and underdevelopment. Science and technology were not only integral to colonial power but also reproduced through postcolonial relationships of enduring discipline and even resistance (see Bonneuil 2000; Tilly 2011).

Agrarian studies scholars are perhaps most aware of the longstanding marginalization of rural populations where claims to land are fundamental to agrarian livelihoods. Such perspectives open up avenues for the ways in which agrarian studies scholarship can contribute to STS. In Actor-Network Theory, ontological categories shed hierarchical organization, subject-object dichotomy and, instead, take on agency as either actors or actants. Such symmetrical networks, or "assemblages," attempt to shield away classical social analytical categories such as class, power and hierarchy (see Mills 2017). This has led to numerous critiques to Latour's strong influence in the discipline as supplying neoliberal ideologies of science (Fuller 2012). *Critical* agrarian studies can texture the social study of science by privileging perspectives "from and for the margins."

The "assemblage" of land for different uses for different groups of people is inherently social and power laden (Li 2014). Over the last decade, new research in critical agrarian studies has focused increasingly on knowledge politics as an important site of struggle where claims to land and territory are taking place on the ground. The "global land grab" was one such moment when a convergence of crises led to a massive and widespread push to commodify vast tracts of land (Borras et al. 2011). New scholarly and activist communities mobilized regionally around seemingly unprecedented levels of expropriation, exclusion and dispossession (Schoenberger et al. 2017). This necessarily demanded new analytical tools to understand how and in what ways land becomes "grabbable" within distinct historical, geographical, social and political contexts. Scientific knowledge claims can serve a politics of land suitability for those with a vested interest. Or as Jenny Goldstein (2016) shows in Indonesia, scientific research can also be mobilized in ways to generate "divergent expertise" or cast doubt on determining how land should be used and by whom. The revelation that there is "scientific uncertainty" is nothing new to STS, even if the political mobilization of that uncertainty has left some wondering what the role of critical scholars – agrarian or otherwise – should be (Latour 2003).

Questions of scientific authority in spaces dominated by capitalist and imperial exploitation are then at the heart of understanding how and why particular scientific facts reign supreme (again, questions of contingency). As Tsing (2015, 218) put it, "uneven development shows us science as a postcolonial translation." Different scales of analysis – from the test tube to transnational knowledge flows – and locations – from the laboratory to multilateral research institutions – are all part of STS scholarship, which speaks to its multi- and cross-disciplinary nature. More recent scholarship has included political economy perspectives of STS (Tyfield et al. 2017; see also Goto 2013) and national and transnational questions of technoscientific politics (see Carney 2001; Jasanoff and Kim 2015; Tsing 2015).

"KNOWING" AGRICULTURE AND AGRARIAN TRANSFORMATIONS

Agronomy is perhaps one of the most useful fields of study to explore productive linkages between STS and critical agrarian studies. The field of agronomy is where plant breeders, soil scientists, geneticists and other scientific "experts" apply their expertise to agricultural production. However, like any other academic field, not all agronomists share the same understanding of science or explicitly engage with the political and social nature of their work (see Ajl 2018). If scientific facts are contingent on social, cultural and political forces then they can and should be contested. The field of agronomy is no exception.

Those who follow and contribute to the agroecological movement (see McCune and Rosset, this volume) are well aware of its battle for legitimacy as a science. The differences between the (crudely put) extremes of agroecological and industrial models of agriculture reveal the inherent political and contingent nature of agronomy specifically, and science more generally. A more privileged account of how perspectives from the margins shape and are shaped by scientific knowledge will hopefully further linkages between STS and agrarian studies. How might Latour's famous study of circulating reference in the Amazon look different with the inclusion of knowledges from Indigenous populations? And how might such an inclusion even be enacted and under whose terms? These are some of the broader epistemological questions at the heart of questioning the multiple scales and relations of power in knowledge production. "Political agronomy analysis" is one emerging area in which methods from STS and political economy are being applied to agronomic sciences (Sumberg 2012). It provides one such "call for research" to further our understanding of agronomy as inherently political, contested and a contingent "world of sciences" (see Harding 2011).

Well-documented cases of agricultural modernization were fueled by the mobilization of science and technology as so-called correctives for the social and economic ills of the countryside. Such was the case of the Green Revolution, which was the deployment of United States experts and expertise throughout the world as a counterrevolutionary force to support agricultural modernization (Perkins 1997). Despite a differentiation in agrarian structures, the pursuit of scientific modernization in the countryside has had remarkable similarities and technical relations between both socialist and capitalist countries (Fitzgerald 2003, 157–183) and agrarian contexts (Olsson 2017). Yet, understanding whose science counts as big "S" Science is also racialized (Eddens 2017; Anderson and Roque 2018), gendered (Keller 1985; Harding 1991) and bounded by space and place over time (Hecht 2011; Medina et al. 2014). Critical agrarian studies scholars are well aware of the importance of historicizing the Green Revolution as an ongoing terrain of contestation. As Patel (2013, 4) claims, "in pushing for a 'second Green Revolution,' the first Green Revolution needs to be sold as a success."

Problems such as underdevelopment and poverty were, and continue to be, framed in technical terms with technical solutions. Such is the case with attempts to "close the yield gap," which argues for technologically driven solutions to realize potential versus actual agricultural yields (see Sumberg 2012). The motives to expand commodity relations in the developing world have been left out of the "official" narrative written by the architects of the Green Revolution. Research that centers on agrarian perspectives has shown that the expansion of commodity relations was not just a consequence of the Green Revolution but a strategic goal by design (Harwood 2019). The so-called biotechnological revolution was not only a marked leap in a scientific approach to farming but it also opened new frontiers for the commodification of nature (Kloppenburg 2005). Yet, science and technology are not fixed or path dependent but subject to competing subjectivities, interests and relations of power.

Critical agrarian studies has shown the importance of centering the rural and agrarian life to more fully understand broader issues such as modernization, globalization and state formation. As such, scholars in the field rightfully contest historically dominant narratives of agrarian societies as backward or primitive. STS provides lessons of how and why knowledge is always incomplete, power-laden, contingent and situated or partial. Both critical agrarian studies and STS can work together "from and for the margins" to contest dominant forms of science and technology from the countryside to the city and even collectively imagine new agrarian futures.

NOTES

1. Critiques of STS from scientific realists played out in the "Science Wars," which marked an important moment for the field to articulate its political implications. For an introduction to the debate see Ashman and Baringer (2001).

2.   Progressive meaning an inevitable march towards truth and enlightenment.

FURTHER READING

Donovan, K.P. (2014), Development as if we have never been modern: Fragments of a Latourian development studies, *Development and Change*, 45(5), 869–894.
Hackett, E.J.; Amsterdamska, O.; Lynch, M.; Wajcman, J. (eds) (2008), *The Handbook of Science and Technology Studies*, third edition, Cambridge, MA: MIT Press.
Pritchard, S.; Wolf, S.A.; Wolford, W. (2016), Knowledge and the politics of land, *Environment and Planning A: Economy and Space*, 48(4), 616–625.
Sumberg, J.; Thompson, J. (eds) (2012), *Contested Agronomy: Agricultural Research in a Changing World*, New York: Routledge.

REFERENCES

Ajl, M. (2018), Auto-centered development and Indigenous technics: Slaheddine el-Amami and Tunisian delinking, *Journal of Peasant Studies*, 46(6), 1240–1263.
Anderson, W. (2009), From subjugated knowledge to conjugated subjects: Science and globalisation, or postcolonial studies of science?, *Postcolonial Studies*, 12(4), 389–400.
Anderson, W.; Roque, R. (2018), Imagined laboratories: Colonial and national racializations in Southeast Asia, *Journal of Southeast Asian Studies*, 43(9), 358–371.
Ashman, K.M.; Baringer, P.S. (eds) (2001), *After the Science Wars*, London: Routledge.
Bernstein, H.; Byers, T. (2001), From peasant studies to agrarian change, *Journal of Agrarian Change*, 1(1), 1–16.
Bonneuil, C. (2000), Development as experiment: Science and state building in colonial and postcolonial Africa, 1930–1970, *Osiris*, 15, 258–281.
Borras, Jr., S.M.; Hall, R.; Scoones, I.; White, B.; Wolford, W. (2011), Towards a better understanding of global land grabbing: An editorial introduction, *Journal of Peasant Studies*, 38(2), 209–216.
Carney, J. (2001), *Black Rice: The African Origins of Rice Cultivation in the Americas*, Cambridge, MA: Harvard University Press.
de Vries, G. (2016), *Bruno Latour*, Cambridge: Polity Press.
Eddens, A. (2017), White science and Indigenous maize: The racial logics of the Green Revolution, *Journal of Peasant Studies*, November 27.
Edelman, M.; Wolford, W. (2017), Critical agrarian studies in theory and practice, *Antipode*, 49(4), 959–976.
Fitzgerald, D. (2003), *Every Farm a Factory: The Industrial Ideal in American Agriculture*, New Haven, CT: Yale University Press.
Fuller, S. (2012), CSI: Kuhn and Latour, *Social Studies of Science*, 42(3), 429–434.
Goldstein, J. (2016), Knowing the subterranean: Land grabbing, oil palm, and divergent expertise in Indonesia's peat soil, *Environment and Planning A*, 48(4), 754–770.
Goto, K. (2013), STS and Marxist study: Where do we stand now?, *Social Epistemology*, 27(2), 125–129.
Hackett, E.J.; Amsterdamska, O.; Lynch, M.; Wajcman, J. (eds) (2008), *The Handbook of Science and Technology Studies*, third edition, Cambridge, MA: MIT Press.
Harding, S. (1991), *Whose Science? Whose Knowledge? Thinking from Women's Lives*, Ithaca, NY: Cornell University Press.
Harding, S. (ed.) (2011), *The Postcolonial Science and Technology Studies Reader*, Durham, NC: Duke University Press.
Harwood, J. (2019), Was the Green Revolution intended to maximize food production?, *International Journal of Agricultural Sustainability*, 17(4), 312–325.
Hecht, G. (ed.) (2011), *Entangled Geographies: Empire and Technopolitics in the Global Cold War*, Cambridge, MA: MIT Press.

Jasanoff, S.; Kim, S.-H. (2015), *Dreamscapes of Modernity: Sociotechnical Imaginaries and the Fabrication of Power*, Chicago, IL: University of Chicago Press.

Keller, E.F. (1985), *Reflections on Gender and Science*, New Haven, CT: Yale University Press.

Kloppenburg, J. (2005), *First the Seed: The Political Economy of Plant Biotechnology*, second edition, Madison, WI: University of Wisconsin Press.

Kuhn, T.S. (1962), *The Structure of Scientific Revolutions*, Chicago, IL: University of Chicago Press.

Latour, B. (1987), *Science in Action: How to Follow Scientists and Engineers through Society*, Cambridge, MA: Harvard University Press.

Latour, B. (1999), *Pandora's Hope: Essays in the Reality of Science Studies*, Cambridge, MA: Harvard University Press.

Latour, B. (2003), Why has critique run out of steam? From matters of fact to matters of concern, *Critical Inquiry*, 30(2), 225–248.

Latour, B.; Woolgar, S. (1979), *Laboratory Life: The Construction of Scientific Facts*, Beverly Hills, CA: Sage.

Li, T. (2014), *Land's End: Capitalist Relations on an Indigenous Frontier*, Durham, NC: Duke University Press.

Medina, E.; Marques, I. da C.; Holmes, C. (2014), *Beyond Imported Magic: Essays on Science, Technology, and Society in Latin America*, Cambridge, MA: MIT Press.

Mills, T. (2017), What has become of critique? Reassembling sociology after Latour, *British Journal of Sociology*, 69(2), 286–305.

Mitchell, T. (1991), *Colonizing Egypt*, Berkeley, CA: University of California Press.

Olsson, T. (2017), *Agrarian Crossings: Reformers and the Remaking of the US and Mexican Countryside*, Princeton, NJ: Princeton University Press.

Ong, A.; Collier, S.J. (eds) (2005), *Global Assemblages: Technology, Politics, and Ethics as Anthropological Problems*, Malden, MA: Blackwell Publishing.

Patel, R. (2013), The long Green Revolution, *Journal of Peasant Studies*, 41(1), 1–63.

Peluso, N.L.; Lund, C. (2011), New frontiers of land control: Introduction, *Journal of Peasant Studies*, 38(4), 667–681.

Perkins, J. (1997), *Geopolitics and the Green Revolution: Wheat, Genes, and the Cold War*, New York: Oxford University Press.

Pritchard, S.; Wolf, S.A.; Wolford, W. (2016), Knowledge and the politics of land, *Environment and Planning A: Economy and Space*, 48(4), 616–625.

Schoenberger, L.; Hall, D.; Vandergeest, P. (2017), What happened when the land grab came to Southeast Asia?, *Journal of Peasant Studies*, 44(4), 697–725.

Scott, J.C.; Bhatt, N. (2001), *Agrarian Studies: Synthetic Work at the Cutting Edge*, New Haven, CT: Yale University Press.

Sumberg, J. (2012), Mind the (yield) gap(s), *Food Security*, 4, 509–518.

Tilly, H. (2011), *Africa as a Living Laboratory: Empire, Development, and the Problem of Scientific Knowledge, 1870–1950*, Chicago, IL: University of Chicago Press.

Tsing, A. (2015), *The Mushroom at the End of the World: On the Possibility of Life in Capitalist Ruins*, Princeton, NJ: Princeton University Press.

Tyfield, D.; Lave, R.; Randalls, S.; Thorpe, C. (2017), *The Routledge Handbook of the Political Economy of Science*, New York: Routledge.

68. The Capitalocene response to the Anthropocene

Kees Jansen and Joost Jongerden

INTRODUCTION

Farming and eating are both social and natural, connecting soils, water, body, labour power, capital (sometimes), culture, hunger, identity, plants, pests, animals, photosynthesis, agricultural knowledge, science (sometimes), seeds, power and so on. Scientists, intellectuals, policy-makers and activists are searching for concepts through which to understand changing dynamics in farming and eating practices, or more generally, agrarian change, thereby crossing disciplinary boundaries between the natural and social sciences. Contemporary awareness of environmental crises seems an important driving force behind this search. This chapter reviews two of those concepts – the Anthropocene and the Capitalocene – and the debate around and between them. One unresolved and hotly debated issue is how to interpret the linkages between, or the totality of, nature and society, or for critical agrarian studies, nature and capitalism. Divergent views exist as to whether it should be termed capitalism *and* nature, nature-capitalism or nature-*in*-capitalism/capitalism-*in*-nature. This chapter works on the premise that critical agrarian studies, one way or another, has to include nature in its core theoretical framework. The discussion around Jason Moore's (2015) book *Capitalism in the Web of Life: Ecology and the Accumulation of Capital* is used here as a platform to stimulate such theoretical engagement. This discussion partly evolves around whether to think in terms of *in, and* or -. A closer look reveals that this semantic strife is based upon quite some different views as to how to conceptualize nature and society (or *in* or -) in the field of critical agrarian studies, on what capitalism is and on how to approach human action.

FROM ANTHROPOCENE TO CAPITALOCENE

With the declaration of mankind as an environmental or geophysical force, Crutzen (2002) inaugurated the concept of the Anthropocene almost two decades ago. Since then, the Anthropocene became a signifier for a new interval of geological time (Ellis et al. 2016; Fremaux and Barry 2018). Though scientists have not yet definitively decided when exactly the Anthropocene began (Ellis et al. 2016; Waters et al. 2016), most trace its origins to the latter part of the eighteenth century, when analyses showed a growing global concentration of carbon dioxide and methane. This coincides with James Watt's design of the steam engine in 1784. Industrialization and expansion in the use of fossil fuels mark the early Anthropocene (Steffen et al. 2007; Trischler 2016). The most recent period in the Anthropocene is referred to as the Great Acceleration (Steffen et al. 2015) and refers to the post-1945 increase of population and the economy, resulting in an explosive growth of fossil energy consumption. Since then, scientists identify a set of converging earth system and socio-economic trends, including, among others, sharp rises in emissions of greenhouse gases, stratospheric ozone, ocean acidification and tropical forest loss as earth system trends, and rising population, gross domestic product, water use, transportation and agrochemical consumption as socio-economic trends (Bai et al. 2016).

In the Anthropocene discourse, the accumulation of knowledge and technical innovation are considered important drivers of humankind as an environmental force. However, in this same discourse, the growing awareness of the apocalyptic dimensions of human impact on the environment may turn technological ingenuity from a force of destruction into a force of salvation. Through its ability to articulate alternative science–practice relationships and integrate various perspectives the upcoming crisis may be averted (Steffen et al. 2015; Bai et al. 2016). This salvation takes place through three interventions, namely (1) mitigation, (2) adaptation and (3) geo-engineering. While mitigation has to realize a decarbonization of our energy systems, adaptation measures aim at reducing the negative consequences, and geo-engineering at offsetting the impact, of humankind on climate change (Brasseur and Granier 2013). Thus, although the Anthropocene discourse identified humankind historically as an environmental force of a destructive kind, the same Anthropocene discourse also produced a future-oriented technological optimism. Through technological intervention the spectre of an apocalypse might be averted.

While several authors have argued that climate change is universal and a threat to humanity as a whole (Crutzen 2002; Chakrabarty 2009), others have pointed out that elevating the frame of analysis to humanity as a whole erases the political history of climate change (McEwan 2018) and obscures how global capitalism continues to produce differentiated vulnerabilities (Malm and Hornborg 2014). In *Capitalism in the Web of Life* (2015), the environmental historian and historical geographer Jason Moore builds on this idea that it was not a unitary subject named humankind that brought the world to the brink of collapse, but capitalism. Moore argues that the Anthropocene is not only one of the most important, yet one of the most dangerous concepts of our time, because when highlighting the pressing nature of climate change it mystifies the relational context in which this potential catastrophe has been produced. The Anthropocene argument has become an easy, not to say easy-going, story, because it does not consider the relations of production and inequality inscribed in our production system. Moore thus argues that the Anthropocene is a quasi-empty signifier and therefore comfortably fits neo-Malthusian arguments on the relationships between fossil fuels, population pressures and the environment (ibid.).

Moore not only delivers a critique of the Anthropocene, but, importantly, offers a new perspective to understand the current environmental crisis through the development of a nature-centred approach to capital accumulation. Fundamental to his analysis is a critique of what Moore refers to as Cartesian dualism, or Green Arithmetic; namely, the distinction between nature and society (ibid., 1–2, 78–81). This distinction, Moore argues, is capitalism's organizing principle (Patel and Moore 2017, 51). The invention of nature as a distinct and separate entity, its setting apart, is functional to capital's domination and exploitation of nature, which is at the foundation of the environmental crisis. The possibility to understand and move beyond the current environmental crisis is dependent on our ability to make an analytical shift from humans and environment to environment-making: 'the ever-changing, interpenetrating, and interchanging dialectic of humans and environments in historical change' (Moore 2015, 45). The environmental crisis is thus at the same time a crisis of capitalism. This brings us to his key proposition: namely, that capitalism does not *have* an ecological regime, but capitalism *is* an ecological regime. Moore understands the idea of capitalism as a World-Ecology and the environmental crisis as a crisis of capitalism by using the concept of 'double internality' (ibid., 1). The notion of double internality holds that capitalism is part of nature and nature part of capitalism. Moore refers to capitalism-in-nature/nature-in-capitalism as a relational approach, emphasizing the unity of capitalism and nature. The current environmental crisis, therefore, can only be overcome through an overcoming of capitalism.

Crucial to the understanding of capitalism as a World-Ecology working toward its own destruction is the relationship between Marx's 'law of value' and Moore's 'law of Cheap Nature'. Following Marx, Moore defines a 'law' as a 'durable pattern of power and production' and 'value' as abstract social labour determined by socially necessary labour time (ibid., 52). However, Moore argues, in order for capital to accumulate it ceaselessly searches for and is in need of 'a rising stream of low-cost food, labour power, energy, and raw materials to the factory gates' to reduce socially necessary labour time. He calls these the Four Cheaps. So nature, Moore argues, is at the foundation of the production of value in capitalism. Therefore, the law of value in capitalism is simultaneously a law of 'Cheap Nature' (ibid., 53) and value is not only produced in a social relation but co-produced by 'human bundled with the rest of nature' (ibid., 63).

How does this create the contemporary environmental crisis? Moore explains this crisis referring to a dialectic between two processes: capitalization and appropriation (ibid., 292). He defines capitalization as the reduction of socially necessary labour time through commodification, while appropriation he defines as the maximization of unpaid work in the service of capitalization (ibid., 300). Elsewhere, he defines these two processes as the exploitation of labour power in commodity production and the appropriation of nature's life-making capacities (ibid., 95). Capital needs a balance between capitalization (or exploitation) and appropriation (ibid., 292), and an increased capitalization is dependent on new forms of appropriation. The accumulation regime of capitalism, Moore argues, is dependent on the dialectic between productivity and plunder. So, in order to sustain exploitation, defined as the production of surplus-value, capital needs the appropriation of Cheap Nature. This demand for Cheap Nature results in an obsessive search to turn the biosphere into capital, driving geographical expansion and creating new frontiers through which new Cheap Nature can be produced.[1] Moore then suggests 'that capitalism has entered an era of epochal crisis' (ibid., 298) as the options to find new frontiers have been reduced.

CONTRASTING POSITIONS

In the following we identify three types of contrasting views: (1) following from the previous section, Moore's critique on the Anthropocene; (2) the differences between the Capitalocene or World-Ecology approach and ecological Marxism, mainly by reviewing a discussion between Jason Moore and John Bellamy Foster; and (3) some other criticisms raised concerning Moore's *Capitalism in the Web of Life* (2015).

Moore raises three interrelated objections to the concept of the Anthropocene. Firstly, the idea of humanity as an undifferentiated whole, 'a homogeneous acting unit' working on nature, removes inequality, commodification, imperialism, patriarchy, racial formations and so on from consideration (ibid., 170). The notion of the Capitalocene, instead of unduly prioritizing environmental consequences and its proximate drivers (industrialization, urbanization, rising population), proposes a methodological shift by incorporating capital and imperialism and producer/product relations (ibid., 172) in any explanation. Secondly, while the Anthropocene concept suggests that historical change is simply driven by technology-resource complexes and population (as perceived from a neo-Malthusian perspective), the concept of the Capitalocene approaches modern history differently, with capitalism as a way of organizing nature. The issue of population, for example, is seen by Moore as the 'modern world-system's patterns of family formation and population movement' (ibid., 171) that are part of the capitalist mode of production. What Moore considers absent from the Anthropocene is a relational conception of *technics*. His notion of technics stands in contrast to an isolated technology. A capitalist technics is specific 'crystallizations of tools and ideas, power and nature, to appropriate the wealth of uncommodified nature in service to advancing labor productivity' (ibid., 59). Thirdly, for Moore these conceptual and methodological problems stem from Cartesian dualism.

According to Moore, Cartesian dualism is not only the problem of the Anthropocene and mainstream environmentalism but also of the ecological Marxist approaches that he is criticizing, or is at least ambivalent. This is visible in the difference in approach of Moore and thinkers like John Bellamy Foster. Moore criticizes ecological Marxism for embracing philosophically and discursively a relational ontology (humanity-in-nature) in a very superficial form only, while accepting practically and analytically, a nature/society dualism (humanity *and* nature). Foster's concept of *metabolic rift* signifies a hard distinction between nature and society, Moore argues, by conceptualizing the rift as 'a disruption in the exchange between social systems and natural systems' (ibid., 77). In other words, 'social systems *disrupt* natural systems' (ibid., 77) and 'capitalism acts upon nature' (ibid., 43). Moore considers this very different from his concepts of double internality, *oikeios* and the web of life. Instead of lamenting humanity's separation *from* nature, he emphasizes humanity's place *within* the web of life, which offers 'the possibility of discerning the conditions of capitalist renewal (if any) and crisis in the twenty-first century' (ibid., 78). For Moore it is capitalism-in-nature/nature-in capitalism; he insists upon substituting *in-* for *and*. He substantiates this argument about a singular metabolism with a reference to Marx, who, Moore argues, referred to the interdependent processes of social metabolism, and not to the metabolism between the two entities nature and society (ibid., 75).

In contrast, Foster considers it unjustified that Moore sets aside thinkers and ideas he disagrees with by referring to Cartesian dualism (in Foster and Angus 2016; see also Watson et al. 2016). Foster also disagrees with Moore's representation of Marx's interpretation of dialectics and argues that Marx's dialectics are a process that both separates *and* unites individuals and society, humanity and nature, parts and wholes (for similar arguments, see also Watson et al. 2016). This is a form of dialectical thinking that allows one to analyse:

> the *separation* of humanity and nature, on the degradation of natural processes and life, because that is the concrete reality of society, life and nature under the current alienated system of production, capitalism … There is no contradiction in seeing society as both separate from and irreducible to the Earth system as a whole, and simultaneously as a fundamental part of it. (Foster and Angus 2016)

Marx starts from the unity of living and active humanity with nature but states that this requires little explanation. Instead, what requires explanation is the *separation* between the 'inorganic conditions of human existence and this active existence, a separation which is completely posited only in the relation of wage labour and capital' (Marx in *Grundrisse* as cited by Foster). Foster's ecological Marxism acknowledges the possibility of distinguishing different forms of ecological crisis, some of which already existed in the past and only intensified under capitalism. Furthermore, 'economic crises and ecological crises do not necessarily determine each other', whereas for Moore there is only a singular crisis of 'capitalism as a way of organizing nature' (Moore 2015, 198). For Foster it is important to analyse what capitalism *does* to nature rather than how nature *works* for capital as in the monist view of Moore.[2] In Moore's monist view, which he refers to using the term 'singular metabolism', capital and nature 'cannot be separated even by abstraction' (Foster and Angus 2016). Foster turns this into the political argument that Moore 'eliminates the very possibility for an ecological critique of capitalism'. By reducing capitalism and nature to one substance (let us call it naturecapitalism or capitalismnature), the contradictions between capitalism and nature are dissolved. Foster expresses concern about Moore attacking 'the Green movement and ecological Marxists wholesale as apocalyptic dualists for being concerned about the growing rifts in the planetary boundaries of the Earth System' and excluding the perspectives of ecological movements. While Moore expects a transition of capitalism in the near future since the end of Cheap Nature is coming – the world-ecological limit of capital is capital itself, now facing an 'epochal crisis' – Foster emphasizes the political project of socialism as the source for change.

Besides the Anthropocene-Capitalocene dichotomy and the differences between Moore and Foster a third set of disagreements between thinkers exists. Firstly, Moore argues that capitalism started in the long sixteenth century (1451–1648) as a consequence of the transition from land to labour productivity, the globalizing character of creating and appropriating cheap nature and cheap labour (the Great Frontier) and, as a condition for this expansion, the identification, mapping, measuring, quantification and coding of human and extra-human natures (a process labelled as 'abstract social nature' by Moore). Hence, in his view capitalism did not start with the expansion of wage labour in factory production in the nineteenth century, building on a longer process of manufacturing in the preceding centuries. In one stroke Moore rejects here both the Anthropocene view of history as well as Marxist positions that take the typical capital(-free) labour relationship as the central notion and driving force of capitalism. The latter puts class, production and the political discourse used to legitimize exploitation (as produced in the modern state) as central to capitalism, rather than the world system, appropriation at the frontier and global trade.

Secondly, Nayeri (2016) discusses Moore's emphasis on capitalism as 'a way of organizing nature', which means that Moore focuses 'attention on what is shared with all other modes of production, the exact opposite of Marx's method that focuses attention on what is unique to capitalist production'. Nayeri argues that since humans started to practice agriculture, they have been controlling and dominating nature, and appropriating it. This raises the question: what then is unique to capitalism in its relation with nature? We consider that Nayeri has a point about Moore's focus, but also that Moore contains at least a partial answer to this question, namely the 'annihilation of space by time' (Moore 2015, 61) in capitalism; that is, the time-discipline on all production with labour productivity as both a metric of wealth and being required for competitiveness. This expanding system transforms all life and space. In short, it is not so much the appropriation of nature but the speed of it, resulting from the 'whip of competition' (ibid., 231), that could be seen as specific for capitalism. For critical agrarian studies the implication is that historically there may be more of a continuity as humans appropriate nature than an absolute break resulting from capitalism.[3] It is the pace and scale of appropriation that has changed over time.

Thirdly, a relevant question is how much detailed knowledge of nature should be developed to analyse capitalism *in/and/*-nature. Ted Benton (in Watson et al. 2016, 108) finds in the web of life little acknowledgement that there is any such thing as natural mechanisms, natural substances, processes, causal mechanisms and so on that exist independently of their being bound together with human economic practices. This is not strange given Moore's condemnation of dualism. Benton argues that this makes it impossible to analyse what human social practice, possibly unintentional and unforeseen, such as climate change, may disrupt. Benton's position requires a concept of 'asymmetry, that persistent externality of large aspects of the whole complex that you can use the word nature to refer to, that you have to have in your metaphysic if you're going to understand how ecological crisis occurs' (Benton in Watson et al. 2016, 109). Benton makes the point that a rejection of dualism should not hinder us in making distinctions; an argument that seems in line with Foster's critique of Moore's representation of dialectics (see also Benton 1991). Making distinctions does not throw away relational thinking, such as the relation between labour and capital, or between the properties of phosphate and how the amount of applied phosphate fertilizer is regulated in environmental law. To talk about relations without distinct, possibly asymmetric, elements is probably impossible.

LOOKING FORWARD

Although this chapter has little space to develop a comprehensive guide to critical agrarian studies, we need as a minimal point of reference an outline of the kind of research for which the World-Ecology approach is relevant. After outlining that point of reference, we synthesize the contribution of Moore and present several directions to overcome some of the limitations of his World-Ecology approach.

The origin of critical agrarian studies lies in peasant studies, agrarian political economy and debates about social change and social struggles in rural societies. 'Critical' in this sense could mean 'critical of social practices it studies as well as of other theories' and realizing that social science 'has an emancipatory potential' (Sayer 2000, 18). Critical studies contrast with approaches that take the totality and historical specificity of society as given, and the necessity to comply to its logic (Horkheimer 1972). On the one hand, critical approaches aim to develop alternative ways of being in the world and of knowing from everyday life experiences (Lefebvre 1991); on the other hand, they identify when and where ways of knowing hide or falsely represent oppressive relationships. Critical thus refers to a gamut of meanings: that social science has an emancipatory potential; that it can reveal implicit and misleading assumptions about the world; and that it has the potential to be self-reflexive about science (and knowledge in general). Critical in critical agrarian studies also refers to its contribution to a critique of political economy, a normative critique of the consequences of capitalism and a refusal to take capitalism as a naturally given fact of life. A second important element of contemporary critical agrarian studies, developed over the last few decades in particular, are its efforts to find new ways of conceptualizing intersections between class relationships and other social relationships, tensions, contradictions and forms of power such as gender, ethnicity and identity. A third development, though far from being turned into a consensus, concerns proposals for less deterministic approaches that lean towards practice, looking at ruptures and resistance, hegemony and autonomy.

The World-Ecology approach is certainly a form of critique of political economy and Moore's *Capitalism in the Web of Life* contributes several important notions to critical agrarian studies. The notion of the Capitalocene is interesting as it emphasizes that we are living in an historical era which privileges the endless accumulation of capital. This accumulation of capital is not to be seen as independent from its effects on nature but as a process of interacting with nature.[4] Capitalism has thrived on the appropriation of unpaid labour and cheap nature. Capitalism searches and benefits from new frontiers,[5] leading to a 'ceaseless transformation of the earth in the endless accumulation of capital – and vice versa' (Moore 2015, 34). Another notion with methodological significance is how such transformation of the earth and economic development in different parts of the world are becoming connected over time; for example, cheap grain from Poland and cheap timber from Norway, paid for with silver from the Andes, for the growth of the economy in the Dutch Republic in the sixteenth century. Moore thus proposes to study how capital accumulation in one place may 'stand on' exploitation, environmental degradation and the appropriation of unpaid labour and nature elsewhere. While this insight is not new, Moore consistently argues the need to look at these as integrated connections, as one totality.[6] Such connections have been revealed in historical studies of commodity chains or in food regime theory, but could be more present in the numerous case studies offered by critical agrarian studies. Thirdly, Moore (2015, 9) invites us to look at human history as a co-produced history 'through which humans put nature to work – including other humans – in accumulating wealth and power'. Co-production is not a new insight for those familiar with technology studies, but Moore stretches our minds by arguing that putting nature to work is not simply connected to capitalism but that it *is* capitalism. Putting nature to work *is* the accumulation of wealth and power; it is the interlocked history of capital, empire (power) and science in the modern world.

Having said that, in its drive to picture nature in capitalism as one totality, it might be asked: how much does World-Ecology thinking contribute to the aim of critical agrarian studies in understanding agrarian *change*? In the web of life, *change* in capitalism is basically capitalism's expansion (the appropriation of Cheap Nature plus labour exploitation). As discussed above, the singular metabolism and rejection of the distinction between nature and society (implied in Moore's rejection of dualism and his particular use of the term 'dialectics') is at the core of Foster's critique. For the claim that his idea of a 'double internality' re-establishes Marx's non-dualistic approach of nature-society interdependences, Moore (2015, 10–11) mobilizes Lefebvre, known for his rejection of Cartesian dualism (Lefebvre 1991, 1). However, both Marx and Lefebvre would probably invite us to study internal contradictions, divergent class interests and social struggle, to a far greater degree than what we find in Moore's analysis, which presents an almost smooth development of the law of value. There is no contradiction between thinking of society as a totality and understanding such totality as composed of interacting parts (Lefebvre 1991, 33; Merrifield 1993, 517–519). Change occurs not as a natural law (or as capitalism's law) but as an outcome of multiple social and natural processes (with different crisis and counter-crisis tendencies). Moore (2015, 4) instead, however, offers us a monist view: 'The crisis today is therefore not multiple but singular and manifold'.[7] Moore's singular monism, with capitalization and appropriation as the pivotal elements, seems to have but one direction: the approaching ending of the frontier (the 'epochal crisis') as the moment of change.

This relates to a second shortcoming: an insufficient recognition of the shaping of society by social struggle, of which class conflict is one, but not the only, form. Foster and Angus (2016) already noticed that Moore attacks the thinking of radical ecological movements, when he argues that 'many Greens, unduly focused on what capitalism *does to* nature (the degradation question)' ignore 'how nature *works for* capitalism (the work/energy question)' (Moore 2015, 280). Green thought provokes changes in how humans interact with nature and it is therefore relevant to study its multiple reformist, progressive and radical expressions and their diversified effects, rather than usurping it in a single capitalist totality (even though the outcome may still be a capitalism with all its tendencies). In a similar way, Moore's understanding of the web of life neglects to a large extent the role of social struggle in *constituting* capitalism and leading to varieties of capitalism. His revised law of value appears for the most part as a natural law. Only casually is some contestation mentioned; for example, when he identifies a 'revolt of extra-human natures' (ibid., 127) in the form of superweeds that emerge as a consequence of monocultures of genetically modified soy. If this line of reasoning would have been followed more strongly, the importance of human revolts in shaping the world would have had a more central place in the analysis of concrete capitalism. Such revolts, whether large or small, change the world, though not necessarily in a way that pleases its initial agents. A worrying effect of representing capitalism as a unitary substance is the emphasis on its self-sustaining character. This may have the performative effect of underscoring its strength while rendering invisible the cracks (Holloway 2010) while agency and imaginations of alternatives turn irrelevant and unrealizable (Gibson-Graham 2008). Instead of a capitalism that is beyond any control and for which we just have to wait until it destroys itself, critical agrarian studies could conceptualize capitalism as constituted by a set of rules and practices which are produced, reproduced as well as distorted and disrupted through enactments (Holloway 2011). This opens a research agenda which includes social struggles, creative practices and possibilities for different futures; and an openness of the future that takes the notion of politics and alternatives seriously (Massey 2005, 11).

The notion of different forms of capitalism and diverse practices brings us to our third rethinking of the World-Ecology approach. The nature of capitalism as an endless frontier process (Moore 2015, 107) to create the Four Cheaps – labour power, raw materials, energy and food – suggests a unified strategy or teleology in capitalism (Patel and Moore (2017) extend the Four Cheaps to Seven Cheaps).[8] This representation of capitalism seems to have only one kind of capitalist, and runs the risk of leading to a neglect of strategies and class fraction interests in the real world. Raw material suppliers, energy companies, large food producers or service firms that organize the supply of labour do not necessarily benefit from going cheap. For critical agrarian studies it is important not to presume a unified capitalist going-cheap strategy, but to also study how groups of capital try to make the commodities they sell expensive: creating monopolies by pushing for certain state regulations (e.g. quality criteria, import barriers), demanding stricter law enforcement that excludes price-reducing competitors (Jansen 2017), reducing production through cartels and so on. A single drive for cheap food is too simple an abstraction to understand diversified capitalist strategies.

This brings us back to the whole and the parts. Though it seems that Moore's singular monism and Foster's view on dialectics are not compatible with one another, there is a way to reconcile the approaches. Harvey's (2014, 9) distinction between capital and capitalism can be instructive here. While capital is value in motion, capitalism is a social formation in which capital accumulation is hegemonic in shaping the material basis of social life. However, this social formation encompasses various contradictions and inequalities, among them gender, ethnicity and (cultural) identity, co-determining outcomes. Intersections between gender and capital or 'race' and capital are historically important, yet have to be distinguished analytically from the logic of capital accumulation. To cut the argument short, Moore's use of the double internality to understand the expansion of capital through the processes of capitalization (or commodification) and appropriation can still be combined with a nature-society duality in capitalism as well as an analysis of multiple contradictions and inequalities that work around gender, ethnicity or (cultural) identities.

CONCLUSION

The World-Ecology approach yields several illuminating insights. It formulates a powerful critique of the concept of the Anthropocene and the idea of a singular humanity. By replacing the Anthropocene with the Capitalocene, Moore is able to show how the capitalist mode of production, and its internal contradictions, have produced the environmental crisis. Furthermore, Moore's analysis foregrounds the idea of the co-production of nature and society within a specific historical context. However, together with a radical rejection of dualistic thinking, Moore's analysis also tends to obscure: (1) contradictions between capital and its antagonists; (2) social struggles around these contradictions; and (3) the possibility of change. His monism, which is enthusiastically put forward in his work, runs the risk of reducing everything to the singular. To this, we may need to restore a notion of dialectics, but not as a rejection of distinctions (therefore labelled as dualisms) but as a process in which social change occurs as a result of contradictions between the parts from which the whole emerges; some parts, such as elements of nature, have to be distinguished analytically and not fully turned social. Moore (2015, 4) mentions the risk of collapsing distinctions, or what he calls 'the danger of Greek holism', but systematically rejects reflections of nature *and* society by other thinkers as dualisms. Yet a dialectical approach necessitates a language in which we distinguish nature and society, labour and capital, etc. This implies that we cannot define the development of capitalism in terms of two internal processes to capital. This effaces contradiction in society, and not only the contradiction between capital and labour but also gender- and (ethnic) identity-based contradictions, and struggles organized around these contradictions. This will allow in turn an understanding of change beyond that of an expansion of capitalism through the opening up of new frontiers of appropriation that will bring about its end when all frontiers are exhausted. It creates room for conceptualizing change as more complex and problematic than the idea of capitalism progressively working towards its epochal crisis.

We have offered a reinterpretation of Moore's analysis, from, it might be said, capitalism in the web of life to capital in the web of life, so as to distinguish between capital and its logic of accumulation, and capitalism as a historic formation marked by a range of contradictions. This could create fertile ground for the further development of critical agrarian studies as it requires viewing capital as one process within the context of multiple determinations.

NOTES

1. One such expansion, Moore argues, has been the development of biotechnology as a means to extend the Cheap Nature quest, though it failed to tame nature (Moore 2015, 273).
2. Moore (2015, 85) himself uses the term monism. He states: 'Instead of asking what capitalism *does to* nature, we may begin to ask how nature *works for* capitalism?' (ibid., 12).

3. This argument could be extended to Moore's correct observation that appropriation is being made possible through the process of coding, quantifying and rationalizing nature. It is probably true that the advancement of science and technology to measure converges with the emergence of capitalism and has been an important driver, but this does not mean that rationalizing as such was not essential to earlier forms of agriculture. The scale and pace may have changed, and therefore the impact, but rationalization itself is not unique to capitalism. Is it possible to imagine an alternative agriculture without it?

4. We slightly depart here in wording from Moore, in line with the criticism that in abstract terms a distinction can be made between humanity and the rest of nature.

5. Here we use a slightly different wording, leaving open the possibility that capitalism can exist without new frontiers. The latter is an impossibility for Moore; the end of capitalism comes because the required frontiers have been exhausted.

6. The use here of the term 'integrated' could be read either as necessary relationships (as Moore does) or as a more contingent, though not less driving, set of interactions (as we do).

7. The casual use of the term 'manifold' could speak in defence of Moore and put him in line with our argument, but in our reading this 'manifold' does not find expression in the rest of his book. The same with the label 'singular metabolism of many determinations' (ibid., 81): the many determinations remain unspecified and not discussed.

8. Moore also writes about the appropriation of unpaid labour/nature. Cheap food (like cheap housing) functions to cheapen labour power. Furthermore, energy can be seen as raw material (e.g. as fuel). Hence, analytically this implies, in fact, two categories: cheap labour and cheap raw material (bringing us back to Marx). We consider the concept of Cheap Food (a commodity produced in capitalism, amongst others by petty commodity producers) and Cheap Nature, as appropriated and not yet fully commoditized (not yet 'capitalized' as Moore would say), as being different in character.

FURTHER READING

Benton, T. (1989), Marxism and natural limits: An ecological critique and reconstruction, *New Left Review*, 178, 51–86.

Foster, J.B.; Clark, B.; York, R. (2010), *The Ecological Rift: Capitalism's War on the Earth*, New York: Monthly Review Press.

Harvey, D. (2014), *Seventeen Contradictions and the End of Capitalism*, Oxford: Oxford University Press.

Malm, A. (2018), *The Progress in this Storm: Nature and Society in a Warming World*, London: Verso.

Moore, J.W. (2015), *Capitalism in the Web of Life: Ecology and the Accumulation of Capital*, London: Verso.

REFERENCES

Bai, X.; Van Der Leeuw, S.; O'Brien, K.; Berkhout, F.; Biermann, F.; Brondizio, E.S.; Cudennec, C.; Dearing, J.; Duraiappah, A.; Glaser, M. (2016), Plausible and desirable futures in the Anthropocene: A new research agenda, *Global Environmental Change*, 39, 351–362.

Benton, T. (1991), Biology and social science: Why the return of the repressed should be given a (cautious) welcome, *Sociology*, 25(1), 1–29.

Brasseur, G.P.; Granier, C. (2013), Mitigation, adaptation or climate engineering?, *Theoretical Inquiries in Law*, 14(1), 1–20.

Chakrabarty, D. (2009), The climate of history: Four theses, *Critical Inquiry*, 35, 197–222.

Crutzen, P.J. (2002), Geology of mankind, *Nature*, 415(23).

Ellis, E.; Maslin, M.; Boivin, N.; Bauer, A. (2016), Involve social scientists in defining the Anthropocene, *Nature*, 540(7632), 192–193.

Foster, J.B.; Angus, I. (2016), In defense of ecological Marxism: John Bellamy Foster responds to a critic, accessed 11 October 2018 at https://climateandcapitalism.com/2016/06/06/in-defense-of-ecological-marxism-john-bellamy-foster-responds-to-a-critic/.

Fremaux, A.; Barry, J. (2018), The 'good Anthropocene' and green political theory: Rethinking environmentalism, resisting ecomodernism, in Biermann, F.; Lövbrand, E. (eds), *The 'Anthropocene' in Green Political Theory: Rethinking Environmentalism*, Cambridge: Cambridge University Press, 171–190.

Gibson-Graham, J.K. (2008), Diverse economies: Performative practices for 'other worlds', *Progress in Human Geography*, 32(5), 613–632.

Harvey, D. (2014), *Seventeen Contradictions and the End of Capitalism*, Oxford: Oxford University Press.

Holloway, J. (2010), *Crack Capitalism*, New York: Pluto Press.

Holloway, J. (2011), Stop making capitalism, accessed 10 December 2019 at www.johnholloway.com.mx/2011/07/30/stop-making-capitalism/.

Horkheimer, M. (1972), Traditional and critical theory, in *Critical Theory: Selected Essays*, New York: Herder and Herder, 188–243.

Jansen, K. (2017), Business conflict and risk regulation: Understanding the influence of the pesticide industry, *Global Environmental Politics*, 17(4), 48–66.

Lefebvre, H. (1991), *The Production of Space*, Malden, MA: Blackwell.

Malm, A.; Hornborg, A. (2014), The geology of mankind? A critique of the Anthropocene narrative, *The Anthropocene Review*, 1(1), 62–69.

Massey, D. (2005), *For Space*, London: Sage.

McEwan, C. (2018), *Postcolonialism, Decoloniality and Development*, second edition, London: Routledge.

Merrifield, A. (1993), Place and space: A Lefebvrian reconciliation, *Transactions of the Institute of British Geographers*, 18(4), 516–531.

Moore, J.W. (2015), *Capitalism in the Web of Life: Ecology and the Accumulation of Capital*, London: Verso.

Nayeri, K. (2016), On Jason W. Moore's 'capitalism in the web of life', accessed 11 October 2018 at http://forhumanliberation.blogspot.com/2016/07/2379-on-jason-w-moores-capitalism-in_18.html.

Patel, R.; Moore, J. (2017), *A History of the World in Seven Cheap Things: A Guide to Nature, Capitalism and the Future of the Planet*, Oakland, CA: University of California Press.

Sayer, A. (2000), *Realism and Social Science*, London: Sage.

Steffen, W.; Crutzen, P.J.; McNeill, J. (2007), The Anthropocene: Are humans now overwhelming the great forces of nature?, *Ambio*, 36(8), 614–621.

Steffen, W.; Broadgate, W.; Deutsch, L.; Gaffney, O.; Ludwig, C. (2015), The trajectory of the Anthropocene: The great acceleration, *The Anthropocene Review*, 2(1), 1–8.

Trischler, H. (2016), The Anthropocene, *NTM Zeitschrift für Geschichte der Wissenschaften, Technik und Medizin*, 24(3), 309–355.

Waters, C.N.; Zalasiewicz, J.; Summerhayes, C.; Barnosky, A.D.; Poirier, C.; Gałuszka, A.; Cearreta, A.; Edgeworth, M.; Ellis, E.C.; Ellis, M.; Jeandel, C.; Leinfelder, R.; McNeill, J.R.; Richter, D.d.; Steffen, W.; Syvitski, J.; Vidas, D.; Wagreich, M.; Williams, M.; Zhisheng, A.; Grinevald, J.; Odada, E.; Oreskes, N.; Wolfe, A.P. (2016), The Anthropocene is functionally and stratigraphically distinct from the Holocene, *Science*, 351(6269), 8 January.

Watson, J.; Benton, T.; Dean, K.; Devine, P.; Hindley, J.; Kuper, R.; Peters, G.; Sharp, G.; Dickens, P. (2016), Disentangling capital's web, *Capitalism Nature Socialism*, 27(2), 103–121.

69. Degrowth in agrarian and fisheries studies

Arnim Scheidel, Irmak Ertör and Federico Demaria

INTRODUCTION

'Degrowth' is an activist slogan and a new academic concept that has emerged in response to the vast adverse ecological and social impacts caused by economic growth. It challenges the obsession with growth as an unquestioned development paradigm and calls to abandon the underlying principles of *Citius, Altius, Fortius* (Latin for 'faster, higher, farther').[1] The emphasis is not only on less economic production and consumption, but also on exploring different forms of society–nature interactions. Degrowth proponents seek a democratically led redistributive downscaling of economic production and consumption in industrialized countries to move towards environmental sustainability, social justice and individual and collective well-being (see Demaria et al. 2013).

Agriculture and food systems have been important topics in degrowth since early debates (Videira et al. 2014). In many places around the globe, agriculture has turned into a major consumer of non-renewable resources and a cause of environmental degradation and greenhouse gas emissions. Capitalist, growth-driven agriculture has also provoked social concerns over questions of access to food and land, or exposure of agricultural workers to toxic agrochemicals. Key questions in degrowth are therefore: which forms of agriculture and food systems can lower resource use and reduce environmental pressures? And what kind of socio-economic institutions and forms of resource governance support not only ecological sustainability but also social justice and well-being in the food and agricultural sector?

Degrowth activists and scholars have sought answers to these questions in ongoing debates concerned, for instance, with the material and energy use in agricultural systems, agroecology, food sovereignty or the role of food cooperatives. Despite the importance of food and agriculture as a primary sector, surprisingly few academic studies have addressed related issues systematically from a degrowth perspective (Weiss and Cattaneo 2017; Gomiero 2018), or within the framework of post-growth economies (Roman-Alcalá 2017). Fisheries, a key but sometimes forgotten component of food systems, have long been a blind spot and entered the debate only recently under the term 'blue degrowth' (Hadjimichael 2018).

After a brief introduction to the concept, this chapter provides an overview of how a degrowth perspective applies in agriculture, fisheries and food studies. Some common concerns and complementary perspectives with critical agrarian studies are outlined, which may form the basis of further dialogue with degrowth studies.

WHAT IS DEGROWTH?

Over the last couple of decades, the triumph of the ideology of growth has become apparent in the seemingly consensual policy concept of sustainable development – a rather obvious oxymoron. Sustainable development tried to save economic growth by tweaking it 'eco' and 'green', against the backdrop of an emerging ecological crisis in the 1970s. Critical scholars and activists, however, questioned whether this approach could truly achieve sustainability and social justice. The Club of Rome report 'The limits to growth' (Meadows et al. 1972) had identified the objective of unlimited economic growth on a limited planet as the fundamental cause of environmental degradation and potential socio-economic collapse. Could sustainable development – a paradigm that continued to rely on economic growth – really overcome the world's emerging environmental and social crises? Critics demanded a radically different imaginary to envision the future. Calls for alternatives to development were voiced under the term 'post-development' in the global South (Escobar 2012) and by the emerging degrowth movement in the global North.

Social philosopher and political ecologist André Gorz was the first to use the term degrowth in 1972, to ask whether the capitalist system was compatible with the earth's balance that needed no growth or even degrowth of material production.[2] In 1979, the term was used to entitle a book with the French translation of essays by Nicholas Georgescu-Roegen, one of the intellectual fathers of ecological economics. French environmental activists launched then in 2001 the provocative slogan degrowth to repoliticize environmentalism and to break with the doublespeak, often meaninglessness, of sustainable development. Thus, the word was originally not a concept (at least not symmetrically to economic growth) but rather a defiant political slogan that reminded people of the meaning of limits.

Although integrating perspectives from the field of ecological economics, degrowth does not focus merely on economic aspects. Degrowth is also not the same as recession or simply negative growth. On one hand, degrowth certainly implies the reduction of the socio-economic metabolism, that is, the energy and material used within the economy (Fischer-Kowalski and Haberl 2015). This is necessary to face the existing biophysical constraints, in terms of sources (the natural resource availability) and sinks (ecosystems' capacities to assimilate waste). On the other hand, degrowth is an attempt to challenge the omnipresence of market-based relations in society and the growth-based roots of the social imaginary by replacing them with the idea of frugal abundance. Degrowth is also a call for deeper democracy applied to issues outside the mainstream democratic domain, like for example the use of technology. Finally, degrowth implies an equitable redistribution of wealth within and across the global North and South (Kerschner 2010).

Degrowth proponents envision degrowth transitions as pathways towards societies in which sharing, simplicity, conviviality, care and the commons are primary significations (D'Alisa et al. 2015). Serge Latouche (2009) proposed eight 'Rs' to guide degrowth transitions: re-evaluate, reconceptualize, restructure, relocate, redistribute, reduce, reuse and recycle. These eight interdependent objectives must constitute a rupture with development as usual to move towards an autonomous society of sustainable and convivial sobriety. In practice, this may include the strengthening of community-centered initiatives such as co-housing, social enterprises and cooperatives, as well as the adoption of larger reforms like basic income schemes (Sekulova et al. 2013). In France, for instance, the experience of community-supported agriculture through the *associations pour le maintien d'une agriculture paysanne*[3] (associations for the maintenance of peasant agriculture) has frequently been presented as an example of degrowth in practice.

The attractiveness of degrowth emerges from its power to draw from diverse streams of thought, including those focusing on justice, democracy and ecology, and to formulate political strategies at various levels, including oppositional activism, grassroots alternatives and institutional politics. It brings together a heterogeneous group of actors who focus on different issues, from agroecology to climate justice. Degrowth aims to complement and reinforce these areas by going beyond one issue-oriented research and politics. It aims to be a connecting thread and a network of networks.

DEGROWTH PERSPECTIVES IN FOOD, AGRICULTURE AND AGRARIAN STUDIES

A degrowth perspective in agriculture and food systems considers pathways to lower resource use, while seeking alternative governance forms capable of addressing social concerns of the people working in and depending on the sector. Degrowth attempts to reverse what Karl Marx had called the 'metabolic rift' (Anguelovski 2015). The metabolic rift refers to the rupture between humanity and nature that is caused by capitalist production methods. The maximization of rents through resource extraction – yields, in the case of industrial agriculture – is higher than the rate these resources regenerate by only ecological processes. Consumption is furthermore increasingly disconnected from production due to a growing divide of town and countryside, and globalized food chains.

This metabolic rift has both ecological and social implications. High yields are sustained by the large use of harmful and non-renewable external inputs to increase land and labor efficiency. Chemical fertilizers and pesticides, for instance, replace natural soil fertility and pest control based on nutrient cycling and crop diversity. Fossil-fueled machineries boost labor productivity and are required to transport food to distant areas. Industrial agriculture has consequently turned into a massive resource consumer on the input side, and a major source of environmental pollutants, including greenhouse gas emissions, on the output side. Biodiversity loss, declining soil fertility and contamination, greenhouse gas emissions and exposure of farmworkers to harmful agro-toxics are just some of the adverse consequences. The need to buy agricultural inputs to sustain the high yields has also pushed many farmers into debt crises, who subsequently lost their land to the creditors. Urban consumers, on the other side, often suffer a 'social rift' (Anguelovski 2015): they lack knowledge about where and under which conditions their food is produced.

To reverse the socio-metabolic rift in agriculture, degrowth proposals draw on biophysical analyses that measure material and energy use in food systems. A frequently used indicator is the 'energy return on investment' that assesses how much energy is invested in the agricultural process (through labor, machineries, manure, electricity used in irrigation and so forth) to obtain a certain amount of usable energy (such as the calories contained in the produced food) (Galán et al. 2016). In asserting that industrial agriculture is highly energy inefficient, both La Via Campesina (Martinez-Alier 2011) and degrowth proponents (Latouche 1993; see Gomiero 2018) have demanded to promote less industrialized and more small-scale and subsistence-based forms of agriculture. Furthermore, transportation, processing, packaging, sale, storage and food preparation in homes account too for a large share of energy use in the food system and must be accordingly changed to achieve a downscaling of energy and material use (Infante Amate and González De Molina 2013). Such a vision of agriculture is comparable with a Chayanovian approach in agrarian studies that sees the future of farming based on small-scale, peasants and family farms (van der Ploeg 2013). Some agrarian economists would be critical whether this is a feasible pathway to actually feed the world (Bernstein 2014).

Degrowth scholars argue that degrowth in food and agriculture must be based not only on organic production and on the principles of agroecology, but also on a shift in consumption patterns and the economic and social institutions governing the sector (Boillat et al. 2012; Infante Amate and González De Molina 2013; Gomiero 2018). To understand how respective changes in the food sector affect other economic sectors, more research is needed. Different quantitative methods for the analysis of the socio-economic metabolism have been proposed here (Gerber and Scheidel 2018; Gomiero 2018). Gomiero (2018) explains why biotech-based agriculture such as genetically modified crops, often marketed as being able to reduce environmental impacts, are not suitable for a degrowth society: they are a product of the current growth economy, based on the formation of an economic monopoly, and they reduce the autonomy and choice of farmers and consumers. Boillat et al. (2012, 600) see in Cuba the 'largest real-life experience of agroecological "degrowth"', however, they argue that the country has to overcome its tradition of central planning while providing more autonomy to small producers. In this context, small farmer cooperatives are seen as important alternative socio-economic models for agricultural producers, workers and consumers (Boillat et al. 2012; Johanisova et al. 2015; Scheidel et al. 2018).

Current niche forms of agriculture, such as urban gardening, are also recognized to make important contributions to reverse the ecological and social rift: urban gardening reconnects people with their metabolic needs, relinks places of production and consumption, claims public spaces under threat of capitalist enclosures as commons, provides affordable food within communities and closes nutrient cycles through reuse of organic waste (Anguelovski 2015). More generally, Infante Amate and González de Molina (2013, 32) outline an overall degrowth strategy for agriculture and food. In paraphrasing the guiding principles for degrowth transitions, they propose the following four 'Rs' for food and agriculture: 'Re-territorialization of production, re-localization of markets, re-vegetarianisation of diet, re-seasonalisation of food consumption'.

BLUE DEGROWTH FOR FISHERIES AND MARINE SPACES

Not only agriculture but also seafood production is a vital component of local and global food systems, providing many coastal communities and urban populations with key nutrients. Until recently, degrowth and agrarian studies have paid relatively less attention to marine spaces, fisheries and aquaculture, despite an urgent need for critical perspectives on the sector. New investments on the seas are currently at the center of the exploitation targets of a range of industries and countries. 'Blue growth' has become a new buzzword referring to policies, initiatives and strategies striving for substantial economic growth in the marine space (see EC 2012; ECA 2016; WB 2016). Within this discourse, the marine space is imagined as a new frontier not yet exploited to its limits. This new rush to the sea emphasizes the emerging sectors such as marine biotechnology, marine energy, coastal and marine tourism and seabed mining, and focuses on (intensive) marine aquaculture for seafood production (Ertör and Hadjimichael 2020). Marine aquaculture was initially proposed to solve the problem of globally declining fish stocks and has become a growing component of global seafood production (Ertör and Ortega-Cerdà 2019). However, this shift from capture fisheries towards intensive aquaculture within ongoing capitalist production relations further intensifies the marine metabolic rift and adds to the oceanic crisis (Clausen and Clark 2005).

The blue degrowth concept emerges from the need to confront these ambitious capitalist plans for marine growth and expansion, usually taken for granted in many political spaces and debates (Ertör and Hadjimichael 2020). A blue degrowth lens aims to uncover the interests behind the marine growth imperative, the ecological limits of marine ecosystems, as well as the social consequences that growth brings with it. From this perspective, the blue degrowth framework challenges blue growth strategies and points to alternatives based on the principles of social justice, environmental sustainability and individual and collective well-being.

A major link between blue degrowth and critical agrarian studies is the study of how the strategies of green growth and green revolution have transformed and shaped access to and control over land, and how their marine counterpart – blue growth and the blue revolution – currently shape social and ecological dynamics within marine spaces. Even though they sometimes occur materially and socially differently, they have many commonalities worth exploring. The following four research themes comprise common concerns for blue degrowth and critical agrarian studies.

First, the transformation of seafood production from capture fisheries to intensive marine aquaculture implies a change from seafood production modes of hunting (including the industrial capture fisheries) and gathering (traditional aquaculture) to a model of cultivation. This model is one that jumps directly to an industrial method. It relies on the use of a vast amount of inputs such as feed, chemicals, antibiotics as well as on capital-intensive production methods based on capital accumulation that leave small players out of the sector (Saguin 2016; Ertör and Ortega-Cerdà 2019). Second, recent debates on ocean grabbing (Bennett et al. 2015; Barbesgaard 2018) indicate a similar phenomenon as it happened on land with enclosures and land grabbing (Borras et al. 2011).

Third, both blue degrowth and critical agrarian studies focus on the role of small-scale fisher communities as the main actors confronting the blue growth paradigm. Their claims for social justice, environmental sustainability (respecting ecological limits and the reproduction of marine species for future generations) and individual and collective well-being, have been summarized sometimes under the banner of 'fisheries justice' (Mills 2018). Finally, another shared perspective between blue degrowth and critical agrarian studies is the struggle for food sovereignty together with peasants, pastoralists or beekeepers, promoting fisher cooperatives, local production and consumption of seafood, and equal access to and control over marine spaces and marine commons. These aims require the discussion of a decentralized and participative governance approach, based on a deeper democracy on how to use marine areas.

In summary, blue degrowth studies enter into a dialogue with both the wider degrowth literature as well as with critical agrarian studies. They challenge and problematize the current growth ambition within marine spaces and point out that issues of ocean grabbing and fisheries (in)justice are not only related to globalized food systems, but also to the rise of blue growth agendas and the capitalist turn within marine spaces in general. All these concerns and inquiries give room for further dialogue between two fields of investigation not yet sufficiently explored.

FERTILE GROUND FOR DIALOGUE BETWEEN DEGROWTH AND CRITICAL AGRARIAN STUDIES

Critical agrarian studies and degrowth share that they call into question some of the most dominant and hegemonic development paradigms of our times. Critical agrarian studies question the role of modernization in rural development and power relations around it, while degrowth challenges the obsession with economic growth and productivism as overarching goals.[4] In doing so, both fields aim to better understand those forms of agriculture and fisheries that offer alternatives to the dominant capitalist and industrial model, which has produced severe pressures on people and the planet.

Both fields discuss similar overarching questions. For instance, if, and under which conditions, locally produced and consumed organic food could feed a growing world population; what kind of resource governance forms offer suitable alternatives to tackle the emerging social concerns over access to land and marine spaces; and, maybe most importantly, which current political, social, economic and ecological barriers hinder transitions to more sustainable and just alternative food systems. 'Scholar activists' (Borras 2016), who pursue transformative research towards socially just and environmentally sustainable societies, have found fertile intellectual ground in both critical agrarian studies and the degrowth academic movement.

Beyond these overlapping concerns, the two fields offer complementary perspectives. Critical agrarian studies, coming largely from social sciences, have become well known for their fine-grained analysis of the social relations in agrarian systems. That is, how social, economic, political and cultural dynamics relate to social differentiation and social justice concerns across class, ethnicity, gender and generation. Critical agrarian studies may help degrowth scholars to sharpen their view on the specific needs and potential roles of different social groups within degrowth transitions. Gerber (2020) argues furthermore that the knowledge accumulated in longstanding debates on the feasibility and desirability of different pathways in agriculture and food production may prevent degrowth proposals from falling into the trap of 'agrarian myths': the pursuit of alternative rural futures that are based on too simple and romantic assumptions of the conditions of rural life, (non-industrialized) small farms or agrarian cooperatives.

Degrowth and related currents within the fields of ecological economics and political ecology offer much to address the ecological relations of different production systems. That is, how environmental factors and biophysical limits actively shape and are shaped by agrarian dynamics. We may expand and 'green' some of the classic questions in agrarian political economy – who owns what, who does what, who gets what and what do they do with it (Bernstein 2017) – to include biophysical and ecological aspects, for example, by asking who does what to the environment and how does the resulting environmental change affect the social relations of production? Or who gets which environmental benefits and burdens, such as fertile soils, clean water and air, and who is exposed to pollution, contamination and environmental degradation? Ecological economics and political ecology offer concepts as well as methodological tools to address such questions. Degrowth may also prevent critical agrarian studies from falling into the trap of the 'myth of green growth', 'according to which the constant development of the productive forces ultimately leads to more welfare and can decouple from ecological impacts with appropriate technologies' (Gerber 2020, 236).

Environmental concerns are becoming more and more relevant in critical agrarian studies. The convergence of environmental, agrarian and marine concerns is further increasing as climate change and climate change politics unfold, as ecological degradation such as soil fertility loss or overfishing continues to shape the country and seaside and as diverse agrarian, fisheries and environmental movements ally more deeply to call for alternatives to development as usual (Borras et al. 2018). A closer dialogue between degrowth and critical agrarian studies will be fruitful to integrate complementary insights from both fields on the future of food, agriculture and fisheries.

ACKNOWLEDGEMENTS

The authors acknowledge funding from the European Research Council advanced grant ENVJUSTICE (Grant-No. 695446). Arnim Scheidel acknowledges support from the Beatriu de Pinós postdoctoral program of the Government of Catalonia's Secretariat for Universities and Research of the Ministry of Economy and Knowledge (2017 BP 00023). Federico Demaria is Serra Húnter Fellow and acknowledges support from the project PROSPERA ERC project (GA947713), and the Maria de Maeztu Unit of Excellence ICTA UAB (CEX2019-0940-M). Irmak Ertör acknowledges the support by Boğaziçi University Research Fund Grant Number 17562.

NOTES

1. See www.degrowth.info/en/what-is-degrowth/.
2. See 'A history of degrowth', www.degrowth.info/en/a-history-of-degrowth/.
3. See www.reseau-amap.org/.
4. Note that not all currents within agrarian studies would critically question the role of agricultural modernization for rural development. Scholars coming from a more Leninist tradition would be critical regarding the viability of small-scale, peasant and family farming, while arguing in favor of modernized, large-scale agriculture. See van der Ploeg (2013, ch. 1) for a brief summary of the historic origins of this divide.

FURTHER READING

D'Alisa, G.; Demaria, F.; Kallis, G. (2015), *Degrowth: A Vocabulary for a New Era*, London: Routledge.
Ertör, I.; Hadjimichael, M. (2020), Blue degrowth and the politics of the sea: Rethinking the blue economy, *Sustainability Science*, 15, 1–10.
Gerber, J.F. (2020), Degrowth and critical agrarian studies, *Journal of Peasant Studies*, 47(2), 235–264.
Gomiero, T. (2018), Agriculture and degrowth: State of the art and assessment of organic and biotech-based agriculture from a degrowth perspective, *Journal of Cleaner Production*, 197, 1823–1839.
Infante Amate, J.; González De Molina, M. (2013), 'Sustainable de-growth' in agriculture and food: An agro-ecological perspective on Spain's agri-food system (year 2000), *Journal of Cleaner Production*, 38, 27–35.

REFERENCES

Anguelovski, I. (2015), Urban gardening, in D'Alisa, G.; Demaria, F.; Kallis, G. (eds), *Degrowth: A Vocabulary for a New Era*, London: Routledge.

Barbesgaard, M. (2018), Blue growth: Savior or ocean grabbing?, *Journal of Peasant Studies*, 45(1), 130–149.

Bennett, N.J.; Govan, H.; Satterfield, T. (2015), Ocean grabbing, *Marine Policy*, 57, 61–68.

Bernstein, H. (2014), Food sovereignty via the 'peasant way': A sceptical view, *Journal of Peasant Studies*, 41(6), 1031–1063.

Bernstein, H. (2017), Political economy of agrarian change: Some key concepts and questions, *RUDN Journal of Sociology*, 17(1), 7–18.

Boillat, S.; Gerber, J.F.; Funes-Monzote, F.R. (2012), What economic democracy for degrowth? Some comments on the contribution of socialist models and Cuban agroecology, *Futures*, 44(6), 600–607.

Borras, S.M.J. (2016), Land politics, agrarian movements and scholar-activism, Inaugural Lecture.

Borras, S.M.; Hall, R.; Scoones, I.; White, B.; Wolford, W. (2011), Towards a better understanding of global land grabbing: An editorial introduction, *Journal of Peasant Studies*, 38(2), 209–216.

Borras, S.M.; Moreda, T.; Alonso-Fradejas, A.; Brent, Z.W. (2018), Converging social justice issues and movements: implications for political actions and research, *Third World Quarterly*, 39(7), 1227–1246.

Clausen, R.; Clark, B. (2005), The metabolic rift and marine ecology: An analysis of the ocean crisis within capitalist production, *Organization and Environment*, 18(4), 422–444.

D'Alisa, G.; Demaria, F.; Kallis, G. (2015), *Degrowth: A Vocabulary for a New Era*, London: Routledge.

Demaria, F.; Schneider, F.; Sekulova, F.; Martinez-Alier, J. (2013), What is degrowth? From an activist slogan to a social movement, *Environmental Values*, 22(2), 191–215.

EC (2012), *Blue Growth Opportunities for Marine and Maritime Sustainable Growth*, Brussels.

ECA (2016), *Africa's Blue Economy: A Policy Handbook*, Addis Ababa.

Ertör, I.; Hadjimichael, M. (2020), Blue degrowth and the politics of the sea: Rethinking the blue economy, *Sustainability Science*, 15, 1–10.

Ertör, I.; Ortega-Cerdà, M. (2019), The expansion of intensive marine aquaculture in Turkey: The next-to-last commodity frontier?, *Journal of Agrarian Change*, 19(2), 337–360.

Escobar, A. (2012), *Encountering Development: The Making and Unmaking of the Third World*, Princeton, NJ: Princeton University Press.

Fischer-Kowalski, M.; Haberl, H. (2015), Social metabolism: A metric for biophysical growth and degrowth, in Martinez-Alier, J.; Muradian, R. (eds), *Handbook of Ecological Economics*, Cheltenham, UK and Northampton, MA, USA: Edward Elgar Publishing, 100–138.

Galán, E.; Padró, R.; Marco, I.; Tello, E.; Cunfer, G.; Guzmán, G.I.; Gonzalez de Molina, M.; Krausmann, F.; Gingrich, S.; Sacristán, V.; Moreno-Delgado, D. (2016), Widening the analysis of Energy Return on Investment (EROI) in agro-ecosystems: Socio-ecological transitions to industrialized farm systems (the Vallès County, Catalonia, c.1860 and 1999), *Ecological Modelling*, 336, 13–25.

Gerber, J.F. (2020), Degrowth and critical agrarian studies, *Journal of Peasant Studies*, 47(2), 235–264.

Gerber, J.F.; Scheidel, A. (2018), In search of substantive economics: Comparing today's two major socio-metabolic approaches to the economy – MEFA and MuSIASEM, *Ecological Economics*, 144(July), 186–194.

Gomiero, T. (2018), Agriculture and degrowth: State of the art and assessment of organic and biotech-based agriculture from a degrowth perspective, *Journal of Cleaner Production*, 197, 1823–1839.

Hadjimichael, M. (2018), A call for a blue degrowth: Unravelling the European Union's fisheries and maritime policies, *Marine Policy*, 94(May), 158–164.

Infante Amate, J.; González De Molina, M. (2013), 'Sustainable de-growth' in agriculture and food: An agro-ecological perspective on Spain's agri-food system (year 2000), *Journal of Cleaner Production*, 38, 27–35.

Johanisova, N.; Suñach-Padilla, R.; Parry, P. (2015), Co-operatives, in D'Alisa, G.; Demaria, F.; Kallis, G. (eds), *Degrowth: A Vocabulary for a New Era*, London: Routledge.

Kerschner, C. (2010), Economic de-growth vs. steady-state economy, *Journal of Cleaner Production*, 18(6), 544–551.

Latouche, S. (1993), *In the Wake of the Affluent Society: An Exploration of Post-Development*, London: Zed Books.

Latouche, S. (2009), *Farewell to Growth*, Cambridge: Polity Press.

Martinez-Alier, J. (2011), The EROI of agriculture and its use by the Via Campesina, *Journal of Peasant Studies*, 38(1), 145–160.

Meadows, D.H.; Meadows, D.L.; Randers, J.; Behrens, W.W. (1972), *The Limits to growth; A Report for the Club of Rome's Project on the Predicament of Mankind*, New York: Universe Books.

Mills, E.N. (2018), Implicating 'fisheries justice' movements in food and climate politics, *Third World Quarterly*, 39(7), 1270–1289.

Roman-Alcalá, A. (2017), Looking to food sovereignty movements for post-growth theory, *Ephemera: Theory and Politics in Organization*, 17(1), 119–145.

Saguin, K. (2016), Blue revolution in a commodity frontier: Ecologies of aquaculture and agrarian change in Laguna Lake, Philippines, *Journal of Agrarian Change*, 16(4), 571–593.

Scheidel, A.; Lim, B.; Sok, K.; Duk, P. (2017), Leapfrogging agricultural development: cooperative initiatives among Cambodian small farmers to handle sustainability constraints, in Fraňková, E.; Haas, W.; Singh, S. (eds), *Socio-Metabolic Perspectives on the Sustainability of Local Food Systems: Human-Environment Interactions*, vol. 7, Springer, Cham.

Sekulova, F.; Kallis, G.; Rodríguez-Labajos, B.; Schneider, F. (2013), Degrowth: From theory to practice, *Journal of Cleaner Production*, 38, 1–6.

van der Ploeg, J.D. (2013), *Peasants and the Art of Farming: A Chayanovian Manifesto*, Halifax: Fernwood Publishing.

Videira, N.; Schneider, F.; Sekulova, F.; Kallis, G. (2014), Improving understanding on degrowth pathways: An exploratory study using collaborative causal models, *Futures*, 55, 58–77.

WB (2016), *Toward a Blue Economy: A Promise for Sustainable Growth in the Caribbean*, Washington, DC: World Bank.

Weiss, M.; Cattaneo, C. (2017), Degrowth – taking stock and reviewing an emerging academic paradigm, *Ecological Economics*, 137, 220–230.

70. Reconfiguring the intersection between urban food movements and agrarian struggles: Building an urban political agroecology praxis

Chiara Tornaghi and Severin Halder

INTRODUCTION

In the past decades, food has become the focus of an increasing number of grassroots initiatives in urban contexts that can be broadly defined as the 'urban food movement'. Smallholders' struggles in the middle of the townships of Cape Town, rooftop gardens with beehives on skyscrapers in New York City, new farmer-consumer alliances through Community Supported Agriculture in Tokyo, community gardens on a former airport site in the middle of Berlin, school gardens in Rosario, Argentina and collecting surplus harvest in Manchester are just a few examples; others include neighbourhood kitchens, food reskilling initiatives and urban homesteading. The trend has been far from a purely grassroots phenomenon, to the point that a whole range of municipal policies, non-governmental organization projects, enterprises and even national and international pacts and coalitions are now largely part of the 'alternative food network'. These latter actors have been intersecting, supporting or sometimes undermining and co-opting the more spontaneous initiatives, through a range of tools such as grant funding, food policy councils, food strategies and so on.

In a world in which food has been progressively taken for granted with the increasing hegemony of the corporate food regime, the emergence of urban food movements, and particularly urban agriculture, has attracted the curiosity and switched on the imagination of a range of professions. Planners and architects, for example, are increasingly facing insurgent planning practices and demands to plan for climate-proof transport and infrastructure. They are coming to realize that the mainstreaming of the modernist idea of urbanization (i.e. the one popularized in the Athens Charter, the manifesto of a group of architects led by Le Corbusier gathered in the 'Congrès Internationaux d'Architecture Moderne') (see CIAM 1933) that popularized the vertical and dense city completely excluded agriculture from urban plans, and thus neglected the spatial, ecological and environmental dimensions of feeding cities. This realization led to the rise within the planning community of the 'food planning' sub-discipline around the year 2005 (van der Valk and Viljoen 2014), immediately followed by the emergence of food policy councils and plans. Changing post-industrial economies and the rising interest in 'green growth' and 'closed-loop' economies have also become popular, alongside concerns for sustainability and climate change. A bit later, the urban food movement also captured the attention of critical scholars interested in food justice and food sovereignty. A number of studies have pointed out both the potential of grassroots initiatives to become sources of new social solidarities and human/non-human relationships, which can reclaim rights to food and the city, while at the same time acknowledging the risks of new forms of capital expansion, 'green washing', communities' self-exploitation, green gentrification and welfare state withdrawal wrapped up in a media image of urban gardens saving the world (McClintock 2014; Tornaghi 2014; Halder 2018). Urban agriculture, the figurehead of the urban food movement, is especially characterized by these contradictions, being 'a form of actually existing neoliberalism and a simultaneous radical counter-movement arising in dialectical tension' (McClintock 2014, 148).

In this chapter, we argue that despite its ambivalence and striking diversity – ranging from gentrifying middle-class gardening clubs to survival-led farming in slums and at the urban fringe – urban food movements and practices should have a central role in critical agrarian studies, for three reasons. Firstly, because the issues and debates that have long been at the centre of agrarian studies, for example food regimes, agroecology, land grabbing, social reproduction, political ecology and the metabolic rift, are highly relevant for understanding the specific conditions that frame both rural and urban food movements, and where the commonalities between the two lie. Secondly, because understanding the extent to which agrarian and urban food movements are shaped (at least partially) by the same logics and dynamics opens up opportunities for rethinking the articulation between the urban and the rural context, moving away from what has often been an artificial and outdated separation between producers and consumers (as exemplified, among other things, by the 'urban bias' debates in critical agrarian studies that oppose food-producing countrysides to draining and extractive urban contexts and populations). Thirdly, because these new understandings of commonalities for struggles and conditions open the ground for new political strategies, and for what is emerging as an urban political agroecology praxis.

This chapter is structured as follows. In the next section, we illustrate a number of key definitions that we use throughout the chapter. We then proceed with the unfolding of our argument in three sections, which discuss: (1) the intersection between urban food movements and critical agrarian studies; (2) the commonalities between urban and rural struggles and a proposal for a reconceptualization of urban–rural links; and (3) the illustration of an emerging urban political agroecology praxis, with which we urge critical agrarian studies to engage. Finally, we conclude with a short summary of the key messages.

THEORETICAL FRAMEWORK AND KEY DEFINITIONS

This chapter is informed by theories and concepts widely used within both critical agrarian studies and critical urban studies. We provide below some succinct definitions, alongside some references that will guide readers to more in-depth reading if necessary.

The 'urban food movement' is an expression used in the literature of both critical agrarian studies and critical urban studies to refer to a broad range of social movements and practices that engage with food in urban contexts in critical ways. They include initiatives that promote alternative food networks – that is to say, alternative ways to improve consumers' access to good food – as well as more radical initiatives such as direct action by food producers (for example, farmers engaging with urban policies), urban agriculture or campaign groups engaged with a number of issues such as food justice and food sovereignty (Jarosz 2008; Block at al. 2012).

'Food sovereignty' and 'food justice' are two key issues promoted by food movements (not only 'urban' movements). Broadly speaking, food justice has roots in the United States environmental justice movement and engages with issues of race, class and gender inequality in terms of access to food. Food sovereignty has roots in the mobilization of peasant farmers in the Global South claiming the right for control over the means and conditions of their subsistence and thriving (including control over seeds, land and water; staking claims for fair salaries and working conditions; demanding control over their sale prices and access to markets; and so on). Many urban food movements are engaged with either food justice or food sovereignty claims, and sometimes with both (see Wekerle 2004; Jarosz 2014; Tornaghi 2017).

'Agroecology' is defined simultaneously as a critical scholarship, a social agricultural practice and a political movement (Wezel et al. 2009; Peterson 2012). It can therefore be understood as an interface of different forms of agricultural knowledge production, helping us to understand, investigate and (if necessary) intervene in social, political, organizational, cultural and ecological processes. In contrast to organic farming, agroecology contradicts in its essence the capitalist development model as it breaks with its hegemony based on monocultures, large-scale land ownership and agribusiness (Articulação Nacional de Agroecologia 2007).

'Urban political agroecology praxis' is a term that refers to politically oriented agroecological practices in urban and peri-urban contexts. This approach has increasingly been taken up by the food sovereignty movement and agroecology practitioners are increasingly politicized, reflecting on the political significance of their practices. With 'praxis', we refer precisely to the enacting of ideas; in other words, to practices that are informed by an active and conscious reflection on their underlying principles, values and theories (Deh-Tor 2017; Tornaghi and Dehaene 2020).

'Urban-rural hybrid' is a concept that refers to the former existence of radically separated urban and rural worlds. The metabolic, spatial, cognitive and epistemic separation between humans and nature has been increasing, and has been increasingly normalized, with urbanization processes (Schneider and McMichael 2010). Yet as we have been famously reminded by David Harvey, 'there is in the final analysis nothing unnatural about New York City' (cited in Heynen et al. 2006, 1), it being the manifestation of a living environment of the human species as much as a nest would be for a bird. But in the age of planetary urbanization, rural and urban lifestyles are increasingly intertwined and hybridized and their realms mutually dependent (see also Bernstein 2014; Jacobs 2018).

'Agroecological urbanism' is both an idea and a live project. It aims to be a series of concepts and principles to transform processes of urbanization in a way that is not resource-depleting, food deskilling and ecologically unsustainable. Rather, urbanization processes should be built around the centrality of the agroecological farmers as stewards of the soil, around a strong citizen engagement with food production, and around community control over the resources of social reproduction (Deh-Tor 2017; Tornaghi and Dehaene 2020).

'A feminist, de-colonial, post-capitalist and political ecology' perspective, such as the one developed by authors such as Silvia Federici (2018), is a framework for reflection and action that would be particularly productive for multiplying political agroecology practices. This perspective builds on a critique of patriarchal, extractive and technocratic approaches to life and environmental management, and instead develops ideas on how communities can engage politically with the governance of resources and empower local communities (Clement et al. 2019; Sato and Soto Alarcón 2019).

MAPPING THE INTERSECTIONS BETWEEN URBAN FOOD MOVEMENTS AND CRITICAL AGRARIAN STUDIES

The experiences and struggles of urban food movements – or at least their more progressive and radical arms, and more often in the Global South than in the North – mirror in many respects the rural struggles that have been at the core of critical agrarian studies. In this overview, we point out two important overlaps: (1) questions of social reproduction, residualization and livelihoods; and (2) questions of food sovereignty and autonomy.

Many urban and peri-urban food initiatives bear issues of marginalization, residuality – or their unfolding within interstitial places and with limited resources – and a fundamental precarity that undermines their capacity to provide the means for social reproduction and livelihood. There is abundant evidence of urban food growing being undertaken by people in various situations: by those marginalized due to their gender, class or race (or a mix of all three); by those who grow food for survival; by those who aim to provide for their families through livelihoods aligned to their values; and by those aiming to rebuild their communities and/or reproduce knowledge-through-practice from one generation to another (Hovorka et al. 2009; Shillington 2013; Jacobs 2018; Siebert 2020). Some of these people left their agricultural lands in rural areas due to new land grabs and enclosures, while others migrated to flee war or poverty (Müller 2002; Hammelman 2018), only to find precarious working conditions in urban contexts. Food growing is thus an imperative to complement their diet. The process of urbanization gives rise to multiple survival strategies, and marginality perpetuates challenges that some of these newcomers knew from their previous rural realities, namely the struggle for land (Bagli 2006). Others defend their positions as agricultural producers in urban or peri-urban contexts, facing expanding urbanization and changing economies, supermarket-led food economies and the decreasing value of urban food, all of which progressively undermine their capacity to operate as micro farmers on residualized and interstitial urban lands. All of these urban dwellers rely on urban agriculture to maintain their day-to-day lives, and must face up to the alliance of neoliberal market forces and geopolitical trade regulations typical of the latest food regime, which goes against their capacity to establish alternative livelihoods.

The second issue that is shared between urban and rural food movements is the question of food sovereignty and autonomy. Subsistence economy forms the core and dominant part of urban agriculture in the Global South. As it follows the fundamentally different logic of producing for self-sufficiency in contrast to commodity production, it sheds light on different forms of urban autonomy. Experiences from cities in the Global South like Bogotá (Rodríguez 2019) and Maputo (Raimundo et al. 2014; Chikanda and Raimundo 2016) prove that a significant level of food sovereignty can be achieved even within an urban or peri-urban context. But urban food movements are also confronted with municipal regulations, land speculation, environmental mismanagement and the metabolic and epistemic rift (Schneider and McMichael 2010), all of which impact on the ability and effectiveness of these movements to build food sovereignty and autonomy. High land prices often result in precarious rent leases; difficult access to water, or municipal regulations against composting, livestock and biological pest and/or soil fertility management, pose great difficulty in terms of establishing ecologically sound means of food production (Tornaghi 2017). And perhaps more than anything, the difficulties in reproducing agricultural and food knowledge, due to the disembedding of these practices from broader networks and agroecological contexts, pose great limitations to the ability of urban food producers and movements to establish food sovereignty.

As Schneider and McMichael (2010) have shown with reference to the history of imperialism, and more recently Sato and Soto Alarcón (2019) with examples from Mexico, healing the knowledge and epistemic rift caused by imperial and colonial dynamics, which drain communities of their knowledge and deprive them of contexts where this knowledge can be reproduced, is no easy task. Both of these issues of sovereignty and livelihood call for feminist, post-capitalist and decolonial political ecology perspectives (such as some that generated the comments above) for their full unpacking, because they are entrenched with issues of patriarchy, power, capitalism and colonialism, that have generated and normalized them over the past centuries.

RECONCEPTUALIZING URBAN-RURAL ARTICULATIONS

From the examples in the previous section, it should be clear that urban food initiatives are often subject to the same logics that affect rural/agrarian food producers. This is not surprising given the strong link between capitalist urbanization, cheap food and the food regime. Literature on planetary urbanization (Brenner 2014) has shed light on the fact that rural lands are often an integral part of urban lifestyles and their economies. In rethinking rural–urban linkages and the potential synergies between agrarian and urban food movements, we are called to focus our attention not on the geographical dislocation of rural and urban, but on the homogeneity of the forces that shape their precarity and residuality as viable sources of alternative livelihoods. Land speculations, socio-economic inequality, disempowerment around the issue of social reproduction (its labour and knowledge) and exposure to the regulating forces of the food regime are unifying tracts that require unified strategies of resistance. International trade agreements, and the power of multinational organizations over price setting, seeds and soil management, all of which devalue agroecological stewardship of the land and impact the livelihoods of rural farmers, are part of the same logic that shapes consumption styles, land values and the commodification of food in urban settings. A reconceptualization of the urban-rural articulation within the critical agrarian debate should go beyond a simplistic view of producers and consumers attached respectively to the rural and urban contexts.

The history of urban agriculture tells us that urban development itself is closely interlinked with growing food in or nearby the urban edge, and presents the city to us as an urban-rural hybrid. We have learnt from historians that medieval European cities often had a population that lived in the city for only part of the year; the rest would be spent cultivating fields outside of the urban area/in the rural surroundings. Furthermore, the initial European settlements around fortresses – the origins of the *burgus*, from which many early cities developed – were temporary markets where rural producers and merchants would meet. So Tenochtitlan, the capital city of the Aztecs, with its floating gardens and self-sufficiency within walking distance, was no exception, as other historical examples from Africa, India and China show us (Smit et al. 1996, 28). But also today – and contrary to the popularity of the dense and vertical city – the horizontal metropolis, where residualized farming coexists with commercial and industrial activities, is the most common type of urbanization on earth. This hybridity helps us to deconstruct the (largely imaginary) divide between urban and rural, and it paves the way for blurring not only the boundaries between producers and consumers, but also those between periphery and centre. Especially in times where most people live in cities, we should look at the dynamics of urbanization as processes that transform both rural and urban contexts into something new (Alentejano 2003). Cities draw and concentrate rural people away from the countryside and into their boundaries but do not offer equal opportunities to everyone. This results in multiple forms of survival strategies, some of which perpetuate the reality of the rural place of origin, or lead to patterns of commuting and multiple belonging. So the urban expands over the rural, but the rural also reproduces itself in different ways in the urban, including through the articulation of new struggles for land in both urban and peri-urban contexts (Bagli 2006).

Urbanization is, within critical agrarian studies, often considered to be the cause of farmers' displacement, rural population drain and poverty (Lipton 1982; Bezemer and Headey 2008; for a critique of the 'urban bias' tradition see Reis 2019). Nevertheless, a reconceptualization of urban-rural articulations and a deeper understanding of peri-urban transformation should be the basis for exploring how a food-enabling, agroecological urbanism can become the foundation for a world that can accommodate a growing population, that accepts and entrusts collective interdependencies and which is set to enlarge collective participation to land stewardship and agroecological food production (Deh-Tor 2017).

Such a rearticulation, we argue, should consider the political-economic dynamics of metropolitan contexts, land protection and land access policies, soil health, farming infrastructure (for nutrients, water, energy and markets) and the existence (or not) of agroecological pedagogies to promote transitions and solidarities with and among farmers (Tornaghi and Dehaene 2020). Fundamental to building such a rearticulation of urban and rural relations is the construction of bridges, dialogue and shared struggles across agrarian and urban food movements, fostering mutual learning processes and solidarity.

AN URBAN POLITICAL AGROECOLOGY PRAXIS

Our call for a stronger consideration of urban food movements in critical agrarian studies is rooted in the understanding of these commonalities as a ground for struggle, and the related tactics and political strategies. This is slowly emerging as an urban political agroecology praxis. Currently, agroecology is far less articulated than its sister, food sovereignty, in terms of political demands, particularly if we consider the urban context (De Molina 2013). On an urbanizing planet, the urban food movement could become a strategic partner for rural struggles and discussions, providing spaces and communities for agrarian struggles to resonate, gain visibility, recruit support and claim positions. In short, in order to bring politicizing trajectories outside of isolated rural contexts.

In the case of the Zapatistas in Chiapas, Mexico, for example, such solidarities have been crucial to avoiding the brutal violence which threatened to wipe out the peasant uprising (Holloway and Pelaetz 1998). Cecosesola – an umbrella organization and network of 50 cooperatives founded in 1967 in Barquisimeto, Venezuela – is an impressive example of strong urban–rural linkages, which connects hundreds of rural farmers with local markets, and thus provides food for thousands of urban families. Furthermore, as these rural and urban dwellers are members of the same cooperative network, they also support and use the same cooperative hospital, bank and funeral service (Wolter et al. 2016). The expanding food sovereignty movement of La Via Campesina, with actors based (at least partially) in urban and peri-urban contexts, and who are partly organized within the Nyèlèni Movement, is another example. On another level, agrarian practices and knowledges find their ways into the city through solidarity movements and urban food-growing initiatives. Here, they help to dismantle the 'illusions of urban self-containment' (Bloom et al. 2016, 16) – that food comes 'from nowhere' – and to distinguish between urban peasant practices and the growing number of urban agricultural practices and discourses built around concepts of intensification, agro-industry and technology (Schmutz 2017).

These solidarities and cross-fertilizations, however, still reproduce a dichotomy between rural and urban. A further, deeper and transformative step is the germination of an urban political agroecology, which is necessary to understand the way in which the specific urban condition qualifies, shapes and transforms the issues at stake. The dynamics of urbanization, the logics of neoliberal urbanism, land value speculation and pollution are just some examples (Tornaghi and Dehaene 2020). Struggles around land tenure for urban agriculture and peri-urban food-based livelihoods, for example, have a lot in common with the struggles against enclosures typical of the agrarian tradition. As Jacobs (2018, 899) points out:

> the land and agrarian question is in part being shifted spatially to the urban areas. Rather than being dismissed as agrarian populism, the self-activity of the urban proletariat with peasant characteristics should be understood as a central component of both contemporary agrarian and urban struggles ... today, urban bias and a linear reading of history continue to obscure the relevance of the agrarian question.

In these contexts and struggles, trajectories of empowerment, such as the commoning of urban resources, encounter specific urban challenges, as Huron (2015) has so beautifully illustrated with reference to the problem of building meaningful relationships of trust in a context saturated by human density and strangers.

Despite the challenges, an urban political agroecology praxis – that is, the joining of critical thinking and politically oriented agroecological practice – is taking shape. For example, the coalition of movements and groups in London, United Kingdom, around the Just Space project is an ensemble of theory-informed tactics of appropriation, political lobbying and pre-figurative planning, placing territorial and ecological solidarities and use values before exchange values, and in so doing shaping and investing in the construction of alternative (urban) livelihoods. In Cape Town, South Africa, in the struggle to preserve the Philippi Horticulture Area (PHA) – 3000 hectares of highly productive urban farmland producing around 100,000 tons of fresh produce per year (Battersby-Lennard and Haysom 2012) – smallholders, farm workers, activists and researchers have united to resist and to raise questions not only about the role of PHA in a resilient urban food system, but also about its importance for groundwater renovation in times of severe drought. Furthermore, this coalition of actors is proposing alternative urban development models in alliance with the 'reclaim the city' movement. The urban garden movement in Berlin, Germany, is influencing urban planning policy, for instance by actively supporting one of the biggest referenda in the city's history against the development of the former Tempelhof airport. The airport site has become a role model for urban commons and serves as a home to one of the city's most emblematic community gardens, Allmende-Kontor, as well as a herd of grazing sheep. The coalition of gardeners, activists and researchers is also involved in the production of critical knowledge; they published an urban gardening manifesto, signed by more than 180 gardens from across Germany and Europe, and are fighting for a 99 year lease for the famous urban agriculture project Prinzessinnengarten (Halder, 2018). Finally, in Rosario, Argentina, activists have successfully taken up positions inside the administration to build 20 years of urban agroecological policies, which include seed-saving and sharing initiatives, training, urban nutrient recovery, soil care and access to markets. All of this makes it possible to establish urban agrarian livelihoods and to build important alternatives to the aggressive genetically modified organism-oriented agribusiness that drains and poisons the peri-urban soils.

There is much to do and learn in order to build alternative worlds, regain control over the processes of social reproduction, enact food sovereignty, steward the land and make more-than-human solidarities thrive. Urban political agroecology projects navigate the difficult waters of social arrangements that have completely dispossessed people from knowledge, awareness and solidarities. Our call here is not only and simply for mutual learning between critical agrarian studies and urban food movements, but rather for taking up the joint challenge of reclaiming urban livelihoods and transforming the urban condition, from one of alienation to a condition built around the wisdom of small agroecological farmers. This would be a necessary step in order to imagine and build an 'agroecological urbanism' (Deh-Tor 2017).

CONCLUSION

In this chapter, we have argued that despite their enormous diversity, urban food movements and practices should play an important role in critical agrarian studies. Firstly, this is because the issues that have long been at the centre of agrarian studies are very relevant for an understanding of the specific conditions that frame food movements in a rural and urban context, and for knowledge of where they are interlinked. The most important intersections at the core of critical agrarian studies debates are questions of social reproduction, residualization and livelihood, as well as questions of food sovereignty and autonomy. We need to understand these overlaps in order to gain an understanding of common rural-urban problems. Critical agrarian studies should be also more aware of its urban counterparts, because understanding the extent to which agrarian and urban food movements are shaped by the same logics and dynamics opens up a field of possibilities for reformulating the articulation between urban and rural, and thus abandoning the artificial and outdated separation between producers and consumers. Last but not least, urban food movements should be more visible in critical agrarian studies, because a new understanding of commonalities for struggles and conditions helps us to acknowledge the emergence of hybrid practices. This ultimately opens the ground for new political strategies and the fostering of common trajectories between agrarian and urban movements, as illustrated by the emergence of an urban political agroecology praxis.

FURTHER READING

RUAF Urban Agriculture Magazine, 33, on urban agroecology, accessed 26 February 2020 at https://ruaf .org/document/urban-agriculture-magazine-no-33-urban-agroecology/.

Schneider, M.; McMichael, P. (2010), Deepening and repairing the metabolic rift, *Journal of Peasant Studies*, 37, 461–484.

Tornaghi, C. (2017), Urban agriculture in the food-disabling city: (Re)defining urban food justice, reimagining a politics of empowerment, *Antipode*, 49(3), 781–801.

Van Dyck, B.; Tornaghi, C.; Halder, S.; von der Haide, E.; Saunders, E. (2018), The making of a strategizing platform: From politicising the food movement in urban contexts to political urban agroecology, in Tornaghi, C.; Certomà, C. (eds), *Urban Gardening as Politics*, London: Routledge, ch. 10.

WinklerPrins, A. (ed.) (2018), *Global Urban Agriculture: Convergence of Theory and Practice between North and South*, Oxford: CABI.

REFERENCES

Alentejano, P.R. (2003), As relações campo-cidade no Brasil do século XXI, *Terra Livre*, 21, 25–39.

Articulação Nacional de Agroecologia (2007), Construção do Conhecimento Agroecologico, Novos Papeis, Novas Identidades. Caderno do II Encontro Nacional de Agroecologia. Grupo de Trabalho sobre Construção do Conhecimento Agroecológico da Articulação Nacional de Agroecologia (GT-CCA/ANA), Recife, 6 February–6 June 2006.

Bagli, P. (2006), Rural e Urbano – harmonia e conflito na cadência da contradição, in Sposito, M.E.B.; Whitacker, A.M. (eds), *Cidade e Campo. Relações e Contradições entre Urbano e Rural*, São Paulo: Expressão Popular, 81–109.

Battersby-Lennard, J.; Haysom, G. (2012), Philippi Horticultural Area: A city asset or potential development node? Rooftops Canada Foundation; Foundation Abri International; African Food Security Urban Network, accessed 13 January 2020 at www.sustainabilityinstitute.net/si-library/1626-philippi-horticultural-area-summary-report.

Bernstein, H. (2014), Food sovereignty via the 'peasant way': A sceptical view, *Journal of Peasant Studies*, 41(6), 1031–1063.

Bezemer, D.; Headey, D. (2008), Agriculture, development and urban bias, *World Development*, 36(8), 1342–1364.

Block, D.R.; Chavez, N.; Allen, E. (2012), Food sovereignty, urban food access and food activism: Contemplating the connections through examples from Chicago, *Agriculture and Human Values*, 29, 203–215.

Bloom, B.; Clausen, M.; Fortune, B.; Sonjasdotter, Å. (2016), Food Futures: Conversations about the future of food and agriculture in the Berlin-Brandenburg bioregion. Neighbourhood Academy at Prinzesinnengarten, Berlin, accessed 13 January 2020 at https://halfletterpress.com/food-futures-conversations-about-the-future-of-food-and-agriculture-in-the-berlin-brandenburg-bio-region/.

Brenner, N. (2014), *Implosions/Explosions: Towards a Study of Planetary Urbanization*, Berlin: Jovis.

Chikanda, A.; Raimundo, I. (2016), *The Urban Food System of Maputo, Mozambique*, Hungry Cities Report, No. 2, Waterloo, ON: Hungry Cities Partnership.

CIAM (1933), *The Athens Charter*, accessed 13 January 2020 at https://modernistarchitecture.wordpress.com/2010/11/03/ciam's-"the-athens-charter"-1933/.

Clement, F.; Harcourt, W.; Joshi, D.; Sato, C. (2019), Feminist political ecologies of the commons and commoning, *International Journal of the Commons*, 13(1), 1–15.

De Molina, M.G. (2013), Agroecology and politics: How to get sustainability? About the necessity for a political agroecology, *Agroecology and Sustainable Food Systems*, 37(1), 45–59.

Deh-Tor, C.M. (2017), From agriculture in the city to an agroecological urbanism: The transformative pathway of urban (political) agroecology, *Urban Agriculture Magazine* (RUAF Foundation), 33, 8–10.

Federici, S. (2018), *Re-Enchanting the World: Feminism and the Politics of the Commons*, Oakland, CA: PM Press.

Halder, S. (2018), *Gemeinsam die Hände dreckig machen – Aktionsforschungen im aktivistischen Kontext urbaner Gärten und kollektiver Kartierungen*, Bielefeld: transcript.

Hammelman, C. (2018), Urban migrant women's everyday food insecurity coping strategies foster alternative urban imaginaries of a more democratic food system, *Urban Geography*, 39(5), 706–725.

Heynen, N.; Kaika, M.; Swyngedouw, E. (2006), *In the Nature of Cities: Urban Political Ecology and the Politics of Urban Metabolism*, London: Routledge.

Holloway, J.; Pelaez, E. (1998), *Zapatista! Reinventing Revolution in Mexico*, London: Pluto Press.

Hovorka, A.; DeZeeuw, H.; Njenga, M. (2009), *Women Feeding Cities: Mainstreaming Gender in Urban Agriculture and Food Security*, Rugby: Practical Action.

Huron, A. (2015), Working with strangers in saturated space: Reclaiming and maintaining the urban commons, *Antipode*, 47(4), 963–979.

Jacobs, R. (2018), An urban proletariat with peasant characteristics: Land occupations and livestock raising in South Africa, *Journal of Peasant Studies*, 45(5–6), 884–903.

Jarosz, L. (2008), The city in the country: Growing alternative food networks in Metropolitan areas, *Journal of Rural Studies*, 24, 231–244.

Jarosz, L. (2014), Comparing food security and food sovereignty discourses, *Dialogues in Human Geography*, 4(2), 168–181.

Lipton, M. (1982), Why poor people stay poor, in Harriss J. (ed.), *Rural Development: Theories of Peasant Economy and Agrarian Change*, London: Hutchinson University Library, 66–81.

McClintock, N. (2014), Radical, reformist, and garden-variety neoliberal: Coming to terms with urban agriculture's contradictions, *Local Environment*, 19(2), 147–171.

Müller, C. (2002), *Wurzeln schlagen: Die internationalen Gärten und ihre Bedeutung für Integrationsprozesse*, Munich: Oekom.

Peterson, P. (2012), Agroecologia em construção: Terceira edição em um terceiro contexto, in Altieri, M. (ed.), *Agroecologia. Bases Científicas para uma Agricultura Sustentável*, São Paulo: Expressão Popular, 7–14.

Raimundo, I.; Crush, J.; Pendleton, W. (2014), *The State of Food Insecurity in Maputo, Mozambique*, Kingston, ON and Cape Town: African Food Security Urban Network.

Reis, N. (2019), A farewell to urban/rural bias: Peripheral finance capitalism in Mexico, *Journal of Peasant Studies*, 46(4), 702–728.

Rodríguez, F.B. (2019), Territorios agroalimentarios de Bogotá – Abastecimento alimentario por la economía campesina y popular, in Hoinle, B.; Rodríguez, F.B.; Soto, C.L.; Pérez, M.C. (eds), *Construyendo Territorio de Paz entre el Campo y la Ciudad. Agroecologías Urbanas y Circuitos Agroalimentarios para la Paz*, Bogotá: Universidad Externado de Colombia, 53–122.

Sato, C.; Soto Alarcón, J.M. (2019), Toward a postcapitalist feminist political ecology approach to the commons and commoning, *International Journal of the Commons*, 13(1), 36–61.

Schmutz, Ulrich (2017), Urban agriculture or urban agroecology?, *RUAF*, 33, 7–10.

Schneider, M.; McMichael, P. (2010), Deepening and repairing, the metabolic rift, *Journal of Peasant Studies*, 37, 461–484.

Shillington, L.J. (2013), Right to food, right to the city: Household urban agriculture and socionatural metabolism in Managua, Nicaragua, *Geoforum*, 44, 103–111.

Siebert, A. (2020), Transforming urban food systems in South Africa: Unfolding food sovereignty in the city, *Journal of Peasant Studies*, 47(2), 401–419.

Smit, J.; Ratta, A.; Nasr, J. (1996), *Urban Agriculture: Food, Jobs and Sustainable Cities*, New York: UNDP.

Tornaghi, C. (2014), Critical geography of urban agriculture, *Progress in Human Geography*, 38(4), 551–567.

Tornaghi, C. (2017), Urban agriculture in the food-disabling city: (Re)defining urban food justice, reimagining a politics of empowerment, *Antipode*, 49(3), 781–801.

Tornaghi, C.; Dehaene, M. (2020), The prefigurative power of urban political agroecology: Rethinking the urbanisms of agroecological transitions for food system transformation, *Agroecology and Sustainable Food Systems*, 44(5), 594–610.

van der Valk, A.; Viljoen, A. (2014), AESOP's thematic groups – Part 3: The sustainable food planning thematic group, *disP – The Planning Review*, 50(4), 78–82.

Wekerle, G.R. (2004), Food justice movements: Policy, planning and networks, *Journal of Planning Education and Research*, 23, 378–386.

Wezel, A.; Bellon, S.; Doré, T.; Francis, C.; Vallod, D.; David, C. (2009), Agroecology as a science, a movement and a practice: A review, *Agronomy for Sustainable Development*, 29(4), 503–516.

Wolter, G.; Bach, P.; Arnold, A.; Rath, G. (2016), *Auf dem Weg. Gelebte Utopie einer Kooperative in Venezuela*, Berlin: Die Buchmacherei.

71. Radical transformation: Creating alternatives to capitalism in the countryside

Kristina Dietz and Bettina Engels

INTRODUCTION

In the twentieth century, a series of social upheavals led to significant changes in class structures as well as social and political institutions in the rural world.[1] Up until the 1970s, as a result of persistent rural struggles or their impending emergence, different variants of agrarian reforms were carried out in many countries in Latin America, Asia, Africa and Southern and Eastern Europe. In some cases, rural social upheavals contributed to revolutionary transformations, for instance in China and Vietnam. In virtually all these struggles, peasants and peasant movements played a central role, either as a driving force or in support of revolutionary movements or parties. Even though in many cases, such as in Cuba, Mozambique, Vietnam and China, more far-reaching aims such as the liberation from feudal, colonial or imperial rule propelled the struggles, land-based claims regarding rights, access, distribution, autonomy, political power and tenure were also essential. However, not all of these claims were successfully enforced, and of those that were it was often the case that they were not enforced in a comprehensive and enduring way. For example, after the Mexican Revolution of 1910–1917, the post-revolutionary ruling class was obliged to launch an agrarian reform which radically transformed rural class relations, due to the massive participation of the peasantry in the revolutionary overthrow of the old regime (Wolf 1969; Vergara-Camus 2012).

Examples from various geographical and historical contexts demonstrate that the peasantry can be a subject and driver of social transformation. The social relations that characterize rural societies today are the result of both capital's insinuation into the countryside and of social action, namely class struggles (Edelman and Wolford 2017). The increased interest in peasant studies and critical agrarian studies in the second half of the twentieth century refers to the rural class struggles of the previous decades. In light of these struggles and of the emergence of peasant guerrilla organizations in countries such as Colombia, Ethiopia and the Philippines, by the 1970s the peasantry was considered an important historical agent for change (Paige 1975; Skocpol 1982).

In this chapter, we explore strategies of radical, that is emancipatory, social transformation in the countryside. Which actors strive to challenge dominant rural social structures? What strategies do they deploy in order to do so? To answer these questions, we introduce the theoretical basics to which scholars in critical agrarian studies refer with regard to the peasantry's potential to drive forward a radical transformation in social and political-economic structures, and we sum up how this has been discussed recently in the field. Subsequently, we present three different strategies applied by actors who are engaged in creating alternatives to capitalism in the countryside. In the concluding section, we discuss these strategies with regard to their scope, premises and interlinkages. We argue that radical transformation is occurring through the gradual change of institutions, which in the long run may have considerable effects on the structures upon which capitalism is built.

OVERCOMING CAPITALISM IN THE COUNTRYSIDE: CLASSICAL AND CONTEMPORARY DEBATES

Questions related to how capitalism in rural societies can be overcome have been at the centre of both classical and contemporary debates within critical agrarian studies. The political agency of rural dwellers, particularly the peasantry, and alliances between rural and urban classes in bringing forth social, political and economic change have been central to these debates.

In classical Marxism, many writers (see Akram-Lodhi and Kay, this volume) considered the peasantry as 'a form of social life over which changes pass but which contributes nothing to the impetus of these changes' (Moore 1996, 453). Most prominently, this view was expressed by Karl Marx himself in his well-known portrayal of French peasants, whom he compared to a 'sack of potatoes':

> The small-holding peasants form an enormous mass whose members live in similar conditions but without entering into manifold relations with each other ... Thus the great mass of the French nation is formed by the simple addition of homologous magnitudes, much as potatoes in a sack form a sack of potatoes. In so far as there is merely a local interconnection among these small-holding peasants, and the identity of their interests begets no community, no national bond and no political organization among them, they do not form a class. They are consequently incapable of enforcing their class interest in their own name ... They cannot represent themselves, they must be represented. (Marx (1978 [1852]), VII, 126)

Similarly, Friedrich Engels (1993 [1894]), in his reflection on the peasants' contribution to the achievement of socialism in France and Germany, considered the peasantry as being a sharply differentiated yet isolated and apathetic population. Peasants did, however, constitute an essential share of the population, and a force of production and power at the end of the nineteenth century. Thus, Engels noted that without the support of the peasantry, a lasting radical transformation towards socialism would not be feasible (ibid., 498). In order to obtain political power, the task for the socialist parties was thus to organize the peasants and mobilize their support with a political programme reflecting the needs and interests of the agrarian population, therewith facilitating the creation of a worker–peasant alliance.

Karl Kautsky (1899) and Vladimir Lenin (1899) also emphasized the structuring forces of capitalism on rural social transformation, but recognized the agency of the rural classes themselves in transformation processes. For Lenin (2017 [1917]), the one and only pathway to transformation was a strong workers' party that would seize power, build a government and lead the revolution. Party members, trained in revolutionary tactics, would be the principal actors to put transformation into effect. Although Kautsky (1899) did not assign an active role to the peasants in a coming revolution, he nevertheless argued that due to their double identity as workers and property-owning smallholders, peasants might under certain circumstances join revolutionary movements and proletarian parties (see Watts, this volume).

Nowadays, the time for revolutions seems to be over. A revolution is a rapid and fundamental transformation of dominant class and state structures that is mostly carried out by class-based revolts from below; it occurs particularly in moments of crisis and the breakdown of the pre-existing social and political order (Skocpol 1979). Revolutions are profound and wide-reaching; but they are difficult to accomplish and maybe even more difficult to maintain. Historical evidence points out that the efforts of revolutionary transformations are likely to be contested by powerful adversaries from both inside and outside.

Nonetheless, in view of recent struggles over land and labour, debates are vibrant within critical agrarian studies over the potential for emancipatory social transformation and the peasantry's capacity to bring it about. Henry Bernstein (2010), for instance, emphasizes that rural life in times of capitalist globalization is highly precarious, and that rural social classes are fragmented due to the differentiation of economic positions, gender, caste, generation, ethnicity and race. In consequence, Bernstein argues, the peasantry – as a rural class and a political force for transformation – has virtually disappeared. The contradictions that permeate the fragmentation of the rural classes hamper the emergence of class consciousness and class struggle. Accordingly, Bernstein raises a doubt that claims for land and labour can unfold the systemic significance and strength needed for transformations of the capitalist mode of production in agriculture (Bernstein 2006, 456).

In contrast, other scholars emphasize that many of the most visible alternatives to capitalism in the countryside stem from land-related issues and agrarian struggles against neoliberalism, dispossession and the further commodification of land, food and labour (for example, McMichael 2006; Edelman and Wolford 2017). They argue that the rise of peasant movements in the late twentieth century and the increasing struggles over land in response to land grabbing and the resource boom is not a game of mortal combat played by a doomed-to-die peasantry, but an indication 'of the incompleteness of the transition to capitalism in agriculture' (Edelman and Borras 2016, 3). Collective claims in current rural class struggles span from demanding land rights and redistributive agrarian reforms to other pressing issues of rural life: access to decent work, autonomy, political rights, environmental justice and the recognition of ethnic and gendered identities and rights. Within these struggles, alternatives are created in multiple ways and by various actors: by establishing cooperative forms of rural labour through the introduction of new socially and ecologically just modes of production or by promoting food sovereignty (see Calvário and Kallis 2017); and by alliances between urban and rural classes within and across national boundaries, global networks of peasant movements and/or regional autonomy movements.

ERODING CAPITALISM IN THE COUNTRYSIDE

The authors whose work builds the fundamentals of critical agrarian studies were concerned with the political-economic development of societies in general, i.e. how social transformation occurs and particularly how capitalism has emerged and shall be overcome. In this chapter, by contrast, we deal with concrete present attempts to create alternatives in the countryside. Overcoming capitalism is not confined to revolutions, but can be accomplished by a variety of strategies, depending on the respective context. It involves conscious and combined efforts to build a new kind of economic reality. It can be engaged in the here and now, in any place or context. It requires an expansive vision of what is possible, a careful analysis of what can be drawn upon to begin the building process, the courage to make a realistic assessment of what might stand in the way of success and the decision to go forward with a mixture of creative disrespect and protective caution (Gibson-Graham 2006, xxxvi).

Of course, strategies vary in scope and depth, and they are by no means exclusive. Though not all are compatible in equal ways, a promising track might be flagged by a multiplicity of often interlinked strategies. Erik Olin Wright has written comprehensively on strategies for overcoming contemporary capitalism. According to him, 'the central task of emancipatory politics is to create social institutions ... that eliminate forms of oppression' (Wright 2010, 5) in all areas of society: economy, social coexistence and politics. With regard to the economy, an emancipatory alternative would consist of the creation of non-hierarchical relations of production. This implies overcoming class relations manifested in differentiated positions in the production process and thus differentiated access to and ownership of resources (such as land, machinery and technology, seeds and labour). Cooperatives or collectives set an example for institutions that build on the principle of non-hierarchical relations of production. On a societal level, institutions to promote emancipatory alternatives are founded on a radical egalitarian idea of justice, namely the dismantling of inequalities of access to the necessary material and social means of life, not only based on class but also on gender, ethnicity, caste, generation and race. Wright (2010, 11) highlights the importance of equal access to education and health care, as discrimination and exclusion based on status can lead to economic marginalization and inequalities. He also underlines that an emancipatory alternative to capitalism needs to be radically democratic: political institutions need to guarantee equal access to democratic decision-making processes that are collectively defined in the first place.

We understand institutions as relatively enduring social arrangements. Institutions constrain or enable social action and human well-being. There is always variable scope for actors to engage in institutional innovation, reinforcement or transformation. Institutions also involve generally unquestioned routines and practices, formal and informal norms, political rules, regulations and sanctioning mechanisms (such as the legal protection of property rights). Institutions that push forward radical transformation in the countryside to the effect of dismantling capitalism are, for instance, collective land use rights, restrictions of private property and of capitalist market regulations, and cooperative labour processes. Institutions do not change on their own, but their alteration is brought about by social and particular collective action. Whether, in which way and with which outcomes institutional change occurs depends on the interaction of the political context, the social actors and the institutions themselves (Mahoney and Thelen 2010). Radical institutional reconfigurations provoked by exogenous shocks or by a revolution that creates new institutions through a sharp break with the existing structures and institutions are the exception rather than the rule. Even in case of considerable shifts of political power, institutions are generally not abolished and new ones created; rather, most commonly, existing institutions are transformed. So, the disillusioning observation is that revolutions similar to prominent historical cases such as Mexico and Vietnam, which radically reconfigure agrarian social structures and institutions, hardly occur any more. The encouraging finding is that institutional change unfolds incrementally, with considerable effects in the long run (Mahoney and Thelen 2010, 2–3).

In the following, we present three kinds of strategies that are of particular importance for anti-capitalist struggles in the countryside: changing institutions and discourses at transnational scales, resisting and building alternatives and escaping and creating alternatives in the interstices. These strategies are certainly not unique; we have selected them as they represent three distinct variants of how actors presently engage to create alternatives to capitalism in the countryside.

CHANGING INSTITUTIONS AND DISCOURSES AT TRANSNATIONAL SCALES

An important strategy of social movements and civil society organizations to expand the 'room for manoeuvre' for antagonizing capitalist logics in rural economies has been the transformation of existing institutional forms (such as land rights and food regimes) and the creation of new models and discourses in order to counter dominant views and concepts. This strategy aims to enhance well-being and living conditions for rural dwellers within capitalism, to advance autonomy and democratic power and thus to expand the potential for building alternatives beyond capitalism. Since the 1990s, social movements and their organizations are increasingly pursuing this strategy in transnational action networks.

La Via Campesina is presently the best-known transnational agrarian movement campaigning for agrarian reform and peasant rights. It was created in 1993 by agrarian movements from around the world. Today, the movement has 182 member organizations from 81 countries; land and peasant rights represent their common ground (LVC 2018). La Via Campesina advocates for peasants' rights in all areas of rural life: land and territory, housing, standards of living, freedom from discrimination and oppression, seeds and traditional agricultural knowledge and access to the means of production. Key demands also address gender equality, climate justice, the right to biological diversity, the dignity of migrant workers, international solidarity and food sovereignty. La Via Campesina's principal strategies are campaigning and lobbying for institutional change, particularly within the United Nations (UN), mobilization for protest events (marches, sit-ins and so on) and creating and diffusing alternative agricultural knowledge.

Around the turn of the century, La Via Campesina, together with other allies, launched the Global Campaign for Agrarian Reform as a counter-campaign to market-led agrarian reforms promoted by the World Bank, the International Monetary Fund and others. The campaign succeeded in bringing land issues and land reforms back onto the international agenda, though in many countries it failed to shift land policies away from the neoliberal paradigm (Borras 2008). Another strategic element of this campaign was the introduction and politicization of a new perspective on food questions that offers the possibility to challenge the narratives of the ineffectiveness of small-scale farming and the promotion of market-led solutions to accomplish food security: 'food sovereignty'. With the concept of food sovereignty, La Via Campesina politicizes the corporate food regime and offers an alternative way to interpret and solve food crises. The movement associates the concept with the promotion of peasant farming as a socio-ecological alternative and necessity for food security (McMichael and Schneider 2011).

In November 2018, after six years of negotiation in an Open-Ended Intergovernmental Working Group, the UN Declaration on the Rights of Peasants and Other People Working in Rural Areas (UNDROP) was adopted by the Human Rights Council. One month later it was ratified by the UN General Assembly (UN 2018). In this way, with its strategies of cross-national campaigning and international lobbying, La Via Campesina has successfully promoted the creation of new institutions at the transnational scale. UNDROP functions as an important frame that actors can refer to in order to promote institutional change at the national and local scales; such institutional change may then allow for the general enhancement of rural life, and for the consolidation of the peasantry as a collective actor that can challenge dominant rural social structures.

RESISTING AND BUILDING ALTERNATIVES

A ubiquitous response to the adverse effects of capitalism on rural well-being is to resist it. Resistance generally means the mobilization of social protest action. It may aim to disrupt the processes of capitalist valorisation, to challenge the raising of costs by political and economic elites, to defend one's own rights or to prevent a particular project or programme (such as the expansion of monocultural agro-industrial production) or the enactment of a law. Social protest occurs when antagonistic interests clash and when rural dwellers perceive, interpret and assess these antagonisms to be unjust or a threat to their existence. Although often stated, not every act of resistance leads to social and political change in an emancipatory sense. However, there are many examples of resistance that are combined with strategies of empowerment, politicization and the creation of economic alternatives, which do contribute to promoting alternatives.

A well-known example is the resistance of the Brazilian Landless Rural Workers Movement (*Movimento dos Trabalhadores Rurais sem Terra*, MST). The MST was founded in 1984 in response to an increasing rural exodus and unequal land distribution. Its members are landless people, small farmers without secure access to land, wage labourers and urban poor without a solid income or access to the labour market. The movement's principal aims are access to land and the redistribution of land ownership. Its central means of action are occupations of large landholdings. At present, the MST has achieved the settlement of more than 400 000 families on more than 7 million hectares of land nationwide. Another 90 000 families live and work on occupied land (Karriem 2009).

For the MST, land occupations are not just a means of distributing land, but are embedded in class struggles and the creation of alternatives. In addition to securing access to land for landless families, the creation of a collective consciousness through education and politicization are central pillars of the MST's struggle. Self-administered schools enable members to benefit from (political) education and to develop political leadership skills. In broad alliances, the MST mobilizes against free trade agreements, the World Trade Organization, the use of genetically modified seeds and for food sovereignty. Regarding the latter, the MST promotes the development and dissemination of alternative, cooperative and agro-ecological forms of production that build the basis for an alternative rural economy.

Though the MST has not yet achieved any effective change in formal institutions regarding land tenure and agrarian politics in Brazil, through the occupations it has significantly improved the lives of nearly half a million families by securing access to land for them. In addition to this, through political education and the promotion of agro-ecological and collective forms of production, the MST has, with its combined strategy of resistance, substantially contributed to the establishment of alternatives to capitalism in rural areas.

ESCAPING AND CREATING ALTERNATIVES IN THE INTERSTICES

In a commentary on a controversy between Henry Bernstein and Philip McMichael on the relevance of food and agriculture in relation to capitalist development today, Harriet Friedmann (2016, 682–683) has argued that alternative ways of living in the countryside might emerge in the interstices of decaying capitalist societies. In fact, escaping – the creation of new forms of social empowerment and social life in the niches and margins of capitalist societies – has historically been an important response to capitalism in the countryside. Examples of utopian communities or rural cooperatives that aim for self-sufficiency, equity and reciprocity exist worldwide. They emerge where people want change and transformation but the balance of power hardly allows it, and where they do not pose a direct threat to dominant classes and elites, at least initially. Escaping does not necessarily entail efforts to transform capitalism. However, there are many examples of 'escaping' where people create alternatives to demonstrate that such alternatives can exist and are feasible, and to act out of the interstices in cooperation with others for the accomplishment of radical transformation and the erosion of capitalism's constraining conditions.

An example of this is the European cooperative Longo Maï (Provençal for 'May it last long'), which was created in the aftermath of the congress 'European Pioneer Settlements', held in Basel, Switzerland, in December 1972. In the adopted resolution, the participants declared that they would leave capitalist industrial society to its fate and build a social alternative beyond the logics of capital, markets and alienated labour in those remote rural areas of Europe particularly hit by capitalism in terms of the decimation of farms and the disappearance of peasants. An example of this was large parts of the French Haute-Provence.

Today about 200 people live and work in Longo Maï cooperatives in France, Austria, Germany, Switzerland, Costa Rica and the Ukraine. Together they cultivate several hundred hectares of land, produce food and wine and run a sheep's wool-spinning mill as well as various smaller facilities for processing their own agricultural products. Longo Maï's approach includes strengthening self-sufficiency and grassroots democracy, and building micro-economies. In a radical departure from the capitalist system, it advocates social and ecological agriculture as well as equitable working conditions, and aims to overcome the separation of productive and unproductive labour (Schwab 2013).

Longo Maï's aim was never to confine itself to the creation of enclaves where the rules of capitalism are suspended; rather, it also strives to intervene socially in order to change the conditions outside. In 1978, the cooperative created the crisis fund for the European mountain regions, with the aim of stopping out-migration from these areas. In 1981, an independent radio station was established in Provence in order to create a counter-public voice. An important field of action is European agricultural policy. In 2008, together with other initiatives, Longo Maï initiated a campaign for free seeds: 'Sowing the Future – Harvesting Diversity'. The campaign was a reaction to a European Union draft law, according to which only registered seed could be used in the Union. As a result of the campaign, international and regional platforms for seed exchange were initiated that continue to operate to this day.

CONCLUSION

Our endeavour in this chapter has been to explore strategies of radical, that is emancipatory, social transformation in the countryside. The three strategies presented reveal that the potential of agrarian struggles to promote alternatives to capitalism is anything but limited to peasant revolts and to seeing the peasantry as an alleged homogeneous actor spurring revolution. In contrast, more often than not, social change happens over time through the gradual change of institutions, which may be more or less radical, and is brought forth by different actors who deploy a variety of strategies, with varying premises, outcomes, scales and scope.

Through its transnational campaigns, the lobbying of international organizations, the creation of counter-discourses and mobilization for trans-local protest events – namely the coordination of protest action at different localities at the same time – La Via Campesina contributes to institutional change both at the transnational and national levels, as new international institutions function as a reference for demands and frames at the national scale. Through (media) campaigns, the network demonstrates that alternatives to agrarian capitalism exist and are feasible. For this strategy of changing institutions to be effective, it depends on a broad network of actors and groups worldwide that are able to build up sufficient political pressure. Furthermore, at least some supporters from within existing institutions are needed in order to achieve change. Although such changes and demonstrations might not shake the very base of the capitalist system and sometimes even run the risk of stabilizing it through legitimization, they nevertheless change the rules of capitalism, so that the room for manoeuvre for rural social actors who strive for emancipatory transformation expands.

In order to secure livelihoods and income for landless people and to achieve a socially just distribution of land, land occupations, combined with the creation of economic alternatives and the politicization of its members, have become tools of resistance for the MST. As with La Via Campesina, this strategy of resisting and building alternatives from below will also not contribute to any profound changes in rural social structures. It can, however, help to enable people to try out strategies for change in the first place, which can then be disseminated and learned by others. Resisting and applying alternative practices of production require patience, and the strength to withstand periods of uncertainty and to ward off counter-attacks by political and economic elites. Alliances and cooperation with the wider public – including parts of the media, political parties and other strong member organizations – are therefore necessary. In the case of the MST, a long-lasting and strong relationship with the Brazilian Workers' Party did exist, though this has declined in recent years, in part due to the co-optation of MST leaders.

In contrast, creating alternatives in the interstices of capitalist societies seems to be more feasible, as niches are perceived as not posing any significant risk to existing political and economic power relations. Independent of how this strategy of escaping and building alternatives is perceived by political and economic elites, it fulfils an important role model function, demonstrating that alternatives can and do exist and are – with limitations – feasible, and thereby they challenge the institutions of agrarian capitalism. Furthermore, out of the interstices, cooperatives intervene directly at various scales in order to bring forth institutional change and push for new practices (such as seed exchange platforms), which contribute to changes within existing institutions and to the conditions of production and reproduction in rural societies.

The three strategies and examples discussed in this chapter do not operate in isolation, but are interlinked. Organizations such as the MST and Longo Maï are, for instance, members of La Via Campesina. This applies to many other initiatives at the local or national level that strive for transformation, and which are also linked to broader networks. In this sense, numerous actors all over the world are engaged in what Wright (2019) calls 'eroding capitalism', namely building emancipatory alternatives in the countryside using different strategies that combine grassroots-centred initiatives with transnational movement actions, and in some cases more top-down state-centred strategies.

In light of these examples, it is clear that eroding agrarian capitalism is not confined to the profound disruption of an existing political and economic system (revolution), but is facilitated by changing discourses and reference frames; by the de facto improvement of access to and control over the means of production (particularly land); and in the form of niches that have radiating impacts. Obviously, these are just three examples of what is possible, each with its strengths and weaknesses.

In whatever way, radical transformation towards alternatives to capitalism occurs, and it has an impact on rural social relations and well beyond. One might argue that at present political-economic power relations are more in favour of transformation towards authoritarianism than towards emancipation. But conditions, though they are hard to change in the short run, are not set in stone; they can be transformed through social action. After all, social change, in the true sense of the word, is not a state of affairs but a never-ending process.

NOTE

1. We are grateful to participants of the *Handbook*'s author workshop in Berlin in May 2019; the debates and comments on a previous version of this chapter that took place within this workshop were enormously helpful. We owe special thanks to Christian Lund for his comprehensive suggestions and advice.

FURTHER READING

Gibson-Graham, J.K. (2006), *Postcapitalist Politics*, Minneapolis, MN: University of Minneapolis Press.
Mahoney, J.; Thelen, K. (eds) (2010), *Explaining Institutional Change: Ambiguity, Agency, and Power*, New York: Cambridge University Press.
Wright, E.O. (2010), *Envisioning Real Utopias*, London: Verso.
Wright, E.O. (2019), *How to be an Anti-Capitalist for the 21st Century*, London: Verso.

REFERENCES

Bernstein, H. (2006), Is there an agrarian question in the 21st century?, *Canadian Journal of Development Studies/Revue canadienne d'études du développement*, 27, 449–460.
Bernstein, H. (2010), *Class Dynamics of Agrarian Change*, Halifax: Fernwood.
Borras, S.J. (2008), La Vía Campesina and its global campaign for agrarian reform, *Journal of Agrarian Change*, 8, 258–289.
Calvário, R.; Kallis, G. (2017), Alternative food economies and transformative politics in times of crisis: Insights from the Basque Country and Greece, *Antipode*, 49, 597–616.
Edelman, M.; Borras, J. (2016), *Political Dynamics of Transnational Agrarian Movements*, Winnipeg: Fernwood.

Edelman, M.; Wolford, W. (2017), Introduction: Critical agrarian studies in theory and practice, *Antipode*, 49, 959–976.

Engels, F. (1993 [1894]), *The Peasant Question in France and Germany*, Moscow: Progress Publishers.

Friedmann, H. (2016), Commentary: Food regime analysis and agrarian questions: Widening the conversation, *Journal of Peasant Studies*, 43, 671–692.

Gibson-Graham, J.K. (2006), *Postcapitalist Politics*, Minneapolis, MN: University of Minneapolis Press.

Karriem, A. (2009), The rise and transformation of the Brazilian landless movement into a counter-hegemonic political actor: A Gramscian analysis, *Geoforum*, 40, 316–325.

Kautsky, K. (1899), *Die Agrarfrage: Eine Uebersicht über die Tendenzen der modernen Landwirthschaft und die Agrarpolitik der Sozialdemokratie*, Stuttgart: Dietz.

Lenin, V.I. (1899), *The Development of Capitalism in Russia: The Process of the Formation of a Home Market for Large-Scale Industry*, Moscow: Progress Publishers.

Lenin, V.I. (2017 [1917]), *The State and Revolution*, London: Aziloth Books.

LVC (2018), Members, La Via Campesina.

Mahoney, J.; Thelen, K. (2010), A theory of gradual institutional change, in Mahoney, J.; Thelen, K. (eds), *Explaining Institutional Change: Ambiguity, Agency, and Power*, New York: Cambridge University Press, 1–37.

Marx, K. (1978 [1852]), *Eighteenth Brumaire of Louis Napoleon*, Beijing: Foreign Languages Press.

McMichael, P. (2006), Reframing development: Global peasant movements and the new agrarian question, *Canadian Journal of Development Studies/Revue canadienne d'études du développement*, 27, 471–483.

McMichael, P.; Schneider, M. (2011), Food security politics and the Millennium Development Goals, *Third World Quarterly*, 32, 119–139.

Moore, B.J. (1996), *Social Origins of Dictatorship and Democracy*, Boston, MA: Beacon.

Paige, J.M. (1975), *Agrarian Revolution: Social Movements and Export Agriculture in the Underdeveloped World*, New York: Free Press.

Schwab, A. (2013), *Landkooperativen Longo Mai. Pioniere einer gelebten Utopie*, Zürich: Rotpunkt.

Skocpol, T. (1979), *States and Social Revolutions: A Comparative Analysis of France, Russia, and China*, Cambridge: Cambridge University Press.

Skocpol, T. (1982), What makes peasants revolutionary?, *Comparative Politics*, 14, 351–375.

UN (2018), *United Nations Declaration on the Rights of Peasants and Other People Working in Rural Areas*, United Nations.

Vergara-Camus, L. (2012), The legacy of social conflicts over property rights in rural Brazil and Mexico: Current land struggles in historical perspective, *Journal of Peasant Studies*, 39, 1133–1158.

Wolf, E. (1969), *Peasant Wars of the Twentieth Century*, New York: Harper and Row.

Wright, E.O. (2010), *Envisioning Real Utopias*, London: Verso.

Wright, E.O. (2019), *How to Be an Anti-Capitalist in the 21st Century*, London: Verso.

72. Feasible utopias

Ray Bush

A map of the world which does not include Utopia is not worth even glancing at, for it leaves out the one country at which humanity is always landing. And when humanity lands there, it looks out, and, seeing a better country, sets sail. Progress is the realisation of Utopias.
(Oscar Wilde 2001 [1891], 141)

INTRODUCTION

It is both timely and important to explore feasible utopias as an integral part of critical agrarian studies. The centenary of the great Bolshevik Revolution of 1917 reminded us of the fiercely contested debate about the relationship between industry and agriculture, the role of the peasantry in the strategy of socialist accumulation and how structural transformation can be promoted to deliver utopia, in the form of justice, equality and democracy. In the Third World,[1] utopia was the alternative to Western dominance and the imperialism of the internationalization of capital, the consequences of the second and third global food regimes; it was related to agrarian questions of agricultural production, (socialist) accumulation and class alliances to promote an alternative to capitalist barbarism.

In the following, I present some essential elements of the intervention that can be made by critical agrarian studies towards the promotion of a socialist transition towards a feasible utopia. A feasible utopia is, at a minimum, a 'form of society which could generally provide for its members the material and social bases of a tolerably contented existence, or (put otherwise) from which the gravest social and political evils familiar to us have been removed' (Geras 1996, 259). The feasible utopia is anti-capitalist and it is achievable and deliverable. It is not merely an imagined subjectivist abstraction from reality, but a strategy for a classless society grounded in an analysis of the contemporary brutality of peasant lived experience. It is a utopia that is forged from a rejection of domination by the international law of value and the local merchant and other classes that benefit from it. A feasible utopia seeks transcendence of rural power relations that subordinate the peasantry and reproduce inequality. It recognizes the struggle for communism as an attainable achievement; a future social formation that shares the collective aims that emerge from contemporary livelihoods.

A feasible utopia is obtainable because it is produced by rural and urban social movements in struggle. The outcome of struggle, however, is constantly being shaped, and reshaped, by clashes with dominant social forces. This includes struggles with the dominant ideology that asserts the permanence of neoliberalism and tries to shut down discussion of alternatives to capitalist hegemony. Class struggles shape agendas for change, and political contestation creates unintended consequences that threaten movements towards a feasible utopia. Yet this is not a reason to reject the battles for utopia, as they will, and do, embrace the 'tension between dreams and practice' (Wright 2010, 6).

There have been a number of important interventions that can directly help us to fathom policy initiatives aimed at promoting and mapping relationships between the feasible utopia and critical agrarian studies. I will explore some of these and set them in the context of struggles for food sovereignty and agro-ecology (Akram-Lodhi 2015; Amin 2017; Wright 2010). I argue for a democratically organized and ecologically structured strategy of accumulation from below. In its early phases, this is likely to be state-centralized and therefore part of an immensely problematic conflict between competing interests. Local conflict, moreover, is overlaid by the contemporary crisis-ridden and financialized world food system. In exploring the possibility of a feasible utopia, I argue for the need to defend and extend the role of the commons. While production and social reproduction in the countryside is not all shared, rural production does often involve collective space and institutions and socially organized production. This both preceded and continues alongside, albeit in a transformed way, commodified market exchanges, and it is within this arena that seeds for utopia can emerge.

Struggles and competition over the commons are, however, contradictory. While the commons offer potential for the alternative utopia, they also provide a certain functionality for capitalism. Capitalism has been advancing on the commons in the wake of the 2008 financial crisis. The commons are a frontier where capital is seeking to benefit from the shared and collective organization of production and the social reproduction of rural communities. Commons production devalues the costs for capital of labour reproduction, and it holds areas of surplus labour power and environmental assets. At the same time, however, the commons are perhaps the final space for capital to capture, transform and generate private accumulation. The contradiction of capitalism is that the eradication of indigenous production, and the commodification of land and labour, provide only short-term productivity gains for capital. A key feature of the neoliberal capitalist crisis is the failure of the system to deliver strategic inputs that reduce rather than increase the costs of production. Cumulative costs of production are driven by resource depletion and financialization that derive profitability from accelerated investment in land grabs; environmental asset stripping then fuels new rounds of speculation and volatile commodity markets (Moore 2010).

Struggles in agriculture are the most fiercely contested of any in capitalism; indeed, agriculture is at the deepest point of struggles within global capitalism, because it is essential to the reproduction of labour. Access to cheap food has always been, and remains, at the core of capitalist development. The neoliberal explanation for the rise in grain and rice prices after 2008 was that it had been caused by the financial crisis, as well as by increased demand from wealthier populations in India and China. This explanation is, however, a product of dominant ideology. The food crisis was the result of decades of underdevelopment of peasant agriculture, the fall in per capita grain production from the mid-1990s on and speculation by traders on futures markets (Chakraborty 2015). As a political economic system, capitalism has always sought to access cheap food. This is necessary to keep the wage bill as close as possible to the cost of the social reproduction of labour power: if agricultural production is destroyed, so too is the working class. It is unsurprising that although agriculture accounts for less than 5 per cent of world trade, World Trade Organization negotiations for the sector remain unresolved and disputed. Managing global movements of grain and food runs alongside contemporary capitalism's struggles to deal with 'surplus populations', migration and refugee 'crises' and the limited containment of working-class and middle-class debt. Low wage bills for employers may no longer be so dependent upon the importance of cheap food in the Global North. Even as 'surplus populations' are promoted as threats to national security, they also provide a means to socially reproduce 'bare life' at minimum cost to capital. The period of financial-ized post-industrial capital accumulation and attempts to manage rivalry between the imperial triad of the United States (US), the European Union (EU) and Japan and China's rise (Amin 2017) obscure the relative simplicity of the necessary measures to transform, and improve, the wellbeing of small farmers in the Global South. Many policy initiatives have been rehearsed in failed attempts to promote alternative (utopian) visions to the mainstream: land reform and cheap peasant credit to enable some assisted technical changes relating to, among other things, cultivation, cropping patterns and choice, irrigation and farming inputs (Kalecki 1993; Ghosh 2011).

FOOD SYSTEM IN CRISIS

A manifesto for a feasible utopia, grounded in local practices and struggles, challenges the violence of late capitalism's construction of persistent and recurrent food insecurity in most of the Global South. The world food system has impacted local struggles for a feasible utopia. Following World War II, Washington used food surpluses to subordinate Third World gov-ernments, and to do so increasingly through the promise of aid in return for client support for US geo-strategic interests. China, as well as many countries in Latin America and Africa during periods of national liberation struggle in the 1970s and 1980s, and South East Asia when it directly repelled imperialist intervention in Viet Nam, have all posed challenges to US hegemony. For example, rural poverty and peasant mobilizations – in different and often uneven ways – in Chile, Ecuador, Peru and Nicaragua, and for a short time in Nasser's Egypt, led to concessions for family farming as well as political representation. Nevertheless, the structural constraints created by the internationalization of capital, including pressures placed on many Third World states to commercialize agricultural production and liberalize govern-ment intervention, dismissed claims for special needs that took into account either the local particularities or the specific claims of national food systems. There may have been short-term engagements with Soviet-style state farms, villagization and co-operatives, but agricultural modernization was mostly and simply seen as a mirror of Western development.

Local food systems in the Global South were subordinated to the demands of international financial institutions, in particular the World Bank and the International Monetary Fund, to maximize the movement of food around the world by promoting export-led growth, by adopting a standardized US farm model of capital-intensive agriculture, fed by agribusiness and fossil fuel-derived inputs, and disciplined by 'the market' through the imposition of economic structural adjustment programmes. The important qualitative shift to the third global food system after 1973 was the neoliberal revolution, which transformed the ways in which Third World political economies in general, and rural political economies in particular, could socially reproduce themselves. The export model for the South and the neoliberal trade regime failed to generate income to pay for and sustain food security. Instead, heavily subsi-dized Northern agriculture flooded the South, and in so doing undermined small-scale family farming. In 1961–1963, the Third World had an aggregate agricultural trade balance of US\$6.7 billion. This had disappeared by the 1990s, and the projection for 2030 is that the agricultural trade deficit for the Global South will be US\$31 billion. For the poorest developing countries, the situation is even worse: by the 1990s, food imports were twice the level of exports.

Changes in net agricultural trade reflect a crisis for the importing country under existing patterns of global inequality. This remains the case even where the trend in agricultural trade balances may mask some basic food production in non-tradable items. There is a heavy toll to pay if production shrinks and is unable to meet local demand. This is reflected in the increased number of people suffering from hunger (Patnaik 2008). Import dependence reduces national autonomy and narrows the space for a feasible utopia. This is especially the case when the national economy is susceptible to the vagaries of international market fluctuations or environmental hazards. These are a very evident and persistent feature of many post-World War II food regimes, as more than 40 countries in the Global South remain dependent upon a single commodity such as coffee, cocoa or sugar to provide more than 20 per cent of their total merchandise export revenue and more than 50 per cent of their total agricultural export revenue.

The mechanism that led to the underdevelopment of Third World agriculture was the second global food regime, which lasted from the 1940s up to 1973, and the third food regime that replaced it. A food regime is one that is governed by rules and operates globally. The first regime, from 1870 to 1914, shaped patterns of agricultural industrialization in the North and crop specialization in the South. The subsequent food regimes affirmed a world of structural food imbalances shaped by producers in the Global North. US and EU subsidies lowered international prices for wheat, soybeans and rice to less than costs of production, promoting depeasantization and deagrarianization in the South. Northern subsidies protected Northern agribusiness and allowed for the flooding of the market with grain and other food surpluses that were also outside many market channels because of US Public Law 480. Public Law 480 was the Agricultural Trade Development and Assistance Act passed by Eisenhower in 1954 which became a mechanism of US imperial foreign policy (Sorenson 1979).

The twin patterns of social transformation, and depeasantization and deagrarianization, pose major challenges as well as opportunities for struggles for a feasible utopia. On the one hand, displaced farmers are added to the 'wasted lives' of humanity: this leads to a rise in unemployment and informal sectors and communities, as well as in recent attempts to enter Europe as migrants (though migration remains largest within continental borders). The displaced are made abject by a financialized capitalism that is in terminal decline; yet in these labour-surplus economies, development and policy alternatives nevertheless remain capital-intensive. On the other hand, the intensification of rural crises helps to explain why social movements such as La Via Campesina LVC (2010) have become so important in mobilizing small farmers against displacement. Food riots are evidence of this, as are the now well-documented spontaneous and independent farmer protests against dispossession and inflated food prices since 2008.

It was not meant to be like this. The post-World War II food system settlement was intended to ensure the dependence of the Global South upon Northern supplies of grain and other agricultural commodities. Peasants and workers in the South were to be kept in a situation of 'bare life', but the food regime jeopardized even that limited delivery. After 1973, the third food regime reflected increased competition in agricultural trade, partly as a result of the end of the Cold War and the increased role of agribusiness. Nation states' abilities to manage and regulate food and grain production were destroyed by the imperialist neoliberal revolution in the 1970s. The North's advocacy of neoliberalism demanded deregulation, and an end to capital controls and any residual national sovereignty. Neoliberal ideologues in the imperialist triad demanded cheap food and continued markets for Northern subsidized producers, which led to austerity and state collapse in the Global South driven by economic and structural adjustment programmes. The triad also demanded continued cheap energy, raw materials and labour power.

The period after the 1970s has been dogged by capitalism's inability to ensure a persistent fall in the costs of inputs to the economic system. This has led to crises of profitability for capitalism that have been driven by worker and farmer protest, resource scarcity and the failure of investors to generate increases in labour productivity. Investors have a range of strategies to promote their accumulation of capital. These include the promotion of out-grower schemes, plantations and other interventions in the food supply chain. The precise strategy is dependent upon local and global conditions, but many have preferred to seek gains from speculation in commodities, including land, rather than to invest in productive assets. The consequence for farmers in the South has been calamitous (Hall et al. 2015).

Contemporary capitalism no longer creates conditions for financing development, but instead for developing finance (Bracking 2016, 16). The realm of agriculture is no exception and the struggles for a feasible utopia involve the transformation of financialized capitalism, which will involve the need to reinstate the financing of development with a democratized state. The struggle here is enormous and we will indicate some of the necessary policy dimensions to do this in a moment. Meanwhile, it is important to be reminded that late capitalism is underpinned by the financialization of food and agriculture. The separation between the 'farm and the plate' and the extended food chain ensures many points of intervention and profitability for capital. Financialization influences how and where food is produced, distributed and consumed. Since 2008, though actually it was already benefiting from the earlier deregulation of markets and speculation in prices, agriculture has become a source of capital accumulation. New investment projects have emerged, like Blackstock's COW funds in companies such as Archer-Daniels-Midlands Co, Tyson Food Inc and Bunge, and Van Eck's MOO investments in Potash Corporation, Syngenta and Deere (Clapp and Isakson 2018).

An obvious scandal is that the demand for food is highly inelastic. Perhaps it needs to be more publicly stated that people need to eat, but food is like any other commodity. Food has a use value and an exchange value, hence consumers need to have the wherewithal to access it. A feasible utopia will directly address the reasons why the producers of food are usually the first to suffer from food insecurity, hunger and structural malnutrition. We need to remind ourselves that capitalism is 'a historically specific and contradictory mode of production that systematically produces class inequality and crisis and conditions state forms and politics' (Levien et al. 2018, 858).

FAMILY FARMING AND THE ART OF THE POSSIBLE – THE FEASIBLE UTOPIA

The twenty-first century has been marked by fiercely contested struggles over land and raw materials. The struggles have been linked to mining and land grabbing for rents derived from the extraction of raw materials and natural resources, which are often generated through rural dispossession, yet which mostly go to Northern corporate actors (Hall et al. 2015; Wengraf 2018). Farmers and rural workers, defended and advocated for by La Via Campesina, among others, provide a counterpoint to the power of international capital, particularly agribusiness, with their agendas of food sovereignty, peasant autonomy and agro-ecology. This constitutes a strategy of repeasantization – countering dispossession and marginality with strategies to bolster peasant farming – and involves a myriad of strategies and programmes orchestrated from the countryside to promote improved rural livelihoods.

One of the most internationally well-known examples of such a programme comes from Zimbabwe, where the state consolidated and then advanced fast-track land reform following persistent rural pressure. After 20 years of stonewalling behind the Lancaster House December 1979 agreement, which tied Robert Mugabe's ruling Zimbabwe African National Union-Patriotic Front (ZANU-PF) into a 'willing seller, willing buyer' arrangement for land transactions, 'war vets', the landless and the state's security forces seized white-owned farmland in the promotion of the third *Chimurenga* or revolutionary struggle (Moyo 2011).

Zimbabwe's Fast Track Land Reform (FTLR) highlights a successful mobilization for land and farming assets and improvements to rural livelihoods, which have resulted from rural struggles for land. However, the FTLR highlights more than just the successful occupation of white-owned commercial farms by many landless in Zimbabwe. It also highlights the persistent and recurrent way in which land and its formal ownership and cropping patterns and pricing mechanisms are politicized, how state power is central – alongside rural and working-class mobilization for redistribution of the means of production – and how international actors remain vigilant to take any opportunity to reverse farmer gains. The FTLR also highlights fierce contestation around the commons, around the encroachment of communal grazing areas by landless peasants, who sometimes employ weapons of the weak to extend their 'plots illegally into areas that were technically designated as common grazing lands' (Mkodzongi 2018, 204). Other rural struggles have highlighted ways of skirting around land use plans, challenging new tenure regimes and problematizing membership of the ruling party ZANU-PF and the bureaucratization of land and farming policy. The Zimbabwe case offers both a glimpse of the radical possible in the ways that the FTLR created conditions for a rural revolution embedded in socially promoted and shared commons activity, and it has also highlighted the political difficulties of agreements to formalize land occupation, to work with local officials to deliver a degree of socialized production and the challenges of maintaining areas for communal grazing in the face of accelerated petty commodity production among peasants.

At the core of La Via Campesina, Zimbabwe's FTLR and other examples of repeasantization is the defence and advancement of family farming. Family and small-scale farming is central to the creation of a feasible utopia. The term may be a 'catch all', but it captures the widespread and significant:

> means of organising agricultural, forestry, fisheries, pastoral and aquaculture production which is managed and operated by a family and predominantly reliant on family labour, including women's and men's. The family and the farm are linked, co-evolve and combine economic, environmental, social and cultural functions. (FAO 2013, 5)

The Food and Agriculture Organization of the United Nations (UN) declared 2014 the year of family farming. In doing so, it generated a publicity boost for peasant and farming communities across the Global South, which was resisted by the US. It also led to the declaration by the UN General Assembly in December 2017 of a Decade of Family Farming 2019–28 (UN 2017). The declaration is meaningful, affirming the role and importance of family farming globally for, among other things, food security and nutrition. However, it was a resolution that affirmed the significance of family farming 'within existing structures and available resources' (UN 2017, 3–4). Almost in recognition of this limitation, in 2018 the General Assembly declared the rights of peasants and other people working in rural areas (UN 2018). This latter declaration was more forthright in its promotion of a peasantry confronted by poverty, climate change, migration and forced displacement, and its recognition of the uneven impact on women of economic crisis, as well as farmer suicides and child welfare.

Movements towards a feasible utopia will require international solidarity and the initiatives of the UN, driven by social activism and debate around food sovereignty and agro-ecology. However, a 'shopping list' approach set in the context of farmer 'rights' will not address the crisis of family farming. International agencies can readily lament the impacts of climate change, land fragmentation and fluctuating levels of agricultural productivity, as well as high levels of rural poverty. In doing so, the tendency is to promote food security via the time-weary agenda of market liberalization, the expansion of trade networks and support for larger, more 'competitive' farms. This neoliberal path does little, however, to address the status quo that has generated the rural crises in the first place. It certainly does not address the reasons why some rural dwellers are poor and others are wealthy. The failure to grasp a relational view of poverty creation is at the core of international financial institutions' inability (reluctance) to mitigate rural impoverishment. The agencies' silences are deafening and a feasible utopia will address them directly: unequal land access and quality, irrigation, rural social differentiation, rural gender dynamics, employment practices and opportunities and the subordination of national agricultural strategies to global grain markets.

The feasible utopia will only be delivered if it valorizes indigenous farming knowledge, and penalizes investors for exercising control over local farming or for trying to take land out of production, often for cash cropping or urbanization, without democratic decision making or any guarantee of local retention of the income generated. The feasible utopia will also promote rural wages and income to restrict rural-to-urban migration, but for that it will be necessary, as I indicate below, to develop a policy to protect local farmers and farming from the international law of value and its most deleterious impact: the dumping of agricultural food imports at prices well below the costs of production. To establish this policy framework, we need to have a strong sense of what it is that rural producers want and how this links to the transformation not only of rural markets, production techniques and cropping, but also, and fundamentally, to the reform of monoculture and 'the active appropriation of farming systems by peasants' using 'local knowledge, ingenuity, and [the] ability to innovate' (LVC 2010, 3).

The two central parameters for the delivery of the feasible utopia, beyond the pressure of the world market, is an understanding of the 'peasant condition' and 'peasant principle'. Family farmers, peasants and the landless struggle for autonomy. They do this in '*a context characterised by dependency relations, marginalization and deprivation*' (Van der Ploeg 2009, 23, emphasis original). Indeed, peasant struggles seek the '*creation and development of a self-controlled and self-managed resource base*' (ibid.) and this creates the promise, although not always delivery, of socialized production. The overwhelming challenges for family farming are access to productive land and the navigation of markets. The peasant principle builds on the possibility for socialized co-production because it places an emphasis on world views of working and living with nature, on confidence in farming practices and a recognition of the pitfalls of the market power of traders and the tyranny of farmgate prices.

Whereas the script of entrepreneurial farming increasingly fails to outline a convincing trajectory for development and survival, the peasant principle, with its focus on the construction of an autonomous and self-governed resource base, clearly specifies ways forward (ibid., 276).

In many ways, it was precisely this peasant principle that proved so successful in the ascendance of radical governments in Latin America. Bolivia, Ecuador and Venezuela, for instance, established legal and political frameworks for a Via Campesina model of rural development based upon food sovereignty and *buen vivir* (good living). Yet while mobilizations brought left-wing governments to power, and there were anti-poverty measures that improved rural livelihoods, at least while commodity prices remained high, there was an absence of redistributive land reform that could have cemented and deepened progressive, and sustained, rural development. Policy backsliding in the case of Ecuador and Bolivia resulted from the failure of social movements to control the state with strong political alliances, which then led simply to the reaffirmation of agribusiness models of development (Clark 2017; Vergara-Camus and Kay 2017a, 2017b).

Social mobilization is dependent upon political class alliances that recognize and advocate for small farmer rights. Perhaps the most appropriate and deliverable mechanism for deepening and then extending the dynamics of family farming, of advancing the interests of small-scale farmers, women and the landless, is the promotion of the commons. I define the commons as common goods that are not valorized by an economic market controlled by an entrepreneur, trader, merchant or agribusiness company. The commons are not 'goods' with an exchange value 'but a social practice that generates, uses and preserves common resources and products' (Meretz 2012, 28). The commons can be managed by the producers themselves, and for this to be successful, in line with the notion of the 'peasant principle', there needs to be agreement among peasant and other social movements. Unlike markets that empower the wealthy, that shape social relations of production and reproduction in a way that constantly generates poverty and inequality, the idea, and practice, of the commons – which I am expressing as central for the delivery of a feasible utopia – are a product of self-management and inclusion. The process of centring the commons on all farming practices requires organization. This is in direct contradiction to the reification of individualism that is the hegemonic neoliberal mantra. The definition of the commons that I promote will be challenged at every turn, not least because it defies the idea that people are inherently selfish rather than co-operative (Hardin 1968; cf. Ostrom 1990) and it promotes a non-binary view of the world.

The neoliberal claim is that there is either the (efficient) individual or the (inefficient) collectivity, people or nature, state or market, property rights or chaos. The view of the commons, however, is to embrace the complexity and dynamics of peasant production and social reproduction, to recognize gendered divisions of labour, to celebrate the collective, labour and resource sharing and to do so with democratic practice. There are difficulties with this, of course, easier to resolve perhaps within a village setting than between two or more villages where the agro-ecological differences, and therefore the productivity of labour, may vary considerably, and with it local wealth creation. The point, however, is that the commons can embrace and advance a non-individualistic market-organized lifestyle. This can form a counterpoint to the ways in which commodification has historically generated social differentiation, uneven development and class power among landed elites.

There are commons not only in terms of access to land and farming inputs, and to agro-ecological products to enhance and develop productivity. The commons involve a multiple range of practices and social and geographical spaces: the successful autonomy of indigenous practices, households and social centres from the influence of capital 'depends on the *contingent* power relations within the commons; on the power of networked commons; and on forces *outside* the commons, such as capital. The commons therefore represent a field of *possibilities* in the struggle against capital' (De Angelis 2012, 186, emphasis original).

Struggles for the feasible utopia seek the extension and deepening of the commons and the recognition that competition between Southern and Northern farmers will never be resolved in favour of those in the Global South. The 'modernization' of farming, tractorization, the increased chemicalization of inputs, the privatization of the commons and improved marketing may benefit a small proportion of family farmers; yet such improvements in wellbeing for the minority will not help the half of humanity that currently generates a living from agriculture. Improved productivity for 50 million farmers in the Global South (200 million with family members) contrasts with the abjection of 3 billion who are excluded from capitalist modernization. As Samir Amin noted in one of his last published essays:

> Capitalism has entered its phase of declining senility: the logic of the system is no longer able to ensure the simple survival of humanity. Capitalism is barbaric and leads directly to genocide. It is more than ever necessary to replace it by other development logics which are more rational. (Amin 2017, 156)

The struggle to promote the feasible utopia is the strategy to avoid genocide in Amin's sense. It is a strategy that will involve the regulation of the global market and the control of powerful local market intermediaries such as merchants and traders. This is necessary to protect and boost local production in order to advance food sovereignty. Essential for this is the delinking of local prices from the dominant world market. The aim of doing this is twofold. The first is to counter imperialist intervention through the continued dominance of global value chains. The second is to boost peasant incomes, which in addition to boosting farmer health and livelihood will begin to reduce rural-to-urban migration to counter a Global South of continued slums rife with unemployment and poverty. The feasible utopia will require, early on, not only the political and social forces to drive this revolutionary strategy and political alliances to sustain newly constituted state power, but also inter-regional connectivity and solidarity to promote local, and deliver national, economies of scale and inclusion.

The sovereign popular project is a major feature of the path towards the feasible utopia. This path involves the promotion of common property rights – land tenure – that is guaranteed by the state. The mechanisms for allocating land will be transparent and contested, but they will not be in the hands of notables and merchants. The democratized state is the only institution that is able to deliver the management of land access. While historically the state's role has been flawed and often corrupt and corrupting, the allocation of land cannot be done through the market, as this has always advanced social inequality.

Underpinning the sovereign popular project is democratic farmer and worker participation in the transformation of unequal access to the means of production, and the recognition of the special character of food and agriculture in the national and global political economy. Democratic farmer organization and activism is central to the global success of La Via Campesina and the agenda for food sovereignty and agro-ecological alternatives to the third food regime. In fact, the agenda of the rights of people to food and land, which also emphasizes ecological methods of production, is becoming embedded in struggles over the commons as well as the alternative food sovereignty agenda. Struggles for the feasible utopia are struggles over material access to geographical spaces. These have been contested dimensions in post-Somoza reconstruction in Nicaragua and post-Ben Ali development at Jemna in Tunisia, for example (Hamouchene 2017; Ruccio 1988). The struggle is also an ideological contest that critiques agribusiness and industrial agriculture as a continuing and inevitable feature of late capitalism.

The struggle is played out in the oasis of Jemna, southern Tunisia, where family farmers reclaimed land from the state after the toppling of Ben Ali in 2011. Farmers created their own organization to manage all aspects of agricultural production and to use farm revenue to promote local development projects, which included building a local market and renovating school buildings and health facilities. There has been a tough battle between farmers seeking to retain control over the land and the income generated from it, as earnings that can be collectivized for the community, and the post-dictatorship state that continues to exert pressure to liberalize the agricultural market and control farm production. Jemna, and many other cases in post-Ben Ali Tunisia, is an illustration of farmer mobilization to reappropriate land that was taken by the state at the time of decolonization. Jemna does not therefore illustrate a challenge to the private ownership of land, as was the case in Zimbabwe (at least where land was held by large-scale white farmers). There has instead been, among other things, a contestation of the legal status of public lands and the reach of the commons, and a fascinating political mobilization to debate the distribution of farm revenue for the collectivity or community.

There have also been challenges in Nicaragua, a country that could become self-sufficient with regard to food. After 1979, the Sandinistas tried to deliver food self-sufficiency through a strategy that combined a reformed agro-export sector inherited from the Samoza dictatorship with agrarian reform to boost poor farmers' incomes. However, the combination of slowly enacted land reform, US-backed military intervention and Washington's co-ordinated trade embargo, that also reduced Nicaragua's access to aid and loans, paved the path towards structural adjustment in 1991 and undermined the state's and farmers' anti-systemic agendas.

Agro-ecological farming methods, namely the promotion of 'diversified farming systems based on the integrated management of functional biodiversity' (Rosset and Martinez-Torres 2012, n.p.), embrace two central elements. The first is the understanding of the essential systemic relationship between people and nature, the inseparable unity that generates the possibility of creating a sustainable alternative to contemporary environmental chaos. The second follows from this, namely that repeasantization is driven by farmers themselves, sharing experiences in farmer-to-farmer patterns of mobilization, learning and sharing. This creates conditions for the recognition of the mutual benefits and gains of environmentally enhancing agro-ecological farming techniques, and of doing so with democratic participation and engagement. Hence La Via Campesina organizes local and international farmer exchanges to share lessons regarding land struggles and innovative indigenous agricultural practice.

The extension of agro-ecology and food sovereignty embraces and promotes decentralized agriculture. This is necessary to advance the withdrawal of farmer domination by the international law of value. In proposing pathways towards the feasible utopia, we have been helped by the work of Samir Amin (2017) and A. Haroon Akram-Lodhi (2015). The latter promotes a doable agenda to advance food sovereignty by identifying the need for redistributive agrarian reform, the control of land markets and the management of agricultural surpluses that serve the interests of those most in need, and to do this with the promotion of agro-ecological farming. Akram-Lodhi (2015) recognizes the importance of a pro-poor sympathetic state machine and the need for international civil society (whatever that is) to advance a new 'common sense' to rein in the power of agribusiness. He also recognizes the importance of rural–urban alliances to bring about political transformation that can deliver this reforming agenda.

We now have a clearer picture of the feasible utopia. One that is anti-capitalist and that delivers on advancing a relationship between a 'global strategy' necessary at the world scale and a 'limited strategy' that addresses local, national or regional policy (Bensaïd 2007). What brings these two strategies together is the specificity of food and the character of the international food regime. Despite all the mayhem I have noted in the current world food system and its consequences in the Global South, is it possible that we are transitioning into a fourth regime, one that can become increasingly dominated by food sovereignty, the political ascendency of La Via Campesina and the broadening of the idea that agro-ecology can feed the world and undermine the ideological hegemony of the financialized agricultural sector.

The continued delivery of the alternative, namely moving towards the feasible utopia, involves a paradigmatic shift away from a capital-centred development perspective that advances the interests of elites while stressing that policy is actually helping the poor. The shift is towards development that is labour-centred, and which is focused on the urban and rural poor, the use of existing wealth to promote real human development for the labouring classes and the creation of a political context in which this development can be delivered (Selwyn 2017, 2018). I have indicated that one of the central spaces in which the feasible utopia can be fought is the commons. This is where shared interests and actions can be mobilized to ultimately promote an alternative view of labour and its engagement with a newly conceived idea of markets. Perhaps we need to return to the intervention of Fernand Braudel (1979; 1982; 1984), who interrogated the changing character and definition of capitalism and the market. He argued for a non-linear idea of capitalist development and the challenge of monopolies that are inefficient, corrupt and corrupting, generating inequality and marginality. Instead, he countered his understanding of 'real capitalism' with a sense of 'liberation through self-controlled economic activities within a complex of competitive markets', where people's activities are 'barely distinguishable from ordinary work' (Wallerstein 1991, 360–361). This would be a competitive market where supply and demand would impact prices without monopoly controls exacted by landed interests and merchants, and where a democratically controlled state would help shape and guide what is produced, where and how it is produced, and with what kind of impact, the level of surplus generated and mechanisms for its distribution. In short, it would be a key element in the struggle for a democratic, probably centralized and definitely ecologically embedded accumulation from below: a feasible utopia.

ACKNOWLEDGEMENTS

Huge thanks to the editors and to Max Ajl, Leo Zeilig and Leandro Vergara-Camus for their comments on an earlier draft of this chapter.

NOTE

1.   I use the terms Third World and Global South interchangeably. I use them as collective terms to identify countries that have been underdeveloped due to colonial transformation and uneven incorporation into the contemporary world capitalist system.

FURTHER READING

Amin, S. (2017), The agrarian question a century after October 1917: Capitalist agriculture and agricultures in capitalism, *Agrarian South: Journal of Political Economy*, 6(2), 149–174.

De Angelis, M. (2012), Crises, capitalism and cooperation: Does capital need a commons Fix?, in Bollier, D.; Helfrich, S. (eds), *The Wealth of the Commons: A World Beyond Market and State*, Amherst: Levellers Press.

Moore, J. (2010), Cheap food and bad money: Food, frontiers and financialisation in the rise and demise of neoliberalism, *Review*, 33(2–3), 225–261.

REFERENCES

Akram-Lodhi, A.H. (2015), Accelerating towards food sovereignty, *Third World Quarterly*, 36(3), 563–583.

Amin, S. (2017), The agrarian question a century after October 1917: Capitalist agriculture and agricultures in capitalism, *Agrarian South: Journal of Political Economy*, 6(2), 149–174.

Bensaïd, D. (2007), On the Return of the politico-strategic question, *International Viewpoint Online*, 4(386), February.

Bracking, S. (2016), *The Financialisation of Power: How Financiers Rule Africa*, London: Routledge.

Braudel, F. (1979; 1982; 1984), *Civilization and Capitalism, 15th–18th Century*, 3 vols, *Structure of Everyday Life*; *The Wheels of Commerce*; *The Perspective of the World*, Berkeley, CA: University of California Press.

Chakraborty, S. (2015), Explaining the rise in agricultural prices: Impact of neoliberal policies on the agrarian economy, *Agrarian South: Journal of Political Economy*, 4(2), 232–258.

Clapp, J.; Isakson, S.R. (2018), *Speculative Harvests*, Winnipeg and Rugby: Fernwood Press and Practical Action Publishing.

Clark, P. (2017), Neo-developmentalism and a 'Vía Campesina' for rural development: Unreconciled projects in Ecuador's Citizen's Revolution, *Journal of Agrarian Change*, 17, 348–364.

De Angelis, M. (2012), Crises, capitalism and cooperation: Does capital need a commons Fix?, in Bollier, D.; Helfrich, S. (eds), *The Wealth of the Commons: A World Beyond Market and State*, Amherst: Levellers Press.

FAO (2013), *International Year of Family Farming 2014 Master Plan (final version)*, 30 May, Rome: Food and Agriculture Organization of the United Nations, accessed 24 October 2016 at www.fao.org/fileadmin/user_upload/iyff/docs/Final_Master_Plan_IYFF_2014_30-05.pdf.

Geras, N. (1996), Socialist hope in an age of catastrophe, *The Socialist Register*, 32, 239–263.

Ghosh, J. (2011), Michal Kalecki and the economics of development, *Monthly Review OnLine*, 27 May, accessed 26 March 2019 at https://mronline.org/2011/05/27/michal-kalecki-and-the-economics-of-development/.

Hall, R; Scoones, I.; Tsikata, D. (2015), *Africa's Land Rush: Rural Livelihoods and Agrarian Change*, Woodbridge: James Currey.

Hamouchene, H. (2017), Jemna in Tunisia: An inspiring land struggle in North Africa, *Open Democracy*, 13 April, accessed 20 April 2019 at www.opendemocracy.net/en/north-africa-west-asia/jemna-in-tunisia-inspiring-land-struggle-in-north-africa/.

Hardin, G. (1968), The tragedy of the commons, *Science*, 162(3859), 1243–1248.

Kalecki, M. (1993), *Developing Economies*, vol. 6 of *Collected Works*, edited by Jerzy Osiatynski, Oxford: Clarendon Press.

Levien, M.; Watts, M.; Hairong, Y. (2018), Agrarian Marxism, *Journal of Peasant Studies*, 45(5–6), 853–883.

LVC (La Via Campesina) (2010), *Sustainable Peasant and Family Farm Agriculture can Feed the World,* accessed 10 April 2019 at https://viacampesina.org/en/sustainable-peasant-and-family-farm-agriculture-can-feed-the-world/.

Meretz, S. (2012), The structural communality of the commons, in Bollier, D.; Helfrich, S. (eds), *The Wealth of the Commons: A World Beyond Market and State*, Amherst: Levellers Press.

Mkodzongi, G. (2018), Peasant agency in a changing agrarian situation in central Zimbabwe: The case of Mhondoro Ngezi, *Agrarian South: Journal of Political Economy*, 7(2), 188–210.

Moore, J. (2010), Cheap food and bad money: Food, frontiers and financialisation in the rise and demise of neoliberalism, *Review*, 33(2–3), 225–261.

Moyo, S. (2011), Land concentration and accumulation after redistributive reform in Zimbabwe, *Review of African Political Economy*, 38(128), 257–276.

Ostrom, E. (1990), *Governing the Commons: The Evolution of the Institutions for Collective Action*, Cambridge: Cambridge University Press.

Patnaik, U. (2008), *The Republic of Hunger and Other Essays*, London: Merlin.

Rosset, P.M.; Martinez-Torres, M.E. (2012), Rural social movements and agroecology: Context, theory and process, *Ecology and Society*, 17(3), 17.

Ruccio, D.F. (1988), The state and planning in Nicaragua, in Spalding, R.J. (ed.), *The Political Economy of Revolutionary Nicaragua*, Boston, MA: Allen and Unwin.

Selwyn, B. (2017), *The Struggle for Development*, Cambridge: Polity.

Selwyn, B. (2018), A manifesto for socialist development in the 21st Century, *Economic and Political Weekly*, 53(36), 47–55.

Sorenson, D.S. (1979), Food for peace – or defence and profit? The role of P.L. 480 1963–79, *Social Science Quarterly*, 60(1, June), 62–71.

UN (2017), General Assembly Resolution adopted by the General Assembly on 20 December, UN Decade of Family Farming 2019–2018, United Nations, accessed 9 April 2019 at https://digitallibrary.un.org/record/1479766.

UN (2018), General Assembly 73rd Session Resolution Adopted by the General Assembly, United Nations, 17 December, accessed 8 April 2019 at https://viacampesina.org/en/wp-content/uploads/sites/2/2019/03/UN_Declaration_on_the_rights_of_peasants_and_other_people_working-in-rural_areas.pdf.

Van Der Ploeg, J.D. (2009), *The New Peasantries: Struggles for Autonomy and Sustainability in an Era of Empire and Globalization*, London: Earthscan.

Vergara-Camus, L.; Kay, C. (2017a), Agribusiness, peasants, left wing governments, and the state in Latin America: An overview and theoretical reflection, *Journal of Agrarian Change*, 17(2), 239–257.

Vergara-Camus, L.; Kay, C. (2017b), The agrarian political economy of left-wing governments in Latin America: Agribusiness, Peasants, and the limits of neo-developmentalism, *Journal of Agrarian Change*, 17(2), 415–437.

Wallerstein, I. (1991), Braudel on capitalism, or everything upside down, *Journal of Modern History*, 63(2), 354–361.

Wengraf, L. (2018), *Extracting Profit: Imperialism, Neoliberalism and the New Scramble for Africa*, Chicago, IL: Haymarket Books.

Wilde, O. (2001 [1891]), The soul of man under socialism, in Wilde, O. (2001), *The Soul of Man under Socialism and Selected Critical Prose*, London: Penguin, 125–162.

Wright, E.O. (2010), *Envisioning Real Utopias*, London: Verso.

Index